WARMAN'S
ANTIQUES
AND THEIR PRICES
16th Edition

*The Standard Price Reference for antiques
and collectibles, for collectors, dealers
and professionals in the trade.*

Edited by
Harry L. Rinker

**Completely illustrated
and authenticated**

Warman Publishing Co., Inc.
Elkins Park, PA 19117

ISBN: 0-911594-02-7
ISSN: 0-196-2272
Library of Congress Catalog Card No. 79-4331
Printed in the United States of America

Additional copies of this book may be obtained from your bookstore or directly from the publisher, Warman Publishing Co., P.O. Box 26742, Elkins Park, PA 19117. Enclose $10.95 plus $1.50 for postage and handling. Pennsylvania residents please add 66¢ state sales tax.

EDITORIAL STAFF, 16th EDITION

Donald C. Koehn
5100 Johnson Ave. S.W.
Cedar Rapids, IO 52404
(319) 396-3836
  *Agata, Amberina, Plated Amberina,
  Crown Milano, Kew Blas, Lutz,
  Paleton, Royal Flemish, Smith Bros.*

Ron Lieberman
The Family Album
R.D. #1
Glen Rock, PA 17327
(717) 235-2134
  Books

Robert A. Limons
R.D. #1, Box 162
Hellertown, PA 18055
(215) 838-8931
  *Firearms, Pewter, Nautical Items,
  Scientific Instruments*

James S. Maxwell, Jr.
Box 5039
Neffsville, PA 17601
(717) 569-7717 or 569-0719
  Mechanical Banks

Mollie Helen McCain
400 J Peppertree Circle
Jackson, MI 49203
(517) 784-5795
  Pattern Glass

Dave Rago
P.O. Box 3592, Station E
Trenton, NJ 08629
(609) 585-2546
  *Fulper, Grueby, Marblehead,
  Newcomb College*

Roy C. Repsher
256 N. Chestnut St.
Bath, PA 18014
(215) 837-0138
  Pocket Knives

George Rinsland
4015 Kilmer Ave.
Allentown, PA 18104
(215) 395-3939
  Autographs, Campaign Items

Barbara J. Roche
20 Elinor Ave.
Stratford, NJ 08084
(609) 784-4379
  Graniteware

Rick and Linda Ronalter
Noble Peddler Antiques
P.O. Box 582
Torrington, CT 06790
(203) 482-3948
  Fenton

Allan B. and Helen B. Smith
The Country House
15 Thomas Ave.
Topsham, ME 04086
(207) 729-8941
  Open Salts

Carolyn Sunstein
P.O. Box 26734
Elkins Park, PA 19117
(215) 884-6171
  Antique Miniatures

William and Carol Warfel
58 Snyder St.
Manheim, PA 17545
(717) 663-4855
  *Butter Prints, Redware, Spatterware,
  Stoneware*

Neil and Clodogh Wotring
Box 745, Mill Rd.
Coopersburg, PA 18036
(215) 282-3677
  Oak Furniture

INTRODUCTION

WARMAN'S is designed to be a helpful tool for both collector and dealer. As such, the following suggestions on organization, pricing, use, buying and selling will prove valuable.

ORGANIZATION

WARMAN'S is organized into two major units—the American Pattern Glass section and the General Collections section. The General Collections section lists categories alphabetically.

The American Pattern Glass section is divided into three groups—clear, colored and opalescent. This year we have devoted considerable attention to clarifying pattern names, enhancing the quality of the identification drawings, and listing those patterns most in market demand. We have moved Pattern Opalescent Glass from the General Collections section, where it has appeared in past editions, to a new and larger section to designate the importance it enjoys in the field.

Every collector should know something about the history of his object. We have presented a capsule background for each category. In many cases the backgrounds contain references to museum collections, buying hints, current market trends or directions to reference texts. We hope you find this new feature useful.

In assigning prices we assume the object is in very good condition. If otherwise, we note this in our history. It would be ideal to suggest that mint, or unused, examples of all objects do exist. The reality is that objects from the past were used, whether they be glass, china, dolls or toys. Because of this use, some normal wear must be expected. In fact, if an object such as furniture does not show wear, its origins may be more suspect than if it does show wear.

PRICE GUIDE

Our book is a price *guide.* It is not absolute. Whenever possible, we have tried to provide a broad listing of prices within a category so you have a "feel" for the market. We emphasize the middle range of prices within a category, while also listing some objects of high and low value to show the market spread.

We do not use ranges because they tend to confuse rather than help a person. How do you determine if your object is at the high or low end of the range? There is a high degree of flexibility in pricing in the antiques field. If you want to set ranges, add or subtract 20% from our prices.

One of the hardest variants with which to deal is the regional fluctuation of prices. Victorian furniture brings widely differing prices in New York, Chicago, New Orleans or San Francisco. We have tried to strike a balance. Know your region and subject before investing heavily. If the best prices for cameo glass are in Montreal or Toronto, then be prepared to go there if you want to save money or add choice pieces to your collection. Research and patience are key factors to building a collection of merit.

Another factor that affects prices is a sale by a leading dealer or private collector. We have tempered both dealer and auction house figures.

USER'S GUIDE

A great deal of effort has been expended to make our index useful. Always try to find the most specific reference. For example, if you have a piece of china, look first for the maker's name and second for the type. The key is to ask the right questions of yourself.

You may encounter a piece you cannot identify well enough to use the index. Consult the photographs and marks. If you own the last several editions of WARMAN'S, you have assembled a valuable photo reference to the antiuqes field.

In comparing your object to our listing, be conscious of all aspects of the listing — size, description, color and condition. Variations in size and color can greatly influence price. Further, variations in size or material can help you spot originals from reproductions. [Reproduced items in the listings are indicated by an asterisk (*).]

It is not possible for us to list everything. Make your own notes in the margins as you encounter objects in your search. WARMAN'S is not designed to sit on your shelf, but to withstand heavy use. Thumb wear is our guage to success.

WARMAN'S is concerned about market trends. For this reason we occasionally repeat an object so its increase or decrease can be traced in the marketplace.

PRICES

Everyone asks — where do we get our prices? They come from many sources.

First, we rely on auctions. Auction houses and auctioneers do not always command the highest prices. If they did, why would so many dealers buy from them? The key to understanding auction prices is to know when a price is high in range, or low. We think we do this and do it well.

Second, we work closely with dealers. We screen our contacts to make certain they have a full knowledge of the market. Dealers make their living or significant side income from selling antiques. They cannot afford to have a price guide which is not in touch with the market.

Over thirty antique magazines, newspapers and journals come into our office regularly. We read them thoroughly and extract price information from them. They are excellent barometers of what is moving and what is not. We don't hesitate to call an advertiser to ask if their listed merchandise sold. Teams from WARMAN'S are in the field at antique shows, flea markets, and country auctions recording prices and taking photographs.

Collectors work closely with us. They are specialists whose devotion to research and accurate information is inspiring. Generally, they are not dealers. Whenever we have asked for help from them, they have responded willingly and admirably.

A major source of price information is our readers. We receive hundreds of letters from readers giving data on sales or objects they have encountered. We eagerly look forward to these letters. The volume prevents us from acknowledging all of them; however, each is considered and its information placed in our files.

BOARD OF ADVISORS

This issue marks a new addition to our price collecting team. Our Board of Advisors are specialists, both dealers and collectors, who feel a commitment to accurate information. Several have authored a major reference work on their subject. You'll find their names listed in the front of the book.

Members of the Board of Advisors file lists of prices in the categories for which they are responsible. They help select and often supply the photographs used. If you wish to buy or sell an object in their field of expertise, drop them a note. If time or interest permits, they will respond.

BUYER'S GUIDE

WARMAN'S is designed to be a buyer's guide, a guide to what you would have to pay to purchase an object on the open market from a dealer or advanced collector. **It is not a seller's guide to prices**. People frequently make this mistake; in doing so, they deceive themselves. If you have an object listed in this book and wish to sell it to a dealer, you should expect to receive approximately fifty percent (50%) of the listed value. If the object is not expected to be resold quickly, expect to receive even less.

A private collector may pay more, perhaps seventy to eighty percent of our list price. Your object will have to be something needed for his or her collection.

If you have an extremely rare object or an object of exceptionally high value, these guidlines do not apply. Examine your piece as objectively as possible. As an antique appraiser, I spend a great deal of time telling people their treasures are not 'gold' at all, but items readily available in the marketplace.

In respect to buying and selling, a simple philosophy is that a good purchase occurs when both the buyer and seller are happy with the price. Don't look back. Hindsight has little value in the antiques field. Given time, things tend to balance out.

ACKNOWLEDGEMENTS

Connie A. Moore has more than put up with my joys and frustrations. I keep promising her the next book will be easier. But both of us know the desire to improve and expand will keep the pressure on us. I hope we can continue to thrive on it.

Virginia Rile and Joyce Clement have worked harder than I have any right to expect from a staff. The Board of Advisors was a source of encouragement and inspiration.

In the field we talked with hundreds of dealers and collectors and have received warm cooperation. To attempt to list all their names would only lead to omissions. Therefore, my sincere thanks is extended to the group as a whole.

Finally, I must thank Stanley and Katherine Greene. They have encouraged me, supported me, and made my task pleasant and possible.

Editorial Office
Warman Publishing Co., Inc.
P.O. Box 265
Zionsville, PA 18092
February, 1982

HARRY L. RINKER

STATE OF THE MARKET

In 1981 the sluggish economy caught up with the antique marketplace. Middle and low price range buyers stayed away from the market. Many weekend and part-time dealers folded. A number of flea markets were canceled; others lost a high percentage of their dealers. The major auction houses experienced modest growth, but not at the same level as in the mid-1970's.

The inflation spiral of the mid-1970's and American Bicentennial fever attracted many to antiques in search of a good investment and quick profit. 1980 and 1981 witnessed these individuals trying to sell off and finding that antiques are risky at best if viewed solely as short term investments.

The market demonstrated that it is quality that retains value in hard times. There were many record prices set in 1981 as leading collectors concentrated on the unique and aesthetic. The year saw the price range in many categories widen between top quality and the middle-lower range. A good example is Fraktur. In the mid-1970's, a museum quality example would sell for $7,000 to $10,000 tops. The middle range was $1,000 to $2,000. In 1981 the top range moved to $25,000 to $30,000, while the middle only advanced to $2,000 to $4,000. Samplers, furniture, quilts, and paintings are also examples of where this is happening.

In addition, other groups of antiques achieved a high value level. Art Glass, Historic Staffordshire, and certain types of porcelain, especially oriental, rose to levels where the collector with a hundred dollars or less to spend found the door closed to collecting these objects. This market requires new middle and high income collectors to sustain itself. They did not materialize in 1980 and 1981.

At the other end of the spectrum, a number of collectibles, e.g., collector's plates and beer cans, weakened as speculators dropped from the market. The collectibles market is the one being most actively pursued by collectors with modest amounts to invest. Time will dictate which forms will retain their value. Cowboy items, Disneyana, and toys are just a few examples of those now firmly established.

Any antique which held its own or declined only slightly in value during 1981 did well. Nevertheless, there were those categories which showed unusual strength or weakness. The following list indicates current trends:

Gaining	*Declining*
Advertising Art	Avon Items
Autographs	Beer Cans
Cambridge Glass	Collector's Plates
Disneyana	Folk Art
Furniture, Country, painted	Lalique
Furniture, English	Oriental Rugs
Pewter	Redware
Quimper	Silver Items
Sandwich Glass	Whiskey Bottles
Staffordshire, Historic	
Toys	

Remember, these are general trends. The high quality items, even in a declining category, continue to command top dollar.

Another major impact on the antique marketplace in 1980 and 1981 was the large number of reproductions and outright fakes. This has been a common problem in the field; however, it now seems to be reaching epidemic proportions. Large warehouses supply dealers with this merchandise. They advertise openly in the trade papers and journals. Legal remedies are almost non-existent. Some dealer organizations are beginning to develop codes of ethics for their members; they deserve the highest praise.

In summary, if you have funds and are willing to take the time to study the market, now is the time to enter the antique arena. Buy quality, first and foremost. Buy your antiques because you plan to live with them. Over an extended period of time, you will gain both from the pleasure you receive and their rise in value.

AUCTION HOUSES

The following auction houses cooperated with Warman Publishing Co., Inc., by providing catalogues of their auctions and price lists. In addition, Bourne, Butterfield's, Oliver, Rinsland, and Roan provided photographs for use in the General Section. This effort is most appreciated.

Richard A. Bourne, Co. Inc.
Corporation St. (P.O. Box 141)
Hyannis, Mass. 02647
(617) 775-0797

Butterfield's
1244 Sutter St.
San Francisco, CA 94109
(415) 673-1362

Christie's
502 Park
New York, N.Y. 10002
(212) 546-1000

Mike Clum
P.O. Box 147
Thornville, Ohio 43076
(614) 246-6851

William Doyle Galleries, Inc.
175 E. 87th St.
New York, N.Y. 10028
(212) 427-2730

Early Auction Co.
123 Main St.
Milford, Ohio 45150
(513) 831-4833

Fine Arts Company of Philadelphia
2317 Chestnut St.
Philadelphia, Pa. 19103
(215) 564-3644

Garth's Auctions, Inc.
2690 Stratford Rd.
P.O. Box 369
Delaware, Ohio 43015
(614) 362-4771 and 369-5085

Morton's Auction Exchange, Inc.
643 Magazine St.
P.O. Box 30380
New Orleans, LA 70190
(504) 561-1196 or (800) 535-7801

Richard W. Oliver Auction & Art Gallery
P.O. Box 337
Kennebunk, Maine 04043
(207) 985-3600

Phillips
867 Madison Ave.
New York, N.Y. 10021
(212) 570-4830

Rinsland's Americana Mail Auction
P. O. Box 265
Zionsville, Pa. 18092
(215) 966-3939

Roan Bros. Auction Gallery
R. E. 3, Box 118
Cogan Station, Pa. 17728
(717) 494-0170

Sotheby's
1334 York Ave.
New York, N.Y. 10021
(212) 472-8424

Sotheby's - Arcade
1334 York Ave.
New York, N.Y. 10021
(212) 472-4701

Verlon Webb Auctions
311 N. Spruce
Centerville, Ind. 47330
(317) 855-5542

Wilson Galleries
Box 102
Fort Defiance, Va. 24437
(703) 885-4292

AMERICAN PATTERN GLASS
Introduction

HISTORY

Two events chronicled the initial production of pattern glass for the mass market. In 1825 Deming Jarvis founded the Boston and Sandwich Glass Company. In 1829 the technique of pressing glass into hinged molds was patented. Housewives now had inexpensive table glass in unlimited quantities.

From the 1860's through the first decade of the 20th century, hundreds of companies produced thousands of intricate patterns that pictured in glass the elements of everyday life as it was in the late 1800's—flowers, animals, portraits, famous actresses, historical figures, Victorian frills, and whimsies. Production of pattern glass was not without its tribulations. There were rapid changes in public taste, strikes and fires at factories, and involvement in our nation's first energy crisis— the absence of enough natural gas to maintain production.

FLINT GLASS

Until 1865 many patterns, e.g., Ashburton, Bigler, Excelsior and Eureka, were made of lead glass, or bell-tone glass. When struck lightly, the object emitted a clear, bell tone. After 1865, glass of high lead content was slowly replaced by glass made with a soda lime formula. Soda lime glass has no ring. The change was gradual, extending over twenty years.

As a result, some patterns can be found in two or three glass types—flint, semi-flint and non-flint. The flint pieces are most desirable. We have indicated those patterns which fit into a dual or triple classification.

RESEARCHERS

Ruth Webb Lee, Dr. S. T. Millard, and Minnie Watson Kamm were pioneer researchers in pattern glass. They attempted to standardize the names of patterns by adopting those names used by manufacturers in their catalogues. Confusion began because two manufacturers would use a different name for the same pattern. Further, manufacturers' catalogues circulated primarily among the wholesale trade, rarely being seen by the average retail buyer.

The number of manufacturers' catalogues available to the pioneer researchers was limited. If the catalogue name did not seem to suit the pattern a totally new name was created. Not only did the researchers create names at random, but dealers and collectors quickly joined the naming craze. Alice Hulett Metz, a later glass researcher, summed up the problem by noting the "endless confusion" which collectors now face.

Today, William Heacock leads a movement to study the catalogues of manufacturers and bring standardization to pattern glass names. Mollie Helen McCain has helped by more accurately illustrating patterns than has been done in the past. *Pattern Glass Preview* is a bimonthly publication by Mr. Heacock that no serious collector should be without. (William Heacock, ed., 1185 A Fountain Lane, Columbus, Ohio, 43213.)

PATTERN NAMES

Being the nation's leading authority on the prices of pattern glass, *Warman's* lends its support to this standardization. For example, authors, collectors, and manufacturers have given the name "Virginia" to five different patterns. Each of these patterns has also been classified under other designations. We have chosen simply to number the "Virginia" pattern 1 through 5. The results are as follows:

No.	Old Pattern Name	Manufacturer
1	*Banded Portland*	U. S. Glass Company
2	*Galloway*	U. S. Glass Company
3	*Henrietta* or *Big Block*	Findlay Glass Company
4	*McKee's Virginia*	McKee Glass Company
5	*Tarentum's Virginia* or *Many Diamonds*	Tarentum Glass Company

A similar catalogue change has been made for the two "Pennsylvania" patterns.

State of the Market

The current market in pattern glass fluctuates. The older, flint glass patterns remain the most collectible, expensive, and hard to find. Reflecting the withdrawal of flint examples from the marketplace, we reduced the listings for these patterns in the 16th Edition.

Other patterns have increased in popularity. This is due in part to the modest cost still encountered by individuals wishing to build a comprehensive collection in a single pattern. We have added over forty new patterns to the 16th Edition.

There has been a general downward trend in prices since publication of the last *Warman's* edition. The 16th Edition reflects this in several categories. The market currently is in a very stable position.

Price changes occur within a pattern for many reasons. As a pattern is better researched, it becomes more "collectible." Availability of examples is another key element. Certain patterns are "in fashion" among collectors at any given moment. Today the "States" patterns enjoy this position.

REPRODUCTIONS

The pattern glass field has been plagued by reproductions, some made from the original molds. The collector is advised to do three things: (a) read and study as much pattern glass literature as possible, (b) deal with a reputable dealer [found by asking other collectors], and (c) handle and examine as many good examples as you can find.

We have marked items for which reproductions are known to exist with an asterisk (*). We encourage collectors to inform us of any we may have missed so they can be added to future editions.

Using Warman's Listing

The Pattern Glass section is divided into three catagories—Clear, Colored and Opalescent. The Clear Pattern Glass section contains patterns made primarily in clear glass. The one exception is patterns which come in only two colors—clear and emerald green. If a pattern is in three or more colors, it is found in the Colored Pattern Glass section. The clear pattern may be one of these colors. Therefore, if you have a piece of clear pattern glass, **check both sections.**

Opalescent glass has a cloudy or opal look. It is found in both clear and colored patterns. In the past, opalescent patterns were found in categories throughout the General section. We feel opalescent patterns deserve special attention because of their increased collectibility.

We have returned to the word "vaseline" in the Colored section. The present manufacturers of vaseline petroleum jelly have changed the color of their product. The current milky white, transparent material is no longer descriptive of anything. But collectors know what vaseline looks like. It is not yellow, it is not canary—it is vaseline. Lets keep it that way!

We have crossed-indexed pattern names. When a pattern has several names, we have retained only those currently in use. We have no desire to perpetuate names loosing favor among collectors.

Many illustrations in this edition are new. We are committed to giving you the best representation of each pattern. Line drawings, rather than photographs, allow the details of a pattern to show clearly.

YOU, THE COLLECTOR

Pattern glass collectors represent our most important source for prices, market trends and research. Sharing your information with us will enable other collectors to benefit. We welcome what data you can send.

CLEAR PATTERN GLASS

ACORN VARIANTS
(Acorn, Acorn Band, Acorn Band with Loops, Panelled Acorn Band).

Non-flint, c. 1870's.

Butter, covered	35.00
Celery	40.00
Creamer	40.00
Compotes	
Covered	62.00
Open	42.00
Egg Cup	22.00
*Goblet	32.00
Pitcher, water	60.00
Sauces	
Flat	8.00
Footed	14.00
Spooner	22.00
Sugars	
Covered	45.00
Open	28.00
Wine	75.00

ACTRESS
(Theatrical)

Made by LaBelle Glass Co., Bridgeport, Ohio, c. 1870's. Prices listed are for clear and frosted.

Bowl, 6" footed	45.00
Butter, covered	80.00

Cake Stand, 10"	115.00
Celery, ftd., H. M. S. Pinafore	140.00
Cheese dish, covered, "The Lone Fisherman"	180.00
Candlesticks, pr.	175.00
Compotes	
Covered, 7", high standard	65.00
Covered, 8", high standard	100.00
Open, 7", low standard	80.00
Open, 10", high standard	90.00
Open, 12", high standard	110.00
Creamer	55.00
*Goblet	80.00
Honey dish, covered	60.00
Marmalade Jar with cover	75.00
Mug, Pinafore	40.00
*Pickle Dish, "Love's Request is Pickles"	37.50
Pitchers	
Milk, oval, "Pinafore"	175.00
Water, "Miss Neilson"	180.00
Sauces	
Flat	20.00
Footed	22.00
Salt and Pepper, pair	60.00
Spooner	60.00
Sugar	75.00
Tray, bread "Give Us This Day Our Daily Bread," "Pinafore"	55.00

ALABAMA
(Beaded Bull's Eye and Drape)

Circa 1898. U. S. Glass Company (One of the States' patterns).

Butter	35.00
Celery	25.00
Compote, open, 5"	30.00
Creamer	32.50
Cruet, with stopper	35.00
Honey dish	22.00
Nappy	18.00
Pitcher, water	45.00
Relish	15.00
Sauce, flat, 5"	14.00
Salt Shakers, pair	50.00
Spooner	22.00
Sugar, covered	30.00
Syrup	40.00
Toothpick	25.00

ALASKA
(See Colored Pattern Glass Section)

ALMOND THUMBPRINT
(Pointed Thumbprint, Finger Point)

An early flint glass pattern with variants in flint and non-flint. The prices are for flint. Non-flint items are approximately 50% less.

Butter, covered	80.00
Celery Vase	62.50
Champagne	60.00
Compotes	
Covered, 4¾", high standard . . .	55.00
Covered, 7", high standard	45.00
Covered, 10", high standard	50.00
Covered, 4¾", low standard	30.00
Covered, 7", low standard	35.00
Cordial	18.00
Creamer	62.00
Cruet, footed	40.00
Decanter	70.00
Egg Cup	30.00
Goblet	25.00
Punch Bowl	100.00
Salts	
Individual	15.00
Large, flat	22.50
Footed, covered	35.00
Sugar, covered	60.00
Sweetmeat Jar, covered	75.00
Tumbler	40.00
Wine	35.00

AMAZON
(Sawtooth Band)

Non-flint made by Bryce Brothers, Pittsburgh, Pa., late 1870's–1880.

Banana Stand	60.00
Butter, covered	55.00
Bowl, open in silver frame	60.00
Bowl, waste	25.00
Cake Plate, 9¼"	37.50
Cake Stand	42.50
Celery	30.00
Creamer	27.50

Creamer, children's toy	18.00
Cruet, with original stopper	40.00
Champagne	30.00
Cordial, etched "Jacksonville Fla." .	22.50
Compotes	
Jelly, 5½"	22.50
Open, 9½", high standard	35.00
Egg Cup	10.50
Goblet	30.00
Nappy, round	18.00
Nappy, with lion handles, oval	
(Sometimes with lid, lion finial) . . .	40.00
Pitcher, water	47.50
Salts	
Flat	18.00
Footed	20.00
Sauces, flat	7.50
Footed	10.00
Shakers, pair	30.00
Sugar, covered	30.00
Sugar, covered, children's toy	20.00
Spooner	22.00
Spooner, children's toy	19.00
Toothpick	25.00
Tumbler	21.00
Wine	32.50
Syrup	47.00

AMBERETTE
(See KLONDIKE, Colored Pattern Glass Section.)

ANTHEMION

Non-flint made by Model Flint Glass Co., Findlay, Ohio, c. 1890–1900.

Bowl, 8"	15.00
Butter, covered	40.00
Cake Plate, 9½"	32.50
Celery	16.00

Creamer	20.00
Marmalade Jar	25.00
Pitcher	
Water	45.00
Milk	40.00
Plates	
10″	15.00
10″ with curled rim, triangular	
shape	25.00
Sauce, square	10.00
Spooner	20.00
Sugar, covered	37.50
Tumbler	25.00

APOLLO

Non-flint first made by Adams and Co., Pittsburgh, Pa., c. 1870's. Later by McKee Brothers, Pittsburgh, Pa., about 1895. Clear and frosted. Frosted increases price 10%, red stained pieces, 20%.

Bowls	
8″, sometimes etched	20.00
9″, also with red stain	28.00
Butter, covered	45.00
Cake Stand	35.00
Celery Vase	30.00
Cheese Dish	40.00
Compotes	
Covered, high standard	50.00
Open, low standard	35.00
Creamer	35.00
Egg Cup	21.00
Goblet	45.00
Lamp, 10″	45.00
Pickle Dish	25.00
Pitcher, water	45.00
Sauce	
Flat	10.00
Footed	12.50
Spooner	25.00
Sugar, covered	40.00
Sugar Shaker	45.00
Syrup	40.00
Water Tray	45.00
Tumbler	25.00
Wine	24.00

ARABESQUE

Non-flint produced by Bakewell, Pears and Co., Pittsburgh, Pa., c. 1870's.

Butter, covered	45.00
Celery	35.00
Compotes	
Covered, 6″, high standard	47.50
Covered, 8″, high standard	55.00
Covered, 8″, low standard	40.00
Creamer, applied handle	45.00
Goblet	30.00
Pitcher, water, applied handle	45.00
Sauce, flat	7.50
Spooner	22.50
Sugars	
Covered	45.00
Open	30.00

ARCHED GRAPE

Flint and non-flint of the 1870's — late 80's. Prices listed for flint.

Butter, covered	50.00
Celery	37.50
Compotes, covered	
High Standard	50.00
Low Standard	45.00
Cordial	25.00
Creamer	40.00
Goblet	35.00
Pitcher, water, applied handle	60.00
Sauce	15.00
Spooner	25.00
Sugar, covered	45.00
Wine	30.00

ARGUS

Bakewell Pears & Co. made this thumbprint type pattern in flint glass in Pittsburgh, Pa., in the early 1870's.

Bitters Bottle	60.00
Bowl, 5½"	50.00
Butter, covered	70.00
Ale Glass	95.00
Celery, cut	75.00
Champagne	52.50
Cordial	29.00
Creamer, applied handle	65.00
Decanters	
Pint	68.00
Quart	70.00
Egg Cup	29.00
Goblet	42.50
Lamp, footed	75.00
Mug, applied handle	75.00
Pitcher, water, applied handle	150.00
Salt, open	30.00
Sauce	22.00
Spooner	50.00
Sugar, covered	70.00
Tumblers	
Footed	45.00
Handled Whiskey	50.00
Wine	30.00

ART

(Teardrop, Job's Tears.)

Non-flint produced by Adams and Co., Pittsburgh, Pa., in the 1870's. Reissued by U. S. Glass Co. in the early 1890's.

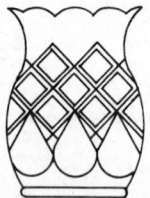

Banana Stand	100.00
Basket, fruit	60.00
Bowl, berry, 8"	30.00
Butter, covered	52.50
Cake stand, 10"	55.00
Celery	35.00
Compotes	
Covered, footed, 7"	60.00
Open, 7½" and 10"	35.00
Cracker Jar	37.50
Creamer	
Regular	35.00
"Hotel" (a large round-shaped creamer)	40.00
Cruet	32.50
Goblet	35.00
Mug	22.50
Pitcher, water	65.00
Plate, 10"	40.00
Relish	20.00
Sauce, footed	15.00
Spooner	25.00
Sugar, covered	40.00
Tumbler	20.00
Vinegar Jugs	
Half pint	40.00
Three pints	50.00
Wine	25.00

ARTICHOKE

Non-flint, c. 1890. Clear, approximately 50% less than frosted. Reportedly no goblet originally produced, but reproductions exist.

Bowl, 8"	35.00
Rose	30.00
Finger Bowl, with underplate	35.00
Bobeche	15.00
Butter, covered	55.00
Cake Stand	47.50
Celery	38.50
Compotes	
Covered	50.00
Open, scalloped edge	45.00
Creamer	45.00
Lamp, large	100.00
Pitcher, water tankard	70.00
Sauces	
Flat	10.00

Footed	12.50
Spooner	22.00
Sugar, covered	55.00
Tray, water	50.00
Tumbler	28.00

ASHBURTON

A popular pattern produced by several factories from the 1840's to the late 1870's with many variations. Originally made in flint by Bakewell, Pears, New England Glass Co. and others. Later produced in non-flint. Prices are for flint.

Ale Glass, 5″	55.00
Bitters Bottle	57.50
Celery	90.00
Champagne, cut	55.00
Claret, 5¼	45.00
*Cordial	50.00
Creamer, Applied handle, (Scarce)	160.00
Decanters	
Pint, stoppered	80.00
Quart, bar lip	85.00
Egg Cup, single	25.00
Egg Cup, double	32.50
*Goblet	50.00
*Jug, pint, quart and three pint	80–100.00
Lamp	75.00
*Lemonade Glass	55.00
Mug	25.00
Sauce	20.00
Spooner	30.00
*Sugar, covered	95.00
Tumblers	
Jelly	30.00
Water	42.50
Whiskey, handled, applied handle	45.00
Whiskey, straight sides with Grape Band at top (Rare)	48.50
Wine bottle with tumble up	50.00
*Wine	30.00

ASHLAND
(Snowdrop)

Non-flint Portland Glass Co., Portland, Maine, c. 1863–1874.

Bowl, 8″	20.00
Goblet	30.00
Ice Cream Tray, with shells in corners (rare)	50.00
Sauce, square	15.00
Sauces, shaped like shells to match above, 5″	25.00

ASHMAN
(Crossroads)

Pieces are square in shape. There are frequent variations within pieces.
    Non-flint c. 1880's. Made in clear and amber, increases price 10%.

Bowls, many sizes	18–26.00
Butter, covered, conventional finial	38.00
Butter, covered, large ball type finial sometimes with flowers within the ball	45.00
Cakestands	
7″	35.00
9″	45.00
Compotes, covered	
6″	40.00
12″	47.50
Compote, open	37.00
Creamer	32.50
Goblet	35.00
Pitcher, water	58.00
Relish	14.00

Sauce	10.00
Spooner	20.00
Sugars	38.00
Covered	38.00
Open	35.00
Tray, water	38.00
Tumbler	18.00
Wine	10.00

ATLANTA
(Square Lion)

Produced by Fostoria Glass Co., Moundsville, West Virginia, c. 1890's. Clear and frosted. Frosted pieces are 20% more. Pieces are square in shape.

Bowl, Berry 8½"	22.50
Butter, covered	48.50
Cake Stand, large	60.00
Celery	32.50
Compotes	
Covered, 7"	47.50
Open, 7"	37.50
Open, 5", jelly	28.00
Creamer	40.00
Goblet	38.50
Marmalade Jar	65.00
Relish	16.00
Salt, individual	12.50
Sauce	12.00
Spooner	26.50
Sugars	
Covered	48.50
Open	35.00
Tumbler	35.00
Toothpick	27.50

ATLAS

Non-flint clear glass pattern and occasionally ruby-stained, made by Bryce Brothers, Mt. Pleasant, Pa., in 1889. Ruby stained pieces 100% more.

Bowl, 7"	15.00
Butter, covered	35.00
Cake Stand, 10"	28.00

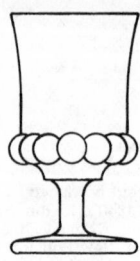

Celery	12.00
Champagne	16.00
Claret	12.00
Compotes	
Covered, 8", high standard	80.00
Covered, 5", jelly	27.50
Open, 7", low standard	30.00
Cordial	20.00
Creamer	20.00
Goblet	24.00
Marmalade Jar, covered	50.00
Pitcher, water	35.00
Salt, master	20.00
Sauce, flat	10.00
4" on a collared base	12.00
Spooner	27.00
Sugar, covered	25.00
Toothpick	15.00
Tumbler	20.00
Wine	25.00

AUSTRIAN
(Finecut Medallion)

Made by Indiana Tumbler and Goblet Co., Greentown, Indiana, c. 1897-1898. Made in clear, milk white, chocolate, canary. A few experimental pieces in green, amber blue, and opaque Nile green. Rare in color. Prices given are for clear glass; color 20% more; caramel or chocolate, 100% more.

Butter, covered	35.00
Celery	18.00

Creamer	35.00
Compote, covered	45.00
Goblet	28.00
Nappy	15.00
Pitcher, water	45.00
Sauce	10.00
Sugar, covered	27.50
Spooner	22.50
Toothpick	25.00
Tumbler	20.00
Wine	20.00

AZTEC

Made by McKee Glass Co., c. 1894 to 1915 (Late imitation cut pattern.)

Bowl	12.50
Butter, covered	15.00
Cake Stand	14.00
Celery Tray	9.50
Compote, open	12.00
Nappy, handled	8.00
Pitcher, water	20.00
Sauce	7.50
Relish	8.00
Sugars	
Covered	10.50
Open	9.00
Tumbler	12.00
Wine	8.00

BABY FACE

Non-flint, c. 1870.

Butter, covered	165.00
Cake Stand	125.00
Celery Vase	75.00
Compotes	
Covered, 5¼", high standard	125.00
Open, 8", high standard	95.00
Creamer	125.00
*Goblet	95.00
Knife Rest	45.00
Lamp	200.00
Pitcher, water	225.00

Salt	35.00
Sauce, footed	35.00
Spooner	72.50
*Sugar, covered	150.00
*Wine	60.00

BABY THUMBPRINT
(See DAKOTA, This Section.)

BALL AND SWIRL

Made in Ohio, c. 1890's.

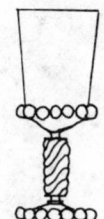

Bowl, Finger	20.00
Butter, covered	25.00
Cake Stand	28.00
Celery	20.00
Compote, open high standard	30.00
Cordial	25.00
Creamer	22.00
Decanter, quart	30.00
Goblet	22.50
Mugs, large and small	15–20.00
Pitcher, water	30.00
Sauce, footed	20.00
Spooner	20.00
Sugar, open	22.50
Tumbler	13.50
Wine	17.50

BALTIMORE PEAR

Non-flint, originally made by Adams and

Company, Pittsburgh, Pa., in the 1880's. Also made by U.S. Glass Company in 1890's. Heavily reproduced.

Bowl, Berry, 9″	28.50
*Butter, covered	45.00
*Cake Stand, 9″	45.00
*Celery	32.50
Compotes	
Covered, 7″, high standard	80.00
Covered, 8½″, low standard	75.00
Open, large	50.00
*Creamer	35.00
*Goblet	35.00
Pickle	20.00
Pitchers	
Milk	50.00
*Water	75.00
Plates	
8½″	35.00
10″	50.00
Sauces	
Flat	10.00
*Footed	13.50
Spooner	22.50
Sugars	
*Covered	37.00
Open	20.00
Tray, 10½″	50.00

BAMBOO

Made in the late 1800's by Pioneer Glass Co., Pittsburgh, Pa. Ruby stained indentations add 100%.

Butter, covered	35.00
Celery	17.50
Compotes, covered, 7″, 8″ and 9″	35-45.00

Creamer	25.00
Pitcher, water	35.00
Relish, 8″	12.50
Sauce	8.50
Shakers, pair	27.50
Spooner	15.00
Sugars	
Covered	30.00
Open	15.00
Tumbler	20.00

BANDED PORTLAND
(Virginia #1)

States' pattern c. 1901. Made by U. S. Glass Company and named by them as one of the States patterns, "Virginia." This state has been given five different pattern names. The reason for these names has become rather obscure, and since Banded Portland seems to be recognized most readily by collectors and dealers as "Virginia," it seemed wise to leave it as such. See further explanation in Introduction.

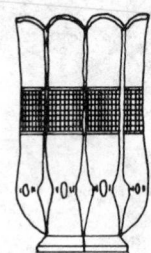

Bowls, various sizes	12-15.00
Boxes	
Powder or puff	18.00
Sardine rectangular	16.00
Bureau Bottle, silver top	27.50
Butter, covered	32.00
Butter Pats	9.00
Cake Stand	35.00
Candlesticks, rare	105.00
Celery	
Vase	25.00
Tray, boat shaped	30.00
Claret	30.00
Creamers	
Large, regular	38.00
Individual, boat shaped	20.00
Compotes	
Covered	75.00
Open, scalloped rim	45.00
Jelly, covered, 6″	30.00
Cruet	38.00
Cup, Punch	8.50

Decanter, handled	40.00
Goblet	30.00
Lamp	
Flat	45.00
Tall	50.00
Marmalade Jar, with cover	35.00
Mug	48.00
Pitcher, water, tankard	50.00
Pitcher, tankard, child's toy	27.50
Punch Bowl, on standard	110.00
Relish, boat shaped	20.00
Long tray	30.00
Round handled nappy	15.00
Spooner	22.00
Salt and Pepper, pair	30.00
Sauces	
Round	10.00
Boat shaped	12.00
Sugars	
Large, covered	28.00
Individual, boat shaped, open	20.00
Sugar shaker, original top	35.00
Syrup	38.00
Toothpick	20.00
Tray, for bureau set	50.00
Tumbler	25.00
Water Carafe	45.00
Wine	25.00
Vases, various sizes	12–18.00

BARBERRY

Non-flint made in Ohio in the early 1880's.

Butter, covered	65.00
Butter Pats	9.00
Cake Stand	35.00
Celery	25.00
Compotes	
Covered, 8", low standard	42.00
Open, 8¼", high standard	30.00
Creamer	45.00
**Cup Plate	17.50
Egg Cup	16.00
Goblet	22.00
Pitcher, water, applied handle	75.00
Plate, 6"	26.50
Relish	20.00
Salt, footed	20.00

Sauces	
Footed	10.00
Flat	13.50
Spooner	22.50
Sugar, covered	55.00
Syrup	95.00
Wine	27.00

**These small plates were designed as individual butter dishes, or butter pats. (RWLee)

BARLEY

Non-flint, originally made by Campbell, Jones and Co., c. 1882 in clear and colors. Possibly by others in varied quality. Add 100% for color.

Butter, covered	30.00
Cake Stand, 9"	29.50
Celery	20.00
Compotes	
Covered	47.50
Open	20.00
Goblet	22.50
Honey Dish	7.50
Marmalade Jar. (scarce)	50.00
Pitcher, water	35.00
Plate, 6". (scarce)	22.50
Salt, Master. Wheelbarrow, pewter wheels	55.00
Sauces, footed 4" and 5"	8.50
Spooner	13.50
Sugar	
Covered	32.00
Open	15.00
Wine	20.00

BARRED FORGET-ME-NOT
(See Colored Pattern Glass Section.)

BASKETWEAVE
(See Colored Pattern Glass Section.)

BEADED ACORN

Non-flint, c. 1860's–1870's.

Butter, covered	50.00

Champagne	35.00
Compotes, covered, high and low standard	45-55.00
Creamer	50.00
Egg Cup	27.50
Goblet	30.00
Pitcher, water	55.00
Plate, 6″	25.00
Relish	18.00
Salt, footed	17.50
Sauce, flat	10.00
Spooner	20.00
Sugar, covered	50.00
Wine	20.00

BEADED BAND

Circa 1884.

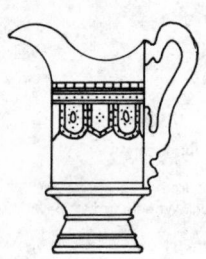

Butter, covered	35.00
Cake Stand	30.00
Compote, covered	55.00
Creamer	25.00
Goblet	25.00
Pickle, covered	45.00
Pitcher, water	50.00
Relish, double	18.00
Sauces	
Flat	7.00
Footed	12.00
Spooner	22.00
Sugars	
Covered	35.00
Open	20.00
Syrup	40.00
Wine	20.00

BEADED DEWDROP
(Wisconsin)

Non-flint made in Pittsburgh, Pa., in the 1880's. Later made by U. S. Glass Co. in Indiana, 1898–1899. (One of States' patterns).

Bowls, 7½″	20.00
Covered, oblong, 6″ and 8″	35.00
Covered, round 7″ and 8″	35.00
Butter, covered, handled	55.00
Cake Stand, 10″	40.00
Bottles, oil and vinegar	20.00
Condiment Set, 4 pieces in holder	85.00
Celery, vase and flat dish	17.50-25.00
Creamer, large and small	25-37.50
Compote, covered 7″	48.00
Compote, open, 10½″	45.00
Cruet	25.00
Candy Dish, handled	20.00
Sweetmeat Dish, on stand, covered	37.50
Goblet	35.00
Mug, large	27.50
Cup and saucer	30.00
Pitchers, water and milk	30-35.00
Syrup, with lid	45.00
Plate, 7″, square	22.50
Salt, Master	25.00
Sauce, flat	10.00
Salt and Pepper Shakers, two types	30.00
Sugar Shaker	40.00
Spooner	25.00
Sugar, large covered, and small	25-40.00
Toothpick Holder	25.00
Tumbler	30.00
Wine	35.00
Vase	25.00

BEADED GRAPE
(California)

Non-flint made by U. S. Glass Co., Pittsburgh, Pa., c. late 1880's. Emerald green 60% more than price of clear. (One of States' patterns.)

| Bowl, 5½″ | 20.00 |
| Bowl, 8″ | 35.00 |

Butter, covered	**40.00**
Cake Stands	
9"	**55.00**
10"	**65.00**
Celeries	
Tray	**25.00**
Vase	**35.00**
Compotes, covered	
6½", high standard	**45.00**
3½", high standard	**55.00**
Compotes, open	
4¾", low standard	**40.00**
7", high standard	**35.00**
4¾", rare with lid, made for jelly .	**50.00**
Creamer	**45.00**
Cordial	**42.50**
Cruet, stoppered	**35.00**
Dish	
Olive dish with handle	**20.00**
Oblong, 6¼ x 8¼"	**18.00**
Square, 7¼ x 8¼"	**20.00**
Egg Cup	**15.00**
*Goblet	**30.00**
Pickle	**16.00**
Pitchers, water	
Round	**65.00**
Square	**70.00**
*Plate	
8¼", square	**22.50**
Platter, 7 x 10" (Originally termed a	
bread tray)	**25.00**
*Sauces	
4"	**10.00**
4½", handled	**14.00**
Shakers, pair	**30.00**
Shaker, Sugar	**35.00**
Spooner	**25.00**
Sugar, covered	**35.00**
Toothpick	**25.00**
*Tumbler	**28.00**
*Wine	**45.00**
Vase, 6"	**20.00**

BEADED GRAPE MEDALLION

Non-flint made by Boston Silver Glass Co., Cambridge, Mass., c. 1869.

Bowl, 7"	**35.00**
Butter, covered (Acorn finial)	**50.00**
Celery	**35.00**
Castor Set	**90.00**
Compotes, covered on high and low	
foot, various sizes	**75.00**

Covered, on a collared base	**60.00**
Cordial	**27.50**
Creamer, applied handle	**45.00**
Goblet, various sizes	**25–30.00**
Egg Cup	**19.00**
Honey Dish, 3½"	**8.50**
Pitcher, water, applied handle	**80.00**
Plate, 6"	**22.50**
Relish, marked "Mould Pat'd May	
11, 1869." Originally had a lid. . . .	**25.00**
Sauce, flat	**10.00**
Salts	
Footed, master	**20.00**
Oval, flat	**13.50**
Round, flat	**12.50**
Sauce	
Spooner	**20.00**
Sugar Bowl, acorn finial	
Covered	**50.00**
Open	**35.00**

BEADED LOOP
(Oregon)

Non-flint. First made in the 1880's. Reissued in 1907 as one of the State series.

Bowls	
6"	**12.00**
7"	**12.00**
8"	**18.50**
Bowl, Berry, covered	**22.50**
Butter, covered, flat and footed	**40.00**

Cake Stand	32.00
Celery	22.00
Compote, open, 9"	25.00
Cordial	15.00
Creamer, flat and footed	22.50
Goblet	30.00
Mug	21.00
Pitcher, milk and water	30–32.00
Syrup	30.00
Relish	10.00
Sauce, flat	6.00
Salt and Pepper Shakers, pair	30.00
Spooner, flat and footed	45–50.00
Sugar bowl	
Covered, flat and footed	22–28.00
Footed, open	15.00
Toothpick	16.00
Tumbler	24.00
Wine	25.00

BEADED SWAG
(Beaded Yoke)

Made by Heisey Glass Company, c. 1895. Comes in red stained, custard glass; some pieces made in opalescent glass. Prices are for clear glass; red stained, 25% more; custard and opalescent, 50% more.

Bowl, Berry	20.00
Butter, covered	30.00
Compote, open	40.00
Creamer	25.00
Mug, souvenir type	30.00
Sauce	10.00
Spooner	25.00
Sugar, covered	30.00
Toothpick	35.00

BEADED TULIP
(Andes)

Non-flint made by McKee Brothers, Pittsburgh, Pa., c. 1894. Very rare piece may be found in emerald green.

Bowl, oval	20.00

Butter, covered	38.50
Compote, covered high standard	45.00
Cake Stand	45.00
Creamer	25.00
Goblet	30.00
Marmalade Jar	30.00
Pickle, oval	18.00
Pitchers	
Milk	40.00
Water	45.00
Plate, 6"	25.00
Sauces	
Flat, irregular leaf-shaped edges	10.00
Footed	12.00
Spooner	20.00
Sugar, covered	35.00
Tray, water	40.00
Wine	22.00

BELLFLOWER

A fine flint glass pattern first made in the 1830's and attributed to Boston and Sandwich. Later produced by other firms for many years. There are many variations of this pattern — single vine and double vine, fine and coarse, rib, knob and plain stems, rayed and plain bases. Type and quality must be considered when evaluating.

Abbreviations:
DV   double vine
SV   single vine
FR   fine rib
CR   course rib

Butter, covered. SV-FR	80.00
Caster Set, 5-bottle pewter stand	225.00
Celery. SV-FR	125.00
Champagnes	
DV-FR with cut bellflowers	250.00
SV-FR knobbed stem, rayed base, barrel shaped.	120.00
Compotes, open	
6½"dia. SV-FR	75.00
7" dia. SV-FR. Scalloped top, low standard	85.00
8" dia. SV-CR. High standard	60.00

Cordial. SV-FR. Knob stem, rayed base, barrel shaped	75.00
Creamer. SV-FR	150.00
Egg Cups	
DV, with cut bellflowers	225.00
SV-CR	22.00
SV-FR	30.00
Decanter, pint. SV-FR. Bar lip	125.00
Goblets	
DV-FR with cut bellflowers	250.00
SV-CR. Barrel shaped	32.00
SV-CR. Straight sides	32.00
SV-FR. Knob stem, barrel shaped	50.00
*SV-FR. Plain stem, rayed base, barrel shaped	30.00
Hat. SV-FR (made from tumbler mold). Rare	350.00
Honey Dish. SV-FR	10.00
Lamp, Whale Oil. SV-FR. Brass stem, marble base	125.00
Mug. SV-FR	200.00
Pitchers	
Milk. DV-FR	400.00+
*Milk, quart. SV-CR	175.00
Syrup, with lid. SV-FR applied handle	225.00
*Water. SV-FR	250.00
Plate, 6″. SV-FR	75.00
Salt, Master. SV-FR. Footed	25.00
*Sauce, flat. SV-FR	7.50
Spooner. SV-FR	33.00
Sugars	
Covered. SV-CR	60.00
Open. DV-CR	45.00
Open. SV-FR	32.00
Tumblers	
DV-CR	75.00
SV-FR. Footed	150.00
SV-FR with cut bellflowers	250.00
Whiskey, 3½″. SV-FR	95.00
Wines	
DV-FR with cut bellflowers, Barrel shaped	250.00
SV-FR. Knob stem, rayed base, barrel shaped	75.00
SV-FR. Straight sides, plain stem, rayed base	65.00

BIGLER

Flint, c. 1850's.

Celery	75.00
Champagne	85.00
Cordial	80.00
Decanter, quart	60.00
Egg cup, double	50.00
Goblet	40.00
Mug, applied handle	65.00
Plate, Toddy	40.00
Sauce	12.00
Tumblers	
Water	50.00
Whiskey	55.00
Wine	45.00

BIRD AND STRAWBERRY
(Bluebird)

Non-flint, c. 1890's. Made by Beatty and Indiana Glass Company, Dunkirk, Indiana. Rare pieces sometimes flashed with color.

Bowls	
5″	22.50
7½″, footed	45.00
9½″, footed, oval	50.00
10½″, footed	50.00
Butter, covered	75.00
Candy, heart shaped	50.00
Cake Stand, 10″	45.00
Celery Vase	55.00
Compotes, covered	
High standard, 6½″	85.00

Low standard, 6", ruffled top ...	75.00
Creamer	45.00
Goblet	40.00
Pitcher, water	150.00
Plate, 12"	125.00
Punch Cup	20.00
Sauces	
Flat	16.00
Footed	20.00
Sugars	
Covered	65.00
Open	35.00
Tumbler	38.00
Wine	32.00

BLACKBERRY
(See Colored Pattern Section.)

BLAZE

Flint made by New England Glass Co., c. 1860.

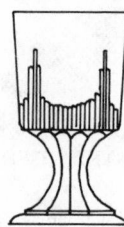

Bowl, 8"	35.00
Butter, covered	65.00
Celery	65.00
Champagne	55.00
Cheese, covered	60.00
Compotes	
Covered, low standard, 6"	65.00
Open, High standard, 8"	65.00
Open, Low standard 8", 9"	50.00
Cordial	55.00
Creamer	75.00
Egg Cup	35.00
Egg Cup, handled	45.00
Goblet	50.00
Plate, 6"	30.00
Plate, 7"	32.50
Salt, rectangular	30.00
Sauces, 4" and 5"	12.50
Spooner	39.50
Sugar, covered	65.00
Tumblers	
Footed	45.00
Lemonade	40.00
Wine	55.00

BLEEDING HEART

Non-flint, c. 1870-80's.

Bowl, Waste	30.00
Butter, covered	55.00
Cake Stand, 10"	58.00
Compotes	
Covered, high standard, 8½" ...	65.00
Covered, low standard, oval	50.00
Open, low standard, 8½"	25.00
Creamer, applied handle	50.00
Egg Cup	35.00
Goblets	
Knob stem	35.00
Plain stem	30.00
Mug 3¼"	
Pitcher, water, applied handle	125.00
Platter, oval	65.00
Relish, divided into four sections ...	65.00
Sauces	
Flat	8.50
Flat, oval	25.00

BLOCK AND FAN

Non-flint made by Richard and Hartley Glass Co., Tarentum, Pa., late 1880's. Ruby stained pieces, add 100%, but rare.

Bowls	
7¼ and 10" berry bowls	25.00
Finger	21.00
Rose	22.50
Butter, covered	35.00

Cake Stand, 10″	35.00
Celery Tray	15.00
Vase	17.50
Cracker Jar	40.00
Creamer	27.50
Cruets with Stoppers	
Small	25.00
Large	30.00
Condiment set with salt and pepper and cruet on tray	65.00
Goblet	60.00
Ice Tub	65.00
Pitchers	
Milk	27.50
Water	35.00
Plate, 10″	25.00
Relish, oblong	15.00
Sauces	
Flat, 3¾″	7.00
Footed	8.00
Square	7.00
Shakers, pair	30.00
Sugar	30.00
Spooner	25.00
Sugar, covered	40.00
Tray, Ice Cream, rectangular, with sauces to match	45.00
Sauces, each	9.00
Tumbler	25.00
Water Bottle	40.00
Wine	35.00

BOSWORTH
(Star Band)

Non-flint, c. 1895–1905. Maker unknown.

Butter, covered	20.00
Bowl, Berry	12.00
Cake Plate	14.50
Creamer	18.00
Goblet	13.50
Pitcher, water	25.00
Relish	12.00
Sauce, flat	8.50
Spooner	20.00
Sugar, covered	22.50
Wine	25.00
Tumbler	25.00

BLOCK AND PALM
(Eighteen-Ninety)

Made by Beaver Falls Glass Company, Beaver Falls, Pa., in the 1890's. Also made in milk glass, 20% more.

Bowl, 8″ deep	15.00
Butter, covered	25.00
Celery	15.00
Creamer	17.50
Pitcher, water	25.00
Shakers, Salt and Pepper pair	20.00
Sugar	18.50
Spooner	13.50
Sugar, open	12.50

BOUQUET
(Narcissus Spray)

Made by Indiana Glass Company, c. 1918. Clear glass with flowers and leaves flashed with cranberry or amethyst color. Prices are for all clear. Color flashed 20% more.

Bowl, Berry	18.00
6″	14.00
5″	10.00
Butter, covered	38.50
Cake plate	25.00
Creamer	22.50
Nappy, handled	12.50
Pitcher, water	37.50
Sauce	5.00

Spooner	18.00
Sugar, covered	30.00
Tumbler	11.50
Tray, water	40.00

BOW TIE

Non-flint made by Thompson Glass Co., Uniontown, Pa., c. 1888-1890.

Bowls		
4"		25.00
8"		35.00
10" deep		65.00
Punch bowl		100.00
Butter, covered		65.00
Cake Stand, large, 9" dia.		75.00
Compotes, open		
High standard, 10", Orange bowl on high stand.		55.00
Low standard, 6½"		45.00
Creamer		45.00
Goblet		45.00
Honey, covered		55.00
Marmalade Jar		45.00
Pitchers		
Milk		40.00
Water		65.00
Relish, rectangular		25.00
Salt, Individual		12.00
Sauce, flat		15.00
Spooner		30.00
Sugars		
Covered		65.00
Open		40.00

BRITTANIC

Non-flint, c. 1898. Pieces are clear with red or yellow stain. Color 20% more.

Bowl, Berry	20.00
Banana Stand	75.00
Butter, covered	40.00
Cake Stand	45.00
Compote	

Covered	55.00
Open	45.00
Creamer	35.00
Goblet	30.00
Pitcher, water	50.00
Relish	18.00
Spooner	25.00
Sugar, covered	30.00
Tumbler	20.00
Wine	22.50

BROKEN COLUMN
(Irish Column, Rattan, and Notched Rib)

Made in Findlay, Ohio, about 1891-1892 by Columbia Glass Co. Later made by U.S. Glass Co. Red notches add 100%.

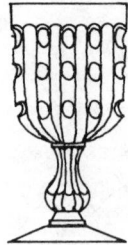

Banana Stand		75.00
Basket, applied handle, 12" x 15"		85.00
Bowls		
6", covered		35.00
7½"		35.00
Butter, covered		55.00
Cake Stand, 9"		55.00
Carafe, water		50.00
Celery, oval		15.00
Celery Vase		35.00
Champagne		55.00
Compotes		
Covered, 10", high standard		50.00
Open, 7", high standard		30.00
Cracker Jar, covered		60.00
Creamer		30.00

Cruet	35.00
*Goblet	40.00
Marmalade Jar, covered	55.00
Mug	40.00
Pickle Castor and Tongs	75.00
Pitchers	
Syrup	50.00
Water	55.00
Punch Cup	20.00
Relish, 5″ x 8″	18.50
Shakers, pair	30.00
Sugar, covered	45.00
Tumbler	25.00
Wine	45.00

BRYCE
(Ribbon Candy)

Non-flint, made by Bryce Brothers, Pittsburgh, Pa., 1880's. Reissued by U.S. Glass Co. in 1890's.

Bowls	
7″, covered	16.00
8″, open	12.00
Butter, covered	28.00
Goblet	22.50
Cake Stands	
8″	23.00
10½″	45.00
Creamer	28.00
Cruet, stoppered	35.00
Cup and Saucer	20.00
Relish	11.00
Oil Lamp	75.00
Plates	25.00
Sauce, Flat	6.50
Honey, covered	30.00
Shakers, pair	40.00
Spillholder	22.50
Pitcher	40.00
Spooner	19.00
Syrup	85.00
Sugars	
Covered	30.00
Open	18.50
Tumbler	20.00
Wine	14.00

BUCKLE

A flint and non-flint made by Gillinder and Sons in Philadelphia, Pa., in the 1870's. Possibly made earlier by Sandwich Glass Co. in Massachusetts. Add 50% more for flint. Prices given are for non-flint.

Bowl, Berry, large (originally had a	
wire basket frame)	60.00
Butter, covered	55.00
Compotes, covered	
High standard	75.00
Low standard	65.00
Creamer, applied handle	25.00
Egg Cup	18.00
Goblets, various styles	18.00
Pickle	11.00
Pitcher, water, applied handle	50.00
Salts	
Master footed	25.00
Flat, oval shape, (very rare)	45.00
Sauce	8.00
Spooner	25.00
Sugars	
Covered	30.00
Open	22.00
Tumbler	37.50
Wine	22.00

BUCKLE, BANDED

Flint and non-flint made by King, Sons and Co., c. 1875. Add 50% for flint. Prices are for non-flint.

Butter, covered	50.00
Compote, covered	60.00
Cordial	22.50
Creamer	22.50
Egg Cup	22.00
Goblet	28.50
Pickle, oval	15.00
Pitchers	
Syrup	35.00
Water	65.00
Salt, Master. Footed	18.50
Sauce	10.00
Spooner	18.50
Sugar, open	20.00
Tumbler, Bar	32.50
Wine	25.00

BUCKLE, LATE
(Belt Buckle, Jasper)
Non-flint, c. 1880.

BUCKLE WITH STAR

Non-flint, c. 1880. Prices for both patterns same value.

BUCKLE, LATE　　**BUCKLE WITH STAR**

Bowls	
6″, covered	20.00
8″, oval	15.00
10″, oval	25.00
Butter, covered	32.50
Cake Stand	30.00
Celery	25.00
Compotes	
Covered, 7″, high standard	50.00
Open, 9½″, high standard	30.00
Open, 9″, low standard	25.00
Creamer	35.00
Goblet	25.00
Pitchers	
Syrup (Buckle with Star), handle applied, with pewter or Brittania lid, with head of man as finial	45.00
Water	65.00
Relish	10.00
Salt, footed	15.00

Sauces	
Flat, 4″	6.00
Footed	12.00
Spooner	20.00
Sugar Open	15.00
Tumbler, handle applied	20.00
Wine	24.00

BUDDED IVY

Non-flint, c. 1870. Stippled Ivy is a contemporary of Budded Ivy. Prices are comparable.

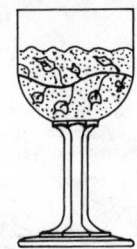

Butter, covered	42.50
Compotes	
Covered, high standard	45.00
Open, high standard	25.00
Creamer	40.00
Egg Cup	20.00
Goblet	30.00
Pitchers	
Syrup	30.00
Water, applied handle	50.00
Relish	17.50
Salt, footed	17.50
Sauce, flat	7.50
Spooner	25.00
Sugar, covered	45.00

BULL'S EYE

Flint made by the New England Glass Co. in the 1850's. Prices are for flint.

Butter, covered	150.00
Carafe, quart	60.00
Castor Bottle	30.00
Celery	65.00
Champagne	85.00
Cordial	25.00
Cologne Bottle	85.00
Creamer	125.00
Decanter, quart, bar lip	125.00
Egg Cups	
Covered but very rare	165.00
Open	45.00

Goblet	65.00
Pitcher, Water	85.00
Lamp	80.00
Mugs	
Large size whiskey tumbler	75.00
Small size with applied handle, 3⅜″	45.00
Relish, oval	45.00
Salt Dip	35.00
Salts, Master. Footed. Also made with covers but rare.	100.00
Open	20.00
Spooner	45.00
Sugar, covered	110.00
Tumbler	85.00
Whiskey	87.50
Water Bottle with tumble up	100.00
Wine	45.00

BULL'S EYE WITH DIAMOND POINT #1

Flint, c. 1850. Prices are for flint.

Butter, covered	200.00
Celery	100.00
Champagne	125.00
Cologne Bottle	125.00
Cordial	100.00
Creamer	175.00
Decanters	
Bar lip, quart	175.00

With stopper, quart	200.00
Egg Cup	85.00
Goblet	95.00
Honey Dish	35.00
Pitcher, 10¼″ tankard	225.00
Sauce	10.00
Spooner	65.00
Sugar, covered	150.00
Tumbler	55.00
Tumble-up	150.00
Wine	65.00

BULL'S EYE WITH FLEUR DE LYS

Flint, c. 1850.

Bowl, Fruit	85.00
Butter, covered	175.00
Celery	87.50
Cordial	75.00
Creamer	250.00
Decanter, quart, bar lip	85.00
Goblet	95.00
Lamp, with marble base	275.00
Mug, handled	150.00
Pitcher, water (scarce)	275.00
Salt, Master. Footed	45.00
Sugar, covered	135.00
Wine	35.00

BUTTON ARCHES

Clear and clear with ruby stained tops, non-flint, c. 1890. Ruby stained items demand approximately 25% more than clear. Some pieces are also seen in clamwater, trimmed in gold. These are known as "Koral," usually souvenir type. There were other patterns made in "Koral" but Button Arches seems most prevalent. Same value as ruby stained.

Bowl, 8″	20.00
Butter, covered	45.00
Cake Stand, 9″	32.50
Compote, Jelly	18.00

Creamer	18.00
Custard Cup	8.00
Goblet	35.00
Mug, small	20.00
Pitchers	
Milk	30.00
Water, tankard	55.00
Shakers, original tops, pair	20.00
Sauce	8.50
Sugar, covered	35.00
Toothpick	14.00
Tumbler	20.00
Wine	15.00

BUTTON BAND
(Umbilicated Hobnail, Wyandotte)

Non-flint, c. 1880's.

Bowl	22.00
Butter, covered	40.00
Cake Stand, 10″	45.00
Castor Set, 5 bottles in glass, stand	100.00
Compote, open, small	45.00
Creamer	32.50
Goblet	30.00
Pitcher, water, tankard	45.00
Salt, Master	12.00
Sauce, footed	10.00
Spooner	20.00
Sugar, covered	35.00
Tumbler	20.00
Wine, (rare)	38.00
Tray, water	40.00

CABBAGE LEAF (CLEAR)

Non-flint, c. 1880's. Add approximately 20% for frosted. Heavily reproduced in both forms and also in color.

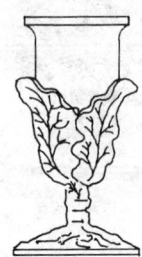

Butter, covered	85.00
Celery	55.00
Cheese, covered	75.00
Compote, covered, high standard	100.00
Creamer	65.00
Pickle, leaf shaped	30.00
Pitcher, water	75.00
Plate, 8″, rabbit center	45.00
Sauce, 3½″	15.00
Spooner	30.00
Sugar, covered	75.00

CABBAGE ROSE

Non-flint made in Wheeling, W. Va., c. 1870–1881.

Basket, handled, 12″ x 14″	75.00
Bowl, Berry, 8½″, oval	27.50
Butter, covered	45.00
Cake Stands	
9″	35.00
11″	62.50
Celery Vase	38.00
Champagnes	27.50
Compotes, (Rose finials on lids)	
Covered, high standard, 6″, 7″	75.00
Covered, high standard, 8″, 9″	65.00
Open, high standard, 7½″	35.00
Creamer, applied handle	57.50
Custard Cup, (rare)	75.00
Egg Cup	22.00

*Goblet	60.00
Pitcher, water	100.00
Relish Dish, (In center, a design of horn of plenty, filled with roses.)	
5″ x 8½″	25.00
Salt, Master. Footed	22.00
Sauces	
Flat, 4″	7.50
Flat, 7″	12.50
Spooner	35.00
Sugars	
Covered	57.50
Open	25.00
Tumbler	40.00
Wine	40.00

CABLE

Flint, c. 1850's. Rare in opaque colors.

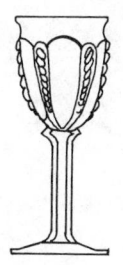

Bowl	25.00
Butter, covered	85.00
Celery	75.00
Champagne	125.00
Compote, open	45.00
Creamer, (rare)	350.00+
Decanters	
Pint	100.00
Quart, ground stopper	175.00
Egg Cups, covered, (rare)	225.00
Goblet	60.00
Lamps	
All glass	125.00
Hand lamp	100.00
Marble base	85.00
Pitchers	
Syrup	125.00
Water (rare)	300.00+
Plate, 6″	75.00
Salts	
Flat	15.00
Footed	45.00
Sauce, flat	10.00
Spooner	30.00
Sugar, covered	85.00
Tumbler, footed (rare)	150.00+
Wine	22.00

CANADIAN

Non-flint, c. 1870's.

Bread Tray	43.00
Butter, covered	50.00
Celery	37.50
Compotes	
Covered, 7″, high standard	50.00
Open, 7″, high standard	30.00
Creamer	55.00
Goblet	45.00
Marmalade Jar	35.00
Pitcher, water	75.00
Pitcher, milk	55.00
Plates	
6″	25.00
10″, handled	55.00
Sauce, flat	10.00
Spooner	32.50
Sugars	
Covered	50.00
Open	22.50
Wine	35.00

CANE
(See Colored Pattern Glass Section.)

CANE AND ROSETTE
(Flowered Panelled Cane)

Non-flint, c. mid-1880's.

Bowl, covered, octagonal	25.00
Butters	
Covered, footed	30.00
Flat	20.00
Cake Stand, large	25.00
Compote, covered, 8", high standard	40.00
Creamer	25.00
Egg Cup	17.50
Goblet	14.00
Pitcher, water	30.00
Sauce, footed	7.50
Spooner	20.00
Sugar, covered	30.00
Wine	15.00

CAPE COD

Non-flint, c. 1870's.

Bowl, 6", handled	20.00
Butter, covered	50.00
Celery	30.00
Compotes	
Covered, 7", high standard	50.00
Covered, 12", high standard	75.00
Open, 7", high standard	25.00
Creamer	27.50
Cup and Saucer	27.50
Goblet	45.00
Cordial	32.50
Marmalade Jar	40.00
Pitchers	
Milk	35.00
Water	50.00
Plates	
8", open handles	25.00
10", handled	40.00
Sauces	
Flat, 4"	10.00
Footed, 4"	12.00
Spooner	27.50
Sugar, covered	50.00
Wine	30.00

CARDINAL BIRD

Non-flint, c. 1870. There has been discussion
as to whether this is a cardinal or blue jay. It
definitely is a cardinal. There were two butter
dishes made — one in the regular pattern and
one with three birds in the base — a cardinal,
pewit, and titmouse. The later is rare and valued at twice the regular piece.

Butter, covered	42.00
Three Birds (Pictured in base of	
butter, See Intro.)	65.00
Regular	55.00
Cake Stand	45.00
Creamer	37.50
*Goblet	35.00
Pitcher, water	100.00
Sauces	
Flat, 4"	15.00
Footed, 4½"	17.50
Footed, 5½"	20.00
Spooner	30.00
Sugars	
Covered	55.00
Open	22.00

CATHEDRAL
(See Colored Pattern Glass Section.)

CHAIN

**Non-flint made by R. B. Curling and Sons,
Fort Pitt Glass Works, Pittsburgh, Pa., in the
1880's.**

Butter, covered	42.00
Cake Stand, 9"	28.50
Compote, covered	35.00

Cordial	25.00
Creamer	17.50
Goblet	20.00
Pitcher, water	35.00
Plate, 7"	15.00
Relish, oval	15.00
Sauces	
Flat	10.00
Footed	14.00
Spooner	18.50
Sugar, covered	40.00
Wine	25.00

CHAIN AND SHIELD

Non-flint, c. 1870.

Butter, covered	35.00
Cordial	20.00
Creamer	27.50
Goblet	25.00
Pitcher, water	37.50
Platter, oval, Bread Tray, handled	32.50
Spoon Holder	18.00
Sugar Bowl, covered	30.00
Sauce Dish, 4"	10.00

CHAIN WITH STAR

Non-flint, c. 1880.

Butter, covered	35.00
Cake Stand, 10½"	30.00

Cordial	20.00
Compotes	
Covered, high standard	45.00
Open, low standard	27.50
Creamer	20.00
Goblet	18.50
Pickle, oval	15.00
Pitcher, water	40.00
Plates	
7"	18.50
13½", handled, round Bread Plate	20.50
Relish	4.50
Sauces	
Flat	8.50
Footed	12.50
Spooner	20.00
Sugars	
Covered	35.00
Open	18.00
Wine	20.00

CHANDELIER
(Crown Jewels)

Non-flint. O'Hara Glass Co., Pittsburgh, Pa., c. 1880.

Bowls	
Berry	20.00
Finger	16.50
Butter, covered	40.00
Cake Stand, 10"	27.50
Celery	27.50
Compotes	
Covered, high standard	40.00
Open, high standard	35.00
Creamer	25.00
Goblet	30.00
Ink-well, (rare)	40.00
Pitcher, water	50.00
Salt	18.00
Sauces	
Flat	10.00
Footed	12.00
Shakers, pair	40.00
Spooner	25.00
Sugars	
Covered	35.00
Open	30.00

Tray, water	50.00
Tumbler	22.50
Wine	40.00

CHECKERBOARD
(Bridal Rosette)

Non-flint made by the Westmoreland Glass Co. and Specialty Co., Pennsylvania, in the 1900's. Heavily reproduced in clear and colors. Also made in milk glass. Prices are for clear; milk glass 10% more.

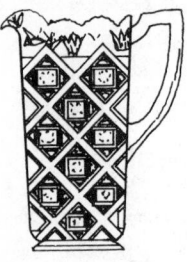

Butter, covered	20.00
Celery Tray	12.00
Celery Vase	15.00
Cheese, covered	22.00
Creamer	18.00
Goblet	15.00
Honey Dish, square footed, covered	20.00
Pitchers	
Milk	20.00
Water	25.00
Plate, 10"	11.50
Sauce, flat	6.00
Shakers, pair	18.00
Sherbet	9.00
Spooner	15.00
Sugar, covered	22.50
Tumbler, water	12.50
Wine	11.50

CLASSIC

Clear and frosted non-flint produced by Gillinder and Sons, Philadelphia, Pa., in the late 1870's–1880's. If pieces carry the log feet instead of a flat or collared base, they are worth more.

Bowl	125.00
Butter, covered on stippled log feet	175.00
Celery Vase	125.00
Compotes, covered. Can be on log feet or collared base.	150.00
Compotes, open	100.00

Creamer	100.00
Goblet	185.00
Jar, Sweetmeat	175.00
Pitcher, water	295.00
Plates	
Jas. G. Blaine	165.00
President Cleveland	165.00
Thomas H. Hendricks	165.00
John A. Logan	165.00
Warrior	150.00
Sauce	35.00
Spooner	85.00
Sugars	
Covered	150.00
Open	95.00

CLEAR DIAGONAL BAND

Non-flint, c. 1880's.

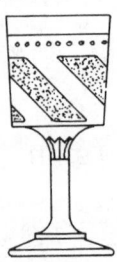

Butter, covered	37.50
Celery	22.00
Compotes	
Covered, high standard	38.50
Covered, low standard	30.00
Cordial	20.00
Creamer	20.00
Goblet	17.50
Marmalade Jar	25.00
Pitcher, water	27.50
Plate	16.50
Platter. Originally meant to be bread tray. Carries the word "Eureka"	

across it. Commemorative of Gold
Rush. 40.00
Sauce, footed 3.00
Shakers, pair 25.00
Spooner 18.50
Sugar Bowl 37.50
Wine 15.00

CLEAR RIBBON

Circa 1880's.

Bread Tray. "Give us This Day our
Daily Bread" 25.00
Butter, covered 27.50
Cake Stands
9" 20.00
10" 22.50
Celery Vase 17.50
Compote, covered, large 35.00
Creamer 27.50
Dish, oblong, covered
6" 25.00
7" 27.00
8" 28.50
Goblet 17.50
Pickle 10.00
Pitcher, water 32.50
Sauce, footed 10.00
Spooner 15.00
Sugar, covered 30.00

CLEMATIS

Non-flint, c. 1876.

Butter, covered 35.00
Creamer 35.00
Goblet 27.50
Lamp, 12", iron base 35.00
Pitcher, water, applied handle 42.00
Relish 12.00
Sauce, flat 10.00
Spooner 25.00
Sugars
Covered 40.00

Open 25.00

COIN—COLUMBIAN

**Non-flint, c. 1890. Prices listed for clear;
frosted demands approximately three times
that of clear.**

Butter, covered 125.00
Cake Stand 40.00
Celery 75.00
Compotes
Covered, 8" 75.00
Open, 7" 55.00
Creamer 65.00
Cruet 100.00
*Goblet 55.00
Pitchers
Syrup 65.00
Water 65.00
Sauce 12.00
Shakers, pair 50.00
Spooner 45.00
Sugars
Covered 60.00
Open 35.00
*Toothpick 25.00
Tray, water 40.00
*Tumbler 25.00
Wine 70.00

COIN—U.S.

Non-flint frosted and clear pattern made in Wheeling, W. Va., in 1892 for three or four months. Production was stopped by U. S. Treasury because real coins were used in the molds.

Bowls	
6″	300.00
9″	500.00
Waste	250.00
Cake Stand, 10″	360.00
Celery	
Tray	200.00
Vase	325.00
Champagne	300.00
Claret	300.00
Compotes	
Covered, 7″, high standard	400.00
Open, 7″, high standard (Quarters and halves)	225.00
Open, 7″, high standard (Quarters and dimes)	195.00
Open, 8″, high standard	325.00
Creamer	375.00
Cruet, stoppered	525.00
Epergne	500.00
Goblets	
Flair top	350.00
Regular	230.00
Lamps	
Round font	300.00
Square font	350.00
Mug, handled	350.00
Pickle	150.00
Pitchers	
Water	425.00
Syrup	475.00
Sauces	
Flat	110.00
Footed	150.00
Shakers, original tops, pair	325.00
Spooner	225.00
Sugars	
Covered	300.00
Open	125.00
*Toothpick	65.00

Trays	
Bread, 7″ x 10″	175.00
Water, 8″, rectangular	300.00
Tumbler (Dollars)	135.00
Wine	250.00

COLORADO
(See Colored Pattern Glass Section.)

COMET

Flint made by Boston and Sandwich Glass Co. in the late 1840's and early 1850's. Horn of Plenty is sometimes referred to by the same name, but is not related in design.

Butter, covered	200.00
Creamer	175.00
Goblet	75.00
Mug	130.00
Pitcher, water	375.00
Spooner	100.00
Tumblers	
Water	130.00
Whiskey	130.00

CONNECTICUT

Non-flint. One of the States' patterns made by U. S. Glass Company, c. 1895.

Bowls	
4″	10.00
6″	14.00
8″	15.00
Butter, covered	22.50
Cake Stand	30.00

Celery Tray	15.00
Celery Vase	15.00
Cracker Jar	22.50
Creamer	18.00
Dishes	
8", oblong	16.50
Olive Dish	15.00
Pitchers	
Half gallon water	30.00
Milk	22.50
Relish	10.00
Shakers, pair	15.00
Tumblers	
Lemonade, handled	10.00
Water	8.50

CORD AND TASSEL

Non-flint of the early 1870's was made by various companies, one of which was Central Glass Company.

Butter, covered	45.00
Cake Stands	
8½"	30.00
9½"	40.00
Celery	32.50
Compotes	
Covered, 10" high standard	65.00
Open, low standard	35.00
Creamer	40.00
Egg Cup	25.00
Dish, oval	12.50
Goblet	27.50
Lamp, handled	60.00
Pitcher, water, applied handle	55.00
Syrup	60.00
Sauce, flat	8.00
Spooner	22.00
Sugar, covered	42.00
Tumblers	
Whiskey, applied handle (very rare)	65.00
Water Tumbler	45.00
Wine	30.00

CORDOVA

Non-flint made by the O'Hara Glass Co., Pittsburgh, Pa., in the early 1890's. (December 16th). Some pieces have been seen in emerald green, which is rare; add 50% more to prices for green.

Bowl, Berry, covered	22.00
Bowl, Finger	16.00
Bureau Bottle	20.00
Butter, covered, handled	28.50
Celery	20.00
Compotes	
Covered, high standard	30.00
Open, low standard	25.00
Creamers	
Regular	22.50
3½" high, green	27.50
Cruet	18.50
Mug, handled	20.00
Pitchers	
Milk	28.00
Water	35.00
Punch cup	
Syrup	25.00
Nappy, handled, 6" dia.	12.00
Salt and Pepper Shaker	18.00
Salts, Individual	8.00
Sauce, Flat	7.50
Spooner	15.00
Sugar, covered	25.00
Toothpick	15.00
Tumbler	15.00

COSMOS
(See General Section.)

COTTAGE
(Dinner Bell)

Non-flint made by Adams and Company, Pittsburgh, Pa., in the late 1870's. Known to have been made in emerald green but very scarce. Add 50% more to prices for green.

Banana Stand	25.00
Bowls	
Waste or Finger	12.50

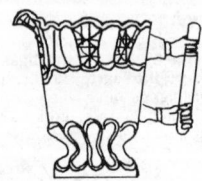

7"	20.00
9½" oval	22.50
Butter, covered	28.50
Cake Stand, 9"	30.00
Celery Vase	20.00
Compotes	
Jelly	17.50
Covered, low standard	35.00
Open, high standard	25.00
Creamer	18.50
Cruet	25.00
Cup and Saucer	30.00
Goblet	18.50
Pitcher	
Water	35.00
Milk	27.00
Syrup	30.00
Dish, oval, deep	20.00
Plates	
6", 7"	15.00
8", 9"	20.00
Relish	10.00
Sauces, flat and footed	6.50–10.00
Shakers, pair	20.00
Spooner	18.00
Sugar, covered	27.50
Tray, water	25.00
Tumbler	22.50
Wine	18.00

CROESUS
(See Colored Pattern Glass Section.)

CROW'S FOOT
(Turkey Track, Yale)

Non-flint made by McKee Glass Co., c. late 1880-1890.

Butter, covered	30.00
Cake Stand	30.00
Celery	20.00
Compotes	
Covered	35.00
Open	20.00
Cordial	15.00
Creamers	
Regular	22.50
Individual	16.00
Goblet	25.00

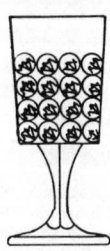

Pitcher, water	35.00
Syrup	22.50
Sauce, 5½"	9.50
Shakers, pair	25.00
Spooner	18.50
Sugar, covered	30.00
Tumbler	15.00

CRYSTAL

A flint glass pattern made by McKee Glass Company, Pittsburgh, Pa., in the early 1860's. Transitional pattern also made in non-flint. Prices given are for flint; non-flint 20% less.

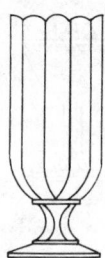

Ale glass	35.00
Bowls	
8"	50.00
10"	65.00
Butter, covered	65.00
Celery	36.00
Champagne	35.00
Compotes	
6", covered, high standard	50.00
8", covered, high standard	65.00
10", open, high standard	60.00
Cordial	32.50
Creamer	65.00
Decanter, quart	60.00
Egg Cup	30.00
Goblet	35.00
Pitcher, water	85.00
Sauce	15.00
Spooner	35.00

Sugar, covered	**75.00**
Tumblers	
Bar	**28.50**
Footed	**50.00**
Wine	**40.00**

CRYSTAL QUEEN

Non-flint made by Northwood Company, Indiana, Pa., later by Cambridge Glass Co., c. late 1890's.

Bowl, 8″	**18.50**
Butter, covered	**40.00**
Celery Tray	**18.50**
Celery Vase	**22.50**
Compote, covered, 9″, high standard	**45.00**
Creamer	**20.00**
Cruet, stoppered	**22.50**
Pitcher, water	**30.00**
Syrup	**20.00**
Spooner	**16.50**
Sugar, open	**22.00**
Tumbler	**12.00**

CRYSTAL WEDDING
(Collins)

Non-flint made by Adams Glass Co., Pittsburgh, Pa., in the late 1880's. Also found frosted and ruby stained. Heavily reproduced in clear, milk and enamel trim. Ruby pieces are valued 20% more.

Banana Stand	**55.00**
Bowl, Berry, 8″	**25.00**
Butter, covered	**39.50**
Cake Stand, 10″	**55.00**

Cake Plate, flat, large with wide edge	**45.00**
Compotes	
Covered, high and low standard	**70.00**
Open, low standard	**50.00**
Creamer	**30.00**
Goblet	**30.00**
Plates, 8″ and 10″	**25.00**
Pitcher, water	**45.00**
Salts, Individual	**18.00**
Sauces, flat	**7.50**
Shakers, pair	**30.00**
Table salt, square, large	**12.50**
Spooner	**25.00**
Sugar, covered	**40.00**
Toothpick	**30.00**
Tumbler	**35.00**

CUPID AND VENUS

Non-flint made by Hartley Glass Co., Tarentum, Pa., in the late 1870's.

Bowls		
8″, covered, footed		**75.00**
9″, oval		**32.00**
10″, footed, scalloped rim		**124.00**
Butter, covered		**50.00**
Cake plate		**32.00**
Celery Vase		**42.50**
Champagne, (rare)		**95.00**
Compotes		
Covered, 8″, high standard		**60.00**
Covered, 9½″ low standard		**48.00**
Open, 7½″ low standard		**29.00**
Open, 9¼″ high standard		**50.00**
Cordial		**50.00**
Creamer		**37.50**
Cruet, stoppered		**60.00**
Goblet		**65.00**
Marmalade Jar		**45.00**
Mugs, 2½″ and 3½″	**27.50**	**32.50**
Pitchers		
Milk		**50.00**
Water		**65.00**
Plate, 10″, round		**35.00**
Relish		**18.00**
Sauces, flat		**6.00**
Footed, 3½″, 4″ and 4½″	**7.50**	**10.00**

Spooner	35.00
Sugar, covered	55.00
Tray, Bread	32.00
Wine (scarce)	70.00

CURRANT

Non-Flint, c. 1870's.

Butter, covered	55.00
Cake Stand, 9½"	55.00
Celery Vase	42.50
Compotes	
8", high standard, covered	55.00
8", low standard	50.00
Cordial	32.50
Creamer, applied handle	50.00
Egg Cup	22.50
Goblet	23.50
Pitcher, water, applied handle	60.00
Plates, oval, 5" x 7" and 6" x 9"	25–30.00
Relish	12.50
Salt, footed	20.00
Sauces	
Flat	8.50
Footed	12.50
Spooner	27.00
Sugar, covered	50.00
Tumbler, footed	20.00
Wine	25.00

CURRIER AND IVES

Non-flint made by Bellaire Glass Co. in Findlay, Ohio in the late 1880's. Although named after the famous printmaker of its era, there was no connection between the companies. Known to have been made in color but rare. Also made in milk glass. Pieces in milk, add 20%; color, add 300%.

Bowl, oval 10" Canoe shaped	32.00
Butter, covered	50.00
Compotes	
Covered	50.00
Open	40.00
Cordial	22.00

Creamer	25.00
Cup and saucer	30.00
Dish, oval, boat shaped, 8"	30.00
Egg Cup	18.50
Goblet, plain and knob stem	18–26.00
Lamp, 9½", high standard	65.00
Pitchers	
Milk	30.00
Water	65.00
Plates	
8"	20.00
10", round with handles	30.00
Relish	12.00
Sauces	
Flat	8.50
Oval	15.00
Shakers, pair	35.00
Spooner	20.00
Sugar, covered	45.00
Syrup	43.00
Tray, water, "Balky Mule"	50.00
Water Bottle or Wine Bottle, about 12" tall, original stopper	85.00
Wine	17.50

CURTAIN

Non-flint produced by Bryce Brothers, Pittsburgh, Pa., in the 1870's through early 1880's.

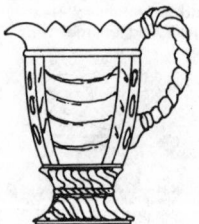

Bowl, Berry	
8"	15.00
Waste	16.50
Butter, covered	45.00
Cake Stand, 9½"	24.00
Celery Vase	27.50

Celery boat	30.00
Compotes	
Covered, high standard	40.00
Open, high standard	25.00
Creamer	35.00
Goblet	26.00
Mug, large	17.50
Pitchers	
Milk	25.00
Water	50.00
Plate, 7", square	19.50
Sauce, collared foot	12.50
Shakers, pair	25.00
Spooner	27.50
Sugars	
Covered	38.50
Open	17.50
Tumbler	23.50
Water Tray	40.00

CUT LOG
(Cat's Eye and Block)

Non-flint, c. 1880's.

Bowls
7" and 10"	12-15.00
10", deep, footed and scalloped	50.00
Butter, covered	50.00
Cake Stands	
large	85.00
small	40.00
Celery Vase	40.00
Compotes	
Covered, 5½"	40.00
Covered, 7¼"	55.00
Open, 7", low standard	20.00
Open, 8", high standard	35.00
Open, 10", high standard	47.50
Cracker Jar	30.00
Creamers	
3"	12.50
5"	42.00
Cruet, original patterned, stopper	40.00
Goblet	35.00
Honey Dish, square	30.00
Mug	21.00
Mustard Jar	22.50
Nappy, handled	13.00
Pitcher, water, applied handle	85.00
Relish	22.50
Sauces	

Flat	7.50
Footed	25.00
Shakers, pair	60.00
Spooner	25.00
Sugar, covered	50.00
Tumbler	25.00
Vase, 16½"	40.00
Wine	25.00

DAHLIA
(See Colored Pattern Glass Section.)

DAISY AND BUTTON
(See Colored Pattern Glass Section.)

DAISY AND BUTTON WITH CROSS BARS
(See Colored Pattern Glass Section.)

DAISY AND BUTTON WITH NARCISSUS
(Daisy and Button with Clear Lily)

Sometimes found with flowers flashed with cranberry flashing and pieces trimmed in gold. Non-flint made in late 1890's. Later made by Indiana Glass Company, Dunkirk, Ind., into 1920's. Color 25% more.

Bowl, 6" x 9¼", oval footed	40.00
Butter, covered	35.00
Celery	22.50
Compote, open	27.00
Creamer	18.00
Decanter, stoppered	32.00
Goblet	20.00
Pitcher, water	60.00
Punch cup	8.00
Sauces	
Flat	6.00
Footed, 4"	8.50
Shakers, pair	25.00
Spooner	20.00
Sugar, covered	28.50
Tray, water or wine, 10"	27.50
Tumbler	15.00
*Wine	15.00

DAISY AND BUTTON WITH "V" ORNAMENT
(See Colored Pattern Glass Section.)

DAKOTA
(Baby Thumbprint; Thumbprint Band)

Non-flint made by Ripley and Company, Pittsburgh, Pa., in the late 1880's and early 1890's. Later reissued by U. S. Glass Company as one of the States patterns. The prices listed are for etched fern and berry. Often found with Oak Leaf etching. Sometimes comes with ruby stain on pieces. Some very rare pieces were made in cobalt blue, which would be 300% more. Plain items command 50% less than prices given.

Bowl, Berry	
8"	27.50
Finger	30.00
Butter, covered	37.50
Cake Stand, 10½"	55.00
Castor Set, wire frame and handle, 2	
oil bottles and salt and pepper	165.00
Celery	35.00
Compotes, covered	
5" and 6", Jelly Compotes	40–50.00
12" (used in bakery trade)	85.00
Creamer	60.00
Cruet	45.00
Egg Cup	22.00
Goblet	32.50
Mug	30.00
Pitcher, water	72.50
Sauces	
Flat	10.00
Footed	12.00
Salt Shakers, pair	65.00
Spooner	26.00
Sugars	
Covered	50.00
Open	25.00
Tumbler	30.00
Tray, water (scarce)	55.00
Wine	30.00

DEER AND DOG

Non-flint, c. 1870's. Frosted Dog finial and comes with etching.

Butter, covered	125.00
Celery Vase	75.00
Compotes	
Covered, 13", high standard	125.00
Open, 7½", high standard	65.00
Creamer	65.00
Goblet, straight sided and U-shaped	45–50.00
Marmalade Jar, covered	100.00
Mug	35.00
Pitcher, water, applied handle	150.00
Sauce, footed	20.00
Spooner	55.00
Sugar, covered	125.00
Wine	40.00

DEER AND PINE TREE
(Deer and Doe)

Non-flint pattern, made in the Pittsburgh area in the 1880's. Although this pattern has been reported to have been made in colors, it is seldom encountered except in the platters. Add approximately 50% more for colors.

Bowl, Waste	30.00
Butter, covered	50.00
Cake Stand	70.00
Celery Vase	50.00
Compotes, open	
7" and 9" high standard	55.00
8" square, high standard	45.00

Creamer	50.00
*Goblet	37.00
Marmalade Jar, covered	45.00
Mugs	
large	26.00
small	14.00
Pickle	22.50
Pitcher, water	75.00
Platter, 8″ x 13″	82.00
Sauces	
Flat	12.50
Footed	20.00
Spooner	40.00
Sugars	
Covered	50.00
Open	35.00
Tray, water, 9″ x 15″	75.00

DELAWARE
(See Colored Pattern Glass Section.)

DEW AND RAINDROP

Non-flint, made in the 1880's. In the 1890's reissued by the Kokomo Glass Co., Kokomo, Ind., of lesser quality without tiny dew drops on stem. Prices listed for the earlier, 1880 pattern.

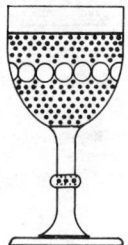

Bowl, Berry	39.50
Butter, covered	52.50
Cake Stand, 9″	40.00
Compote, covered, small	45.00
Creamer	35.00
*Goblet	35.00
Pitcher, water	60.00
Punch Cup	6.00
Sauce, flat	10.00
Shakers, pair	40.00
Spooner	25.00
Sugar, covered	35.00
Tumbler	12.00
*Wine	25.00

DEWDROP
(See Colored Pattern Glass Section.)

DEWDROP IN POINTS

Non-flint made by Brilliant Glass Works, Brilliant, Ohio, in the late 1870's, and Greensburg Glass Co., Greensburg, Pa., after 1889.

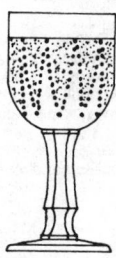

Cake Stand, rimless	35.00
Compotes	
Covered	35.00
Open	22.50
Creamer	20.00
Goblet	25.00
Pickle	15.00
Pitcher, water	35.00
Plate, 12″, handled with vine border	27.50
Platter, handled, 9″ x 11¾″	28.00
Sauces	
Flat	7.50
Footed	10.00
Spooner	17.50
Sugars	
Covered	32.50
Open	18.00
Wine	17.50

DEWDROP WITH STAR

Non-flint made by Campbell, Jones and Co., Pittsburgh, Pa., in the late 1870's. There was no Goblet made originally with this pattern.

Bowls, on collared bases, 7"	18.50
Butter, covered	55.00
Cake Stands	
9"	55.00
Very large	65.00
Compotes, covered with large domed lids	
High standard	75.00
Low standard	65.00
Open, high standard	50.00
Cheese Dish, covered, large domed	75.00
Creamer, applied handle	38.00
Honey Dish, plate with large domed cover	75.00
Lamp, patented, 1876	100.00
Pitcher, water, applied handle	85.00
*Plates	
*4¼"	16.50
*7"	20.00
9"	25.00
Relish	12.50
*Salts, footed	20.00
Sauces	
Flat	10.00
Footed	12.50
Spooner	20.00
Sugar, covered, domed lid as on Compotes and Butter	32.50
*Tray, Bread, sheaf of wheat in center	25.00

DEWEY
(See Colored Pattern Glass Section.)

DIAGONAL BAND WITH FAN

Non-flint, c. 1880's.

Butter, covered	35.00
Celery	20.00
Champagne	18.00
Compotes	
Covered, high standard	45.00
Open, low standard	25.00
Creamer	25.00
Goblet	19.00

Marmalade Jar	20.00
Pickle	15.00
Pitchers	
Milk	25.00
Water	50.00
Plates	
6"	10.00
7"	15.00
8"	18.00
Sauces, footed	3.00
Shakers, pair	25.00
Spooner	20.00
Sugar, covered	32.00
Wine	15.00

DIAMOND AND SUNBURST

Non-flint, c. 1874.

Butter, covered	35.00
Butter Pat	8.00
Cake Stand	30.00
Celery	20.00
Compote, covered, high standard	40.00
Creamer, applied handle	30.00
Egg Cup	15.00
Goblet	20.00
Relish	12.00
Salt, footed	12.00
Sauce, flat	7.50
Spooner	16.00
Sugar, covered	30.00
Tumbler	15.00
Wine	15.00

DIAMOND CUT WITH LEAF

Non-flint, c. 1880. Scarce in color; add 100% more.

Butter, covered	35.00
Cordial	22.00
Creamer	20.00
Goblet	22.00
Mug, 2½", handled	21.00
Plates	
7"	15.00

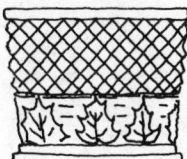

9½"	20.00
Spooner	15.00
Sugars	
Covered	30.00
Open	17.50
Wine	22.00

DIAMOND MEDALLION
(Grand)

Non-flint, c. 1880's.

Butter, covered	
Flat	25.00
Footed	35.00
Cake Stand	
8"	20.00
10"	35.00
Celery Vase	18.50
Compotes	
7", high standard, covered	35.00
9", high standard, open	25.00
Creamer	21.00
Goblet	20.00
Pitcher, water	35.00
Plate, 10"	15.00
Relish, 7½", oval	10.00
Syrup	50.00
Sauces	
Flat	7.50
Footed	10.00
Spooner	17.50
Sugar, covered	20.00
Wine	20.00

DIAMOND POINT

Flint originally made by Boston and Sandwich

Glass Co., in the 1830–1840 period. Rare in color, add 400%. Add 200% for milk white.

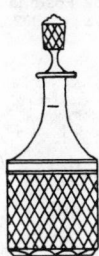

Bowls	
7", covered	55.00
8", covered	55.00
7", open	40.00
8", open	40.00
Butter, covered	80.00
Cake Stand, 14"	185.00
Candlesticks	150.00
Celery, K-S	65.00
Champagne	65.00
Claret, K-S	60.00
Compotes	
Covered, 6", high standard	85.00
Covered, 8", high standard	100.00
Open, 7½", low standard	48.00
Creamer	85.00
Decanters	
Bar lip, pint	55.00
Bar lip, quart	75.00
Stoppered, pint	75.00
Stoppered, quart	100.00
Egg Cup	18.00
Goblet	45.00
Honey	20.00
Mustard, with Brittania cover	18.00
Pitchers	
Half pint	55.00
Pint	75.00
Quart	145.00
Three pints	100.00
Plates	
6"	30.00
8"	50.00
Pepper, with cut neck, Brittania screw cap	20.00
Salt, Master	50.00
Sauce, 5¼"	15.00
Spooner	40.00
Syrup	75.00
Sugar, covered	70.00
Tumblers	
Bar	60.00
Jelly	35.00
Whiskey, handled	55.00
Wine	40.00

DIAMOND PYRAMIDS

Non-flint made by Fostoria Glass Company, Moundsville, W. Va., c. 1902.

Bowl, Berry	12.50
Butter, covered	18.50
Celery Vase	16.00
Creamer	17.50
Cruet, with facetted stopper	20.00
Pitcher, water	30.00
Salt Shakers, pair	18.00
Spooner	12.00
Sauce	6.00
Sugar, covered	18.50
Toothpick	15.00
Tumbler	12.50

DIAMOND QUILTED
(See Colored Pattern Glass Section.)

DIAMOND THUMBPRINT

Flint attributed to Boston and Sandwich Glass Co. and other factories from 1840 to the 1850's.

Bowl, waste	85.00
Butter, covered	145.00
Celery	175.00
Champagne, (scarce)	225.00
Compotes	
Plain, open, 8″, low standard	45.00
Scalloped, open 8″, low standard	95.00
Cordial	175.00

Creamer	150.00
Decanters	
Pint, no stopper	75.00
Quart, original stopper	150.00
*Goblet, (rare)	350.00+
Honey Dish	15.00
Pitcher, water, (scarce)	300.00+
Sauce	15.00
Spooner	75.00
Sugar, covered	160.00
Tumblers	
Water	95.00
Whiskey, 3″	125.00
Whiskey, handled	300.00
Wine, (scarce)	225.00

DOLPHIN

Non-flint, c. 1880.

Bowl, 8″	100.00
Butter, covered	150.00
Candlestick	125.00
Compote, open, high standard	85.00
Creamer	100.00
Goblet	95.00
Pitcher, water	150.00
Spooner	75.00
Sugar, covered	100.00
Toothpick	35.00

DOUBLE RIBBON

Non-flint, c. 1870. Made by King Glass Co.

Butter, covered	40.00
Celery	27.50
Compotes	
Covered, high standard	45.00
Open, high standard	25.00
Creamer	27.50
Egg Cup	22.50
Goblet	32.50
Pitcher, water	45.00
Relish	15.00
Sauce, footed	10.00

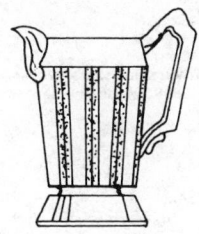

Spooner	27.50
Sugar, covered	28.50
Tray, Bread	22.00

DOUBLE SPEAR

Non-flint, c. 1880's.

Butter, covered, flat	27.50
Celery	20.00
Compote, covered, high standard	40.00
Creamer	25.00
Egg Cup	16.50
Goblet	18.50
Pickle	12.50
Pitcher, water	40.00
Sauce, footed	12.50
Spooner	17.50
Sugar, covered	25.00

DOUBLE WEDDING RING

Flint, c. 1860.

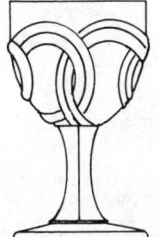

Champagne	75.00
Decanter	125.00
*Goblet	55.00
Syrup, original top	75.00
Tumbler, Bar	67.50
*Wine	65.00

DRAPERY
(Lace)

Non-flint made by Doyle and Co., Pittsburgh, Pa. in the 1870's. Reportedly made by Sandwich Glass Company at an earlier period.

Butter, covered	45.00
Creamer	
Applied handle	45.00
Molded handle	25.00
Egg Cup	18.50
Goblet	30.00
Pitcher, water	45.00
Plate, 6"	20.00
Sauce, flat	8.50
Spooner	35.00
Sugar, covered	37.00

EGG IN SAND

Non-flint, c. 1880's. Has also been seen occasionally in amber, but rare. Add 10% for amber.

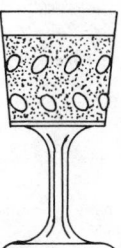

Butter, covered	40.00
Cake Stand	40.00
Compote, covered	45.00

Creamer	22.50
Goblet	30.00
Jam Jar	35.00
Pitchers	
Milk	30.00
Water	42.50
Punch Cup	20.00
Relish	17.50
Sauce, flat	7.50
Shakers, pair	35.00
Spooner	25.00
Sugar, covered	33.50
Tray	
Bread	25.00
Water	37.50
Tumbler	17.50
Wine	20.00

EGYPTIAN

Non-flint, c. 1870.

Butter, covered	55.00
Celery Vase	40.00
Compotes	
Covered, 7", high standard	75.00
Open, 6", low standard	50.00
Creamer	32.00
Goblet	45.00
Honey	14.50
Pickle, oval	28.00
Pitcher, water	100.00
Plate, 12", handled, Pyramids	45.00
Relish	25.00
Sauce, footed, 4½"	12.00
Spooner	35.00
Sugars	
Covered	45.00
Open	25.00
Trays, Bread	
9" x 12", "Cleopatra"	42.00
"Salt Lake Temple"	250.00 +

EMERALD GREEN HERRINGBONE
(See GREEN HERRINGBONE.)

EMPRESS
(Double Arch #2)

Made by Riverside Glass Works, Wellsburg, W. Va., c. 1898. Made in clear and emerald green.

Bowl, Berry	25.00
Butter, covered	50.00
Celery Tray	40.00
Creamer	42.50
Cruet	25.00
Nappy, handled	15.00
Relish	30.00
Salt and Pepper Shakers	30.00
Pitcher, water	80.00
Sauces	18.00
Sugar Shaker	25.00
Tumbler	20.00

ESTHER #2
(Tooth and Claw)

Non-flint made by Riverside Glass Works of Wellsburgh, W. Va., c. 1896. Add 100% for emerald green.

Bowl, 8"	25.00
Butter, covered	65.00
Cake Stand, 10½"	45.00
Celery Vase	35.00
Compotes	
Covered, 5", low standard (Jelly)	40.00
Open, 6", high standard	30.00
Creamer	85.00
Cruet, stoppered	18.00

Goblet	35.00
Pitcher, water	100.00
Sauce, footed	15.00
Salt and Pepper Shakers, pair	70.00
Spooner	30.00
Sugar, covered	45.00
Toothpick	30.00
Tumbler	20.00
Wine	25.00

EUGENIE

Flint made by McKee Glass Co., Pittsburgh, Pa., c. 1850.

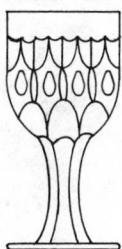

Butter, covered	75.00
Castor Bottle	25.00
Celery	75.00
Champagne	55.00
Compote, covered, on high standard	100.00
Cordial	45.00
Dish, covered, 7″ and 9″, collared base	95.00
Egg Cup	45.00
Goblet	50.00
Sauce, flat	18.50
Sugar, covered, Dolphin finial	75.00
Tumbler	40.00
Wine	45.00

EUREKA

Flint made in Pittsburgh, Pa., in the late 1860's.

Bowl, 8″	30.00
Butter, covered	65.00
Compotes	
7″ and 8″, covered, high standard	85.00
7″ and 8″, open, low standard	45.00
Cordial	35.00
Creamer	50.00
Egg Cup	32.50
Goblet	30.00
Plate, Bread	40.00

Salt, footed	20.00
Sauce	12.50
Spooner	30.00
Sugar, covered	55.00
Tumbler, footed	25.00
Wine	35.00

EXCELSIOR

Flint made by several firms from 1850's–1860's. Quality and design vary.

Bowl, 10″, open	125.00
Bitters Bottle	25.00
Butter, covered	100.00
Candlestick	125.00
Celery Vase	95.00
Claret	45.00
Compotes	
Covered, low standard	125.00
Open, high standard	85.00
Cordial	40.00
Covered Pickle Jar	45.00
Creamer	70.00
Egg Cups	
Double	30.00
Single	35.00
Goblets	
plain, either size	45.00
with Maltese Cross	50.00
Pitchers	
Milk, (scarce)	200.00+
Water, (scarce)	150.00
Salt, footed	35.00
Spooner	75.00
Sugar, covered	85.00
Tumblers	

Bar	35.00
Footed	55.00
Jelly	35.00
Whiskey with Maltese Cross	65.00
Wine	40.00

EYEWINKER

Non-flint made in Findlay, Ohio, in 1889. This pattern reportedly made by Dalzell, Gilmore and Leighton Glass Co., who were organized in 1883 in West Virginia, moved to Findlay, Ohio in 1888. It was made originally only in clear glass; colors have been reproduced. A goblet was not made originally in this pattern.

Banana Dish	95.00
Bowl, 9"	35.00
Butter, covered	65.00
Cake Stand	62.50
Celery	42.50
Compotes	
Covered, 6"	28.50
Open, 7¼", with fluted edge	55.00
Jelly	20.00
Compote with turned up side	45.00
Creamer	30.00
Cruet	30.00
Lamp, Kerosene	75.00
Nappies	9.00
Pitchers	
Milk	35.00
Water	50.00
Plate	
7½"	25.00
Square, with upturned rims	30.00
*Sauce, flat	9.00
Syrup, with pewter top	75.00
*Shakers, pair	35.00
*Spooner	19.50
Sugars	
Covered	50.00
Open	22.50
*Toothpick	15.00
*Tumbler	17.50

FAN WITH DIAMOND

Non-flint, c. 1870.

Butter, covered	35.00
Compotes	
Covered, high standard	45.00
Covered, low standard	35.00
Cordial	17.50
Creamer	17.50
Egg Cup	17.50
Goblet	22.00
Pitcher, water	35.00
Relish	15.00
Sauce, flat	10.00
Spooner	22.50
Sugars	
Covered	28.50
Open	17.50
Wine	35.00

FEATHER
(Doric)

Non-flint made in Indiana in 1896. Later the pattern was reissued with variations and quality. Also rare in green, approximately three times the price of clear.

Banana Dish	60.00
Bowls	
8", square	18.00
9½", oval	15.00
Butter, covered	38.00
Cake Stands	

8″	27.00
9½″	30.00
Compotes	
Covered, 8¼″, low standard	50.00
Open, high standard	35.00
Jelly, 4½″	16.50
Cordial	65.00
Creamer	22.50
Cruet, stoppered	38.50
Goblet	50.00
Marmalade Jar	75.00
Pitchers	
Milk	40.00
Water	50.00
Plates, 10″, 8″ and 6″	18.00
Honey Dish, 3½″	15.00
Relish	15.00
Sauces	
Flat, 4″	10.00
Footed, 5½″	17.50
Spooner	17.50
Sugar, covered	28.00
Toothpick	35.00
Tumbler	30.00
Wine, straight and scalloped border	25–40.00

FESTOON

Non-flint, c. late 1880's. No goblet was made originally in this pattern.

Bowls	
4¼″	10.00
7″	16.50
9″, rectangular	20.00
Butter, covered	40.00
Cake Stand, 10″	30.00
Compotes	
Covered, high standard	50.00
Open, high standard	28.50
Creamer	20.00
Pickle Jar	40.00
Pitcher, water	50.00
Plates, 7¼″, 8¼″ (scarce)	35.00
Sauce, flat	8.50
Spooner	20.00
Sugars	
Covered	50.00
Open	30.00
Tray, water, 10″	32.00

Tumbler	20.00
Wine	17.50

FINE CUT
(See Colored Pattern Glass Section.)

FINE CUT AND PANEL
(See Colored Pattern Glass Section.)

FINE RIB

Flint made by New England Glass Co. in the 1860's. Later made in non-flint. Prices listed are for flint.

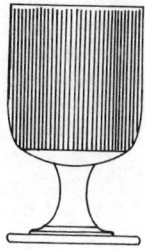

Bitters Bottle	65.00
Bowl, 7″, covered	85.00
Butter, covered	100.00
Castor Bottle	25.00
Celery	50.00
Champagne	50.00
Compotes	
Covered, 7″, 8″, high standard	125.00
Covered, 7″, 8″, low standard	100.00
Open, 8″, low standard	65.00
Open, 9″, 10″, low standard	75.00
Cordial	60.00
Creamer, applied handle	125.00
Decanters	
Bar lip, pint	55.00
Bar lip, quart	65.00
With stopper, pint	100.00
With stopper, quart	135.00
Egg Cup	33.50
Goblet	50.00
Lamp	150.00
Mug	55.00
Pitcher, water	175.00
Plates, 6″ and 7″	50.00
Salts	
Covered, footed	85.00
Individual	20.00
Sauce	16.50
Spooner	60.00
Sugar, covered	85.00
Tumbler, Bar	40.00

Tumble-up	125.00
Whiskey, handled	85.00
Wine	38.00

FISH SCALE
(Coral)

Non-flint made by Bryce Brothers, Pittsburgh, Pa., in the mid-1880's.

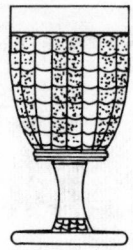

Bowls		
Covered, 7¾″		37.50
Open, 8″		16.00
Waste		15.00
Butter, covered		45.00
Cake Stand, 9″ and 10½″		35.00
Celery		25.00
Compote, Jelly		13.50
Compote, open, 7″		25.00
Creamer		30.00
Goblet		26.00
Lamp, Finger		75.00
Mug, large		35.00
Pitchers		
Water		30.00
Milk		28.00
Plates		
7″, round		25.00
8″, square		30.00
Sauces		
Footed		10.00
Flat, round		5.00
Flat, square		6.00
Shakers, pair		40.00
Spooner		20.00
Sugar, covered		40.00
Tumbler		22.50

FLAT DIAMOND

Non-flint, c. 1870's.

Butter, covered	47.50
Celery	35.00
Creamer	36.50
Goblet	10.00

Pitcher, water	45.00
Sauces	
Flat	8.50
Footed	12.50
Spooner	26.50
Sugars	
Covered	35.00
Open	25.00
Wine	20.00

FLEUR DE LYS AND DRAPE
(Fleur de Lys and Tassel)

Non-flint made by U. S. Glass Co., c. 1892. Comes in clear and emerald green, with occasional gold trim. Also made in milk glass but rare. Made in many pieces and forms. Add 20% more for green.

Bowls	12.00
Butter, covered	38.00
Cake Stand	45.00
Compotes	
Covered	25.00
Open	18.00
Dish, Honey, square, covered	40.00
Goblet	30.00
Cruet, stoppered, various sizes	37.50
Syrup, with metal top	40.00
Creamer	22.50
Pitcher, water	50.00
Plates, 8″	22.50
Sauces	
Flat	10.00
Footed	12.00
Nappy	12.00

Relish, boat shaped	15.00
Mustard Jar, covered	18.00
Water Bottle	38.00
Tumbler	22.50
Wine	20.00

FLOWER POT
(Potted Plant)

Non-flint, c. 1880's.

Butter, covered	50.00
Cake Stand, 10½"	45.00
Compote, 7", covered	45.00
Creamer	35.00
Goblet	25.00
Pitchers	
Milk	35.00
Water	50.00
Sauces	
Footed	8.50
Square	10.00
Salt Shaker, (1)	23.00
Spooner	25.00
Sugars	
Covered	40.00
Open	25.00
Tray, Bread	40.00

FLUTE

Research has proven there were more than 15 Flute variants produced in flint and non-flint glass from the 1850's through 1880's. Some of the flint variants are Banded Flute, Bessimer Flute, New England Flute, etc., all with comparable prices. Prices listed are for flint.

Ale Glass	28.00
Candlesticks, 4", pair	35.00
Champagne	26.50
Compote, open, 8½", low standard	30.00
Creamer	35.00
Decanter, Bar lip, quart	45.00
Egg Cups	
Double	25.00
Single	17.50
Goblet	25.00
Lamp, Whale Oil	65.00
Mug	40.00
Pitchers	
Milk	30.00
Water	50.00
Sauce, flat	8.50
Sugar, open	25.00
Tumbler	20.00
Whiskey, handled	20.00
Wine	20.00

FROSTED CIRCLE

Produced by Bryce Bros., Pittsburgh, Pa., in the late 1870's. Later by U. S. Glass Co. in the late 1890's.

Bowls	
Covered, 7", 8"	30.00
Open, 8", 9"	20.00
Butter, covered	55.00
Cake Stand, 10"	50.00
Compotes	
Covered, 7", 8", high standard	65.00
Open, 10", high standard	45.00
Creamer	45.00
Cruet, stoppered	55.00
*Goblet	35.00
Pitcher, water	65.00
Plates	
4"	16.50
7"	25.00
9"	28.50
Relish, oval	20.00
Sauces	
Flat	10.00
Footed	12.50

Shakers, pair	50.00
Spooner	22.00
Sugar, covered	45.00
Tumbler	20.00
Wine	35.00

FROSTED LEAF

Flint, c. 1850's. Listed as being produced by Portland Glass Co. later, between 1863 and 1874.

Butter, covered	150.00
Celery Vase	125.00
Champagne	175.00
Compote, covered	250.00
Creamer	125.00
Decanter, stoppered, quart	250.00
Egg Cup	95.00
*Goblet	79.50
Pitcher, water, (very scarce)	350.00+
Salt	50.00
Sauce	25.00
Spooner	75.00
Sugars	
Covered	125.00
Open	65.00
Tumbler	150.00
Wine	20.00

FROSTED RIBBON

Non-flint made by Bakewell, Pears and Co., Pittsburgh, Pa., in the 1870's. Later made by George Duncan and Sons, Pittsburgh, Pa.

Butter, covered	30.00
Celery	27.50
Champagne	22.50
Compotes	
Covered, high standard	35.00
Open, low standard	17.50
Creamer	43.00
Egg Cup	22.50
*Goblet	25.00
Pitcher, water	27.50
Salt, footed	12.00

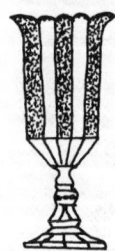

Sauce, footed	15.00
Spooner	35.00
Sugar, covered	55.00
Tumbler	22.50
Wine	20.00

FROSTED STORK

Non-flint made by Crystal Glass Co., Bridgeport, Ohio, c. 1880. Now reproduced.

Bowl, waste	42.00
Butter, covered	65.00
Creamer	50.00
Goblet	55.00
Marmalade Jar	55.00
Pitcher, water	125.00
Platter, 9″	43.00
Sauce, flat	15.50
Spooner	55.00
Sugar, covered	40.00
Trays, Bread, 9″, oval	50.00
Water Tray	35.00

GALLOWAY
(Virginia #2)

Non-flint made by United States Glass Co., 1904. Clear glass with gold trim, sometimes with cranberry flashing. See Introduction for more about this pattern.

Bowls	
Berry	15.00
Punch, 15¼″	100.00

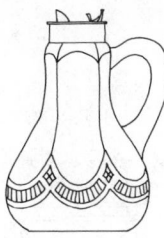

Butter, covered, large and small . . .	25–32.00
Cake Plate	25.00
Carafe, water	48.00
Celery	25.00
Creamer	35.00
Dish, oval	30.00
Dish, oblong	18.00
Goblet	30.00
Lemonade, handled	27.50
Nappy, handled	15.00
Punch Cup	8.50
Plate, round	12.00
Pitcher, water	
Two quart	45.00
Small milk tankard	40.00
Salt and Pepper Shakers, pair	30.00
Sugar, covered	28.00
Sauces	
4¼″, footed	10.00
3½″, flat	6.00
Spooner	22.00
Toothpick	20.00
Tumbler	25.00
Wine	25.00

GARDEN OF EDEN
(Lotus and Serpent)

Non-flint, c. 1870's.

Bowl, 4½″ x 7″, oval	17.50
Butter, covered	75.00
Cake Stand, 11½″	50.00
Celery	25.00
Compotes	

Covered, 10″, high standard	75.00
Open, 10″, high standard	45.00
Creamer	38.00
Cup	18.50
Goblet	60.00
Mug	48.00
Nappy, handled	9.50
Pickle, oval	20.00
Pitcher, water	40.00
Plate, 6½″, handled	20.00
Salt, Master	30.00
Sauce, flat	12.00
Spooner	22.00
Sugars	
Covered	45.00
Open	28.00
Toothpick	21.00
Tray, Bread	50.00

GARFIELD DRAPE

Non-flint pattern issued in 1881 by Adams and Co., Pittsburgh, Pa., after the assassination of President Garfield.

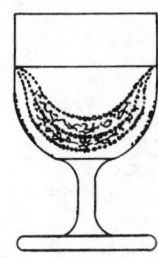

Bowl, 6″	25.00
Butter, covered	65.00
Cake Stand, 9½″	55.00
Celery	35.00
Compotes	
Covered, 8″, high standard	70.00
Open, 8½″, low standard	32.50
Creamer	40.00
Goblet	32.50
Pitchers	
Milk	65.00
Water	70.00
Plates	
11″, Memorial (Plume border. "It	
is God's Way")	50.00
11″, Star center	37.00
Bread Plate	35.00
Relish, oval	18.00
Sauces	
Flat	9.50
Footed	12.00
Spooner	25.00

Sugars		
Covered		50.00
Open		17.50
Tumbler		22.50

Sugars		
Covered		35.00
Open		29.00
Tumbler		29.50

GIBSON GIRL

Non-flint, early 1904. Made by Kokomo Glass Company.

Butter, covered	65.00
Creamer	50.00
Pitcher, water	235.00
Plate, 10″	75.00
Salt Shaker, single	40.00
Spooner	50.00
Sugar, covered	55.00
Tumbler	65.00

GOOD LUCK
(See HORSESHOE.)

GOOSEBERRY

Non-flint of the 1880's. Made at Boston & Sandwich Glass Co. and others in clear and milk glass. Reproduced in milk glass.

Butter, covered	42.50
Compote, covered, 8″, high standard	50.00
Creamer	32.00
Goblet	22.00
Mug	22.50
Pickles	15.00
Pitcher, water	55.00
Sauce, flat	8.00
Spooner	22.50
Syrup, applied handle	57.50

GOTHIC

Flint made by McKee & Bros. in the 1860's. Possibly reissued in the 1870's.

Bowl, 8″	50.00
Fruit Bowl	95.00
Butter, covered	85.00
Castor Bottle	20.00
Celery Vase	80.00
Champagne	75.00
Compotes	
Covered, 8″	150.00
Open, 7″	65.00
Cordial	55.00
Creamer	75.00
Egg Cup	42.00
Goblet	35.00
Sauce, flat	18.00
Spooner	35.00
Sugars	
Covered	75.00
Open	40.00
Tumbler	45.00
Wine	85.00

GRAPE AND FESTOON WITH STIPPLED LEAF

Non-flint made by Doyle & Company, Pittsburgh, Pa., in the early 1870's.

Bowl	14.50
Butter, covered	40.00
Celery Vase	39.50
Creamer, applied handle	35.00
Egg Cup	18.50
Goblet	15.00
Lamp, Oil, 7½″	50.00
Mug	18.00
Pitchers	
Milk, applied handle	50.00

Water, applied handle	65.00
Plate, 6″	8.00
Relish	12.50
Salt, footed	17.50
Sauce, flat, 4″	8.00
Spooner	22.50
Sugar, covered	35.00
Wine	20.00

GRAPE BAND

Issued in flint in the late 1850's; non-flint in late 1860's. Prices listed are for non-flint glass. Flint glass prices are approximately 100% more.

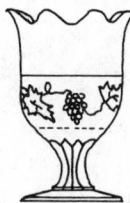

Butter, covered	35.00
Compotes, covered	
High standard	40.00
Low standard	25.00
Low, open, high standard	35.00
Creamer	25.00
Egg Cup	15.00
Goblet	18.50
Pickle	12.50
Honey Dish	7.50
Pitcher, water	50.00
Salt, footed	12.50
Sauce, flat	7.50
Spooner	20.00
Sugars	
Covered	35.00
Open	17.50
Wine	17.50

GRAPE WITH THUMBPRINT BAND

Non-flint, c. 1890's.

Bowl	35.00
Butter, covered	35.00
Celery	22.50
Creamer	25.00
Goblet	33.00
Pitcher, water	37.50
Sauce, flat	7.50
Spooner	15.00
Syrup	27.50
Sugar, covered	30.00

GRASSHOPPER
(Long Spear)

Not all pieces carry the grasshopper on the side in the motif. Pieces with insect bring more in price, 20% less without insect.

Bowls	
Covered	27.50
Footed	26.00
Butter, covered	50.00
Celery	27.50
Compote, covered, 8½″, high standard	55.00
Creamer	27.50
Marmalade Jar, covered (with insect)	115.00
Pickle	16.00
Pitcher, water	65.00

Sauce, footed	13.50
Spooner	22.50
Sugars	
Covered	40.00
Open	20.00

GREEN HERRINGBONE
(Panelled Herringbone, Florida States' pattern.)

Non-flint made by U. S. Glass Co., c. late 1880's–1890's. Found in emerald green, clear and milk glass. Should always be called Green Herringbone. Prices for clear; add 150% more for green and milk.

Bowls	
6″	22.00
9″	30.00
Butter, covered	25.00
Cake Stand	30.00
Celery	15.00
Compotes, open	
5½″	22.50
6½″, square, high standard	35.00
Cordial	22.50
Creamer	17.50
Cruet	30.00
Goblets	
Buttermilk	20.00
Regular	15.00
Pitchers	
Milk	18.50
Water	40.00
Plates	
7½″, square	10.00
9¼″	18.00
Relishes	
6″, square	12.00
8½″, square	14.00
Shakers, pair	25.00
Sauce	6.50
Spillholder	22.50
Spooner	22.50
Syrup	25.00
Sugars	
Covered	22.00
Open	15.00

Tumbler	12.00
Wine	14.00

HAIRPIN

Flint made by Boston & Sandwich Co. in the 1850's. Add 100% for milk glass.

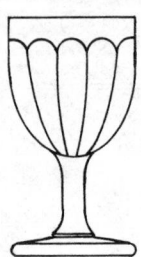

Butter, covered	75.00
Celery	60.00
Champagne	50.00
Compote, open, low standard	25.00
Compote, covered	85.00
Creamer	72.50
Decanter	35.00
Egg Cup	28.50
Goblet	35.00
Pitcher, water	125.00
Salt, footed	18.50
Sauce, flat	12.50
Spooner	35.00
Sugars	
Covered	60.00
Open	35.00
Wine	25.00

HAMILTON AND HAMILTON WITH LEAF

Flint, c. 1869. Both have same values.

Butter, covered	75.00
Celery	65.00

Compotes
Covered, high standard	100.00
Open, low standard	55.00
Cordial	50.00

Creamers
Applied handle	75.00
Molded handle	50.00
Egg Cup	25.00
Goblet	40.00
Honey	15.00
Pitcher, water	150.00
Plate, 6″	45.00
Salt, footed	30.00
Sauce, flat	15.00
Spooner	24.00
Sugar, covered	65.00

Tumblers
Water	65.00
Whiskey, handled	95.00
Wine	100.00

HAND
(Pennsylvania #2)

Made by O'Hara Glass Co., Pittsburgh, Pa., c. 1880's. Covered pieces have a hand holding bar finial, hence the name. Pieces with original lids are rare.

Bowls
8″	22.50
10″	27.50
Butter, covered	50.00
Cake Stand	38.00
Celery	50.00

Compotes
Covered, high standard	85.00
Open, high standard	43.00
Creamer	40.00
Goblet	30.00
Marmalade Jar, covered	38.50
Pickle	17.50
Pitcher, water	75.00
Platter, 8″ x 10½″, or Bread Tray	30.00

Sauces
Flat	10.00
Footed	12.50
Spooner	25.00

Sugar, covered	85.00
Wine	38.00

HARP

Flint glass made by Bryce Bros., Pittsburgh, Pa., in the late 1840's and early 1850's.

Butter, covered	125.00
Compotes, covered, 6″, low standard	175.00
Goblet, (rare)	350.00 +
Honey	20.00
Lamp, Hand	75.00
Salt, footed	38.50
Spillholder	60.00

HEART WITH THUMBPRINT
(Bull's Eye in Heart)

Non-flint, c. 1899. Occasionally found in emerald green. Extremely rare in cobalt blue. Prices are for clear. Add 100% for emerald green; 200% for cobalt blue.

Banana Boat	37.50

Bowls
7″	25.00
8″	30.00
9″	35.00
Barber Bottle, (rare)	60.00
Butter, covered	40.00
Carafe, water	48.50
Card Tray	17.50
Celery	39.00
Compote, 8½″, high standard	48.00

Creamers	
Individual	18.00
Regular	35.00
Goblet	42.00
Hair Receiver, metal lid	28.50
Ice Bucket	65.00
Lamps	
Finger	65.00
8″	45.00
Nappy, with turned up edges	15.00
Pitcher, water	45.00
Plates	
6″	22.00
10″	32.00
12″	37.50
Punch Cup	15.00
Rose Bowl	25.00
Sauces, flat	8.50
Syrup	32.50
Sugars	
Individual, open	18.00
Regular, covered	50.00
Boat shaped, open	.00
Toothpick	20.00
Tumbler	40.00
Vases	
6″	17.50
10″	35.00
Wine	35.00

HEAVY PANELLED FINECUT

Made by Geo. Duncan & Sons, Pittsburgh, Pa., c. 1880's. This pattern is same as Sequoia. Some handled pieces, such as platter or bread tray, carry small leaves on handles.

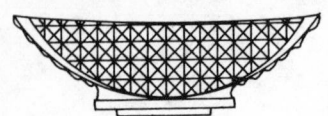

Bowls, Berry	
8″	17.50
10″	22.00
Butter, covered	25.00
Castor Set, 5-bottle	100.00
Celery Vase	20.00
Compote, covered, 8″, high standard	35.00
Creamer	15.00
Goblet	14.50
Pitcher, water	60.00
Platter, handled, or Bread Tray	16.50
Spooner	18.00
Sugar, covered	22.50
Tumbler	15.00
Tray, small, shaped like large platter, with leaves on handles, 6½″ x 4⅜″	11.50

HERRINGBONE
(See GREEN HERRINGBONE.)

HICKMAN
(La Clede)

Non-flint pattern made by McKee Bros. Glass Co., Pittsburgh, Pa., c. 1897. Comes in clear glass and emerald green. Made in 189 pieces. Add 20% more for green.

Bottle, water	40.00
Bowls, Berry	30.00
Butter, covered	40.00
Cake Plate, flat	32.50
Cake Stand	40.00
Bon Bon Dish, 9″, square	12.00
Cologne Bottle, facetted stopper	32.50
Mustard, flat with cover	35.00
Dish, Jelly, 7″, flat	9.50
Compote, Jelly, 4½″, open	15.00
Dish, Olive, 4″ with long-end handle	12.00
Salt, Individual	10.00
Shakers, pair	
Tall, straight	15.00
Round, squatty	20.00
Round with long neck, cut on neck	20.00
Sugar Shaker	30.00
Creamer	25.00
Goblet	30.00
Champagne	25.00
Sauces	
Round, 4″	10.00
Square, 4″	12.00
Spooner	25.00
Toy Set, child's condiment set, oil bottles, cruet on tray	55.00
Tumbler	25.00
Pitcher, water	50.00
Toothpick	20.00
Vase, 6″	15.00

HIDALGO
(Frosted Waffle)

Non-flint made by Adams and Co., Pittsburgh,

Pa., in the early 1880's. This pattern comes etched and clear, and also with part of pattern frosted. Add 20% for frosted.

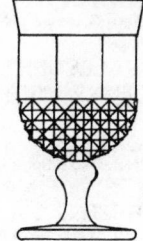

Bowls
7½", square	15.00
10", square	17.50
Waste	20.00
Bread Boat, large	45.00
Butter, covered	40.00
Celery Vase	27.50

Compotes
Covered, high standard	35.00
Open, low standard	20.00
Cruets, 2 sizes	20-40.00
Goblet	16.50

Pitchers
Milk	30.00
Water	40.00
Plate, 10"	22.50

Sauces
Flat	7.50
Footed	10.00
Handled	10.00
Pickle or Olive Dish	9.50
Boat shaped	12.00
Cup and Saucer	35.00
Nappy, handled, square	18.00

Salts
Shakers, pair	20.00
Master, square	12.50
Sugar Shaker	30.00
Syrup	45.00
Spooner	20.00
Sugar, covered	30.00
Tray, water	55.00
Tumbler	25.00

HINOTO
(Diamond Point with Panel)

Flint made by Boston & Sandwich Co. in the 1850's.

Butter, covered	75.00
Celery	65.00
Champagne	40.00
Creamer	70.00
Egg Cup, handled	28.00
Goblet	25.00

Spooner	30.00
Sugar, covered	65.00
Tumbler, footed	30.00
Whiskey, handled, footed	50.00
Wine	40.00

HOBNAIL BAND

Non-flint, c. 1900's. Sometimes hobnails are ruby-flashed. Add 20%.

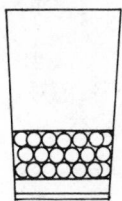

Bowls
8½"	16.00
9¼"	18.50
Butter, covered	30.00
Candlesticks, ball top, pair	35.00
Celery Tray	22.50
Champagne	17.50
Coaster	7.50
Creamer	22.00
Cup and Saucer	18.00
Custard Cup	10.00
Goblet	16.00
Pitcher, water	32.00

Plates
7⅜"	12.00
8", handled	15.00
11"	20.00
Relish, divided	12.50
Sauce, flat	8.50
Shakers, in matching holder	25.00
Spooner	16.50
Sugar, covered	25.00

Tumblers
Juice	8.50
Water	10.00

HOBNAIL, FAN TOP
(See Colored Pattern Glass Section.)

HOBNAIL, OPALESCENT
(See Opalescent Glass, General Section.)

HOBNAIL, POINTED
(See Colored Pattern Glass Section.)

HOBNAIL, PRINTED
(See Colored Pattern Glass Section.)

HOBNAIL, THUMBPRINT BASE
(See Colored Pattern Glass Section.)

HOLLY

Non-flint made by Boston & Sandwich Glass Co., late 1860's, early 1870's.

Butter, covered	125.00
Cake Stand, 11"	85.00
Celery Vase	75.00
Compotes	
Covered, high standard	125.00
Open, low standard	50.00
Creamer, applied handle	55.00
Egg Cup	55.00
Goblet	65.00
Pitcher, water	100.00
Salt, footed	25.00
Sauce, flat	15.00
Spooner	55.00
Sugar, covered	100.00
Tumbler	90.00
Wine	45.00

HOLLY AMBER
(See Colored Pattern Glass Section.)

HONEYCOMB

A popular pattern made in flint and non-flint glass by numerous firms, c. 1860–1900. The prices recorded below are for non-flint glass. Prices for flint glass are considerably higher.

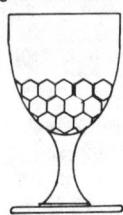

Ale Glass	15.00
Bottles	
Barber	22.50
Castor	15.00
Bowls	
6", covered	18.50
8"	15.00
10"	22.50
Butter, covered	35.00
Celery Vase	27.50
Champagne	25.00
Compotes	
Covered, high standard	55.00
Covered, low standard	40.00
Open, low standard	25.00
Creamer, applied handle	25.00
Decanter	
Pint	18.50
Quart, stoppered	29.50
Egg Cup	16.50
Goblet	24.00
Honey, covered	25.00
Lamps	
All glass	45.00
Marble base	30.00
Mug, half pint	15.00
Pitcher, water, applied handle	40.00
Plate, 6"	12.50
Pomade Jar	15.00
Salts	
Covered, footed	20.00
Open, footed	15.00
Sauce	7.50
Shakers, pair	22.50
Spooner	15.00
Sugar, covered	45.00
Tumblers	
Flat	12.50
Footed	15.00
Lemonade	16.50
Wine	12.50

HONEYCOMB WITH FLOWER FLANGE
(Vermont)

Non-flint made by Indiana Tumbler & Goblet Co., Greentown, Ind., c. 1899 as States' pattern. Made in clear with gold, green with gold, custard, chocolate, caramel, and novelty items in slag. Add 20% for green, 100% for custard and opaque.

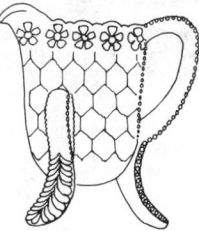

Bowl, Berry	22.00
Butter, covered	30.00
Creamer	25.00
Sugar, covered	30.00
Spooner	20.00
Pitcher, water	40.00
Toothpick	20.00
Tumbler	20.00
Sauce	12.50

HONEYCOMB AND STAR
(Starred Honeycomb)

Non-flint made by Fostoria Glass Co., c. 1905. Clear and gold trimmed.

Butter, covered	30.00
Cake Stand	30.00
Celery	15.00
Compote, covered, high standard	35.00
Creamer	20.00
Cruet	30.00
Sauce, flat	7.50
Nappy, handled	12.50
Spooner	18.00
Sugars	
Covered	25.00
Open	15.00
Tumbler	18.00

HORN OF PLENTY

A fine flint glass pattern reputed to have been first made by Boston & Sandwich Co. in the 1850's. Later made in flint and non-flint by other firms. Prices are for flint.

Bowl, 8½", flat	100.00
Butters, covered	
Conventional, finial	125.00
Head of Washington	400.00
Shape of Acorn	130.00
Cake Stand, (extremely rare)	350.00+
Celery	100.00
Champagne	150.00
Compotes, open	
7", low standard	65.00
7", scalloped rim	125.00
8", high standard	100.00
10½", high standard	135.00
Cordial	95.00
Creamers	
Large, applied handle	130.00
Regular	200.00
Decanters	
Pint	100.00
Quart, stoppered	125.00
Egg Cup	50.00
*Goblet	70.00
Honey, covered, rectangular	500.00
Lamps	
*All glass	165.00
Marble base	100.00
Mug, small, handled, (rare)	155.00
Pitcher, water	300.00
Plate, 6"	42.00
Relish, 5" x 7"	30.00
Salt, Master, oval, flat, (extremely rare)	75.00
Sauces	
3½"	7.50
4¼"	15.00
5"	52.50
Sauce, bottles	175.00
Spillholder	40.00
Spooner	45.00
Sugar, covered	60.00
Tumblers	
*Water	65.00

Whiskey, 3″	**52.00**
Wine	**125.00**

handles	**35.00**
Single, horseshoe handles	**28.50**
Wine (rare)	**150.00**

HORSESHOE
(Good Luck, Prayer Rug)

Non-flint made by Adams & Co. and others in the 1880's.

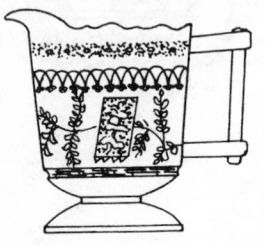

Bowls	
Finger	**20.00**
Waste	**40.00**
Covered, 7″ and 8″ x 5″, oval, (rare)	**125.00**
Open, 7″ and 9″ x 6″, oval	**20.00**
Butter, covered	**65.00**
Cake Stands	
8″	**30.00**
9″	**48.00**
10″	**65.00**
Celery, plain stem	**45.00**
Cheese, covered, scenic base	**175.00**
Compotes	
Covered, 7″, high standard	**50.00**
Open, 8″, high standard	**35.00**
Creamer	**40.00**
Goblet	
Plain stem	**25.00**
Knob stem	**35.00**
Marmalade Jar, covered	**25.00**
Pitcher, water	**75.00**
Plates	
7″	**35.00**
9″	**45.00**
10″	**45.00**
Relish, 5″ x 7″	**12.50**
Salts	
Individual, shape of horseshoe . .	**17.50**
Master, shape of horseshoe	**50.00**
Sauces	
Flat, 4½″	**27.50**
Footed, 5″	**10.00**
Spooner	**27.00**
Sugars	
Covered	**48.50**
Open	**20.00**
Trays, Bread	
Double, 10″ x 14″, horseshoe	

HUBER
(Straight Huber)

Flint made by Boston & Sandwich Glass Co., and Bakewell, Pears & Co., Pittsburgh, Pa., in the 1860's. Barrel Huber has the same values.

Bottle, Bitters	**25.00**
Bowls	
6″	**20.00**
7″, covered	**35.00**
Butter, covered	**50.00**
Celery	**28.50**
Compotes, covered	
8″ high standard	**65.00**
10″ high standard	**50.00**
8″ low standard	**75.00**
Cordial	**25.00**
Creamer	**45.00**
Decanters	
Bar Lip, pint	**35.00**
Bar Lip, quart	**50.00**
Stoppered, pint	**50.00**
Stoppered, quart	**65.00**
Egg Cups	
Handled	**35.00**
Regular	**20.00**
Goblet	**22.00**
Mug	**20.00**
Pitcher, water	**50.00**
Plate, 7½″	**22.50**
Salts	
Footed	**20.00**
Individual	**7.50**
Sauce, flat	**10.00**
Spooner	**20.00**
Sugars	
Covered	**40.00**
Open	**18.50**
Tumblers	
Jelly	**15.00**
Lemonade	**17.50**
Water	**15.00**
Whiskey	**32.50**
Wine	**25.00**

HUMMING BIRD
(See Colored Pattern Glass Section.)

ICICLE

Non-flint, c. 1870's. Add 100% for milk glass.

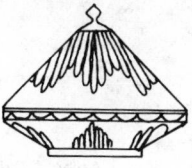

Butters	
Covered, flat	45.00
Covered, footed	55.00
Compotes	
Covered, 6", high standard	50.00
Covered, 8", high standard	60.00
Open, 8", low standard	35.00
Creamer	35.00
Goblet	35.00
Lamp, Hand, 5", complete	50.00
Pickle	20.00
Pitcher, water	50.00
Salt, Master	20.00
Sauce, flat	12.50
Spooner	30.00
Sugar, covered	45.00

ILLINOIS

Non-flint. One of the States' Patterns made by U. S. Glass Co. in 1907. Add 20% for clear glass and emerald green.

Bowls	
6"	18.50
8"	15.00
Butter, covered	45.00
Candlestick	15.00
Celerys	
Tray, 11"	27.00
Vase	25.00
Cheese, covered	35.00
Creamers	

Large	20.00
Small	14.00
Cruet	15.00
Olive	12.00
Pitchers	
Milk	32.00
Water, square	75.00
Water, tankard	62.00
Plates	
7", round	15.00
7", square	17.50
Relish	10.00
Salt and Pepper Shakers, pair	22.50
Sugar Shaker	16.50
Spooner	15.00
Straw Holder, with metal top	55.00
Sugar, open	15.00
Syrup, with pewter top	45.00
Toothpick	28.00
Tray, Ice Cream	20.00
Tumbler	10.00
Vase	40.00

INVERTED FERN

Flint, c. 1860.

Butter, covered	50.00
Compote, open, 8"	55.00
Creamer, applied handle	85.00
Egg Cup	30.00
Goblets	
Plain base	35.00
Rayed base	40.00
Honey	12.50
Pitcher, water	200.00
Salt, footed	25.00
Sauce, flat	5.00
Spooner	25.00
Sugars	
Covered	50.00
Open	25.00
Tumbler	60.00
Wine	32.00

INVERTED STRAWBERRY

Non-flint, c. 1890.

Bowl, 9″	35.00
Celery Tray, handled	35.00
Compote, open, 5″, high standard	38.00
Cruet	45.00
Cup, Punch	15.00
Goblet	23.00
Mug	18.50
Nappy	27.50
Pitchers	
Milk	55.00
*Water	75.00
Plates	
9½″, rolled rim	30.00
10″	35.00
Relish, 4½″ x 7″	17.50
Rose Bowl	40.00
Salt Dip	20.00
Sauce, flat, 4″	8.50
Sugars	
Individual	35.00
Regular, covered	35.00
Regular, open	35.00
Toothpick	10.00
*Tumbler	45.00
Tumbler, ruby stained, Souvenir type.	45.00
Toy Punch Bowl to child's play set	42.00

IOWA
(Panelled Zipper)

Non-flint made by United States Glass Co., c. 1902. Part of the States' Pattern series. Clear glass with gold trim, often found with cranberry flashing. Also in colors, amber, green, and blue, but rare. Add 20% for color.

Bowl, Berry	12.00
Butter, covered	25.00
Cake Stand	22.50
Compote, covered, 8″	35.00
Creamer	18.50
Pitcher, water	30.00
Relish	10.00
Sauces	7.50
Toothpick	15.00
Tumbler	18.00

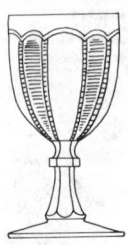

IVY, ROYAL
(See ROYAL IVY in Colored Pattern Glass Section.)

IVY IN SNOW

Non-flint made by Cooperative Flint Glass Co., Beaver Falls, Pa., in the late 1880's and continued by other firms. Reproduced in clear and milk glass.

Bowl 8″	26.50
Butter, covered	50.00
Cake Stand, large	50.00
Celery	30.00
Compotes, covered, high standard	
Small	32.50
Medium	50.00
Large	65.00
Creamer	20.00
Goblet	20.00
Marmalade Jar	30.00
Pitcher, water	40.00
Plates	
6″	20.00
8″	25.00
10″	30.00
Relish	12.00
Sauce, flat, 4″	10.00
Spooner	25.00
Sugars	
Covered	40.00
Open	25.00

Tumbler	20.00
Wine	24.00

JACOB'S COAT

Non-flint, c. 1880. Add 50% for amber and other colors. Colors are very rare.

Bowl, 8″	20.00
Butter, covered	30.00
Celery	25.00
Creamer	20.00
Goblet	28.50
Pitcher	40.00
Relish	15.00
Sauce, flat	6.50
Spooner	18.00
Sugar, covered	25.00

JACOB'S LADDER
(Maltese)

Non-flint made by Bryce Bros., Pittsburgh, Pa., in the 1870's. Reissued in 1890 but of inferior quality.

Bottle, Castor	12.50
Bowls	
7¼″, footed	20.00
10″	30.00
Butter, covered	75.00
Cake Stand, 9½″	32.50
Celery	30.00
Compotes, open	
7″, low standard	25.00
9″, high standard	40.00

12″, low standard	70.00
Dolphin standard, (scarce)	250.00
Creamer	35.00
Goblet	55.00
Honey	6.00
Honey, covered	65.00
Marmalade Jar	75.00
Pickle	20.00
Pitchers	
Syrup, Knight's head finial	85.00
Syrup, plain top	40.00
Water	125.00
Plate, 6½″	28.00
Platters	
8″	18.50
9¾″	25.00
Relish, Maltese Cross handles	29.00
Salt, Master	
Sauces	
Flat, 3½″	8.00
Footed, 4″	12.00
Spooner	28.00
Sugars	
Covered	34.00
Open	25.00
Tumbler, Bar	50.00
Wine	32.50

JEWEL AND DEWDROP
(Kansas)

Non-flint originally produced by Cooperative Flint Glass Co., Beaver Falls, Pa. Later produced as part of the States' Pattern series by U. S. Glass Co. in 1907. Comes clear, with jewels flashed with color. Add 20% for color.

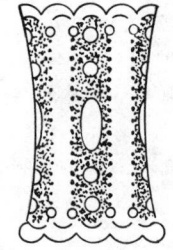

Banana Stand	45.00
Bowls	
6½″	19.00
7¼″	22.50
Butter, covered	50.00
Cake Stands	
8″	35.00
10″	38.00
Celery	32.50
Compotes, open	

6½", low standard	20.00
9½", high standard	40.00
Cordial	28.50
Creamer	22.50
*Goblet	30.00
*Mug	20.00
Pitchers	
Milk	28.00
Water	45.00
Relish	18.00
Sauce, flat	10.00
Syrup	60.00
Shakers, pair	55.00
Spooner, (scarce)	35.00
Sugar, covered	40.00
Toothpick	45.00
Tray, Bread	55.00
Tumbler	26.50
Wine	36.00

JEWEL BAND
(Scalloped Tape)

Non-flint, c. 1870–1880's. Maker unknown.

Butter, covered	35.00
Cake Stand	30.00
Compotes, open and covered	40.00
Creamer	18.50
Dish, rectangular, vegetable, covered	40.00
Egg Cup	15.00
Goblet	28.50
Pitcher, water	45.00
Plate, 6"	12.00
Relish Dish	9.00
Sauces, flat and footed	6–10.00
Salt	12.00
Spooner	15.00
Sugars	
Covered	25.00
Open	20.00
Tray, Bread	38.50
Wine	20.00

JEWEL WITH MOON AND STAR
(Shrine)

Non-flint made by Beatty & Indiana Glass Co., Dunkirk, Ind., c. late 1880's. Design is clear glass with cranberry and yellow flashed moon and stars. Add 20% for color.

Bowls, many sizes, 9½"	30.00
Butter, covered	40.00
Cake Stand	45.00
Celery	45.00
Creamer	30.00
Goblet	32.50
Mug, handled	20.00
Pitcher, water	50.00
Relish Dish	18.50
Spooner	22.50
Sugar Bowl, covered	40.00
Tumblers	
Iced tea size	35.00
Regular	30.00

JUMBO

A non-flint novelty pattern made by Canton Glass Co., Canton, Ohio, in the 1870's. The unique motif was used to commemorate P. T. Barnum's famous elephant, "Jumbo."

Butters	
Covered, with Barnum's head . . .	300.00
Oblong, plain Jumbo	225.00
Castor Set, Elephants' head holder, with bottles	325.00
Compote, covered, 7", plain Jumbo	350.00 +
Creamer, Plain Jumbo	200.00

Goblet, (rare)	350.00+
Spooner, Barnum's head	100.00
Spoon Rack, Barnum's head	125.00
Sugars	
Covered, Barnum's head	250.00
Open, plain Jumbo	65.00
Toothpick, with box on back	55.00

KENTUCKY

Non-flint made by U. S. Glass Co., c. 1897 as part of the States' Pattern series. Rare pieces sometimes found in emerald green. Add 20% for color.

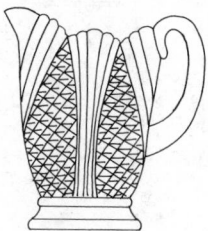

Bowl	18.00
Butter, covered	25.00
Goblet	22.50
Pitcher, water	40.00
Spooner	20.00
Sugar, covered	25.00
Tumbler	18.00
Wine	20.00

KING'S CROWN
(When this pattern is ruby-stained, it is known as Ruby Thumbprint.)

A non-flint pattern made by Adams and Co. and others from the 1890's. Made in clear, clear with gilt, ruby-stained and green and blue (rare). Clear and ruby-stained are the most prevelant. Practically every piece has been reproduced. Add approximately 30% for gilt or ruby-stain. It also came with pieces etched. For a rare piece in cobalt blue, add 100%.

Banana stand	100.00
Bowls	
7½", Berry	42.50
10", oval, scalloped	60.00
Butter, covered	55.00
Cake Stand, 9"	35.00
Castor Set, all glass, complete with	
4 bottles	75.00
Celery Vase	27.50

Champagne	35.00
Cheese, covered	150.00
Compote, open, 7", high standard	45.00
Compote, Jelly, 6"	40.00
Creamer, regular	150.00
Creamer and Sugar, individual	45.00
Cup and Saucer	45.00
Goblet	28.00
Olive Dish, round handled	20.00
Pitchers, water	
Bulbous	125.00
Tankard	100.00
Plate, 8", square	35.00
Punch Cup	6.50
Sauces	
Boat shaped	17.50
Scalloped top	15.00
Shakers, pair	50.00
Spooner	25.00
Sugar, covered	45.00
Toothpick	17.00
Tumbler	24.00
Wine	10.00

LATE BUTTERFLY
(Mikado)

Non-flint made by the Indiana Glass Co., Dunkird, Ind., in the early 1900's.

Bowls, various sizes	15–18.00
Butter, covered	25.00
Celery	15.00
Compotes, various sizes	20–30.00
Creamer	17.50
Goblet	15.00
Pitchers	

Water	25.00
Milk	20.00
Punch Cup	7.50
Sauce	5.00
Spooner	13.50
Sauces	5.00
Sugars	
Covered	17.50
Open	12.50
Tumbler	10.00
Wine	12.00

LATTICE
(Diamond Bar)

Non-flint made by King, Son and Co., Pittsburgh, Pa., c. 1880.

Bowl, 9½"	20.00
Butter, covered	40.00
Cake Stand, 12½"	45.00
Celery	25.00
Compote, covered, 7½", high standard	40.00
Creamer	30.00
Egg Cup	18.50
Goblet	25.00
Pitchers	
Milk	30.00
Water	40.00
Plates	
6"	10.00
7"	15.00
Platter or Bread Tray, oblong, handled, "Waste Not, Want Not"	25.00
Relish	15.00
Sauces	
Flat	8.50
Footed	15.00
Spooner	18.50
Sugar, covered	22.00
Syrup, top dated	40.00
Wine	18.50

LIBERTY BELL
(Centennial)

Made by Gillinder and Co., Philadelphia, Pa., for the Centennial Exposition, 1876.

Bowls, footed	
6"	95.00
8"	95.00
Butter, covered	135.00
Compote, open, 8"	90.00
Creamer, applied handle	100.00
Goblet	55.00
Mug, snake handle, (rare)	195.00
Pickle, 5½" x 9½", with 13 colonies	55.00
Pitcher, water, applied handle	500.00 +
Plate, with 13 colonies	
6"	55.00
8"	75.00
10"	100.00
Platters, Bread	
Clear, 9½" x 13⅜", no signatures	75.00
"John Hancock"	200.00
Milk White, 9½" x 13½"	300.00 +
Salt, individual	26.50
Sauces	
Flat	23.00
Footed	35.00
Shakers, pair	100.00
Spooner	90.00
Sugars	
Covered	94.00
Open	38.00

LILY OF THE VALLEY

Non-flint pattern made in the 1870's in two forms, plain stem and three-legged. Attributed to Boston & Sandwich Glass Co.

Butter, covered, either type	55.00
Cake Stand	55.00
Celery	25.00
Compote, covered, 8", high standard	75.00
Creamer, either type, applied handle	60.00
Cruet, stoppered	50.00
Egg Cup	39.50
Goblet	37.50
Pitchers	
Milk, plain type	75.00

Water, plain type	85.00
Relish, 5" x 8"	16.50
Salt, covered, legged	185.00
Spooner	25.00
Sugar, covered, legged	60.00
Wine, (scarce)	50.00

LINCOLN DRAPE

LINCOLN DRAPE WITH TASSEL

Flint pattern made originally by Boston & Sandwich Glass Co., probably continued by other companies, c. 1860. Commemmorative of Lincoln's death. Clear flint, and some very rare pieces in cobalt blue, are 200% more. Any piece is becoming rare.

LINCOLN DRAPE   **LINCOLN DRAPE, WITH TASSEL**

Butter, covered	100.00
Compotes, open, 6", low standard	65.00
Covered, 8½", high standard	150.00
Open, 8", high standard	85.00
Creamer, applied handle	125.00
Egg Cup	55.00
Goblet	80.00
Honey	20.00
Lamp	
Marble base	125.00
Miniature	45.00
Pitchers, water, applied handle	350.00
Syrup, applied handle	100.00
Sauce, flat, 4"	20.00
Salt, footed	35.00
Spillholder	50.00
Spooner	50.00

Sugar, covered	125.00
Wine	50.00

LION

Clear and frosted pattern made by Gillinder & Sons, Philadelphia, Pa., in the 1870's. Many reproductions. Add 50% for frosted pieces.

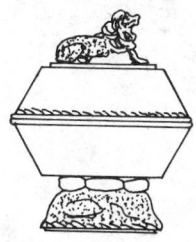

Butters, covered	
Lion's head finial	95.00
Rampant finial	100.00
Celery	75.00
Champagne	100.00
Cheese, covered, rampant lion finial	295.00
Compotes, covered	
6", rampant finial, low standard	85.00
7", rampant finial, high standard	125.00
9", rampant finial, oval, collared base	100.00
10", rampant finial, low standard	100.00
Open, 8", low standard	65.00
Creamer	65.00
Egg Cup	45.00
Goblet	55.00
Marmalade Jar, rampant finial	85.00
Paperweight	150.00
Pitchers	
Milk	350.00+
Water	200.00
Plate, Bread, 10"	75.00
Relish, frosted, lion handles	50.00
Salt, Master, footed	150.00
Sauces, footed	
4"	15.00
5"	25.00
Spooner	50.00
Sugars, covered	
Lion head finial	65.00
Rampant finial	85.00
Sugar, open	38.50
Wine, frosted	150.00

LOG CABIN

Non-flint made by Central Glass Co., Wheeling, W. Va., c. 1875.

Butter, covered	80.00
Compote, covered, 4″ x 6″, high standard	225.00
Creamer	55.00
Pitcher, water	275.00
Sauce, flat	35.00
Spooner	90.00
Sugar, covered	185.00

LOOP
(Seneca Loop)

Flint, of the 1850's–1860's. Made by several firms. Later produced in non-flint. Yuma Loop is a contemporary with comparable values. Prices listed are for flint.

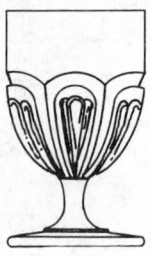 

SENECA LOOP   **YUMA LOOP**

Bowl, 9″	50.00
Butter, covered	65.00
Cake Stand	75.00
Celery	50.00
Champagne	27.50
Compotes	
Covered, 8″, high standard	60.00
Open, 8″, low standard	35.00
Creamer	60.00
Egg Cup	27.50
Flip Glass	40.00
Goblet	25.00
Pitcher, water	75.00
Salt, Master	20.00
Spooner	30.00
Sugars	

Covered	60.00
Open	35.00
Wine	30.00

LOOP AND DART

Non-flint clear and stippled pattern of the 1860's with many variants: Loop and Dart with Diamond Ornaments, Loop and Dart with Round Ornaments, Double Loop and Dart. Leaf and Dart and others. Prices for all are comparable.

LOOP AND DART   **LOOP AND DART WITH DIAMOND ORNAMENTS**

 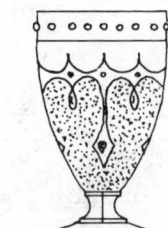

DOUBLE LOOP AND DART   **LOOP AND DART WITH ROUND ORNAMENTS**

LEAF AND DART

Bowl, 6″ x 9″, oval	20.00
Butter, covered	38.00
Cake Stand, 10″	35.00
Celery	45.00
Compotes	
Covered, 8″, high standard	60.00
Open, 8″, low standard	30.00
Creamer, applied handle	35.00
Cruet	75.00
Egg Cup	25.00
Goblet	35.00
Pitcher, water	65.00
Plate, 6″	25.00
Relish	15.00
Salt	
Covered	65.00
Master	30.00
Sauces	
Flat	7.50
Footed	10.00
Spooner	25.00
Sugars	
Covered	37.00
Open	22.50
Tumbler, footed	28.00
Wine	30.00

LOOP AND JEWEL
(Jewel and Festoon)

Non-flint made by Beatty Glass and National Glass Company, then continued by Indiana Glass Company. Made until 1915. Clear, with few rare pieces in milk white.

Bowls, 6″, 7″ and 8″	12.00
Butter, covered	22.50
Compote, 6½″	12.50
Creamer	12.00
Cup, Sherbet	6.50
Pitcher, water	25.00
Plate, square	10.00
Relish, rectangular	10.00
Salt and Pepper Shakers	20.00
Salt, footed	17.00
Sauce 4″	8.50
Sugar, covered	18.00
Syrup	25.00

LOOP WITH DEWDROPS

Early maker unknown. Reissued by U. S. Glass Co. in 1892 and later in 1898.

Bowl, 8″	18.50
Butter, covered	35.00
Cake Stand, 10″	42.00
Celery	25.00
Compotes, covered	
7″, high standard	65.00
8″, high standard	45.00
Creamer	30.00
Cup and Saucer	25.00
Goblet	22.50
Mug	12.50
Pickle Jar	20.00
Pitcher, water	32.50
Sauces	
Flat, 4″	7.50
Footed, 4″	12.00
Shakers, pair	25.00
Spooner	20.00
Sugar, covered	32.00
Tumbler	16.50
Wine	25.00

MAGNET AND GRAPE, FROSTED LEAF

Flint, c. 1860's. Reproductions reported.

Butter, covered	200.00
Celery Vase	175.00
Champagne	120.00
Compote, open, 7", high standard	95.00
Cordial	100.00
Creamer	110.00
Decanter, quart, original stopper	200.00
Egg Cup	75.00
Goblets	
American Shield, (rare)	150.00 +
Knob stem	40.00
Low stem	65.00
Salt, footed	37.50
Sauce, flat	15.00
Sugar, covered	120.00
Tumblers	
Water	95.00
Whiskey	100.00
Wine	85.00

MAGNET AND GRAPE, STIPPLED LEAF

Non-flint, c. 1870's.

Butter, covered	40.00
Creamer, applied handle	37.50
Egg Cup	20.00
Goblet	22.50
Mug	22.50
Pitcher, water, applied handle	70.00
Relish, oval	15.00
Salt, footed	15.00
Sauce, flat, 4"	7.50
Syrup, spring lid	45.00
Spooner	22.50
Sugar, open	22.50
Tumbler	19.50
Wine	22.50

MAINE

(Panelled Stippled Flower)

Non-flint made by U. S. Glass Co., Pittsburgh, Pa., c. 1890's. Goblets were not made originally. Found in clear and green, sometimes

with enamel trim. Add 100% for green.

Bowls	
6" x 8"	22.50
8"	27.50
Cake Stand	50.00
Celery	28.50
Creamer	22.50
Mug	20.00
Sauce, flat	11.50
Sugars	
Covered	27.50
Open	18.00
Syrup	
Toothpick	18.50
Wine	30.00

MAIZE
(See Colored Pattern Glass Section.)

MANHATTAN

Non-flint made by U. S. Glass Company, c. 1902. It has been reproduced in clear and color.

Bowls	
7"	10.00
8½"	12.00
10"	15.00
12½"	20.00
Cake Stand, 10"	30.00
Celery	12.50
Compote, covered, 9½", high standard	30.00
Creamers	
Individual	10.00
Regular	16.00
Goblet	12.50
Lamp	80.00
Pitcher, water, tankard	40.00

Plates
   5″ and 6″ **10.00**
   8″ and 10½″ **15.00**
Punch Cup **5.50**
Punch Set, 14 pieces **95.00**
Sauce, flat, 4½″ **6.00**
Strawholder, with lid for drug store
   trade **45.00**
Sugars
   Covered **25.00**
   Open, individual **12.50**
Toothpick **25.00**
Tumbler **12.00**
Wine **12.00**

MAPLE LEAF
(See Colored Pattern Glass Section.)

MARQUISETTE

Non-flint made by Cooperative Glass Company, Beaver Falls, Pa., c. 1880.

Butter, covered **60.00**
Celery **32.50**
Champagne **30.00**
Compotes
   Covered, high standard **60.00**
   Open, low standard **35.00**
Creamer, applied handle **45.00**
Sauce, flat, 4″ **12.00**
Spooner **25.00**
Sugar, covered **55.00**
Wine **25.00**

MASCOTTE

Non-flint made by Ripley and Co., Pittsburgh, Pa., in the 1870's. Reissued by U. S. Glass Co. in 1898. Pattern comes clear and, with etching, 20% more.

Bowl, 8″ **18.00**
Dishes or bowls, 7″– 8″ diameter,
which fit one into another, and
form tall jar-type containers. Three

sizes with lids. . . . . **each 20.00**
Butter, covered
   Regular **45.00**
   Special (See note) **75.00**
Cake Basket, with a handle **80.00**
Cake Stand, 10¼″ **35.00**
Celery Vase, plain **25.00**
Cookie Jar, bail handle **27.50**
Cheese, covered **50.00**
Dishes, round **10.00**
Compotes
   Covered, 8″, high standard **65.00**
   Open, 8″, low standard **40.00**
Creamer, etched **30.00**
Goblet, etched **25.00**
Marmalade Jar, covered, Pat'd May
   20, 1873 . . . .   **55.00**
Pitchers
   Milk **17.50**
   Water **37.50**
Sauces
   Flat **7.50**
   Footed **8.00**
Shakers, pair **30.00**
Spooner, etched **30.00**
Sugar, covered **37.50**
Tray, water, etched **45.00**
Tumbler **17.50**
Wine **25.00**

Note: The butter dish shown on Plate 77 of Ruth Webb Lee's ''Victorian Glass'' is said to go with the Mascotte pattern. It has a horseshoe finial, and was named for the famous ''Maude S.,'' ''Queen of the Turf'' trotting horse during the 1880's. Made by Ripley Bros. The pattern was named ''Mascotte'' in honor of this event.

MASONIC
(Inverted Prism)

Non-flint made by McKee Glass Co., Jeannette, Pa., c. 1894.

Bowl, 8″ **25.00**
Bowl, Salad, 9″ **30.00**
Butter
   Covered **40.00**

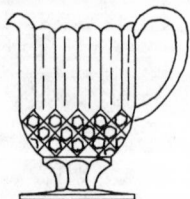

Flat, open butter dish	30.00
Cake Stand, 10″	37.50
Celery	17.50
Creamer	18.00
Handle, for a salad fork	20.00
Honey Dish, flat, square, covered	40.00
Nappy, heart shaped, handled	15.00
Pitcher, water, tankard	40.00
Sardine Box	12.50
Sauces	
Flat	10.00
Footed	10.00
Spooner	15.00
Sugar, covered	37.50
Tumbler	18.50

MEDALLION
(See Colored Pattern Glass Section.)

MELROSE

Non-flint made by Brilliant Glass Works, Brilliant, Ohio, c. 1887. Etched pieces add approximately 25%.

Banana Stand	30.00
Bowl, 8″	20.00
Butter, covered	32.50
Cake Stand, 10″	35.00
Celery	29.00
Compotes	
Covered, 6″, high standard	13.50
Covered, 8″, high standard	20.00
Open, 7″, low standard	18.00
Creamer	15.00
Goblet	15.00

Mug	12.50
Pickle	12.50
Pitchers	
Milk	30.00
Water	40.00
Plates	
8″	10.00
9″	10.00
10″	13.50
Sauce, footed	7.50
Spooner	15.00
Sugars	
Covered	22.50
Open	15.00
Tray, water	35.00
Wine	12.50

MICHIGAN
(Panelled Jewel)

Non-flint made by U. S. Glass Co., c. 1893, one of the States' Pattern series. Often seen clear with cranberry flashing, and rarely with yellow and blue stain. Add 100% for color.

Bowls	
8½″	18.50
10¼″	25.00
Butter, covered	35.00
Champagne	27.50
Creamers	
Individual	16.00
Regular	20.00
Cruet, stoppered	25.00
Goblet	25.00
Mug	25.00
Pitchers	
Milk	35.00
Water	45.00
Sauce	8.50
Shakers, pair	30.00
Spooner	20.00
Sugar, covered	30.00
Syrup, with lid	55.00
Toothpick	20.00
Tumbler	25.00
Vase, tall trumpet shaped	21.00
Water Bottle	28.50
Wine	25.00

MINERVA

Non-flint made by Boston and Sandwich Glass Co.

Butter, covered	80.00
Cake Stands	
9"	65.00
13"	110.00
Compote, covered, 7", high standard	85.00
Creamer	45.00
Goblet, (rare)	85.00
Marmalade Jar, covered	75.00
Pickle, inscribed "Love's Request is Pickles"	28.50
Pitcher, water	100.00
Plates	
9", closed, handles	50.00
11"	55.00
Platter, 9" x 13"	60.00
Sauces	
Flat	15.00
Footed	30.00
Spooner	30.00
Sugar, covered	75.00

MINNESOTA

Non-flint made by U. S. Glass Co., c. late 1890's. One of the States' Patterns. Comes in clear and emerald green, sometimes gold trimmed. Add 20% for green.

Bowl, 8½", round, flared edge	30.00
Butter, covered	45.00
Celery Trays	
10"	14.00
13"	16.00

Compotes, open	
9", square, low standard	55.00
10", flared edge, high standard	60.00
Creamer	30.00
Goblet	24.00
Mug	12.50
Nappy	10.00
Pitcher, water, tankard	40.00
Relish	15.00
Sauce, flat 4"	8.50
Spooner	22.50
Sugar, covered	37.50
Toothpick, 3-handled	27.50
Tumbler	15.00
Wine	18.50

MISSOURI
(Palm and Scroll)

Non-flint made by U. S. Glass Company, c. 1880's, in the States' Pattern series. Clear and emerald green. Add 20% for green.

Bowl, Berry	18.00
Butter, covered	35.00
Cake Stands	
8"	25.00
9"-10"	35.00
Creamer	27.50
Compote, open	30.00
Dish, 5"	18.00
Goblet, (scarce)	30.00
Salt Shakers, pair	30.00
Syrup	40.00
Relish	18.00
Sugar, covered	32.50
Sauce, flat	10.00
Tray, Bread, oval	32.50
Wine	25.00

[OLD] MOON AND STAR
(Palace)

Non-flint made by several manufacturers over a long period of time. Heavily reproduced in clear and color.

Bowls

6″	16.00
8″	22.50
12½″	32.50
Butter, covered	50.00
Cake Stand, 9″	50.00
Celery	35.00
Champagne	45.00
Cheese, covered	60.00

Compotes

Covered, 7″, low standard	37.50
Covered, 8″, high standard	65.00
Covered, 10″, high standard	70.00
Open, 9″, high standard	35.00
Creamer	55.00
Cruet	60.00
Egg Cup	35.00
Goblet	35.00
Lamp, tall	60.00
Pickle, oval	25.00
Pitcher, water	95.00
Salt Dip	7.50

Sauces

Flat	8.50
Footed	12.50
Shakers, pair	45.00
Spooner	25.00
Sugar, covered	45.00
Toothpick	17.50
Tray, water	45.00
Tumbler, footed	37.50
Wine	30.00

NAILHEAD
(Gem)

Non-flint, c. 1830's.

Butter, covered	32.50

Cake Stands

9″	28.00
12″	38.00
Celery	25.00

Compotes

Covered, 8″, high standard	55.00
Open, 9½″, high standard	45.00
Cordial	25.00
Creamer	25.00
Goblet	22.50
Pitcher, water	40.00

Plates

Round, 9″	17.50
Square, 7″	22.50
Sauce, flat	8.00
Sugar, covered	30.00
Spooner	22.50
Tumbler	18.00
Wine	16.00

NEVADA

Non-flint made by U. S. Glass Co. as a States' Pattern. Pieces are sometimes partly frosted and have enamel decoration. Add 20% for frosted.

Bowl, 8″	15.00
Butter, covered	25.00
Cake Stand, 10″	25.00
Celery	17.50

Compotes

Covered, 8″, high standard	32.50
Open, 6″, low standard	22.50
Creamer	17.50
Cruet	20.00
Pickle, oval	10.00
Pitcher, water, tankard	30.00

Salts

Individual	5.00
Master	8.50
Sauce	6.50
Shakers, pair	20.00
Sugar, covered	22.50
Toothpick	15.00
Tumbler	10.00

NEW ENGLAND PINEAPPLE

Flint made by Boston and Sandwich Glass Co. in early 1860's. Continued by other companies in non-flint. Prices are for flint. Non-flint is 50% less.

Bottle, Castor	28.50
Castor Set, 4 bottles, complete	300.00
Champagne	100.00
Compotes, open	
7", high standard	65.00
8½", high standard	80.00
Cordial	70.00
Creamer	150.00
Decanters	
Pint, no stopper	75.00
Quart, stoppered	100.00
Egg Cup	37.50
*Goblet, either size	39.50
Mug	95.00
Pitcher, water	295.00
Plate, 6"	85.00
Salt, Master	40.00
Sauce, flat	15.00
Spooner	35.00
Sugars	
Covered	80.00
Open	35.00
Tumblers	
Bar	80.00
Water	70.00
Whiskey, handled	100.00
*Wine	70.00

NEW HAMPSHIRE
(Bent Buckle, Modiste)

Non-flint made by U. S. Glass Co. in the States' Pattern series. Pieces found in clear with gold trim and some with cranberry flashing. Add 20% for color.

Bowls	
Flared	
6½"	15.00
7½"	15.00

8½"	15.00
Round	
6½"	17.50
7½"	17.50
8½"	17.50
Square, same sizes as above	25.00
Butter, covered	30.00
Celery	22.50
Champagne	17.50
Creamers	
Individual	6.00
Regular	16.00
Goblet	18.50
Mug, large	12.00
Nappy, square	8.50
Pitcher, water tankard	30.00
Punch cup	10.00
Sugars	
Covered	27.50
Individual	20.00
Toothpick	20.00
Wine	15.00
Tumbler	16.50

NEW JERSEY
(Loops and Drops)

Non-flint made by U. S. Glass Co. in States' Pattern Series. Sometimes flashed in red; mostly clear with gold trim. Add 50% to clear prices for red.

Bowls	
8", flared	25.00
10", oval	25.00
Butter, covered	50.00

Cake Stand, 8″	30.00
Celery Tray	15.00
Celery Vase	25.00
Compotes	
Jelly, covered, 5″	45.00
Open, 8″, high standard	35.00
Creamer	28.00
Cruet	20.00
Goblet	35.00
Pickle	12.00
Pitchers, water	
One gallon, applied handle	65.00
Half gallon, molded handle	35.00
Plates	
8″	10.00
10½″	25.00
12″	21.00
Relish	10.00
Sauce, 4″	7.50
Shakers, pair	35.00
Sherry, flared	45.00
Spooner	20.00
Sugar, covered	30.00
Toothpick	20.00
Tumbler	18.50
Wine	25.00

OAK, ROYAL
(See ROYAL OAK in the Colored Pattern Glass Section.)

ONE HUNDRED ONE

Non-flint made by the Bellaire Goblet Co., Findlay, Ohio, in the late 1870's.

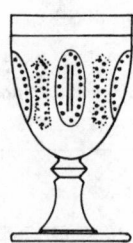

Butter, covered	60.00
Cake Stand, 9″	50.00
Celery	55.00
Compote, covered, low standard	60.00
Creamer	32.00
Goblet	40.00
Lamp, Hand	85.00
Pitcher, water	100.00
Plates	
7″	17.50

9″	22.50
11″	40.00
Relish	15.00
Sauces	
Flat	10.00
Footed	13.50
Spooner	40.00
Sugars	
Covered	45.00
Open	25.00

OPALESCENT HOBNAIL
(See Opalescent Glass Section.)

OPEN ROSE

Non-flint, c. 1870's.

Bowls	
Berry, scalloped, handled	30.00
Oval, 6″ x 9″	22.50
Butter, covered	55.00
Celery	35.00
Compotes	
Covered, 9″, high standard	60.00
Open, 7½″, low standard	30.00
Creamer	40.00
Egg Cup	20.00
Goblet	25.00
Pitcher, water, applied handle	95.00
Relish	15.00
Salt, Master	17.50
Sauce, flat, 4″	7.50
Spooner	22.50
Sugar, covered	48.50
Tumbler	30.00

OVAL MITRE

Flint, late 1850's.

Bowl	35.00
Butter, covered	75.00
Creamer, applied handle	55.00
Compotes	

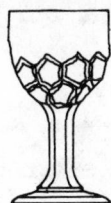

Covered, 6″, high standard	**55.00**
Open, 7″, high standard	**45.00**
Open, 10″, high standard	**65.00**
Goblet	**40.00**
Sauce, 4″	**10.00**
Spooner	**35.00**
Sugar, covered	**65.00**

PALMETTE

Non-flint, late 1870's.

Bowl, 8″	**12.50**
Butter Chip, 2″	**7.50**
Butter, covered	**55.00**
Cake Stand	**38.50**
Castor Bottle	**15.00**
Celery Vase	**30.00**
Compotes	
Covered, 8½″, high standard . . .	**55.00**
Open, 7″, low standard	**25.00**
Cordial	**25.00**
Creamer, applied handle	**45.00**
Egg Cup	**27.50**
Goblet	**28.00**
Lamp, Oil	**60.00**
Pitcher, water, applied handle	**65.00**
Relish Scoop	**14.00**
Salt, Master, footed	**18.50**
Sauces	
4″	**7.50**
6″	**14.00**
Syrup, applied handle	**45.00**
Spooner	**25.00**
Sugar, covered	**35.00**
Tumblers	
Bar	**45.00**
Footed	**30.00**
Wine	**22.50**

PANELLED CHERRY

Non-flint, late 1880's. Some pieces are with colored fruit; add 20%.

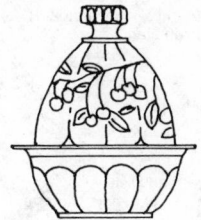

Bowls, 7″ and 8″	**25.00**
Butter, covered	**40.00**
Creamer	**32.50**
Goblet	**30.00**
Pitcher, water	**45.00**
Sauces	
Flat	**6.50**
Footed, ruby stained	**15.00**
Spooner	**22.00**
Syrup	**28.50**
Sugar, covered	**32.50**
Toothpick	**10.00**
Tumbler	**16.00**

PANELLED DAISY
(Brazil)

Non-flint made by Bryce Bros., Pittsburg, Pa., in the late 1870's.

Bowls	
5″ x 7″, oval	**10.00**
9″, square	**20.00**
10½″, open	**12.50**
Waste	**20.00**
Butter, covered	**40.00**
Cake Stands	
8″ and 9″	**40.00**
10¼″ and 11″	**45.00**

Celery Vase	35.00
Compotes	
Covered, 5″, 6″, high standard,	
Jelly	37.50
Covered, 7″, 8″, high standard ..	42.50
Covered, 10″, 11″, high standard	60.00
Open, 11″, high standard	45.00
Creamer	35.00
*Goblet	30.00
Mug	30.00
Pickle, handled	17.50
Pitcher, water	60.00
Plates	
Round, 7″	22.00
Square, 9″, Bread Dish	27.00
Relish, 5″ x 7″, fish shaped, wider at	
one end	15.00
Sauces	
Flat	10.00
Footed	15.00
Shakers	
Salt and Pepper, pair	38.00
Sugar	35.00
Spooner	25.00
Sugar, covered	40.00
Tray, water	45.00
*Tumbler	26.00

PANELLED DEWDROP
(Stippled Dewdrop)

Non-flint, c. 1870's.

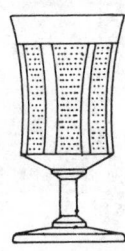

Bowls	
6½″	15.00
8½″, oval	17.00
11″, oval, panelled, footed	22.00
Butter, covered	57.50
Celery Vase	32.50
Cheese, covered	62.50
Compote, covered, 8″, high standard	55.00
Creamer, applied handle	35.00
Goblets	
Dewdrops on base	36.00
Plain base	32.00
Lemonade Glass, applied handle ..	40.00
Marmalade Jar, covered	47.00

Mug, applied handle	35.00
Pitchers	
Milk	32.00
Water	37.50
Relish, 5″ x 7″	12.50
Plates	
6″	16.00
10″	20.00
Platter, Bread, ''Give us this day our	
Daily Bread''	45.00
Sauces	
Flat	6.00
Footed	8.00
Spooner	35.00
Sugar, covered	35.00
Wine	15.00

PANELLED DIAMOND POINT #1

Flint, c. 1860's.

Butter, covered	80.00
Celery Vase	55.00
Creamer	50.00
Goblet	25.00
Pitcher, water	85.00
Sauce	15.00
Spillholder	35.00
Spooner	35.00
Sugar, covered	60.00

PANELLED FORGET-ME-NOT
(See Colored Pattern Glass Section.)

PANELLED "44"
(Reverse "44")

Non-flint made by U. S. Glass Co., c. 1912. Some pieces bear intertwined U. S. Glass Co. mark in base. Also comes trimmed in gold and in untarnishable platinum. Has been seen with cranberry and green flashing.

Butter, covered	55.00
Bowls	

Berry, 8", flat	12.00
Finger Bowl	15.00
Oval, footed	14.00
Candlestick, 7"	20.00
Cruet	40.00
Dish	
Bon Bon, footed with cover	32.50
Olive	15.00
Goblet	30.00
Pitcher, water	
Tall tankard on foot	60.00
Flat, bulbous	65.00
Creamer	35.00
Sugars	
Covered, with handles	40.00
Powdered Sugar, covered, no handles	30.00
Syrup, with Brittania top	55.00
Salt and Pepper Shakers, pair	60.00
Toothpick	35.00
Tumblers	
Iced Tea	35.00
Regular	30.00
Wine	40.00

PANELLED GRAPE
(Heavy Panelled Grape)

Non-flint made in Indiana, Pa., c. 1880–1900. This pattern has been heavily reproduced.

Ale Glass	25.00
Bowl, 12", crimped	25.00
Butter, covered	40.00
Celery	25.00
Compotes	

Covered, 5"	30.00
Open, 6½", low standard	26.00
Creamer, vine handle	40.00
Goblet	16.00
Mug	18.50
Pitcher, water	60.00
Plate, 10"	25.00
Salt	15.00
Sauces	
Oval	15.00
Round, 4¼"	13.50
Sherbet	15.00
Spooner	17.50
Sugar, covered	40.00
Toothpick	20.00
Tumblers	
Jelly	25.00
Lemonade	25.00
Water	30.00

PANELLED GRAPE, LATE

Non-flint made by D. C. Jenkins Glass Co., Arcadia and Kokomo, Ind., c. 1913 to 1932.

Bowl, 12", covered	29.50
Butter, covered	45.00
Creamer	22.50
Goblet	25.00
Pitchers	
Milk	30.00
Water	40.00
Sauce	12.50
Spooner	22.50
Syrup	37.50
Sugar, covered	27.50
Tumbler	15.00
Wine	18.00

PANELLED THISTLE

Non-flint made by J. P. Higbee Glass Co., Bridgeville, Pa., in the early 1900's. This pattern has been heavily reproduced. The Higbee Glass Co. often used a bee as a trade mark.

PAVONIA
(Pineapple Stem)

Non-flint made in Pittsburgh, Pa., c. 1880's. This pattern comes both plain and with etching; also with ruby flashing on pieces. Add 50% for ruby and etched pieces.

Banana Stand	50.00
Basket	35.00
Bowls	
7¼"	12.00
8", with Bee	18.00
Butter, covered	38.50
Cake Stand, 9"	22.50
Celerys	
Trays	18.50
Vase	25.00
Compotes, open	
5", low standard	18.00
8", high standard	25.00
Cordial	25.00
Creamer, with Bee	27.50
Cruet, stoppered	32.00
Egg Cup	20.00
Goblet	35.00
Honey, covered, square, with Bee	45.00
Pitchers	
Milk	40.00
Water	50.00
Plates	
7"	25.00
9"	20.00
10", with Bee	27.50
Punch Cup, with Bee	23.00
Relish, with Bee	22.00
Rose Bowl, large	42.50
Salts	
Dip	9.00
Master, with Bee	12.50
Sauces	
Flared, with Bee	14.00
Flat	10.00
Footed	12.00
Shakers, pair	35.00
Spooner	18.00
Sugars	
Covered	35.00
Open	18.00
Toothpick, with Bee	30.00
Tumbler, water	25.00
Vases	
5"	15.00
9", trumpet shaped	20.00
Wine	25.00
Wine, with Bee	30.00

Bowls	
9"	28.50
Finger Bowl and Underplate	50.00
Waste	32.00
Butter, covered	65.00
Cake Stands	
Large	50.00
Small	30.00
Compotes	
Covered, 6", high standard	45.00
Open, 8", high standard	32.00
Creamers	18–45.00
Goblets	22–35.00
Pitchers	30–55.00
Salt, Individual	
Sauces, flat and footed	8.50–12.00
Spooner	20.00
Sugar, covered	45.00
Tumblers	10–24.00
Wines	18.50–30.00

PEACOCK FEATHER
(Georgia)

Originally a Sandwich pattern, but reissued by several glass companies, including U. S. Glass Co. in 1907 as part of their States' series.

Bowl, 8"	18.50
Butter, covered	25.00
Cake Stand, 11"	40.00
Celery Tray	20.00
Compotes	
Jelly	20.00
Open, 8", high standard	25.00
Creamer	23.50
Cruet, stoppered	25.00
Lamps	
7", hand	40.00

9″	60.00
Pitchers, water	55.00
Plate, 5¼″	25.00
Relish, 8″, oval	15.00
Sauces	
4½″	3.50
6½″, flared	12.50
Shakers, pair	40.00
Spooner	22.50
Sugar, covered	35.00
Tumbler	25.00

PENNSYLVANIA #1
(Balder)

Non-flint issued by U. S. Glass Co., 1898. This pattern comes in clear with gold trim and in emerald green. Add 50% for green.

Bowls	
Berry, 8″	20.00
Punch, 12″	65.00
Square, 8″	22.00
Butter, covered	55.00
Carafe	22.50
Celery Tray	15.00
Celery Vase	20.00
Champagne	17.50
Cheese, covered	35.00
Cracker Jar, covered	25.00
Creamers	
Small, breakfast set	12.50
Large	20.00
Cruet, stoppered	15.00
Goblet	20.00
Pitchers, water, tankard	40.00
Plate, 6½″	9.00

Punch Cup	6.00
Sauces	
Boat shaped	9.50
Flat, 4″	7.50
Spooner	25.00
Sugars	
Individual, breakfast set	12.50
Regular, covered	25.00
Tumblers	
Juice	9.50
Water	10.00
Wine	15.00

PICKET

Non-flint made by the King Glass Co., Pittsburgh, Pa., in the late 1800's.

Butter, covered	50.00
Celery	30.00
Compotes	
Covered, 6″, high standard	40.00
Covered, 8″, high standard	50.00
Open, 8″, high standard	35.00
Creamer	32.50
Goblet	30.00
Marmalade Jar, covered	35.00
Pitcher, water	50.00
Salts	
Individual	10.00
Master	14.00
Sauces	
Flat	8.00
Footed	10.00
Sugar, covered	35.00
Toothpick	22.00
Tray, water	40.00
Waste Bowl	25.00

PINEAPPLE AND FAN #2
(Cube with Fan, Holbrook)

Non-flint mady by Adams & Co., Pittsburgh, Pa., later made by U. S. Glass Co. in 1891.

Bowls	
8″	20.00

Punch, 12″	60.00
Waste	15.00
Bucket, ice	35.00
Butter, covered	35.00
Cake Stand, 9″	22.50
Celery Vase	27.50
Creamers	
Individual	20.00
Regular	25.00
Cruet, stoppered	25.00
Goblet	20.00
Pitchers	
Milk	25.00
Water, tankard	35.00
Plate, 6½″	14.50
Sauce, 4″	7.50
Spooner	18.50
Sugars	
Individual	20.00
Regular, covered	27.50
Toothpick	27.50
Tumblers	
Water	12.50
Whiskey	14.50
Wine	18.50

PLEAT AND PANEL
(Derby)

Non-flint made by Bryce Bros., Pittsburgh, Pa., c. 1870–1880.

Bowls	
5″ x 8″, covered	45.00
Waste	37.50
Butter, covered	45.00
Candy Jar, covered	50.00

Cake Stands	
9″	40.00
10″	44.00
Celery Vase	35.00
Compotes	
Covered, 6″, high standard	40.00
Covered, 8″, high standard	45.00
Open, 8″, high standard	28.00
Creamer	27.00
*Goblet	26.00
Marmalade Jar, covered	50.00
Pitchers	
Milk	35.00
Water	45.00
Plates	
6″	14.50
*7″	15.00
8″	22.50
Relish, 5″ x 8½″	28.00
Salt, Master	20.00
Sauces	
Flat	8.00
Handled	10.00
Shakers, pair	50.00
Spooner	22.50
Sugar, covered	40.00
Trays	
Bread, closed, handled	30.00
Bread, open, handled	25.00
Water, (scarce)	50.00
Wine, (scarce)	50.00

PLUME

Non-flint made by Adams Glass Co., Pittsburgh, Pa., c. 1874.

Bowls	
6″	25.00
8″, shallow	17.50
Butter, covered	47.50
Cake Stand, 10″	38.50
Celery	30.00
Compotes, open	
6″, low standard	22.50
7″, high standard	27.50
9″, high standard	38.00
Creamer	22.50

*Goblet	30.00
Lamp, Hand	60.00
Pickle	15.00
Pitcher, water	45.00
Sauces	
Flat	6.00
Footed	10.00
Spooner	20.00
Sugar, covered	25.00
Tumbler	17.50

POLAR BEAR

Non-flint made by Crystal Glass Co., Bridgeport, Ohio, c. 1880. Pattern made in clear and frosted.

Bowls	
Ice, clear	85.00
Waste, frosted	85.00
Goblets	
Clear	85.00
Frosted	100.00
Pitchers, water	
Clear	150.00
Frosted	185.00
Trays, bread	
Bread, frosted	100.00
Water, frosted, oval	125.00

POPCORN

Non-flint, c. late 1860's. Maker unknown. Pieces were made with a large outstanding ornament, somewhat like an ear of corn, on bowl of pieces. It was probably continued by another company. The "popcorn ears" were made by a flat oval, filled with lines. Pieces with an outstanding ear should read "With ear" and the others "Lined ear." Add 20% with ear.

Butter, covered	65.00
Cordial	50.00
Creamer	50.00
Goblets	
Lined ear	22.50

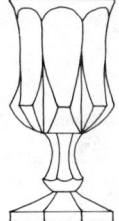

With ear	50.00
Pitcher, water	95.00
Sauce	17.50
Spooner	30.00
Sugar, covered	60.00
Wine, with ear	65.00

PORTLAND

Non-flint pattern said to have been originated by Portland Glass Co., Portland, Maine, between 1863 and 1874. It was continued by several companies and also by U. S. Glass Co. in the early 1900's. Clear with gold trim, sometimes with cranberry flashing. Add 20% for color.

Bowl, berry	15.00
Butter, covered	35.00
Basket, with handle of glass, (rare)	65.00
Cake Stand, 10½"	40.00
Candlesticks, (rare)	105.00
Compotes	
Covered, 6"	35.00
Open, 7"	40.00
Open, 9¼"	35.00
Creamer, 2 sizes, (small and child's)	22.00
Cruet, stoppered	27.50
Bureau Jar, with silver lid	27.50
Pomade Box, with cover	18.00
Puff Box	18.00
Pitchers	
Water, straight sides, ½ gallon	45.00
Tankard type	50.00

Pickle or Relish
  Boat Shaped 20.00
  Oval 15.00
Salt and Pepper Shakers 30.00
Sugar Shaker 35.00
Tumbler 25.00
Wine 25.00
Vase
  7" 12.50
  10½" 18.00
Sauces
  Boat shaped 12.00
  Round, flat 10.00
Water Carafe 45.00

POWDER AND SHOT

Flint and non-flint made by Boston & Sandwich Glass Co., c. 1870's.

Bowls, 5" footed and handled 45.00
Butter, covered 85.00
Castor Bottle 35.00
Celery 50.00
Compotes
  Covered, high standard 85.00
  Open, low standard 50.00
Creamer, applied handle 70.00
Egg Cup, flint 65.00
Goblet, flint and non-flint 35–55.00
Salt, footed 27.50
Sauce 10.00
Spooner 30.00
Sugars
  Covered 65.00
  Open 35.00

PRESSED LEAF

Non-flint first made by Sandwich Glass Co. and McKee Bros. in 1868, Central Glass Co., Wheeling, W. Va., in 1881. Prices are for non-flint. Add 50% for flint.

Butter, covered 40.00
Champagne 42.00
Compotes, covered
  6" high standard 50.00

  7", 8", high standard 60.00
  7", 8", low standard 30.00
Cordial
Creamer, applied handle 50.00
Egg Cup 19.50
Goblet 19.50–22.50
Lamp, Hand 40.00
Pitcher, water, applied handle 75–85.00
Salt, Master 20.00
Sauce, flat 9.50
Spooner 20.00
Sugar, covered 35.00
Wine 35.00

PRIMROSE
(See Colored Pattern Glass Section.)

PRINCESS FEATHER
(Rochelle)

Non-flint made by Bakewell, Pears, & Co. in the late 70's, later by U. S. Glass Co. in 1880. Add 100% for milk glass.

Bowl, 7¼", covered 35.00
Butter, covered 65.00
Cake Stand, 8" 27.50
Celery Vase 35.00
Compotes
  Covered, 6", high standard 45.00
  Covered, 8", high standard 50.00
  Open, 8", low standard 25.00
Creamer, applied handle 50.00
Plates

6″	25.00
7″	25.00
9″	32.50
Relish, 5″ x 7″	18.50
Salt, Master	22.50
Sauce, flat	8.50
Spooner	22.00
Sugars	
Covered	50.00
Open	30.00

PRINTED HOBNAIL
(See Colored Pattern Glass Section.)

PRISCILLA

Non-flint made by Dalzell, Gillmore & Leighton, Findlay, Ohio, in the late 1890's. Heavily reproduced in clear, colors, and opalescent.

Biscuit Jar, covered	60.00
Bowl, 10¼″	20.00
Butter, covered	45.00
Cake Stand	55.00
Celery	55.00
Compotes	
Jelly, covered	35.00
Open, 9″, high standard	39.00
Creamer	25.00
Cruet, stoppered	35.00
Cup and Saucer	35.00
Goblet	25.00
Mug	
Plates	
Regular	15.00
10½″, turned up edge	30.00
Relish	20.00
Rose Bowl	22.50
Sauce, 4½″	12.50
Spooner	20.00
Salt Shaker, 1	25.00
Sugar, open	20.00
Syrup	45.00
Toothpick	50.00
Tumbler	21.00
Wine	26.00

PRISM AND FLUTE

Non-flint made by Bakewell, Pears, Pittsburgh, Pa., in the late 1870's. Can be found in flint; add 20%.

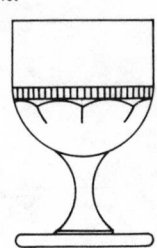

Butter, covered	50.00
Cake Stands	
9″	35.00
10½″	40.00
12¼″	45.00
Celery Vase	30.00
Compotes	
Covered, 8″, high standard	50.00
Open, 8″, low standard	32.50
Cordial	30.00
Creamer	35.00
Egg Cup	25.00
Goblet	12.50–17.50
Pitcher, water	60.00
Salt, Master	12.50
Sauce, flat	7.50
Tumbler, footed	20.00
Wine	25.00

PRISM WITH DIAMOND POINTS

Flint made by Boston & Sandwich Glass Co.

Butter, covered	75.00
Compote, covered, 6″, high standard	95.00
Creamer	65.00
Egg Cups	
Double	45.00
Single	35.00

Goblet	45.00
Pitcher, water	95.00
Salt, Master	25.00
Sauce	15.00
Sugar, covered	50.00
Tumbler	35.00
Wine	40.00

PSYCHE AND CUPID

Non-flint, c. 1870's.

Butter, covered	60.00
Celery	40.00
Creamer	35.00
Goblet	40.00
Pitcher, water	60.00
Sauces, footed	
3¾"	10.00
4½"	12.50
Spooner	35.00
Sugars	
Covered	42.50
Open	22.50
Wine	25.00

PURPLE SLAG
(See Colored Pattern Glass Section.)

QUEENE ANNE
(Bearded Man)

Non-flint made by LaBelle Glass Co., Bridgeport, Ohio, c. 1879.

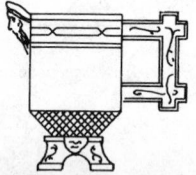

Butter, covered	50.00
Celery	25.00
Compotes	
Covered	45.00
Open, oval	17.00
Creamer	30.00
Egg Cup	45.00
Pitcher, water	50.00
Punch Cup	9.00
Sauce, footed, 4½"	20.00
Spooner	19.50
Sugars	
Covered	35.00
Open	20.00

RAINDROP
(See Colored Pattern Glass Section.)

RED BLOCK

Non-flint with red stain made by Doyle and Co., later by U. S. Glass Co. in 1892.

Bowl, 8"	60.00
Butter, covered	65.00
Celery	45.00
Creamers	
Individual	40.00
Regular	50.00
Decanter, 12", stoppered	80.00
*Goblet	40.00
*Mug	35.00
Pitcher, water	90.00
Rose Bowl	45.00
Sauce, flat, 4½"	25.00
Shakers, pair	75.00
Spooner	40.00
Sugars	
Covered	50.00
Open	35.00
Tumbler	30.00
*Wine	30.00

REVERSE TORPEDO
(Bull's Eye Band, Bull's Eye and Diamond Point #2.)

Made by Dalzell, Gillmore & Leighton Glass Co., Findlay, Ohio, c. 1888–1890.

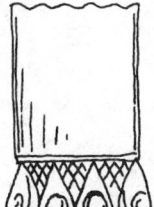

Banana Stand	90.00
Bowls	
6″	30.00
7½″, crimped	50.00
Butter, covered	65.00
Cake Stand, 9½″	60.00
Compotes	
Jelly, covered	65.00
Open, 6″, high standard	45.00
Goblet, (rare)	80.00
Pitcher, water, tankard	90.00
Sauce	12.50
Sugar, covered	50.00
Tumbler	25.00

RIBBED GRAPE

Flint, c. early 1862's.

Butter, covered	85.00
Celery	50.00
Compotes	
Covered, 6″	125.00
Open, 8″, low standard	65.00
Creamer, applied handle	125.00
Goblet	40.00
Pitcher, water, applied handle	150.00
Plate, 6″	50.00
Sauce	22.50
Spooner	55.00
Sugar, covered	85.00

RIBBED IVY

Flint, c. late 1850's.

Butter, covered	90.00
Castor Bottle	35.00
Celery, (rare)	300.00+
Champagne	100.00
Compotes	
6″ Jelly, covered	125.00
8″, open, low standard, scalloped edge	50.00
9″, open, high standard, scalloped edge	60.00
Creamer	125.00
Decanters	
Half pint, without stopper	75.00
Quart, stoppered	100.00
Egg Cup	28.00
Goblet	40.00
Hat	350.00
Honey	15.00
Salts	
Master, covered	130.00
Master, open, beaded	45.00
Open, scalloped rim	40.00
Sauce	12.50
Spooner	26.00
Sugar, covered	85.00
Sweetmeat, covered, on stand	125.00
Tumblers	
Water	65.00
Whiskey, handled	65.00
Wine	90.00

RIBBED PALM

Flint made by McKee Glass Co., Pittsburgh, Pa., c. 1868.

Bowl, 8″	40.00
Butter, covered	85.00
Castor Set, pewter base	150.00
Compotes	
Covered, 6″	125.00
Open, 8″	60.00
Open, 10″	80.00
Open, 7″, low standard	45.00

Creamer, applied handle	110.00
Egg Cup	16.00
Goblet	37.50
Lamp, all glass	85.00
Pitcher, water, applied handle, (rare)	125.00
Plate, 6″	50.00
Salt, footed	30.00
Sauce, flat	16.00
Spillholder	40.00
Spooner	35.00
Sugar, covered	60.00
Tumbler	75.00
Wine	50.00

RIBBON

Non-flint made by Bakewell, Pears, Pittsburgh, Pa., in the late 1860's. Other Ribbon patterns are Clear Ribbon, Frosted Ribbon, Double Ribbon, Fluted Ribbon, Grated Ribbon. It seems logical to use "Ribbon" to denote this one, the oldest and best known. (Lee — EAPG — pl. 67) It has been erroneously called "Frosted Ribbon" at times, which can be confusing.

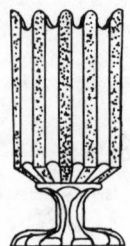

Butter, covered	65.00
Cake Stand, 8½″	35.00
Celery	25.00
Cheese, covered	75.00
Compotes, covered	
7″, low standard	30.00
7½″, high standard	40.00

Compotes, open	
7″, low standard	40.00
10½″, silverplated, Dolphin stand	100.00
Oblong Dolphin stand, small	175.00
Oblong Dolphin stand, large	300.00
Creamer	45.00
*Goblet	35.00
Pitcher, water	65.00
Platter, 9″ x 13″, oblong, cut corners	62.50
Sauces	
Flat	10.00
Footed	18.50
Handled	20.00
Spooner	30.00
Sugar, covered	65.00
Tray, water, 15″ x 16¼″	100.00
Waste Bowl	40.00
Wine, (scarce)	85.00

ROMAN KEY

Flint glass pattern of the 1860's made in several variants by different companies. Sometimes erroneously called "Greek Key" because of the typical Greek band. Prices recorded are for flint glass. Non-flint variants are approximately 50% less.

Bowl, 8″	35.00
Butter, covered	35.00
Cake Stand, 12″	50.00
Celery Vase	45.00
Champagne	45.00
Compote, open, 7″, low standard . .	45.00
Creamer, applied handle	65.00
Decanter, stoppered	90.00
Egg Cup	30.00
Goblet	45.00
Pitcher, water	200.00
Salt, footed	40.00
Sauce	12.50
Spooner	40.00
Sugar, covered	50.00
Tumbler	45.00
Wine	50.00

ROMAN ROSETTE

Non-flint made by Bryce, Walker and Co. 1875–1885. Reissued by U. S. Glass Co. in 1892 and 1898. Add 20% for ruby stained.

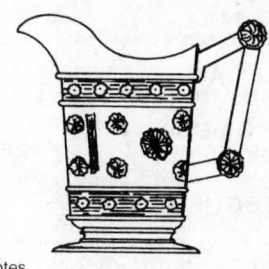

Bowls	
6½"	18.00
8½"	20.00
Butter, covered	40.00
Cake Stand, 9"	80.00
Castor Set, glass	50.00
Celery	32.50
Compotes	
Covered, 6", high standard	65.00
Open, 7½", high standard	35.00
Cordial	40.00
Creamer	32.50
*Goblet	27.50
Mug, 3"	14.00
Pickle	20.00
Pitchers	
Milk	35.00
Water	40.00
Plate, 7½"	35.00
Sauces	
Flat	8.00
Footed	10.00
Shakers, pair	30.00
Spooner	60.00
Sugar, covered	60.00
Tray, bread	30.00
Wine	30.00

ROSE-IN-SNOW
(See Colored Pattern Glass Section.)

ROSE SPRIG
(See Colored Pattern Glass Section.)

ROSETTE

Non-flint made by Bryce Bros., Pittsburgh, Pa., in the late 1870's. Continued by the U. S. Glass Co. Later made in Ohio in 1898.

Bowl, 7½", covered	30.00
Butter, covered	32.50
Cake Stand, 11"	30.00
Celery	25.00

Compotes	
Jelly	15.00
Covered, 6", high standard	40.00
Open, 7", high standard	35.00
Creamer	22.50
Goblet	26.50
Pitchers	
Milk	25.00
Water	40.00
Plates	
7"	18.00
9", handled	22.50
Relish (fish shaped) wider at one end	14.00
Sauce, flat	8.00
Shakers, pair	35.00
Spooner	20.00
Sugar, covered	25.00
Wine	18.50

ROSETTE AND PALM

Non-flint, c. late 1880's.

Banana Stand	35.00
Butter, covered	28.00
Cake Stand, 9½"	22.50
Celery	20.00
Goblet	17.50
Plate, 9"	9.00
Relish	10.00
Sauce	6.50
Spooner	15.00
Sugar, covered	22.50
Wine	18.00

ROYAL IVY
(See Colored Pattern Glass Section.)

ROYAL OAK
(See Colored Pattern Glass Section.)

RUBY THUMBPRINT
(See KING'S CROWN.)

SAWTOOTH

An early flint glass pattern made in the late 1850's by the New England Glass Co. Later made in non-flint. Prices given are for flint.

Butter, covered	85.00
Cake Stand, 10″	85.00
Celery Vase, 10″	55.00
Champagne	65.00
Compotes	
Covered, 8″, low standard	75.00
Covered, 9½″, high standard . . .	95.00
Open, 8″, low standard	65.00
Creamer	85.00
Cruet, Acorn finial	100.00
Decanter, quart stoppered	125.00
Egg Cup	45.00
Goblet	45.00
Pitchers	
Milk	65.00
Water	95.00
Pomade Jar, covered	50.00
Salts	
Covered, footed	40.00
Open, smooth edge	25.00
Sauce, flat, 4″	15.00
Spooner	35.00
Sugar, covered	80.00
Tumblers	
Flat	35.00
Footed	45.00
Wine	50.00
Spillholder	30.00

SAWTOOTH AND STAR
(OHara's Diamond)

Non-flint, c. 1890's. Add 20% for pieces with red stain.

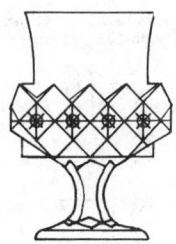

Butter, covered	30.00
Banana Stand	28.00
Creamer	20.00
Compote, 7″	40.00
Cruet	20.00
Cup and Saucer	20.00
Goblet	22.50
Lamp Oil	30.00
Pickle	17.50
Pitcher, syrup	25.00
Plate, 10″	17.50
Sauce, flat	7.50
Shakers, pair	25.00
Salt, Master	10.00
Sugar Shaker	20.00
Spooner	20.00
Sugar, covered	25.00
Tumbler	30.00
Wine	20.00

SAWTOOTHED HONEYCOMB
(Serrated Block and Loop)

Non-flint pattern made by Steimer Glass Co., Buckhannon, W. Va., 1904-1908. Molds sold to Morgantown Glass Co. about 1921. Clear, sometimes with red stain.

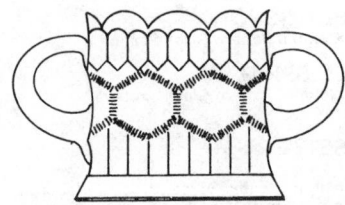

Bowls, Berry	
8″	22.50
9″	25.00
Butter, covered	35.00
Compotes, 9½″, high standard . . .	40.00
Creamer	20.00

Cruet 30.00
Goblet 18.50
Nappy 18.50
Pitchers
   Milk, 7″, bulbous, applied handle   40.00
   Milk, 8″, tankard 35.00
   Water, 10″, bulbous, applied han-
   dle 45.00
Sugar, covered 27.50
Toothpick 20.00

SAXON

Non-flint made by Adams & Co., Pittsburgh, Pa., c. 1870's. Often seen with red stain.

Bowl, 8″ 25.00
Butter, covered 45.00
Cake Stand, 2 sizes 32–35.00
Celery 32.00
Creamer 27.50
Egg Cup 25.00
Goblet 22.50
Mug, handled 27.50
Pitcher, water 40.00
Plate, 6″ 22.50
Relish 12.50
Salt 10.00
Sauce, flat 7.50
Syrup, with metal top 25.00
Spooner 20.00
Sugar, covered 35.00
Sweetmeat Jar, covered 40.00
Tumbler 18.50
Toothpick 22.50
Water Tray 40.00
Waste Bowl or Finger 22.50
Wine 18.50

SCROLL

Non-flint of the 1870's.

Butter, covered 35.00
Celery 27.50

Compotes
   Covered, high standard 35.00
   Open, high standard 25.00
Creamer 20.00
Egg Cup 18.50
Goblet 20.00
Pitcher, water 40.00
Relish 20.00
Salt, footed 12.00
Sauce, flat 7.50
Spooner 18.50
Sugar, covered 35.00
Tumbler, footed 15.00
Wine 15.00

SCROLL WITH FLOWERS

Non-flint made by Central Glass Co. in the 1870's; then later by Northwood. Occasionally found in color.

Butter, covered 35.00
Cake Plate, handled 18.50
Celery 25.00
Cordial 30.00
Creamer 24.00
Egg Cups
   Double, handled 25.00
   Single 12.00
Goblet 25.00
Mustard Jar, covered 30.00
Pickle, handled 17.50
Pitcher, water 75.00
Salt, footed 15.00
Sauce, double-handled 10.00
Spooner 20.00
Sugar, covered 35.00
Wine 20.00

SHELL AND JEWEL
(Victor)

Non-flint made by Westmoreland Glass Co., c. 1893. Clear and rare in blue and green. Add 100% for color.

Banana Stand	36.50
Bowl, 8″	28.00
Butter, covered	42.50
Cake Stand, 10″	40.00
Compote, open, 7″, high standard	35.00
Creamer	25.00
Pitcher, water	35.00
Relish	18.50
Sauce, flat	10.00
Spooner	20.00
Sugar, covered	27.50
Tray, water	30.00
Tumbler	14.00

SHELL AND TASSEL
(Shell and Spike)

Non-flint made by George A. Duncan & Sons, Pittsburgh, Pa., in the 1880's. Two forms were issued, square with shell shaped finials, and later, round with frosted dog finials. Also made in azure blue, amber, and canary, but extremely rare. Add 100% for color.

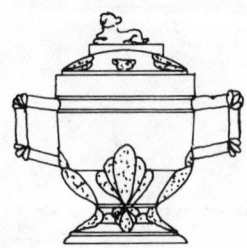

Round
Bowls

10¼″, oval	45.00
12″, oval, deep	60.00
Butters	

Covered	45.00
Pat	23.50
Celery Vase	75.00
Creamer	32.50
*Goblet	35.00
Marmalade Jar	50.00
Pitcher, water	40.00
Sauce, footed	12.50
Shakers, pair	100.00
Spooner	25.00
Sugar, covered, Dog finial	110.00
Tray, 9″ x 13″	45.00
Vase	135.00
Square	
Bowl, 5″ x 8″	20.00
Butter, covered	75.00
Cake Stands	
8″	45.00
12″	65.00
Celery Vase	35.00
Compotes	
4½″, jelly	45.00
8″, open	40.00
10″, open	50.00
Creamer	45.00
*Goblet	65.00
Pitcher, water	55.00
Platter, 9″ x 13″	65.00
Salt, shell shaped	15.00
Sauces	
Flat, shell shaped	10.00
Footed	12.50
Spooner	35.00
Sugar, covered	85.00
Oyster Plate, large, (very rare)	110.00

SHERATON
(See Colored Pattern Glass Section.)

SMOCKING

Flint, c. 1850's.

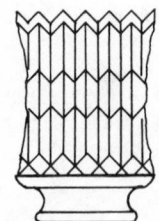

Bottle, Bar, blob top	100.00
Bowl, Berry, 9″	75.00
Butter, covered	75.00
Compote, covered, 7″, low standard	50.00

Creamer, applied handle	85.00
Egg Cup	50.00
Goblet	60.00
Lamp, 9″	125.00
Spillholder	45.00
Spooner	18.00
Sugars	
Covered	75.00
Open	50.00
Tumblers	
Water	50.00
Whiskey	75.00
Vase, 10″	75.00
Wine	35.00

SNAIL
(Compact, Idaho)

Non-flint made by George Duncan & Sons, Pittsburgh, Pa., c. 1880, in the States' Pattern series. This pattern is sometimes stained with red, but rarely.

Banana Stand	100.00
Bowls	
Berry, 8″	35.00
Open, 6″ x 9″	28.00
Butter, covered	53.00
Cake Stand	75.00
Celery Vase	32.00
Cheese, covered	65.00
Compotes, high standard	
Covered, 10″	43.00
Open, 8″	35.00
Creamers	
Individual	25.00
Regular	35.00
Cruet, stoppered	40.00
Finger Bowl	25.00
Goblet	85.00
Pitchers	
Syrup	45.00
Water, tankard	85.00
Plate, 7″	23.00
Punch Cup	20.00
Relish, 7″, oval	25.00
Rose Bowl	42.00
Salt	12.00

Sauce, 4″	15.00
Shakers	
Salt and Pepper, pair	40.00
Sugar	35.00
Spooner	28.50
Sugars	
Individual, covered	20.00
Regular, covered	45.00
Open	30.00
Tumbler	35.00
Wine	30.00

SOUTHERN IVY

Non-flint, c. 1880's.

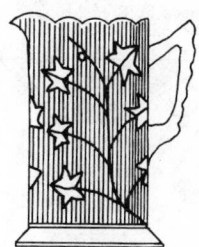

Bowl, 8″	18.50
Butter, covered	25.00
Creamer	25.00
Cruet, stoppered	25.00
Pitcher, water	30.00
Sauce, flat	17.00
Spooner	17.00
Sugars	
Covered	25.00
Open	15.00

SPIRALED IVY

Non-flint, c. 1880's.

Butter, covered	39.50
Creamer	25.00

Pitchers
Milk 35.00
Water 45.00
Sauce, flat 7.50
Spooner 20.00
Sugars
Covered 30.00
Open 18.50
Tumbler 18.00

SPIREA BAND
(See Colored Pattern Glass Section.)

SPRIG

Non-flint made by Bryce, Higbee & Co., Pittsburgh, Pa., c. mid-1880's.

Bowls
5″ x 7″ 20.00
10″, footed, scalloped 35.00
Butter, covered 40.00
Cake Stand, 8″ 28.00
Celery 30.00
Compotes
Covered, high standard 40.00
Open, high standard 32.50
Open, low standard 28.50
Creamer 22.00
Goblet 30.00
Pickle 15.00
Pitcher, water 45.00
Platter 35.00
Sauces
Flat 8.00
Footed 12.00
Spooner 25.00
Sugar, covered 35.00
Tumbler 20.00
Wine 45.00

STAR ROSETTED

Non-flint made by McKee Bros., Pittsburgh, Pa., c. 1875.

Butter, covered 35.00
Compotes

Covered 48.00
Open 30.00
Creamer 28.50
Goblet 22.50
Pickle 10.00
Pitcher, water 40.00
Plates
7″ 15.00
10″, bread plate, "A Good Mother
Makes a Happy Home" 40.00
Relish, 9″ 15.00
Sauces
Flat 6.50
Footed 10.00
Spooner 18.50
Sugars
Covered 35.00
Open 25.00

[THE] STATES
(Cane and Star Medallion)

Non-flint made by the U. S. Glass Co. in 1905. Clear with gold trim, found also in emerald green. Add 20% for green.

Bowl, 9″ 32.50
Butter, covered 35.00
Celery Vase 17.50
Compote, open, 7″, high standard . . 42.00
Creamer 18.50
Goblet 22.00
Pitcher, water 50.00
Plate, 10″ 22.50
Punch Cup 9.75

Punch Bowl	80.00
Relish, 6½", three-handled	25.00
Sauces, 4", flat, shaped like little tubs with handles	8.00
Sugar, covered	25.00
Syrup	65.00
Tumbler	15.00
Toothpick, handled	26.00
Wine	24.00

STEDMAN

Flint glass c. 1860.

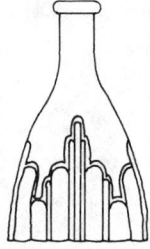

Celery	60.00
Champagne	30.00
Cheese, covered	60.00
Compotes	
Covered, 7", 8", high standard	75.00
Open, 8", low standard	50.00
Creamer	75.00
Decanter, unstoppered	72.50
Egg Cup	35.00
Goblet	50.00
Plate, 6"	30.00
Salt, Master	12.50
Sauce	12.50
Spooner	30.00
Sugar, covered	85.00
Tumbler	35.00
Wine	50.00

STIPPLED BAND
(Panelled Stippled Bowl)

Non-flint, c. 1870's.

Butter, covered	40.00
Celery	25.00
Compotes, high standard	
Covered, 9"	45.00
Open, 8"	35.00
Creamer, applied handle	30.00
Goblet	18.50
Pitcher, water, applied handle	40.00
Salt, footed	15.00
Sauce, flat	6.50
Spooner	18.50
Sugars	
Covered	30.00
Open	18.00
Tumbler, footed	20.00

STIPPLED CHAIN

Non-flint made by Gillinder & Sons, c. 1870's.

Biscuit Jar	75.00
Butter, covered	45.00
Creamer, applied handle	15.00
Egg Cup	18.50
Goblet	20.00
Pickle	15.00
Pitcher, water, applied handle	42.50
Salt, footed	15.00
Sauce	8.00
Spooner	20.00
Sugar, covered	35.00

STIPPLED CHERRY

Non-flint reportedly made by Lancaster Glass Co. in the 1880's.

Bowl, 8"	25.00
Butter, covered	40.00
Celery	25.00
Creamer	25.00
Pitcher, water	35.00
Plates	
6"	18.50
9¼", bread	30.00
Sauce, 4"	10.00

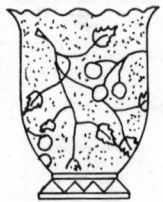

Spooner	15.00
Sugar, covered	28.50
Tumbler	18.50

STIPPLED DAISY

Non-flint, c. 1890's.

Compote, open, 8¼", high standard	24.00
Creamer	25.00
Pickle	15.00
Pitcher, water	40.00
Sauce, flat, 4¼"	8.50
Spooner	18.50
Sugar, covered	30.00

STIPPLED FORGET-ME-NOT

Non-flint made by Bryce Bros. in the 1880's, and after 1891 by the Model Flint Glass Co., Findlay, Ohio.

Butter, covered, Acorn finial	50.00
Cake Stands	

9"	35.00
12"	55.00
Celery	45.00
Compotes, covered	
6", low standard	45.00
8", high standard	60.00
Creamer	30.00
Cup and Saucer	35.00
Goblet	30.00
Mug	20.00
Pitchers	
Milk	42.50
Water	50.00
Plates	
7", Star center	30.00
9", Kitten center	40.00
Relish, oval	16.50
Salt, Master	25.00
Sauces	
Flat	10.00
Footed	15.00
Spooner	25.00
Sugar, covered	35.00
Toothpick, hat shaped	75.00
Trays	
Bread	35.00
Water, Aquatic center	45.00
Tumbler	30.00
Wine	35.00

STIPPLED GRAPE AND FESTOON

Non-flint made by Doyle & Co., Pittsburgh, Pa., c. 1870.

Butter, covered	50.00
Celery	40.00
Compote, covered, 9", low standard	55.00
Creamer, applied handle	50.00
Egg Cup	22.50
Goblet	25.00
Pickle	15.00
Pitcher, applied handle	
Milk	60.00
Water	85.00
Sauce, flat	12.00
Spooner	30.00
Sugar, covered	45.00
Wine	25.00

STIPPLED PEPPERS

Non-flint made by Boston & Sandwich Glass Co. in the 1870's.

Creamer, applied handle	32.50
Egg Cup	20.00
Goblet	27.50
Pitcher, water, applied handle	45.00
Salt, footed	15.00
Sauce	8.50
Spooner	25.00
Sugar, covered	35.00
Tumbler, footed	18.50

STIPPLED STAR

Non-flint made by Gillinder & Sons in the 1870's.

Butter, covered	35.00
Celery	29.00
Compotes, high standard	
Covered, 12"	65.00
Open, 8"	45.00
*Creamer	45.00
Egg Cup	25.00
*Goblet	27.00
Pickle	15.00
Pitcher, water	75.00
Sauces	
Flat	9.00
Footed	15.00

Spooner	22.00
*Sugar, covered	45.00
Tumbler	20.00
*Wine	25.00

STRAWBERRY
(Fairfax)

Non-flint pattern first made in the late 1860's and attributed to Boston & Sandwich Glass Co. Add approximately 100% for milk glass.

Bowl, oval	29.50
Butter, covered	55.00
Compotes, covered	
8", high standard	75.00
8", low standard	65.00
Creamer, applied handle	40.00
*Egg Cup	25.00
*Goblet	25.00
Pitchers, applied handle	
Syrup	40.00
Water	65.00
Relish, oval, scoop-shape	20.00
Salt, footed	25.00
Sauce, flat	15.00
Spooner	25.00
Sugar, covered	40.00

STRAWBERRY AND CURRANT

One of a non-flint series of fruit patterns which has become known as Multiple Fruits, (Cherry and Fig, Loganberry and Grape). They were made in Findlay, Ohio. All pieces carry the same design around the base. There is also a variation in the goblets in this series, made without the interlocking design, and they are of inferior quality. They were originally made to contain jelly and had a tin lid. The goblets to the set are of better glass, and carry the design which identifies them.

Butter, covered	50.00
Celery	40.00
Cheese, covered	50.00
Creamer	40.00

*Goblet	30.00
Pitchers	
Milk	40.00
Water	50.00
Sauce, footed	12.00
Spooner	30.00
Sugars	
Covered	40.00
Open	30.00
Syrup	45.00
Tumblers	30.00

SUNBURST

Non-flint c. 1880's.

Bowl, 5"	15.00
Butter, covered	40.00
Cake Stand, 9"	30.00
Celery	30.00
Cordial	18.50
Creamer	25.00
Cruet, stoppered	25.00
Egg Cup	15.00
Goblet	13.00
Marmalade Jar, covered	28.50
Pitchers	
Milk	35.00
Water	45.00
Plates	
6"	13.50
11"	20.00
11", Bread, with motto	30.00
Relish, double	20.00
Salts	

Individual	6.50
Master	18.00
Sauce, handled	10.00
Spooner	20.00
Sugar, covered	30.00
Tumbler	12.00
Wine	15.00

SWAN
(See Colored Pattern Glass Section.)

SWIRL
(See Colored Pattern Glass Section.)

TEARDROP AND TASSEL
(See Colored Pattern Glass Section.)

TEXAS
(Loop with Stippled Panels)

Non-flint made by U. S. Glass Co., c. 1900 in the States' Pattern series. Pieces are clear, trimmed in gold, sometimes cranberry flashed.

Bowls	
Flat, 7¼", 8½", 9½"	25.00
Footed, 7½", 8½", 9½"	30.00
Scalloped, 6", 7", 8"	25.00
Butter, covered	40.00
Cake Stand, 10"	35.00
Celery	
Tray	15.00
Vase	25.00
Compotes	
4", open, low standard	22.50
5", open, high standard	30.00
8", covered, high standard	50.00
*Creamers, individual and regular	15–25.00
Cruet, stoppered	25.00
Goblet	25.00
Pitcher, water	40.00
Plate, 9"	20.00
Relish	15.00
Salt, Master	22.50
Sauce, 4"	10.00
Spooner	20.00

*Sugars
Individual		20.00
Regular, covered		35.00
Regular, open		20.00
Toothpick		50.00
Tumbler		25.00
Wine		20.00

TEXAS BULL'S EYE
(Filley, Bull's Eye Variant)

Originated by Bryce Bros., Pittsburgh, Pa., and continued by Findlay Glass, Findlay, Ohio. Originally made in semi-flint, (not bell tone, but some lead content), c. 1850–1870 and later.

Bowl, Berry	18.50
Butter, covered	30.00
Sugar, covered	25.00
Spooner	20.00
Creamer	25.00
Pitcher, water	40.00
Tumblers	
Footed	22.50
Regular	20.00

TEXAS STAR
(Swirl and Star, Snowflake Base)

Non-flint pattern made by Steimer Glass Co., Buckhannon, W. Va., c. 1903–1908. Body of pieces are panelled. Pattern appears on the base, which is frosted around the design.

Bowls	
6"	30.00
9½"	45.00
Creamer and Sugar, open, bulbuous	45.00
Cup, Punch	12.00
Nappy, 5"	35.00
Pitchers	
Milk, bulbous, applied handle	50.00
Water, tankard, applied handle	60.00
Plates	
8"	30.00
11", cake	40.00

Salt and Pepper Shakers, pair	25.00
Syrup	50.00
Sugar Shaker	40.00
Toothpick	15.00
Tumbler	12.50

THISTLE

Non-flint c. 1870.

Bowl, 8"	30.00
Butter, covered	50.00
Cake Stand	45.00
Compotes	
High, covered	50.00
Low, covered	40.00
Low, open	20.00
Cordial	40.00
Creamer, applied handle	55.00
Cruet	45.00
Egg Cup	30.00
*Goblet	30.00
Pitcher, water	50.00
Relish	20.00
Salt, footed	18.50
Sauce, flat	15.00
Spooner	22.00
Sugars	
Covered	45.00
Open	35.00
Tumbler	30.00
Wine	35.00

THOUSAND EYE
(See Colored Pattern Glass Section.)

THREE-FACE

Non-flint made by George E. Duncan & Son, Pittsburgh, Pa., c. 1872. Designed by John E. Miller, a designer with Duncan, who later became a member of the firm. Companies in the Pittsburgh area produced many patterns in expectation of the 1876 Philadelphia Centennial Exposition. It has been heavily reproduced.

Butter, covered	150.00
Cake Stands	
8″, 9″	110.00
10″, 11″	150.00
Celery	100.00
Champagnes	
Hollow stem	250.00+
Saucer type	150.00
Claret	125.00
Compotes	
Covered, 4″	115.00
Covered, 6½″	150.00
Open, 8″	100.00
Cracker Jar, (rare)	500.00+
Creamer, with face	100.00
Goblet	80.00
Lamp, Oil	140.00
Marmalade Jar	100.00
Pitchers	
Milk	300.00
Water	295.00
Salt Dip	35.00
Sauce, footed	25.00
Shakers, pair	75.00
Spooner	75.00
Sugar, covered	95.00
Tumbler	55.00
Wine	85.00

THREE IN ONE
(Fancy Diamonds)

Non-flint, c. early 1900's.

Bowl, fluted, 8″	22.50
Butter, covered	38.50
Cake Stand, 9″	28.50
Celery	26.50

Compotes	
Covered, 6″, high standard	25.00
Open, 10″, fluted, high standard .	40.00
*Cracker Jar	55.00
Creamers	
Individual	18.50
Regular	25.00
Goblet	13.50
Pickle	17.50
Pitcher, water	35.00
Shakers, pair	25.00
Spooner	20.00
Sugars	
Individual	18.50
Regular, open	25.00
Tumbler	9.50
Toothpick	15.00
Wine	15.00

THREE-PANEL
(See Colored Pattern Glass Section.)

THUMBPRINT, EARLY
(Giant Baby Thumbprint)

Flint originally produced by Bakewell, Pears, & Co., Pittsburgh, Pa., c. 1850-1860's. Made by several factories in various forms.

Castor Bottle	30.00
Celery Vases	
Patterned base	100.00
Plain base	90.00
Compotes	

4", covered	75.00
8", open, flared and scalloped top base patterned	95.00
8½", open, patterned base	150.00
12¼", extremely large, spherical shape, with cover, (very rare, only two known)	350.00
Creamer	65.00
Egg Cup	40.00
Goblet, barrel shaped, baluster stem	50.00
Honey Dish	18.00
Plate, 8"	55.00
Salt, Master, footed	35.00
Sugars	
Covered	90.00
Open	40.00
Tumbler	50.00
Tumble-Up	350.00
Wine, barrel shape, baluster stem .	60.00

TORPEDO
(Pygmy)

Non-flint made by Thompson Glass Co., Uniontown, Pa., c. 1889. Clear; rare pieces with red stain.

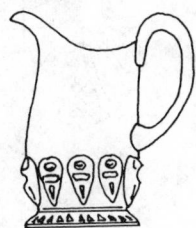

Banana Stand	75.00
Bowls	
7", open, flared rim	30.00
8", covered	38.50
9½", flared rim, open	35.00
Butter, covered	75.00
Cake Stand, 10"	65.00
Celery, scalloped top	40.00
Compotes	
4", covered Jelly	50.00
5", open, flared rim	35.00
6", covered, high standard	60.00
8", covered, high standard	95.00
9", open, flared rim, high standard	50.00
Creamer	40.00
Cruet, stoppered	45.00
Cup and Saucer	55.00
Decanter, stoppered	65.00
Goblet	50.00
Honey, 6", covered	50.00
Lamps	

3⅜", handled	45.00
8", plain base, pattern on bowl ..	85.00
Marmalade Jar, covered	55.00
Pitchers	
Milk, 8½"	60.00
Water, 10½"	95.00
Rose Bowl	60.00
Salts	
Individual	12.00
Master	20.00
Shakers, pair	50.00
Sauces	
3½", flat	12.50
3½", collared base	16.50
4½", collared base	20.00
Spooner, scalloped top	35.00
Syrup	55.00
Sugar, open	55.00
Trays, water	
10", round	95.00
11¾", clover shaped	75.00
Tumbler	40.00
Waste Bowl	40.00
Wine	28.50

TREE OF LIFE WITH HAND

Non-flint made by Duncan & Sons, Pittsburgh, Pa., c. 1884.

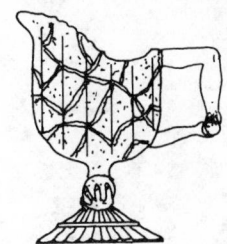

Bowls, oval, 8", 10"	25–35.00
Butter, covered	75.00
Cake Stands	
8¾"	60.00
10"	100.00
Celery	40.00
Compote, covered, 6", high standard	95.00
Compotes, open	
5", low standard	50.00
9", high standard	65.00
10½", high standard	80.00
Creamer	50.00
Finger Bowl	16.50
Goblet	40.00
Mug	30.00
Pitcher, water	75.00
Plate, 7"	20.00
Punch Cup	17.50

Sauce, footed	15.00
Sauces, flat, shaped like shells	15.00
Spooner	35.00
Sugar, covered	65.00
Tray, Ice Cream	40.00
Tumbler	27.50
Wine	30.00

TRUNCATED CUBE
(Thompson's #77)

Non-flint made by Thompson Glass Co., Uniontown, Pa., c. 1892. Clear and sometimes stained with ruby. Add 20% for ruby.

Butter, covered	35.00
Cordial	25.00
Creamers	
Individual	22.50
Regular, open	35.00
Spooner	25.00
Sugars	
Individual	22.50
Regular open	27.50
Syrup	45.00
Toothpick	20.00
Tumbler	28.50
Waste Bowl	30.00
Wine	25.00

TULIP

Flint, c. late 1850's.

Butter, covered	125.00
Celery Vase	75.00

Compotes	
Covered, 7", high standard	135.00
Open, 7", high standard	100.00
Creamer	85.00
Cruet, stoppered	85.00
Decanters, stoppered	
Pint	85.00
Quart	150.00
Egg Cup	35.00
Goblet	50.00
Honey	20.00
Mug	65.00
Pitcher, water	250.00
Plate, 6"	65.00
Salt, Master	30.00
Spooner	50.00
Sugar, covered	100.00
Tumbler	38.00
Wine	28.00

TULIP WITH SAWTOOTH

Originally made in flint glass by Bryce Bros., Pittsburgh, Pa., c. 1860's. Later made in non-flint. Prices represent flint.

Butter, covered	125.00
Celery	60.00
Champagne	75.00
Compotes	
Covered, 6", high standard	90.00
Open, 9", high standard	75.00
Open, 9", low standard	55.00
Open, 7", low standard	40.00
Creamer	100.00
Cruet	60.00
Decanters, handled	
Pint, bar lip	55.00
Quart, stoppered	100.00
Egg Cup	40.00
Goblet	45.00
Mug	80.00
Oil Bottle, stoppered	75.00
Pitcher, water	150.00
Plate, 6"	60.00
Pomade Jar	45.00
Salt, Master, plain edge	25.00
Sauce, flat	15.00

Spooner	35.00
Sugars	
Covered	95.00
Open	45.00
Tumblers	
Footed	50.00
Footed, semi-flint	35.00
Bar, non-flint	30.00
*Wine	42.50

TWO PANEL
(See Colored Pattern Glass Section.)

UTAH
(Frost Flower)

Non-flint made by U. S. Glass Co. in 1901 in the States' Pattern series.

Bowls	
Covered, 6", 7", 8"	20.00
Open, 6", 7", 8"	18.00
Butter, covered	30.00
Cake Plates	
9"	20.00
11"	25.00
Cake Stands	
8"	20.00
10"	27.50
Celery	17.50
Compotes	
Covered, 6", Jelly	25.00
Open, 6", Jelly	20.00
Goblet	27.50
Pickle	12.00
Pitcher, water	32.00
Sauce, 4"	7.50
Salt and Pepper Shakers, pair	25.00
Salt and Pepper Shakers, in holder, pair	32.50
Spooner	13.50
Sugar, covered	25.00
Tumbler	15.00

VICTORIA

Flint made by Bakewell, Pears, & Co., c. early 1860's.

Butter, covered	100.00
Cake Stands	
9"	75.00
15"	120.00
Compotes	
Covered, 6", high standard	55.00
Covered, 8", high standard	65.00
Covered, 8", low standard	55.00
Open, 10", high standard	60.00
Open, 10", low standard	55.00
Creamer	80.00
Spooner	50.00
Sugar, covered	95.00

VIKING

Non-flint, c. 1880's.

Bowls	
7"	25.00
8", oblong	
9"	35.00
Butter, covered	55.00
Cake Plate, 10", footed	45.00
Celery Vase	40.00
Compotes	
Covered, 8", low standard	82.00
Covered, 8", oval, low standard	55.00
Creamer	30.00
Custard Cup	9.00
Egg Cup, (rare)	45.00
Mug	45.00
Pickle	25.00
Pitcher, water	75.00
Salt, Master	18.00
Sauce, footed	9.00

Spooner	40.00
Sugars	
Covered	55.00
Open	27.50
Tray, Bread	45.00

WAFFLE

Flint made by Boston & Sandwich Glass Co. in the mid-1880's. Later by Bryce, Walker & Co., Pittsburgh, Pa.

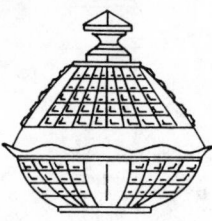

Butter, covered	125.00
Celery, 9½", footed	100.00
Champagne	100.00
Compotes	
Covered, high standard	125.00
Open, high standard	65.00
Cordial	75.00
Creamer	110.00
Decanter, stoppered	100.00
Egg Cup	32.50
Goblet	55.00
Lamps	
All Glass	175.00
Marble base	125.00
Plate, 6"	20.00
Salt, Master	30.00
Sauce, flat	15.00
Spooner	50.00
Sugar, covered	95.00
Tumblers	
Water	75.00
Whiskey, handled	85.00
Wine	65.00

WAFFLE AND THUMBPRINT

Flint made by the New England Glass Co. and Boston & Sandwich Glass Co., c. 1850–1860. Later by Bryce Walker & Co., Pittsburgh, Pa.

Butter, covered	150.00
Celery, knob stem	82.50
Champagne	38.00
Claret	85.00
Compotes	
Covered, high standard	150.00

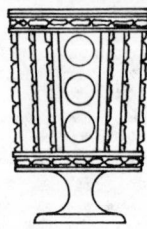

Open, high standard	125.00
Open, low standard	85.00
Creamer	125.00
Decanter, quart, stoppered	125.00
Egg Cup	45.00
Goblet, knob stem	60.00
Lamp, 9½"	100.00
Pitcher, water, (rare)	250.00 +
Salt, Master	40.00
Spillholder	55.00
Spooner	65.00
Sugar, covered	125.00
Sweetmeat, 6", covered, high standard, (rare)	150.00
Tumblers	
Water, footed	75.00
Large Flip Glass	145.00
Whiskey	65.00
Wine	60.00

WASHINGTON CENTENNIAL
(Chain with Diamonds)

Non-flint made by Gillinder & Co., Philadelphia, Pa.

Butter, covered	85.00
Cake Stands, 8½", 10"	60–75.00
Celery Vase	60.00
Champagne	65.00
Compotes	
Covered, 9"	65.00
Open, 8"	35.00
Creamer, applied handle	70.00
Egg Cup	45.00
Goblet	45.00
Pitcher, water	85.00
Platters	

"Carpenter's Hall"	100.00
"George Washington"	125.00
"Independence Hall"	85.00
Relish, Bear Paw handled, dated	55.00
Salt, Master	45.00
Sauce, 4″	12.00
Spooner	50.00
Sugars	
Covered	70.00
Open	40.00
Wine	50.00

WASHINGTON (EARLY)

Flint made by New England Glass Co., c. 1860's.

Bowl, 6¼″ x 9¼″, oval	75.00
Bottle, Bitters	75.00
Butter, covered	175.00
Celery	95.00
Champagne	100.00
Compotes	
Covered, 6″, high standard	95.00
Covered, 10″, high standard	175.00
Cordial	150.00
Creamer	200.00
Decanter, stoppered	150.00
Egg Cup	75.00
Goblet	75.00
Pitcher, water	250.00+
Relish	55.00
Salt, Master	55.00
Sauce, 4½″	25.00
Spooner	65.00
Sugar, covered	100.00
Tumbler	85.00
Wine	65.00

WASHINGTON (LATE)

Non-flint made by U. S. Glass Co., c. 1900 in the States' Pattern series. Clear. This pattern is often found with ruby stain as a souvenir of a place or event. Add 20% for ruby.

Bowls	
Covered, 5″, 6″	13.50

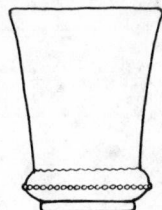

Covered, 7″, 8″	15.00
Open, 8″	13.00
Butter, covered	22.50
Cake Stands, 8″, 11″	22.50-27.50
Celery Tray	16.00
Champagne	13.00
Claret	13.00
Compotes	
Covered, 6″	27.50
Open, 8″	25.00
Cordial	13.50
Creamer	18.50
Cruet, stoppered	15.00
Goblet	15.00
Pickle	8.50
Pitchers	
Milk	30.00
Water	27.50
Water, ½ gallon	32.50
Plates, 6″, 8″, 10″	10-15.00
Sauces, 3″, 4″	7.50-9.50
Spooner	13.50
Sugar, open	18.50
Toothpick	8.50
Tumbler	13.50
Wine	13.50

WESTWARD HO

Non-flint made by Gillinder & Sons, Philadelphia, Pa., c. late 1870's. Has been reproduced in clear and colors.

Butter, covered	165.00
Celery Vase	105.00

Champagne, (rare)	250.00
Compotes, covered	
4", low standard	125.00
5", high standard	250.00
5", low standard	175.00
6", low standard	150.00
8", high standard	225.00
8", open	75.00
Cordial	150.00
Creamer	85.00
Goblet	85.00
Marmalade Jar, covered	175.00
Pitcher, water	200.00
Platter, Bread, oval	100.00
Sauces, footed	
3½"	23.00
4⅛"	40.00
Spooner	85.00
Sugar, covered	145.00
Wine	135.00

Spooner	25.00
Sugar, open	25.00
Tumbler	25.00
Wine	30.00

WISCONSIN
(See BEADED DEWDROP.)

WYOMING
(Enigma)

Made by U. S. Glass Co., in the States' Pattern series, c. 1890.

Butter, covered	30.00
Cake Stand	35.00
Goblet	30.00
Creamer, 2 shapes	25.00
Sugars	
Covered	35.00
Open	30.00
Spooner	20.00

WHEAT AND BARLEY
(See Colored Pattern Glass Section.)

WILD FLOWER
(See Colored Pattern Glass Section.)

WILLOW OAK
(See Colored Pattern Glass Section.)

WINDFLOWER

Non-flint, c. late 1870's.

Butter, covered	50.00
Celery	32.50
Compotes	
Covered, high standard	65.00
Open, low standard	35.00
Cordial	38.00
Creamer	17.50
Egg Cup	22.50
Goblet	30.00
Pickle	20.00
Pitcher, water	45.00
Salt, Master	25.00
Sauce, flat	8.50

X-BULL'S EYE
(Summit)

Non-flint made by Thompson Glass Co., Uniontown, Pa., in the early 1890's.

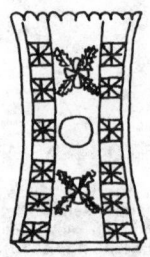

Bowl, 7½", pie crust edge	28.50
Butter, covered	65.00
Celery	35.00

Compote, open, 8", high standard, pie crust edge	55.00
Creamers	
Individual	25.00
Regular	40.00
Pitcher, water, tankard	75.00
Relish, handled	25.00
Spooner	28.50
Sugar, open	40.00
Tumbler	26.50

ZIPPER
(Cobb)

Non-flint made by Richards & Hartley, Tarentum, Pa., c. 1880's.

Banana Stand	50.00
Bowl, 7"	15.00
Butter, covered	30.00
Celery	18.50
Compote, covered, 8", low standard	35.00
Creamer	18.50
Cruet, stoppered	25.00
Egg Cup	18.50
Goblet	15.00
Lamp, Oil	35.00
Marmalade Jar, covered	28.00
Pitchers	
Milk	25.00
Water	35.00
Relish	12.50
Salt Dip	10.00
Sauces, flat and footed	6.00
Spooner	16.50
Sugars	
Covered	22.50
Open	15.00
Salt and Pepper Shakers	15.00
Sugar Shaker	26.00
Toothpick	15.00
Toy, child's banana stand	22.50
Wine	15.00

COLORED PATTERN GLASS

AMBERETTE
(See KLONDIKE)

ARCHED OVALS

Made by U.S. Glass Co., c. 1908. Cobalt is
very rare.

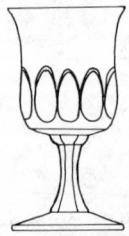

	Clear	Geeen	Red	Cobalt
Bowl, Berry	15.00	20.00	20.00	
Butter, covered	30.00	35.00	35.00	
Cruet	25.00	30.00	30.00	
Celery	20.00	25.00	25.00	
Dishes, various shapes and sizes	7.50	10.00	10.00	
Dish, Olive, with handle	12.00	14.00	14.00	
Pitcher, Water	30.00	35.00	35.00	
Syrup, with cover	35.00	38.00	38.00	55.00
Goblet	30.00	32.50	32.50	
Salt and Pepper Shakers	20.00	22.50	22.50	
Mugs	15.00	18.00	18.00	36.00
Spooner	18.00	18.00	18.00	
Sugar, covered	25.00	28.00	28.00	
Tumbler	28.00	32.50	32.50	55.00
Toothpick	20.00	25.00	25.00	48.00
Vase	15.00	18.00	18.00	36.00

BARRED FORGET-ME-NOT

Made by Canton Glass Co., Canton, Ohio, c.
1883.

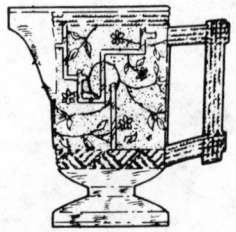

	Clear	Amber	Blue	Milk	Vaseline	Apple Green
Butter, covered	35.00	45.00	48.00	45.00	45.00	60.00
Cake Stand, large	45.00	55.00	58.00	55.00	55.00	75.00
Celery	30.00	50.00	53.00	50.00	50.00	60.00
Compotes						
Covered, high standard	35.00	50.00	53.00	50.00	50.00	60.00
Open, low standard	25.00	45.00	48.00	45.00	45.00	42.50
Creamer	27.50	40.00	43.00	40.00	40.00	48.00

	Clear	Amber	Blue	Milk	Vaseline	Apple Green
Goblet	30.00	52.00	55.00	52.00	52.00	60.00
Pitcher, Water	40.00	60.00	63.00	60.00	60.00	80.00
Plate, 9", handles	28.50	45.00	48.00	45.00	45.00	40.00
Relish, handles	12.00	23.00	26.00	23.00	23.00	25.00
Sauce, flat	10.00	19.00	22.00	19.00	19.00	20.00
Spooner	20.00	28.00	30.00	28.00	28.00	40.00
Sugar, covered	30.00	40.00	43.00	40.00	40.00	60.00
Wine	20.00	30.00	32.00	30.00	30.00	40.00

BASKETWEAVE

Non-flint c. 1880's.

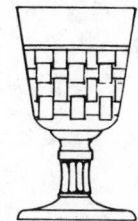

	Clear	Canary	Amber	Blue	Vaseline	Apple Green
Bowl, 9", covered	18.00	21.00	21.00	23.00	25.00	36.00
Butter, covered	32.00	35.00	35.00	37.50	39.00	60.00
Cordial	22.00	25.00	25.00	27.50	29.00	38.00
Creamer	27.50	30.00	30.00	32.50	36.00	47.50
Cup and Saucer	30.00	33.00	33.00	35.00	37.00	60.00
Egg Cup, single	15.00	18.00	18.00	20.00	25.00	30.00
*Goblet	25.00	28.00	28.00	30.00	32.50	50.00
Mug	20.00	23.00	23.00	25.00	27.50	40.00
Pickle	14.00	17.00	17.00	19.00	21.00	30.00
Pitcher						
Milk	40.00	43.00	43.00	45.00	47.00	65.00
Water	45.00	48.00	48.00	50.00	32.00	75.00
Plate, 9"	20.00	23.00	23.00	25.00	27.50	38.00
Salt Dip	7.50	10.00	10.00	12.00	12.00	10.00
Sauces	7.50	10.00	10.00	12.00	12.00	14.00
Shakers, pair	25.00	28.00	28.00	32.50	30.00	35.00
Spooner	18.50	21.00	21.00	23.00	25.00	35.00
Sugar, covered	30.00	33.00	33.00	35.00	37.50	60.00
Syrup	45.00	48.00	48.00	50.00	52.00	70.00
Tumbler	15.00	18.00	18.00	20.00	20.00	30.00
Tray, Water	28.50	32.50	32.50	33.00	45.00	45.00
Wine	25.00	28.00	28.00	30.00	30.00	50.00

BEADED SWIRL
(Swirled Column)

**Made by George Duncan & Sons, c. 1890. The
dual names are for the two forms of the pattern. Beaded Swirl stands on flat bases and
is solid in shape. Swirled Column stands on
scrolled, sometimes guilded, feet, and the
shape taped towards the base. Both forms in
clear and emerald green, trimmed in gold.**

Some also in milk white. Flat type pieces produced in greater quantity than footed. Footed pieces in Berry bowl, compote, creamer, cruet, sauces, spooner, covered sugar and water pitcher. Prices for both forms are equal.

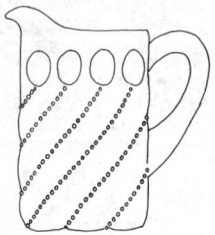 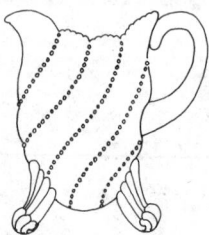

	Clear	Emerald Green	Milk
Butter, covered	35.00	45.00	45.00
Cake Stand	35.00	45.00	45.00
Bowls			
Flat	18.00	23.00	23.00
Footed, round	18.00	23.00	23.00
Footed, oval	18.00	23.00	23.00
Compotes			
Covered	42.00	52.00	52.00
Open	37.00	45.00	45.00
Goblet	35.00	40.00	45.00
Mug, handled	25.00	35.00	35.00
Pitcher, Water	40.00	50.00	50.00
Creamer			
Flat	30.00	40.00	40.00
Footed	30.00	40.00	40.00
Dish, oval flat	12.00	18.00	18.00
Relish	12.00	20.00	20.00
Sugar, covered			
Flat	35.00	45.00	45.00
Footed	35.00	45.00	45.00
Spooner			
Flat	30.00	45.00	45.00
Footed	30.00	45.00	45.00
Syrup, with Brittania top	45.00	55.00	55.00
Sauces			
Flat	18.00	23.00	23.00
Footed	18.00	23.00	23.00
Tumbler	20.00	30.00	30.00
Wine	30.00	35.00	35.00

BLACKBERRY

Non-flint made by Hobbs, Brockunier & Co. in the late 1870's. Later reissued by Phoenix Glass Co. Has been reproduced in milk glass.

	Clear	Milk
Butter, covered	60.00	85.00
Celery vase	60.00	85.00
Compote, covered, 8″, high standard	75.00	90.00
Creamer	55.00	80.00
Egg Cup, double	40.00	75.00
Goblet	30.00	40.00
Honey Dish	16.50	40.00
Pitcher, Water, (scarce)	150.00	500.00+
Relish	25.00	55.00
Salt, Master	28.50	65.00
Sauces	15.00	30.00
Spooner	50.00	85.00
Sugar, covered	60.00	110.00
Tumbler	25.00	45.00
Wine	18.00	35.00

CANE

Non-flint made by Gillinder Glass Co. and McKee Glass Co., c. 1875–1885.

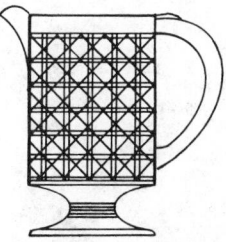

	Clear	Apple Green	Amber	Vaseline	Blue
Bowl, 7½″	20.00	22.00	23.00	27.00	30.00
Butter, covered	40.00	42.00	43.00	47.00	50.00
Celery	20.00	—	23.00	—	—
Creamer	22.50	24.00	25.00	30.00	32.50
Cruet, with original stopper	25.00	—	—	—	—
Finger Bowl	15.00	17.00	20.00	22.50	25.00
Goblet	20.00	22.00	25.00	27.00	30.00
Kettle, Matchholder	31.00	—	32.00	35.00	40.00
Pickle	12.50	14.00	14.00	19.00	22.50
Pitcher, Water	30.00	32.00	32.00	37.50	45.00
Plate, Toddy, 4½″	10.00	12.00	12.00	17.00	20.00
Salt Dip	7.50	10.00	10.00	12.00	16.00
Sauce,					
Flat	7.50	10.00	10.00	12.00	16.00
Footed	8.50	10.00	12.00	13.50	17.00
Shakers, pair	27.50	35.00	30.00	34.00	37.50
Slipper, whimsey	30.00	—	—	—	37.50
Spooner	18.50	21.00	20.00	25.00	27.50
Sugar, covered	47.50	50.00	50.00	52.50	55.00
Toothpicks	20.00	22.00	23.00	27.00	30.00
Tray, Water	30.00	32.00	33.00	37.00	45.00
Tumbler	18.50	21.00	20.00	25.00	27.50
Wine	20.00	22.00	22.50	27.00	30.00

CANDLEWICK
(Cole, Banded Raindrop)

Non-flint c. 1880's.

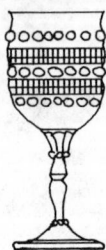

	Clear	Amber	Milk
Bowls	15.00	18.00	18.00
Butter, covered	35.00	42.00	42.00
Celery	20.00	24.00	24.00
Compote			
Covered	45.00	54.00	54.00
Open	35.00	42.00	42.00
Creamer	22.50	27.50	27.50
Cup and Saucer	25.00	30.00	30.00
Goblet	20.00	24.00	24.00
Plate, some with turned up edges	10.00	12.50	12.50
Relish, square	20.00	24.00	24.00
Salt and Pepper Shakers	28.50	34.00	34.00
Sauce, flat	6.50	8.00	8.00
Sugar			
Covered	35.00	42.00	42.00
Open	20.00	24.00	24.00
Spooner	18.50	21.00	21.00
Wine	19.50	22.50	22.50

CARAMEL SLAG
(See GREENTOWN, General Section)

CATHEDRAL

Non-flint pattern made by Bryce Bros., Pittsburgh, Pa., in the 1880's.

	Clear	Amber	Canary	Vaseline	Blue	Amythyst
Bowl, Berry, 7", 8"	25.00	28.00	28.00	30.00	32.00	50.00
Butter, covered	55.00	58.00	58.00	60.00	62.00	110.00
Cake Stand	38.50	41.00	41.00	43.00	45.00	75.00
Celery	30.00	33.00	33.00	35.00	37.00	60.00
Compote						
Covered, 8", high standard	50.00	53.00	53.00	55.00	57.00	100.00
Open, 7", low standard	25.00	28.00	28.00	30.00	32.00	50.00

	Clear	Amber	Vaseline	Blue	Green	Amethyst
Creamer	40.00	43.00	43.00	45.00	47.00	80.00
Cruet, stoppered	—	90.00	90.00	—	—	—
Egg Cup	25.00	28.00	28.00	30.00	32.00	50.00
Goblet	35.00	38.00	38.00	40.00	42.00	70.00
Pitcher, Water	55.00	58.00	58.00	60.00	62.00	110.00
Sauce						
Flat, 4″	10.00	13.00	13.00	15.00	17.00	20.00
Turned in-ruffled edge with ruby						
Stain, unusual	25.00	—	—	—	—	—
Footed	15.00	15.00	15.00	20.00	22.00	30.00
Spooner	25.00	28.00	28.00	30.00	32.00	50.00
Sugar, covered	32.00	35.00	35.00	37.00	39.00	65.00
Tumbler	15.00	18.00	18.00	20.00	22.00	30.00
Wine	24.00	27.00	27.00	29.00	31.00	47.50

COLORADO
(Lacy Medallion)

Non-flint made by U.S. Glass Co. in 1891 for States' pattern. Made in ruby, clear and amethyst (rare) besides green and blue. The State pieces (Colorado) usually have feet. Lacy Medallion is flat on base.

	Clear	Green	Blue	Amethyst
Banana Stand	25.00	37.00	40.00	58.00
Bowl, 6″	12.50	25.00	28.00	46.00
Bowl				
7½″, footed	20.00	32.00	35.00	53.00
8½″, footed	45.00	57.00	60.00	78.00
10″, footed, flared	55.00	67.00	70.00	88.00
Butter, covered	50.00	62.00	65.00	83.00
Cake Stand	55.00	67.00	70.00	88.00
Candy, 6″	15.00	27.00	30.00	48.00
Celery	32.50	45.00	48.00	66.00
Compote				
Open, 6″, low standard	27.50	39.00	42.00	60.00
Open, 9½″, low standard	35.00	47.00	50.00	68.00
Creamer				
Individual	20.00	32.00	35.00	53.00
Regular	32.50	45.00	48.00	74.00
Mug	18.50	30.00	33.00	50.00
Nappy	20.00	32.00	35.00	53.00
Plate, 6″, square	22.50	45.00	48.00	66.00
Punch Cup	12.00	26.00	30.00	48.00
Salt	10.00	22.00	25.00	43.00
Sauce, footed	15.00	27.00	30.00	48.00
Spooner	22.00	35.00	38.00	56.00
Sugar				
Individual	22.50	35.00	38.00	56.00
Regular, covered	45.00	57.50	60.00	78.00

	Clear	Green	Blue	Amethyst
Toothpick	22.00	35.00	38.00	56.00
Tray, Card	16.50	28.00	31.00	48.00
Tumbler	18.00	30.00	33.00	51.00
Vase				
12″	35.00	47.50	50.00	68.00
14″	40.00	52.00	55.00	73.00

CROESUS

Made in clear by Riverside Glass Works, Wheeling, W. Va., in 1897. Produced in color by McKee in 1899.

	Clear	Green	Amethyst
Bowl, 6¼″, footed	75.00	152.50	225.00
*Butter, covered	100.00	175.00	300.00
Celery Vase	65.00	135.00	195.00
Compote, Jelly	85.00	165.00	250.00
Creamer			
Individual	35.00	72.00	105.00
Regular	65.00	140.00	200.00
Cruet, stoppered	75.00	155.00	230.00
Cruet, Salt and Pepper Shakers, on small tray as set	195.00	330.00	355.00
Pitcher, Water	90.00	185.00	265.00
Relish	35.00	72.00	100.00
Sauce	20.00	39.50	60.00
Shakers, pair	45.00	95.00	150.00
Spooner	40.00	75.00	120.00
Sugar, covered	85.00	175.00	250.00
*Toothpick	40.00	82.50	125.00
*Tumbler	30.00	65.00	95.00

DAHLIA

Non-flint c. 1880's.

	Clear	Blue	Green	Amber	Vaseline
Bowl, 5″ x 7″	15.00	22.50	22.50	28,50	28.50
Butter, covered	32.50	68.00	68.00	80.00	80.00
Cake Stand, 10″	30.00	46.50	46.50	75.00	75.00

	Clear	Blue	Green	Amber	Vaseline
Champagne	80.00	65.00	65.00	80.00	80.00
Compote					
Covered, 7″, high standard	55.00	85.00	85.00	100.00	100.00
Open, 8″, high standard	30.00	45.00	45.00	57.00	57.00
Cordial	30.00	46.50	46.50	55.00	55.00
Creamer	22.50	32.50	32.50	40.00	40.00
Egg Cup					
Double	45.00	65.00	65.00	80.00	80.00
Single	16.50	36.00	36.00	52.00	52.00
Goblet	40.00	55.00	55.00	65.00	65.00
Mug					
Large	37.50	55.00	55.00	65.00	65.00
Small	30.00	42.50	42.50	55.00	55.00
Pickle	18.00	27.50	27.50	32.50	32.50
Pitcher					
Milk, applied handle	35.00	55.00	55.00	66.00	66.00
*Water, applied handle	60.00	95.00	95.00	110.00	110.00
Plate, 7″	22.00	37.50	37.50	45.00	45.00
Plate, Cake, 9″, closed handles	24.00	45.00	45.00	60.00	60.00
Platter 8″ x 12″	28.00	42.00	42.00	50.00	50.00
Salt, footed	5.00	30.00	30.00	35.00	35.00
Sauce					
Flat	5.00	8.50	8.50	10.00	10.00
Footed	10.00	15.00	15.00	18.50	18.50
Spooner	17.50	40.00	40.00	50.00	50.00
Sugar, covered	40.00	58.00	58.00	72.00	72.00
Wine	30.00	52.00	52.00	62.50	62.50

DAISY AND BUTTON

Non-flint pattern made in the 1870's by several companies in many different forms. Practically every piece in this pattern has been reproduced in a variety of colors.

	Clear	Amber	Yellow	Blue	Vaseline	Apple green
Bowl						
9″, octagonal	30.00	33.00	33.00	38.00	45.00	45.00
11″, scalloped	60.00	63.00	63.00	68.00	75.00	75.00
Butter Chip	5.50	8.50	8.50	13.50	21.50	21.50
Butter, covered						
Round	65.00	68.00	68.00	73.00	80.00	80.00
Square	100.00	105.00	105.00	110.00	117.00	117.00
Canoe						
4″	7.50	10.00	10.00	15.00	22.00	22.00
8½″	15.00	18.00	18.00	23.00	30.00	30.00
12″	20.00	23.00	23.00	28.00	35.00	35.00
14″	25.00	28.00	28.00	33.00	40.00	40.00
Castor Set						
Glass holder, 3-bottle	50.00	53.00	53.00	58.00	65.00	65.00
Metal holder, 5-bottle	100.00	103.00	103.00	108.00	115.00	115.00

	Clear	Amber	Yellow	Blue	Vaseline	Apple green
Celery, square	25.00	28.00	28.00	33.00	41.00	41.00
Compote						
Covered, 6", high standard	20.00	23.00	23.00	28.00	35.00	35.00
Open, 8", high standard	50.00	53.00	53.00	58.00	65.00	65.00
Creamer	20.00	23.00	23.00	28.00	35.00	35.00
Cruet, stoppered	25.00	28.00	28.00	33.00	40.00	40.00
Egg Cup	15.00	18.00	18.00	23.00	30.00	30.00
Goblet	16.00	19.00	19.00	24.00	31.00	31.00
Hat, various sizes	10–13.00	14–35.00	14–35.00	36–50.00	51–57.00	51–57.00
Inkwell	30.00	33.00	33.00	38.00	45.00	45.00
Parfait	20.00	23.00	23.00	28.00	35.00	35.00
Pickle Castor, complete	75.00	78.00	78.00	83.00	90.00	90.00
Syrup	30.00	33.00	33.00	38.00	45.00	45.00
Pitcher, Water						
Bulbous	95.00	98.00	98.00	103.00	110.00	110.00
Tankard	50.00	53.00	53.00	58.00	65.00	65.00
Plate						
5", leaf shaped	8.00	11.00	11.00	16.00	23.00	23.00
6", round	6.50	10.00	10.00	15.00	22.00	22.00
7", square	10.00	13.00	13.00	18.00	35.00	35.00
10½", 2" deep	—	28.00	28.00	—	—	—
Platter, handled, 9" × 13", oval	22.00	25.00	25.00	28.00	35.00	35.00
Punch Bowl, with stand	85.00	88.00	88.00	93.00	100.00	100.00
Powder Horn	45.00	48.00	48.00	53.00	60.00	60.00
Salt, Master	10.00	13.00	13.00	18.00	25.00	25.00
Sauces, various sizes and shapes	7.50–15.00	10–18.00	10–18.00	19–27.00	28–35.00	28–35.00
Shakers, pair	20.00	23.00	23.00	28.00	35.00	35.00
Slipper						
5"	18.50	21.00	21.00	26.00	33.00	33.00
Scuff type, 11½"	100.00	103.00	103.00	111.00	118.00	118.00
Spooner	15.00	18.00	18.00	23.00	30.00	30.00
Sugar						
Covered	35.00	38.00	38.00	43.00	50.00	50.00
Open	25.00	28.00	28.00	33.00	40.00	40.00
Toothpick						
Urn shape	10.00	13.00	13.00	18.00	25.00	25.00
Round, silver rim and base	40.00	43.00	43.00	48.00	55.00	55.00
Trays, various sizes and shapes	20–35.00	36–50.00	36–50.00	51–65.00	66–80.00	66–80.00
Tumbler	12.00	15.00	15.00	20.00	27.00	27.00
Wine	10.00	13.00	13.00	18.00	25.00	25.00

DAISY AND BUTTON WITH CROSSBARS

Non-flint pattern made by Richards and Hartley, Tarentum, Pa., c. 1888.

	Clear	Yellow	Vaseline	Blue
Bowl				
6", open	18.50	26.00	26.00	30.00
9", open	22.50	32.50	32.50	38.50
Butter, covered				
Flat	75.00	100.00	100.00	125.00
Footed	85.00	120.00	120.00	138.50
Celery	30.00	35.00	35.00	50.00
Compote				
Covered, 8", high standard	45.00	65.00	65.00	78.50
Open, 8", high standard	30.00	45.00	45.00	50.00
Creamer				
Individual	20.00	28.00	28.00	35.00
Regular	28.50	40.00	40.00	48.00
Cruet, stoppered	32.50	45.00	45.00	55.00
Goblet	25.00	36.50	36.50	37.50
Pitcher				
Milk	35.00	52.50	52.50	60.00
Water	55.00	80.00	80.00	90.00
Sauce				
Flat	10.00	15.00	15.00	20.00
Footed	15.00	22.50	22.50	25.00
Shakers, pair	25.00	38.50	38.50	42.50
Spooner	22.50	32.50	32.50	45.00
Sugar, covered	40.00	55.00	55.00	65.00
Syrup	35.00	50.00	50.00	58.00
Toothpick	15.00	22.50	22.50	27.50
Tray, Water	35.00	50.00	50.00	58.00
Tumbler	15.00	22.50	22.50	28.50
Wine	20.00	28.50	28.50	35.00

DAISY AND BUTTON WITH "V" ORNAMENT

Made by A. J. Beatty & Company, 1886–1887.

	Clear	Amber	Yellow	Blue	Vaseline
Bowl					
9"	22.50	35.00	35.00	42.50	55.00
10"	25.00	38.50	38.50	45.00	45.00
Butter, covered	75.00	110.00	110.00	125.00	90.00
Celery	30.00	42.00	42.00	50.00	50.00
Creamer	28.50	40.00	40.00	48.00	50.00
Goblet	25.00	36.50	36.50	45.00	50.00
Mug	15.00	22.50	22.50	27.50	35.00
Pickle Castor, complete	85.00	122.00	122.00	135.00	100.00
Pitcher, Water	40.00	55.00	55.00	68.50	60.00
Punch Cup	7.50	12.50	12.50	18.00	27.50
Sauce, 5"	10.00	15.00	15.00	18.50	30.00
Spooner	22.50	32.50	32.50	40.00	45.00

	Clear	Amber	Yellow	Blue	Vaseline
Sugar, covered	40.00	60.00	60.00	75.00	75.00
Toothpick	12.50	18.50	18.50	45.00	48.00
Tray, Water	35.00	50.00	50.00	65.00	55.00
Tumbler	15.00	24.50	24.50	28.00	35.00

DELAWARE
(Four-Petal Flower)

Non-flint pattern made by U.S. Glass Company circa 1899. Amethyst is very scarce.

	Clear	Green with Gold	Rose with Gold
Bowl, 9"	25.00	45.00	58.00
Bowl, Banana	40.00	48.50	55.00
Butter, covered	75.00	100.00	125.00
Celery	—	65.00	—
Creamer	20.00	40.00	50.00
Cruet, stoppered	42.50	50.00	60.00
Cup and Saucer	35.00	45.00	50.00
Pitcher, Water	60.00	75.00	100.00
Punch Cup	10.00	15.00	18.00
Sauce	20.00	25.00	30.00
Spooner	20.00	50.00	75.00
Sugar, covered	65.00	85.00	100.00
Toothpick	20.00	30.00	40.00
Tray, Water	18.00	—	—
Tumbler	30.00	35.00	45.00
Vase	—	44.00	—

DEWDROP

Non-flint c. 1870.

	Clear	Vaseline	Amber	Blue
Butter, covered	40.00	50.00	50.00	75.00
Cake Stand, 9½"	30.00	42.50	42.50	55.00
Compote, covered, 9¼", high standard	50.00	55.00	55.00	75.00
Creamer	30.00	40.00	40.00	50.00
Goblet				
Dewdrop base	35.00	40.00	40.00	55.00
Plain base	14.00	26.00	26.00	35.00
Mug, applied handle	20.00	32.50	32.50	40.00
Pitcher, Water	40.00	55.00	55.00	75.00

	Clear	Vaseline	Amber	Blue
Relish, double	20.00	25.00	25.00	35.00
Salt Shaker, footed (1)	18.00	20.00	20.00	22.50
Sauce, flat	7.50	12.00	12.00	17.50
Sugar, covered	35.00	50.00	50.00	57.50
Wine	10.00	15.00	15.00	20.00

DEWEY
(Flower Flange)

Made by Indiana Tumbler & Goblet Co., Greentown, Ind., 1894. Later by U.S. Glass Co. until 1904.

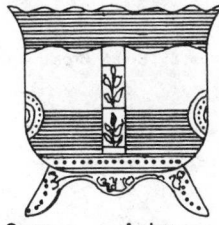

	Clear	Green	Amber	Caramel
Butter, covered	30.00	61.00	61.00	151.00
Creamer	25.00	56.00	56.00	146.00
Cruet, stoppered	27.50	58.50	58.50	148.50
Mug	32.50	63.50	63.50	153.50
Pitcher, Water	42.50	73.50	73.50	163.50
Plate, 7½″, footed	20.00	41.00	41.00	131.00
Relish dish, serpentine shape	25.00	56.00	56.00	146.00
Sauce	10.00	31.00	31.00	121.00
Shakers, pair	30.00	51.00	51.00	141.00
Spooner	20.00	41.00	41.00	131.00
Sugar, covered	30.00	51.00	51.00	141.00
Tumbler	25.00	56.00	56.00	146.00

DIAMOND QUILTED

Non-flint c. 1880.

	Clear	Vaseline	Amber	Blue	Amethyst
Butter, Covered	40.00	80.00	125.00	125.00	125.00
Celery	27.50	60.00	75.00	75.00	75.00
Champagne	25.00	65.00	78.00	78.00	78.00
Compote					
Covered, high standard	45.00	87.50	120.00	120.00	120.00
Open, high standard	30.00	65.00	78.00	78.00	78.00
Creamer	25.00	55.00	75.00	75.00	75.00
*Goblet	25.00	52.50	65.00	65.00	65.00
Pitcher, Water	35.00	72.50	85.00	85.00	85.00
Sauce					
Flat	9.00	25.00	9.00	9.00	9.00
Footed	18.00	37.50	25.00	25.00	25.00

	Clear	Vaseline	Amber	Blue	Amethyst
Spooner	25.00	55.00	38.00	38.00	38.00
Sugar, covered	30.00	62.50	75.00	75.00	75.00
Tray	30.00	65.00	80.00	80.00	80.00
*Tumbler	15.00	32.50	40.00	40.00	40.00
Wine	15.00	35.00	42.00	42.00	42.00

FINECUT

Non-flint made by Bryce Bros., Pittsburgh, Pa., c. 1879.

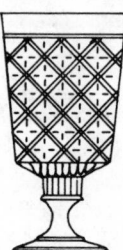

	Clear	Amber	Vaseline	Blue
Butter, covered	40.00	55.00	55.00	68.50
Creamer	26.50	37.50	37.50	45.00
Finger Bowl, footed	16.50	25.00	25.00	28.50
Goblet	25.00	34.00	34.00	42.50
Pickle	15.00	20.00	20.00	25.00
Pitcher, Water	40.00	52.00	52.00	65.00
Plate				
6"	20.00	28.50	28.50	35.00
7"	22.50	30.00	30.00	38.00
10"	30.00	42.00	42.00	50.00
Sauce	8.50	12.50	12.50	14.50
Spooner	30.00	39.50	39.50	48.00
Sugar				
Covered	32.50	45.00	45.00	55.00
Open	25.00	38.00	38.00	45.00
Tray				
Bread	25.00	35.00	35.00	42.00
Water	35.00	48.00	48.00	55.00

FINECUT AND PANEL

Non-flint pattern made by many Pittsburgh factories in the 1880's. Reissued in the early 1890's by U.S. Glass Co.

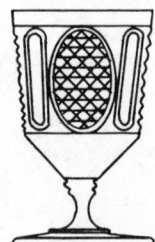

	Clear	Amber	Vaseline	Blue
Bowl, 7"	17.50	26.50	26.50	35.00
Butter, covered, square	40.00	60.00	60.00	75.00
Cake Stand, 10"	30.00	48.00	48.00	55.00
Compote, open, high standard	35.00	55.00	55.00	60.00

	Clear	Amber	Vaseline	Blue
Cordial	20.00	32.50	32.50	37.50
Creamer	25.00	37.50	37.50	45.00
Goblet	24.00	35.00	35.00	50.00
Pitcher, Water	35.00	42.50	42.50	65.00
Plate				
6¼"	15.00	20.00	20.00	27.00
7¼"	17.50	22.50	22.50	30.00
Platter	45.00	50.00	50.00	75.00
Relish	17.50	22.00	22.00	27.50
Sauce				
Flat, square	10.00	15.00	15.00	22.00
Footed, square	10.00	15.00	15.00	22.00
Spooner	25.00	32.00	32.00	45.00
Sugar, open	22.50	30.00	30.00	40.00
Tray, Water, 12"	45.00	60.00	60.00	75.00
Tumbler	13.50	20.00	20.00	27.50
Wine	20.00	25.00	25.00	28.00

FRANCESWARE

Made by Hobbs, Brokunier & Co., Wheeling, W. Va., c. 1880's. A clear frosted hobnail or swirl pattern galss with amber stained top rims. It may be pressed or mold blown. (Swirl pieces are noted, otherwise they are hobnail.)

	Clear	Frosted
Bowl		
4"	28.50	45.00
7½"	50.00	75.00
Box, 5¼", round, covered	45.00	65.00
Butter, covered	80.00	110.00
Creamer	50.00	70.00
Pitcher		
8½"	90.00	150.00
11"	150.00	200.00
Syrup, swirl	65.00	80.00
Sauce, 4", square	22.50	32.00
Sugar Shaker, swirl	65.00	78.00
Shakers, pair	50.00	65.00
Shakers, pair, swirl	60.00	75.00
Spooner	45.00	52.00
Sugar		
Covered	60.00	75.00
Open	40.00	60.00
Tumbler	35.00	42.00
Toothpick	40.00	50.00
Tray, leaf shaped, 12"	75.00	100.00

GREEN HERRINGBONE
(See PANELLED HERRINGBONE, Clear Pattern Glass Section.)

HOBNAIL, FAN TOP

Non-flint c. 1880.

	Clear	Amber	Blue
Bowl, Berry	25.00	45.00	50.00
Butter, covered	40.00	65.00	70.00
Celery	30.00	35.00	40.00
Creamer	25.00	40.00	45.00
Goblet	20.00	35.00	40.00
Salt, individual	8.50	12.00	17.00
*Sauce	10.00	18.00	23.00
Sugar, covered	30.00	45.00	50.00
Tray, 8″ x 12″	20.00	30.00	35.00

HOBNAIL, OPALESCENT
(See Opalescent Glass Section.)

HOBNAIL, POINTED

Non-flint c. 1880. Rare in Apple Green, Dark Green and Vaseline.

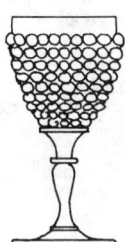

	Clear	Amber	Blue
Bone Dish	18.00	23.00	28.00
*Bowl	20.00	25.00	30.00
Butter, covered	30.00	35.00	40.00
Cake Stand, 10″	35.00	40.00	45.00
Celery Vase	25.00	30.00	35.00
Compote, open, 8″, high standard ..	35.00	40.00	45.00
Cordial	20.00	25.00	30.00
Creamer	25.00	30.00	35.00
Goblet	25.00	30.00	35.00
Inkwell	25.00	30.00	35.00
Pickle	12.00	17.00	22.50
*Pitcher, Water	20.00	25.00	30.00
Plate, 7″	17.50	22.50	27.50
Salt			
Individual	5.00	10.00	15.00
*Shakers, pair	16.00	20.00	25.00
*Sauce, flat	10.00	15.00	20.00
Spooner	18.00	23.00	28.00
*Sugar, open	15.00	20.00	25.00

	Clear	Amber	Blue
Toy Mug, child's	9.00	—	14.00
Tray			
Pen	15.00	20.00	25.00
Water, 11½"	30.00	35.00	40.00
*Wine	14.00	20.00	25.00

HOBNAIL, PRINTED

Non flint c. 1880–1890's

	Clear	Amber	Vaseline	Canary	Blue
Butter, covered	30.00	35.00	35.00	35.00	50.00
Celery Vase	25.00	30.00	30.00	30.00	45.00
Creamer	20.00	25.00	25.00	25.00	35.00
Goblet	20.00	25.00	25.00	25.00	40.00
Mug	15.00	20.00	20.00	20.00	35.00
Pitcher, Water	30.00	35.00	35.00	35.00	50.00
Sauce	8.50	12.00	12.00	12.00	22.50
Spooner	20.00	25.00	25.00	25.00	27.50
Sugar, covered	25.00	30.00	30.00	30.00	40.00
Tumbler	15.00	20.00	20.00	20.00	35.00
Wine	16.00	21.00	21.00	21.00	30.00

HOBNAIL, THUMBPRINT BASE

**Non-flint pattern originally made by Doyle &
Co., Pittsburgh, Pa., c. 1880's. Later, by several other companies between 1893–1898.**

	Clear	Amber	Blue
Bowl, Berry, 9", 10"	25.00	35.00	50.00
Butter, covered	25.00	35.00	50.00
Celery	20.00	30.00	45.00
Creamer	25.00	35.00	45.00
Mustard Jar	14.00	24.00	38.50
Pitcher, Water	35.00	45.00	58.00
Salt, Individual	10.00	20.00	27.50
Spooner	25.00	35.00	42.50
Sugar, covered	27.50	37.50	45.00
Tray, Water	30.00	40.00	45.00

HOLLY AMBER
(Golden Agate)

Made by Indiana Tumbler & Goblet Co., Greentown, Ind. from January 1 to June 12, 1903. Original pieces are very rare. Prices given are for genuine pieces.

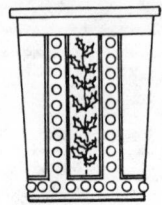

	Amber		Amber
Bowls		Plate, 7½", round	500.00
7"	650.00	Relish	500.00
9½"	750.00	Sauce, 4"	200.00
*Butter, covered	1400.00	Spooner	500.00
Cake Stand	1700.00	Sugar,	
*Compote, Jelly, 4¼", covered	750.00	Covered, 4½"	500.00
*Creamer	600.00	Open	400.00
*Cruet, stoppered	1250.00	Toothpick	
*Mug, 4", handled	500.00	*Flat	225.00
*Nappy	550.00	Footed rare	750.00
Parfait, 6"	550.00	Tray, Water, 9½"	1000.00
Pitcher, Water, 10"	2250.00		
Syrup	700.00		

HUMMING BIRD
(Flying Robin)

Non-flint c. 1880's.

	Clear	Canary	Vaseline	Amber	Blue
Bowl, Finger	20.00	28.00	28.00	35.00	35.00
Butter, covered	45.00	65.00	65.00	70.00	70.00
Celery	45.00	48.00	48.00	55.00	55.00
Compote, high standard	48.00	51.00	51.00	48.00	48.00
Creamer	27.00	48.00	48.00	58.00	58.00
Goblet	30.00	40.00	40.00	45.00	45.00
Pitcher, Water	40.00	65.00	65.00	70.00	70.00
Sauce					
Flat	10.00	15.00	15.00	20.00	20.00
Footed	15.00	20.00	20.00	26.50	26.50
Spooner	29.50	35.00	35.00	37.50	37.50
Sugar, covered	40.00	55.00	55.00	65.00	65.00
Tray, Water	50.00	60.00	60.00	75.00	75.00
Tumbler	27.50	30.00	30.00	35.00	35.00
Wine	30.00	42.50	42.50	45.00	45.00

JERSEY SWIRL
(Swirl)

Non-flint pattern made by Windsor Glass Co.,
Pittsburgh, Pa., c. 1887. Heavily reproduced
in color.

	Clear	Canary	Vaseline	Amber	Blue
Butter, covered	40.00	50.00	50.00	55.00	55.00
Cake Stand, 9″	45.00	55.00	55.00	60.00	60.00
Celery	26.50	36.00	36.00	41.00	41.00
Creamer	30.00	40.00	40.00	45.00	45.00
Marmalade Jar, original glass lid . . .	50.00	60.00	60.00	65.00	65.00
*Goblet					
Small	25.00	35.00	35.00	40.00	40.00
Large, wide bowl	28.50	38.50	38.50	43.00	43.00
Pitcher, Water	35.00	45.00	45.00	50.00	50.00
Plate					
6″	12.00	15.00	15.00	18.00	18.00
8″	14.00	17.00	17.00	20.00	20.00
10″	16.00	19.00	19.00	22.00	22.00
Salt,					
Individual	8.50	12.00	12.00	15.00	15.00
Master	12.00	14.00	14.00	16.00	16.00
Sauce	10.00	15.00	15.00	20.00	20.00
Spooner	20.00	25.00	25.00	28.00	28.00
Sugar, covered	27.50	32.50	32.50	37.50	37.50
Tumbler	16.50	22.50	22.50	26.00	26.00
Wine	45.00	50.00	50.00	52.50	52.50

KLONDIKE
(Amberette, English Hobnail Cross)

Non-flint pattern issued in the 1880's to commemorate the Alaskan Gold Rush. Frosted
panels depict snow; amber bands, gold. It
can be found clear and frosted, with or without scrolls, depending on the maker. Prices
listed are for frosted. Clear panels, approximately 30% less.

	Frosted		Frosted
Bowl, Berry, 8″	95.00	Sauce, flat	75.00
Butter, covered	250.00	Shakers, pair original tops	95.00
Cake Stand, 8″, square	500.00	Sugars,	
Celery	200.00	Covered	300.00
Champagne	400.00	Open	225.00
Creamer	175.00	Syrup, pewter lid	500.00
Cruet, stoppered	550.00	Toothpick	225.00
Goblet	250.00	Tray, 5½″, square	150.00
Pitcher, Water	600.00	Tumbler	135.00
Punch Cup	85.00		

LEAF MEDALLION

Made by Northwood Glass Co., c. 1880's. With gold trim, beading and medallions. Cobalt blue and amethyst are hard to find.

	Clear	Green	Cobalt	Amethyst
Bowl, Berry	12.00	24.00	48.00	48.00
Butter, covered	30.00	60.00	120.00	120.00
Cake Stand, 10"	35.00	70.00	140.00	140.00
Compote, open, Jelly, 5", 6"	27.50	55.00	100.00	100.00
Creamer	30.00	60.00	100.00	100.00
Pitcher, Water	50.00	100.00	150.00	150.00
Spooner	25.00	50.00	95.00	95.00
Sauce, 4½"	15.00	30.00	50.00	50.00
Sugar, covered	35.00	70.00	140.00	140.00
Tumbler	25.00	50.00	95.00	95.00

MAIZE

A milk white novelty glass designed by Joseph Locke and made by Libbey & Sons, Toledo, Ohio, c. 1889.

	Milk		Milk
Bowls			
5"	125.00	*Pitcher, Water	275.00
9"	175.00	Sauce	45.00
Butter, covered	295.00	*Shakers, pair	165.00
Celery Vase	85.00	Spooner	95.00
Creamer	165.00	Sugar, covered	250.00
Cruet, stoppered	175.00	Toothpick	160.00
Mustard, covered	95.00	*Tumbler	125.00

MAPLE LEAF

Non-flint pattern made by Gillinder & Sons, c. 1880. Heavily reproduced in clear and colors.

	Clear	Frosted	Amber	Vaseline	Canary	Blue
Bowl, 6" x 9"	20.00	25.00	30.00	30.00	30.00	34.00
Butter, covered	65.00	70.00	75.00	75.00	75.00	79.00
Cake Stand, 11"	40.00	45.00	50.00	50.00	50.00	54.00

	Clear	Frosted	Amber	Vaseline	Canary	Blue
Celery	30.00	35.00	40.00	40.00	40.00	44.00
Compote						
Covered, 9″, high standard	75.00	80.00	85.00	85.00	85.00	89.00
Jelly	30.00	35.00	40.00	40.00	40.00	44.00
Creamer	35.00	35.00	40.00	40.00	40.00	44.00
Goblet	35.00	40.00	45.00	45.00	45.00	49.00
Pitcher						
Milk	35.00	40.00	45.00	45.00	45.00	49.00
Water	50.00	55.00	60.00	60.00	60.00	64.00
Plate "Grant Peace," 10″	35.00	40.00	45.00	45.00	45.00	49.00
Platter, 10½″	30.00	35.00	40.00	40.00	40.00	44.00
Relish	12.00	15.00	18.00	18.00	18.00	22.00
Sauce						
5″	10.00	12.00	14.00	14.00	14.00	18.00
6″, footed	10.00	12.00	14.00	14.00	14.00	18.00
Spooner	20.00	25.00	30.00	30.00	30.00	34.00
Spooner	20.00	25.00	30.00	30.00	30.00	29.00
Sugar, covered	35.00	40.00	45.00	45.00	45.00	44.00
Tumbler	20.00	25.00	30.00	30.00	30.00	29.00

MARBLE GLASS

Made by Challinor, Taylor & Co., Tarantum, Pa., 1870's–1880's. Small quantities also made by other companies. Purple marble glass was also made in England, and all English pieces are marked. There are 8″ lattice-edged plates, never made in this country. A few of the better known patterns are Oval Panel, Flying Swan, Sunflower, Slabsides, Acanthus Leaf, Acanthus Basketweave, Raindrop, Flower and Panel and Flute. Purple is found most often, but there were other color combinations which are rarely seen today. Often referred to as "slag" glass, a term that has become obsolete, as it denotes it was made from waste material which was not the case.

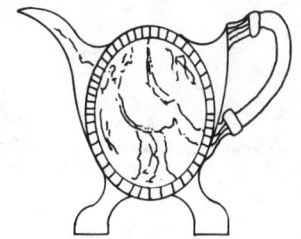

	Purple Marble
Bowls	
5½″ x 8″	125.00
5″	50.00
Celery Vases	125.00
Compotes	

	Purple Marble
7″, open, high standard	150.00
8″, covered, high standard	225.00
Match Holder	75.00
Pitcher, Water	225.00
Plates	

	Purple Marble		Purple Marble
8½	85.00	Spooner	90.00
10″	125.00	Sugar, open	100.00
Sauce, flat	50.00	Toothpick	75.00

MEDALLION

Non-flint c. 1880's.

	Clear	Amber	Canary	Vaseline	Blue	Green
Butter, covered	35.00	40.00	40.00	45.00	50.00	50.00
Castor Bottle	10.00	15.00	15.00	20.00	30.00	30.00
Celery	20.00	25.00	25.00	30.00	40.00	40.00
Compote, covered, high standard ...	40.00	45.00	45.00	50.00	60.00	60.00
Creamer	25.00	30.00	30.00	35.00	45.00	45.00
Egg Cup	18.00	23.00	23.00	28.00	38.00	38.00
Goblet	25.00	30.00	30.00	35.00	45.00	45.00
Pickle	15.00	18.00	18.00	20.00	30.00	30.00
Pitcher, Water	45.00	50.00	50.00	55.00	65.00	65.00
Sauce						
Flat	7.50	9.50	9.50	12.00	24.00	24.00
Footed	10.00	12.00	12.00	14.00	25.00	25.00
Spooner	18.00	20.00	20.00	22.00	30.00	30.00
Sugar, covered	25.00	30.00	30.00	30.00	40.00	40.00
Tumbler	18.50	22.50	22.50	25.00	35.00	35.00
Wine	20.00	25.00	25.00	25.00	35.00	35.00

NESTOR

Non-flint pattern made by National Glass Co., Indiana, Pa., c. 1903. Decorated with enamel.

	Clear	Green	Blue	Amethyst
Bowl, Berry	25.00	30.00	45.00	45.00
Butter, covered	35.00	40.00	55.00	55.00
Cake Plate	35.00	40.00	55.00	55.00
Compote, open, Jelly, 5″, 6″	40.00	45.00	60.00	60.00
Creamer	35.00	40.00	55.00	55.00

	Clear	Green	Blue	Amethyst
Cruet, with stopper	40.00	45.00	60.00	60.00
Pitcher, Water	50.00	55.00	70.00	70.00
Salt Shakers, pair	50.00	55.00	70.00	70.00
Spooner	30.00	35.00	50.00	50.00
Sugar, covered	35.00	40.00	55.00	55.00
Toothpick	30.00	35.00	50.00	50.00
Tumbler	40.00	45.00	60.00	60.00

OPALESCENT HOBNAIL
(See Opalescent Glass Section.)

PANELLED FORGET-ME-NOT

Non-flint pattern made by Bryce Bros., Pittsburgh, Pa., c. 1870's. Amethyst is rare, add 200% to clear.

	Clear	Amber	Vaseline	Blue	Green	Amethyst
Butter, covered	35.00	40.00	50.00	60.00	60.00	105.00
Cake Stand, 9½"	20.00	25.00	35.00	45.00	45.00	65.00
Celery	45.00	50.00	60.00	70.00	70.00	135.00
Compote, covered, 8" high standard	50.00	55.00	65.00	75.00	75.00	150.00
Creamer	25.00	30.00	40.00	50.00	50.00	75.00
Goblet	35.00	40.00	50.00	60.00	60.00	105.00
Marmalade Jar, covered	35.00	40.00	50.00	60.00	60.00	105.00
Pickle	12.00	17.00	18.00	35.00	35.00	36.00
Pitcher, Water	35.00	40.00	50.00	60.00	60.00	105.00
Sauce, Flat	8.50	10.00	12.00	30.00	30.00	25.50
Footed	10.00	12.00	18.00	15.00	15.00	30.00
Spooner	20.00	25.00	30.00	40.00	40.00	60.00
Sugar, covered	30.00	35.00	45.00	50.00	50.00	90.00
Wine	30.00	35.00	45.00	50.00	50.00	90.00

PRIMROSE

Non-flint pattern made by the Canton Glass Co., Canton, Ohio, c. 1880's. Apple Green is 100% more than clear.

	Clear	Amber	Vaseline	Canary	Blue
Bowl, 8"	22.50	26.50	26.50	26.50	32.50
Butter, covered	40.00	50.00	50.00	50.00	68.50
Cake Stand, 10"	35.00	45.00	45.00	45.00	55.00
Celery	25.00	30.00	30.00	30.00	40.00
Compote, covered, 6" low standard	28.00	32.50	32.50	32.50	45.00

	Clear	Amber	Vaseline	Canary	Blue
Creamer	30.00	35.00	35.00	35.00	47.00
Egg Cup	20.00	25.00	25.00	25.00	32.50
Goblet					
Plain stem	19.50	25.00	25.00	25.00	32.50
Knob stem	26.50	36.00	36.00	36.00	45.00
Pickle	12.50	16.50	16.50	16.50	20.00
Pitcher					
Milk	35.00	45.00	45.00	45.00	55.00
Water	32.00	42.00	42.00	42.00	50.00
Plate					
4½"	10.00	12.00	12.00	12.00	14.50
6"	15.00	14.00	14.00	14.00	25.00
Sauce, footed	12.00	15.00	15.00	15.00	18.50
Spooner	18.00	22.00	22.00	22.00	30.00
Sugar, covered	30.00	40.00	40.00	40.00	55.00
Toothpick	17.50	22.00	22.00	22.00	28.50
Tray, Water	30.00	40.00	40.00	40.00	50.00
Waste Bowl	20.00	30.00	30.00	30.00	32.50
Wine	28.00	32.00	32.00	32.00	32.00

PRINTED HOBNAIL
(See HOBNAIL, PRINTED)

PURPLE SLAG
(See MARBLE GLASS, This Section)

RAINDROP

Non-flint c. 1880's. Scarce in apple green.

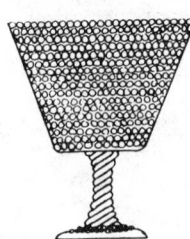

	Clear	Amber	Vaseline	Blue
Compote, open, 8", low standard	20.00	35.00	35.00	45.00
Creamer	20.00	35.00	35.00	45.00
Cup and Saucer	25.00	40.00	40.00	50.00
Egg Cup, double	25.00	35.00	35.00	45.00
Finger Bowl	15.00	25.00	25.00	35.00
Lamp, miniature	—	95.00	95.00	—
Pickle	16.00	22.50	22.50	32.50
Pitcher, Water	35.00	45.00	45.00	55.00
Plate, Cake	26.00	40.00	40.00	50.00
Sauce,				
Flat	8.00	12.00	12.00	14.00
Footed	10.00	15.00	15.00	18.00
Syrup	35.00	50.00	50.00	60.00
Tray, Water	35.00	45.00	45.00	55.00

ROSE-IN-SNOW

Non-flint pattern made by Bryce Bros., Pittsburgh, Pa., in the square form, c. 1880. Also made in the round form by Ohio Flint Glass Co.

	Clear	Amber	Canary	Vaseline	Blue
Bowl, 4″	10.00	13.00	13.00	13.00	20.00
Butter, covered					
Round	40.00	10.00	10.00	10.00	65.00
Square	50.00	60.00	60.00	60.00	75.00
Cake Stand 9″	80.00	90.00	90.00	90.00	125.00
Compote, covered					
8″ high standard	65.00	75.00	75.00	75.00	100.00
7″ low standard	50.00	60.00	60.00	60.00	75.00
Open, low standard	25.00	35.00	35.00	35.00	45.00
Creamer					
Round	35.00	45.00	45.00	45.00	55.00
Square	28.00	38.00	38.00	38.00	60.00
*Goblet	25.00	35.00	35.00	35.00	50.00
Marmalade Jar, covered	50.00	60.00	60.00	60.00	75.00
*Mug, "In Fond Remembrance"	35.00	45.00	45.00	45.00	55.00
Pickle					
'8½″ x 7″, double, (scarce)	85.00	95.00	95.00	95.00	125.00
Oval, handles at ends	21.50	31.50	31.50	31.50	32.50
Pitcher, Water, applied handle	95.00	105.00	105.00	105.00	150.00
Plate, 6½″	18.00	22.50	22.50	22.50	38.50
*10″ handled	35.00	40.00	40.00	40.00	55.00
Powder Jar	30.00	—	—	—	—
Sauce					
Flat	9.00	14.00	14.00	14.00	16.00
Footed	7.00	10.00	10.00	10.00	22.50
Spooner					
Round	25.00	35.00	35.00	35.00	40.00
Square	32.50	42.50	42.50	42.50	48.00
Sugar, covered					
Round	40.00	50.00	50.00	50.00	60.00
Square	45.00	55.00	55.00	55.00	70.00
Tumbler, applied handle	38.00	48.00	48.00	48.00	50.00
Vegetable, 7″ x 10″	65.00	70.00	70.00	70.00	105.00
Wine	28.00	35.00	35.00	35.00	42.50

ROSE SPRIG

Non-flint pattern made by Campbell, Jones & Co., Pittsburgh, Pa., 1886.

	Clear	Amber	Canary	Vaseline	Blue
Cake Stand, 9″	26.00	65.00	65.00	65.00	55.00
Celery	30.00	38.50	38.50	38.50	47.50
Creamer	32.50	40.00	40.00	40.00	50.00
Goblet	35.00	37.50	37.50	37.50	45.00

	Clear	Amber	Canary	Vaseline	Blue
Lemonade Glass	35.00	42.50	42.50	42.50	50.00
Nappy, 6", square	15.00	18.50	18.50	18.50	22.50
Pitcher, Water	45.00	55.00	55.00	55.00	65.00
Plates					
8"	25.00	30.00	30.00	30.00	37.50
10"	30.00	37.50	37.50	37.50	45.00
Relish, boat shaped	25.00	32.50	32.50	32.50	38.00
*Salt, Sleigh	22.50	30.00	30.00	30.00	40.00
Sauce, footed	10.00	15.00	15.00	15.00	20.00
Spooner	22.50	27.50	27.50	27.50	32.50
Sugar, covered	42.50	50.00	50.00	50.00	60.00
Tray, Water	45.00	55.00	55.00	55.00	68.50
Tumbler	25.00	30.00	30.00	30.00	37.50
Wine	30.00	37.50	37.50	37.50	45.00

ROYAL IVY

Non-flint made by Northwood Glass Co. in 1889 and 1890. Made clear and frosted, with cranberry flashing. Also made in cased spatter, cracquelle (clear and frosted), amber stained and clambroth. These last mentioned were experimental pieces, and not made in collectible sets.

	Clear	Frosted
Bowl		
Finger	120.00	120.00
Rose	85.00	100.00
Butter, covered	170.00	195.00
Creamer, applied handle	50.00	60.00
Jam or Marmalade Jar, silver cover .	115.00	125.00
Pitcher, Water, applied handle	90.00	100.00
Salt and Pepper Shakers, pair	100.00	125.00
Spooner	50.00	60.00
Sugar, covered	110.00	150.00
Syrup, silver cover	110.00	125.00
Toothpick	60.00	75.00
Tumbler	50.00	75.00

ROYAL OAK
(Acorn)

Non-flint made by Northwood Glass Co., Martins Ferry, Ohio, c. 1899. Made in clear and frosted with cranberry flashing. In early 1900

it was made in opaque, white with colored tops, and colored acorns and leaves. Milk white pieces are rarer, and are more expensive.

	Clear	Frosted	Milk glass
Bowl, Berry	135.00	145.00	155.00
Butter, covered	200.00	215.00	250.00
Creamer	50.00	60.00	70.00
Cruet, stopper	200.00	215.00	225.00
Mustard Jar, covered	85.00	90.00	95.00
Pitcher, Water	85.00	100.00	125.00
Salt and Pepper Shakers, original tops	125.00	135.00	150.00
Spooner	35.00	45.00	55.00
Sugar, covered, acorn finial	150.00	160.00	175.00
Sugar shaker, metal top	75.00	90.00	100.00
Syrup, metal top	125.00	135.00	150.00
Tumbler	75.00	85.00	95.00

RUBY THUMBPRINT
(See KING'S CROWN in Clear Pattern Glass Section.)

SHERATON

Non-flint pattern mady by Bryce, Higbee & Co., Pittsburgh, Pa., c. 1880's.

	Clear	Amber	Blue
Bowl, 8" x 10"	13.50	35.00	40.00
Butter, covered	25.00	40.00	50.00
Celery Vase	20.00	30.00	35.00
Compote, open, 7", low standard	20.00	25.00	30.00
Creamer	20.00	28.00	32.00
Goblet	35.00	37.50	40.00
Pitcher			
Milk	20.00	27.50	35.00
Water	28.00	35.00	40.00
Relish, handled	16.00	23.00	28.00

	Clear	Amber	Blue
Sauce, flat	10.00	15.00	18.00
Spooner	16.00	22.00	25.00
Sugar, covered	27.50	35.00	45.00
Tray, Bread	13.50	27.00	32.00
Wine	15.00	25.00	30.00

SPIREA BAND

**Non-flint pattern mady by Bryce, Higbee &
Co., Pittsburgh, Pa., c. 1885.**

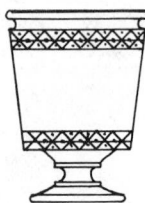

	Clear	Vaseline	Amber	Blue
Bowl, 8″	15.00	27.00	27.00	37.00
Butter, covered	32.00	44.00	44.00	54.00
Cake Stand, 11″	30.00	42.00	42.00	52.00
Celery	25.00	37.00	37.00	47.00
Compote, covered, 7″, high standard	32.00	44.00	44.00	54.00
Cordial	20.00	32.00	32.00	42.00
Creamer	22.00	34.00	34.00	44.00
Goblet	22.00	34.00	34.00	44.00
Pitcher, Water	35.00	47.00	47.00	57.00
Platter, 10½″	20.00	32.00	32.00	42.00
Relish	15.00	27.00	27.00	39.00
Sauce				
Flat	8.50	12.00	12.00	16.00
Footed	10.00	14.00	14.00	18.00
Spooner	20.00	24.00	24.00	30.00
Sugar, Open	18.00	30.00	30.00	37.00
Wine	16.00	28.00	28.00	32.00

SWAN

Non-flint c. 1880's.

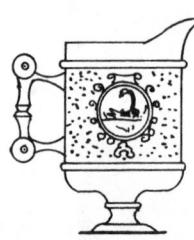

	Clear	Amber	Canary	Vaseline	Blue
Bowl, covered, 7½″ x 10″, oval	40.00	50.00	50.00	53.00	60.00
Butter, covered	75.00	85.00	85.00	88.00	94.00
Celery	35.00	45.00	45.00	48.00	54.00
Creamer	40.00	50.00	50.00	53.00	59.00
Goblet	40.00	50.00	50.00	53.00	59.00
Pitcher, Water	135.00	140.00	140.00	143.00	149.00
Sauce					
Flat	12.00	15.00	15.00	18.00	24.00

	Clear	Amber	Canary	Vaseline	Blue
Footed	15.00	18.00	18.00	21.00	27.00
Spooner	40.00	50.00	50.00	53.00	59.00
Sugar					
Covered	45.00	52.00	52.00	55.00	61.00
Open	35.00	40.00	40.00	43.00	49.00

TEARDROP AND TASSEL
(Sampson)

Non-flint pattern made by the Indiana Tumbler & Goblet Co., Greentown, Ind., c. 1890.

	Clear	Green	Cobalt	Green milk glass
Bowl, 7½"	40.00	45.00	55.00	75.00
Butter, covered	41.00	46.00	56.00	76.00
Compote,				
Covered, 7", high standard	75.00	80.00	90.00	110.00
Open, 8", low standard	28.00	33.00	43.00	63.00
Creamer	18.00	25.00	33.00	53.00
Goblet, (scarce)	60.00	65.00	75.00	95.00
Pickle	15.00	20.00	30.00	50.00
Pitcher, Water	70.00	75.00	90.00	110.00
Sauce, flat	9.00	14.00	24.00	44.00
Shakers, pair	75.00	80.00	90.00	110.00
Spooner	30.00	35.00	45.00	65.00
Sugar, covered	50.00	55.00	65.00	85.00
Tumbler	30.00	35.00	45.00	65.00
Wine, (scarce)	65.00	70.00	80.00	95.00

THOUSAND EYE

Non-flint pattern made by Adams and Co., 1875, and by Richards & Hartley, c. 1888, and New Brighton Glass Co., New Brighton, Pa., at about the same time. It was made in two forms, with the plain stem, and with a three-knob stem. Covered pieces of this type have three-knob finials. Three knob should be 50% more than plain.

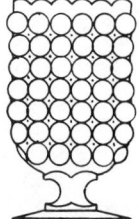

	Clear	Amber	Vaseline	Blue	Apple Green
Butter, covered	50.00	65.00	65.00	70.00	90.00
Celery, hat shaped	40.00	48.50	48.50	53.00	73.00
Cologne Bottle	25.00	32.50	32.50	37.50	57.00
Compote, covered, 6", high standard	65.00	72.00	72.00	77.00	97.00
Cordial	25.00	32.00	32.00	37.50	57.00
Creamer	40.00	47.00	47.00	52.00	72.00

	Clear	Amber	Vaseline	Blue	Apple Green
*Cruet	30.00	37.00	37.00	42.00	62.00
Egg Cup, (rare)	50.00	60.00	60.00	70.00	90.00
*Goblet	30.00	37.00	37.00	42.00	62.00
*Hat	15.00	22.00	22.00	27.00	47.00
Lamp					
Handled	55.00	62.00	62.00	67.00	87.00
High standard	85.00	92.00	92.00	97.00	117.00
*Mug	15.00	22.00	22.00	27.00	47.00
Pickle	25.00	32.00	32.00	37.00	57.00
Syrup, pewter top	55.00	62.00	62.00	69.00	89.00
Pitcher, Water	65.00	72.00	72.00	79.00	99.00
*Plate					
6″	15.00	22.00	22.00	27.00	47.00
*8″	20.00	27.00	27.00	34.00	54.00
*10″	25.00	32.00	32.00	39.00	59.00
Platter, 11″, oblong	35.00	42.00	42.00	49.00	69.00
Sauce,					
Flat	8.50	12.00	12.00	16.00	36.00
Footed	10.00	14.00	14.00	17.00	37.00
Shakers, pair	35.00	42.00	42.00	49.00	69.00
Spooner	20.00	27.00	27.00	34.00	54.00
Sugar, covered	40.00	47.00	47.00	54.00	74.00
Toothpick	16.00	23.00	23.00	30.00	50.00
Tray, Water					
14″, oval	55.00	62.00	62.00	64.00	87.00
12½″	50.00	57.00	57.00	64.00	84.00
*Tumbler, Water	22.00	27.00	27.00	34.00	54.00
*Twine holder	25.00	32.00	32.00	37.00	57.00
*Wine	20.00	27.00	27.00	30.00	50.00

THREE PANEL

Non-flint pattern made by Richards & Hartley Co., Tarentum, Pa., c. 1888.

	Clear	Amber	Vaseline	Blue	Apple Green
Bowl					
8½″	17.50	25.00	40.00	45.00	50.00
10″	25.00	35.00	50.00	55.00	60.00
Butter, covered	35.00	45.00	60.00	65.00	70.00
Compote					
7″, open, low standard	25.00	30.00	45.00	50.00	55.00
10″, open, low standard	30.00	42.00	57.00	62.00	67.00
Creamer	25.00	32.00	47.00	52.00	57.00
Goblet	25.00	32.00	47.00	52.00	57.00
Mug	17.50	25.00	40.00	45.00	50.00
Pitcher, Water	37.50	48.00	63.00	68.00	73.00
Sauce, footed	12.00	18.00	24.00	29.00	34.00
Spooner	20.00	30.00	45.00	50.00	55.00
Sugar, covered	35.00	45.00	60.00	65.00	70.00
Tumbler	18.00	25.00	32.50	40.00	45.00

TWO PANEL

Non-flint pattern made by Richards & Hartley
Glass Co., Tarentum, Pa., early 1880's.

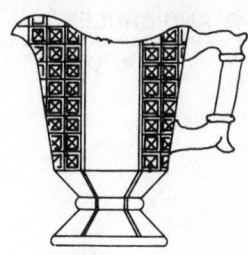

	Clear	Vaseline	Apple Green	Amber	Blue
Bowl					
5½" x 7"	15.00	25.00	30.00	35.00	35.00
8" x 10"	17.50	27.50	32.50	37.50	37.50
Butter, covered	30.00	40.00	45.00	50.00	50.00
Celery	25.00	35.00	40.00	45.00	45.00
Creamer	22.50	32.50	37.50	42.50	42.50
*Goblet	22.50	32.50	37.50	42.50	42.50
Lamp	45.00	55.00	60.00	65.00	65.00
Mug, large	20.00	30.00	35.00	40.00	40.00
Pitcher Water	40.00	50.00	60.00	65.00	65.00
Relish 4½" x 7"	10.00	15.00	20.00	25.00	25.00
Salts					
Individual	5.50	8.50	12.00	16.00	16.00
Master	12.00	14.00	16.00	18.00	18.00
Sauces					
Flat	8.50	10.00	12.00	14.00	14.00
Footed	10.00	12.00	14.00	16.00	16.00
Shakers, pair	25.00	30.00	35.00	40.00	40.00
Spooner	25.00	35.00	40.00	45.00	45.00
Sugar, covered	30.00	40.00	45.00	50.00	50.00
Tray, Water	35.00	45.00	50.00	55.00	55.00
Tumbler	15.00	25.00	30.00	35.00	35.00
Waste Bowl	22.50	32.50	37.50	42.50	42.50
*Wine	20.00	30.00	35.00	40.00	40.00

U.S. RIB

Made by U.S. Glass Co., c. 1900-09. Comes in
square shaped pieces in clear and emerald
green with lavish gold trim.

	Clear	Emerald Green
Bowl, Berry, 9½"	15.00	30.00
Butter, covered	25.00	50.00
Creamer		
Breakfast size	22.50	45.00
Regular	25.00	50.00
Cup, Punch or Sherbet	22.50	45.00
Pitcher, Water	40.00	75.00
Spooner	20.00	40.00
Sauce, square	12.50	18.00
Sugar		
Breakfast size	28.00	40.00
Covered	35.00	48.00

WHEAT AND BARLEY

Non-flint pattern made by Bryce Bros., Pittsburgh, Pa., in the late 1870's. Later by U.S. Glass Co.

	Clear	Amber	Vaseline	Blue
Bowl, covered, 8″	22.00	34.00	34.00	44.00
Butter, covered	35.00	47.00	47.00	57.00
Cake Stand				
8″	18.50	30.00	30.00	40.00
10″	30.00	42.00	42.00	52.00
Compote, covered				
7″ high standard	32.50	45.00	45.00	55.00
8″ high standard	32.50	45.00	45.00	57.00
Open, Jelly, high standard	35.00	47.00	47.00	57.00
Creamer	25.00	37.50	37.50	47.50
Goblet	18.50	30.00	30.00	40.00
Mug	18.50	30.00	30.00	40.00
Pitcher				
Milk	27.50	40.00	40.00	50.00
Water	45.00	55.00	55.00	65.00
Plate				
7″	18.00	23.00	23.00	33.00
9″, closed, handled	22.00	27.00	27.00	37.00
Sauce				
Flat	9.00	12.00	12.00	15.00
Footed	10.00	14.00	14.00	16.00
Shakers, pair	30.00	42.00	42.00	52.00
Spooner	20.00	30.00	30.00	40.00
Sugar, covered	30.00	40.00	40.00	50.00
Toothpick	12.00	20.00	20.00	30.00
Tumbler				
Regular	18.00	25.00	25.00	35.00
Footed	15.00	20.00	20.00	30.00

WILDFLOWER

Non-flint pattern made by Adams & Co., Pittsburgh, Pa., c. 1874 and by U.S. Glass Co., c. 1898. This pattern has been heavily reproduced.

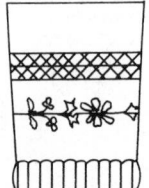

	Clear	Amber	Vaseline	Blue	Green
Bowl					
6″ round	12.00	19.00	19.00	29.00	29.00
8″ square	18.00	25.00	25.00	35.00	35.00
Butter, covered					
Collared Base	35.00	42.00	42.00	52.00	52.00
Flat	30.00	37.00	37.00	47.00	47.00

	Clear	Amber	Vaseline	Blue	Green
Cake Stand 9½″	47.50	52.00	52.00	62.00	62.00
Celery Vase	28.00	35.00	35.00	45.00	45.00
Champagne	30.00	37.00	37.00	47.00	47.00
Compote, covered					
8″, high standard	40.00	47.00	47.00	57.00	57.00
8″, low standard	35.00	42.00	42.00	52.00	52.00
Cordial	25.00	32.00	32.00	42.00	42.00
Creamer	20.00	27.00	27.00	37.00	37.00
*Goblet	25.00	32.00	32.00	42.00	42.00
Syrup	42.00	47.00	47.00	57.00	57.00
Pitcher, Water	45.00	52.00	52.00	62.00	62.00
Plate					
8″	15.00	18.00	18.00	21.00	21.00
10″, square	25.00	28.00	28.00	31.00	31.00
Platter, 10″, oblong	30.00	37.00	37.00	47.00	47.00
Relish, 8″	18.00	25.00	25.00	35.00	35.00
*Salt, Turtle	37.50	42.50	42.50	52.50	52.50
Sauce					
Flat, round or square	8.50	12.00	12.00	16.00	16.00
Footed, 4″, round	12.00	14.00	14.00	18.00	18.00
Shakers, pair	40.00	47.00	47.00	57.00	57.00
Spooner	17.00	24.00	24.00	34.00	34.00
Sugar, covered	30.00	37.00	37.00	47.00	47.00
Tray, Water	40.00	47.00	47.00	57.00	57.00
Tumbler	20.00	27.00	27.00	37.00	37.00
Wine	28.50	35.00	35.00	45.00	45.00

WILLOW OAK
Non-flint pattern made by Bryce Bros., Pittsburgh, Pa., c. 1880's.

	Clear	Amber	Blue
Bowl			
7″, covered	35.00	45.00	50.00
8″	22.00	35.00	40.00
Butter, covered	48.00	50.00	55.00
Cake Stand, 8½″	24.00	37.50	42.50
Celery Vase	30.00	40.00	45.00
Compote, covered 7½″, high standard	42.50	48.00	52.00
Creamer	26.00	35.00	40.00
Goblet	34.00	40.00	45.00
Mug	35.00	42.50	47.50
Pitcher			
Milk	45.00	50.00	55.00
Water	45.00	50.00	55.00
Plate,			
7″, (rare)	20.00	35.00	40.00
9″, closed handled	26.00	38.00	43.00
Sauce,			

	Clear	Amber	Blue
Flat, square, handled	8.50	14.00	20.00
Footed, 4″	15.00	22.00	27.00
Shakers, pair	40.00	45.00	80.00
Spooner	27.50	37.50	42.50
Sugar, covered	35.00	45.00	50.00
Tray, Water, 10½″, round	25.00	35.00	40.00
Tumbler	20.00	28.00	33.00
Waste Bowl	32.00	35.00	40.00

X-RAY

Non-flint made by Riverside Glass Works, Wellsburg, W. Va., 1896 to 1898. Found with gold trim.

	Clear	Emerald Green	Canary
Bowl, Berry, 8″, with beaded edge ..	25.00	50.00	60.00
Butter, covered	30.00	55.00	65.00
Compotes			
Covered, high standard	35.00	60.00	70.00
Open, high standard	30.00	55.00	65.00
Creamer	25.00	50.00	65.00
Pitcher, Water	50.00	75.00	85.00
Plate, Bread	45.00	70.00	80.00
Salt Shakers, pair	20.00	35.00	45.00
Spooner	20.00	45.00	55.00
Sugar, covered	25.00	50.00	60.00
Sauce, 4½″	8.50	15.00	25.00
Tumbler	10.00	14.00	24.00

OPALESCENT PATTERN GLASS

ALASKA
(Lion's Leg)

Non-flint opalescent made by Northwood Glass Company, from 1897 to 1910.

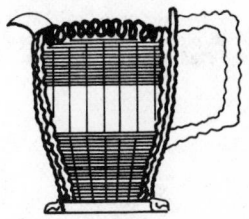

	White opal.	Vaseline opal.	Blue opal.
Bowl, Berry	65.00	70.00	75.00
Banana Boat	180.00	195.00	190.00
Butter, covered	290.00	295.00	300.00
Cruet, facetted stopper	165.00	170.00	175.00
Creamer	90.00	95.00	100.00
Celery Tray	110.00	115.00	120.00
Pitcher, Water	290.00	295.00	300.00
Salt and Pepper Shakers	75.00	70.00	85.00
Spooner	90.00	95.00	100.00
Sugar, covered	120.00	125.00	130.00
Sauces	40.00	45.00	50.00

ARGONAUT SHELL
(Nautilus)

Non-flint opalescent made by Northwood Glass Co., c. 1897.

	Vaseline opal.	Blue opal.	Custard
Bowl, Berry	125.00	150.00	325.00
Butter, covered	225.00	250.00	250.00
Compote, Jelly	250.00	275.00	155.00
Creamer	175.00	200.00	110.00
Cruet	225.00	250.00	300.00
Pitcher, Water	325.00	350.00	500.00
Salt and Pepper Shakers	95.00	100.00	300.00
Sauces	55.00	55.00	65.00
Sugar, covered	225.00	250.00	225.00
*Toothpick (only in custard)	—	—	165.00
Tumbler	250.00	290.00	125.00

BEADED SWAG
(Beaded Yoke)

Made by Heisey Glass Co., 1895. Limited
number of pieces made in opalescent glass.
(See also Clear Pattern Glass Section).

	Clear opal.	Vaseline opal.	Clear Green	Clear and Ruby	Custard
Bowl, Berry	18.00	20.00	22.00	25.00	40.00
Butter, covered	50.00	55.00	60.00	65.00	85.00
Creamer	40.00	45.00	55.00	45.00	65.00
Goblet	27.50	30.00	32.50	35.00	65.00
Pitcher, Water	35.00	40.00	37.50	65.00	85.00
Salt and Pepper Shakers	35.00	45.00	40.00	60.00	75.00
Sauces	12.00	15.00	18.00	20.00	35.00
Spooner	20.00	25.00	22.50	25.00	40.00
Sugar	30.00	40.00	55.00	35.00	75.00
Toothpick	30.00	37.50	40.00	45.00	80.00
Tumbler	25.00	30.00	30.00	35.00	50.00

BEATTY'S HONEYCOMB

Non-flint made by Beatty Glass Co., Tiffin,
Ohio, c. 1888. Made in white, blue, and vaseline opalescent.

	White opal.	Vaseline opal.	Blue opal.
Bowl, Berry	50.00	75.00	100.00
Butter, covered	90.00	105.00	115.00
Celery	75.00	75.00	95.00
Creamer			
Individual	20.00	25.00	35.00
Regular	25.00	25.00	30.00
Cruet	85.00	90.00	100.00
Mug	25.00	30.00	35.00
Sauces	25.00	30.00	35.00
Spooner	25.00	35.00	40.00
Sugar, covered			
Individual	55.00	60.00	65.00
Regular	65.00	70.00	70.00
Toothpick	25.50	30.00	35.00
Tumbler	40.00	42.50	45.00

BEATTY'S RIBBED OPALESCENT
(Ribbed Opal)

Made by Beatty and Sons Glass Co., Tiffin, Ohio, c. 1888 1889. Rare in vaseline opalescent.

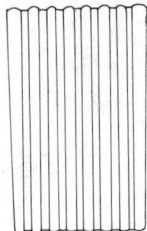

	Clear opal.	Blue opal.	Vaseline opal.
Bowl, Berry			
Rectangular	55.00	60.00	65.00
Round	50.00	55.00	60.00
Finger	40.00	55.00	60.00
Celery	75.00	80.00	82.50
Cracker Jar	150.00	165.00	165.00
Creamer			
Regular	30.00	40.00	45.00
Small	25.00	35.00	35.00
Dish, covered, round	90.00	100.00	110.00
Match Holder	25.00	35.00	35.00
Mug	32.50	37.50	40.00
Salt and Dip	25.00	30.00	30.00
Salt and Pepper Shakers	85.00	90.00	95.00
Sauces			
Rectangular	25.00	35.00	37.50
Round	25.00	35.00	37.50
Spooner	37.50	40.00	42.50
Sugar, covered	65.00	75.00	75.00
Toothpick	30.00	40.00	40.00
Tumbler	40.00	50.00	45.00

BEATTY'S SWIRLED OPALESCENT
(Swirled Opal)

Made by Beatty and Sons Glass Co., Tiffin, Ohio, c. 1889.

	White opal.	Blue opal.	Vaseline opal.
Bowl, Berry	95.00	100.00	110.00
Butter, covered	105.00	115.00	120.00
Celery	75.00	85.00	95.00
Creamer	30.00	40.00	50.00
Mug	27.50	35.00	45.00
Pitcher, Water	150.00	175.00	200.00

	White opal.	Blue opal.	Vaseline opal.
Sauces	30.00	35.00	35.00
Spooner	60.00	70.00	80.00
Sugar, covered	65.00	75.00	85.00
Syrup	115.00	125.00	150.00
Tray, Water	105.00	125.00	130.00
Tumbler	40.00	50.00	55.00

COIN SPOT

Made by various companies over a period of
time, c. 1870's–1890's.

	Clear opal.	Blue opal.	Cranberry opal.
Bowl, Berry, 9½", cranberry	60.00	65.00	75.00
Cruet, with stopper	60.00	65.00	75.00
Pitcher, Water, ruffled rim	200.00	230.00	250.00
Sauces	25.00	25.00	28.00
Syrup Pitcher	65.00	75.00	85.00
Sugar Shaker	30.00	30.00	35.00
Tumbler	35.00	40.00	45.00

DOLLY MADISON
(Jefferson's #271)

Made by Jefferson Glass Co., Follansbee, W.
Va., c. 1907.

	Clear	Blue	Green	Clear opal.	Blue opal.	Green opal.
Bowl, Berry	25.00	30.00	35.00	95.00	105.00	115.00
Butter, covered	20.00	30.00	35.00	100.00	110.00	175.00
Creamer	25.00	25.00	35.00	80.00	85.00	90.00
Pitcher, Water	35.00	40.00	45.00	125.00	150.00	195.00
Sauces	12.00	22.00	20.00	40.00	45.00	48.00
Spooner	20.00	20.00	30.00	75.00	80.00	85.00
Sugar, covered	30.00	35.00	40.00	85.00	90.00	100.00
Tumbler	30.00	30.00	30.00	35.00	40.00	55.00

EVERGLADES

Made by Harry Northwood Co., Wheeling, W. Va., c. 1903. Rare occasional custard piece. Add 200% for green opalescent.

	White opal.	Canary opal.	Blue opal.
Banana Dish, boat shaped	165.00	170.00	175.00
Bowl, Berry	90.00	95.00	100.00
Butter, covered	140.00	145.00	150.00
Compote, Jelly	85.00	90.00	95.00
Creamer	48.00	52.00	58.00
Cruet	165.00	170.00	175.00
Pitcher, Water	225.00	230.00	250.00
Salt and Pepper Shakers	55.00	55.00	65.00
Sauces	30.00	30.00	35.00
Spooner	65.00	70.00	75.00
Sugar, covered	85.00	90.00	95.00
Tumbler	22.50	24.00	24.00

FLUTED SCROLLS

Made by Harry Northwood & Co., Indiana, Pa., c. 1898–1900. Sometimes with burnished gold trim.

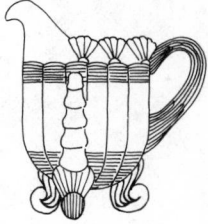

	Canary opal.	Sapphire blue opal.
Bowl, Berry	95.00	100.00
Butter, Covered	100.00	125.00
Creamer	40.00	45.00
Cruet	90.00	95.00
Epergne, tiny, 2-piece	100.00	125.00
Pitcher, Water	155.00	175.00
Puff Jar	40.00	45.00
Salt and Pepper Shakers	95.00	95.00
Sauces, 4½"	25.00	25.00
Spooner	50.00	50.00
Sugar, covered	75.00	75.00
Tumbler	45.00	55.00

HOBNAIL IN SQUARE
(Vesta)

Made by Aetna Glass & Mfg. Co., Bellaire, Ohio, c. 1887.

	Clear glass	Clear opal.
Barber Bottle	50.00	
Bowl, Berry	40.00	20.00
Butter, Covered	65.00	35.00
Celery	25.00	25.00
Compotes, various sizes	40.00	30.00
Creamer	35.00	25.00
Pitcher, Water	65.00	50.00
Sauce, flat	18.00	15.00
Spooner	20.00	20.00
Sugar, covered	50.00	40.00
Tumblers	25.00	20.00

HOBNAIL OPALESCENT

Made by several companies with variations in forms of pieces, c. 1880–1900. Pieces are found round in shape, with frilled tops, pieces on three feet, pieces on four feet, square in shape, octagonal in shape.

	White opal.	Blue opal.	Vaseline opal.	Cranberry opal.
Butter, covered				
Flat	82.00	100.00	105.00	110.00
Four-footed	85.00	102.00	107.00	112.00
Celery	85.00	85.00	100.00	115.00
Creamer				
Flat	90.00	95.00	110.00	115.00
Four footed	95.00	97.50	112.00	120.00
Mug	30.00	35.00	50.00	55.00
Pitcher, Water	95.00	100.00	120.00	125.00
Sauces	18.00	20.00	30.00	35.00
Spooner				
Flat	20.00	22.50	30.00	37.50
Four footed	22.00	22.50	30.00	37.50
Sugar, covered				
Flat	30.00	40.00	55.00	60.00
Four footed	35.00	42.50	57.50	62.00
Toothpick	20.00	25.00	40.00	50.00
Tumbler	28.50	35.00	50.00	55.00

INTAGLIO

Made by Northwood Co., Indiana, Pa., c. 1899.

	White opal.	Blue opal.	Vaseline opal.
Bowl, Berry, on stands like compotes	100.00	150.00	175.00
Butter, covered	150.00	200.00	210.00

	White opal.	Blue opal.	Vaseline opal.
Compote, Jelly	40.00	50.00	75.00
Creamer	50.00	70.00	90.00
Cruet	95.00	100.00	110.00
Pitcher, Water	200.00	250.00	275.00
Sauce	25.00	30.00	40.00
Spooner	70.00	75.00	80.00
Sugar, covered	90.00	95.00	100.00
Tumbler	40.00	50.00	55.00

INVERTED FAN AND FEATHER

Made by Northwood Co., Wheeling, W. Va., c. 1900. (Asterisk: reproduced in custard glass.)

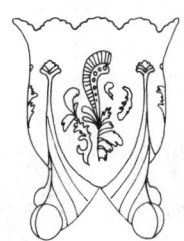

	Clear opal.	Clear Green with gold	Blue opal.	Custard
Bowl, Berry	100.00	110.00	125.00	225.00
Butter, covered	195.00	195.00	275.00	—
Compote	195.00	195.00	200.00	---
Creamer	65.00	65.00	85.00	175.00
Cruet	195.00	195.00	200.00	—
Pitcher, Water	200.00	200.00	325.00	500.00+
Punch Bowl and Cups (rare)	—	—	—	
Sauces	30.00	30.00	35.00	85.00
Spooner	75.00	75.00	95.00	100.00
*Sugar, covered	100.00	100.00	145.00	125.00
*Toothpick, (rare)	100.00	100.00	125.00	---
*Tumbler	65.00	65.00	75.00	80.00

IRIS WITH MEANDER

Made by Jefferson Glass Co., Steubenville, Ohio, c. 1903. This pattern also comes in

clear, blue, apple green, amethyst with gold
trim.

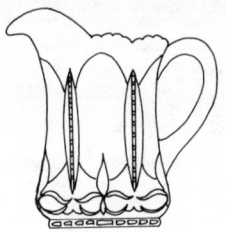

	White opal.	Vaseline opal.	Blue opal.
Bowl, Berry	80.00	90.00	95.00
Butter, covered	95.00	100.00	125.00
Compote, Jelly, 5–6″	75.00	80.00	85.00
Creamer	80.00	80.00	85.00
Cruet, with stopper	100.00	100.00	125.00
Pickle	20.00	22.50	25.00
Pitcher, Water	200.00	175.00	225.00
Plate	80.00	90.00	95.00
Salt Shakers, pair	90.00	100.00	100.00
Sauces, 2 sizes	27.50	27.50	30.00
Spooner	85.00	80.00	85.00
Sugar, covered	80.00	90.00	95.00
Toothpick	50.00	68.00	75.00
Tumbler	27.00	28.00	32.00
Vase, tall	22.00	25.00	25.00

JEWEL AND FLOWER
(Beaded Oval and Leaf)

Made by Northwood Glass Co., c. 1908.

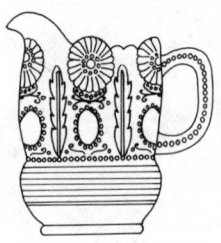

	Clear opal.	Blue opal.	Vaseline opal.
Bowl, Berry	55.00	75.00	85.00
Butter, covered	75.00	95.00	110.00
Creamer	60.00	80.00	100.00
Cruet	75.00	95.00	100.00
Pitcher, Water	125.00	140.00	150.00
Salt and Pepper Shakers	55.00	75.00	80.00
Spooner	70.00	90.00	100.00
Sugar, covered	75.00	90.00	100.00
Tumbler	30.00	50.00	75.00

JEWELLED HEART

Made by Northwood Glass Co., Indiana, Pa., c. 1897–1900. Made in blue and apple green opalescent; might occasionally be found in clear.

	Clear opal.	Green opal.	Sapphire Blue opal.
Bowl, Berry, ruffled edges	95.00	110.00	125.00
Butter, covered	100.00	125.00	135.00
Cake Stand	110.00	120.00	120.00
Compote			
Covered	120.00	130.00	130.00
Open	110.00	110.00	110.00
Creamer	90.00	95.00	100.00
Cruet	85.00	90.00	128.00
Lamp	95.00	95.00	100.00
Pitcher, Water	100.00	110.00	120.00
Salt and Pepper Shakers	85.00	85.00	85.00
Sauces	25.00	25.00	28.00
Spooner	50.00	50.00	50.00
Sugar, covered	55.00	75.00	85.00
Syrup	125.00	130.00	135.00
Toothpick	30.00	35.00	35.00
Tumbler	18.00	25.00	25.00

MONKEY

Non-flint made by George Duncan & Son, Washington, Pa., c. 1880's. Opalescent is 75% more than clear.

	Clear	Clear opal.
Bowl, 8½"	100.00	175.00
Butter, covered	150.00	270.00
Creamer	100.00	175.00
Mug	65.00	100.00
Pitcher, Water	175.00	295.00
*Spooner	95.00	150.00
Sugar		
Covered	150.00	270.00
Open	75.00	125.00
*Toothpick	65.00	110.00
Tumbler	75.00	145.00
Waste Bowl	85.00	160.00

NORTHWOOD'S DRAPERY

Made by Harry Northwood Co., Wheeling, W.
Va., c. 1905. Usually signed "N" in circle.

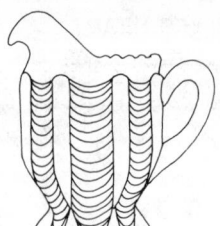

	White opal.	Blue opal.
Bowl, Berry	80.00	100.00
Butter, covered	145.00	165.00
Creamer	55.00	75.00
Pitcher, Water	185.00	200.00
Sauces	20.00	28.00
Spooner	45.00	65.00
Sugar, covered	75.00	85.00
Tumbler	50.00	70.00

PALM BEACH

Reportedly made by U.S. Glass Co., Pittsburgh, Pa., c. 1905.

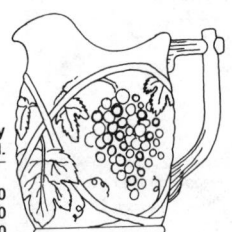

	Blue opal.	Canary opal.
Bowl, Berry	90.00	100.00
Butter, covered	140.00	150.00
Compote, Jelly	60.00	65.00
Creamer	50.00	50.00
Finger Bowl	45.00	45.00
Pitcher, Water	200.00	225.00
Sauces	28.00	28.00
Spooner	65.00	65.00
Sugar, covered	70.00	75.00
Tumbler	48.50	50.00

POINTSETTA

Orginally made by Hobbs and Brocunier, later
by Northwood Glass Co., c. 1903.

	Green opal.	Blue opal.	Cranberry opal.
Pitcher, Water	200.00	210.00	225.00
Sugar Shaker	—	95.00	125.00
Syrup	—	95.00	125.00
Tumbler	28.00–30.00	—	40.00

SWAG WITH BRACKETS

Made by Jefferson Glass Co., Steubenville, Ohio., c. 1904.

	Blue opal.	Green opal.	Vaseline opal.
Butter, covered	145.00	150.00	152.00
Compote, Jelly	25.00	28.00	30.00
Creamer	45.00	50.00	52.00
Cruet, with original stopper	85.00	85.00	87.00
Pitcher, Water	195.00	200.00	205.00
Salt and Pepper Shakers	80.00	90.00	90.00
Spooner	58.00	62.00	65.00
Sugar, covered	85.00	90.00	92.00
Tumbler	45.00	50.00	52.00

TOKYO

Made by Jefferson Glass Co., Steubenville, Ohio, c. 1905.

	White opal.	Blue opal.	Green opal.
Bowl, Berry	85.00	95.00	95.00
Butter, covered	90.00	100.00	100.00
Compote, Jelly	35.00	40.00	45.00
Creamer	75.00	85.00	90.00
Cruet	90.00	100.00	110.00
Dish, 6½"	40.00	50.00	75.00
Pitcher, Water	195.00	200.00	210.00
Salt and Pepper Shakers	40.00	50.00	50.00
Sauces	25.00	28.00	28.00
Spooner	65.00	75.00	80.00
Sugar, covered	90.00	100.00	100.00
Toothpick	40.00	50.00	50.00
Tumbler	35.00	45.00	50.00
Vase	45.00	60.00	60.00

WATER LILY AND CATTAILS

Mady by Fenton Glass Co., Williamstown, W. Va., and Northwood Glass Co., Wheeling, W. Va., c. 1900-1905.

	Clear opal.	Blue opal.	Green opal.	Amethyet opal.
Bowl, Berry	35.00	45.00	55.00	55.00
Butter, covered	65.00	75.00	90.00	100.00
Creamer				
Individual	25.00	30.00	35.00	35.00
Regular	45.00	55.00	65.00	75.00
Dish, bon bon, tri-cornered	35.00	45.00	50.00	55.00
Pitcher, Water	100.00	125.00	200.00	225.00 +
Plates	25.00	28.00	30.00	32.00
Relish, handled	30.00	32.00	35.00	40.00
Sauces	25.00	30.00	35.00	35.00
Spooner	35.00	35.00	40.00	40.00
Sugar, covered				
Regular	30.00	35.00	40.00	40.00
Individual	50.00	60.00	95.00	95.00
Tumbler	30.00	30.00	35.00	35.00

WILD BOUQUET

Made by Northwood Glass Co., Wheeling, W. Va., c. 1900-1905.

	White opal.	Green opal.	Blue opal.
Bowl, Berry	75.00	80.00	
Butter, covered	185.00	190.00	
Creamer	40.00	50.00	
Cruet	175.00	195.00	195.00
Cruet Set on tray	300.00 +	300.00 +	300.00 +
Pitcher, Water	235.00	245.00	245.00
Salt and Pepper Shakers	100.00	100.00	100.00
Sauces	25.00	25.00	30.00
Spooner	80.00	90.00	90.00
Sugar, covered	120.00	125.00	130.00
Toothpick	100.00	120.00	125.00
Tumbler	38.00	38.00	40.00

GENERAL COLLECTIONS

ABC PLATES

These plates were made especially for children with the alphabet around the outer rim. Center decorations often consisted of animals, great men, maxims and nursery rhymes. They were made of various materials including glass, pewter, porcelain, pottery and tin.

China, Staffordshire style, 8½" dia. $15.00

GLASS

Child's head, 6", amber	35.00
Child's head, 6", frosted	45.00
Clock face, 7", amber	35.00
Clock face, 7", amethyst	55.00
Daisy, 6", clear	32.50
Deer, house and pinetree, frosted design	50.00
Dog's head, 6", blue	35.00
Dog's head, 6", clear	28.50
Ducks, 6", amber	35.00
Elephant, clear	25.00
Floral bouquet with bow, clear	45.00
Hen and chicks, clear	25.00
Heron, palm trees, clear and frosted	30.00
"Little Bo-Peep," with numerals, clear	45.00
Milk Glass, white with blue beaded edge	30.00
"Mary had a little lamb," clear	45.00
Numbers, one to ten, clear	25.00
Rabbit, house and tree, frosted . . .	50.00
Sancho Panza and Dabble, clear and frosted	40.00
Star, clear	28.00

PORCELAIN OR POTTERY

"A Timely Rescue," brown transfer, soldier, maiden and lion. C. and A. Sons, England	25.00
"B is for Billy," 7"	32.50
Bathing scene at the beach, 6¼"	60.00
Birds, three, 6"	35.00
Boatman, England, 7"	30.00
Boy and girl in red car, Germany . .	55.00
Canary, bullfinch and goldfinch, Staffordshire, 6"	37.50
Cat lapping milk, in color, 7½"	25.00
Cat and four kittens, 7¼"	35.00
Children, 6¾", four, transfer, Germany	55.00
Clock, months, 8", Allertown	55.00
Cow, 7"	32.50
Dancing master, 7½"	28.50
David and Goliath, 5"	30.00
December, old man, holly, 7"	35.00
"The Flower Garden," 8¼"	40.00
Girl rolling hoop, early	225.00
Horse racing, 7"	30.00
Hunters and dogs, 7¼"	35.00
"The Little Bear," 7¼"	45.00
"Little Bo-Peep," 8"	45.00
Little boys playing marbles, 6"	28.50
Little Jack Horner, 7½"	40.00
Little Jockey, 7½"	35.00
The Lord's Prayer, transfer	45.00
Miss Muffet, 6½"	35.00
"Mother and Daughter, Dear to Each," transfer, early Staffordshire	65.00
New Pony, transfer, Staffordshire . .	35.00
"Not to Oversee Workmen is to Leave Your Purse Open," polychrome, black transfer	65.00
Our Donkey and Foal, 6"	30.00
Owl, sign language around border, 6½"	45.00
Playing Lovers, 7¾"	35.00
"Plough Deep while Sluggards Sleep," polychrome, black transfer	85.00
The Potter's Art, 7"	35.00
Punctuality, 8"	30.00
Puss in Boots, 7"	35.00
Rabbit, sign language around border, 8"	50.00
Red Riding Hood, 8½", late Delft . .	30.00
Red Riding Hood meets the Wolf, 7¼"	35.00
Robinson Crusoe, England, 8"	68.00
Rooster, three chickens, color transfer	40.00
"See-Saw, Marjorie Daw," 7½", blue transfer	40.00
Those Children, etc., 6"	30.00
Whittington and his Cat, 8"	35.00
Youth, woman, child and fowl, 8" . .	35.00

TIN

Bird, animals, 8″	25.00
Cock Robin, 7″	35.00
Girl on swing, 6″	25.00
Hey, Diddle, Diddle, 9″	35.00
Jumbo, 6¼″	60.00
Liberty, 5½″	50.00
Numerals, 6½″	50.00
Victoria and Albert, 5½″	30.00
Washington, 5½″	60.00

ADAMS
See FLOW BLUE, JASPERWARE, STAFFORDSHIRE.

ADAMS ROSE

This ware is decorated with brilliant red roses, green leaves on a white background. It was made by Adams and Son, c. 1820–1840, in the Staffordshire district of England. A variant of the pattern was made later by G. Jones and Son, England, until 1908. The colors are not as brilliant, and the background is a "dirty" white. This type is known as Late Adams Rose and commands less than the price of the early pattern.

Cup and Saucer, late, plain edge, saucer 6″ dia. $60.00

Bowls	
6″, early	300.00
6″, late	100.00
Creamers	
Early	325.00
Late	100.00
Cups and Saucers, early, scalloped edge	250.00
Pitcher, 7″, late	125.00
Plates	
7½″, early	175.00
7½″, late	40.00
8½″, early	200.00
8½″, late	50.00
9½″, early	250.00
9½″, late	75.00
10½″, soup, early	250.00
10½″, soup, late	125.00
Sugar, covered, Impressed "Wood"	500.00
Teapots	
Early	650.00
Late	225.00
Wash Bowl and Pitcher, early	1000.00

ADVERTISING SIGNS

"Green River Whiskey," lithograph on cardboard, copyright 1899, 20 x 30″ $175.00

"Baxter's Drum 5¢ Cigar," 10 x 14″, tin, red white and blue, c. 1910	25.00
"Big 6 Gin," 13 x 16″, wooden, barroom scene in color, c. 1910	300.00
Bull Durham	
17 x 7″, paper, 1940	20.00
14 x 22″, cardboard	35.00
"Burger Brewing Co.," 14½ x 11½″, hand-worked copper and hand-cast aluminum, beautiful sculptured sign, "Burger Beer — A Finer Beer," 2 Irish setters, pointing in grass	36.00
"Buster Brown Bread," 22 x 30″, tin, embossed frame, c. 1920	200.00

"Campbell's Soup," 16 x 24", porcelain **145.00**
Coke. See Coca Cola Items.
"Columbian Beer," 12 x 16", tin, "Columbia" on label, c. 1915 . . . **30.00**
"Cook's Beer," 12 x 21", tin, cop, horseless carriage **75.00**
"Cunard Line," 1920's **125.00**
"Dan Patch," tin, c. 1915 . . . . **40.00**
"Diamond Wedding Whiskey," 12", self framed, lady in red, c. 1905 . **150.00**
"D. W. Donald Co.," blue and white Delft porcelain sign, shaped like mug, pineapple frappe **125.00**
"DuBois Budweiser," 13 x 21", tin, c. 1920 . . . . **25.00**
"Enjoy Bacardi Rum and Coca Cola," 72", cardboard, blonde in swimming pool **60.00**
"Fairy Soap," 11 x 21", c. 1920 . . . **65.00**
"Fill 'em Fast Gasoline," 9 x 16", porcelain, orange and yellow . . . **20.00**
"Gayoso Gin," 15 x 5", tin, c. 1900 **95.00**
"Hasson Cigarettes," 7", tin **35.00**
"Harvard Brewery," tin, beautiful lady drinking beer, c. 1890 . . . . . **90.00**
"Hires Root Beer," 12 x 28", paper, framed, c. 1926 . . . . **40.00**
"Honeymoon Tobacco," tin **65.00**
"Hudepol Beer," 8 x 12", tin, bottle of beer, c. 1930 . . . . **45.00**
"Ice Card," 9", cardboard **3.00**
"Kellogg's Corn Flakes," 13 x 9", tin, baby in wicker basket, c. 1910 **75.00**
"Kools," 4 x 12", tin, c. 1930 . . . . . **12.00**
"Korbel Sec," 13 x 9", girl holding grapes, c. 1910 . . . . **135.00**
"Lipton's Tea," 9 x 19", tin, two sided, c. 1915 . . . . **30.00**
"Mail Pouch Tobacco," 2¾ x 12", porcelain **35.00**
"Mail Pouch Tobacco," 11 x 36", "Treat Yourself to the Best" **75.00**
"Moxie," 8 x 18", two sided, steel, c. 1940 . . . . **50.00**
"Moxie," 8½ x 18", square, cardboard, soda fountain table top . . **50.00**
"Nehi Soda-Pop," 4 x 18", tin, c. 1920 . . . . **15.00**
"Nehi," 14 x 20", cardboard, ladies, c. 1930 . . . . **20.00**
"Old Dutch Cleanser," 9 x 13", cardboard, c. 1930 . . . . **20.00**
"Paul Jones Whiskey," large, tin . . **35.00**
"Popsicle," 12 x 28", tin, embossed, c. 1930 . . . . **30.00**
"Providence Washington Insurance Co.," tin, good color **35.00**
"Prudential Insurance Co. of America," 12 x 15", brass **75.00**
"Quaker Oats," 30 x 60", tin, framed, c. 1910 . . . . **250.00**

"Red Indian Cut Plug," 8 x 12", tin . **40.00**
"Sleepy Eye, the Meretorious Flour, Sleepy Eye Milling Co., Sleepy Eye, Minn." portrait of American Indian, tin **500.00**
"St. Paul Fire Insurance Co.," porcelain, c. 1920 . . . . **65.00**
"Swift's Washing Soda," 10 x 24", cardboard, framed, little girl with large hair ribbon in kitchen, c. 1909 . . . . **45.00**
"Tiger Hay Rake," tin, colors worn, c. 1910 . . . . **100.00**
"Henry Tetlow," "Gossamer for the complexion," wooden, c. 1900 . . **110.00**
"E.R. Wetthee, Bootmaker," 32", wooden, original red paint **150.00**
"Welch," 13 x 19", tin, c. 1931 . . . **30.00**
"Whitman's Chocolates," 13 x 18", velvet, c. 1920 . . . . **50.00**
"John Wilson and Sons, Tobacco," tin **50.00**

ADVERTISING TRADE CARDS

These cards are small, thin cardboard, extolling the merits of a product and bearing the name and address of a merchant.

With the invention of lithography, colorful trade cards became a popular advertising media in the late 19th and early 20th centuries. They were made to appeal to children, especially. Young and old alike collected and treasured them in albums and scrapbooks. Very few are dated; 1880 to 1893 were the prime years for trade cards; 1810 to 1850 can be found, but rarely. Most range in price from $1.00 to $7.50. A few command higher prices because of subject matter, artist or scarcity.

Many were made in sets, and collectors still seek to complete them today. Cards taken from old albums should be handled with care, as there is often valuable information on the reverse side.

CLOTHING

G. H. Curtis, Wholesale and Retail Clothier, Hatter, and Furnisher, Springfield, Mass., picture, two little girls with doll carriages **1.50**
Celluloid Waterproof Collars, Cuffs, and Shirt Bosoms, picture of man showing these to three Chinese laundrymen **5.00**
Vogel Brothers, Shoe Department, picture of large, ladies' high-buttoned shoe **3.00**
W. H. Kunsman, Dress Goods, Cloaks, Carpets, Oil Cloth, 436 Northampton St., Easton, Pa., pic-

ture of two little girls with shopping baskets 1.50

Sweet, Orr & Co., eight men playing Tug-O'-War, with pair of overalls, factory in background, "Guaranteed Never to Rip, Orr's Pantaloon Overalls." 5.00

Union Clothing Co., Rochester, N. Y., embossed, boy leaving train at station with tasselled graduation cap and girl in typical 1870's clothing, snow-covered background 3.50

FOOD PROCESSING

Enterprise Manufacturing Co., Philadelphia, Pa., picture, Uncle Sam demonstrating Enterprise Meat Chopper to foreign dignitaries ... 5.00

Independence Hall, Philadelphia, and Enterprise Sausage Stuffer .. 3.50

Enterprise Raisin Seeder, picture .. 3.50

FOOD PRODUCTS

Atlantic and Pacific Tea Co.
Three children at tea table, with Punch and Judy dolls, "Compliments of the Great Atlantic and Pacific Tea Company—200 Stores in the U.S." 5.00
Boy washing his sister's hair in front of old standing mirror 2.50
Monkey in uniform, playing cards with bull dog in top hat 2.00
Large figural-shaped card, father pushing boy and girl in wheelbarrow, dog running along, "Going to the Great Atlantic and Pacific Tea Company" 4.00

B. T. Babbitt's Baking Powder, little girl standing on baking powder crate, holding her cat 2.50

Wilson Packing Co., Cooked Meats, picture, 1890's lady and man on train, "Makes an Excellent Lunch for Travellers" 3.00

Heinz Co., card shaped like a pickle, little girl inside, holding a can of tomato soup 5.00

Holmes and Coutts, Biscuit Manufacturers, N. Y., picture, one-pound decorated fruit cake tin ... 1.50

Quaker Oats, picture three little girls in bonnets, "We eat Quaker Oats" 2.00

COFFEE

Chase and Sanborn, souvenir, Montreal Winter Carnival, enormous coffee pot being pulled on sled

"Arbuckle Ariosa Coffee," from "Judge" $1.00

with double-harnessed horses, "Presented by Chase and Sanborn Company, 1885" 7.50

Lion Coffee Co.
Large figural frog dressed in derby, with walking stick, swallow-tail coat and monocle, "Compliments of Lion Coffee Company, 1874" . 7.50
"Sleeping Beauty" 5.00
"Babes in the Woods" (These are Fairy Tale series, story on reverse) McLaughlin & Co. 5.00
Small boy savage, with war paint and shield "Malay Islands" 3.00
Boy with fez, smoking water pipe, minerets in background, "Turkey" (part of a series). 3.00

CONDENSED MILK

"The Little Doctor," boy dressed as a doctor, treating girl's sick doll, in small iron dollbed, patchwork quilt, "Yes Ma'am, the child wouldn't be sick had you fed it on Highland Brand Evaporated Cream" 5.00

C. H. Eddy & Co., Manufacturers Standard Flavoring Extracts, Bay Rum and Jamaican Ginger, picture, Spanish lady in mantilla 1.50

Washburn-Crosby Mills, picture, girl sitting on flour barrel, holding loaf of bread. 2.50

National Biscuit Co., large card, picture of lady in beautiful plumed hat, with cupids holding box of "Nabisco" cookies. 5.00

Huyler's Milk Chocolate, picture, baby in old fashioned carriage, looking through fence at cows ...

Chinaman in store buying Chinese tea 2.00

FARM MACHINERY AND WAGONS

"Compliments of McCormick Harvesting Machine Company," Chicago, Ill. "The Improvements of 55 years, 1831-1886," five colorful medallion pictures of farm machinery **7.50**

Picture of "The New Reindeer Rake, manufactured by John Dodds. Dayton, Ohio" **4.00**

Picture of Randall Harrow, manufactured by Warrior Mower Co., Little Falls, N. Y. **4.00**

Kentucky Wagon Manufacturing Co., Louisville, Ky., picture of "Old Hickory" open wagon, pulled by two horses, going past Capitol in Washington, cows grazing in field beside it. **10.00**

GUM AND CANDY

Robert Clark, Pure Candy, picture of donkey dumping boy head first in watering trough **2.00**

Kis-Me Gum Co., little tailor, sewing, with cat beside him, "As with my shears, I cut my fabric stout, so Kis-Me Gum cuts all her rivals out." **3.00**

MEDICINE

Boschee's German Syrup, "Cures Coughs, Colds and Consumption," little girls and their granny **2.50**

Brown's Iron Bitters, "The Best Tonic," "Mrs. Langtry, the Jersey Lily," picture of the actress in one of her roles **8.50**

Brown's Eisen Bitters, picture, two puppies in barrel **2.50**

Carter's Little Nerve Pills, baby and a frog **5.00**

Dr. Harter Medicine Co., marriage puzzle card **5.00**

H.T. L. Pills, little girl at window . . . **2.50**

Kennedy & Co., Pittsburgh, Pa., "Dr. Radcliffe's Great Remedy," picture, mother and child with book . **3.00**

Lash's Bitters Co., "Lash's Bitters Tonic Laxitive" **1.50**

Lydia Pinkham Co., Lydia Pinkham's granddaughters, two little girls . . . **2.50**

Porter's Cough Balsam, "Rich and Poor Use it," picture, rich home and poor home **3.00**

Scott's Emulsion, picture Turkish boy, leaning on crate of bottles, "The Little Turk" **3.00**

Warner's Log Cabin Remedies, large card, picture of log cabin, and lists all their products **7.50**

Mrs. Winslow's Soothing Syrup, "For children Teething," picture mother and baby **3.00**

MUSICAL

Esty Piano Co., New York
"The First Music Lesson," large card, Colonial decor, picture, little boy meeting his music teacher . . **2.50**
"Prospective Purchasers of Esty Pianos," picture, four little girls playing piccolo, triangle, cymbols and drum **5.00**
"Esty Phonorium," girl playing organ **2.50**

J. and C. Fischer, "Grand and Upright Pianos," picture, two little girls in woods **1.50**

SOAPS AND CLEANERS

Banner Soap, with pictures, flags of the world, Series, "Egypt" **3.00**

Colgate and Company, "New Soap," picture, newsboy and his dog . . . **2.00**

Grandpa's Wonder Soap, Grandfather and three children, blowing soap bubbles **3.00**

J. S. Larkin and Co., little girl with umbrella, "Boraxine Makes Everyone Happy" **5.00**

Kendall Manufacturing Co., R. I.
Picture of train "Look out for Soapine" **5.00**
"Soapine, the Dirt Killer," picture of a whale washed up on beach, being scrubbed with Soapine **5.00**

Pearline Soap Co.
Little girl with umbrella, crying, surrounded by flock of geese, "Highway Robbery" **2.50**
Woman bending over wash tubs and washboard, cupids arriving with "Pearline Soap" to rescue her **5.00**
Three little girls in white dresses, cut-out figural card, "Our Mamas use Pearline" **5.00**

THREAD

Corticelli Silk Thread Co., picture of three young ladies lasso-ing a young man through church door, "The Perils of Leap Year" **6.50**

O. N. T. Co., card shaped like spool of thread, picture of mother and baby, "Nothing stronger can there be, than Mother love and O. N. T." **7.50**

Williamantic Thread Co., picture of circus parade, and "Jumbo," "Jumbo must go because drawn by Williamantic Thread" 10.00

TOBACCO

C. A. Jackson and Co., Petersburg, Va., two rhinos meeting Stanley in Africa, ask him for some tobacco . 6.50
Lovell and Buffington Tobacco Co., Covington, Ky., picture of a pretty girl, through snow-laden window . 3.00
Owl Cigars, card shaped like cage, with owl inside 3.50

TRANSPORTATION

North German Lloyd Steamship Co., picture, one of their liners at sea . 8.50
State Line, for Europe, picture, ship anchored in foreign harbor 8.50

MISCELLANEOUS

J. M. Sauder's Cholera Balm; the reverse of this card is a puzzle, scene, within picture there is hidden a bull, two deer, camel, chicken, shrimp, face, monkey and old man smoking pipe. 5.00
Patented Granite Iron Co., (Granite Ware), picture of girl holding graniteware tureen, "Turkey soup for dinner" 5.00
Tacony Iron and Metal Co., Tacony, Philadelphia, postcard size, steel engraving of plant site. Reverse: sepia picture of statue of William Penn, (now atop City Hall) and "Made in Bronze Department of Tacony Iron and Metal Company, 1892, Largest Bronze Statue in America" and gives list of dimensions. 10.00
Indian Rock Hotel, four page card, booklet type, picture, artist signed, of Indian Chief of Delawares, Tudyuscumb, and "Legend of Indian Rock." Souvenir of Indian Rock Hotel, Wissahickon Drive, Fairmount Park, Philadelphia, c. 1890–1900. . . . . 10.00
Unusual child-sized afghan, made from advertising cards, (Victorian) crocheted together, blue and tan wool between cards, 37" x 56" . . 85.00

ADVERTISING TRAYS

It was the custom, in the 1880's to 1900, for businesses, bars, country hotels and general stores to issue colorful trays advertising their place of business or product. Beer com-panies gave these trays to hotels and bars, and general stores issued them, especially at Christmas. They were usually colorful and a popular means of advertising. They have become very collectible today.

"De Laval Cream Separators," 4¾" dia. $40.00

"Bergdoll Brewing Company," brass, engraved, floral 12 x 15", 1917 . .	50.00
"Camel Cigarettes," tip	7.50
"Coke," See Coca Cola items	
"Coors," See Coors items	
"Cortex Cigars," 1905–1930	30.00
"Pabst," 12 x 17", factory scene, 1900	45.00
Eagle Breweries, portrait, center . .	45.00
"Fairy Soap"	22.50
"Franklin Life Insurance," Ben Franklin, tip, 1915	25.00
"Gloria Ice Cream," Palmer Cox and Brownies, 1905–1915	35.00
"Hanley Bull Dog Beer"	30.00
Hess, Ely, General Store, New Holland, Pa., 16½", floral	80.00
"Hires Root Beer," brunette, 1910 .	85.00
"Liberty Ice Cream," round, 1900–1910	25.00
"Moxie," tip, 1900–1910	25.00
"Moxie," 6", lady with violets	35.00
"Muriel Cigars," tip, gypsy girl	35.00
"Old Reliable Coffee," tip, 1907 . . .	20.00
"Orange Julep," rectangular, 1920 .	30.00
"Piels," 1961	7.50
"Red Raven Splits," Victorian lady hugging red raven, 1910	65.00
"Resinol Soap," tip, girl with red roses	45.00
"Schlitz," 1955	7.50
"Stemaier Brewing Company," tip,	

hand with four bottles	25.00
"Sweetwater Ice Cream," lady eating ice cream, 1921	110.00
"Universal Stoves," tip, 1910–1920	15.00
"Wrigley's Gum," glass, change, in shape of arrow	20.00
"Yuengling's Bottles Beer, Porter, and Ale," change	8.00

ADVERTISING ITEMS, MISCELLANEOUS

In the days before television put a manufacturer's product before the public instantly, merchants used many different methods of advertisement. The first and most effective were advertising cards. People collected them avidly and carefully pasted them in scrapbooks and albums. There were also give-aways; calendars were very popular, as were plates, kitchen utensils and spoons, which were collected in sets. There is hardly an object which was useful to a householder which was not utilized in this way. We know today, it is still a popular method of advertising and will, no doubt, produce many of tomorrow's antiques and collectibles.

Advertising Mirror, "La Clef Aperitif," wooden case, oval mirror, 5½ long $17.50

Ashtray, "Security National Bank, Trenton, N. J.," c. 1927, brown glaze	15.00
Calendars	
"Alka Seltzer," 10 x 13", 1942 ..	3.50
"Blatz Beer," Victorian girl in pink dress, 1904	150.00
"Jacob Rupert Beer," 10 x 15", elves and beer cans, 1937	10.00
Corkscrew, "Anheuser Busch," 3" ad on brass plate, 1900	20.00
Crate, wooden, "Asco, American Stores Co., Phila. Pa.," 8 x 5 x 4½", "Fancy Apricots from California," varnished and dovetailed .	15.00
Dish, "Kraft Cheese," cobalt blue, with underplate	20.00
Doll, "Kellogg's Daddy Bear," 12", c. 1920	35.00
Flashlight, Winchester	20.00
Fountain Pen, "Pepsi Cola," c. 1930	65.00
Glasses	
"Clarksville Cider"	17.50
"National Lager," raised stem ...	40.00
"Peerless Ginger Ale"	10.00
"Richardson's Liberty Flair"	22.00
"Welch's Grape Juice," etched ..	12.50
Mugs	
"Anheuser Busch," 6", 1930–1940, emblem monogramed	15.00
"Iroquois Brewing Co., Buffalo N. Y.," c. 1900, sepia Indian head ..	45.00
Lemonade mug, Austrian, pink flowers	55.00
Opener, "Duquesne Beer," 4", tin, bottle shaped, c. 1940	3.00
Picture, sheet metal automotive poster on a wooden frame, old brown, black, silver paint, old auto picture, 30 x 53"	165.00
Pin, "Heinz Pickle," green	3.00
Perfume Bottle, "Larkin Company," 4", square, "Modjeska Bouquet," ground stopper, with label, impressed in bottle, "1916"	5.00
Pitchers	
"Hennesy's Cognac," head	30.00
Wild Turkey Mustard	50.00
Plates	
"Roberts, the Home Furnishers, Market and Locust Sts., Johnstown, Pa.," monk center, dark green, gold trim, Dresden in wreath	30.00
"Waltham Watch Co.," 8", Wedgwood, dated 1904	60.00
Salt and Pepper shakers, "Schlitz Beer," miniature bottles, pair	25.00
Spoons	
"Banner Buggies,"	30.00
"Rolex Watches"	5.50
Statue, "Miller's Beer," 6½", girl,	

1930	30.00
Thermometers	
" Dr. Pepper," 17"	25.00
"Landis Leaf Tobacco Co.," 5½ x 24", wood, shape and color of leaf	140.00
"Mail Pouch Tobacco," 8 x 39", porcelain	50.00
"Old Dutch Rooth Beer," 7 x 26", two windmills	25.00
Thimbles, metal	
"Harniss Co."	5.50
"Tastykake Co."	5.50
Watches	
Trade sign, form of a pocket watch, face on each side, old black and white paint, 20¾"	725.00
Trade sign, large watch, cast iron frame, zinc face, old black paint .	280.00

AGATA GLASS

Joseph Locke of the New England Glass Co., Cambridge, Mass., is credited with producing this art glass in the 1880's. Agata is usually an opaque pink shading to dark rose. The surface was left glossy and coated with a metallic stain which was spattered with alcohol and fired. Gloss finish predominates. It is rarely found in satin finish.

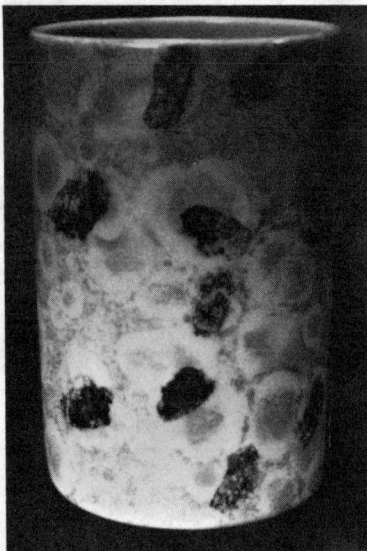

Tumbler, blue with black oil spots and gold $1100.00

Bowls	
5" dia., tricorne shape, fingerbowl	1250.00
5½" dia., ruffled fingerbowl	1500.00
Celery	
6½", square, scalloped top	1500.00
6½", crimped top	1750.00
Cruet, bulbous, three lip top, opaque handle and matching stopper . . .	1750.00
Pitcher, 9", ruffled top, reeded handle	3500.00
Toothpick Holders	
Crimped top	850.00
Square top	600.00
Tumbler, water	750.00
Vases	
5½", bulbous, four lip top, rare matte finish	3500.00
6", four lip pinched top, dimpled sides	1750.00
8½", Morgan vase, (rare shape) .	2500.00
9", Lily shape	1250.00

AKRO AGATE GLASS

The Akro Agate Co. was formed in 1911, first as jobbers, selling marbles made by the Navarre Glass Marble Specialty Co. to chain stores and wholesalers.

In 1914 the owners moved from near Akron, Ohio, to Clarksburg, W. Va., where cheap labor and a plentiful supply of natural gas were available. They opened a factory, known as the Akro Agate Co., for production of marbles which continued in profitable operation until 1929.

In 1932 the company was diversified and started making bowls, ashtrays, flower pots, etc., in green, red and blue onyx. Operations continued successfully until 1948. Finally, because of the lack of profits, the firm was dissolved and the factory was sold in 1951 to the Clarksburg Glass Co.

Ashtrays	
3 x 4", leaf shaped, blue	11.00
Square, cobalt and white	15.00
4", rectangular, orange marblized	15.00
Baskets	
Two handles, opaque white	25.00
6", blue in metal frame	40.00
Bowls	
Green slag	13.00
9", orange marblized	12.00
Opaque white	12.00
Children's Toy Dishes	
13 pieces, stippled band, transparent green	35.00

"The Little American Maid Tea Set,"
No. 335, opaque, 3 colors, octagonal,
set $110.00

6 pieces, water set	35.00
4 pieces, lustre jade green, 2 cups and saucers, 2 plates	35.00
8 pieces, set in original box	45.00
Creamer, 3", blue	13.00
Dish, shell shaped, blue	10.00
Jar, covered, 4½", Mexicali Sombre Ru lid	50.00
Match Holder	
Green, black and white	15.00
Horn of Plenty shape, orange and white	20.00
Marbles	
Set of 10, original box	15.00
Set of 50, original box	45.00
Set of 50 in bag	45.00
Planters	
3 x 6", oval, blue and white	18.00
Metal frame with bail handle, opaque white	35.00
8", rectangular, scalloped top, opaque yellow	40.00
Powder Jar, opaque white dog	35.00
Smoker's Set, holder and two ash-trays, opaque cobalt, set	50.00
Souvenir, "Watkin's Glen," shell shaped, orange and white	35.00
Toothpick, blue and white, urn	

shape	35.00
Tumbler, green and white	32.50

ALMANACS

An almanac is a small booklet containing cal-culations and other pertinent facts regarding astronomical data, weather forecasts and other useful information. They have been published for several centuries; in the late 18th and early 19th century, people used al-manacs for determining their activities, such as when to plant and harvest, much as we now depend on weather forecasters.

In addition to useful facts, almanacs are enjoyable to peruse. Although the very early ones are the most valuable, there are many late ones, printed in the 20th century, avail-able today at very reasonable prices.

"Home Almanac," Ford Motor Co.,
Dearborn, Mich., 48 pp, 1937 ...$3.00

1752, Astronomical, Astrological, Meterological Diary, John Brad-bury	25.00
1781, Connecticut Almanac	22.50
1783, Bickerstaff's New England Al-manac, Norwich	28.50
1794, Astronomical Diary, Nathanael Low, Boston	25.00

1795, New England Almanac, New London 28.50

1799, Farmer's Leap Year Issue, In Old Kyng's English 25.00

1805, New England Almanac, Nathan Daboll, New London 30.00

1809, New Hampshire and Vermont Almanac, Worcester 30.00

1810, New England Almanac, Nathan Daboll, New London 30.00

1813, Clergyman's Almanac or an Astronomical Diary and Serious Monitor 18.00

1828, The Farmer's Dairy or Ontario Almanac, Oliver Loud, Canandaiqua 19.00

1833-1840, Farmer's Almanac, Robert B. Thomas, set 35.00

1834, Poor Richard's Almanac, Tobias Ostrander 20.00

1839, American Almanac and Repository of Useful Knowledge ... 15.00

1841, Keystone Agricultural Almanac 15.00

1843, Presbyterian Almanac, Pittsburgh 9.00

1849, The Universalist Companion with Almanac and Register 12.00

1853, Ayers American Almanac ... 10.00

1864, Leavitt's Farmer's Almanack and Miscellaneous Year Book, Dudley Leavitt 10.00

1867, Pinney's Calendar or Western Almanac, George R. Perkins 15.00

1868, Old Farmer's Almanac, Brewer and Tileston 12.00

1869, Hagerstown Town and Country Almanac 7.50

1871, Miner's Almanac, Pittsburgh . 10.00

1872, Tarrytown Argus Almanac ... 10.00

1873, Farmer and Mechanics Almanac, A.L. Scovill & Co. 10.00

1874, Hostetter's United States Almanac, Pittsburgh 10.00

1880, Hagerstown Town and Country Almanac 7.00

1882, Dykman and Mott Almanac, Catskill, N.Y. 8.00

1883, Great Rock Island Railroad .. 30.00

1885, John Baers' Sons Agricultural Almanac, Lancaster 10.00

1889, Pocket Almanac and Account Book, Brown's Iron Bitters 22.50

1894, August German Flower and Syrup Almanac 12.00

1894, Herrick's Almanac 10.00

1895, Ayer's American Almanac ... 15.00

1897, Ladies Birthday Almanac ... 15.00

1900, Barker's Illustrated Farmer's Guide and Household Cook Book, with cartoons 25.00

1908, Diamond Dye #6 .... 9.00

1909, International Harvester Almanac 25.00

1916, Polish Almanac, religious and war foldout, colored pictures and calendar 25.00

1918, Dr. Miles New Weather Almanac 7.50

1922, Swamp Root Almanac 10.00

1927, Rawleigh's Good Health Guide Almanac Cook Book 8.50

1939, Ford Home Almanac and Facts Book, Ford Motor Co. 8.50

1939, Watkin's Almanac and Cook Book 8.50

ALUMINUM, HAND WROUGHT

Aluminum is a light weight, malleable silvery metal that resists corrosion. In the mid 20th century, hand wrought aluminum tablewares were made by several manufacturers in various patterns. These accessaries became acceptable to the modest, modern homemaker and were popular gifts. Due to the lack of present day production, hand wrought aluminum wares are becoming collectible and are still relatively inexpensive to obtain.

Coaster, 3¼", dia., Flying Geese decor, unmarked $4.00

Ashtray, 7", "Chrysanthemum," Continental 3.00

Baskets

9½", Buenulum 3.50

13", "Raspberry," Farberware ... 5.00

Bowls

"Dogwood," 11", Everlast 4.00

Embossed roses, panelled edge, World Hand Forged 6.50

"Leaf Scroll," Admiration 6.00
Candle Holder, saucer type,
stemmed cup, holder, beaded
around base, castle mark and
B.W. Buenulum 6.50
Candy dish, 7", underplate 10", cov-
ered, with glass insert, bail handle,
fruit and flowers, hand finished . . 7.50
Casserole holder and lid, 9¼",
Buenulum 4.00
Coasters
Six, in holder, 3¼", "Tulip,"
Hodney Kent, set 5.00
Eight, monogrammed K, 3¼", no
mark 5.00
Cocktail Shaker, "Chrysanthemum,"
Continental 15.00
Ice Bucket
Open, bail handle, 5", unmarked . 3.50
With lid, "Chrysanthemum," Conti-
nental 10.00
Lazy Susan, 14½", fruits and flow-
ers, Cromwell 7.50
Percolator, lucite handles, original
cord, "Chrysanthemum," Conti-
nental 30.00
Pitcher, quart size, loop handle,
plain, Buenulum 6.50
Plate, 8", plain, Hodney Kent 2.50
Server, two-tiered, 17½", Acorn,
Continental 10.00
Silent Butler, fruits and flowers,
Cromwell 3.50
Trays
Bread, bail handle, Chrysanthe-
mum, Continental 8.50
Flying geese decor, unmarked . . . 15.00
Pines and mountains, cylinder
handles, Arthur Armour 10.00
Bird, 11½ x 16½", two handles,
Lehman 5.00
Center dip dish and cover, 11",
"Tulip," Hodney Kent 8.50
Fruit tree, two handles, 14",
unmarked 7.00
Two-handled, 15", Acorns, Conti-
nental 7.50
Two-handled, full length rose,
marked Wild Rose, Silvertone,
Brilliantone 11.50
Two-handled, full length Chrysan-
themum, open work, applied
leaves on handles, Hand Wrought
Silverlook 755, Continental 12.00
Daffodils, unmarked, 20" 10.00

AMBERINA GLASS

The New England Glass Co. of Cambridge,
Mass., introduced Amberina Glass in 1883 under a patent granted to Joseph Locke.

Amberina is a transparent glass shading from
deep ruby to amber in color. The colors were
produced by adding small amounts of gold to
an amber glass batch and reheating portions
of the piece (generally the top) to bring out
the deep red. The Mt. Washington Glass Co.
called their similar ware Rose Amber. Most
early Amberina is of flint quality glass, blown
or pattern molded in the familiar diamond
quilted pattern. Some pieces are found in the
pressed Daisy and Button pattern and have
been attributed to Sandwich.

Amberina Glass was made by several Mid-
western factories, circa 1890. The shading
from cranberry to amber was produced by
giving the amber glass a thin flashing of
cranberry on upper portions of the piece.
This gave the piece a sharp line of demarka-
tion between the two colors. This less expensive version caused the death knell for the
New England variety.

In the 1920's Amberina Glass was revived
for a short time by Edward D. Libbey at his
factory which was then situated in Toledo,
Ohio. These pieces are signed and are included under the New England listing since
they were of that quality.

Amberina Glass has been widely reproduced.

Toothpick Holder, 2¼" high . . $75.00

NEW ENGLAND

Bowls
4¼", four cornered, amber wish-

bone feet, berry pontil	750.00
4½", diamond quilted, tricorner .	225.00
5½", finger, ruffled	195.00
7½", swirl, enamel and gold decor, ruffled, footed	325.00
7⅞", round, diamond quilted	295.00
9", square, pressed Daisy and Button, bell tone	395.00
Butter, covered, diamond quilted, ruffled edge base, reeded amber finial	595.00
Butter Pat, square, pressed Daisy and Button	125.00
Canoes	
8½", pressed Daisy and Button, bell tone	160.00
14", pressed Daisy and Button, bell tone	395.00
Celery	
6½", diamond quilted, scalloped square top	325.00
6½", IVT, crimped top	395.00
Cologne Bottle, 8", matching stopper, pedestal base, signed Libbey	595.00
Compote, 5", signed Libbey	495.00
Creamers	
4", bulbous, square mouth, IVT, amber reeded handle	350.00
Tankard shape, pressed Daisy and Button, amber handle, bell tone	395.00
Cruet, 7", bulbous, IVT, amber handle and faceted handle	395.00
Cup, punch, diamond quilted, amber reeded handle	175.00
Mustard, IVT, original pewter top . . .	165.00
Pitchers	
6", tankard, diamond quilted, amber handle	375.00
7", bulbous, IVT, amber reeded handle	450.00
Tankard, crackle glass, amber handle	425.00
RoseBowl, 3", diamond quilted, crimped top	350.00
Sauces	
4", round, diamond quilted	75.00
5", square, pressed Daisy and Button, bell tone	110.00
Syrup, IVT, silver plated top and handle	395.00
Toothpicks	
Square top, diamond quilted	165.00
Tricorn shape	225.00
Pressed Daisy and Button, footed	225.00
Tray, Ice Cream, 8½ x 13½", pressed Daisy and Button, bell tone	595.00
Vases	
5¼", diamond quilted, fluted top, amber applied rigaree around neck	395.00

7¼", lily	350.00

MIDWESTERN

Bowls	
4½", diamond optic	60.00
4¾", hobnail	250.00
9", fan shape, swirl, gold leaf and berry decor, footed	225.00
Celery, IVT, round scalloped top . . .	165.00
Creamer, 4¼", bulbous, square mouth, IVT, amber reeded handle	195.00
Cruets	
6½", bulbous, IVT, amber handle and stopper	225.00
6¾", mellon, herringbone, amber handle and bubble stopper	225.00
9", swirl, amber handle and bubble stopper	225.00
Cups, punch, IVT, amber handle . . .	95.00
Pitchers	
7", bulbous, IVT, clear applied handle	175.00
8", honeycomb, clear applied reeded handle	175.00
9", bulbous, swirl, enamel white flowers, green leaf decor	225.00
Salt and Pepper, IVT, enamel decor, original pewter tops, pair	165.00
Sugar Castor, IVT, original pewter top	225.00
Toothpicks	
IVT, pedestal foot	95.00
IVT, barrel, enamel floral decor . .	165.00
Tumblers	
Juice, IVT	70.00
Water, IVT, enamel floral decor . .	95.00
Water, IVT	65.00
Vases	
5¾", IVT, ruffled top, amber rigaree around neck, footed	245.00
6⅛", crackle glass, crystal applied leaves and loop feet	395.00
7", square top, scalloped rim, expanded diamond	225.00
10", swirl, jack-in-the-pulpit top . .	295.00
13", lily, amber serpentine trim around base, enamel decor	195.00

AMBERINA GLASS—PLATED

Plated Amberina glass was patented by Edward Libby in 1889 for the New England Glass Co., Cambridge, Mass. Its characteristic coloring of deep amber shading to deep ruby is enhanced by vertical ribbing and a fiery opalescent lining. A cased Wheeling glass of similar appearance has an opaque white lining, but is not opalescent and the body is not ribbed. Plated Amberina was made in a limited quantity, was susceptible to breakage, is consequently rare.

Tumbler, some "soot"
specks $1900.00

AMPHORA

The dictionary defines amphora as a two-handled vessel with a narrow neck used by the ancient Greeks to hold wine, water or oil. The Amphora wares found on today's market were made in Austria in the late 1880's. They are usually marked "Amphora" with a crown. Occasionally a piece is cross-indexed with "Tillowitz" and signed twice.

Statutes with green dresses & pink roses, (left) 19″ high, (right) 20¼″ high; marked Amphora, Austria, with crown, pair $875.00

Bowls
  5½″ dia., 3⅜″ high, fluted edge,
  fingerbowl **2250.00**
  8″ dia., 3½″ high, squatty bulbous, crimped top **6000.00**
Celery, 7½″, round top with slightly
  tapered waist **3000.00**
Cruet, 7″, bulbous, 3-pinch top, amber handle and cut, faceted amber
  stopper **3500.00**
Cup, Punch, amber handle **2500.00**
Pitchers
  4″, bulbous, scoop shape top, amber handle **3800.00**
  7″, bulbous, amber handle **6500.00**
  10″, tankard, amber handle **7500.00**
Shaker, Salt, original silver plated
  top **550.00**
Toothpicks
  2¼″, bulbous with tapered round
  top **1500.00**
  2″, barrel shape, (very rare) **2000.00**
Tumbler **2000.00**

Baskets
  6 x 7″, incised with flowers in relief, predominately blue **65.00**
  7 x 11″, floral and cupid decor,
  signed "Amphora" with crown .. **195.00**
Bowls
  5″ diam., 5″ high, owl decor in relief, blue signed **75.00**
  10″, Bird's nest with pheasant, all-
  over embossing earth tones,
  signed **375.00**

Bust of woman, pastel colors, signed "Amphora"	175.00
Ewer, oversized green and gilt leaves, stem rises to form handle, mottled blue and green background, impressed marks and 3853/42	400.00
Figurines	
12", full figured lady and bowl	390.00
16", half sized figure of woman, signed	850.00
Hen and egg, sculpted	175.00
Urns	
9 x 9½", figure of boy with couldron decor	150.00
12 x 14", green glaze, purple highlights, gold flowers, signed "Amphora" with crown	275.00
Vases	
Two handled vase, bulbous, narrow neck, beige glaze dripped over deep blue mottled background, gilt handles and detail, incised designer mark, P. D.	375.00
Cylindrical body, applied slender stemmed buds, blossoms and leafage, on avocado and brown textured background, two foliatte handles and gilt, Amphora, Austria	275.00
Gourd shaped vase, gilt rim, sunflowers, matte brown and peach mottled background, Amphora, Austria	250.00
Elongated oval form, lug handles, stylized peonies in polychrome enamels with gilt, impressed mark	290.00
7¼", four gold handles, yellow roses with black decor	90.00
7¼", bird shaped handles, brown matte finish	145.00
8¾", ducks in flight, moon, surface decor	180.00
8 x 8", bulbous, bunches of grapes in high relief	250.00
10½", flower-form neck, multi colored enamel decor, signed	265.00
11½", pink flowers and branches, pair	235.00

ANIMAL DISHES, COVERED

Covered animal dishes became popular in the late 1800's and continue their popularity today.

Among the leading American manufacturers were McKee Glass Co., Pittsburgh, Pa., and Atterbury Glass Co., also of Pittsburgh, which made the famous Atterbury duck covered dish, which was patented on March 15, 1887. The most popular collectible in this category was hen on nest, as collectors concentrated on size, color and type of glass.

Reproductions are found in almost every form. Collectors must use caution and discretion in purchasing these articles.

Also see MILK GLASS and VALLERYSTAHL for added listings.

References given are: *Milk Glass* by Belknap; *Early American Pattern Glass* by A. H. Metz.

Hen, 4½ x 5½" long, blue with white base **$22.00**

Camel, resting, white milk glass, B-183A	90.00
Bull's head mustard	110.00
Cats	
8", cobalt carnival, limited edition	40.00
White milk glass, Atterbury	150.00
5½", white milk glass, blue ribbed base	85.00
Chicken on sleigh, white milk glass	50.00
Chicken and eggs on nest, white milk glass, Atterbury	150.00
Chicks with chicken, round basket base, frosted	100.00
3½", Cockatoo, painted, Staffordshire	85.00
Cows	
6", amber glass, ribbed base	40.00
6", amber glass, ribbed base, frosted	95.00
Dogs	
5½", blue milk glass, white head	125.00
5", amber on wide ribbed base	90.00
5", green milk glass, fringed mat, embossed flowers	85.00
5", white milk glass	100.00
Doves	
6", amber, ribbed base	35.00
4 x 4½", white milk glass,	

basketweave base, McKee 250.00

Ducks
5", clear aqua 75.00
Blue milk glass, white head 22.50
Blue milk glass, without eyes,
Atterbury, (rare) 500.00
6½", clear glass 50.00
8", cobalt carnival, limited edition 40.00
White milk glass in natural bull
rush base 90.00
6½", frosted 60.00
7½", frosted 65.00
*White milk glass, amethyst head,
Atterbury 225.00
*White milk glass, Atterbury 150.00

Eagles
6⅛", ovoid, white milk glass, "The
American Hen," Puerto Rico,
Cuba, Phillipines 125.00
Jar, standing 125.00
White milk glass 125.00

Fish
White milk glass, Atterbury 175.00
Frosted, sea base, Flaccus 90.00

Hens
5½", amber, marked Vallerysthal 15.00
6½", dark amber 50.00
6½", light amber 75.00
Cobalt carnival, limited edition . . . 20.00
6½", custard 100.00
7", Parian 175.00
6½", purple carnival, limited edi-
tion 25.00
6½", white milk glass 100.00

Hens, Staffordshire
2½", painted 50.00
3½", painted 75.00
6½", painted 125.00
8", white, brown basket base . . . 150.00

Lamb
White milk glass, McKee 175.00
White milk glass, split rib base,
McKee 90.00

Lions
Blue milk glass, white head, on
blue ribbed base 100.00
White milk glass, lacy base,
Atterbury 165.00
White milk glass, split rib base,
unsigned 90.00

Owls
White milk glass, red eyes,
Atterbury 150.00
Jar 140.00
3¾", creamer 9.00

Quail, 5", white milk glass 75.00

Rabbits
*White milk glass 75.00
White milk glass, Atterbury 175.00
White milk glass, blue ribbed base 175.00
White milk glass, split rib base,
McKee 90.00

White milk glass, Greentown 225.00

Robins
White milk glass, blue head 75.00
*White milk glass, ribbed base . . 75.00

Roosters
White milk glass, blue head 75.00
*White milk glass, ribbed base . . 75.00
10", clear, Atterbury 75.00

Squirrel, white milk glass, ribbed
base, McKee 150.00

Swans
*5", white milk glass 125.00
6½", clear glass, frosted head
and neck, Sandwich 150.00
6", Staffordshire 225.00
5", white milk glass, closed neck . 85.00
7", white milk glass, open neck,
Atterbury 125.00
5½"white milk glass, spread wings 150.00
Black, B-186, Atterbury 200.00

Turkeys
9", Leeds 275.00
5", white milk glass, McKee 175.00
8", white with brown nest, Staf-
fordshire 200.00
8", clear glass 12.00

Turtle, 6", clear 25.00

APOTHECARY ITEMS

Yesteryear's apothecary shop was quite removed from today's version of the modern drug store which sells everything from gift items to prescriptions from corporate manufacturers. Early pharmacists concocted shotgun prescriptions in a mortar and pestle, rolled pills by hand, percolated cough syrup, sold over-the-counter remedies and acted as the country doctor, neighborhood psychiatrist and checker partner. Bygone apothecary items are being collected for nostalgia, especially by those in the medical field.

Bottles
6", with stopper 12.50
6½", emerald, ribbed, recessed
panel for label, glass stopper . . . 35.00
6½", embossed, Fayette Drug
Co., Uniontown, Pa. 7.50
7½", round, glass stopper, finger-
pull type, recessed label, gold . . . 26.00
7½", free blown, clear 30.00
8", recessed label, ribbed emer-
ald, "Tinc. OPII," ground stopper . 30.00
8¼", tam-o-shanter stopper, inset
label, marked on base, "Pat'd
April 2, 1889, W. T. and Co." . . . 35.00
8½", clear, stopper 25.00
8½", square, clear, ground stop-
per, "Tinc. OPII Camph." 30.00
9½", round, clear, label, wide red

Bottle, "Potassium Nitrate Salt Petre," 10″ high, recessed label; ground stopper $20.00

border	32.50
10½″, tam-o-shanter stopper, blown, cobalt, gold-edged label, "Tinc. OPII"	45.00
10″, round thumbprint stopper, label "Ed Peps e Bis"	35.00
10½″, tam-o-shanter stopper, inset labels, marked on base "W.T. &Co."	35.00
10½″, clear, blown, mushroom	

stopper	30.00
10½″, tam-o-shanter stopper, amethystine, pontil, gold label, "Tinc. Iodini"	45.00
11″, stopper, wide mouth	40.00
12″, ground stopper	50.00
14″, bulbous, fancy ITP pedestal base	65.00
15″, round, slender, thumbprint base and cover	75.00
18″, blown, ground tam-o-shanter stopper	75.00
Container, ice cream topping, 7″, white ceramic with nickel plated hinged top	25.00
Cork Press, 8¼″, lever-type, black cast iron, 4 different size corks ..	50.00
Display Cases	
"B. D. Thermometers," wood and glass front, original lining	30.00
"Parke Davis," tin, two drawers ..	75.00
Funnels, 24½″, clear glass mounted on 9″ square wooden base, pair .	100.00
Globes	
Hanging, 22″, clear, glass, three chains, c. 1891	195.00
Standing, 13″, three-tier, top section green glass, bottom clear ...	50.00
Labels, blank, early 1900's, set of 12	1.00
Label Dispensers	
Cabinet, oak, 4 drawers, 12 brass labels per drawer	150.00
McCourt Label Cabinet Co., oak and brass, holds 48 labels	75.00
McCourt Label Cabinet Co., Bradford, Pa., Pat'd June 11, 1912, 3 x 6 x 6″ brass, top hinges open, dispenses roll of labels ...	50.00
Literature	
"American Druggists Journals," 1932–1937, ads and illustrations, ea.	2.00
"Druggist Catalogue,"1911	5.00
"Handbook of Pharmacy and Theuraputics," Eli Lily, hardback c. 1897	35.00
"The Pharmaceutical Era," complete list of drugs and preps, from 1905 USP, 1st ed. pocketsize ...	20.00
"The Pharmacapeia of the U. S." and "National Formulary with Comments," leather covers, c. 1916, set	35.00
Brass, 4	
Brass, 5″	70.00
Lignum Vitae	80.00
Maple, 6″, hand turned	70.00
Pine, 5″, hand turned	40.00
Porcelain, 5″	35.00
Pill Roller, 7 x 14″, 2 piece walnut and brass, makes 24 pills	85.00
Scales	

Counter top-type, cast iron with porcelain pans, American 75.00
Counter top-type, wood base, marble top, brass pans and weights 135.00
Suppository Mold, brass, "S. Maw and Son" and "Thompson," London 75.00
Tumbler, "Ace Tumbler Cover and Dose Indicator," Pat'd Nov. 17, 1896 .... 20.00

ART DECO

The Art Deco period was named for an exhibition held in Paris in 1927, "L'Exposition Internationale des Arts Decoratifs." It is a later period than Art Nouveau but sometimes crosses since they were relatively close in time and are often confused with the flowing and sensuous female forms of the earlier era.

The designs of Art Deco are angular and of simple lines. This was the period of skyscrapers, movie idols and the cubist work of Picasso and Legras. It was used for every conceivable object being produced in the 1920's–1930's, including ceramics, furniture, glass and metals, not only in Europe, but in America as well.

This is a special market for the "new" collector and the best of this style is now commanding prices comparable to earlier periods.

Statue, 11", white metal on marble base, signed Denis $355.00

Andirons, brass, square column, tapering to step tops, pair 250.00
Ashtrays
  5½", square, bronze, footed base, kneeling Egyptian woman nude girl, holding tray 95.00
Atomizer, 3 x 3", cut crystal, signed "Marcel Franck" 75.00
Biscuit Jar, 6", off-white, "Valamour" 35.00
Bookends, 6 x 8", bronzed metal, nude girl sitting on open book, signed "K and Co.," pair 75.00
Bottles, Perfume
  5", emerald green, stylized cut, stoppered 25.00
  6", crystal 25.00
  6½", cobalt, geometric cutting .. 40.00
  10", crystal, cone-shaped with 7", twisted and pointed stopper 85.00
Bowl, 8", square, black enamel, hand painted red flowers, gold edge 100.00
Box, 6", powder, frosted pale green glass, molded cubic designs 25.00
Bust, 7", mouth is cigarette lighter, signed "Arturo Levi" 85.00
Candelabra, 15", bronze, three light,

straight line, signed, E. Hurley ... 500.00
Cigarette Cases
  Chrome trim on simulated tortoise shell 10.00
  With attached lighter, "Ronson," simulated tortoise, chrome trim, original flannel bag 20.00
Compacts
  3", sterling and 14K gold, hangs from 6" chain 75.00
  3½", enameled, turquoise and lime green, simulated diamond in center, fitted interior 20.00
  4", enameled, black with bust of woman on cover in relief, chain handle 35.00
  4", sterling, all over engraving ... 50.00
Demitasse Set, 4 cups and saucers, creamer and sugar, geometric pattern of leaves in green, black, platinum on white ground, marked Empire Ivory Ware, "Grosvenor," set 100.00
Desk Calendar, 6⅜", bronze finish, ornate initial in circle, c. 1939 ... 50.00
Desk Set, inkwell, paper clip, rocking blotter, triple stamp box, signed

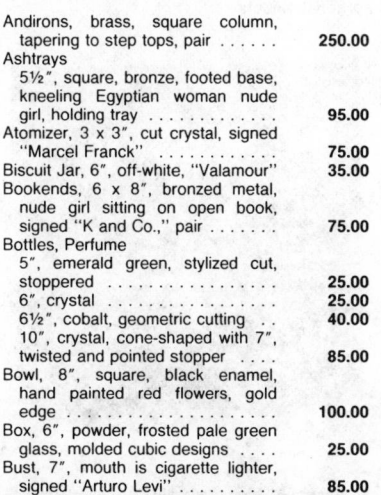

Tea Set, 3 pieces, chrome, signed Chase **$355.00**

"Bradley Hubbard," set	250.00
Figurines	
11¼", nude, carved French ivory, (Chryselephantine sculpture)	650.00
12¾", woman, porcelain, yellow, blue, brown, Austria	200.00
Flower Frogs	
6½", seated nude, light blue glass	35.00
8", woman in long dress, trailing flowers, 2 piece, white porcelain .	50.00
Furniture — See "Furniture"	
Lamps	
15", marble drum base, figure atop, outstretched arms, wearing blue cape	300.00
8¾", gilded metal nude, afghan hound, Hobnail glass shade	100.00
9", gilt bronze, oriental dancer, holds Millefiore globe, (Chryselephantine Sculpture)	1,500.00
10½", bronze, mushroom-shaped with silver decor, "Henitz"	300.00
11", bronze, dancing girl on marble plinth, brass shade, crystal prisms, signed "Braved, Austria" .	650.00
13", bronzed metal with three standing nudes, arms raised, holding globe-shaped marigold shade with geometric sculptured design .	175.00
13½", galleon, silvered metal base, shade of multicolored glass fruit	175.00
15½", desk type, adjustable, brass	195.00
Plate, butterfly center	19.00
Porringer, 5½", sterling, handle set with carnelian stone, "Greif"	175.00
Radiator Screen, 52 x 27", three-panelled, pierced brass, wood frame	500.00
Shoe Buckles, 1½", steel backs and clips, late 1930's, assorted styles,	

pair	10.00
Smoking Set, one side holds cigarettes, other, three ashtrays, match box, sterling trim on bronze	95.00
Tazza, 4½ x 6", pierced border, set with three cabachon jade stones, "Greif"	300.00
Vases	
6", pear-shaped, flared rim, enamel blue and yellow, stylized pussy willows on clear ground, signed "Groupy"	250.00
8½", flying geese, blue, green, yellow, signed "Boch"	175.00
12", parrot, all-over enamel, marked "Keramis, Made in Belgium"	150.00

ART NOUVEAU

The French term for the new art, "Art Nouveau," had its beginning in the 1890's and swept the continent and America for almost 40 years. Some of its more recognized artists were Galle, Lalique and Tiffany. But there were other artists of the period, not as proficient or promoted, and knowledgeable collectors are now searching out their works. Art Nouveau can be identified by its flowing, sensuous lines, floral forms, insects and the feminine form. These designs were incorporated on almost everything produced at that time, from art glass to furniture, to silver, to personal objects.

Vases, 6" high, calla lily, leaf handles, painted bronz metal, pair $75.00

Ashtray, 26½", figural floor type, bronzed pot metal 95.00

Bag, or dance purse, Whiting and Davis, sterling silver, lady's head . 165.00

Bookends
Brass, reclining nudes with arched backs and flowing hair, pair 100.00
Brass, frog in tailcoat, carrying top hat, pair 75.00
Bronze nude, 6¼", pair 100.00

Boxes
Collar Button, 2½", silver plated, lady's head, flowing hair, Victor S. Company 48.00
Collar Button, silver plated, Parke S. Company 22.00
Pewter design on top, 3 x 5", red acid finish, signed "M. Hess" . . . 100.00
Ring, gold plated, lined 20.00

Button hook, 6½", sterling 30.00

Candlesticks
Free Form, 6" base, applied leaves, flower shaped cup for candle, signed "CPR" 110.00
Flowers with intertwined stems, 10¼", silverplated 40.00
Man, woman, butterflies, 15", silver plated, pair 175.00
Battery operated, bronze finish, "Candle," Pat. 1915 . . . . 35.00

Card Holder, 13 x 15½", 22K gold on pewter, nude seated on leaf . . 385.00

Centerpiece Compote, with matching candlesticks, black enamel on amber glass and intaglio-cut, set . . . 295.00

Compote, 2 x 6", chintz, black and green striped on clear background, clear base, signed, "Nash" 135.00

Comb, 7½", sterling silver, ornate . . 95.00

Dresser Set, two brushes, comb, mirror, sterling, Unger Bros., set . 250.00

Figurine, 9", girl dancing, bronze, ivory face and hands 300.00

Hand mirror, sterling, sculptured woman's head with flowing tresses, irises, swans, and rising sun, Unger Bros. 125.00

Hair brush, sterling 9¼", handle in form of woman, roses and cupid at top 125.00

Hat Pin, 7½", three faces, sterling silver 55.00

Knife Sharpener, bronze stylized bird 35.00

Lamps
Small, four-footed pedestal, large flame-shaped globe, pair 150.00
Musical jester, frosted globe 95.00
Roman chariot and soldier 95.00
Branched, candle shaped, gold washed stem and branches and base, stems ending in small pink, ceramic blossoms, electrified 175.00
Gilded nymph supporting pedestal with ball shade of cased spatter glass in red, yellow and white . . . 150.00
Cobra-shaped base, 15", jewelled shade, gilded metal 300.00
Red lustre glass in bronze holder, shape of flowers, 16", leaves and vines 300.00
Bronzed base with three medallions of woman's head, 18", art glass shade, 10" dia., amber mottling on yellow background 375.00
Six-panel glass shade, panels of blue and white 285.00

Letter Holder, 2 sections, four ladies, side profiles with long, flowing hair, long stemmed, floral decor, bronzed 60.00

Match Holder, lady smoking 100.00

Mirror, three sections, each 10 x 10" figure of women, ivory celluloid . . 150.00

Pitcher, pewter, female figure-form handle, bearded man decor, signed 300.00

Stamp case, sterling 20.00

Tea Strainer, pierced corner, 7", fits over cup, sterling 35.00

Trays
Flowing haired woman, flowers in relief, sterling 35.00
Girl watching sunrise, 4 x 8", bronze "Maxim" 175.00
Oval, 6 x 7", sterling 50.00

Vases
Cluthra, female form, light blue . . 295.00
Dragon, 8", "Hawkes" 85.00
Floral motif, pewter, 8", "Kayserzinn" 150.00
Floral decor, signed "Corona-Holland" 250.00
Ceramic, brown, 9¼", hand painted floral on bulbous base, floral rim, impressed, "Germany" . 60.00
Girl with flowing hair, flowers, handled metal 75.00
Bronze, dark patina, 10", high relief grapes, in darker bronze 250.00
Female figure wrapped around vase, signed "VanBriggle, Colorado Springs" 225.00
Panelled blue opalescent to green, 10½", heavy enamelled poppies 125.00
Lady with flowing hair, signed "Asch, Royal Bonn" 250.00
Angels, 17½", green and maroon leaves, Dore female figures, bronze, signed 500.00

Wax letter seal, sterling 35.00

AURENE GLASS

AURENE

This type of art glass was invented by Frederick Carder for the Steuben Glass Works of Corning, New York. The name Aurene was given to the glass by the originator from the Latin "Aureus," a Roman gold coin. Aurene glass has a smooth, uniform, iridescent surface in gold, blue or silvery blue. It was made by the Steuben Glass Works from 1904 to 1933. Some items were marked with "Steuben" or "Aurene" or both scratched in the base, others have the name and the factory number. Many pieces were unmarked and had only a paper label. Unmarked pieces are difficult to distinguish from Tiffany's "Favrile."

Vase, 5¾" blue, optic rib, signed "Steuben, Aurene 6299," . . . $1775.00

Bottles
4¼", cologne, gold, acorn stopper, signed	375.00
7", cologne, gold and blue, blue stopper, signed	395.00

Bowls
8", blue, loop decor	350.00
12", gold and calcite, bulbous base	365.00
Finger, ruffled with ruffled underplate, signed and numbered	375.00
Box, 4" dia., covered, blue, signed	475.00

Candlesticks
8", gold, signed, pair	585.00
10", blue, twisted stem, signed and numbered, pair	1250.00
Chalice, 6½", trumpet shape, gold, footed	285.00

Compotes
5½ x 5¼", gold, signed and numbered	225.00
7", gold, signed	275.00
8", gold and calcite	245.00
Creamer, 4", gold and blue, clover shape, signed	450.00
Lamp Shades—See "Lamp Shades"	
Nut Dish, 3½", gold, ruffled, signed and numbered	115.00
Salt, 2½", gold	100.00
Sherbet, gold, with underplate, signed	215.00

Vases
2⅜", gold and blue, signed	225.00
5", gold with stretched ruffled top, signed	210.00
6", gold	300.00
6½", gold, signed and numbered	350.00
6½", blue, signed and numbered	430.00
8", gold, signed	375.00
8⅞", blue, flared bottom, ruffled rim top	550.00
12", gold and blue, signed	400.00
12", gold, green leaf and vine decor, with off white, millefiori, signed and numbered	2950.00

AUSTRIAN WARE

During the late 19th and early 20th centuries, much fine porcelain and pottery were produced in Austria. Although Carlsbad, known as Karlsbad after World War I when Austria became part of Czechoslovakia, was the center of the industry, other factories existed. These factories were either owned or supported by Americans, thus, their wares were produced mainly for export to the United States. The U. S. firm of Lazarus and Rosenfeldt imported large amounts of porcelain from Czechoslovakia after World War I, marked "Victoria." For additional listings, see specific manufacturers listed alphabetically in this book.

Bowl, 5¾", hand painted border of yellow roses, artist signed	25.00
Butter Pats, marked "Vienna, Austria," set of 8	9.00
Cache Pot, 6½" dia., 3¼" high, handled fluted, small sprays in pink, lustre touches	35.00
Cake Set, 9¾" serving plate, six 6¾" plates, hand painted vintage decor, gold trim, pierced rims, artist signed, set	165.00

Cake Plate, 11½″ dia., including handles, Carlsbad, multicolored daisies on white ground $85.00

Creamer, 3″, floral decor, lattice handle, "M.Z. Austria" 7.00

Cream and Sugars
Egg shell porcelain with pale blue and shaded red fruit decor, gold trim 40.00
White with pink roses, green leaf trim, Imperial 12.50

Demitasse, six cups and saucers, green with white, gold floral, set . 65.00

Dresser Set, 4 pieces, bluebird under glaze, Victoria 60.00

Egg Cups, figurals of chick, bunny, rooster, and duck, set of 4 . . . . . 25.00

Fish Set, 15 pieces, Imperial Crown China, Austria 595.00

Hair Receivers
Gold scroll edging, tiny rose decor, Victoria 60.00
Rust to yellow with roses, Victoria 18.50

Pitcher, syrup, 5½″ high, rose decor, underplate, Victoria 40.00

Plates
8¾″, geese flying against white moon, pale blue background, dark blue rim, M. S. Austria 20.00
6″, handled, sailing scene, gold handles, artist signed 12.00
9½″, hand painted, pink, yellow roses, tinted background, Victoria 25.00
Sardine, pink floral, Sardine handles, Victoria 25.00

Ramekins with underplates, white porcelain, gold trim, Victoria, set of 6 . . . . 35.00

Salt and pepper shakers, hand painted florals, pair 20.00

Salt Dips, hand painted with pink roses, gold feet and trim, set of 6 35.00

Vases
8½″, floral decor on medallion, green and white, pair 75.00
12″, pink and yellow floral decor on ivory background, gold trim, footed and handled, bisque finish 75.00
Woman in yellow dress, gold handles, brown, orange, and green with gold, gold handles, artist signed, Victoria, Austria 225.00

AUTOGRAPHS

Autographs occur in a wide variety of formats — letters, documents, photographs, autograph books and cards, etc. Most collectors focus on a particular person, country, or category, e.g., opera singers.

The condition and content of letters and documents bears significantly on value. Collectors should know their source since forgeries abound and copy machines compound the problem. Further, some signatures of recent Presidents and movie stars are done by machine rather than by the person themselves. A good dealer or advanced collector can help one spot the differences.

The following abbreviations denote type of autograph material:

ADS	Autograph Document Signed
ALS	Autograph Letter Signed
AMsS	Autograph Manuscript Signed
CS	Card Signed
DS	Document Signed
LS	Letter Signed
MCS	Magazine Cover Signed
PS	Photograph Signed
TLS	Typed Letter Signed
TMsS	Typed Manuscript Signed

GENERAL

Anthony, Susan B., woman's rights leader, PS, 4 x 5½″, 1904 . . . . . 550.00

Boone, Daniel, frontiersman, AMsS, 1p, 1783, legal 2525.00

Dali, Salvador, Spanish American Artist, sketch, 1944 . . . . 350.00

Edison, Thomas, inventor, check, 1928 . . . . 100.00

Lindbergh, Charles A., aviator, TLS, 1p, 1965 . . . . 285.00

Peary, Robert E., artic explorer, TLS, 1½p, 1910, financial 185.00

Vanderbilt, Cornelius, DS, railroad

bond, c. 1882 . . . .   100.00
Washington, Booker T., teacher, LS, 1p, 1911 . . . .   65.00
Wright, Frank Lloyd, architect, book signed, 1949 . . . .   300.00

LITERATURE

Buck, Pearl S., Nobel prize winner, TMsS, 15 pages 145.00
Cooper, J. Fennimore, author, check, 1972 . . . .   45.00
Gray, Zane, western author, AL, 1p, 1931 . . . .   165.00
Hemingway, Ernst, author, CS, 4¼ x 3¼" 240.00
Howe, Julia Ward, author, AMsS, 1p, 1871, poem 80.00
Pasternack, Boris, Russian Nobel prize winner, envelope addressed by him 120.00
Steinbeck, John, Nobel prize winner, ANS, 1p 200.00
Whitman, Walt, poet and author, SO, 10 x 8" sheet, 1872 . . . .   205.00

MUSIC

Blake, Eubie, composer, PS, 10 x 8"   24.00
Caruso, Enrico, opera singer, LS, 1p, 1916, medical 120.00
Cohan, George M., song writer, PS, 6 x 9" 65.00
Gadski, Johanna, opera singer, PS, 10 x 8", 1920 . . . .   50.00
Grieg, Edvard, Norwegian composer, ALS, 2p, 1888 . . . .   375.00
Sousa, John Philip, composer and bandmaster, PS, postcard size, 1905 . . . .   185.00

ROYALTY

George III, King of England, DS, 1p, 1767, military commission 115.00
George IV, King of England, DS as Prince Regent, 1812 . . . .   110.00
James II, King of England, DS as Duke of York, 1p, 1660, financial   400.00
Louis XIV, King of France, DS, 1p, 1707, commission 335.00
Peter I (The Great), Czar of Russia, DS, 2p, 1721 . . . .   1400.00
Victoria, Queen of England, DS, 1p, 1707, commission 150.00

SHOW BUSINESS

Arbucille, Roscoe (Fatty), silent movie star, ALS, 2p, 1924, personal . .   140.00
Beatles, singers, MCS *People*, 11 x 8", 1976 . . . .   625.00

Walter Lanz, cartoon drawing framed & matted, crayon & ink, 10⅝ x 12½" $75.00

Blackstone, Harry, magician, DS, program (Lyceum Theatre), 6 x 9", 1948 . . . .   145.00
Garland, Judy, actress, TDS, 1p, 1959, financial 100.00
Gish, Lillian, actress, TLS, 2p, 1942   45.00
Karloff, Boris, actor, PS, 5 x 7" 75.00
Mostel, Zero, actor, CS with Jack Rosen caricature, 1968, 14 x 11"   80.00
Oakley, Annie, wild west show actress, pamphlet signed, 4p, 1918 .   750.00
Presley, Elvis, singer, DS, 1947, contract 250.00
Tracy, Spencer, actor, PS, sepia tone, 7 x 5" 85.00
Wood, Natalie, actress, DS, 41p, 1965, contract, signed with real and stage name 75.00

SPORTS

Ali, Muhammad, boxer, PS, 10 x 8" .   25.00
Clemente, Roberto, baseball, CS, 1970 Topps #350 . . . .   125.00
Dempsey, Jack, boxer, CS, postcard "Dempsey knocks out Willard" . .   13.00
Musical, Stan, baseball, CS, 1953

Bowman #32	40.00
New York Yankees, baseball, team signed baseball, 1932 world series champs	450.00
Paige, Satchel, baseball, CS with Jack Rosen caricature, 13 x 11″	115.00
Postal, Bernard, signed book, *Encyclopedia of Jews in Sports*, 1965	18.00

STATESMEN, AMERICAN

Buchanan, James, President, DS, 1p, 1860 appointment	350.00
Davis, Jefferson, President of Confederacy, ALS, 1p, personal	385.00
Ford, Gerald R., TLS, 2p, 1980, thanks for support	75.00
Franklin, Benjamin, signer and inventor, ALS, 1p, 1779, scientific experiments	8500.00
Hayes, Rutherford B., President, ANS, 1872	35.00
Hoover, Herbert, President, TLS, 1p, 1947, financial	50.00
Hughes, Charles Evans, Chief Justice, TLS, 1p, 1906	50.00
Jefferson, Thomas, signer and President, ALS, 1p, 1822	1700.00
Lincoln, Abraham, President, DS, 1864, commission	1750.00
McKinley, William, President, TLS, 1p, 1896	250.00
Stevenson, Adlai E., Statesman, TLS, 1p, 1965	40.00
Truman, Harry S., signed book, *Mr. Citizen*, 1960	50.00

STATESMEN, EUROPEAN

Disraeli, Benjamin, English Prime Minister, ALS, 4p, 1869	200.00
Gladstone, William E., English Prime Minister, ALS, 1p, 1874	50.00
Kruger, Stephanns, President of South Africa, DS, 1p, 1899, commission	250.00
Menshikov, Mikail, Soviet diplomat, PS, 1961	25.00
Napoleon, Emperor of France, LS, 1p, 1806	500.00
Pitt, William (The Younger), English Prime Minister, ALS, 1p, 1766	575.00

AUTOMOBILE ITEMS

Carbide Tank, for running board, brass plated	175.00
Clock, dash, Stevens Duryea, brass, beveled case, 8 day, key wind, Hoffecker Co., Boston	75.00
Emblems, each	15–25.00

Hood ornament, Louis Varonson, 1915, (arms rotate) $250.00

Engines	
Chrysler, 28, 4 cyl.	150.00
Ford, 29, Model A	200.00
Gear Shift Knobs	
Orange and white, marbleized	20.00
Red and white agate	45.00
Hood ornaments	
Buick, blue glass	50.00
Mack Truck, Bulldog	20.00
Nude, Chrome	65.00
Pontiac, Chief	30.00
Horns	
English, No. 34, brass, "King of the Road"	150.00
Plunger type, early	60.00
Jack, Ford, Model T	50.00
Lamps	
Adlake Balanced Draft, 8½″, original brackets	65.00
Dietz Eureda, 7½″, clear lens in front, red glass in rear, brass	125.00
Everready Mazada, original bulbs, c. 1910	30.00
Interior, electric car, 2¾ x 5″,	

brass, bevelled glass panels, pair	175.00

License Plates

California World's Fair, 1939, pair	35.00
Enameled, each	10 25.00
Porcelain, each	25 60.00

Lights

Cadillac, 1913, headlights, pair	200.00
Ford, Model T, 1915, tail light, brass, pair	60.00
Lucas Fog, SFT 576	100.00

Literature

Cadillac, Shop Manuel, Brougham, 1957 58	69.50
Chevrolet, Shop Manuel, 1961 Corvair	16.50
Chrysler, Shop Manuel, 1935	42.50
Ford at the San Francisco Exposition, 1915, brochure	40.00
Hudson, Sales Literature, 1916, 32 pages	60.00
Jewell, Sales Literature, 1927, 16 pages	30.00
Lincoln, Body and Chassis Shop Manuel, 1952	20.00
Motors Air Conditioning/Heater Manuel, 1970 76	15.00
Plymouth, Shop Manuel, 1957	17.50

Magneto, Ford, Model "N", 4 cyl. engine	100.00

Motor Meters

1916 Boyce	50.00
1916 Dodge	50.00
Pump, Tire, Ford	35.00
Radio, Silvertone, 6 volt, 1930's	85.00

Seats

Packard Coupe, 1922, set of two	200.00
Toledo, 1905 06, front, original upholstery	300.00
Spark Coil, early, each	50.00
Steering Wheel, 1925 Durant	80.00
Tools, Ford, set of 12	35.00

Vases (used to hold flowers for electric cars)

Black Satin Glass, Tiffin, pair	35.00
Pink glass, no bracket	20.00

AUTOMOBILES

Automobiles can be classified into several categories. In 1947 the Antique Automobile Club of America (AACA) devised a system whereby any motor vehicle (car, bus, motorcycle, etc.) made prior to 1930 is an "antique" car. The Classic Car Club of America (CCCA) expanded the list focusing on luxury models from 1925 to 1948. The Mile Stone Car Club (MSC) developed a list for cars in the 1948 to 1964 period.

Some states, such as Pennsylvania, have devised a dual registration system for older cars antique and classic. Models from the 1960's and 1970's, especially convertibles and limited production models, fall into the "classic" designation depending on how they are used.

The cost to own cars made prior to 1940 has risen dramatically. New collectors are focusing on those makes and models which have the potential to become tomorrow's antiques. The list reflects the wide variety of the market place.

The prices here are based upon a car in running condition, with a high percentage of original parts, and somewhere between 60 and 80% restored. *Prices can vary by as much as 30% in either direction.*

Before buying, new collectors are advised to attend several antique car shows, seek out specialized collector clubs in the makes and models they find appealing, and secure the advise of a mechanic and body restorer familiar with old cars. Especially helpful are the catalogues and sale bills of Kruse Auctioneers, Inc., Auburn, IN, 46706.

Monza, 1963, "Spyder," convertible, 6 cyld. $3750.00

Adams-Farewell, 1910, Model 40/45, Touring	5000.00
Alfa-Romeo, 1950, Model 2500, Cabriolet	4500.00
Auburn, 1929, Model 8-90, Roadster	9500.00
Austin, 1954, Princess, Sedan	2600.00
Buick, 1914, Model B-25, Touring	7200.00
Buick, 1926, Model 50, Coupe	4800.00
Buick, 1942, Special, Sedan	2500.00
Buick, 1967, Electra 225, Convertible	2300.00
Cadillac, 1917, Model 55, Touring	9500.00
Cadillac, 1928, Fisher, Town Sport	6250.00
Cadillac, 1934, Model 370D, Convertible Sedan	30000.00
Cadillac, 1941, Model 63, Sedan	3500.00
Cadillac, 1952, Coupe de Ville, Hardtop	2300.00
Cadillac, 1966, Eldorado, Convertible	2500.00
Chevrolet, 1920, Model 490, Sedan	4250.00
Chevrolet, 1933, Eagle, Sport Roadster	11000.00

Chevrolet, 1934, Master, Sedan . . . 3600.00
Chevrolet, 1946, Fleetmaster, Convertible 4250.00
Chevrolet, 1950, Fleetline Deluxe, Sedan 900.00
Chevrolet, 1955, Bel Air, Hardtop . . 3250.00
Chevrolet, 1958, Corvette, Roadster, Fuel Injection 9000.00
Chevrolet, 1962, Corvair Monza, Convertible 2800.00
Chevrolet, 1967, Camaro SS, Sport Coupe 2400.00
Chrysler, 1929, Model 75, Sedan . . 4100.00
Chrysler, 1942, Town & Country, Station Wagon 10500.00
Chrysler, 1954, New Yorker, Hardtop 1800.00
Columbia, 1919, Six, Touring 11500.00
Cord, 1931, Model L-29, Sedan . . . 23000.00
DeSota, 1932, Model SC, Convertible Sedan 11000.00
DeSota, 1949, Model 5-13, Club Coupe 1700.00
DeSota, 1957, Fireflite, Convertible 2100.00

Duesenberg, 1932 Murphey convertible coupe, restored . . . . . $185,000+

Dodge, 1936, Model D2, Sedan . . . 2600.00
Dodge, 1953, Coronet, Convertible, 8 cyl. 3250.00
Duesenberg, 1931, Model J, Phaeton 145000.00
Edsel, 1958, Citation, Hardtop 1600.00
Edsel, 1960, Ranger, Convertible . . 2700.00
Essex, 1931, Challenger, Coach . . . 3400.00
Ford, 1916, Model T, Coupe 6200.00
Ford, 1924, Model T, Touring 3900.00
Ford, 1928, Model A, Sport Coupe . 5500.00
Ford, 1931, Model A, Station Wagon 9400.00
Ford, 1936, Model 68, Deluxe Sedan 4900.00
Ford, 1941, Deluxe, Club Coupe . . . 2700.00
Ford, 1952, Customline, Country Squire 1500.00
Ford, 1956, Thunderbird, Roadster . 8200.00
Ford, 1958, Fairlane 500, Convertible 3000.00
Ford, 1961, Thunderbird, Convertible 4500.00
Ford, 1965, Mustang, Fastback 2900.00
Franklin, 1931, Model 15, Sedan . . . 9000.00

Hudson, 1921, Model Six, Coach . . 4800.00
Hudson, 1954, Hornet, Convertible . 5200.00
Jaguar, 1949, Mark V, Sedan 4600.00
Jaguar, 1955, Mark VII, Sedan 2600.00
Jaguar, 1966, Model XKE, Sport Racing 2800.00
Jordan, 1928, Playboy, Cabriolet . . . 7000.00
Kaiser, 1954, Manhatten, Sedan . . . 2300.00
LaSalle, 1935, Model 350, Coupe . . 5200.00
Lincoln, 1925, Model L, Sedan 8200.00
Lincoln, 1933, LeBaron, Coupe 12000.00
Lincoln, 1940, Zephyr, Sedan 6400.00
Lincoln, 1951, Cosmopolitan, Sport Sedan 1700.00
Lincoln, 1958, Mark III, Convertible . 3000.00
Lincoln, 1967, Continental, Convertible 4500.00
Mercedes-Benz, 1935, Model 170V, Limousine 15000.00
Mercedes-Benz, 1957, Model 300SL, Roadster 17500.00
Mercury, 1947, Station Wagon 1800.00
Mercury, 1955, Monterey, Sedan . . 3500.00
Nash, 1932, Model 1060, Sedan . . . 2700.00
Nash, 1950, Ambassador, Brougham 2200.00
Nash, 1960, Metropolitan, Convertible 3400.00
Oldsmobile, 1912, Autocrat, Touring 13500.00
Oldsmobile, 1948, Futuramic, Station Wagon 3400.00
Oldsmobile, 1957, Model S-88, Convertible 3700.00
Oldsmobile, 1963, Starfire, Coupe . . 1750.00
Packard, 1929, Model 626, Speedster 25000.00
Packard, 1938, Model 1603, Touring Sedan 6200.00
Packard, 1955, Carribean, Convertible 5800.00
Pierce-Arrow, 1931, Model 42, Rumble Seat Coupe 9300.00
Pierce-Arrow, 1937, Model 1702, Sedan, 12 cyl. 12000.00
Plymouth, 1932, Model PA, Roadster 8500.00
Plymouth, 1954, Belvedere, Convertible Coupe 2300.00
Plymouth, 1957, Fury, Hardtop 3500.00
Pontiac, 1936, Deluxe, Sedan 2800.00
Pontiac, 1957, Bonneville, Convertible 7000.00
Pontiac, 1964, Model GTO, Convertible 3400.00
Rambler, 1910, Touring 10000.00
Reo, 1927, Flying Cloud, Sedan . . . 4100.00
Rolls Royce, 1929, Brewster, Touring 22000.00
Rolls Royce, 1948, Silver Wraith, Touring Sedan 9300.00
Rolls Royce, 1952, Silver Wraith, Sedan 11000.00
Rolls Royce, 1963, Silver Cloud, Limousine 16000.00

Stanley, 1922, Roadster	15000.00
Studebacker, 1929, President, Cabriolet	10500.00
Studebacker, 1941, President, Sedan	4700.00
Studebacker, 1958, Golden Hawk, Coupe	3100.00
Studebacker, 1963, Avanti, Coupe .	6200.00
Stutz, 1913, Bearcat, Speedster . . .	45000.00
Stutz, 1930, Black Hawk, Speedster	25000.00
Willys, 1930, Model 6-87, Roadster .	8500.00

MISCELLANEOUS

Fire Engines

Diamond T, 1947, Pumper	2300.00
Dodge, 1932, Pumper	3500.00
Ford, 1929, Model AA	4000.00
La France, 1934, Pumper	1800.00
La France, 1939, 85' Aerial Ladder Truck	5000.00

Motorcycles

Harley, 1948, Model 45	2950.00
Harley-Davidson, 1956, Model K .	3500.00
Indian, 1941	11500.00
Indian Chief, 1951	4900.00

Trucks

Acme, 1924, 1½ ton Pick-up	2500.00
Chevrolet, 1936, Master, Pick-up .	12000.00
Ford, 1924, Model T	7600.00
Ford, 1925, Model T, Cattle Truck	4750.00
Ford, 1932, Pick-up	7000.00
Ford, 1941, ½ ton Pick-up	2000.00

Willys

Jeepster, 1947, Convertible	3500.00
Military Jeep, 1943, French Service Vehicle	7000.00

AUTUMN LEAF PATTERN

The only exclusive premium line pattern produced by Hall China, East Liverpool, Ohio. The "Autumn Leaf" pattern was designed for the Jewel Tea Company in 1933 by Arden Richards. At first this Hall-Jewel design had no name and in the early years was called "Hall-Jewel" or "Autumnal." Then in April, 1942, it was designated "Autumn." Finally in 1960 it was called "Autumn Leaf."

It still is a Jewel property. Although the Jewel catalog has not listed any "Autumn Leaf" since 1977, the pattern has not been officially discontinued.

Bowls

6½"	10.00
9"	10.00
Cream soup	12.00
Mixing, 3 pieces, set	35.00

Pitcher, 5½" high, Jewel Tea, Hall's
Superior $5.00

Cake Plate, footed, metal base . . .	12.00
Cake Server, metal	30.00
Candle Warmer Base	75.00
Canister, round, plastic cover	9.00
Casserole, covered, tab handles . .	20.00
Clock	210.00
Coffee Pot, 8 cup, dripolator	35.00
Coffee Server, 8 cup	25.00
Cookie Jars	
Covered, tab handles, early	70.00
Late	45.00
Creamers & Sugars	
Early	30.00
Late	10.00
Cup & Saucer	6.50
Gravy Boat with underplate	22.50
Marmalade Jar, covered with underplate	45.00
Pitchers	
Milk, small	12.50
Water, with ice lip	20.00
Plates	
7¼"	6.00
10"	8.00
Platter, 13"	15.00
Salt & Pepper, pair	14.00
Tea Pot, Aladdin, with insert	22.00
Trivets (Hot Plates)	
Metal	8.00
Oval	12.00
Round	10.00
Tumbler, 14 oz. frosted	13.00

BACCARAT GLASS

Baccarat glass was established by royal decree from Louis XV in 1764. The factory was located in Alsace-Lorraine, France. From its very beginning, Baccarat glass has always been of the finest quality and highly regarded by all connoisseurs of crystal.

During the Classic Era of Paperweights (1845–1860), Baccarat was one of the major producers of exquisite weights. In 1953 Baccarat again re-entered the paper weight market with an assortment of limited editions. Also see PAPERWEIGHTS.

Bobeches, signed, pair	**50.00**
Bottles, perfume	
4″, crystal, "Guerlain"	**48.00**
5¼″, porcelain, inverted heart stopper, signed	**35.00**
6″, gold stripes, gold star, cut stopper	**65.00**
Bowls	
3¼″, rose cut, enamel floral decor	**145.00**
7″, lacy with underplate	**65.00**
8″, cut	**150.00**
Box, 4 x 4″, crystal, covered, angular designs	**125.00**
Candlesticks, 8″, serpents coiling . .	**150.00**
Champagne, 7″, engraved	**30.00**
Compotes	
3″, open, crystal, swirl	**30.00**
etched, oak leaves and grapes, gold trim	**130.00**
Cordial, set of 6	**150.00**
Creamer and Sugar, handled tray, crystal	**90.00**
Cruet, Amberina Swirl	**100.00**
Cup and Saucer	**75.00**
Decanter	
7½″, opaque and clear swirled, red and white latticino ring at shoulder and lip	**100.00**
8½″, lacy	**90.00**
Dish, 9½″, Rubina	**55.00**
Fairy Lamps, see Fairy Lamps	
Ginger Jar, cranberry on frosted, brass handle and bail	**150.00**
Inkwells	
Crystal bowl with green leaves, brass top	**150.00**
Crystal, swirl, sterling top	**150.00**
Jam Jar, Amberina Swirl, covered .	**75.00**
Knife Rest, 4″, crystal, signed	**40.00**

Perfume Atomizer, 6″ overall height, Amberina $50.00

Letter Opener, 9″, signed	**35.00**
Pitchers, 10¼″, taupe and white mottling	**175.00**
Relish, 3½ x 9½″, rose to light amber	**90.00**
Rocker Blotter, brass, crystal handle	**65.00**
Toothpick, crystal	**35.00**
Tray, Pin, crystal	**25.00**
Tumblers	
Blue swirl	**40.00**
Clear swirl	**30.00**
Ruby swirl with plate	**90.00**

Tumble-Up with plate	175.00
Vases	
5″, Lacy	150.00
6¼″, crackle, cranberry, footed .	150.00
6½″, cameo cut, gold washed	
metal base, pair	225.00
7″, tear drop shape bud, polished	
base, signed	50.00

BANKS—GLASS

Snoopy Bank, 6″ $12.00

Barrel, embossed staves, bands . .	7.50
Baseball, Mobil giveaway	5.00
Bear, 8″	12.00
Beehive Coke oven, green, com-	
memorative	15.00
Brick, "Pittsburgh Paints"	10.00
"Charlie Chaplin," 3¾″	50.00
House, 3″, "Save with Pittsburgh	
Paints"	20.00
Independence Hall, 7½″	85.00
Kewpie	65.00
Liberty Bell, carnival glass, marigold	22.50
Liberty Bell, 5″, tin screw base,	
marked "Robinson and Loeble,	
Phila. Pa.," amber and milk glass	35.00
Lincoln bottle, tin top	15.00
Lincoln "Pure Fruit Flavored Orange	
Syrup," tin top	15.00
Log Cabin Syrup	15.00
Lucky Joe, painted	25.00
Radio	15.00

BANKS, MECHANICAL

Banks which display some form of action while utilizing a coin are considered mechanical banks. Although mechanical banks are known which date back to ancient Greece and Rome, the majority of collectors center their interests in those made between 1867 and 1928 in Germany, England and the United States. Recently there has been an upsurge of interest in later types, some of which date into the 1970's.

Initial research suggested that approximately 250 to 300 different or variant designs of banks were made in the early period. Today that number has been revised to 2,000–3,000 types and varieties. Within the past year, eighteen previously unknown variations have been identified. The field remains ripe for discovery and research.

Over 80% of all cast iron mechanical banks produced between 1869 and 1928 were made by J. E. Stevens Co., Cromwell, CT. Tin banks tend to be German in origin.

Reproductions, fakes, and forgeries exist of many banks. Forgeries of some mechanical banks were made as early as 1937, so age alone is not a guarantee of authenticity. In our listing two "**" indicate banks for which serious forgeries exist and one "*" banks for which causual reproductions have been made.

While rarity is a factor in value, appeal of design, action, quality of manufacture, country of origin, and history of collector interest also are important. Radical price fluctuations may occur with an inbalance of these factors. Rare banks may sell for a few hundred dollars while one of more common design with greater appeal will sell in the thousands.

The prices on our list represent fairly what a bank sells for in the specialized collectors market.

The prices listed are for original old mechanical banks with no repaired, missing, or replaced parts, in sound operating condition, and with the vast majority of the original paint intact.

**Acrobats, iron	750.00
African Bank	1250.00
Alligator, grabs coin in mouth, tin . .	1000.00
**American Sewing Machine, iron . .	1250.00
*Artillery, four-sided block house . .	275.00
Atlas, lead & wood	450.00
Australian William Tell, brass, wood	
& tin	300.00
Automatic Coin Savings, tin, strong	
man in leopard skin holding man	

Eagle and Eaglets **$325.00**

by hair	900.00
*Bad Accident, iron	500.00
Bank of Education & Economy	550.00
Barking Dog, wood & steel	850.00
**Bear, iron, sulky bruin	200.00
**Bear Standing, iron	350.00
**Billy Goat, iron	1000.00
**Bismark, iron	850.00
Bonzo, tin	750.00
Bowing Man in Cupola, iron	3000.00
**Boy & Bull Dog, iron	300.00
**Boy on Trapeze, iron	400.00
*Boy Scout Camp, iron	550.00
**Boys Stealing Watermelons, iron .	500.00
British Lion, tin	700.00
**Bull & Bear, iron	3000.00
*Bull Dog, iron, coin on nose	250.00
Bull Dog Savings, iron, key wind ..	1000.00
Bull Tosses Boy in Well, brass	250.00
Bureau, Freedman's, wood	400.00
Bureau, tin, Ideal	125.00
Bureau, wood, Serrill Pat. Appld. For	250.00
Bureau, wood, stenciling on front ..	200.00
**Butting Buffalo, iron	700.00
Butting Ram, man thumbs nose ...	1250.00
**Calamity, iron	2000.00
**Called Out, original unpainted iron	3000.00
Called Out, lead master pattern ...	750.00
Calumet with Calumet Kid, tin can .	100.00
Calumet with Soldier, tin can	350.00
Calumet with Sailor, tin can	350.00
**Cannon, U. S. & Spain	1500.00
Cat & Mouse, iron & brass, cat standing upright	1750.00
Cat Chasing Mouse in Building, tin .	300.00
Chandlers, iron	200.00
Child's Bank, Clark Thread	400.00
**Chimpanzee, iron & tin	450.00
Chinaman, iron, reclining	600.00
Chocolat Menier, tin	75.00

**Circus Ticket Collector, man at barrel	600.00
Clown & Dog, tin	750.00
Clown, tin, black face	350.00
**Clown, Harlequin, Columbine, iron	7500.00
**Clown on Globe, iron	450.00
Coin Registering, iron, domed building	350.00
Confectionery, iron	1750.00
Cresent Cash Register, iron	225.00
Crowing Rooster, tin	400.00
Dapper Dan, tin	250.00
Darky Bust, tin	450.00
**Dentist, iron	1500.00
Dinah, aluminum	90.00
Dog Goes Into House, lead & brass	500.00
Dog, pot metal, spring jawed	200.00
**Dog With Tray, iron, oval base ...	900.00
Ducks, lead, two	400.00
Electric Safe, steel	100.00
Elephant Baby, lead, with clown at table	2000.00
**Elephant With Howdah, iron, man pops out	175.00
**Elephant With Locked Howdah, iron, oval base	600.00
**Elephant, iron, "Light of Asia" on wheels	800.00
Elephant, tin, Royal Trick	1000.00
**Elephant On Wheels, iron, trunk moves	700.00
**Elephant, iron, trunk moves, raised coin slot	50.00
Face, wood	75.00
**Feed The Kitty, iron	200.00
**Ferris Wheel, iron & tin, marked	

Organ Bank, with monkey .. **$275.00**

"Bowen's Pat."	500.00
Fire Alarm, tin	150.00
Flip The Frog, tin	700.00
Football, iron, black & watermelon	7500.00
Fortune Teller Safe, iron	350.00
**Forty-Niner, iron	200.00
Frog On Arched Track, tin	2500.00
Fun Producing Savings, tin	400.00
Germania Exchange, iron, tin & lead	3500.00
**Giant Standing, iron	3500.00
**Girl in Victorian Chair, iron	1750.00
Give Me A Penny, wood	900.00
**Glutton, brass, lifts turkey	150.00
Golden Gate Key, aluminum	125.00
Grasshopper, tin, wind-up	5000.00
Guessing, lead & iron, man's figure	850.00
Hall's Excelsior, iron & wood, no figure	75.00
Hall's Excelsior, iron & wood, policeman figure	350.00
Hall's Lilliput, Type II	150.00
Hall's Yankee Notion, brass	350.00
Harold Lloyd, tin	1250.00
Hillman Coin Bank, wood, iron, & glass	2500.00
**Hold The Fort, iron, five holes	750.00
Home, iron	125.00
Home With Dormer Windows, iron	200.00
**Horse Race, iron with tin horses, flanged base	750.00
**Humpty Dumpty, iron	175.00
**I Always Did 'Spize a Mule, black sitting on bench in front	275.00
Huntley And Palmers Readings	450.00
*Indian And Bear, iron, white bear	350.00
**Initiating First Degree, iron	2000.00
Jack on Roof, tin	200.00
Joe Socko, tin	175.00
John R. Jennings Money Box, wood	150.00
Jolly Joe Clown, tin	700.00
**Jolly Nigger, aluminum	90.00
**Jolly Nigger, aluminum, moves ears	150.00
**Jolly Nigger, aluminum, string tie	100.00
**Jolly Nigger, iron	100.00
**Jolly Nigger, iron, high hat	125.00
Jonah And Whale, iron, footed base	7500.00
Key, iron, World's Fair	300.00
Kick Inn, paper on wood	275.00
**Leap Frog, iron	450.00
**Lighthouse, iron	300.00
Lion Hunter, iron	900.00
Little High Hat, iron	500.00
Little Jocko Musical, tin	800.00
Little Moe, iron, tip hat	450.00
Long May It Wave, iron & wood	200.00
Lucky Wheel Money Box, tin	325.00
**Magic Safe, iron	175.00
**Magician, iron	575.00
**Mama Katzenjammer, iron, 1930's	550.00
Mama Katzenjammer, iron, 1905-08, low cut dress with white fringe	1500.00

Man on Chimney	200.00
**Mason, iron	550.00
Merry-Go-Round, mechanical	4500.00
Metropolitan, iron	150.00
Mikado, iron	3500.00
Minstrel, tin	150.00
Model Railroad Stamp Dispenser, tin	1500.00
Model Railroad Sweet Dispenser	1750.00
Model Savings, tin	800.00
*Monkey & Coconut, iron	475.00
Monkey & Parrot, tin	175.00
Monkey With Tray, tin	275.00
Moonface, iron	15000.00
Mosque, iron	250.00
*Mule Entering Barn, iron	250.00
Musical Church, wood, rotating tower	475.00
Musical Savings, tin	800.00
Musical Savings, wood house	1200.00
New, iron, lever in center	350.00
New Creedmoor Bank, iron	175.00
**Novelty, iron	175.00
Octagonal Fort, iron	750.00
*Organ, iron, cat & dog	250.00
**Organ, iron, miniature	350.00
**Organ Grinder With Performing Bear, iron	900.00
Owl, iron, slot in head	250.00
*Paddy & Pig, iron	350.00
Pascal Savings, tin	250.00
**Peg Leg Begger, iron	600.00
**Pelican With Mammy, iron	300.00
**Pelican With Rabbit, iron	450.00
**Piano, iron, old conversion to musical	1500.00

Frog on round lattice base, .$225.00

Pig In High Chair, iron	250.00
Pistol, stamped metal	275.00
Postman, tin, English	100.00
Presto, iron, penny changes to quarter	2500.00
Presto, paper on wood, mouse on roof	2500.00
Pump & Bucket, iron	475.00
*Punch & Judy, iron	400.00
Punch & Judy, tin	800.00
Queen Victoria Bust, iron	3000.00
**Rabbit, iron, large	175.00
Rabbit In Cabbage	200.00
**Red Riding Hood, iron	4000.00
Rival, iron	3500.00
Rollerskating, iron	3000.00
Safety Locomotive, iron	475.00
Saluting Sailor, tin	500.00
Sam Segal's Aim To Save Target, iron	1500.00
Savo, tin, round drum	125.00
Savo, tin, rectangular with children	200.00
Savo, tin, round with children	125.00
Scotchman, tin	175.00
Sentry, tin, raises rifle	575.00
Sentry, wood, c. 1910	300.00
Shoot The Hat, brass	1500.00
Signal Cabin, tin	275.00
Snake & Frog In Pond, tin	2000.00
*Speaking Dog Bank	250.00
Sportsman, iron, fowler	400.00
**Squirrel & Tree Stump, iron	600.00
Stollwerk, tin, Victoria	150.00
Sweet Thrift, tin	150.00
*Tammany, iron	125.00
*Tank & Cannon, aluminum	200.00
Target, iron, fort and cannon	2750.00
Ten Cent Adding Bank, iron	400.00
Thrifty Tom's Jigger, tin	300.00
Tiger, tin	1200.00
Time Lock Savings, iron	1500.00
Toboggan, silver plated Britannia metal	325.00
Treasure Chest Music, pot metal	750.00
**Trick Dog, iron, solid base	100.00
*Trick Pony, iron	275.00
Trick Savings, wood, front drawer	125.00
Try Your Weight Scale, tin	750.00
**U. S. & Spain (see Cannon)	
**Uncle Remus, iron	1000.00
**Uncle Sam Bust, iron	425.00
Uncle Tom, iron, star base	100.00
United States Bank, iron, picture pops up	675.00
Viennese Soldier, lead	1500.00
Volunteer, iron	200.00
Watch Dog Safe, iron	175.00
Weeden's Plantation, tin, wind-up	375.00
Wimbledon, iron	1750.00
Wireless, iron & tin	150.00
Wishbone, brass	2500.00
Woodpecker, tin, 1920's	1400.00

World's Banker, tin	850.00
**Zoo, iron	575.00

BANKS, STILL

Banks with no mechanical action are known as Still Banks. They are usually made of cast iron, with tin as the second most prominent metal. Within the past year (1981-2), this category has shown a marked increase in prices.

Battleship Maine $140.00

METAL STILL BANKS

Animals

Bears	
Sitting	55.00
With staff, 6", brass	90.00
*Buffalo, standing	85.00
Camel, standing, small	92.50
*Cat With Ball	225.00
Deer with Antlers	75.00
Dogs	
*Bull, standing	65.00
Scotty	165.00
Shepherd, with pack, 5¼ x 8"	75.00
Donkey with Saddle	85.00
Elephants	
*Standing	90.00
Wheels	150.00
Goose, large	125.00
Horses	
Prancing	75.00
Standing	90.00
Lions	
Large	90.00
Tub	65.00

Owl	150.00
*Pigs, sitting	50.00
*Rabbit, large	65.00
*Rooster, standing	75.00
Squirrel With Nut	55.00
Turkey, small	45.00

Other

Auto	325.00
Banks	
E. River Savings Bank, Rochester	65.00
Home Savings Bank, dog head finial	75.00
Rival Bank	60.00
Trader's Bank, Canada, 1891	90.00
*Billiken	50.00
Boy Scout	85.00
Buildings	
Independence Hall, Enterprise Mfg. Co., Philadelphia, 1875	350.00
Skyscraper, six towers	65.00
Washington Mansion, Mt. Vernon, 3″	75.00
Woolworth, 7″	95.00
Cabin, tin	45.00
Captain Kidd	275.00
Clock	105.00
Clown, painted, tin	65.00
Dutch Boy, sitting on keg	45.00
Gas Pump	350.00
General Eisenhower	40.00
Golliwog	225.00
Heatrola	50.00
Indians	
*Head	60.00
*Standing	80.00
Little Daisy	60.00
*Mail Box	70.00
Mary and Lamb	450.00
Mutt & Jeff	80.00
Negro Man	105.00
*Policeman, Irish	90.00
Radio	72.50
Safes	
Burglar Proof House safe with key	125.00
Royal Safe Deposit	60.00
Sport, 3″, 1882	65.00
Union Bank Safe	70.00
6″, combination lock	55.00
Santa Claus	150.00
Satchel, 3 x 6″	65.00
Soldier, World War I	110.00
Steamboat "Arcade"	135.00
Teddy Bear	65.00
Telephone, wall type	70.00
Two-faced Woman	80.00

POTTERY STILL BANKS

Acorn, "Acorn Stoves," 3″, light brown glaze	40.00

Pig, 5½″ **$35.00**

Barrel, gilt hoops	25.00
Beehive, 4¼″, brown mottled slipware	40.00
Bird	27.50
Black Face With Turban, 4½″	75.00
Cash Register, white/yellow glaze	45.00
Cat, white and yellow, on green and white cushion	60.00
Corn	55.00
Dwarf Head, brown enameled	50.00
Frog, 4″, coin goes in mouth	37.50
Gourd, 4″	45.00
Lion, 6″	40.00
Monkey, mottled yellow and brown	30.00
Pig In Green Pocketbook	55.00
Poodle Head, Staffordshire-type, ¾ x 4½″	75.00
Rooster, standing	40.00
Shoe, high button, 5″, tan	80.00
Turnip, marked "Charity"	40.00
Watermelon Slice, 4 x 9½″, hanging type	60.00

BAROMETERS

A barometer is an instrument for measuring atmospheric pressure which, in turn, aids in the forecasting of weather. For example, low pressure indicates the coming of rain, snow, or a storm, while high pressure indicates fair weather. They were popular home accessories in Victorian England and later in America.

Banjo Type

Berringer, John, mahogany	350.00
English, rosewood	300.00
Desk Type, English, 4″ dia. brass dial	65.00

Stick Type

J. G. Bowesmith and Co., Mans-	

F. Aprile, New Market, 39", mahogany, swan neck crest, hydrometer dial, Fahrenheit thermometer, silvered dial, c. 1860 . . . . **350.00**
G. Bianchi, Salisburgy, 22", inlayed mahogany, swan neck crest, hydrometer, thermometer, and barometer dials, c. 1860 . . . . **350.00**
Dominick Dotty Co., London, mahogany, thermometer to left side of dial, early 19th Century **700.00**
Georgian style, English, 36", mahogany, broken arch crest, silvered dial, thermometer **650.00**
Short and Mason, London, 12", inlayed mahogany, Fahrenheit and centigrade **1250.00**

BASALT

This type of black viteous pottery was originally made in ancient times and rediscovered in the latter part of the 18th century by Josiah Wedgwood. It was later produced by other English potters.

Cup and Saucer, undecorated, signed Wedgwood only **$65.00**

Short and Mason, London, #2404, **26½"** **$225.00**

field, OH, 20th C., tiger maple . . . **275.00**
J. G. Bowesmith and Co., Mansfield, OH, 19th C., walnut **225.00**
H. A. Clum, Rochester, NY, c. 1860, double column, mahogany . **900.00**
Hayden and Gibbard, Auburn, NY, walnut **650.00**
E. Kendall, New Lebanon, walnut and veneer **675.00**
Queen and Co., Philadelphia, oak **275.00**
J. Westscott & Co., Montreal, walnut **650.00**
C. A. Wheeler, Peterboro, NH, walnut **275.00**
Woodruff's Patent, June 5th, 1860, Charles Wilder, Peterboro, NH **900.00**
Wheel Type
Air Guide, 18", walnut, brass dial, vertical thermometer **175.00**

Atomizer, 4", including sterling top, classical decor in white, Wedgwood, England **125.00**
Bowls
   8 x 3½", EPNS rim, Wedgwood . **125.00**
   8", figures in relief, Wedgwood . . **395.00**
   9½", acorn border **225.00**
Box, cherubs on front and back . . . **185.00**
Busts

Byron, 18", c. 1860 . . . . 1000.00
Churchill, Winston, 7", impressed
W, Made in England 40.00
Mercury, 18", c. 1800 . . . . 1200.00
Washington, 9" 195.00
Candlesticks, 12", pair 250.00
Chalice, 3"deep, beaded, pedestal
base, Wedgwood 275.00
Coffee Pot, 8½", engine-turned . . . 195.00
Creamers
2¼", glazed interior, molded han-
dle, Wedgwood 25.00
3¼", drape decor, c. 1800–1820 . 95.00
4½", classical decor, Wedgwood 150.00
6", cream jug, engine-turned
basketweave, impress Wedgwood 70.00
Cups and Saucers, classical decor,
Wedgwood 65.00
Figurines
Bear, Polar, 8½", ebonized base,
artist signed 400.00
Bear, striding, 4⅝", impressed
Wedgwood 250.00
Bulldog, standing, glass eyes, impressed Wedgwood 200.00
Foo dog, 3"on base 50.00
Inkwell, Wedgwood 175.00
Medallions
2¼ x 2¾", Wedgwood and Bent-
ley 750.00
Scipio and Brutus, 4¾", im-
pressed Wedgwood and Bentley,
c. 1780 . . . . 750.00
Paperweight, Liberty Bell, modern . . 25.00
Pitchers
5¼", helmet shape, c. 1880 . . . . 150.00
6½"relief Flaxman figures around
base, leaves and grapes, Wedg-
wood 195.00
Sugar, covered, glubular, engine-
turned fluting, impress Wedgwood,
c. 1800 . . . . 110.00
Teapot, 4¾", "widow" finial, Wedg-
wood 85.00
Teaset, 4 pcs., teapot, stand, cov-
ered sugar, creamer, classical figure decor, acanthus leaf border,
impressed Wedgwood, made in
England 275.00

BASKETS

Baskets are often classified as hard textiles
and are a form of textile art in that they are
woven.

Baskets were invented when man first required containers to gather, store, and transport goods. Thus, basketry is probably one
of the earliest indigenous crafts of all cultures. There are baskets for every use — egg
baskets, cheese baskets, market baskets and
even bed baskets for infants.

Baskets were made in a variety of shapes
and sizes to fulfil specific needs. Methods
and techniques used in construction — coil-
ing, plaiting, wicker type, rib cage, etc. —
mainly depended on the raw materials available or intended usage. Enthusiastic collectors of baskets prefer to view basketry more
of an art form than a craft.

Decorated, 15" dia. $9.00

Baby cradle with hood, 36", splint . 175.00
Cheese, 25" diam. 9" deep 425.00
Clothes basket, two handles, 21"
diam. 75.00
Egg, Central Pa., 10 x 13", 12" high
including handle 65.00
Fruit, oval, ½ bushel 35.00
Gathering
Handleless, painted white 37.50
Open weave bottom 65.00
Splint, braided rim, round shape,
with handle 250.00
Split hickory, open handles on
sides, 9 x 21" 65.00
Split oak, four decorative bands of
blue under rim 100.00
Splint, circular, stationary oak han-
dle, 9¾" 80.00
Indian
Apache, 8 x 9¼" 165.00
California, 3¼ x 7" 35.00
Circular, covered, coiled, 3¾ x
7¼" 250.00
Circular, rust green and gold de-
sign 70.00
Southwest Indian, coiled storage,
brown geometric design, 13½ x
10¾" 225.00
Maine
Splint, red painted flowers, 7 x
11½ x 16" 100.00
Splint, sweet grass, woven, red
and green bands around top, lid,
with ring handle, work or sewing

basket, 8" diam., 3½" deep 55.00
Splint, covered, painted with stencils of red, yellow circles, 11 x 13 x 22" 150.00
Nova Scotia, eel trap 145.00

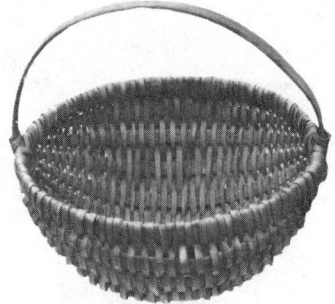

Splint, Center Rib $95.00

Papago
Pot shaped, 10" diam., top, 8" deep 195.00
Drying type, two handles, 12" . . . 45.00
Shallow dish type, coiled construction, 36" 100.00
Japanese, brown and tan finely woven reeds, 7¼" diam. 75.00
Lunch, double handles, 5 x 8" 35.00
Nantucket
Brass ears, 7" 300.00
Handled, 14" 150.00
Shaker type, splint with quartered bracing into base and up sides, swing handle, 12½" diam. 120.00
Suit case type, split hickory, dark brown, hinged lid, brass handle and fastenings, c. 1890 . . . . 150.00
Wall type
Three compartments, early, 10 x 29" 250.00
Wicker type, handles on sides, for mail, 6" long, 8" deep, late 25.00
Willow, darning basket, 12" diam. 30.00

BATTERSEA ENAMELS

Battersea enamel is a generic name for painted enamels on metal.

Stephen T. Janssen first demonstrated this method of transferring prints from engraved copper plates onto enamelled surfaces in the early 1750's at the York House, in Battersea, London. In 1756, financial difficulties forced the enterprise to be discontinued. All materials, including the copper plates were sold and subsequently used by other firms, mainly in the Staffordshire district.

Small gift boxes of Battersea-type enamels are currently being produced in France and available in fine retail outlets at a fraction of the cost of the earlier examples.

Patch Box, 1⅞" oval, "May Nature Paint the Cheek and Virtue The Mind," White base $395.00

Boxes
"And tighter the knot, the farther apart," heart shaped, yellow base 500.00
"Angel," 1¾" x 3" 400.00
"Coaching," shield shape, pink base 500.00
"Esteem the Giver," yellow with rust colored bird on nest 500.00
"Fishing Scene" 450.00
4", square, blue and yellow 350.00
"Fox Hunt," 2" x 4" 500.00
"Garden Scene," 1½" x 2" 395.00
"Lay hold on Time while in your Prime," 2" dia., blue base 500.00
"Love is Eternal," blue base 600.00
"Pixies," 2" x 3" 600.00
"Racing and You See the Race," 1½" x 2½", robin's egg blue base 500.00
"Success to the Fleet," blue base, heart shaped 500.00

BAVARIAN CHINA

Bavaria was an important porcelain production center in Germany, similar to the Staffordshire districts in England. However, very little of the production from this area was imported into the United States before 1870. The term covers the products of several companies operating there.

Vase, 6", artist signed, iridescent $32.00

Bowls
7", green, pink roses, gold trim, reticulated sides	35.00
9¾", fruit decor	10.00
9¾", cobalt blue border, pink roses, white center, six 4½" bowls to match, gold trim, set ...	69.00
9", roses, hand painted	29.00
9½", cobalt with roses in center .	29.00
9", orchids, roses and lustre	45.00
10", rose decor on white	48.00
Box, 6", lavender base, white cover, Oriental woman, seated on cover, lavender trim	90.00
Cake Set, 11" plate, six serving plates, 7½", floral center, pierced edges, gold and green trim, set .	100.00
Celery, 5" wide, 14" long, pink roses, cobalt background, gold edge	35.00
Cream and Sugar, covered, hand painted, peony decor and leaves, heavy gold trim, set	50.00
Cup and Saucer, cream and maroon, "Baker's Chocolate" portrait decor	25.00
Dinner Set, white with small pink roses, and green vine trim around piece, light touches of gold, scalloped edges, marked "Hutchendreuther," 42 pieces	200.00
Fruit dishes, Carmen, Bavaria "R C," set of 12	84.00
Gravy or Sauce boat, with attached tray, matching ladle, blue floral decor, with gold trim, Crown mark, Bavaria	50.00

Plates
7¼", fruit plate, gold, rose decor on black ground, gold trim, made in Germany	10.00
8½", purple grapes, pink floral border around entire plate, most of surface covered fruit and floral	30.00
8¼", fruit and flowers in multicolors, covers surface	50.00
8½", apples, "J. L. Louise"	45.00
9½", scalloped, pierced border, fruit decor, gold trim, Crown mark, Bavaria	55.00
13", dark green shading to lighter green, with white and peach colored flowers, gold trim, Royal Rudulstadt, Bavaria	95.00

Shakers
3" high, salt and pepper, pink and cream roses, gold tops	25.00
3" high, green bases, shading up to pink and cream, pair	25.00
Syrup, covered, fancy handle, cream, peach and gold	45.00
Tea Set, teapot, sugar and creamer, divided panels, hand painted violets, marked Z. S. Mignon, set ...	85.00
Tray, gold border, center floral design, medallions of flowers on inner surface, pierced border, Schumann	15.00

BEER CANS (AMERICAN)

Beer cans are one of the newest collectibles and after a little over ten years of interest, it is reported that there are over a half million collectors in the United States alone. How or why this "fad" began will remain as much a mystery as the reason for any collection.

Beer in cans is a relatively new phenomenon. Before prohibition, beer was stored and shipped in kegs and dispensed in returnable bottles. When the Prohibition Act was repealed in 1933, only 700 of 1700 breweries resumed operation. Expanding distribution created the need for an inexpensive container that would permit beer to be stored longer and shipped safely. Cans were the answer.

The first patent for a lined can was issued to the American Can Co. on Sept. 25, 1934, for their "Keglined" process. Gottried Kruger Brewing Co., Newark, N.J., was the first brewery to use the can. Pabst was the first major company to join the canned beer movement.

Continental Can Co. introduced the cone-top beer can in 1935. Schlitz was the first brewery to use this type of can. The next major change in beer can design was the aluminum pop-top in 1962.

The following abbreviations are used in the listings: CT-cone type, FT-flat top, PT-pull top, ML-malt liquor.

Union Cream Ale Rodger Williams Brewing Corp. Providence, R.I. $250.00

7 oz.

Coors, Gold Band, Golden, Co., (FT)	2.00
National Bohemian, Baltimore, (FT)	12.00
Rolling Rock, Spring label, Latrobe, Pa., (PT)	2.00

8 oz.

Colt 45 M.L. National, 4 cities, (PT)	1.00
Miller, 3 cities, (PT)	1.00
Schlitz M.L. (1963), paper label, Milwaukee, Wi., (FT)	5.00

10 oz.

Budweiser, Anheuser-Busch, 4 cities, (PT)	4.00
Tuborg, Carling, Baltimore, Md., (PT)	8.00

12 oz.

Acme Beer, Acme Brewing Co., (PT)	2.00
Andy's Beer, New Ulm, Minn., (PT)	1.50
American, Baltimore, Md., (CT)	50.00
Ballantine Ale, Newark, N.J., (1935), (FT)	15.00
Bavarian's Select, Associated, 3 cities, (PT)	6.00
Black Label, Carling, Cleveland,	

Oh., (PT)	2.50
Blatz Pilsener, Milwaukee, Wi., (1945), (FT)	7.00
Brickskeller Beer, Endangered Species Series, Pittsburgh, Pa., (PT), each	4.00
Bub's Beer, Eau Claire, Wi., (PT)	1.50
Budweiser, (ML), 9 cities, (PT)	7.00
Cook's, Associated, 3 cities, (PT)	3.00
Dixie, New Orleans, La., (PT)	1.00
Encore, Schlitz, 8 cities, (1970), (PT)	4.00
Falstaff, 8 cities, (PT)	2.00
Fort Pitt, Smithton, Pa., (PT)	8.00
Horlacher, Limited Edition, hex signs, Allentown, Pa., (PT), each	3.00
Iron City, 1974 Barnegat Light House, N.J., Series, Pittsburgh, Pa., (PT), each	2.00
Iron City, 1974 Sport Series, Pittsburgh, Pa., (PT), each	3.00
Lucky Lager, Falstaff, 6 cities, (PT)	1.00
Metz, Red Label, Omaha, Neb., (FT)	12.00
National Bohemian Bock, 4 cities, (PT)	10.00
Old Frothingslosh, Pittsburgh, Pa., (PT), blue	8.00
Old Milwaukee, 6 cities, (PT)	2.00
Old Milwaukee (1962) Schlitz, Milwaukee, Wi., (PT)	4.00
Ortlieb's, 1976 Bicentennial Series, Phila., Pa., (PT), each	5.00
Pfeiffer, 1960, Outdoor Series, Detroit, Mi., (FT), each	30.00
Pocono Mountain Series, Pottsville, Pa., (PT), each	3.00
Point Bicentennial Beer, Stevens Point, Wi., (PT)	3.50
Schaefer, New York, (FT)	15.00
Schmidt Draft-Wildlife Series, Associated, St. Paul, Minn., (PT), each	10.00
Schmidt's Drafting-Bicentennial Series, 2 cities, (PT), each	2.00
Shell's Beer, Multicolored with deer, New Ulm, Minn., (PT)	5.00
Sterling, Gold, Evansville, IN (FT)	12.00
Sunshine Premium, Reading, Pa., (CT)	40.00
Topper Pilsner Beer, Hammonton, N.J., (PT)	1.50
Valley Forge, Norristown, Pa., (FT)	15.00
Ye Tavern, Lafeyette, Ind., (CT)	60.00
Zodiac, (ML) Chicago, Ill., (PT)	2.00

14 oz.

Old Milwaukee, 6 cities, (PT)	2.00

16 oz.

Ballantine Ale, Newark, N.J., (PT)	6.00
Champagne Velvet, Associated, 3 cities, (PT)	5.00

Left: Croft Champagne Ale, Crown Brewing Co. Cranston, R.I. ...$75.00 Right: Genessee Ale, Genessee Brewing Co. Rochester N.Y. $50.00

Heidelberg, Carling, Tacoma, Wa., (PT)	8.00
Narragansett, 1966, Cranston, R.I., (PT)	7.00
Ortlieb's, 1976 Bicentennial, Phila., Pa., (PT), each	2.50
Rheingold, 2 cities, (PT)	2.00
Shell's Golden 16, multicolored with deer, New Ulm, Minn., (PT)	3.50
32 oz.	
Ballentine's Ale, Newark, N.J., (CT)	60.00
Pabst Blue Ribbon, Milwaukee, Wi., (CT)	12.00
Schmidt's Light, Phila., Pa., (CT)	50.00
Gallons	
Ballantine Draught Beer, Newark, N.J.	30.00
National Draft, Baltimore, Md.	60.00
102 Draught, Maier, Los Angeles, Ca.	100.00
Sterling Draught Ale, Associated, Evansville, Ind.	80.00

BELLEEK

Belleek is a thin, ivory colored, almost iridescent-type porcelain made in County FermanIreland, from 1857. The company continued production until World War I, discontinued operation for a period of time, then resumed operations until today. The Shamrock pattern may be most familiar, but other patterns were made, such as Limpet, Tridacna, etc.

Several different identifying marks were used including the Harp and Hound (1865–1880) and Harp, Hound and Castle (1863–1891). Some items are marked "Belleek Co., Fermanagh." After 1891 the word Ireland, or Eire was added. Serious collectors can identify the circas by these marks.

A Belleek-type porcelain was made in America by several firms. The first was Ott and Brewer Co., Trenton, N. J., in 1884. Another early manufacturer was Willets. Other American firms and their years of establishment were the Ceramic Art Co. (1889), American Art China Works (1892), Columbian Art Co. (1893) and Lenox, Inc., (1904).

There is an Irish saying . . . if a newly married couple receive a gift of Belleek, their marriage will be blessed with lasting happiness.

Abbreviations: 1BM — 1st Black Mark; 2BM — 2nd Black Mark; 3BM — 3rd Black Mark. See also LENOX.

Bowl, 8½" dia, handled $25.00

Baskets	
Trefoil, applied florals	175.00
Heart shaped, 4-strand petal decor, 7"	350.00
Bowls	
Coral, 2BM	195.00
Fruit, gold paste, Thistle	795.00
Hand painted white dogwood blossoms, pink shaded to green background 2 gold handles, ruffled rim, Willets, 9"	125.00
DQ, colored dots, rose bowl, center of diamonds	75.00
Cake Set, plate and six matching cups and saucers	1100.00
Coffee Pot, Limpet, 3BM	184.00
Chalice	
Grape decor, Willets, 11"	175.00
Portrait, monk drinking tea on green background, Willets, 11"	325.00
Creamers	
Hawthorne, white, gold trim	225.00
Hexagon, 2BM	110.00

Pansies, enameled, Ott and Brewer, 3¼" 165.00
Shamrock, green mark, 4½" ... 60.00
Shell and Coral, 2BM 65.00
Tridacna, pink with gold trim, 1BM 180.00

Creamers and Sugars
Pure white, molded design, set .. 150.00
Limpet, 3BM 100.00
Neptune 2BM 150.00
Cup, Tridacna 25.00

Cups and Saucers
Bacchus 110.00
Handleless, D460 1BM 80.00
Floral on ivory, demitasse, set of
six 125.00
Leprechaun, no color 237.50
Nautilus 115.00
Shamrock, harp handle, 1BM ... 69.00
Three Leafed clover 1 green mark 50.00

Dish
Lemon or mints, handled, Irish
mark 30.00
Shamrock basketweave, brownish
twig handle, 2BM 38.00
Egg Cup, Shamrock, 2BM 125.00
Figurine, "Girl with Basket," 1BM, 9" 950.00
Flower Pot, applied roses and
leaves, 3⅝" 195.00
Footed sherbet, fluted edge, egg
shell, with gold paste, 3½" 150.00
Hat Pin Holder, swirled floral, silver
overlay, Willets, 5" 100.00
Jam Pot, Aberdeen 295.00
Juice Set, pitcher, 4 matching tumblers, raised enameled fruit, flowers, Willets 350.00
Marmalade Jar, Shamrock, 3BM .. 80.00

Mugs
Hand painted, tankard shape,
blackberry decor, Lenox 85.00
Corn decor, Ceramic Art Co., 5" . 50.00
Dark brown Art Deco designs on
tan, Willets 75.00
Rope-handle, 2BM, 2" 65.00
Hand painted, tankard shape,
"Gambling Ladies," signed "M.
Hunter," Ceramic Art Co. 150.00
Shamrock, green mark 295.00

Pitchers
Cider, ocean scene, artist signed,
1910 .... 175.00
Raised gold leaves, blossoms, solid gold embellishments on body,
American Art China Works 450.00
Grape cluster decor, ornate handle, artist signed, dated 1906, 14" 175.00
Red berries, green leaves, on tan,
Ceramic Art Co. 150.00
Tankard, green berries, leaves,
German verse, artist signed, dated
1898, Ceramic Art Co. 175.00

Plates

Bread, 9" 95.00
Bacchus, 10" 110.00
Cone, green trim, 2BM 65.00
Echinus, green trim, 1BM 62.00
Gold, green enameled rim, Willets . 42.00
Hexagon, bread plate, 2BM 75.00
Shamrock, basketweave, 3BM, 8" . 55.00

Platters
Hawthorne 195.00
Twig handles, 2BM 85.00
Shamrock, basketweave, 3BM ... 75.00

Salts
Floral decor, cream background,
gold rim and ball feet, Willets, pair 35.00
Heart shaped, pansy center, ruffled edge, gold trim, Willets 15.00
Master, Shell and Coral, 2BM ... 40.00

Sugars
Etruria, blue and white, late 35.00
Neptune, 2BM 85.00
Shamrock, basketweave, 3BM ... 65.00

Teapots
Peach-color roses with gold vines
and leaves, signed, Ceramic Art
Co. 98.00
Bamboo, 1BM, 8½" 500.00
Hexagon, green trim, 2BM 250.00
Neptune, green trim, 2BM 250.00
Roses, hand painted, pink, cream,
jewelled scrollwork, gold handle
and finial, Lenox 175.00

Vases
Open water lily, Willets, 3" 100.00
Ruffled rim, pink, lavender florals,
gold leaves and trim, Lenox 125.00
Pink, yellow, blue florals, green
leaves, Lenox, 6" 125.00
Pearl, 3BM, 6½" 125.00
Gold handles, crimped rim, salmon pink, yellow rose decor,
Willets, 7" 160.00
Shamrock, panel 2BM, green petals, 8½" 235.00
Nile, pearl lustre, yellow leaves,
3BM, 13" 350.00
Hand Painted, Morning Glory decor, Willets, 13½" 175.00

BELLS

**Bells have been used for centuries for many
different purposes, and have in the last twenty years, become a very popular collectible
item. There are many types of materials of
which bells have been made; almost as many
materials, as there are uses for them. See
also specific categories, such as GLASS, etc.**

Animal
Camel Brass 35.00
Cow, 3½", sheet iron 32.50

Sheeps Bell, brass, leather strap $25.00

Goat, heavy tin	11.50
Horse, Set of 4 medium to large rump bells on leather strap	45.00
Sheep, brass with iron clapper, leather strap loop	30.00
Church steeple bell, signed "Vanduzen and Tift, Cincinnati"	555.00
Door Bell, brass, "Connell's Pat. 1873"	55.00
Farm yard bell, cast iron with yoke, #2	100.00

Figurals

Brass, windmill	50.00
Bronze, lady with dolphin atop her head	45.00
Bronze, wrought iron stand, rampant lion, probably Alpine	65.00
Man holding bell on his head ...	175.00
Sterling silver, Dutch woman wearing hoop skirt, with "Repouse" flowers and swags, hands holding small cup overhead	195.00
Fire engine bell, chromed bronze ..	250.00

Horse Hames

Set of four	350.00
Set of 5, Swedish	125.00

Hand bells

Brass, 6¾", embossed animals and Latin inscription on side	100.00
Figural, Napoleon handle, army figures and soldiers in relief	225.00
School teacher's, 7", brass with turned wood handle	40.00
Sterling silver, 4½", Art Nouveau style	88.00
Sterling silver, chased and cast with frieze of revelers at merry celebration and with figural fiddler handle	440.00
Sterling silver, Old Florentine pattern by Gorham with ivory handle, c. 1888	195.00
Locomotive bell, large, cast iron ...	425.00
Ship's bell, brass, U. S. N. and cast with florals on armature	350.00

Sleigh

8 Brass crotal-type bells on leather strap, dated 3/14/78	75.00
14 Brass crotal-type bells, graduated in size from #1 to #13, 71¼" leather strap	200.00
18 Brass bells in graduated sizes from #0 to #11, on leather strap with cotter keys	195.00
27 Brass crotal-type bells riveted to leather strap, c. 1870	100.00
30 Brass bells riveted to original double leather strap	150.00
36 Brass crotal-type bells riveted to 89" leather strap	175.00

Tap Bells

Brass, with twist ring	65.00
Nickel plated brass on marble base, Patent date 2-74	25.00
Trolly Car Bell, foot operated marked "Star Bros. Bell Co." ...	90.00

BELLS—GLASS

Although bells made of metal are more practical, glass bells were produced in England and the United States in the early 1800's. They can be found in clear or colored glass, large or small. Some were made for use on the tea tray or dining table, while others were purely decorative, an example of the glass blower's talent and the glass manufacturer's product.

Glass bells are still being manufactured. Be careful of the reproductions which are coming in from Europe.

Amber, 5", clear handle, etched floral decor	22.50
Bristol, 11½"	100.00
Bristol, 13¼", wedding bell, red barrel in swirl pattern, clear swirl handle, 4-ball finial, with clapper .	125.00
Columbian Exposition, 1893, swirled handle, metal clapper	75.00
Cranberry, 11", clear applied handle, English	175.00
Cranberry, 4⅝", with opaque white handle, clear clapper	125.00
Custard, souvenir, "Seaside Pavillion, Corpus Christie"	35.00
Cut glass, 5½", overall cut hob stars, handle with facetted knob .	285.00

Amber, 6⅝", Pattern Glass $7.50

Milk glass, 5½", chain links form handle, metal clapper	65.00
Nailsea-type, 12", cranberry opaque and white loopings, clear handle and clapper	195.00
Ruby, 12", clear handle	50.00
Venetian, latticinio, 4¼"	150.00

BENNINGTON POTTERY

The two potteries located in Bennington, Vt., were Norton Pottery and Fenton Pottery, owned and operated independently. When Capt. John Norton began making pottery in 1793, he offered only crocks and jugs. Later, Parian, stoneware, colored porcelains and much more were produced. They were marked with several different names: J. and E. Norton, E. and L. P. Norton, L. Norton Co., and others. The pottery existed as a family business until 1894.

In 1845, Christopher Fenton entered the business. He introduced additional lines, including the "Rockingham Glaze," which had been produced originally in England. The American "Rockingham Glaze" as known today, was developed by the Jersey City Pot-

tery in 1829. It was peddled door to door throughout the country and was common tableware for two generations, being made between 1830 and 1900 by some 150 potteries in 11 states, most of them in the Middle West. The hound-handled pitcher was also made by some 30 other potteries in the United States, and there are approximately 55 variations of it.

Bennington also produced a beautiful line of Parian ware, sometimes called "Statuary Ware." First made by Copeland in England in 1842, it is translucent and vitreous, and Parian proper is unglazed. It is usually molded and uncolored, but Bennington added color to the slip, and this is known as Parian on a colored background.

American ware included pitchers, vases, boxes, animal and human figures (which are seldom marked). Bennington Parian is considered to be the earliest and finest made in America.

Bennington also made a ware known as "Scroddled Ware," which was different colored clay, mixed with cream colored clay, put into a mold, turned on a potter's wheel and coated with feldspar and flint glaze. It was a slow and costly process, therefore very little was made at Fenton. When marked, it has the United States Pottery oval mark "H," or Fenton "E."

Creamer, 4" high, flint Enamel, blue, green, brown $60.00

NORTON

Beer Bottle, 8", Joe Norton	35.00
Butter Crock, grey stoneware, with	

cobalt blue, stylized leaf decor, impressed, "E. and L. P. Norton, Bennington, Vt." 185.00

Chamber Pot, grey stoneware, Julius Norton 100.00

Cream Pot, covered, 1 qt., cobalt floral, J. & E. Norton 125.00

Crocks
4-gal., yellow-brown with "4" impressed with cobalt blue, L. Norton and Co. 280.00
5-gal., blue cobalt on incised flower, J. Norton 150.00

Inkstand, 6", J. Norton and Co. . . . 160.00

Jars
1 gal., grey stoneware, cobalt blue, "Butterfly" and floral decor, impressed E. and L. Norton, Bennington, Vt. 95.00
Covered, 1-gal., preserve-type, blue cobalt 200.00

Jugs
2-gal., grey stoneware, cobalt blue, floral decor, impressed "E and L. P. Norton, Bennington" . . 125.00
2-gal., blue maple leaf impressed, J. & E. Norton 150.00
2-gal., two handled blue cobalt rabbit, J. Norton and Co. 650.00
4-gal., blue cobalt floral decor, E. Norton and Co. 100.00

Pitcher, 11", hexagonal, brown birds and flowers, Norton and Fenton . 250.00

FENTON

Boxes
5¾", square, all white Parian, shell finial 85.00
4⅜", square, Parian, top with figure, Lion of Lucerne 100.00

Bowls
6", bell-shaped, Rockingham glaze 80.00
15", flared sides, milk-pan type . . 110.00

Butter, covered, molded design, Rockingham glaze 100.00

Coffee Pot, 13", peaked cover, finial, 8-sided tapering body, flint enamel glaze 1300.00

Compote, on low footed base, molded design on body 100.00

Creamer, 5½", cow, with cover, Rockingham glaze 150.00

Croup Kettle, 4½", baluster form, Rockingham glaze 350.00

Cuspidors
Honey color, 4 x 9½", Lyman and Fenton 50.00
Tortoise shell, 3¾ x 8¼" 75.00
Shell pattern, mottled brown, Rockingham glaze 75.00

Figurines
Bust, George Washington 50.00
Dog, 7" poodle, with basket of fruit in his mouth, head, ears and mane of "coleslaw" porcelain . . . 350.00
Parian, 4½", girl praying 280.00
Parian, 5", Red Riding Hood 300.00
Parian, "The Tight Shoe," 80.00
Spaniel, lying, 3", white graniteware 125.00
Standing woman with grapes, 10", Parian 400.00

Flasks
Book shaped, "Comin' through the Rye," Rockingham 350.00
Book shaped, "For the Ladies," flint enamel 400.00

Inkwell, cylindrical, Rockingham glaze 90.00

Pitchers
Parian, 8½", molded grape cluster, leaves, blue and white 100.00
Parian, acorn and leaf, blue background, tree trunk handle and pouring spout, Bennington ribbon mark 450.00
Parian, 10", Pond Lily pattern, polychrome glaze, U. S. Pottery ribbon mark 275.00
Parian, Paul and Virginia, molded figures on blue background 350.00
Rockingham glaze, 8½", molded floral 250.00
Scroddle, 10", molded handle, reddish brown and grey on cream background 450.00

Plate, Pie, 10½", Rockingham glaze 125.00

Snuff Jar, 3⅞", flint enamel, flat bottom 680.00

Soap Dish, 2½ x 5 x 4" 55.00

Toby Jugs
6", "General Stark," seated, Rockingham, 1848 mark 375.00
6¼", long haired man, seated, glass in one hand, pipe in the other, loop handle, grape vines, Rockingham glaze 275.00
9¾", Toby holding mug, Rockingham glaze 225.00

Vase, 10", Tulip, flint enamel, blue olive green, ochre glaze 450.00

BENNINGTON-TYPE

Flower Pot, 6", Rockingham glaze, raised eagles on sides 25.00

Jar, covered, 6⅝", Rockingham glaze 70.00

Pitcher, 8", peacock pattern, Rockingham glaze

Tea Pot, 7¾", "Rebecca at the Well" 65.00

Tobacco Jar, 7½", scroll handle, gothic arches, flower finial **80.00**

BISCUIT JARS

The biscuit or cracker jar was the forerunner of the cookie jar. They were made of various materials by many major glass makers and potteries. All items listed have silver plated mountings unless otherwise noted.
See also individual categories.

Wavecrest, 7½" overall height, not signed $200.00

Bristol Glass
  Soft green, enamel floral decor . . **100.00**
  Turquoise, enamel floral and heron decor **135.00**
  White opaque, enamel floral decor **70.00**
Cased Glass, rose and white, mottled overlay **85.00**
Crown Milano, enameled pansies and medallion decor, embossed lid, butterfly handle **850.00**
Cut Glass, hobstars, strawberry diamond and fan, sterling lid **185.00**
Moriage, green, heavy orchid decor, double handle **230.00**
Opaline, green to brown, hand painted monk portrait, metal lid Handel **385.00**
Porcelains
  Austrian, portrait of Victorian lady

decal **75.00**
Limoge, pastel, enamel floral decor, gold handles **145.00**
Royal Doulton, Dickensware, "Old Peggoty" **225.00**
Satin Glass
  Pink, "Shell and Seaweed," enamel decor **240.00**
  Pink, "Fleurette" **200.00**
  Yellow shading to white, enamel floral decor **150.00**
Mt. Washington, yellow, pastel enamel floral decor, satin finish . . **450.00**

BISQUE

Bisque or biscuit china is the name given to wares that have been fired once and are not glazed. Some were decorated with colors, and the body is soft and porous. Bisque figurines and busts were popular during the Victorian era. They were made by numerous potteries in the United States and abroad. Bisque wares are being produced today in Japan.

Fairy Lamp, 4⅝" high Austrian $215.00

Box, egg-shaped, footed, windmill scene in relief **45.00**
Bust, 5½", girl with blonde hair, blue hat, blouse, gold trim **75.00**
Figurines
  Baby in a basket, 5¼" **70.00**
  Bathing beauties, Germany **35.00**
  Boy and girl, boy with fishing pole, pair **100.00**
  Boy and girl, dressed in parents' clothing, c. 1840, pair **165.00**
  Boy and girl, 8½", carrying tod-

dlers on shoulders, pair 425.00
Boy, dressed in nightgown, hold-
ing doll, Germany 50.00
Cherub on sleigh, pink, white, gold
trim 65.00
Farmer, 12¼″, with scythe,
Heubach 165.00
Hunter, 8″, with gun and dog 65.00
Tennis players, 15″, decorated,
pair 150.00

Match Holders
Dutch girl holding pitcher, 3½″ . . 35.00
Girl holding doll, 5½″ 45.00
"Happy Hooligan," 8″ 55.00
*Piano Babies, See Dolls
Boy, reclining, 5½″ 125.00
Girl lying on stomach, 6″, Germa-
ny 150.00
Holding Toy doll, decorated, 8″ . . 125.00
Girl sitting, 13″ 275.00

Shoes
Blue flower, yellow center, laven-
der frill 50.00
White love birds at top, three blue
birds on side, 6¼″ 65.00
Tobacco Jars, boy's head, 4⅞″ . . . 135.00
Toby, hanging, 3 x 3″ 40.00
Toothpick, boy with bottle 20.00

Vase
Blossoms and leaves, 5″ 40.00
Two molded peaches and leaves
on outside, oval, 6″, wishbone
handles, color and gold trim,
Crown mark, Vienna, Austria 35.00

BLOWN THREE MOLD GLASS

Although the method of producing blown
mold glass objects was known to the an-
cients, it was not practiced in America until
the early 1800's. The glass maker placed a
quantity of molten glass on the tip of a rod
or tube and literally blew air into it to form
the article.

Free blown glass did not use a mold.
Blown molded glass used a pre-designed
mold that usually consisted of two, three or
more hinged parts. The term Blown Three
Mold (BTM), indicates a three-part mold.

The impressed decorations on blown mold
glass are usually reversed, i.e., what is raised
or convex on the outside will be concave on
the inside. This is one of its identifying factors. New methods for producing glass items
continued to be developed. By 1850, American made glasswares were in relatively common usage which necessitated greater production by mechanical means. Small glass
producers either abandoned the trade or became large industrial factories. Two important firms were Boston and Sandwich and

the New England Glass Co.
The numbers used refer to *American Glass*
by George L. and Helen McKearin.

Decanter, miniature, no stopper $365.00

Bird Drinking Fountain, 7″, clear, fit-
ted with amethyst blown glass ball
top, free blown 250.00
Bottles
Castor, geometric, (GI-13) 45.00
Castor, Shaker, baroque, (GV-19) 45.00
Bowls
5″, folded rim, geometric, rough
pontil, (GIII-6) 100.00
Geometric, design, clear 110.00
Castor Set, four bottle, geometric
pewter frame, "Eben Smith,"
(GI-14) 350.00
Celery vases, geometric, 7″, pair,
(GIII-34) 1125.00
Decanters
Quart, clear, with stopper, geo-
metric, (GI-29) 150.00
Quart, clear, produced at Keene,
N.H. 400.00
Quart, with original stopper, geo-
metric, clear, (GII-21) 150.00
Quart, with stopper, arch clear,
(GIV-5) 70.00
Flip glass
5½″, clear 200.00
6¼″, clear, geometric, (GIII-22) . 200.00

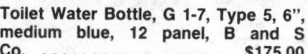

**Toilet Water Bottle, G 1-7, Type 5, 6",
medium blue, 12 panel, B and S
Co.** $175.00

**Toilet Water Bottle, G 1-7, Type 5,
medium blue, ribbed** $165.00

Hat, geometric, clear, (GII-5)	125.00
Ink bottles	
Olive amber, geometric, (GII-18) .	150.00
Green, Keene glass, (GII-29) ...	175.00
Mug, 4", clear, enameled decor, applied handle, (GI-6)	55.00
Ointment Jar, 3¾", Clear, brass lid, "Glenn and Co, Phila.," (GI-19) ..	45.00
Salts	
Cobalt blue, (GII-21)	400.00
Clear, (GIII-3)	100.00
Clear, (GIII-20)	100.00
Brilliant green	250.00
String Holder, 4½", clear with applied cobalt blue rim at top, attributed B. and S. Co.	225.00
Tumbler, clear, geometric, (GII-18) .	145.00
Whiskey Tasters	
3½", aqua blue-green, rough pontil	45.00
3½", sapphire blue, rough pontil .	45.00
12 rib, medium blue, slightly flared rim	45.00
Sunburst, clear	200.00
Wine, clear, geometric, (GII-19) ...	275.00

BOHEMIAN GLASS

The once independent country of Bohemia, now a part of Czechoslovakia, produced a variety of fine glassware-etched, cut, overlay and colored. Their glasswares were first imported into America in the early 1820's and continue today. Perhaps Bohemia is known for their "flashed" glass that was not only produced in the familiar ruby color, but also in amber, green, blue and black. Common patterns include "Deer and Pine Tree," "Deer and Castle" and "Vintage." Most of the Bohemian glass encountered in today's market is of the 1875-1900 period. A Bonemian type glass was also made in England, Switzerland and Germany.

*Bell, 4½", "Deer and Castle," ruby, clear glass handle, clear clapper on chain	85.00
Bottles	
Cologne, "Vintage," ruby, original stopper	85.00
Cologne, "Deer and Castle,"	

Decanter, 14", vintage, ruby . . $85.00

green, original stopper	85.00
Cologne, 8", amber, floral etched	100.00

Bowls

Finger, "Vintage," ruby	50.00
Tree, amber, three legged, 3½" x 9", "Deer and Pine Tree"	75.00
Butter, covered, "Deer and Castle," ruby	150.00
Caster Set, 14½", ruby and clear, frosted, three bottles, stoppered, Sheffield holder	175.00
Celery, "Deer and Castle," ruby, c. 1875	75.00
Chalice, 10", enameled overlay, amber	150.00

Compotes

Open, "Deer and Castle," 7", ruby	75.00
Covered, "Vintage," ruby	35.00
Covered, "Deer and Pine Tree," ruby, 10"	150.00
Covered, "Deer and Pine Tree," ruby	175.00
Cordials, 6½", blown, large pontil on base, Vintage etching, applied ring on stem, six, red, each	30.00

Cordial Sets

Decanter and 4 cordials, "Deer and Castle," ruby	200.00
Decanter, tray, 4 cordials, "Lily of the Valley," amber . . . . . ,.	300.00

Decanters, 11¼", "Deer and Castle," ruby with clear stoppers, pair	135.00
Decanter, amber, deer scene . . .	100.00
"Vintage," ruby, 10"	50.00
"Vintage," ruby, 12½"	75.00
"Deer and Castle," 15", ruby stoppered, c. 1850	150.00
Door Knobs, ruby, set	75.00
Epergne, 14¾"	110.00

Lamps

Pair fine etched bases, with brass and marble, each	70.00
12", cobalt overlay	175.00
Pitcher, water, "Vintage," ruby	150.00
Plate, 8¾", "Deer and Castle, ruby .	60.00
Salt, "Vintage," ruby, three-ribbed, scroll feet, gold trim	20.00
Salt and Pepper shakers, "Deer and Castle," ruby, ornate silverplated frame, set	200.00

Sugars, covered

Etched, hunting scene, amber . . .	150.00
"Tower and Deer," Princess Feather design	60.00
Tumble-Up, "Vintage," ruby	95.00

Tumblers

Juice, "Bird and Castle," ruby . . .	30.00
Water, "Deer and Pine Tree," green	40.00
"Flowers and Birds," amber	45.00
"Vintage," ruby	35.00
"Vintage," ruby, footed	50.00
Urn, covered, 14", "Deer and Pine Tree," ruby	150.00

Vases

"Castle and Deer," 5", ruby	75.00
"Wildlife," ruby 5¼"	100.00
"Deer and Castle," ruby, tapered, gourd shaped	125.00
"Castle and Bird," ruby, cone shaped	125.00
"Flowers and Birds," ruby	120.00
"Castle and Deer," ruby, 12¼ . . .	150.00
"Deer and Pine Tree," 12", pair .	175.00
Amethyst to clear, with heavy gold overlay	250.00
Green, enameled grapes, gold leaves fluted top, pedestal base .	125.00
"Deer and Castle," ruby, 19½ . . .	175.00
Wine, "Vintage," ruby	30.00
Wine Set, "Deer and Castle," ruby, decanter and six glasses	300.00

BONE

**Items carved from dried animal bones are
desirable collector's items. Some bone items
are being misrepresented as ivory on today's
market and buyers should use caution.**

Apple Corer, 4", early	25.00
Back Scratcher, Chinese, late	25.00

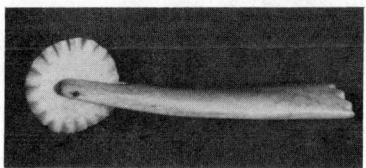

Crimper, 6" long $65.00

Clothes Pin, early	15.00
Crochet Hooks, 11", two-part, screws together in center, elaborately carved to center, then plain to hook, set of 5, different sized hooks	25.00
Letter Opener, carved figure at top .	25.00
Napkin Rings	
Ornate	15.00
Plain	10.00
Pickle fork, sterling silver handle ...	21.00
Scoop, flour, early	30.00
Sled, 6", leather lacing	30.00
Spoons	
5¼"	15.00
8"	20.00

BOOKENDS

Bookends have been, and are made of every conceivable shape, size, form and material imaginable. Very popular in the early 1900's, those of Art Nouveau and Art Deco designs are highly collectible and command high prices.

Cast Iron, Halloween Cat, 1925, signed D. A. L., pair $65.00

Brass

Art Nouveau decor, 27", expansion type	75.00
Dog, marble base, pair	100.00
Owl, expandable, pair	75.00

Bronze

Buffalo, 5" x 5", pair	195.00
Geisha Girl, 4½", pair	150.00
Lily pad with frogs, pair	150.00
Napoleon Bust, armour, artist-signed	75.00
Oriental figurine, on green marble base, pair	185.00
Scottie dog, signed Edith Parsons, pair	225.00
German Shepherd, 5", c. 1900–1920, pair	50.00

Cast Iron

Elephant, pair	50.00
Lincoln Cabin, pair	100.00
Pirate, 7", painted light green, pair	50.00
Pirate ship, painted, pair	50.00
Figures, bookshelves and Shakespearian quotation "My library is dukedom large enough," pair ...	75.00

Glass, molded

Rearing horses	40.00
Frosted horse head	15.00
Clear horse heads	35.00
Horses with riders	50.00
Running horse on base	35.00
Jade, 3" x 5", Foo dog, ebony bases, pair	850.00
Mahogany with brass bases, 6", carved jade inserts, pair	150.00
Plaster of Paris, bronzed, female, Art Nouveau, pair	100.00
Porcelain, 5½", male and female figures, Japan, c.1930, pr.	40.00
Pottery lion, 5" x 7", Ohio pottery, late 19th century, pr.	250.00
Rose Quartz, bird on stepped brass bases, hand carved, pr. ...	200.00
Soapstone, Urn and flowers, pair .	65.00
Teakwood, 10", elephant head, ivory trim, pair	100.00
Petrified Wood, 5½" x 8", cut and polished bases, 12 lbs., pair	75.00

BOOKS, MODERN AMERICAN FIRST EDITIONS

Collecting modern American first editions can be both rewarding and hazardous. The value of first editions has withstood fluctuations in the market.

There is no easy method to identify a first edition. Collectors are urged to consult Blank's *Bibliography of American First Editions* or Tannen's *How to Identify & Collect*

American First Editions.

Modern first editions must be in fine condition and complete with dust jacket to be of value. The latter is very important. If the dust jacket does not exist, the book is worth substantially less.

Most collectors will automatically reject book club editions.

The following prices are for books in fine condition *and with* dust jackets. Occasionally hints are given to identify the first edition from subsequent editions.

Agee, James, *A Death in the Family*, NY:1957, first issue with "walking" on page 80 .... 25.00

Algren, Nelson, *A Walk on the Wide Side*, NY:1957 .... 15.00

Baldwin, James, *Nobody Knows My Name*, NY:1961 .... 15.00

Barth, John, *Floating Opera*, NY:1956, signed by author 200.00

Barth, John, *Giles Goat Boy*, NY:1966 .... 15.00

Bellow, Saul, *The Adventures of Augie March*, NY:1953 .... 17.50

Benet, Stephen Vincent, *We Stand United. . .*, NY:1945 .... 10.00

Bradbury, Ray, *The Martian Chronicles*, Garden City:1953, author presentation copy 40.00

Brooks, Van Wyck, *The Flowering of New England*, NY:1936 .... 7.50

Brown, Elijah, *The Real Billy Sunday*, 1914, signed by Billy Sunday ... 35.00

Buck, Pearl, *The Good Earth*, NY:1931, first issue with "flees" for "fleas" in line 17, page 100, top edges stained brown 75.00

Burroughs, Edgar Rice, *Tarzan of the Apes*, Chicago:1914, acorn device at foot of spine 2000.00

Burroughs, Edgar Rice, *Warlord of Mars*, Chicago:1919 .... 120.00

Cabell, James Branch, *Jurgen*, NY:1919
First issue with line rules on page 114 intact 220.00
Without dust jacket 75.00

Caldwell, Erskine, *God's Little Acre*, NY:1933 .... 50.00

Capote, Truman, *Breakfast at Tiffany's*, NY:1958 .... 40.00

Cather, Willa, *Sapphire & the Slave Girl*, NY:1940 .... 15.00

Dahlberg, Edward, *Do These Bones Live?*, NY:1941 .... 25.00

Fast, Howard, *The Proud & the Free*, Boston:1950 .... 7.50

Faulkner, William, *Intruder in the Dust*, NY:1948 .... 75.00

Faulkner, William, *The Unvanquished*,

NY:1938, first trade edition, signed by author 450.00

Fitzgerald, F. Scott, *Tender Is the Night*, NY:1934 .... 400.00

Frost, Robert, *A Masque of Mercy*, NY:1947 .... 10.00

Gorey, Edward, *The Blue Aspic*, NY:1966 .... 12.00

Hemingway, Ernest, *Across the River & into the Trees*, NY:1950 ... 20.00

Hemingway, Ernest, *The Green Hills of Africa*, NY:1935 .... 65.00

Kennedy, John F., *Profiles in Courage*, NY:1956 .... 75.00

Kent, Rockwell, *N by E*, NY:1930 .. 15.00

Kerouac, Jack, *The Dharma Bums*, NY:1958 .... 50.00

Kesey, Ken, *One Flew Over the Cuckoo's Nest*, NY:1962 ...... 60.00

Lewis, Sinclair, *Elmer Gantry*, NY:1927, binding with spine title resembling "Cantry" 65.00

Lovecraft, H. P., *Best Supernatural Stories of. . .*, Cleveland:1945 ... 25.00

Mailer, Norman, *Cannibals and Christians*, NY:1966 .... 15.00

Mencken, H. L., *A Treatise on the Gods*, NY:1930 .... 40.00

Mitchell, Margaret, *Gone With the Wind*, NY:Published May 1936 ... 500.00

Moore, Marianne, *Predilections*, NY: 1955 .... 40.00

Morley, Christopher, *Where the Blue Begins*, Garden City:1922 ...... 22.00

Morris, Wright, *Man & Boy*, NY:1951 25.00

Nin, Anais, *Ladders to Fire*, NY:1946 30.00

Newton, A. E., *End Papers*, Boston:1933 .... 20.00

Oates, Joyce Carol, *Wonderland*, NY:1971 .... 10.00

O'Hara, John, *Lovely Childs: A Philadelphia Story*, NY:1969 .... 6.50

O'Neill, Eugene, *The Iceman Cometh*, NY:1946 .... 50.00

Patchen, Kenneth, *Sleeper's Awake*, NY:1946 .... 25.00

Paettie, Donald Culross, *Immortal Village*, Chicago:1945, limited to 500 copies, signed by author and illustrator 25.00

Porter, Katherine Annie, *The Leaning Tower & Other Stories*, NY: 1944 .... 20.00

Purdy, James, *Cabot Wright Begins*, NY:1964 .... 10.00

Pynchon, Thomas, *V*, Philadelphia:1963 .... 150.00

Queen, Ellery, *The Spanish Cape Mystery* 50.00

Remington, Frederic, *Crooked Trails*, NY:1898 .... 200.00

Roberts, Kenneth, *Boon Island*, Gar-

den City:1956 . . . . 8.00
Robinson, Edwin Arlington, *Cavender's House*, NY:1929 . . . . 10.00
Roth, Philip, *Letting Go*, NY:1962 . . 18.00
Schulberg, Budd, *The Harder They Fall*, NY:1947 . . . . 20.00
Sinclair, Upton, *Depression Island*, Pasadena, CA:1935 . . . . 22.50
Saroyan, William, *The Daring Young Man on the Flying Trapeze & Other Stories*, NY:1935, first book by author 55.00
Salinger, J. D., *Franny and Zooey*, Boston:1961 . . . . 15.00
Sandburg, Carl, *Remembrance Rock*, NY:1948, signed by author 50.00
Santayanna, George, *Wide Is the Gate*, NY:1943 . . . . 15.00
Steinbeck, John, *Bombs Away: The Story of a Bomber Team*, NY:1942 22.50
Steinbeck, John, *The Long Valley*, NY:1938 . . . . 60.00
Steinbeck, John, *The Wayward Bus*, NY:1947 . . . . 35.00
Stryon, William, *Lie Down in Darkness*, Indianapolis:1951 . . . . 30.00
Updike, John, *Couples*, NY:1968 . . . 12.50
Van Vogt, A. E., *Out of the Unknown*, Los Angeles:1948 . . . . 20.00
Vonnegut, Kurt, *Cat's Cradle*, NY: 1963 . . . . 40.00
Williams, Tennessee, *The Roman Spring of Mrs. Stone*, NY:1950 . . 25.00
Wilson, Edmund, *A Piece of My Mind: Reflections at Sixty*, NY:1956 . . . . 5.00
Wright, Richard, *Native Son*, NY: 1940 . . . . 15.00

BOOT JACKS

Various types of boot jacks were made to facilitate the removal of boots. Some were constructed of wood while others were made of metals such as brass or iron. Two of the popular designs were "Beetle" and "Naughty Nellie."

Brass
10″, "Beetle" 85.00
"Naughty Nellie" 85.00
Cast Iron — Advertising
13″ Center design, Downs and Co. 30.00
"Try It" 25.00
"Use Musselman's Boot Jack Plug" 35.00
*11½″, "Beetle" 50.00
Bowed type, 7″, "C. Hull, Birmingham" on back and "Regd. Boot Jack" 25.00

Cast Iron, lyre shaped, 10¼″ long $45.00

Buggy Wrench, Pittsburgh Novelty Works 50.00
Cap Pistol, 8½″, double barrel. Legend "American Bull Dog Boot Jack" 65.00
Double, Ornate Pat. 1869 . . . . . . 50.00
Horseshoe 25.00
Horse, stylized 105.00
Mechanical, carpet covered, movable jaws to grip boot, Pat. 1850 . 50.00
*Naughty Nellie 50.00
15″, Shoe sole, with maple wood, Pat. 1859 . . . . 35.00
Wooden
13″ long, advertising type, "Fye & Co. The popular shoe for men, Zanesville, Ohio" 25.00
Cow horns 40.00
7″ long, maple 25.00
25″ long, pine, oval ends with square nails 25.00
Portable
2½ x 5″, brass riveted 35.00
8″ Pine 40.00
16″ Primitive 25.00
Walnut, cast iron frame, carpeted top 45.00

BOTTLES

APOTHECARY—SEE APOTHECARY ITEMS

AVON BOTTLES

David H. McConnell founded the California Perfume Co. in 1886. He hired saleswomen, a radical concept for that time. They sold door-to-door their first product, "Little Dot," a set of five perfumes; thus was born the "Avon Lady" of whom in 1979 there were more than

one million. In 1929 they became the Avon Company. A tiny perfume company became a giant corporation, and their bottles are of interest to collectors today. Prices are for full containers.

Clock, white, 5 oz, "Charisma Foaming Bath Oil" 5.00

Bay Rum, 1 pint, 1878, mushroom stopper	225.00
Brilliantine, 1923	115.00
Bubble Bath, Christmas trees, 1968, ea.	2.50
Christmas Surprise Cologne, green boot, red cap ea.	2.00
Indian Chieftan, 4 oz., 1972, amber	4.00
Lavender Salts, 1893	200.00
Liberty Bell, amber, 1971	5.00
Perfume	
1908, Heliatrope	150.00
1914, with wooden holder	225.00
1917	120.00
1925, flaconette, ...	75.00
1926, flaconette, ...	75.00
1928, atomizer	150.00
Powder Sachet, 1915, American Ideal label, metal top	85.00
Violet Water, old label, applicator top, 1906	170.00

Avon Figurals

Alladin's Lamp, bath oil, 1971 ...	10.00
Athena, bath urn, 1974	7.50
Baby Basset, amber, 1974	7.00
Bath Treasure, snail, 1973, ...	7.00
Bud Vase, garnet, with stopper,	
1973	5.00
Butterfly, clear, 1972	4.00
Cannon Ball Express, locomotive, 1976	6.00
Fairy Tale Frog, 1976	2.00
Flamingo, 1971	8.00
Inkwell, 1969	9.00
Just Two, black glass, 1965, set .	32.00
Lanterns	
Casey's, 10 oz., 1966	6.00
Country, 4 oz., 1979	7.00
Mallard, silver head, 6 oz., 1967 .	12.00
Pointer, dog, 1973	5.00
Rolls Royce, 1972	8.00
Sea Trophy, sailfish, blue, 1972 .	7.00
Stein, stoneware, numbered, 1976	22.00
Straight Eight, 1969, ...	6.00
Viking Horn, 1966	22.00
Volkswagen, black, 1970, ...	6.00
Warrior, frosted	6.00

BARBER BOTTLES

Barber bottles are disappearing from the American scene, as the old time barber shop has been replaced by its modern counterpart. The barber, in days gone by, was a very important person in town, and he often took the part of doctor and dentist. His "bench bottles" as they were called, were cared for and replenished by him when his supplies ran low, and he knew what each bottle contained by its color and form. The older barber bottles were usually imported from Europe, and American bottles were made from the 1860's through 1900. The earliest American bottles were Hobnail, the rarest of which were crystal or clear Hobnail, opalescent hobnail, swirl, and striped, and amberina. These bottles are being reproduced, especially in the opalescent colors.

Bohemian, 8½", ruby, enamel floral decor	75.00
Blown	
Amber, DQ	75.00
Amethyst, enamel decor	100.00
Blue, sapphire thumbprint	100.00
Blue, cobalt, enamel decor	150.00
Canary	30.00
Clear, panelled	50.00
Green, DQ	75.00
Green, olive, enamel decor	65.00
Blue, donut shape, "Life Saver," black lettering	40.00
Bristol, 9½", black enamel decor ..	50.00
Camphor, "Witch Hazel"	80.00
Cranberry	
Opalescent, Stars and Stripes ...	115.00
Cranberry ITP, pair	175.00
Iridescent Cranberry, mottled finish	30.00

Blown, vaseline, 8½" thumbprint, porcelain stopper, smooth pontal mark 45.00

Crystal, sterling topped, cork with pull ring	50.00
Cut Glass	
Pewter top, 5"	45.00
Sterling top	135.00
Frosted glass, pottery dispensers, "Water" and "Witch Hazel," pair .	120.00
*Hobnail	
Amber	85.00
Cobalt	100.00
Cranberry	75.00
Vaseline	95.00
Mary Gregory-type	
Amethyst, girl	185.00
Cobalt, boy playing tennis	185.00
Milk Glass	
"Bay Rum," label on painted surface	40.00
"Bay Rum," name in tall letters, painted flowers	50.00
"Witch Hazel," tall tapering, fluted base, space for label	50.00
Opalescent	
*Stripes	85.00
*Swirl	85.00
Satin Glass	

10½", Cranberry with white looping, pewter stopper	225.00
10½", DQ, MOP, one pink, one blue, original pewter stoppers, pair	800.00
*Spanish Lace, 8½", cranberry ...	85.00
Wedgwood, tri-color, four cameos of classical scenes	750.00

BEER BOTTLES

Beer was bottled in the United States as early as 1860. Perhaps the earliest beer containers were hand thrown pottery, later blown glass and eventually mass produced machine made.

Embossed "Fayette Brewing Co. Uniontown, Pa." 9½" high, brown .7.00

Blatz, Milwaukee, 12 oz. embossed, clear	7.50
Bock, quart, stoneware	65.00
Carnival-type, 16 oz.	20.00
Coors, miniature	7.50
Ginger-beer, stoneware c. 1915 ...	20.00
Home-brew, pint, amber	2.50
Home-brew, quart, light green	10.00
Milk glass, 16 oz.	15.00
Miller's High Life, c. 1935	7.50

Schlitz, 7 oz., ruby red **15.00**
Tennessee Brewing Co., 12 oz., paper label **7.50**

BITTERS BOTTLES

Our forbearers did not have the medical treatment that we are lucky enough to have today, so they leaned very heavily on patent medicines. Bitters, a "remedy," made from natural herbs and other mixtures, had an alcoholic base, and was said to cure anything. It was made by hundreds of different makers, put in most intriguingly-shaped and colored bottles, and highly advertised by almanacs, advertising cards, and other methods used in those days. Their names were imaginative, (though seldom did what their makers claimed for them), but people had faith in them. Alcohol was never mentioned, and in 1907, when the Pure Foods Regulations went into effect, "an honest statement of content on every label," put most of these manufacturers out of business, but some of the bottles still remain.

References: "Bitters Bottles," Richard Watson, 1965, (RW); "Bitters Bottles," J. H. Thompson, (JHT)

"Doyles," 1872. 9¾" high, amber, raised fruit decor **95.00**

Acorn Bitters, amber, 5-star, JHT . .   **200.00**
Alpine Herb Bitters, amber, 5-star, JHT **200.00**
Amazon Bitters, amber, 5-star, JHT .   **200.00**
American Celebrated Stomach Bitters, amber, 5-star, JHT **200.00**
Arabian Bitters, amber, 5-star, JHT .   **200.00**
Argyle Bitters, dark amber, 5-star, JHT **200.00**
Atherton's, Dr., Dewdrop Bitters, lt. honeyamber **125.00**
Ayola Mexican Bitters, amber **100.00**
Baker's, E. Premium Bitters, aqua, oval **100.00**
Ball's, Dr., Vegetable Stomach Bitters, aqua **100.00**
Barber's Indian Vegetable Jaundice Bitters, aqua **100.00**
Barto's Great Gun Bitters, olive, (Reading, Pa.) **125.00**
Bavarian Bitters, amber **75.00**
Bell's, Dr., Blood Purifying Bitters, amber **125.00**
Belmont Tonic Herb Bitters, amber .   **75.00**
Bender's Bitters, aqua **50.00**
Bengal Bitters, amber **75.00**
Ben Hur Bitters **50.00**
Bennet's Wild Cherry Bitters, ...   **45.00**
Best Bitters in America, roofed, amber **200.00**
Birmingham's, Dr., Anti Bilious Purifying Bitters, medium green **100.00**
Bishop's, Dr., Wahoo Bitters, amber   **125.00**
Blake's, Dr., Aromatic Bitters, aqua .   **75.00**
Blue Mountain Bitters **50.00**
Boerhane's, Dr., Stomach Bitters, lt. olive green **75.00**
Boerhane's Holland Bitters, aqua . .   **50.00**
Boneset Bitters **35.00**
Botanic Bitters, amber **45.00**
Botarici Stomach Bitters, amber . . .   **45.00**
Brady's Family Bitters, olive amber .   **50.00**
Brown's Aromatic Bitters, aqua **50.00**
Brown's, Dr., Berry Bitters, clear . . .   **35.00**
Bull's Genuine Wild Cherry Bitters, embossed, clear, extremely rare, (one to five specimens known), c. 1890, JHT, P.21, #54 . . . .   **350.00**
Burgundy Bitters, amber **100.00**
Burton's Stomach Bitters, amber . . .   **100.00**
Calabash Bitters, aqua **75.00**
California Fig and Herb Bitters, lt. amber **80.00**
California Wine Bitters, olive green .   **75.00**
Carey's Grecian Bend Bitters, puce .   **100.00**
Carson's, Dr., Stomach Bitters, aqua   **75.00**
Carter's Liver Bitters, amber **75.00**
Carver's Tonic Bitters, aqua **75.00**
Castilian Bitters, lt. honey amber . . .   **100.00**
Celebrated Berlin Stomach Bitters, olive-amber **100.00**
Celebrated Crown Bitters, (Cheva-

lier), amber	125.00
Chalmer's Catawba Wine Bitters, aqua	75.00
General Frank Cheatham's Bitters, olive amber, ...	100.00
Clark's Stomach Bitters, golden amber	100.00
Clark's Compound Mandrake Bitters, aqua	75.00
Clark's Sarsaparilla Bitters, aqua . . .	75.00
Excelsior Aromatic Bitters, smoky amber	100.00
Fowler's Stomach Bitters, lt. amber .	100.00
Gilbert's, Dr., Rock and Rye Bitters, bluish-green	100.00
Green Mountain Cider Bitters, aqua .	75.00
Hanlon's Tuna Bitters, clear amethystine	50.00
Hentz's Curative Bitters, pale green	100.00
Horseshoe Bitters, amber	80.00
Hungarbuehler's Swiss Alpine Bitters, amber	100.00
Indian Vegetable Sarsaparilla Bitters	100.00
Jackson's Stonewall Bitters, amber .	85.00
Johnson's Indian Dyspeptic Bitters, aqua	75.00
Jones' Indian Specific Herb Bitters, aqua, 1868	100.00
Kaufmann's Celebrated Anti-Cholera Bitters, puce	125.00
Kickapoo Bitters, Indian Sagwa, (part of label still on), aqua	150.00
Keystone Bitters, barrel shaped . . .	200.00
Kline, J. M. Co., Aromatic Digestive Cordial, cobalt	225.00
Old Homestead Wild Cherry Bitters, amber, shape of tall log cabin . . .	200.00
Old Jamaica Stomach Bitters, handled jug	175.00
Scott's, General, Artillery Bitters, amber	100.00
Stanley's, Dr., South American Indian Bitters, amber	85.00
Turkish Bitters, amber	75.00
Uncle Tom's Bitters, lt. amber	75.00
Whitwell's Temperance Bitters, aqua or clear green, very early, 1847, 5-star, one of top ten	350.00
Wishart's Pine Tree Cordial, pine-green, Phila., Pa.	100.00

COLOGNE BOTTLES

The cologne bottles listed are mainly early American pressed glass (unless noted) made prior to 1850 at the Boston and Sandwich Glass Co., and in the Pittsburgh area.

Amethyst

4¾", twelve-panel, McKearin, 243 –4	175.00
6⅞", bulbous, twelve-panel	275.00

Light Amethyst, 11" high, 12 panel 225.00

11", twelve-panel	250.00
Amethyst, bright, 5", applied salamander and white enamel and gold leaf decor, French	175.00
Amethyst, light, 5", twelve-panel . . .	90.00
Aqua, 10½", hexagonal, with Gothic Arch, ...	110.00
Clear, 5⅛", Loop, with gold presentation decoration c. 1840–50	150.00
Cobalt Blue "Violin"	225.00
4¼", bulbous, ten-panel	175.00
7½", twelve-panel	245.00
7⅜", bulbous, twelve-panel	175.00
Cobalt blue, brilliant, 5⅞", hexagonal shape, fine gold decoration, French	150.00
Cobalt blue, deep 4¼", replaced clear stopper	75.00
5¾", eighteen panels, replaced stopper, BTM	150.00
Emerald Green "Violin"	275.00
4¼", waisted B & S	275.00
4¾", twelve-panel, McKearin 342	

−4	165.00
4⅞″, twelve-panel, B & S	185.00
5″ bulbous, twelve-panel	245.00
5⅝″, twelve-panel	185.00
Fiery opalescent, 5½″, decor of large rose and other flowers, original stopper	100.00
Blue opalene, cream decoration, gold trim, blown stopper, late . . .	175.00
Ruby glass, 6¾″, floral decoration, jewelled, late	135.00

11½″	50.00
Pickwick, coat, and spectacles, vinegar	50.00
Poodle, sitting on a hassock	35.00
Potato, 5″, embossed, "World's Fair, 1893"	35.00
St. Nicholas, tall, stippled	45.00
St. Nicholas, small, with sack	40.00
Shoe, 5″, perfume	35.00
Washington, bust, cobalt blue, Joachim's Blackberry Brandy, Phila.	40.00

FIGURAL BOTTLES

Bottles which are shaped in any recognizable form, such as animals, objects, people, are known as figural bottles. Such bottles, in the past, could have held anything from perfume to vinegar, and many new ones are coming on the market, which in time, will become collectible.

Fish, 9″ long, Bennington, brown 450.00

Antelope, 15″, horn-shaped, twisted	40.00
Baby crying, bust	40.00
Bennington-type, book	60.00
Bear, black, Kummel type	60.00
Carrie Nation, with satchel, clear . . .	100.00
Cat, porcelain	30.00
Cigar, 6″, amber	50.00
Cucumber, 6″, pottery, green	35.00
Dog, 13″, standing on hind legs, clear	20.00
Ear of Corn, 6½″, good old paint, metal screw top	20.00
Goblet-shaped candy measure, cork in base, 2½″	25.00
Grapes, bunch, 4½″, reads "Frucht Rein," not old	5.00
Hand, frosted, 4½″, lotion bottle, (Pat'd June 21, 1874, T.S.P. Co.) .	50.00
Japanese man, kimona and clogs . .	15.00
Leprechaun	20.00
Monkey, wrapped around green bottle	20.00
Nude, frosted, French, 13½″, standing in foliage	40.00
Pagliacci, clown costume, Delft,	

FOOD BOTTLES

Milk, "Miller's Dairy," ½ pint, c. 1892 . . . . .4.00

Heinz Ketchup, urn shaped, blob top	10.00
Jumbos	
Bank type, figural, Castle Products, Neward	15.00
Peanut Butter, 1 lb., embossed elephant	10.00
Lee and Perrins, 11½″, glass stopper	7.50
Milk	
Baby Face, quart embossed	7.50
Cream Top, embossed, quart . . .	7.50
Embossed, pint and quart, ea . . .	1.00
Garner Dairy Co., ½ pint	1.00

Pepper Sauce
  Cathedral Arches, 7½" aqua **35.00**
  Goofus, 10½", embossed floral,
  ground mouth **20.00**
  Cathedral Arches, square, 11"
  rolled lip, aqua **125.00**

INK BOTTLES

Early ink bottles were made of ceramics and glass, designed to be "tip-proof." Most were imported. They were first used in America in the early 1800's.

Light-green, 2½" high, applied lip. c.
1910 ....**5.00**

Aqua, 3", round, applied lip and col-
  lar, c. 1880 .... **8.50**
Billing and Co., 2", embossed B ... **15.00**
Carter's
  Label, 2¼", aqua **5.00**
  "Ma and Pa," 3⅝", pair **75.00**
  Cathedral, pint, embossed, cobalt **45.00**
  Machine made, label, 32 oz., co-
  balt **15.00**
  Farley's, 2 x 2", deep olive green,
  open pontil, c. 1850 .... **200.00**
  Hover, Phila., umbrella shape, 2⅛
  x 2¼", 8 panels, aqua **200.00**
Improved Process Blue Company
  Cone, aqua 2½" **6.50**
  Label, clear, 2¼" **3.00**
  Round, cobalt, 2¼" **5.00**
  Square, cobalt, 2¼" **5.00**
Sanford's, 2 x 2", machine made .. **7.50**
Turtle, 2 x 4", travel, aqua **75.00**

Travel, umbrella, blue, no pontil ... **25.00**
Underwood, 9¾", pinch spout, co-
  balt **40.00**

MEDICINE BOTTLES

Not all medicines were patented in early America. During the 1880's, the "medicine show" which introduced American's first traveling salesmen, was very popular, and for one dollar small town residents could see a traveling show and buy a bottle of medicine which was said to cure anything. Luckily for today's collectors, some of the bottles still exist. The 1907 Pure Food and Drug Act ended this era, but remedies of the 1890's and early 1900's are still interesting to collectors. Some of these early bottles were made in the South Jersey glass manufacturing area and are good specimens of early bottle manufacture. It is said that "Turlington's Balsam" had been carried by soldiers in the Revolution.

"Warner's Safe Kidney & Liver
Cure," Rochester, N.Y., amber,
9½" high **300.00**

Angier Petroleum Emulsion **12.00**
Brandt's Indian Pulmonary Balsam . **20.00**
Baker's Specific, "clear, impressed
  on glass, full length figure of Un-
  cle Sam, one foot on box marked
  "Bakers," looking at bottle in his
  hand, and "R. Hurd, Prop., N.
  Brunswick, Maine" **25.00**
Barker's Poison Panacea **20.00**

Bateman's Drops	7.50
Buckout Dutch Liniment	7.50
Carter's Spanish Mixture	7.50
Cole's Cough Balsam	15.00
Chamberlain's Cough Remedy	7.50
"Cinot, The Herbal Tonic, Prepared for Stomach, Kidney, Bowels, and Rheumatism," T. G. Walton Co., Bridgeport, Conn., clear, 8½", 4 leaf clover impressed on bottle	25.00
Osgood's India Cholagogue	50.00
Clickmer's Purgative Pills	15.00
Cherokee Liniment, (bottle made in South Jersey)	50.00
Daniel's Triple Homallis	12.00
Dalley's Magic Pain Extract	20.00
Drake's Croup Remedy	7.50
Elderkin's Egyptian Balsam	8.00
Fahrney's Reliable Old Time Preparation	20.00
Fenner's Kidney and Backache Cure	8.00
Fellow's Syrup of Hypophos, aqua	7.50
Forni's Alpenkrauter Blubelader	20.00
Flander's Grecian Oil and Drops, (bottle made in South Jersey)	50.00
Guysott's Yellow Dock and Sarsaparilla	35.00
Hoofland's German Tonic	10.00
Heine's Golden Specific	7.50
Hobo Medicine	12.00
Haine's Arabian Milk Cure	15.00
Haarlem Oil	15.00
Jordon's Cholera Remedy	20.00
St. Jacob's Oil, aqua	7.50
Kilmer's Female Remedy	20.00
Mile's Restorative Nervine	7.50
Modac Indian Oil	20.00
McMinn's Elixir of Opium	30.00
Moxie Nerve Food	12.50
Opodeldoc, (bottle made in South Jersey)	50.00
Phillip's Emulsion Cod Liver Oil, N.Y., dark amber	11.50
Paul's Russian Oil, (bottle made in South Jersey)	50.00
Porter's Pain King, aqua	6.00
Sanitol, embossed on one side, other side "For the Teeth," white milk glass 5"	8.00
Schenk's Pulmonic Syrup, cylindrical, aqua	7.50
Swain's Panacea, aqua	7.50
Schoop's Family Medicine, cylindrical, aqua	7.50
Turlington's Balsam, (bottle made in South Jersey)	50.00
Wood's Elixir	25.00

MINERAL WATER BOTTLES

Mineral water is the natural spring water found beneath the earth's surface. In the 1850's to 1900's, health conscious people favored this water for drinking. Many resorts were built around a natural spring. Several establishments had special bottles produced to ship and store their mineral water.

Superior Mineral Water, Twitchel, Phila., 7⅛", graphite bottle 35.00

Buffalo Lithia, embossed, ½ gal.	20.00
Buffalo Lithia, paper label, aqua, ½ gal.	10.00
Clark and White, olive green, pint	30.00
Congress and Empire Spring Co., olive green, quart	30.00
Empire Spring Co., E. Saratoga, N.Y., dark green, quart	30.00
Hathorn Spring, Saratoga, N.Y., blue-green, pint	28.50
Middletown Springs, amber, quart	35.00
Oak Orchard Acid Springs, H. W. Bostwick, teal green, quart	45.00
Saratoga Red Spring, dark green, quart	40.00
Veronica, California, amber, quart.	10.00
Watchung Spring, N.Y., green, quart	20.00

NURSING BOTTLES

Early nursing bottles were of the blown-type. They were first used in the mid-19th century. Increased popularity and demand necessitated improved design and production — machine made, embossed, graduated and disposable.

prevent accidental intake or misuse of their poisonous substances, especially in the dark of the night. Poison bottles were generally made of colored glass, embossed with the word "POISON," a skull and crossbones, ribbed, ghastly-shaped, anything to call attention to their deadly contents.

Blown, 8¾", without glass nipple 250.00

"Not To Be Taken," green, 4⅛" high, Embossed "Cash/Boots/Chemist" around bottom 10.00

"Acme Nursing Bottle," 6½", with monogram and star, W.T. & Co., (Whitall, Tatum Co., Millville, N. J.)	100.00
"Normandie Nursing Bottle," clear, flat oval, raised neck, early nurser	50.00
"Sunny Babe," 4 oz., full length figure of baby on his tummy, embossed	10.00
"Empire Nursing Bottle," 6½", bent neck	45.00
"Handy Nurser," 8", (Pat'd. Feb. 24, 1891)	50.00
"Three Star Nurser," 6½", (Pat'd. June 19, 1894)	45.00
Shoe-shaped nurser, 6½", bent neck	95.00

POISON BOTTLES

Poison bottles were designed to warn and

Coffin-shaped, 5", amber	95.00
Poison, embossed	
Diamond shaped, amber, 3⅝" . . .	10.00
Lattice, green, 11½"	50.00
Flask-type, 8½", cobalt blue, heavily ribbed	50.00
Deep blue, covered with sharp diamond-shaped points, tastefully arranged, Whitall Tatum Co., c. 1896	40.00
Skull and crossbones, 8", clear, Germany	20.00
Skull and crossbones, 3¼", light amber, "Tincture of Iodine"	10.00

SARSAPARILLA AND SODA BOTTLES

Sarsaparilla was a soft, sweet drink, made from natural roots of plants for flavoring. It was the fore-runner of the currently popular soda or "cola" drinks. Early bottles for carbonated drinks dated from approximately 1840; the first were, no doubt, stoneware. Glass bottles date from about 1850. A group of them may all look the same, but all are different, being made by many companies. Closures were of different types, some had glass marbles in sliding grooves as stoppers. Others had pull-out sealers with hooks that were pushed in to open. They must be studied closely to mark their differences.

Ayer's Compound Extract, pint	7.50
Babcock's	50.00
Beard, Luke, Boston, green, pontil .	50.00
Bristol's, quart, aqua	25.00
Brown, H. L. and J. W., Conn. blob top, dark green	75.00
Brown's Jamaica Ginger, 9", aqua .	12.50
Canada Dry Ginger Ale, carnival glass	10.00
Coca-Cola, See Coca-Cola items	
Dr. Green's, pint, aqua	18.50
Dr. Larahah's	15.00
Dr. Pepper	
Baylor Bears	8.50
Embossed	3.50
Fat Stack Show	7.50
Miami Dolphins	15.00
Texas versus Oklahoma	7.50
Foley's Sarsaparilla	15.00
Grapette, painted	3.00
Hood's	25.00
Jay's	25.00
Kuck, Henry, green, c. 1898	25.00
Moxie	
Embossed, pat'd stopper	20.00
Labeled	15.00
Nehi Lemon	2.50
Nugrape	2.50
Orange Crush, embossed	7.50
Pepsi Cola	
Amber, 16 oz., embossed	6.50
Cincinatti Reds, World Champs . .	7.50
Dallas Cowboys	8.50
#1, Mountain State, W. Va.	7.50
State Bicentennial, ea	7.50
Perkiomenville Brewery, Green Lane, Pa., clear, metal stopper, (bottled beer and soda)	25.00
Ranier Soda and Bottling Works, Seattle, stoppered	22.50
Royal Crown	
12 oz.	3.50
Governor Cup #1 and #2, ea . .	5.00
Kentucky Derby	10.00
Pittsburgh World Champs	

Empty	7.50
Full	10.00
Raft Race, Michigan	3.50
Schlieper, C. W., St. Louis, Mo. pontil	20.00
Seven-Up	
Cincinatti Bengals	5.00
Cleveland Browns	5.00
Farm Fest, Minn.	5.00
Indiana University, 1976	5.00
Ohio State Buckeyes	5.00
Oklahoma Sooners, 1976	5.00
U.C.L.A.	
Soda and Mineral Co., Warren, Pa. .	15.00
Standard Bottling Co., Boston, Mass., leather top, spring cap, imprint of 10-star flag on side, aqua	50.00
Witner and Helt, squat, Lykens, Pa., teal blue	45.00

SCENT BOTTLES

Some of the scent bottles listed are early American pressed glass, made prior to 1850, mainly originating in New England. Later it became fashionable to have small, rather fancy bottles of scent, or smelling salts to carry in women's purses, if a sudden fainting spell, or "the vapors" overcame them. These bottles, also called vinaigrettes, are prized collector's items when found today.

Fiery Opalescent, white Gothic shape, paneled 75.00

Crystal, 2½", all-over finecut, ground stopper, cut star top	25.00
Cut to clear blue, 3", double cut overlay, gourd shaped	125.00
Cylindrical, 3½", milk glass, silver top, (vinaigrette)	30.00
Fiery opalescent, with brown slag, tin top	110.00
Opaque opalescent, 2⅝", original pewter screw top, rosetted molding around lower edge, embossed eagle on top, Boston and Sandwich	150.00
Seahorse form, clear with white stripes	95.00
Shoe shape, neck of bottle at toe, marked on base, B&L	30.00
Slag, dark blue, eagle top	110.00
Smelling salts, or (vinaigrette) 3½", emerald, ribbed and fluted, matching stopper	35.00
Stiegel-type, cobalt blue, ribbed, c. 1765	225.00
Long bottle, (vinaigrette), 5½", emerald green, ribbed, with ground stopper, pointed end, to fit in handbag	30.00
Violin, amber, pewter top	125.00
Violine, powder blue, pewter top . . .	175.00

SNUFF

Tobacco usage spread from America to Europe to China during the 17th century. Europeans and Chinese preferred to grind the dried leaves into a powder and sniff it into their nostrils. The elegant Europeans carried their snuff in boxes and took a pinch with their finger tips. The Chinese upperclass, because of their lengthy fingernails, found this inconvenient and devised a bottle with a fitted stopper and attached spoon.

In the Chinese manner, these utilitarian objects soon became objects d'art. Snuff bottles were fashioned from precious and semi-precious stones, glass, porcelain and pottery, wood, metals, and ivory. Glass and transparent stone bottles often were enhanced further with delicate hand paintings, some done in the interior of the bottle.

Collecting snuff bottles has enabled collectors to explore the varieties of Chinese art without large capital expenditures or consuming a large amount of space.

Snuff bottles of superior quality still are being made today and command relatively high prices.

Agate, applied ivory paint with mother of pearl	250.00
Agate, translucent blue gray, polished	140.00

Snuff Jar, Bennington Pottery, c. 1850 . . . . $375.00

Amber	
Carved	90.00
Smooth finish, early 19th century	200.00
Amethyst, 2", carved	175.00
Beetlenut, carved, bird and flower motif	125.00
Chalcidony, carved, tapered	350.00
Cinnabar, red with white jade top . .	250.00
Cinnabar, 3½", red with persimmon decor, late 19th century	100.00
Cloisonne	
Autumn foliage on blue ground, stopper	200.00
Dragons, 2½"	225.00
Mongolian, 2¾", marked "China"	175.00
Coral, oviform, carved	275.00
Crystal, carved monkey, tiger eye stopper	225.00
Famille Rose, 19th century	300.00
Hornbill, 2½", carved, 19th century	650.00
Ivory	
Figures and flowers, 2½", rings on each side	125.00
Shape of man's head, 2½"	175.00
Jade	
2", white, teakwood stand	350.00
2½", carved landscape, mottled brown, seal button, 19th century	500.00
3", pebble shaped, coral stopper, wooden spoon	300.00
Lapis Lazuli	
Carved	275.00
Oviform, flattened	200.00
Malachite	
2¼", carved Bonsai tree	275.00
2½", carved bird	300.00

Mother of Pearl	
Carved	150.00
Oviform, scenic	95.00
Opal, carved	395.00

Painted Interiors
3¾″, birds and flowers, unsigned, 19th century	400.00
3¾″, landscape, artist signed, c. 1895	650.00

Peking
2½″, bird and flowers, red on white	300.00
3″, carved with flora and fauna, black and white to deep red, 19th century	500.00

Porcelain
3½″, white ground with green and copper red	175.00
Two Poems, blue, gray, and red underglaze	400.00
Blue and white, vase shaped, teakwood stand	275.00
Dragons, yellow ground, c. 1850 .	350.00

Rose Quartz, 3½″, carved mother and child	800.00
Turquoise, 2½″, carved Chinese decor	350.00
Wood, black lacquered, Mother of Pearl inlay	50.00

WHISKEY

EARLY

The earliest whiskey bottles made in America were blown by pioneer glass makers in the 18th century. The Biningers (1820–1880's) were the first bottles specifically designed for whiskey. After the 1860's, distillers favored the cylindrical 'fifth' form.

The first embossed brand name bottle was the amber E. G. Booz Old Cabin Whiskey bottle which was issued in 1860. Many stories have been told about this classic bottle; unfortunately, most are not true. Research has proved that "booze" was a corruption of the words "bouse" and "boozy" from the 16th and 17th centuries. It was only a coincidence that the Philadelphia distributor also was named Booz. This bottle has been reproduced extensively.

Prohibition (1920–1933) brought the legal whiskey industry to a stand still. Whiskey was marked "medicinal purposes only" and distributed by private distillers in unmarked or paper label bottles.

The size and shape of whiskey bottles is standard. Colors are limited to amber, amethyst, clear, green, and cobalt blue (rare). Corks were the common closure in the early period, with the inside screw top being used in the 1890–1910 period.

Bottles made prior to 1880 are the most desirable. In purchasing a bottle with a label, condition is a critical factor. In the 1950's, distillers began to issue collectors' bottles to help increase sales.

Currently the bottle market, both in early whiskey and collectors' bottles, is down with the exception of the true rarities.

"Warrented Flask," amber, molded 6⅜″ h., c. 1891–1900 . . . . $5.00

Bininger & Co., A. M., Old Kentucky Bourbon, 9½″, amber, New York	125.00
Bininger & Co., A. M., Traveler, ½ pint flask, honey amber	160.00
Caspers Whiskey, quart, cobalt blue	225.00
Cedarhurst, ½ pint, amber	7.00
Cheatham & Kinney, Chestnut Bottle, 4″, amber, machine made . . .	10.00
Dallemand & Co., 2¾″, amber, Chicago	8.00
Duffy Malt, quart, amber, Baltimore, machine made	4.00
Fitzgerald, John F., quart, amethyst	10.50
Golden Wedding, fifth, carnival glass, label	12.00
Hall, Luhrs & Co., 6¾″, amethyst, Sacramento	15.00
Hollywood, 12″, amber	15.00
Jesse Moore-Hunt Co., 11¾″, amber, San Francisco	9.00
Lone Creek, quart, amber, Kentucky	12.50
Mount Vernon Pure Rye Whiskey, 4¼″, amber, patented 1890	17.50
Old Kentucky, Taylor Bland, quart, clear	10.00

Old Time, 9½″, clear, first prize	
1893 World's Fair	**12.50**
Paul Jones, quart, amber, label	**17.50**
Roth & Co., quart, amber, San	
Francisco	**20.00**
Taylor & Williams, 3¼″, amethyst	**4.00**
Vinol, violin, 8½″, amber, label	**17.50**
Wharton, ½ pint, clear, label	**3.00**

Barsottini

Antique Carriage	**10.00**
Antique Automobile, Open Car	**6.00**
Colosseum, Roman	**12.00**
Eiffel Tower	**10.00**
Floretine Steeple	**12.00**
Fruit Basket	**10.00**
Love Birds	**18.00**
Monk With Wine Glass	**15.00**
Santa Claus With Bag of Toys	**18.00**

BEAM, JIM

Jacob Beam established the Beam Distillery in Kentucky in 1788. About 1880, Colonel James "Jim" Beam, whose name the distillery adopted, began to work making bourbon.

The company began the novelty bottle business in 1953 for the Christmas trade. It was an immediate success. The Executive Series, decorated with 22 Karat gold, was first issued in 1955 to celebrate the 160th anniversary of the company. Other series followed; Beam also issued many customer specials. As a result, the number of bottles available now is approaching 450.

**Jim Beam, States Series,
Michigan $12.00**

Centennial Series, First Issue, 1960

1960, Santa Fe	**175.00**
1960, Civil War, South	**40.00**
1966, Alaska Purchase	**40.00**
1968, Laramie	**6.00**
1968, San Diego	**5.50**
1969, Lombardi Lilac	**7.00**

1970, Preakness	**5.00**
1971, Great Chicago Fire	**20.00**
1972, Colorado Springs	**6.50**
1973, Reidsville	**8.00**
1973, Phi Sigma Kappa	**7.50**
1976, Washington, Bicentennial	

Executive Series, First Issue, 1955

1955, Black Porcelain	**350.00**
1957, Royal DiMonte	**65.00**
1959, Tavern Scene	**55.00**
1961, Chalice, God	**60.00**
1963, Royal Rose	**35.00**
1965, Marbled Fantasy	**50.00**
1967, Prestige	**15.00**
1969, Sovereign	**7.50**
1971, Fantasia	**12.50**
1973, Phoenician	**10.00**
1975, Reflections	**15.00**
1977, Golden Jubilee	**17.50**
1979, Mother of Pearl	**20.00**

Glass Specialities, First Issue, 1953

1953, Cocktail Shaker	**5.00**
1955, Ducks & Geese	**6.00**
1957, Royal Opal	**8.50**
1962, Cleopatra, yellow	**7.50**
1963, Delft Rose	**6.00**
1963, Dancing Scot, tall	**8.00**
1965, Cameo Blue	**5.00**
1967, Pressed Crystal Ruby	**12.00**
1969, Pressed Crystal Opaline	**6.50**
1972, Crystal Marbleized	**5.00**
1973, Sapphire	**6.50**
1975, Sunburst(s), amaritto, azur-glo, multi-glo, & smoke glo	**4.50**

Regal China Series, First Issue, 1955

1955, Ivory Ashtray	**15.00**
1962, Seattle World's Fair	**25.00**
1966, Turquoise Jug	**6.50**
1968, Antique Trader	**7.00**
1970, Bell Ringer, Plaid #1	**8.00**
1970, London Bridge	**6.50**
1971, New Hampshire Eagle	**25.00**
1974, Hawaii Aloha	**7.50**
1975, Bonded, Silver	**5.00**

State Series, First Issue, 1958

1958, Alaska	**70.00**
1959, Colorado	**30.00**
1960, Kansas	**55.00**
1963, Montana	**75.00**
1963, New Jersey, yellow	**42.50**
1964, North Dakota	**80.00**
1966, Ohio	**15.00**
1967, Kentucky, White	**17.50**
1967, New Hampshire	**12.50**
1968, Arizona	**7.50**
1968, Illinois	**10.00**
1970, South Carolina	**7.50**
1972, Delaware	**8.00**
1975, Washington	**10.00**

Trophy Series, First Issue, 1957

1957, Duck	**35.00**
1959, Dog	**47.50**

1961 thru 1968, Horse(s), each ..	**12.50**
1965, Fox	**27.50**
1967, Cat(s), each	**12.50**
1968, Cardinal, male	**40.00**
1970, Poodle, Gray	**5.00**
1971, Texas Rabbit	**7.50**
1976, Great Dane	**8.00**

Non-Series Bottles

AHEPA 50th Anniversary	**9.00**
Antioch	**7.00**
Black Katz	**8.00**
Bob Hope, 15th Desert Classic, 1974	**12.50**
Broadmoor Hotel	**6.00**
Cable Car	**6.00**
Churchill Downs, Pink Roses	**5.00**
Conventions	
First, Denver	**15.00**
Third, Detroit	**22.50**
Fifth, Sacramento	**17.50**
Seventh, Louisville	**17.50**
Ninth, Houston	**20.00**
Donkey, Campaigner, 1960	**17.50**
Donkey, Clown, 1968	**7.50**
Elephant, Campaigner, 1960	**17.50**
Elephant, Clown, 1968	**7.50**
Emmett Kelly	**12.50**
Fiesta Bowl	**15.00**
First National Bank of Chicago ..	**(Rare)**
Foremost, 1956, black and gold ..	**85.00**
Foremost, 1956, gray and gold ..	**90.00**
Germany, Weisbaden	**7.50**
Golden Gate Las Vegas, 1969 ...	**55.00**
Green China Jug	**6.50**
Grey Slot Machine	**7.00**
Hannah Dustin	**15.00**
Harold's Club, Man in a Barrel, 1957	**300.00**
Harold's Club, Nevada, Silver ...	**125.00**
Harold's Club, VIP, 1967	**47.50**
Harold's Club, VIP, 1969	**80.00**
Harold's Club, VIP, 1971	**60.00**
Harold's Club, VIP, 1975	**20.00**
Hawaiian Open, 1973	**7.50**
Hemisphere	**11.00**
Jackalope	**12.00**
Kaiser International Open, 1971 .	**5.00**
Las Vegas	**7.00**
Mark Anthony	**15.00**
Nebraska Football	**12.00**
Pearl Harbor Memorial, 1972	**17.50**
Ponderosa Ranch	**10.00**
Pony Express	**8.50**
Prima Donna	**6.00**
Redwood	**4.50**
Ruidoso Downs, 1968, pointed ears	**12.50**
Shriners	
El Kahir Temple	**15.00**
Moila with Camel	**15.00**
Rajah Temple	**17.50**
Submarine Redfin	**12.50**

Thailand	**5.00**
Twin Bridges	**37.50**
V. F. W.	**14.00**
Yosemite	**10.00**
Zimmerman Blue Beauty	**12.50**
Zimmerman Peddler	**16.00**

BISCHOFF

African Head	**11.00**
Bell House	**27.50**
Canteen, floral	**12.50**
Cat, black	**10.00**
Chariot, urn	**17.50**
Clown, low/tall, each	**30.00**
Dog, alabaster	**12.00**
Duck	**20.00**
Fish, ashtray	**15.00**
Geese	**22.50**
Pirate	**12.50**
Spanish, boy/girl, each	**27.50**
Vase, black/gold, each	**27.50**
Watchtower	**10.00**

BOLS

Bols, Ballerina $15.00

Animals, miniatures, each	**8.00**
Crock(s), each	**10.00**
Dutch, boy/girl, each	**15.00**
Lobster Claw, miniature	**10.00**
Pitcher, Delft	**12.50**
Tea Pot, Delft	**12.50**

BROOKS, EZRA

Ezra Brooks, Ram $16.00

American Legion	20.00
American Legion, Illinois	15.00
American Legion, Texas	40.00
Arizona	10.00
Basketball Player	9.00
Big Bertha, Elephant	12.00
Birthday Cake, 100th Award	15.00
Brahama Bull	14.00
Bulldog	7.00
CB Convoy	10.00
Cable Car, set of 3	15.00
Cheyenne	10.00
Cigar Store Indian	10.00
Club Bottle(s), each	10.00
Conquistador's Drum & Bugle	11.00
Dead Wagon	7.50
Elk	17.50
Flintlock Pistol, Heritage	10.00
Florida Gators, three variations, each	17.50
Fresno Grape, with gold	42.50
Go Big Red, football	20.00
Go Big Red, rooter	10.00
Gold Prospector	10.00
Golden Rooster	27.50
Hambletonian	8.00
Hereford	10.00
Idaho, Skier on Potato	12.50
Indianapolis 500	20.00
Jack of Diamonds	9.00
Kachina Doll #1	140.00
Kachina Doll(s), #3 to #7, each	20.00
King of Clubs	6.50
Liberty Bell	10.00

Maine Lobster	17.50
Missouri Mule	12.50
Mr. Foremost	14.00
New Hampshire State House	7.50
Oil Gusher	10.00
Panda	12.50
Penny Farthington High-Wheeler	10.00
Pirate	8.00
Queen of Hearts	7.50
Razorback Hog	10.00
Sailfish	12.50
Sea Captain	12.00
Silver Dollar, black/white base, each	6.00
Silver Spur	15.00
Slot Machine	12.00
Sprint Car	15.00
Telephone	12.00
Texas Longhorn	10.00
Tonopah	16.00
Tractor	12.00
U.S.C. Trojans	12.50
Vermont Skier	15.00
West Virginia Mountaineer	90.00
Zimmerman's Hat	16.00

DANT, J. W.

J. W. Dant, Field Bird Series,"Mountain Quail" $8.00

Alamo	5.00
Atlantic City	5.00
Boeing 747	9.00
Burr & Hamilton Duel	7.00
Constitution	7.50

Field Birds, each 8.00
Indianapolis 500 . . . .   6.50
Patrick Henry 4.00
Pot Belly Stove 6.00
Washington Crossing Delaware . . .   5.50

DICKEL, GEO.

George Dickel, powder horn . . . $6.00

Golf Club 7.00
Golf Club, miniature 3.50
Powder Horn, miniature 3.50

DOUBLE SPRINGS

Bentley 22.00
Bicentennial States Series 12–16.00
   California (exception) 40.00
   Iowa (exception) 35.00
Bull, red 17.00
Cale Yarborough 14.00
Duesenburg, S. J. 20.00
Ford, 1910 . . . .   20.00
Golden Coyote 10.00
Matador 12.00
Mercer 20.00
Peasant Boy and Peasant Girl, each   7.00
Rolls Royce 30.00
Stutz Bearcat 27.50
Wild Catter 6.00

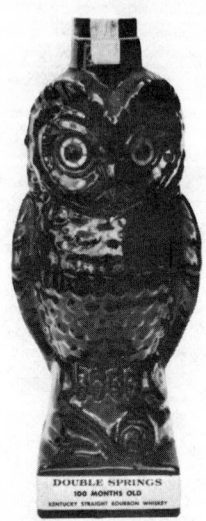

Double Springs, owl, brown . . . $10.00

GARNIER (FRANCE)

Garnier, trout, c. 1967 . . . . $15.95

Alladins Lamp	20.00	New York Policeman	13.00
Alfa Romeo, 1929	6.00	Paris Taxi	21.00
Aztec Vase	9.00	Scarecrow	11.00
Bacchus	12.50	Snail	25.00
Bedroom Candlestick	10.00	SS France, large	75.00
Bird Series, each	10–15.00	Teapot, 1961	10.00
Boquet	12.00	Watering Can	12.50
Canadian Mountie	11.00		
Cannon	30.00		
Cars, each	9.00		

GIN

Bininger DeWitt, ¾ quart, tapered square, olive green	500.00
Bininger, Old London Dock, No. 17, ¾ quart, yellow amber	60.00
Blown, 9″, olive amber, flared mouth	30.00
Burnett, Sir Robert, miniature, aqua case, applied seal, olive	55.00
Case., 10″, no label, deep olive	15.00
Gordon & Co.'s Dry Gin, bear head	10.00
Imperial Gin, H. S. & Co., I & W in base, case shape, amber	12.00
Morley's Buchlin, 12″ square	20.00
Tipstaff, Stephen, 9″, stoneware	100.00

Cat, gray	10.00
Chimney	15.00
Chinese Statuette, Man/Woman	12.50
Clock	15.00
Coffee Mill	22.50
Duckling	17.50
Eiffel Tower	15.00
Empire Vase	8.00
Giraffe	12.50
Harlequin With Mandolin	14.00
Horse Pistol	9.00
Indian	16.00
Locomotive	8.00
Montmartre Jug	12.50

GRENADIER

Gin Bottle, 7¾″, amber, 681 pressed in bottom, applied lip $25.00

Grenadier, (left) Baylor's 3rd Continental, 1969, American Revolution Series $25.00
(right) Eugene, Napolean Series, 1970 . . . . $24.00

Bicentennial Series, set of 12	**200.00**
Colonial Soldier Series	
Baylors 3rd	**30.00**
Connecticut Foot Guards	**25.00**
First Georgia	**15.00**
Second Maryland	**45.00**
General Series	
Custer, George	**20.00**
Lafayette	**25.00**
MacArthur, Douglass	**20.00**
Washington, George	**25.00**
Horse Series, each	**25.00**
Napoleon Series	
Eugene	**24.00**
Lassal	**30.00**
Napoleon	**65.00**
Pancho Villa with second figure, each	**25.00**
Pancho Villa, Historical, set of 6 . . .	**100.00**

HARPER, I. W.

I. W. Harper barrel and case, c. 1975, top of barrel comes off $15.00

Flag of Nations	**8.00**
Man, blue/gray, each	**5.00**
Roman Coins	**6.00**

HOFFMAN

Bicentennial Series, each	**25.00**
Decoy Ducks Series, each	**15.00**
Doggie Series, miniature, musical, each	**12.50**
Leprechaun Series, 6 per set, each .	**45.00**
Mr. Lucky Series, 6 per set, minia-	

Hoffman, Wildlife Series, Deer, musical $27.50

ture, each	**65.00**
Pistol Series, each	**22.50**
Race Car Series, each	**25.00**
Rodeo Series, each	**22.50**
Russell, C. M., Series, each	**17.50**
Wildlife Series, musical, each	**27.50**
Exceptions:	
Eagle, 1976	**65.00**
Eagle, 1977	**37.50**

HOUSE OF KOSHU

Angel With Book, 7 oz.	**5.00**
Boy, Naughty	**22.50**
Geisha Series, floral, each	**17.50**
Lantern, stone	**35.00**
Mask, Noh/Okame	**27.50**
Playboy	**12.50**

LIONSTONE

Al Unser #1	**17.50**
Annie Oakley	**25.00**
Bar Scene, #2, frame with nude . .	**650.00**
Baseball	**20.00**
Basketball	**17.50**
Betsy Ross	**20.00**
Blue Jay	**25.00**
Boxer (dog)	**12.50**
Buccaneer	**30.00**
Calamity Jane	**35.00**
Camp Follower	**17.50**
Chinese Laundryman	**15.00**
Cocker Spaniel	**12.00**
Cowgirl	**40.00**
Egg Merchant	**30.00**

Lionstone, Wild West Series, gold panner, 1969 . . . . $75.00

Fireman, #1, yellow hat	75.00
Fireman, #3, down pole	35.00
French Poodle	10.00
Gambel's Quail	17.50
George Washington	25.00
Golfer	27.50
Hockey Players	17.50
Indian Weaver	30.00
Johnny Lightning	37.50
Lonely Luck	40.00
Madame	60.00
Meadowlark	30.00
Molly Pitcher	32.50
Paul Revere	37.50
Proud Indian	15.00
Rain Maker	27.50
Riverboat Captain	20.00
Rose Parade	55.00
Sheepherder	60.00
Sod Buster	27.50
Stage Coach Driver	30.00
Tea Vendor, oriental	25.00
Trapper	32.50
Turbo Car, STP, red	20.00

LUXARDO (ITALY)

Ampulla	20.00
Apple Figural	12.50
Babylon	9.00
Bacchus	17.50
Bizantina	20.00
Buddha Goddess	20.00
Candlestick, alabaster	22.50
Cellini, 1968	15.00
Chess Horse, quartz	40.00
Cocktail Shaker	15.00
Curva Vaso	30.00
Diana	15.00
Dolphin	45.00
Duck	27.50
Egyptian	20.00
Euganean Bronze	27.50
Faenza	30.00
Fish, alabaster	25.00
Fish, ruby murano	35.00
Gambia	17.50
Gondola	20.00
Mayan	17.50
Opal Majolica	22.50
Pheasant, red and gold	40.00
Puppy, Cucciolo	32.50
Silver Blue Decanter	25.00
Sir Lancelot	20.00
Suden	17.50
Tower of Flowers	15.00

MCCORMICK

McCormick, Passenger Railroad Car, 1970 . . . . $75.00

Air Race, propeller	17.50
Austin, Stephen	30.00
Barrel, with stand	15.00
Bicentennial Series, each	30.00
Confederate Series, each	30.00
Confederate Series, miniature, each	15.00
Famous Americans Portrait Series, each	30.00
Football Mascot Series, each	15.00
Frontiersman Series, each	30.00
Gunfighter Series, each	22.50
Rogers, Will	32.50
Train Series, each	75.00

O.B.R. (OLD BLUE RIBBON)

O.B.R., Transportation Series, River Queen, 1968 . . . . $10.00

Fields, W. C., Top Hat	15.00
Football, NFL	15.00
Hockey Series, each	12.50
Transportation Series	
Balloon	10.00
Fifth Avenue Bus	15.00
Train	17.50
Wagon, covered	15.00

OLD FITZGERALD

Old Fitzgerald, Tournament Decanter, Wedgewood Green $7.00

America's Cup	27.50
Blarney Stone	17.50
Cabin Still	
Hillbilly, pint	40.00
Hillbilly, gallon	250.00
Candlelite, 1961	9.00
Executive	7.50
Gold Coaster	12.50
Golden Bough	5.00
Jewel	9.00
L. S. U.	20.00
Memphis Sesquicentennial	15.00
Old Cabin Still, 1958	12.50
Rip Van Winkle	32.50
Sons of Erin	12.50
Tree of Live	5.50
West Virginia Forest Festival	17.50

SKI COUNTRY

Ski Country, Barnum Festival Series, elephant, 1973 . . . . $48.00

Barnum, P. T.	48.00
Baby Snow Owl	40.00
Bonnie/Clyde, each	30.00
Canadian Goose	45.00
Dove	35.00
Ducks	
Bluetail	40.00
Red Head	42.50
Wood	90.00
Eagles	
Majestic, gallon	350.00

On Drum	75.00
Hawk Eagle	40.00
Horse, Palomino	40.00
Indian on Horse, #1 and #2, each	35.00
Mountain Goat	37.50
Peacock	50.00
Ringmaster	25.00
Skiers, blue	90.00
Skiers, miniature, each	15.00
Tom Thumb	25.00
Woodpecker, Ivory Bill	37.50

WHEATON-NULINE

In 1888, the Wheaton firm was organized and began producing hand blown and pressed glass bottles. As automation of the industry took hold, they added a line of molded containers for pharmaceutical and food suppliers as well as "antique" bottles for gift shops.

Wheaton-Nuline entered the field of limited edition collectors' bottles in 1975. The firm also produced the Holly City Bottles. In 1979, Wheaton-Nuline became Millville Art Glass.

Wheaton-Nuline, Christmas series, The Poinsetta Legend, green, 1974 . $10.00

Astronaut Series

Apollo 11	17.50
Apollo 13	10.00
Apollo 15	10.00
Apollo 17	12.50

Christmas Series

1971, green	10.00

1973	5.00
1975	7.50

Great Americans Series

Bogart, Humphrey, green	5.00
Franklin, Benjamin, aqua	10.00
Kennedy, Robert, green	7.00
Lee, Robert E., green	10.00
Revere, Paul, blue	7.00

Presidential Series

Washington, frosty mint	7.00
Lincoln, topaz	7.00
Eisenhower, green	7.00
Kennedy, blue	30.00
Saint Series, each	12.00
Sky Lab Series, each	6.00

WILD TURKEY

Wild Turkey #3, on wing $175.00

No. 1, male, 1971	300.00
No. 5, with flags	40.00
No. 7	20.00

BOTTLES, WHISKEY PITCHERS

Small water pitchers bearing the product's name were given as premiums to tavern keepers by whiskey salesman. These were placed on the bar for the convenience of the patron and also as an advertising media.

Ballentine	12.50
Bischoff	10.00
Black Velvet	12.50
Boodle Gin	22.50
Four Roses	7.50
Hennessey	10.00
Imperial	12.50
Kentucky Tavern	7.50

Hennessey pitcher, Captain Richard **$25.00**

Old Grandad	12.50
Teachers	10.00
W. C. Fields	20.00
Wild Turkey	25.00

WINE (ITALIAN)

Angel, ½ gallon	10.00
Baby Bottle, miniature	6.50
Bagpiper	7.50
Bird, Red	10.00
Cannon, Floretine	12.50
Cat, Black	8.00
Dog, Poddle, leather covered	20.00
Eiffel Tower	11.00
Harlequin	8.00
Lamp, Hurricane, round	5.00
Leaning Tower	10.00
Manger Scene	25.00
Penquin With Hat	7.50
Rooster, white, red specks	12.50
Santa Maria Ship	8.00
Turkey, ceramic	12.50
Vase, Artisca series, each	14.00

BRANDING IRONS

A branding iron is used to brand or mark animals for identification purposes. They were first used by early ranchers in the western part of the United States. Branding livestock still is being practiced today. The early hand forged irons are the most desirable.

Iron, 16½″ l. **$42.00**

Wrought Iron, initials, early	30–50.00
Wrought Iron, initials, late	15–30.00
Wrought Iron, symbol, early	45–75.00
Wrought Iron, symbol, late	25–35.00

BRASS

Brass is a durable, malleable and ductile metal alloy consisting mainly of copper and zinc. It was and continues to be used by many cultures to make a variety of utilitarian and decorative objects.

See also specific categories, e.g., BELLS, CANDLESTICKS, FIREPLACE EQUIPMENT, etc.

Anvil, 5″ long, 2¼″ high	25.00
Ashtrays	
5″, ball feet, foliage decor, "India"	7.50
Hunter's scene	35.00
Baby's Bed, brass, ornate, c. 1900	285.00
Bed Warmers	
Natural finish, long walnut handle, 18th century	225.00
Turned handle	250.00
9½″, including handle	75.00
46″, pine handle	250.00
Bird cages	
15″ high	65.00
Bird cage and stand, Hendryx	95.00
Bowls	
7¾″, Dragon decor, impressed, "Made in China"	50.00
12″, etched dragon design, teak-	

Vase, 8¾", 3 handles, triangle shape, flared $50.00

wood base and stand	85.00
14", hand hammered, early	150.00
Box, 2½ x 7 x 7", three compartments for stamps, marked "Austria"	37.50
Buckets	
10", dated 1866	100.00
11", iron bail, polished	95.00
13½", iron bail, "E. Miller and Co., Meriden, Conn."	125.00
18½", iron bail	200.00
Candelabras	
11", three branch	125.00
18", seven branch, arms turn separately	200.00
20", seven branch, adjustable ..	250.00
*Candleholder, chamber type, 4½", saucer	50.00
*Candle Snuffer, with scissors and tray	50.00
*Candlesticks	
7¾", heavy, "India," pair	20.00
8", Bradley and Hubbard	125.00
7¾", Victorian with push ups, pair	125.00

8", single, Colonial style, very heavy, marks on base	100.00
9", Beehive, burnished, push ups, pair	225.00
10", Facetted, push ups, English, pair	160.00
11½", push ups, "The 1901," pair	200.00
11½", "Queen of Diamonds," pair	225.00
Chafing Dish and tray, 2 quart	125.00
Chestnut Roasters	
20", English, 19th century	140.00
18", brass handles	125.00
Coffee Pot, 7¼", tankard shape ..	120.00
Cuspidors	
8½", granite liner	65.00
12"	85.00
Turtle shaped	100.00
Dipper, 6"	125.00
Door Latches	
Chippendale style, scrolled	80.00
Wallace Nutting	85.00
Easel, floor, 62", triangular shape, c. 1880	150.00
Ferner, three ball feet	65.00
Fireplace Items, See FIREPLACE EQUIPMENT	
Foot Warmer, oval shape	90.00
Forks	
18", Shakespeare on handle, English	45.00
20", owl on handle	40.00
Hand Warmer, 5 x 7", wood handle, French	50.00
Heel plates, Pennsylvania Dutch, heart cut outs, pair	50.00
Horns	
24", Canal polished and lacquered, horse bit	60.00
12", Butcher's	50.00
Horse Brasses	
American symbols	15.00
English Diamond Jubilee	40.00
Edward VIII	40.00
George V	45.00
Golden Jubilee	45.00
Ice Tongs	40.00
Jardinieres	
5 x 5", hand hammered	50.00
8", three ball feet, polished	75.00
10", stag head handle	150.00
Kettle, footed, 17", ball and claw feet, globular body, loop handles .	400.00
*Key, Large	7.50
*Ladles	
3½" bowl, 15" handle	35.00
5½" bowl, 14" iron handle, "F. B. Co., Canton, Ohio, Pat'd Jan. 20, '88"	50.00
Mortor and Pestle	
5¾", with cast dragon's head handles	100.00
4", signed	50.00

Mustache Curling Iron, alcohol burner, repousse decor on handle and stand 50.00

Pot, handled, 12″ dia., American $180.00

*Pans
9″, two open handles 65.00
18″, two handles 85.00
Paper Clips
Bird, "China" 20.00
Hand shaped 35.00
Plaques
22 x 24″, William Shakespeare, bust in high relief, inlaid ornamented ebony frame 100.00
24″, tavern scene in center, ornate border 125.00
Powder Horns, see POWDER FLASKS AND HORNS
Roasting Jack, iron wheel hooks, English 170.00
Scales, sand and gravel scale 25.00
Sconces, two candle sconce, King's Crown design, pair 250.00
Scoops
Candy, brass 25.00
3 x 5½″, 3″ handle 45.00
5¼ x 8¾″ 60.00
Skimmer, 7¾″ 65.00
Slide Bolt, embossed decor 25.00
Stove, hand warming, portable, charcoal burning 100.00
*Teakettles
Acorns and raised leaves decor, stand and burner 125.00
Dovetailed, early American 250.00
Gooseneck, button feet, wooden handle 75.00
Trays
6¼″, desk tray, Chinese figures on bridge, marked "China" 30.00
11¼″, etched decor, figures, foliage, "India" 20.00

14 x 21″, open handles 65.00
15″ diam. 50.00
*Umbrella Stand, lion ring handles . 75.00
Urns, 16″, ornate, pair 200.00
Whistle, steamboat, 10¼″ high 150.00

BREAD PLATES

From the mid 1880's, special serving plates were made for serving bread and rolls, and many were made in the different table sets in pattern glass. There were also special large plates made by certain glass companies to expand their lines, and these would honor heroes, special events, and historical events. There are 10″ plates in some patterns, designated as bread plates, but bear no mottoes which mark them as such. Plates were also made in porcelain, milk glass and silver, and were very popular on the Victorian dining table.

References: Alice Hulett Metz, "Much More Early American Pattern Glass," Bk.II; "Give Us This Day Our Daily Bread," (GUTDODB)

See also Pattern Glass Section for various patterns.

"Give us this day . . ." 7 x 10½″, rectangular, clear $30.00

Actress, scene from "Pinafore" . . . 55.00
American Eagle, 8½″, Centennial, sheaf of wheat handles,

(GUTDODB)	25.00
Bible	50.00
Clear Diagonal Band, says "Eureka" in commemmoration of Gold Rush	40.00
Clear Ribbon, (GUTDODB)	25.00
Cleveland, (Classic pattern)	165.00
Cupid and Venus, 10", round	32.00
Continental platter, clear	45.00
Dancing Bears, Teddy Roosevelt	125.00
Dewdrop in Points, 10" round, vine border	35.00
Egyptian	
Cleopatra	42.00
Salt Lake Temple, (rare)	250.00+
Elaine	65.00
Faith, Hope and Charity	65.00
Flower Pot	40.00
Frosted Stork, 9"	50.00
Garden of Eden, (Lotus), log handles, (GUTDODB)	50.00
Garfield, star border	50.00
Garfield Memorial, 11"	65.00
Gladstone	30.00
G.O.P. Commemorative	100.00
Grant, General, Patriot and Soldier	55.00
Thomas H. Hendricks, (Classic)	165.00
Heavy Panelled Finecut	16.50
Hidalgo, (Frosted Waffle), bread boat	45.00
Horseshoe, (Good Luck), horseshoe handles	55.00
In Remembrance	55.00
"It is Pleasant to Labor for Those We Love," grape center	42.00
Jewel Band or (Scalloped Tape) "Bread is the Staff of Life"	40.00
Jewel and Dewdrop, with colored jewels	55.00
*Last Supper	25.00
Liberty Bell	
Clear, no signers	75.00
Milk white, with signers	300.00+
McCormick Reaper, (Reaper tray), (MII 1462)	75.00
McKinley Campaign plate, star border, c. 1895	50.00
Minerva, traces of old gold paint	50.00
Mitchell, John	150.00
Nellie Bly	175.00
Niagara Falls, frosted and clear	125.00
Old Statehouse, Phila. Pa.	75.00
Peerless, handled	20.00
Pleat and Panel	30.00
Pope Leo XIII	25.00
Prescott, Stark, Warren, Putnam, 1776–1876	50.00
Railroad, Transcontinental	85.00
Rock of Ages, milk glass center	125.00
Star Rosetted, "A Good Mother Makes a Happy Home," (MII, 1206)	50.00
Sheraton	
Clear	13.50
Amber	27.50
Blue	32.00
Sheriden Memorial, (MII 1206)	50.00
U. S. Thumbprint, (Carolina), double handled, beaded edge	30.00
Warrior, (Classic)	150.00
Washington Centennial	
Carpenter's Hall	85.00
"First in War, First in Peace," Washington	125.00
Independence Hall	85.00
"Waste Not, Want Not," (Lattice pattern)	45.00
Wheat, Sheaf of, oval, hat-shaped, rolled edge, "GUTDODB" on edge	48.00
Plate, porcelain, with rolled edge, oval, hand painted roses and GUTDODB in gold, raised impressed sword, "Germany" on base, open handles	50.00

BRIDE'S BASKETS

The bride's basket derived its name because it was a popular wedding gift of the 1880–1910 era. The glass bowls, usually with a ruffled edge, were made by many American and European glass makers. . .from the finest art glass to the style of the day glass. The metal holders, most often silverplated, were fitted with a bail handle, thus, resembling a basket. Reproductions exist, especially the glass bowls.

Prices listed include accompanying silver plated holder unless otherwise noted.

Amber, ribbon edge, floral decor	130.00
Burmese bowl, signed Pairpoint frame	1500.00
Cased	
Apricot	150.00
Blue interior, white outside ruffled rim, enameled floral decor	205.00
Pink, enamel decor	260.00
Red to light pink inside, clear outside, clear crimped edge	375.00
Rose, enamel scroll decor, brass frame	195.00
Rose and ivory, crimped edge	165.00
Cranberry	
Hobnail	250.00
Undecorated	120.00
Hobnail, blue	240.00
Peachblow, New Martinsville	90.00
Rubina, Pointsetta	185.00
Satin Glass	
Blue, enamel floral decor	185.00
Pink, enamel floral decor	175.00
Vasa Murrhina, blue, silver mica	225.00

Pink cased bowl, silver-plated frame, blackberry decor, 11½″ dia. . $185.00

BRISTOL GLASS

Bristol glass was made in several glass-houses in Bristol, England, and in the U.S. in the 18th and 19th centuries. The name has become generic and to collectors it means glass of semi-opaque nature, usually decorated with enameling.

Biscuit Jars
  6½ x 4¾″, blue translucent, silverplated top, rim and handle, floral decor 100.00
  Blue, satin finish, blue and white, silver rim, handle and lid, floral decor 95.00
  Blue, Bird of Paradise and floral decor, silver top and base 120.00
  Turquoise, with white enameling, resilvered rim, bail handle 110.00
Bottles
  Cologne, stoppered, bulbous slender neck, gold designs on, pale green, pontil mark 75.00
  9½″, Dresser, blue and white, enameled florals and butterfly, pair 40.00
  7½″, covered, hand painted, white flowers on pink 45.00
  Set, gold decor on white, enamel design, pair 125.00
Bowl, Rose, egg shaped, pinch pleated expanded top, light to dark blue, white lining 50.00,
Cuspidor, Ladies′, 9½ x 4″, translu-

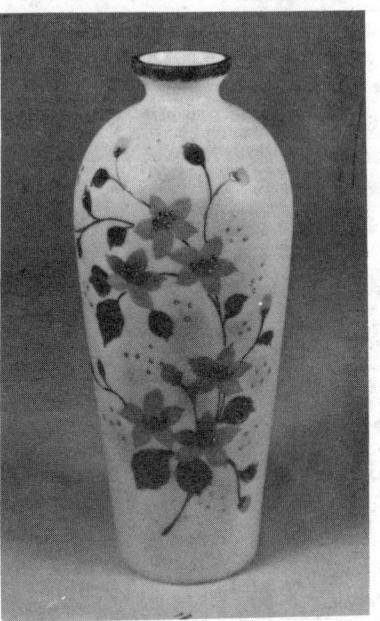

Vase, 8½″, cream with beige, splashes of turquoise flower, brownish green leaves and stems, raised enameled gold trim, c. 1880 . . .$65.00

  cent blue with folded rim 125.00
Easter Egg, 6½ x 4″, hand painted, blown, lavender and green floral, lettered "Easter" in gold 25.00
Mugs
  Hand painted, lettered "Remember Me" 40.00
  4″ blue, "Think of Me" 45.00
Pitcher, 7¾″, square top, shades of brown and orange 80.00
Powder Box, 7″, enameled flowers . 35.00
Rolling Pin, 14½″, early, blue 52.50
Salt Dip, 2⅝″, bucket-shaped, metal rim and handle, enameled storks and rushes, decor 35.00
Smoke Bell, plain white, ruffled edges 27.50
Tumbler, hand painted, roses and leaves, gold rim 30.00
Tobacco Jar, oyster white, autumn colored decor 70.00
Vases
  5½″, ruffled top, gold red, black

enameling, heraldic design	35.00
5½", ruffled overlay pink edge hand painted bird on branch	40.00
7", enameled florals on opaque blue-green	47.50
7", hand painted dark red roses on white	65.00
7" goblet form, hand painted decor on paque grey	82.50

BRONZE

Bronze is an alloy of copper, tin and traces of other metals. It has been used since Biblical times not only for art objects but also for utilitarian purposes.

After a slump in the Middle Ages, bronze was revived in the 17th, 18th, and 19th centuries. Today bronzes have become a highly sophisticated collectible in the antique trade. Prices have reached new heights.

Do not confuse a "bronzed" object with a true bronze. A bronzed object is usually made of white metal and then coated with a reddish-brown material to give it a bronze appearance. A signed bronze commands a higher price than an unsigned object. There are also "signed" reproductions on the market. It is terribly important to know your dealer, the history of the mold and the background of the foundry.

Bull with Piccolo Pete astride carrying basket $175.00

ANIMALS

Bear, 6¾", marble ball and base . .	400.00
Bear and bull fighting, 4½ x 9½", A. Phimistor, Proctor Gorham Co. . .	650.00
Bird, 5 x 7", Pautrot	600.00
Bird, partridge, 6½ x 7", Moigniez .	600.00
Bird, fish in mouth, 5 x 6½", DeLabrierre	600.00
Bisons Battling, 25", DeLabrierre . .	600.00
Bulls	
3½ x 5¼", Perrin	400.00
5½ x 7½", Bayre	800.00
13", Rosa Bonheur	650.00
Bull fighting dog, 4½ x 7½", DeLabrierre	500.00
Bull, signed Paul Hertzel	125.00
Camel, 9 x 10"	300.00
Chickens, seven, 6½ x 10", basket, Cain	650.00
Cow, 1½ x 3½", Bonheur	650.00
Dogs	
1½ x 3½", Tail in mouth, Savago, Gorham	400.00
5 x 8½", Moigniez	600.00
Greyhound, 8 x 11", Mene	550.00
Manchester, Mene	600.00
Pointer, 8 x 11½", Mene	700.00
Retriever, 14", Moigniez	600.00
Scottie, 5 x 7", E. B. Parsons . . .	550.00
Weiderkin, Dachshund, foundry mark, signed Jenson	425.00
Elephants	
5 x 7", Fratin	495.00
6½ x 8", Valton	700.00
18"	550.00
Kneeling temple elephants, Chinese, c. 1765	1850.00
Fox, 4½ x 5", peeking over a rock at rabbit, Masson	650.00
Goat, 6 x 10", Mene	600.00
Horse, 10 x 10½", with saddle, Geschuetzt Foundry	700.00
Jaguar, 7½ x 9½", A. L. Bayre . . .	900.00
Lion, 12 x 22", holding rabbit in jaws, DeLabrierre	1700.00
Lizard, Bayre	500.00
Pheasant, 7", Mene	595.00
Ram, 8 x 10", Lanceray	1550.00
Reindeer, 2 x 2"	200.00
Seal on Rocks, 5", E. Angela, Gorham and Co.	550.00
Stallion, 1 x 2"	100.00
Tiger and two cubs, 8½ x 14", Valton	850.00
Wolf, and Romulus and Remus . . .	275.00

BUSTS

Dante 3½", Marble plinth, c. 1880 .	175.00
Indian Head, 4 x 4", head dress, mouth open, Renevez	800.00
Joan of Arc, 18", Chapu	1400.00
Lincoln	
7", G. O. Bissell	500.00

11", L. Volk, Gorham	650.00
Man 10", marble column	275.00
Napoleon, larger than life size	275.00
Rafael, 3½", marble plinth, c. 1880	175.00
Tiziano, 3½", marble plinth, c. 1880	175.00

FIGURINES

Arab, Boy riding donkey	160.00
Arab Boy selling	160.00
Arab on camel 5 x 5"	235.00
Arab on carpet, 5 x 6"	235.00
Blacksmith, 20", Rere Gewso	1600.00
Boxer, 19¼", Greugante B. Boschetti	1950.00
Boy Fishing 17", Lavergue	900.00
Farmer, leaning against fence, Polychrome	225.00
Discus Thrower, 19½", Greugante B. Boschetti	1950.00
Girl, Nude, 9", Paul Herz	135.00
Knight, 11"	135.00
Lincoln, 8¼", Bissel	800.00
Napoleon, on horse	1000.00

Vase, 11¼", mottled green, sterling overlay, pat. Aug. 27, 1912 . . . $350.00

Shepherd, Lanceray	1950.00
Tutanckamon, The Boy Pharoah	375.00

MINIATURES

Antelope, 1¼", Tiffany Studios	150.00
Camel, 2½", Tiffany Studios	150.00
Cat, 3", arch back, Vienna	150.00
Kitten, with boot, 2½"	150.00
Seal, 3½", tree trunk, mouse crawling up with bird sitting on top of trunk, unsigned	65.00
Young Black Boy, lying prone and looking at kettle hanging from tripod, Vienna	220.00

MISCELLANEOUS

Ashtray, marble base, Gregoire	350.00
Bowl, 11¼", aqua marbled, grape handles, Soreneson	75.00
Door Knocker, eagle	125.00
Letter Opener, Art Nouveau	95.00
Planter, 6½", W. Henning	140.00
Salver, 5 x 13", footed, "John the Baptist," c. 1880, Emile Picault	950.00
Vases	
9", Clewell, green drip patina, signed, pair	300.00
10", Art Nouveau	250.00
13½", shape of tree trunk, nude women on side	1100.00

BUFFALO POTTERY

The Buffalo Pottery Co., Buffalo, N.Y., was founded in 1901 by John D. Larkin of the Larkin Co. (soap manufacturers) to produce pottery and ceramics for premium use and for general sale. From the beginning the company produced a superior semivitreous ware. Unfortunately, production records for all types of ware and processes used are scanty.

Some of the earliest wares were dinner sets used as premiums. An early pattern produced was "Blue Willow" in 1905, the first American production of that familiar pattern. Also produced at that time was "Gaudy Willow," a colorful version of "Blue Willow," the

series of Historical Plates, Commemorative and Advertising Pieces and Historical Jugs.

In 1908 the company introduced "Deldare Ware," probably its most highly prized line today. "Deldare Ware" has an olive-green body tone with vivid decorative scenes. Two of the decoration series most commonly found are "The Fallowfield Hunt" and "Ye Olden Times." In 1911 "Emerald Deldare" was introduced, with the most common decoration being the Dr. Syntax scenes (they also appeared on blue plates). Emerald ware was produced on Deldare blanks with the chief difference being the Art Nouveau border on the Emerald ware. In 1911 "Abino" Ware was introduced. This is usually rust and pale green in color with sailing and windmill scenes most often used.

In 1915 the company changed from production of semivitreous ware to a vitrified china and pieces were then stamped "Buffalo China." Some pieces were still made in the semivitreous ware and were stamped "Buffalo Pottery."

Commercial production ceased in World War I; after the war commercial, institutional and dinnerware lines were produced. In 1956 the firm's name was changed to Buffalo China, Inc.

Collectors consider pieces stamped "Buffalo Pottery" with an early date to be most desirable.

Jug, Mason, 8¼″ h., emerald green, signed, 1907 . . . . $300.00

Bowls
6″, Roosevelt Bears	120.00
7½″, Campbell Soup Kids	65.00
7½″, Tea Rose	9.00
Butter Pats, Willow, 8	65.00
Compote, Roycroft Inn	40.00
Cream and Sugar, Forget Me Not .	30.00

Cups and Saucers
Glendale	10.00
Kenmore	9.00
Game Set, Deer at Pond	225.00
Gravy Boat, Tea Rose	15.00

Jugs
New Bedford	250.00
Robin Hood	255.00
Rip Van Winkle	225.00
Luncheon Set, bluebird, service for 6	225.00

Pitchers
4½″, Bluebirds	40.00
6½″, Deer Hunt, 1907	225.00
6½″, Blue Geranium, bulbous, 1905	85.00
8″, Roosevelt Bears, 1907	395.00
9¼″, Blue Gloriana 1907	275.00
9¼″, Wild Ducks, green	55.00
12″, Flora	37.50
Buffalo Hunting Scene, green and white	250.00

Plates
7¼″, Gaudy Willow	45.00
7½″, Grant's Tomb	35.00
7½″, Niagara Falls	28.00
7½″, Trinity Church, N.Y.	53.00
9″, The Gunner	50.00
10″, Faneuill Hall, green and white	40.00
10″, Independence Hall, green and white	40.00
10″, Mount Vernon, green and white	40.00
10″, White House	40.00
1959, Christmas Plate	40.00
Platter, white, medium	20.00
Sugar Bowl, Gaudy Willow	30.00

Teapots
11″, old ivory, English scene . . .	85.00
Argyle, blue and white	115.00
Toddy Set, silver plate holder	75.00
Vegetables, covered, Wedding Band	40.00

DELDARE WARE

Bowls
6½″, "Ye Olden Days"	150.00
8″, nut, "Ye Lion Inn"	365.00
9″, "Fallowfield Hunt"	300.00
9″, "Fallowfield Hunt—the Death"	440.00
9″, "Village Scene"	300.00

Candlesticks
9½″, "Village Scenes," pair	565.00
Emerald, shieldback	490.00
Card Tray, "Dr. Syntax Robbed of His Property"	300.00
Cream and Sugar, "Scenes of Village Life"	365.00
Cups and Saucers, "Ye Olden Days"	150.00
Hair Receiver, "Ye Village Street" . .	250.00

Humidor, Tobacco
"At Ye Lion Inn"	665.00

Deldare, bowl, "Ye Village Tavern," 9"
dia. 3¾" h., 1908 ....$400.00

"There Was an Old Sailor"	850.00
Mugs	
"At the Three Pigeons"	240.00
"Breaking Cover"	225.00
"Ye Lion Inn"	275.00
Pitchers	
7", "Dr. Syntax Soliloquizing" ...	375.00
7", "Advise Me in a Whisper," P. Hall	325.00
7", "Breaking Cover"	350.00
8", "Demand the Annual Rent" ..	395.00
8", "Fallowfield Hunt — The Return"	400.00
8½", "Go Collect My Annual Rent"	440.00
9", octagon, "With a Cane Superior Air"	470.00
Plates	
6¼", "At Ye Lion Inn"	105.00
7", "Dr. Syntax Soliloquizing" ...	310.00
7", "Fallowfield Hunt — Breaking Cover"	275.00
7", "Fallowfield Hunt"	185.00
7", "Ye Village Street"	115.00
8⅜", "Ye Town Crier"	150.00
9¼", "Dr. Syntax Disputing Bill" .	275.00
9¼", "Fallowfield Hunt — the Start"	180.00
9¼", Emerald, "Introduction to Courtship"	300.00
10", "Breaking Cover"	190.00
10", "Ye Village Gossips"	200.00
12½", "Breakfast at the Three Pigeons"	375.00
14", "Ye Olde Lion Inn," signed .	450.00
Saucer, "Ye Olden Days"	95.00

Teapot, 5¾", "Village Life in Ye Olden Days"	320.00
Tile, "Breaking Cover"	195.00
Tray, 9¼ x 12¼", "Rural Sports" ..	780.00

BURMESE GLASS

Burmese glass is a translucent art glass originated by Frederick Shirley and manufactured by the Mt. Washington Glass Co., New Bedford, Mass., from 1885 to approximately 1891. Burmese glass shades from a soft lemon yellow to a salmon pink. Uranium was used to attain the yellow color and gold was added to the batch so that upon reheating one end turned pink. Upon reheating again the edges would revert to the yellow coloring. The blending of the colors was so gradual that it was difficult to determine where one color ended and the other began.

Although some of the glass has a surface that is glossy, most of it is acid finished. The majority of items were free blown but some were blown molded in a ribbed, hobnail or diamond quilted design. American-made Burmese is quite thin, fragile and brittle.

The only other factory licensed to make it was Thos. Webb & Sons in England. Out of deference to Queen Victoria, they named their wares "Queen's Burmese."

Reproductions abound in almost every form. Since uranium can no longer be used, some of the reproduction is easy to spot. In the 1950's Gunderson produced many pieces in imitation of Burmese. Since these pieces now have a collectible value they have been included in the listing.

Bon-Bon, ribbed, tricorn, acid finish	175.00
Bottle, Cologne, floral decor, pair ..	225.00
Bowls	
2¼ x 4", diamond quilted, pansy decor	210.00
2½ x 3½", signed Webb	250.00
2⅝ x 4", ruffled, glossy finish ...	235.00
5¼", tricorn, acid finish, Mt. Washington	295.00
2 bowls, acid finish, butterfly and floral decor, hallmark silver holder, signed "Webb"	1500.00
Condiment Set, 3 pieces, ribbed, glossy finish, Pairpoint holder ...	725.00
Cruet, melon ribbed, glossy finish, Mt. Washington	695.00
Cup, punch, applied, acid finish ...	375.00
Cup and Saucer, 3 applied feet and handle on cup, Mt. Washington with original label	650.00
Epergne, Fairy lamp, 8⅝ x 9¾", 3 shades on Clarke bases, 2 vases, acid finish	1650.00

Jack-in-Pulpit vase, 10¾" h. , New England Glass Co., glossy finish $950.00

Fairy Lamps. See Fairy Lamps.

Goblet, Gunderson 125.00

Jars
 Mustard, 4 ⁵/₁₆", vertical ribbed, silver plated, hinged top, handle and fittings 165.00
 Rose Petal, 4", floral decor, Mt. Washington 525.00

Lamps. See Lamps.

Pitchers
 3½", acid finish 435.00
 5¼", acid finish, crimped top ... 300.00
 5½", hobnail, acid finish 450.00
 Tankard, acid finish, applied glossy handle, hood verse Mt. Washington 1300.00

Rose Bowls
 Miniature, acid finish, floral decor 170.00
 2½", acid finish, 8 crimp top, Webb 220.00
 2½", floral decor 275.00

6 x 6", acid finish 250.00

Salt and Pepper Shakers, ribbed, acid finish, pair 550.00

Toothpicks
 Tricorn, diamond quilted, floral decor, Mt. Washington 275.00
 Tricorn, acid finish 200.00

Tumblers
 2", acid finish, folded top 300.00
 2½", acid finish, floral decor ... 250.00
 Lemonade, handled, glossy finish 150.00
 Glossy finish, Gunderson 115.00

Vases
 2¾", 6 sided top, floral decor ... 225.00
 3", oval, ruffled foot 375.00
 3½", columbine decor, signed Webb 485.00
 3¾", acid finish, brass tripod holder 525.00
 4½", pedestal, signed Webb ... 295.00
 5", lavender 5 petal floral decor, signed Webb 795.00
 5⅛", Gunderson 85.00
 6", lily, glossy finish 375.00
 7½", hobnail, 5 sided opening, Gunderson 115.00
 11½" stick, heavy floral decor, acid finish 600.00
 12", Egyptian style, acid finish ... 785.00

BUSTS

The portrait bust originated from pagan and Christian traditions. The first were mainly of Roman heroes. Later, images of Christian saints were made for reliquaries. It was not until the Renaissance that is was deemed proper that 'ordinary' man should be represented. Busts of notable persons were popular adornments in 18th and 19th century home libraries. Considering the number of library pieces produced, a collector can still find excellent examples at reasonable prices based on artist, subject and material.

By the very nature of their simplicity, busts can add a very spectacular image to the most modern setting. Also see "Bronzes" and "Parian."

Burns, Robert, 13", parian 195.00
Clytie, parian 125.00
Duke of Wellington, 6", wax, framed, green velvet background 95.00
Edward VII and Alexandra, 6½", parian on marble base, impressed "Prince and Princess of Wales," pair 250.00
Franklin, Ben, parian 185.00
Gladstone, 25½", terra cotta 150.00
Goethe, 22½", Philosopher, parian . 275.00
Judith, 7", bronze, Art Nouveau ... 125.00

George Washington, 8¼″ h., Stafford-shire $95.00

King George V, 7½″, clay, by L. Harradine, Doulton-Lambeth	150.00
Lady, 20½″, "Mitchell," c. 1856 . . .	300.00
Mozart, 6″, square pedestal, parian, Herco	35.00
Onenone, Crystal Palace Art Union, "Copeland"	495.00
Penn, William, parian	75.00
Queen Alexandra, 10½″, 1884, Crystal Palace Art Union, terra cotta, "Copeland"	550.00
Queen Victoria, 23″, "Copeland" . .	550.00
Rebecca at the Well, 16½″, bronze, "Villanis," French	650.00
Scott, Sir Walter, 6″, parian, Germany	35.00
Shakespeare, 6″, parian	50.00
Sumner, Charles, 12¾″, polychrome, Emblem of Boston Sculpture Co.	85.00
Washington, George, 7″, parian . . .	35.00
Washington, George, 8″, modeled by Enoch Wood, impressed "Washington" on base, c. 1800–1810	350.00

BUTTER PRINTS

Butter prints are made up of two categories —butter molds and butter stamps. Butter stamps are of one piece construction, sometimes two piece if the handle is from a separate piece of wood. Butter molds are generally of three piece construction: the design, the screw-in handle, and the case. Stamps decorate the top of butter after it is molded; molds both mold and stamp the butter at the same time.

The earliest prints were one piece and hand carved, often thick and deeply carved. Later prints were factory made with the design force into the wood by a metal die.

Some of the most common designs are sheaves of wheat, leaves, flowers, and pineapples. Animal designs and Germanic tulips are difficult to find. Rare prints include unusual shapes, such as half-rounded and lollipop, and those with designs on both sides.

Thistle, semi-circle, 3¼ x 7″ dia. $165.00

Cow	
Stamp, 4″ dia., one piece	185.00
Stamp, half round, 6¾″ long, shallow carving, applied handle . .	260.00
Eagle and Star, stamp, 4½″ dia., one piece, turned handle	250.00
Leaf	
Mold, 3¾″ dia., round case	40.00
Stamp, round, one piece, machine carved	35.00
Pineapple	
Mold, 3¼″ dia., round case	45.00
Stamp, 3½″ dia., one piece, turned handle	60.00
Stamp, half round, 7″ long, applied handle	300.00

Sheaf of Wheat

Mold, 3½″ dia., round case	45.00
Stamp, 4½″ dia., one piece, turned handle	65.00
Stamp, double image, 2½ x 4¾″, block	55.00
Stamp, half round, 7″ long, applied handle	275.00
Star Flower, stamp, lollipop form, deeply carved, one piece	525.00
Swan, mold, 3½″ dia., round case .	65.00
Tulip with Star and Leaves, stamp, 4¾″ dia., deeply carved, one piece, turned handle, PA	275.00

BUTTONS

The collecting of buttons is one of the most fascinating of hobbies, as there is a wealth of historical material in their development. Caspar Wister was making brass buttons in Philadelphia as early as 1750 and the Shaker colony at New Lebanon, N. Y. was making them in 1789. The most popular of the Victorian period were the story buttons. They were usually brass or gilt, and the subjects were from well-known stories, fairy tales, heroes, nursury rhymes, nature subjects and literary characters.

Also collectible are tole or painted tin buttons, which were done by the Pennsylvania Dutch. Most buttons found today are of the later two-piece variety of late 19th century.

The term "pearl," refers to the inside of fresh-water shells. In small towns along the Mississippi River, small industries turned out the fresh water pearl shell which was used in button manufacture.

References: Button Heritage, (BH); Button Classics, (BC); Button Sampler, (BS).

Museums: Cooper Union Museum for the Art of Decoration, New York, N. Y.

Victorian Jewel, 2 pc. brass, embossed edge with blue facetted stone in center, 1½″	2.50
Cut pewter, open work figure of gazelle leaping through foliage, self, shank, 1″	2.50
Embossed head of "Hercule," French, flat brass, wide steel rim, 1½″, (BC, p. 80)	5.00
Bandmaster or musician's uniform button, embossed lyre, 2 pc. brass, set of eight	3.00
(Diminutive), needlepoint covered, small rosebud, ⅜″	.50
"Chateau" center, heart and fleur de lys border, 2 pc. brass, 1¼″	2.50
"Cupid at Rest," wide steel rim, brass, 1½″, (BC, p. 93)	8.00

"Hector," pewter head, Roman gladiator, brass rim, (BC p. 31)	5.50
"Pierrot and Pierrette," pressed brass, steel half moon, brass inset figures, 1⅜″	5.00
"Boy at Window," 2 pc. brass, scarce, ⅜″	3.50
"Gardens at Karnak, Egypt," 2 pc. brass, 1″, (BC p. 93)	5.00
"Garden of Eden," or "Thehion and the Snake," from fable by La Fontaine, 2 pc. brass, 1⅜″, (BH) .	15.00
"Grapes and Leaves," black glass, brass shank, Pat'd date, 1899 . . .	1.50
Embossed leaves and grapes, brass background, steel bits, crimped steel edge, self shank, 1¼″	2.50
Pennsylvania Dutch, "tinsel type," spherical, brass shank, good green color	1.00
Liberty Bell, painted, cut-out plastic "Goofie"	.75
Painted porcelain, orange, strawberries, and apple, "Goofies," set of three	2.50
Pearl in brass filagree frame, 2 pc. brass, ¾″	2.00
Brass, with iridescent pearl and brass maple leaf inset, brass shank, 2½″	3.00
Iridescent pearl, grillwork center, plain edges, brass shank, 1¾″ . .	3.50
Victorian black glass, gold lustre, all-over-stippled flower, 1″	1.75
Large brass base, celluloid ovoid top with brass inset, c. 1890	2.00
Paperweight-type, "Millville Rose," brass shank, ½″	18.00
Porcelain, hand painted, rose garlands, artist signed, 1¼″	6.00
Carved ivory, square stylized bird, Japanese type, ¾″	7.50
Strawberries, filagree design, 2 pc. brass, 1″	2.00
Iridescent blue steel, inverted-bowl shaped, brass filagree with blue iridescent cut steel bits, c. 1890 . .	4.50

CALENDAR PLATES

Calendar plates were first made in England in the late 1880's. They became popular in the United States after 1900, their peak years being between 1909 and 1915. The majority of the advertising type were made of porcelain or pottery. Occasionally, some were made of glass or tin.

1907, 9¼″, Santa and holly	55.00
1907, tin, girl's head	45.00
1908, girl in old-time bathing suit . .	50.00

1908, 9″, advertising type, child's portrait $30.00

1909, 9″, pink rose center, "Compliments, C.C. Smith, Marshall, Michigan," calendar border 50.00
1909, painted roses and flowers in center, calendar border 40.00
1909, mountain scene in wreath of flowers 40.00
1909, painted fruit in center 30.00
1909, 9¼″, gold calendar in center with three roses and bud border . 30.00
1910, 8″, dog with calendar 25.00
1910, 9½″, Betsy Ross center 35.00
1910, holly with gold trim 35.00
1910, Niagara Falls, and horseshoe 35.00
1911, "Should Auld Acquaintance be Forgot" 40.00
1911, red roses and cupid border .. 35.00
1911, sailboat and harbor scene .. 30.00
1912, cherries and cherubs 35.00
1912, country farm scene 30.00
1912, 8″, airplane in center 40.00
1913, 8½″, house and rural scene, calendar border 35.00
1913, girl on rock, gazing at water . 30.00
1914, Betsy Ross center 35.00
1914, Washington's tomb
1915, Panama Canal, with flags, calendar border 45.00
1916, Indian in canoe 30.00
1916, calendar and birds in center, floral border 40.00
1918, calendar border, peaches in center 30.00
1918, two deer, trees, stream and birds 35.00

1919, calendar border, flags of France, Belgium, England, and U. S., large U. S. flag in center 50.00
1920, War and Peace flags 50.00
1921, flag in center, bluebirds and floral 35.00
1921, 9″, five flags of Allies in WW1, dove of peace, dated Nov. 11, 1918. .... 55.00
1923, 8½″, calendar with blue, yellow, red flowers at top, trees and stream in center 35.00
1928, roses, red, pink, and yellow, marked "Harker" 30.00
1929, Boy with dog, center 25.00

CALLING CARD CASES

During the Victorian era, leaving a personal calling card was the social custom. The engraved cards were carried in a proper case. Card cases were made of various materials— silver, gold, ivory, mother of pearl, etc.; many were handsomely monogrammed. This gracious custom passed into oblivion after World War I.

Silver with blue enamel, 3⅛ x 3⅞″, Art Deco style $225.00

Ivory, 2½″ x 4½″, carved flowers and vines 75.00
Lacquer, black 25.00
Mother of Pearl and tortoise, monogrammed 50.00
Mother of Pearl 50.00
Silver
  Chinese, applied dragon, signed . 100.00
  Coin 50.00
  English, 2¾″ x 4″, embossed scroll work 145.00
  Plated 35.00
  Sterling, embossed 65.00

Sterling, embossed, chain handle	75.00
Sterling, enameled	85.00
Tortoise Shell	
Monogrammed	65.00
With ivory separator, c. 1900	50.00

CAMBRIDGE GLASS

Cambridge Glass Co., Cambridge, Ohio, was incorporated in 1901. In the beginning their main line was clear tableware. Later they expanded into colored, etched and engraved glass. Over 40 different hues were produced in their fine blown and pressed glass. Five different marks were employed during the production years, but not every piece was signed.

The plant closed in 1954. Some of the molds were later sold to the Imperial Glass Co., Bellaire, Ohio.

Box, pink with dolphinfeet, 4¾ x 4" **$25.00**

Ashtray Set, 8 pieces, shell, original box and labels	75.00
Basket, 7", Georgian, amethyst	37.50
Berry Set, 7 pieces, Marjorie	60.00
Bowls	
7½", ebony	25.00
8¾", gold band, helio	55.00
10", Diane, crystal	35.00
10", Honeycomb, amethyst	38.00
10", jade	40.00
10", Crown Tuscan, flying lady decor	235.00
11¾", gold band, helio	65.00
12", Everglades, clear amber, dolphin footed	40.00
12", Diane, 4 footed	40.00
13", amber with swans	62.75
16", 10 panels, pink	65.00
Berry, Wheat and Sheaf	8.00

4"Farberware holder, cobalt	12.00
Console, Honeycomb, rubena	105.00
Butter, round, Near-cut	135.00
Candlelabras	
Alpine, 2-lite, keyhole stem, single	30.00
Carmen, 2-lite, Farberware, pair	55.00
Diane, crystal	35.00
Dolphin, green, pair	145.00
Candlesticks	
Calla Lily, emerald green, pair	40.00
Caprice with prisms, pair	50.00
Hexagon, jade with gold, pair	55.00
Vintage, etch, single	20.00
Castor Set, amber vinegar and oil jugs, 8" Farberware tray	18.50
Champagnes	
Caprice, crystal	20.00
Chantilly	15.00
Rosepoint	25.00
Cocktail, Crown Tuscan, nude stem	22.50
Cocktail Set, 12½" shaker, 6 green cordials in Farberware holders, Farberware tray	120.00
Cocktail Shakers	
Wildflower, etch	38.00
King Edward, cut crystal	45.00
Console Set, 12" bowl, 2 candlesticks, amber with heavy gold decor	125.00
Compotes	
5½", Crown Tuscan, nude stem, flat shell	135.00
6", Primrose, gold engraved trim	45.00
7½", jade	40.00
7½", Feather, footed, Near-cut	38.00
8½", Carmen, nude stem, crystal	95.00
Amber, nude, Farberware	40.00
Cordials	
Caprice, crystal	17.50
Rosepoint, crystal	38.00
Wildflower, crystal	20.00
Cream and Sugar	
Caprice, small	16.00
Rosepoint, gold decor	47.00
Cruet, Feather, crystal, Near-cut	68.00
Cups and Saucers	
Caprice, crystal	10.00
Ruby with luncheon plate, set	25.00
Cup, Colonial, Near-cut	4.50
Decanter, 5 cordials, amethyst, Farberware holders	60.00
Flower Figures (Frogs)	
9", Bashful Charlotte, amber	95.00
9", Heron, crystal	68.00
9½", Gull, crystal	50.00
9½", 2 Kids, crystal	65.00
11", September Morn, crystal	150.00
12¾", Draped Lady, crystal	135.00
13", Draped Lady, green	225.00
Goblets	
Apple Blossom, etch	12.00
Caprice, crystal	9.00

Chantilly	20.00
Georgian Peachblow	20.00
Martha Washington, heather	18.00
Rosepoint, crystal	27.50

Ice Buckets

Caprice, crystal, with tongs	32.50
Roselyn with tongs	38.00
Tally Ho	135.00
Ivy Ball, Rosepoint	45.00

Jars

64 oz., ball, amethyst, clear handle	28.00
80 oz., Doulton, Rosepoint, etch	250.00
Dessicator, 11½ x 10½", clear, original label	120.00
Mayonnaise Server, Chantilly, 3 piece, gold encrusted	45.00
Mug, Carmen, ruby, crystal handle	38.00
Nut Set, Crown Tuscan, 5-piece	125.00
Pepper Shaker, Wildflower	12.00
Pitcher, water, 6 tumblers, amber, Farberware, paper labels	85.00

Plates

7", amber, angel border	15.00
7½", Caprice, crystal	6.00
8¾", Cleo, pink	8.75
12", Rosepoint, cheese	27.50
12½", Rosepoint, handled	45.00
14", Sandwich	40.00
Punch Bowl and Stand, Feather, Near-cut	95.00

Relishes

7½", Rosepoint, gold	32.50
8½", Caprice, crystal, 3 part	13.00

Salt and Peppers

Amber, Farberware holders	15.00
Carmen, Farberware holders	45.00
Chantilly, etch, sterling base and tops	27.50
Gloria, topaz	75.00
Rosepoint, salt	18.00
Wildflower, salt	18.00
Sandwich Server, 10½", heliotrope, center loop handle	75.00
Shell Dish, 10", Crown Tuscan, 3 footed	65.00

Sherbets

Apple Blossom	8.00
Caprice, crystal	6.00
Rosepoint	20.00
Sugar, Everglades	15.00

Swans

3", crystal	12.50
3", light pink, signed	35.00
3¼", yellow	32.00
8", peachblow	22.50
8½", Mandarin gold, signed	85.00
Toothpick, Colonial	14.00

Tumblers

Caprice, crystal	20.00
Georgian, signed	25.00
Near-cut	18.00

Rosepoint	20.00

Vases

6", Rosepoint	27.50
6", Caprice, pink, blown	25.00
10", Crown Tuscan, cornucopia, sea shell base, pair	85.00
10", Horn of Plenty, mandarin gold, calla lily candlesticks, set	85.00
10", Keyhold, apple green	35.00
10", Portia	70.00
12", ebony, bird and floral etching	55.00

Wines

Amber, flared, Farberware holder	6.00
Caprice, blue	14.00
Rosepoint	30.00

CAMBRIDGE

CAMBRIDGE POTTERY

The Cambridge Art Pottery was incorporated in Ohio in 1900. Between 1901 and 1909, the firm produced the usual line of jarinieres, tankards, and vases with underglazed slip decorations and glazes similar to other Ohio potteries. Their line names included "Terrhea," "Oakwood," "Otoe" and others. In 1904, the company introduced Guernsey kitchenwares. It was so well received that it became the plant's primary product and in 1909 the name was changed to Guernsey Earthenware Com-

Vase, 6½", green, acorn mark .$60.00

pany. All wares were marked.

Bowls
8", berry motif, glossy brown
glaze 65.00
8", Terrhea, standard glaze 55.00
9½", floral slip decor, glossy
brown glaze 75.00
Candlesticks, 4" Terrhea, standard
glaze, pair 30.00
Cookie Jar, 14", high, brown glaze . 60.00
Tankard, 12", Oakwood 125.00
Vases
3½", bulbous, floral decor, stan-
dard glaze 65.00
8", berry motif, two-handled, artist
signed 175.00
8", Otoe 75.00
8", Terrhea 100.00
10", Acorn 85.00
10¾", cherry spray, high brown
glaze 125.00
11", floral slip decor, standard
glaze 95.00
11", Oakwood 100.00
13", bulbous base, slender neck,
artist signed 250.00

CAMEO GLASS

Cameo glass is a form of cased glass. A shell
of glass was prepared; then another layer or
more of glass of a different color(s) was
faced to the first. A design was then cut
through the outer layer(s) leaving the inner
layer(s) exposed.

This type of art glass originated in Alexan-
dria, Egypt, 100–200 A.D. The oldest and
most famous example of Cameo glass is the
Barberini or Portland vase which was found
near Rome in 1582. It contained the ashes of
Emperor Alexander Serverus who was assas-
sinated by his own soldiers in 235 A.D.

Emile Gallé, son of a French glassmaker, is
probably one of the best known artists of
Cameo glass. He established his factory at
Nancy, France in 1884. Although much of the
glass bears his signature, some he only
designed while his many assistants did the
actual work, even to signing his name. Glass
made after his death in 1904 has a star before the name Gallé. Other makers of Cameo
glass located in France included D'Argental,
Daum (Bros.) Nancy, LeGras and DeLatte
(1920's). The best known English maker was
Thomas Webb & Sons.

The majority of Cameo glass found on the
market today was made in the 1884–1900 period. It is being reproduced in limited quantities in France but is inferior in quality.

Bottle, cologne, pink with ornate sil-

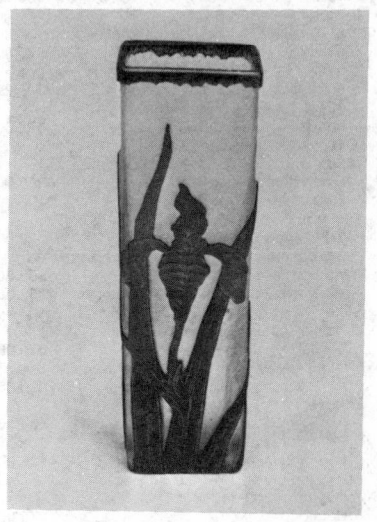

Vase, Daum Nancy, iris, rectangular,
7¼" $490.00

ver base, Daum Nancy 1700.00
Bottles, perfume
3", avocado with white florals,
Gallé 245.00
3¼", yellow with white florals,
hinged silver cap and stopper,
Webb 425.00
Bowls
4½ x 7", frosted yellow and white
with pink and red flowers and
leaves, Gallé 1500.00
8", butterflies, Gallé 525.00
9½ x 5", white and blue with flo-
rals and butterflies, silver rim and
feet, Webb 1485.00
Boxes
3" dia., tangerine, winter scene,
Daum Nancy 595.00
4½" dia., lavender to deep purple,
floral. DeLatte Nancy 574.00
scenic, Gallé 1295.00
Charger, 20", orange, stylized floral 875.00
Compote, Chardu 450.00
Cordial, 3", frosted with yellow flowers, cutback gold rim 195.00
Creamer, 3½", yellow, white floral
and butterfly, Webb 425.00
Decanter, 9½", frosted, purple vio-
lets and leaves, clear stopper, Val
St. Lambert 670.00
Dish, 6¾", leaf shape, frosted with

yellow daffodil, Gallé 300.00

Lamps

8½", night, black and dark pink, scenic 975.00

night, 2½" dome, burgundy butterflies, metal base, Gallé . . . 325.00

12¾", candle, blue with Venetian boat scene, Daum Nancy 375.00

14", base and shade, clear frosted with topaz, yellow, peach, green floral decor 5000.00

23", table, florals, Gallé 2100.00

Pitchers

2½", snow scene, Daum Nancy . 700.00

3", frosted pink with purple bleeding hearts, Gallé 850.00

Rose Bowl, 2¾", pink, white frosted 1850.00

Salts

Raisin color with white flowers, English 600.00

Oval, green with gold enamel decor 295.00

Tumblers

3½", snow scene, Daum Nancy . 500.00

3¾", brown glass, orange with tree landscape, Limaral 175.00

4", amethyst to clear, carnation design, orange peel surface, Degue 275.00

Vases

3½", gold, scenic, maroon and gold, D'Argental 550.00

4", orange ferns, Gallé 389.00

4", apricot with red cherries and leaves decor, sterling leafed collar and base 600.00

4½", lime green, scenic, Gallé . . 775.00

5¾ x 2¾" lavender, scenic, shades blue and coral, Muller Fres Luneville 650.00

5⅞", scenic, blue, green, white, DeVez 500.00

6", blue, scenic, sailboats, mountains, 4 colors, DeVez 695.00

6", white and red, florals in shades of red, Muller Croismare-Depot Nancy 950.00

7", white, scenic, light blue and royal blue, Gallé 1250.00

7", gold, roses and butterflies, white and red 3500.00

7¼", citron, florals, vines and leaves, Webb 1640.00

8", scenic, trees, mountains, dark brown, russet, amber 1185.00

8⅝", "L'Meteor Village," scenic, DeVez 1100.00

8¾", cylinder, redish-purple iridescence, raised enamel roses, Daum Nancy 525.00

9½ x 5½" citron, white leaves, berries 850.00

9½", blue-gray, pink and chartreuse, florals, outer layer polished, Gallé 1750.00

9¾", oak leaves and acorns, apricot, green and green-brown 1250.00

10", pink, dark blue florals, DeVeare 1150.00

10", white, floral and leaves design in shades of orange signed "CP" (Cristallerie de Pantin) 450.00

11", scenic, cut and enameled, Daum Nancy 1350.00

12", dark pink, thistle and blossom in white and shades of pink, C. Vessiere Nancy 1000.00

12½", orange-yellow, green leaves and vine, enameled red poppy, LeGras 650.00

13½", bun shaped base, straight neck, 3 colors, floral and leaf cutting 1600.00

14½", dragon fly and floral, F. Delatte 1700.00

16¼", pink, scenic, blue, yellow, DeVez 2250.00

18", yellow and green foliage, Gallé 1795.00

CAMERAS

Photographica, the collecting of cameras and related items, is still in its infancy. The current market in photographs as an art form has brought attention to the instruments and equipment used to make them.

Any camera older than twenty years is considered collectible. Among the makers, the most desirable are Leica and Zeiss. The two key elements are good exterior condition and good working condition. The original box does not add greatly to the value.

Tenax, focusing panel with pack adapter, 4½ x 6 cm., film pack, early 1900's $100.00

Ansco
Memo, f 6.3	60.00
Photo-Vanity	800.00
Anthony View Camera, 5 x 8"	150.00

Argus
A, f 4.5	20.00
K, f 4.5	175.00
Blair No. 7 Weno Hawk-Eye	45.00
Century Folding Plate Camera, 4 x 5"	65.00
Conley Folding Plate Camera, 5 x 7"	100.00
Daguerreotype, quarter-plate	5000.00

Eastman Kodak
Bantam Special, f 2, Compur-Rapid Shutter	115.00
Brownie, Box Camera, No. 2A	5.00
Bull's Eye No. 2	35.00
Cirkut, No. 10	1000.00
Folding Pocket Kodak, No. 4	60.00
Ordinary, Model C	900.00
Original, cyclindrical shutter	3500.00
Retina, IIIc, f 2	125.00
Stereo Brownie, No. 2	200.00
Vest Pocket Kodak	25.00
Ermanox, f 2, 4.5 x 6 cm	1200.00
Exakta VX, f 2.8	70.00
Expo Watch Camera	100.00
Forth Derby, f 3.5	40.00
Graflex Series B, 3¼ x 4¼"	80.00
Leica II(D), f 3.5	200.00
Minox III-S	60.00
Pearlette	40.00
Perfex 101	40.00
Petal, round	85.00
Pilot 6	60.00
Plaubel Makina II	175.00
Polaroid 95 (first model)	20.00
QRS Kamra	50.00
Robot I	100.00
Rolleiflex Standard	65.00

Rochester Optical
New Model Improved, 6½ x 8½"	150.00
The Premier	140.00
Seneca Chautauqua, 4 x 5"	45.00
Voigtlander Avus, 9 x 12 cm	50.00
Zeiss Contax I, f 2.8	400.00

CAMPAIGN ITEMS

Since 1800 the American presidency always has been a contest between two or more candidates. Initially, souvenirs were issued to celebrate victories. Items issued during a campaign to show support for a candidate were actively being distributed in the William Henry Harrison election of 1840.

Campaign items cover a wide variety of materials — badges, bandannas, bumper stickers, buttons, tokens, etc. The only limiting factor seems to be a promoter's imagination.

Items selling below $100.00 move frequently enough to establish firm prices. Items above that price fluctuate according to supply and demand. This past year a record price was set for a campaign button — $30,000 was paid for a Cox-Roosevelt item. Many individuals now recognize the value of political items, acquiring them and holding them for future sale. As a result, modern material has a relatively low market value.

Badges
1876, Hayes, eagle top, flag ribbon, disk with eagle and ferrotype portraits of Hayes and Wheeler	400.00
1884–1892, Cleveland, eagle top, red, white, and blue striped ribbon, star with cardboard photo	40.00
1904, Roosevelt, inauguration, metal top, flag ribbon, portrait of Roosevelt	65.00
1924, Davis, button with ribbon labeled "Davis, Smith, and Victory"	100.00
1948, Dewey, button with "God Bless America" and "1944–1948," red, white and blue striped ribbon, and horseshoe	10.00
1952, Eisenhower, Inaugural Committee, metal and ribbon	15.00

Bandannas
1876, Tilden, "Centennial Election/The Democratic Nominees"	200.00
1888, Harrison, "The Old Flag and Protection," oval portraits and metal within field of flag	65.00
1912, Roosevelt, "The Roosevelt Bandanna/Progressive Party"	30.00

Books, Song
1865, Lincoln	60.00
1880, Garfield	30.00

Bumper Stickers
1960, Nixon	5.00
1972, McGovern	4.00

Buttons
1896, McKinley-Hobart, Republican Phalanx, 1⅛"	20.00
1896–1900, Bryan, colored, 2"	12.00
1900, McKinley-Roosevelt, 4 Years of Full Dinner Pail, 1⅛"	75.00
1912, Roosevelt-Mead, flag style border, 1⅛"	15.00
1912, Taft, "New Hampshire's Choice," multicolored, 1⅛"	8.00
1916, Wilson, name in white stripe with red above and blue below, ¾"	4.00
1916, Hughes, black and white portrait, ¾"	9.00
1920, Harding, oval portrait in flag shield flanked by elephant heads, 1⅝"	65.00
1920, Cox, "Coxsure" on blue	

ground, ½"	15.00
1924, Coolidge and Dawes, sepia portrait, 1⅛"	300.00
1924, Coolidge, "Keep Coolidge," black and white portrait, 1"	10.00
1924, Teapot in blue with "DOOM" on white ground, ⅞"	30.00
1928, Hoover, black and white portrait with blue border with "A Democrat for Hoover," 1"	20.00
1928–1932, Hoover and Curtis, blue letters on white ground	2.00
1928, Smith, black and white portrait, beaded brass band, 1⅛"	18.00
1932–1936, Roosevelt and Garner, portraits in oval on black ground, ¾"	50.00
1932–1944, Roosevelt, colored portrait, 1⅞"	8.00
1940–1944, Roosevelt, portrait with white border "Re-elect Roosevelt," 1⅛"	3.50
1936, Landon and Knox, sunflower pedal border, GOP elephant, 1⅞"	3.50
1940, Wilkie, white ground, portrait, "Wilkie/For President," 1¾"	5.00
1940, Joe Louis for Wilkie, sepia, 1⅜"	17.50
1940, half red, half white ground, white letters "All's Well With Wilkie," ⅞"	2.00
1948, Dewey and Warren, red, white, and blue ground, portraits, "Vote Republican/For/Dewey Warren," 3"	2.50
1948, Truman, gold ground, "Minnesota/Truman/Club," 2"	25.00
1952–1956, Eisenhower, blue tone, portrait, border with "Eisenhower/For President," 1⅛"	3.00

Note: A range of from $1.00 to $7.00 will cover ninety percent of all buttons relating to the campaigns of 1960 to 1980.

Cane, wood with paper label, 1904, Roosevelt and Fairbanks	50.00
Catalogue, 1904, Roosevelt, campaign supplies	125.00

Cigars

1952–1956, Eisenhower, DeLuxe, "I Like Ike"	5.00
1968, Nixon, El Bubble, DeLuxe, "Win With Dick"	2.50
Cigarettes, 1952, Stevenson	12.50

Flashers

1952, Stevenson, portrait on tie bar	2.00
1956, Eisenhower, portrait with White House in background	5.00
1960, Kennedy, bell, portrait and letters	12.50

Plate, 9½", 1908 campaign, William Howard Taft and James Schoolcraft Sherman **$65.00**

Fobs

1908, Bryan and Kern, shield	10.00
1912, National Progressive Party/ New York State Convention	25.00
1912, Wilson, Lock to White House, swing tab over word Wilson	30.00
1928, Smith and Robinson, shield	22.50

Hats

1892, Top Hat, Harrison and Reid label inside	150.00
1892, Glass Hat, toothpick, "The Same Old Hat"	50.00
1952, Cloth, baseball style, "Let's Back Ike"	7.50
Invitation, Inaugural, 1904, Roosevelt	30.00

Lanterns

1856, Fillmore, tin with punched stars and "Fillmore/Donelson"	800.00
1876, Tilden and Hendricks, paper	150.00
1880, Garfield, paper	65.00
Tin Parade, three outlets, shield, late 19th	95.00

License Plates

1932–1944, Roosevelt, Uncle Sam with hand on shoulder of Roosevelt, "Drive Ahead with Roosevelt"	40.00
1944, Dewey, stipe border with star corner blocks, "Dewey/We are DUE for a change"	15.00
1964, Goldwater, "Goldwater in 64/AuH₂0"	8.00
1968, Humphrey, "Vote Demo-	

cratic/Humphrey—Muskie'' 7.00
Matchbooks, 1952 to present 1.00

Mugs
1860–1864, Lincoln, half portrait, black and white, 3¼" 450.00
1880, Garfield, pressed glass, portrait, racoon on reverse, 2¼" ... 100.00
1896–1900, McKinley and Bryan, beer premium 135.00
1928, Hoover, ceramic, toby type, 7" 95.00

Pencils
1932, Hoover, "Hoover for President 1932," metal bust instead of eraser 15.00
1944, Dewey, two eagles aside of portrait 7.00
1952, Stevenson, mechanical, waist portrait in plastic bubble at top 20.00

Pins
1888, Harrison, Whisk Broom with portrait 35.00
1896, Bryan, Gold Bug 17.50
1912, Roosevelt, "Bullmoose" ... 10.00
1920, Cox, Rooster 20.00
1928, Smith, Donkey with "Al & Joe" 10.00
1952, Eisenhower, Bust, "I Like Ike" 5.00
1960, Kennedy, PT 109 .... 10.00

Pipes
1884–1892, Cleveland, clay, "A Public Office is a Public Trust," 6¼" 65.00
1904, Roosevelt, clay, face with glasses 40.00

Plates
1836–1840, Harrison, center portrait medallion, "Hero of the Thames," brown and white, 9½" . 325.00
1880, Garfield, portrait and signature on white ground, 8" 25.00
1900, McKinley and Roosevelt, lithograph tin, Columbia with outstretched arms on medallions of candidates, 12" 150.00
1936, Landon, glass plate, "Elect Landon/Save America," 7" 45.00

Razors
1848, Taylor, "General Taylor" manufactured by Woreaves & Sons 125.00
1884, Blaine and Logan 75.00
1920, Cox and Roosevelt 850.00

Ribbons
1840, Van Buren, "Van Buren/ Johnson/and an Independent Treasury" 325.00
1856, Buchanan, "For President/James Buchanan" 100.00
1880, Hancock, "Hancock/and/

English" 65.00
1908, Bryan, "The Commoner/ Wm. Jennings Bryan/Denver, July 1908" 30.00

Stickpins
1896–1900, Bryan 10.00
1908, Taft and Sherman, colored portraits in medallions with flag and shield, oval 75.00
1920, Harding, colored portrait .. 25.00

Studs
1888, Harrison, celluloid with metal frame 20.00
1904, McKinley-Roosevelt 22.50
1920, Cox, "I will crow in November" (raised letters) 30.00

Tabs
1948, Roosevelt and Truman, white ground, red and blue top and bottom 4.00
1948, Dewey, blue letters on white ground.................... 1.00
1952–1956, Eisenhower, half red, half blue, "Eisenhower/Nixon" .. 1.00
1952, Stevenson, "Volunteer for Stevenson" 3.00

Tie-Bars
1940, Wilkie, enamel shield on open wire bar 5.00
1964, Johnson, map of U.S. with "LBJ for USA" 2.00

Ties
1944, Roosevelt, portrait 12.50
1944–1948, Dewey, name repeated five times with cut of Dewey at base 10.00

Tokens
1828–1832, Jackson, "Hero of New Orleans," brass 40.00
1868, Grant, bronze 45.00
1904, Parker-Davis, gilt metal ... 30.00
T-Shirt, 1972, Nixon, "Nixon's Out Front" 7.50

Umbrellas
1904, Parker, portrait 250.00
1964, GOP Party 20.00
1968, Humphrey, name on six panels 17.50

CAMPHOR GLASS

Camphor glass derives its name from its color. It has a cloudy, white appearance, similar to gum camphor. This was accomplished by treating the glass with hydrofluoric acid vapors.

Basket, 4" 20.00
Bookends, 7", horses heads, pair .. 80.00
Bottles
4", stoppered 15.00

Powder Box, 5″ dia., salmon pink, embossed florals, c. 1920 ....$40.00

6½″, stoppered	30.00
8½″, pinch type, mushroom stoppered, perfume	35.00
Boxes	
Scroll design	35.00
Powder, hinged cover, 4½″	35.00
Hair receiver, scroll design	50.00
Hinged, 5″, holly spray	75.00
Candlesticks, 7″, Centennial Expo. Phila., 1876, pair	150.00
Compote, 7″, embossed, running horses	75.00
Console Set, compote and candlesticks, stems are seated cherubs, set	150.00
Cruet, stoppered, hand painted enameled roses	30.00
Hands, grapes and leaves at wrists	35.00
Hen-on Nest, 7 x 4½″, basketweave camphor base, No. 2 in base	35.00
Owl, standing, green glass eyes	35.00
Pitchers	
Water, hobnail, applied handle, ground pontil	125.00
7¾″, enameling	25.00
Plates	
6½″, Easter Greeting	25.00
7¼″, Fleur-de-lis decor	25.00
7¼″, Owl	25.00
Playing Card Holder, ftd., 3¾″	16.00
Rose Bowl, hand painted, blue forget-me-nots, gold trim	40.00
Shoes	
Boot, 2½″	22.50
Lady's, 5″, Libbey Glass Co., Toledo, Ohio, for 1893 World's Fair	40.00
Lady's shoe, with bow, from Centennial Expos. marked "Gillinder"	45.00
Table Set, "Wild Rose and Bowknot," covered sugar, covered butter, creamer, spooner, 4 pieces	150.00
Toothpick holder, swirled, ruffled top	27.50
Trays, 8 x 10½″, "Wild rose, and Bowknot"	28.50
Vases	
8″, Fan shaped, clear leaf design and trim	75.00
10½″, Tall, Grecian shape, double handled, clear base	100.00

CANARY LUSTER
See ENGLISH YELLOW GLAZED EARTHENWARE

CANDLE MOLDS

Candles were a necessity of life in the past and candle making a major household chore. First, a supply of animal fat had to be collected. The fat was then purified by boiling with water. The resulting tallow rose to the top and was then skimmed off.

There were two methods used to make the final product, dipping and molding. Dipped candles were made by repeatedly dipping the wick in and out of the tallow until the desired size was formed. Molded candles were made in a tubular mold. The wick was threaded through the center of the tube and securely fastened. Then, the tallow was poured into the mold and allowed to harden. Candle molds were usually made of tin in various sizes, from a single candle mold to a grouping that made dozens of candles at a single time.

6-Candle, handled, tin $70.00

1-Candle, 9¾"	50.00
1-Candle, 15"	100.00
4-Candle	60.00
6-Candle	80.00
8-Candle	100.00
12-Candle	125.00
16-Candle, pewter with wood frame	900.00
18-Candle	225.00
18-Candle, pewter with wood frame	1000.00
24-Candle	200.00
24-Candle, pewter, signed Webb . . .	2000.00
48-Candle	350.00
50-Candle	450.00

CANDLESTICKS

A candlestick or candleholder is a portable holder with a hollow cup or spike to support a single candle. These very necessary implements have developed over the centuries into a myriad of shapes, sizes and types of materials. Candelabra, or candelabrum, is a large candlestick which has more than one branch or arms. These decorations have become very collectible and may be made of various materials. See specific categories for different types.

Brass
Candelabrum, 10½", 5-light	125.00
Candelabra, 3-light, brass with marble base, entwined grape clusters on cups, arms and shakes, pair	150.00
Candle Holders, 5", saucer-type . . .	30.00
Candle Holders, 11", saucer-type with push up, single	40.00
Candle Holders, 5½", brass, chamber type, oval boat shape with ring handle	45.00
Candlesticks, 3⅝", beehives, square bases, miniature, pair	150.00
Candlesticks, 7½", with push ups, mid-18th century	350.00
Candlesticks, 17", beehives, with drip trays, Birmingham, pair	260.00
Candlesticks, rectangular bases on bracket feet, baluster stems, circular knozzles, early 19th century, pair	225.00
Candlesticks, 18½", twisted stems 18th century, pair	125.00

Glass
Amber, 9¾", twisted hollow stems, wide bebeche-like tops, signed Sinclaire	200.00
Iridescent deep blue, 7", pair . . .	50.00
Celeste blue, attributed to Boston and Sandwich Glass Co.	300.00
Cut Glass, 9", cut scrolls, leaves and flower buds, single	120.00

Corinthian colum, blue, 9", acid finish, square base $190.00

Cut Glass, 12½", delicate cut, sterling bases, signed Hawkes . .	475.00
Cut Glass, engraved flower basket pattern, green pair, signed Hawkes	125.00
Cut Glass, 8", twisted stems, signed Libbey	185.00

Iron
With hogscraper, with lip and lift, dated 1855	65.00
Iron spiral twist stem, on turned wooden base, with lifting tab to raise candle, 18th century	350.00

Miscellaneous
Tole, 4½", saucer-type with ring handle and push ups	75.00
Tole, with push up, (single)	54.00
Candlesticks, 16½", carved gilt wood, form of kneeling angels carrying candlestick on elongated bases, 19th century, pair	350.00

CANDY CONTAINERS

Candy containers were small glass toys, holding tiny pellets of sugar candy when purchased, in the shape of boats, cars, trains, dogs, etc.; when the child had eaten the candy, he still had a toy to remember. Some had small metal cap, and the earlier ones had corks for stoppers. They were very popular for gifts and stocking stuffers at Christmas time. Today they are very popular for collectors, and ones made in commemoration of movie stars and well known characters are quite expensive.

Santa	75.00
Soldier and Tent, 3⅜″	1700.00
Soldier on monument base, 5⅝″	500.00
Spirit of St. Louis, airplane, pink glass and tin	275.00
Station Wagon, woody, 4⅞″	25.00
Suitcase	22.50
Telephone	20.00
Train	25.00
Turkey	25.00
Van	10.00
Wheelbarrow	27.50
Whistle	10.00

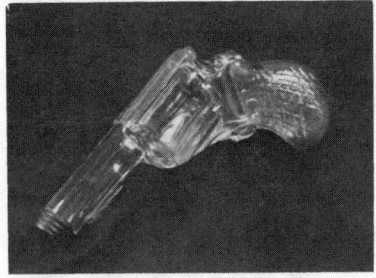

Revolver, 8″, clear glass, screw cap $30.00

Airplane, tin wings	25.00
Auto Lamp, 5¾″	30.00
Auto, Pierce Arrow	35.00
Armored Tank, 4¼″	60.00
Battleship on waves, 5¼″	90.00
Bear beside tree trunk, with honey, paper mache	85.00
Babe Ruth on the bag	625.00
Betty Boop	30.00
Buses	
Greyhound	38.50
Victory Bus	35.00
Chicken on Nest	15.00
Colorado, S. S., 6½″	325.00
Charlie Chaplin, barrel bank 4⅛″	250.00
Jackie Coogan, 5″	875.00
Duck	40.00
Fire Engine	100.00
Gun, 4″	20.00
Horn	60.00
House	25.00
Independence Hall	250.00
Jack-O-Lantern, wire bale, 3⅞″	45.00
Motorboat	15.00
Phonograph with glass record and tin horn, 4½″	250.00
Radio	28.00
Rabbit running on log, 4¼″	100.00

CANES

Cane handle, ivory $95.00

Bottle Cane, 36″ long, glass inside liner for holding liquor, removable head exposes cork 150.00

Glass
39″, amber color and gold encircles stripes	95.00
35″, clear glass with blue-red swirl ribbon inside	165.00
48″, green	65.00
60″, green	85.00
Horn handle, personalized	75.00
Horseman's Special, English	85.00
Parade, political type, elephant head	50.00

Sword Canes
35″, horn handle in shape of dog's head	150.00
38″, bone and wooden handle	75.00
34″, umbrella cane, black umbrella, wood case	85.00

Walking Sticks
Gold head, 14K, scrolled and monogrammed	100.00
Hickory, carved dog's head	135.00
Sterling Silver head	125.00

Silvered top and tip, Briar	30.00

Wooden

Turned shaft, carved goose head handle	165.00
Carved face handle	55.00
Carved tiger head handle	95.00

Handles Only

12½", amethyst, cut glass with tortoise shell	195.00
Gold, 14K Plain	75.00
MOP and gold	60.00
Sterling, walking stick top	30.00

CANTON CHINA

Canton china is a type of oriental porcelain made in Canton, China, for export to America from the 1820's to the present. These wares were hand decorated in light to dark blues underglaze on white, with simple scenes of houses, mountains and a bridge in the center panel. Borders on earlier Canton feature a rain and cloud motif while later pieces usually have a straight line border. The Canton pattern has the second greatest variety of forms found in Chinese export porcelain. The markings "Made in China" and "China" indicates wares made after 1891.

Plate, 10" dia., water edge scene, 1800–1820 . . . .**$60.00**

Bottle, water	
8½"	325.00
9", 19th century	425.00
10"	375.00
Bowls	
4½", waste	85.00
6"	100.00
9¼", fruit with underplate, reticulated	550.00

9½", scalloped edge, "China", 19th century	500.00
Punch, 14", Chinese, 19th century	2700.00
Rice, with saucer	45.00
Butter Dish, three pieces	800.00
Cache Pot, 5 x 8"	800.00
Coffee Pot, 9", dome lid	800.00
Creamer, 3", Chinese, 19th century	150.00
Cups and Saucers	
Cross handle	80.00
Loop handle	45.00
Curry dish, on high base, 13¾", Chinese, 19th century	850.00
Dishes	
Fish shaped, 6", late	85.00
Oblong, deep, Chinese, 19th century	300.00
Garden Seat, 19", octagonal	1250.00
Ginger Jars, covered	
3"	80.00
6"	180.00
9"	360.00
Hot Water Dish, octagonal	250.00
Lamp, 6½", ginger jar base, brass fittings	
Mug	250.00
Pitchers	
4"	150.00
8"	280.00
10"	450.00
Plates	
7"	70.00
8"	65.00
8½", soup	65.00
9½"	100.00
9⅞", oval, 19th century, Chinese	170.00
10¼", square	255.00
Platters	
7 x 10"	160.00
8 x 10½"	180.00
14½ x 17½"	280.00
16¼ x 20¼"	355.00
Footed, 16¾", well and tree, Chinese	400.00
Posset Cup, 3", Polychromed	155.00
Sugars, covered	
Chinese, 19th century, intertwining strap handles	200.00
Intertwining handles	250.00
Tea Caddy, hexagonal	800.00
Teapots	
4", 4" square base	600.00
Intertwining handle, 6"	350.00
6¼"	650.00
Tile, 6" square	225.00
Tray, oblong, 8 x 5⅝", 19th century	225.00
Vegetable Dishes, covered	
8", oval, late	100.00
10⅛", 19th century	200.00
11½", oval, strawberry finial, scalloped rims	475.00
12", oval, boar head handles, c.	

1810	900.00

Vases
15¼", Baluster form, Chinese, 19th century	900.00
10⅜", cylindrical, 19th century	500.00

CAPO-DI-MONTI CHINA

The Capo-di-Monti factory in Naples started production in 1736. In 1743, King Charles of Naples established a factory there that made relief decoration. The molds were acquired by the Doccia factory of Florence in 1886, and they have since made reproductions of original Capo-di-Monti pieces, with the "N" mark beneath a crown. Very early pieces are extremely valuable but most of these are in museums. Pieces found today are considerably lower and should be known as "Capo-di-Monti-type."

Figurine, child with comb, signed G. Armanis, late **$150.00**

Boxes
9¾" x 6", 18th century	525.00
Patch, hunting scene decor	100.00

3½", Patch, King Neptune and horses breaking through waves on hinged cover	135.00
Trinket, classical figures on hinged cover, cherubs and lions' heads on base, late	165.00
Carriage, with lady and gentleman	125.00

Compote
7", garden scene, nudes and cherubs	65.00
6½", gold and blue trim, figures in classical scene, pair	125.00
Creamer, 3½", Bacchus	160.00

Cups and Saucers
Farm scene, blue	100.00
Floral decor, matching pair	45.00
Floral, with twisted branch handle	65.00
Ewer, 14⅜", Dolphins frolicking, figural satyr handle, bright colors and gilded scrollwork, 4 feet	200.00

Figurines
3½", Man holding bowl of vegetables	120.00
Peasant girl by Guisseppi Gricci	21100.00
3½", Woman, seated with flower basket	110.00
6½", Soldier on horse	125.00
Lamp, 37", Man, woman and children, nudes in high relief, handled, dolphins on corners	160.00
Pitcher, 8", figures in relief, branch handle	225.00
Plaque, 8 x 6½", molded seated Venus and Cupid, black wood, gilt metal frame inlaid with oval colored marbles, late 19th century, pair	1200.00

Plates
8½", center, allegorical scene, embossed figures at rim	85.00
11", Napolean and soldiers	140.00

Teapot
Nude woman in relief, animal spout, coral branch handle, peach finial	200.00
Figure of lady with mirror, her maiden in relief, serpent spout	275.00
Tea Set, teapot, four cups and saucers, portrait front, scenic backs, high relief, jewelled, set	375.00
Urn, with cover, footed, pistol grip handles, battle scene decor, c. 1860	190.00

CARLSBAD CHINA

This porcelain was made at Carlsbad, Austria, by a number of factories. Most of the items

found in shops and collections today were made after 1891.

Vase, 9 ½" h. 2 handles, portrait center, deep pink with gold trim, marked Victoria, Carlsbad, Austria, artist signed Fr. Stahl $85.00

Bowls
3¼", Cream ground with flowers in red, green and gold	35.00
6", Classic figures, decor	45.00

Chocolate Pot, 9", blue bachelor's buttons on violet ground, gold trim 115.00

Cups and Saucers
Demitasse, lady and gentlemen decor	45.00
Demitasse, portrait "Meditation," heavy gold trim	100.00
Tea, pink and yellow roses on white, 1" gold scroll with blue border	40.00

Dinner Set, 45 pieces, small rosebuds, vines, marked "H. C. Carlsbad, Austria," 8 serving pieces, plus service for eight 225.00

Ewer, 11", picnic scene, tan ground 50.00

Mayonnaise Set, portrait, green with gold	50.00

Pitchers
11", pink with cobalt blue band at top and bottom, gold trim	85.00
Helmet type, cream ground, white lilies, gold handle and trim, signed, "Austria"	75.00

Plates
7¼", hand painted rosebuds, and gold trim, marked "A. C. Carlsbad, Austria"	25.00
8¼", Oyster, scalloped gold rim, violet decor	35.00
10", Turquoise rim, gold trim, unsigned, portrait, "Austria"	40.00
11½", hanging type, dark green border, gold trim, two ladies at tea, gentleman visitor	75.00
11½", scenic decor, green and gold trim, signed "A. Kauffman" .	100.00

Platter, 15¼", blue floral decor, gold trim	35.00

Tea Caddies
Pink to white background, women with cupid decor	75.00
Portrait of lady on side	85.00

Tray, 6½ x 9", pin compartments, crimped border with sepia, green floral on white, gold trim	30.00
Tureen, covered, 7½", violets, daisies, and leaves, gold trim	52.50
Vase, 7", Cupids, gold trim	65.00

CARNIVAL GLASS — AMERICAN

Carnival Glass, sometimes referred to as "Taffeta Glass" or "Poor Man's Tiffany," was made during the 1900–1925's. The majority was manufactured near Wheeling, W. Va. Carnival glass has been reproduced profusely in various patterns and colors. Imperial Glass Co., of Ohio, one of the largest producers of "new" Carnival glass, was purchased by the Lenox China Co., who in turn, has sold it to a private investor. What Carnival patterns will be produced in the future is not known, but the discontinued patterns are collectible.

ACORN BURRS (NORTHWOOD)

Bowls
5", Marigold	30.00
10", Purple, signed	145.00

Butter, covered
Marigold	125.00
Purple	225.00

Punch bowl and base
Purple	560.00
White	800.00

Pitcher, Water, marigold 220.00

Rose Bowl, 3½″ d. x 4½″ h., mari-gold $22.00

Spooner, purple 90.00
Tumbler, purple 70.00

APPLE TREE (FENTON)

Pitcher, Water
  Marigold 150.00
  Purple 300.00
Tumblers
  Marigold 40.00
  Purple 50.00

BEADED SHELL (NORTHWOOD)

Bowls
  Large, footed, marigold 65.00
  Large, footed, purple 90.00
  Small, footed, marigold 30.00
Butter, covered
  Marigold 35.00
  Purple 110.00
Creamers
  Marigold 65.00
  Purple 170.00
  Pastel 90.00
Pitcher, water
  Marigold 350.00
  Purple 450.00
Sugar, covered
  Marigold 75.00
  Purple 100.00
Tumblers
  Amethyst 45.00
  Marigold 60.00
  Purple 85.00

BIRDS AND CHERRIES (FENTON)

Bon-Bon Dish
  Marigold 38.00
  Purple 60.00
Bowls
  5″, (rare), marigold 60.00
  5″, purple 85.00
  9″, marigold 200.00
  9″, purple 300.00
Compotes
  Marigold 45.00
  Purple 60.00
Chop Plate, 10″, either color 1000.00

BLACKBERRY (NORTHWOOD)

Bowl, 10″, footed, purple 58.00
Compotes
  Marigold 50.00
  Purple 65.00

CHERRY (NORTHWOOD)

Bowls
  5″, flat, marigold 30.00
  5″, flat, purple 45.00
  8½″, flat, marigold 50.00
  8½″, flat, purple 65.00
  8½″, footed, marigold 65.00
Butter, covered, purple 290.00
Compote, purple 95.00
Plate, 6″
  Marigold 185.00
  Purple 195.00

CHERRY AND CABLE (NORTHWOOD)

All Marigold

Bowls
  5″ 38.00
  9″ 85.00
Butter, covered, (rare) 300.00
Creamer 155.00
Pitcher, Water 1700.00
Spooner 155.00
Sugar 155.00
Tumbler 210.00

CIRCLED SCROLL (DUGAN)

Bowls
  5″, marigold 30.00
  5″, purple 40.00
  11″, marigold 55.00
  11″, purple 70.00
Butter, covered
  Marigold 125.00
  Purple 175.00
Creamers
  Marigold 45.00

Purple	55.00

Pitcher, Water

Marigold, (rare)	2600.00
Purple, (rare)	4000.00

Tumblers

Marigold	325.00
Purple	500.00

DAHLIA (NORTHWOOD-DUGAN)

Bowls

5", marigold, footed	90.00
5", purple, footed	127.00
5", white, footed	100.00
10", marigold, footed	35.00
10", purple, footed	100.00
10", white	200.00

Butter, covered

Marigold	100.00
Purple	140.00
White	310.00

Creamers

Marigold	70.00
Purple	90.00
White	250.00

Sugar, covered

Marigold	75.00
Purple	100.00
White	275.00

Pitcher, water

Marigold	295.00
Purple	450.00
White	650.00

Tumblers

Marigold, (rare)	75.00
Purple	110.00
White	275.00

Water set, pitcher 8½" h. 6 glasses, "Diamond Lace," purple and blues, ...$475.00

DANDELION (NORTHWOOD)

Mugs

Marigold	345.00
Purple	320.00

Pitcher, Water

Marigold	395.00
Purple	595.00
White	975.00

Tumblers

Marigold	47.00
Purple	52.00
White	140.00
Tankard pitcher, four tumblers, purple, set	450.00

FASHION (IMPERIAL)

Bowls

9", marigold	35.00
Fruit and base, marigold	54.00

Bride's Basket

Marigold	97.00
Pastel	100.00

Creamer or Sugar

Marigold	95.00
Pastel	42.00

Punch Bowl and base

Marigold	67.00
Pastel	70.00
Red	1800.00

Punch Cup

Marigold	20.00
Pastel	22.00
Red	260.00

Pitcher, Water

Marigold	160.00
Purple	900.00
Pastel	700.00
Tumbler, marigold	40.00

FLUTE (NORTHWOOD)

Bowls

5", marigold	32.00
10", marigold	60.00

Pitcher, Water

Marigold, (rare)	385.00
Purple, (rare)	545.00
Ringtree, marigold, (very rare)	165.00

Sherbet

Marigold	30.00
Purple	45.00
Pastel	40.00

GRAPE AND CABLE (NORTHWOOD, N)

All Purple

Banana boat, footed	220.00
Berry Set, large bowl, six matching sauces	115.00

Bon Bon Dish	50.00
Bowls	
5½"	40.00
10"	85.00
11", ice cream	295.00
Butter, covered	210.00
Candlesticks, pair	260.00
Compotes	
Large, covered	700.00
Large, open	500.00
Cologne Bottle, with stopper	195.00
Cookie Jar, covered	420.00
Creamer	125.00
Cup and Saucer, (rare)	450.00
Fernery, footed, (rare)	1000.00
Hatpin holder	125.00
Nappy	75.00
Pitcher, Water, tankard	850.00
Plates	
6"–9½", flat	90.00
Footed	90.00
Handgrip	80.00
Turned up sides	80.00
Powder Jar, with lid	110.00
Punch Bowl and base	
Banquet	1450.00
Small	450.00
Punch Cup	36.00
Spooner	60.00
Sweetmeat Jar, covered	280.00
Tobacco Jar with lid	400.00
Trays	
Dresser	300.00
Pin	135.00
Tumblers	
Regular	60.00
Jumbo	70.00

HEART AND VINE (FENTON)

Bowls	
8½", marigold	36.00
8½", purple	42.00
8½", pastel	58.00
Plates	
9", marigold, (rare)	175.00
9", purple	42.00
9", pastel	58.00

HORSE'S HEADS (FENTON)

Bowls	
7½", flat, marigold	525.00
7¼", flat, purple	78.00
7¼", flat, pastel	100.00
7¼", flat, red	600.00
7"–8", footed, marigold	58.00
7"–8", footed, purple	85.00
7"–8", footed, pastel	120.00
7"–8", footed, red	600.00
Rose, footed, marigold, (rare)	95.00
Rose, footed, purple	125.00
Rose, pastel	180.00

Cracker jar, Inverted Feather, 6" d. x 6½" h., green $185.00

INVERTED STRAWBERRY (CAMBRIDGE)

Bowls	
5", marigold	37.00
5", purple	50.00
9"–10", marigold	60.00
9"–10", purple	85.00
Candlesticks, pair	
Marigold, (rare)	250.00
Purple	325.00
Celery, marigold	300.00
Compotes	
Large, marigold	250.00
Small, marigold	175.00
Small, purple	250.00
Small, pastel	400.00
Creamer, either color	90.00
Pitchers	
Milk, either color	2000.00
Regular, water, marigold	1000.00
Regular, water, purple	1300.00
Spittoon, ladies'	
Marigold	500.00
Purple	625.00

KITTENS (FENTON)

Bowls	
4", marigold	120.00
4", purple	140.00
4", marigold, turned up edge	120.00
4", purple, turned up edge	140.00
Cereal, marigold, (scarce)	140.00
Cereal, purple, (scarce)	165.00
Cup and Saucer, complete	
Marigold	120.00
Purple	185.00

Plate
4½″, marigold	....	120.00
4½″, purple	....	140.00

LUSTRE ROSE (IMPERIAL)

In Marigold or Green.

Bowls
4¾″–5½″	....	16.00
7″–11″, flat	....	28.00
8″–9″	....	32.00
9″–12″, footed	....	38.00
Butter, covered	....	54.00
Creamer	....	40.00
Fernery, footed	....	37.00
Pitcher, Water	....	70.00
Tumbler	....	18.00

OCTAGON (IMPERIAL)

Butter, covered		
Marigold	....	80.00
Purple	....	120.00
Creamers		
Marigold	....	46.00
Purple	....	60.00
Decanter, with stopper		
Marigold	....	90.00
Purple	....	250.00
Pitcher, water		
Marigold	....	115.00
Purple	....	225.00
Tumblers		
Marigold	....	28.00
Purple	....	50.00
Wine		
Marigold	....	26.00
Purple	....	54.00

ORANGE TREE (FENTON)

Bowl, 5½″, footed		
Marigold	....	28.00
Purple	....	32.00
Bowl, 8″–10″, flat		
Marigold	....	24.00
Purple	....	40.00
Bowl, 10″–11″, footed		
Marigold	....	70.00
Purple	....	100.00
White	....	110.00
Rose, marigold	....	45.00
Purple	....	60.00
White	....	85.00
Red	....	450.00
Butter, covered		
Marigold	....	130.00
Purple	....	150.00
White	....	400.00
Creamers		

Marigold	....	45.00
Purple	....	65.00
White	....	125.00
Cups		
Marigold	....	20.00
Purple	....	28.00
White	....	35.00
Goblet, (all)	....	90.00
Hatpin Holder		
Marigold	....	120.00
Purple	....	165.00
White	....	250.00
Mugs		
Marigold	....	30.00
Purple	....	45.00
Pastel	....	70.00
Red	....	185.00
Pitcher, water, 2 styles (either)		
Marigold	....	195.00
Purple	....	250.00
White	....	390.00
Powder Jar, with lid		
Marigold	....	65.00
Purple	....	85.00
White	....	110.00
Punch Bowl and base		
Marigold	....	190.00
Purple	....	255.00
White	....	350.00
Tumbler, footed		
Marigold	....	35.00
Purple	....	40.00
White	....	60.00

ORIENTAL POPPY (NORTHWOOD)

Pitcher, Water, tankard		
Marigold	....	395.00
Purple	....	600.00
White	....	900.00
Tumblers		
Marigold	....	32.00
Purple	....	48.00
White	....	140.00
Bowls		
5″, green	....	50.00
5″, white	....	60.00
9″, green	....	200.00
9″, white	....	210.00
Butter, covered		
Green	....	200.00
White	....	210.00
Creamers		
Green	....	110.00
White	....	120.00
Pitcher, Water		
Green	....	575.00
White	....	650.00
Tumblers		
Green	....	75.00
White	....	90.00

PEACOCK AT FOUNTAIN (NORTHWOOD)

Bowls

5", marigold	28.00
5", purple	35.00
5", pastel	50.00
9", marigold	64.00
9", purple	35.00
9", pastel	260.00
Orange, footed, marigold	140.00
Orange, footed, purple	260.00
Orange, footed, pastel	1400.00

Butter, covered

Marigold	120.00
Purple	165.00
Pastel	210.00

Creamers

Marigold	60.00
Purple	255.00
Pastel	290.00

Punch Bowl and base

Marigold	165.00
Purple	370.00
Pastel	2500.00

Spooners

Marigold	60.00
Purple	80.00
Pastel	95.00

Pitcher, Water

Marigold	260.00
Purple	395.00
Pastel	560.00

SODA GOLD (IMPERIAL)

Bowls

4½"	20.00
9½"	36.00
Plate, 9"	57.00

STAR MEDALLION (IMPERIAL)

All in Marigold

Bowl, 7-9", round or square	26.00
Butter, covered	80.00
Celery	
Handled	38.00
Tray	45.00
Compote, large	45.00
Creamer	45.00
Goblet	42.00
Pitcher, Water	56.00
Plate, 5"	28.00
Tumbler	28.00
Vase, 6"	34.00

STRAWBERRY (NORTHWOOD)

Bowls

5", marigold	24.00
5", purple	30.00

5", pastel	32.00
8"-10", marigold	45.00
8"-10", purple	57.00
8"-10", white	150.00

Plates

7", handgrip, marigold	75.00
7", purple,	90.00
9", marigold	85.00
9", purple	95.00
9", white	170.00

CARNIVAL, MISCELLANEOUS AND SPECIAL ITEMS

Basket (Northwood), footed, marigold	58.00
Barnyard, bowl, blue	1800.00
Butterfly and Tulip (Northwood), square footed bowl, purple, (rare)	1350.00
Cherries and Blossoms, water pitcher, blue	105.00
Frolicking Bears, water pitcher, green	1000.00
God and Home, water pitcher, and one tumbler, blue	1200.00
Good Luck (Northwood)	
Bowl, pie crust edge, green	125.00
Plate, green	170.00
Memphis (Northwood), white punch cup	45.00
Persian Medallion (Fenton), marigold candy dish	50.00
Raspberry (Northwood), water pitcher, ice blue	1800.00
Tumbler to match	80.00

CAROUSEL FIGURES

When, where or how the carousel originated is truly unimportant when compared to the excitement and joy of riding the Merry-Go-Round. Prancing steeds, snarling tigers and graceful swans set to calliope music and bright lights can transfer all, young and old into the Magic Kingdom.

Early figures were usually hand crafted by superior craftsmen and artists. The prices listed can only serve as a guide as condition is extremely important.

Camel, French	3000.00
Cat, French	3500.00
Dog, Spillman	2000.00
Goat, Spillman	3000.00
Giraffe, Looff, original park paint, 2 glass eyes, parrots on saddle	14000.00
Horses	
Dentzel, stationary, jumping, carved saddle	2650.00
Muller	3000.00
Parker, jeweled	1500.00

Horse, 38″ long $1500.00

Spooner	2000.00
Spillman, jumper, jeweled	1350.00
Stein and Goldstein	3500.00
Unknown Maker, American, re-painted, c. 1910	750.00
Pig, French, pink, leaping, with saddle, 19th century	1550.00
Roosters	
American, steeplechase, two seater, 19th century	3800.00
English, roundabout, two seater, 19th century	2500.00

CASTLEFORD

Castleford is a soft paste porcelain made in Yorkshire, England in the early 1800's for the American trade. The ware has a warm, white ground, scalloped rims, (resembling castle tops) and trimmed in deep blue. Occasionally, pieces were further decorated with a coat-of-arms, eagles, or "Liberty." Few pieces, if any, are marked.

Tea pot, 7 x 10½″ d. salt glaze, cobalt trim $145.00

Bowl, 5″	175.00
Creamer	275.00
Spill Holder	150.00
Sugar, covered	225.00

CASTOR SETS

A castor set is a set of matched condiment bottles, held within a frame or holder. Most castor sets consisted of three to five pressed glass bottles in a silverplated frame. Some consisted of cut glass bottles and a sterling silver holder. Occasionally, an all-glass set is encountered. Although castor sets were known as early as the 1700's, most found today are from the Victorian period when they were quite popular.

3 bottle, milk glass, fan-shaped base, pink with hand-painted floral decor, pewter tops $55.00

3-bottle, square cut glass, in silverplated Sheffield holder, square mustard pot, pepper shaker and rectangular salt dish	125.00
3-bottle, ribbed, silverplated holder, English	50.00
3-bottles, Ribbed Palm, pewter tops, frame	100.00
3-bottles, Gothic	65.00
4-bottle, cut glass, silverplated frame	150.00
4-bottle, milk glass, plain pattern bottles, metal holder	100.00
4-bottle, pressed glass, in glass holder, metal ring post	65.00

4-bottle, miniature, revolving tin base	75.00
4-bottle, Rubina cut glass, footed square silverplated holder, with center post	195.00
4-bottle, cut glass, square, silverplated holder	150.00
5-bottle, Button Band, pattern glass stand	100.00
5-bottle, cut shield pattern	100.00
5-bottle, clear bottles, blue glass base with center post, 11" high to top of handle	175.00
5-bottle, 15", cut and etched bottles in silverplated holder, ground stoppers	145.00
5-bottle, cut and etched, silverplated Reed and Barton holder	125.00
5-bottle, early flint bottles with pewter holder	200.00
5-bottle, Gothic, pewter holder, "Israel Trask"	175.00
5-bottle, Honeycomb, resilvered holder, Meriden #39	175.00
5-bottle, matching, replated tops and holder	145.00
6-bottle, cut diamond, oval, silverplated holder	175.00
8-bottle, cut glass, sterling tops and holder, ground stoppers, hallmarked and documented c. 1733	3500.00
8-bottle, pressed glass, silverplated tops and holder, Simpson H. Miller Co.	225.00

CATALOGUES AND MAGAZINES

These old publications are of great value to collectors in all fields because they contain valuable information as to prices and items formerly in great demand. Catalogues give vital information as to what products were manufactured, year, date of manufacture, and names of companies who made them.

Magazines, especially older ones, have many ads of items which are today highly collectible, which antique buffs find very useful in their search for their particular item. Magazine covers, taken for granted in the 1920's to 1940's, are valuable today for the art work by their famous originators; lithographs of these artists' work are very much in demand today.

CATALOGUES

Allied Radios, 1925	8.00
American-LaFrance, fire fighting equipment	20.00
Bausch and Lomb, scientific instruments, 1940, 250 pp	15.00
Belknap's Hardware, c. 1910, 3784	

pp	45.00
Chevrolet Parts, 4-cylinder models .	10.00
Columbia Bicycle Co., 1896	28.00
Crane Plumbing Supplies, 1086 pp .	25.00
DeLaval Cream Separators, 1916, 72 pp	12.00
Deming Co., pumps and hydraulic machinery	45.00
Diamonds and Precious Stones, S. C. Scott Co., 1900, 72 pp	15.00
Farm Wagons, Peter Schuller Co., Chicago, leather bound, 113 pp .	20.00
Frost, wood implements, 63 pp . . .	12.00
Griswold and Palmer Co., Ladies coats and outer garments, 1885 .	25.00
Hartman Furniture, oak furniture, 422 pp	25.00
Keuffel and Esser, drawing and surveying instruments, hard back . .	24.00
(Lalique), DesVerreries de Rene Lalique, photocopy of original publication, 1932	42.00
Larkin catalogues, 1920-21-26-27, 228 pp ea.	30.00
Marlin Co., repeating rifles and shotguns, 1918, 24 pp	24.50
Nat'l Bellas Hess Co., Fall and Winter, 1929-30	12.00
Parke-Davis, 1914, 18 pp	42.00
Singer Sewing Machine Company, 1920	10.00
Sleighs, Sullivan Bros., Rochester, N. Y., 24 pp	17.50
Walter Wood Co. Machines and Implements for the Farm	7.00
Mowing and Reaping Machines, Hoosick Falls, N. Y.	25.00
Whitall Tatum Glassware, Sundry Pharmaceuticals	35.00
Winchester Firearms, 1908, 180 pp	25.00
Winters Art Litho. Co., Chicago 32 pp	25.00

MAGAZINES

American Home, 1940's, each	3.00
American Printer, 1913	12.00
Atlantic Monthly, July, 1932	8.00
Antiques Magazine	
1922–1940	10.00
1941 to present	5.00
Ballou's, 12 issues, 1956	10.00
Barron's June 1934 to August 1935, 58 issues	50.00
Collier's 1899 to 1952, mixed years, 147 issues	130.00
Cosmopolitan, three issues 1900, ea.	6.00
Delineator	
October, 1855	10.00
June, 1926	7.50

"Stamps" vol. 26, #12, whole #341, March 25, 1939, H.L. Lindquist, publisher $2.50

Esquire, 1941, Vargas centerfold ..	7.00
Etude, 1920's, 1930's, 10 issues mixed	25.00
Frank Leslie's Popular Monthly, September, 1877	12.00
Fortune, February, 1930, Vol I	125.00
Harper's Bazaar, September 5, 1874	9.00
Harper's Monthly, April, 1909	5.00

Ladies' Home Journal

April and November, 1892, ea. ..	12.00
January, 1925, paper doll page ..	20.00

Life

First issue through December 1937, 58 issues	250.00
July 1940 through June 1941, 53 issues	65.00
Liberty, 1920's, 1930's, ea.	2.00
Literary Digest, 1900, ea.	2.50

McCalls

1913 to 1940, with paper doll pages	15–25.00
1941 to 1959	5.00
1960 to present	1.00

National Geographics

1899 through 1900, ea.	15.00
1900–1930	10.00
1931–1950	3.50
1951 to present	1–5.00
Note: Special editions and supplements may have varying prices.	
Peterson's, 1875 and 1876, 12 issues, bound, each	15.00
Popular Radio, 1920's, ea.	3.00

Playboy

December 1953 through December 1980, complete set, 27 years, 324 issues	2995.00
Single issues, ea.	3.00
St. Nicholas, November, 1891	3.00
Saturday Evening Post	
1888 to 1981, ea.	10–50.00
Rockwell and Leyendecker covers, add per issue	25–37.00

CELADON

Celadon is an Oriental porcelain with a characteristic of pale grey-green glaze. The name was taken from the character Celadon in D'Urfe's "L'Astree" of the 17th century. The ware has been made for centuries in China, Japan and Korea.

Brush washer bowl, 2" h., 2" dia. $65.00

Bowls

10", 19th century	650.00
15¾", Turned-up rim, 5" high ...	1250.00
Charger, 14½", birds, insects, mums	375.00
Condiment, 5½", shaped like fish ..	100.00
Creamer and Sugar, covered, foliage design with gold, pair	200.00
Cup and Saucer, demitasse, foliage design	35.00
Inkwell, 2 x 3½" x 3¾", openwork sides, simulated bamboo cross pieces	45.00

Plates

7", bird, flowers, butterfly decor, early	80.00
7", collared base, scalloped rim, 19th century	160.00

10", peony and daisies, butterflies, Chin Lang mark	250.00
11", leaf shape, pastel florals, bug decor, ribbing	275.00
Soap Dish, 3½", hanging type	85.00
Sugar, 5", loop handles	150.00
Teapot, 5", bulbous covered, raised pastel floral decor, late	75.00
Umbrella Holder, 8½", flowering tree	800.00

Vases

7¼", underglaze decor panels, ears, late	200.00
9", applied Foo Dog and small animal near top, early	700.00
9½", hexagonal shape, bird and floral decor, late	175.00
11", hexagonal, pink and white flowers, 19th century	400.00
12¼", Iris, wall vase	185.00
14", sea bottom decor	225.00

CELLULOID ITEMS

Celluloid is the trade name for a material made of nitrocellulose and camphor invented just before 1870. It was used mainly in making toilet articles and also as an inexpensive material for figurines, jewelry, vases, etc. to simulate the more expensive amber, bone, ivory or tortoise shell.

Brooch, 2½" d. yellow and black, art deco style $15.00

Album, photo, 8½ x 12"	27.50
Baby Rattle, 2½"	6.50
Bank, "My Own Bank," clock shaped	15.00

Boxes

Collar, lined	25.00
Glove, mottled green with decor of flowers, original lining	42.50
Jewelry, hinged lid, 2½"	14.50
Powder, 2 x 4"	6.50

Trinket

Covered, picture on lid and front, man and woman	15.00
Hinged lid, lined, has picture of woman in canoe on lake, continues around box, metal fastening	17.50

Combs

8⅝", ivory color	8.00
Black, set with red stones, ornamental	8.50
Crumb Set, crumber and tray	6.00
Doll, 5", moveable arms and legs, to dress	15.00

Dresser Sets

Five pieces, tray, mirror, hair receiver, comb and brush	37.50
Eight pieces, long box, round box with glass insert, nail buffer, nail file, button hook, scissors, shoe horn and mirror	50.00
Elephant, 6", nodding, natural color with beige blanket on back	20.00
Fan, pierced frame, "Germany"	12.00
Hair brush	3.50
Hair Pin, 5⅛", amber, fancy openwork	6.00
Hair Receiver, 3 pieces	6.50
Hand Mirror, 4", ring handle	8.50
Manicure Set, 14 pieces, leather roll case	35.00
Mule, standing, "German"	25.00
Napkin Ring, ivory color	8.00
Ram, 3½ x 4½"	15.00
Reindeer, removable antlers, set of 8	35.00
Shoe Horn	5.00
St. Nicholas, figurine, with sack, "Germany"	25.00
St. Nicholas, 8½", with light inside (Xmas)	27.50
Tray, dresser, 7½"	10.00
Vase, 6½"	10.00

CHALKWARE

Chalkware figurines are made of Plaster-of-Paris and decorated with water base paints. The animal forms are imitations of the Staffordshire and other European models.

There is a discrepancy concerning the origin of chalkware. Some say that it was developed from the folk art of the Pennsylvania Dutch or Germans; others insist that the figurines were made and sold in America by Italian immigrants during the mid-nineteenth century.

Bust, 11½″ h. woman on pedestal, "Micaela," MFO,270 on back, black **$125.00**

Cat, 4½″	175.00
Dogs	
3″ base, white, black trim, red dots	135.00
4″, reclining, original black and brown paint, early, pair	460.00
8½″, with sparkly, red ribbon, late	50.00
12″, Staffordshire-type, white with black markings	325.00
Deer, old dark polychrome paint, antlers painted yellow	45.00
Dove, 6″	135.00
Eagle, spread, 9″, late	225.00
Ewe and Lamb, 7″	325.00

Hen	
6½″	250.00
On cardboard nest	15.00
Lamb, 8½″, grey body, tail and ears, red inside ears	325.00
Lincoln, bust, 13″, signed Boston Sculpture Co., 1909, Melrose, Mass.	85.00
Pig Bank, fanciful decoration, original paint	15.00
Rabbit, sitting, 8½″	180.00
Roosters	
6½″, multicolored gold trim, late .	50.00
11″, painted, late	250.00
Shepherd and Pig	12.50
Squirrel, 9″	250.00
Stag, 15″	475.00
"Thinker," "Kewpie"	22.00

CHARACTER AND PERSONALITY ITEMS

Children raised in the age of radio, television, and comic strips looked forward to their favorite programs and the premiums they offered and/or products they promoted. Fictional characters assumed very real personalities.

This area of collectibles is rapidly growing. Collectors are advised to specialize early. Because of the abundance of these items, garage sales have been a fruitful and inexpensive way to add to a collection.

See also COWBOY COLLECTIBLES and DISNEYANA

Shirley Temple pitcher, 4½″ . . **$22.50**

Andy Gump, figural light bulb, white milk glass, 3″	30.00
Batman, thermos, 1966	5.00

Beatles, textured mesh seamfree nylons, heads and signatures printed on fabric at top 80.00

Betty Boop and Bimbo
Ashtray, three dimensional figures on rim, orange dress and blue hat 100.00
Hanky, white with pictures of characters in corners 30.00

Brownies
Book, "The Brownies in the Philippines," 144 pages 30.00
Cup and Saucer, porcelain 35.00
Paper Dolls, set of 12 . . . . 40.00
Spoon, demitasse, enameled Brownie, sterling 25.00

Buck Rogers
Battle Cruiser, Tootsietoy, blue and white, 4½" 65.00
Big Little Book, Whitman, 1935 . . 17.50
Telescope, 1½ diameter, 14" long 125.00
Water Pistol, red and yellow design 85.00
Buffalo Bill, trade card, 1910 . . . . . 7.50

Buster Brown
Camera 35.00
Clicker 5.00
Figurine, cast iron 20.00
Knife, Fork, and Spoon, silver plate 45.00

Campbell Kids
Mug 20.00
Salt and Pepper 17.50

Captain Marvel
Iron-Ons, eight tissue sheets, two colors 25.00
Pennant, dark blue felt with maroon picture 20.00
Wrist Watch, original box 110.00

Captain Midnight
Flight Patrol Badge 10.00
Glass, Ovaltine 17.50
Membership Badge 10.00

Davy Crockett
Doll, beige soft covering, vinyl face, 19" 20.00
Glass, green picture and white lettering, 4" 8.00
Mug, bright yellow plastic, black illustration 15.00
Notebook binder, three ring, vinyl cover 10 x 12" 12.50

Dick Tracy
Camera, Seymore Products, Chicago, black plastic, 3 x 5" 40.00
Card Game, Whitman, 1934, thirty-five cards 25.00
Pistol, click, litho tin, "Junior" . . . 30.00
Salt and Pepper, plaster, Dick and Junior 32.50

Dionne Quintuplets
Sheet Music, "Fifty Chubby Tiny Toes — Quintuplets Lullaby," 1935 25.00

Thermometer, wall, shows girls eating, notes about each girl, 1935 . . . . 35.00
Elsie, pull toy, "Cow Who Jumps Over The Moon," 1944 . . . . 37.50
Felix, post card, English, 1924, being chased by ostrich 17.50

Flash Gordon
Magazine, *Look*, beginning March 15, 1938, three issues devoted to new movie serial 45.00
Photo, Dixie premium, color, 9 x 11" 25.00
Fred Flintstone and Dino Marx Wind-Up Toy, lithographed tin, 1963, 5½ x 8" 80.00
Froggy the Gremlin, rubber squeeze toy, J. E. McConnel 32.50

Spoon, "Tony the Tiger," Kellogg Co., old company plate 1965 . . . . $8.00

Howdy Doody
Bandanna, Howdy and bucking horses, 18 x 18" 35.00
Cookie-Go-Round, litho tin container, clear glass knob, 8" high . 35.00
Salt and Pepper set, shape of Howdy's head 27.50
Wallet, picture of Dilly Dally, Clarabell and the Air-O-Doodle, 3 x 7" 12.50
Wash Cloth Glover, terry cloth, picture of Mr. Bluster 15.00
Umbrella, blue vinyl top with pictures of Howdy, Mr. Bluster, Clarabell and Flubadub 50.00
Jetsons, tin wind-up figure, Marx, litho tin, 1963, 4" 32.50
Jiggs' lunch box, oval shape, color litho, tin, 1930's 45.00

Little Orphan Annie
Big Little Book, Whitman, 1934, 7 x 9½", 316 pages 50.00
Cup, Ovaltine, green oval ground, Annie and Sandy running for more

Ovaltine 35.00
Manuel, "Official 1936 Secrets for Silver Star Member," green four page folder, 3 x 6½″ 80.00
Tea Set, dark green depression glass, four place settings, original box 135.00
Stove, red metal, Annie holding a tray with cake, 5 x 4″ 45.00
Moon Mullins and Kayo, salt and pepper shakers, seated on yellow chairs 27.50

Planters Peanut
Clock, alarm, original box, 1960's special offer 35.00
Cookie Cutters, plastic, two different shapes, blue 7.50
Jar, 15″, four peanuts in relief, peanut finial, embossed 110.00
Mug, baby, silver plated 35.00
Pencil, mechanical, figure at end is floating in oil 12.50

Popeye
Eagle Pencil Box, pink, red, and black design, pictures of Popeye and others, 1929 .... 32.50
Pop-up Book, "Popeye Among the White Savages," Blue Ribbon Press, 1934, 60 pages, 4 x 5″ ... 100.00
Puzzle, Jaymar, Popeye punching a heavy set person while others look on, 1940 .... 27.50
Olive Oyl, walking toy, composition material, 5″ 80.00
Ring Toss Game, cardboard figures of Popeye and Olive, 1933, original box, 10½ x 15½″ 60.00
Raggedy Ann Planter, glazed china, "Rubens Originals, Los Angeles, Made in Japan," 4 x 4 x 6″ 27.50

Shirley Temple
Bathing Suit, Forest Mills, original box 140.00
Book, Heidi, hardback 15.00
Book, Little Rebel 12.50
Creamer 25.00
Figurine, flocking on dress, paper flowers, 7″ 50.00
Glass, blue, decal 16.00
Paper Dolls and Dresses, Saalfield, 1934 .... 60.00

Space Patrol
Diplomatic Pouch, Top Secret, brown and white cardboard folder, 11½″ square 80.00
Gun, plastic, fires darts, Space Patrol emblem on grip 120.00
Space Patrol Card, Wheat Chex premium 17.50
Video, Capt., leather belt and holster, decorated with silver metal studs 37.50

Video, Capt., Puzzle, two men flying rocketship, 10½ x 14½″ 40.00

Superman
Hand Puppet, cloth body, vinyl head, 1956, 10″ 20.00
Muscle Building Set, Golden, Milton, contains handles, springs, hand grippers, jump rope, etc., original box, 11½ x 18″ 85.00
Snorkel, Super, blue plastic, original box, 29″ 30.00
Tarzan, Better Little Book, Whitman, 1945 .... 17.50
Uncle Wiggley, magazine, lot of seven issues, 1943 .... 21.00

Yellow Kid
Button, No. 10 .... 15.00
Button, No. 46, for Yale College . 27.50
Stickpin, die-cut metal, pale yellow nightshirt, flesh tones on face, 1896 .... 60.00

CHELSEA

Chelsea is a fine English porcelain which was made to compete with Dresden. The factory began operating in the Chelsea area of London, England, in the 1740's. Chelsea products can be divided into four periods: (1) Early period, 1740's, with incised triangle and raised anchor mark, (2) The 1750's, with red raised anchor mark, (3) The 1760's, the gold anchor period, (4) The Derby period from 1770–1783. In 1924, a large number of the molds and models of figurines were found at the Spode-Copeland Works and many items were brought back into circulation.

Plate, 9⅞″ floral decor on white ground $85.00

Bowl, 6½″, molded leaves on exterior, floral spray in center, red an-

chor	1000.00
Candlesticks, 10¾", birds, gold anchor, pair	2000.00
Cup and Saucer, ladies, late	17.50
Figurines	
4⅜", Pantaloon, Italian comedy, red anchor	1500.00
7", Tyrolean Dancers, red anchor	2500.00
8½", Woman with tray, white background with rust, red and blue decor, late	250.00
9", Woodsman and Milkmaid, late, pair	500.00
Jardiniere, 11", covered, hexagonal shape, red anchor	1275.00
Plates	
7½", floral decor, late	40.00
8½", fruit decor, late	75.00
9⅜", floral decor, red anchor	875.00
Tureens, covered	
5¼", molded as cauliflower with natural coloring, red anchor	1000.00
15", blue, gold anchor	1800.00

"CHELSEA" GRANDMOTHER'S WARE

Wares decorated with the familiar grape, sprig, or thistle pattern in relief and lustred are erroneously called Chelsea. These wares were not made in Chelsea, but in the Staffordshire district of England in the early 1880's. There is a movement to rename this decorated porcelain "Grandmother's Ware."

Plate, 7" dia., Vintage, copper lustre decor $18.00

Bowl, 10", grape	50.00
Butter Pat, grape	7.50

Creamers	
Grape	25.00
Thistle	45.00
Cups and Saucers	
Grape, bouillon	20.00
Grape, handled	20.00
Thistle, handled	27.50
Egg Cup	16.50
Plates	
Grape, 4"	9.50
Grape, 7"	15.00
Grape, 9"	25.00
Sauce boat, grape	25.00
Sugars, covered	
Grape	75.00
Sprig	135.00
Teapots	
Grape	125.00
Thistle	150.00
Set, coffee pot, creamer, covered sugar, purple lustre decor	325.00

CHILDREN'S BOOKS

Collectors have always been attracted to children's books, because there's a bit of the child in all of us. Books in the 18th century were popular gifts for children, and unlike today, there were not so many of them published. They were treasured momentoes and in many cases, kept throughout a lifetime. The early art work in these books, by the artists and illustrators of the day, make them interesting and valuable collectibles.

ABC, linen, 12 pages	10.00
Aesop's Fables, large, color plates and illus. by Milo Winter, c. 1930	35.00
Alice's Adventures in Wonderland, Lewis Carroll, illus. by Tennial, 1st ed. 1886, red cloth	800.00
Arabian Night's Stories, color plates and illus. by Milo Winter	27.50
Big Circus, W. W. Denslow, illus. by author, 1903	50.00
Book about Animals, woodblock prints by Rufus Merrill	12.50
Brownies	
Brownies Abroad, Palmer Cox, dust jacket	50.00
Brownies and the Goblins, 1915	10.00
Brownies and the Farmer	40.00
Brownies, Their Book, Century Co., 1887	60.00
Bunny Brown and his Sister Sue, series, ea.	15.00
ChatterBox	
1887	15.00
1910	10.00
Child's Book of Myths, large, color plates and black and white illus.	

"Zauberlinda: the Wise Witch" by Eva Katharine Gibson, Chicago, 1901 . . . . $40.00

by Milo Winter, c. 1930	35.00
Child's Book of Songs, 7 woodblock prints	25.00
Frog Who Would A-Wooing Go, McLaughlin, Fairy Moonbeam Series, 1870	25.00
Henty, Alfred, Series, Boy's adventure books, various titles, ea. . . .	10.00
Honeybunch, series, ea.	10.00
Kids of Many Colors, McLaughlin, 1888, color illus.	50.00
Little Engine that Could, retold by Watty Piper & illus. by Lois Lensby	10.00
Mother Goose Nursery Rhymes, illustrated, G. M. Burdt, Violet Moore Higgins	18.50
Mother Goose, pamphlet, Metropolitan Life Insurance Co., 1925	11.50
Merry Adventures of Robin Hood, written and illus. by Howard Pyle, Scribner's leather binding, 1883 .	40.00
Oliver Optic series, Lee and Shepherd, Boston, 1860–1890	15.00
Out and About, Woods, 1882	15.00
Pinnochio, A. Collodi, illus. by Tony Sarg	25.00
Poppy Ott, series, Leo Edwards, 1924, ea.	15.00
Potter, Beatrix, Animal Stories, color	

plates by author, small books, any of original series, ea	35.00
Raggedy Ann, series, Johhy Gruelle, color plates, c. 1916, ea.	28.50
Rollo series, Jacob Abbott, 1840–1850, ea.	20.00
Sleepy Time Stories, 17 plates, Maude Humphrey, c. 1911	55.00
St. Nicholas, bound volumes, six months, 1889, 1890, red cloth, ea.	18.00
Two bound volumes, 12 months, 1880–1881, leather spine, marbleized covers, ea.	35.00
Tin Woodsman of Oz, Frank Baum, 1918	25.00
Tuck's Play and Pleasure Series, Raphel Tuck and Sons, linen, c. 1890, Robinson Crusoe	50.00
T'was the Night Before Christmas, illus. by Jesse Wilcox Smith	50.00
Uncle Wiggly series, small, illus. in color, c. 1927, ea.	10.00
"Winnie-the-Pooh," A. A. Milne, illus. by author, 1st. ed. 1927	50.00
Youth's Companion, Perry Mason and Co., bound, weeklies, year 1888	25.00

CHILDREN'S FEEDING DISHES

During the late 19th century and into the 20th, tablewares designed especially for children's personal use were very much in vogue. Even major pottery firms catered to the demand. Today these children's items are very collectible and sometimes command very high prices.

Also see CHILDREN'S TOY DISHES, GLASS, PORCELAIN AND TIN.

Bowls	
6¾", "Beach Baby," P. K. Unity, Germany	35.00
7½", "Campbell Kids," Buffalo Pottery Co.	50.00
6½", "Kewpie"	40.00
9", "Sing and Song of Sixpence," warming type	35.00
Creamers	
4", "Bunnykins," Royal Doulton . .	35.00
5", "Cow Jumping over the Moon," U. S.	20.00
"Jack and Jill," Germany	30.00
"Kewpies," playing in yard	30.00
Cup and saucer, Crown Staffordshire China, floral decor	30.00
Mugs	
Alphabet and dog chasing rabbit decor	25.00
3½", "Bunnykins," Royal Doulton	35.00
Silver, dated 1854	95.00

**Feeding Dish "Baby Bunting,"
5¼"** $39.00

Napkins Ring, design in metal	20.00
Plates	
6½", "Bunnykins," Royal Doulton	35.00
6½", "Frolicking Animals," James Kent, Ltd.	35.00
7½", "Mother Goose," animals . .	20.00
7", "Puss in Boots," red and white porcelain	15.00
"Sunbonnet Girl," Roseville Pottery	45.00
7½", "Winnie-the-Pooh," color decor	14.50
7", "Three Little Kittens," heart border	18.50

CHILDREN'S TOY DISHES

From the Victorian era up until after World War II, children's toy dishes were made by many pottery companies and toy manufacturers. Toy tea sets were made in Japan, occupied Japan, Europe, and in the United States, and today, these items are quite collectible. As distinguished from the utilitarian Feeding Dishes, Toy Dishes were used with dolls and doll houses.

PORCELAIN

Candlestick, 2¾", Staffordshire . . .	3.00
Chamber Pot, "The Family Physician," Japan	4.00
Casserole, "Blue Willow"	39.50
Condiment Sets	
Transfer, children and dolls, Germany, 3", cannisters, 15 pcs., set	150.00

Teapot, 2 cups and saucers, white porcelain with colorful transfer of woman and children, Germany $27.00

Four bottles, in pewter stand, flat, not castor set	60.00
Demitasse set, 21 pieces, white porcelain, Germany	165.00
Plate, 4", Spongeware, decorated, blue and white, c. 1820	30.00
Platters, 5 x 3½", black and white fish in center, gold trim, no mark .	18.50
Tea Sets	
6 serving pieces, blue and white country scene	85.00
10 pieces, on round tray, Occupied Japan	23.50
21 pieces, white with gold decor, lavender flowers, six cups and saucers, creamer, covered sugar, covered teapot	55.00
Orange, with hand painted design, tea set	65.00
18 pieces, blue and white transfer, Spode mark, covered teapot, coffee pot, sugar, creamer, water pitcher, six cups and saucers . . .	165.00
Sugar Bowl, creamer, teapot, cups and saucers, pink roses, green leaves, Spode mark	175.00
15 pieces, Nippon, little girl, puppy, and duck	275.00
17 pieces, Noritake, "Azalea" . . .	200.00
28 pieces, blue and white transfer, center scene, little boy with very large dog, creamer, covered sugar and teapot, 8 plates, 8 cups and saucers, c. 1900	200.00
15 pieces, "Blue Willow," Japan .	125.00
Water Set, 4½", pitcher, "Red Riding Hood and Wolf," six tumblers	175.00

TIN

Mugs	
3½", "Little Bo-Peep"	10.00

Nursery Rhymes	**32.00**

Tea Sets

13 pieces, hand painted, animals, original box	**15.00**
6 pieces, Ohio Art Co., plate, tea-pot, 2 cups and saucers, c. 1940	**18.00**
9 pieces, red and blue, Germany, cats and dogs	**55.00**
10 pieces, "Cinderella"	**25.00**
15 pieces, "Little Bo-Peep"	**45.00**

CHILDREN'S TOY GLASS DISHES

Children's glass dishes evolved in the 1900's by a recycling process. Glass manufacturers had a surplus problem stemming from producing only two new patterns a year. To remedy the waste, the manufacturers began to produce dishes for children. The dishes were used as premiums with grocery items and were also sold to the Sears Roebuck and Montgomery Ward catalog houses.

Tulip and Honeycomb: Covered Butler, oval $35.00
Cream $18.00
Sugar $22.00

Berry Sets

Amazon (or Sawtooth Band), 6 pieces	**85.00**
Lacy Daisy, 7 pieces	**82.00**
Tappan, 6 pieces	**80.00**

Bowls

Hawiian Lei, (Bee mark)	**25.00**
Kokomo (Bar and Finecut)	**22.50**
Portland, with gold	**27.50**

Butter, covered

Aztec	**20.00**
Galloway (Virginia #2)	**50.00**
Tappan	**42.50**
Wee Branches	**125.00**

Cake Stands

Beautiful Lady	**35.00**
Carltec	**35.00**
Rexford	**30.00**
Strigil	**30.00**

Carafe, Water, 4⅛", Truncated Prisms (Thompson's #77), pair	**100.00**

Castor Sets

English Hobnail, 3-bottle, tin stand	**35.00**
Milk glass, plain bottles, metal stand	**40.00**
Palmette, 2-bottle, metal stand	**27.50**
Saxon, 3-bottle, pewter tops and stand	**90.00**

Condiment Sets

English Hobnail, cruet, salt and pepper on tray	**50.00**
Hickman, oil bottle and cruet on tray	**55.00**

Creamers

Amazon (Sawtooth Band)	**27.50**
Arrowhead	**20.00**
Daisy and Button	**18.00**
Hobnail	**20.00**
Inverted Strawberry	**45.00**
Sweetheart	**45.00**

Cups and Saucers

Cherry Blossom, pink	**19.50**
Doric and Pansy, ultramarine (part of Pretty Polly set)	**22.50**
Grape design, set of six	**75.00**
Lion	**50.00**

Mugs

Butterfly	**25.00**
Grape, with leaves and vine, clear	**20.00**
Liberty Bell, milk glass	**210.00**
Plain, ribbed base, candy-dip type	**25.00**

Punch Bowls

Arrowhead in Ovals	**25.00**
Nursery Rhymes, milk glass	**125.00**

Punch Bowl Sets

Inverted Strawberry, bowl and six cups	**175.00**
Nursery Rhymes, clear, bowl and six cups	**75.00**
Tulip and Honeycomb, bowl and six cups	**110.00**
Wild Rose, milk glass, bowl and six cups	**100.00**

Spooners

Button Panel	**25.00**
Clear and Diamond Panels	**45.00**
Nursery Rhymes	**70.00**
Pennsylvania #1	**22.00**

Sugars, covered

Colonial (Heisey)	**45.00**
Flute (Heisey)	**28.00**
Lion, frosted	**350.00**
Sweetheart, with gold	**35.00**

Table Sets, (four pieces, creamer, covered sugar, covered butter and spooner.)

Akro-Agate, green marbleized	**65.00**
Tappan	**85.00**
Tulip and Honeycomb	**120.00**

Water Pitchers

Galloway (Virginia #2)	**70.00**

Pattee Cross	50.00
Portland with Diamond Band (Virginia #1)	75.00
Sheep and ram design	67.50

CHILDREN'S ITEMS— MISCELLANEOUS

Block puzzle, six views, lithograph scenes $85.00

Blocks
Design, different colors and sides in box make designs, set	50.00
Paper over wood, Victorian girls playing with pets and dolls	45.00
Brownie Stamping Set, "The Funny Brownie Stamps"	45.00
Bubble Pipe, tin, c. 1880	100.00
Coal bucket, on stand, tin	10.00
Coloring Book, early, "Buster Brown"	10.00
Curling iron, for doll	3.00
Doll Coach, leather seat and back, cast iron body	295.00
Flat iron, or Sad iron, for doll's clothes, and two interchangeable handles	28.00
Ice Cream Freezer, 5 x 7", wooden barrel, iron handle	45.00
Iron coal stove, 4 cast iron pots	100.00
Kiddie Kar, all wood, stencil-decor and dated, three wheels	75.00
Parasol, child's, red and white with	

ruffles	20.00
Rattles	
Celluloid, souvenir, 1893 Columbian Exposition	65.00
Wooden, hand-hewn box-type, overlapping sides, 18th century	35.00
Marbles, Akro Agate, set of 50, original box	40.00
Noah's Ark, paper on wood, with animals, c. 1900	125.00
Piano, Schoenhut, 9¾" high	75.00
Sewing Machine, 5 x 7", "Betsy Ross"	75.00
Sleds	
36", wooden, railing around back, handle for pushing	225.00
Painted flower decor	185.00
Wash Tub, tin, blue and white, with small washboard	15.00

CHRISTMAS ITEMS

There are many reasons why individuals collect Christmas decorations and related items from the past . . . nostalgia, return to the basics, acceptance of traditions. Perhaps they seek assurance that in this contemporary world, an old fashioned Christmas will always be in vogue.

Light, Bell, Santa decor, all glass $10.00

Books
"Miracle of Christmas," Hallmark, 1968	6.00
"The Life and Adventures of Santa Claus," Julie Lane, Santa Claus Publishing Co., 1932	25.00
Pop-Up Santa Claus, 1949	8.00

Cards, "Greetings for Christmas," in
good condition 3–5.00
Santa Claus, 47", wooden, hand
painted 150.00
Santa (filled with straw), in wooden
sleigh, 8 celluloid reindeer, remov-
able antlers, "Germany," c. 1900,
set 100.00
Santa Claus glass ornament and
planter, combination 16.00
Santa Stocking, 31", printed cotton,
c. 1900 . . . . 35.00
Tree Lights, candleholders, 3½"
Amber 10.00
Amethyst 15.00
Cobalt 12.50
Tree Lights, electric
Ball with holly 4.00
Ball with stars 4.00
Basket of fruit, milk glass 5.00
Birdcage 5.00
Blue Bird 4.00
Child, milk glass 6.00
Clown, milk glass 6.00
Elephant 3.00
Gingerbread Man 8.00
Grapes 8.00
Humpty Dumpty, milk glass 8.50
Lantern, Occupied Japan 3.00
Rose 4.00
Santa, head 8.50
Santa, standing 15.00
Showman, milk glass 8.50
Terrier 11.00
Zepplin, with flag 10.00
Tree Lights, sets
Bubble-lite, original box 15.00
Lights by Noma, c. 1936, original
box 15.00
Tree, 11½", with fixtures for
Noma Bubble Lights, by Noma
Mfg. Co., Brooklyn, N. Y., original
box 35.00
Tree Ornaments
Angel, wax figural, 6" long, in
flight, with hair and spun glass
wings, blowing horn, "Germany" . 65.00
Balls
5", amber glass, original wire . . . 15.00
7", covered with silver twine, like
a balloon, hanging basket be-
neath, pink satin color, "Germa-
ny" 10.00
Football player, celluloid 6.00
Fruit shapes, blown glass, each . . 8.00
Icicles, 8", double, each 2.50
Icicles, twisted metal, all colors,
each 1.50
Mercury glass, very heavy, brass
collar and hanger c. 1890 . . . . . . 10.00
Reindeer, 5", blown amber glass,
"Germany" 20.00

Spider, blown glass, in strands of
blown glass web, "Germany" . . . 25.00
Peacock, blown glass, brush tail . 15.00
Pinecone, silver blown glass 10.00
Saxophone, trumpet, tuba, and
English horn, all colors, set 35.00
Santa, blown glass 21.50
Tree Stands
Tin shaped, tin with decals, Noma 55.00
Musical, revolving and lighted,
"Lador," c. 1935 . . . . 250.00

CIGAR CUTTERS, POCKET

**Pocket-type cigar cutters were not only utili-
tarian to a smoking man but often a fine
piece of jewelry that was attached to his
watch chain. With the return of the vested
suit and watch chain, cigar cutters have regained their popularity. They are again being
made and sold in tobacco shops and jewelry
stores.**

Man, arm swings, 1⅝" h., metal $75.00

Bottle-shaped, 2", brass 20.00
Combination cigar cutter, and pen
knife, MOP sides with ring for
chain 30.00
Combination cigar cutter and watch
fob, 10K gold 70.00
Elks emblem, 1915 . . . . 20.00
Horseshoe shaped with buckle 40.00
Knife types
Gold, 10K, engraved 55.00
Goldplated Loop 20.00

MOP and silver loop, 2½", leather holder	35.00
Silverplated	20.00
Sterling, embossed	50.00
Scissors type	
Gold, 10K	55.00
Nickelplated	35.00
Silverplated	35.00
Sterling, embossed	50.00

CIGAR STORE FIGURES

Cigar store Indians, squaws or turks were familiar sights in front of cigar stores and tobacco shops. These figures are now scarce and command a good price when offered for sale. They are being reproduced in various sizes, styles and materials.

Indian, 108" **$9500.00**

Indian, 24½", original paint, bone embellishments, leather belt, and metal earrings 2000.00

Indian Brave, 60"	6000.00
Indian Chief, 60"	5000.00
Indian Chief, "Strobel"	7000.00
Indian, 6 ft. original paint, "Frank"	7000.00
Indian Squaw, tall	7500.00
Indian Maiden, half life size, on base with wheels, 5' 8", painted	7000.00
Statue of Lincoln, life size, carved wood	8000.00
Standing figure, cap, ruffled collar, red and blue costume, holding box of cigars in left hand, 5' 9"	8000.00

CINNABAR

Cinnabar is a ware made of numerous layers of a heavy mercuric sulphide, often referred to as vermillion. It was carved into boxes, buttons, snuff bottles, and vases. The best of this ware was made in China.

Bracelet, 7½", plus clasp marked "China" **$80.00**

Boxes	
Floral carvings on red, black interior, 2 x 3"	75.00
Carved bird on lid, marked "China"	50.00
Carved, scenic decor, brass bound edges	75.00
Garden scene, 2½"	50.00
Chinese figures in garden with flowers and trees	75.00
Figurine, horses, 10½", jade with turquoise inlay	2500.00
Plate, 9", carved scene of people	250.00
Snuff bottle, red, carved	125.00
Tray, 8 x 12", scenic decor	200.00
Vases	
Carved, 7", people	100.00
Floral design, 4", red, marked "China"	50.00
Carved floral design, brown, 6½"	75.00
Dragon design, early, 10½"	225.00

CIVIL WAR AND RELATED ITEMS

Civil War items listed here consist mainly of military items issued and used from 1861–1865.

Union artifacts are the most plentiful. If the artifact is Confederate, the price will increase four to ten times over a similar Union artifact. Beware of reproductions. Everything is reproduced, from swords and rifles to clothing and badges. Due in part to the reenactment units, reproductions began inundating the market in the early 1950's.

Stereoscope cards, "The War for the Union," each $10.00

Badge, Helmut, brass shield and eagle, company number in center ..	40.00
Bags	
Carpet, 18 x 18", leather handles, iron lock, double compartments .	65.00
Doctor's, 9 x 11½", black leather, two flapped pockets on front, brass mounts, lock with star and eagle	250.00
Bayonet and Scabbard, .58 cal., 1861 musket	45.00
Belt, waist, leather, brass buckle with eagle imprint, Union	95.00
Boots, Cavalry, pair, black leather .	150.00
Bullet Mold, iron, four .44 cal., Colt Army Revolver	85.00
Buttons, brass, U. S. eagle imprint, each	7.50
Canteens	
Tin, drum shape	100.00
Wood, cloth covered	65.00
Cap, Kepi, blue wood, black leather bill, brass insignia	125.00
Cartridge Box, pistol, brown leather, .36 cal., "W. C. Mclallan & Co.," Springfield, MA	85.00
Cartridge Box, rifle, black leather, .58 cal., stamped "U.S."	110.00
Casket Plate, silver on copper	25.00

Chin strap, Officer's	25.00
Daguerreotypes	
Confederate, 2 x 2½"	125.00
Union, 2¾ x 3¼"	75.00
Union, 2 x 2½"	50.00
Discharge Papers, 1st Ohio, dated 1863	80.00
Drum, 17" dia., 15" high, eagle motif on side	500.00
Envelope Covers	
Confederate	100.00
Union	25.00
Enlistment Papers, Union, signed ..	75.00
Eye Glasses	
Clear, adjustable frames	25.00
Sun, Sharpshooter's	30.00

Confederate cap box, found at Antietam $200.00

Flags	
6' x 9', United States, 36 stars, 1864–1867 period	500.00
22 x 28", 19th Corps, 159 New York State Volunteer's, swallow tail, silk, two ties	1000.00
Field Glasses, 7½" closed, brass, made by Lemaire Fabt., Paris ...	85.00
Gloves, Officer's, leather	100.00
Helmet, Dress, cavalry, brass trim with eagle badge, spike	150.00
Holsters, Pistol	
Brown leather, iron flap fastener, Confederate	300.00
Brown leather, push through flap fastener, brown leather belt, Confederate	450.00
Horse Bit, iron	65.00
Jacket, Shell, Union cavalry, complete with buttons, lining, and inspector's marks	350.00

Knife and Spoon, combination	25.00
Knives, Bowie	
Bone handle, scabbard	275.00
Stag handle, Wostenholme, "IXL," etching of eagles and flags, leather scabbard	600.00
Wood handle, brass guard, no scabbard	125.00
Leggings, black leather	125.00
Letters and Numbers, Regimental, brass, each	8.50
Mess Kit, bone handles, original leather case	150.00
Musket, Union, Model 1863, rifle, .58 cal., marked "U. S. Springfield," walnut stock	400.00
Pistols	
Colt, Model 1860 Army Revolver, 6 shot, .44 cal., 8" barrel	650.00
Colt, Model 1861, Navy Revolver, 6 shot, .36 cal., 7" barrel	500.00
Single Shot Boot, 3" barrel, .40 cal.	150.00
Plume, Shako, Cavalry and Artillery, horse hair	25.00
Razor, U. S. and eagle impressed in gutta percha handle	75.00
Ribbon, 1861–1865, Lincoln's head surrounded by "With Malice Toward None, With Charity For All," blue gray	75.00
Saddle, Cavalry, McCullem and Militia types	295.00
Saddle Bags	
Allegheny Arsenal, 1864	250.00
Virginia, 1st Cavalry	500.00
Shoulder Sling, brass buckle, carbine	60.00
Slave	
Bill of Rental, 1865	175.00
Bill of Sale, entire family, 1862 . .	250.00
Spurs	
Brass, Officer's	125.00
Teardrop, 1" rowels with chins . .	50.00
Spy Glass, 16", four sections, leather wrapped	250.00
Sword Belt Plate, Union, Non-Commissioned Officer	60.00
Swords (also see SWORDS)	
Confederate Cavalry Saber, 40" .	450.00
Light Cavalry Saber, Union, 42", Model 1860	150.00
Naval Cutlass, Model 1860, leather scabbard, brass grip	350.00
Officer's Sword, Model 1850, iron scabbard	200.00
Tarpot	125.00

CLAMBROTH GLASS

Clambroth glass derives its name from the color of the glass. The semi-opaque greyish-white color resembles the broth from clams. This type of glass ware was popular in the Victorian period.

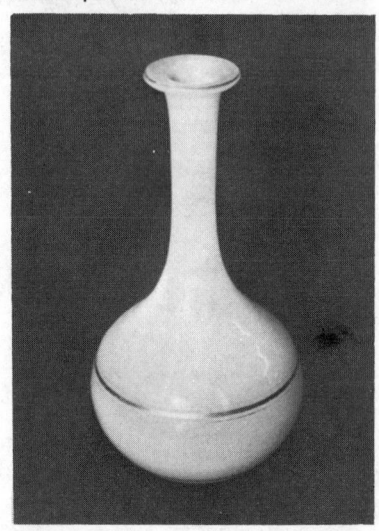

Barber Bottle, 6", gold trim line decoration, possibly Sandwich . . .$37.50

Bottle, barber, "Bay Rum," stoppered	30.00
Buttons, rounded tops, 1", brass shanks, set of six	3.50
Candlesticks, Dolphins, pair	500.00
Cruet, applied blue rope handle . . .	50.00
Goblet, souvenir type, "Koral Ware," with red lettering, gold trim	35.00
Mugs	
Birds and wheat, fence post handle	
Swans, ring handle, 3"	35.00
Shaving, floral enamel decor, gold rim	35.00
Plate, 8"	30.00
Sterilizer, 5"	15.00
Toothpick, souvenir	25.00
Tumbler, souvenir, "Atlantic City, N. J.," floral enamel decor	35.00
Vases	
Crimped top, pontil, hand painted flowers, pair	75.00
Floral, 9¾"	25.00
Whimsey, 2", green serpent entwining cylinder	45.00

CLEWELL POTTERY

Charles Walter Clewell was first a metal worker and second a potter. In the early 1900's he opened a small shop in Canton, Ohio, to produce metal overlay pottery.

Metal on pottery was not a new idea, but Clewell was perhaps the first to completely mask the ceramic body with copper, brass, "silvered" and "bronzed" metals. One result was a product whose patina added to the character of the piece over time.

Most of the wares are marked with a simple incised "CLEWELL" along with a code number. Because Clewell used pottery blanks from other firms, the names "Owens" or "Weller" are sometimes found.

A limited quantity of his art work exists, because he operated on a small scale with little outside assistance. He retired at the age of 79 in 1955, choosing not to reveal his technique to anyone else.

Vase, 7½", marked #351-24 . .$195.00

Bookends, monogramed, dark brown patina, pair	275.00
Bowl, 4", blue-green patina	100.00
Tankard and Mug Set, seven pieces, hammered & riveted design, dark brown patina	600.00

Tobacco Jar, covered, 6 x 8", hammered & riveted design, dark brown patina	275.00
Vases	
4", twisted shape, raised floral decoration, marked "Clewell and Owens Pottery"	275.00
7", slender, blue-green patina . . .	150.00
8", bulbous base with slender neck and flared top, blue-green patina	195.00
10", jug shaped, copper with brass inlaid design of butterflies . .	550.00
16", blue-green patina	150.00

CLIFTON POTTERY

The Clifton Art Pottery, Newark, N.J., was established by William A. Long, once associated with Lonhuda Pottery, and Fred Tschirner, a chemist.

Production consisted of two major lines: "Crystal Patina," that resembled 'true porcelain' with a subdued crystal-like glaze, and "Indian Ware" or "Western Influence," an adaptation of the American Indians' unglazed and decorated pottery, but with a high glazed black interior. Other lines included "Robin's Egg Blue" and "Tirrube." Robin's Egg Blue is a variation of the crystal patina line but in blue-greens instead of straw colored hues and with a less prominent "crushed crystal" effect in the glaze. Tirrube is on a terra cotta background but features brightly colored, slip decorated flowers and is often artist signed.

Marks were incised or impressed. Early pieces may be dated and shape numbers impressed, and Indian wares were further identified by tribes.

Bowl, 8", Indian Ware, "4 mile run" inscription	65.00
Jar, covered, 7½", Indian Ware . . .	85.00
Candleholder, 7 x 4", 2 handled . . .	100.00
Mug, 4", Arkansas Tribal Design, signed W. A. Long, c. 1905	65.00
Pitcher, with lid, Crystal Patina, 5½"	110.00
Vases	
5 x 4", bulbous gourd shape, 1906	85.00
8 x 5", poppies clustered to form a jagged opening	150.00
9 x 6", bulbous base, 2 handled	175.00
9 x 12", black painted geometric design on terra cotta, marked Clif-	

Vase, 8½", 1905, marked #164 $75.00

ton, CAP mark and "4 mile run" .	175.00
Corset shape, Robin's Egg Blue, Art Nouveau silver overlay	375.00

CLOCKS

The sundial was the first man-made device for measuring time. Its basic disadvantage is well expressed in the saying: "Do like the sundial, count only the sunny days."

With the need for greater dependability, man developed the water clock, the oil clock and the sand clock respectively. All these clocks worked on the same principle — time was measured by the amount of material passing from one container to another.

The wheel clock was the next major step toward more accurate time. These clocks can be traced back as far as the 13th century. Many improvements on the basic wheel clock were made and they continued to be the most accurate time piece available until the quartz crystal movement was introduced in 1934.

Recently an atomic clock, that measures time by the frequency of radiation, that only varies one second in a thousand years, has been invented.

Condition of works is a critical factor in collecting clocks. Examine the works to see how many original parts remain and examine the clock in running condition. If repairs are needed, try to include this in your estimate of purchase price. Few clocks are purchased purely for decorative value.

ALARM CLOCKS

Ansonia, Peep-O-Day, 4" dia. dial, Pat. 3/27/1877, independent second dial	**32.50**
Ben Ben, nickeled case, 4" black dial and luminous numbers	**90.00**
German, ornate oak round case with brass spandrels, strikes on half hour and hour, 30 hour	**150.00**
Gilbert, Wm. L., Blossom Alarm, 4" dia. dial, independent second dial, floral decor on side	**45.00**
Musical, 4 x 5 x 6", nickeled case, Swiss movement, 2 tune	**200.00**
New Haven, Tat-Too, Art Alarm, 4¼" dia. dial, c. 1930	**12.50**
Terry Clock Co., One Day Time Alarm, 2½" dia. dial, 6" high case, iron case, model No. Z	**135.00**
Thomas, Seth, Echo-Alarm, 4½" dia. dial, c. 1885	**40.00**

BANJO CLOCKS

Howard #4, signed on dial	**2250.00**
Howard & Davis, #2, weight driven, signed dial, mint condition	**4500.00**
Ingraham, No. 1, eagle finial, floral decor on neck, river scene in glass, 6" dia. dial, c. 1930	**150.00**
Ingraham, Nile, mahogany case, turned wood columns and wood finial, open light to view pendulum, 39" high, 8" dia. dial	**350.00**
New Haven, mahogany case, 30" high, brass eagle and spandrels, 8 day spring movement	**325.00**
New Haven, miniature case, 16" high, 8 day spring movement . . .	**300.00**
Noyes, L., mahogany case, 7" dia. dial, weight driven, brass spandrels and eagle, original glass tablets, time only	**750.00**
Sessions, Lexington, eagle finial, diamond inlay on waist, sailing ship, 6", dia. dial, c. 1930	**150.00**
Sessions, Salem eagle finial, naval geometric waist, full rigged sailing ship, 8" dia. dial, c. 1930	**250.00**
Stennes, Elmer O., bird's-eye maple veneer case, oval medallion with two female figures and eagle,	

Banjo, 34″ h. mahogany, repainted dial, 8-day, dial marked John Sawin, Boston $1100.00

34½″ **1400.00**

Statzell, A. & Sons, mahogany case, 7″ dial, signed, 8 day weight driven, restored, Charlestown, Mass. **950.00**

Tifft, H., weighted, wooden bezel and wood throat, early **1575.00**

Unsigned, Federal, mahogany and eglomise, New England, 19th century, Federal mansion scene in base, 33½″ **750.00**

Unsigned, Federal mahogany and eglomise, New England, Willard's patent, brass urn finial, 23″, c. 1830 .... **2100.00**

Waltham, No. 1525, mahogany case, gold gilding, Waltham design glasses, 40½″ high **1500.00**

Waltham, No. 1554, walnut case, conical finial, gable end house in rural scene, 21″ high, miniature .. **300.00**

Waterbury, mission oak case, weighted, heavy porcelain dial, black, gold glasses **1500.00**

Waterbury, Williard style, porcelain dial, standard size, 8 day weight movement **1250.00**

Williard, A. "Patent", mahogany case, gilt rope molding, 7″ dial, repainted tablets, 8 day weight driven, time only **2000.00**

Willard, S., "Patent", Federal inlaid mahogany and eglomise, case eagle finial, 33¾″, c. 1830, Boston . **1700.00**

Williard type, 8 day spring driven ... **400.00**

Shelf, Eli Terry & Sons, 8-day, stencil decor, claw feet, Plymouth, Conn. $450.00

BEEHIVE SHELF CLOCKS

Brown, J.C., walnut case, ripple front, 8 day, original **925.00**

Pratt, Daniel, mahogany case, frosted tablet, 8 day **200.00**

Terry and Andrews, 8 day, restored condition **250.00**

Thomas, Seth, column, walnut case, painted dial, 8 day, alarm **295.00**

Thomas, Seth, Grecian, mahogany

case, 8 day, alarm **275.00**
Waterbury, walnut case, frosted
glass, 30 hour **125.00**

BRACKET CLOCKS

Boulle, ornate gilt case, 18″ high,
porcelain dial, full strike, double
fuzee, 8 day, mint condition, c.
1730 . . . . **4250.00**
English, baroque oak case, 29″,
double fuzee, strikes hours **1500.00**
English, double fuzee, 8 day **750.00**
German, inlaid rosewood case, full
columns, two train, quarter chime **450.00**
Vienna, ebony case with basket top,
bracket verge, single strike **850.00**

CALENDAR SHELF AND WALL CLOCKS

Ansonia, Carlos, ornate wood case,
8 day strike, 24½″ **300.00**
Burwell & Carter, wall, #2, rose-
wood case, 31″, B.B. Lewis calen-
dar, 8 day weight, time only **950.00**
Gilbert, Benworth, oak or walnut, 8
day strike, 27″ **500.00**
Gilbert, Maine, oak, battleship Maine
on glass, 8 day strike, 49½″ **2500.00**
Ingraham, Lyric, oak, 8 day strike,
27″ **275.00**
Ingraham, Mosaic, wall, B.B. Lewis
calendar, original dials, 8 day . . . **1000.00**
Ithaca, shelf, No. 11, octagon, 21″ . **700.00**
Ithaca, shelf, mahogany case, sim-
ple pediment top, straight lines,
38½″ **900.00**
Ithaca, shelf, No. 4½″ Favorite, wal-
nut case, 32″ **1500.00**
New Haven, 12″ Drop Octagon,
rosewood, 8 day strike, 24″ **300.00**
Prentiss, Standard, oak case, 30
day, 47″ **1750.00**
Sessions, Eclipse, wall, oak case, 17
x 38″, regulator type, 8 day, time
only **375.00**
Thomas, Seth, Dixie, oak, 8 day
strike, 28″ **600.00**
Thomas, Seth, Parlor Calendar #4,
patent date 12/12/1875, burled
walnut case, brass works, original
label, 25″ **1000.00**
Waterbury, Buffalo Calendar, walnut,
8 day strike **375.00**
Waterbury, English Drop No. 2, ve-
neer and inlay, half hour strike,
27¾″ **400.00**
Welch, E.N., wall, rosewood case
and gold trim, calendar dial, 8 day,
24″ short drop **350.00**

CARRIAGE CLOCKS

Ansonia, 8 day, duplex movement,
8½″ **225.00**
English, Dent, London, French
works, gilt metal, 5½″ **800.00**
French, metal and porcelain, white
dial with landscapes, gilt, repeat-
ing, 6½″ **2750.00**

**Carriage, French brass with 4 beveled
glass panels, 2½ x 3¼ x 4½″, patent
French make** **$450.00**

French, gilt metal, repeating alarm,
7″ **900.00**
French, brass, white enamel dial,
alarm, 6½″ **300.00**
German, brass with leather case, 3″
square **85.00**
Musical, "Pepoday", metal case,
6½″ **300.00**
New Haven, Pilgrim, beveled glass
front, 1 day, alarm, 6″ **150.00**
Repeater, 5 minute, rare **1000.00**
Waterbury, miniature brass case, 8
day, time only **165.00**

CHINA CASED CLOCKS

Ansonia, La Gironde, floral design, 13¾"	275.00
Ansonia, La Layon, ornate case, 14½"	350.00
Ansonia, Royal Bonn case, open escapement, 8 day	400.00
German movement, delft blue decor on white, 7¾"	200.00
Gilbert, blue, gold, and pink flowers, c. 1905, 11"	300.00
New Haven, Waldorf, three female profiles, one day, 8¼"	125.00
Waterbury, white china case, 5" porcelain dial, floral decor, 8 day	175.00

COTTAGE STYLE CLOCKS

Ithaca, No. 9, walnut case, 8 day, calendar, 23"	750.00
Jerome, miniature, painted tablet, 30 hour, 9"	80.00
Jerome, walnut case, label and good tablet, 30 hour, 11"	120.00
New Haven, rosewood case, 8 day	100.00
Thomas, Seth, rosewood case, 30 hour	90.00
Thomas, Seth, walnut case, miniature, mirror tablet, Seth Thomas Hands, 30 hour	75.00
Waterbury, rosewood case, 30 hour	85.00
Welch, E.N., rosewood case, miniature, 30 hour, 9"	100.00

CRYSTAL REGULATOR CLOCKS

Ansonia, Crystal Palace No. 1, No. 802, 8 day strike, mercury pendulum, 18½"	550.00
Ansonia, Symbol No. 1, silver finish, open escapement, mercury pendulum, 15½"	500.00
Ansonia, Symbol No. 2, four columns with acorn finials, open escapement, mercury pendulum, 15½"	450.00
French, alabaster top and base, enameled columns, mercury pendulum, ornate top, open escapement, mint condition	1900.00
New Haven, Thoreau, antique verde case, beveled glass, 8 day, half hour strike, 15"	450.00
Thomas, Seth, Empire, No. 2, brass, beveled glass, porcelain dial	375.00
Tiffany, heavily detailed case, mercury pendulum	475.00
Waterbury, plain case, porcelain dial, beveled glass, 9½"	250.00

ELECTRIC (BATTERY) DRIVEN CLOCKS

Brille, wall, oak case, Master regulator, 14" dial, sweep seconds, battery driven, 8 day, time only	550.00
Bulle, Duchesse, shelf, glass case, gold metal, spun silver background 9¾"	325.00
Bulle, Denver, shelf, mahogany case, brass dial, 9" high, 20" long	85.00
Eureka, shelf, wood and glass case, battery driven, 8" high	450.00
Self Winding Clock Co., wall, carved mahogany case, Gallery type, dry cell battery movement, 8 day, time only, 20"	500.00

GALLERY CLOCKS

Ansonia, oak case, wood bezel, seconds bit, 30 day, time only, 24"	475.00
Atkins, rosewood case, octagon shape, ripple front, 2 fuzee, 30 day, 26"	1250.00
May, S. Elwood, Ideal D, gold plated, 30 hour, 4½"	165.00
New Haven, Hidalgo, mahogany, dull finish, 8 day strike, 17¾"	165.00
Thomas, Seth, mahogany case, square, 11" dial, 8 day, all original	225.00
Thomas, Seth, oak case, 14" dial, 8 day, 19"	300.00

KITCHEN SHELF CLOCK

Ansonia, Artic, oak case, 8 day strike, 22"	150.00
Davis, H. J., Morning Star, walnut case, 8 day, restored	250.00
Gilbert, Egyptian Series, Cairo, 8 day, hour and half hour strike, 23"	175.00
Gilbert, Navy Series, Missouri, oak, 8 day, hour and half hour strike, 24"	200.00
Ingraham, Mt. Vernon, oak case, octagon door, 8 day, half hour strike, 22"	250.00
Ingraham, Oneida, oak case, octagon door, highly embossed, 8 day, half hour strike, 22"	185.00
Ingraham, New River Series, Wabash, oak, 8 day, half hour strike, 23"	175.00
New Haven, Samson, fitted with thermometer, barometer and spirit level, 8 day, half hour strike, calendar, 23¾"	200.00
Sessions, Hiawatha, oak case, 8 day	225.00
Thomas, Seth, College Series, Yale, oak, 8 day, three cathedral bell strike, alarm, 23"	225.00
Thomas, Seth, Fleet Series, oak, 8 day, half hour strike, 23"	200.00

Waterbury, Pattern No. 9093, oak case	175.00
Welch, Maine, oak case, ship on glass and top, 6" dial	300.00
Welch, Pattern No. 66, oak case, octagon door	150.00

MARINE CLOCKS

| Chronometer, Ulysee Nardin, original wooden box | 1150.00 |

Deck

Hamilton, outer protective box	325.00
Longines, complete	250.00
Thomas, Seth, nickled case, 6" silvered dial, side winder, lever action	225.00
Waltham, in gimbaled box	425.00

Ships Bell

Chelsea, heavy brass, 8 day	450.00
Chelsea, outside bell, 8 day	550.00
Thomas, Seth, heavy brass case, outside bell, 8 day	425.00

MIRROR SIDE SHELF CLOCKS

Ansonia, concave sided frame, floral and bird border, silver plated, 22½"	1250.00
Gilbert, Wm., walnut case, original cherubs, R&A pendulum, 8 day, 23" restored	375.00
New Haven, walnut case, drawer front, 8 day, all original	350.00

NEW ENGLAND WALL AND SHELF CLOCKS

Ives, Joseph, wall, walnut case, mirror clock, Conn., 36", (rare)	2700.00
Morill, B., wall, wheelbarrow movement, New Hampshire, mint condition	2000.00
Stennes, shelf, Mass.	1750.00
Tappen, wall, mirror clock, 2 weight movement, time only, New Hampshire, mint condition	2250.00

O. G. SHELF CLOCKS

Ansonia Brass Co., rosewood case, good tablet, 30 hour weight driven	150.00
Brown, J. C., iron dial, 8 day, all original	325.00
Burch, Thomas, 30 day, Pittsburgh	165.00
Davis Clock Co., 30 hour weight driven, all original	175.00
Gilbert, Wm. L., square molded case, bird in branch on panel, o.g. spring, 30 hour, 11¾"	110.00
Jerome, Chauncey, original tablet, rare weight alarm	275.00

Miniature Shelf, O. G. Seth Thomas, 9" $80.00

Long and Jones, mirrored tablet	165.00
New Haven, mahogany, weight driven, 8 day strike, 30"	175.00
Terry Clock Co., molded veneer case, beehive on glass, 8 day, 18"	225.00
Thomas, Seth, miniature, original tablet, 8 day spring driven, alarm, 16"	225.00
Thomas, Seth, stylized floral tablet in gold, 30 hour weight driven, Thomaston, Conn.	125.00

PILLAR AND SCROLL SHELF CLOCKS

Hopkins and Alfred, mahogany case, brass finials, painted wood dial, 30 hour wood movement	950.00
Ives, Chauncey, cherry case, wooden finials, wooden movements, weight driven, labeled Bristol, Conn.	1000.00
Terry, Eli & Sons, mahogany case, brass finials and original glass, 2 weights, 30 hour wood movement	1250.00
Wadsworth, Longsbury and Turner, walnut case, standard size, brass finials and original tablet, 2 weight, wood movement	875.00

POT METAL AND IRON CASE MANTEL CLOCKS

Ansonia, La Duchess, seated female figure, beveled glass, white porcelain dial, half hour strike, 10½"	**200.00**
Art Nouveau, statue clock, marble base, porcelain dial, hand painted, 8 day French movement, 18"	**650.00**
Flash Light, Deposit Box, pressed steel, alarm	**125.00**
Jennings, B2513, cupid figure to left, ormolu gold plated case, ivory porcelain dial, 30 hour, 6½"	**65.00**
Kroeber, F., iron case, patented 1859, 8 day	**175.00**
Mueller, ornate iron case, 8 day	**150.00**
Ornate case, iron front, 30 hour, 16"	**165.00**
River Boat, no animation, pot metal, side wheeler	**90.00**
Ship's Wheel, F.D.R., animated bartender, pot metal, c. "Repeal of Prohibition"	**125.00**
Welch, E. N., iron front case, labeled, 8 day	**175.00**

RECTANGULAR SHELF CLOCKS (early 1900)

Gilbert, Anniversary, black marble case, bell on top, 8 day	**225.00**
Ingraham, mantle, black marble case, 8 day	**165.00**
Thomas, Seth, black paint, 8 day	**150.00**

REGULATOR WALL CLOCKS

Ansonia, Regulator A, black walnut, 8 day strike, roman dial, 32"	**400.00**
English Parliament, walnut burl case, 11" painted dial, heavy brass movement, weight driven, time only	**475.00**
Gilbert, Regulator No. 4, walnut, 8 day, glass sides, dead beat escapement 51"	**1250.00**
Gilbert, Regulator B, oak case, time and strike, 29"	**350.00**
Howard, #85, oak case, 8 day	**4500.00**
Ingraham, Landau, solid oak case, rubbed finish, 8 day strike, 38¼"	**275.00**
New Haven, Barometer Regulator, oak case, 8 day strike, 37"	**425.00**
New Haven, Regulator D.R., calendar, oval base, 8 day, 31"	**275.00**
New Haven, Rutland, oak case, 8 day strike, 48"	**500.00**
Nolting, Oskamp Co., Regulator, No. 746, oak case, 8 day weight, dead beat pin escapement, 83"	**3000.00**
Pinwheel, porcelain face, lyre pendulum, sweep second hand, weight driven	**3200.00**
Sessions, Regulator No. 2, square case with fluted sides, 12" dial	**175.00**
Thomas, Seth, #3, rosewood case, 8 day, 40", used in railroad station at Saybrook Junction, CT	**1300.00**
Thomas, Seth, #16, walnut case, 8 day, weight, 75"	**2500.00**
Thomas, Seth, #63, oak case, Graham dead beat escapement, 8 day weight, 76"	**2000.00**
Thomas, Seth, Umbria, oak case, 15 day, 40½"	**500.00**
Sempire Clock Co., Jewelers' Regulator, electric, oak, 72"	**2500.00**
Waterbury, Freeport, walnut case, 8 day, half hour strike, 45½"	**600.00**
Waterbury, Perth, cherry case, 8 day, half hour strike, 41½"	**900.00**
Waterbury, oak case, 30 day spring driven, time only	**350.00**
Waterbury, Pinwheel, walnut case, porcelain dial, sweep second hand, lyre pendulum, weight driven, time only, can be mounted on 36" base for floor standing, 60"	**3700.00**

SCHOOL HOUSE CLOCKS

American, cherry case, 8 day spring movement, short drop, 22" octagonal, refinished	**225.00**
Ansonia, walnut case, long drop, seconds bit, 8 day spring movement, all original	**400.00**
Ball, walnut case, short drop, original glass, 11" dial, 8 day, time only, Regulator type	**325.00**
Gilbert, Standard Admiral, oak case, 8 hour strike, 26¼"	**300.00**
Ingraham, Boston, oak case, 8 day time, 32"	**300.00**
Miniature, cherry case, round top, 8 day spring movement, mint condition	**225.00**
New Haven, Mosaic Drop, 8 day time, 24"	**200.00**
New Haven, Imperial, rosewood case, 8 day strike, 32½"	**300.00**
Prentiss, School Gallery, square wooden case, 14" dial, 20"	**235.00**
Thomas, Seth, Brighton, mahogany case, 8 day strike, 22¼"	**250.00**
Waterbury, Octagon, 10" drop, rosewood veneer case, 8 day, half hour strike, 22"	**250.00**
Waterbury, Digby, oak case, 8 day, time, 27¼"	**225.00**
Welch, miniature, original label, 8 day spring movement	**275.00**
Welch, Verdi, rosewood case, painted dial, strikes gong on hour	

and bell on ½ hour, labeled, 8 day
spring movement **475.00**

SHELF CLOCKS

Ansonia, Triumph, oak case, silver
cupid, plate glass mirrors, 8 days,
24½" **350.00**
Brewster and Ingraham, walnut
case, round gothic onion top with
4 columns and frosted tablet, 8
day **750.00**
Gilbert, Comet, semi-octagon top, 8
day spring, 14¾" **80.00**
Ingraham, E., Doric Mosaic, 8 day
strike, 16" **115.00**
Ingraham, E., Venetian No. 2, 8 day
strike, gilt columns, 18" **160.00**
New Haven, Countess, black walnut
case, solid metal head, 12 mirrors,
8 day strike, 26" **375.00**
New Haven, Mantel Mission, San
Pedro, oak case, brass numbers,
8 day, half hour strike, 19" **150.00**
Thomas, Seth, walnut case and
painted dial with Seth Thomas
hands, 8 day, alarm, original **250.00**
Welch, E. N., Patti, rosewood case,
6¼ x 12¼ x 19" high, 8 day, all
original **900.00**

STEEPLE SHELF CLOCKS

Ansonia, Sharp Gothic, M.P., 8 day
strike, 19½" **180.00**
Birge and Fuller, steeple on steeple,
wagon spring movement, 8 day,
all original **2250.00**
Brewster and Ingraham, cuvered
gothic steeple, original brass
springs, 8 day **875.00**
English, Clement-Royal Exchange,
London, stepped fretwork, full columns, oak with brass works, Goth-
ic Revival fuzee bracket, 27" **850.00**
Gilbert, W. L., Sharp Gothic, 8 day,
17½" **150.00**
Jerome and Co., miniature, mahoga-
ny case, painted dial and tablet, 3
o'clock wind, 30 hour **165.00**
New Haven, Sharp Gothic, zebra
striped case, 8 day strike, 20½" . **200.00**
New Haven, Verda, oak case, pol-
ished, 8 day, striking hour and half
hour, cathedral gong, 20½" **150.00**
Sessions, Coplay, No. 32229, mahogany case, 8 day strike, oval
ship medallion, 15½" **150.00**
Terry and Andrews, walnut case,
double steeple, lyre movement, 8
day **775.00**
Welch, E. N. miniature steeple,

painted dial and tablet, 30 hour,
time and alarm **135.00**

SWINGER CLOCKS

Ansonia, Diana, small size **325.00**
Ansonia, Fortuna, ball movement, 8
day, time only **2100.00**
Ansonia, Huntress, ball movement . **1100.00**
Ansonia, Juno, tin can, 8 day move-
ment **1000.00**
Jughans, Elephant, original **375.00**
Kroeber, F., Swinging Doll, walnut
case, labeled, 17" **525.00**

TALL CASE CLOCKS

Aiten, mahogany case, painted dial,
8 day, Glasgow, Scotland **1650.00**
American, cherry case, moon dial,
center sweep second hand, Hill,
Ohio **4750.00**
Cummens, William, mahogany case,
Federal style, molded and inlaid
door and base, brass stop-fluted
quarter columns, bracket feet, 8
day, painted face, 98", Roxbury,
MA **4500.00**
Edson, Jonah, mahogany case with
French feet and arched hood top
(finials missing), 8 day, painted
face, c. 1815–1830, Bridgewater,
MA **5000.00**
English, mahogany case with fluted
quarter columns, 8 day, brass
moon dial, arched hood with
pierced crest and brass ball finials **2600.00**
English, oak case, plain, painted
dial, wood works, 1 weight, 30
hour, c. 1780 . . . . **1000.00**
Empire, tiger maple case, 8 day,
painted face, 93", probably N.E. **1750.00**
Federal style, mahogany case, broken arch, moon phase, 8 day
brass movement, unsigned, c.
1820 . . . . **2250.00**
Godshalk, Jacob, walnut case, Chip-
pendale, molded swan's neck
pediment, flame formed finials,
fluted quarter columns, shaped
panel on base, ogee bracket feet,
brass and silvered dial, moon register, 8 day, 96", c. 1770, Phila.,
Pa. **14000.00**
Hoff, John, mahogany and cherry
case, Federal, swan's neck pediment ending in rosettes, wood urn
finials, chamfered corners on
waist, flaring bracket feet, painted
face with moon dial, 8 day, 97", c.
1805, Lancaster, Pa. **5500.00**
Parry, John J., mahogany, Federal,

molded swan's neck pediment ending in rosettes, brass finial, painted face with rocking ship, fluted quarter columns waist and base, 95", c. 1795, Phila., Pa. ... **4750.00**

Pennsylvania, walnut, Chippendale, molded swan's neck pediment, fluted quarter columns, molded base centering on applied panel, ogee bracket feet, one day, 85½" **2100.00**

Pennsylvania, walnut case with inlay, moon phase, 8 day **4500.00**

Scottish, mahogany veneer and inlay case, moon dial, calendar and second hand, mint dial, c. 1800 . . **2500.00**

Shriener, Martin, cherry case, moon dial, calendar and sweep second hand on center arbor, 8 day movement, very rare, American . . **6500.00**

Willard, Simon, mahogany, Federal, hood with pierced crest, brass ball finials, brass stopped fluted corner columns, bracket feet, painted face, 8 day, 92", c. 1785, Roxbury, MA **17500.00**

Watz, George, walnut, Chippendale, molded swan's neck crest on bonnet, panelled base, 8 day, painted face, 99", Hagerstown, MD **1250.00**

TAMBOR SHELF CLOCKS

New Haven, carved walnut case, Westminster chime, brass dial, 8 day spring driven **170.00**

Sessions, Westminster chime, 8 day **150.00**

Thomas, Seth, carved mahogany case, Giant, Senora chime, plays tune on 5 bells **325.00**

VIENNA REGULATOR WALL CLOCKS

1 weight, porcelain dial, 8 day, original **325.00**

1 weight, black case, 8 day, early . . **300.00**

1 weight, mahogany case, fancy top, porcelain dial, center sweep second hand, 8 day, time only, rare . **700.00**

3 weight, serpentine walnut case, porcelain dial, seconds bit, 8 day, 50" **1450.00**

3 weight, dark mahogany case, fancy porcelain dial, seconds bit, 42", all original **2100.00**

R&A, spring driven, rosewood case, fancy, porcelain dial and pendulum bob, 8 day, 27" **300.00**

MISCELLANEOUS

Advertising

Calumet Baking Powder, wall, oak case, 8 day, time only **475.00**

EverReady, wood case **225.00**

Sauer's Extracts and Flavorings, regulator, oak case, 8 day, New Haven **450.00**

Black Forest

Ansonia, Bobbing Doll, original doll, time only, 13" **600.00**

Carved clock peddler, whistles and head turns **300.00**

Wall, highly carved deer and bird finial, 2 weights, c. 1840–1850, 44 " **2200.00**

Gaslight, 5⅛" dia. porcelain face, Theodore B. Starr, N.Y., original letter case $150.00

Gas Light, Waltham **185.00**

Gravity, Ansonia, good condition . . . **225.00**

Railroad, hanging type, brass, faces on opposite sides, French **575.00**

Rotary (Briggs)

Early **395.00**

Welch, E. N., glass dome, 30 hour spring driven, time only **395.00**

Skeleton

Double fuzee, glass dome, 8 day,

English, 11" 850.00
Triple fuzee, shelf, glass dome, 8
day, English, rare 8750.00
Tavern, painted dial, 8 day, time
only, English, c. 1790, 13" 550.00

Time Recorders
Cincinnati, oak case, 8 day, time
only, 42" 300.00
International, ornate oak case, 8
day, time only, all original and
working, restored 575.00

Tower
Marbier, pinwheel movement only,
short pendulum 1500.00
Thomas, Seth, movement only,
weights and pendulum not original 1100.00
Wag on Wall, 2 weights,
handpainted face, Germany, c.
1825 .... 350.00

CLOISSONÉ

**Cloisonné is a form of enameling on metal.
The technique originated in the orient many
centuries ago. The work is done by pouring
liquid enamel colors (smalt) into a pattern
which has been outlined with bent wire fil-
lets, secured to the ground before firing. By
using this fine wire, very delicate designs can
be made. Less expensive metals such as
brass later came to be used instead of gold.
Most cloisonné found today is from the Victorian era, 1870–1900, and came from China
or Japan.**

**Powder Jar, covered, 3¾" dia., yellow
background $65.00**

Boxes
2", stamp box 68.00
4", egg-shaped, dark green 495.00
4¾", floral and butterflies 495.00
Round, covered 75.00

7", Foo dog finial, yellow, pink,
blue floral, and green leaves decor 200.00
Chargers
12", two cranes and pink peonies 425.00
14½", bluebird, flowers in red,
pink and white, copper edge 400.00
Incense Burner, 4", with goldstone,
in green 275.00
Jars
Cache, small, with lids, c. 1870,
pair 450.00
5 x 5", shaped like swans, Chinese, c. 1900, pair 2000.00
6", enamel, with cover, on metal
feet, panels in red, grey green,
and light blue background 1200.00
7", rust background, white flowers, pair 125.00
7", blue with green edging, overall
floral decor, marked "China" 85.00
Plates
Bowl-shaped, red florals on blue
background, c. 1790 .... 200.00
7¾", green plum tree, buds, blossoms, no mark 150.00
8¼", butterflies, fans, blossoms,
multicolored, pair 350.00
8½", florals and birds on blue
background, Japanese 175.00
Sake cup and saucer 325.00
Tea Pots
4½", Egg shaped, tri-footed, floral
and butterflies on amethyst background with goldstone 275.00
Miniature, dome shape, pink, blue
and white floral on green background 165.00
5 x 6", Floral decor on white 295.00
Miniature, Dragon on yellow background, cane handle 165.00
6", Robins, pink and orchid blossoms on turquoise background,
geometric borders on cover 150.00
Tea Set, Teapot, creamer, covered sugar, one cup and saucer,
green border, and detailed motif
on rust background Set 400.00
Trays
Rectangular, pin, blue jay on
peach branch 45.00
Round, pin, blue and white blossoms on terra cotta background . 45.00
8 x 4½", butterflies and florals on
brick red background, with four
knob feet 200.00
11⅜", square with rounded corners, birds perched on snowy
branch on pale blue shading to
grey background, underside with
white florals and green leaves on
black background, Japanese, c.

1900 .... 475.00
14½" x 8¼", multicolored Chinese florals and oriental design on outer edge, brass bamboo edging all around 350.00

Vases

3½", bud, stylized florals on green 350.00
4⅞", baluster form, brown, turquoise and yellow butterflies hovering above band of lappets, mustard yellow background, c. 1900 . 320.00
5", peach colored florals and bright green leaves, on electric blue fishscale background 185.00
5", large dragon in shades of blue, red and purple on turquoise, white and green background 200.00
5⅞", double gourd shape, blue, red, lavender and green pattern of flying bats, and repousse gilt metal cloud scrolls on turquoise background, Ch'ien Lung period 900.00
6⅛", stylized floral motif inset with copper goldstone panels, and multicolored decor 150.00
6¾", floral on black with turquoise banding 125.00
7", waisted neck fitted with gilt metal drop handles, Foo lion panel enclosed by foliage, Japan ... 275.00
7½", red crane among bamboo trees in deep blue, white and gold, 19th century 295.00
9", pink flowers, green trees, Japanese, marked Sato 150.00
10", pod-shaped, 5-toed Imperial dragons on black 180.00
11", hydrangea, wild flowers and insects 350.00
14½", baluster form, polychrome panels of stylized serpents, Japan 375.00
15", red, yellow, green and peach, lotus scrolls on blue background, 19th century, pair 900.00
15", pigeon blood birds in bamboo trees, on silver-colored background, Japanese 500.00
25⅛", baluster form, flowers and insects on blue background, elaborate diaper and brocade reserves, 19th century 600.00
36½", baluster-shaped, pink and white wisteria blossoms on blue background 700.00
45¼", wood pigeons in flowering cherry tree, on blue background . 1000.00
Enamel, and cover, multicolored flowers and birds, on dark blue background, silver mounts, Hirasuke, late 19th century 2500.00

CLOTHING AND HANDBAGS

Clothing worn in past decades has become highly collectible, especially the dramatic styles of the late 1930's and early 1940's. Evening gowns; beaded bags; cloche hats of the "Flapper Age;" beaded dresses, which were so highly fashionable in the age of the "Charleston;" are all very eagerly sought by collectors. Laces, lawn petticoats, camisoles, cambric underthings, are all collectible today. Old furs and other accessories are making a come-back that their creators never dreamed of.

The mesh and beaded handbags, which were in vogue in the 1920's and 1930's, are very much in demand right now. They are quite fashionable with evening clothes and cocktail wear. Sterling silver bags, and those set with precious stones, are valuable; the intricate bead work on beaded bags are very popular with collectors.

Man's silk top hat $28.00

CLOTHING

Apron, blue and white kerchief, ruffled bottom 7.50
Boa, 70", ostrich feathers 50.00
Blouse
White batiste, long sleeves, round neck, tucks and lace inserts 25.00
Blue, tucked 20.00
Victorian, black lace 25.00
Bonnet, Dutch type, pleated lace, ribbon ties 30.00
Camisole, white cotton, lacy trim .. 15.00
Capes
Black taffeta, 16", Ruffled collar,

c. 1900 .... 20.00
Seal, Finger tip length 100.00
Brown plush, with monkey fur ... 35.00

Coats
Caracul, woman's grey, trimmed in black Hudson Seal collar and across bottom, c. 1932, size 14–16 .... 85.00
Persian Lamb, ¾ length 100.00
Raccoon, man's 850.00
Sheared Raccoon, small size ... 125.00

Collars
Lace, Ecru 7.50
Mink, 7" wide 20.00
Mink dyed squirrel, collar, and cuffs, pom-poms for hat trim 45.00

Dresses
Beaded, black on black net, V-neck, sleeveless, floor length c. 1925 .... 65.00
Black crepe, short, flapper style, low waist, black beaded yoke, and beads on part of skirt, c. 1922 .. 75.00
Taffeta, green, ankle length, round neck, puffed sleeves, flounced skirt, c. 1925 .... 35.00
Silk Chiffon, with red carnations, and leaves, knee length, flounced skirt, bertha collar, sleeveless, c. 1925 .... 35.00

Hats
Flapper, black felt 5.00
Flapper, pink felt, gold braid band, and sparkly gold ornament on each side 10.00
Black straw, pearl ornaments, c. 1918 .... 20.00

Jackets, Ladies
Brown Beaver on camel's hair, tuxedo style, ¾ length, c. 1957 .. 150.00
Mink, matching pill box hat, c. 1950 .... 100.00
Muskrat 65.00
Ocelot 85.00
Sheared raccoon 75.00
Kimono, all-over hand embroidered, c. 1880 .... 180.00
Mantilla, black lace, triangular shape, Italian 45.00

Petticoats
Long, white 50.00
Short, white cotton, flounce bottom 12.50

Shawls
46 x 46", fringe, silk, hand embroidered 95.00
Black cashmere, with fringe 125.00
Woven Paisley, c. 1860 .... 110.00
Skirt Hoop 20.00
Shirt waist, white, with blue, lace bollar, tucks 20.00

HANDBAGS

Beaded
Blue and black beads, fringed bottom, drawstring top 25.00
Beige and white beading overall, pouch drawstring type 25.00
Beaded, Czeckoslovakian, c. 1920 25.00
Blue, beaded 30.00
Beaded, 6½", 5" wide, deep royal blue, cobalt and silver beads, with roses in pink and yellow, on body, deep beaded fringe on bottom, silver chain, c. 1925, Whiting and Davis frame 125.00
Teal blue, beige, maize and forest green beading in stylized floral pattern, gilt sterling silver frame chased with foliate scrolls and marked Gorham 100.00

Mesh
Cream colored mesh, pink and purple, floral decor, silver frame and handle 35.00
Geometric design mesh, blue, cream, salmon and black with silver trim, Whiting and Davis frame 85.00
Silver mesh with fringe and drawstring closing 27.50
Sterling silver mesh, engraved frame, silver chain 30.00

COALPORT

Coalport porcelain has been made by the Coalport Porcelain Works in England since the late 1700's. It is currently being produced at Stoke-on-Trent. One of their more popular patterns, is "Indian Tree." See "Indian Tree Pattern."

Platter, 14½" w. x 19 ½" l., "Urn and Florals," orange and blue on white, c. 1800 ....$350.00

Boxes
Fan shaped, hinged lid, floral decor, 2 x 1¼" **65.00**
Pink background, jewelled, with gold trim, 2¼ x 4" **175.00**
Chocolate Pot, 6", tankard, bird and flowers **65.00**
Cups and Saucers
Black, orange floral on white, gold trim, late **15.00**
Demitasse, blue flowers on gold, gold interior, c. 1891 .... **95.00**
Demitasse, jewelled **125.00**
Mug, 2½", can shaped **50.00**
Plates
8½", green border, castle scene in center, gold trim **35.00**
11½", scalloped edge, cobalt border, floral center, gold trim **125.00**
Vases
4", shell shaped, oyster coloring . **50.00**
5½", cobalt with gold trim, handled, pair **175.00**
6", blue, gold handles, hand painted scenic, reverse designs on each side, gold trim, pair **225.00**

COCA COLA ITEMS

The originator of Coca Cola was John Pemberton, a pharmacist from Atlanta, Ga. In 1886, Dr. Pemberton introduced a patent medicine to relieve headaches, stomach disorders and other minor maladies.

Unfortunately, his failing health and meager finances forced him to sell his interest. In 1888, Asa G. Candler was the sole owner of Coca Cola. Candler improved the formula, increased the advertising budget and widened the distribution. Accidentally, a 'patient' was given a dose of the syrup mixed with carbonated water instead of the usual still water. The result was a tastier, more refreshing drink. As sales increased in the 1890's, Candler recognized that the product was more suitable for the soft drink market and began advertising as such. From the beginning a myriad of advertising items have been issued to invite all to "Drink Coca Cola."

Dates of interest: The first unauthorized Coca Cola tray was issued in 1900. "Coke" was first used in advertising in 1941. The distinctive shaped bottle was registered as a trademark on April 12, 1960.

Paperweight, clear with red carpet, white lettering $42.50

Ash Tray set, playing-card shapes, ruby glass, set of 4 .... **40.00**
Banks
Cooler-shaped, 1948 .... **35.00**
Red, tin **14.00**
Binoculars, 1910 .... **135.00**
Blotter, 3½ x 8", teen-age girl with Coca Cola, "I think it's swell," dated 1942 .... **10.00**
Bottle-carrier, 6 pack, wooden **40.00**
Bear, battery-operated **55.00**
Bookmarks, cardboard, 1899–1904 **100.00**
Calendars
Lillian Nordica, 1909 .... **500.00**
"Betty," framed, 1914 .... **130.00**
"Autumn Girl" **130.00**
Boy with dog, N. C. Wyeth, 1931 **150.00**

Beautiful girl each month, 1947 . . **60.00**
Cards
  Set of Nature cards, original box . **25.00**
  Playing Cards, WW II planes **45.00**
  Trade Cards, picture of boy, signed Thomas, 1930 . . . . **30.00**
Cigarette Case, 50th Anniversary, 1936 . . . . **135.00**
Cigarette Lighter, shaped like bottle **20.00**
Crock, fountain dispenser, c. 1890, porcelain **1200.00**
Fans, 1920–1940 . . . . **30.00**
Glasses
  Clear, with enameled emblem, 5¢ size, each **10.00**
  6 oz., 1920's **12.00**
  12 oz. gold colored **14.00**
Ice Pick, "Things Go Better with Coke" **8.50**
Keg, 21", paper advertising, "Coca Cola" on top **95.00**
Letter Opener, 1920 . . . . **32.50**
Mechanical Pencil, 1930 . . . . **27.50**
Pencil Box, with contents **40.00**
Pocket Mirror
  "Coca Cola Girl," 1909 . . . . **110.00**
  Girl in bonnet, 1914 . . . . **110.00**
Post Card, "Duster Girl," 1910 . . . . **175.00**
Route pads, ea. **5.00**
Signs
  10 x 24", cardboard, girl with Coca Cola bottle and refrigerator, c. 1940 . . . . **25.00**
  10 x 24", porcelain, bottle shaped **45.00**
Thermometer
  December, 25, 1923 . . . . **50.00**
  17", bottle-shaped **18.50**
Trays
  10", Vienna Art, 1905 . . . . **150.00**
  "Relieves Fatigue," 1906 . . . . . . **225.00**
  "Elaine," oval, change **80.00**
  Bathing beauty, 1924 . . . . **80.00**
  Girl on telephone, 1930 . . . . **75.00**
  Madge Evans, movie star, 1935 . **40.00**
  Woman in evening gown, 1936 . . **39.50**
  Girl in yellow bathing suit, 1937 . **40.00**
Trucks
  12", cast iron, red **75.00**
  Smith, Miller, six original cases and bottles in box **450.00**

COFFEE MILLS

Coffee mills or grinders were made in a variety of shapes and sizes, from the large cast iron store models to the table top, lap and wall models for the home. The first home-size coffee mill was introduced in the 1890's, and large store sized grinders have recently been traded. They command good prices.

Crescent #705, Superior Coffee Mill, Crescent Mfg. Co., Louisville, Ky. **$40.00**

Arcade, wall type, cast iron and glass **45.00**
Crystal, wall type, glass container . . **30.00**
Elgin, 27", cast iron 2 wheels **325.00**
Elgin Nat'l Coffee Mill, Woodruff and Edwards Co., 6 x 6", store model **275.00**
Enterprise Mfg. Co.,
  7", square wood base with bottom drawer, painting of buck deer holding powder horn **375.00**
  5½", store floor model, 2 wheels, cast iron, red and blue paint, stenciling all original, eagle finial, tin coffee holder, dated 1873 . . . . . . **1000.00**
  18", cast iron, crank handle wheel, set in 33" plank bench with peeled log legs **275.00**
  21", store counter type, 2 wheels, cast iron, original paint **160.00**
Lap type, black tin, brass hopper, c. 1886 . . . . **45.00**
National Specialty Co., Phila., Pa., wall type, cast iron, original red scroll with gold decor **75.00**
"Patent Applied For," wall type, cast iron, glass jar **35.00**

Peugeot, Brevetes, S.G.D.G., 17", cast iron wheel and cup one drawer, store type	200.00
Pride, wood, one drawer, iron handle, lap type	45.00
Universal	
Table type, with clamp	35.00
Wall type, cast iron, metal container	45.00
Unmarked Wooden	
2½ x 2½ x 3", Iron cup and crank, one drawer	50.00
4½ x 7 x 10", wall type glass dome	40.00
5 x 5½ x 5⅞", brass fittings, refinished	55.00
6" square, dovetailed, embossed iron top	75.00
6" square, dovetailed, early pewter cup, iron crank, one drawer, refinished	85.00
7½ x 13", table type with cast iron, one drawer	75.00
Wall type	
1876 Parker Co.	45.00
Cast iron with panelled glass jar	35.00

COIN OPERATED ITEMS

A wide variety of coin operated machines have been made in the past. Games of skill and chance have always held a fascination for many people; candy and gum machines have a well known fascination for children. People are collecting the earlier coin operated machines for entertainment as well as investment value.

GAMES

Advance Electric Shock, c. 1920	250.00
Bally Hoo, Pinball, c. 1931	450.00
Booz Barometer, 5-cent	150.00
Charger Target Game, 1-cent	200.00
Genco, hand strength tester	75.00
Grand Tour, Bally pinball, c. 1964	350.00
Hi Score Pool	500.00
Kicker Katcher, 1-cent wood	200.00
Merry-Go-Round, pinball, Gottlieb, c. 1964	450.00
Smiley, 1-cent counter game	150.00
Steeple Chase, 1-cent counter game	350.00
Turf, Champ, one player pinball, Williams, c. 1958	650.00

VENDING MACHINES

Advance, 1-cent gumball, c. 1912	110.00
Advance, 5-cent nut, c. 1923	80.00
Advance, 5-cent package gum, c.	

Vending Machine, Ajax 5¢ Nut, 3 units, aluminum, Newark, N.J. $55.00

1924	60.00
Belvend, 1-cent candy vendor	45.00
Columbus, 1-cent gumball	80.00
Dixie, 1-cent paper cup dispenser, c. 1913	400.00
Ford, 1-cent gumball, chrome	50.00
Gas Pump, 1-cent lighter fluid dispenser, card holder	200.00
Hawkeye, 1-cent gumball with bell	75.00
Hershey, 1-cent candy	95.00
Imp, 1-cent game with gumball	150.00
National, 5-cent mint and gum	95.00
Northwestern, 1-cent, 5-cent peanut machine	65.00
Postcard, 25-cents, 3 cards prestamped	100.00
Rosebud Ohio match	85.00
Silver Comet, 1-cent cigarette	125.00
Silver King, 5-cent hot nuts	95.00
Spitfire gumball	125.00
Stamp, vends 1-cent and 3-cent stamps	80.00
Stampmaster, vends 4-cent stamps	45.00
Star, 1-cent candy	80.00
Victor, 1-cent candy	70.00
Zeno, Gum, wood case, c. 1908	400.00

MISCELLANEOUS

Cash Registers
Michigan, 1-cent to 50-cents	300.00

National, rings from 1-cent to $3.00, ornate brass 550.00
Duo-Scope Flip Card, 13x14x19", spring wound, electrified 400.00
Juke Boxes
AMI, Model C, c. 1949 . . . . 450.00
Seeburg, 100-selections, 45RPM, c. 1958 . . . . 450.00
Seeburg, 100-selections, 78RPM, Model M-100-A 550.00
Wurlitzer, 48-selections, 78RPM, Style 1600 . . . . 750.00
Mutoscopes (Peep Shows)
64" high, cast iron stand, c. 1920's 850.00
76" high, ornate cast iron stand, "American Mutoscope Reel Co." c. 1905–10 . . . . 1400.00
Parking Meter, 1-cent with key 50.00
Scale, Vending operator's 65.00

Slot Machine Mills, "Jackpot" c. 1930's $1500.00

Slot Machines
Caille, "Doughboy," 5-cent, c. 1930 . . . . 850.00
English, vertical wood case, ornate cast iron trim, 1-cent 250.00
Jennings, "Chief," 3-reels, 10-cents 1400.00

Mills, "Black Knight," 25-cents . . 900.00
Mills, "Special Award 7-7-7," 1-cent, restored 1000.00

COIN SPOT GLASS
See OPALESCENT GLASS

COLLECTORS' PLATES

The first collectors' plates were made by Bing and Grondahl in 1895. Royal Copenhagen issued their first Christmas plate in 1908.

In the late 1960's and early 1970's several potteries, glass factories, mints and artists began issuing plates commemorating events, people, animals, etc. Christmas plates were supplemented by Mother's Day plates, Easter plates, etc. A sense of speculation swept the field, fostered in part by flamboyant ad in newspapers and flashy direct mail promotion.

The bubble burst in the last two years. The old standbys have weathered the price drop well. The newer plates still are in a state of flux in respect to price. Some plates have held value; many have dropped considerably.

Collectors often favor the first plate issued in a series above all others. Condition is a prime factor. Having the original box also influences price.

Collector's plates, more than any other object in Warman's guide, should be collected for design and pleasure and only secondarily for rise in value.

ANRI (ITALY)

Christmas Plates
1971-FE 95.00
1972 . . . . 110.00
1973 . . . . 275.00
1974 . . . . 80.00
1975 . . . . 70.00
1976 . . . . 110.00
1977 . . . . 80.00
1978 . . . . 55.00
1979 . . . . 95.00
1980 . . . . 95.00
1981 . . . . 125.00
Figurines 6"
Girl in Egg 200.00
Hurdy Gurdy 230.00
Journey 250.00
Spring Arrivals 150.00

BAREUTHER (GERMANY)

1967-Christmas. FE 100.00
1968-Christmas 27.50

1969-Christmas	**15.00**
1970-Christmas	**12.50**
1971-Father's Day	**17.50**
1971-Mother's Day	**17.50**
1972-Christmas	**37.50**
1972 Thanksgiving	**17.50**
1973-Christmas	**22.50**
1973-Father's Day	**22.50**
1973-Thanksgiving	**20.00**
1974-Christmas	**20.00**
1975-Christmas	**22.50**
1976-Christmas	**22.50**
1976-Mother's Day	**20.00**
1977-Mother's Day	**22.50**
1978-Christmas	**20.00**

BERLIN (GERMANY)

1970-Christmas. FE	**125.00**
1971-Mother's Day. FE	**25.00**
1972-Bell. FE	**20.00**
1973-Christmas	**35.00**
1974-Father's Day	**37.50**
1975-Christmas	**35.00**
1976-Christmas	**30.00**
1976-Stein. Annual	**70.00**
1976-Stein. Nautical	**140.00**
1977-Historical	**30.00**
1978-Christmas	**35.00**
1979-Christmas	**35.00**

Bing and Grondahl, 7¼″ dia., "The Fir Tree and Hare," 1964 . . . .$50.00

BING AND GRONDAHL (DENMARK)

Christmas Plates

1895-Frozen Window. FE	**3250.00**
1896-New Moon	**2475.00**
1897-Sparrows	**1275.00**

1898-Star and Roses	**695.00**
1899-Crows	**1975.00**
1900-Church Bells	**695.00**
1901-Three Wise Men	**300.00**
1902-Gothic Church Interior	**290.00**
1903-Expectant Children	**245.00**
1904-Frederiksberg Hill	**125.00**
1905-Christmas Night	**142.50**
1906-One Horse Sleigh	**90.00**
1907-Little Match Girl	**120.00**
1908-St. Petri Church	**90.00**
1909-Yule Tree	**95.00**
1910-The Old Organist	**95.00**
1911-Angels and Shepherds	**95.00**
1912-Going to Church	**95.00**
1913-Bringing Home the Tree	**95.00**
1914-Royal Castle	**90.00**
1915-Dog Outside Window	**135.00**
1916-Sparrows at Christmas	**90.00**
1917-Christmas Boat	**90.00**
1918-Fishing Boat	**90.00**
1919-Outside the Window	**90.00**
1920-Hare in the Snow	**90.00**
1921-Pigeons	**70.00**
1922-Star of Bethlehem	**70.00**
1923-The Ermitage	**75.00**
1924-Lighthouse	**70.00**
1925-Child's Christmas	**85.00**
1926-Churchgoers	**80.00**
1927-Skating Couple	**100.00**
1928-Eskimos	**75.00**
1929-Fox Outside Farm	**90.00**
1930-Town Hall Square	**115.00**
1931-Christmas Train	**90.00**
1932-Lifeboat	**90.00**
1933-Korsor-Nyborg Ferry	**75.00**
1934-Church Bell in Tower	**75.00**
1935-Lillebelt Bridge	**85.00**
1936-Amalienborg Castle	**80.00**
1937-Guests Arrival	**90.00**
1938-Lighting the Candles	**130.00**
1939-Old Lock-Eye, the Sandman	**180.00**
1940-Christmas Letters	**145.00**
1941-Horses	**300.00**
1942-Danish Farm	**150.00**
1943-Ribe Cathedral	**160.00**
1944-Sorgenfri Castle	**105.00**
1945-The Old Water Mill	**125.00**
1946-Commemoration Cross	**90.00**
1947-Dybbol Mill	**100.00**
1948-Watchman	**80.00**
1949-Landsoldaten	**90.00**
1950-Kronborg Castle	**145.00**
1951-Jens Bang	**110.00**
1952-Thorvaldsen Museum	**90.00**
1953-Royal Boat	**80.00**
1954-Snowman	**105.00**
1955-Kalundborg Church	**110.00**
1956-Christmas in Copenhagen	**120.00**
1957-Christmas Candles	**130.00**
1958-Santa Claus	**100.00**
1959-Christmas Eve	**120.00**

1960-Village Church	195.00
1961-Winter Harmony	105.00
1962-Winter Night	80.00
1963-The Christmas Elf	125.00
1964-The Fir Tree and Hare	50.00
1965-Bringing Home the Tree	50.00
1966-Home for Christmas	45.00
1967-Sharing the Joy	45.00
1968-Christmas in Church	42.50
1969-Arrival of Guests	25.00
1970-Pheasants in Snow	23.00
1971-Christmas at Home	15.00
1972-Christmas in Greenland	15.00
1973-Family Reunion	20.00
1974-Christmas in the Village	15.00
1975-Old Water Mill	20.00
1976-Christmas Welcome	27.50
1977-Copenhagen Xmas	25.00
1978-B&G Xmas Tale	30.00
1979	30.00
1980	37.00
1981	45.00

Mother's Day Plates

1969-Dog. FE	395.00
1970-Bird	35.00
1971-Cat	15.00
1972-Horses	15.00
1973-Duck	17.50
1974-Bear	15.00
1975-Doe	17.50
1976-Swans	17.50
1977-Squirrels	25.00
1978-Heron	22.50
1979	28.50
1980	28.50
1981	34.00

Miscellaneous

1974-Bell, Annual. FE	175.00
1976-Bicentennial U.S.A.	55.00
1978-Thimble. FE	15.00

BOEHM (LENOX)

Annuals

1970	225.00
1978	50.00

Bird Series

1970-Wood Thrush. FE	295.00
1971-Goldfinch	80.00
1972-Mountain Bluebird	50.00
1973-Meadowlark	50.00
1974-Hummingbirds	70.00
1975-Redstart	45.00
1976-Cardinals	40.00
1977-Robins	40.00
1978-Mockingbirds	50.00
1979	55.00
1980	70.00

Wildlife Series

1973-Raccoons. FE	85.00

1974-Fox	27.50
1975-Rabbits	80.00
1976-Chipmunks	50.00
1977-Beaver	50.00
1978-Whitetail Deer	60.00
1979	65.00
1980-Bobcats	80.00

DISNEY, WALT (SCHMID)

1973-Christmas. FE	230.00
1974-Christmas	60.00
1974-Christmas Ornament. FE	10.00
1974-Mother's Day. FE	40.00
1975-Christmas	15.00
1975-Christmas Bell. FE	12.50
1976-Bicentennial	16.50
1977-Mother's Day Bell. FE	10.00
1978-Mickey Mouse. 50th Birthday	30.00
1978-Christmas	6.00
1979-Mother's Day	7.00
1980-Mother's Day	15.00

**Franklin Plate, crystal,"Snow Flake,"
1977, boxed $27.50**

FRANKLIN MINT

Audubon Series (Younger)

1972 thru 1973. Each	100.00

Mother's Day (Spencer)

1972. FE	120.00
1973	95.00
1974	110.00
1975	135.00
1976	140.00
Presidents Series. Each	125.00

Rockwell, See ROCKWELL, NORMAN

Thanksgiving
1972 thru 1975. Each 100.00
Western Americana
1972 thru 1973.
Gold. Each 1500.00
Silver. Each 100.00
Wyeth, James
1972 . . . . 125.00
1973 . . . . 110.00
1974 . . . . 125.00
1975 . . . . 135.00

GORHAM
Christmas Items (other than plates)

Bells
1976 thru 1978. Each 15.00
Ornaments
Angel 20.00
Drummer Boy 20.00
Three Wise Men 22.50
Snowflakes
1970-Sterling 65.00
1971-Sterling 40.00
1974-Sterling 25.00
1976-Sterling 25.00
1977-Sterling 27.50
1978-Crystal 22.50
Spoons, Sterling
1972 . . . . 20.00
1973 . . . . 20.00
1975 . . . . 20.00
Santa, demi 25.00

Figurines
Beguiling Buttercup 80.00
Fishing 80.00
Four Seasons, See Rockwell, N.
Gay Blades 77.50
Grace Before Meals 90.00
Independent 70.00
Missed 105.00
Skating 60.00

Plates
1971-Quiet Waters 20.00
1972-Rembrandt 30.00
1972–1978-Four Seasons. See
ROCKWELL, NORMAN
1973-Moppets. Christmas. FE 27.50
1973-Moppets. Mother's Day. FE . . 20.00
1974-Moppets. Christmas 10.00
1975-Dear Child 100.00
1976-Promises to Keep 50.00
1977-Johnny and Duke 20.00
1977-Patient Ones 35.00

HAVILAND & CO.

1970-Christmas. FE 190.00
1971-Christmas 35.00

1971-Christmas Ornament. FE 8.00
1972-Gaspee 10.00
1973-Mother's Day, Breakfast. FE . . 9.00
1975-Christmas 27.50
1975-Mother's Day 25.00
1976-Christmas 32.50
1976-Mother's Day 25.00
1977-Christmas 37.50
1977-Mother's Day 30.00
1978-Christmas 37.50
1978-Mother's Day 32.50

HAVILAND-PARLON (FRANCE)

1971-Unicorn Captivity. FE 150.00
1972-Madonna. FE 175.00
1973-Madonna 110.00
1974-Madonna 55.00
1976-Mother's Day. Mother and
Child. FE 60.00
1977-Lady and Unicorn. FE 90.00
1978-Madonna 55.00
1979-Sound 50.00
1980-Touch 80.00
1981-Scent 60.00

HUMMEL, (SCHMID)

1971-Christmas. FE 55.00
1972-Christmas 35.00
1973-Christmas 220.00
1974-Mother's Day 35.00
1975-Christmas 35.00
1975-Mother's Day 30.00
1976-Mother's Day 28.50
1977-Christmas 35.00
1978-Bell. FE 275.00
1978-Christmas Cup 20.00
1978-Paperweight. Crystal. FE 165.00
1978-Christmas 35.00
1979-Christmas 35.00
1980-Christmas 27.00

HUMMEL, GOEBEL (GERMANY)

1971 . . . . 700.00
1972 . . . . 65.00
1973 . . . . 185.00
1974 . . . . 90.00
1975 . . . . 90.00
1976 . . . . 60.00
1977 . . . . 75.00
1978 . . . . 90.00
1979 . . . . 60.00
1980 . . . . 55.00
1981 . . . . 60.00

HUTSCHENREUTHER (GERMANY)

Figurines
Beagle. 4¼ x 5½" 50.00
Chihuahua. 4 x 4" 55.00

Hummel, christmas ornament, 3¼" dia., 1974, "The Guardian Angel" $10.00

Cocker Spaniel. 4¼ x 5½"	55.00
Colt, lying. 3 x 5½"	65.00
Donkey, lying. 3¼ x 4"	47.50
Donkey, standing. 5 x 6½"	55.00
Fawn, spotted, lying. 4 x 4¾" ...	80.00
Fawn, spotted, standing. 5 x 5½"	110.00
Fawn, standing. Colored foal. 4¾ x 5½"	47.50
Foxes. 7 x 11"	200.00
Hummingbird, flower. 2¾ x 4" ..	65.00
Hummingbird, nest with egg. Matte finish. 2¼ x 3"	77.50
Lizard, 2 x 3½"	50.00
Stallion. 4 x 4¼"	40.00
Tammy "Tiger Eye" Cat. 4¼ x 6¼"	90.00

Miscellaneous

Birthday	135.00
Christmas Bell. 1978. FE	20.00
Christmas 1978. FE	225.00
Floral Bell. 1978 FE	40.00
Friendship	65.00
Months. Set of 12	600.00
Mother and Child 1978. FE	45.00
"Pansies in a Coffee Tin." Carroll. 1978. FE	62.50
"Princess Snowflake." Valenza. 1978 FE	40.00
Wedding	175.00
"Zinnias in a Sugar Bowl." 1978 FE	57.50
Zodiac. Set of 12	1100.00

NORITAKE (JAPAN)

1971-Easter Egg. FE	80.00
1972-Christmas Bell. FE	15.00

Noritake, Easter egg, 1978 ....$20.00

1973-Easter Egg	22.50
1973-Valentine Heart. FE	10.00
1974-Christmas Bell	20.00
1974-Easter Egg	17.50
1974-Valentine Heart	6.00
1975-Christmas Bell	15.00
1976-Easter Egg	12.50
1976-Mother's Day Cup	17.50
1977-Irish Setter	35.00
1978-Easter Egg	20.00
1979-Easter Egg	17.50
1979-Valentine	20.00

Peanuts, "Christmas 1973" ...$40.00

PEANUTS (SCHMID)

1972-Christmas. FE	45.00
1972-Mother's Day. FE.	10.00
1973-Christmas	40.00
1973-Christmas Bell. FE	15.00
1973-Mother's Day	12.50
1974-Christmas	40.00
1975-Christmas	8.00
1975-Mother's Day	10.00
1976-Bicentennial	8.00
1976-Christmas	8.00
1977-Christmas	6.00
1977-Mother's Day Bell. FE	6.00
1977-Valentine. FE	5.00
1978-Christmas	6.00
1978-Mother's Day	5.00
1979-Valentine	5.00
1979-Mother's Day	6.00
1980-Christmas	5.00
1980-Anniversary	10.00

ROCKWELL
See ROCKWELL, NORMAN

ROYAL COPENHAGEN (DENMARK)

Christmas Plates

1908-Madonna and Child	1500.00
1909-Danish Landscape	135.00
1910-The Magi	120.00
1911-Danish Landscape	150.00
1912-Christmas Tree	130.00
1913-Frederik Church Spire	145.00
1914-Holy Spirit Church	120.00
1915-Danish Landscape	130.00
1916-Shepherd at Christmas	90.00
1917-Our Saviour Church	85.00
1918-Sheep and Shepherds	90.00
1919-In the Park	90.00
1920-Mary and Child Jesus	100.00
1921-Aabenraa Marketplace	80.00
1922-Three Singing Angels	80.00
1923-Danish Landscape	80.00
1924-Sailing Ship	95.00
1925-Christianshavn	100.00
1926-Christianshavn Canal	80.00
1927-Ship's Boy at Tiller	195.00
1928-Vicar Family	85.00
1929-Grundtvig Church	85.00
1930-Fishing Boat	100.00
1931-Mother and Child	110.00
1932-Frederiksberg Gardens	110.00
1933-Great Belt Ferry	125.00
1934-The Hermitage Castle	125.00
1935-Kronborg Castle	140.00
1936-Roskilde Cathedral	140.00
1937-Main Street Copenhagen	140.00
1938-Round Church Ostelars	265.00
1939-Greenland Pack Ice	255.00
1940-The Good Shepherd	340.00
1941-Danish Village Church	335.00

Royal Copenhagen, "Aabenraa Market Place," 1921 ....$80.00

1942-Bell Tower	340.00
1943-Flight into Egypt	415.00
1944-Danish Winter Scene	180.00
1945-A Peaceful Motif	335.00
1946-Zealand Village Church	165.00
1947-The Good Shepherd	220.00
1948-Noddebo Church	220.00
1949-Our Lady's Cathedral	220.00
1950-Boeslunde Church	250.00
1951-Christmas Angel	400.00
1952-Christmas in Forest	140.00
1953-Frederiksborg Castle	130.00
1954-Amalienbord Palace	150.00
1955-Fano Girl	185.00
1956-Rosenborg Castle	230.00
1957-The Good Shepherd	125.00
1958-Sunshine Over Greenland	150.00
1959-Christmas Night	170.00
1960-The Stag	225.00
1961-Training Ship Danmark	220.00
1962-The Little Mermaid	195.00
1963-Hojsager Mill	100.00
1964-Fetching the Tree	90.00
1965-Little Skaters	75.00
1966-Blackbird	65.00
1967-The Royal Oak	50.00
1968-The Last Umiak	35.00
1969-The Old Farmyard	35.00
1970-Christmas Rose and Cat	30.00
1971-Hare in Winter	30.00
1972-In the Desert	27.50
1973-Train Homeward Bound	27.50
1974-Winter Twilight	27.50
1975-Queen's Palace	25.00
1976-Waterfall	30.00

1977-Hunter-Hound	22.50
1978-Greenland Scenery	35.00
1979	35.00
1980	35.00
1981	44.00

Mother's Day Plates

1971-American Mother. FE	45.00
1972-Oriental	15.00
1973-Danish	10.00
1974-Greenland	15.00
1975-Bird in Nest	17.50
1976-Mermaids	17.50
1977-The Twins	20.00
1978-Mother and Child	20.00
1979	20.00

VENETO FLAIR (ITALY)

1970-Madonna. Bellini	550.00
1971-Christmas. Three Kings. FE	100.00
1972-Mother's Day. Madonna and Child. FE	80.00
1972-Christmas. Shepherds	70.00
1972–1976. Dog Series	
1972-Shepherd	75.00
1973-Poodle	30.00
1974-Doberman	27.50
1975-Collie	30.00
1976-Dachshund	30.00
1972–1976. Last Supper Series. Set of 5	250.00
1973-Easter. Rabbits. FE	80.00
1975-Candleholder. FE	9.00
1975-Christmas Bell. FE	19.00
1975-Diana	55.00
1975-Easter Egg. FE	7.00
1976-Christmas Card. Old North Church	32.50
1976-Mother's Day	40.00
1976-Stein. FE	50.00
1977-Valentine	55.00
1978-Christmas Card. Dutch Christmas	40.00
1978-Easter Egg	10.00
1978–1979. New Years Bell	25.00
1979-Flower Children. FE	40.00
1979-Valentine. FE	37.50

WEDGWOOD (ENGLAND)

1969-Christmas. FE	285.00
1970-Christmas	25.00
1971-Children's Story. FE	15.00
1973-Christmas	29.50
1973-Mother's Day	15.00
1974-Christmas	29.50
1974-Mother's Day	15.00
1975-Christmas	15.00
1975-Christmas Mug	30.00
1975-Mother's Day	20.00

1976-Christmas	15.00
1977-Easter Egg. FE	25.00
1977-Christmas	16.00
1978-Christmas	22.50
1979-Easter Egg	12.00
1979-Mother's Day	22.00
1979-Christmas	30.00
1980-Easter Egg	12.00
1980-Mother's Day	30.00
1980-Christmas	30.00
1981-Easter Egg	25.00
1981-Mother's Day	30.00
1981-Christmas	42.50

COMIC BOOKS

Throughout history drawings and cartoons were important visual images for learning, political and social satire and entertainment. The advent of mass circulation newspapers opened the way for Sunday and daily comic features. The first comic Sunday feature appeared in the New York World in Feb., 1896.

Some of these comics were extracted into pulp magazine form in the 1915 to 1930 period. However, these pulps contained reprints of comics from the newspapers and did not appear on a regular basis.

By the late 1930's comic books achieved their own identity. Initially, the characters chosen were those familiar to comic strip readers—Captain Easy, Maggie and Jiggs, Orphan Annie, etc. As the comic book idea caught hold, publishers hired artists to create new characters and special adventure plots. Bulletman, Capt. Marvel, Plastic Man, Spy Smasher, and Superman arrived upon the scene.

Disney and the early cowboy heroes saw the comic book as a way to increase popularity and make a handsome profit. Today the comic book helps promote movies and television programs.

Comic books are collected for a variety of reasons—aesthetic (some artwork is avant-guard or classic), social commentary (one professor used comics to study the image of science in popular culture), and rarity. Although the price of most comic books of the 1950 to 1970 period is one to three dollars, rare and first editions command hundreds of dollars.

Comic books are printed on poor quality paper. Serious collectors must spend substantial sums to protect their investment. Condition is a prime factor in price. Tears, missing pages or corners of pages, signs of heavy use, and dirt lower prices quickly.

The prices below are for books in fine condition, showing some use but still crisp and clean. The numbers represent issue numbers, i.e. #1 is first issue, #2 is second issue, etc.

Comic books have been reissued; and, different publishers published the same title in different years. Check carefully.

Action Comics, #1, June 1938, Superman	6000.00
Amazing Spider-Man, #1, March 1963, Marvel Comics Group	300.00
Archie Comics, #1 Veronica, Winter 1942–43, MLJ Magazines	375.00
Batman, #1, Spring 1940, DC	1750.00
Better Publications, #1, 1944, 196 pages (biggest comic known), The Grim Reaper, The Silver Knight, Zudo, The Jungle Boy, Commando Cubs, Thunderhoof	25.00
Buck Rogers, #1, October 1964, Golden Key	5.00
Captain Marvel Adventures, #1, 1941, Fawcett	1800.00
Classic Comics, #1, October 1941, The Three Musketeers	230.00
Detective Comics, #1, March 1937, DC, origin of Fu Manchu	750.00
Dick Tracy, #1, 1939, black and white, Dell Publ.	180.00
Donald Duck Beach Party, #1, 1954, Dell Publ.	10.00

Tarzan #137, August 1963, Edgar Rice Burroughs, K.K. Publications .. $6.00

Frankenstein Comics, #1, 1945, Frankenstein begins by Dick Briefer	35.00
Hopalong Cassidy, #1, 1943, Fawcett	60.00
Journey Into Unknown Worlds, #36, Atlas Comics	10.00
The Lone Ranger, #1, 1948, Dell Publ.	60.00
Polic Comics, #1, 1941, Quality Comic Group, origin of Plastic Man	500.00
Popeye, #1, 1937, David McKay Publ.	500.00
Santa Claus Funnies, four color, Kelly Art, each	25.00
Shadow Comics, #1, March 1940, Street & Smith Publ., Shadow and Doc Savage	150.00
Uncle Scrooge, #495, four color, March 1952, Dell Publ.	50.00
Wheaties Premiums, Walt Disney, 32 titles, 1950–1951, 32 pages each, Sets A-1 to A-8 (four to a set), per set	50.00

COMMEMORATIVE AND HISTORICAL GLASS

Collectors have always sought commemorative and historical items made of glass, and since the bicentennial celebration in 1976, there has been an increase in demand for them. Consequently, there has been a substantial increase in the price of such things as "Liberty Bell" pattern glass, the commemorative trays and bread plates, as well as many new collectibles which were made expressly for the 1976 event. Collectors should be aware of this and separate new items from the old glass when it is available. There also are many other collectible items which are commemorative, but not especially historical.

Bottles

6½", Henry Ward Beecher, embossed, "T. P. Spencer, N. Y."	50.00
½ pt., General Douglas MacArthur, aqua, 1942	35.00
1 qt., Mail Box, 1891, clear	25.00
1 qt., "Moses," Poland Water, clear	30.00
24 oz., Santa Claus, "M. S. Husted" on base	250.00
9½", "Uncle Sam," clear	150.00

Bread Plates

10½ x 7½", Bible, Curtain Tie-

Plate, 7½″ dia., George Washington-200th Birth. $23.00

back pattern	50.00
10″, round, "Cleveland Reform" plate, hobnail border	35.00
10″, round "Golden Rule" plate, inscribed with Golden Rule	75.00
10½ x 7½″, "President Taylor" plate, successor to Brigham Young, also Curtain Tieback pattern	50.00
10¼ x 7¾″, Teddy Roosevelt, clear with frosted portrait, also known as the "Teddy Bear Platter"	105.00

Butters, covered

7½ x 5¼″, "Banner" or "Three Shields," novelty Daisy and Button, pattern, clear, shield finial . .	100.00
Bullet Emblem, covered	100.00
Liberty Bell, clear	135.00
"Maude S" (Mascotte pattern), horseshoe finial	75.00

Compotes

8″, "Jenny Lind," clear, open . . .	150.00
12⅜″, "Rebecca at the Well" . .	350.00

Goblets

"Actress," Lotta Crabtree and Kate Claxton, clear	80.00
Emblem Centennial goblet, Keystone and Shield	80.00
G.A.R., issued 1887, 21st Encampment	95.00
Garfield Drape, clear	32.50
Greeley, Brown, clear, ball stem .	200.00
Lincoln Drape, clear flint	80.00

Jars

3¾ x 2″, "Tehcumseh," mustard

jar, with cover, clear, log cabin shape	50.00
7½″, "Lafayette," aqua, profile embossed	75.00

Lamps

8″, "Coolidge Drape," oil lamp . .	150.00
Dotted American Shield, hand lamp, clear	100.00
Fine Rib and Star	150.00
8″, Lincoln Drape, cobalt blue, flint	300.00
3⅛ x 2¾″, log cabin shaped, with side handle, embossed "Pat'd, April 18, 1875"	75.00

Paperweights

3½ x 2″, Doorknob type, portrait in glass	100.00
3¼ x 4⅜″, King Edward VII, background frosted	95.00
4⅜ x 6⅛″, Memorial Hall, inscribed "1776–1876," Memorial Hall sculptured in glass, all frosted, mirror glass beneath, black opaque glass base, (rare)	150.00
3¾″, "Plymouth Rock," on base, "Inkstand Co., Providence, R. I."	50.00

Pitchers

"Dewey," cannonballs around base, portrait	75.00
Garfield Drape, clear	70.00
"Gridley, You May Fire When Ready," around body of pitcher, mortar shells around base, portrait	75.00

Trays

11½ x 9½″, "Columbia," shield shaped, head of Columbia in center	100.00
11 x 8″, "Flag," early, made for the Centennial, 38 stars in circle, plain border	100.00
"Flag," later made with 48 stars, sometime prior to 1912	50.00
10¾ x 7¾″, "McKinley Gold Standard," pattern surrounding full length figure, is Huckel or Feather Duster	75.00

Tumblers

Civil War, clear glass, cannon and eagle	35.00
Pittsburgh liquor tumbler, Arms of city of Pittsburgh, from family arms of William Pitt, inscribed "1708–1908— Sesquicentennial, Oct. 3, 1908," clear with red flashing . . .	45.00
"Louisiana Purchase," milk glass .	45.00
4½″, Wilkie, etched	35.00

COMMEMORATIVE AND SOUVENIR PLATES

Commemorative, historical and souvenir items, celebrating special events, places or

people, have always ranked high with collectors. Since the Bicentennial in 1976, interest in these items has increased greatly. Back in the 1880's, collectors were equally zealous, and their interests embraced both new and old objects and places.

Jones, McDuffee and Stratton, of Boston, were an extensive importing firm dealing in fine china, and they sponsored the making of the first Historic Wedgwood U. S. Calendar Tiles. Amazed at the enthusiastic acceptance of the idea, (which reawakened public interest in our social history), they thought the re-issue of "Historic Old Blue" plates, with traditional Wedgwood borders, but with new scenes and portraits, would be a great success.

With the Wedgwood firm's collaboration in making 78 different historic dessert-size plates, distributed exclusively in the United States, by Jones, McDuffee and Stratton in 1910, collectors had a new goal in trying to acquire a complete set. It is believed that besides these 78, there are scenes of the American South and West also, and that perhaps there are close to 300 of these subjects around.

From the Philadelphia Centennial in 1876 to the New York World's Fair in 1939, a series of American scenes on plates were also made by Rowland and Marcellus (R & M), of Staffordshire, England, like "Old Blue," with a wide, rolled edge which differentiates them. All of these plates are marked, and should not be confused with the actual old soft paste plates made by early Staffordshire potters.

Plates were also made by other potters in England and United States, see: COPELAND-SPODE, BUFFALO POTTERY, etc.

In the listing below, the Wedgewood are all 7½", the Rowland and Marcellus (R & M) are 10½".

"Souvenir of Carlisle" (Pa.) 10" dia., Rowland & Marsellus Co., Staffordshire, Eng. $22.00

Asbury Park, N. J., R & M, vignette border and rolled rim	32.00
Atlantic City, N. J., R & M, vignette border and rolled rim	32.00
Boston Hospital, Ridgeway, Staffordshire	110.00
Boston Tea Party, Wedgwood	50.00
Birthplace of Longfellow, Portland, Maine, Wedgwood	50.00
Capitol, Wash., D. C., Wedgwood . .	32.00
City Hall, N. Y., J. and W. Ridgeway, (Beauties of America series)	110.00
Declaration of Independence, signing of, Wedgwood	50.00
Faneuil Hall, Cradle of Liberty, Wedgwood	55.00
Fort Ticonderoga, N. Y., Wedgwood	32.00
Grant's Tomb, Riverside Drive on the Hudson, Wedgwood (rare) . . .	100.00
George Washington, Wedgwood . . .	32.00
Green Dragon Tavern, Boston, Wedgwood	50.00
Grover Cleveland, Wedgwood	45.00
"Half Moon" on the Hudson, Wedgwood	60.00
Hermitage, home of Andrew Jackson (rare), Wedgwood	100.00
Independence Hall, Phila., Pa., Wedgwood	32.00
King's Chapel, Boston, Wedgwood .	32.00
Longfellow, R & M, vignette border, rolled rim	55.00
Morman Temple block, (Utah) (rare), Wedgwood	100.00
Monticello, home of Thomas Jefferson, Wedgwood	35.00
Mount Vernon, Wedgwood	32.00
Niagara Falls, R & M, vignette border, rolled rim	40.00
Old Feather Store, Boston, Wedgwood	32.00
Old Corner Bookstore, Boston, Wedgwood	50.00
Old Man of the Mountains, N. H., Wedgwood	35.00
Park Street Church, Boston, Wedgwood	35.00
Pike's Peak, Wedgwood (rare)	100.00
Pilgrim Exiles, Wedgwood	50.00
Priscilla and John Alden, Wedgwood	40.00

Rear View of Independence Hall, Phila., Pa., Wedgwood	35.00
Return of the Mayflower, Wedgwood	45.00
Saratoga, New York, R & M, vignette border rolled rim	50.00
State House, Boston, Wedgwood . .	35.00
Taft, William Howard, 9½", tin, campaign plate, showing G. O. P. candidates prior to 1908 on border . .	65.00
Trinity Church, Copley Square, Boston, Wedgwood	40.00
Union Station, Wash., D. C., Wedgwood	32.00
Van Renssalaer Manor House, N. Y., Wedgwood, Blue Bell border Albany series, (rare)	100.00
Williamsburg scene, Wedgwood . . .	32.00

COMMEMORATIVE AND SOUVENIR SPOONS

These spoons were made as mementos of special events, personages or places of interest, reaching their highest peak of popularity in the 1880's–1890's. Commemorative spoons are currently being made and spoon collecting is regaining favor.

The spoons listed are 800–900 silver unless otherwise noted. Abbreviation in regards to size D-demitasse; all others are teaspoons. Reference numbers refer to *American Spoons, Souvenir and Historical* **by Rainwater and Felger.**

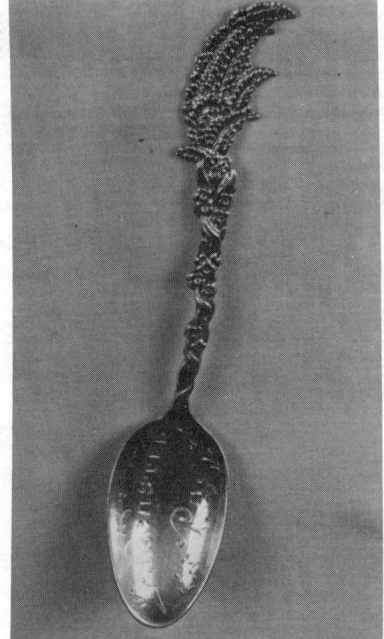

Admiral Dewey, Manila Bay	14.50
American Flag, enameled red, white and blue, eagle and shield on handle	35.00
American Indian, tusk beads, sailing vessel	25.00
Brooklyn, Rogers, silver plate	10.00
Cadillac, Michigan	40.00
California, capitol, state seal, Golden Gate	40.00
Canada, 1967, Niagara Falls	7.50
Charter Oak	50.00
Chicago	
Public Library, Indian, (D)	10.00
Chicago World's Fair, 1933	10.00
Chicago World's Fair, A Century of Progress, "Science and Court"	7.00
Cheyenne, Wyoming	16.00
Chief Kasko, totem pole, Victoria, B. C.	10.00
Columbian Exposition	
Goddess on globe	35.00
Exposition	35.00
Columbus, statue in relief in bowl,	

Lancaster, Pa., sterling $17.00	
gold washed	45.00
Cuyahoga County, Soldiers and Sailors Monument, floral handle	25.00
Denver, Prospector and Burro, Indian, state seal, gold bowl	50.00
Florida, Old City Gate, St. Augustine	16.00
Fort Dearborn	10.00
Fresno, California, 4 buildings, fruit	15.00
Havre, Montana, Indian	12.50
Hudson-Fulton Celebration, 1909, Tiffany Co.	40.00
Indian, headdress and beads	35.00
Landing of the Pilgrims	40.00
Los Angeles, dated 1905	25.00
Louisiana Purchase Exposition	40.00
Maine, Portland, Longfellow, (D) . . .	20.00
Maryland	35.00
Miles Standish	60.00
Nantucket Windmill	50.00
New York skyline	48.00
New Orleans	40.00
Niagara Falls, American Indian	25.00

Our Martyred Presidents	35.00
Palm Beach	45.00
Pan American Exposition	35.00
(Penna.) Willow Grove Park, P. and B.	8.00
Philadelphia	20.00
Pittsburgh Court House	20.00
Quebec, Duquet, scenic of houses, handle has horse and buggy	30.00
Queen Mary, painted bowl	15.00
Red Cross Society, "Clara Barton"	15.00
St. Paul	10.00
St. Augustine, "Sunny South"	10.00
Texas	
Texas Centennial, 1839–1936	50.00
Texas eagle, seal, capitol	20.00
Trinity Church, Philips Brooks, (D)	16.00
Utah	10.00
Washington Irving's home, Sleepy Hollow, Old Dutch church, Tarrytown, N.Y.	25.00
Whittier birthplace	50.00
White House, Mt. Vernon and cannon	25.00
World's Fair, Columbus, Santa Maria in bowl	40.00
Yellowstone Park, deer in handle	16.00
Yerkes Observatory, ornate twisted fish handle	45.00

today carry the late Spode mark, and pieces prior to 1843 should be attributed to Spode.

Plate, 10¼", white center, cream border with blue floral decor, gold trim, "Marathon" $20.00

COPELAND

COPELAND AND SPODE CHINA

Josiah Spode, a pupil of Thomas Whieldon, started the Spode Works in Stoke-on-Trent in 1770, with the help of William Copeland, a banker and tea merchant of London. The original idea was that the new-found beverage of tea would find more patrons if associated with a teapot to enhance its flavor. The firm has been handed down through the two families and W. T. Copeland and Sons have operated the works since 1847.

The company emphasizes the fact that Spode designs are hand engraved on imperishable copper. Every design is recorded in pattern books; no design is ever discontinued or lost; every Spode pattern is always available. This may or may not be entirely true today, but Spode patterns that are available are quite collectible. Most pieces found

Basket, Fruit, 8 x 6", handled, pierced "Blue Willow," c. 1830	200.00
Bowls 5", "Armorial," grey, cobalt blue, gold, c. 1890	50.00
Butter Dish, stoneware, grapevines, acanthus leaves, c. 1850	155.00
Chocolate Set, pot, 6 cups and saucers, "Indian Tree," set	200.00
Coffee Pot, 18", "Brown Delft," brown borders, with yellow floral decor, scenes of ruins of old English castles and abbeys	175.00
Creamer, "Indian Tree"	20.00
Cups and Saucers	
Cobalt blue and floral decor	85.00
"Christmas Holly"	75.00
Imari-type decor, Orange Blossoms	45.00
"Seasons," late Spode mark, blue and white	35.00
"Tobacco Leaf," Spode's Newstone mark, c. 1820	50.00
Egg Server, 4½ x 6", 4 egg cups and center salt dip, 4 silverplated spoons, salt spoon, "Pink Willow,"	275.00
Figurine, 13", unglazed, cherub holding a bellflower	60.00
Jugs	
5½", molded figures on body, molded vines at rim, c. 1810	150.00
4", floral decor on white ground, c. 1830	95.00

Pitchers
   5", molded water lily leaf and floral, blue and white, c. 1870 .... 75.00
   6½", golfing figures 40.00
Plates
   10", "Buttercup," yellow on ivory
   ground, late 25.00
   9", Floral center, cobalt blue and
   gold, scalloped edge 55.00
   10", "Fairy Dell," swirl-patterned
   edges, late 25.00
   8", Peacock, hen, peonies, blue
   transfer, gold trim, c. 1815 ..... 90.00
   10", "Peplow," Oriental decor and
   style of shape 25.00
   8", "Rosebud Chintz," all-over
   rosebud design, late 20.00
   6½", "Spode's Tower" 15.00
   8", soup, "Wicker Dale," late ... 30.00
   7", soup, "Wicker Lane," wide
   rim, late 30.00
   9", Willow, transfer for Tiffany and
   Co. N. Y., gold trim 25.00
Platter
   Large, Imari-type, colorful decor . 175.00
   16", "Gainsborough," floral, blue,
   crimson, purple, yellow on ivory
   ground over sepia print, late 200.00
Teapots
   "Billingsley Rose," (8 cup), late . 125.00
   6½", with cover and stand, scroll
   handle and feet, pink and cream,
   c. 1825, Spode Felspar marks .. 200.00
   "Pink Tower," 6-cup, late 130.00
Tureens
   Brown transfer, underplate and ladle 225.00
   7½", covered, on stand, "Japan,"
   c. 1822 .... 175.00
   "Spode's Tower," with underplate 150.00

COPPER

**Copper has been an important metal
throughout the centuries. Buckets, pots and
pans were few of the applications. It was
also used for jewelry, plaques, lighting fixtures, weather vanes and decorative items.**

Apple Butter Kettle
   Dovetailed, with iron handle,
   35-gal. 295.00
   Straight sided with rounded bottom, wrought iron bail handle ... 300.00
Bowl and tray, Art Nouveau style,
   sterling silver mounts of fish, birds
   and foliage, signed Gorham Mfg.
   Co. 1000.00

Measure, 1 gal., handled $75.00

Bucket, 11½", two pouring lips, 2
   handles at base, one handle at
   top 120.00
Candle holder, handled, hand hammered, signed 30.00
Coffee Pots
   10", with handle at right angle,
   American 125.00
   9", covered, sheet copper 100.00
   Covered, wooden handle and
   knob, brass fittings, tin lining 150.00
Coffee Set, zinc-lined coffee pot,
   covered sugar bowl and tray, shell
   designs and some brass trim 180.00
Dipper, 4¾", burnished bowl, handled 85.00
Dishes
   Charger, 10½", reticulated rim,
   shield-shaped silver inset, in cen-
   ter with monogram, signed 50.00
   Hand hammered, circular forms,
   flattened rims, signed Gustav
   Stickley, c. 1910 .... 235.00
Funnel with brass thumblift 35.00
Measures, ½ gal. to 1 gal., Ameri-
   can, one dated 1872, matched set
   of 7 .... 500.00
Measuring Pitcher, handled, flaring
   sides 85.00
Milk Pail, 6¼", with wire bail handle 65.00

Mug, 4¾", dovetailed seam, cast
handle 35.00
Pans
  5", wirebail handle 75.00
  9", dovetailed bottom and side
  seams, applied long heart-shaped
  handle 130.00
  2 qt., sauce pan, dovetailed con-
  struction, hammered copper han-
  dle, 18th century 100.00
  With cover, 6", pouring lip, front,
  handle at back, with wire bail han-
  dle 85.00
  5 qt. sauce pan, with cover, iron
  handle, marked "Lewis and
  Congor" 150.00
Pen tray and letter opener, applied
monogram, signed, Dirk Van Erp,
c. 1915 . . . . 200.00
Skillet, 13", hand hammered 85.00
Tea Kettles
  11", brass legs, handle and spout 90.00
  8", gooseneck spout, copper strap
  handle 120.00
  11", gooseneck spout, marked
  "Brittons, Pat. Aug. 9, 1870" 150.00
  Domed lid, gooseneck spout,
  strap handle, marked "D. Bentley," Philadelphia, early 19th cen-
  tury 800.00
  Covered, beehive finial 9¼",
  scrolling spout, rigid handle 135.00
  Covered, brass finial, deep
  straight sided base, for inserting
  into stove lid opening, copper bail
  handle 155.00
Tea Pot, gooseneck spout, strap
handle, with dove tailing, Alaska,
1800 . . . . 275.00
Vase, 8", with silver inlaid floral de-
signs 80.00
Wash boiler, with galvanized tin
cover 55.00

COPPER LUSTRE

**Copper lustres wares were first made in the
early 1800's by potters in the Staffordshire
district, England. A copper compound added
to the glaze resulted in the fine metallic-like
surface. Quantities were imported into the
United States during the 19th century. Reproductions are on the market, especially creamers and the so-called "Polka Jug." The new
wares are heavier in appearance and weight
when compared to the earlier.**

Bowls
  4", blue band with red roses 55.00

Pitcher, 4", blue decor $35.00

  5", pedestaled, blue band 50.00
  5½", covered, plain 75.00
  6", blue band, leaf decor 65.00
  6", rice, white cherubs in relief . . 55.00
Box, Comic, black transfer, 2¾ x
  3¼ x 5" 85.00
Cups and Saucers
  Blue band, c. 1820–40 . . . . 55.00
  Handpainted design 65.00
  Scalloped rims 60.00
Figurine, dog, 8" 85.00
Goblets
  Blue band, floral decor 65.00
  Blue band, boy and girl decor . . . 75.00
  Cream band, green and pink lustre
  vines 55.00
Mugs
  3", plain 50.00
  3", decorated blue band 55.00
  3¾", orange band, floral decor . . 60.00
  4", pink lustre on rim, tan band . . 65.00
  Shaving mug, cream band, lustre
  floral decor 70.00
Pitchers
  2½", plain 25.00
  3½", plain 32.50
  3½", blue band, with figure of girl
  and cat 45.00
  4½", white band, red scrolls 75.00
  5", bulbous, plain 50.00
  5", bulbous, band with blue flow-
  ers 85.00
  5½", sanded band 85.00
  5½", embossed figures, figural
  spout 50.00
  5½", stag decor, dark blue band 135.00
  5½", pink lustre band, "House
  Pattern," pink lustre lining, wish
  bone handle, c. 1840 . . . . 135.00
  6½", lustre lining, c. 1840 . . . . . 125.00

6¾", children dancing on blue band	75.00
7", white band, floral decor	125.00
7½", plain	80.00
8", floral decor, c. 1820–40	175.00
Salts	
Blue band, pedestaled	32.50
Plain, pedestaled	30.00
Sanded band, pedestaled	35.00
Sugar Bowl, open, raised floral and leaf design on 2" blue band	85.00
Teapots	
5½", plain, c. 1820–40	225.00
6", floral and leaf design on 2" blue band, same on lid	175.00
Toby Jug, c. 1820–40	250.00
Toothpick, sanded band	45.00
Urn, 8½", green band	175.00

CORALENE

Coralene is a type of art glass made in the 1880's by several American and English companies. The name Coralene was actually given to a type of decoration rather than a specific kind of glass. The design was painted on the surface of the piece, then tiny glass beads were applied by hand and adhered to the enamel paint. The object was then placed in a muffle to fix the enamel and set the beads. The design most commonly used resembled seaweed or coral — thus the name Coralene. Other designs were "Wheat Sheaf" and "Fleur-de-Lis." Most of the base glass used was satin finished.

    Reproductions are on the market. Some reproductions have been made using old glass. The beaded decoration on new Coralene has been glued on and can be scraped off.

Bowl, 6¾" dia., pink satin glass, "Seaweed," footed	375.00
Compote, 9½", pink satin glass, "Seaweed," ornate metal base, signed Webb	350.00
Ewers, 9", butterfly decor, pair	600.00
Rose Bowls	
5⅛", diamond quilted, "Star"	295.00
6¾", diamond quilted, "Fleur-de-Lis"	650.00
Sugar Castor, pink satin glass, "Seaweed"	125.00
Tumbler, 4", pink satin glass, "Seaweed"	240.00
Vases	
3", satin glass, "Seaweed," signed Webb	240.00
5", yellow satin glass, "Wheat Sheaf"	250.00

6¾", peachblow satin glass, 2 handled	550.00
7½", peachblow satin glass, "Seaweed"	440.00
7½", yellow satin glass, "Seaweed"	525.00
8½", blue satin glass, "Seaweed"	365.00

Vase, 5¾", rainbow, Mt. Washington $350.00

CORKSCREWS

The corkscrew is a utilitarian device used to draw a cork from a bottle. It continues to be made in a variety of shapes, styles and materials.

    As early as the 17th century, the figural corkscrew was favored. Mechanical models were popular in the Victorian era. Elaborate examples with handles of Mother of Pearl, ivory and sterling proliferated throughout the Art Nouveau period for people with champagne tastes.

Brass, Cheshire cat, 6¼"	45.00
Commemorative, inscribed "Chicago's World's Fair, 1893"	12.50
Figural, Scottie, bronzed metal, German	15.00

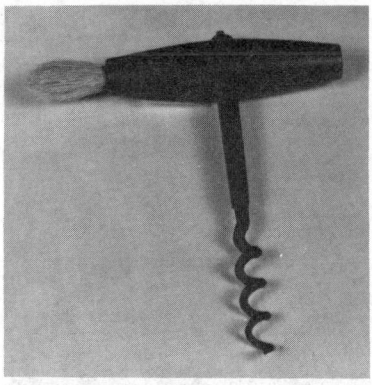

Wood handle, brush end, 5″, marked
Warrenty $75.00

Plate, 8½″ square, Edward VIII,
1937 . . . .$35.00

Horn, 4¼″, capped with continental silver, English	40.00
Steel	
2¾″, ring top, American	8.00
3″, bar top, American	15.00
4½″, flat ring top, American	25.00
7″ Captain's Key, Germany	35.00
Wood	
4″, walnut with ring top, American	20.00
4¼″, hand turned walnut handle, English	35.00
4½″, hand turned, black stain, English	30.00
5″, hand turned cherry, American	25.00
5½″, hand turned walnut with ring top, American	28.50
6″, black stained handle, brass cap, English	35.00
6″, black stained handle, long skirt, spring plunger, marked "Hercules," English	55.00
6″, burl	25.00

CORONATION ITEMS

**From the time of Queen Victoria's coronation
to the present ruling monarch of England,
souvenir items commemorating the occasions have been made. Although china mugs
and plates were the most prevalent, tin boxes, glasswares, silver spoons and a variety of
other items were also made and are considered collectible.**

Beaker, Royal Doulton, Edward VII, 1901–1910, "Presented by His Majesty" and "Coronation Dinner"	35.00
Bottle, 9½″, Copeland-Spode, George V, for wine	140.00
Candy Tins	
Edward VIII	25.00
Elizabeth II	25.00
Creamer and Sugar, George VI, 1936–1952, pair	54.00
Cheese Dish, pottery, Elizabeth II . .	50.00
Cup and Saucer, Portrait of Victoria and Albert, purple transfer with touches of pink and green lustre trim	130.00
Cups	
George V, portrait of George and Mary, Royal Doulton	40.00
Edward VIII, 4″	25.00
Edward VIII, 3″, pottery, portrait of Edward, flags and lions	20.00
George VI, designed by Dame Laura Knight	75.00
George VI, loving cup, 2 handled, portraits of George and Elizabeth, Royal Doulton, No. 429 of 2,000 .	225.00
Decanter, Elizabeth II, squat shape	45.00
Dish, George VI, 5″, pottery	25.00
Door Knocker, brass, Elizabeth II . .	35.00
Mugs	
Edward VIII	25.00
Edward VIII, shaving mug, scuttle type	75.00
George VI, portraits of George and Elizabeth	35.00

Elizabeth II, pottery 18.00
Elizabeth II, crystal, etched crown
and date, original label 75.00
George V, 6", Royal Doulton . . . 85.00
George VI, portraits of George
and Elizabeth 35.00
George V, 3½", with portrait . . . 35.00
Edward VIII, 3", full face portrait
with Abbey and Windsor Castle
background, Aynsley China 52.00
George VI, portraits of George
and Elizabeth, artist signed, Dame
Laura Knight 55.00
Elizabeth II, portrait, flags and
crown, W. Adams and Sons 60.00
Pitchers
Edward VII, Portrait medallion of
Edward and Alexandra, on medi-
um brown background, chocolate
banded rim, Doulton Lambeth . . . 185.00
Edward VIII, 4", Lancaster and
Sons, Ltd 55.00
Elizabeth II, 4", Raised yellow por-
trait on brown glaze, Dartmouth
Pottery, Devon 66.00
Elizabeth II, 5½", Mask spout,
Worcester Bone China 55.00
Pipe, Edward VII, Biscuit clay with
figural head of Edward 50.00
Plates
George V, Portrait of George and
Mary, and floral garland center,
cobalt blue and gold border with
crest 85.00
George V, Portrait of George and
Mary with crest, "May Their Reign
be Glorious", reticulated rim 60.00
Edward VIII, Bust portrait with
crown and flags, gold scalloped
edge, J. and G. Meakin 35.00
George VI, Portrait of George and
Elizabeth 48.00
Elizabeth II, Portrait, Meakin 25.00
Edward VII, Portraits of Edward
and Alexandra 60.00
George V, 6¼", Portraits of
George and Mary center, em-
bossed rim with flags 45.00
George V, Portraits of George and
Mary center, roses on rims 55.00
Edward VIII, 10", Brown glaze pro-
file 35.00
George VI, 10", Scalloped rim,
beading "God Save the King" . . . 65.00
Elizabeth II, 8½" 30.00
Portraits, Edward VII and Alexandra,
woven silk, by W. H. Grant, black
and white, with flag and coat of
arms in red, blue and gold thread,
original frames 400.00
Trays
Edward VIII, 7", ash tray, brass

with bronze medallion of Edward
in center 52.20
Elizabeth II, pin tray, portraits of
Elizabeth and Phillip, tin 8.50
Tumblers
Edward VII, 4", porcelain 35.00
Edward VIII, Wedgwood 55.00
Elizabeth II, glass, with coat of
arms 25.00

COSMOS GLASS

**Cosmos glass is pressed milk glass decorat-
ed with cosmos flowers in relief. The flowers
were "stained" or "flashed" with pale shades
of blue, pink and yellow. It is attributed to
Dithridge & Son, New Brighton, Pa., c. 1900.**

Syrup, 6½" $120.00

Butter, covered 200.00
Condiment Set, salt, pepper, mus-
tard 190.00
Creamer 125.00
Creamer and Covered Sugar 200.00
Lamps
7½", base only 45.00
Mini base, panelled, chimney 80.00
16" base, Eagle burner 250.00
Pickle Castor, no lid, no tongs 175.00
Pitcher, bulbous with 8 tumblers (2
chipped) 275.00

Shakers, pair	95.00
Spooner	100.00
Sugar, covered	150.00
Tumbler	85.00

COWAN POTTERY

R. Guy Gowan founded the Cowan Pottery in 1913 in Cleveland, Ohio. The establishment remained in almost continuous operation until 1931 when financial difficulties forced closure.

Early production was redware pottery. Later a porcelain-like finish was perfected with special emphasis placed on glazes. Lustreware is one of the most common types. Commercial type wares marked "Lakeware" were produced from 1927 to 1931.

Early marks include an incised "Cowan Pottery" on the redware (1913–1917), impressed "Cowan," and impressed "Lakewood." The imprinted stylized semi-circle with or without the initials R.G. was later.

Bookends, 7½", Sunbonnet girls, ivory glaze, pair	200.00
Bottle, figural of Queen from Alice in Wonderland, Chinese red glaze	450.00
Candlesticks, 4¼", seahorse base, jet black glaze, pair	65.00
Flower Frogs	
5", cluster of mushrooms, ivory glaze	55.00
6", Figural #701, nude bent backwards, ivory glaze	100.00
6½", Figural #686, nude dancer with scarf, ivory glaze	100.00
7½", Figural #685, double nudes, ivory glaze	150.00
11½", Figural #687, nude dancer with tambourine, ivory glaze	175.00
Pitcher, quart size, pink lustre glaze	45.00
Vases	
6½", blue lustre	45.00
8 x 7", fan shape with floral handles, ivory glaze	45.00
8 x 8", fan shape with seahorse base, jet black glaze	95.00
11", cyclindrical, Chinese red glaze	125.00
12", molded design of squirrel, bird, and foliage, light blue glaze	150.00

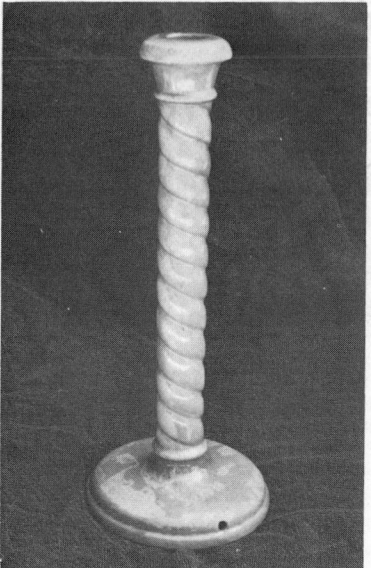

Lamp Base, 17", yellow lustre, 1920's $65.00

13", footed urn shape with flared top, marigold lustre glaze	75.00

COWBOY COLLECTIBLES

The dime novel and the yellow press helped promote the cowboy hero. In the early 20th Century novelists, silent films, and Wild West shows continued the tradition.´

With the advent of television, the cowboy hero reached the masses. Bill Boyd, Hopalong Cassidy, demonstrated the power and profit of star endorsement. Hopalong Cassidy's logo appeared on over 2,000 items. The peak period of the cowboy hero was 1948 to 1955. As television developed, the cowboy was replaced with the comic and urban heros.

Cowboy collectibles were generally of high quality. As treasured possessions of childhood, they have been guarded and saved by many. There is a good supply available. However, the number of serious collectors is growing, and competition is strong for rare items.

UNEXPECTED GUEST

Bubble Gum card, 22 cards in set, black, 1950 .... $20.00

Gene Autry
Belt Buckle, brass, Autry's name and figure outlined in red, 1950's   32.50
Button, blue, 1½", Sunbeam Bread — Gene Autry's Bread ...   8.00
Cap Pistol, cast iron, Kenton, red grips, 6½" c. 1940 ....   40.00
Cereal Box, Wheaties, 6 x 8" ...   25.00
Galoshes in shape of cowboy boot, rubber, red and white 40.00
Guitar, wood, Melody Ranch, western decals 75.00
Plate, white china, border of brands, Autry with Champ in middle, 9½" 25.00
Publicity Photo, 5 x 7" 7.50
Thermos Bottle, 1950's 12.00

Hopalong Cassidy
Boy's Playsuit 30.00
Box Camera, Gaiter Products Co., 1940, flash attachment, original boxes 60.00
Ear Muffs, maroon plush with oval tin picture 22.50
Galoshes in shape of cowboy boots, rubber, black and white with die-cut rubber spur, 10" high   80.00
Jigsaw Puzzle, Whitman, color, 9 x 11½" 12.50
Mechanical Shooting Gallery, litho tin, original box 75.00
Pocket Knife, Imperial Knife Co. .   25.00
Radio, Arvin, red or black case . .   70.00
Range Rifle, Marx Toy Co., red tin, 30" 150.00
Throw Rug, biege chenille, red and brown with design with Topper in center, 25 x 49" 67.50

Lone Ranger
Binoculars, red plastic with two color decal 20.00

Deputy Sheriff Secret Folder, came with secret badge, 2½ x 5½", folded in three sections 15.00
Frontier Town, premium from Cheerios, four paper sections, fifty plus buildings 140.00
Game, Parker Bros., 1938, original box, 10 x 19" 40.00
Harmonica on original card, c. 1960 ....   12.00
Lobby Card, "Lost City of Gold," 1957 ....   5.00
Paint Book, Whitman, 1938, 11 x 13½" 35.00
Record Player, wood case, c. 1950 ....   55.00
Ring Toss, Rosebud Art Co., 1946   25.00

Tom Mix
Bandanna, "Best Wishes — Tom Mix," multicolored, Mix on horseback 67.50
Periscope, blue cardboard tube, inscribed "Ralston Straight Shooters," 9" long 60.00
Postal Telegraph Signal Set, 5 x 7½" 55.00

Roy Rogers
Bandanna, "Many Happy Trails — Roy Rogers & Trigger," red ground, 18" square 35.00
Bathrobe, terry cloth, Polly Prentiss, illustrations of cowboy on horse 40.00
Book, "The Brasada Bandits," Whitman, 1955 ....   8.00
Cut Out Dolls, Rogers and Dale Evans, 1953, Whitman 15.00
Lunch Box, Trigger, dark blue ground, 6 x 8½" 25.00
Record Album, songs from eight Rogers' movies, four 78 rpm records, seven black and white photos 40.00
School Bag, Dale Evans, red 32.50
Wrist Watch, Rogers and Trigger, 1950's 50.00

Others
Bonanza, wedge of Ponderosa pine with color photo of Lorne Greene as Ben Cartwright 15.00
Cheyene, Clint Walker, Harland cowboy figure 60.00
Cisco Kid, advertising sign, 10 x 18" 30.00
Dillon, Matt, hat, brown felt, picture of James Arness 17.50
Earp, Wyatt, white milk glass plate, 7" 9.00
Have Gun Will Travel, holster set,

original box, 12 x 14"	**65.00**
Hayes, Gabby, Treasure Chest of Tall Tales, Wilson-Hill, 128 pages, 1952	**27.50**
Jones, Buck, premium kerchief, yellow with blue picture of cowboy on bucking horse, triangular, 26" long side	**75.00**

CRANBERRY GLASS

Cranberry is the color of the glass and not the ware. The color was achieved by adding a small amount of gold to a pot of molten glass. The blown or molded objects were first amber in color. When reheated at a low temperature, the cranberry or ruby color developed. Cranberry glass was made by many glass factories in America and Europe. It was often decorated with gold or enamel decoration. Cranberry glass has been widely reproduced but the new is not of the same quality or color as the old.

Miniature Lamp, 5¾", cranberry font, opalescent chimney, silver plated base $525.00

Atomizer, throat, panelled, cut, polished base	**95.00**
Biscuit Jar, covered, rib	**95.00**
Bobeches, ruffled, opalescent, pair .	**50.00**
Bottles, Perfume	
4¾", white lacey enamel decor, crystal stopper	**110.00**
5", gold floral decor	**120.00**
6", gold intaglio cut, deer in meadow scene, gold trim stopper	**120.00**
7", enamel decor with gold outlining, crystal ball stopper	**225.00**
Bowls	
5", finger	**45.00**
5¼", crystal, applied petals and feet	**225.00**
7¼", in Sheffield holder	**155.00**
10", crackle, ribbed feet, pinched sides	**95.00**
10½", silver plated holder	**195.00**
Boxes	
2¾" square, covered, crackle, gold finial	**85.00**
3" dia., hinged, enamel decor . . .	**125.00**
3¼" dia., hinged	**95.00**
Butter, covered, 6", crystal ball finial, 6½" underplate	**170.00**
Castor Set, 3 bottles, silver plated holder	**150.00**
Celery, 6⅞", IVT, scalloped top, enamel decor	**105.00**
Cream and Sugar, crystal applied handles	**145.00**
Cruets	
7¼", lacy foliage, daisies and scrolls decor, crystal handle and ball stopper	**145.00**
8", applied crystal handle	**85.00**
8", flattened bulbous, 3 petal top, white and gold enamel decor, crystal applied handle	**175.00**
Decanters	
7½", bird with brass feet, legs, neck and head	**175.00**
8", floral enamel decor, crystal applied handle and bubble stopper .	**150.00**
9", Hobnail, enamel floral decor .	**220.00**
9", applied clear handle, clear swirl stopper, star cut bottom . . .	**90.00**
11", enamel floral decor, steeple bubble stopper	**125.00**
Hat, 2 x 3½"	**55.00**
Lamp Chimney, 10½", swirl	**125.00**
Pickle Castors	
Fancy footed frame, lid, tongs . . .	**165.00**
Flower form frame, enamel decor	**195.00**
Thumbprint, tongs, Meridian silver plated holder	**195.00**
Pitchers	
6", hexagonal top, white and gold decor	**65.00**
6", bulbous with swirls, clear ap	

plied handle	120.00
6½", dragonfly and leaves in gold	160.00
7", bulbous, overshot	100.00
9", tankard, overshot	135.00
9½", candy ribbon top, applied clear reeded handle, 6 matching tumblers, set	250.00
11½", tankard with ice bladder, overshot	195.00
Tankard	110.00
Ring Tree, 2¾", gold bands, floral decor	65.00
Rose Bowl, 6½", crimped top, gold and enamel floral decor, pedestal foot	150.00
Salt, ruffled rim, 5 circular applied feet	45.00
Salts, Master	
Vaseline shell applique, silver plated holder	90.00
Vaseline applied rigaree, silver plated holder, claw feet	110.00
Brass holder, fancy open work . .	110.00
Salt Shaker, opalescent swirl	60.00
Smoke Bell, 8¾", opalescent swirl .	60.00
Spooner, 5⅞", overshot, scalloped top	75.00
Sugar Castors	
Panelled	55.00
IVT, original top	75.00
Syrup, IVT, silver plated spring lid . .	80.00
Table Set, covered butter, creamer, covered sugar, floral decor	195.00
Tumblers	
Heavy enamel decor	175.00
Honeycomb, enamel floral decor .	50.00
IVT, floral decor	40.00
Overshot	35.00
Tumble Up	65.00
Vases	
7", overshot, diamond shape top, blown out pears design	165.00
7", drape, ruffled top, clear applied feet	110.00
7⅛", melon sectioned, crystal leaves and feet	85.00
7½", IVT, bulbous, tri-corner top .	150.00
7½", ruffled top, enamel floral decor, fancy ormulu feet	195.00
9", enamel floral decor, large gold flowers	165.00
12", lacy gold leaves and scrolls decor, pair	295.00
15", ewer, clear applied handles, gold scrolls, enamel floral decor, clear foot, pair	550.00
16", gold floral decor, clear base .	125.00
Wine Decanter, clear stopper and handle, 6 wines with clear stems .	225.00

CROCKS
See STONEWARE

CROWN DERBY
See ROYAL CROWN DERBY

CROWN MILANO

Crown Milano is an American Art Glass produced by the Mt. Washington Glass Works at New Bedford, Mass. The original patent was issued in 1886 to Frederick Shirley and Albert Steffin.

Normally it is an opaque white satin glass finished with light beige or ivory color background embellished with fancy florals, decorations and elaborate heavy raised gold. When marked, pieces carry an entwined CM with crown in purple enamel on the base. Sometimes paper labels were used. The silver plated mounts often have MW impressed or the Pairpoint mark as they supplied the mountings.

Vase, 6" high, white with pink and gray mottling, gold decor, paper label $1395.00

Bride's Basket, 8", cream opaque, beige shadow foliage, heavy coin gold raised florals, ruffled, silver plated holder marked Pairpoint . .	2000.00
Biscuit Jars	
Squatty bulbous, water lilies and foliage in pastel colors outlined in raised gold, silver plated top, ruffled, signed	895.00
Square, jewelled flowers and heavy raised gold decor, silver plated top with MW under lid	895.00
Slightly bulbous, spring flowers decor, heavy gold scrolls and trim, silver plated mounts, signed	850.00
Squatty bulbous, elaborate jewelled starfish and heavy gold decor, signed, top also marked MW .	950.00

Cruet, 7½", bulbous, beige, pastel flowers heavily outlined in raised gold, twisted rope opaque applied handle, very rare 2500.00

Cup and Saucer, demitasse, pink with gold scalloped edge, ribbed effect, gold shadow scrolls, gold flowers in heavy gold, opaque handle, signed, rare 1500.00

Ewers
  10", pastel flowers with heavy raised gold, rope handle 1500.00
  12", large fish and net heavily outlined in gold, twisted rope handle 3000.00

Hatpin Holder, mushroom shape, 5½" dia., beige, pastel flowers . . 250.00

Jardiniere, 12", pastel flowers heavily outlined in gold with shadow foliage, fancy gold scrolls, signed . . 1500.00

Mustard Pot, silver plated hinged top, shaded blue, white with heavy gold flowers, marked MW 325.00

Pitcher, water, mellon sectioned, water lilies in pastel outlined in heavy raised gold, green leaves, rope handle, signed 2500.00

Sweetmeat Jars
  4¼", mellon sectioned, burmese color, autumn leaves and acorns outlined in heavy raised gold, marked MW under silver plated lid 795.00
  4½", swirled beige, heavy florals and trim, silver plated mounts marked MW, turtle finial . . 750.00

Syrup, 7", hinged metal top, pink, pastel flowers outlined in gold, opaque applied handle, very rare . 895.00

Tray, 7 x 9½", glossy opaque white, pastel thistles with heavy raised gold trim, signed 1150.00

Vases
  8", beige satin, shadow leaves and heavy gold roses, two small leaf applied gold trim handles . . . 1495.00
  13", bulbous, mellon sectioned, long thin neck lipped top, cream, pastel blossoms, heavily outlined in gold, signed 1650.00
  14", beige, heavy gold flowers, jewelled, fancy scalloped and pointed top 1600.00

CRUETS

Cruets are small bottles used for storing or serving vinegar and oil. They were introduced to England from Italy in the 17th Century and entered the American homes in the 19th Century. Practically every glass manufacturer produced cruets.

Also see specific wares such as Amberina,

Amber, 4½", Cambridge $18.00

Cranberry Glass, Cut Glass, Pattern Glass, etc.

Amethyst, amber handle and stopper, melon-shaped 95.00
Blue
  Reverse swirl 100.00
  Ribbed handle, Overshot 70.00
  Sapphire, amber handle 70.00
Cut Glass
  Pineapple 120.00
  Hobstars, fans 75.00
Fostoria, American 35.00
Green
  Emerald, Sunbeam 145.00
  Clear 25.00
Milk Glass, late 20.00
Mt. Washington, cream and tan, enamel decor of leaves and blueberries 750.00
Opalescent, blown, Daisy and Fern, blue 75.00
Ruby Glass
  Honeycomb, World's Fair, 1893 . 125.00
  Pillow Encircled, small 110.00

CUP PLATES

Many early cups and saucers were handleless, with deep saucers. The hot liquid was poured into the saucer and sipped from it. This necessitated another plate for the cup . . the cup plate.

The first cup plates made of pottery were of the Staffordshire variety. In the mid-1830's to 40's, glass cup plates were favored. Boston and Sandwich Glass Co. was one of the main contributors to the lacy glass type.

The numbers listed refer to *American Cup Glass Plates* by Ruth Webb Lee, and James H. Rose. Reproductions are on the markets.

Glass, clear, log cabin with flag $25.00

GLASS

LR-11, clear, Eastern	25.00
LR-46, black amber, unique	1200.00
LR-62, clear, Eastern	35.00
LR-65, clear, Eastern	25.00
LR-79, clear, New England Glass Co.	25.00
LR-82, acorn and leaves, silver opaque blue, fiery opalescent . . .	550.00
LR-147 A, flower, bull's eye border, clear, Midwestern	30.00
LR-159 A, clear, Midwestern	45.00
LR-197 B, lacy, clear, Midwestern . .	25.00
LR-230 A, lacy, clear, Eastern	45.00
LR-262, 12 sides, white fiery opalescent	250.00
LR-343 B, clear, Eastern	35.00
R-394, beehive, clear	25.00
LR-440 B, valentine, cobalt blue . . .	300.00
LR-455 B, heart, clear	25.00
LR-458 A, heart, fiery opalescent . .	95.00
LR-465 J, heart, lacy opalescent . . .	150.00
LR-467 A, heart, canary	500.00
LR-522, sunburst, amethyst	150.00
LR-531, sunburst, vaseline	150.00
LR-562 A, Henry Clay, clear	175.00
LR-565 B, Henry Clay, peacock blue	350.00
LR-568, Harrison, clear	45.00
LR-576, Victoria, clear	50.00
LR-592, Log Cabin, clear	350.00
LR-610 B, Cadmus, cobalt blue . . .	150.00
LR-610 B, Cadmus, peacock blue . .	300.00
LR-612 A, steamboat, clear, Mid-	

western	150.00
LR-628, Livingston, blue green	500.00
LR-635, Maid of the Mist, light green, Midwestern	300.00
LR-651 A, eagle, fiery opalescent . .	500.00
LR-654 A, eagle, cobalt blue	350.00
LR-670, eagle, clear, Midwestern . .	50.00
LR-679, eagle, clear	35.00
LR-692, Lyre, clear, Midwestern . . .	25.00
LR-699, hound, clear	125.00

PORCELAIN OR POTTERY

American Villa, dark blue	95.00
Battery, wood	150.00
Cadmus, wood	165.00
Canova	40.00
Cathedral, brown	40.00
Franklin Kite	65.00
King's Rose	95.00
Pink Lustre	30.00
Spatterware, floral	50.00
Vintage, alcock, light blue	50.00

CUSTARD GLASS

Custard glass, as we know it, was made first in England in the early 1880's. Among the English makers who came to America, Harry Northwood brought custard glass to his factory in Indiana, Pa., in 1898. It has become very popular and collectible, the demand having increased the price, and it is still desirable to collectors today.

Two patterns which have been heavily reproduced are Argonaut Shell (Nautilus) and Grape and Cable (Grape with Thumbprints). This glass gets its "custard" color from uranium salts which were added to the molten glass.

Berry Sets

Chrysanthemum Sprig, 5 pcs., bowl and 4 sauces	600.00
Chrysanthemum Sprig, 5 pcs., bowl and 4 sauces in blue opaque	1000.00
Beaded Circle, enameled florals, bowl and 4 sauces, gold trim	500.00
Cherry and Scale, bowl and 5 sauces, nutmeg stain	375.00
Diamond with Peg, bowl and six sauces, roses decor, gold trim . . .	500.00
Everglades, gold trim	500.00
Fluted Scrolls, bowl and six sauces, gold trim	300.00
Georgia Gem, enameled flowers .	225.00
Geneva, bowl and six sauces, oval shape, gold trim	295.00
*Grape and Cable, bowl and six sauces, nutmeg stain, plain rim . .	575.00

Vase, 4″, vintage decor with basket weave $65.00

Berry Bowls

*Argonaut Shell (Nautilus)	325.00
Fan (Northwood)	175.00
Georgia Gem	95.00
Intaglio	180.00
Inverted Fan and Feather, footed	145.00
Louis XV	145.00
Ring Band	140.00

Butters, covered

Chrysanthemum Sprig	250.00
Diamond with Peg	195.00
Everglades	300.00
Geneva	150.00
Grape and Gothic Arches	195.00
Inverted Fan and Feather	245.00
Intaglio	200.00
Maple Leaf	225.00
Wild Bouquet	350.00

Celeries

Chrysanthemum Sprig	700.00
Ring Band, roses, gold trim	290.00
Victoria (Tarentum's)	225.00
Winged Scroll (Ivorina Verde)	265.00

Compotes, Jelly

*Argonaut Shell (Nautilus)	110.00
Beaded Circle	110.00
Cherry and Scale, nutmeg stain	90.00
Chrysanthemum Sprig, gold decor	115.00
Everglades, green and gold decor	115.00
Fan (Northwood's)	95.00
Fluted Scrolls	80.00
Geneva	80.00
Georgia Gem, with gold	60.00
Intaglio	100.00
Inverted Fan and Feather	175.00
Iris, gold decor	110.00
Louis XV	80.00

Maple Leaf, gold decor	100.00
Winged Scroll (Ivorina Verde)	70.00

Cruets

*Argonaut Shell (Nautilus), original stopper	300.00
Beaded Scroll, gold trim, original stopper	600.00
Chrysanthemum Sprig, gold trim, original stopper	220.00
Everglades, gold decor, original stopper	700.00
Fluted Scrolls	175.00
Inverted Fan and Feather	600.00
Louis XV	200.00
Maple Leaf, good decor, original stopper	900.00
Winged Scroll (Ivorina Verde), undecorated	100.00

Goblets

Beaded Swag	65.00
Diamond with Peg, souvenir	40.00
*Grape and Cable	70.00
Grape and Gothic Arch, nutmeg stain	60.00

Mugs

Diamond with Peg, souvenir, roses decor	40.00
Punty Band, souvenir	30.00
Strawberry-Diamond, rose decor, souvenir, Nash, Oklahoma	35.00

Pitchers

*Argonaut Shell (Nautilus)	500.00
Chrysanthemum Sprig	380.00
Diamond with Peg, tankard, with roses	150.00
Everglades, good decor	600.00
Fan, (Northwood's)	200.00

Salt and Pepper Shakers

*Argonaut Shell, (Nautilus) original tops, pair	300.00
Beaded Circle, original top, single	200.00
Chrysanthemum Sprig, good decor, single	70.00
Chrysanthemum Sprig, good decor, pair	170.00
Diamond with Peg, good decor, original tops, pair	80.00
Everglades, good decor, original tops, pair	250.00
Fluted Scrolls, original tops, pair	110.00
Geneva, original tops, pair	110.00
Intaglio, original tops, pair	170.00
Inverted Fan and Feather, original tops, pair	420.00
Louis XV, original tops, pair	170.00
Maple Leaf, good decor, original tops, pair	500.00
Winged Scroll, (Ivorina Verde), decorated, pair	155.00

Sauces

*Argonaut Shell (Nautilus)	65.00
Beaded Circle	50.00

Beaded Swag, souvenir	35.00
Chrysanthemum Sprig	50.00
Diamond with Peg, roses	45.00
Diamond with Peg, souvenir	45.00
Fan (Northwood's)	45.00
Fluted Scrolls	35.00
Geneva, oval	32.00
Geneva, round	35.00
Georgia Gem, souvenir	25.00
Georgia Gem, regular	25.00
Intaglio	50.00
Inverted Fan and Feather	85.00
Louis XV, oval, 5"	42.50
Maple Leaf, decorated	85.00
*Grape and Cable, nutmeg stain, flat	38.00
*Grape and Cable, nutmeg stain, footed	42.50
Ribbed Drape, decorated, roses .	38.00
Ring Band, roses, gold trim	35.00
Winged Scroll (Ivorina Verde), decorated	38.00

Spooners

*Argonaut Shell (Nautilus)	110.00
Beaded Circle	110.00
Beaded Swag	35.00
Cherry and Scale, nutmeg stain ..	85.00
Chrysanthemum Sprig	95.00
Diamond with Peg	70.00
Everglades	120.00
Fan (Northwood)	85.00
Geneva	60.00
Intaglio, gold and blue, decor ...	110.00
Louis XV	75.00
Maple Leaf	110.00
*Grape and Cable, nutmeg stain .	145.00
Ribbed Drape, roses decor	145.00
Ring Band, roses gold trim	80.00
Ring Band, chrysanthemum decor	90.00

Sugars, covered

*Argonaut Shell (Nautilus)	255.00
Beaded Circle	165.00
Cherry and Scale, nutmeg stain ..	125.00
Chrysanthemum Sprig, gold decor	165.00
Chrysanthemum Sprig, undecorated	125.00
Diamond with Peg, rose decor ...	145.00
Everglades, decorated	165.00
Fan (Northwood's)	120.00
Fluted Scrolls	115.00
Grapes and Gothic Arch	95.00
Winged Scroll (Ivorina Verde) ...	170.00

Toothpicks

*Argonaut Shell, (Nautilus)	125.00
*Chrysanthemum Sprig, decorated	240.00
Diamond with Peg, roses, decor .	50.00
Geneva	140.00
Georgia Gem, enamel decor, souvenir	75.00
Georgia Gem, gold decor	75.00
*Inverted Fan and Feather	545.00
Maple Leaf, decor	600.00

Ring Band, roses gold	80.00
Ring Band, gold souvenir	80.00
Winged Scroll (Ivorina Verde) ...	100.00

Tumblers

*Argonaut Shell (Nautilus)	85.00
Beaded Circle, gold and floral decor	70.00
Beaded Swag, souvenir	50.00
Chrysanthemum Sprig	45.00
Diamond with Peg	42.50
Everglades, green and gold	145.00
Fan (Northwood's)	75.00
Intaglio, gold worn	55.00
*Inverted Fan and Feather	80.00
Louis XV	75.00
Maple Leaf	60.00
Ring Band	60.00
Winged Scroll (Ivorina Verde) ...	90.00

Miscellaneous Custard Items

Dish, Peacock with Urn, nutmeg stain	195.00
Napkin Ring, "Republic, Kansas," souvenir	16.00

Plates

*Grape and Cable, 7", nutmeg stain	35.00
Prayer Rug, 7½"	22.50

Powder Jars

*Grape and Cable, nutmeg stain .	210.00
Winged Scroll (Ivorina Verde) ...	80.00

Punch Bowls

*Grape and Cable, nutmeg stain, 2 pieces	900.00
Inverted Fan and Feather	2000.00
Sunburst Cane	500.00

Punch Cups

Diamond with Peg, roses decor ..	42.50
*Grape and Cable, nutmeg stain .	200.00
Ring Band, roses, gold	35.00
Shaving Mug, Georgia Gem, souvenir	50.00

Syrups

Geneva, original lid	200.00
Winged Scroll, (Ivorina Verde), original lid	300.00

CUT GLASS

Cut Glass is the process of grinding decorations into glassware by means of a metal or stone cutting tool. A very ancient craft, it was revived in 1600 by Bohemians, and it spread through Europe, Great Britain and to America.

Our cut glass came of age at the Centennial Exposition in 1876 and the World Columbian Exposition in 1893, and the American public realized American cut glass to be exceptional in quality and workmanship. Our country's greatest output was during years of 1890 to well into the 1900's, and this is

known as the "Brilliant Period," when companies such as, Libby, Dorflinger, Tuthill, Hawkes, Clarke and others were making this beautiful glass.

During those years, the ideal wedding present was a piece of cut glass, and most of the pieces found today are from this period or later.

Finger Bowl, 2½ x 5″ dia., with underplate, American **$195.00**

Baskets, Handled
5 x 10 x 15″ to top of double-notch cut handle, flowers, leaves, Harvard border, sixteen point rayed base	350.00
8¼ x 12″, butterflies, flowers, foliage, ornate silver plated frame, signed Hawkes	395.00
8″, "Eldorado," Pitkins and Brooks	295.00

Bells
Large size, cut body and handle, T. B. Clarke Co.	142.00
Call, Buzz-Star	150.00
Tea, 5½″, plain handle, cut body	143.00
Bobeches, unsigned, pair	75.00

Bon-Bon Dishes
6″, "Evelyn"	60.00
6″, "Beverly," triangular shape . .	100.00
7″, Olive or bon-bon	55.00
7½″, "Myrtle," oblong	40.00
7½″, "Rahjah," ornate cut	90.00

Bowls
8″, "Arbutus," round	126.50
9″ "Drape"	225.00
8″, "Harvard," signed Hawkes . . .	125.00
"Intaglio Rose," signed Tuthill . . .	295.00
8″, "Lovebirds," signed Libbey . .	600.00
8″, "Millicent," signed Hawkes . .	175.00
9″, "Manhattan," on footed base, T. B. Clarke	205.00
9″, "Peerless," with matching tray	190.00
9″, "Pinwheel," salad	150.00
10″, "Rahjah," salad	195.00

10″, "Sunburst," Pitkins and Brooks	205.00

Boxes
3½″, all-over cut	150.00
4″, "Garland," covered, round, late cut	55.00
5″, "Hobstar," rayed base, silver rim	165.00

Butters, Covered
"Electric"	255.00
Fans, stars, and strawberry, diamond-cut	225.00
"Orland"	255.00

Butter Pats
3½″, "Ashland"	33.00
3½″, "Canton"	24.00
3½″, "Lady Curzon"	24.00
3½″, "Priscilla"	24.00
3½″, "Saratoga"	24.00
3½″, "Spruce"	24.00

Butter Tubs, open
"Boston," plate to match	144.00
"Manhattan," plate to match, T. B. Clarke	216.00
"Napoleon," plate to match	222.00
"Seaside," plate to match	216.00
Cake Stand, 12″, with gallery, "Hobstar and Fan"	325.00

Candelabra
3-light, J. D. Bergen	252.00
5-light, J. D. Bergen	276.00

Candlesticks
10″, "Albert," pair	384.00
10″, "Victoria," pair	384.00
Canoe, Persian-cut	375.00

Carafes
Qt., "Arlington"	108.00
Qt., "Acme," notched neck	180.00
"Ansonia"	120.00
"Diamond and Fan," Higgins-Seiter	66.00
"Heart Globe," notched neck . . .	160.00
"Lady Curzon," Averbeck	99.00
"Venetian," signed Hawkes	285.00

Celery Trays
"Diamond," Averbeck	143.00
10″, "Nordica," T. B. Clarke	60.00
4 x 11½″, "St. Cloud," Higgins and Seiter	85.00

Cheese Dish, Covered
6″, high over cover, "Glenwood" .	315.00
5″, "Manhattan," T. B. Clarke . . .	305.00

Cigar Jars
50 cigars, "Glenwood"	305.00
Jar in frame of antique oak	355.00

Cologne Bottles
4½″, sterling enameled stopper . .	90.00
5 oz., "Berry," tall slim with ground stopper	37.00
6 oz., "Bermuda"	40.00
12 oz., "St. George," square, T. B. Clarke	57.00

12 oz., "St. Julien," Higgins and Seiter 36.00

Compotes

"Arcadia," covered 265.00
"Carmen," high standard 305.00
5", "Crete," double handled, on foot 140.00
"Empire," bowl on footed standard, 2 pcs. 280.00
6", "Manhattan," low standard, T. B. Clarke 90.00
5", "Raynor," Empire 98.00
Various designs, signed Maple City 200.00

Cordial Sets

Tall wine cruet, stoppered, six cordials and matching tray 355.00
"Concord," bulbous, handled cruet, 6 flat tumbler-type cordials, handled, matching tray, Higgins and Seiter 250.00
6" cruets, stoppered (2) in "Dewey" pattern, in handled, wooden, oak frame, Higgins and Seiter . . . 355.00

Creamers and Sugars

"Belmont," sugar tub and creamer, Pitkin and Brooks, set 126.00
"Byrns," on foot, set 107.00
"Carolyn," Pitkins and Brooks, set 140.00
"Duchess," set 210.00
"Harvard," all-over cut, set 150.00
"Heart," oval shaped, set 225.00
"Northern Star," set 102.00
"Prism," set 132.00
"Venus," T. B. Clarke, set 181.00

Cruets

Tall, on stand, facetted stopper, signed Hawkes 85.00
All-over cut, facetted stopper 350.00
Harvard-cut, and Cosmos, stopper 350.00
Hobstar and Cane, stopper 250.00
"Waverley," ½ pint, oil, stopper . 104.00

Decanters

1 qt., "Ansonia," stoppered, J. D. Bergen 209.00
1 qt., "Clarion," jug shaped, handled and stopper 200.00
Delmar, tall bottle-shaped, stopper 145.00

Dishes

"Chrysanthemum," rectangular dish, signed Hawkes 395.00
7", "Lotus," signed Egginton . . . 135.00
7 x 4", Star-cut, pickle 72.00
9", Curio-type, waved-edge, deep cut 115.00
12", "London," sloping sides 115.00
9", square, "Oriole," fancy 258.00
"Jubilee," handled pickle 71.00
9", "Venus," rounded, T. B. Clarke 262.50
Ferner, 8", "Hiawatha," fern dish and liner, footed 135.00

Finger Bowls

5", "Electric" 40.00
"Lorraine," signed Dorflinger 75.00
"Strawberry, Diamond and Fan," Higgins and Seiter 44.00
"Winola," T. B. Clarke 58.00
"Electric," low stem, J. D. Bergen . 47.00
"Florentine," Higgins and Seiter . 55.00
"Marie," J. D. Bergen 60.00
"Priscilla," signed 60.00
"Star in Pinwheel," signed Tuthill . 55.00
"Strawberry, Diamond and Fan," signed 50.00

Ice Buckets

5¾ x 7¾", "Florida," plate to match 195.00
"Ivanhoe," tub with drainer 185.00
"Jewel," on foot, double handled, T. B. Clarke 160.00

Knife Rests

Hobstars, signed Hawkes 95.00
2½", "Prism" 24.00

Lamps

17", "Chrysanthemum," electric, round shade 1030.00
23", "Chrysanthemum," cut base, Gone-With-The-Wind type, 32 prisms, Higgins and Seiter 1070.00
"Delmar," electric, rock-crystal effect, with or without prisms 1070.00
24½", lamp and shade, cut to match 2400.00
13¼", boudoir lamp 495.00
21", "Harvard," 40 original prisms 2700.00
22", "Kenwood," bulbous base, ornate cut, round top globe matching cut, silver plated mountings and fount 1220.00
17", Pansy-cut, base and round shade, 32 prisms 1220.00
Muffineer, "Henry VIII," sterling top, T. B. Clarke 130.00

Napkin Rings

"Harvard" 65.00
"Saratoga" 57.00

Nappies

"Clover," leaf-shaped, handled . . 29.00
6", "Diamond" 89.00
6", "Frisco," double handled 68.00
6", "Marietta," all-over cut, handle 55.00
10", "Webster," J. D. Bergen . . . 238.00

Pitchers

3-pint, "Alabama," Averbeck 192.00
3-pint, "Amazon," sterling silver mounting around top, Higgins and Seiter 122.00
2 qt., "Federal," Bergen 255.00
8", "Harvard," signed Libbey 225.00
3-pint, "Lakeland," claret, sterling silver mounting around top, Higgins and Seiter 230.00
2-pint, "Maine," claret, sterling sil-

ver mounting 180.00
3-pint, "Strawberry, Diamond and
Fan," bulbous 150.00

Plates
7", "Boston" 63.00
7", "Capetown" 82.00
4-lobed, "Lawton" 220.00
9", "Oriole" 258.00
9", "Venus," rounded, triangular
shape, T. B. Clarke 262.50
Powder Jar, "Notched Prisms," sil-
ver lid 75.00

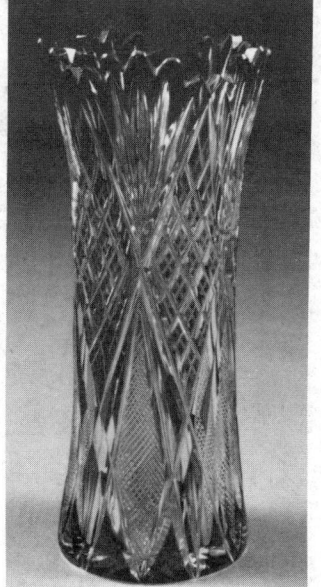

**Vase, 8", flashed red and clear, T. B.
Clark** $300.00

Punch Bowls
"Ceres," signed Fry 150.00
12", "Crete," Pitkins and Brooks . 451.00
14", "Leader," Higgins and Seiter 341.00
"Wabash" bowl, 12 handled, footed cups, footed tray, cut-handled
ladle, set 2310.00

Punch Cups
Cup, with underplate, signed
Clarke 69.00
"Heart," notched handle 60.00
"Occident," handled, on foot 55.00

Relish Dish, "Adonis," 2-handled,
signed Clarke 300.00

Spooners and Spoon Dishes
7¼", "Chrysanthemum" 47.00
"Jewel," signed Clarke 92.00
"Manhattan," 2 handled, rectan-
gular 67.00
"Napoleon," Higgins and Seiter . . 97.00
"Prism," Averbeck 102.00
"Rahjah," oval, flat 59.00
"Webster," Higgins and Seiter . . . 102.00

Trays
Bread, "Hobstar, Strawberry,
Diamond and Fan," signed Libbey 285.00
Bread, 8½", signed Sinclaire 275.00
Comb and Brush, "Electra," all-
over cut 289.00
Ice cream, "Hobstar, Hobnails,
Crosshatch" 150.00
10", "Rossacre," round, signed
Tuthill 750.00

Tumblers
"Cut Star," Higgins and Seiter . . . 35.00
"Florida" 29.00
"Florentine" 27.00
"Honeycomb" — cut 20.00
"Manhattan," Clarke 37.00
"Strawberry, Diamond and Fan" . 24.00

Vases
4", bud, "Belmont" 78.00
5", violet, cut stars, engraved
flowers, signed Hawkes 175.00
8", cuspidor-shape, with rim 236.00
8", Persian-cut 170.00
9", corset-shaped, ornate cut . . . 375.00
10", "Teck," on foot, slender . . . 131.00
12", "Eyes," tall, cylindrical, on
foot 141.00
14", Trumpet-shaped, "Strawber-
ry, Diamond and Fan," signed with
Maple Leaf 200.00
15", Presentation piece, "Herring-
bone, Hobstar, Bullseye and Fan,
Pineapple, and Strawberry" 2975.00
18", tall, cylindrical, flat 325.50

Water Sets
"Ruth," buzz-star-type cutting, tall
tankard, six tumblers, and tray,
unsigned 250.00
Pitcher, ten matching tumblers,
each piece signed "Libbey" 1000.00

CUT VELVET

**Cut Velvet is a satin finished art glass made
with two layers of glass — the outer layer in
color with a white liner. The ribbed or
diamond shaped designs were cut in high relief, exposing the white interior. The name
Cut Velvet is a descriptive name given to this
glass because of its velvet like appearance. It**

was a product of several glass manufacturers in the Victorian era, 1870–1900.

Vase, 7½", pink, ribbed $225.00

Biscuit Jar, pink, silver plated mountings	200.00
Cruet, blue, diamond	295.00
Ewer, 4⅝", rose, diamond	185.00
Jar, jam, 4⅛", rose, diamond	295.00
Rose Bowls	
3¼", blue, diamond, 4 crimp top	165.00
4", pink, diamond	180.00
Vases	
6", stick, blue	100.00
6¼", bulbous base, blue, diamond	80.00
6¾", ruffled, pink, diamond	195.00
7¼", ruffled, blue, diamond	150.00
9", ruffled, blue, diamond	235.00
10", ruffled, blue, diamond	275.00

CZECHOSLOVAKIAN ITEMS

Objects marked "Made in Czechoslovakia" were produced after 1918, when the country claimed its independence from Austria Hungary. The people became more cosmopolitan, liberating and expanding their scope of life. They approached the arts on the principle "art for art's sake." Their porcelains, pottery and glassware reflect many influences. A specific manufacturer's mark may be identified as being much earlier than 1918 but indicates that the factory existed in the Bohemian or the Austrian-Hungarian Empire period.

Plate, 10" dia., porcelain, white with floral decor, "Epiag" Royal, made in Czech. $25.00

Ashtrays	
4½", orange lustre with multicolored Indian-type design, yellow lustre interior	12.00
2½ x 3 x 5", with cigarette box, 1¾ x 3½ x 4½", orange and white lustre transfer of matches and cigarettes, set	15.00
Basket, 4 x 5", tan lustre, black trim	20.00
Bridge Set, four cups and saucers, card suit shapes, black and red	55.00
Coffee Service, demitasse, 16 pieces, white background with cobalt and rust, gold lined cups, heavy gold trim, open handled tray marked "Pirkenhammer," set	200.00
Creamer, grey blue lustre background, with gold checkerboard trim around top, gold lustre lining, black handle and trim, marked "Czechoslovakia"	20.00
Cream and Sugar, Creamer, 4½", sugar, 6½", peach iridescent, pearlized interior, black handles, finial, set	35.00
Cup and Saucer, demitasse, multicolored, set of four	25.00
Invalid Feeder, Alladin's lamp-shape	15.00
Pitcher, 3½", bulbous, ribbed, blue and white lustre	18.00
Plates	
White porcelain, 6", gold initial "N", gold trim, marked "M. Z. Attroulea, CMR, Czechoslovakia"	15.00

10¾", hand painted "Rembrandt," heavy gold trim 80.00

Ramekin, semi-porcelain, molded fruit design lids 20.00

Tea Set, light blue lustre, gold lining in interior, gold handles and finials, teapot, covered sugar, creamer, six cups and saucers 185.00

Vases

4", barrel shaped, brown lustre exterior with applied flowers, leaves, rings, buff lustre interior . .   15.00

5¼", yellow and blue parrot on brown stump, three openings, matte finish 20.00

6", footed, with two handles, grey, pink and blue lustre, black trim . .   15.00

8", pottery frog on tree trunk with bug 30.00

8½", black and tangerine, with snake wrapped around center . . .   65.00

10", black and tangerine decor . .   85.00

Wall Pocket, red and blue bird perches on green and brown tree, matte finish 15.00

DAGUERREOTYPES

The earliest attempts to project images involved the camera obscura, a device known to the Greeks and Romans. The Scientific Revolution of the 17th Century, especially in chemistry, opened the way to capturing images on plate and film.

In 1839, J. M. Daguerre of France patented a process consisting of covering a copper plate with silver salts, sandwiching the plate between glass for protection and exposing the plate to light and mercury vapors to imprint the image. The process produced Daguerreotypes.

Fox Talbot of Britain patented the method for making paper negatives and prints (calotypes) in 1841. Frederick Scott Archer introduced the wet collodian process in 1851. Dr. Maddox developed dry plates in 1871. When George Eastman produced roll film in 1888, the photographic industry reached maturity.

Ambrotypes and tin types are contemporaries of the daguerreotype. Ambrotypes are photographs made on glass by backing a thin negative with a black surface. Tintypes, or ferreotypes, are positive photographs made on a thin iron plate having a darkened surface.

Daguerreotypes were generally housed in embossed gutta percha cases padded and lined with fabric and ornamented with metal mounts. These cases have some collecting value independent of the prints they house.

The subject matter has the greatest effect on value. Next comes the photographer, if known, followed by condition, size, and finally, style of case. The following prices are guidelines. If a daguerreotype has that extra something, e.g., a pet with the child, value should be increased.

Small = 1⅝ x 2⅛" to 2 x 2½"
Medium = 2⅛ x 3¼" to 3¼ x 4¼"
Large = 4¼ x 6½" to 6½ x 8½"
Photographer Identified — Add 20 to 40%

Gentleman, 3¼ x 3¼" $35.00

Building or Outdoor Scene

Small 40.00
Medium 50.00
Large 65.00

Boy or Girl

Small 10.00
Medium 15.00
Large 20.00

Coffin or Funerary

Child 35.00
Adult 45.00

Man or Woman

Small 15.00
Medium 25.00
Large 35.00

Soldier, Confederate

Small 45.00
Medium 60.00
Large 75.00

Soldier, Union

Small 30.00
Medium 45.00
Large 60.00

Soldier, other

Small 20.00
Medium 25.00
Large 30.00

Tradesman with tools

Small 50.00
Medium 75.00
Large 100.00

CASES

Basket of Fruit 10.00
Cupid and Wounded Stag, gutta-

percha	65.00
Fireman saving child	50.00
Geometric, Littlefield and Parsons	22.50
Scrolled, Littlefield and Parsons, gutta-percha	30.00

DAVENPORT CHINA

DAVENPORT
LONGPORT
STAFFORDSHIRE

John Davenport opened a pottery in Longport, Staffordshire, England in 1793. His ware was of high quality, light-weight, cream colored, with a beautiful velvety texture. The firm made soft-paste (Old Blue), lustre trimmed ware, pink lustre with black transfer and there have been pieces of Gaudy Dutch and Spatter ware found with the Davenport mark. Later on he became one of the best makers of ironstone and early flowing blue. His famous "Cyprus" pattern in mulberry became very popular and is highly collectible today. The factory was carried on by his heirs until it was closed in 1886.

Plate, 8¾", white with blue and orange florals, "Chantilly," impressed Davenport with red anchor ... $50.00

Bowls

9½", Stoneware, floral decor, c. 1850	25.00
13", 4½" deep, English scene, floral border, "Old Blue"	150.00

Cup Plates

Light blue, pagoda decor	30.00
Teaberry, pink lustre	30.00

Cups and Saucers

Cyprus, mulberry, handleless	50.00
Imari, can shaped, c. 1815	50.00

Dish, in plated holder, Imari colors, c. 1875	85.00
Gravy Boat, blue and white flowers, bird band	95.00

Pitchers

Squat, gold trim and monogram, c. 1810	225.00
6¾", blue, pink floral decor, c. 1840	95.00
8", Cathedral, pink lustre, black transfer	195.00

Plates

7", Blue Willow, c. 1820	30.00
8½", floral border, woman milking cow, "Old Blue"	100.00
9", hand painted fruit center, green border, c. 1885	35.00
10½", green transfer, 1850	40.00
10½", Cyprus, mulberry	50.00

Platters

9 x 12½", Cyprus, mulberry	95.00
9 x 10½", Blue Willow, c. 1810	75.00
11 x 4", blue and white, oriental decor, reticulated border	85.00

Sugar, covered, Cyprus, mulberry, shell handles, pagoda shape	150.00
Tea Pot, with lid, pink lustre decor	225.00

Tureens

Castle scene, in blue, shell handles, early	125.00
10½", Cyprus, mulberry	100.00
Sauce, with cover and ladle, creamware, molded leaves, lime green veining, early	400.00

Wash Bowl, pitcher, toothbrush holder, soap dish with drain, Cyprus, mulberry, set	600.00

DECOYS

Carved wooden decoys, used to lure ducks and geese to the hunter, have in the past several years become widely recognized as an indigenous American folk art form. Demand for them has increased dramatically as have prices.

Many decoys are from the 1880–1930 period when commercial gunners commonly hunted over rigs of several hundred decoys. Many other fine carvers also worked through the 1930's and 1940's.

The value of a decoy is based on several factors: (1) the fame of the carver, (2) the quality of the carving, (3) the species of wild fowl — the most desirable are herons, swans, mergansers, shorebirds, (4) the condition of the original paint (o.p.)

The inexperienced collector should be aware of several facts. The age of a decoy, per se, is usually of no importance in determining value. Since very few decoys were ever signed, it will be quite difficult to attribute most decoys to known carvers. Anyone who has not examined a known carver's work will be hardpressed to determine if the paint on one of his decoys is indeed original.

Repainting severely decreases a decoy's value. In addition, there are many fakes and reproductions on the market and even experienced collectors are occasionally fooled.

Shorebird, blue bellied plover, Cape May, N.J. **$325.00**

Black Duck, coastal N.J., hollow carved, o.p., c. 1920	175.00
Black Duck, Delaware River, carved raised wings, o.p., c. 1920	300.00
Black Duck, Long Island, cork body, o.p., c. 1900	35.00
Black Duck, Rozwell Bliss, Stratford, CT., o.p., c. 1930	350.00
Bluebill Drake, Kan Anger, Dunnville, Ontario, o.p., c. 1940	450.00
Bluebill Drake, Ken Harris, Woodville, N.Y., o.p., c. 1950 ...	150.00
Bluebill Drake, Ira Hudson, Chincoteaque, VA. banjo tail, old repaint, c. 1930	250.00
Bluebill Drake, Mason Decoy Co.,	

Detroit, MI, standard grade, excellent o.p., c. 1910	225.00
Bluebill Drake, Mason Decoy Co., standard grade, old repaint	50.00
Bluebill Drake, Stevens Decoy Co., Weedsport, N.Y., old repaint, c. 1880	250.00
Bluebill Hen, Frank Coombs, Alexandria Bay, N.Y., o.p., c. 1920	375.00
Brant, Joe Dickerson, Lolita, CA., o.p., c. 1930	175.00
Brant, Ira Hudson, o.p., c. 1930 ...	650.00
Brant, Lloyd Parker, N.J., old repaint, c. 1910	200.00
Canada Goose, A. Elmer Crowell, East Harwich, MA., slat style, signed, o.p., c. 1930	700.00
Canada Goose, Dodge Decoy Co., Detroit, MI., o.p., c. 1880	1200.00
Canada Goose, Joe Lincoln, Accord, MA., old repaint, c. 1930	350.00
Canada Goose, Madison Mitchell, Havre de Grace, MD., o.p., c. 1950	250.00
Canada Goose, Wildfowler Decoy Co., Old Saybrook, CT., signed, o.p., c. 1940's	350.00
Canada Goose, Nova Scotia, flat stickup, o.p., c. 1940	50.00
Canvasback Drake, Bob McGaw, Havre de Grace, MD, o.p., c. 1940	175.00
Canvasback Drake, Madison Mitchell, o.p., c. 1950	110.00
Canvasback Drake, Ben Schmidt, Centerline, MI., o.p., c. 1940	375.00
Canvasback Drake, Wildfowler, o.p., c. 1940	125.00
Crow, Charles Perdew, Henry, Ill., o.p., c. 1930	750.00
Eider Drake, Monhegan Island, ME	1800.00
Eider Drake, coastal Maine, o.p., c. 1920	150.00
Goldeneye Drake, Frank Lewis, Ogdensburg, N.Y., humpback style, o.p., c. 1940	125.00
Goldeneye Drake, Mason Decoy Co., standard grade, o.p.	300.00
Goldeneye Hen, Down East Decoy Co., Freeport, ME, o.p., 1940's ..	125.00
Mallard Drake, Animal Trap Co., Passagoula, Miss., o.p., 1950's ..	75.00
Mallard Drake, Dodge Decoy Co., Detroit, MI, o.p., 1880's	275.00
Mallard Drake, Mason Decoy Co., challenge grade, hollow, o.p.	600.00
Mallard Drake, Heck Whittington, Oglesby, Ill., o.p., c. 1950	450.00
Merganser Drake, Mason Decoy Co., premier grade, hollow, o.p. ..	3000.00
Mergansers, Hen and Drake, Hurley Conklin, Manahawkin, N.J., unused. 1970, pair	400.00

Mergansers, Hen and Drake, Alvin Meeks, Hooper's Island, VA., o.p., c. 1960, pair 375.00
Oldsquaw, Gene Hendrickson, Lower Bank, N.J., unused, 1950's . . . 150.00
Oldsquaw Drake, coastal Maine, o.p., c. 1930 . . . . 125.00
Owl, Herter's Decoy Co., Waseca, Minn., o.p., c. 1950 . . . . 275.00
Pintail, Wildfowler Decoy Co., o.p., c. 1940 . . . . 225.00
Redhead Drake, Ward Brothers, Crisfield, MD., unused, c. 1960 . . 750.00
Swan, Chesapeake Bay, o.p., c. 1900 . . . . 2000.00
Swan, Herter's Decoy Co., o.p., c. 1950 . . . . 250.00
White-winged Scoter, Hans Berry, Gross Island, ME., old repaint, c. 1880 . . . . 900.00
Wood Duck, Herter's Decoy Co., o.p., c. 1950 . . . . 150.00

DEDHAM POTTERY

The business was originally established as Chelsea Pottery in Chelsea, Mass., in 1860 by Alexander W. Robertson. In 1872, it was known as the Chelsea Keramic Art Works.

In 1895, the pottery moved to Dedham, Mass., and the name was changed to Dedham Pottery. The famous Crackleware, or Dedham Pottery, has an unusual spiderweb effect of blue in the glaze. The rabbit pattern was their most popular design. Other patterns include apple, azalea, bird-orange tree, butterfly, chicken, clover, crab, dolphin, duck, elephant, grape, horse chestnut, iris, lion, lobster, magnolia, owl, polar bear, snowtree, swan turtle, and water lily.

The following marks can be used to determine the approximate age of items made by the company: (1) Chelsea Keramic Art Works, name Robertson impressed, 1876–1889. (2) C. P. U. S. impressed in a clover leaf, 1891–1895. (3) Foreshortened rabbit, 1895–1896. (4) Conventional rabbit, with Dedham Pottery stamped in blue, 1897. (5) Word "Registered" added to rabbit mark, 1929–1943.

Bowls
Rabbit, 4½" 100.00
Rabbit, 6" 110.00
10" 200.00
Turtle, 7½" 200.00

Plate, 10", "Snow Tree" $150.00

Butter Dish, Rabbit 200.00
Candlesticks
  Azalea, pair 175.00
  Rabbit, pair 200.00
Celery dishes
  Elephant 150.00
  Rabbit 180.00
Chocolate pot, Rabbit 200.00
Creamers
  3", Magnolia 100.00
  4", Rabbit 100.00
Cups and Saucers
  Duck 95.00
  Elephant 95.00
  Polar Bear 110.00
  Pond Lily 95.00
  Rabbit 95.00
  Rabbit, large 120.00
Egg Cup, 4", double, Rabbit 120.00
Jug, Azalea, 5" 175.00
Mug, 4½", fruit band top, Rabbit base 150.00
Plates
  6", Duck 65.00
  6", Horse Chestnut 65.00
  6", Magnolia 65.00
  6", Mushroom 95.00
  6", Pond Lily 75.00
  6", Puppy in center 210.00
  6", Rabbit 55.00
  6", Snowtree 65.00
  6", Turtle 145.00
  7½", Azalea 65.00
  7½", Elephant 120.00
  8½", Butterfly 95.00
  8½", Duck 95.00
  8½", Horse Chestnut 95.00
  8½", Magnolia 85.00

8½", Pond Lily	145.00
8½", Rabbit	75.00
8½", Snowtree	110.00
8½", Turkey	95.00
10", Azalea	120.00
10", Butterfly	120.00
10", Duck border	145.00
10", Grape	110.00
10", Iris	125.00
10", Mushroom	145.00
10", Polar Bear	185.00
10", Pond Lily	135.00
10", Rabbit	110.00
12½", Crab	260.00
12½", Rabbit	175.00
Platter, 6 x 10", Rabbit border	185.00
Salt and Pepper shakers, Rabbit, pair	160.00
Sugar Bowl, covered Rabbit	135.00

Tiles

Horse Chestnut	100.00
Magnolia	105.00
Rabbit	130.00
Swan	140.00

DEGENHART GLASS

John and Elizabeth Degenhart founded Crystal Art Glass in Cambridge, Ohio, in 1947. Their privately owned company produced a wide variety of pressed glass objects and John became famous for his paperweights.

After John's death in 1964, the operation continued under the personal direction of his widow. Elizabeth Degenhart made many innovations, adding new molds and introducing a wide spectrum of colors (many of her own creation). There are 150 official colors in the Degenhart glass listing, but the actual list of colors is much longer (over 214) because of numerous variations of some colors. Only a few of the available colors can be listed in Warman's.

Elizabeth died in 1978 and the Crystal Art Glass plant was closed. The molds were bought by Island Mold Co. and the familiar trademark of a "D" within a heart was removed. A few molds were left intact and glass will be pressed in these molds specifically to support the new Degenhart Museum in Cambridge, Ohio.

The Degenhart plant recently has been sold to Bernard Boyd who is producing glass in the molds not kept for the Museum. The mark on this glass is a "B" inside a diamond.

Animal Dishes, covered, Hen, Lamb, Robin, Turkey, 5"

Amberina	350.00

Cat Slipper, amber	**$38.00**

Amethyst	175.00
Crown Tuscan	200.00
Custard, dark	200.00
Milk blue	100.00
Sapphire blue	100.00
White milk glass	60.00

Bicentennial Bells

Canary	40.00
Ivorine	40.00
Opalescent	25.00
Pearl gray	40.00
Sapphire Blue	25.00
Seafoam	50.00
Vaseline	25.00

Candleholders, Bird

Basic colors, crystal	20.00
Opaques	60.00

Candy Dishes, covered, Wildflower, 4"

Basic colors, crystal	30.00
Opaques	40.00

Creamers and Sugars, Daisy and Button

Crystal	80.00
Iridescent crystals	90.00
Opaques	125.00

Doll, "Priscilla." 7"

April Green	80.00
Amber	75.00
Crystal	75.00
Daffodil	85.00
Dark amethyst	80.00
Degenhart green	125.00
Milk white	55.00
Vaseline	75.00

Drawer Pulls, "Sandwich"

Crystals	10.00
Opaques	15.00

Owls, 3"

Amber	27.00
Champagne	175.00
Cobalt	75.00
Crystal clear	20.00
Lavender blue	65.00
Lemonade	30.00
Opal	45.00
Red carnival	125.00
Tiger ivory	48.50

Vaseline	27.50
Violet	55.00

Paperweights

Crystal, colored, controlled bubbles	175.00
Diamond mold from bridge set, opaques	45.00
Name weight with First Lady of Glass	200.00
Name weights painted by Herbert Burris, D in Heart mark	150.00
Rose, yellow	300.00
Scent bottles in any color	350.00

Pooch Dog, 2½"

April green	35.00
Amber	25.00
Crystal	15.00
Daffodil	32.00
Elizabeth blue	100.00
Golden glo	20.00
Orchid	40.00

Plate, 5½", Elizabeth Degenhart portrait, blue $52.50

Portrait Plate (Elizabeth Degenhart)

Amberina	60.00
Canary	50.00

Salt Dips, Salt and Pepper Shakers, Bird Candleholders, various patterns

Crystals	20.00
Opaques	60.00

Shoes, all types

Crystals	20.00
Opaques	35.00

Slippers, Bow and Cat

Crystals	20.00
Opaques	35.00

Texas Boots

Crystals	30.00
Opaques	25.00

Toothpicks, various patterns

Amber	20.00
Blue Bell	30.00
Crystal	20.00

Custard	35.00
Emerald	25.00
Milk blue	35.00

Wines, "Buzz Star," "Daisy and Button"

Amethyst	15.00
Cobalt	35.00
Cobalt, iridescent	45.00
Crystal	12.00
Custard	30.00
Rose moire	15.00
Vaseline	15.00

DELDARE WARE
See BUFFALO POTTERY

DELFT WARE

Delft ware is a kind of pottery first made in Belgium and Italy as early as the 16th century. Dutch traders made the city of Delft, in Holland, a world trade center, and it became synonymous with the pottery made and exported there.

The body is of soft red clay with a coating of tin glaze. Blue designs on white ground were the first coloring, but polychrome coloring was perfected and used. Most English potteries made this ware. The Delft ware found in the market today will also include other tin-glazed pottery produced in England and on the Continent. Delft, faience, and majolica are all tin-glazed pottery.

Charger

13½", blue and white peacock pattern, c. 1765	300.00
13½", blue and white basket of flowers center, stylized scrolls and flower heads, border, early 18th century	300.00

Dishes

Polychrome oriental flowering shrub center, rim with border of flutes, tassels, etc., Bristol, England, c. 1760	700.00
11½ x 8½", blue and white, floral decor with bouquet in center, England, c. 1850	320.00
Blue and white center, painted with lion flanked by columns, the rim with alternating Chinese figures and floral panels. De Porceleyne Claeuw factory, 18th century	500.00
Vase and Tulips design	100.00
Ewer, 6½", blue and white applied flowers	50.00
Inkwell, 4", heart shaped, three-holder, blue and white late	40.00

6½", ginger jar shape, blue and white, three panels of Oriental figures, separated by panels of crisscross design **275.00**

12½", sepia monochrome medallion of lion beneath tree, inscribed "Hier Rustikveyiig" below, pair .. **1000.00**

13⅜", blue and white, three masted sailing ship **350.00**

14½", tulip vase, nine tulip spouts, fan shaped body with grotesque serpents at each side, in iron-red, green and blue, Dutch, early 18th century **950.00**

14", fishing vessel scene, within medallion c. 1900 .... **225.00**

17", covered, with parrot knob, fluted form, blue floral **400.00**

Vegetable dish, covered, 12", windmill scene **50.00**

DEPRESSION GLASS

Depression glass is a general term used to describe the glassware manufactured primarily during the "Depression" years, 1929–1940. It was an inexpensive machine-made glass manufactured by several major glass factories in a wide variety of patterns, and in green, pink, blue, red, yellow, white and crystal. It was sold through variety stores, given as premiums, or packaged with certain products. Movie houses gave it away from 1935 until well into the 1940's.

Interest in collecting Depression glass has risen, including the later hand-made colored glass of the 1950's and 1960's. As with most antiques and collectibles, where demand exceeds the supply, reproductions appear on the market. The majority of the reissued patterns are marked accordingly, but there are some deceivers.

ADAM

Jeanette Glass Co., 1932–34.

Green

Ashtray, 4½"	**12.00**
Bowls	
5¾"	**12.00**
9", covered	**20.00**
10", oval	**13.00**
Butter, covered	**185.00**
Candlestick, 4"	**40.00**
Cake Plate, footed	**14.00**
Cream and Sugar, covered	**22.50**
Cup and Saucer, square	**14.00**
Platter, 12"	**11.75**
Salt and Pepper, footed, pair ...	**65.00**
Tumblers	

Miniature Lamp, 10½", Dutch scene, blue and white $220.00

Jugs

9½", blue and white, painted flowering branches and sprigs, pewter mounted strap handle and cover, Germany **500.00**

12", rope handle, portrait decor, blue and white Dutch, 18th century **225.00**

Lamp, miniature, with original clear chimney **200.00**

Plates

4½", windmill decor **50.00**

7½", Dutch farm scene **55.00**

8½", blue and white, with central diamond shaped panel, five floral medallions, diaper ground, Dutch, c. 1720 pair **350.00**

8⅞", blue and white vase of flowers, England, c. 1760 .... **250.00**

8¼", soup plate, polychrome, island pavillion center, Bristol England, c. 1770 .... **225.00**

Shoe, 4½", scenic, basketweave body **35.00**

Vases

6", windmill, cottages, sailboat, marked J. T. and L. **75.00**

Ruby Hobnail, pitcher, 8″, glasses, 4¾″ **$65.00**

4½″	10.00
5½″, iced tea	18.00
Vase, 7½″	22.50

Pink
Bowls
5¾″	15.00
10″, oval	12.00
Butter, covered	60.00
Butter, Sierra, (rare)	375.00
Candy Jar, covered	35.00
Cream and Sugar, covered	19.50
Cup and Saucer, round	35.00
Pitcher, quart, round base	20.00

Plates
7¾″, round	22.50
7¾″, square	5.00
9″, grill	8.00
Platter, 12″	8.00
Relish, divided, 8″	8.00
Sherbet, 3″	7.50
Vase, 7½″	40.00

AMERICAN PIONEER

Liberty Works, 1931–34.

Crystal
Bowls
5″, handled	5.00
10¾″, console	17.50
Candlestick, 6½″	12.00
Cream and sugar, 3½″	12.00
Cup and Saucer	8.50
Goblet, 6″	18.50
Ice Bucket, 6″	22.50
Pitcher, covered, 5″	50.00

Plates
8″	4.50
11½″, handled	5.00
Rose Bowl, footed, 4½″	18.50

Green
Candy, covered, 1 lb.	40.00
Cream and Sugar, 3½″	20.00
Cup and Saucer	8.50
Dresser Set, 3 pcs.	8.50
Lamp, 8½″	55.00

Tumblers
4″	7.50
5″	7.50
Vase, 7″	25.00

AMERICAN SWEETHEART

MacBeth-Evans Glass Co., 1930–36. Comes in pink, monax, cremax, red & blue.

Blue
Cream and Sugar, open	165.00
Cup and Saucer	125.00

Plates
8″	85.00
15½″	300.00
Salver	140.00
Server, 2 tier, 8″ and 12″ plates .	250.00

Cremax
Bowls
6″	10.00
9″	30.00

Monax
Bowls
6″	8.50
9″	18.00
Console bowl	275.00
11″, oval	30.00
Creamer, footed	6.50

Plates
6″	3.25
8″	6.00
9″	6.50
9¾″–10″	12.50
Platter, 13″	30.00
Salt and Pepper, footed	150.00
Sugar, open	5.75
Sugar, covered	135.00
Server, 3-tier	75.00

Pink
Bowls
9″	10.00
11″, oval	18.00
Cream and Sugar, open	10.00
Cup and Saucer	10.00

Plates
6″	3.00
10½″	12.00
Pitcher, 8″	185.00
Salt and Pepper, footed	175.00
Tumbler, 4½″	20.00

Red

Cream and Sugar	175.00
Cup and Saucer	115.00
Plates	
8"	75.00
15½", wedding	270.00
Server, 3-tier	650.00

BLOCK OPTIC (BLOCK)

Hocking Glass Co., 1929–33. Comes in green, pink, yellow, crystal.

Pink and Crystal

Bowls	
5¼"	5.00
8½"	9.00
Cream and Sugar	12.00
Cup and Saucer	6.00
Goblet	12.50
Ice bucket	15.00
Pitcher	20.00
Mug	15.00
Plates	
6"	1.35
8"	2.00
9"	6.00
9", grill	6.00
Salt and Pepper, pair	15.00
Sugar	3.00
Tumbler, footed	5.00

Green and Yellow

Bowls	
5½"	5.75
8½"	9.50
Cream and Sugar	4.50
Goblet	15.00
Ice bucket	16.00
Mug	20.00
Plates	
6"	1.50
8"	2.25
9"	8.50
9", grill	7.00
Salt and Pepper, squatty, pair	20.00
Sandwich server, center handle	25.00
Sherbet, 6 oz.	9.00
Tumbler, flat	5.00

BOWKNOT

Unknown manufacturer. Made only in green, as far as known.

Green

Bowls	
4½"	7.00
5"	9.00
Cup	5.50
Plate, 7"	5.00
Sherbet, low foot	6.50
Tumblers	
10", flat	8.50

10", footed	7.00

BUBBLE

Anchor Hocking, 1934–1965. Comes in crystal, dark green, pale blue and pink, ruby red and milk white, made in 1960's. Green, ruby & milk, 20% more.

Crystal

Bowls	
Berry, 9"	3.00
Cereal	2.00
Creamer	2.50
Cup	2.00
Plate, dinner	2.00
Platter, 12", oval	3.00
Sugar, open	2.50

Blue & Pink

Bowls	
Berry, 9"	6.00
Cereal	4.00
Creamer	15.00
Cup	2.50
Plate, dinner	3.50
Platter, 12", oval	5.50
Sugar, open	8.00

CAMEO (DANCING GIRL, BALLERINA)

Hocking Glass Co., 1930–1934. Comes in green, yellow, pink, and crystal with platinum rim.

Crystal

Bowl, 4½"	4.50
Cocktail Shaker, metal lid, (crystal only)	150.00
Tumbler, 8 oz. footed	12.00

Green

Bowls	
Cereal	10.00
Berry, 8¼"	20.00
Three-legged console	30.00
Butter, covered	120.00
Cake Plate, three legs	11.00
Candlesticks, 4", pair	66.50
Candy Jar	
Low, covered	35.00
Tall, covered	77.50
Cookie Jar, covered	25.00
Cream Soup	44.75
Creamer, 2 sizes	12–13.50
Decanter, stoppered	20.00
Goblet	27.50
Ice bucket	90.00
Pitcher, water	30.00
Plates	
6"	2.50
8"	4.50
8½", square	18.00
10½", grill, closed handles	6.50

Platter, 12″	10.00
Relish, 3 sections, footed	12.00
Sugar, 2 sizes	8–12.00
Wine	5.50
Vase	
5¼″	90.00
8″	15.00

Yellow & Pink

Bowl	
Cereal	12.00
Berry	20.00
Console, 3 legs	45.00
Butter, covered	600.00
Cake Plate, 3 legs	15.00
Creamer, 2 sizes	11–13.50
Pitcher, milk	250.00
Plates	
6″	1.75
8″	4.00
8½″, square	50.00
10″ grill, closed handles	5.00
Platter, 12″, closed handles	17.50
Sugar, 2 sizes	7.50–12.00
Tumbler, footed	12.00

CHERRY BLOSSOM

Jeanette Glass, Co., 1930–39. Comes in Delphite (blue opaque), pink, green and crystal. Crystal, 10% less than pink; Delphite (rare) 50% more than pink.

Pink

Bowls	
4¾″	7.00
9″, handled	13.00
*Butter dish, covered	55.00
Cake Plate, 3 legs, 10¼″	13.00
Candy, covered	25.00
Coaster	9.00
Creamer	9.00
Mug	115.00
Pitcher, water	27.50
Plates	
6″	3.75
7″	11.00
9″	9.50
Platters	
9″, oval	500.00
11″, oval	14.00
13″, plain	15.00
13″, divided	27.50
Salt and Pepper, pair	1000.00
Sugar, covered	17.50
Tumblers	
Flat	11.00
Footed	10.00

Green

Bowls	
4¾″	8.25
9″, handled	14.00
*Butter Dish, covered	70.00

Cake Plate, 3 legs, 10¼″	15.00
Coaster	8.00
Creamer	10.00
Mug	
Regular	125.00
Toy, child's	130.00
Pitcher, water	35.00
Plates	
6″	4.25
7″	11.00
9″	12.00
Platters	
Oval, 11″	18.50
Divided, 13″	32.50
*Salt and Peppers, pair	700.00
Sugar, covered	18.00
Tumblers	
Flat	11.00
Footed	14.00

CIRCLE

Hocking Glass Co., 1930. Comes in green, crystal, and pink. Prices are for green. Crystal, pink, 10% less.

Green

Creamer	3.50
Cup	2.50
Decanter, handled	15.00
Pitcher, 80 oz.	15.00
Plate, sherbet, 6″	1.50
Saucer	1.00
Sherbet	3.00
Sugar	3.50
Tumblers	
Juice	3.00
Water	3.50
Vase, hat shape	15.00
Wine	1.50

CLOVER LEAF

Hazel Atlas Glass Co., 1930–1936. Comes in pink, green, yellow, black. Pink & green are 20% less.

Black

Ashtray	
4″	45.00
5¾″	60.00
Creamer	7.50
Cup	5.00
Cup and Saucer	7.50
Plates	
6″	12.00
8″	5.00
Salt and Pepper	25.00
Saucer	2.00
Sherbet	1.25
Sugar	7.50

Green and Pink
Bowls
4″	8.00
8″	15.00
Candy dish, covered	30.00
Cream and Sugar, footed	15.00
Cup and Saucer	10.00
Plate, 8″	3.50
Salt and Pepper, pair	30.00
Sherbet, footed	5.00
Tumbler	16.00

Yellow
Bowls, 5″	15.00
Creamer	10.00

Plates
8″	5.00
10¼″, grill	10.00
Salt and Pepper, pair	75.00
Sherbet	8.00
Tumbler, footed	17.50

COLONIAL (KNIFE AND FORK)

Hocking Glass Co., 1934–38. Comes in green, pink, and crystal. Prices are for green. Crystal and pink are 20% less.

Green
Bowls
Regular	6.50
Large	10.00
Butter, covered	37.50
Celery	95.00
Creamer	12.00
Goblet	15.00
Mug, (rare)	300.00

Plate
8½″	4.00
10½″	30.00
Platter, oval, 12″	11.00
Salt and Pepper, pair	95.00
Spooner	50.00
Sugar, covered	18.00

Tumbler
Juice	10.00
Water	11.00
Iced Tea	22.00
Lemonade, 15 oz.	32.50

COLONIAL BLOCK

Hazel Atlas Glass Co., late 1920's to early 1930's. Green only.

Green
Bowl
4″	3.00
7″	7.00
Butter, covered	27.50
Candy, covered	17.50
Creamer	4.00
Sugar, covered	7.50

COLUMBIA

Federal Glass Co., 1938–1942. Comes in crystal and pink.

Crystal
Bowls
5″	5.00
8″, soup	6.50
8½″	6.00
10½″, ruffled edge	9.00
Butter, covered, with ruby flashing	15.00
Cup	3.00

Plates
6″	1.50
9½″	3.00
11¾″	5.00
Snack plate	4.00

Pink
Cup	6.50

Plates
6″	3.00
9½″	10.00
9½ x 11¾″	12.00

DAISY (NUMBER 620)

Indiana Glass Co., 1933–40. Comes in crystal and amber. Dark green and milk glass, made in 1960's, are 10% less.

Crystal
Bowls
4½″	2.00
6″	5.00
7″	3.00
9″	6.00
10″, oval	5.00
Creamer, footed	2.50
Cup	2.00

Plates
6″	1.00
7⅜″	2.00
8⅜″	2.00
9⅜″	2.50
10⅜″, grill	4.00
11½″, cake	5.00
Platter, 10¾″	5.00
Relish, 3-sectioned	8.00
Saucer	.75
Sugar, footed	2.50

Tumblers
9 oz., footed	5.00
12 oz., footed	9.00

Amber
Bowls
4½″	6.00
6″	6.00
7″	6.00
9″	18.00
10″, oval	11.00
Creamer, footed	4.00

Cup	3.25
Plates	
6″	2.00
7⅜″	5.00
8⅜″	5.50
9⅜″	6.00
10⅜″	7.00
11½″, cake	6.00
Platter, 10¾″	9.00
Relish, 3-sectioned	12.00
Saucer	1.25
Sugar, footed	4.00
Tumblers	
9 oz.	10.00
12 oz.	22.00

DIANA

Federal Glass Co., 1937–1941. Prices are for pink; crystal, 20% less; amber, 20% more.

Pink

Ash Tray	2.50
Bowls	
5″	3.00
9″	6.25
12″ scalloped edge	7.00
Candy Jar, covered, round	16.00
Coaster	3.00
Creamer, oval	3.00
Cup	3.50
Cup, demitasse set	4.00
Plates	
6″	1.00
9½″	3.00
11¾″	4.00
Platter, oval 12″	5.00
Salt and Pepper, pair	25.00
Sugar, oval	3.00
Toy, child's plate	2.50
Tumbler, 9 oz.	6.00

DOGWOOD (APPLE BLOSSOM, WILD ROSE)

MacBeth Evans Glass Co., 1929–32. Comes in pink and green.

Pink

Bowls	
5½″	4.00
8½″	25.00
10¼″	90.00
Cake Plates	
Solid foot, 11″	100.00
Solid foot, 13″	50.00
Creamer	8.00
Cup	6.00
Pitcher, Water	
80 oz.	90.00
"American Sweetheart" style	425.00
Plates	

6″ or 8″	3.00
9¼″	12.50
12″ Salver	15.00
Platter, oval, 12″ (rare)	65.00
Sugar	9.50
Tumblers	
5 oz., decorated	60.00
10 oz., decorated	17.00
11 oz., decorated	22.00
12 oz., decorated	25.00

Green

Bowls	
5½″	12.50
8½″	50.00
10¼″	75.00
Creamer	30.00
Cup	12.50
Pitcher, 80 oz.	400.00
Plates	
6″	3.00
8″	3.50
10½″	9.00
Sugar	30.00
Tumblers	
10 oz.	40.00
11 oz.	45.00
12 oz.	50.00

FLORAL AND DIAMOND BAND

U. S. Glass Co. 1927–31. Crystal, pink and green; crystal is 20% less.

Pink and Green

Bowls	
4½″	4.00
8″	8.00
Butter, covered	60.00
Compote, 5½″ tall	6.50
Creamer, 2 sizes	5–9.00
Pitcher, 42 oz.	60.00
Plate, 8″	10.50
Sugar, 2 sizes	15–20.00
Tumblers	
Water	7.50
Iced Tea	12.50

GEORGIAN (LOVE BIRDS)

Federal Glass Co., 1931–36. Comes in green and crystal. Prices are for green; crystal 10% less.

Green

Bowls	
4½″	4.25
5¾″	8.00
6½″	30.00
7½″	23.00
Oval vegetable	32.50
Cold cuts server, 18½″, wood, with seven 5″ openings for 5″	

coasters	375.00
Creamer, 2 sizes	6.50–8.00
Cup	5.00
Hot Plate	25.00
Plates	
6″	2.00
8″	5.00
9¼″	13.00
Platters, 11½″	32.50
Sugar, covered, 2 sizes	15–17.00
Tumblers	
9 oz.	25.00
12 oz.	35.00

HEX OPTIC (HONEYCOMB)

Jeanette Glass Co., 1928–1932. Comes in pink and green.

Pink and Green

Bowls	
4¼″, ruffled	2.00
7½″	4.50
Butter, covered, rectangular, 1 lb. size	15.00
Creamer—2 style handles	2.50
Cup	2.50
Ice Bucket, metal handle	7.50
Pitchers	
32 oz., sunflower motif in bottom	10.00
48 oz., footed	25.00
Plates	
6″	1.25
8″	4.50
Platter, 11″	4.00
Refrigerator Dish	4.00
Salt and Pepper, pair	15.00
Sugar, 2 style handles	2.50
Tumblers	
9 oz.	3.50
5¾″, footed	4.00
7″, footed	5.00
Whiskey	3.00

HOMESPUN (FINERIB)

Jeanette Glass Co., 1939–40. Comes in pink and crystal.

Pink or Crystal

Bowls	
4½″	4.00
5″	7.00
8¼″	8.00
Butter, covered	35.00
Coaster/Ashtray	3.50
Creamer	5.50
Cup	3.25
Plates	
6″	2.00
9¼″	6.00

Platter, 13″	6.50
Saucer	1.75
Sugar	5.50
Tea Set, child's toy, cup, saucer, plate, teapot with lid, 14 pcs.	185.00
Tumblers	
9 oz., water	6.00
13 oz., iced tea	10.00
5 oz., footed	6.50
9 oz., footed	8.00
15 oz., footed	12.00

IRIS AND HERRINGBONE

Jeanette Glass Co., 1928–32, made again in 1950. Prices are for crystal; iridescent, 10% more.

Crystal

Bowls	
4½″	15.00
5″	4.00
6″	15.00
7½″	55.00
8″	9.00
9″	8.00
11″, ruffles	20.00
Butter, covered	22.50
Candlesticks, pair	13.00
*Candy Jar, covered	45.00
Coaster	25.00
Creamer	3.50
Cup	5.50
Demitasse cup and saucer	30.00
Goblet	11.00
Pitcher, water	15.00
Plates	
5½″	4.00
8″	24.00
9″	7.50
11¾″	2.50
Sugar, covered	9.00
Tumblers	
4″ flat	23.00
6″, footed	8.00
7″, footed	11.50
Wine	9.00
*Vase, 9″	10.00

MISS AMERICA

Hocking Glass Co., 1933–1937. Made in crystal and pink originally; green, red-amberina type color, ice blue, are reproductions. 50% less for reproductions.

Crystal

Bowls	
6¼″	4.00
8″, curved in at top	32.00
8¾″, straight, deep	20.00
10″, oval, vegetable	7.50

Plate, 9″, Petalware, Monax Macbeth Evans **$3.00**

Butter, covered	185.00
Cake Plate, footed, 12″	12.00
Candy Jar, covered	40.00
Celery, oblong	6.00
Coaster	10.00
Compote, 5″	7.50
Creamer	5.50
Cup	6.00
Goblet	15.00
Pitcher, ice lip	55.00
Plates	
5¾″	2.50
8½″	4.50
10½″	8.00
10½″	8.00
10¼″ grill	6.50
Platter, oval, 12″	9.50
Relish	
4-part	6.00
Round, divided	11.00
*Salt and Pepper, pair	20.00
Sherbet	6.00
Sugar	5.00
Tumblers	
Juice	12.00
Water	10.00
Iced Tea	18.00
Wine	14.00
Pink	
Bowls	
6¼″	8.50
8″, curved in at top	37.50
8¾″ straight, deep	33.00
10″ oval, vegetable	11.00
*Butter, covered	350.00
Cake Plate, footed	20.00
Candy Jar, covered	72.50

Celery	9.50
Coaster	17.50
Plates	
5¾″	4.00
8½″	8.50
10½″	13.50
10¼″	9.50
Platter, oval 12″	11.00
Relish	
4-part	9.00
Round, divided	50.00
Salt and Pepper, pair	30.00
Sherbet	3.25
Sugar	9.00
Tumblers	
Juice	28.00
Water	18.00
Iced Tea	35.00

NORMANDIE (BOUQUET AND LATTICE)

Federal Glass Co., 1933–40. Comes in iridescent, amber and pink. Prices given are for pink; amber is 10% less; iridescent is 10% more.

Pink

Bowls	
5″	4.00
6½″	7.00
8½″	9.00
10″ oval, vegetable	15.00
Creamer	5.00
Cup	4.00
Pitcher, water, 80 oz.	60.00
Plates	
6″	2.00
8″	6.00
9¼″	7.50
11″	25.00
11″, grill	8.50
Platter, 11¾″	10.00
Salt and Pepper, pair	35.00
Sugar, covered	88.00
Tumblers	
Juice	20.00
Water	15.00
Iced Tea	22.00

OVIDE

Hazel Atlas Co., 1930–1935. Comes in green, black, and milk white.

Black and White

Bowls	
4¾″	6.59
5½″	6.50
8″	13.50
Candy, covered	20.00
Cocktail fruit, footed	6.00
Creamer	7.50

Cup	5.00
Plates	
6"	2.50
8"	5.00
Salt and Pepper, pair	17.50
Sugar, open	7.50

Green

Candy, covered	12.00
Cocktail fruit, footed	1.50
Creamer	2.50
Cup	1.50
Plates	
6"	1.00
8"	1.50
Salt and Pepper, pair	7.50
Sugar, open	2.00

Server, 10½" dia., apple green handled $24.00

PARROT (SYLVAN)

Federal Glass Co., 1931–1932. Prices are for green; amber and crystal are 20% less.

Green

Bowls	
5"	9.00
7"	16.00
8"	40.00
10", oval, vegetable	20.00
Butter, covered	200.00
Creamer	12.00
Cup	13.00
Hot Plate, 5"	175.00
Jam Dish, 7"	20.00
Pitcher, 80 oz.	500.00
Plates	
5¾"	7.59
7½"	10.00
9"	15.00

10½", grill, round	10.00
11", grill, square	10.00
10½", plain, square	15.00
Platter, oblong, 11¼"	20.00
Salt and Pepper, pair	140.00
Sherbet, cone shaped	10.00
Sugar, covered	50.00
Sugar, covered in amber, (rare)	112.00
Tumblers	
12 oz.	60.00
footed, heavy	65.00

PINEAPPLE AND FLORAL

Indiana Glass Co. 1932–1937 Comes in crystal, crystal with fired-on red, and amber. Prices are for crystal, with fired on red; amber is 10% more.

Crystal, crystal with fired-on red

Ashtray, handled	12.50
Bowls	
6"	14.00
7"	4.00
10" oval, vegetable	12.00
Compote, diamond-shaped	1.00
Creamer	12.50
Cream Soup	12.50
Cup	5.00
Plates	
6"	2.00
8⅜"	3.50
9⅜"	6.00
11½"	8.00
Platter, 11"	8.00
Relish, divided, 11½"	12.00
Sauce, footed, diamond shaped, open	6.00
Sugar, diamond shaped	6.00
Tumblers	
8 oz.	14.00
10 oz.	18.00
Vase, cone shaped, large	20.00

RING (BANDED RINGS)

Hocking Glass Co., 1927–1932. Comes plain crystal, crystal and green with colored rings. Prices are for plain crystal; color and decorated rings are 50% more.

Crystal

Bowls	
5"	1.75
8"	3.00
Butter Tub or Ice Bucket	8.00
Cocktail Shaker	7.00
Cup	2.50
Creamer	2.50
Decanter, stoppered	12.00
Goblet, 9 oz.	6.00
Pitchers, water	

60 oz.	8.00
80 oz.	10.00
Plates	
6"	1.50
8"	10.00
Salt and Pepper, pair	12.00
Sandwich server, center handle	9.00
Sherbet, 2 sizes	3–4.50
Sugar	2.50
Tumbler, 4 sizes	2–4.00
Whiskey	2.50

ROYAL LACE

Hazel Atlas Glass Co., 1934–1941. Comes in pink, cobalt blue, crystal and green. Prices are for pink and cobalt; green is 10% more than pink; crystal is 10% less.

Pink

Bowls	
4¾"	9.00
5"	9.00
10"	10.00
10", three legged, straight edge	13.50
10", three legged, rolled edge	14.00
10", three legged, ruffled edge	15.00
11", oval, vegetable	12.00
Butter, covered	85.00
Candlestick, pairs	
Straight edge	20.00
Rolled edge	25.00
Ruffled edge	27.50
Cookie Jar, covered	27.50
Creamer, footed	7.00
Cup	5.25
Pitchers, water	
54 oz., straight sides	32.50
68 oz.	32.50
56 oz.	50.00
96 oz.	55.00
Plates	
6"	2.75
8½"	5.50
10"	7.00
9⅞", grill	8.00
Platter, oval, 13"	15.00
Salt and Pepper, pair	32.50
Sugar, covered	16.00
Tumblers	
5 oz., 3½"	12.00
9 oz., 4⅛"	9.00
12 oz., 4⅞"	12.00
13 oz., 5⅜"	14.00
Cobalt Blue	
Bowls	
4¾"	17.00
5"	15.00
10"	25.00
10", 3 legged, straight edge	28.00
10", 3 legged, rolled edge	55.00
10", 3 legged, ruffled	35.00

11", oval, vegetable	22.50
Butter, covered	265.00
Candlesticks pairs	
Straight edge	55.00
Rolled edge	65.00
Ruffled edge	60.00
Cookie Jar, covered	145.00
Creamer, footed	17.50
Cup	15.50
Pitchers, water	
54 oz., straight sides	60.00
68 oz.	80.00
96 oz.	95.00
96 oz.	125.00
Plates	
6"	6.00
8½"	15.00
10"	21.50
9⅞", grill	16.00
Platter, oval, 13"	26.00
Salt and Pepper, pair	140.00
Sugar, covered	55.00
Tumblers	
5 oz., 3½"	22.00
9 oz., 4⅛"	18.00
12 oz., 4⅞"	25.00
13 oz., 5⅜"	29.00

ROYAL RUBY

Anchor Hocking Glass Co., 1939–1960's.

Green and red

Ashtray, square	2.50
Bowls	
4¼"	3.00
7½"	7.50
8", oval, vegetable	8.50
Creamers	
Flat	4.50
Footed	5.50
Cup, round or square	3.00
Goblet, ball stem	8.50
Lamp	17.50
Pitchers, water	
42 oz., tilted or upright	15.00
3 qt., tilted or upright	20.00
Sherbet	1.50
Plates	
6½"	1.50
7"	3.00
7¾"	3.25
9¼"	5.00
Punch Bowl, with stand	30.00
Sugar, flat or footed	4.50
Tumblers	
5 oz., juice	4.00
9 oz., water	4.00
10 oz., water	4.50
13 oz., iced tea	6.50
Footed, wine	7.00
Vases, 4 shapes and sizes	3.50–8.50

STRAWBERRY

U. S. Glass Co., 1928–1931. Prices are for pink or green; iridescent is 10% more.

Pink or green

Bowls
4″	5.00
6½″	8.00
7½″	10.00
Butter dish, covered	100.00
Compote, 5¾″	10.00

Creamers
Small	8.00
Large	12.00
Olive dish, handled	7.50
Pickle dish	8.00
Pitcher, water, 7¾″	100.00

Plates
6″	4.75
7½″	7.00

Sugars
Small, open	10.00
Large, covered	25.00
Tumbler, 9 oz.	17.50

SWIRL (PETAL SWIRL)

Jeanette Glass Co., 1937–1938. Comes in pink, ultramarine, Delphite. Prices are for ultramarine; pink is 10% less and Delphite, (rare), is 50% more.

Ultramarine

Bowls
5¼″	6.00
9″	11.00
10″, footed	17.50
10½″, console	185.00
Candleholders, double branch, pair	17.50

Candy Dishes
Open, 3-legged	5.00
Covered	60.00
Coaster	6.00
Creamer	6.50
Cup	4.50

Plates
6½″	2.50
7¼″	5.00
8″	8.00
9¼″	6.50
12½″	9.00
Salt and Pepper, pair	20.00
Soup, tab handles	12.50
Sugar, covered	5.50

Tumblers
9 oz.	9.50
12 oz.	22.00
9 oz., footed	15.00

Vases, footed
6½″	12.00
8½″	14.00

TEA ROOM

Indiana Glass Company, 1926–1931. Comes in pink and green; crystal is 20% less. Prices are for pink or green.

Pink or green
Banana Split dish	8.50

Bowls
8½″	10.00
8¾″	30.00
9½″, oval, vegetable	32.50
Candlesticks, low, pair	25.00
Creamer	10.00
Cream and sugar on glass tray, ring handle	30.00
Cup	12.50
Goblet, 9 oz.	15.00
Ice bucket	27.50
Lamp, 9″, electric	27.50
Mustard, covered	42.50
Parfait	9.00
Pitcher, water, 64 oz.	75.00

Plates
6½″	6.50
8¼″	16.50
10½″, double handled	18.00
Relish, divided	7.50
Salt and Pepper, pair	30.00
Sherbets, 3 styles, all	10.00
Sugar, covered	20.00

Tumblers
8½ oz.	15.00
6 oz. footed	11.00
9 oz. footed	10.50
11 oz. footed	13.00
12 oz. footed	20.00
Vase, 9″	22.50

WATERFORD WAFFLE

Hocking Glass Co., 1938–1944. Prices are for crystal; pink is 100% more.

Crystal
Ashtray	2.50

Bowls
4¾″	3.50
5½″	6.00
8¼″	5.50
Butter, covered	12.50
Coaster	1.50
Creamer, oval	2.50
Cup	3.25
Goblet	8.50

Pitchers, water
42 oz., tilted	14.00
80 oz., ice lip, tilted	22.50

Plates
6″	1.75

7⅛"	2.00
9⅝"	4.00
10¼", double handles	4.00
13¾"	4.50
Salt and Pepper, 2 styles, both	5.00
Sugar, covered, oval	3.75
Tumbler, footed	6.00
Vase, 6¾"	8.00

DESIGN SPATTERWARE

Design Spatterware marks the transition period that bridged Spatterware and Spongeware. Early examples are often confused with Spongeware because they are similar to some degree. The earliest patterns were carefully arranged and generally covered the entire piece. In the next period of this ware, various motifs were created such as a decorated border with a tulip in the center.

In the 1850's, Elsmore and Foster in England created the noted Holly Leaf pattern in red and green, and also in purple and green; blue bands divide the primary motif arranged in broader bands. Design Spatterware progressed to more definitive designs and finally was limited to only floral, much of which is attributed to Adams.

Design Spatterware is primarily in blue. Modes of decoration were applied in several ways, including the so-called 'cut-sponge.' Some were hand painted while other pieces were transferred in an endless variety of colors and designs.

Bowls

Earthenware, heavy, greens and ochre, large	250.00
Rainbow, blue and red, small	150.00
Serrated Rim, blue, white, black 9½", (rare)	275.00
Tulip and Pretzels, small, damaged	95.00
Butter, covered, holly leaf, lion finial, drain	275.00
Charger, 15", elaboration of Adam's Rose	180.00

Cups and Saucers

Adam's Rose, red rosette border	185.00
Blue	185.00
Poppies, red, blue and green Mush	145.00
Red	225.00

Jugs

Diamonds and bands, blue, very early form, 5¾"	185.00
Geometric design, red, green and brown, 4"	65.00
Leaf, green, early form, 5½", damaged	95.00
Rosettes, blue, rare barrel-shaped,	

Sugar, 5" high, closed ring and shell handles, white with blue and red flowers, green leaves, soft paste, c. 1820–1840 ....$65.00

fern prongs, 7", repaired	125.00
Tulip, blue, 3⅞"	165.00

Mugs

Blue and purple, large	125.00
Holly Leaf, red and green	100.00
Rosettes, blue; green bands	72.00
Tree, blue	65.00

Plates

Colombine with rose bud and thistle, 8½", green, rosette border	165.00
Holly Leaf, 8¾", red and green Elsmore and Foster	92.00
Peony, 8¾", red and green	125.00
Tree border, 8¾", red flowers, green leaves	75.00
Tulip, 8½", blue	225.00
Plate, Soup, six tulips in 6 pointed star, red, blue and purple	155.00

Platters

Dragoon and Awkward Squads, red, 14"	200.00
Holly Leaf, red and green Elsmore and Foster, 12"	185.00
Holly Leaf, red and green, Elsmore and Foster, 16"	225.00

Sugars

Large, red and green	85.00
Small, red and green	65.00
Teapot, blue, early form, repaired	265.00

DISNEYANA

Walt Disney and the creations of the famous Disney studio hold a place of fondness and enchantment not only in the hearts of Americans, but people throughout the world. The release of "Steamboat Willie" in 1928 harolded an entertainment empire.

Walt and his brother showed shrewd business acumen. From the beginning they licensed the reproduction of Disney characters in products ranging from wrist watches to clothing. Ceil Munsey's *Disneyana* chronicles this material.

Disney collectors are devoted. The products from the 1930's command the most attention. Animated celluloids range in value from $50 to $300 depending on subject and complexity of scene. The Disneyana market now is so firmly established that Phillips in New York held a sale devoted exclusively to Disneyana in October, 1981.

Hoppity Mickey Mouse, 23″ high, Walt Disney Productions, Sun Products Corp. $35.00

Disney Studio
Christmas Card, 1937, 7 x 10″ ...	100.00
Menu, Disney Studio Restaurant, 9 x 12½″	75.00

Donald Duck
Alarm Clock, Westclox, made in Mexico, green metal case	150.00
Book, flip, "Donald Duck and Pluto Movie Book in Five Reels," Random House, 1942, 10 pages .	75.00
Figure, plaster, Donald with hands on hip and head turned up, 6½″ .	75.00
Marionette, Madame Alexander, 1938, 11″	300.00
Paint Box, Transogram, litho tin, 1946, 3 x 8″	50.00
Sand Pail, Ohio Art Co., Donald as capt. of boat	85.00

Mickey Mouse
Alarm Clock, Ingersoll, white plastic case, 4½″	185.00
Bank, aluminum, painted, 1930's .	750.00
Book, "Mickey Mouse Alphabet Book," Whitman, 1936, 32 pages, 7 x 9″	130.00
Book, Big Little, "Mickey Mouse and the Bat Bandit," Whitman, 1935, 428 pages	35.00
Drum, Ohio Art Co., tin litho, 6½″ diameter, 4″ high, 1930's	45.00
Hairbrush, wood, decal in center, rectangular, 1930's	25.00
Mug, Salem China Co., Mickey dressed as fireman	160.00
Package Sticker, Dennison, embossed silver foil, 3½″	15.00
Sheet Music, "Mickey Mouse 'Theme Song'," first Mickey Mouse Club, 1930	65.00

Minnie Mouse
Cardboard cut from sign advertising Post Toasties Disney cut-outs, 1935	17.50
Dolls—Minnie and Mickey, 50th Anniversary, Lars (Italy), 1978 ...	400.00
Figure, bisque, with mandolin, dress blue, 3½″	50.00
Dolls, Minnie and Mickey, 50th Anniversary, Lars, 1978, made in Italy	400.00
Figure, bisque, with mandolin, dress blue, 3½″	50.00
Figure, celluloid, original paper label, moveable head and hands, c. 1930	275.00
Figure, china, glazed, feet orange, dress yellow, hat blue, 4″	150.00

Pinocchio
Bookplate, 3 x 4″	8.00
Doll, Ideal, wood jointed, 8″	135.00
Figure, china, National Porcelain Co., Trenton, NJ, green glaze, 1940	25.00
Valentine, mechanical, Pinocchio, pull feather to make nose move, 1939	22.50

Valentine, mechanical, Wiley Fox, arm moves, 1939	20.00

Snow White and the Seven Dwarfs

Dime Register Bank, Snow White, litho tin, 1938, 2½" square	65.00
Figure, bisque, Sleepy, 5"	30.00
Glass, drinking, Snow White, 4½"	37.50
Marionette, Grumpy, Madame Alexander, 9"	100.00
Pillow Cover, 16" x 16"	80.00
Planter, Leeds China Co., 6" x 6½"	25.00
Puzzle, two scenes, 7½ x 10", original box	35.00
Record Album, Dennis Day and Ilene Woods, two 78 rpm, 1949 . .	50.00
Wall Plaque, cardboard, raised image of Bashful, 5 x 7"	20.00
Watering Can, Ohio Art Company, litho tin, 4" dia., 7" high	60.00

Miscellaneous

Bambi, figure, Thumper, Goebel .	85.00
Ferdinand the Bull, wind-up toy, Marx	80.00
Nutcracker, glazed designed by Vernon Kilns, 6" dia.	40.00

DOLL HOUSE ACCESSORIES AND TOY FURNITURE

Although most toy and doll house furniture of the past was of primitive construction made by doting relatives, exquisitely detailed furniture was also made. These fine examples are sometimes placed in the category of salesman's samples or miniatures of the cabinet maker's skill.

Doll houses are primarily enjoyed by children, but it was not unusual in the Victorian era for ladies to amuse themselves by furnishing a doll house for themselves. Today there are many women who collect doll's things; they are extremely popular and frequently bring handsome prices in today's antique market.

Bathroom Set, tub, pedestal sink, toilet; made in Japan	42.00

Beds

Cast iron, 26", gilt with hand painted scene and prayer on headboard	300.00
Mahogany, 24 x 33 x 18", four poster; coverlet and pillow	110.00
Victorian Oak, 22"	45.00
Walnut, 20 x 22 x 15", two mattresses, hand quilted spread and bolster	98.00
Wooden, 10 x 13½", low poster rope type, headboard with "rolling pin" crest	160.00

Chest, 2 drawer, mirror top . . $125.00

Wooden, "tester" type, with tall turned and carved wooden posts; floral chintz mattress and canopy	325.00
Birdcage and Candlestand, 4¼" . .	170.00

Bureaus

Oak, Victorian style	48.00
Tin mirror on back, Victorian style	35.00

Chairs

Cast lead, cane seat, 3½", original green, gold, white and red paint, European	310.00
Painted wood, spindle back cushion seat, original stencil decor . .	90.00

Chaise Lounge

Chaise and two chairs, bamboo .	22.50
Oak, 35", shaped legs, molded apron, original grey, black and yellow upholstery, c. 1900	70.00
Coffee Grinder, 1¼", brass	25.00
Crib, 13", white wood, brass tips . .	30.00
Cupboard, wooden, 13", painted light blue; two shelves, upper level; pull out counter; two shelves lower level; hand crafted, c. 1932	65.00

Doll Houses

Cardboard, with furniture, original carton, c. 1930	25.00
Colonial style, 22 x 15", twenty pieces original furniture, original box	75.00
Federal style, 10 x 19 x 20¼", log cabin, roofed porch, 2 fireplaces,	

6 glass windows, shake roof	350.00
Schoenut House, 15 x 13 x 17", top removes	195.00
Highchair, 25", oak	60.00
Lawn Swing for garden, wooden . .	19.00

Living Room Sets

Art Deco style, 6 pieces, original box	40.00
Wicker, 3 pieces	165.00

Parlor Sets

Cast lead, three pieces, (The Fairy Furniture), settee and two chairs .	50.00
Cast Lead, four pieces, settee, 2 chairs, rocking chair	35.00
Parlor Stove, 4¼", cast lead, c. 1900	160.00
Sideboard, 22 x 14½", oak, mirror back, drawer and double doors, dated in pencil "1892" and "321"	70.00
Stroller, iron with heavy linen seat, c. 1920	32.50

Table and Chairs

Bamboo, table and two chairs . .	13.00
Metal table and five chairs	40.00
Table and three plank bottom Lyre chairs, decorated	32.50
Tea Cart, 2", iron, Germany	25.00
Trunk, wooden, with doll clothes . .	24.00
Wardrobe, 19 x 12 x 4", pier mirror, 2 doors and 8 drawers	75.00
Washbowl and Pitcher Set, doll house size, ironstone	55.00
Wicker lounge, arm chairs, basket, sunshade, phonograph and spinning wheel, set	125.00
Wheelbarrow, pine, painted red	28.00

DOLLS

Dolls have existed as children's play toys as well as important figurines in the ceremonies of life in all cultures from pre-historic times. The earliest known examples date from the Babylonians, 3000 B.C.

From the 14th through the 18th century, doll making was centered in Europe, namely Germany and France. French dolls were not primarily play toys but were elaborately dressed in the latest couturier designs. All these dolls had one thing in common: they represented adults.

In the mid-19th century the child or baby doll was introduced in England. The famous Jumeau doll with swivel head and sawdust-filled kid body had its beginning in France in that era.

The Bye-lo, designed by Grace S. Putnam, was introduced in the 20th century; it was made by firms in Germany and the United States. Doll making in the United States began to flourish in the 1900's with names like

Horsman, Effanbee, Alexander, Ideal and others.

Composition, 11½", Dutch girl, blond hair, original clothing in shades of purple, no marks $30.00

A.B.G. (Alt, Beck and Ghottschalk)

Girl, bisque head, 19", blue sleep eyes, ball jointed, composition body, dressed	210.00
Character, bisque head, 14", open mouth, sleep eyes, dressed	195.00

Alexander

Baby Victoria, composition body, dressed, with white wooden highchair	65.00
21", Cornelia, composition, dressed	185.00
Margaret O'Brien, composition, dressed	500.00
17½", Scarlett O'Hara, compo., dressed	250.00

A. M. (Armond Marsielle)

Girl, bisque shoulder and head, 15", blue sleep googlie eyes, closed mouth, kid body, bisque hands, cloth lower legs, voice box, dressed	850.00
Girl, bisque head, 26", brown sleep eyes, long blonde human hair in curls, ball jointed, compo., dressed	245.00
Toddler, bisque head, 19", brown	

sleep eyes, open mouth, two upper teeth, original lambs' wool wig, composition 175.00

Betty Boop, 18", Rag stuffed 120.00

Bisque head girl, 17", marked "E. G. Germany," brown stationary eyes, jointed compo. body 400.00

Bisque head girl, marked "Mascotte," brown paperweight eyes, closed mouth, pierced ears, brown human hair wig, ball jointed compo. body, dressed 2100.00

Bisque head girl, marked "Paris Bebe Tete Depose," brown paperweight eyes, closed mouth, pierced ears, blonde human hair wig, body marked with Eiffel Tower 2500.00

Buddy Lee, advertising doll for H. D. Lee Company 100.00

Bye-los
  5", all bisque, marked "Grace S. Putnam," swivel neck, jointed arms and legs, dressed 285.00
  18", bisque head, marked "Grace S. Putnam," blue sleep eyes, closed mouth, cloth body, celluloid hands, dressed 585.00

Charlie Chaplin, composition 300.00

Campbell Kid, in English wicker doll buggy 150.00

Disney Dolls
  Dwarfs, set of seven, marked "Walt Disney" 850.00
  "Doc," from Snow White, all original except hat 15.00
  Pinocchio, 8", Compo. fully jointed, molded hat 50.00
  Pinocchio, 12", all wood, jointed . 150.00

Deanna Durbin, 21", compo., original clothes 400.00

Effanbee, "Skippy," original sailor suit 150.00

French Fashion
  18", bisque swivel head, blue glass eyes, blonde human hair wig, articulated wooden body, swivels at waist 2950.00
  Bisque swivel head, blue stationary inset eyes, closed mouth, pierced ears, original human hair wig, kid leather body 800.00

Frozen Charlie, 11½" 575.00

Frozen Charlotte, 5", China, red eyelines, molded blonde hair, molded shoes and socks 100.00

Fulper
  14", bisque head baby, blue sleep eyes, open mouth, human hair wig, jointed compo. body 290.00
  25", bisque head girl, blue stationary eyes, long human hair wig, ball

Flexo Toys, Indian boy, 11½", composition head, cloth body, pot metal hands and large feet, Pat. applied for **$25.00**

jointed compo. body 700.00

Handwerk
  Boy, bisque head 800.00
  Child, bisque head, brown sleep eyes, open mouth, dimpled chin, ball jointed compo. 165.00

Heubach
  Girl, bisque head, 8½", blue intaglio eyes, closed mouth, molded blonde hair with exposed ears, ball jointed compo. 310.00
  Character Boy, bisque head, 16", brown sleep eyes, original auburn human hair wig, ball jointed compo. 450.00
  Character Baby, Koppelsdorf bisque head, 19", dark sleep eyes, open mouth, bent limbs, compo. body 325.00

Jumeau
  Girl, bisque head, head marked "E. J.," 10", brown paperweight eyes, closed mouth, blonde mohair wig, jointed body, marked "Medaille D'Or" 1600.00

Girl, bisque head, stationary eyes, open mouth with molded teeth, jointed compo. body **700.00**

Girl, bisque head, marked "Emile," brown paperweight eyes, closed mouth, applied ears with original earrings, straight wrists, original clothes **6300.00**

Lady, bisque swivel head, brown stationary paperweight eyes, closed mouth, applied pierced ears, kid body **1115.00**

Kemmer & Reinhart, Kay Star, flirty eye, mold #126, 1910 ......$750.00

K (star) R (Kammer and Reinhardt)

Girl, 7½", bisque head marked "101," 7½", intaglio eyes, closed mouth, ball jointed compo. **925.00**

Kaiser Baby, bisque head, blue intaglio eyes, open-closed mouth, painted hair, 5-piece bent-limb body **350.00**

Kathe Kruse girl, 14", all cloth, smoke grey eyes, blonde human hair wig, muslin body stitched fingers and toes, original clothes ... **625.00**

Kestner

Baby, bisque socket head baby, 19" circumference head, flirty eyes, open mouth with teeth and moveable tongue, blonde human hair wig, bent limb compo. body . **650.00**

Boy, bisque head, dressed **500.00**

Twins, bisque socket head, sleep

eyes, open-closed mouth, mohair wig, compo. body, pair **760.00**

Lenci girl, 14" felt, original cloth and paper labels, Italian costume, c. 1930 .... **100.00**

Minerva, 14", tin head girl, kid body, bisque hands, dressed **100.00**

Paper Mache

Composition French doll, closed mouth, inset eyes, mohair wig, original corset, kid body, c. 1880 . **87.50**

Girl, paperweight glass eyes, closed smiling mouth with painted teeth, cloth body, straw-stuffed, paper mache hands and feet **190.00**

Girl, shoulder and head, 43", blue painted eyes, molded blonde hair with vertical curls, cloth body, leather arms **325.00**

Parian

Girl, 4", blue painted eyes, short curly blonde wig, jointed at shoulders and hips **148.00**

Bonnet head girl, 17", molded white bonnet trimmed in pink flowers, and blue bows, original body, parian arms and legs **650.00**

Paratrooper Doll, World War II, with parachute, in original box created by Antrix Elvy Kalep, dist. by Geo. Borgfeldt Co., c. 1942 .... **20.00**

Paper Dolls

Baby Bonnie, Whitman, 1960, 4 uncut sets of clothes **18.00**

Eva Gabor and Eddie Albert, 1968, clothes, boxed (cut) **20.00**

Little Women, 6 dolls on stands; clothes (cut); in original box **40.00**

Raphael Tuck, 10", complete with four changes, artist series, c. 1894 **95.00**

Tillie the Toiler, cut from Phila. Inquirer comic sections, c. 1930, 12 different dolls pasted on cardboard, plus clothes; in box, well preserved **100.00**

Pincushion Dolls

2½", blonde hair girl, flowers in hand, Germany **50.00**

4¾", gray hair, one arm raised, Germany, #5022 .... **23.00**

5", flapper, Germany **23.00**

Rag Dolls

Boy, 13", printed cloth face, original blue jumper suit, c. 1890 .... **25.00**

Cat, 12", dressed like a person, c. 1920 .... **35.00**

Raggedy Ann, original clothes, c. 1930 .... **36.00**

Raggedy Andy, original overalls and hat **36.00**

Aunt Jemima, stuffed, c. 1927 ... **40.00**

Uncle Mose, stuffed, c. 1927 .... **40.00**

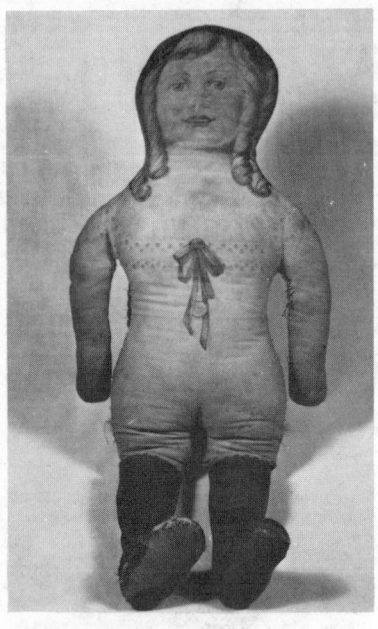

Grown-Up Paper Dolls, Merrill # 3408, 1936, uncut $20.00

Rag, girl, painted, c. 1900 .....$85.00

Shirley Temple, 15″, composition, Ideal, c. 1930 .... 67.50
Simon and Halbig
  Girl, bisque head, 36″, brown glass inset eyes, open mouth with upper row of teeth, pierced ears, original brown wig, ball jointed body, jointed wrists, original clothes 1250.00
  Girl, bisque head, 27″, dressed .. 735.00
Wax shoulder head girl; 5″; black inset bead eyes; painted black hair with bun at back; cloth body, wax arms and legs; dressed, c. 1800 . 220.00

DOLLS—PAPER

Within the past several years, paper dolls have become highly collectible. When buying paper dolls the collector should make sure that the set is complete, that all clothes and accessories are there. Uncut, unused, paper dolls are the most desirable.

Adele, *Delineator Magazine*, Carolyn Chester, April, 1912 .... 16.00
Barbara Britton, 1954 .... 15.00
Rosemary Clooney (Pollard) Bonnie Child Craft Series, 1958 .... 15.00
Dolly Dingle, *Pictorial Review*, June, 1929, peach and brown colors .. 10.00
Dolly Dingle, *Pictorial Review*, any date, full color 15.00
Dixie Dugan, Sunday Comics, 1940 3.50
Faye Emerson, Saalfeld #1557, 1952, uncut 15.00
Gone with the Wind, 18 doll set, Merrill, 1940, cut but complete .. 75.00
Gone with the Wind, 18 doll set, Merrill, 1940, mint condition 150.00
Gone with the wind, 5 doll set, Merrill, 1940, mint condition 250.00
Grown Up Paper Dolls, Merrill # 3408, Gladys O'Rourke, 1936, uncut 20.00
Elizabeth Taylor, Whitman, 1957, uncut 35.00
Walking Paper Doll Family, Saalfeld #1074, Ruth Upham, 1934, uncut 25.00
Who Are They? Patten Beard Presents Peter Pan's Movie Contest,

Delineator Magazine Series, Corwin Krapp Linson 1917, each **18.00**

10", parrot, figural, painted	**30.00**
10", scrolls, with flowers	**30.00**
Spur	**35.00**

DOOR KNOCKERS

Before the advent of the mechanical bell, electric buzzer and chimes, a door knocker was considered an essential door ornament to announce the arrival of visitors. Metal was used to cast or forge the various forms.

DOOR STOPS

Door stops were usually made of cast-iron and painted. They were and are used, of course, to hold doors in an open position.

Iron, 4" dia., basket of flowers, painted $24.00

Cat, 7¼" high, cast iron $15.00

Brass

Atlantis, head of, dolphin and shell motif	**55.00**
Bust of Will Rogers	**65.00**
Bust of Shakespeare, 4"	**65.00**
4", deer	**40.00**
Dolphin, figural	**45.00**
Eagle, figural, large	**55.00**
4", Lion's head with ring knocker, c. 1880	**75.00**
Pistol	**50.00**
Standing bear	**55.00**

Bronze

Lion's head, loose ring knocker .	**50.00**
Charles Dickens	**85.00**
Woodpecker, figural	**45.00**

Cast Iron

4", ladies's hand, ring on finger, lace cuff, has round ball in hand which does knocking, hinged at wrist	**38.00**
11", head of Mercury	**45.00**

Baskets	
Basket of flowers, 9½"	**20.00**
Basket of tulips, 8½"	**22.50**
Dogs	
Airdale, with worn paint, 14¾" ..	**100.00**
Boston Bull, worn paint	**55.00**
Bull Dog, 9", white and black ...	**50.00**
Shepherd, poor paint	**30.00**
St. Bernard, with keg, no paint, 11"	**50.00**
Elephant, 6", old grey paint	**55.00**
Flapper, old worn paint	**70.00**
Geese, three, marching in a row ..	**42.50**
Horses	
7¾", Black with red saddle	**55.00**
12½", brass; bridle, and saddle, standing on grass	**55.00**
Kitten, 7½", standing	**40.00**
Monkey, reading Darwin, 7", worn black paint	**12.50**
Owl, 10"	**40.00**
Penguin, 10¼"	**185.00**

Rooster, heavy solid iron, polychrome paint	**160.00**
Sunbonnet Baby, 6″, lead, old worn paint	**35.00**
Teddy Roosevelt, "Rough Rider," dated 1899	**65.00**
Woman with basket of fruit, worn paint	**75.00**
Woman holding skirt out, 11⅜″, old worn blue and white paint, marked, B. & H.	**105.00**

DORCHESTER POTTERY

George Henderson founded the Dorchester Pottery Works near Boston, Mass., in 1895. At first, bean pots, jugs, jars and industrial containers, all of stoneware, were produced. In 1940, a line of decorated pottery in blue and white made from New Jersey clay was introduced. Some of the patterns are: "Blueberry," "Colonial Lace," "Pinecone," "Pussy Willow" and "Scroll."

Since 1940, the potters and decorators sign each piece and the name Dorchester is on each example. This helps dating for collectors, as most earlier wares are marked with the name of the company only.

The pottery is still in operation today using the traditional methods of production to maintain the high quality of Dorchester. The stoneware is available only at the pottery; it is never shipped or sold in other commercial outlets.

Bowl, 5¾″, 2″ deep, "Scroll," Artist signed	**50.00**
Creamers and Sugars	
"Colonial Lace," creamer, 3″ high, sugar 3½″ high, artist signed, set	**95.00**
"Scroll," 3″ high with underplates, 4¾″ diam., artist signed, set	**150.00**
Crock, covered, 10″, signed Dorchester	**65.00**
Cups and Saucers, coffee	
"Grape"	**30.00**
"Scroll"	**50.00**
Cups and Saucers, demi	
"Blueberry"	**40.00**
"Pussy Willow"	**50.00**
Dish, 8 x 5½″, shell shaped, brown	**40.00**
Foot Warmer, 4 x 6 x 10¾″, jug-shaped, brass screw cap, impressed Dorchester	**125.00**
Mugs, 4″ high	
"Pear"	**45.00**
"Stripes and Codfish"	**50.00**
Pitcher, 9″, batter-type, signed Dorchester	**85.00**
Plates	
"Blueberry," 8″	**60.00**

"Blueberry," 10″	**75.00**
"Scroll," 10½″, artist signed . . .	**95.00**

DRESDEN (MEISSEN)

In 1710, Johann Frederick Boettger, an alchemist, accidently discovered a white clay in the area of Dresden, Germany. When he replaced his red stoneware pots with the white kaolin clay product, he produced the first true porcelain in Europe and Meissen Porcelain Works had its beginning.

Meissen porcelain is finely molded, decorated with applied floral motifs, enameled and gilded. In the 19th century, the factory reissued versions of their earlier examples. These debased wares are referred to as Dresden to differentiate them from the original Meissen porcelains.

Many marks were used to identify the porcelain. The first was a pseudo-oriental mark in a square. The famous crossed swords mark was adopted in 1724. The crossed swords mark with a small dot between the hilts was used in the 1763–1774 period. The following years, 1774 to 1814, the dot between the hilts was changed to a star. It has been reported that two new marks are appearing on the modern market — swords with a hammer and sickle and swords with a crown.

Bowls	
9½″, female portrait	**200.00**
9¼″, reticulated rim, hand painted decor	**215.00**
Boxes	
7¼″, turtle shape	**250.00**
4½ x 3″, covered; Birds and flowers on cover, red mark	**275.00**
Candelabra, 10″, scenic with children	**125.00**
Chocolate Pot, and five cups and saucers, flowers and figures, set .	**350.00**
Compote, 11″, applied flowers and cupids	**450.00**
Cups and Saucers	
Blue and gold decor with miniatures	**75.00**
Floral, with gilding	**50.00**
Blue and white panels, with flowers and figures, c. 1860	**100.00**
Cakestand, 4″, paneled floral border	**160.00**
Figurines	
Birds, 4″, pair	**100.00**
Coach and horses, 16″, colors . .	**225.00**
George Washington on horse-	

back, 17½", by Schreiber	450.00
Shepherd boy playing flute, 2 lambs and goat, 4½ x 6½"	225.00

Plaques

The Goddess Pysche, peering into stream, 6½ x 5", artist signed ...	750.00
Zither Player, 7", peasant scene, sepia	325.00
Madonna Della Sedia, after Raphael, 9¾", artist signed, early 20th century	600.00

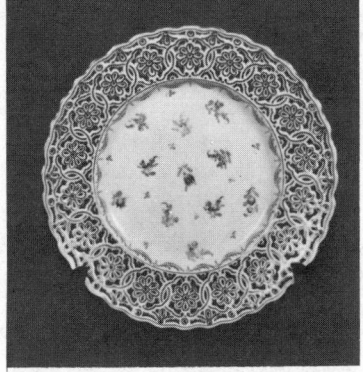

Plate, 11", scalloped and reticulated edge, gold trim, floral center decor $100.00

Plates

Cupid, openwork, 7¾", colored border, set of six	250.00
Three cherubs, pierced edge, 9" .	115.00
Woman and child, 12", pierced for hanging	130.00
Portrait of Lady Bingham Reynolds, blue, heavy gold, signed Vorberger	255.00
Place Card Holder, roses around the edges, signed A. Lamb, set of 12	85.00
Shoe, 6½", floral decor, signed ...	68.00

Snuffbox, Hardstone, by Johann Chrstian Neuber, c. 1770	15000.00

Tea Caddy

Blue courting scene, 6", c. 1896 .	200.00
Traditional Dresden flowers, 5¼"	175.00

Tea Pots

5", footed, floral decor on white .	150.00
8", cobalt, white with 2 scenic medallions, rose finial	225.00
17", relief molded hot water kettle, on stand, burner, gold on white	150.00

Tea Service, two pots, cream, sugar, 12 cups and saucers, white, cobalt, with gold trim	1250.00

Tea Sets

Teapot, sugar and creamer, floral and gold decor, swan finial	375.00
Teapot with dragon spout, creamer, sugar, bowl, 8 demitasse cups and saucers, fluted rims, hand painted, gold trim, set	400.00
Toast Rack, white and gold	75.00

Vases

5½", floral decor on white, scalloped tops, collared base, pair ...	200.00
7½", turquoise, jewelled, portrait, signed Richtner, "Voluptos"	395.00
9¼", covered, dragon handles, Foo Dog finial, birds, flowers	250.00
10½", portrait Marie Antoinette, butterflies, gold	2050.00
12", white handles, cobalt blue background, florals on white	150.00

DUNCAN AND MILLER GLASS

The firm began in Pittsburgh, Pa., in the late 1860's under the name of George Duncan and Sons. In 1893-94 the glass works moved to Washington, Pa. where they manufactured some of the finest handmade glassware in America for sixty-three years.

George Duncan, the founder, recognized the talents of his designer, John Ernest Miller, encouraged his growth, and made him one of the owners, thus the name Duncan and Miller.

A specialty of the firm was the reproduction of early American Sandwich Glass, but probably the most famous Miller design was "Three Face" and probably the most beautiful is the Duncan and Miller "Swan."

Production ceased in June 1955. The U. S. Glass Co. purchased the molds, equipment and machinery in 1956.

Ashtrays

Dogwood	12.50
Duck, clear	15.00
Duck, ruby	9.00

Animals

7", Heron	70.00
12", Swan, clear, wings spread ..	40.00

Bowls

10", Canterbury, chartruse	25.00
12", Ivy, hobnail, pink opalescent	35.00
12", Ivy, hobnail, ruby	85.00
Finger, Sandwich, green	15.00

Boxes

Cigarette, duck on lid	40.00
Cigarette, Passion Flower	25.00
Puff, Astair, amber	25.00

Butter, covered, Double Snail	**125.00**
Candlelabras	
Granada, 3-lite, pair	**55.00**
Hobnail, yellow, pair	**25.00**
Indian Tree, etch, 2-lite, pair	**45.00**
Magnolia, 2-lite, pair	**60.00**
Candlesticks	
American Way, pink opalescent, pair	**55.00**
Hobnail, pink opalescent, pair . . .	**45.00**
Murano, frosted, pair	**45.00**
Champagne, Adoration	**14.00**
Coasters	
3¼", Hobnail, green	**8.50**
5", Sandwich, crystal	**7.50**
Hobnail, Schraft's	**6.00**
Cocktail Shaker, Chanticleer, ruby .	**110.00**
Compotes	
5", Canterbury, vaseline	**38.00**
5", Canterbury, green	**25.00**
5½", First Love, crystal, etched .	**45.00**

Console Set, bowl, 2¾ x 12" dia., candle holders, 5½", "Canteberry," frosted, set $125.00

Console Set, Caribbean, Cape Cod blue	**145.00**
Creamers	
Amberette	**65.00**
Whirligig, individual	**15.00**
Creamer and Sugar	
Canterbury, crystal	**12.00**
Sandwich, crystal	**15.00**
Cruet, Caribbean, crystal, cobalt stopper	**32.00**
Goblets	
Daisy and Button, panelled, vaseline	**18.00**
Sandwich, amber or light amber .	**16.00**
Hat, 4", Hobnail, blue opalescent . .	**20.00**
Ice Tub, Block	**20.00**
Nappies	
4½", Flower Scroll	**12.50**
6", Sanibel, Cape Cod, blue opalescent	**26.00**
Pitchers	
Water, Heavy Panel, fine cut . . .	**100.00**
Water, Mardi Gras, silver plate spout	**125.00**

Water, Sandwich, crystal	**45.00**
Plates	
6", Cambria	**12.50**
7", Sandwich, amber	**12.00**
8", Sandwich, green	**17.50**
8½", Canterbury, crystal	**4.50**
13", Sanibel, pink opalescent . . .	**32.75**
Punch Cups, Ivy, hobnail	**6.00**
Relishes	
Canterbury, pink opalescent	**40.00**
Caribbean, round, 4 part	**20.00**
Sanibel, jasmine yellow opalescent, 2 part	**47.00**
Rose Bowl, Hobnail, footed, crimped top	**20.00**
Sherbets	
Charmain Rose	**16.00**
Cretan	**16.00**
Indian Tree	**16.00**
Swans, Open Back	
3", crystal	**25.00**
7½", ruby bowl	**28.00**
8", ruby bowl	**35.00**
13½", crystal	**45.00**
Swans, Solid Back	
3"	**18.00**
4½"	**20.00**
Toothpicks	
Teepee	**45.00**
Two Ply Swirl	**28.00**
Tumblers	
Arliss, ruby	**25.00**
Hobnail, pink opalescent	**20.00**
Sandwich, vaseline	**20.00**
Vases	
3½", Canterbury, pink opalescent, crimped	**16.00**
4", pink opalescent	**28.00**
4", Hobnail, blue opalescent	**28.00**
5 x 5", Canterbury, pink opalescent	**30.00**
8½", blue opalescent	**40.00**

DURAND

Victor Durand, Sr., reputed to be a descendant of the French family which made Baccarat glass, started a factory in Vineland, N.J., in 1925.

The art glass resembles Tiffany in some respects, especially the iridescent sheen. Much of Durand glass was not marked, some bore a sticker labeled "Durand Art Glass," some had the name Durand scratched in the pontil and a few had the name inside a large V. The factory closed in 1932.

Box, 3½" dia., covered, green lustre glass, gold lustre King Tut decor .	**950.00**
Bowl, 5" high, gold, King Tut decor, footed	**375.00**
Candlesticks, 10", blue, signed	**375.00**

Champagne, 6½", ruby and amber . 225.00
Compotes
2¾ x 4½" dia., miniature, blue, lily pad decor 400.00
6½ x 7¾" dia., gold blue, signed 395.00
Goblet, green with feather decor, flared 175.00
Ginger Jar, 10½", covered, gold and green, King Tut decor 1850.00
Plate, 8", ruby, white pulled feather decor 295.00
Rose Bowls
3½", blue, ruffled rim, signed . . . 400.00
4", clear, controlled bubbles, signed 225.00
5½", blue, gold threads, gold foot, signed 375.00
Sherbet, low, cranberry, white feather decor 150.00

ery 350.00
8½", beige and pink, green threaded leaves to middle 300.00
8½", opalescent gold, gold and white pulled feather and spider webbing decor, blue edge 750.00
9½", crackle glass, blue-gold aurene lining 600.00
9½", blue lustre, King Tut decor . 785.00
10", oviform, blue iridescent, engraved signature and numbered . 900.00
11⅛", peacock blue, green lily pads, signed and numbered 750.00
12", gold iridescent, pale green leaf and vine decor 700.00

END-OF-DAY GLASS
See SPATTER GLASS

ENGLISH YELLOW-GLAZED EARTHENWARE

This ware has been called Canary Lustre. It dates back to the early 1800's and is identified with the Staffordshire district of England. The body of the piece is yellow (canary) colored, the transfer picture is usually in black and the decoration in lustre.

Developed at the highest technical moment in English pottery history, English Yellow-Glazed Earthenware embraces the finest quality creamware found toward the end of the century of experimentation and into the nineteenth century. Documented pieces date from the 1780's to 1840, including Wedgwood wares as early as 1785.

While many pieces have silver and, more rarely, copper lustre, some items have none. Examples may be painted in a colorful, free-form manner, or transfer decor in black or brick red, with or without lustre. Pieces without any decoration are uncommon. The yellow overglaze varies in intensity from canary to a very pale yellow.

This category has also been called "Canary Lustre."

Vase, 7", iridescent blue with white webbing **$325.00**

Vases
7", bulbous, Kimbel Cluthra, lemon, white, orange, light green, flared rim, signed 595.00
7½", threaded feather pattern, original label 700.00
8", green, cut to clear, silvery trac-

Jug, "Faith and Hope" transfer in black, canary-colored body 800.00
Mugs
"A Present for a Good Boy," 2¼" 300.00
"Want of care does thee more damage than want of knowledge," Franklin Maxim, 2¼" 300.00
Babies, transfer in black, 7" 650.00
Child's red churchyard scene . . . 300.00
Pitcher, 4½", "Faith and Hope" . . . 500.00
Plate, 7", rose in center, embossed fruit around rim 600.00

Cup and Saucer, black transfer of woman and children at piano, black rim $250.00

17″ high, 12″ dia. base, opalescent blue, ruffled tops $325.00

EPERGNES

An epergne is an elaborately designed centerpiece for a table, consisting of a number of receptacles for fruits, flowers, candies and/or candles. Epergnes were made by many of the glass manufacturers, both American and European.

See also specific glass categories.

9″ high, cranberry, ruffled bowl, 3 lilies	325.00
10″ high, amethyst, ruffled footed bowl, single lily	75.00
10″ high, clear glass, 3 lilies	50.00
10″ high, cased, pink and white floral decor, single lily	160.00
10½″ high, vaseline, applied leaves, single lily	220.00
11″ high, opaque turquoise, 2 piece, Fenton	125.00
12″ high, vaseline, clear edge on base, 3 opalescent lilies	260.00
14½″ high, cranberry, milk white bowl, single lily	180.00
15″ high, cranberry, round metal base with mirror, 3 lilies	225.00
15½″ high, nailsea, green and white, single lily	275.00
21″ high, venetian, opalescent, green and blue, 4 lilies	180.00
22″ high, green opalescent, 2 twisted crystal arms, 3 lilies	360.00

FAIRY LAMPS

Fairy Lamps are candle-burning night lights. They were first introduced by the Samuel Clarke Co., England, in 1857, but were made by many other firms in England, Europe and the U.S. from then on.

A wide array were produced, from pressed glass to fine art glass. There are two main classifications: The Fairy Pyramid has a clear glass base and a dome shaped shade that measures approximately 3½″ high when assembled. Others are 5″ or more high and may have in addition to the clear glass candle insert, a saucer that matches the shade.

Brass	
Etched and enameled, glass inserts, blue stylized leaf design ..	350.00
Rose on ormalu stand	185.00
Baccarat, wine to clear, swirl, signed	220.00
Bisque	
Castle	300.00
Woman's head, flowing hair, Austrian	195.00
Bohemian, red, cut back, matching base	150.00

Overshot, blue, "Crown," Clarke base $125.00

Bristol
Pink, lighthouse, ivory carrying ring marked Depose	150.00
White, on white matching base, enamel floral decor	170.00

Burmese
Clarke base, small	165.00
5⅝", square folded over base, green ivy leaf decor, Clarke insert, signed Webb	1200.00

Clarke, clear ribbed dome, matching base, signed dome	80.00
Crackle Glass, rainbow, Clarke base	125.00
End of Day, yellow and red, Clarke base	130.00
Lithophane, 3 colored lithophane panels in dome	800.00
Overshot, Crown pattern, cranberry, Clarke base	85.00
Parian, ram's head, matching base .	200.00

Pressed
Waffle pattern, Clarke base	160.00
Diamond point, clear, Clarke base	105.00

Satin Glass
Apricot, lighthouse	120.00
Rainbow, diamond quilted, mother-of-pearl, matching base, signed Clarke	700.00
Rose, diamond quilted, mother-of-pearl, Clarke base	165.00

Vaseline

Ribbed dome on green pressed Clarke base	150.00
Frosted, matching handled base .	150.00

Verre Moire (Nailsea)
White, upturned matching base, Clarke insert	220.00
Yellow, Clarke base	100.00
Blue, matching base	180.00
Rose, upturned matching crimped	

FAMILLE ROSE

Famille Rose is Chinese export enameled porcelain in which the pink color predominates. It was made primarily in the 18th and early 19th century. Other porcelains in the same family group are Famille Jaune (yellow), Famille Noire (black), and Famille Verte (green).

Decorations include courtyard and home scenes, birds, and insects. Secondary colors are yellow, green, blue, aubergine, and black.

Mid to late 19th century Chinese export wares similar to Famille Rose are identified as Rose Canton, Rose Mandarin, and Rose Medallion.

Snuff Bottle, 2½ x 2" wide . . . $125.00

Basin, rose-robed lady, turquoise robed lady, 16⅛" dia.	400.00
Beaker Vase, figures in pavilion, 10¼"	425.00

Bowls
10", peonies and blossoms, c. 1750	600.00

10¼", Judgment of Paris, lotus sprays	675.00
10½", peonies and magnolia, birds	1750.00

Chargers

13⅛", octagonal, c. 1740	350.00
15", cluster of flowers	450.00

Garden Seat, phoenix bird amidst peonies, 18¾" high	2000.00
Ginger Jar, ovoid, floral sprays, 8¾"	700.00

Mugs

5", Dutchman motif, c. 1780	350.00
5½", floral motif, c. 1800	300.00

Plates

8¾", figure on pink horse	225.00
8⅞", bouquet with lappet border	250.00
9", peony spray, multi-colored	175.00
10⅛", six sprays of fruit and flowers on rim	425.00

Teapot, Judgement of Paris, 5⅝", c. 1775	450.00
Tureen, Soup, cover, fishing scene	1750.00

Vases

9⅜", balustered, figures with scroll work panel	550.00
10⅜", two peasants on rockwork, mounted as lamp	950.00
16½", seven sages on mountain plateau, floral decoration on neck and base	3000.00

Wig Stand, 11½" high	500.00

FANS

Fans have been used for generations and early ones were painted by hand. The hand fan was a necessary 'coolant' before the electric fan and central air conditioning. Utilitarian fans made of paper and wood were a popular advertising media distributed to churches, social organizations, meetings, etc. An elaborate fan, fashioned of lace or silk, was an important accessory to womens' costumes in the Victorian era. Fans were very ornate, and some were even set with jewels. Cheaper paper fans were turned out by the carload in the last century.

Advertising

"Keen Kutter Kutlery," 1904, St. Louis, hatchet shaped handle	10.00
"Moxie" Lillian MacKenzie	18.00
Celluloid, hand painted blue florals on white, c. 1910, opens to 12⅝"	20.00
Chiffon fan with ivory ribs and hand painted birds	18.00
Feathers, white, hand painted Japanese warriors center, and multi-colored florals, reverse	45.00

Ivory

Marked "Hotel Atlantic, Hamburg"

on one side and "Der Kaiserhof, Berlin," on the other	45.00
Louis XV style, classical scene and couple in landscape on parchment, carved, pierced, painted, ivory spokes	65.00
Hand painted birds, floral butterfly decor, ivory spokes	37.50

Lace, 8½", black with sequins, celluloid sticks	**$35.00**

Lace

White, with ivory spokes, in Japanese fan box	42.50
Black, ebony pierced spokes, tortoise shell handle	50.00
on satin, MOP slats	35.00
White embroidered florals, MOP sticks, gold tassel, original satin covered fan box	75.00
Lacquered fan, black, cut out gothic ribs, hand painted country scene with rushing water	50.00
Ostrich feather, black, tortoise shell sticks	80.00

Paper

Round, with velvet handles and trim	20.00
13" radius, panorama of Columbian Exposition, advertising cigars	37.50

FENTON GLASS

The Fenton Art Glass Company was founded at Martin Ferry, Ohio, by Frank L. Fenton in 1907. They began production with carnival, chocolate, custard, pressed and mold blown

opalescent glass. In the 1920's stretch glass, Fenton dolphins, jade green, ruby and art glass were added to their line.

In the 30's boudoir lamps, "Dancing Ladies," and various slags were produced. The 40's saw crests of different colors being added to each piece by hand. Hobnail, opalescent, and two-color overlay pieces were popular items. Handles were added to different shapes, making the baskets they created as popular today as then.

Through the years, Fenton has added beauty to their glass by decorating it with hand painting, acid etching, color staining and copper wheel cutting. Several different paper labels have been used. However, in 1970 an oval raised trademark was also adopted. Located today in Williamstown, West Virginia, Fenton is recognized as one of the foremost glass companies in the United States.

See also CARNIVAL GLASS.

Bell, 7", "Rosaline," made from 1969–1971 . . . . $29.00

Baskets

5", blue overlay	36.00
5½" high, cranberry hobnail	34.00
8", blue hobnail opalescent, footed	38.00

Bowls

3½", Kittens, carnival, marigold .	68.00
6½", Mandarin red, cupped	62.00
7½", charcoal grey, stretch, shal-	

low cupped	34.00
8", Dancing Ladies, cobalt	100.00
8½", Dolphin, pink, handled	25.00
9½", Dragon and Lotus, carnival, marigold, fluted	40.00
10½", periwinkle blue, footed . . .	68.00
11", blue hobnail, crimped, footed	60.00

Candlesticks

3½", Dolphin, pink, pair	32.00
3½", Dolphin, red, pair	42.50
5", cobalt, cornucopia, pair	52.00

Compotes

6", jade green	17.00
6", Persian Medallion, carnival, marigold	27.00
Flowerpot, 4½" high, Snowcrest, green, attached saucer	42.00

Hats

4" dia., peach crest	34.00
6" dia., French opalescent, ribbed	45.00
7½", green opalescent, ribbed . .	62.50
Lemon Server, 2¼" high, yellow, stretch	24.00

Nappies

5", Dolphin, green	10.00
5", Panther, carnival, marigold . .	45.00
5", Sailboats, carnival, marigold .	26.00
Paperweight, 3½" high, Bicentennial, chocolate slag	32.00

Plates

7", Bicentennial, Mandarin red, slag	27.00
8", leaf dish, French opalescent .	34.00

Pitchers

5½", green hobnail, handled . . .	40.00
8", 80 oz. cranberry opalescent, hobnail	80.00
8½", white with blue overlay . . .	37.00
Rose Bowl, 5" dia., periwinkle blue	58.00

Slippers

6", Cat, blue opalescent hobnail .	24.00
6", Cat, French opalescent	18.00

Tumblers

Carnival, marigold, Floral and Grape	21.00
Carnival, marigold, Milady	30.00
Carnival, cobalt, Butterfly and Berry	36.00
Coinspot, green opalescent, late .	17.00
Fenton Drapery, blue opalescent	24.00

Vases

2", aqua crest, miniature	22.00
3½", hand, topaz opalescent . . .	24.00
4", blue opalescent hobnail	18.00
4½", green opalescent	25.00
5¼", fan shape, velva rose, stretch	42.00
5½", fan shape, Mongolian green	55.00
6", fan shape, aqua crest	18.00
6", flared, Mandarin red	65.00
6½", cranberry opalescent rib . . .	48.00
7½", Mongolian green peacock . .	110.00

7½", periwinkle blue peacock . . .	**115.00**
8", fan shape, green jade	**32.00**
11", blue opalescent, optic, rib . .	**52.00**

FIESTA WARE

Fiesta ware is a pottery dinnerware made by the Homer Laughlin China Co. in 1936, redesigned in 1969 and discontinued in 1973.

It can be distinguished from other brightly colored dinnerware of the same period by its characteristic band of concentric circles beginning at the rim and the full circle handle on the cups. In 1969, a partial circle handle was used. Most of the wares were incised "Fiesta."

Coffee Pot, cobalt $25.50

Ashtrays	
Cobalt blue	14.00
Red	25.00
Bowls	
4¾", cobalt blue	6.50
4¾", forest green	7.50
4¾", light green	4.50
5½", chartreuse	7.50
5½", ivory	7.25
5½", turquoise	8.00
Flat fruit, ivory	82.00
Salad, green, yellow	40.00
Cake Server, red	30.00

Carafe	
Ivory	40.00
Red	60.00
Casserole, covered, green	60.00
Coffee Pot, forest green	42.00
Creamers	
Ivory, ring handle	3–6.00
Red	15.00
Turquoise	3–5.00
Creamer and covered sugar, pair, turquoise	15.00
Cups and Saucers	
Chartreuse	14.50
Cobalt blue	10–14.00
Forest green	13.00
Grey	12.00
Demitasse, yellow, set	16.50
Egg Cups	
Chartreuse	15.00
Cobalt blue	12.00
Turquoise	11.50
Mugs	
Green	5.00
Grey	15.00
Ivory	16.00
Mustard Jars, covered	
Cobalt blue	55.00
Yellow, unsigned	40.00
Nappy, 8½", forest green	7.50
Pitchers	
Ivory, water	22.50
Red, juice	80.00
Yellow, juice	17.50
Plates	
10½", cobalt blue	10.00
10½", red, grey and rose	20.00
Large grill, cobalt blue	22.00
Large grill, red	26.00
Pie plate, red	22.00
Salt and Pepper shakers	
Green, single	2.50
Ivory, turquoise, pair	22.50
Red, pair	65.00

FIRE EQUIPMENT

The volunteer fire company has played a central social and functional role in numerous towns and rural areas throughout America. Each company prided itself on its individual uniforms and equipment. Firemen conventions and parades allowed each company to "show off" as well as produced additional memorabilia such as presentation trophies, ribbons, etc.

Fire museums have arisen across America. In addition, many fire houses and local historical societies have a room devoted to old equipment and accouterments. The literature

in the field is extensive, enhanced by the collection and publications of the Insurance Company of North America, Philadelphia, Pa.

Helmet, tin, "N.F.D.," "1st Asst.," white with gold and red trim, Pat'd. '87–'89 . . . . $150.00

Alarms
Gamewell alarm gong, brass bells, oak case	500.00
Repeater, brass mechanism, glass case, 33″ marble base	1000.00
Wooden ratchet rattle	75.00
Axe, blade and pick, painted wooden handle, 20″	35.00

Belts
Axeman, black leather, white letters	45.00
Augusta, ME, No. 1, Cushnoe, white leather	70.00
Protection, black leather with red and white trim, 40″	110.00

Buckets, leather
1806, Providence, No. 2, Ezra Wheeler	250.00
1812, pair, Portsmouth, NH, Hall Varrell, No. 1 and No. 2, repainted early 19th c.	1750.00
Concord, NH, early 19th c., rough condition	500.00
Decorated, general design	175.00
"Phoenix" in scroll, picture of fire chief, rough condition	625.00

Extinguishers
Brass, 14″	20.00
Brass, 24″	40.00

Fire Marks
Germantown National Fire, 1843 .	125.00
Hydrant, F. A., 1817	200.00
United Fireman's Ins. Co.	140.00

Helmuts, aluminum	45.00
Helmuts, brass	
American, eagle finial	200.00
English, c. 1860	135.00
Helmuts, leather	
Chief, AFD, white painted leather .	140.00
HSDC, AFD, black leather	160.00
Firemans Active, Phila., red painted leather	375.00
Plain, black leather	40.00
Shield, Pioneer Fire Co., No. 1 . .	60.00
Nozzles, Hose	
12½″, brass, Eureka	60.00
20″, brass, Eastern Coupling Co., Camden, ME	125.00
25½″, copper with brass fittings, B. C. Co.	85.00
36″, brass, adjustable by small wheel	300.00
Play pipe nozzle holder	60.00
Pin, CT, 1836, Firemen's convention, ribbon	15.00
Speaking Trumpets	
Presentation, brass, 16½″	550.00
Presentation, silver plated, 19″ . .	1000.00
Presentation, silver plated, 21″ . .	1150.00
Presentation, silver plated, 23½″ .	1600.00
Presentation, Warren Hose Co. by Bunkerhill Assembly, October 5, 1857, silver plated, ornately decorated	2600.00
Working, brass	425.00
Working, brass, collapsible, 13″ . .	850.00

FIREARMS

The value of any particular type of antique firearm will cover a very wide range. For instance, a Colt 1849 pocket model revolver with a 5″ barrel could be priced from $100.00 to $700.00 depending on whether or not all the component parts are original, whether some are missing, how much of the original finish (bluing) remains on the barrel and frame, how much silver plating remains on the brass trigger guard and back strap and the condition and finish of the walnut grips. Thus, condition is one of the two variables controlling value. The other is rarity. A rare type of Colt firearm such as a Paterson belt revolver in just fair condition will command a much higher price than the Colt pocket model in very fine condition because of the rarity. Values listed below are for firearms in good, complete condition.

FLINTLOCK PISTOLS—SINGLE SHOT

British military, 7½″ round, steel barrel, lockplate marked "Tower & 1772" with British crown, full walnut stock with steel trigger guard

36, Navy Revolver, "E. Whitney/N. Haven" Powder & Ball pattern, 6 cyl. $450.00

and ramrod pipes **550.00**

British, 8″ half round-half octagon, steel barrel, marked "D. Egg & London," full walnut stock with steel trigger guard and ramrod pipes, lockplate also marked, "D. Egg & London" **600.00**

British officer's, 7″ round, brass barrel marked "London," lockplate marked "Sharpe," full oak stock with brass trigger guard and ramrod pipes **425.00**

British pocket, 2½″ round steel barrel, hammer mounted on top of steel frame, frame marked "H. Nock" and "London," rosewood grips with silver wire inlay **275.00**

British sea service, 9½″ round steel barrel, full oak stock with brass butt plate, trigger guard and ramrod pipes, lockplate marked "Tower and London" with British crown, distinctive steel belt hook attached to left side of pistol ... **950.00**

Kentucky, 10″ octagonal iron barrel, 48 cal., full curly maple stock with brass fore-end cap, brass trigger guard and ramrod pipes, lock marked "Ashmore/Warranted" .. **2500.00**

U.S. Model 1805 (Harper's Ferr), 10″ round iron barrel with ironrib underneath holding ramrod pipe, lockplate marked "Harper's Ferry & 1808," with spread eagle and shield over U.S. stamping, 54 cal., walnut half stock with brass butt plate and trigger guard **2500.00**

U.S. Model 1816, 9″ round barrel, 54 cal., lockplate marked "S. North & Midl^{tn} Conn.," with spread eagle stamping, full walnut stock with steel double barrel band, steel butt plate and trigger guard **750.00**

U.S. Model 1819, 10″ round barrel, 54 cal., lockplate marked "S. North & Midl^{tn} Conn.," with spread eagle stamp, dated 1822, full walnut stock, swivel ramrod attached to barrel, all iron parts **1000.00**

U.S. Model 1836, 8½″ round barrel, 54 cal., lockplate marked "A. Waters-Milbury, Ms.," and dated 1838, half walnut stock, swivel ramrod attached to barrel, all iron parts **800.00**

U.S. Model 1836, 8½″ round barrel, 54 cal., lockplate marked "R. Johson Midd^{n} Conn.," and dated 1838, half walnut stock, swivel ramrod attached to barrel, all iron parts **800.00**

PERCUSSION PISTOLS—SINGLE SHOT

Note: Conversion of flintlock pistols to percussion was common practice. Most British and U.S. Military flintlock model pistols listed above can be found in percussion. Values for these percussion converted pistols may be from 40 to 60% of the flintlock values as given.

Belt, 5½″ octagonal barrel, 45 cal., back action lock with lockplate marked "Tryon, Philadelphia," walnut full stock, brass trigger guard, c. 1860 .... **475.00**

Deringer, 3½″ barrel flattened on top and marked "Deringer/ Philadel^a," identical marking appears on lockplate, 41 cal., checkered walnut stock, German silver trigger guard and butt cap **600.00**

Kentucky, 8″ octagonal brass barrel, 45 cal., full curly maple stock with brass fore-end cap, brass trigger guard and ramrod pipes, lock marked "Golcher" **1200.00**

U.S. Model 1842, 8½″ round barrel, 54 cal., lockplate marked "H. Aston" & Midd^{tn} Conn., 1848," walnut half stock, swivel ramrod attached to barrel, brass butt cap and trigger guard **500.00**

U.S. Model 1855 pistol-carbine, 12″ round barrel, 58 cal., three quarter walnut stock, swivel ramrod attached to barrel, lock marked "U.S. Springfield & 1856," distinguishing feature is walnut carbine stock fitted to rear of pistol . **1000.00**

U.S. Navy Box Lock Model 1843, 6″ round barrel, 54 cal., locked marked "N.P. Ames, Springfield, Mass.," and "U.S.N. 1844," walnut three quarter stock, swivel ramrod attached to barrel, brass butt and trigger guard **600.00**

PERCUSSION PISTOLS—MULTI SHOT (REVOLVERS)

Colt

Iver Johnson, Arms & Cycle Works, 1895, Fitchburg, Ma., 38 cal. with MOP grips, Ser. # 181 ....$225.00

1860 Army Model, 8″ round barrel marked "Address Col. Sam¹ Colt New York U.S. American," 6 shot, 44 cal., cylinder engraved with naval battle scene, walnut grips ... **600.00**

Dragoon
  First Model (c. 1849) 7½″, part octagon, part round barrel marked "Address Sam¹ Colt, New York City-Colt's Patent," 6 shot, 44 cal., cylinder engraved with Indian fight scene, square backed trigger guard, walnut grips **3000.00**
  Third Model, (c. 1855), very similar to above with rounded trigger guard **2500.00**

Navy
  1851 Model, 7½″ octagonal barrel marked "Address Sam¹ Colt New York U.S. America," 6 shot, 36 cal., cylinder engraved with naval battle scene, round trigger guard, walnut grips **575.00**
  1861 model, very similar to Army model, with 7½″ round barrel and 36 cal. **550.00**

Paterson Belt Model (c. 1840), 5½″ octagon barrel marked "Patent Arms Mfg. Co. Paterson N.J. Colt's Pt," 5 shot, 31 cal., engraved cylinder, disappearing trigger, no trigger guard, flared walnut grips **2800.00**

Pocket Model, 1849, barrel lengths of 3″, 4″, 5″ & 6″, octagonal with attached loading lever, 5 or 6 shot, 31 cal., barrel marked "Address Col. Sam¹ Colt New York U.S. America," cylinder engraved with stagecoach holdup scene, walnut grips, round trigger guard . **400.00**

Police Model, 1862, 5½″ barrel with Colt, New York address, 36 cal., 5 shot half-fluted cylinder, walnut grips **600.00**

Sidehammer (Root) Model 1855, 3½″ octagonal barrel marked "Address Sam¹ Colt. Hartford CT," 28 cal., cylinder engraved with Indian fight scene, hammer mounted on right side of frame, walnut grips **500.00**

Remington
Army Model 1861, 8″ octagonal barrel, 6 shot, 44 cal., barrel marked "Patented Dec. 17, 1861 — Manufactured by Remington's, Ilion, N.Y.," walnut grips **450.00**

Navy Model, 1861, very similar to 1861 Army model, 7⅜″ octagon barrel and 36 cal. **650.00**

New Pocket Model (c. 1870), 3½″ octagon barrel, 5 shot, 31 cal., barrel marked with Remington address plus "New Model," walnut grips and spur trigger — no guard .. **800.00**

Remington-Beals 1st model, 3″ octagonal barrel marked "F. Beal's Patent & date," frame marked "Remingtons, Ilion, N.Y.," 5 shot, 31 cal., gutta percha grips, round trigger guard **400.00**

Other
Allen & Thurber "Pepperbox," 6 shot, 5″ barrel, bar type hammer mounted on top of frame, hammer marked "Allen & Thurber, Norwich, Ct. Pat. 1837," umbrella handle type wood grips, many variations **500.00**

Bacon Mfg. Co., 5″ octagonal barrel, 5 shot, round cylinder, 31 cal., barrel marked "Bacon Mfg. Co.— Norwich, Conn.," round trigger guard, walnut grips **325.00**

Butterfield Army Model 1861, 7″ octagonal barrel marked "Butterfield's Patent Dec. 11, 1855-Philada.," 5 shot, 41 cal., hammer mounted on top of brass frame, walnut grips, round trigger guard . **2000.00**

Cooper Pocket Model, 5″ octagonal barrel, 5 shot, 31 cal., barrel marked "Address Cooper Fire Arms Co. Frankford Phila-Pat. 1863," walnut grips, round trigger guard **400.00**

Freeman Army Model 1863, 7½″ round barrel, 6 shot, 44 cal., barrel marked "Freemans Pat. Dec. 9, 1862-Hoards Armory, Watertown, N.Y.," walnut grips, round trigger guard **650.00**

Joslyn Army Model 1862, 8″ octagonal barrel marked "B.F. Joslyn Patd 1858," 5 shot, 44 cal., side hammer mounted on right side of frame, walnut grips, round trigger guard 750.00

Metropolitan Navy Model (c. 1862), 7½" octagonal barrel marked "Metropolitan Arms Co. New York," 6 shot, 36 cal., walnut grips, round trigger guard, direct copy of Colt 600.00

Rogers & Spencer Army Model (c. 1864), 7½" octagonal barrel marked "Rogers & Spencer"— Utica, N.Y.," walnut grips, round trigger guard 650.00

Savage Navy Model (c. 1864), 7¼" octagonal barrel, 6 shot, 36 cal., solid frame marked "Savage Co. Patented 1856," distinguished by double trigger inside large trigger guard, walnut grips 550.00

Starr Army Model 1858, 6" round barrel marked "Starr Arms Co. New York" 6 shot, 44 cal., double action revolver, walnut grips, round trigger guard 400.00

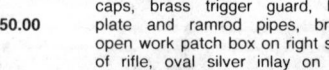

10 gauge, pin-fired shotgun, French, Lefaucheux, Damascus steel barrel, heavily gold inlayed, cased . 1,200.00

FLINTLOCK LONGARMS

British "Brown Boss" Musket (c. 1760–1770), 42" round barrel, 80 cal., lockplate marked "Tower" with British crown stamp, full length walnut stock pinned to barrel, brass trigger guard, butt plate and ramrod pipes, the major weapon of British infantry troops during the Revolutionary War ... 900.00

French Model 1763 Musket, 44½" round barrel, 75 cal., lockplate marked "St. Etienne," full length walnut stock with three iron barrel bands, iron trigger guard and butt plate, the major weapon of French infantry troops during the Revolutionary War 950.00

Kentucky Rifle (c. 1820), 40" octagonal barrel, 45 cal., lock marked "London/Warranted," curly maple full stock with brass fore-end

caps, brass trigger guard, butt plate and ramrod pipes, brass open work patch box on right side of rifle, oval silver inlay on left cheek piece, four silver inlays on each side of stock 2800.00

U.S. Model 1806–1809 Musket, 44¾" long round barrel, 69 cal., lockplate marked "U.S." and "Springfield" with American eagle, dated 1808, full walnut stock, three barrel bands, all iron fittings 1400.00

U.S. Model 1803 Musket, 36" half octagon, half round barrel, 54 cal., lock marked "U.S." and "Harpers Ferry" with eagle, dated 1816, walnut half stock with brass patch box on right side 2200.00

U.S. Model 1814 Musket, 33" round barrel, 54 cal., lock marked "U.S." and "H. Deringer," walnut full stock with large oval, round patch box on right side 1000.00

U.S. Model 1840 Musket, 42" round barrel, 64 cal., lock marked "U.S." and "Springfield," dated 1841, walnut full stock, all fittings iron, Caution: most of these muskets were converted to percussion by government arsenals. Original flintlock values to 3000.00

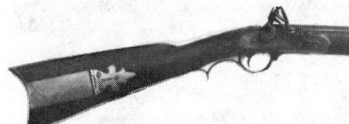

Pennsylvania Long Rifle, Peter Moll, Hellertown, Warrented No. 58, artifically striped stock, c. 1830, 55½" 1250.00

PERCUSSION LONG ARMS

Note: Conversion of flintlock long arms to percuss was common practice. Most British, French and U.S. military flintlock model longarms listed in the previous section can be found in percussion. Values for these percussion converted pistols may be from 40 to 60% of the flintlock value noted previously.

Kentucky Rifle (c. 1845), 39" octagonal barrel, 38 cal., full curly maple stock with brass fore-end cap, lock marked "Joseph Golcher," large brass open work patch box on right side of butt, silver star inlay on left cheek piece, twelve silver inlays on each side of stock, brass trigger guard and ramrod pipes 1750.00

U.S. Model 1841 Rifle (Missippi Rifle) c. 1850, 33″ round barrel, 54 cal., lockplate marked "Harpers Ferry" and "U.S. 1850," full walnut stock with two barrel bands, large brass patch box on right side of butt, brass trigger guard and butt plate **750.00**

U.S. Model 1855 (Maynard Tape Primer), 40″ round barrel, 58 cal., full walnut stock with brass fore-end cap, three iron barrel bands, lock marked "U.S./Springfield" and "1858," American eagle stamped on lid of tape primer compartment **750.00**

U.S. Model 1861, 40″ round barrel, 58 cal., full walnut stock with three iron barrel bands, lock marked "U.S./Springfield" and "1862," American eagle stamp **500.00**

FIREPLACE EQUIPMENT

The fireplace was a gathering point in the colonial home for heat, meals, and social interaction. It maintained its dominate position until the introduction of central heating in the mid-19th century.

Because of the continued popularity of the fireplace, its accessories still are manufactured, usually in an early American motif. Modern blacksmiths are reproducing the old iron implements; examine any item most carefully before purchasing.

Firebox, 14 x 20 x 22″, iron, ornate handles, feet $125.00

Andirons (pair)

Adams style, brass, 18″ **125.00**
Chippendale, brass, urn top, spurred arch, penny foot, 17¼″ .. **800.00**
Federal, brass, steeple top, ball feet, 22¼″ **600.00**
Federal, brass, Richard Wittingham (signed), spurred arch, ball feet, 17¾″ **1750.00**
Firedogs, wrought iron, 19th c. .. **250.00**
Hessian soldiers, cast iron, 20″ .. **500.00**
Queen Anne, wrought iron and brass, knife blade standard, 18¼″ **450.00**
Queen Anne, brass, ball finial, penny feet, rectangular base, RI, 17¼″ **1600.00**

Bellows, wood
15½″, turtle back, yellow ground with stencil border **110.00**
17¾″, turtle back, yellow ground with red roses **90.00**
17⅞″, red ground with gold fruit . **70.00**
24¾″, advertising, "Bellows Made and Repaired," iron nozzle, leather trim **175.00**

Boxes, Coal
Brass, slanted lid, ball feet, "Repousse," 12 x 16 x 17″ **250.00**
Brass, plated, hinged slanted lid, paper picture on front, 11½ x 14 x 15″ **75.00**
Cast iron, green with floral decoration, trimmed in gold, English, 19 x 20″ **150.00**

Fenders
31″, iron base, brass rail **250.00**
49½″, Federal, wirework and brass, c. 1800 .... **350.00**
52½″, Federal, wirework and brass, NY, D shape with hexagonal finials, c. 1810 .... **575.00**

Firebacks
22½″, cast iron, arched crest and tulips, dated 1794 .... **450.00**
40″, cast iron, two pieces, Gothic Revival, Whitehead and Law **1500.00**

Grate, cast iron, 9 x 17½″, mid-19th c. **50.00**

Hods
Brass, Chinese **45.00**
Brass, helmut type, scoop, burnished and lacquered **150.00**
Copper, iron feet, handle and bail **95.00**

Lighter, brass, engraved with scroll design **160.00**

Screens
Federal, maple and mahogany, rectangular top, carved, NY, c. 1820 .... **250.00**
George III, painted and gilded, dual screen inset with Chinese wallpaper, early 19th c. **200.00**
Oriental, lacquered, black with

gold stencilling, tripod feet	450.00
Victorian, wood, three sections, arch design on center section . . .	150.00
Tongs, wrought iron, spring action, 15"	75.00
Tongs, wrought iron, engraved, NE, 20¾", c. 1780	900.00
Tool set, brass, three pieces, holder, mid-19th c.	140.00

Trammels

26½", hand forged, sawtooth, late 18th c.	200.00
28½", hand forged, early	350.00
37", hand forged, 10 holes for adjustment	280.00

Trivets, wrought iron

Rams horn scroll work, pad feet .	70.00
Round, three legs with pad feet, three point center	45.00
Tulip and leaf pattern, round legs, 5½"	55.00
Tulip shape, pad feet, long handle, 11½"	160.00

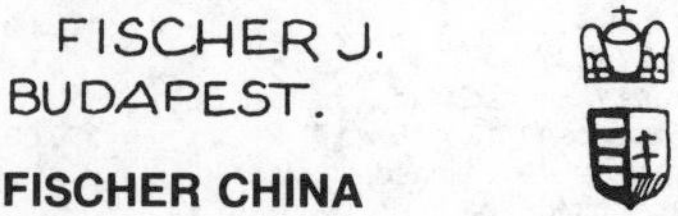

FISCHER J. BUDAPEST.

FISCHER CHINA

Moritz Fischer founded his factory in Herend, Hungary, in 1839. Herend has been a center of porcelain production from the 1790's, but collectors are interested only in porcelain produced after 1839.

There has been much confusion about this porcelain because of its quality and resemblence to the finest wares of Meissen, Chantilly, Sevres, and even Oriental Export wares. Knowingly or unknowingly, it was often bought and sold as the product of these other potteries. It is said that often forged marks of other potteries are found on Herend pieces. The mark "MF," often joined, is the mark of Moritz Fischer's pottery.

Fischer's Herend is very hard paste ware, of lovely luminosity, and exquisite decoration. These pieces are designated by certain pattern names, and the best known of these are Chantilly Fruit, Rothschild Bird, Chinese Bouquet, Victoria Butterfly, and Parsley.

He also made figural birds and animal groups, Magyar figures, individually and in groups, and Herend eagles, poised for flight. It is collectible among advanced collectors, and is not too well known because of its close resemblence to other famous china products.

Cachepot

5", handled, Rothchild Bird pattern	150.00
5", handled, Victoria Butterfly pattern	150.00

Dishes

5⅞", covered, on collared base, Parsley pattern	200.00
4½", triangular shaped, Victoria Butterfly, gold trim	125.00

Plates

7½", luncheon plate, Chantilly Fruit pattern	85.00
10½", dinner plate, Chantilly Fruit pattern	110.00
10¼", dinner plate, Parsley pattern	110.00
Sauce Boat, Chantilly Fruit pattern, with underplate and matching china ladle	225.00

Tureens

Covered, 8½" diam., two handled, Chantilly Fruit pattern with natural fruit molded finial	300.00
Covered, 8½", two handled, Victoria Butterfly, with large molded finial	300.00

Vases

3", gold top, cream bottom, hand painted florals	75.00
7¼", reticulated, decorated with blue florals, green foliage, gold handles	150.00
8¼", multicolored enameling, reticulated, gold rim	300.00
8½", reticulated barrel shaped vase in a holder	350.00
9", triangular top and base, polychromed, gold trim	300.00
10", reticulated, ornate handles, multicolored with heavy gold trim	300.00
12", reticulated, urn shaped, blue decor	350.00
15", reds, blues, gold trim, reticulated, top and bottom	395.00
Vegetable dish, open, 9½", Chantilly Fruit pattern	125.00

FISH SETS
See GAME PLATES

FITZHUGH

Fitzhugh is one of the most recognized Chinese Export porcelain patterns. It was named for the Fitzhugh family for which the first dinner service was made. The peak period of production was 1780 to 1850.

Fitzhugh features an oval center medallion or monogram surrounded by four groups of flowers or emblems. The border is similar to that on Nanking china. Occasional border variations are found with butterfly and honeycomb among the rarest.

Blue is the common color. Color is a key factor in pricing with rarity in ascending order of orange, green, sepia, mulberry, yellow, black, and gold. Combinations of colors are scarce.

Spode Porcelain Company, England, currently is producing a copy of the Fitzhugh pattern in several colors.

used mainly for liquids. Some whiskey flasks are shaped to fit a pocket. The historical flasks are very desirable collectors' items and, therefore, demand a good price. The numbers used refer to *American Glass* by George L. and Helen McKearin.

Platter, 15¾″ long, blue $425.00

Basin, blue, 16½″	475.00
Basket, reticulated, blue, 10¼″ . . .	575.00
Basket, reticulated, covered, brown, 10⅜ x 10⅞″	1750.00
Bowl, green, cuaterfoil rim, 9½″, c. 1820	800.00
Brush Box, blue	525.00
Butter Tub, cover and stand, blue, 5¼ x 6⅜″	550.00
Garden Seat, green, 18½″ high, c. 1850	4000.00
Plates, 10″	
Black	1000.00
Blue	200.00
Green	325.00
Orange	275.00
Sepia	425.00
Yellow	500.00
Platter, blue, oval, well and tree, 17½″	450.00
Platter, orange, oval, American eagle, 12″	4000.00
Soup, yellow, peony and beast medallion, 7⅞″	2000.00
Vegetable, covered, blue, 9⅝″ long	425.00

FLASKS

A flask is a container with a narrow neck,

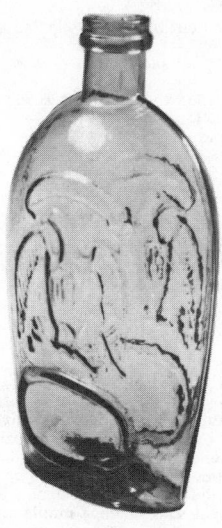

Eagle, pint, aqua $75.00

Anchor, quart, amber	35.00
Chestnuts	
5″, amber	100.00
6½″, 16 Swirled ribs, aqua	75.00
6½″, vertical ribs, aqua	85.00
Coventry Glass Works, Coventry, Conn.	
Pint, olive green	125.00
Quart, olive green	135.00
Eagles	
With cornucopia, light golden amber	120.00
For Pike's Peak, aqua	75.00
Double eagle, quart, aqua, (GII-31)	85.00
Ravenna Glass Co. on reverse side	400.00
Stoddard on reverse side, pint, amber	85.00
Union, ½ pint	75.00

Flag, American, twenty stars, eagle, aqua, pontil mark	300.00
Granite Glass Co., Stoddard, N. H., pint, olive	150.00
Pitkin type	
Broken swirl, 36 ribs, olive green, blown; Keene, Conn.	150.00
Broken swirl, 30 ribs, tubular pontil	155.00
Three swirled ribs, 7⅛″, tubular pontil	150.00
Thirty-two right hand swirls, 3 ribs, olive amber	150.00
Thirty-six left hand swirls, yellow green	75.00
Stiegel-type, vertical and swirled ribbing to the left	125.00
Scroll, two stars, pint, amber (GIX-10)	350.00
"Success to the Railroad," Double, pontil, olive green	175.00
Sunburst, yellow-green, pontil	450.00
"Traveler's Companion," pint, "Ravenna Glass Co.," on reverse, 8-point star	350.00
Vertical ribs, 25, ½″, pint, tiny, light green	125.00
Washington and Taylor, quart, aqua	85.00

FLOWING BLUE

Flowing Blue or Flow Blue, as it is sometimes called, is a cobalt blue, on white earthenware or ironstone, that had been let "flow" in the firing, producing a deep, flowing or smudging effect in the pattern. Its designs were copies of Japanese and Chinese motifs and carried names suggesting Oriental places. It was made from 1825–1850, by various potters in the Staffordshire district — Adams and Co.; Davenport, Podmore and Walker; Alcock (Samuel); Wedgwood; Ridgeway, etc.

About 1880 to 1890 and well into the 1900's, flowing blue again was made, this time a little more to the Victorian taste. The "flowing" was not quite so pronounced, ware was lighter than ironstone, but not so fine as porcelain, patterns were daintier and gold trim was added. Henry Alcock, Samuel's son, made "Touraine," one of the later patterns that is most popular among collectors today.

The older ware is becoming quite scarce and expensive. Collectors have been concentrating on the later patterns, although older pieces are still much sought-after, when available. These older patterns were also made in colors other than blue, one of them being a "flowing," deep brown, almost black which is commonly known as "mulberry." Prices would be about the same for older blue and mulberry.

See also MULBERRY CHINA.

Plate, 8½″, "Non Pareil", Burgess & Leigh, Middleport Pottery $45.00

EARLY PATTERNS — C. 1825–1850

Bowls	
Chapoo, 6 x 9″ oval, Wedgwood .	165.00
Chapoo, waste or gravy bowl, deep flow blue	150.00
Kin Shan, 8½″, Phillips and Sons, c. 1840–1850	95.00
Manilla, 8″, Podmore and Walker .	90.00
Butters, covered	
Amoy, Davenport, c. 1840–1850 .	125.00
Athens	75.00
Brunswick, Wood and Sons	125.00
Chusan	100.00
Coburg	125.00
Khyber, J. Meir and Son	150.00
Oregon	175.00
Pelew, Challinor, c. 1840–1850 . .	195.00
Scinde, Alcock	200.00
Chamber Pot, Khyber, Adams, & Co.	175.00
Creamers	
Corean, Podmore and Walker, c. 1850	95.00
Ferrarra, Wedgwood	100.00
Formosa	85.00
Hong Kong	75.00
Indian Jar, T. F. & Co., (Thomas Ford), c. 1840	175.00
Leipsic, Clementson, octagonal . .	157.50
Lugano, Ridgeway	75.00
Manilla, Podmore and Walker . . .	85.00
Penang, Ridgeway	85.00
Simla	75.00
Cups and Saucers	
Jeddo, Adams and Co., handle-less, c. 1840	75.00
Khyber, J. Meir and Son, handle-	

less	75.00
Khyber, Adams and Co., handle-	
less	75.00
Pelew, Challinor, handleless, c.	
1740–1850	85.00
Sobraon, T. W., handleless	125.00

Gravy Boats

Amoy	225.00
Cashmere	225.00
Damascus, T. F. and Co.	175.00
Gothic, T. E. Mayer	200.00
Jeddo	145.00
Madras	100.00
Manilla, Podmore and Walker . . .	200.00
Mongolia	150.00
Oregon	225.00
Poppy, Wedgwood	215.00

Plates

Birmah,"C," 7¼"	35.00
Cashmere, 7¼"	50.00
Chusan, 7¼"	35.00
Formosa, Ridgeway, 7¼"	42.50
Indian Jar, 8½"	50.00
Khyber, 9½"	50.00
Pelew, 9½"	50.00
Scinde, 10"	55.00
Sobraon, 10"	55.00
Temple, 10"	60.00
Tonquin, 10"	55.00
Wamphoa, 10"	55.00

Platters

Cashmere, 16", Morley	350.00
Chusan, 18 x 14"	200.00
Coburg, 18 x 14"	195.00
Scinde, 20"	295.00
Sauce Boat, Gothic, T. E. Mayer . . .	160.00

Sauces

Alhambra	15.00
Amherst-Japan, Minton	15.00
Atlanta, Wedgwood	25.00
Chapoo	25.00

Soup Plates

Amoy, wide rim	60.00
Arabesque	60.00
Athens	50.00
Tea Pot, Ferrara, Wedgwood	225.00
Tureen, covered, Chusan	150.00
Wash Bowl and Pitcher set, Cam-	
bridge, Meakin	550.00

LATER PATTERNS — C. 1880–1900's

Bone Dishes

Alaska . . . . **ea.**	12.00
Andora	14.00
Touraine	18.00

Bowls

Conway, 9", New Wharf Pottery	
Co.	28.00
Del Monte, 10", Johnson Bros. . .	32.50
Dorothy, 10½", Grindley	32.50

Butter Pats

Marachal-Neil, Grindley	12.50
Touraine	18.00

Creamers

Alaska	32.50
Argyle	20.00
Beaufort	28.00
Cecil	30.00
Chiswick, Ridgeway, c. 1897	35.00
Conway	35.00
Dorothy, Grindley, c. 1897	35.00
Hafburg, Grindley, gold trim	32.50
Irene	28.00
Cup and Saucer, Hafburg, Grindley,	
gold trim and handle	40.00
Dinner Set, Lorne, Grindley, 45	
pieces	1350.00

Gravy Boats

Claremont	55.00
Eclipse, Johnson Bros.	55.00
Janett-#292398, Grindley	50.00
Lancaster, New Wharf Pottery Co.	65.00
Lotus, Grindley, gold trim	60.00

Pitchers

Beaufort, 6", Grindley	69.00
Cecil, 6", Till and Sons	69.00
Conway, 10", New Wharf Pottery	
Co.	95.00
Dorothy, 10", Grindley, c. 1897 . .	95.00

Plates

Andora, 6", Johnson Bros.	15.00
Beaufort, 6", Grindley	10.00
Cecil, 7", Till and Sons	8.00
Clarence, 7", Grindley	8.00
Clifton, 7", Grindley	8.00
Conway, 9½", New Wharf Pottery	
Co.	19.00
Del Monte, 9½", Johnson Bros. .	20.00
Florida, 10", Johnson Bros., with	
gold	30.00
Hafburg, 10", Grindley, with gold .	25.00
Jewel, 10"	22.50
Kenilworth, 10", Johnson Bros. . .	22.00
Normandy, 10", Johnson Bros. . .	30.00
Richmond, 10", Grindley	25.00
St. Louis, 10", Johnson Bros. . . .	30.00

Platters

Florida, 12", Grindley	60.00
Lorne, 14 x 10", Grindley	60.00
Lotus, 14", Grindley, with gold trim	60.00

Soup Plates

Conway, 9"	20.00
Dorothy, 9"	22.50
Duchess, 9"	20.00
Eclipse, 9"	15.00
Irene, 9"	15.00

Sugars, covered

Carleton	50.00
Cecil, Till and Sons	52.50

Tureens, covered

Florida, 12 x 8"	160.00
Lancaster, New Wharf Pottery Co.	175.00
Lorne	160.00

Platter, 10½ x 14", "Holland," Johnson Bros., England $50.00

Lotus, Grindley, with gold trim ...	150.00
Vegetables Dishes, covered	
Florida, 10"	40.00
Touraine, 9¾"	42.50
Waldorf, New Wharf Pottery Co. .	40.00

FOOD MOLDS

Decorative food molds were made for a variety of foods — butter, cakes, candles, puddings, etc. Their main object was to present the food in a pleasing and appetizing manner. Most early food molds are collected today for decorative purposes, but also they are used for their original purpose.

See also BUTTER PRINTS.

Cake Mold, 2# size, Lamb, No. 866 ....$55.00

BUTTER MOLDS

Acorn, one pound, rectangular	45.00
Cloverleaf, one pound, rectangular .	50.00
Cows	
Cylinder type	95.00
Hexagon barrel, pewter bands ..	130.00
Daisy, 4"	50.00
Ferns	
Rectangular	45.00
Round, 4½"	45.00
Letters	
L., Rectangular	35.00
W., Round	35.00
Maltese Cross, hinged	65.00
Maple Leaves, two, rectangular ...	75.00
*Pineapple	60.00
Plain, glass	35.00
*Sheaf of Wheat	
Rectangular	65.00
Round, two stars	185.00
Star	45.00
Strawberries, two, rectangular	65.00
Swan, one pound	85.00
Thistle, 1½"	30.00

CANDY MOLDS (TIN, TIN AND COPPER, ETC.)

Basket, 3½ x 6"	30.00
Bridge set, heart, spade, diamond .	55.00
Clown, 10", 4 pieces	40.00
Duck	22.50
Frog, 5"	25.00
Groom, 3½"	17.50
Humpty Dumpty, 5½", two side, locks embossed	70.00
Jenny Lind, 3 pieces	70.00
Lion	25.00
Pineapple	25.00
Rabbits	
5¾", tin	27.50
7½"	30.00
10", standing, holding egg	40.00
Rooster, 5¼"	30.00
Rose	20.00
Santa Claus, 6½"	55.00
Snowman, 4"	30.00
Three Wise Men on Horses, 8 pieces	85.00
Witch on Broom, 6"	25.00

ICE CREAM MOLDS (PEWTER, IRON, ETC.)

Apple	20.00
Artichoke	25.00
Banana	25.00
Bell	35.00
Bride and Groom	50.00
Camel, 2¼ x 6¼"	30.00
Champagne Bottle in Ice Bucket ..	55.00
Colonial Lady	30.00
Corn	25.00
Eagle, American	70.00
Elk's Head	30.00
Fire Engine, 4½"	40.00
Fish, 4"	30.00

Football, 3"	22.50
Grapes, 5"	30.00
Hatchet, G. W.	35.00
Heart	25.00
Heart and Cupid	30.00
Hen	20.00
Hen on Basket	30.00
Hobby Horse	35.00
Kiwanis	20.00
Leaf	25.00
Lincoln	65.00
Pumpkin	30.00
Rings	
Engagement	20.00
Wedding	20.00
Rooster	25.00
Santa Claus	50.00
Sea Shell	20.00
Shield with Stars and Stripes	50.00
Star	20.00
Stork	30.00
Strawberry	25.00
Tulip, 3"	20.00
Turkey, 4"	30.00
Uncle Sam	40.00
Vintage Car	55.00
Washington George, bust	55.00
Watermelon	25.00

POTTERY MOLDS (PUDDING, CUSTARDS, ETC.)

Asparagus, 3½ x 6 x 8"	35.00
Nelon	25.00
Pea Pods	35.00

MISCELLANEOUS MOLDS

Fish, copper	35.00
Grape, 4", glass, c. 1897	25.00
Pear, 2 x 7¾", copper	25.00
Rabbit, 4½", copper	25.00
Santa Claus, 12", iron	70.00
Sunburst, 2¼ x 8¼", copper	25.00
Horseshoe, 5½ x 6", tole	70.00

FOSTORIA GLASS   FOSTORIA

Fostoria Glass Co. began operations at Fostoria, Ohio, in 1887. A few years later they moved to Moundsville, W. Va., where they continue to manufacture quality glassware. Many of their discontinued patterns and items are being collected today.

Bowls

4½", Fairfax, amber	7.50
7½", Queen Anne, fluted top	20.00
8", American, handled	35.00
13", Holly	20.00
Console, Grape Brocade, green	49.00

Cream and Sugar, each 4¾" long, pink opalescent, set $42.50

Console, Vesper, amber	25.00
Box, cigarette, American	30.00
Cake Stand, 10" square, American	32.00
Candlelabra, Baroque, 3-lite, pair	35.00
Candlesticks	
2", June, pair	25.00
5", Fairfax, pair	25.00
Trindle, Romance, pair	65.00
Champagnes	
Chintz, etch	18.00
Meadow Rose, crystal, each	15.00
Trojan, topaz	16.00
Compotes	
6½", Vesper	28.00
Colony	10.00
Creamers and Sugars	
American, individual	12.00
Meadow Rose, crystal, each	19.00
Versailles	42.50
Cruet, American	22.50
Cups and Saucers	
Colony	8.50
Meadow Rose, crystal, each	15.00
Royal, amber	15.00
Jar, dresser, elephant on lid, crystal	15.00
Jug, June, azure, optic, footed	130.00
Goblets	
Chintz, each	20.00
Colony	7.75
June, topaz	25.00
Versailles, azure	25.00
Plates	
7", Mayfair, topaz	4.00
7½", June, blue	8.50
9½", American	6.00
10", Colony	12.00
10½", Royal, amber	15.00
Punch Ladle, clear	42.00
Relishes	
8½", Virginia	9.00
Midnight Rose, 5 part	25.00
American, divided	10.00
Colony, handled, 3 part	15.00
Salt and Peppers	
Fairfax	25.00
June, pink	95.00
Versailles	95.00

Goblet, 7½", "Mother of Pearl" with vaseline stem and base, c. 1925, set of 6 .... $72.00

Sherbets
  American 4.00
  Baroque, yellow 6.00
  June, topaz 23.00
Spooner, Colony 25.00
Syrup, Priscilla, green with gold ... 70.00
Toothpicks
  Sylvan, all over diamond 22.00
  Brazilian 24.00
Tumblers
  June, footed 10.00
  Meadow Rose, souvenir, footed,
  crystal 12.00
  Priscilla, green with gold 40.00
  Romance, crystal, each 6.50
  Trojan, topaz 10.00
  Versailles, pink 10.00
Vases
  6", Spool, azure 22.00
  8", American 25.00

FRAKTUR

Fraktur, the calligraphy associated with the Pennsylvania Germans, is named for the elaborate first letter found in many of the handdrawn examples. Throughout its history printed, partially printed-handdrawn, and fully handdrawn works existed side by side. Fraktur often were made by the school teachers or ministers living in the rural areas of Pennsylvania, Maryland and Virginia. Many artists are unknown.

Fraktur exists in several forms—geburts and taufschein (birth and baptismal certificates), vorschrift (writing example, often with alphabet), haus sagen (house blessing), bookplates and marks, rewards of merit, illuminated religious text, valentines, and drawings. Although collected for decoration, the key element in Fraktur is the text.

Fraktur prices rise and fall along with the American Folk Art market. Currently prices are one-quarter to one-half their level of the mid-1970's. The key market place is Pennsylvania and the middle Atlantic states. The major study collection of Fraktur is found in the Rare Book room of the Free Library of Philadelphia.

Birth Certificate, 15⅜ x 18⅜ overall including frame, dated 1834, Penn. Dutch $65.00

HANDDRAWN

Brechall, Martin, birth and baptismal, Northampton Co., Pa., 13½ x 15¾" 700.00
Cross Legged Angel artist, birth and baptismal, S.E. Pa., 12½ x 15", 1813 .... 1200.00
Faber, Wilheminus, birth and baptis-

mal, cut work, Berks Co., Pa., 7½
x 9½" 1250.00

Flying Angel artist, birth and baptismal, Northampton Co., Pa., 13½ x
16" 850.00

Hoevelman, Arnold, birth and baptismal, Lancaster Co., Pa., 13½ x
16" 750.00

Krebs, Frederick, birth and baptismal
combined with marriage, 12¼ x
15½", 1804 .... 1350.00

Mt. Pleasant artist, birth and baptismal, Lancaster Co., Pa., 7½ x
9½", 1808 restored 1500.00

Peterman, Daniel, birth and baptismal, York Co., Pa., 13½ x 15½" . 2500.00

Unknown, birth and baptismal, S.E.
Pa., bright red, yellow, and blue
flowers and geometric designs,
7¾ x 12½", dated 1765 .... 17500.00

Unknown, bookplate, Berks Co., Pa.,
6½ x 3¾", 1834 .... 1000.00

Unknown, drawing, Pa., bird, 5½ x
6" 350.00

Unknown, drawing, Pa., floral, 6¾ x
4¼" 125.00

Unknown, Vorschrift, S.E. Pa., Men-
nonite, 7½ x 13" 675.00

Young, Henry, birth and baptismal,
Center Co., Pa., couple, 12 x 8" . 1350.00

Young, Henry, birth and baptismal,
Lycoming Co., Pa., single woman,
10½ x 7¾" 2500.00

HANDDRAWN-PRINTED

Dulheuer, Henrich, birth and baptismal, 13¼ x 17" 800.00

Krebs, Frederick, birth and baptismal, two parrots, Reading form, 13
x 15" 750.00

Otto, Henrich, birth and baptismal,
13 x 15¾" 1250.00

Pseudo-Otto artist, birth and baptismal, Md., 13¼ x 16¼" 950.00

Speyer, Frederick, birth and baptismal, Reading form, 12¾ x 15½" . 750.00

PRINTED

Adam and Eve
Baumann, Ephrata 275.00
Sage, H., Reading 145.00

Birth and Baptismal
Baumann, J., Ephrata 750.00
Baumann, S., Ephrata 425.00
Blumer & Bush, Allentown 47.50
Currier and Ives, New York 17.50
Dreisbach, Bath 80.00
Eagle Bookstore, Reading 20.00
Ebner, Allentown 75.00
Hantsch, Reading 95.00

Lutz & Scheffer, Harrisburg 20.00
Peter, Harrisburg 45.00
Ritter, Johann, Reading, late form 40.00
Schnee, Jospeh, Lebanon 375.00
*Note: If signed by Scrivener, in-
crease value by 50%*

Haus Sagen
Blumer & Bush, Allentown 95.00
Ritter, Reading 55.00

FRAMES
See FURNITURE

FRANKOMA POTTERY

**John N. Frank, an instructor of ceramics at
the University of Oklahoma, founded the
Frankoma Pottery at Sapulpa, Ok., in 1936.
After a fire in 1938, the pottery was inactive
until its reactivation in 1943. Modern pieces
are marked with "FRANKOMA."**

**The recent interest in American Art pottery
has focused attention on Frankoma pottery.
Collectors should concentrate on early examples, many of which still are available at reasonable prices.**

**Cider Pitcher and 6 Mugs, green,
brown, set $42.00**

Bean Pot, green-brown, block caps,
lidded, 6½ x 8½" 20.00
Bowl, mottled brown-yellow, early
Leopard mark, 11" 60.00
Bowl, mottled brown-yellow, 12" ... 17.50
Candlesticks (pair), light brown 12.50
Christmas Plate, 1969 .... 6.00
Console Set, brown-cream glaze,
loop shaped candleholders, boat
shaped bowl 25.00
Cookie Jar, mottled blue 37.50
Creamer, brown-green, 8" 7.50
Cup and Saucer, demitasse 6.00
Honey Pot, hive with embossed bee 10.00
Jug, handled, green-brown, raised
letters "The Gardens Country
Store," 5½" 20.00

Leaf Dish, green-brown, impressed "226," 12" ... **8.00**

Mugs, political, elephant, red or black ... **15.00**

Pitchers
3⅛", covered, mottled blue ... **5.00**
8", green-brown, ice lip, impressed "5-D" ... **15.00**

Sugar, Aztec, block caps, one handle ... **7.00**

Vases
4½", mottled blue, ball shape ... **8.00**
6", brown-green, ram's head handles ... **12.00**
6", blue-brown, bulbous shape ... **9.00**
7½", rose, bulbous shape, paper label ... **10.00**
9", brown-green, signed ... **10.00**

Wall Pockets
Acorn, tan ... **6.50**
Girl, green ... **7.50**
Indian Brave and Squaw, pair ... **20.00**

Water Set, powder blue glaze, lidded pitcher and six tumblers ... **40.00**

FRUIT CRATE ART

Fruit crate art had its beginning in the 1880's when orange growers in California began using lithographed labels on their wooden crates. Soon other fruit growers followed suit. The earlier labels were romantic and sentimental. Later, the labels became more masculine to appeal to the male wholesale buyer.

Cardboard boxes replaced the wooden crates in the 1940's, marking the end of the colorful labels. These labels, however, have regained their popularity and are now being framed and displayed in homes and even in museums as a part of the history of American art.

Airship, Oranges, old transport plane descending at night, Fillmore ... **7.50**

America's Delight, Apples, orchard scene ... **10.00**

Arab, Lemons, Arab with gun, on horseback, San Dimas ... **7.50**

Barbara Worth, Grapefruit, cowgirl heroine, Riverside ... **15.00**

Basketball, Lemons, Girls playing basketball in 1920's uniforms, Claremont ... **5.00**

Big Ben, Oranges, Tower with Big Ben clock, Villa Park ... **15.00**

Black Hawk, Oranges, fierce-looking Indian, Riverside ... **17.50**

Blue Goose, Oranges, candy-box style lettering, San Francisco ... **5.00**

California Dream, Oranges, two gold

Depend-On, C.M. Kopp Co., Yakima, Wash. ... **$2.50**

peacocks, enchanted house, c. 1928, Placentia ... **7.00**

Dixie Boy, Grapefruit, black boy eating fruit, Florida ... **3.50**

Evergreen Lemons, Mountain and lemon grove, Villa Park ... **5.00**

First American, Lemons and oranges, Indian girl, teepee, c. 1905, Los Angeles ... **50.00**

Florigold, Oranges, gold coin, Indian head, Florida ... **2.00**

Golden Bowl, Lemons, golden ornate footed bowl, Santa Paula ... **18.00**

Golden Trout, Oranges, large trout jumping out of water, c. 1945, Orange Cove ... **10.00**

Hiawatha, Oranges, face of Indian brave, Strathmore ... **7.50**

Honeymoon, Lemons, black orange and white castle in moonlight, Los Angeles ... **15.00**

Sunkist emblem, 2", c. 1916, Porterville ... **35.00**

Lincoln, Oranges, full color bust, Riverside ... **2.00**

Magnolia, Oranges, large magnolia blossom, Porterville ... **3.00**

Mercury, Oranges, Mercury sitting on box of fruit, Redlands ... **12.00**

Mission, Lemons, Santa Barbara Mission, Santa Barbara ... **7.50**

New Deal, Apples, Bee playing cards ... **3.50**

Old Mission Oranges, three monks by mission, Fullerton ... **3.50**

Red Skin, Oranges, Indian at camp, Rialto ... **7.50**

Rooster, Oranges, crowing rooster, c. 1927 ... **5.00**

San Francisco, Oranges, Golden Gate Bridge, yellow bird, San

Francisco 35.00
Sea Cool, Lemons, green stylized
waves, Oxnard 1.50
Sea Gull, Lemons, three flying gulls,
Uplant 3.00
Shamrock, Lemons, green shamrock
over orange grove, Placentia ... 2.50
Squirrel, Oranges, Squirrel on
branch, Riverside 6.00
Stonewall Jackson Oranges, full col-
or portrait, Placentia 8.00
Sunkist, Apples, Sunkist emblem, c.
1912 .... 20.00
Sunkist, Apples, Ranch scene with
sun shining on apples, c. 1912,
Watsonville 16.00
Tom Cat, Lemons, black cat, Orosi.. 5.00
20th Century, Apples, futuristic
scene 5.00

FRUIT JARS

**Fruit or canning jars for preserving food
have become very collectible. Thomas W.
Dyott, one of Philadelphia's earliest and most
innovative glass makers, was promoting his
glass canning jars in 1829. John Landis Mason patented his screw-type canning jar on
November 30, 1858. This date refers to the
patent date, not age of jar. There are thousands of types of canning jars in many colors, types of closures, and embossings.**

Atlas Improved Mason, c. 1890,
glass lid metal screw band, aqua
or green 2.50
Atlas Mason's Patent Nov. 30, 1858,
½ gal., zinc lid, olive green 15.00
Atlas Mason's Patent Nov. 30, 1858,
quart, screw top, olive green 15.00
Baker Bros., pint, wax sealer, groove
ring, green or aqua, c. 1885 .... 28.00
Baltimore Glass Works, quart, aqua 95.00
Banner Trademark warranted, quart,
glass top, aqua 7.50
B.B.G.M. Co., quart, glass lid, metal
screw band, blue, green, aqua, c.
1887 .... 28.00
Borden's Milk Co., pint, c. 1885,
hexagonal, metal band, glass insert 7.50
Clarke Fruit Jar Co., 7¼″, Cleveland, Oh., aqua 18.50
Climax, pint, full wire bail, green
glass lid 8.50
Cohansey Glass Mfg. Co., Pat.
MCH2077 under bottom, barrel
shaped, aqua 15.00
Dalbey's Fruit Jar, quart, c. 1866,
glass lid, deep aqua 42.50
The Dandy, 7½″, amber 12.00

Crown Imperial, quart, aqua, glass insert top with zinc screw band . $12.00

The Dunkley Celery Co., Kalamazoo,
quart, four piece mold, ground top,
amethyst 15.00
The Eclipse, quart, c. 1868, wax
seal, aqua 27.50
E. G. Co., imperial, quart, monogram, clear 7.50
The Empire, quart, c. 1860, glass
stopper, deep blue 48.00
Eureka, Pat. Feb. 9, 1864, quart,
Dunbar, W. Va., aqua 12.50
Flaccus Co., E. C. Trade Mark, elk
and floral design, milk glass 80.00
Franklin Dexter Fruit Jar, quart, c.
1865, zinc lid, aqua 13.50
The Gem, quart, Pat. Nov. 26, 1867,
clear 5.00
Glassboro, three sizes, c. 1880-
1900, zinc band and glass insert,
light to dark green 12.00
Hansee's Place Home Jar, 7″, Pat.
Dec. 19, 1899 .... 22.50
E. C. Hazard Co., quart, Shrewsbury,
N. J., wire clamp, aqua 5.00
Hazel-Atlas Lightning Seal, quart, full
wire bail and glass lid 7.50
Holz, Clarke and Taylor, quart,
screw on glass lid, aqua, c. 1878 . 48.00
Hudson Bay, quart, clear, picture of

a beaver on side, coat of arms, rawhide clamp top, square 15.00

The Ideal, quart, c. 1890, zinc lid, clear 7.50

Independent Jar, quart, c. 1888, screw on glass lid, clear or amethyst 22.50

Ivanhoe, quart, glass lid and wire bail 5.00

J. and B. Fruit Jar, quart, c. 1898, zinc lid, clear or amethyst 22.50

Lightning, Putnam 824 under bottom, sheared top, aqua 10.00

P. Lorillard & Co., pint, 6½″, sheared top, amber 12.00

Masons Patent, Nov. 30, 1858, quart, aqua, screw top 7.50

Mason's Patent, 1858, quart, zinc top 6.00

Mason's Patent, November, 1858, quart, amber or yellow 13.50

Mason's Patent, Nov. 30, 1858, C. F. J. Co., pint, monogram, aqua . .   5.00

Mason's, quart, under name an arrow and Patent, Nov. 30, 1858, sheared top 15.00

Miller's Fine Flavor, quart, three bees in circle, aqua 14.50

Millville Atmospheric Fruit, jar, Whitall's Patent, June 18, 1861, clamp top 40.00

National, quart, c. 1885, metal top .   5.00

N Star, quart, metal top and wax seal, blue 15.00

Ohio Quality Mason, quart, clear . . .   5.00

Potter and Bodine, Phila., quart, in script, glass top and clamp, aqua .   37.50

The Queen, quart, circled by Pat. Dec. 28, Pat. June 16, 1868, wax seal, green 15.00

Quong Hop and Co., 12 oz., glass lid wire bail Chinese writing, clear . . .   7.50

Root Mason, quart, c. 1910, zinc screw on lid, aqua, green or blue .   5.00

The Rose, three sizes, c. 1920, screw on lid, clear 8.50

Safety Wide Mouth Mason, Salem Glass Works, Salem, N. J., ½ gal., zinc lid, aqua or green 12.50

Schram, 4″, Schram St. Louis on bottom, clear or amethyst 7.50

J. P. Smith Son and Co., Pittsburgh, quart, clear 15.00

Spencer's Patent, quart, wax dipped cork, aqua 27.50

Stone Mason Fruit Jar, Union Stoneware Co., Red Wing, Minn., ½ gal., sand crock 13.50

Suey Fung Yuen Co., quart clear, Chinese writing 7.50

Swazyee's Fruit Jar, quart, pint, zinc

top, aqua 10.00

Telephone Jar, quart, full wire bail, green glass top 14.50

Union Fruit Jar, quart, c. 1866, wax seal and metal top, aqua 15.00

The Valve Jar Co., Phila., 1½ pint, Pat'd Mar. 10, 1868, glass lid wire coil clamp, sheared top, aqua . . .   110.00

W and Co., quart, green 15.00

Joshua Wright, Phila., pontil barrel type 90.00

FRY GLASS

The H. C. Fry Glass Co., Rochester, Pa., began operating in 1901, and ceased production in 1933. At first, their main products were cut glass. Later, an art-glass type of ware was made, but only for a few months during 1926 and 1927. This was known as "Foval." It is primarily pearly blue in color, and other than a simple Delft blue or Jade green contrasting color trim, the items were no further decorated. These were the only two colors produced commercially by Fry. Fry Foval was seldom, if ever signed. Fry also made a silky opalescent ovenware which is now quite collectible.

Note: **Some of Fry's rarer pieces were produced on Fry blanks, which were sold to the Rockwell Co. and marketed under their name.**

Creamer, 4⅝″, oval; sugar, 4½″, oval, blue opalescent, set $95.00

Bowl, 9½″, fruit, delft blue on flared rim and stem, footed, Foval 300.00

Cake pan, 8½″, square, ovenware .   16.00

Candlesticks, blue wafers and threading on opalescent white, Foval, pair 195.00

Casserole, covered, dated, ovenware 20.00

Compote, 12″, Foval, pale green with white rim and wafer stem . . .   250.00

Cup and Saucer, with jade green handle, Foval 55.00

Goblets

4½″, opal with sterling bowl with green foot 45.00

Opalescent base and stem, pink cone top, Foval 60.00

Juice reamer, ovenware	16.00
Perfume bottle, with blue capped dauber, petticoat shape, Foval . . .	110.00

Pitchers

9", cobalt blue handle, opalescent stripe on vaseline	100.00
9½", crackle, transparent lime green handle	65.00

Plates

8½", light green border rim, Foval	35.00
9½", Delft blue rim, Foval	45.00
9", pie plate, ovenware	16.00
Punch cup, clear deep blue handle, crackle	20.00
Sugar bowl, Foval, festoon pattern, green handles	175.00
Tea Set, miniature tea pot, creamer, sugar bowl, 2 cups and saucers, 2 plates, 2 underplates, Foval, 11 pieces	400.00
Tea Pot, Foval, with jade green handle and spout	110.00
Toothpick Holder, Foval, blue handles	55.00
Tray, 8", ovenware dated 1959	8.50

Vases

5¼", silver overlay, signed "Rockwell" at rim, green base	395.00
6¼", clear crackle with three applied green leaves	55.00
10½", blue with cream bases, Foval, pair	200.00
12", opalescent with pink dragloop designs, Foval	200.00
12", transparent blue with solid ball at base	110.00
Water Set, tankard pitcher, 5 footed tumblers, Foval, fiery opalescense with jade base and handle	450.00

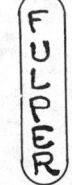

FULPER POTTERY

The American Pottery Company of Flemington, N.J., made pottery jugs and housewares from the early 1800's. They made Fulper Art Pottery from approximately 1910 to 1930.

Pieces made between 1910 and 1920 are products of a less production oriented period and subsequently are of a better quality. Almost all pieces are molded.

Vase, 7¾", Flambé glaze $125.00

Bowls

2 x 8", mottled green glaze	50.00
3 x 7", yellow to green matte . . .	40.00
6" high, 13" wide, blue flambe to white matte glaze, 1910	150.00

Boxes, covered

Cleopatra curled up on lid, pink and yellow	150.00
Stylized Art Deco woman on lid, black and white	100.00
Candleholder, hooded, 3 leaded glass inserts at the front-top, c. 1910 .	450.00
Flask, 9", 3 sided, stoppered opening, unusual circular mark, 1910 .	150.00
Flower Frog, 4 x 4½", green and brown	50.00

Perfume Lamps

Kneeling ballerina, red and beige, with base	125.00
Perched robin, brown, with base .	175.00
Pitcher, 5¼", coiled form, brown, tan and grey glaze	125.00

Vases

4 x 2", cabinet vase, deep brown, gun metal finish, c.1912	65.00
5", bud vase, tan and brown, mirror glaze	45.00
5", green snowflake, crystalline glaze	50.00
6 x 6", bulbous, green crystalline glaze, 2 handles, c. 1920	40.00
8", bulbous, beige, steel blue and gray, flambe glaze	155.00

9", green shaded to turquoise, crystalline glaze	125.00
12 x 6", 2 handles at top, brown to blue glaze, c. 1912	200.00
18 x 9", flair vase, blue flambe crystalline, c. 1915	400.00
Wall Pocket, 7 x 5", incised decor, blue glaze	55.00

FURNITURE

Prices vary considerably on furniture. The original quality, style, desirability and condition, i.e., original finish, amount of restoration and the quality of the workmanship in the restoration, are all influencing factors in determining prices.

Region also is critical. Victorian furniture is popular in New Orleans, and unpopular in New England. Oak is in demand in the Northwest, not so much in the Middle Atlantic States. Learn your area before you buy.

Collectors are urged to shop around before buying. Furniture is plentiful unless you are after a truly rare example. Find a piece which fits your needs, is pleasant, and has a price you can afford. An attempt has been made to arrive at an average price on each item listed. This list should only serve as a guide. The above enumerated factors must be taken into consideration in arriving at a final price.

FURNITURE STYLES
APPROXIMATE DATES

William and Mary	**1688–1710**
Queen Anne	**1710–1750**
Chippendale	**1754–1780**
Hepplewhite	**1786–1800**
Sheraton	**1790–1810**
Empire	**1810–1830**
Duncan Phyfe	**1800–1840**
Victorian	
Early	**1840–1850**
Rococo or Louis XV	**1845–1870**
Louis XVI	**1865–1880**
Renaissance	**1860–1885**
Eastlake	**1875–1895**

BEDS

Art Deco, headboard 43¼", burled demilune contour, stylized mask decor	350.00
Art Nouveau, single, inlaid mahogany, molded cornice, carved supports; attributed to Louis Marjorelle, c. 1890	2000.00
Brass, Double size.	
Ornate fan-shaped headboard, 62"	

Sheraton, mahogany, canopy, turned posts, fully footed, detailed carving $5000.00

high, footboard 42" high complete with rails, polished	1200.00
Standard tubular styling, burnished	750.00
Brass, single size, standard tubular styling	400.00
Brass and Iron, double size, ornate headboard and footboard, complete	500.00
Cannon Ball, double size, maple, all original	700.00
Cannon Ball, single size, rope-type, pine, original red stain	450.00
Day Beds	
American Empire, 22 x 71", pine, sleigh front end, upholstered	200.00
Chippendale, carved mahogany, shaped crestrail, N.E., c. 1780, length 76"	3500.00
Queen Anne, cherry, cabriole legs with pad feet, c. 1750, length 66½"	4500.00
Eastlake, Victorian, double size, 7' headboard, walnut with burled veneer panels, applied carvings	500.00
Empire, double size, mahogany, elaborately turned posts with leaf carving and flame finial, recessed panel headboard with turned top column, 1830	2000.00
Field	
Double size, simple slopped headboard with bulbous tapered posts, rear posts with checkered carving, rope, c. 1820	2250.00

Single size, maple, c. 1820, Sheraton style 1350.00
Tiger maple and poplar, original finish, Connecticut, 18th century . 3500.00
Jenny Lind-style
Double size, maple, original finish 650.00
Single size, walnut .... : 300.00
¾-size, walnut 500.00
Oak, double size, arched headboard and footboard, some carving ... 600.00
Pencil-Post tester, carved walnut and pine, octagonal headboard, probably Pa., c. 1800, 75½ x 55¼" 1750.00
Renaissance, Victorian
Double size, highly carved architectural headboard and footboard, c. 1860 .... 1250.00
Rococo, Victorian, double size, walnut, finely carved arches, pediments, detailed carvings of people, c. 1840–1850 .... 3000.00
Rope
Turned posts, plain headboards, pegged side rails, modern green paint, 50½ x 77" 250.00
Turned posts with vase finials, scalloped panel headboards, pegged side rails, brown flame graining, 52½ x 72" 400.00
Spool, single, maple, Pa. or N.E., late 18th century 1250.00
Tester, Chippendale, pine, arched headboards, Ct., c. 1780, 81 x 80" 4750.00

BENCHES

Carver's, 72" long, maple 700.00
Church
36 x 48" long, pine 250.00
36 x 60" long, oak 375.00
Cobbler
Three drawers, pine with leather seat, all original 750.00
12 x 16½ x 19" long, splayed sides, four drawers, hand forged strappings, pine 275.00
17 x 44" long, pine, one piece construction, refinished 450.00
Deacon (see SeHee)
Fireside, 18 x 59" high back, scalloped top and base, pine 750.00
Kneeling, 6½ x 48" long, (from church) 75.00
Kneeling, 7½ x 8 x 20" long, Pa. ... 45.00
Mammy
44", half spindle back, shaped crest, repainted and stenciled ... 750.00
72", 4-chair back, restenciled with original design, complete with

Bench, 36" long, 11½" wide, 18" high $45.00

keeper 950.00
Park, 54" long, pine with wrought iron supports, Pa. 200.00
River Boat-type, 98" long, mixed woods, metal arms, turned spindle back, plain crest 500.00
SeHee (Deacon)
Bamboo-turned, 22 spindle back, incised apron, c. 1800, length 68¾" 1500.00
Bamboo-turned, rectangular stepped crest rail, plank seat, Pa., early 19th cent. length 80" 2000.00
Tinsmith's, 34 x 70" long, oak 500.00
Water
7½ x 30 x 32", pine, two shelves, zinc lined, old paint 300.00
18 x 43 x 68" high, cupboard above shelves, shelf and 2 panelled doors below 1250.00
35 x 46", pine, boot jack ends, old paint 175.00

BENTWOOD

In 1856, Michael Thonet of Vienna perfected the process of bending wood using steam. Shortly after, Bentwood furniture became popular. Other manufacturers of Bentwood furniture were Jacob and Joseph Kohn, Philip Strobel and Son, Sheboygan Chair Co. and Tidoute Chair Co. Bentwood furniture is still being produced today by the Thonet firm and others.

Chairs
Arm, cane seat and high back ... 175.00
Arm, wooden seat, signed Thonet 200.00
High Chair, child's 150.00
Rocker, child's, 22" 100.00
Rocker, child's, signed Thonet ... 300.00

Rocker, nursing, replaced cane
seat 250.00
Rocker, sleigh, recaned back and
seat 500.00
*Rocker, sleigh, signed Thonet . .   850.00
*Side, cane seat 80.00
*Side, wood seat 50.00
Side, wood seat, signed Thonet . .   75.00

Cradles
22″ high 300.00
50″ high, on stand with bonnet
top, swing-type, all original 1300.00
Easel, Artist's 75.00

Hat Racks
9 x 36½″ long, 5 swivel pegs,
brass fittings 95.00
28 x 32″ long, 7 pegs, glove hold-
er 175.00
62″ high, floor model with umbrel-
la holder, 6 shaped hangers 300.00
Stool, 26½″ high, cane seat 60.00

BOOK CASES

Empire, three sections each with 2
doors, rope twisted columns, paw
feet, Winthrop style glass division
in doors, reeding at top molding .   2750.00
Federal, mahogany, inlay, bracket
feet, mullioned doors, N.Y., c.
1810, 51 x 32″ 750.00

Oak
17½″ square, 42½″ high, 5 slots,
6 shelves, revolving-type 400.00
29 x 32 x 59½″ wide, open, cop-
per hardware, c. 1910, signed L. &
J. G. Stickley 850.00
46 x 74″ high, with desk, shaped
glass doors; desk has pigeon
holes and drawers, mirror on side   600.00
Oak, Golden, 48 x 58″ high, 4
shelves, 4 lifting glass doors, c.
1920's 300.00

Walnut
13¼ x 48 x 74″ high, 2 drawers
below, 5 shelves, c. 1870 . . . . . .   450.00
92″ x 102″ high, carved cornice, 4
glazed arched doors above and 4
paneled doors below, adjustable
shelving, early Victorian 2000.00

BOXES

Ballot
6 x 8 x 12″, maple, dovetailed,

**Bride's, 22″ long, 14¾″ wide, oval,
Bentwood $150.00**

sliding top 150.00
6 x 7 x 11″, pine with brass fitting,
Pa. 75.00
7 x 7½ x 18¼″, pine, dovetailed,
carved wooden handles, c. 1850 .   100.00
8½ x 11 x 16″, walnut, wide
dovetailing, brass hardware 125.00

Band
New England, printed paper, rural
country scene, yellow, 10½ x 15″   350.00
New York, printed paper, Grand
(Erie) Canal, blue, 16½ x 20¼″ . .   475.00
Pennsylvania, printed paper, floral
print, pink, 12 x 16″ 250.00

Bride's
5½ x 6 x 12″ long, dome top,
original paper cover, c. 1810 . . . .   275.00
27″ long, sponge decor, c. 1840 .   350.00

Candle
5 x 5 x 12″, pine with sliding lid,
dovetailed 80.00
5 x 5 x 12″, red ground, floral mo-
tif in yellow and white, Pa. Ger-
man, c. 1840 . . . .   950.00
5 x 7½ x 15¼″, wall-type,
dovetailed, original blue paint . . .   250.00
8½ x 14¼ x 16″, oak, shaped
crest, hinged lid 125.00
10 x 13½″ long, walnut, sliding lid,
refinished 75.00
Cigar, 4 x 7½ x 12″, mahogany,
stripe inlay on lid and base, zinc
lined, nickelplated hardware 75.00

Deed
Leather cover, brass studding, pa-
per liner, iron lock, key, c. 1850 . .   100.00
Pennsylvania, painted, floral motif,
bail handle, c. 1820, 7½ x 10″ . .   2250.00
Tinware, painted, dome lid, possibly N.E., early 19th cent., length
9½″ 250.00

Hat

9½ x 12", cardboard, covered with floral paper, c. 1880 . . . . **50.00**
16" square, pine, domed top with strap handle **180.00**

Knife, mahogany

Serpentine front, inlaid, pair **1500.00**
Sheraton, pair **1750.00**
Urn-shaped, pair **1000.00**

Pantry

5¾", hand stitched **40.00**
7", splint wood **50.00**
14" oval, dark wood **65.00**
14½", 7" deep, splint wood, original stain **80.00**
25½" oval, splint wood, stained . **95.00**
Sewing, chinese export, black lacquer, gold decorated, 19th cent., length 14¼" **275.00**

Spice

Oak
4 drawers, brass pulls **125.00**
8 drawers, brass pulls **225.00**

Pine
4 drawers, labeled **100.00**
4 drawers, slant lid, all dovetailed, 18th century **450.00**
5 drawers, painted white, black trim, porcelain knobs, labeled Germany **90.00**
8 drawers, brass pulls, refinished **100.00**
8 drawers, original green paint . **195.00**
8 drawers, porcelain fronts **125.00**
9 drawers, wall-type, old paint . **150.00**

Rosewood
8 drawers, wood pulls **150.00**

Tin
Cylindrical, 6 cans with grater and 2 shakers, all original including stenciling **85.00**
Rectangular, hinged lid, 6 containers, original paint **65.00**
Tobacco, brass, oval, engraved eagle, c. 1800, length 3⅜" **400.00**

Trinket
3 x 4½ x 6", pine, carved, one piece construction **95.00**
3¼ x 6¾ x 10", mahogany, paper lined, reverse painting on glass inside lid **75.00**

CABINETS

China
Chippendale, Chinese, English,
elaborate fretwork, Centennial . . **1300.00**
Victorian, Golden oak, paw feet, two columns with leaf carving on top, rounded glass sides, c. 1900 **850.00**

Dye

Peerless, 10½ x 18½ x 32", oak, tin front **400.00**
Putnam, slant front, metal and wood, lithograph of General Putnam **250.00**
Hardware, hexagonal on rotating base, 8 drawers and 2 open shelves per unit, porcelain pulls . **650.00**
Kitchen, Hoosier, oak with glass doors, porcelain work surface, flour bin, etc. **375.00**
Liquor, bronze, filigree with medieval knights and other ornamentation, marble top, c. 1920 . . . . **950.00**

Medicine

Pine, 3 shelves, primitive, open . . **65.00**
5½ x 16 x 24½", painted pine, glazed door, 3 shelves, shaped crest **95.00**

Pie Safe (see also Cupboards)

Hepplewhite, pine, extended tapered legs, punched tin of circle and stars, c. 1850 . . . . **900.00**
Walnut, short tapered legs, punched tin of geometric design, single drawer across bottom, c. 1860 . . . . **650.00**

Serving

35 x 37½" wide, Art Deco, mirrored glass top, bronze hardware; one drawer over double cupboard with 3 shelves **750.00**
Silver, 18 x 28 x 30", Oriental-style, black lacquer, MOP Coramandel decor, fitted interior, lined with felt, brass fittings, including puzzle locks **1250.00**

Spool

Clarks Spool, 4 drawers, original pulls **375.00**
Cortecilli, 5 drawers **350.00**
Goffs Best Braid, 3 drawers, original melon-shaped pulls **275.00**
Leonard Silk Co., 10 glass front drawers, 2 wooden front doors, beveled mirror sides **900.00**
Merrick's, Six Cord, 2 large drawers over 2 small drawers, cherry, refinished **350.00**
Richardson's Spool Silk, 2 drawers **150.00**
Williamantic, 2 drawers, original pulls **150.00**
Watchmaker's, 17 x 18¾ x 31" long, 10 drawers complete, 6 drawers with 42 scooped out pockets, 4 undivided drawers, sin-

gle board construction 400.00

CANDLE SHIELDS

21″, brass with needlepoint and beaded shield, angel with cherubs decor, French, pair 500.00
22″, brass with floral needlepoint shields, pair 300.00
53″, mahogany, fabric screen, 18th century 2500.00

Cherry, 8 sided, 14¾ x 17¾″ top, 27 ½″ high $450.00

CANDLE STANDS

Ash, 35½″ high, ratchet-type, adjustable standard, block support, N.Y., c. 1710 . . . . 1000.00
Cherry
15″ dia., ring and vase standard, arched tripod with snake feet . . . 500.00
16½″ square top, 26½″ high, Hepplewhite-style, N.Y. 750.00
Queen Anne, bird cage, possibly N.Y., c. 1750–1770, 19″ dia. top, 26″ high 800.00
Curly Maple
16″ dia., dish top 650.00
16″ oblong top, one drawer, vase turned standard, arched tripod base 750.00
Mahogany
21″, tilt-top, inlay, ring-vase stan-

dard, N.E., c. 1800 . . . . 1500.00
21¾″, tilt-top, inlay, oval top, snake feet, Pa., c. 1780 . . . . 2000.00
27″ dia., dish top, Philadelphia, c. 1760 . . . . 2500.00
28″ dia., bird cage, Pa., c. 1770 4000.00
Maple, tripod base with snake feet, hexagonal and turned column, one board top with tapered edges and cut out corners, 13¼ x 13¾ x 27″ 800.00
Pine
16½″ square, Hepplewhite-style . 500.00
27″ square, tapered legs 350.00
Walnut
Chippendale, dish top, carved, Phila., 21⅛″ dia., 29″ high, c. 1780 . . . . 2500.00
Queen Anne-style, dish top and bird cage support, Pa. 1750.00

CHAIRS

Children's, hickory splint seat . $45.00

Arrowbacks
Full, plank seat 225.00
Half, plank seat, original stenciling 200.00
Writing Arm, dark green paint with green and yellow decoration 850.00
Art Deco
Arm, 3″ high, tiger eye maple, brown leather inserts, red lacquered fretwork 500.00

Side, walnut and black stain, shaped back, scrolled side rails, 2 straight legs, 2 cabriole legs, upholstered seat, Viennese, c. 1930 — 350.00

Barber Chairs

Cast iron and oak, upholstered in velvet, refinished, c. 1890 . . . . . . — 700.00

Cast iron and porcelain, upholstered, rough condition . . . . — 275.00

Belter, side, rosewood, pierced, carved grapes and roses, upholstered needlepoint seat and back — 3500.00

Biedermeier-style, arm, fruitwood, lyre splat, shaped seat, c. 1850 . . — 275.00

*Captain's, pine, roll-back, refinished — 325.00

Children's

Arm, ladderback, cane seat . . . . . — 100.00

Arrowback, plank seat . . . . — 160.00

Captain's, plank seat, hickory, original finish . . . . — 225.00

High Chair, maple and pine, solid shaped back rail, 8 spindles, c. 1875 . . . . — 200.00

High Chair with stroller, pine, spindle back, cane seat, refinished . . — 200.00

Ladderback, red paint, rush seat, oak, early . . . . — 225.00

Morris, oak, upholstered . . . . — 85.00

New England, maple, ball finials, simple tapered supports, reed seat, c. 1820 . . . . — 150.00

Potty, pine, painted and stenciled — 135.00

Side, rush seat, ring turned legs, ball feet, American, c. 1910 . . . . . — 90.00

Chippendale-style

Arm, mahogany, pierced slat, knuckle arms, Phila., c. 1770 . . . . — 1750.00

Arm, wing, mahogany, serpentine crest, scrolled wings and arms, c. 1800 . . . . — 4000.00

Corner, mahogany, horseshoe rest, turned posts, solid splats, molded seat . . . . — 750.00

Corner, maple, carved, N.E., c. 1780 . . . . — 1100.00

Country, slat back, rush seat, 18th century . . . . — 750.00

Side, cherry, leather upholstery, N.E., c. 1770 . . . . — 900.00

Side, cherry, slip seat, N.E., Centennial . . . . — 500.00

Side, mahogany, shell, leaf carved top rail, baluster splat, Philadelphia . . . . — 3000.00

Side, walnut, carved, baluster splat, Phila. . . . . — 2500.00

Eastlake, Victorian

Arm, walnut, upholstered back and seat . . . . — 300.00

Side, walnut, small arms, cane seat . . . . — 200.00

Side, walnut, upholstered, tufted

Side, upholstered slip seat, walnut, stretcher base, set of 4 . . . . $3200.00

back, castors on front legs, small arms . . . . — 260.00

Empire-style

Arm, mahogany, square back, upholstered seat, brass castors, eagle terminals on arms, c. 1825 . . — 800.00

Side, mahogany and mahogany veneer, fiddleback, serpentine seat, saber leg . . . . — 180.00

Folding, carpet back and seat, late Victorian . . . . — 125.00

George II-style, corner, mahogany, slip seat, upholstered with crewel work, c. 1740 . . . . — 1500.00

Gothic-style, side, walnut, upholstered seat . . . . — 425.00

Hepplewhite-style

Arm, mahogany, carved, upholstered seat, c. 1800 . . . . — 1500.00

Arm, wing, mahogany, canted back, arched cresting, N.Y., c. 1820 . . . . — 900.00

Side, painted, cane seat, turned legs, MD, early 19th cent. . . . . . . — 250.00

Side, set of 6, mahogany, carved, c. 1790 . . . . — 3100.00

Hitchcock, plank seat, original paint and stencil, c. 1840 . . . . — 600.00

*Hitchcock-style, rush seat, original paint and stenciling 175.00

Ladderback
Cherry, rush seat, c. 1880 . . . . . . 375.00
Queen Anne, arm, shaped arms, turned legs, c. 1780 . . . . 1200.00
Mahogany, pierced slats, rush seat 500.00
Maple, rush seat, ball turned stretcher 450.00

Louis XV-style
Arm, walnut, finger carved, upholstered seat, Victorian 750.00
Side, walnut, finger carved frame, scroll and rose carved crest, upholstered 350.00

Morris
Oak, lion's paw feet and arms, adjustable back 250.00
Walnut, ball and claw feet, brass rod, adjustable back 300.00
Office, (Desk) Arm, oak, flat spindles, revolving seat, tilt back, c. 1910 . . . . 250.00

Oriental
Arm, ornately carved teakwood, c. 1860 . . . . 1250.00
Side, heavy carvings, arched top with finials, carved seat, Japanese, c. 1900 . . . . 600.00
Plank Bottom, 4 half turned spindles, pillow crest, original paint and stenciling 175.00
Pressed Back, side oak 50.00

Queen Anne-style
Banister back with scroll top, ball finials, turned columns, reed seat 550.00
Corner, tiger maple and pine, pierced slats, scalloped apron . . . 1000.00
Corner, walnut, slip seat 1200.00
Country, maple; bulbous stretcher, block legs with Spanish feet, N.E. 650.00
Side, walnut, cabriole legs, pad feet, English 1500.00

Renaissance, Victorian
Arm, lady's, walnut, upholstered, refinished, c. 1870 . . . . 500.00
Side, walnut with maple inlay, upholstered back and seat, c. 1870 . 350.00

Rococo, Victorian
Arm, gentleman's, finger molded and pierced, reupholstered, c. 1860 . . . . 700.00
Arm, lady's, refinished and reupholstered 400.00
Side, cherry, balloon back, slip seat 250.00
Side, walnut, balloon back, upholstered seat 200.00

Windsor style, side, 5 spindles, bamboo turned, plank seat, refinished $150.00

Sheraton Country, arm, cherry, rush seat 350.00
William and Mary, banister back, N.E., c. 1740 . . . . 1500.00

Windsor-style
Arm, bow back, 7 spindles, bamboo turned, black with gold trim . . 950.00
Arm, brace back, 9 spindles, bulbous turnings, shaped seat, original paint 2000.00
Arm, comb back, Rhode Island, c. 1780 . . . . 3500.00
Side, set of 6, Conn., bow back, saddle seats 7200.00
Side, bow back, signed Wallace Nutting 550.00
Side, bow back, bamboo turnings, shaped seat, 7 spindles, old paint 375.00
Side, brace back, 9 spindles 750.00
Side, dove cote, 7 spindles, bamboo turned legs, original paint . . . 425.00
Side, fan back, 7 spindles, saddle seat 550.00
Writing Arm, 7 spindles, Conn., c. 1780 . . . . 3500.00

**Blanket Chest, tulip wood, 31½″ long
17½″ wide x 19¼″ high, dovetailed,
Ohio legs** **$275.00**

Blanket
Pine, 20 x 24 x 42″ long, cannon-
ball feet, refinished 400.00
Pine, painted, unicorn motif,
bracket feet, elaborate strap
hinges, Pa., c. 1780 .... 20000.00
Poplar, 19 x 26¾ x 39¼″, original
graining, ball feet, Pa., c. 1840 ... 500.00
Chippendale-style
18 x 38 x 45″, 2 drawers over 4,
tiger stripe maple 2200.00
19½ x 55½ x 41½″, carved birch,
molded cornice, 6 drawers, N.E.,
c. 1770 .... 1750.00
22 x 29 x 49″, blanket, pine, strap
hinges, Pa., c. 1780 .... 1500.00
22½ x 33 x 37″, carved mahogany, rectangular top, 4 drawers,
Pa., c. 1780 .... 2600.00
38 x 60¾″, mahogany, molded
cornice, 3 freize drawers, 5 graduated drawers, bracket feet, replaced brasses 3000.00
81 x 42″, highboy, cherrywood,
bonnet-top, fan carved, Ct. River
Valley, c. 1780 .... 15000.00
80½″, highboy, cherry, bonnet
top, centennial 450.00
Commode
Mahogany, English Chippendale-
style, c. 1820 .... 750.00
Pine, refinished 350.00
Oak, machine carvings, one drawer over 2 doors, towel racks 275.00
Walnut, white marble top, back
splash, candle shelves, one drawer over 2 doors, c. 1860 .... 500.00
Dower, 22¼ x 29 x 50″, 3 drawers,
original finish, inscribed and dated
1808, Pa. 5500.00

Eastlake, Victorian
30″, oak, 3 drawers, machine carvings, white marble top 300.00
32″, walnut, 3 drawers, candle
stands, attached mirror, white
marble top, machine carved 500.00
48″, oak, 2 drawers over 1 drawer
over 2 door cupboard, back
splash, machine carved 450.00
Empire
46 x 43″, mahogany, wood pulls,
scroll feet, c. 1840 .... 400.00
47″, cherry, 4 drawers, inlaid, c.
1840 .... 500.00
Hepplewhite
37 x 40½ x 18″, inlayed cherrywood, 4 graduated drawers,
stringing, c. 1800 .... 950.00
37¾ x 41¾″, bow-front, inlayed
mahogany, cherrywood, valanced
apron, Mass., c. 1800 .... 1200.00
40″, mahogany, band inlaid, 4
graduated drawers, fluted columns, Mass., c. 1820 .... 1750.00
46″, cherry with mahogany strip
inlay and shield escutcheons, 5
drawers, French feet, original
brasses 2750.00
Ice, 36 x 50½″, golden oak, 4
paneled doors, original ornate
brasses 325.00
Pine
39 x 48½″, 2 drawers over 4,
original brasses, dovetailed, c.
1810 .... 1450.00
40 x 42″, 4 drawers, plank sides . 550.00
42 x 46½″, 4 drawers, plank
sides, maple pulls 650.00
Queen Anne-style
Blanket, cherry and tulip wood, on
frame, N.E. 3000.00
Chest on Chest, 41¼″ wide, 6′
11″ high, cherry, flat top, molded
cornice; 3 small drawers above 5
graduated drawers, lower section
with 3 small drawers over 4 graduated drawers, molded apron, cabriole legs, pad feet, N.E., c. 1760–
80 .... 7500.00
Chest on frame, walnut, carved, 3
short and 4 long drawers, frame
with drawer, c. 1750 .... 3000.00
Highboy, cherrywood, bonnet top,
swan's neck cresting, cabriole
legs, pad feet, c. 1770, 88 x 39″ . 8000.00
Lowboy, mahogany, notched cor-
ners, shell carved legs, Phila., c.
1760, 28¼ x 34 x 19½″ 10500.00
Rococo, Victorian, walnut, 2 small
drawers, marble insert over 4
graduated drawers, attached oval
mirror, leaf pulls, c. 1870 ...... 650.00

Queen Anne, tiger maple, flat top, original hardware **$15000.00**

Sea Chest, 12½ x 14½ x 25½",
strap hinges, handles, fitted for
bottles, early 19th century **450.00**
Sheraton
  19 x 22½ x 40", blanket, curly
  maple **1400.00**
  21 x 40½ x 44⅞", cherry, 2 split
  drawers over 3 graduated drawers, inlaid escutcheons, replaced
  brasses, c. 1830 .... **1000.00**
  Silver Chest, 8 x 18 x 24", mahogany, hinged lift top, 1 drawer below, silk lined fitted interior, brass
  hardware **450.00**
William and Mary, pine, painted, 2
  small drawers, 3 long drawers,
  ball foot, Ct., 39 x 37¾ x 21" ... **4500.00**

CRADLES

Cherry, 17 x 40", shaped ends,
  handholds **325.00**

**Mixed woods, 37" long, 31½" high, 5
spindle ends, 8 on sides, Pat. 1869,
replaced cushion** **$275.00**

Maple
  22 x 38 x 40", Windsor-style **400.00**
  26½ x 32 x 51", folding-type, c.
  1880 .... **225.00**
Mixed Woods, 38" long, spindled,
  arched bentwood top and bottom,
  straight spindled sides, feather
  mattress **140.00**
Pine
  13 x 34", open sides **225.00**
  14 x 37", hooded, dovetailed **475.00**
Walnut
  42", spindle-type, refinished, c.
  1900 .... **300.00**
  44", bonnet top **400.00**
Walnut and walnut burl veneered, 16
  x 37", on platform, c. 1877 ..... **475.00**

CUPBOARDS

Chimney
  9¼ x 38", hanging-type, 4
  shelves, original paint **1000.00**
  14 x 17 x 74", 2 doors, original
  paint, brass hardware **1500.00**
Corner
  Cherry, 33 x 83" high, swan neck,
  urn-shaped wood finials; cathedral
  door with glazed panels, one
  drawer over single cupboard door,
  bracket feet **4000.00**
  Cherry, 45 x 86" high, Primitive, 2
  pieces, Pa., c. 1844 .... **2750.00**
  Cherry and pine, dentiled cornice,
  flaring bracket feet, c. 1790, 62½
  x 33" **2250.00**
  Cherry, 92" high, cathedral door,
  blown glass panes, butterfly
  shelves, original brass hinges, 2

Cherry and walnut, American, refinished with interior repainted, 41 x 20 x 82½", c. 1800 ....$1250.00

pieces	6500.00
Cherry and Tiger Maple, 96" high, cathedral door with blown glass panes, 3 drawers over 2 doors, bracket feet	5000.00
Curly Maple, 86" high, glazed panel door, 16 panes, 2 drawers over cupboard, c. 1810	4500.00
Pine, barrel back, arched opening, painted, N.E., c. 1780, 82 x 49 x 32½"	1800.00
Pine, carved, two parts, glazed doors over solid doors, c. 1800, 88½ x 42 x 26½"	2000.00
Pine, grain painted, projecting molded cornice, late 18th c., 96 x 56½"	5000.00
Poplar, 40 x 77" high, simple cornice, 4 panels on single upper door with single paneled door ...	1250.00
Walnut, carved, 2 parts, glazed doors, cupboard, Pa., c. 1790, 93 x 53 x 27½"	2750.00

Flat Wall

Cherrywood, 2 parts, glazed doors, drawers, Pa., c. 1800, 84 x 50¾ x 18¾"	4250.00
Honduras Mahogany, 5 x 12 x 16", curved glass sides, glass door, c. 1930's	125.00
Oak, curved glass sides, glass door, mirrored back, glass shelves	900.00
Oak, 16½ x 37 x 68", 2 glass doors over 2 drawers, over 2 blind doors, machine carved	600.00
Pine, 2 parts, 2 glazed doors, red and white paint decoration, c. 1810, 74 x 51½"	2250.00
Pine, 2 parts, painted, molded cornice, primitive, 2 panelled cupboard doors, early 19th c., 74 x 43½"	1100.00
Walnut, Eastlake, single panel glazed doors, 2 drawers over 2 blind doors, machine carvings ...	700.00

Hanging

Cherry, 19¾ x 25", 2 doors with glass panes, brass and porcelain fittings, orig. condition, c. 1900 ..	125.00
Pine, panelled door, drawer, possibly Pa., mid-19th c., 27¼ x 17¾"	600.00
Poplar, 20 x 29" high, painted graining, one shelf, blind door ...	475.00
Walnut, English, 3 drawers across bottom, shaped door, corner style, early 19th c.	450.00

Jelly

15 x 33 x 57½" high, 2 doors, 4 shelves, gallery top, original red paint, c. 1850	650.00
27 x 34 x 58" high, single door, simple molding, stripped of old paint	300.00
Kas, 53½" high, 54½" wide, pine, diamond inlay on doors, Canadian	1850.00

Pie Safe (see also Cabinets)

Pine, eagle tins	750.00
Pine, straight cornice, 2 pierced tin doors, drawer, 2 cupboard doors, 71½ x 40 x 14½"	475.00
Poplar, flower basket tins, refinished	400.00
Poplar, pinwheel tins	375.00
Walnut, pinwheel tins	450.00

DESKS

Chippendale-style

Block-front, mahogany, carved fan, Ma., c. 1765, 45¼ x 41¾" .	7000.00
Slant-front, early maple, 4 graduated drawers, c. 1760, 41½ x 35½ x 18"	4750.00
Slant-front, carved mahogany, serpentine, fitted interior, c. 1770, 44 x 42 x 23 1/3"	4750.00

Lap Desk, mixed woods, 10½″ deep, 11¾″ high, 15¾″ wide **$155.00**

Slant-front, walnut, shell carved drawers, Phila., c. 1770, 45¼ x 38 ¼ x 21¾″ . . . . | 6500.00

Davenport
Walnut, inlaid top, front . . . . | 450.00
Walnut, spring operated structure, brass gallery . . . . | 700.00

Eastlake, Victorian, 35 x 62″, drop front, machine carvings, gallery top, fitted interior, walnut, c. 1890 | 600.00

Empire, mahogany, inlayed, bookcase, butler's drawer, glazed doors, 88 x 42¼″ . . . . | 550.00

Hepplewhite, mixed woods, 3 graduated drawers, drop lid top drawer, interior all drawers (butler's desk), French feet, c. 1810 . . . . | 2250.00

Lap Desks
8½ x 11½″, child's, walnut, drawing slate, green felt writing surface, original label, c. 1877 . . . . . | 100.00
9 x 12½″, walnut, blue velvet lining, secret compartment, 19th century . . . . | 125.00
9½ x 14″, oak . . . . | 75.00
10 x 12″, mahogany, brass fittings and filigree decorations . . . . . . | 200.00

Partner's desk, walnut, 3 drawers across and 3 drawers on each side, c. 1880 . . . . | 2500.00

Queen Anne, slant-front, walnut, stepped interior, 4 graduated drawers, c. 1760, 43 x 39¼ x 20¾″ . . . . | 6250.00

Renaissance, Victorian, walnut, cylinder front, fitted interior, 3 small drawers, c. 1876 . . . . | 1750.00

*Roll Tops
Mahogany, 48″, "C" curved . . . . | 900.00
Oak, "S" shaped roll top, 3 drawers on each side, plain interior . . | 1000.00

Schoolmaster's Desk, 23″ deep, 30″ wide, 35″ high, dovetailed, porcelain knobs, brass escutcheons, restored **$235.00**

Oak, "S" shaped roll top, Victorian, wooten type doors on sides, elaborate carving, fancy interior . | 2750.00
School, child's, pine with iron, folding seat, c. 1930 . . . . | 25.00

Schoolmaster's
Flat top, 26 x 31 x 36″, oak, one drawer . . . . | 200.00
Kneehole-type, 25 x 59″, mahogany, veneered drawers, 4 drawers in each pedestal, fitted interior . . | 650.00
Slant top, 33 x 37½″, painted pine, pigeon holes . . . . | 375.00
Sheraton, Country, 32″ wide, pine, slant front, one deep drawer, gallery back . . . . | 1500.00

Store, Country
7½ x 19 x 24″, pine, counter top-type . . . . | 250.00
72″ wide, pigeon holes, walnut . . | 800.00

DOUGH TROUGHS

Cherry, 29 x 32″, dovetailed, turned legs, original finish . . . . | 750.00
Chestnut, 18 x 28 x 28″, pine legs . | 400.00
Maple, 33 x 38″, set in legs, sliding top . . . . | 500.00

**Dough Trough, table top, 32″ long,
16″ wide x 9½″ high $50.00**

Pine
13 x 24″, table top-type	125.00
23 x 9″, carved, covered, tapering sides, mid-19th c.	275.00
30 x 32″, splayed legs with stretcher, covered	650.00
34 x 29½″, dovetailed, turned legs	300.00

Walnut, 20 x 27 x 39″, dovetailed, splayed legs **425.00**

DRY SINKS

Pine and Poplar, late Victorian adaptation, 42½″ long $300.00

Butternut, 20 x 35 x 42″, 2 doors, one shelf inside, original stippling and finish **425.00**

Maple, 60½ x 30½″, rectangular top, single drawer, 2 doors, painted, Pa. German **750.00**

Oak, 19 x 34 x 44″, zinc lined, 2 doors **500.00**

Pine
28½ x 26″, rectangular top with gallery, early 19th cent.	350.00
42 x 48″, one drawer, 2 doors below, copper lined, redecorated ...	325.00
43¼ x 36½″, rectangular top, primitive, 2 drawers, 2 cupboard doors, mid-19th cent.	300.00
66″, painted, all original, Lancaster, Pa	1500.00

Pine and Poplar, 50″, 2 drawers, 2 doors below **450.00**

Poplar, 36 x 42″, single drawer, 2 paneled doors, painted graining .. **550.00**

Walnut, 33 x 44″, one drawer with 2 doors **425.00**

FRAMES

Brass
7 x 12″, Art Nouveau-style, 2 oval openings, easel back	110.00
8 x 14″, Florentine styling, easel back	60.00

Brass Plated
2½ x 3½″, blue enameled decor .	20.00
7¾ x 10¾″, pierced, scrolled, easel back	30.00

Cinnabar, oriental scene, 6 x 9″ ... **140.00**

Curly Maple, 15 x 17″ **150.00**

Empire, wide molding, mahogany veneer, 20 x 26″ **40.00**

Gold Gilt
10½ x 12¾″, berries and leaves in relief	60.00
24 x 28″, shadow box-type, scrolled, c. 1900	80.00

Leather over wood, 6 x 6½″, birds, animals, etc. in relief, Folk Art ... **350.00**

Mahogany, gold liner, 35″ square .. **100.00**

Oak
10½ x 38½″	50.00
20 x 77″, medallions and bulleyes, 19th century	275.00

Pine
Flat, block corners with metal stars, 15 x 18″	55.00
Flat, beveled toward center, feather graining, red ground, 16 x 20″ .	125.00

Porcelain, 10 x 12″, double openings, handpainted pansy decor, gold trim, T & V France **65.00**

Silver, Sterling
4 x 6″, easel-type	30.00
5⅝ x 7″, plain rim	50.00
8 x 9″, ornate	80.00

Walnut
8¾ x 11″, oval	30.00
8 x 12″, cross bar corners	40.00
16 x 19″, oval	60.00
18¼ x 27½″, leaves in relief, gold liner	90.00

28 x 32", shadow box-type, double liner 115.00

HAT RACKS AND HALL TREES

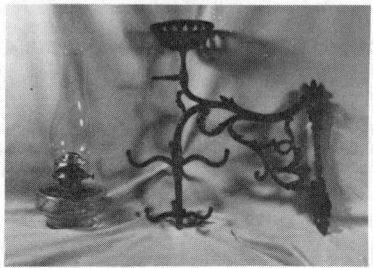

Iron, 8 prongs, lamp, 16¾",
1869 . . . . $125.00

Iron, cast, 10" beveled mirror, 12 hooks, umbrella holders, 4 arched legs, c. 1880 . . . . 250.00
Oak, 60" high, 8 brass hooks, c. 1910 . . . . 95.00
Oak, beveled mirror, seat with lid, iron hooks, umbrella holder, 90" . 450.00
Pine, accordion-type, 7 porcelain pegs 50.00
Pine, accordion-type, 9 turned wooden pegs 60.00
Walnut, accordion-type, wooden pegs, porcelain tips, c. 1860 . . . . 95.00
Walnut, 27" long mirror with 3 pegs below 50.00
Walnut, Hall Trees, 96½" high, beveled mirror with wooden pegs, white marble insert, umbrella holders, c. 1870 . . . . 800.00

ICE CREAM PARLOR FURNITURE

Chairs
Heart back, refinished 70.00
Spectacle, refinished 80.00
Arm, wood seat 125.00
Stools
26½" high, refinished 50.00
30" high, 12" dia., seat, refinished 60.00
Tables
27" square, oak top 200.00
30" dia., oak top 250.00
Table and 2 chairs, child's, table 18" dia.; chairs, 9½" dia. seat, set 200.00
Table and 4 chairs, table, 30" dia., wood top; Chairs, 14" dia. replaced seats, refinished, Set 550.00

LOVE SEATS

Adams, triple oval back, bellflower painted satinwood, c. 1770 . . . . . 4000.00
Art Nouveau, 62", carved mahogany frame, upholstered 1000.00
Eastlake, purple velvet upholstery . 300.00
Hepplewhite, walnut, spade feet, bellflower inlay, refinished and re-upholstered 1250.00
Oriental, elaborately carved teakwood, interlocking dragons with mouths at end of arms, China, mid-19th c. 1750.00
Rococo, Victorian, walnut frame with rose carving on 3 crests, refinished and re-upholstered 650.00
Sheraton, 52", refinished, reupholstered in velvet, nailhead trim . . . 700.00
Victorian, early, walnut, mirror back 850.00
William and Mary-style, 48", loose cushion, turned baluster legs, stretcher 600.00

MAGAZINE RACKS

Magazine Rack, walnut, 17¼" deep, 22¾" wide x 23¼" high, acorn finials, brass castors, American Canterbury $600.00

Canterbury
American, 14½ x 18½ x 20", walnut 500.00
American, 17 x 17½ x 22½", acorn finials, one drawer, brass castors 750.00
English, 15½ x 19½ x 25", mahogany 750.00
Eastlake, Victorian
13½ x 18", walnut, machine carved 50.00
13½ x 26", turned posts, machine carved, pierced sides 85.00

Rococo, Victorian, 13½ x 23", walnut, carved leaves, flowers **150.00**

MANTELS

Marble, Carrara, 70" shelf, Adams-style **1350.00**
Oak, 66 x 78" high, carved and scalloped columns **750.00**
Pine
  44 x 47" high **250.00**
  60 x 70½" carved, painted, dentilled frieze, reeded pillasters, Pa., c. 1800 . . . . **900.00**
  68", curved top section, c. 1820 . **500.00**
  82", carved rosettes, round columns, c. 1790 . . . . **1100.00**
Poplar, 76½ x 52½", architectural with strong molding and reeding, original light blue paint **550.00**

MIRRORS

Dresser swing mirror, mixed woods, 7½ x 13½ x 21" high, original finish **$350.00**

Cheval, 30 x 57½", oak, S-supports, paw feet, castors **250.00**
Chippendale
  Mahogany, carved, J. Elliot, Phila., c. 1780, 40¾" **1850.00**
  Mahogany, inlayed, parcel gilded, scroll-carved cresting, c. 1780, 38½" **600.00**

  Mahogany, parcel-gilded, scrolled cresting with phoenix, c. 1790, 39" **875.00**
Convex, 27" wide, 34" overall height, carved, gilted, eagle finial **3000.00**
Dresser
  Applewood, oval, one drawer, English **450.00**
  Brass, 15 x 16" oval, cupid and floral decor **150.00**
  Cherry, 13½ x 33 x 34½", oval mirror on set drawer with lift-top lid **300.00**
  Chippendale, walnut and parcel-gilt, rectangular, molded supports, late 18th c., 18 x 12" **275.00**
  Federal, mahogany, bow-front, pivoting mirror, N.E., early 19th c., 19" **150.00**
  Hepplewhite, mahogany, inlaid stripes, two drawers, glass knobs **650.00**
  Iron, cast, 14½" high, tilt-type, ornate base and crest **50.00**
Empire, wide molding, mahogany veneer, c. 1830–1850, 36" **65.00**
Federal-type
  11¾ x 22", reverse painting, black half columns, rosettes at corner . **200.00**
  12 x 13", cherry, string decor, shoe foot, all original **325.00**
  15 x 30", gold leafed, scenic reverse painting, replaced mirror . . . **175.00**
  15¾ x 27¾", gilded, reverse painting of mother and child, label for James Todd, Portland **550.00**
Gilt, gesso, eglomise, early 19th c., 39" **400.00**
Mantel, 23 x 69" long, 3 sections, gilted metal, ornate crest, c. 1910 **250.00**
Pier, 42 x 8½" high, gilted, ornate shell-type crest, fluted columns, marble shelf **1000.00**
Plateau
  6", gilted metal **30.00**
  10", silverplated ornate base, beveled mirror **75.00**
  14", silverplated ornate base, beveled mirror **95.00**
Queen Anne
  Walnut, inlayed, shaped cresting, 57¾ x 20½" **1500.00**
  Walnut, inlayed, parcel-gilt applied flowers and scrolls, 34¼ x 14¼" . **1100.00**
Sheraton, 21 x 29", maple, reeded pilaster, cornice **400.00**

ROCKERS

Arrowback, child's, pine and maple, 4 splats, N.E., c. 1830 . . . . **300.00**
*Bentwood, sleigh-type, signed Thonet **700.00**

Slat back rocker, mixed woods, replaced basketweave seat $135.00

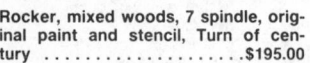

Rocker, mixed woods, 7 spindle, original paint and stencil, Turn of century $195.00

*Boston

Cane seat	250.00
Saddle seat, painted black, stenciled	500.00

Eastlake, Victorian, oak, platform, upholstered seat and back 275.00

Ladderback

Child's rush seat, original paint . .	275.00
Double bearing arms, 4 slats, splint seat	450.00
Mammy Rocker, pine, 9 spindles, flat headboard, southern	450.00

Oak

Cane seat, back, refinished, c. 1920	150.00
Full pressed back, upholstered spring cushion seat, 20th century	250.00

Rococo, Victorian, finger carved frame, ornate crest and apron, fully upholstered, tufted back 500.00

Windsor-style

Comb back, 8 spindles, bamboo style legs and arm supports, c. 1825	1000.00
Fan back, 5 spindles, bamboo style, maple and pine, N.E., c. 1840	250.00
7-spindles, saddle seat, bamboo turnings	750.00
7-spindles, child's	250.00

SECRETARIES

Connecticut, Secretary-Bookcase, walnut, 18th c., bookcase in sections with 2 dovetailed drawers and cove molded cornice, desk with slant front lid and 6 dovetailed drawers, signed S. Hale, 39 x 20¾ x 30¼"	29000.00
Eastlake, Victorian, walnut, flat top, 2 glass doors, cylinder front desk, bureau below, machine carved . .	1750.00
Empire, mahogany, molded cornice, slant front, convex drawer, c. 1820, 93 x 44"	750.00
Hepplewhite, mahogany, swan's neck cresting, inlayed American eagle, c. 1795, 96 x 41"	3250.00
Renaissance, Victorian, walnut, arched pediment over 2 glazed doors, fitted interior, bureau base	1500.00
Rococo, Victorian, walnut, scrolled cornice above 2 glazed doors, slant front, paneled cupboard doors below	2250.00
Sheraton, Mahogany, 2 glazed, mullioned doors, fold-out writing surface, 4 drawers below, shaped crest with 3 brass finials, 40 x 74" high	2750.00
Victorian, Secretary-Bookcase,	

Hepplewhite, mahogany veneer, English $4500.00

mid-19th c., grained mahogany and mahogany veneer, reeded moldings on glass and base door panels, single drawer, Fretwork inside glass door, simple bracket feet, 42 x 21½ x 68" **3250.00**

SETTLES
See, BENCHES

SIDEBOARDS

Chippendale-style, 23 x 38 x 81", cherry, original brasses, Virginia .   **12500.00**
Empire
  Mahogany and cherry, pie crust molding, drawer at base, 21 x 45 x 48" **1000.00**
  Maple and cherry, inlayed, 3 drawers, 4 field cupboard doors, c. 1820, 42 x 66" **375.00**
Federal
  Mahogany, inlay, shaped top, drawers, cupboards, c. 1800, 41½ x 75⅜ x 28¼ **2250.00**

Hepplewhite, inlayed mahogany, serpentine front, American, 75½" long, 40" high $4250.00

Mahogany, inlay, serpentine front, 3 drawers, cupboard doors, c. 1810, 39 x 65" **1600.00**
Mahogany, bow-front, 3 bowed frieze drawers, oval medallions, late 18th c., 44¼ x 71½ x 29¾" .   **3250.00**
Renaissance, Victorian
  41 x 72", walnut with walnut burl panels, white marble top, c. 1860–1870 . . . .   **1000.00**
  5 x 8', walnut, high back with open shelves, large mirror, marble top over drawers and cupboard doors below, c.1870 . . . .   **1750.00**
Sheraton-style, 68", mahogany, 3 drawers over 4 doors, scalloped base, gallery top **750.00**

SOFAS

Chippendale, carved mahogany, camel back, bowed front, scrolled arms, upholstered back, c. 1790 .   **4750.00**
Eastlake, Victorian, 76", walnut frame, machine carvings, refinished and re-upholstered **550.00**
Empire, straight back with leaf carving at ends, scrolled arms, elaborate carving, bulbous feet **1500.00**
Empire, carved mahogany, Duncan Phyfe school, paw feet with winged eagle supports, length 85", c. 1815 . . . .   **3250.00**
Federal, curly maple, tall back, upholstered, N.E., length 74½", c. 1810 . . . .   **2000.00**
Louis XV, Victorian, walnut, 3 semicabriole legs, swelled back with carved board in center, fruit and leaf motif, c. 1870 . . . .   **1500.00**
Mission, 72", pullman-style, upholstered **300.00**
Renaissance, Victorian, 68", carved walnut frame **650.00**

Rococo, Victorian, 72", nut and finger carved walnut frame, re-
upholstered in ivory brocade **1250.00**
Sheraton, straight back, reeded
arms and accent rail on back, ta-
pered fluted legs, N.E., c. 1815 .. **2500.00**

SPINNING WHEELS

Flax Wheels
Maple, N.E., c. 1830 .... **250.00**
Mixed woods, turned, Pa., c. 1840 **275.00**
Mixed woods, nice turnings, in-
cised heart decoration, painted,
Pa., c. 1810 .... **450.00**
Wool Wheels
Mixed woods, turned, Pa., c. 1840 **325.00**
Walnut, Pa., mid-19th c. **375.00**

STANDS

**Shaving Stand, Queen Anne style,
mahogany** $350.00

Country, pine, 1 drawer, tapered
legs, blue paint, Pa., c. 1830 .... **325.00**
Empire
Curly maple, 16¼ x 17 x 28" high,
square top, turned columns, tripod
feet **425.00**
Mahogany, 2 drawer, square top,
tapered feet, 28½ x 34½ x 17" .. **275.00**
Federal, 20½ x 28" high, pine,

square top, legs, painted, Primitive **200.00**
Hepplewhite
Birch, 19¼ x 26" high, square
top, plain apron, one drawer **275.00**
Cherry, 20 x 28" high, square one
board top, dovetailed drawer **400.00**
Mahogany, corner washstand, 3
drawers, slightly splayed legs ... **550.00**
Walnut, 21 x 26" high, square top,
one drawer, tapered legs, Red
stain **275.00**

**Wash Stand, walnut, 18½ x 37½
x 36½" high, shaped splat, back
splash** $235.00

Sheraton
Cherry, 21 x 28½" high, 2 draw-
ers, glass pulls, turned legs **275.00**
Cherry and Tiger Maple, 20 x
28¾" high, 2 drawers, beaded,
mushroom pulls **350.00**
Mahogany, rectangular with convex front, 3 drawers top, 2 side
drawers bottom, center drawer
stool, turned legs, c. 1790 ...... **750.00**
Twentieth Century, golden oak, one
drawer, two towel bars **125.00**
Victorian
Brass, 33" high, marble inserts .. **300.00**
Walnut, 22" high, one drawer,
wooden pull, turned legs **150.00**

STEPS

Bed
Sheraton, 2-steps, lift top, walnut . **350.00**
Sheraton, 3-steps, lift top lids,
original carpet **475.00**
Sheraton, 3-steps, 2 lift top lids,

gold tooled red leather tops, walnut 600.00
Library, spiral, 4 steps, leather covers, bamboo turned post, c. 1890 .... 500.00

STOOLS

5 Board Stool, 6¾ x 9 x 17″ long, pine $42.00

Foot
Chippendale-style, 15 x 17½ x 22″, mahogany, slip seat, 18th century 500.00
Country
  Maple, turned, rush seat, N.E., early 19th c. 250.00
  Pine, plank top, red paint, Pa., mid-19th c. 125.00
Empire, 8 x 8 x 12″ dia., mahogany, upholstered 85.00
Iron, 12½″, square, upholstered . 60.00
Pottery, rockingham-type glaze, 5 x 10½ x 12″, carpeted lid opens to spittoon 225.00
Queen-Anne style, cabriola legs with pad feet, centennial, upholstered 175.00
Rolling Pin-type, 18″ long, walnut frame, upholstered 85.00
Sheraton, 7 x 9 x 13″, walnut, reeded legs, needlepoint upholstery 90.00
Victorian, 8 x 12″ dia., walnut, scrolled legs, needlepoint upholstery 85.00
Windsor, maple and pine, turned, painted red, N.E., early 19th c. .. 1500.00
Gout
12 x 13 x 19″, mahogany, English, c. 1890 .... 275.00
12 x 19 x 21″, walnut upholstered, rocking-type, American, c. 1880 .. 150.00
Joint, 18 x 18″, oak, molded frame, baluster turned legs, box stretch-

er, English 250.00
Milking
Cast iron, 12″ high 25.00
Oak, 10″ dia. seat, 3 legs 40.00
Pine, 9½″ dia. seat, 4 legs, Pa., early 60.00
Piano, 14″ dia. seat, adjustable, swivel-type, glass ball feet 95.00

TABLES

Tavern Table, 27¼ x 44 x 28½″ high spade foot, all original, New England $850.00

Card
Adam-style, 17¾ x 29 x 36″, tulip wood, D-shaped 1250.00
Chippendale, cherrywood, rectangular, single drawer, c. 1780, 29¾ x 35¼ x 16⅜″ 3500.00
Duncan Phyfe-style, 18 x 35½″, mahogany, Lyre base, acanthus leaf decor on legs, brass claw feet 750.00
Empire, birch and inlayed burlwood, D shape, trestle shaped feet, 30 x 35″ 400.00
Federal, serpentine, mahogany, inlay, MA, c. 1790, 29½ x 34½″ .. 900.00
Hepplewhite, bird's eye maple, inlaid, N.E. 750.00
Hepplewhite, 37″ wide, mahogany, Phila., c. 1800 .... 1100.00
Queen Anne-style, 30 x 35½″, mahogany 1500.00
Regency, 29 x 36″, satinwood and rosewood, inlaid, c. 1815 ...... 1600.00
Sheraton, 17½ x 30 x 35½″, mahogany, chamfered corners, reeded legs 750.00
Chair, pine, painted blue, rectangular top above seat, hinged lid, c. 1775, 28¾ x 66½ x 36¼″ 2750.00
Dining
Art Deco, 72″ rectangular, maple,

Tea Table, 24″ dia., walnut, bird cage support, ball and claw feet, carved knees, Philadelphia, c. 1780 . $3250.00

ebony, blue mirror top, apron, 3 supports on plinth bases	1500.00
Chippendale, mahogany, drop leaf, claw and ball feet, Phila., 28 x 48 x 54″	4000.00
Duncan Phyfe, 9′4″, mahogany, D-shaped ends, 3 pedestals with reeded tetrapods, brass paw-castors	3500.00
Empire, mahogany, drop leaf, 1 drawer, paw feet, 28 x 51″	400.00
Federal, drop leaf, walnut, N.E., c. 1800, 30 x 61″	700.00
Federal, gate leg, mahogany, drop leaf, c. 1820, 31 x 68″	300.00
Queen Anne-style, 36 x 48″, elm	1500.00
Queen Anne, drop-leaf, walnut, carved, trifed feet, c. 1750, 28½ x 47½″	3250.00
Twentieth Century, 45″ dia., oak,	

pedestal base, scrolled feet	600.00
Victorian, 48″ dia., walnut, pedestal base, paw feet	800.00

Drop Leaf

Chippendale, mahogany, oblong top, cabriole legs, bull & claw feet, Pa., c. 1780, 28¾ x 41½ x 49½″	1600.00
Country, cherry, maple, rectangular top, 2 end drawers, turned legs, 30 x 60 x 45″	375.00
Empire, American, 18 x 48″, 23″ leaves, mahogany	400.00
Hepplewhite, 30 x 60″, walnut . .	800.00
Queen Anne, walnut, oblong top, pad feet, c. 1750, Pa., or N.Y., 26¾ x 37¾ x 44″	900.00
Sheraton, 18¼ x 29 x 46″, 20½″ leaves, walnut	750.00
Victorian, American, mahogany, cylinder, 34 x 36 (open) x 29″ . . .	450.00

Harvest

Drop leaf, plank top, traces of blue paint, c. 1820, 28 x 84″ . . .	700.00
Pine, oblong, X-form legs, N.E., mid-19th c., 28½ x 156″	2250.00
Walnut, oblong, tapered legs, early 19th c., 28 x 72″	1500.00

Library

Empire, mahogany, carved, drop leaf, Allison, N.Y., 28¾ x 39¼ x 48″	2000.00
Oak, one shelf, square legs, 23 x 23 x 29″	350.00

Marble Top

14 x 18″, walnut, finger molded, scrolled legs, castors, white marble	400.00
15 x 20″, walnut, machine carvings, brown marble, Eastlake, c. 1890	300.00
18 x 22″ oval, walnut, finger carved, center pedestal with 4 supports, white marble	400.00
18½ x 23″, walnut, machine carved, black marble insert, c. 1890	250.00
24″, turtle top, walnut, molded apron, scrolled balustered supports, white marble	600.00

Papier Mache

32″ dia., tilt top, wood pedestal, black lacquered floral center, gold trim	700.00
Nest of 3, 15 x 22″ largest, black lacquer, MOP inlay, c. 1890	450.00

Pembroke

Cherrywood, inlayed, Ct. or N.Y., c. 1800, 27¾ x 37¾″	1600.00
Cherrywood, oblong top, square tapering legs, c. 1815, 28¼ x 34¾ x 35″	375.00
Mahogany, D shaped drop leaves,	

tapered legs, N.Y., c. 1810, 28¾ x 36 x 54¼" **650.00**

Satinwood, mahogany, inlayed, drop leaves, J. Shaw, Md., c. 1790, 27¾ x 30¼ x 39" **22000.00**

Poker, 36" dia., oak, swivel iron pedestal base **650.00**

Pool, regulation size, 9' long, oak, slate top, webbed leather pockets **1250.00**

Tavern

Curly maple, turned, oval top, arched apron, N.E., c. 1750, 26 x 35¼" **1750.00**

Pine, primitive, oblong, octagonal legs, N.E., c. 1780, 25¾ x 31¼ x 22½" **600.00**

Pine, 48", cherry turned legs, box stretcher **700.00**

Pine, 60", maple turned legs, single drawer **900.00**

Walnut, oblong top, drawer, ball feet, Pa., c. 1750, 28¾ x 28 x 21¾" **2750.00**

Close-up view of bird cage support on Philadelphia Tea Table.

Tea

18¾" dia., walnut, dish top, inlaid with star and circles, reeded pedestal, serpent feet **700.00**

26 x 30" oval, cherry, splayed legs, pad feet **2250.00**

29" dia., cherry, tilt top, Birdcage, Pa., c. 1760 .... **1750.00**

31" dia., maple, tilt top, pie crust top **750.00**

32¾", walnut, turned, dish top, bird cage support, Pa., c. 1780 .. **3500.00**

36" dia., mahogany tilt top, tripod base, serpent feet **900.00**

37", mahogany, pie crust, tilt top, ball and claw feet, c. 1770 ..... **4600.00**

Work

Empire, mahogany, carved, lyre support, Mass., c. 1830, 28½ x 19½ x 17¼" **350.00**

Federal, mahogany, octagonal case, round tapering legs, N.E., c. 1880, 28 x 20¾" **550.00**

Federal, maple and birch, painted dec., square tapered legs, c. 1800, 28½ x 15½" **2000.00**

Hepplewhite, Country, 28½ x 42", walnut single drawer **300.00**

Oriental, 19 x 26", black lacquered, gold stenciling, ivory fittings **650.00**

Queen-Anne-style, Country, 29 x 45", bread board ends, single drawer, turned legs, pad feet **1750.00**

Regency, 16 x 29 x 32", mahogany, English **1500.00**

Victorian, 17½" dia., walnut, sewing, 1880 .... **300.00**

TEA WAGONS

Walnut, D-shaped drop leaves, one drawer, slide out tray, 2 large wooden wheels **300.00**

Walnut, D-shaped drop leaves, glass lift off tray top, 2 large wooden wheels, castors, Victorian **210.00**

WAGON SEATS

Wagon seats cannot be classified with seats from a wagon. Early wagon seats were usually constructed with a double frame and a basketry-type seat. They served a dual purpose: in the house and in the family wagon for additional seating.

Hickory, spindle back and arms, leather basketweave seat, 6 legs, 18th century **750.00**

Maple, ash, rush seat, N.E., 19th cent. **350.00**

Pine, painted, slat back, rush seat, Connecticut, c. 1830 .... **500.00**

Pine, Windsor-type, spindle back, cut-out heart sides **650.00**

WICKER

Rattan, reed and willow are all known as wicker. Wicker items were produced and imported from the Orient as early as the 18th century. It was not until the mid 19th century that wicker furniture was manufactured in the United States. The elaborate, ornate and

closely woven designs are from this Victorian era. The plainer and coarser reedings are from the early 1900's.

Carriage, toddler type, painted beige, c. 1930 . . . . **$135.00**

Bassinet, 18 x 23" high, ornate, c.1890	250.00
Carriage, large wire wheels, rubber tires, re-upholstered interior, refinished	550.00
Chairs	
Arm, rolled arms, round seat, scrolled curled back	275.00
Arm, spring seat, rolled arms, refinished, c. 1910	150.00
Rocker, Child's, high fan back, rolled arms, upholstered slip seat	175.00
Rocker, Child's, upholstered slip seat, c. 1910	125.00
Rocker, Lady's, ornate, green velvet seat, refinished, c. 1890	350.00
Rocker, spring cushion seat, barrel back	175.00
Side, ornate, c. 1890	500.00
Crib, high back, ornate, early	500.00
Hall Tree, floor model, 12 pegs	225.00
Hamper, Corner, 25" high, hinged lid, c. 1890	55.00
Lamp, floor, 27" dia., shade, 71" high, refinished	275.00
Settee, 23 x 31 x 50", Tete-tete-type	300.00
Sofa, 72" long, 3 spring cushions, closed back	425.00

Tables	
12 x 22¾", c. 1900	125.00
20 x 36" oval, refinished	200.00
Tea Wagon, 31 x 34", removable glass serving tray top	275.00
Tray, 8 x 12" oval, butterfly and fern under glass	40.00

YARN WINDERS

6-Spoke **$55.00**

Double Spool, rare	225.00
Niddy Noddy, maple, hand pegged .	65.00
4-spoke, adjustable, pine	150.00
6-spoke, oak and ash, carved, clock wheel, mid-19th c., 38" . . .	150.00
6-spoke, oak and turned maple, mid-19th c., 37"	110.00
6-spoke, walnut, late 19th c., 37"	150.00

GAME PLATES

A general classification of special plates used to serve game, including fish, is games plates. They were popular in the late 1800's and early 1900's. They were decorated with various species of birds, fish or other game. A set usually consisted of a service platter, individual serving plates and sauce boat. Many sets have been divided and the individual plates used for wall hangings.

Plate, Ducks, burgundy with gold borders, Limoges, signed Vitet .. $125.00

BIRDS

Plates

9", birds, J. and G. Meakin, England 20.00
9", grouse, heavy gold, artist signed, Marked Comte de Artois Limoges 38.50
9½", ducks, Limoge 40.00
10", pheasant, Limoge, signed Max 85.00
10½", bird and 2 water spaniels, crimped gold rim, signed, R. K. Beck..................... 65.00
16", quail chop plate, 2 handles, hand painted gold trim, Limoges, T. and V. France 125.00

Sets

8 pieces, 9⅝", different birds, dark brown borders, gold Royal Vienna 225.00
7 pieces, wild game birds, pastoral scene background, molded edges, shell decor, Fazent Mehlem, Bonn, Germany 215.00
8 pieces, birds in marsh, cobalt and gold fluted edges, Limoges, H. and C. Co. 375.00

DEER

Sets

7 pieces, Buffalo Pottery 225.00
5 pieces, artist signed Beck, Buffalo Pottery 275.00
7 pieces, 18" platter, 6–9¼"

plates, gold trim, unsigned 175.00

FISH

Plates

7", picture of muskie jumping out of water, fluted edge, M.Z., Austria 38.50
8½", hanging type, colorful fish swimming on green shaded background, scalloped border, gold trim, signed "Lancy," "Biarritz, W. S. or S. W. Co., Limoges, France" 30.00
9", trout, cobalt border, signed "Kestle Beehive," (old underglaze mark), M.Z. Austria 45.00
9", underwater scene of fish, clams, plant life, embossed and scalloped rim decorated with green and gold seaweed, "T and V Limoge" 45.00

Platters

14", bass, on lure, signed "R. K. Beck" 85.00
16¼", bass, waterlilies heavily embossed, signed "MAX," Limoge 125.00

Sets

7 pieces, 16" platter, 6–9" plates, seashells and fish, Limoge 225.00
7 pieces, 15" platter, 6–9" plates, signed "R. K. Beck," Buffalo Pottery 325.00
8 pieces, 24" platter, 4 plates, covered tureen and sauce boat with attached underplate, Rosenthal 350.00
9 pieces, 17" platter, 8–8⅞" plates, embossed gilt rims artist signed, Limoges 375.00
10 pieces, 24" platter, 6–9" plates, covered casserole, sauce boat, hand painted, Selb, Bavaria 375.00
12 pieces, 22" platter, white various species of fish in brown, light gold trim, impressed "Frieda" ... 325.00
14 pieces, 22" platter, 12–9" plates, sauce with attached plate, covered tureen, handpainted, heavy raised gold design on edges, gold handles and finial, artist signed, Limoges 750.00
14 pieces, 22" platter, 10–8½" plates, sauce boat with underliner, artist signed, Limoges 400.00
15 pieces, 24" platter, 12–9" plates, sauce with attached plate, covered tureen, handpainted, raised gold design on edges, artist signed, Limoges 750.00

GAMES

Earlier versions of old parlor or home games are being collected for the quality of materials and fine craftsmanship in their making. Until about 1843, in New England especially, the struggle for existence was hard and "games" just to play, were looked upon as "devices of the Devil." The two oldest game manufacturers, Parker and Bradley, had other ideas and the parlor game became a great success. In order to meet the demand, other companies came into being, but merged, or eventually died out completely. Parker and Bradley are still in business today. Many games found now are not especially rare, but are of interest as collectibles of a past era.

Spelling, wood with wood discs, beige with red trim, black lettering on discs, Pat. Feb. 16, 1886 . . . . . $40.00

Across the Continent, Parker, 1927	18.00
Anagrams, Milton Bradley, c. 1940 .	10.00
Authors, Milton Bradley, 1896, original box	18.00
Auto Race, All Fair Games, 1922 . .	19.00
Banking, Parker, 1883	30.00
Battle of Manilla, Parker	27.50
Black Cat, fortune telling game, 1897	22.50
Brownie Horseshoe, original box . .	25.00
Checkered Game of Life, Milton Bradley, 1866, (rare)	75.00
Chess Set, carved ivory pieces, leather covered box, brass hardware	450.00
Cotton Tail and Peter, Parker, 1922	28.00
Cribbage, board, carved ivory, Chinese	75.00
District Messenger Boy, McLaughlin, 1886	35.00
Dominoes, ivory and ebony, brass pegs	50.00
East is East, Parker	30.00
Fan, original box with instructions,	

by Schoenhut	50.00
Fish Pond, McLaughlin	17.50
Grandma's Geographical Game, Milton Bradley	40.00
Hokum, Parker, 1927	30.00
Home and History Game, Milton Bradley	35.00
India, c. 1900	40.00
Innocence Abroad, Parker, 1888 . .	40.00
King's Quoits, McLaughlin, 1893 . .	50.00
Klondike, Parker, 1927	35.00
Lincoln Highway, Parker, 1927	30.00
Little Red Riding Hood, McLaughlin, 1867	30.00
Lotto, McLaughlin, c. 1880	27.50
Maj Jongg, box, 10 x 7", teakwood box, 152 hand-painted game tiles, ivory counting rods, and pair of dice, (imported from China 1920–1935), complete set	400.00
Man in the Moon, McLaughlin, 1901	30.00
Monopoly, Parker, 1932, original edition	50.00
Pick-up-Sticks, tin container	15.00
Pike's Peak or Bust, Parker	25.00
Ping Pong, Parker, 1927	15.00
Race for the North Pole, Milton Bradley, 1901	20.00
Rook	28.00
Round the World Flyer's Game, tin playing board, 1922	35.00
Scouting for Boy Scouts, Milton Bradley, (under license Boy Scouts of America), 1920, original box	25.50
Seige of Havana, Parker	25.00
Tell it to the Judge, McLaughlin, Eddie Cantor game, mid-1930's .	35.00
Touring, Parker, 1927	20.00
Train for Boston, Parker, 1900	35.00
The Old Homestead, Milton Bradley, c. 1870	40.00
Toy Town series, Milton Bradley, 1901 (masks for children to wear in playing game)	35.00
War in Cuba, Parker	25.00
Wide World, Parker, c. 1933, map of the world, 4 metal airplanes 4 ships	60.00
Words and Sentences	15.00

GARDEN FURNISHINGS

Garden Furniture and accessories, mainly from the Victorian Gingerbread era, are being collected for use on patios or for special garden settings. With the current interest in plants, all types of planters and plant stands are being sought by home gardeners and decorators. Many of these items are being reproduced.

**Cast iron, Phila., 1860's A. Bach,
set $450.00**

Benches
44″, cast iron, rustic design	375.00
46″, cast iron, circular design . . .	355.00

Chairs
14″ dia. seat, 31″ high, cast iron, ornate	175.00
17″ dia. seat, 33″ high, cast iron, wire mesh	150.00
Empire style, cast iron, painted, pair	425.00

Fence, 39½″ high, cast iron, ornamental, painted black, per linear foot 30.00

Planters, Urn-shaped
32″ high, cast iron, turned down rim, no handles	350.00
40″ high, white cast iron, ornate .	375.00
42½″ high, cast iron, ornate handles, three swan base	350.00

Settee, cast iron, 48″, foliage and grape design, pair 650.00
Stand, plant, cast iron, painted green, pair 140.00

GAUDY DUTCH

Gaudy Dutch is a hand decorated, opaque soft pasteware made in England's Staffordshire district during the first quarter of the 19th century. Sytlistically it is contemporary and similar to the Imari-type wares being made at Derby and Worcester.

The blue decoration was applied to the bisque, glazed, and fired. Other colors were added, glazed, and refired. There is no lustre on any of the standard patterns. Most Gaudy Dutch is unmarked, although occasionally a piece will be found impressed with Wood or Riley.

Reproductions of these patterns have been reported, especially cup plates. These reproductions have a semi-porcelain body and not earthenware; hence, they can be spotted easily.

The known patterns are: Butterfly (two types), Carnation, Dahalia, Double Rose, Dove, Grape, Leaf (scarce), Oyster, Primrose, Single Rose, Strawflower, Sunflower, Urn (two types . . . also known as Vase or Flower Pot), War Bonnet, and Zinnia.

See also KINGS ROSE

Single Rose, 6½″, plate $85.00

Butterfly
Coffee Pot, 10⅞″	3500.00
Creamer	450.00
Cup and Saucer	700.00

Plates
6⅜″	475.00
8¼″	700.00
9¾″	1250.00
Teapot	2000.00
Sugar Bowl	650.00

Carnation
Bowl, 5½″	600.00
Cup and Saucer	500.00

Plates
6½″	325.00
7½″	375.00
8¼″	475.00
Teapot	1000.00

Dahlia
Creamer	425.00
Cup and Saucer	550.00
Sugar, covered	650.00
Teapot	1250.00

Double Rose
Plate, 7½″	475.00

Dove
Coffee Pot, 11″	3000.00
Cup and Saucer	600.00

Plates
6¾″	350.00

8¼″	500.00
9¾″	700.00
Wash Bowl	650.00

Grape

Cup and Saucer	250.00
Plate, 8″	275.00
Sugar, covered	400.00

Oyster

Cup and Saucer	525.00
Plate, 8¼″	475.00

Primrose

Plates

4¾″	425.00
8⅜″, marked Riley	375.00

Single Rose

Coffee Pot	950.00
Cup and Saucer	275.00
Plate, 8¼″	325.00

Sunflower

Cup and Saucer	275.00
Plate, 8½″	300.00
Sugar, covered	275.00

Urn

Cup and Saucer	425.00

Plates

5⅝″	275.00
8¼″	400.00

War Bonnet

Creamer	325.00
Cup and Saucer	475.00
Plate, 9¾″	650.00
Teapot	1250.00

Zinnia

Plates

8⅜″	250.00
10″	325.00

GAUDY IRONSTONE

Ironstone is an opaque, heavy bodied earthenware containing large proportions of flint and slag. Gaudy Ironstone is decorated with some of the patterns bearing resemblance to Gaudy Welsh. The shape, texture and registry marks indicates that the ware was made in England in the 1850's. Most items are impressed "Ironstone."

Coffee Pot, 10″ high, strawberry	500.00
Compote, 7″, Gaudy, green and orange, Amherst Japan pattern	110.00
Cracker Jar, Imari-type decor, silvered lid and bail	125.00

Cups and Saucers

Blackberry, demitasse	75.00
Imari-type decor	65.00
Seeing Eye, Niagara-shape	125.00
Strawberry	125.00
Pitcher, 8″, Imari-type decor	125.00

Plates

Grape, 9½″	55.00

Cup and Saucer, cup 3½″ dia., saucer, 5¾″ dia., no marks $75.00

Seeing Eye, 9″	95.00
Strawberry, 9″	125.00
Sunflower, 7″	55.00
Urn, 8″	75.00

Platters

Imari-type decor, leaf-shape, 7¼ x 11″	75.00
Polychrome, 13 x 18″	150.00
Sauce, 6¾″, Imari-type decor	35.00
Sugar, covered, 8½″ high, strawberry	395.00

GAUDY WELSH

Gaudy Welsh is a translucent porcelain that was originally made in the Swansea area of England from about 1830 to 1845. Although the designs resemble Gaudy Dutch, the body texture and weight differ. One of the characteristics is the gold lustre on top of the glaze.

In 1890, Allerton made a similar ware. These items are a heavier, opaque porcelain and usually bear the export mark.

Some of the known patterns are: Daisy and Chain, Flower Basket, Grape, Morning Glory, Oyster, Shanghai, Strawberry, Tulip, Urn and Wagon Wheel.

Daisy and Chain

Creamer	75.00
Sugar, covered	125.00
Teapot	165.00

Flower Basket (also known as "Urn" or "Vase")

Bowl, 10½″	175.00
Creamer	85.00
Cup and Saucer	75.00
Mug, 4″	65.00

Plates

7½″	60.00

Creamer, 3¼″ high, 5½″ long . $70.00

9″	85.00
Sugar, covered	95.00
Grape	
Creamer	47.50
Cup and Saucer, handled	65.00
Cup and Saucer, handleless	85.00
Morning Glory	
Cup and Saucer	65.00
Pitcher, 6½″, bulbous, Allerton, c.	
1890	85.00
Plate, 10″	100.00
Teapot, 5½″ to top of finial	150.00
Oyster	
Bowl, 6¼″	60.00
Creamer	75.00
Cup and Saucer	75.00
Mug, 3″	55.00
Plates	
5½″	55.00
7″	65.00
9½″	100.00
Tiles	55.00
Shanghai, Creamer	95.00
Strawberry	
Creamer	95.00
Plate, 8¼″	85.00
Teapot	175.00
Tulip	
Creamer	75.00
Cup and Saucer	55.00
Pitcher, Milk	150.00
Plate, 6″	40.00
Sugar, covered	95.00
Teapot	150.00
Wash Set, miniature; pitcher, 3¼″,	
bowl, 4¼″	200.00
Waste Bowl	75.00
Wagon Wheel	
Cup and Saucer	60.00
Mug, 2¾″	55.00
Plates	
5½″	35.00
7″	47.50
8¼″	65.00

GEISHA GIRL

Geisha Girl is a generic title for ware made by Japan for export to the West, from 1880 until the late 1930's. It was sold as souvenir ware in resort and gift shops. It has become quite popular and has increased in price among collectors. There are over sixty patterns showing activities of the Japanese Geisha. It was made in the Kutani area of Koga province, as well as in Kobe, Tokyo and Nagoya, which were large china-decorating centers. It could be said it is a descendant of Kutani ware; nevertheless, it was designed strictly for Western export and to be sold cheaply.

The designs are typically Japanese, and pieces are bordered in orange-red, dark blue and light green; later pieces show touches of gold. It may be marked "Japan" or "Made in Japan" and carry major Nippon marks, and marks of small Japanese factories. Much of it is not marked at all. It was made in chocolate sets, tea sets, bowls, vases and bureau pieces. It is being reproduced, but copies are decidedly inferior as to design detail and painting of figures.

Bowl and Underplate, bowl 4½″ dia. x 2″ high, marked "Made in Japan" $10.00

Creamer, 5½″, blue border and	
background	8.00
*Cup and Saucer, red border, one	
Geisha in garden	12.50
Nut Cups, 2¼″, footed, blue border,	
set of 5	15.00
Plates, 7¼″, green border with gold	
trim, each	6.00
Plate, 10″, with six 7¼″ serving	
plates, red borders and back-	
ground, two Geishas on bridge,	
set	35.00
*Salt Shaker, 3¼″, one only, red	
background	8.00

Tea Set, covered teapot, creamer and covered sugar, red borders and background, red nobs on covers, red sprouts and handles, 3 pcs. 75.00

Toothpicks
*2½", red trim 10.00
*2½", blue trim 10.00

GIBSON GIRL PLATES

Charles Dana Gibson, an eminent American artist, produced a series of 24 drawings entitled "The Widow and her Friends." The Royal Doulton Works at Lambeth, England, reproduced the drawings on plates. All the plates are 10½" and have the same wide stylized leaf blue border. Life Publishing Co. copyrighted the plates in 1900 and 1901. Prices for the following range from $85.00 to $95.00 each.

Miss Bobbles, "The Authoress Calls and Reads Aloud," 10½" dia. . $85.00

A Message from the Outside World
A Quiet Dinner with Dr. Bottles
And Here Winning New Friends
Failing to Find Rest and Quiet in the Country, She Decides to Return Home
Miss Bobbles Brings a Copy of the Morning Paper
Mr. Waddles Arrives Late and Finds Her Card Filled
Mrs. Diggs is Alarmed at Discovering She Becomes a Trained Nurse
She Contemplates the Cloister
She Decides to Die in Spite of Dr. Bottles
She Finds Exercise does not Improve her Spirits
She Finds Some Consolation in her Mirror

She Goes into Colors
She Goes into Retreat
She Goes to the Fancy Dress Ball as "Juliet"
She is Disturbed by a Vision
She Looks for Relief Among the Old Ones
She Renounces the World; her six Admirers also take Holy Orders
Some Think She Has Remained in Retirement
The Day After Arriving at her Journey's End
They All Go Skating
They Go Fishing
They Take a Morning Run

GIRANDOLES AND MANTEL LUSTRES

Girandole is a highly ornamental candlestick, with marble base and cut glass prisms surrounding the mountings. Mantel lustres are glass vases, with attached cut glass prisms. They are decorative and made of a variety of glass types, enameled or gilded, and were produced in Bohemia and England and various other countries in Europe, and in the United States in the mid-19th century.

GIRANDOLES

Gold leaf, 16", marble base, prisms, girl and boy, birds, pair 355.00
Indian, full figure, spear, three branches 495.00
Man and woman in European attire, double handle, brass, prisms, pair   400.00
Three ornate brass arms, glass prisms, girl and boy on brass base, pair 450.00

Mantel Lustres, 12¼", cream ground, painted pink roses, pink glass cut outs, pair $350.00

MANTEL LUSTRES

Blue with white enameled flowers, cut glass prisms, pair	200.00
Blue with enameled florals, gold trim, white beading, Waterford crystal prisms, pair	225.00
Blue, with 9″, prisms	100.00
Bristol, pink double row of prisms, blue and white floral	140.00
Bristol, camphor with gold at rim, cut glass prisms, single	140.00
Cobalt blue, 10″ with prisms, pair	160.00
Cobalt blue, enameled with prisms	85.00
Cut glass, sunburst base, baluster stem, nine cut prisms, pair	180.00
Overlay, with plain ruby with spear cut prisms	375.00
Pairpoint, green cut glass, signed pair, electrified	500.00
Ruby lustre with long cut prisms, pair	350.00

GONDER POTTERY

Lawton Gonder established Gonder Ceramic Arts, Inc., at Zainsville, Ohio, in 1941. He gained his experience at other factories in the area. The corporation remained in existance until 1957.

Among Gonder's glazes where Chinese crackle, gold crackle, and flambe. The overall design of his products is excellent. Lamp bases were manufactured under the name Eglee at a second plant location.

Gonder's pieces are clearly marked. They remain an inexpensive item, although several dealers have begun to purchase them and put them in storage waiting for a market increase.

Candlesticks, 4¾″ dia., turquoise exterior, pink coral interior, marked "E-14" Gonder $12.50

Bowls	
6½ x 2½″, light blue and pink glossy glaze, ribbed	8.00
7¾ x 7″, blue and brown glossy glaze, swirl, flower frog	17.50
Cornucopia, turquoise and brown, marked E-5, 7″	12.00
Ewers	
6″, mottled blue, pink interior	20.00

12″, swan shaped	27.50
Vases	
5″, dogwood, marked E-3	10.00
7½″, pink and mottled blue glaze, flower shaped	12.50
8″, lavender and brown glaze, swans on base, marked 1-147 USA	25.00
12″, glossy yellow with mottled red glaze, leaf motif	30.00

GOOFUS GLASS

This glass was originally called Mexican Glass, and was first made in the early 1900's. From about 1910 to 1920 it competed with Carnival glass as give-aways or prizes at fairs and carnivals. The glass was pressed with painted design and lustred. Several factories produced it: LaBelle Glass Co., Bridgeport, Ohio; Crescent Glass Co., Wellsburg, W. Va.; Imperial Glass Co., Bellaire, Ohio; and Northwood Glass Co., Indiana, Pa.

Vase, "Rose," 7½″, rose with gold $25.00

Bowls	
Rose design, 4½″, roses cover outside, milk glass, painted	20.00
Carnation, 9″	25.00
Grapes, 9¼″	17.50
Pointsetta, 9¼″	22.50
Roses, 9″, milk glass	25.00

Strawberry, 10½"	22.50
Water Lily, 10½"	22.50
Centerpiece, footed bowl, apples, pears, gold leaves, edge and feet, marked "N" in center	35.00
Flask, Klondyke-type, milk glass, made during the Gold Rush, outstanding molded, zig-zag design, gold paint, metal screw top	45.00

Jars

Aqua, molded, floral design; originally held pickles; gold, blue and red paint	25.00
Peacocks	20.00
Roses	18.50

Lamps

Miniature	40.00
Oil, pedesteled type	35.00
Low, bulged bowl, large "Goofus" Spider Web shade, milk glass, (scarce)	150.00

Plates

Fruit and grape center, gold trim, good paint	25.00
Poppies and leaves, good paint, clear, 8"	25.00
Roses, milk glass, paint worn, 8¼"	20.00
Salt, "Gaudy Rose," flowers protrude ½" from body, large single	25.00
Tray, Chrysanthemum, 8¼ x 11"	35.00

Vases

Daisy and Scroll, 9¼", milk glass, painted	27.50
Roses, 10", outstanding roses and leaves, milk glass, painted	30.00

MARK

GOSS CHINA

W H GOSS

In 1858, William Henry Goss began the production of Parian, ivory-porcelain terracotta, and such at a factory in Stoke-upon-Trent, England. The progress of this company in pure art production was notable. Among its most famous specialties were porcelain, floral jewelry and dress ornaments—brooches, hairpins, scent diffusers, and crosses. Many handpainted scent vases, pomade boxes, rice powder jars, pastil and scented ribbon burners were made, largely for the great Paris and London perfume houses. Goss also produced jewelled porcelain vases, scent bottles, tazzas, and other ornaments, inventing a process for such jewelling.

His ivory-porcelain was soft and mellow in

tone and extremely durable; it is of this ware that the little crest souvenir jugs were made.

The Goss China Co. was sold to Washington Potteries (China Craft) Ltd., in 1951. Some Goss pieces are stamped "W. H. Goss." On others, the crest, a falcon rising, ducally gorged, was used either by itself or with the name.

Goss pieces are sometimes grouped with the small colored figures known as "Fairings," because they were sold at fairs and on market-day galas, very cheaply. However, the quality of Goss items far exceeds that of "Fairings."

CRESTS. All following pieces have name and Falcon mark.

Ashtray with heraldic crest	30.00

Cups

Egg Cup Tynemouth crest	40.00
Three handled, Arms of Glastonburg	30.00
Three handled, Seal of Chichester	30.00
Goblet, Woodbridge crest	20.00
Hat Pin Holder, Bilston crest	35.00
Jug, handled, City of Liverpool crest	40.00

Models

Jersey fish basket, crest	20.00
Pilgrim bottle crest	20.00
Roman ewer, 3½", crest	20.00
Shoe with frilled top, Cambridge crest	30.00
Tumbler, 3½", Stoke on Trent crest	30.00

Vase, 2⅝", No. 382437, model of Roman vase found at Walmar Lodge $25.00

Vases

Mitre shaped, Burnham coat of arms	40.00
Pear shaped, York coat of arms .	40.00
Three handled, matte finish, City of London coat of arms	45.00
Two handled, Edinburgh coat of arms	35.00
Urn shaped, Brighton coat of arms	35.00
Urn shaped, Bolton Abbey seal . .	35.00

OTHER ITEMS

Animals

Cat, Cheshire, England	85.00
Cat, Cheshire, unglazed, c. 1920 .	250.00
Dog, colored, c. 1920	650.00
Lion, standing, c. 1920	500.00
Rabbit, small, Goss, England . . .	65.00
Swan, 2″, c. 1920	195.00

Busts

Burns, Robert, terracotta, c. 1867	400.00
Scott, Sir Walter, 5½″, Parian . . .	195.00
Shakespeare, 3½″, Parian colored	125.00
Shakespeare, 3½″, Parian, white	75.00

Cottages

Dickens, Charles, Gad's Hill	175.00
Hathaway, Ann	100.00
Shakespeare, Full length	85.00
Shakespeare, night light	175.00
Cross, Banbury, white Goss, England	295.00

Figurines, Goss, England

Bride	150.00
Grandmother	200.00
Lady Rose	225.00
Mother-in-law	150.00
Trusty Servant, colored	225.00
Welsh Lady, (Teapot)	125.00

Models

Canterbury Leather bottle	20.00
Chester Roman Vase, large	25.00
Dorchester Jug	15.00
Irish Wooden Noggin	25.00
Lanlawren Urn, small	12.00
Norwegian Wooden shoe	40.00
Swiss milk bucket, 2½″	28.50
Tewkesbury Urn	15.00
Wesh hat	22.50
Yorick's skull, medium yellow . . .	225.00
Yorick's skull, white	125.00
Yorick's skull, night light, white . .	250.00
Jug, cream, 4½″, melon shape . . .	10.00
Marmalade, covered Bag ware	50.00

Mugs

Windsor Castle, 1¼″	25.00
Blenheim, 3″	30.00
Teapot, Bag ware	55.00
Tea Set, Miniature, "Thistle," 8 pieces	300.00
Vase, 1¾″, Bag ware	20.00

MADE IN
Zuid Holland

GOUDA POTTERY

Gouda and the surrounding areas of Holland have been one of the centers of the Dutch pottery industry for centuries. Originally the potteries produced a simple utilitarian Delft-type earthenware with a tin glaze and the famous clay smokers' pipes.

When the pipe making portion declined in the early 1900's, the Gouda potteries turned to Art Pottery. Influenced by the Art Nouveau and Art Deco movements, artists expressed themselves with free-form and stylized designs in bold colors.

With the Art Nouveau and Art Deco revival of recent years, modern reproductions of Gouda pottery currently are on the market. They are difficult to distinguish from the originals.

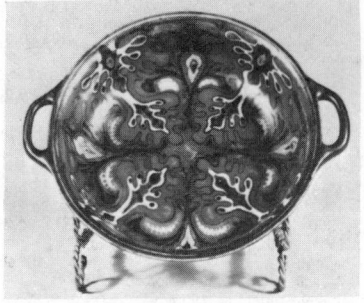

Bowl, 10¼″ dia. including handles, typical colors $135.00

Basket, turquoise, navy, orange, etc., Ingeborg, 5¼ x 8½″	125.00

Bowls

4″, blue and green, handled	40.00
6″, covered, Schoonhaven, stylized leaves	90.00
7½″, multicolored, Canada	60.00
8½″, multicolored, two handled, Pelta, floral decor	70.00
Box, carved, black, gold, white, high glaze, Regina, 4¼″	150.00

Candlesticks

3″, chamberstick, green with yel-

low, blues, and cream, matted finish, 0139 DAM III, floral motif, c. 1885 .... 90.00
4", pair, floral motif 80.00
13", pair, blue, gold, black, c. 1910 .... 150.00
Charger, pierced for hanging, Plazuid, 12" diam., 2" deep 175.00
Coaster, grape, c. 1910 .... 35.00
Compotes
   3" x 10" diam., two handled, multicolored, Sluis 130.00
   7½", handled, multicolored, floral motif, c. 1925 .... 85.00
Ewer
   4¼", canteen shape, multicolored, floral motif 60.00
   6", Art Deco, multicolored, Arnhem 75.00
Inkwell, hexagonal shape, 3", c. 1920 .... 80.00
Jardiniere, multicolored, floral motif, 4½", c. 1930 .... 85.00
Pitchers
   3¼", two handles, multicolor on black base, floral motif 32.50
   5", orange, green, lion design, late 50.00
Plates
   8", multicolored, pastel, c. 1900 . 80.00
   10", Art Deco 110.00
Shoe, multicolored, Lanac, 5" 50.00
Tobacco Jars
   7", Art Deco 150.00
   11", floral motif, c. 1910 .... 180.00
Tray, black ground, high glaze, 12½ x 17" 175.00
Trivet, Damascus, 4", c. 1895 .... 175.00
Vases
   3¼", Bergen 35.00
   4½", rust, cobalt, Art Nouveau, c. 1900 .... 60.00
   6½", high glaze, Art Nouveau, signed 100.00
   7", stick type, multicolored, high glaze, Arnhem, c. 1900 .... 115.00
   7½", coral, Schoonoven 90.00
   8", blue and white 200.00
   10", multicolored, Art Deco, Isolde 160.00
   12¼", Eskroff 175.00

GRANITEWARE

Graniteware is the name given to, usually, iron kitchenware covered with enamel coating. It was featured at the 1876 Centennial Exposition, and became popular because it was light weight and attractive. It is still made, but the earlier pieces are in great demand by collectors. It was made primarily in mottled grey, marbleized green and blue. The green is the earliest color made. It is also made in pure white with red and dark blue and black trim.

Chamberstick, 6" dia. base, marbelized pink and green $67.50

Bundt Pan, fluted grey 12.50
Bowls
   8", blue and white 10.00
   8", green and white 12.00
   8", mottled grey 7.50
Cake Pan, angel food, grey 12.00
Collander, on base, grey 10.00
Coffee Pot, goose neck spout, mottled grey, pewter lid, wooden finial 37.50
Cream can, with lid and bail handle, mottled grey 20.00
Custard cups, white, black trim, "Germany" 7.50
Cuspidor, ladies', grey 15.00
Dish Pan
   17", blue 40.00
   White with black trim 30.00
   White with red trim 30.00
Funnels
   Grey 5.00
   Blue and white, marbleized 8.50
Invalid Feeders
   White with black trim and handle 12.00
   Grey 10.00
Mugs
   Blue 10.00
   Green 12.00
   Grey 10.00
Pitchers
   Blue, tankard type 25.00
   Grey, ½ gallon 22.50
Plates
   Dinner, grey 8.00
   Pie, grey 8.00
   Pie, blue and white 10.00
Pot, covered, 6½", grey 15.00
Pudding Pan, 5¼", grey 12.00
Skillet, 8½", grey 18.00
Soap Dish, blue and white 7.50
Spoon
   Large, grey 8.00

White, black handle	7.50

Teapots
Covered, gooseneck spout, blue and white	25.00
Egg, shaped, grey pewter handle and lid, and handle, tea ball attached	55.00
Water Dipper, 12″, grey	12.00

GREENAWAY, KATE   K.G.

Kate Greenaway, or K.G. as she initialed her famous drawings, was born in 1846 in London. She was naturally talented as an artist. Her father was a prominent wood engraver. She went to art classes at age 12, had her first public exhibition in 1868. She did card illustrations for Marcus Ward, which were all unsigned and would be a good source for collectors today. China companies and potteries in England used her children in all manner of items which were extremely popular at that time, and afford many opportunities for collectors today. Some Greenaway buttons have been reproduced in Europe and sold in the United States and collectors should be aware of this fact.

Book, Frederick Warne & Co., Ltd. $100.00

Books
April Baby's Book of Tunes, MacMillan, 1900 (rare)	100.00
Kate Greenaway's Alphabet	75.00
Kate Greenaway's Birthday Book .	68.50
*Language of Flowers, Edmund Evans	100.00
Marigold Garden, 1885	100.00
Mother Goose, Routledge, 1881 .	100.00
Book Plate, 7 x 9½″, lithographed, c. 1881	15.00
Book Mark, 8″ long, blue silk, handpainted, Greenaway illus. . . .	50.00
Boot Scraper, 4 x 6¼″, cast iron, fence, Greenaway children supporting each end	65.00

Buttons
2 pc. brass, ¾″, from "Under the Window" set of 8 different	57.50
2 pc. brass, 1″ Kate Greenaway girl in straw hat, ea.	5.00
Black glass, lustred ¾″, Pat'd date, 1880, "Child at Well", ea. . .	6.50
Black glass, lustred, ¾″, Pat'd date, 1880, "Girl and Kitten at Stile", ea.	6.50
Cake Stand, 9″, Doulton	150.00
Calendar of the Seasons, 8 tinted pages, signed	65.00
Child's Feeding Set, plate, cup and saucer, Germany	125.00
Children's Toy Dishes, embossed alphabet borders, Greenaway girls sitting on dog, set	100.00
Feeding Dish, 6½″, "This is the Maiden all Forlorn"	60.00

Figurines
6″, "Little Julia"	85.00
5¾″, boy in coat with fur collar and hat	85.00
5 x 6½″, three little girls holding on to each other's skirts black, blue, pink and gold decor	125.00
Match Holder, child with hat, with holder beside her	125.00
Mug, 3½″, figural, silver, little girl, marked Simpson, Hall, Miller and Co.	100.00
Plate, 8″, oval, child's plate, from "Under the Window"	45.00

Salt and Pepper shakers
5″ girl in fur trimmed coat and muff, polychrome, glazed, single .	25.00
4½″, two little girls, old fashioned clothes, silver plate, pair	75.00
Tea Set, 15″ tray, pierced handles, teapot, sugar bowl, two cups and saucers, Greenaway decor, 5 pcs.	350.00

Tiles
"Pipe thee High," little boy with horn, Wedgwood	75.00
Two girls in apple tree, from "Marigold Garden," marked Minton, Hollins Co., Pat'd Tile Works, Stoke-on-Trent	85.00

Toothpick Holders
Bisque, boy behind basket 50.00
Girl with fur collar and muff, silver, Meriden 75.00
Girl in cape and bonnet, sitting beside holder, silver plate 75.00
Vases
3¾", hand painted, Greenaway children, decor 50.00
9", ivory, with silver rim, Greenaway girls 85.00

GREENTOWN GLASS

Greentown glass was first made by the Indiana Tumbler and Goblet Co., Greentown, Ind., in 1894. In 1899, the company was reorganized as the National Glass Co., the second largest glass manufacturer in the U. S. A factory fire in June, 1903, brought an end to Greentown glass.

The concern produced a variety of pressed glass wares in clear and colored, including the limited "Holly Amber." Their "Cactus" pattern has been heavily reproduced in colors not originally made. Also, see Pattern Glass Section for additional patterns.

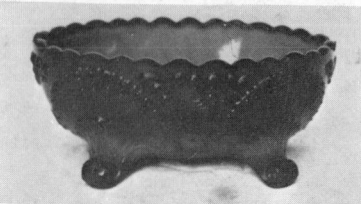

Bowl, berry, "Geneva," chocolate, 4⅛" oval $200.00

Animal Dishes, covered
Cat on hamper, chocolate 250.00
Fighting cocks 1750.00
Hen on nest, golden agate 1410.00
Hen on nest, opaque nile green . 1575.00
Rabbit on nest, amber 125.00
Robin on pedestal nest, milk white 210.00
*Berry Set, Cactus, chocolate, 7 pcs. 250.00
Bowls, Berry
*Cactus, chocolate 200.00
Cord Drapery, amber 52.50
Dewey, (Flower Flange), amber . 52.50
Leaf Bracket, chocolate 225.00
Leaf Bracket, clear 35.00
Herringbone Buttress, chocolate . 250.00
Herringbone Buttress, emerald green 65.00

Butter, Covered
*Cactus, chocolate 250.00
Cord Drapery, amber 61.00
Dewey, (Flower Flange), green . . 61.00
*Cakestand; Cactus, chocolate, (rare) 950.00
*Celery, Cactus, chocolate 150.00
Compotes
*Cactus, sweetmeat, chocolate . . 395.00
Pleat Band, clear 25.00
*Cracker Jar, Cactus, chocolate . . . 275.00
Creamers
Austrian, clear 35.00
*Cactus, chocolate 100.00
Cord Drapery, clear 40.00
Fleur de Lys, chocolate 100.00
Overall Lattice, clear 30.00
Shuttle, (Hearts of Loch Laven), chocolate 90.00
Cruets, stoppered
Dewey (Flower Flange), chocolate 200.00
Cord Drapery, blue 500.00
Goblets
Austrian, clear 28.00
Beehive, clear 50.00
Birds in Swamp, clear 85.00
Brazen Shield, clear 65.00
Cord Drapery, chocolate 75.00
Diamond Prisms 95.00
Hearts of Loch Haven, (Shuttle), clear 35.00
Shovel, clear 15.00
Strigil, clear 10.00
Lamp, "Wild Rose with Festoon," chocolate base 475.00
Mugs
Cactus, chocolate 75.00
Dewey, (Flower Flange), green . . 63.50
Hearts of Loch Laven, (Shuttle), clear 35.00
Serenade, milk white 45.00
Nappies
Austrian, clear 15.00
Masonic, chocolate 175.00
Pitchers, syrup
*Cactus, chocolate 250.00
Cord Drapery 200.00
Herringbone Buttress, clear 85.00
Pitchers, water
Brickwork, clear 39.00
Cord Drapery, chocolate 200.00
Deer Alert, clear 110.00
Deer with Oak Tree 145.00
Dog Hunting 150.00
Herringbone Buttress, clear 85.00
Ruffled Eye, green 150.00
Plates
*Cactus, chocolate, 7½" 90.00
"Austrian," clear, 10" 22.50
"Overall Lattice," clear center . . . 25.00
Shakers, Herringbone Buttress, emerald green, pair 200.00

Spooners
　Austrian, clear 22.50
　Leaf Bracket, chocolate 85.00
Smoking Set, Wild Rose with Bow-
　knot, chocolate 850.00
Stein, lidded, Elves, milk white 50.00
Sugars
　Austrian, clear 27.50
　*Cactus, chocolate 150.00
　Dewey, (Flower Flange), choco-
　late 141.00
　Herringbone Buttress, clear 45.00
Toothpicks
　Boot, chocolate 85.00
　*Cactus, chocolate 125.00
　Herringbone Buttress, clear 45.00
　Wild Rose with Bowknot,
　chocolate 150.00
Tumblers
　Austrian, clear 20.00
　*Cactus, iced tea, chocolate 95.00
　Geneva, chocolate 125.00
　Leaf Bracket, chocolate 125.00
　Uneeda Biscuit tumbler, choco-
　late 95.00
Vase, Herringbone Buttress, emerald
　green, 8½" 90.00

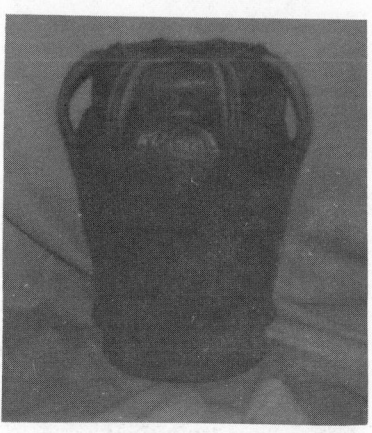

Vase, 8", tooled leaves and buds, green $350.00

　green ground 350.00
　6 x 6", white horses on a blue
　ground 450.00
Tobacco Jar, yellow flowers near top
　on green ground 850.00
Vases
　4 x 4", bulbous, tooled verticle rib-
　bing, brown 250.00
　4½", tooled leaves, blue 300.00
　9", overlapping leaves overall, yel-
　low 550.00

GRUEBY POTTERY

**William Grueby was active in the ceramic in-
dustry for several years before he developed
his own method of producing matte glazed
pottery and founded the Grueby Faience
Company in Boston, Massachusetts, in 1897.**

　**The art pottery was hand thrown in natural
shapes, hand molded and hand tooled. A variety of colored glazes, singly or in combinations, were produced with green being the
most prominent. In 1908, the firm was divided into the Grueby Pottery Company and
Grueby Faience & Title Co.; the latter making
art pottery until bankruptcy forced closure
shortly thereafter.**

Bowl, 3", turned in rim, green 100.00
Candlestick, 5½", blue 250.00
Scarab (paperweight) 150.00
Tiles
　4½ x 4½", white lamb on a green
　ground 225.00
　6 x 6", turtle tile, brown on a

GUTTA-PERCHA

**Gutta-Percha are species of tropical trees
that have a milky latex sap. The sap can be
used to make a rubbery, leather-like material.
Probably the most extensive use of gutta-
percha material in the past has been for daguerreotype cases.**

　**See also DAGUERREOTYPES AND DA-
GUERREOTYPE CASES**

Boxes
　2 x 3¼ x 13", Hinged lid, straw-
　berry decor in relief 45.00
　3¼ x 4¾ x 4¾", Hinged lid, or-
　nate scene of deer in woodland . 40.00
Brooch
　Cameo-type of woman's face in
　relief, c. 1860 . . . . 30.00
　Key design, 3¾", ornate 35.00
Buckle, George and Martha Wash-
　ington decor 75.00
Compote, 7", turned wooden stan-

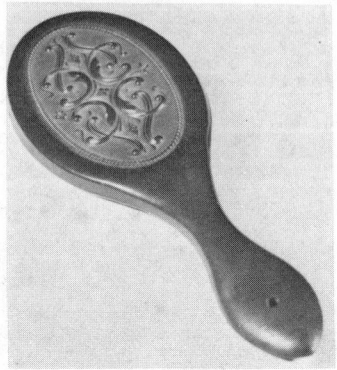

Hand Mirror, 7½", Pat. June 19, 1866 . . . . $22.00

dard, inlaid bands of gutta-percha and wooden decor and medallion	150.00
Cross, 3¾", ornate	60.00
Frame, Daguerreotype, 6 x 8", embossed, lined with red velvet, book type, dated 1868	75.00
Match Safes	
Arm and Hammer	30.00
Garter Crest, Edward VII	80.00
Mirrors	
Folding, 4½ x 7", Greek key border, florals, portrait center	125.00
Hand, 9¾", portrait center, scroll border	35.00
Hand, leaves and berry design, Pat'd. 1868	30.00
Hand, woodland scene, house, dated 1872	30.00
Pencil, mechanical, checkered design with gold filled top and bottom	25.00

HAIR ORNAMENTS

Hair ornaments consist of barrettes, combs and elaborate hair pins to hold or adorn women's hair of all cultures, from the past to the present. They can be in any material, from simple bone or celluloid set with "Brilliants" to precious metals.

Barrette, 4", bar type, tortoise shell type with rhinestones	7.50
Bun Cover, expandable type, metal with beads, c. 1940	10.00
Combs	

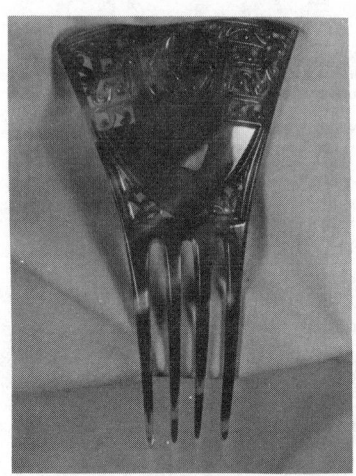

Tortoise type, 6", comb, pierced top $7.50

Gutta Percha and Cetron Turquoise, 8", scrolled and pierced floral	65.00
Silver, coin, 3½", wedge shaped	65.00
Sterling serpent, 4", 2-prong	35.00
Tortoise Shell, 7", 4-pronged, set with beads	45.00
Turquoise set with brilliants, "King Tut"	85.00
Hair pins	
Gold, mounted with small diamond	75.00
Metal, silvered, 6", free swinging bells, Oriental, c. 1960	10.00
Tortoise type, 2", 2 pronged, vine decor	7.50
Tortoise type, 3", 2 pronged, inlaid stones	10.00

HAMPSHIRE POTTERY

James S. Taft founded the Hampshire Pottery Company, Keene, N.H., in 1871. In the beginning redwares and stonewares were produced. Majolica wares decorated with colors entered in 1879. A semi-porcelain ware with the Royal Worcester glaze was introduced in 1883. Also in 1883, the recognizable matte glazes were developed.

The factory made an extensive line of utilitarian and art wares including souvenir items until World War I when the limited demand

for such items forced closure. After the war, the firm resumed operation, but only made hotel dinnerware and tiles. The company was dissolved in 1923.

Creamer, Souvenir "Eastport, Me.," black with gold lettering, Impressed Hampshire, Date 1883–1900 . . . $20.00

Bowls
5 x 4", scroll work in relief, green	**30.00**
6 x 2½" deep, dark blue	**55.00**
9 x 2¼" deep, florals in relief, dark blue	**85.00**
Mug, 4⅛", Landing of the Pilgrims, tan . . . . | **75.00**
Nappy, 9", violet on ivory, artist signed . . . . | **65.00**
Pitchers
6", Roman Key	**35.00**
11½", Yankee Doodle, Royal Worcester glaze, c. 1883	**350.00**
11", tankard, greens	**75.00**
Planter, 4 x 6½", cattails in relief, green . . . . | **50.00**
Vases
3⅜", green	**20.00**
6½", green, blue	**65.00**
7", cylinder, blue	**45.00**
7", spear decor, gray	**65.00**
7½", acanthus leaves in relief, green	**85.00**
9", free-form, mottled blue, brown, green	**95.00**

HAND PAINTED CHINA

Hand painting on china was a very popular pasttime for ladies in the Victorian era. It is currently being revived. It was done in England and the Continent much earlier than in the United States, where it did not become a popular pasttime until after the Civil War.

Many china factories in America made china blanks for the amateur painters, as did the big porcelain factories in Europe; among the American factories that supplied these blanks were A. H. Hews Co., Cambridge, Mass.; Willetts Mfg. Co., Trenton, N.J.; Knowles, Taylor and Knowles, East Liverpool, Ohio.

Prices vary according to origin and type of porcelain blank, and the talent of the artist using it. See also, BAVARIAN, LIMOGES, HAVILAND, GAME PLATES, etc.

Compote, 5½" high, 8⅞" dia., Artist signed, 1907 . . . .$125.00

Bowls
13", burnt orange with gold sketch of trees, mountains and foliage, Hutschenreuther, Selb, Bavaria, Germany **85.00**
14¼", Lenox Art Pottery, Pallette mark, on foot, with Water Lily design, blue green, gold trim on white **57.50**
Candle Holders, Limoge, low wide bases, petal shaped cups, floral, blue and yellow decor, with gold trim, pair **35.00**
Dishes
12", footed, TV Elite, Limoge, Roses, foliage and gold trim **50.00**
14", E. and S. Germany, centerpiece shallow bowl, green and gold decor, swans and castle . . . **75.00**
Jug, Cider, painted with apples and leaves **85.00**
Pitchers
Tall, narrow, with elaborate dragon handle, heavily trimmed in gold, handle, and top rim, fruit, peaches, apples, cherries, decor,

no mark	100.00
Wine, 15″, roses pink on shaded red background, gold trim and handle	90.00
Plates	
8″, shaded pale yellow to rich green, large bunch of grapes and foliage, no mark	25.00
8″, Water Lily medallions around border, pond scene in center ...	27.50
9″, deep blue borders, with ribbon and rosetted medallions, gold medallion center	35.00
13″, white background, strawberries and foliage, Limoge	55.00
Ramekins, 3½″, white background, pink borders, rosebuds decor, gold trim on edges, set of 12, Limoge	135.00
Tea Set, tea pot, covered; sugar, creamer, 12 cups and saucers; 12 8½″ plates; Royal Rudulstadt, Germany; rosebuds, gold band around body, gold handles, gold footed cups, 27 pieces	350.00

HARDWARE
See IRONWARE

HAT PINS AND HAT PIN HOLDERS

Hat pins became popular in the closing decades of the 1800's when the vogue developed for oversize hats. Designers used various materials to decorate the pin shaft: china, crystal, shells, enamel, gem stones, precious metals and coins. Decorative subjects range from commemorative designs to insects.

Porcelain containers, designed to hold a collection of these pins, could be found on most dressing tables in the Victorian period. Familiar names such as Wedgwood, Meissen, Limoge and Satsuma are associated with the production of hatpin holders.

HAT PINS

Abalone	7.50
Brass	
Amber set	10.00
Parrot	15.00
Sailor's hat with enamelled red bow	12.00
Black glass	3.00
Gilt on metal	6.00
Gold metal, initial "E"	6.00
Engraved, on gold, pair	39.00
Four Leaf clover, enameled green	

on gold	50.00
Moonstone, gold filled	16.00
Openwork knot, center diamond chip	75.00
Oriental pearl	50.00
Synthetic pink sapphire	35.00
Tear-shaped pink quartz	30.00
Violets, hand painted on china ...	16.00
Turtle, enameled green with red eyes	22.50
Zig-Zag pattern, Carnival glass, purple	45.00

R.S. Germany, handpainted, 4½″ $35.00

HAT PIN HOLDERS

Austrian, floral decor, gold trim, saucer base	25.00
Haviland, white, undecorated, petal base	18.50
Nippon, 5″, maple leaf mark, delicate pink flowers, surrounded by a circle of gold, green leaves, and gold beading	60.00
R. S. Germany, floral decor, hand painted	48.50
R. S. Prussia, mill scene, brown tones	350.00
Hand painted, signed "J. D.," pink flowers	21.00
Yellow Roses, hand painted	16.00

HAVILAND CHINA

Treasured from generation to generation, Haviland china has never fallen from favor with those who demand the finest in porcelain. The first Haviland was imported in 1842 and production continues to this day. Four generations of the family have maintained a standard of high quality and artistic achievement that is evident in each of many hundreds of patterns and in thousands of variations of those patterns.

The history of Haviland china is complicated and confusing because of the various combinations of partnerships of the Haviland brothers and their sons. David Haviland, a New York china importer, established a china factory at Limoges, France in 1842, under the name of Haviland & Co. Products were sold through the American firm of D.G. & D. Haviland Co., of which David Haviland was a partner.

In 1852, two other brothers were admitted to the firm of D. G. & D. Haviland Co., and the name Haviland Bros. & Co. was established. The firm was discontinued in 1865.

Chronology of the various Haviland firms and partnerships:

1835–36. Edmund and David Haviland, New York china importers.

1837. David Haviland established his own importing business.

1838. David's brother, Daniel, joined him to establish the American firm of D. G. & D. Haviland.

1842. David Haviland established a factory at Limoges, France under the name of Haviland & Co. His brother Daniel was a silent partner and continued to manage the New York importing firm.

1852. Daniel and David admitted two brothers, Robert and Richard, to the D.G. & D. Haviland firm. The name was then changed to Haviland Bros. & Co.

1858. Chas. Field Haviland, a son of David's brother Robert, married the granddaughter of Francois Alluaud, owner of the Alluaud factory.

1859. Chas. Field Haviland established a decorating shop with blanks furnished by the Alluaud Works.

1863. David withdrew from Haviland Bros. & Co. to devote full time to the Limoges factory.

1865. Haviland Bros. & Co. suspended business as importers and distributors.

1866. Daniel G. Haviland withdrew as a partner from the French Limoges factory.

1870. Chas. Field Haviland & Co. was formed in New York between Chas. Field Haviland and Oliver A. Gager.

1874. David Haviland's sons, Charles Edward Miller and Theodore, entered into partnership with their father as Haviland & Co.

1876. Chas. Field Haviland became manager of Casseau Pottery Works, successor to the Alluaud Pottery. He used the mark "Ch. Field Haviland."

1879. David died and his sons, Charles Edward and Theodore, continued business through 1891.

1881. Chas. Field Haviland retired from manufacturing and sold his interest in Chas. Field Haviland & Co. in New York to Oliver A. Gager who continued in the business until 1889 when he died. Firm name was changed to Haviland & Abbott. Operations ended about the time of World War I.

1892. Brothers, Charles Edward Miller and Theodore, dissolved partnership. Charles continued business under the name of Haviland & Co., while Theodore began operations as LaPorcelaine Theodore Haviland at Limoges, France where he acquired a factory. White ware was marked "Theodore Haviland" in a horseshoe with "France" within, all in green. Decoration marks varied. In 1892 the T. H. monogram with "Limoges France" printed in red, and "Porcelaine Mousseline" above was used. In 1914 the mark was "Theodore Haviland" (in italics) with "Limoges" below and "France" underneath. The mark was usually in red with occasional green coloring. In 1920 the italicizing of the name Theodore was discontinued after his death. The business was then conducted by his son, Wm. David Haviland.

1936. Company decided to make chinaware in America because of tariff regulations and rising costs in France.

1941. Assets of Haviland & Co. were obtained from the French heirs of Charles Edward Miller Haviland by Wm. David Haviland for the Theodore Haviland Co. The mark after 1941 was "Theodore Haviland, New York" in a vignette with "Made in America" below.

1946. Wm. Theodore Haviland modernized factory at Limoges, France with electronically controlled kilns.

1963. New line of Haviland giftware introduced in America.

1970. Issued first edition in a series of Christmas collector's plates.

Bone Dish, Ranson. #1 . . . . 12.50

Bowls
Ranson, #24. Cereal 16.50
Ranson, #24. Soup 18.50
Butter Pats
Princess 6.50
Ranson, #1 .... 6.50
Chocolate Pot, H-P blue green flowers, leaves, gold trim 85.00
Cream and Sugar, 3½", H-P florals, gold trim 65.00
Cream Soups, with underplates "Autumn Leaf," set of 6 .... 90.00
Cups and Saucers
Drop Rose 75.00
Norma, coffee 22.50
Princess, coffee 22.50
Ranson, #1, coffee 25.00
Ranson, #24, coffee 35.00
Ranson, #24, tea 30.00
Decanter, 9", with stopper, H-P floral decor 55.00
Dinner Sets
Ranson, #24, service for 12, 120 pieces 2500.00
Ranson, #1, service for 12, 100 pieces 1500.00
Silver Anniversary, service for 12, 80 pieces 1500.00
Dresser Trays
7¾ x 9½", H-P flowers and berries 45.00
8 x 9", leaf-shaped, Baltimore Rose 35.00
Gravy Boats
Princess 45.00
Ranson, #24 .... 65.00
Silver Anniversary 50.00
Mayonnaise, with underplate, H-P florals 40.00
Pitcher, Water, 7½", H-P yellow roses on white ground, gold handle, trim 85.00
Plaque, 13½", Indian chief, full head dress 85.00
Plates
Dorset, 6⅛" 7.50
Princess, 9½" 20.00
Ranson, #1, oyster 37.50
Ranson, #24, 7⅜" (coupe) 18.50
Ranson, #24, 9⅝" 25.00
Roses, hand painted, set of 6 ... 150.00
Silver Anniversary, 9½" 15.00
Platters
Baltimore Rose, 10½" 45.00
Greek Key, 16" 40.00
Handpainted, 23½", yellow roses, satin finish, artist signed 225.00
Ranson, #1, 16" 28.50
Ranson, #24, 11½" 35.00
Ranson, #24, 18", two wells ... 65.00
Ramekin, with underplate, Baltimore Rose 32.50

Plate, 7¼", Limoges $20.00

Relish, Princess 18.50
Sauces
Baltimore Rose 12.50
Moss Rose 6.50
Ranson, #24 .... 10.00
Silver Anniversary 6.50
Soup Plates, 8", cobalt borders with gold, black cherries, set of 7 .... 27.00
Sugars, covered
Ranson, #1 .... 25.00
Ranson, #24 .... 35.00
Teapots
Handpainted. Cupids, florals.
Gold trim 75.00
Moss Rose 50.00
Ranson, #1 .... 65.00
Tea Set. Wedding Ring. 3 pieces .. 125.00
Tureen, 9½" diam., 10" high, H-P blue flowers 125.00
Vegetables, covered
Ranson, #24, Oval 50.00
Silver Anniversary 35.00
Vegetables, open
Norma 30.00
Princess 30.00
Ranson, #24 .... 40.00
Waste Bowl, Ranson, #1 .... 25.00

HEISEY GLASS

The A. H. Heisey Glass Co. began producing glasswares in April, 1896 in Newark, Ohio. Mr. Heisey was not a newcomer to the field having been associated with the craft since his youth.

Hundreds of crystal patterns for table settings were produced. Heisey also employed colored and opal (custard) glass. Glass figurines were introduced in 1933 and continued until 1957 when the factory ceased production.

Some Heisey molds were sold to Imperial Glass of Bellaire, Ohio, and certain items were reissued. These pieces may be mistaken for the original Heisey as they are of the same quality. Some of the reproductions were produced in colors which were never made by Heisey. Not all Heisey glassware is marked with the familiar "H" within a diamond.

Animals	
Chick, signed	55.00
Elephant	140.00
Giraffe, head turned	115.00
*Goose, wings half	85.00
*Goose, wings up	90.00
Pheasant	120.00
*Pouter Pigeon	500.00
Ashtrays	
*3½", Crystolite	11.00
3½", Plantation	14.00
Beer Mugs	
Old Sandwich, Sahara	150.00
Sportsman, etch	125.00
Berry Set, 7 pieces, Pineapple and Fan, emerald	600.00
Bookends, Fish, pair	175.00
Bowls	
5", Octagon, cut, footed	30.00
6½", Empress, Sahara, with underliner	30.00
7", Orchid	25.00
8", Wing Scroll, emerald	120.00
8½", Cross Line Flute	35.00
8½", Pillow	50.00
9", Star and Zipper	150.00
Floral, Fern, oval, footed	30.00
Floral, Queen Anne, dolphin footed, Chateau cutting	75.00
Floral, Thumbprint and Panel, Moongleam	65.00
Floral, Warwick, Horn of Plenty, cobalt	250.00
Box, Cigarette, Ridgeleigh	25.00
Butter, covered	
Etched with applied sterling	40.00
Plantation, ¼ size	65.00
Candlesticks	
Ipswich, cobalt, pair	1150.00
*Orchid, pair	45.00
Stanhope, pair	35.00
Candy Dishes	
Crystolite, 2 part	30.00
Flamingo, handled	15.00
Candy Jars	
Colonial, covered, gold trim	30.00

*Waverly, seahorse handle	115.00
Card Tray, Crystolite, pedestal	22.00
Celery	
12", amber flashed, oval	35.00
Ring Band, Ivorina Verde, gold floral decor	185.00
Champagnes	
Crystolite	10.00
Ipswich	18.00
Cocktails	
Albermarle	18.00
Goose stem, frosted goose	145.00
Tyrolean	37.50
Cocktail Shakers	
Coronation, 3 piece, 11" with cutting in forest	275.00
Country Club with 4 clarets	190.00
Compotes	
Continental	36.00
Queen Anne, Sahara	35.00
Twist, Moongleam	30.00
Cream and Sugars	
Flute	30.00
Saturn	35.00
Stanhope	25.00
*Waverly, individual	50.00
Cruets	
Colonial	18.00
Lariat	28.00
Kalonyal	125.00
Pleat and Panel, Flamingo	65.00
Pleat and Panel, Moongleam	110.00
Ring Band, Ivorina Verde, gold flowers	185.00
Cups and Saucers	
Queen Anne	20.00
Yeoman, Flamingo, diamond optic	15.00
Decanter, Tallyho	150.00
Goblets	
Fairacre, Moongleam stem and foot	20.00
Frontenac	18.00
King Arthur, diamond optic	15.00
New Era	10.00
Plateau, Flamingo	15.00
Sussex, green bowl, crystal base	37.50
Tyrolean, Orchid etch	30.00
Wabash, Pied Piper etch	20.00
*Whirlpool	13.00
Ice Tea Glasses, Zodiac	18.00
Jars, covered	
Crystal, cut and etched	125.00
Greek Key	325.00
Toujours, Minuet cut	150.00
Ice Tubs	
Colonial, Flamingo, silver plated handle	75.00
Narrow Flute	60.00
Mugs	
Pineapple and Fan, green and gold	35.00
Punty Band, souvenir	40.00

Mustard, covered, Colonial, ladle .. 33.00
Nut Dishes
  Empress, Alexandrite, individual .. **60.00**
  Flamingo, dolphin footed **15.00**
  Swan, master and 4 individual ... **75.00**

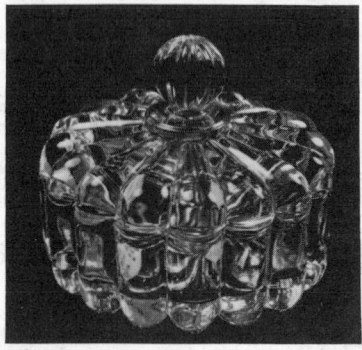

Powder Box, Crystolite, 5″ dia. $35.00

Pitchers
  Beaded Swag, syrup **110.00**
  Ivorina Verde, water **65.00**
  Priscille, 1 quart **85.00**
Parfait, Duquesne, Tangerine **200.00**
Plates
  6″, Diana, etch **7.00**
  7″, Queen Anne **10.00**
  8″, Empress, Sahara **20.00**
  8″, Frontenac **8.00**
  *8″, Waverly **17.50**
  9″, Revere **60.00**
Platter, 15″, Fern, Zircon **75.00**
Punch Cups
  Colonial **5.00**
  Narrow Flute **8.00**
  Prince of Wales **16.00**
  Victorian **8.00**
Punch Sets
  Colonial, 10 pieces **285.00**
  Sunburst, bowl only **250.00**
Relishes
  12″, Lariat **24.00**
  12″, Queen Anne, Sahara **35.00**
Salver, 9″, Locket on a Chain **145.00**
Salt and Pepper, Plantation **40.00**
Sherbets
  Colonial **8.00**
  Greek Key **18.00**
  Lariat **11.00**
  Spanish, Titania etch **23.00**
Soda Glasses
  Country Club with Winchester 73
  etching **120.00**

Spanish, Titania etch **40.00**
Toothpicks
  Fandango **85.00**
  Fancy Loop **80.00**
  Sawtooth Band **35.00**
Tumblers
  New Jersey, no gold **12.50**
  Punty Band, Ivorina Verde, souve-
  nir **55.00**
  Winged Scroll **95.00**
  Yeoman, Moongleam, diamond
  optic, flared **15.00**
Vases
  4″, Waverly, violet **70.00**
  6″, Ridgeleigh **18.00**
  7″, ball vase with mermaid etching **175.00**
Wines
  Jamestown, Barcelona cutting ... **25.00**
  Spanish, Titania etch **50.00**
  Victorian **18.00**

HERCULANEUM CHINA

Before 1796, known as Worthington, Humble and Holland, this factory was taken over by a more ambitious group in that year and by modern methods produced a fine, cream-colored earthenware.

By 1800, the factory was producing bone china, heavier than most bone china of the period but, nevertheless, well potted and with an exceptional glaze. Early examples were rarely marked; but later examples in Liverpool, marked Herculaneum pieces can be found with some frequency. Transfer examples in black and polychrome are appealing and much collected. The factory closed in 1841.

Harvest Jug, 9⅛″, Creamware,
  black transfer print, folk dancers,
  and "The Farmer's Arms" on reverse, American Eagle, above inscription, "Herculaneum Pottery"
  under spout, c. 1800 .... **450.00**
Plate, 9″, Black transfer **190.00**
Soup Plate, 9½″, Black transfer,
  marked **230.00**

HORN

Horns from animals have been used for centuries to make items such as powder horns, drinking cups, small dishes and snuff boxes. The older pieces of horn are bringing substantial prices today.

Bird, made with several pieces of
  horn **25.00**
Letter opener, crocodile head **12.00**

Tablespoon, tapered handle . . .$15.00

Napkin ring	14.50
Snuffbox, mid-1800's, American . . .	35.00
Texas Longhorn Steer Horn	
40″, historical engraving of Washington, Jefferson, Monroe, General Gates, and General Schuyler .	500.00
Velvet in center, ready for mounting	85.00
Chair, with leather seat cushion; arms, back and legs made from Texas Steer horn, shaped to form, Texas style	200.00
Tumblers	
2½″, inset horn bottom	12.50
4″	15.00

HULL POTTERY

In 1905 Addis E. Hull purchased The Acme Pottery Company, Crooksville, Ohio. In 1917 A. E. Hull Pottery Company began making a line of art pottery for florists and gift shops. Also made were novelties, kitchenwares and stoneware.

From 1921 to 1929 the firm also imported European pottery to be sold through their outlets. In 1950 the factory was destroyed by fire and re-established in 1952 as Hull Pottery Company by J. Brandon Hull. The company is currently in operation but the artline has been discontinued.

The pottery is marked "Hull U.S.A.," "Hull Art U.S." paper labeled, and pieces made after 1952 "hull".

Vase, 9¼″, blue base shading to cream to pink, floral decor, marked $22.50

Basket, bow knot	35.00
Bowls, console	
Bow Knot, 11½″	30.00
Woodland	20.00
Candlesticks	
Magnolia	16.00
Seranade	25.00
Cookie Jar, Red Riding Hood	35.00
Cornucopias	
Bow Knot, 7½″	30.00
Magnolia, 8½″	20.00
Parchment Pine, 4¾″	30.00
Wildflower, 8½″	20.00
Creamers and Sugars	
Magnolia, open	22.50
Red Riding Hood	35.00
Rosella	20.00
Demitasse Pot, pine	32.50
Ewer, Woodland, 13½″	50.00
Pitchers	
Magnolia, yellow and brown	15.00
Tokay, 8″	25.00
Wildflower, 5½″	15.00
Planters	
Clown	12.00
Lamb, 8″	20.00
Ostrich	20.00
Penguin	15.00

Swan, 8¾ x 10¼ "	25.00
Salt Box, ribbed, wooden cover . . .	20.00
Shakers, Salt and Pepper, Red Riding Hood, Small, Pair	12.00

Teapots

Magnolia	32.00
Red Riding Hood, 8"	70.00
Tom, The Piper's Son	30.00

Tea Sets

Open Rose, 3 pieces	55.00
Parchment & Pine, 3 pieces	45.00

Vases

Bow Knot, 6½", V-lip	20.00
Butterfly, 10", triangular-shaped . .	32.50
Iris, 4¾", 2 handles	15.00
Magnolia, 8½", 2 handles	28.00
Narcissus, 8½"	25.00
Rosella, 5"	15.00
Tulip, 6"	18.00
Waterlily, 6½"	18.00
Waterlily, 8½"	20.00
Wildflower, 7½", 2 handles	17.00
Woodland, 7½"	17.00

Wall Pockets

Goose, Flying	15.00
Woodland	16.00

1935   1950

1957   ©by W Goebel 1964 W Germany

Goebel   Goebel
1972   1979

HUMMEL ITEMS

Hummel items are the original creations of the German artist, Berta Hummel. Born in 1909 in Massing, Bavaria, into a family where the arts were a part of everyday living, her talents were encouraged by her parents and formal educators from early childhood. At the age of 18, she was enrolled in the Academy of Fine Arts in Munich to further her mastery of drawing and the palette.

She entered the Convent of Siessen and became Sister Maria Innocentia in 1934. In this Franciscan cloister, she continued drawing and painting images of her childhood friends.

In 1935, W. Goebel Co. in Rodental, Germany, conceived the idea of reproducing Sister Berta's sketches into 3-dimensional bisque figurines. John Schmid discovered the German made figurines. The Schmid Brothers of Randolph, Mass., introduced the figurines to America and became Goebel's U.S. distributor.

In 1967, Goebel began distributing Hummel items in the U.S. and a controversy developed between the two companies involving the Hummel family and the convent. Law suits and countersuits ensued. The German courts finally effected a compromise. The convent held legal rights to all works produced by Sister Berta from 1934 until her death in 1964 and licensed Goebel to reproduce these works. Schmid was to deal directly with the Hummel family for permission to reproduce any pre-convent art work.

All authentic Hummels bear both the signature, M.I. Hummel, and a Goebel trademark. Various trademarks were used to identify the year of production.

Recently, certain early Hummel figurines have been 're-instated' by Goebel from the original molds.

Ashtrays

Boy with Bird, #166, stylized bee	100.00
Happy Pastime, #62, 3-line	80.00
Joyful, #33, LB	65.00
Let's Sing, #114, stylized bee . . .	95.00
Singing Lessons, #34, stylized bee	75.00

Bookends

Apple Tree Boy and Girl, #252, full bee	370.00
Bookworms, #14, stylized bee . .	360.00
Friends, She Loves Me, She Loves Me Not, #251, 3-line	200.00
Goose Girl and Farm Boy, #60, LB	210.00
Little Goat Herder and Feeding Time, #250, full bee	390.00
Playmates and Chick Girl, #61, full bee, LB	215.00

Candleholders

Angel Duet, #193, 3-line	120.00
Angelic Sleep, #25-1, full bee . .	215.00
Angel Trio, 3 Ass't. sitting with candle, #111-38-0, full bee, set .	185.00
Christmas Angels, #115-116-117, current, set	75.00
Herald Angels, #37, full bee	150.00
Lullaby, #24-1, full bee	195.00
Silent Night, #54, stylized bee . .	170.00
Watchful Angel, #194, 3-line . . .	190.00

Candy Boxes

Chick Girl, #57, 3-line	100.00
Happy Pastime, #69, stylized bee, LB	80.00
Joyful, #53, current, LB	85.00
Let's Sing, #110, 3-line	100.00
Playmates, #58, LB	85.00
Singing Lesson, #63, 3-line	100.00

Figurines

Accordian Boy, #185, full bee . .	185.00

Adoration, #23-1, stylized bee .. **245.00**
Angelic Song, #144, stylized bee **115.00**
Apple Tree Boy, #142-1, full bee **265.00**
Apple Tree Boy, #142-V, stylized
bee **525.00**
Apple Tree Girl, #141-1, stylized
bee **180.00**
Apple Tree Girl, #141-1, full bee . **270.00**
Auf Wiedersehen, #153-1, LB .. **150.00**
Autumn Harvest, #355, LB **90.00**
Band Leader, #129, full bee **200.00**
Barnyard Hero, #195-1, stylized
bee **220.00**
Birthday Serenade, #218-0, full
bee **275.00**
Blessed Event, #333, 3-line **275.00**
Bookworm, #3-1, stylized bee .. **250.00**
Boots, #143-1, LB **150.00**
Brother, #95, full bee **135.00**
Builder, #305, 3-line **125.00**
Busy Student, #367, 3-line **100.00**

**Figurine, Chick Girl, 3½″, #57/0 styl-
ized bee $125.00**

Chimney Sweep, #12-2-0, full
bee **130.00**
Confidentially, #314, 3-line **350.00**
Congratulations, #17-0, stylized
bee **150.00**
Culprits, #56-A, full bee **225.00**
Doctor, #127, stylized bee **95.00**
Doll Mother, #67, FB **250.00**
Drummer, #240, 3-line **75.00**
A Fair Measure, #345, current,
LB **120.00**
Farewell, #65, LB **110.00**

For Mother, #257, 3-line **100.00**
Friends, #136-1, 3-line **130.00**
Going to Grandma's, #52-0, styl-
ized bee **140.00**
Goose Girl, #47-0, crown **275.00**
Goose Girl, #47-3-0, full bee ... **230.00**
Happiness, #86, stylized bee ... **95.00**
Happy Birthday, #176-0, stylized
bee **150.00**
Happy Days, #150-1, full bee ... **400.00**
Happy Pastime, #69, 3-line **80.00**
Hear Ye! Hear Ye! #15-1, full bee **250.00**
Hear Ye! Hear Ye! #15-0, stylized
bee **140.00**
Heavenly Angel, #21-0, full bee . **140.00**
Heavenly Angel, #21-11, full bee **360.00**
Heavenly Protection, #88-1,
3-line **250.00**
Hello, #124-0, stylized bee **135.00**
Homeward Bound, #334, LB ... **165.00**
Joyful, #53, full bee **140.00**
Joyous News, #27-111, LB **110.00**
Kiss Me, #311, 3-line **150.00**
Knitting Lesson, #256, 3-line ... **290.00**
Let's Sing, #110-0, crown **190.00**
Letter to Santa Claus, #340, LB . **175.00**
Little Cellist, #89, 3-line **215.00**
Little Fiddler, #4, full bee **180.00**
Little Goat Herder, #200-0, full
bee **210.00**
Little Helper, #73, full bee **160.00**
Little Hiker, #16-1, full bee **225.00**
Little Pharmacist, #322, 3-line, LB **100.00**
Little Scholar, #80, full bee **190.00**
Little Shopper, #96, crown **195.00**
*Little Thrifty, #118, stylized bee **125.00**
Mail Coach, #226, 3-line **315.00**
Max and Moritz, #123, 3-line ... **105.00**
Meditation, #13-0, Crown **400.00**
Merry Wanderer, #11-0, 3-line .. **95.00**
Merry Wanderer, #11-2-0, full bee **195.00**
Mother's Helper, #133, stylized
bee **140.00**
Photographer, #178, 3-line **140.00**
Playmates, #58-0, stylized bee .. **125.00**
Playmates, #58-1, stylized bee .. **180.00**
Postman, #119, stylized bee ... **140.00**
Puppy Love, #1, stylized bee ... **125.00**
Retreat to Safety, #201-2-0,
3-line **100.00**
Ride into Christmas, #396, Cur-
rent LB **250.00**
School Boy, #82-0 LB **70.00**
School Boy, #82-2-0, stylized bee **105.00**
School Boys, #170-1, 3-line **600.00**
School Girl, #81-2-0, stylized bee **105.00**
School Girls, #177-111, stylized
bee LB **1250.00**
Sensitive Hunter, #6-0, stylized
bee **120.00**
Signs of Spring. #203-1, stylized
bee **140.00**

Singing Lesson, #63, crown **225.00**
Sister, #98-0, stylized bee **90.00**
Skier, #59, stylized bee, 3-line .. **125.00**
Smart Little Sister, #346, Current,
3-line **125.00**
Stitch in Time, #255, 3-line **125.00**
Telling Her Secret, #196-1, LB .. **230.00**
The Run-a-Way, #327, LB **120.00**
To Market, #49-1, full bee **500.00**
Trumpet Boy, #97, crown **215.00**
Umbrella Boy, stylized bee,
152-A-11 .... **800.00**
Umbrella Girl, #152-B-O, 3-line .. **350.00**
Volunteers, #50-0, LB **135.00**
Wash Day, #321, 3-line **135.00**
Wayside Devotion, #28-11, styl-
ized bee **240.00**
Wayside Harmony, #111-3-0, full
bee **125.00**
We Congratulate, #220, LB **75.00**
Worship, #84-0, full bee **225.00**

Fonts
Angels at Prayer, #91-A & B, pair
stylized bee **65.00**
Angel Cloud, #206, LB **40.00**
Angel with Birds, #22-0, stylized
bee **35.00**
Angel with Flowers, #36-0, LB .. **25.00**
Child Jesus, #26-0, stylized bee . **35.00**
Devotion, #147, crown **115.00**
Good Shepherd, #35-0, crown .. **70.00**
Holy Family, #246, full bee **105.00**
Worship, #164, LB **40.00**

Lamp Bases (Wired)
Apple Tree Boy, #230, LB **170.00**
Apple Tree Girl, #229, LB **180.00**
Culprits, #44-A, full bee **300.00**
Good Friends, #228, LB **175.00**
Just Resting, #225, LB **185.00**
Out of Danger, #44-B, full bee .. **300.00**
She Loves Me, She Loves Me
Not, #227, LB **170.00**
To Market, #223, LB **185.00**
Wayside Harmony, #224-II, LB .. **185.00**

Madonnas
Flower Madonna, Color, #10-1,
full bee **220.00**
Flower Madonna, White, #10-1,
LB **85.00**
Flower Madonna, Color, #10-111,
full bee open halo **600.00**
Madonna with Halo, #45-0, 3-line **40.00**

Music Boxes
Little Band, With Candle, #388M,
3-line **255.00**
Little Band, Without candle,
#392M, 3-line **240.00**

Nativity Components
Angel Serenade, #214-D, stylized
bee **60.00**
Cow, #214-K, LB **40.00**
Donkey, #214-J, LB **40.00**

Flying Angel, Color, #366, LB ... **60.00**
Infant Jesus, #214-A-K, LB **25.00**
King, Keeling on both knees,
#214-N, LB **85.00**
King, Keeling on one knee,
#214-M, LB **85.00**
King, Standing, #214-L, LB **100.00**
Lamb, #214-0, LB **10.00**
Little Tooter, #214-H, full bee ... **130.00**
Madonna and Child, 2 pieces, Col-
or, #214-A, LB **100.00**
St. Joseph, #214-B, stylized bee **140.00**
Shepherd Boy, #214-G, 3-line .. **80.00**
Shepherd with Sheep, 1 piece,
#214-F, LB **105.00**
We Congratulate, LB **65.00**

Nativity Sets
12 pieces, #214 A-O, current ... **680.00**
16 pieces, #260 A-R, with wood-
en stable, current **2800.00**

Plates (See "Collectors' Plates, Etc.")

Wall Plaques
Ba Bee Ring, #30-A&B, full bee,
Set **125.00**
Child in Bed, #137, full bee **95.00**
Little Fiddler, #93, LB **65.00**
Madonna, #48-0, full bee **140.00**
Mail Coach, #140, 3-line **170.00**
Merry Wanderer, #92, crown ... **285.00**
Retreat to Safety, #126, full bee . **225.00**
Vacation Time, #125, 3-line **140.00**

**NOTE: The slash-mark which appears be-
tween numbers on Hummel items has been
set here as a dash.**

IMARI

Imari derives its name from a Japanese port
city. Although Imari ware was manufactured
in the 17th century, the wares manufactured
between 1770 and 1900 are those most commonly encountered.

Early Imari was decorated simply, quite unlike the later heavily decorated brocade pattern commonly associated with Imari. Most
of the decorative patterns are an underglaze
blue and overglaze "seal wax" red supported
by turquoise and yellow.

The Chinese copied Imari ware. Important
differences of the Japanese type include
grayer clay, thicker glaze, runny and darker
blue, and deep red opaque hues.

The pattern and colors of Imari inspired
many English and European potteries, such
as Derby, Meissen, and others, to adopt a
similar style of decoration for their wares.
Reproductions of Imari patterns exist.

See also ROYAL CROWN DERBY.

Bowls
6¾", blue and white **60.00**

14″, typical colors	**275.00**

Fish Dishes

7″, blue and white landscape, gilt	**40.00**
12″, three color ware	**175.00**

Plates

8¼″, blue and white, ribbed, scalloped rim	**50.00**
9″, blue and white, c. 1880	**110.00**
14″, ovoid, bat motif on floral ground, c. 1880	**350.00**
15½″, ovoid, hexagonal panels of flowers, dragons, and courtesans, c. 1875	**375.00**

IMPERIAL GLASS

The Imperial Glass Co., organized in 1901 in Bellaire, Ohio, at first produced mainly clear, pressed glass for the "mass market." In 1910 they began making the popular, inexpensive lustre ware known as Carnival Glass. Then came NUART, an iridescent ware, followed by pressed glass imitations of hand cut glass under the tradename of NUCUT.

In 1916, the company introduced a Lustred Art Glass line, "Free-Hand" and "Imperial Jewels," an exquisite iridescent stretch glass that carried the Imperial-cross trademark. Reorganized as Imperial Glass Corporation, in the 1930's the company continued to produce a great variety of wares.

In recent years Imperial has acquired the molds and equipment of several other glass companies — Central, Cambridge and Heisey. Many of the "retired" molds of these companies are once again in use. The resulting reissues are acceptable as such because they are marked to distinguish them from the originals.

Imperial Glass Co. has recently been sold to a private investor. The last day's run (marked LIG) was Cambridge Dresden dolls, dolls from Heisey molds and bells from an Imperial mold.

For Imperial Carnival see CARNIVAL GLASS.

CUT GLASS (ETCHED OR ENGRAVED)

Bowls

5½″, floral spray, rayed bottom	**22.50**

Ginger Jars, 9¼″ **$225.00**

7″, border of birds and flowers, riverscape center, c. 1900	85.00
8″, fluted panels of flowers, lotus medallion, c. 1900	150.00
9″, octagonal shape, scalloped rim, typical colors, c. 1830	400.00
11½″, fluted rim, border of birds and flowers, dragon medallion, c. 1875	390.00
Box, covered, 2 x 3½″	60.00
Chargers	
12″, blue and white	160.00
12″, typical colors, c. 1850	220.00
14½″, typical colors, four reserves	275.00
18″, typical colors, c. 1850	450.00
24½″, fluted rim with panels of birds, floral center, c. 1875	600.00
Compote, oval shaped, 8 x 9 x 12″	225.00
Cups and Saucers	
Handled	47.50
Handlesless, c. 1850	60.00
Garden Seats	
Cylindrical, blue and white, 19″	1250.00
Octagonal, typical colors, 20″	2200.00
Ginger Jars	
8½″, blue and white	150.00

7", buzz star, rayed bottom 25.00
Candlesticks, 12", etched, signed . 35.00
Console Set, "Susie" green, 11"
bowl, 8¼" candlesticks, etched . 75.00
Pitchers
6", butterfly decor 35.00
9", daisy decor 40.00
Tumbler, 4", buzz star 14.00

JEWELS

Bowls
7" dia., blue iridescent, footed,
signed 45.00
8½" dia., amethyst, signed 60.00
9" dia., pearl amethyst, flaring rim 95.00
10" dia., lemon yellow iridescent . 40.00
Compote, marigold, footed 50.00
Rosebowl, amethyst, green irides-
cent 65.00
Sherbets, 4¾", sapphire blue, 6 . . 88.50
Vases
5", green iridescent 80.00
6", pear shape, amethyst, green
iridescent 95.00
7", gold iridescent with webbing
and jewels, 3 handled, Imperial
crown mark 275.00

LUSTRED (FREE HAND)

**Vase, 6", lustred, "Free Hand," blue
body with white leaf and vine de-
cor $195.00**

Bowl, 11" dia. green loop on clear,
green wafer base 250.00
Rose Bowl, 8", dark green, leaf and
vine decor 95.00
Vases
7", blue with white decor, tri-corner with 3 pull down tabs 325.00
8", cobalt and light blue marbelized, iridescent orange interior 125.00
9¾", orange lustre with iridescent
blue decor, orange interior 125.00
10", green iridescent, white hearts
and vine decor, orange interior . . 175.00
10¾", cobalt, white vine and leaf
decor, pair 300.00
11", yellow orange lustre, white
drag loop decor 375.00

NUART

Ashtray 15.00
Vases
7", bulbous, iridescent green . . . 120.00
7½", green over green transpar-
ent 125.00

NUCUT

Bowls
5½" 12.00
8½" 20.00
12 x 8½" high, flared top 45.00
Compotes
4½" 9.00
9¼" 65.00
Cream and Sugar, open 20.00
Nappy, two handles 15.00
Spooner 18.00
Vases
6" 15.00
10" 25.00

PRESSED (CANDLEWICK)

Ashtray 5.00
Bon Bon, 2 handles 6.00
Bowls
5½", fruit 4.25
8½", fruit, handles 9.00
Console 22.00
Punch set, 15 pieces 75.00
Cake Stand, 11" 15.00
Candleholders, pair 10.00
Cheese and Cracker Set 13.50
Creamer, Sugar and Tray 12.50
Cup and Saucer 10.50
Dish, heart shaped, center handle . . 8.00
Mayonnaise, 2 pieces 11.00
Plates
6" 3.00
10" 8.50
Relish, 8", divided 8.00

Salt and Pepper, pair	**12.50**
Salad Spoon and Fork, set	**23.50**
Tray, oblong	**6.00**

MISCELLANEOUS

Animals-Heisey molds	
Duck, carmel slag	**25.00**
Goose, wings up, carmel slag . . .	**30.00**
Pony, blue, kicking	**20.00**
Pony, blue, standing	**75.00**
Hen on Nest	**18.50**
Milk Glass rabbit	**12.00**
Purple Slag	
Owl	**10.00**
Sugar	**10.00**
Swan	**27.50**

INDIAN ARTIFACTS

American Indian artifacts, for the purpose of this listing, are the objects made on the North American continent during the pre-historic and historic periods. During the historic period there were approximately 350 tribes which are grouped into the following regions: Northern Woodlands, Southeast Woodlands, Plains, Southwest, Northwest Coast, North Athabascan, and Eskimo.

American Indian Art is quite popular. The current high prices reflect this. Northwest Coast artifacts bring the highest prices.

Navajo Rug, colors: grays, red, tan, brown, white, 49 x 84" **425.00**

Arrow, Apache, complete, c. 1890 .	**40.00**
Axe Head, Northern Woodlands, grooved	**65.00**
Baskets	
Apache, 16" dia.	**800.00**
Hupa, 4 x 8"	**250.00**
Pomo, 4" dia.	**500.00**
Washoe by Dasolace	**5000.00**
Woodlands, 15 x 8"	**125.00**
Belts	
34", Sioux, beaded	**450.00**
44½", leather, quill work on both sides, Texas, c. 1900	**150.00**
Blankets, Navajo	
Classic Blanket, 48 x 72", c. 1860	**10000.00**

Germantown Rug, 48 x 72", c. 1890	**1500.00**
Rug, 48 x 84", c. 1930	**450.00**
Saddle, 30 x 36", c. 1920	**125.00**
Blanket, Rio Grande, 42 x 96", c. 1920	**150.00**
Canoe Model	
Eskimo, sealskin, 14"	**125.00**
Northern Woodlands, birch bark, 20"	**50.00**
Celt, Southeast Woodlands	**25.00**
Doll, Sioux, beaded dress, 8"	**250.00**
Eskimo	
Belt, Hide, 42"	**75.00**
Cribbage Board, Ivory	**500.00**
Doll, prehistoric, ivory, 2"	**150.00**
Mask, oval form, wood, 4⅜"	**525.00**
Fetisches	
Bear, black, polished, San Ildefonso, c. 1900	**35.00**
Turtle, polychrome pottery, Cochiti, c. 1900	**25.00**
Headdress, tradecloth, beaded with feathers	**1200.00**
Knife, Plains, c. 1920	**125.00**
Knifecase	
Blackfoot, beaded, c. 1880	**500.00**
Sioux, beaded, c. 1890	**300.00**
Leggings, Kiowa	**150.00**
Moccasins	
Cheyenne, beaded top and bottom	**400.00**
Sioux, leather with beaded tops . .	**250.00**
Woodlands, floral designs	**100.00**
Northwest Coast	
Basket, Tlingit, 4 x 6"	**800.00**
Box, 9 x 14"	**1200.00**
Mask, Bella Coola	**3000.00**
Mask, Tlingit	**25000.00**
Raven Rattle, 13"	**5000.00**
Totem Pole, 8"	**200.00**
Pipe Bags	
Cheyenne, bird quill decoration, 16"	**700.00**
Sioux, beaded decoration, 20" . . .	**425.00**
Pipes	
Eastern Plains, wood and red catlinite	**550.00**
Iroquois, c. 1900	**75.00**
Seminole	**50.00**
Sioux, wood stem with catlinite bowl, 20"	**200.00**
Points, Flint	
2", bird point, Plains	**15.00**
3½", stunner, Penn.	**7.50**
5", turkey tail, Ind.	**45.00**
Points, Stone, Northern Woodlands, 4½"	**6.00**
Pottery, Historic	
Acoma, jar, black, white, and red, 12 x 12", c. 1890	**900.00**
Acoma, jar, 6 x 8", c. 1930	**200.00**

Cochiti, jar, black and white, 6 x 8", c. 1930 . . . . 300.00
Hopi, bowl, signed Nampeyo, 10", c. 1890 . . . . 1000.00
Hopi, bowl, 6", c. 1950 . . . . 15.00
Hopi, jar, wedding, c. 1920 . . . . . 40.00
Zia, jar, 8 x 10", c. 1870 . . . . . . 1000.00
Zia, jar, 10 x 10", c. 1930 . . . . . . 600.00
Zuni, bowl, 6", c. 1940 . . . . 75.00
Zuni, jar, 8 x 10", c. 1920 . . . . . . 400.00
Pottery, Prehistoric
  Casa Grande, 4 x 6" 100.00
  Chaco, cup, black on white, 3" . . 75.00
  Gila, red on tan ground 150.00
  Mimbres, bowl, 6" 600.00
  Mound, Ohio 200.00
  Roosevelt, bowl, black decoration on white ground, 6" 125.00
  Sikyati, bowl, polychrome on tan ground 3000.00
  Tularosa, jar, black on white ground, 8 x 7" 450.00
Pouches
  Apache, beaded with metal cones, 4 x 3" 150.00
  Athabascan, tradecloth with beads, 22" 350.00
  British Columbia, octopus bag, 12" 700.00
Shawl, Winnebago, broadcloth decorated with silk ribbons 650.00
Shields
  Cheyenne, decorated with feathers, 20" dia. 3500.00
  Kiowa, painted eagle, 18" dia. . . . 1000.00
Shirt, Southern Plains, hide, fringed, 32" 700.00

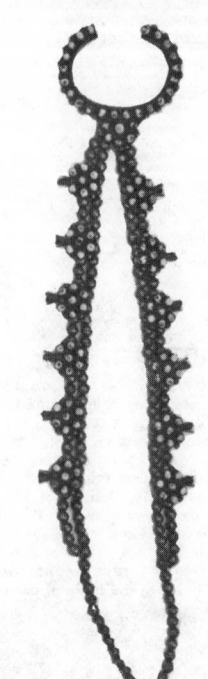

INDIAN JEWELRY

Indian jewelry represents one of the highest standards of native American art. Old Pawn or Pawn is the name given to the jewelry made by the Indians for their personal adornment, wealth, or collateral. It has come into the market through the trading post pawn room.

Current prices are high, reflecting turquoise's role as an investment stone. Some contemporary jewelry sells for as much or more than the antique variety. Antique jewelry can be found at specialized Indian auctions held by America's leading auction houses, e.g., Butterfield and Sotheby. Be alert to reproductions. Buy quality, not only in stones and silver but also in workmanship. If contemporary, try to identify the craftsman and find something about him or her.

All jewelry listed below is understood to be made of sterling silver and the stones to be genuine.

Necklace, 24" chain, 14½" length, silver and turquoise **$500.00**

Beads, trade
  Earthenware, 28" on straw 25.00
  Heische Shell, 30" on straw 40.00
Belt, concha, 6 scalloped pieces with 6 butterfly separators, buckle set with coral 1500.00
Bracelets
Contemporary, Tommy Yellowshoe, large cabochon turquoise stone in center with three coral stones 160.00
Hopi, Pawn
  Jackson, shadowbox with triangular shaped turquoise 125.00
  Lee, T., 5 small oval cabochons of Kingman turquoise 120.00
Navajo, Contemporary
  D.W., cluster of oval cabochons of Royston turquoise 350.00
  Yazzie, C.M., 3 cabochons of Persian turquoise 175.00

Simple reeded band mounted with irregular turquoise stones . **75.00**
Ten blossom shaped mountings set with green turquoise centers, c. 1927 . . . . **240.00**
Navajo, Pawn
  Cluster of 24 baroque nuggets of Gem Mine turquoise set in round bezel, two leaves on each side **375.00**
  Sand cast with Nevada green cabochon turquoise stone and two coral cabochon **85.00**
  Turquoise center stone with raindrop bezel, silver twist and bands **140.00**
Zuni, Contemporary
  Coral inlay cardinal on branch of turquoise, Kingman bands around edges, C. Bowie **200.00**
  Turquoise and coral mounted . **60.00**
Zuni, Pawn
  Cluster of 77 round and tear drop shaped turquoise **350.00**
  Three rows of turquoise stones, needlepoint work, Begay **275.00**
  Three oval baroque turquoise with wire twists, bentwork, raindrops, and bars **150.00**

Buckles, Navajo
  Bowed Rectangle with shaped sides, decorated with stylized flowers, 4⅝" **150.00**
  Square, quartering repousse and chased flower forms, 3⅜" **60.00**

Earings
  Heische, birds suspended on turquoise, 1½" hoop **100.00**
  Navajo, Pawn, blossom shaped mountings with green turquoise . **60.00**
  Zuni, pair, elaborate design, each using 13 turquoise stones **135.00**

Necklaces
  Cheyenne or Canadian Beaded and Trade Silver Cross, two strands of rounded blue and faced black glass beads, double barred cross, 13" **55.00**
  Contemporary, Tommy Yellowshoe, 5 large free form turquoise stones, silver beads **225.00**
  Heische, 14 green serpentine birds, 16 pieces of red coral interwoven **450.00**
  Navajo, squash blossom necklace, single strand of round biconical beads, 6 blossom horseshoe Naja with rope twisted terminals, 25" . . **550.00**
  Northern Plains, eagle claw, blue and pink glass beads with 7 eagle claws, 30" **75.00**

Rattlesnake, faceted amber beads suspending a rattlesnake rattle, figure of rattlesnake with turquoise eyes **60.00**
Zuni
  Squash blossom, turquoise and coral, two strands of beads with 12 stone mounted blossoms, horseshoe Naja, 31" **325.00**
  35 petit point turquoise, signed H.A., c. 1925 . . . . **350.00**
Ring, Navajo, 30 carat Lone Mountain turquoise, leaf design **225.00**

INDIAN TREE PATTERN

The Indian Tree pattern, derived from the Oriental-type shrub or tree that predominates the design, is a popular pattern for porcelain dinnerware from the last half of the 19th century till the present. The pattern was used by several English potteries including Burgess and Leigh, Coalport, Maddox and others.

Gravy Boat with 8" underplate, Coalport **$95.00**

Bowl, 7", Coalport **35.00**
Butter, covered, Coalport **95.00**
Chocolate Set, pot, 6 cups and saucers, 14 pieces **225.00**
Cream and Sugar, open, Coalport . **50.00**
Cups and Saucers
  Bouillon, Coalport **25.00**
  Coffee, Maddox **20.00**
  Coffee, Minton **25.00**
  Demitasse, Coalport **25.00**
Pitchers
  5", Burgess and Leigh **30.00**
  6", Maddox and Sons **40.00**
Plates
  6", Coalport **10.00**
  6", fluted rim **12.00**
  7½", soup, Coalport **12.50**
  8", Coalport **15.00**
  9", fluted **20.00**
  9½", Maddox and Sons **18.50**

10", Johnson Bros.	25.00
10½", square, handled	40.00

Platters

10½", Coalport	35.00
13½", Copeland-Spode	40.00
15½", Burgess and Leigh	60.00
19½", Minton	95.00
Sauce, 5", Coalport	7.00

Shakers, Salt and Pepper, Coalport,

pair	50.00

Tea Set, pot, cream and sugar, 6
cups and saucers, 6–7" plates,

Coalport, 23 pieces	295.00

Tureen, soup, 10" with ladle, Mad-

dox and Sons	125.00

Vegetables, covered

9", Maddox	40.00
11½", Coalport	20.00
Waste Bowl, Coalport	20.00

INKWELLS

**Commercial ink bottles in America date from
the early 1800's; inkwells were made much
earlier. Ever since man began recording his
thoughts and experiences with pen and ink, a
suitable container was needed for the ink.**

**With the advent of the self contained ink
pen, inkwells disappeared from the scene.
The majority of inkwells found in the collector's field today are ornate examples with
Victorian or early 20th century styling.**

**Also see specific categories in regard to
material or manufacturer, e.g., CUT GLASS,
LIMOGES, TIFFANY, etc.**

**Desk Set, 3¾ x 6 x 9¾" long, English
oak, mahogany interior, crystal wells,
green stoppers, brass fittings $135.00**

Agate well, grey vessel carved with
birds on foliate sprays in high relief, gilt metal cover, with jade fini-

al	150.00

Brass

Brass stand, hinged lid, double
porcelain inserts and pen rest,

marked "Austria"	40.00

Brass stand, footed and handled,
ornate high back with fittings for
three quills, 2 diamond point glass

wells, brass covers	95.00

Well, marked "Bradley and Hub-

bard"	32.00

Bronze

Octagon shaped well, hinged cover and original glass insert, Vene-

tian pattern, signed "Tiffany" . . .	275.00

Bronze stand, footed, domed
cover, mask handles, amethyst

glass insert	125.00

Bronze stand, two crystal inserts,
with pen rack and bill holder, dat-

ed 1873	45.00

Bronze well, brass insert, sea life

and basketweave designs	55.00

Cast Iron

Stand, with 4 quill holes and two

glass inserts	40.00

Sitting Bear, cobalt blue insert,

hinged top	42.00

Cut Glass

Cut well, with sterling top,

embossed lady's head, floral . . .	45.00

Cut well, 2½" square base, flat

circular top, brass rims	44.00

Cut well, intaglio, 4", blossoms
with sterling hinged cover, Stevens and Williams Glass, Tiffany

Co.	235.00
Cut well, sterling top and pen . . .	140.00

Cut well, hinged cover with pewter

connections	75.00

Figural

Baby with nursing bottle, & dog,
glass insert, hinged lid, 4 dolphin-

feet, gun metal patina, c. 1900 . .	95.00
Dog, hinged top, signed "Bonzo"	145.00

Dog, Spaniel, with glass eyes, be-

side cast iron well	80.00

Full figure of Professor in carica-

ture, 9½"	39.00

Stag's Head, hinged copper lid,

Art Nouveau	95.00

Glass

Cranberry glass, with silver overlay, Art Nouveau designs, brass

hinged cover, clear glass insert . .	150.00

Loetz, signed, iridescent blue
green, purple, with embossed

brass cover	200.00
Clear, swirled design, with cover .	35.00
Sandwich Star pattern, flint	90.00

Vaseline, Thousand Eye pattern,

covered	175.00

Jade, agate and carnelian stand,
oval jade base, carved with figures, carnelian pen holders in
form of Foo dogs, shaped agate

well, and Foo dog finial	300.00

Mahogany stand, rectangle with brass carrying handle at center, fitted with well in each end, late 18th century 200.00
Marble base stand with brass well, footed, with peacock finial 145.00
Metal well, figural lion's head, porcelain insert 85.00
Pewter well, figural monk with hinged hat, lid 75.00
Soapstone well, 3 x 3", trunk-shaped, with 4 quill holes 48.00
Snail well and pin holder 60.00
Staffordshire well, girl and dog on top, ink pot and sander, place for pens 140.00
Traveling type, brass valise with bottle insert 49.00
Wooden well, carved shape of Tyrolean hat with feather, hinged cap with glass insert 30.00

INSULATORS

Insulators are relative newcomers to the collectible scene; the need for them was created by the invention of the telephone and telegraph. The first patent was issued in 1844. The earliest insulators were threadless, and there has been little modification in their basic style. They have a single function and there is little variation in their design.

Hemingray #9, 3¾" aqua $4.00

American Insulator Co., tall, dome signal 22.50
Armstong, 51-C3, dark amber 10.00

Brookfield
  CD 102, light purple 12.00
  CD 126, green 20.00
  CD 145 .... 8.00
  CD 205, aqua 10.00
  CD 205, green 15.00
Brooks, CPRR, embossed lettering on bottom, August 6, 1867 ..... 35.00
Cable No. 3 aqua 18.00
Canada, B. T., purple 20.00
Corning, Pyrex, T. M. Reg U.S. Patent office, #171, saddle type .. 20.00
California Mickey Mouse, green ... 50.00
California
  Amethyst signal 15.00
  Aqua signal 10.00
  Smokey signal 10.00
CDP Tel. Co. 15.00
Chicago Electric Supply, aqua 20.00
Columbia No. 2, Pat'd. May 12, 1891 aqua 100.00
Fireplug 1003, large style 20.00
Great Northwestern Telegraph Co. around base, CD 144 .... 70.00
Gaynor No. 43–400, aqua 10.00
Hawley, Beehive aqua 7.50
Hemingray, E
  E1, E2 or E3 .... 70.00
  E3, blue 150.00
Sombrero, carnival glass 70.00
Whitall, Tatum and Armstrong, clear 70.00

IRONS (SMOOTHING, ETC.)

Old smoothing irons or hand pressing irons were probably one of the least popular domestic objects in a woman's life. The flat iron is sometimes called a 'sad iron.' It derived this name from the obsolete terminology for solid — sad.

There were four methods for heating these irons: (1) The slug was heated and attached to the iron; (2) The iron was heated directly on the fire; (3) Hot charcoal was contained within the iron; (4) The self-heating gas iron.

Irons can be found in various shapes and sizes, many of which were designed to be used on the current fashions of the day — ruffles, stiff collars, mutton sleeves, etc.

Box Iron, cast iron with wood handle, one slug 40.00
Charcoal Irons
  American, with trivet 55.00
  British, one chimney 65.00
Flat Irons
  Children's 30.00
  Cross Hatch 25.00
  French, mid 1800's 35.00
  Nickel plated 15.00
Fluting Irons
  "American" 65.00

Sad iron, straight back, 4½" high, 5¾" long $12.50

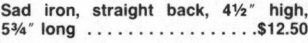

"Geneva"	40.00
Gas iron, Coleman	25.00
Sleeve Iron	20.00
Tailor's Iron	25.00

IRONSTONE
See WHITE PATTERNED IRONSTONE

IRONWARE

Iron, a metallic element that occurs abundantly in combined forms, has been known for centuries. Items made from iron range from the utilitarian to the decorative. Early hand-forged ironwares are of considerable interest to collectors of Americana.

Also see KITCHEN COLLECTIBLES, LAMPS, TOOLS.

Blacksmith tongs, 11", hand forged	100.00
Book Ends, "Constitution"	20.00
Boot Scrapers	
Dachshund, 21½"	65.00
Sling shot type, early	50.00
Buggy Whip Holder	65.00
Bullet Mold, Winchester 32, 1874 ..	35.00
Candle Snuffer, scissors type	35.00
Candle Sticks	
Hog Scraper, with pushup, 7⅛" .	65.00
Phoenix bird, black	12.00
Door Knocker, lady's head	35.00
Door Latches, butterfly	75.00
Door Lock, 4 x 6", turn handle with	
key, c. 1840	100.00
Door Stops/Figurals	
Cat, seated, 7½", black and white	
paint	95.00
Dog, on pillow, 5"	70.00

Skeleton key, 5½" $15.00

Frog, 5¼", green paint	75.00
Snowbirds, 5", pitted surfaces,	
pair	55.00
Eel Spear, hand forged	60.00
Fire Mark, Buckeye Union Fire Ins.	
Co., 1938	55.00
Flag Holder, claw feet, c. 1885 ...	25.00
Hair Curling Iron, 10"	20.00
Harpoon, 58", wooden pole	15.00
Hayfork, 34" long	50.00
Hinges	
12", pair	30.00
18", pair	40.00
36", pair	85.00
Hitching Posts	
Black Boy, 46", painted	950.00
Horse's Head, 8"	100.00
Jockey, 38", painted	350.00
Hooks	
Bailing	7.50
Fireplace, crane, double	65.00
Shutter, 7", "S"	10.00
Horse Collar	60.00
Horse Shoe	7.50
Ice Skates, clamp-ons, pair	35.00
Kettles	
5 x 8" dia.	40.00
5½ x 9" dia., three legs, lid	90.00
11 x 20½" dia., three legs, bail	
handle	150.00
Masonry Tiles, 9½ x 15¼", foliage	
plates, pair	45.00
Mortar and Pestle, 7 x 7"	35.00
Quilt Clamps, pair	30.00
Scales, "Perfection Scales," size 2,	
American Mfg. Co., Philadelphia,	
15", tin plated brass pans, worn	
paint	48.00

Scissors, 8", hand wrought	35.00
Sheep Shears	5.00
Shoes, 7", plain, open sole, red paint	20.00
Shot Gun Shell Pliers	8.00
Spitoon, tin lid	50.00
Sugar Nippers, 9" long, hand wrought	65.00

Tongs

European, 8½" long, c. 1700's . .	75.00
Ice, long handled	15.00
Tractor Seat, c. 1910–20	65.00
Trammel, sawtooth, adjusts from 36"	115.00

Traps

Bear, hand forged	170.00
Beaver, double spring	85.00
Fox, hand forged	125.00
Wolf, double spring	80.00

IVORY

True ivory, a yellowish white organic material, comes from the teeth or tusks of animals. Ivory lends itself well to carving because of its basic structure and has been used for centuries, by many cultures, for artistic and utilitarian items. The Endangered Species Act of 1973 that prohibited the importation and sale of antique ivory and tortoise shell was amended in 1978, with limitations. If you deal or collect ivory, familiarize yourself with this law.

Carved Pendant, 2¼", "Rose" $175.00

Billiard ball, ½lb.	25.00

Boxes

Covered, seated figure, holding fan on top, Chinese, 12"	500.00
Entwined dragons, carved lid, 2" .	50.00
Opium, carved elephants, 4 x 4" .	298.00

Brush Holders

Carved, houses, trees, people, 5"	155.00
Carved scene with figures, early 18th century	550.00
Carved, five-claw dragons, pierced, 3"	175.00
Button, Chinese, carved shank, with figures, shank unscrews, 11" . . .	28.00
Button Hook, Ivory handle, (glove) .	20.00

Card Cases

Carved stag, foliage, red lining . .	90.00
Card case and note case, combined	125.00

Chess Set

King, 4", red and white, c. 1830 .	400.00
Carved, tallest piece 2¾"	265.00

Cigarette Holders

6", carved	25.00
7", engraved dragon	50.00

Doctor's Dolls

6½", on stand	175.00
8", on base, c. 1925	250.00
Lying on carved fire amber couch, holding amber fan	650.00
15", on base	500.00
Nude male figure, on stomach, holding flower, fitted teak stand .	700.00

Figurines — Animals

Bears, Polar, Eskimo carved, pair	355.00
Caribou, Eskimo carved	330.00
Elephant, 1½", Japanese, c. 1890	125.00
Elephant bridge, carved, upraised trunks forming bridge, on wooden base, 17"	645.00
Elephant, 2¾"	350.00
Foo dog, 6", Chinese, c. 1890 . .	500.00
Rabbit, bear and bird, Eskimo carved	185.00
Seals, three, Eskimo carved, 1⅝"	145.00

Figurines — People

Carpenter, planing board, child, and butterfly, 5"	600.00
Chinese in kimono, 4"	35.00
"Flower Woman"	22.00
Girl dressed in kimono carrying flowers, holding fan, late 19th cent.	6.50
Man, holding fish, with basket on head, MOP inlay	400.00
Kwan Yin, rosewood stand	2700.00
Seven Immortals, on base, 18th century	1150.00
Knife Case, stylized dragon in relief, Chinese symbol, ivory-handled knife	190.00
Knife Rest, carved heads, 4½" . . .	50.00

Letter Openers

Carved elephants, 16 on handle .	50.00
Carved, with seal handle	95.00
Primitively carved snake, 6"	25.00
Mug, lobed octagon, domed cover, carved two-8-point stars, scroll-	

work handle with mask, German, mid-17th century, 4⅛″ 100.00

Napkin Rings
Carved, scene of people, trees .. 28.50
Enameled decor 25.00

Pill container, carved, 1¼″ 30.00

Spoon, carved handle, 5″ 70.00

Tankard
Carved battle scenes, elephant standing on hinged lid, ornate handle, Germany, 18th century, 10½″ 3400.00
Carved warriors, heraldic design, female figure-handle, infant Bacchus on top, 8⅞″ 1200.00

Tusk, 8½ x 4″ whole surface carved, figures, animals, temple doors, cranes, Foo dogs, flowers, etc., 19th century 2000.00

JACKFIELD POTTERY

Jackfield pottery originated in England in the early 17th century. It is a red clay pottery with a high black glaze, found both plain and decorated with enamels, or designs in relief. It was made at the Jackfield Pottery in Stropshire, England, and most that is encountered today is from the 19th century. It differs from Basalt, which is black throughout the body.

Teapot and Underplate, 6½″ high $75.00

Creamers
Cow, figural, on stand, black glaze with gold highlights 90.00
7½″, cow, with lid and gold trim . 95.00
7″, fluted gold enameling 100.00

Figurines
7¼″, cats, black and white, red and green bases, pair 100.00
8″, dogs, pair 110.00
9½″, poodles, pair 120.00
12″, rooster 85.00

Pitchers
7½″, floral panels, gold trim 75.00
8″, molasses, on black background 95.00

Syrup Jug, with metal lid, 9″, black glaze with gold leaves decor ... 78.00

Sugar Bowl, handleless, enameled birds 85.00

Teapot, covered, 6¾″, black glaze, c. 1810 .... 160.00

JACK-IN-THE-PULPIT VASES

Vases in the form of a "Jack-in-the-Pulpit" flower were in vogue during the late Victorian period and early 20th century. These vases were made in a wide variety of glass, color and size. See specific categories for additional listings.

Vase, 9″, opalescent swirl stripes with cobalt rim $85.00

Amberina
7″, signed Libbey 350.00
8″, souvenir, 1893 World's Fair .. 180.00

Cased Glass
4½″, squatty, pink 75.00
6″, aqua 58.00

Cranberry

8¼", applied clear rigaree	55.00
10¾"	95.00
Custard	30.00

Opalescent

5½", cranberry and vaseline, rainbow stripe, clear foot	150.00
9¾", cranberry	60.00
Green, applied clear flower and leaf decor	85.00
Blue, yellow and white enamel decor	55.00
Orient and Flume	100.00

Transparent

9⅝", swirl, blue	175.00
12¼", red, signed Steuben	90.00
Aqua, enamel yellow and white floral decor	85.00

JADE

Jade is the generic name for two distinct minerals, nephrite and jadite.

Nephrite, an amphibole mineral from Central Asia, has a waxy surface and ranges in hues from white to almost a black-green. All jade carvings before the 18th century were of nephrite.

Jadite, a pyroxene mineral found in Burma, has a glassy appearance and comes in various shades of white, green, yellow-brown and violet. Most jade carvings from the 18th century to the present are jadite.

Jade is held in high esteem as a gemstone and lends itself well to carving.

Floral Centerpiece, 21½ x 12½" high $315.00

Box, 2¼ dia., 3½" high, covered, light green	350.00
Buckle, 4¾", white, carved dragon .	300.00

Dice

English, pair	50.00
Gold inlaid 'numbers', pair	175.00

Figurines

Bird, 4½", medium green	195.00
Buddha, 6", light green, c. 1850 .	650.00
Carp, 2½", medium green	175.00
Carp, 3½", lavender	250.00
Elephant, 7", medium green	490.00
Foo Dog, 2½", mutton fat	275.00
Foo Dog, 3", green	225.00
Frog, 3", deep green	295.00
God of Longevity, 6½", green . .	650.00
Goldfish, fantail, 3¼ x 3¼", yellow green	190.00
Griffin, 3½ x 5½", medium green	350.00
Horse, 4½", grey, white	500.00
Lion, 2½ x 3", roaring, green . . .	175.00
Raven, 5½", dark green	390.00
Rhinoceros, 5", medium green . .	475.00
Water Buffalo, 3 x 5½", rose . . .	500.00
Incense Burner, 6", carved masks, vines, mutton fat	400.00
Letter Opener, 6", dark green	95.00
Paperweight, 2¾", pale green	225.00
Pendant, 2½ x 3¼", carved florals, medium green	125.00
Screen, 20 x 25", carved birds, lotus flowers, foliage; green; mounted on carved teakwood stand	5000.00

Trees

8½" high, various shades of jadite, c. 1870	325.00
11" high, various shades and hues of jadite, cloisonne planter .	650.00

Vase

7", carved, mutton fat, c. 1810 . .	1250.00
Carved birds, green	315.00

JAPANESE CORALENE
See MORIAGE

JAPANESE EXPORT POTTERY

Japanese Export Pottery (J.E.P.), also known as SUMIDA, was first produced in 1890 at kilns along the Sumida River near Tokyo. J.E.P. wares were made throughout the Nippon and 'Made In' eras and continues in production today.

Most of the Japanese Export Pottery, which is hand thrown pottery with molded and applied porcelain characteristics, has a cartouche (seal) or marking indicating the name Ryosai (a family name, likely the original potter).

For some time, SUMIDA pieces such as vases, baskets and teapots have been mistaken for Korean Banko, but research reveals little resemblance as the latter is much earlier

in origin and does not bear the 'Ryosai' mark.

There is no reason to believe J.E.P. prices will decline, collectors continue to find Japanese Export Pottery very appealing and definitely collectible.

probably the most prolific and recognized maker, other English potteries produced Jasperware. Jasperware continues to be made today.

Saki-set, 4 pieces, tray 6¼″ dia., unsigned, set $170.00

Ashtray, 3¼″ dia., boy climbing into bowl, impressed signed	55.00
Basket, 10½″ high, seal signed . . .	350.00
Humidor, 7¼″, seal signed	275.00
Lamp Base, 13″, unsigned	150.00
Mug, 5″, old man carrying large rock, seal signed	125.00
Teapot, two applied figures, seal signed	325.00
Toothpick, impressed signed	75.00

Vases
8″, figure climbing over a bar, seal signed	175.00
8½″, bottle-shaped, man with beard in ceremonial robe sitting on throne, unsigned	100.00
9″, impressed signed	145.00
12″, three figures in high relief, impressed signed	225.00

JASPERWARE

Jasperware is a hard, unglazed porcelain with a background that varies in colors, from the most common blues and greens to lavender, yellow, red or black. The white designs are applied in relief and often reflect classical tradition. Josiah Wedgwood described Jasperware as "a fine Terra Cotta of great beauty and delicacy proper for cameos."

This ware was first produced at Wedgwood Etruria Works in 1775. While Wedgwood was

Pitcher, brown, 7″, W.T. Copeland & Sons staff, marked J.M.D. & S., Importers $175.00

Biscuit Jars
Blue, classical figures, silver plated lid and bail	90.00
Blue, hunt scene, Adams	180.00
Sage Green, 7¼″, bust medallions of Washington, Jefferson and Franklin, silver plated lid and bail	345.00

Bowls
Light Green, 7″	150.00
Dark Blue, 9″, silver plated rim, Wedgwood	250.00

Boxes
5″, heart shape, Queen Louise on cover, white floral on base	85.00
5″, light blue, classical figures, Wedgwood, England	85.00

Candlesticks
6¾″, blue, classical figures, Wedgwood, pair	220.00
8″, dark blue, classical figures, Wedgwood, pair	250.00

Cheese Dishes, Covered
10″, blue, classical figures	220.00
10½″ underplate, 8½″ cover, blue, classical figures, Copeland .	525.00
Clock, mantel, 8″, blue, gilt metal and ivory dial, Wedgwood, England	375.00
Cream and Sugar, dark blue, Adams,	

set 125.00

Creamers

Dark Blue, 3¾", classical figures, grapes and leaves border 45.00

Slate Blue, sheep, dog, swan, obelisk and urn decor, Neale & Co. 160.00

Cup and Saucer, "Trophy Ware," blue, Wedgwood 425.00

Hair Receiver, green, maidens and cupids 45.00

Jam Jar, dark blue, matching underplate, Wedgwood 150.00

Jardinieres

4", pale green, cherub blowing pipe medallion, vine and scrolls border 75.00

7½", light blue, Landing of Columbus, Copeland 175.00

8", dark blue, hunting scene, Adams 225.00

Jug, covered, bulbous, blue, vines and grapes decor, branch handle 275.00

Medallion, 4¼", black, "Captain Cook" in frame 140.00

Mugs

5½", green, "Fill This Cup and Drink It Up," floral garland 125.00

6", blue, Four Seasons 125.00

Pitchers

4⅛", acorn and leaves, classical figures 110.00

6¾", light blue, classical figures, Wedgwood 75.00

8", dark blue, tankard 195.00

10", dark blue, Adams 135.00

blue, classical figures, Copeland . 110.00

Plaques

7½ x 2⅛", lilac, 7 Vestal Virgins, Wedgwood 220.00

9¾ x 8¾", "Achilles Taking Leave of Lycomodes," Wedgwood 700.00

10", lilac, classical figures, Wedgwood, England 110.00

Ring Tree, 4¼" dia., 2¾" high, green, Wedgwood, England 75.00

Statuette, 10", blue, "Leda and the Swan," white pedestal base, Wedgwood, England 80.00

Sugars, Covered

Blue, classical figures, metal cover, Adams 80.00

Dark Blue, classical figures, Wedgwood 100.00

Yellow, Wedgwood 275.00

Sugar Shaker, dark blue, classical figures 175.00

Syrup, 5", blue, bust portraits Washington, Jefferson, Franklin 165.00

Tea Set, dark blue, Adams, 3 pieces 175.00

Tobacco Jar Covered, tri-color, 8", seated maiden knob, Wedgwood,

England 600.00

Toothpick, light blue, angel head medallion 50.00

Tray, 7¾ x 10", blue classical figures, Wedgwood, England 165.00

Vases

4", green, spill vase. "Muses," Wedgwood, England 90.00

5½", green, classical figures, Heubach 50.00

6⅛", crimson, "Muses," Wedgwood, England 750.00

7", bud vase, yellow and black, Wedgwood 275.00

7", dark blue, classical figures, Adams 120.00

7¾", blue, classical figures, one handle, Wedgwood 180.00

9", Portland, black 525.00

JEWEL BOXES

The jewel boxes listed here are mainly from the late Victorian period. The common variety was made of pot metal, cast in an irregular shape, with scrolls, flowers, etc., in relief and gilded. The interior was lined with satin or velvet.

Glass-amethyst jewel box, enameled decor, silver rim and base, 4⅞" high, 6" dia. $100.00

Carved, Victorian style, with leaf design on top, brass escutheon and lock 35.00

Continental silverplate, 9", musical, form of jewelled crown chased scrollwork, colored glass jewels on outside, velvet interior 200.00

Embossed brass, scene, St. Mark in

Venice, glass floral mosaic design
on hinged lid 30.00
French Bouelle marquetry, bombe
form, feet in form of sea creatures 400.00
French porcelain, 8½″, lozenge
shape, floral, blue and gold decor 300.00
Gilt metal, mounted jewel casket,
7½″, tops and sides bevelled
glass 100.00
Wooden, lithograph under glass as
top, inside painted gold with mirror
and glass in bottom 30.00
Wooden, inlaid and veneered, with
lock 25.00

JEWELRY

Jewelry has been a part of every culture. It was a way of displaying wealth, power, or love of beauty. The metals, stones, and gems used in jewelry have proven endurable over time. Therefore, many examples from the past exist today.

Jewelry items were treasured and handed down as heirlooms from generation to generation. This is still a common practice. Jewelry frequently is given to mark important occasions such as births, weddings, anniversaries, etc. Style and fashions change, but jewelry craftsmen have a knack of redesigning their product to fit any fashion trend.

Jewelry can be reset to modern fashion or treasured for its "antique" value. The choice is sometimes most difficult to make. In examining jewelry from the 19th and 20th centuries, the current value of silver and gold must be taken into consideration.

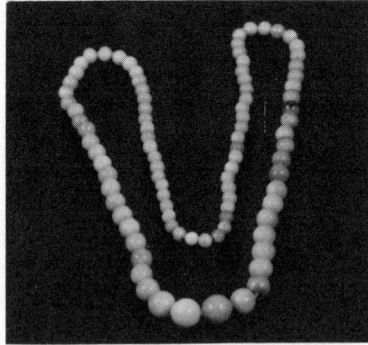

Jade beads, 30″ long $300.00

Beads
Agate, moss, 18″ 40.00
Amber, faceted honey color, 24″ . 125.00
Carnelian, 18″ 45.00
Crystal, faceted, graduated, 18″ . 95.00
Garnets, faceted, 17″ 125.00
Ivory, carved, 24″ 125.00
Jade, green, 14 KT gold clasp,
20″ 225.00
Jet, 30″ 55.00
Pearls, cultured, graduated, 14 KT
y.g. clasp, 18″ 125.00
Pearls, oriental, graduated, 20″ . . 600.00

Bracelets
Bangle, 14 KT y.g., Florentined, ½″
bangles 215.00
Bangle, S.S., repoussed 45.00
Charm, S.S., 22 charms 65.00
Filigree, 14 KT w.g., 5 mm wide, 6
pt. full cut diamond with 2 sap-
phire baguettes 250.00
Garnet, Victorian, S.S., numerous
round and faceted garnets 275.00
Marcasite, S.S., Art Deco, open-
work 20.00
Pearl, cultured, triple strands, 5
and 6 mm., 14 KT y.g. clasp 130.00
Sterling Silver, ornate oval links,
7″ 35.00

Brooches
Cameo, lady in ruffled dress, 18
KT y.g. frame, 1⅝″ 190.00
Bow, Victorian, turquoise and sap-
phire set in garved floral trim with
tassel ends 160.00
Garnet, open floral, 5 garnets, 14
KT y.g. 150.00
Portrait, miniature, young girl, 14
KT y.g., 2″ 200.00
Victorian, scroll design with ropes
and anchor, 6 genuine seed
pearls, 14 KT y.g. 120.00
Victorian, turquoise, 9 pieces, hair
compartment in back, 14 KT y.g.,
2″ 240.00

Buckles
Gold, yellow, 14 KT, plain, 2″ . . . 200.00
Silver, sterling, Art Deco, woman's
face 95.00

Chains
16″, 14 KT y.g., handmade rope . 75.00
18″, 10 KT y.g., filigree 60.00
18″, 14 KT y.g., heavy double
rope 175.00

Chatelains, Sterling
Gorham clip, three implements . . 150.00
Kerr, clip with two ornate imple-
ments, Art Nouveau 100.00

Crosses
Garnet, gold filled, 1½″ 35.00
Gold, yellow, ornate filigree, 2″ . . 90.00
Pearl, 14 KT gold back, 1¼″ . . . 100.00
Silver, sterling, engraved 35.00

Cuff links

Gold, white, machine scored with diamond chips 325.00
Onyx, black, diamond chips, 14 KT y.g. 200.00

Earrings

Amber, dangle 125.00
Diamond, stud, cult of t white mine cut diamonds, 30 pts., 14 KT w.g. 230.00
Gold, white, 14 KT, Art Deco, 18 pt. diamond, engraved 215.00
Pearl, pearl drop, 14 KT y.g. 80.00

Lockets

1″ dia., engraved 14 KT 75.00
1½″ dia., oval, engraved, 14 KT . 125.00
2″, sterling silver, oval, raised design 65.00

Pendants

Gold filled, pink, floral trim, set with 4 garnets 10.00
Pearl, diamond shaped, 5 oriental pearls, 14 KT y.g. 125.00
Silver, sterling, heart, 18 KT y.g. center, Tiffany, 1⅛″ 65.00

Ladies lapel watch, 1½″ dia., sterling case, Croton, marquisite $95.00

Pins

Art Deco, multi-color, 3 floral sections, 14 KT y.g. 75.00
Bar, shaped filigree, 8 pt. center diamond with 2 sapphire baguettes, 14 KT y.g. 185.00

Bar, open, amethyst center, 8 fresh water pearls, 10 KT y.g., 1⅞″ 75.00
Bird in Flight, pearl in beak, 14 KT y.g., 2″ 95.00
Circle, wreath of engraved leaves, 5 one-half mm cultured pearls, 14 KT y.g. 125.00
Crescent moon, 9 garnets, 14 KT y.g., 1⅜″ 135.00
Marcasite, sunburst 35.00

Rings

Art Nouveau, woman with saphire at neck, 14 KT 50.00
Cocktail ring, 14 KT, open work with 3 mine cut diamonds, total weight 3 cts. 1000.00
Gypsy, set with garnet, 14 KT y.g. 70.00
Onyx, black, oval, lady's, diamond chips, 10 KT 45.00
Onyx, black, man's, simple gold mount, 10 KT, ¾″ dia. 120.00
Peridot, 75 pts., 14 KT y.g. 65.00
Silver, sterling, band, 5½ mm . . . 15.00
Wedding band, 14 KT y.g., 6 mm 125.00

Slides, 14 KT y.g.

Heart, mine cut diamond in center, ⁹⁄₁₆″ 75.00
Round, 3 seed pearls, ½″ 50.00

Stick Pins

Cameo, pink, bezel set, 14 KT y.g. 35.00
Crescent Moon, 14 KT y.g. 30.00
Garnet, 6 prong setting, 14 KT y.g. 35.00
Love Knot, 14 KT y.g. 50.00
Sapphire center, 8 fresh water pearls in daisy pattern, 14 KT y.g. 65.00

Watches, see Watches

JUGTOWN POTTERY

Pottery making in North Carolina commenced in the mid 18th century and continued through the 19th and 20th centuries. The Jugtown Pottery encountered today began its colorful and somewhat off-beat operation in 1920. Jacques and Juliana Bushbee decided to leave their cosmopolitan world and return to North Carolina to revive the dying craft of pottery making in their native state.

They located in Moore County, miles away

from any large city and accessible only "if mud permits." They employed a talented young potter, Ben Owen, to turn all the wares. Jacques Bushbee did most of the designing and glazing. Juliana busied herself in promoting.

From 1922 until 1962, with only a few years exception, "Jugtown Ware" was made by Ben Owen under the operation of the founders, Jacques and Juliana Bushbee. Utilitarian and decorative items were produced. Although many colorful glazes were used, orange predominated. A Chinese blue glaze that ranged from light blue to deep turquoise was a prized glaze reserved for the very finest pieces.

Pottery is still being made in North Carolina and marked "Jugtown." At last report, Ben Owen is still turning pottery under his own mark, "Ben Owen, Master Potter."

Bowl, 2½" opening, 4" high, gray and brown $25.00

Bean Pot, covered, orange, late . . .	30.00
Bowls	
3", dark green to blue	35.00
4½", blue with some pink	50.00
5", orange lustre, handled, late . .	15.00
6", green-brown, frogskin glaze .	35.00
Candleholder, Ben Owen marked,	
frogskin glaze	85.00
Mug, orange, Ben Owen	20.00
Pitchers	
5" green	40.00
6½", covered, brown	50.00
7¾", covered, orange	35.00
Redware, orange, late	10.00
Plates	
5¾", orange, Ben Owen	25.00
6", orange	19.00
Pot, frog shaped, handled	50.00
Sugar, covered, Chinese blue, (rare shape)	100.00

Vases

3 x 1½", Chinese blue cabinet vase	60.00
6", white	60.00
6 x 2", frogskin glaze	50.00
6 x 3", black, rare glaze	100.00
6 x 3", cobalt blue, rare glaze . . .	85.00
8 x 4", salt glazed base with Chinese blue drip on the top ¼	125.00
12 x 8", Chinese blue, 2 small handles	225.00

KPM CHINA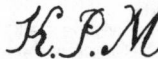

This mark, KPM, had been used by Meissen, but was adopted in 1830 by the Royal Factory, Koniglische Porzellanmanufaktur, in Berlin. This was the factory that worked under the patronage of Frederick the Great in latter part of the 18th century. Other German factories have used this mark also.

Platter, 14 x 19½", white, gold and black trim $65.00

Busts of Diana and Apollo, 4½" on tall waisted stands, pair	150.00
Creamers	
Floral and gold decor, pearlized interior	35.00
Pink roses, gold handles, artist signed	45.00
Cup and Saucer, demitasse, six-footed cup, portait of child and medallions on one side, floral decor other, gold florals all over	85.00
Dish, two compartments, pink floral and wide pink edge	55.00
Figurine, small boy dressed in 18th century style	95.00
Paintings on Porcelain	
18th Century lady, framed	160.00
Moorish lady with turban, oval with gold frame	625.00

Profile portrait of young maiden with dark curling hair, 10⅝ x 5⅝", late 19th or early 20th century .. **650.00**

Winged child in clouds, 9 x 11", framed oval **375.00**

Plates

6", fruit decor **25.00**

10", hand painted center florals, each different, magenta and gold tracery borders, set of 8 .... **250.00**

10", gypsy boy **68.00**

10¼, pierced handles, hand painted roses, gold trim **50.00**

Service for eight, contains 2 oval chop platters, 2 circular vegetable dishes, 12 soups, 15 lunch plates, 12 salads, 3 shallow dishes, flowers, and fruit molded borders, Orb and Scepter mark **1500.00**

Tea Set, Teapot, creamer, sugar, tray, cups and saucers, flowers and butterflies decor **400.00**

Tureen, soup, 16½", oval, covered, and 18" underplatter, gold edges, c. 1870 .... **375.00**

Vase, 9½", fruit decor **160.00**

KAUFFMANN, ANGELICA

Marie Angelique Catherine Kauffmann was a Swiss artist who lived from 1741 until 1807. Paintings copied from her original work often embellished porcelain and those signed with her name have attracted collectors.

Bowl, 9" square, classical scene center, green border with gold edge, (Vienna Austria, and Beehive mark) **70.00**

Box, hinged cover, center scene medallion, gold trim, iridescent background **22.00**

Cups and Saucers

Classical ladies **40.00**

Footed, gold handles, portrait decor (Beehive mark) **55.00**

Ornate handle, claw foot, pastoral scene, cerise with gold **69.00**

Jam Jar, covered, 5¼", pastoral scene, ladies dancing, pale green with gold trim, Beehive mark, signed **100.00**

Pitcher, 6", center medallion, gold borders with roses **80.00**

Plates

6", classical maidens, deep green scalloped border with gold scrolls, "Victoria Carlsbad" **65.00**

7½", classical figures decor, gold shamrock border **40.00**

Tobacco Jar, 7½", dark green muted with orange and yellow, silverplated rim and lid $290.00

8¼", classical musicians decor, uneven edge, gold tracery on green border, "Victoria, Austria, Carlsbad" **70.00**

8½", three maidens serving seated gentleman, gold scallops around center, "Austria Beehive mark" **60.00**

9", classic scene with gold tracery center, cobalt blue, triple cut-out border **60.00**

10" "Venus" **68.00**

10½", three classical figures center, gold border, raised dots **70.00**

Trinket box, Classical scene after Kauffmann on lid, floral decor on body with brass mounts **75.00**

Vases

9¼", two ornate handles, classical scene on pearized background lacy gold decor **75.00**

9¾", portraits on front and reverse, "Victoria Austria"

KEW BLAS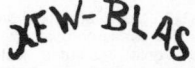

Kew Blas is an iridescent art glass made by

the Union Glass Works, Somerville, Mass. Items, when signed, were signed with the name in the center of the base. The ware was a contemporary of Tiffany at the turn of the century.

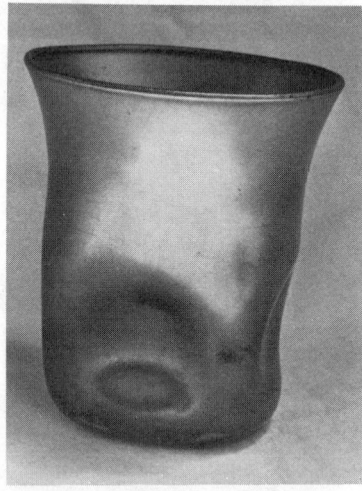

Tumbler, dimpled, 3½", gold irides- cent $225.00

Bowls, 10", green pulled feather on opaque off-white iridescent background, flared edge	1250.00
Candlesticks, 8½", iridescent gold, twisted stems, pair	695.00
Compote, 4½", iridescent gold, fluted top	495.00
Creamer, 5", pulled feather on iridescent off-white background, fancy iridescent handle, (very rare) . .	1250.00
Finger bowl, iridescent gold, fluted edge	295.00
ribbed with scalloped border in metallic lustre gold with platinum highlights, with 6" underplate . . .	325.00
Goblet, 6", iridescent gold, knob stem	350.00
Rosebowl, 4", green feather on iridescent off-white and gold background	895.00
Salt, open, iridescent gold	195.00
Vases	
4¼", green and gold iridescent pulled thread on opalescent body	800.00
6", gold decorated lustre over green feathers on opaque body, fluted top	1250.00

6", iridescent gold, slightly bulbous with gold handles	695.00
7", iridescent rich blue	800.00
7¾", opaque with gold and green iridized rippled designs	1250.00
9½", bulbous bottom, trumpet top, silver lustre background, pulled amber feathers	875.00

KING'S ROSE

King's Rose is a hand decorated earthenware made in the Staffordshire district, England, in the period 1820–1840. It was heavily exported to the Middle Atlantic states.

The central feature is a large, cabbage type rose in red, pale red, or pink. The pink rose often is called "Queen's Rose." Secondary colors are pastels of yellow, pink, and occasionally green. The borders are varied—a solid band, vined, lined, or sectional.

Because of the soft paste, the enameled colors do not hold well. It is not unusual to see portions of the decoration flaked off. Further, the ware is subject to cracking and chipping.

Bowl, 8½" diam., 4½" high . . $135.00

Coffee Pot, dome lid, brick red rose, 10½"	850.00
Creamer, brick red rose, helmet shape	225.00
Cups and Saucers	
Handled, brick red rose	100.00
Handless	
Brick red rose	175.00
Pink rose	150.00
Pale red rose	120.00
Plates	
5¼", brick red rose	120.00
8¼", brick red rose	125.00
8¾", brick red rose	150.00
9⅞", brick red rose	180.00
Sauceboat, brick red rose, 6"	150.00

Soups
9¾", solid border, brick red rose .	**170.00**
10", broken border, brick red rose	**160.00**

Sugars, covered
Brick red rose, scroll work in relief	**225.00**
Pink rose	**160.00**
Teapot, pink rose, bulbous, 5"	**325.00**
Waste Bowl, 5⅝"	**100.00**

KITCHEN COLLECTIBLES

Kitchenwares and allied primitives of any period are very collectible today. From the days when cooking was done on any open hearth, when cooking pots were made of iron, copper or brass, cast iron, and to the days when they were replaced by lighter and easier-to-clean materials, till well into the 1920's, kitchenwares are part of our past history. Wooden ware dishes, and implements are very much sought after today, as are the patented implements used to make the housewifes' duties easier and more efficiently performed.

See various other categories such as, Graniteware, Woodenware, Copper, Brass, Ironware, etc.

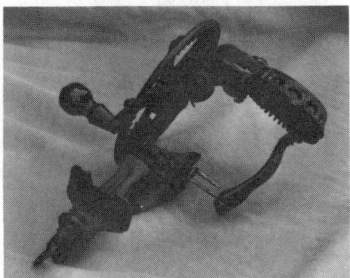

Apple Pealer, cast iron and brass, "Made only by the Reading Hardware Co., Reading, Pa." **$40.00**

Apple Parers
Cast iron, dated 1878	**45.00**
Cast iron, Leominster, Mass., 1904	**35.00**
Cast Iron, Hudson Improved Apple Parer Co., Leominster, Mass., dated 1882	**50.00**
Wooden, two-gear belt-driven model, on chip, carved board	**180.00**

Bowls
8" Graniteware, blue and white	**15.00**
14½", bird's eye maple	**60.00**
10 x 8", wooden, dough bowl	**85.00**
14", yellow ware mixing bowl	**75.00**

Bread Boards
9½", maple, "Bread" carved on border	**40.00**
Shaped like a pig, burnt design	**15.00**
Bread Raiser, with lid, 14", tin	**25.00**

Bread Pan, two loaf, round, tin and sheet iron **30.00**

Butter Churns
25½", wood with iron bandings, with lid and dasher	**195.00**
Drum type, 18½", wooden with iron crank, cow stenciled in red	**80.00**
Stoneware, grey, dark blue, earred handles, c. 1830	**85.00**
18", Dasher type with piggin handle	**120.00**

Cabbage cutting board, 7¼ x 20", three blades and sliding hopper box **45.00**

Cheese ladder, wood, mortised and pegged **25.00**

Cherry Stoner
Enterprise, pat. date 1885	**25.00**
Cast Iron, "Rollman Mfg. Co."	**25.00**

Chopping bowl, turned wood, old mustard paint, early 19th century . **88.00**

Crock, pottery, preserves, 12" high, 8" dia. **$55.00**

Coffee Pot
Graniteware, blue and white	**30.00**
Graniteware, mottled grey with pewter lid	**45.00**
Covered, nickel-plated copper with brass trim, wooden handle	**32.50**

Corn stick pan, cast iron	10.00
Egg Basket, folding type, wire	15.00

Egg Beaters
Rotary, cast iron, dated 1903 . . .	7.00
Two propellers, iron and tin	7.50
Fruit Press, Enterprise, table top model	18.00

Lemon Squeezers
Iron, "Yankee Lid On"	25.00
Wooden, hinged	25.00

Nutmeg Graters
Tin, handled	22.50
Tin with wooden handles, marked, "Edgar Mfg. Co.," dated 1891 . .	27.50
Pastry Crimper, brass and iron, three way, dated 1866	25.00
Pie Peel or Lifter, wrought iron, ring on end with hook	22.50

Raisin Seeder
Enterprise, pat. 1895	30.00
Wire with wooden handle, "Everett," Patd. 1888	30.00

Rolling Pins
Maple, 12″	22.50
White milk glass	50.00
White milk glass, says "Forget Me Not," holds water	55.00
Tiger stripe maple, single handle .	60.00

Salt Box
Wall type, white milk glass, wooden lid	50.00
Wall type, Blue Onion design, with wooden lid	65.00
Salt Bowl, wooden turned, 5″	27.50

Sausage Stuffer
Cast and sheet iron, with gears . .	35.00
Enterprise Mfg. Co., iron	40.00
Scoop, walnut, 12″	45.00
Utensil Rack, hand forged iron	65.00
Washboard (Scrubstick), wooden, 32″	120.00

KUTANI

Kutani, in Kaga province, Japan, is where this ware was made in the mid-1600's. The earliest ware is quite heavy, like stoneware; the next group of collectible ware is somewhat lighter, and is decorated with many colors, such as green, yellow, and purple, with black outlining. The Kutani made since 1875, for Western export, is what is found most often today, and is what most collectors look for. The earlier ware is the most expensive, and is harder to find.

Bowls
Round, flat, on small stand, oriental scene	225.00

Left: Vase, 5¾″, red, 2 men . . $100.00
Right: Vase, 7″, flowers and birds $80.00

Berry, one large bowl, six smaller ones, red and gilt border, coutesans in procession, Mt. Fuji in background, polychrome enamels	150.00
Berry, one large, four smaller, each piece on four legs, deep red border, floral motif	100.00
7″, red design on white, background, One Thousand Faces . . .	65.00
7″, central motif of carp, floral diapered border, foliage	375.00
Cachepot, 11″, three feet, scalloped rim, red ground, polychrome figures in garden setting	250.00

Chargers
23″, gold background, polychrome decor, Seven Gods of Good Luck	250.00
23″, band of birds and floral roundels	225.00
Cup and Saucer, orange border, "One Thousand Faces"	25.00

Dishes
7″, square form, motif of pine branch and perched bird	750.00
10″, polychrome and gold figures against a water scene	100.00
Ginger Jars, 7″, red on white background, birds and flowers, stylized flowers, pair	485.00
Hair Receiver, polychrome, figures .	75.00
Tea Caddy, 8″, covered, red decor, florals, on white background	100.00

Tea Sets
Covered teapot, sugar, creamer, six cups and saucers, six cake plates, orange and red trim, lotus finials	175.00

Covered teapot, open sugar, creamer, four cups and saucers, cobalt blue and gold, red roses .. **225.00**
Tray, 14", polychrome and gilt, garden scene with figures, red orange and gold border **325.00**

Vases
8", red, gold background, and black with birds **325.00**
16", ovoid, polychrome, pastel hues, motif of a waterfall, mountains and lake **375.00**
18", octagonal, panels containing medallions filled with beautiful women, red on white background, pair **800.00**

LALIQUE R.LALIQUE

LALIQUE

Lalique is a quality glass designed in the manner of the Art Nouveau and Art Deco style. It is a combination of blown, molded or pressed and/or engraved glass.

Rene Lalique produced this glass in France from the 1890's until his death in 1945. Pieces from this era are signed "R. Lalique." Items made after 1945 are marked "Lalique." Script and block letters were used alternately.

Forgeries of the signature on Lalique-type glass are not uncommon. In some instances the "R" has been added to "Lalique" to misrepresent the circa.

Vase, 3½", Lion, script signed . $35.00

Ashtray, 6¼", square, band of marguerites highlighted with brown patinated enamel **155.00**

Atomizers
4⅛", maidens, frosted glass, gilt metal, R. Lalique **130.00**
4½", semi-draped figures, glass and metal, R. Lalique **160.00**
5½", female nudes, frosted glass, gilt metal, R. Lalique **225.00**
Blotter, rocker, molded snails on handle, R. Lalique **400.00**

Bottles, Perfume
3½", double poppy, frosted, Lalique, France **110.00**
4", molded sides swallows in flight, frosted, R. Lalique **180.00**
5½", "Bouchon Fleurs de Pommies," R. Lalique **250.00**
6", molded flowering marguerites **250.00**
7", clear, brown stain, overall florals, floral stopper **350.00**

Bowls
6½ x 2½", molded cherries on base, enamel decor, Lalique **250.00**
8⅛", opalescent, 6 nymphs relief molded, wheel cut, R. Lalique ... **325.00**
8½ x 3½", molded leaves and mistletoe, opalescent, berry feet . **375.00**
10", opalescent swirled, R. Lalique **225.00**
10½", octagon shape fruit bowl, 4 frosted and clear art deco table candleholders, relief molded dripguards, Lalique **600.00**
13¾", fish and hobnail decor, Lalique **300.00**
14", opalescent glass centerpiece, 5 sea nymphs molded in high relief, Lalique **850.00**

Bowls
3¼" dia., black glass, molded scarab lid, molded thistles on base, R. Lalique **1300.00**
4" dia., Emiliane, covered, molded flowering marguerites, brown patinated enamel in recesses, R. Lalique **130.00**
4⅛" dia., frosted glass, berry laded mistletoe on cover with green patinated enamel, R. Lalique ... **300.00**
5½" dia., frosted glass, cover ribbed in the form of cluster of stems, base molded with flower heads, wheel cut, R. Lalique **160.00**
6½" dia., seagreen glass, cover intaglio molded with swifts in flight, R. Lalique **600.00**
Carafe, 13½", tear drop form, gray patinated enamel, Lalique **1100.00**

Car Mascots
5", relief molded, frosted horse's head with stylized mane chromium mount, R. Lalique **1300.00**

6¼" long, frosted dragonfly with folded wings, R. Lalique **950.00**

7¾", deep green, standing cockrell, mounted on red marble plinth, R. Lalique **2200.00**

8", clear glass, crouching cock, R. Lalique **550.00**

Charger, 10¼", opalescent, exterior molded with parakeets in blossoming branches, R. Lalique **1300.00**

Clock, 9", arched, dial surmounted by pair doves in flowers and branches, wheel cut, R. Lalique . **1200.00**

Dish, 14½" dia., relief molded with swirling fish, teakwood stand, R. Lalique **1500.00**

Decanter, 7¾", frosted, spherical ribbed with trumpet neck, domical stopper, R. Lalique **350.00**

Figurines

1¾ x 2", blue angel fish, Lalique . **65.00**

3¼", frosted standing sparrow, R. Lalique **140.00**

3¾", frosted sparrow pecking, R. Lalique **190.00**

4⅝", frosted nude and bird, Lalique **125.00**

5½", frosted nudes, Lalique, pair . **175.00**

5½", frosted and clear quail **160.00**

Inkwell, frosted, 4 mermaids molded, intaglio cut, brown stained recesses, R. Lalique **450.00**

Medallion, 3¾" dia., frosted, winged male nudes, Paris International Exposition 1937, R. Lalique **425.00**

Mirror, 11¾" long, hand, molded stylized foliage, nude male, sepia patinated enamel in recesses, R. Lalique **1100.00**

Pendants

1½", triangular, frosted, molded dancing nymph **170.00**

1½" dia., frosted nymph in flower tree, Lalique **200.00**

3⅜", oval, R. Lalique **250.00**

Plate, 6½", clear glass, side plates, R. Lalique, 6 . . . . **110.00**

Statues

21", frosted glass maiden, hands raised, head bowed, Lalique, rare **3500.00**

27½", frosted glass stylized maiden, wooden plinth base, R. Lalique **2800.00**

Vases

5", frosted glass, molded maidens, R. Lalique **425.00**

5¾", tulip form, green enameled decor panels, R. Lalique, pair . . . **350.00**

7", spherical, Formose, molded goldfish, cased red **2860.00**

8", 3 sided, nude woman, Lalique **595.00**

8¾", clear and frosted, molded birds and blossoms **1540.00**

9½", frosted, Art Deco, R. Lalique **250.00**

LAMP SHADES

Art Nouveau art glass shades created by Durand, Quezal, Steuben and other glass makers of the early 20th century have become highly prized. These glass shades will probably never be used as they were originally intended, since most collectors consider them shelf or cabinet pieces.

Carnival Glass, 4¾" high, orange, pair $24.00

Burmese, 2" collar, ruffled edge, acid finish **250.00**

Duncan and Miller, Diamond Ridge . **30.00**

Durand

3½", candle shade, gold iridescent **100.00**

8", lily, threads over opal **225.00**

King Tut, orange iridescent, opal lined **250.00**

White hearts, random threading on white **110.00**

Fostoria

Gold, pulled down, opalescent gold lining **110.00**

Green and gold leaves, vines on opalescent, gold lined **115.00**

Green leaves, vertical vines on opalescent, gold lined, pair **175.00**

Lalique, hanging type

12", amber, shallow, molded shells, R. Lalique **500.00**

13", crystal, molded ivy, R. Lalique **575.00**

14", crystal, frosted, block panels, molded leaves, R. Lalique **650.00**

Leaded, handing dome type

Early 1900's, florals, fruits, birds, etc. **700.00 +**

1940 and later, florals, fruits, birds, etc. **350.00 +**

Slag panels . . . . **250.00 +**

Lustre Art

Calcite, threading	95.00
Blue hooked feather on opalescent, gold lined	225.00
Gold iridescent, ribbed	125.00
Yellow band on white	100.00

Imperial-Nuart

Amberina, grape pattern	30.00
Cameo satin, floral border	30.00
Crystal, etched, electric	15.00
Crystal, 4" collar, gas	25.00
Gold iridescent	34.00
Marigold	50.00
Northwood, 4½ x 5", peach opal	85.00

Quezal

Blue pulled feather on opalescent, gold lined	165.00
Gold hooked feather on opalescent, gold lined	175.00
Green pulled feather outlined in gold on opalescent, ribbed, gold lined	165.00
Lily, 4½", gold iridescent	225.00
Optic rib, 2¼", collar, 7" high	250.00
Pumpkin	120.00
Zipper, 3¾" high, gold on opalescent	150.00

Steuben

Dark green pulled feather on white, 5" high	125.00
Drag loop, brown aurene on calcite, gold lined	150.00
Gold aurent, tulip shape, four	350.00
Green pulled feather on gold aurene	185.00
Student, 3" collar, green, miniature	25.00

Tiffany

Candle lamp shade, ruffled edge	295.00
Diamond optic, silver pulled decor on green iridescent	350.00
Gold draped on brown ground	275.00
Gold iridescent favrile, signed	180.00
Waterford, 4 x 6½", crystal	75.00

LAMPS

Oil lamps evolved from the Stone Age lamps which were nothing more than small hollowed-out stones in which animal fat was burned.

In 1784, Aime' Argand, a Swiss physicist, patented the first 'modern' oil lamp which bears his name; it featured a round, hollow burner with a tubular wick and glass chimney.

After oil was discovered in Titusville, Pa., in 1850,bears his name; it featured a round, holloinvented the electric light bulb in 1879 and his invention marked the beginning of the end of oil lamps even though the full impact was not felt for another quarter century.

Oil lamps are still used today. However, most lamps from the past are collected because of their artistic qualities and not their usefulness.

Lard, tin, 2 handled, skillet $65.00

Aladdin Lamps

Anniversary	200.00
Beehives	
Amber, dark	100.00
Amber, light	85.00
Clear	30.00
Bennington-type base, removable font, 14"	65.00
Lincoln Drape, Alacite	100.00
Washington Drape, clear	90.00

Angle Lamps

Double, nickelplated brass, milk glass chimneys, frosted glass shades	250.00
Single, nickelplated brass, milk glass chimney, frosted glass shade	135.00
Argand Lamp, double, bronzed, etched shades, signed	500.00
Astral Lamp, 34" high, brass base, cut and etched shade with prisms, electrified	400.00
Banner Lamp, 20", clear glass paneled base, drum font, #2 chimney	50.00

Banquet Lamps

25½", iron cutout base, floral, ball shade	250.00
29" high, brass, cherub standing with butterfly in hand, frosted white shade, ornate font, burnished and electrified	350.00

31" high, brass base, stem font, green wreaths with gold leaf ribbons, Handel 695.00
31" high, metal, cutouts, floral shade 340.00
37" high, ornate brass base, opaque white overlay stem, brass font with double wick burner, frosted wheel-cut engraved shade . . . 500.00

Betty Lamps
Iron, wrought, double 50.00
Redware, sponged 135.00
Tin 100.00

Bicycle Oil Lamp 40.00

Bracket Lamps
Brass, blown chimney 125.00
Iron, lacy frame, 9" mercury glass reflector 85.00

Bradley and Hubbard Lamps
Banquet, 28", brass relief base, and font, clematis 325.00
Banquet, 31½", onyx and gilted metal base and stem, complete with shade 650.00
Bracket, Gas, 4" projection, scrolled brass 100.00
Chandelier, 19 x 34", brass, three gas lights 500.00
Hall, brass, 7 x 7", brass and beveled glass light 200.00
Pendant, 20" closed, 80" extended, brass, embosses font, 14" white dome shade 400.00
Piano, extension-type, 54" to burner, cast metal, no shade . . . 500.00
Table, 12" to burner, ornate cast metal, brass finish, detachable font 250.00
Table, 21", Bradley & Hubbard, signed, panelled slag, glass shade with pierced leaf and berry design, polychrome metal, fluted, baluster stem 500.00

Carriage Lamp, 20", painted black metal, four beveled glass panes, brass trim 250.00

Chandeliers
Brass, 31" spread, 42" drop, four glass fonts, electrified 1500.00
Glass, 36" spread, frosted and molded panels on gilted metal supports, molded leaves, signed Sabino 1500.00
Glass, 36" spread, glass arms with five lights, prisms and chains 1000.00

Cruise Lamps
Iron, wrought, 8½", double 85.00
Tin, lapped, 8", double 175.00

Gone With the Wind Lamps
20½" high, green ground, pink and red roses on font and shade, electrified 350.00

23" high, lion's head on base and shade, all original 750.00
25" high, red satin bull's eye, signed Miller, 1895 . . . . 795.00
27½" high, satin glass, puffed iris, white 675.00

Grease Lamps
Iron 100.00
Tin, handled, European 100.00

Hand Lamps
Glass
Aqua, 3", free blown, circular foot, applied handle, attributed to South Jersey 350.00
Blue Bristol, applied handle, all original 90.00
Clambroth, 5", "Waisted Loop," double burners 295.00
Clear, 4" green, diamond 95.00
Cobalt, 3¼", "Three Printie" pewter collar, single drop burner 450.00
Pewter, 3 x 6", single brass tube, early 175.00
Tin, 2 x 2½", drum-shaped, strap handle 65.00

Handel Lamps
7½", hanging lantern, tan slag panels in reticulated metal frame . 750.00
8", tree trunk base, leaded shade 500.00
18", Oriental-style base, Persian border shade 2000.00
18", tripod base, Art Deco-type shade 1750.00
19", patina finished base, leaded green slag 500.00
24", bronze base, leaded floral shade 2500.00
57", floor, patina finished base, "Chipped Ice" shade 2000.00
61", floor, double standard base, 20" dia., leaded shade 3500.00
Bronzed metal, reverse, painted glass, table 1800.00

Hanging Lamps
Central, brass frame and font, 14" handpainted shade, prisms, all original 375.00
Country Store, embossed brass font, 14" dia., tin shade, complete 300.00
Hall, brass frame and chains, cranberry cylindrical shade 175.00
Kitchen, brass frame, milk glass shade 275.00
Kitchen, iron frame, milk glass shade, complete, electrified 175.00
Miniature, 17", jeweled brass . . . 200.00

Jefferson Lamp, bronzed base, 16" dia., domed shade with scenic decor, signed base and shade 1000.00

Lacemaker's Lamps
9¾", clear blown glass, peg-like font, hollow stem, circular foot 16", cranberry overshot, brass base . . 395.00

Pairpoint Lamps

8" high, apricot floral shade **895.00**

8" high, silvered base, puffed rose shade **750.00**

14½", puffy glass shade, with interior painted blossoms, beige with black ribboned lower border, silvered metal base **800.00**

Peg Lamps

4" high, tin asphaltum, petticoat-type with handle **85.00**

5" high, blown molded globular ribbed panels, brass fittings **175.00**

6½", clear, "Thumbprint," brass fittings **75.00**

19½" o.h. shaded pink satin glass, "Beaded Drape," brass candlestick holder **350.00**

Rushlight Holder, 10¼" high, wrought iron with scrolled balance, turned wooded base **175.00**

Sparking Lamps

Black Amethyst, 4½", tin burner, (unique) **1500.00**

Blue, light, wine glass form, knob stem **150.00**

Clear

2⅜", BTM, single drop tin burner, McKearin 110-4 .... **100.00**

3⅜", free blown font, trefoil scalloped pressed base, single drop burner, McKearin 189-19 . **150.00**

4½", free blown globular font, knob stem, waffle cup plate base, single drop burner **325.00**

Student Lamps

24" high, double, brass, green cased shades **750.00**

24" high, single, tin plated brass, 7" milk glass shade **375.00**

40" long, hanging-type, double, 10" dia., cased green shades, burnished, electrified **1200.00**

Tiffany Lamps, see "Tiffany Glass"

Whale Oil Lamps. Also see "Sandwich Glass," Brass, 7", single burner **125.00**

Dolphins

Petticoat (McKee)

Canary, 6½", fiery opalescent sockets **450.00**

Electric Blue, 6½" **425.00**

Electric Blue, 6½", opalescent sockets **475.00**

Scalloped (Mid-West)

Canary

6½", slim **500.00**

8½" **400.00**

Clambroth

6½" **450.00**

8½" **375.00**

Clear, 8½" **125.00**

Jade Green, (one color) 6½" **850.00**

Translucent Blue, 6½", slim . **450.00**

Steps (Boston and Sandwich)

Canary, 10⅛", single **425.00**

Clambroth, 10⅛", single ... **400.00**

Clear, 10⅛"

Double **125.00**

Single **125.00**

Overlay Glass

Amethyst, 11" high, marble base **750.00**

Cranberry, 11½" high, white base **275.00**

Patterned Glass

Acanthus Leaf, 9", brilliant blue font, brass stem, marble base . **300.00**

Bigler, 10¼", cobalt blue, square base, McKearin 198-14 **750.00**

Bull's Eye and Fleur-de-lis, 9" clear, pewter collar, hexagonal baluster stem and base **125.00**

Hearts under glass, 7½" **140.00**

Loop, 9½", cobalt blue, pewter collar, hexagonal base, double drop burners **350.00**

Sandwich Star, 10½", clear, brass collar, hexagonal baluster stem and base **150.00**

Waffle and Thumbprint, 4½", fingertype, clear, mold blown, pewter collar **95.00**

Pewter, 7½", double burner, "Smith and Co." **125.00**

Tole

6½" dia., base, 7½" high, handled **175.00**

11" high, six 3½" wick tubes, bail handle, workshop-type ... **225.00**

LAMPS, MINIATURE

Miniature oil and kerosene lamps, often called "night lamps," are diminutive replicas of larger lamps; they may measure as high as 12" or as small as 2½". Simple and utilitarian in design, these lamps were used primarily as "night lamps" and also in the parlor as "courting lamps" and in sickrooms.

During the Victorian period, beautiful fine art glass shades were introduced in miniatures.

Though elaborate in decor, small glass lamps were usually constructed of several separate parts—base, collar, burner, chimney and shade. A careful study of these individual parts can help determine the age of the lamp, country or origin and also if the miniature is all original or had certain parts replaced.

***Note*: Figure numbers refer to illustration figure number in the book, *Miniature Lamps* by Frank R. and Ruth E. Smith.**

Caution: **More and more reproductions of miniature lamps are appearing on the market. These "new" lamps are similar to the originals in shape, design and color. To date, Smith figure numbers 85, 149, 150, 203, 228, 336, 400, 403, 419, 434 and 482 have been reproduced.**

Santa Claus, 9½" scarlet & black milk glass, Fig. VII $1650.00

Figure #
18 — silver base, cranberry font with enamel decor, opalescent chimney 500.00
40 — Spanish Lace, blue opalescent, finger 220.00
44 — Little Jewel, clear glass 70.00
51 — Shoe, amber 440.00
111 — Bull's Eye, amber, pair 220.00
120 — Time, clear glass, with milk glass beehive shade 130.00
128 — milk glass, pewter base 120.00
174 — milk glass, swirl pattern 180.00
189 — milk glass, ribbed blue to white 200.00

219 — milk glass, Nellie Bly, pink . . 120.00
229 — milk glass, green, Cosmos pattern 330.00
230 — milk glass, Acanthus, green decor 230.00
231 — green satin, Drape pattern . . 245.00
275 — Eagle, pink and green 375.00
276 — "Pineapple in the Basket," clear blue glass 240.00
286 — milk glass, white, Cosmos, painted floral 240.00
339 — milk glass, Bristol, brown painted scenes 180.00
369 — Beaded Swirl, cranberry, embossed 275.00
385 — cased glass, pink, satin finish 270.00
385 — cased glass, yellow, glossy finish 600.00
388 — cased glass, Florette, pink, glossy finish 575.00
432 — Twinkle, amethyst clear glass 250.00
439 — cranberry with matching chimney 290.00
479 — ribbed swirl, blue 300.00
480 — pedestal, amber glass, embossed base 275.00
482 — Daisy & Cube, clear glass . . . 110.00
497 — Owl, green 740.00
517 — blue opalescent with blue applied feet 820.00
529 — cased glass, candy stripe, pink and white 715.00
530 — cased glass, pink, ribbed swirl pattern 770.00
569 — cased glass, deep pink shading to light, satin finish 825.00
601 — Satin glass, mother-of-pearl, raindrop 1200.00
625 — Glow lamp, cranberry 95.00
Fig. III Artichoke, pink and green fired on paint 310.00
No #, brass formalin lamp 65.00
No #, Goofus glass 28.00
No #, finger lamp, blue with torch type burner 105.00

LANTERNS

A lantern is an enclosed, portable light source, hand carried or attached to a bracket or pole to illuminate an area. It allegedly derived its name from early times when candles were placed in thin animal horns and were called "Lantern Horns." They were developed into portable lighting devices with glass sides or chimneys as we know them today.

Auto Lanterns, see AUTO ITEMS
Barn, 22", tin, mercury glass reflector 75.00
Bicycle, brass 65.00
Bicycle, 6", solar 40.00

Miner's, "Patterson Lames, Ltd., Gateshead on Tyne," brass . . . $50.00

Buggy, kerosene-type, Dietz 50.00
Carriage
  15″, beveled glass panes, brass
  trim 200.00
  34½″, painted metal, ornate brass
  trim, eagle finial; 6 beveled glass
  panes 350.00
Candle
  13½″, Paul Revere-type, pierced
  tin, cone-shaped top 150.00
  15″, pierced tin, tri-shape, crimped
  wafer and bail 145.00
  17½″, pierced copper 175.00
Hand, 8½″, brass, round glass door   40.00
Magic Lanterns. See MAGIC LAN-
  TERNS
Policeman's, 3 x 7″, tin 45.00
Railroad Lanterns. See RAILROAD
  ITEMS
Ship Lanterns
  12″, brass, tin reflectors; port and
  starboard, pair 300.00
  22½″, brass and steel, early 19th
  century 185.00
Skater Lanterns
  Brass, all original 65.00
  Brass and tin, 7 x 8″, mold blown
  globe 100.00
  Tole, square, glass panels 85.00
Street Post, 22″ high, 13″ canopy;
  opalescent globe, 11″ high, 8″
  wide; gas burner 175.00

Wagon, tin, square red lense, origi-
  nal oil burner 30.00
Whale Oil, pierced tin with glass
  panel, all original 125.00

LEEDS CHINA

The Leeds Pottery in Yorkshire, England, began production about 1758. It made among
other things, creamware that was competi-
tive with Wedgwoods. The factory there
closed in 1820, but continued under various
owners until about 1880. They made exceptional cream colored ware, either plain or
salt-glazed, or painted with colored enamels,
and glazed and unglazed redware.

Early wares are unmarked, but later pieces
bear marks of "Leeds Pottery" sometimes
followed by "Hartley-Green and Co." or the
letters "LP." Reproductions may also bear
these marks. It is beautiful ware and eagerly
sought in the antique market today.

**Creamware, chestnut bowl, 1790–
1800 . . . . $750.00**

Bowls
Oval, reticulated, footed 150.00
11½ x 8¾″, vegetable, oval, cut
  corners, blue feathered edge . . .   195.00
13″, creamware, plain 200.00
Coffee Pot, covered, creamware,
  pear shaped, leaf molded curved
  spout and entwined rope handle,
  terminating in floral clusters,
  domed cover with flower head fini-
  al, c. 1785 . . . .   400.00
Cups and Saucers
Handleless, white with blue flow-
  ers 125.00
Five color, floral and cross
  hatched decor 75.00

Two color, Gaudy type decor . . . 85.00
Three color decor, miniature size 105.00
Jug, 11¼", orange rope handle and
rim, green and orange floral band
decor, c. 1820 . . . . 500.00

Pitchers

Gaudy floral decor in three colors 165.00
Gaudy floral decor, yellow rim . . . 775.00
Miniature, White twisted handle,
classical figures on blue 100.00
Stoneware, 8½", creamy beige
with incised bamboo leaves, terra
cotta borders, original pewter cover, Leed Burmantofts, c. 1182 . . 500.00

Plates

5½", Toddy plate, green feather
edge, 4-color peafowl on branch . 305.00
7⅛", green molded feather edge,
4-color gaudy decor 295.00
7¾", blue feather edge, 4-color
floral decor 135.00
8¼", blue feather edge, with ea-
gle and 13 stars, 4-color 475.00
9¾", blue feather edge, ochre flo-
ral design 155.00
9½", underglaze blue, Chinese
landscape decor, c. 1780 . . . . . . 450.00
Embossed swag border, 5-color
floral decor 135.00
12¼", charger, blue feather edge,
5-color decor, peafowl in tree . . . 785.00

Platters

4 x 5", miniature, rare size, 3-color
floral decor 275.00
9¾ x 8", creamware, pierced bas-
ket loop border 125.00
15", blue feather edge 100.00
16½", blue feather edge 150.00
Sauce Boat, creamware, silver
shape, with entwined strap han-
dle, and floral terminals, c. 1785 . 275.00
Soup Plate, green feather edge . . . 95.00
Sugar Bowl, covered, draped blue
design with yellow dots 140.00
Tea Kettle, with cover, 4",
creamware, golular form with long
straight spout and overhead strap
handle terminating in flower heads 165.00

Teapots

Flower form finial, twisted handle,
iron red and green decor 575.00
5", octagon shape, white with
embossed feathers, c. 1780 . . . . 400.00
Tea Strainer, Blue Willow pattern, c.
1800 . . . . 100.00

LENOX CHINA

Jonathan Cox and Walter Scott Lenox

established The Ceramic Art Company, Trenton, N. J., in 1889. The factory was best
known for its American Belleek. In 1906, the
factory became the Lenox Co., and they
made quality American porcelain.

Two marks appear on Lenox China, the
'pallette' mark, and a 'green wreath.' The 'pallette' mark appears on many pieces of hand
painted china, which was supplied in great
quantity when it was the vogue for amateur
hand painting of china, as a hobby. The company is still in existance today and the current mark is stamped in gold.

Candlestick, 8", marked Lenox, 930/
E41 . . . .$75.00

Candy dish, 3", silver overlay 35.00
Cookie Jar, Ming pattern, Black
Wreath mark 100.00
Cups and Saucers
Yellow with gold trim, made for
Bailey Banks and Biddle, set 4 . . 100.00
Demitasse, in sterling holder 85.00
Demitasse, black with silver trim,
made for Marshall Field 85.00
Peachtree pattern, 1948 . . . . 35.00
Flower holder, 8½", 4 branch exten-
sions attached to bulbous round
base 95.00
Honey Pot, bee finial, gold bees on
white background, marked 60.00
Plates
8¼", hand painted, game bird in
natural setting, cream, gold border
and trim, artist signed, set of 12 . 200.00

8½", square, Ming pattern	12.00
9¼", Peachtree pattern	18.00
Powder Jar, hand painted violets . .	37.50
Ramekin and underplate, pink with gold border and trim, signed	27.50
Salt, shape of swan, white, with matching spoon	40.00
Teapot and creamer, nested with sterling overlay	100.00
Tea Set, teapot, covered, creamer, sugar, brown glaze, set	125.00
Urn, 5¼", three handled, imbedded silver medallion on dark blue background, presentation inscription	140.00
Vase, 10", stick type, white, pink border neck and base, gold trim .	55.00
12", cylindrical, 4 oval panels, marked	300.00

LIBBEY GLASS

In 1888, the New England Glass Works, W. L. Libbey and Son, Proprietors, Cambridge, Ohio, closed and Edward Libbey established the Libbey Glass Company in Toledo, Ohio. The firm produced quality cut and intaglio cut glass for the "Brilliant Period." In 1930, Libbey's interest in art glass production was renewed. A. Douglas Nash was employed as a designer. Perhaps his "Animal Fair" stemware is best known. The factory continues production today as Libbey Glassware, a division of Owens-Illinois, Inc. For cut glass see CUT GLASS

Candlesticks, 6", made by Nash, acid marked Libbey, pair $700.00

Bowl, 8", vaseline stretch, silver strans	65.00
Candlesticks	
5¼", camel stem	185.00
8", crystal, air twist stem, signed .	125.00
10", intaglio cut flowers on bowl & foot, teardrop stem	110.00
Cup and Saucer, World's Fair, 1893, signed	70.00
Rose Bowl, 8", clear swirl	40.00
Stemware, "Animal Fair," c. 1933	
Claret, bear stem, signed	155.00
Cocktail, kangaroo stem	135.00
Cocktail, deer stem	155.00

LIMOGES

Limoges porcelain has been produced in Limoges, France, for over a century by numerous factories other than the famed Haviland. One of the most frequently encountered marks is "T. & V. Limoges" which is the ware made by Tressman and Vought. Other identifiable Limoges marks are A.L. (A. Lanternier), J.P.L. (J. Pouyat, Limoges), M.R. (M. Reddon), Elite and Coronet.

See also HAVILAND CHINA.

Marmalade Jar with cover and underplate, pale green, strawberry decor $65.00

Boullion cup & saucer, white, heavy gold borders, (J. Pouyat, Limoge), set of 6	118.00
Bowl and underplate, 9½" and 11½", embossed, gilt, irregular rims; pink, lavender, yellow and orange carnations, white background, T. & V. Limoge	290.00
Cake Stand, 4 x 9½" dia., hand-painted portrait center	65.00

Candlesticks, 9", handpainted berries, flowers, foliage, gold trim, artist signed, pair 75.00

Cheese dish, covered, small, mice on rope decor, white with gold trim 65.00

Chocolate Pot, 8½", embossed gold on ivory 85.00

Chocolate Set, covered pot, sugar, creamer, 6 cups and saucers, gold leaves on ivory, heavy gold trim, set 450.00

Cider Set, pitcher, underplate, 3 tumblers, roses decor, T. & V. 120.00

Cream and Sugar, covered, handpainted violets, gold handles, set 45.00

Cups and Saucers
Coffee, 8 oz., handpainted flowers, leaves; gold trim, signed A. Taylor 65.00
Demitasse, handpainted roses, gold trim 25.00

Dinner Set, floral, pink roses, grey-green leaves and vines, embossed irregular edges; service for 12, 3-size platters, 4 covered turreens, butter pats, bone dishes, open vegetables, (no cups & saucers) A. Lanternier 2500.00

Diptych, 12¼ x 19", depicts bishops within architectural setting, 19th century 1250.00

Dresser Sets
3 pieces, handpainted violets, gold trim 100.00
6 pieces, apple blossom decor, J.P.L. 175.00

Fernery, handpainted, autumn leaves 65.00

Fish Set, 24" platter, 10 plates, varied species of fish on plates, gold borders, artist signed, set 475.00

Game Plate, 13½", snipes center, gold border, artist signed 165.00

Hatpin holder, purple violets decor . 75.00

Hair Receiver, handpainted roses on blue ground, artist signed 25.00

Mug, floral decor, artist signed and dated 1911, T. & V. Limoge 37.50

Napkin plate, folded corners, pointsetta decor 35.00

Pitchers
7¾", bulbous, handpainted berry decor, gold trim 150.00
12", tankard, handpainted currants, gold trim, J.P.L. 200.00
13½", tankard, monk pouring wine, artist signed 275.00

Plaques, 9½ x 13", large pink, red and yellow roses, pair 300.00

Plates
8", crossed tennis racquets and balls, six pairs on plate, gold border, D & C, France 35.00
10", asparagus; molded asparagus separate well, irregular gold rims. D & C; set of 6 . . . . 225.00
10", handpainted portrait, signed Dubois 135.00
10" Kitten, playing, butterfly decor, artist signed, coronet 55.00
11", service, 22K gold medallion borders on white, set of 12 . . . . . 750.00

Punch Bowl, 14", 9" high; grape decor interior, portrait medallions on exterior, heavy rococo gold trim, T.V., 2 pieces 500.00

Punch Cup, handpainted grape motif, set of 6 . . . . 180.00

Ramekin, handpainted red roses . . . 25.00

Tea Set, handpainted pink roses, gold trim, T & V, 3 pieces 125.00

Tile, 6½" square, pink and green florals 25.00

Tray, 14", narcissus decor, heavy gold trim, artist-signed, c. 1900–1920 . . . . 120.00

Tureen, covered, 8 x 16" oval, rose decor, gold and green bands 175.00

Vases
3½", handpainted roses 30.00
10", handpainted cherries, signed Burghoff, c. 1895 . . . . 150.00
12½", handpainted red roses, gold ball feet, handles and scrolled top, artist signed 225.00

LITHOPHANES

Lithophanes are highly translucent porcelain panels with impressed designs. The design is formed by the difference in thickness of the plaque. Thin parts transmit an abundance of light while thicker parts represent shadows. They were first made by the Royal Berlin Porcelain Works in 1828. Other factories in Germany, France and England later produced the items. The majority on the market today were probably made between 1850 and 1900. Be careful of reproductions!

Candle Shields
5¾", Pandora's Box, in candle stand 300.00
19½", signed KPM 600.00

Fairy Lamps
One piece top, 4 panels 375.00
Children and animals 425.00

Lamps
4 panels, 4 x 6", brass frame, hanging type 850.00
5 panels, mother and children, iron frame 900.00
6 panels, iron frame, signed KPM 2000.00

Lamp Shade, 4", 4 panels, children's scene 275.00

**Fairy lamp, 9″, Lady in Tower, 3 litho-
phane panels $1100.00**

Matchbox, girl watching boats	90.00
Mug, monk	95.00

Plaques
Castle, turreted, 4 x 4⅝″	95.00
Children and priest, 4 x 5⅛″ . . .	90.00
Children having picnic, 4 x 4¹¹/₁₆″	90.00
Couple and dog, woodland set-
ting, KPM	200.00
Cupid and girl fishing, 4⅛ x 5¹/₁₀″,
P.R. Sickle	150.00
Dog flushing bird, 3¼ x 4¼″,
KPM	250.00
Girl with cat, 7¼ x 9″	125.00
Girl with rose, 6 x 7½″, KPM . . .	250.00
Madonna and Child, 6 x 7½″ . . .	175.00
Monk and girl, 4⅛ x 5¹/₁₀″, P.R.
Sickle	150.00
Rheinstein, colored, 4⅝ x 6¼″,
KPM	300.00
Rural scene, 4⅜ x 5¼″	90.00
View from West Point, 2½ x 3¼″,
KPM	150.00
Woman gazing at sea, 4⅛ x 5¹/₁₀″
, P. R. Sickle	150.00
Woman in flowing robe, 4⅛ x
5¹/₁₀″, P. R. Sickle	150.00

Steins
Regimental	190.00
Snow scene	200.00

Tea Warmers
4 x 5″, 4 panels, nickleplated
holder	350.00
5″ square, 4 panels, brass holder	400.00

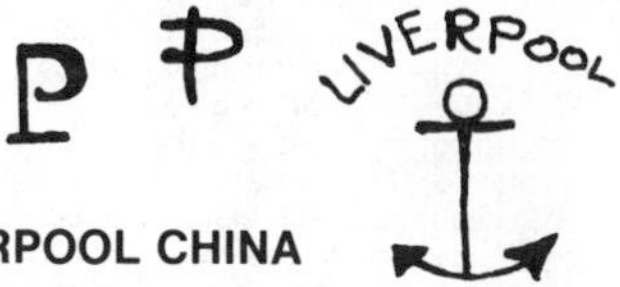

LIVERPOOL CHINA

Liverpool is the name given to products
made at several potteries in Liverpool, England, from 1750 to 1840. Among the early
producers were Seth and James Pennington
and Richard Chaffers who made tin-enam-
elled earthenwares. By the 1780's, the tin
glazed earthenwares gave way to cream colored wares decorated with cobalt, enamel
colors, or blue or black transfers. These are
the Liverpool pieces one is most likely to encounter on the market today.

The Liverpool glaze is characterized by
bubbles and most often there is clouding under the foot rims. Although the late 18th century black transfer bowls and pitchers (many
of historic interest) are eagerly collected,
they are only a small part of the total Liverpool production. By the turn of the century,
about 80 potteries were working in the town
producing not only cream ware, but soft
paste, soapstone and bone porcelain.

**Jug, 7¾″, "The Farmers Arms," multi-
color, c. 1810 . . . . $750.00**

Jugs
Harvest Jug, 9⅛″, black transfer,
oval medallion bust portrait,
George Washington, surrounded
by Victory, Justice, etc., c. 1800 .	900.00

8", Creamware with black transfer, eagle, named states, and "Peace and Prosperity to America," American flag and Miss Liberty, c. 1808 .... 300.00

8¾", Washington Memorial item, black transfer print on creamware, "Washington in Glory, America in Tears," c. 1808 .... 700.00

9", Creamware, with black transfer print, colored in iron-red, yellow, green and blue, British sailing ship and reverse, inscribed portrait, Cornwallis flanked by Justice and Mercy, 1800 .... 400.00

Mugs
  4", Black transfer, Fraternal insignia 110.00
  4⅝", Black transfer of ship's arms, "Success to the Ship's Trade, Industry Procureth Wealth," polychrome enameling 105.00
Plate, 9⅝", creamware transfer print of British sailing ship in black and colored in yellow and green, c. 1825 .... 100.00
Pitcher, 11", colored marine scenes ... 275.00
Sauce Dish, black transfer print of mother playing with child, with pink lustre bands 75.00

LOETZ GLASS

Loetz is a type of iridescent art glass made in Austria by J. Loetz Witwe in the late 1890's. Loetz was a contemporary of L. C. Tiffany and worked in the Tiffany factory before establishing his own operation. Therefore, much of the wares are similar in appearance to Tiffany's. Some pieces are signed "Loetz," "Loetz, Austria," or "Austria." The Loetz factory also produced ware with fine cameo effects on cased glass.

Basket, blue iridescent with silver threading, coin spots, brass holder ... 350.00
Bowls
  9" square, sides form lips, iridescent amber glass dribbled over all .. 575.00
  10" dia., purple-green iridescent, red glass, fluted sides 300.00
  10" dia., purple-blue, iridescent mottling, 3 large impressed dimples 595.00
Inkwells
  3 x 2½", green iridescent, pewter lily pad frame and brass lid and cover, signed 175.00
  5¼" dia., purple iridescent, brass hinged top, signed 350.00

Vase, 4", dark green with blue threading $85.00

Jar, Sweetmeat, 5" dia., 3½" high, iridescent green, dark red threading, silver plated handle and lid, signed 475.00
Rose Bowl, 4", gold iridescent, rose, lavender, blue, pink highlights, silver overlay 425.00
Vases
  3½", Formosa pattern, blue iridescent, threadware 160.00
  4¼", green iridescent, ruffled neck, signed 235.00
  4¼", green-blue iridescent, amber oil spots, 3 pinched sides 175.00
  4½", blue-green iridescent 180.00
  4¾", cranberry iridescent in pewter holder 125.00
  6¼", silvery-blue iridescent, dimpled 180.00
  7", bulbous, blue iridescent, oil spots, 3 dimples, signed 200.00
  7", blue-green iridescent, mottled over deep ruby, 999/1000 fine silver overlay 1195.00
  7½", baluster, transparent blue, bright iridescent blue and purple spider web decor, pedestal base, signed 440.00
  8¾", gold iridescent, leafe and berry decor, sterling silver overlay 1195.00
  9", gourd, gold iridescent, pinch base, signed 500.00
  9½ x 9½", fan, gold, orange, red iridescent 325.00
  10¼ x 6" dia., clambroth, swirled gold-blue iridescent striped, signed 600.00

LOTUS WARE CHINA

Lotus Ware, one of the most sought American ceramics in today's antique market, was made by Knowles, Taylor and Knowles Co. of East Liverpool, Ohio, between 1891 and 1898.

A china as translucent and as thinly potted as Belleek, it was first marked "KTK" China. In 1893, after being exhibited at the World's Columbian Exposition at Chicago, it was christened Lotus Ware, by Col. John T. Taylor, who was then president of the company. He so named it because of the body's resemblance to the petals of the lotus blossom. This was made at the time when China painting was the rage among club women, and pieces were sold from the factory plain and decorated. Pieces of Lotus Ware are hard to find today, and when found, are quite expensive.

Vase, 8", cream with green, blue violet and gold, large gold insect $675.00

Biscuit Jar, 6¾", covered, pale blue background, ivory panels, red and blue flowers, heavy gold leaves and vines, fish net slip in alternate panels, Lotus mark 300.00

Bowls
4", footed, leaves and berries in high relief 350.00

4 x 5 x 6½", gold florals, ornate top, open handles 225.00
5½ x 11", hand painted decor .. 400.00
7½", boat shaped pink and gold openwork, cherry blossoms, KTK 475.00
Chocolate Pot, handpainted sunflowers 395.00
Cup and Saucer, blank for china painting, hand painted violets on white background, KTK 75.00
Cuspidor, footed, pink flowers, gold trim on pale green background .. 300.00
Ewer, 7½", paneled in pastels, pierced and jewelled, signed Lotus mark 495.00
Pitchers
3½", with fish net or slip decor, signed 350.00
Fish net design, small, rose decor 175.00
5", bulbous, handpainted violets in panels, gold fish net 300.00
Sugar, 4 x 6", wide at handles, feather, KTK 300.00
Tea Sets
Blue handpainted flowers, gold fishnet, 3 pieces 650.00
Pink blossoms on white, gold rims and handles, 3 pieces 500.00
Tea Pot, all white, embossed flowers, KTK 450.00
Vases
7", pitcher-type, bulbous, floral decor, with gold, KTK 600.00
9", mazarine blue underglaze, heavily gilded, figures done in pate-sur-pate technique 800.00

LOWESTOFT

This soft paste porcelain was made at Lowestoft, Suffolk, England, from about 1757 to 1803. For many years Lowestoft was a misnomer used to describe Chinese Export porcelain and unfortunately it continues in many instances.

Much Lowestoft resembles Worcester porcelain and the Worcester mark (crescent) was actually copied by the factory. Some of the initials found on examples are: H,S,R,Z,W, and R.P. The earliest examples were decorated in underglaze blue with molded reliefs; later the blue was underglazed and the enamels overglazed. The paintings are often sketchy or crude. Many were in the Chinese 'style' as were most wares of the period.

Box, cricket 140.00
Bowl, 10" dia., polychrome enamel florals 350.00
Cup and Saucer, demitasse, blue underglaze 95.00

Saucer, 4¾" dia., blue decor . . $60.00

LUTZ GLASS

Lutz is an art glass attributed to Nicholas Lutz while he worked at the Boston and Sandwich Glass Co., 1869–1888. Two distinct types of glass have been associated with his name, striped glass and threaded glass. The striped glass was made by using threaded glass rods in the Venetian manner. Threaded glass was blown and decorated by winding threads of glass around the piece. After the Boston and Sandwich Co. closed, Lutz worked for the Mt. Washington Glass Co. and later for the Union Glass Works.

Since this type of glass was popular and there were many capable glass makers it is nearly impossible to distinguish actual Lutz products. They are not signed. The Venetian striped glass and threaded glass have been widely reproduced. Generally the modern pieces are heavier and more brightly colored.

Bottle, 8", ornate threaded panels alternate with opaque stripes and goldstone	350.00
Compote, 6" dia., latticino ribbons with pink threads and goldstone, flared fluted top	195.00
Cup and Saucer, filigree canes in pink, blue and white, cup on pedestal foot	195.00
Ewer, 12", white latticino threads alternate with goldstone, clear fancy applied handle	325.00
Finger Bowls 5" dia., lacy white filigree panels with pink ribbons and goldstone, lion's head prunts on sides	250.00

Bowl, 6", clear with pink and gold threading, fluted edge $110.00

5¾" dia., latticino ribbons interspersed with goldstone	195.00
Pitcher, water, pink swirl ribbons alternating with panels of white threading, fancy filigree handle . .	395.00
Plates 7", goldstone spiral threading . . .	125.00
8", white filigree on clear	125.00
Tumbler, 4", white, pink and goldstone threading	125.00
Vases 6", stick, opaque blue ribbons alternating with goldstone latticino ribbons	145.00
8", bulbous, latticino white, berry prunts, lipped top	195.00

MAASTRICHT WARE

Maastricht ware was made in Holland from about 1835 to near the end of the 19th century. English workmen and methods were employed. The pottery was named De Sphinx and produced ironstone with transfer prints. The product found a ready market in the United States and sold in competition with the English ware of the period.

Bowls

Chinese shape, 4½" and 6¼", cereal or rice, (fit into each other) flowing blue on pale blue background, rose or tulip, feather design on interior rim, marked "Maastricht-Regout-Holland," pair	30.00

Bowl, 6″ dia. x 3″ deep, white background, marked "Vlinder" $29.00

9½″, blue and white floral, wreaths and medallions, marked "Maastricht-Holland" 12.00
Black and tan transfer on white, Pajong pattern 25.00
Cream soup dish, 7¼″ deep, oriental scene decor 15.00
Cup and Saucer
Handleless, deep saucer, flowing blue on pale blue background, rose or tulip, feather design inside cup, marked "Maastricht-Regout, Holland" 18.50
Blue floral on cream background . 13.50
Plate
8″, abbey scene 10.00
8″, oriental scene, artist signed .. 18.50
8¼″, apples on green background 15.00
9½″, stylized bird decor, embossed terra cotta rim, pierced to hang 18.00
9½″, Hong pattern 20.00
Tureen, large, covered, with ladle to match, all white 40.00

MAGAZINES
See CATALOGUES AND MAGAZINES

MAGIC LANTERNS

Magic Lanterns were the forerunners of the home movie projector. Glass slides were inserted between a light source and a lense to project the images on a wall or cloth. The earlier ones used kerosene lanterns which were housed inside the machine. The majority were manufactured in Germany between 1890–1910. Prices for Magic Lanterns vary depending on manufacturer, size and condition. Slides range in price from $2.00 to $5.00 depending on subject matter.

"Lanterna Magica," brass, made in Germany, No. 596 .... $75.00

Cylindrical, 4½ x 9″, tin 50.00
Hand Crank, Bavarian 175.00
Triumph, kerosene with 6 slides ... 60.00
"Triumph Lanterna Magician," 10½″, tin with brass, mounted on wooden base 125.00

MAJOLICA

Majolica is tin-enameled glazed pottery and has been produced by many countries for centuries. It originally took its name from the island of Majorca, where figuline (a potter's clay) is found. The company of Griffin, Smith and Hill (G. S. H.), in Phoenixville, Pa. made this ware in the Victorian era, and while not the earliest manufacturer in the United States, is the most popular and sought-after type today. Their pieces are usually marked "Etruscan" and "G. S. H." in a circle. In 1880, this ware was given away as premium by a large tea company. Most Majolica found today is of 19th or 20th century manufacture.

Basket, branch handle, berry clusters on leaves on basketweave, natural colors, 5¾″ 70.00
Bottle, cucumber shaped, green and tan, 5″ 48.00
Bowls
Floral rosette center, masks separated by foliage, Castle Hedingham, E. Bingham, England, c. 1890 .... 130.00
Leaf shaped, 8″ 45.00
Shell and Seaweed, Etruscan, 8½″ 85.00

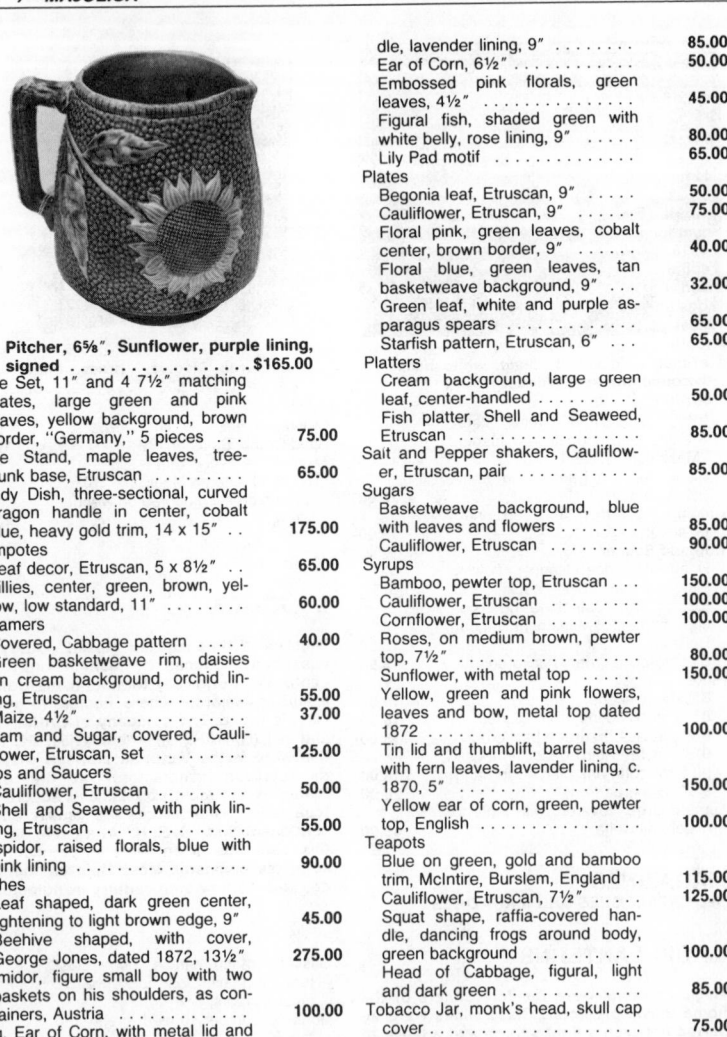

Pitcher, 6⅝", Sunflower, purple lining, signed **$165.00**

Cake Set, 11" and 4 7½" matching plates, large green and pink leaves, yellow background, brown border, "Germany," 5 pieces ... 75.00

Cake Stand, maple leaves, tree-trunk base, Etruscan 65.00

Candy Dish, three-sectional, curved dragon handle in center, cobalt blue, heavy gold trim, 14 x 15" .. 175.00

Compotes
Leaf decor, Etruscan, 5 x 8½" .. 65.00
Lillies, center, green, brown, yellow, low standard, 11" 60.00

Creamers
Covered, Cabbage pattern 40.00
Green basketweave rim, daisies on cream background, orchid lining, Etruscan 55.00
Maize, 4½" 37.00
Cream and Sugar, covered, Cauliflower, Etruscan, set 125.00

Cups and Saucers
Cauliflower, Etruscan 50.00
Shell and Seaweed, with pink lining, Etruscan 55.00

Cuspidor, raised florals, blue with pink lining 90.00

Dishes
Leaf shaped, dark green center, lightening to light brown edge, 9" 45.00
Beehive shaped, with cover, George Jones, dated 1872, 13½" 275.00

Humidor, figure small boy with two baskets on his shoulders, as containers, Austria 100.00

Jug, Ear of Corn, with metal lid and rim, yellow and green, 6½" 90.00

Mugs
Bird in flight, twig handle 50.00
Floral and butterfly 50.00

Pitchers
Begonia leaf, brown, Etruscan .. 55.00
Bird's nest on sides with eggs in it, brown background, ornate handle, lavender lining, 9" 85.00
Ear of Corn, 6½" 50.00
Embossed pink florals, green leaves, 4½" 45.00
Figural fish, shaded green with white belly, rose lining, 9" 80.00
Lily Pad motif 65.00

Plates
Begonia leaf, Etruscan, 9" 50.00
Cauliflower, Etruscan, 9" 75.00
Floral pink, green leaves, cobalt center, brown border, 9" 40.00
Floral blue, green leaves, tan basketweave background, 9" ... 32.00
Green leaf, white and purple asparagus spears 65.00
Starfish pattern, Etruscan, 6" ... 65.00

Platters
Cream background, large green leaf, center-handled 50.00
Fish platter, Shell and Seaweed, Etruscan 85.00

Salt and Pepper shakers, Cauliflower, Etruscan, pair 85.00

Sugars
Basketweave background, blue with leaves and flowers 85.00
Cauliflower, Etruscan 90.00

Syrups
Bamboo, pewter top, Etruscan ... 150.00
Cauliflower, Etruscan 100.00
Cornflower, Etruscan 100.00
Roses, on medium brown, pewter top, 7½" 80.00
Sunflower, with metal top 150.00
Yellow, green and pink flowers, leaves and bow, metal top dated 1872 .... 100.00
Tin lid and thumblift, barrel staves with fern leaves, lavender lining, c. 1870, 5" 150.00
Yellow ear of corn, green, pewter top, English 100.00

Teapots
Blue on green, gold and bamboo trim, McIntire, Burslem, England . 115.00
Cauliflower, Etruscan, 7½" 125.00
Squat shape, raffia-covered handle, dancing frogs around body, green background 100.00
Head of Cabbage, figural, light and dark green 85.00

Tobacco Jar, monk's head, skull cap cover 75.00

Vases
Basketweave, short feet, sanded, maroon, 6½" 55.00
Floral decor, sanded 65.00
Figure of boy on panel, 5½" 45.00
Figural frog musician, 6" 60.00
Tusk shapes, joined, c. 1866, Minton 90.00

MARBLEHEAD POTTERY

This hand thrown pottery had its beginning in 1905 as a therapeutic program introduced by Dr. J. Hall for the patients confined to a sanitorium located in Marblehead, Massachusetts. In 1916, the operation was removed from the hospital to another site and the factory continued under the directorship of Arthur E. Boggs until its closing in 1936.

Most pieces found today are glazed with a smooth, porous, even finish in a single color. The most desirable pieces are decorated with conventionalized design in one or more subordinate colors.

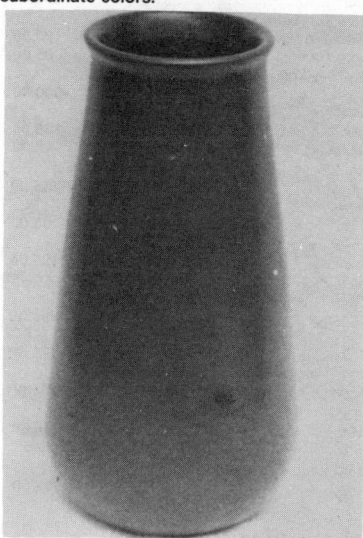

**Vase, 8″, blue matte glaze,
signed $175.00**

Bowl, 5 x 2″, closed rim, 2 colors with stylized floral design, artist signed	350.00
Candleholder, 5 x 4″, with ring handle, blue	100.00
Humidor, covered, 7 x 7″, Artist A.E. Baggs, green design on blue . . .	350.00
Vases	
4 x 2″, pink glaze	40.00
5 x 3″, green glaze	60.00

7 x 5″, grey and blue flowers on a blue ground	550.00

MARBLES

Marbles were known to the Egyptians, the Romans and the American Indians. Early marbles were made from a variety of materials such as unglazed clay, porcelain, semi-precious stones, etc., and varied in size from less than one half inch to five inch carpet balls.

Most marbles were imported from Europe until the early 1900's when commercial manufacturing of "glassies" were produced by glass factories in Ohio and Pennsylvania. Today, millions of glass marbles are made in plants in Clarksburg and St. Mary, West Virginia.

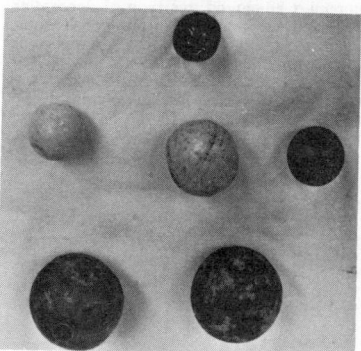

Bennington and China, each $2–$5.00

Akro Agate	
Three sizes in bag, 96 count . . .	100.00
Set of 27, original bag and box . .	6.50
Bennington	10.00
Bennington-type, ¾″, brown	2.00
Clay, painted ½″, set of 10	3.50
Comic Strip type	
"Herbie," c. 1926	30.00
"Kayo," c. 1926	30.00
"Little Orphan Annie," c. 1926 . .	34.00
Glass, clear green 1½″	52.50
Spatterglass, 2″	85.00
Sulphides	
Cat, sitting, large	55.00
Dog, 1¼″	37.50
Eagle, 4½″	55.00
Goat, 1½″	40.00
Horse, 1¼″	45.00
Rooster 2¼″	52.50
Squirrel, ⅞″	27.50

Swirls

Latticinio, 1⅞″	65.00
Lutz-type, candy stripe	65.00
Onionskin, 1¾″	50.00
With cane center	36.00
With goldstone swirl, and 2 red swirls in clear, 1⅝″	70.00

MARINE ITEMS
See NAUTICAL ITEMS

MARY GREGORY GLASS

Mary Gregory (1856–1908) was employed by Boston and Sandwich Glass Co., Mass., as an artist. Her charming designs of children were delicately painted with white enamel on transparent clear and colored glass items. A positive identification of items personally decorated by her is virtually impossible. In the late 1880's and early 1900's other glass companies employed this type of decoration in America, England and Europe and it would be more correct to refer to the wares as "Mary Gregory type."

There are many current reproductions and there have been some reproductions of current painting on old glass.

Vase in Victorian silver stand, cased, 13½″ overall height, 9″ vase . $350.00

Carafe, 7½″, clear, girl in white	110.00
Box, Dresser, hinged, black, girl in	

white on lid, floral band on sides	210.00

Bottles

Barber, cobalt, children playing badminton in white, pair	210.00
Cordial, 9″, green optic, angel and leaves in white, bubble stopper	140.00
Perfume, 4½″, girl in white	95.00
Cruet, 7″, clear, child in snow scene	85.00
Decanter, clear, children in white, trefoil shaped lip, applied clear handle	145.00
Jar, Mustard, covered, clear, boy in white, tinted face	85.00
Perfume Vial, purple, child in white, hinged top	250.00

Pitchers

9″, tankard, cranberry, girl with hoop, birds in white	335.00
11½″, emerald green, children in white, tinted features, 6 tumblers, set	300.00
Water, blue, girl and trees in white, ruffled, ribbed	180.00
Sugar Castor, cranberry, girl in white	65.00
Tray, 9½″ dia., cranberry, children in white	500.00

Tumblers

4½″, cranberry, girl in white	135.00
Juice, green, child in white, ribbed	45.00
Tumble-Up, 9¼″, emerald green, girl in white	195.00

Vases

3⅞″, cranberry, girl in white	95.00
5⅛″, cranberry, girl with balloon in white	95.00
8½″, bulbous, cranberry, boy and girl in white, ribbed, applied clear rigaree	295.00
9⅞″, honey amber, young boy in white, gold trim, reeded handles	195.00
11″, emerald green, girl in white, crystal shell trim down sides	145.00
13¼″, lime green, children and dogs in white, pair	695.00
13⅝″, girls with fancy dresses and hats, cut scalloped top, facing pair	575.00

MASONIC ITEMS

Masonic items are primarily the souvenir type glass and other materials that were made to commemorate the Syria Temple AAONMS organization's important meetings and conventions. These items date from the 1890–1900 period and quite sought after by Masonic collectors.

Cane, Ivory handle	85.00

Chalices

Glass, gold decor, dated June,

**Golden Peacock, jeweled, 6½ x 10½",
Monongahela Valley Shrine #9, 1916–
1969, monogrammed $135.00**

1905, Pittsburgh, Pa.	75.00
Glass, gold, enamel decor, 1908, St. Paul, Minn.	75.00
Champagnes	
Alligator decor on sides, May, 1912, New Orleans	95.00
Alligators, climbing sides of glass, 1910, New Orleans	95.00
Coverlet, double woven, reversible, blue and white	275.00
Cup and Saucer, Orange, Pittsburgh Commandery, 1906	85.00
Gavel, wood, hand carved	38.50
Goblets	
5", Pittsburgh, May, 22, 1900 . . .	75.00
St. Paul, Minn., 1908, round base	70.00
Shrine, Pittsburgh, Pa., 1909, with 2 sword handles	75.00
Mugs	
Atlantic City, July 13, 1904	55.00
Pittsburgh, Pa., 1898, three handles	75.00
Pittsburgh, Pa., 1904, fish handle	60.00
4", Insignia, Knight's Templar, amethyst flashed design, gold trim, ornate handle	85.00
Paperweights	
4", shape of Bible, iron	60.00
Blown, round glass, floral and Masonic emblems	65.00
Plates	
6", Los Angeles, May, 1906	58.50
8½", Shrine	65.00
10", 54th Annual Conclave, Grand Commandery, Knights Templar, Harrisburg, Pa., 1909	85.00
Plaque, 8 x 9", black Masonic design, verse on secrecy, impressed mark	100.00
Razor, Straight, tortoise shell handle, with Masonic symbols on one	

side, pictures of women of period other side; Pat. date Nov., 1879 .	45.00
Ring, Man's, onyx stone, with diamond chip, 14k, Masonic emblem	85.00
Slipper	
Degree, blue leather	58.00
Lapel pin, screw type, for women to wear, Masonic emblem on gold slipper	55.00
Sword, dress sword, Pittsburgh, Pa., 1909	75.00
Trowel, 4", steel, with turned wooden handle, banquet favor	27.50
Tumbler, China, souvenir of Louisville, scene of Confederate Monument, City Hall, Masonic Temple .	95.00
Watch Fob, with chain, 32nd Degree, Masonic Knights Templar	95.00

MATCH HOLDERS

In the days of the so-called "barnburner" matches, match holders were a household necessity. Many styles, types and shapes were made.

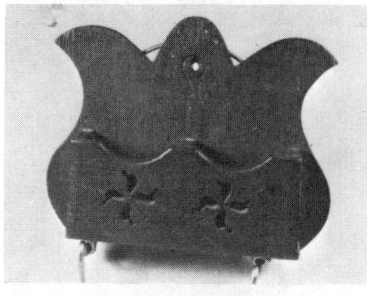

Wall type, 3¾ x 5", mahogany, tulip shaped $38.00

Brass

Bacchus, grape and leaf base . .	50.00
Beetle, hinged lid, 4"	35.00
Fly, hinged	20.00
Indian Chief, engraved	45.00

China & Pottery

Boots, 4 x 4", pink and green on white ground	25.00
Chimney Sweep, flowers, blown out	45.00
Jolly Jester	30.00
Peacock, 6" high, majolica	65.00

Clear Glass

Bear Head	45.00
Goddess of Liberty	35.00

Saddle	20.00	Gold, 9K, English	30.00
Iron, Cast		Gutta Percha, horseshoe, with strik-	
Advertising-type, 4" high	35.00	er	30.00
Boot	30.00	Mother of Pearl	25.00
Coal Scuttle, 4 x 5"	25.00	Silverplated, Columbus Landing	45.00
Dog on lid	30.00	**Sterling Silver**	
Helmet	18.00	Art Nouveau, figure of woman	50.00
Milk Glass		Fisherman	60.00
Butterfly, 5", painted, wall-type	35.00	Flowers, leaves, scrolls, reticulat-	
Jester, black, 4¼", Pat. date,		ed	55.00
June 13, '76,	75.00	Hunter with dogs	65.00
Uncle Sam's Hat, with stars,		Plain, monogrammed	25.00
painted	50.00	Scrolls, embossed	40.00
Urn, Saucer base	25.00	Tin, Japanned, hinged	25.00
Silverplated, picnic basket, Meriden	50.00		
Sterling, egg-shaped, sheaf of wheat			
base	50.00		

McCOY POTTERY

The McCoy Pottery was established in 1899 in Roseville, Ohio. Household objects were the principal products. In 1926 the company had become the Nelson McCoy Co. and began to produce art pottery. The McCoy mark dates from this period. The firm was acquired in 1967 by the Mt. Clement Pottery of Michigan.

Tin	
Advertising-type, 4 x 6", c. 1900's	20.00
Crimped, 8", early	40.00
Wooden, souvenir	15.00

MATCH SAFES-POCKET

Before safety matches, friction matches were carried in a safe. Early jewelry catalogues of the 1890's–1900's offered pocket match safes.

Art Nouveau, silverplated, 2½" $40.00

Advertising and Commemorative	
Arm & Hammer Baking Soda, Gut-	
ta Percha	25.00
Blatz Beer	50.00
BPOE, engraved, sterling	60.00
"St. Louis World's Fair, 1904,"	
sterling	60.00
Brass	
Bull Dog	50.00
Pig, enameled	50.00
Pig, jeweled	85.00
Skull, with striker	150.00
Celluloid, advertising	15.00

Cookie Jar, 10½", Aunt Jemima, white dress, red bandana and letters, impressed script "McCoy" $40.00

Baskets	
9", basketweave, green	17.00
9", pineapple, yellow	22.00
Candlestick, chamber, Zuniart, 7"	65.00
Cookie Jars	
Apple, 1950–64	14.00

Bear, white, 1943–45	30.00
Dog on Basket, 1956	15.00
Honey Bear	25.00
Locomotive	32.50
Mr. and Mrs. Owl, 1953–55	30.00
Windmill, 1961	28.00
Creamer, pine cone	6.50
Jardiniere, Blossomtime, ivory, 4" . .	15.00

Lamp, sculptured berries and leaves,
bulbous, blue high glaze, 6½" . . 40.00

Planters

Baby Shoes, 2¾"	5.00
Frog	10.00
Turtle, 8", 1955	15.00
Wishing Well, 1950	10.00

Tea Sets

English Ivy, 3 pieces	27.50
Pine Cone, 3 pieces	30.00

Vases

6", butterfly, 1956	8.00
6¾", lily, yellow	15.00
7", cornucopia	16.00
9", iris, Loy-Nel	75.00
9½", swan, aqua, 1949	15.00

Wall Pockets

Lily, single bud, 1948	10.00
Oranges	14.00
Violin, 1957	12.00

Wash Sets

Rose, pitcher and bowl	100.00
Sponged, blue on white, Brush McCoy, pitcher and bowl, 1910 . .	125.00

MCKEE GLASS

The name McKee has been associated with glass making since 1843. In 1852, a factory was established in Pittsburgh, Pa., for the production of pressed glass objects. In 1888, the factory relocated to Jeannette, Pa., and continued production until 1951 when the factory was sold to Thatcher Manufacturing Co.

Many types of glass were produced by McKee from the very first — bottles, window panes, pressed glass tablewares (flint and non-flint), Depression glass, Milk glass objects and a variety of bar and utility wares. Also see specific categories, e.g., CANDLESTICKS, LAMPS, MILK GLASS, etc.

Bowls

9½", rainbow, green	40.00
10½", jade	20.00
11", custard	45.00

Creamers

Aztec

Crowsfoot, individual	16.00
Eugenie, flint	65.00
Masonic	15.00
Non-flint	19.50
Star Rosetted	28.50
Egg cup, double opaque green . . .	25.00

Candy Dish, 7¾" to top of finial, orange with gold trim lid, gold finial, clear base $18.50

Goblets

Eugenie, flint	50.00
Gothic, flint	35.00
Rock Crystal, red	25.00

Hen-on Nest, 6½", white milk glass,
marked McKee 100.00

Pitchers

Aldine crystal	30.00
Aztec	20.00
Snowflake, crystal	35.00

Plates

Bread, star rosetted, "A Good
Mother Makes a Happy Home" . . 40.00
7½", scroll and waffle border, milk
glass, bronzed waffles, signed
"McKee" in script on back 35.00

Server, cheese and crackers, Rock
Crystal, red 75.00
Shakers, opaque green, pair 16.00
Tom and Jerry set, custard with
black lettering, 13 pieces 75.00
Toothpick, Aztec pattern 17.50

Tumblers

Beaded Swag, custard souvenir .	50.00
Gladiator, cobalt blue, gold trim .	45.00
Ribbed Palm	75.00

Whiskeys "Bottom-Up"

Caramel	40.00
Custard	50.00
Opalescent green	60.00

MECHANICAL BANKS
See BANKS, MECHANICAL

MEDICAL ITEMS

Early medical instruments and related items are of interest to special collectors, especially those in the professions.

Alcohol Burner, 2½″, brass, sterilizer $36.00

Bleeding Cup, early blown glass . . .	25.00
Bleeding Lance, triggered	25.00
Bottles	
Glass measure on top, amber . . .	40.00
Nursing, glass nipple, early blown glass	40.00
Breast Pump, early blown glass . . .	25.00
Dental Cabinet, 23½ x 35½ x 50″, oak, unrestored condition	750.00
Dental Cabinet, Harvard, 79″ high, golden oak, restored and refinished	1500.00
Dental Drill, foot power-type, workable condition, 20th century, complete	200.00
Dental Forceps, c. 1900	6.50
Dental Tooth Key, iron, wood handle, c. 1889	50.00
Doctor's Bag, 6½ x 11″, grain leather, brass fittings	65.00
Electro Therapeutic Machine, 6 x 7 x 9″, walnut case, nickelplated metal works, c. 1880	75.00
Eye Cups	
Clear glass	5.00
Cobalt	10.00
Milk glass	12.00
Eye Speculum, c. 1915	3.00
Hearing Aids	
Dipper Trumpet	50.00
Long Japanned Ear Trumpet . . .	40.00
Microscopes	
Brass, student-type, English, c. 1880	150.00
Enameled iron and brass, Spencer, c. 1915	200.00
Obstetrical Forceps, c. 1915	25.00

Percussion Hammer, c. 1880's	25.00
Ophthalmic Lamps	
Brass, moveable hand lantern, electric	150.00
Brass with glass font and shade, oil	300.00
Pleximeter, c. 1880's	20.00
Retractor, 11″	3.00
Rinsing Curettes, original box, set of two	35.00
Scissors, silver with spoon bowl, figural stork scissors inside (midwife scissors) c. 1850	190.00
Scarificator, ten-bladed, brass, Tieman & Co., c. 1890	95.00
Stethoscope, mohair tubing, hard rubber bell, nickelplated metal parts	75.00
Table, Boston, golden oak, leather top cushion, c. 1915	800.00
Thermometer Cases	
Gutta Percha	10.00
Silverplated, with chain	35.00
Tongue Depressor, steel, c. 1915 . .	5.00
Tonsillectome, c. 1915	20.00
Trepanning Instruments, c. 1880s	
Hey's Saw	35.00
Pope's Antrum Drill	45.00
Trepanning, Scalpel	30.00
Trephine, Handle and Crown . . .	50.00

MERCURY GLASS

Mercury glass is a light bodied, double-walled glass that was 'silvered' by applying a solution of silver nitrate to the inside of the object through a hole in the base of the formed object.

F. Hale Thomson, London, patented the method in 1849. In 1855, the New England Glass Co. filed a patent for the same type of process. Other glass makers soon followed suit. The glass did not reach popularity until the early 20th century.

Bowls	
6″	30.00
6″, with white painted flowers . . .	32.50
8″, with gilt interior	35.00
Christmas Decorations	
2½″, grapes	10.00
7″, ball with brass collar and hanger, c. 1890	12.50
Compote, 8″, Mercury glass with glass insert	45.00
Curtain Tie Backs, 3½″, pair, vintage engraved	12.00
Figurine, birds, 5″, Germany	20.00
Goblet, 7½″, ivy, grape leaves and grapes engraved, early	130.00
Inkwell, on glass stand, 2 mercury wells, one at each end	50.00

Tie Backs, 3″ dia., vintage decor, pewter shanks, pair $48.00

Pitcher, 12½″ high, clear applied handle 65.00
Rose Bowl, 5″, gilt interior 50.00
Salt, Master, urn-shaped, footed .. 30.00
Spooner, white painted, floral decor 20.00
Toothpick, white painted decor, gilt interior 35.00
Vases
  Bud vase, tall and slender 22.50
  9½″, floral bands, castle scene painted on front 35.00
  10¼″, bulbous, pedestaled, floral decor 50.00
  10″, white, decor, with red and white stripes, top and base 65.00
Witch Ball, green ball on attached base 95.00

METTLACH

Jean Francis Boch founded the pottery at Mettlach, in the Moselle Valley of Germany, in 1809. His father had established a pottery at Septfontaines in 1767. Nicholas Villery began his pottery career at Wallerfangen in 1789.

In 1841 these three factories merged. They pioneered in using coal to fire kilns and the underglaze printing on earthenware using transfers from copper plates. Other factories were developed at Dresden, Wadgassen, and Danischburg.

The castle and Mercury emblem are the two chief marks. Secondary marks also are known. To check price examine the base to determine the shape mark, usually followed by a decor mark. Pieces are assumed to be print under glaze unless otherwise marked.

An excellent reference is R. H. Mohr's *Mettlach Steins*.

See also VILLEROY & BOCH.

Beakers
  2327/1024, ¼ liter, minstrel playing flute 65.00
  2327/1200, ¼ l., state shield of Bremen 60.00
  2368/1033, ¼ l., drinking scene . 75.00
  2368/1108, ¼ l., people drinking and lifting steins to toast 70.00
Plaques
  167A, fairyland castle, 11″ 325.00
  1044/126, hunting dog, 17¼″ .. 375.00
  1044/221, Munchen, 14″ 325.00
  1044/1067, rural scene with millstream, 17½″ 400.00
  1048.5, King slaying dragon, etched, 15½″ 525.00
  1404, floral decor, 9″ 180.00
  1500, pond with two swans, relief, 14″ 275.00
  2003, valley and mountain scene, 24″ 500.00
  2070, two dogs and stag, etched, signed Stocke, 15½″ 650.00
  2148, Schneewisschen (Snow White), etched, signed H. Schlitt, 16¼″ 1350.00
  2299, sailboats and hugh rock, 12½″ 125.00
  2361A, Wartburg Castle, etched, 17½″ 800.00
  2578, town scene, etched, 17½″ . 650.00
  3236, farm scene, 15″ 260.00
  5058, canal scene, rectangular .. 225.00
Punch Bowls
  418, underplate and lid, relief, two quart 600.00
  2226, tavern scene on one side, two soldiers and maiden on reverse, relief, lidded 425.00
Steins
  6, 3 l., justice with shield, man with harp, Noah in ark, relief 500.00
  485, ½ l., ten people at festival, relief, insert lid 250.00
  690, 2 l., barrel shape with staves and hoops, plain 235.00
  insert lid 250.00
  1028, ½ l., brown tree trunk, cream and white, relief 165.00
  1164, ½ l., figures drinking and smoking, silver lid, signed C. Warth, 1883, etched 600.00
  1370, ½ l., figures in white, insert lid, relief 225.00
  1400, ½ l., brown body with insert lid, plain 65.00
  1467, ½ l., four maidens representing four seasons, lid, relief .. 225.00
  1526/592, ½ l., tavern scene, pewter lid 115.00
  1648, ½ l., man drinking, pewter lid, tapestry, etched 380.00

Wine Tureen, no ladle, Castle mark, signed, #2234 ....$750.00

1786, ½ l., St. Florian theme, dragon handle with original head, fish scale lid, etched 750.00

1896, ¼ l., domestic scene, relief .. 140.00

1909, ⁴/₁₀ l. 120.00

1909/83, Falstaff in wine cellar drinking from boot, pewter lid ... 225.00

2001, ½ l., book, architect, glaze . 500.00

2140/1047, 1 l., dwarf scene, pewter lid 180.00

2177/960, ¼ l., jester lying in grass playing mandolin, initialed H. S. 200.00

2180/955, 5 l., cavalier drinking scene, signed H. Schlitt, pewter lid 1350.00

2181/957, ¼ l., lady holding stein, pewter lid 160.00

2182, ½ l., bowling scene, pewter lid, relief 325.00

2271/1055, ½ l., two inebriated cavaliers, "Geschutzt" 200.00

2348/1022, 3 l., man with feathered hat making merry, pewter lid 600.00

2388, ½ l., pretzel body, handle is pretzel, glazed 625.00

3328, ½ l., gentleman drinking mug of beer, "Gesundheit", etched 260.00

Miscellaneous

Planter, Art Deco motif, etched, 5" x 14" 100.00

Vases

10½", castle scene, 2856 .... 200.00

14", blue and white, 2915 .... **230.00**

MILK GLASS

This is opaque-white glass that resembles the color of milk and was used as a substitute for white porcelain in the 18th century. It has been made in England and the United States, and is still being produced today. The popularity of milk glass in this country was prevalent during the Victorian period and it is popular with collectors today. The earlier pieces made between 1870–1890 are most collectible and some have been reproduced.

Animal Dishes, covered, — See ANIMAL DISHES, COVERED.

Bottles, Figural

  Bear, sitting, 11" 175.00

  Columbus Column 150.00

Bowls

  Acanthus Leaf, 10" 85.00

  Beaded Rib, 10½" 50.00

  Dutch Windmill, 8¾" 55.50

  Lattice, open, 8½" 85.00

  Scroll, 7½" 75.00

  Square, lacy edge, 8¼" 75.00

Butter, covered, Scroll, nile green .. 125.00

Cake stand, flowers, 9½" 30.00

Candlestick, crucifix, hexagonal base, 10" 95.00

Celery, Sandwich Loop, flint 85.00

Compotes

  Atlas, open edge, 7¾" 125.00

  Basketweave, 7", blue 85.00

  Sandwich Loop, 4½" 100.00

  Scroll, 8", nile green 175.00

Creamer, Marquis and Marchioness of Lorne, dated 1878 .... 75.00

Dishes, covered

  Battleship, "Dewey" 65.00

  Battleship, "Maine" 65.00

  Battleship, "Uncle Sam" 65.00

  Conestoga Wagon 100.00

  Hand and Dove, Atterbury 150.00

  Moses in the Bullrushes 225.00

Fish Tray, dated June 4, 1872, Atterbury 85.00

Hat, Uncle Sam's, painted 50.00

Mustard Jar, swan 45.00

Pitchers

  George Washington, 7" 85.00

  Owl, glass eyes 225.00

  Scroll, 11½", tankard shape 125.00

Plates

  ABC Alphabet plate, white with blue and beaded edge 30.00

  Angel Head 30.00

  Backward "C" 20.00

  Columbus, club and shell border . 40.00

  Easter Ducks, 7½" 40.00

  Gothic 17.50

Tumblers

Scroll	30.00
Single Rose	40.00
Swirl, beaded	30.00

MILLEFIORI

Millefiori (thousand flowers) is an ornamental glass composed of bundles of colored glass rods fused to become canes. The canes were pulled while still ductile to the desired length, sliced, arranged in a pattern and again fused together. This technique was developed by the Egyptians in the first century B.C. Millefiori glass making was revived in the 1880's. It is again being produced by many companies in articles such as paperweights, cruets, toothpicks, etc.

Decanter, stoppered, 9", blue, Crown with flame $25.00

Yoked Slatted Border, 7½", gold trimmed	45.00
Indian head, 7¼"	27.50
Rabbit and Horseshoe, 7½"	40.00
Rooster and Hens, 7½"	35.00
Scroll and Waffle border, bronzed waffles, signed "McKee" in script	35.00
Spring meets Winter	50.00
*Three Kittens, square	40.00

Platters

Retriever, 13½"	150.00
Rock of Ages, 13"	125.00

Shakers, Salt and Peppers, pair

Apricot Band	45.00
Beaded Fan	40.00
Billiken	175.00
Bird, handled with pewter tops	55.00
Butterfly	40.00
Leaf and grape, footed	45.00
Rabbits, egg shaped	75.00

Shakers, sugar

Acorn (or Royal Oak)	100.00
Beaded Swirl	55.00
Forget-Me-Not	55.00
Roman Cross	60.00
Spooner, Sandwich Loop	75.00

Sugars, covered

Basketweave, Atterbury	125.00
Cherry, blue	25.00
Diamond, Fan and Leaf, (or Block and Palm)	30.00
Swan and Cattail	125.00

Syrups

Beehive, pewter top	95.00
Tree of Life, pewter top, blue	150.00

Miniature lamp, 8½" to top of chimney $350.00

Atomizer	75.00
Bottle, 4½", late	10.00
Box, 3" high, covered	150.00
Cruets	
With cut crystal stopper, 1890's	300.00
Frosted stopper, frosted applied handle, 1930's	95.00
Cup and Saucer	75.00
Goblet, 7½", clear stem and base	175.00
Lamp, umbrella shade, homemade spider	385.00

Rose Bowl, 1890's	150.00
Salt, Master	85.00
Sugar Shaker, 5″	75.00
Syrup, frosted handle	200.00
Toothpick, pinched sides, 1890's	150.00
Vases	
2¾″, blue, paperweight, satin finish	70.00
7″, bud, footed	140.00
8″, bulbous, slender neck, crimped ruffled top, 1950's	80.00

MINIATURE LAMPS
See LAMPS, MINIATURE

MINIATURE PAINTING

Prior to the advent of the photograph, miniature portraits and silhouettes were the principal way of preserving a person's image. Miniaturists were common; and, they often made more than one copy of a drawing. The extras were distributed to family and friends.

Miniaturists worked in watercolors and oil. The surface was paper, porcelain, or ivory. Miniaturists supplemented commission work by painting popular figures of the times and important works of art.

Careful study has divided miniature paintings into schools. Many artists now are being studied. The miniature painting market has not yet reached its full potential.

AMERICAN SCHOOL

Anonymous, Child, N.E., oval, on ivory, c. 1830, 3⅜″	275.00
Anonymous, Gentleman, oval, c. 1800, cloth case, 2⅛″	300.00
Anonymous, Gentleman, rectangular, c. 1830, gilt gesso frame, 3⅛″	120.00
Anonymous, Lady, rectangular, c. 1840, leather covered frame, 2¾″	250.00
Armstrong, William G., William Ellery (Signer), 1840, rectangular, gilt metal frame, 3⅛″	350.00
Brown, John Henry, 1879, Elderly Couple, oval, gilt metal frame, 3½″	750.00
Goodrich, Sarah, Gentleman, rectangular, c. 1840, wood frame, 3⅞″	600.00
Hayward, Gerald S., Lady, c. 1880, oval, gold chased frame, 4⅛″	650.00
Hazlits, John, Samueo Goodwin, Sr., rectangular, c. 1810, leather case, 2¾″	700.00
Peale, Anna Claypoole, Lady, 1827, rectangular, gilt wood frame, 3″	850.00
Peale, Raphael, Gentleman, 1799, oval, gold frame, 2½″	3500.00
Staigg, Richard Morell, Miss Ann	

Portrait on ivory, framed, 4½ x 5″, "Sarah", artist signed $250.00

King, oval, c. 1840, gilt wood frame, 4½″	200.00

CONTINENTAL SCHOOL, ANONYMOUS

Lady, oval, c. 1810, frame with ropework border, 2″	150.00
Narcissus at Well, 19th c., circular, wood frame, 3⅝″	225.00
Officer, circular, c. 1810, 2⅛″	125.00

ENGLISH SCHOOL, ANONYMOUS

Gentleman, late 18th c., oval, gold oval pendant frame, 2⅝″	400.00
Gentleman, holds sword and blue military jacket, rectangular, leather frame, 4⅛″	450.00
Lady, oval, 19th c., 1⅝″	275.00

FRENCH SCHOOL, ANONYMOUS

Lady of Court (dress c. 1775), 19th c., rectangular, gilt metal and enamel frame, 2⅝″	650.00
Marie Antoinette, c. 1870, 2⅝″	150.00
Soldier, 19th c., 3¾″	200.00

GERMAN SCHOOL

Anonymous, Gentleman, oval, c. 1760, gilt metal frame, 2½″	425.00
Muster, E., Boy, c. 1875, circular, wood frame, 3½″	300.00

MINIATURES

Miniature collecting is one of the world's leading hobbies. The leaders in the field were the Europeans who made miniature collecting fashionable during the 19th century.

There are three sizes of miniatures: doll house scale (ranging from ½"to 1"), sample size, and child's size. The most common examples are 20th century, since most earlier material is in museums or extremely expensive.

Many mediums were used for miniatures— silver, copper, tin, wood, glass, ivory, and canvas. Even books were printed in miniature. Prices are broad ranged, depending on scarcity and quality of workmanship.

Chest, pine, 8¾ x 10 x 22", Chippendale, apprentice sample, c. 1770 ....$795.00

DOLLHOUSE SIZE

Armoire, Golden Oak, 1" scale, c. 1900	95.00
Bathroom set, Tootsietoy, 8 pieces, metal, c. 1920	90.00
Beds	
Golden Oak, 1" scale, c. 1890 ..	45.00
Maple, honey, scalloped head and footboard, 6¼", c. 1900	100.00
Petite Princess	20.00
Tynietoy, 4 poster with canopy, all original, c. 1930	150.00
Bird Cages	
Brass, parrot, 2⅛"	120.00
Ormolu, 3", c. 1850	225.00
Pewter-like metal, 1¾", c. 1930 .	25.00
Books	
Bible, 1¼", 20th C.	5.00
History of Bible, 1¼", c.1890 ...	65.00
Small Rain, leather, blue, ¾", c. 1860	45.00
Small Rain, leather, closing case, ¾", c. 1870	50.00
Bronze Seal	
Lady, Art Nouveau, gilded, signed French, 2½"	200.00
Woman, bust, uncut, 2", early	

20th C.	65.00
Buffet, Tynietoy, c. 1930	55.00
Chamber Pots	
1"	4.00
1¼", inscription	10.00
Candlesticks	
Brass, pair, 1", c. 1900	35.00
Pewter, candelabra, three branch, 1½", c. 1900	25.00
Soft metal, candelabra, pair, embossed. c. 1890	75.00

Captains chair, salesman sample, Maine, c. 1870 ....$60.00

Chairs	
Biedermeier, Gothic Arm, c. 1850	350.00
Biedermeier, Side, c. 1850	200.00
Bliss, lithograph, oversize	15.00
Tynietoy, high, painted, c. 1930 .	55.00
Tynietoy, wing, black with roses, c. 1930	55.00
China Cabinet, Golden Oak, mirrored door, c. 1890	125.00
Clocks	
Art Nouveau, gilt	75.00
Golden Oak, pendulum, 2", c. 1880	135.00
Metal, alarm, ½", c. 1920	20.00
Ormolu, cuckoo, ¾", c. 1870 ...	225.00
Tynietoy, mantle, 2", c. 1930 ...	65.00
Commode, Golden Oak, marble top, two drawers, c. 1890	120.00
Couch, Tynietoy, black with roses, c. 1930	75.00
Desk, Biedermeier, marble top, stencilled on black, c. 1860	350.00
Dining Sets	
Golden Oak, 9 pieces, 1" scale, c. 1900	600.00
Tootsietoy, 7 pieces	85.00

Dishes

China with serving pieces, 15 items 125.00

Pitcher, white porcelain with red roses, marked Staffordshire, 1⅜″ 40.00

Treen, vases, and compote, 4 pieces, c. 1850 .... 50.00

Doll Houses

Bliss, lithographed, two rooms, late 19th C. 525.00

Schoenhut, 4 rooms, c. 1930 ... 350.00

Fireplace

Filigree metal, Victorian, tools ... 85.00

Ormolu, mantel and mirror, 2¾ x 2 x 6″ 225.00

Glass

Compote, Bristol, Victorian, ½″ .. 30.00

Goblet, green, Victorian 25.00

Lamp, c. 1930 .... 25.00

Pitcher, Bristol, Victorian, 1″ 40.00

Ice Box, oak, label "Henry Schwartz, Baltimore," 3¼ x 2 x 4¼″ 120.00

Lacquer, Japanese

Bowl with flowers, late 19th C. 22.00

Box, double, 1¼″, c. 1800 ..... 150.00

Table and four pieces, chrysanthemum motif, c. 1800 .... 300.00

Living Room Sets

Schoenhut, 8 pieces 100.00

Tootsietoy, 8 pieces 65.00

Mirrors

Biedermeier, c. 1860 .... 75.00

Golden Oak, standing, bamboo turnings, c. 1890 .... 85.00

Metal, filigree, wall, c. 1890 ..... 20.00

Pewter

Carrier, 6 glasses, c. 1920 ...... 30.00

Platter, 1″, c. 1890 .... 25.00

Piano

Ivory, ¾″ scale, c. 1860 .... 325.00

Petite Princess, plastic, c. 1960 .. 25.00

Pots and Pans

Copper, set of 5, c. 1940 ...... 5.00

Pot, copper, 1½″ dia., c. 1860 .. 65.00

Print, Baxter, 1½″, c. 1840 .... 50.00

Rooms

Victorian, double, empty, original paper 100.00

Victorian, single, 8 pieces of furniture, original 500.00

Serving Carts

Metal filigree, c. 1900 .... 125.00

Tootsietoy 15.00

Sewing

Machine, cast iron, 3″, c. 1930 .. 75.00

Machine, soft metal, filigree, 4″, c. 1880, (rare) 150.00

Machine, tin, painted, 4″, c. 1920 40.00

Table, Golden Oak, 1¼″ scale, c. 1890 .... 75.00

Silver

Cake Plate, stand, 2″, Irish, c.

1800 .... 175.00

Goblet, Meyers, ½″, 20th C. 50.00

Riever Dredger, English, c. 1889 . 75.00

Stick, Continental, 2″, mid 19th C. 150.00

Sugar Shaker, London, 2″, c. 1831 .... 200.00

Teapot, Dutch, turned wood swing handle, 1½″, c. 1790 .... 500.00

Tea Set, Gallery Tray, English, tray 3½″, c. 1880 .... 350.00

Tables

Battersea and gilt, 2″ scale, damage, c. 1890 .... 50.00

Ivory, chess, ¾″ scale, c. 1870 .. 350.00

Ivory, ¾″ scale, c. 1870 .... 275.00

Table and Chairs

Biedermeier, 3 pieces, 1½″ scale, c. 1860 .... 125.00

German, boxed, 5 pieces and two male figures, ¼″ scale, c. 1910 .. 30.00

Golden Oak, 6 pieces, ½″ scale, c. 1890 .... 150.00

Petite Princess, 5 pieces 55.00

Telephones

Metal, upright model, c. 1920 ... 25.00

Wood, wall, c. 1880 .... 65.00

Tub and Washstand, tin, mirror attached to washstand, c. 1900 ... 100.00

Vienese

Bronze, chipmunk, Beatrix Potter, late 19th C., 1″ 125.00

Bronze, flowers in pot, late 19th C., 1½″ 35.00

Enamel, tea set, 8 pieces on tray, c. 1870 .... 3000.00

Washstand, maple, honey, marble top, 3¾ x 1½ x 4¼″, c. 1900 .. 125.00

SAMPLE SIZE

Bedwarmer, copper, Victorian, 8″ .. 35.00

Bureau, oak, swing mirror, c. 1890, 16 x 8¾″, rough 75.00

Chests

Empire, mahogany, 3 drawer, American, 9 x 12″ 350.00

Victorian, copper and brass, 2 drawers, 3¾ x 5″ 300.00

China

21 pieces, German, pink, white gold decoration, c. 1900 .... 125.00

50 pieces, Staffordshire 700.00

Clock, Chippendale style, Centennial, working, 10″ 300.00

Desk, slant front, mahogany, inlayed, 9″, c. 1790 .... 800.00

Dishwasher, plastic, includes plastic dishes, c. 1940 .... 45.00

Fireplace, Victorian, iron, brass, copper, implements, 12″ 250.00

Piano, Philadelphia, 6″ wide, c. 1900 150.00

CHILD'S SIZE

Chair, Hepplewhite, mahogany **350.00**
Chair, wing, upholstered, c. 1800 . .   **3200.00**
Desk, slant front, cherry, N.E. late
18th C.   **2800.00**
Recamier, Victorian, walnut, uphol-
stered, plain **450.00**

MINTON CHINA

**Minton earthenwares were first made by
Thomas Minton in 1793 in the Staffordshire
district of England. Porcelain was introduced
in 1798, but was not made in any quantity until about 1825. Minton also made Parian, used
a Majolica-type glaze and employed the Pate-
sur-Pate technique. Many date marks were
used to identify the year of production, and
Minton is still in operation today.**

Tea Cup and Saucer, cup — 4⅛″, saucer — 6″, "Tree Leaf," signed . . **$25.00**

Bowl, deep blue, vines, and leaves
decor **125.00**
Butter Dish, covered, floral decor . .   **95.00**
Candle Snuffer, double, floral decor,
c. 1846 . . . .   **95.00**
Cups and Saucers
  Demitasse, urns of fruit, serpents,
  and red band **65.00**
  Blue decorated panels, with gold
  rims **60.00**
  Roses, with gold trim, c. 1854 . . .   **65.00**
Dinner set, 84 piece service for 8,
lustre border pattern, c. 1859 . . .   **500.00**

Egg cup, floral decor **22.50**
Pitcher, water, grapes with gold de-
cor, marked **145.00**
Plates, 10″, rose and floral border,
artist signed, set of 12 . . . .   **395.00**
Platters
  Blue Sea Leaf pattern **250.00**
  13″, cobalt blue and orange floral
  decor, Imari type, yellow borders   **195.00**
  15 x 18″, Passion Flower pattern   **200.00**
Punch Bowl, 11″ d., 6″ h., blue,
orange, yellow, copper lustre,
marked **350.00**
Tea Set, Teapot, sugar, creamer,
white with gold trim, red roses,
marked **375.00**
Tile, 6″, blue and white **35.00**
Vases
  5½″, blue and white farm scene .   **200.00**
  7½″, birds and flowers decor . . .   **125.00**
  9″, bulbous, two handled, cream
  background, handpainted flowers
  and butterflies **220.00**
Vegetable Dish
  Covered, leaf decor, 4 classical
  figures in browns, blues and pinks,
  c. 1877 . . . .   **50.00**
  Covered, two handled, floral decor   **50.00**
Wash Bowl and Pitcher
  Bowl and pitcher, blue, leaves and
  flowers, marked **265.00**
  Bowl and pitcher, blue and green,
  embossed design **265.00**

MOCHA

**Mocha decoration is found on basically utili-
tarian creamware or stoneware articles and
is achieved by a simple chemical reaction. A
color pigment of brown, blue, green or black
is given an acid nature by infusion of tobacco or hops. When this acid colorant is applied in blobs to an alkaline ground color, it
reacts by spreading in feathery seaplant designs. This type of decoration is usually ac-
companied by horizontal bands of light color
slip.**

**Types of decoration vary greatly, from
those done in a combination of motifs such
as "Cat's Eye" with "Earthworm," to a plain
pink mug decorated with green ribbed bands.
Most forms of Mocha are hollow, such as
mugs, jugs, bowls and shakers. Majority of
articles are English, and fall into three essential dated groupings: 1780–1820, 1820–1840,
1840–1880. Marked pieces are extremely rare.**

Bowls
  5⅝″, Earthworm, on grey-green
  band **125.00**
  7½″, connected white circles on
  black ground **185.00**

8½", Earthworm, gray, green, brown and white 350.00
9", Seaweed, on white band, yellow ware 195.00
9¼", footed, Earthworm, blue bands 225.00
10", Earthworm, jade on blue . . . 120.00
11", Seaweed decor band 250.00
Chamber Pot
Earthworm on cream glaze 100.00
Large blue decor on white band . 125.00
Cup, 4½", Cat's Eye 150.00
Cup and Saucer, Cat's Eye, ochre and brown with brown bands . . . 135.00
Jugs
4", Seaweed, dark brown on ochre band, green ribbed bands, earthenware 385.00
5", Seaweed 175.00
5⅝", quart, incised plaid design black, blue and yellow on white . 250.00
6", Seaweed 150.00
7½", Earthworm, gray black and ochre 225.00
9", Seaweed, yellow ground, wide white band, blue fern and rose . . 375.00
Mugs
2¾", Baluster, Seaweed, brown and ochre 145.00
3", Seaweed, black on blue ground, no bandings 155.00
3½", strap handle, white and brown bands 185.00
4", Seaweed, green band at top . 125.00
5", Tree, blue bands 150.00
6", Earthworm, dark brown and black 195.00
Mustard Pot, covered, Earthworm, brown and blue 255.00
Pitcher, 6", bands of black, blue and brown on white 150.00
Salts, Master
Footed, Earthworm and Cat's Eye, black blue ochre 185.00
Plain band with 7 white lines, pumpkin shaped 65.00
Sauce, 4½", footed, marbleized brown, black gray and white 135.00
Shakers
Earthworm 85.00
White vertical lines on black and blue ground 125.00
Sugar, covered, 5" high, Tree, black and green 300.00

MONART GLASS

Monart glass is a heavy, simply shaped art glass in which colored enamels are suspended in the glass during the glass making process. This technique was originally developed by the Ysart family in Spain in 1923;

John Moncrief, a Scottish glassmaker, discovered the glass while vacationing there. He recognized the beauty and potential market for such a glass and began production in his Perth, Scotland, glassworks in 1924.

The name "Monart" is derived from the surnames Moncrief and Ysart. Two types of Monart were manufactured: a "commercial" line which incorporated colored enamels and a touch of adventurine in crystal, and the "art" line in which the suspended enamels formed designs such as feathers or scrolls. Monart glass, in most instances, is not marked since the factory used paper labels.

Vase, 8½", green pedestal, brown and clear to green rim $55.00

Basket, 4", mottled orange and green 40.00
Bowls
4", swirled blue, pink, green, green swirls 100.00
6", orange and brown 65.00
10½", spider web radiating from base 90.00
Vases
5½", bulbous, mottled reddish-brown base shading to green . . . 130.00
6½", bulbous, blue and rose mottling 100.00
7½", blue, orange, red, abstract figure 95.00
10", turquoise to orange 90.00

MOORCROFT POTTERY

William Moorcroft established the Moorcroft pottery in 1913 in Burslem, England. The majority of the ware was hand thrown, resulting in a great variation among similarly styled pieces. Moorcroft pottery is still being made. Color is a key to determining the age of older pieces. William Moorcroft died in 1945 at which time his son, Walter, continued the business.

Vase, 12½″, floral decor	**$160.00**
Bowls	
4½ x 2″, panies, relief, blue	40.00
6″, covered, amaryllis, green	70.00
9¼″, floral motif, green iridescent, script signed	85.00
10″, blossoms of red and yellow on white ground, script signed	120.00
Boxes	
3 x 5″, covered, gladiolus, script designed	100.00
3¾ x 5″, floral motif on lid, cobalt	65.00
Biscuit Jar, blue base with cobalt top, silver lid and bail, MacIntyre	350.00
Candlesticks	
3½″, floral motif, dark blue, signed	70.00

7″, fruit and leaf motif, blue, pair	110.00
10″, trees in shades of yellow, cobalt blue ground, script signed	125.00
Chocolate Pot, blue and green motif on tan ground, 7″, MacIntyre, c. 1899	265.00
Cup and Saucer, demitasse, leaves and berries, flambe glaze	60.00
Inkwell, floral motif, blue ground, script signed, 3″ square	90.00
Jar, covered, orchid motif, blue, 5¼″	90.00
Lamp, floral motif, dark to light blue hues, signed, 12″	450.00
Lamp Base, orchid motif, green, paper label, 13″	175.00
Pitchers	
3″, berries and leaves, flambe glaze	100.00
8″, bulbous, poppy motif, blue, script signed	175.00
16½″, cylindrical, floral motif, flambe glaze, script signed	625.00
Plate, stylized floral motif, multi-colored, signed, late, 11½″	35.00
Teapot, plums and lemons, silver rim, cobalt, 4½″, c. 1898	160.00
Vases	
2½″, fruit and leaves, cobalt, c. 1897	110.00
4¾″, blue rose, green flowers, yellow ground, impressed mark	90.00
5″, Wisteria	400.00
5¾″, floral motif, blue to green, script signed, "Potter to the Queen"	175.00
6½″, bulbous, pink and green floral motif	80.00
8″, pomegranate, cobalt, purple grapes	300.00
8½″, poppies, blue, white ground, green leaves and stems	500.00

MORIAGE—JAPANESE

Moriage refers to applied clay (slip) relief motifs and decorations used on certain classes of Japanese pottery and porcelain.

This decorating was done by three methods: Handrolling and shaping, which was applied by hand to the biscuit in one or more layers; the design and effect required determined thickness and shape. Tubing, or slip trailing, which applied decoration from a tube, like decorating a cake. Hakeme, which is reducing the slip to a liquid, and decorating the object with a brush. Color was applied either before or after this process.

Basket, 5″, floral decor	85.00
Bowls	
6″, shades of brown and gold, moriage motif of flying cranes,	

Vase, handled, 9½″, Bending Violets $250.00

blue maple leaf, Nippon	175.00
10″, red roses, green foliage, moriage scroll decor	200.00
11″, lake scene, moriage decor on trees	100.00
Box, with hinged lid, moriage decor over red roses	185.00
Calling card tray, charcoal and turquoise dragons, moriage decor, signed	50.00
Chocolate Pot, grey moriage dragon decor	210.00
Demitasse set, teapot, open sugar, creamer, four cups and saucers, moriage dragon decor, marked "Made in Japan"	55.00
Humidor, 6¼″, moriage motif of owl on branch, blue maple leaf, Nippon	370.00
Mugs	
Rope handle, pink yellow floral on green, heavy white moriage beading decor	95.00
Grey background with red roses, gray moriage motif of scrolls, overall, pre Nippon	150.00
Floral and geometric motifs, moriage decor	100.00
Salt and Pepper shakers, moriage decor, unsigned	18.00
Tea Set, 7″, covered teapot, creamer, sugar, and 5 cups and saucers	85.00
Tray, 12 x 14″, moriage floral center, lots of beading	179.00

MOSER GLASS

The Moser Glassworks, Karlovy Vary, (Carlsbad), Czechoslovakia, began in 1857. It was founded by Ludwig Moser whose specialty was glass engraving. Examples include Cameo, intaglio cut and enameled glass of superior quality. The firm is currently producing two-color engraved glassware.

Vase, 9½″, amethyst, signed . .$400.00

Atomizer, 8″, cut florals, gold trim . .	75.00
Bottles, Perfume	
Amber, 3″, finger type, gold enamel decor	150.00
Cranberry, 6½″, heavy gold enamel decor	265.00
Bowls	
7″, underwater scene with fish, gold enamel decor	300.00
10″, ruby cut to clear	150.00
11″ oval, green cased, ruffled rim, footed, signed	400.00
Boxes	
Patch, enamel floral decor on lid, signed	150.00
Powder, cranberry flashed, enamel floral decor, signed	165.00
Chalice, 5½″, enamel floral decor, gold band	185.00
Champagne, cobalt blue, cabachon panels with heavy gold decor,	

signed	110.00
Compote, 7″, amethyst, gold border	250.00
Cruet, 4″, cranberry, heavy gold enameling and floral decor	150.00
Cups and Saucers	
Amber, gold floral decor, signed .	150.00
Emerald, gold decor	175.00
Decanters	
12¾″, gold grapes, swirl stopper .	160.00
14″, ruby cut to frosted to clear ..	300.00
Ewer, 12″, amber, enameled flower and berries decor, gold trim, blue handle	350.00
Finger Bowls with underplate	
Alexandrite	200.00
Clear, intaglio cut, forest scene, signed	175.00
Goblets	
Jewelled cobalt, enamel decor, signed	200.00
Sea green, hexagonal base, signed	45.00
Jam Dish, 2 x 6″, cranberry, pink and blue forget-me-nots, gold feet and trim	175.00
Mug, alexandrite, etched bird	80.00
Pitcher, 3¾″, gold enamel foliage and bees, signed	300.00
Plates	
9″, intaglio cut green to clear, signed	300.00
Home on the Range	60.00
Rose Bowl, orange cased, mica flecks	160.00
Toothpick, clear crystal	65.00
Tumblers	
3½″, blue shaded to clear, 8 jewels around top, enamel floral decor	225.00
Gold trim, signed	95.00
Vases	
3¾″, blue, heavy white enamel decor	175.00
5½″, barrel shape, clear, gold etch fern decor	265.00
6½″, amber, applied lustre acorns, enamel decor, rigaree at neck, footed	495.00
8″, green, classical decor, gold band	300.00
9″, cranberry, gold flowers	250.00
11″, cranberry, applied bees, enamel floral decor, pair	735.00
17½″, rubena, 4 panels with white, green, gold floral decor, signed	335.00
Wines	
Cased overlay, wide incrusted gold band	195.00
Vaseline, intaglio cut birds and foliage, signed	85.00

MOSS ROSE PATTERN CHINA

The Moss Rose was a common garden flower grown in English gardens, and after the growing china-making business in this country began to tire of Oriental china designs, the makers chose motifs of nature and things around them. English potters had adopted this form as decoration for their wares, and American manufacturers started using it, too.

David Haviland in France, Wedgwood, Meakin, Powell and Bishop, were importing china decorated with this flower to America, and Knowles, Taylor, and Knowles, East Liverpool, Ohio, started making china with this motif and it became very popular here. Many collectors today are still trying to find pieces with which to replace the dinner sets of yesterday.

Plate, 10″ $35.00

Box, covered, oval, 6½″	22.50
Coffee Pot, 9″, E. C. & Co.	68.00
Coffee Mug and Saucer	18.00
Creamer	20.00
Cup and Saucer	22.50
Pitcher	
6″, pink handle	32.00
7¼″, J. M. Co.	50.00
Plates	
7½″	15.00
8½″, KTK	25.00
11″, cakeplate, open handles ...	28.00
Platters	
7 x 11″	22.00
12 x 18″	45.00
Sauces	
4½″	7.50
5″, pink rim, set of four	25.00
Shaving Mug	30.00
Sugar, covered	45.00
Syrup	
8″	40.00
8½″, pewter top, KTK, c. 1872 ..	150.00
Tea Set, covered tea pot, creamer, covered sugar, 4 plates, cups and	

saucers, 15 pieces, no mark	25.00
Teapot, 8½", bulbous, Meakin	65.00
Tureens	
Covered, gold trim, 12"	60.00
Gravy, attached underplate	38.00
Toilet chamber, covered, Meakin . .	50.00

MUFFINEERS
See SUGAR CASTORS.

MUGS

Mugs were a popular gift item in the late 19th century and continue today. They are made of various materials, decorated and/or personalized. Also see CHILDREN'S FEEDING DISHES and specific wares.

Clear, footed and handled, 3¾", "Owl" $37.00

Glass

Actress, scenes from "Pinafore" .	40.00
Beaded Arch Panels, cobalt blue .	35.00
Beaded Loop (Oregon)	21.00
Beaded Swag, souvenir type	30.00
Birds at Fountain, clear	25.00
Bleeding Heart, 3¼"	21.00
Broken Column, clear	40.00
Button Arches, Ruby top, souvenir type, small	20.00
Clear glass, applied handle, blown, reads "Hannah" with engraved wreath	30.00
Cordova	20.00
Jewel and Dewdrop (Kansas), flaring edges, no color	20.00
Monkey, clear opalescent	65.00
Ribbed Opal (Beatty's Rib), clear opalescent	32.50
Ribbed Cherry, clear	35.00
Ribbed Leaves	35.00

Porcelain or Pottery

Bennington-type, 4½"	40.00
Copper Lustre, 3⅜", blue and sanded bands	75.00
Copper Lustre, house pattern, beaded edge, pink lustre interior .	85.00
English, yellow glazed earthenware, 7", "A Trifle from Yarmouth"	100.00
Kate Greenaway decor, china, from "Under the Window"	45.00
China, with Masonic emblems, all seeing eye, square and compass blue star border	50.00
Mocha ware, blue Seaweed pattern	125.00
Portrait of Napoleon, 5½", marked "Belleek, M. M., Trenton, N. J."	70.00
Salt glazed stoneware, 5", four blue bands	50.00
Silver, figural, little girl, Kate Greenaway, from "Under the Window," marked "Simpson, Hall and Miller"	100.00

MULBERRY CHINA

Mulberry china derives its name from the color of the decoration which resembles the stain of mulberry juice. Porcelains decorated as such were made mainly in the Staffordshire district of England in the 1830-50 period by several potteries.

Fruit bowl, fruited, 10½" overall $35.00

Bowls

"Corean," 4"	60.00
"Rose," 4", E. Challinor	55.00
"Temple," 5", Podmore and Walker	65.00

"Vincennes," J. Alcock, waste
bowl **79.50**
Butter, covered
"Coburg" **115.00**
"Vincennes," J. Alcock **125.00**
Coffee Pot, "Udina," J. Clementson,
c. 1850 . . . .   **175.00**
Creamers
"Corean," Podmore and Walker .   **30.00**
"Formosa," E. Challinor **80.00**
"Neva" **85.00**
"Pelew," E. Challinor **85.00**
Cup Plates
"Corean," Podmore and Walker .   **30.00**
"Pelew," E. Challinor **50.00**
"Rose," E. Challinor **25.00**
Cups and Saucers, handleless
"Corean," Podmore and Walker .   **60.00**
"Cyprus," Davenport **60.00**
"Foliage," E. Walley **40.50**
"Washington Vase" **55.00**
Milk Pitcher, ½ pint, "Khyber," J.
Mier and Son **125.00**
Plates
"Albany," 9½", grape and vine
border, 12-sided **50.00**
"Allegheny," 10½", Goodfellow,
c. 1850 . . . .   **45.00**
"Birmah," 9½", "C" **30.00**
"Castle Scenery," 10½" **35.00**
"Corean," 10½", Podmore and
Walker **40.00**
"Cyprus," 10½", Davenport **50.00**
"Delhi," 9½", M. T. and Co. **35.00**
"Jeddo," 10½", Adams and Son .   **40.00**
"Loretta," 10½", octagon shape,
S. Alcock, Hill Pottery, c. 1830-
1859 . . . .   **50.00**
"Neva" **35.00**
"Ning-Po," 9½", R. H. and Co. . .   **35.00**
"Pelew," E. Challinor **37.50**
"Peru," Holdcraft and Co. **35.00**
"Peruvian," 10½", Wedgwood . .   **40.00**
"Temple," Podmore and Walker .   **35.00**
"Udina," 9½", Clementson **40.00**
"Washington Vase" **40.00**
Platters
"Allegheny," 16", T. Goodfellow,
1850 . . . .   **85.00**
"Corean," Podmore and Walker .   **100.00**
"Formosa," E. Challinor **85.00**
"Neva," 16" **85.00**
"Temple," 13", Podmore and
Walker **65.00**
Relish, "Percy," Morley, (shell-
shaped) **29.50**
Sauce dish, 3⅝", "Pelew," E.
Challinor **30.00**
Sauce Tureen
"Peru," Holdcraft and Co., with
matching plate and ladle **150.00**
Shaving Mug, "Washington Vase" .   **89.50**

Sugar, covered
"Bochara" **95.00**
"Cyprus," Davenport, handled and
pagoda shape **100.00**
"Washington Vase" **100.00**
Vegetable Dish, open, "Rose," E.
Challinor **75.00**
Vegetable Dish, covered
"Allegheny," T. Goodfellow **85.00**
"Delhi," M. T. and Co., handled,
on feet **100.00**
Wash Bowl and Pitcher
"Cyprus," Davenport, bowl, pitch-
er, toothbrush holder, soap dish .   **600.00**
"Washington Vase," bowl, pitcher,
toothbrush holder, shaving mug,
soap dish **650.00**

MUSIC BOXES

**Music boxes were invented in Switzerland
around 1825. The instrument contained a cylinder (pin barrel) and a sounding board
encased in a wooden enclosure. Later instruments used metal discs; still later ones had
paper rolls resembling player piano rolls.**

**Mira, restored and cleaned, 20 discs,
19 x 25½ x 14" $2750.00**

Album, photo, 2-tune, tune card,
leather cover **150.00**
Birds
Single, ornate gilted cage **300.00**
Two, brass cage, 12 x 20½",
needs regulating, c. 1890's **1000.00**

Three, brass cage, 10¼ x 15¼ x 22", 19th century **1650.00**

CYLINDER-TYPE

3⅝" cylinder, 4-tunes, mahogany case, tune card and mechanical tune indicator **600.00**

6" cylinder, 8-tunes, 3 bells, walnut case with floral inlay, decorated tune card **850.00**

8" cylinder, 8-tunes, burled wood case with inlay **800.00**

8" cylinder, 10-tunes, mahogany case, tune card **900.00**

10½" cylinders interchangeable-type, 6-tunes, zither attachment, walnut case with inlay of musical instruments, Mermod Freres **2500.00**

11" cylinder, 12-tunes, tune indicator, tune card zither attachment . **1000.00**

13" cylinder, 6-tunes, walnut case, inlay on lid and front, Heller Organ **2250.00**

13" cylinders, 3 interchangeable cylinders included, 8-tunes on each, Allard-Sandoz **3700.00**

14" cylinder, 10-tunes, piccolo zither attachment, Mermod Freres **1100.00**

15" cylinder, 10 tunes, tune sheet, Thibouville-Lampy **1900.00**

16½" cylinder, 24 tune, 6 bells, drum, castanet, butterfly strikers, zither attachment, wood case, tune indicator tune card **3000.00**

17" cylinder, 12 tune, 6 bells, 9 beaters, 8 strikers, castanets wood case, inlay decoration **2800.00**

DISC-TYPE

Criterion, 20½" disc, mahogany case, underlid lithograph **2100.00**

Kalliope

7¼" disc, 4 bells, 6½ x 9 x 10¼" **1250.00**

7¾" disc, walnut cabinet, underlid lithograph **750.00**

9¼" disc, 7 x 11 x 11½" **825.00**

9¼" disc, 6 bells, walnut cabinet with inlaid top, underlid lithograph, 7 x 10¾ x 11½" **1250.00**

13½" disc, 10 saucer bells, walnut case **1750.00**

17¾" disc, zither attachment, walnut cabinet, underlid lithograph . . **2100.00**

Komet, 10¼" disc,"Komet" inlaid in ivory, 7½ x 11½ x 13" **750.00**

Polyphon

6½" disc, 4 bells, 4¾ x 7¼ x 7¼" **650.00**

8¼" disc, walnut cabinet, underlid lithograph, 6¼ x 9½ x 10¼" . . . **750.00**

9¾" disc, walnut cabinet with underlid lithograph, 7½ x 11 x 12¼" **850.00**

11¼" disc, walnut cabinet, floral inlay on lid, underlid lithograph, 7½ x 11 x 12¼" **1150.00**

15½" disc, walnut cabinet with underlid lithograph, 8¾ x 18 x 21" **1500.00**

Regina

8¼" disc, mahogany cabinet, 8 x 9¾ x 12¼" **600.00**

15½" disc, double comb, mahogany case, Style #10 . . . . **2500.00**

15½" disc, double comb, oak case, Style #9 . . . . **1800.00**

15½" disc, single comb, oak case **1500.00**

20¾" disc, short bedplate, banjo attachment, Style #26 . . . . **5500.00**

Stella

9½" disc, double comb, oak case **950.00**

17¼" disc, double comb, console model, oak cabinet, 36" high **3000.00**

Symphonion

5¾" disc, 4¾ x 6¾ x 7½" **450.00**

8¼" disc, walnut cabinet with, decal design on lid, underlid lithograph **750.00**

11¾" disc, Sublime-Harmonic combs, walnut cabinet, carrying handles **1750.00**

14¾" disc, walnut cabinet, 10 bells, underlid lithograph **3000.00**

Troubadour, 8¾" disc, zither attachment, walnut cabinet with "Troubadour" inlaid in ivory on lid, underlid lithograph, 6½ x 9½ x 10½" **8500.00**

PAPER-TYPE

4¼" rolls, (3) "Tanzbar Roll Playing Accordion," case with inlay, 9 x 11 x 11" **650.00**

5¼" roll, "Mignon Organette," 22 reeds, walnut case **650.00**

7¾" roll, Melodia, 14 reeds, walnut case **450.00**

MUSICAL INSTRUMENTS

Down through the ages people have stamped their feet, clapped their hands or were compelled to sit quietly when music was 'in the air.' Musical instruments have changed very little since the original forms. Perhaps the case design, the material used or ornamentation has changed, but a flute is a flute.

Banjo, 5 strings, bird's eye maple, original case, "Howe-Stowe" . . . **75.00**

Banjo, 5 strings, professional, com-

plete with velvet lined case and
tenor tuner, "Vega" 200.00
Bugle, Boy Scout, brass 35.00
Bugle, Military, brass 45.00
Clarinet, ebony, leather case, French 80.00
Concertina, German with leather
case 75.00
Drum, 15", gold papered sides with
American flag decor, wooden
bands, complete, c. 1905 . . . . . . 85.00
Dulcimer, walnut 125.00
Fife, rosewood and brass 100.00
Flute, carved ivory 450.00
Glockenspiel, two rows of steel bars
supported on brass posts, tubular
brass harp with 14 bars 175.00
Guitar, "National Triolan," c. 1929 . 350.00
Harmonica, brass, c. 1875 . . . . 75.00
Harmonica, Marine Band, original
box, "Hohner" 15.00
Harp, enamel and gold 2500.00
Harp, Lap, c. 1880's 200.00
Mandolin, Kay, c. 1930 . . . . 90.00
Ocarina, wooden 20.00
Organs
Aeolian Grand, 73 keys, 20 stops,
mahogany cabinet, nickelplated
hardware, needs restoring 1500.00
Chicago Cottage, ornate cabinet
including spindled back, lamp
holders, c. 1900, restored 3000.00
Mason & Hamlin, 61 notes, 17
stops, c. 1900 . . . . 600.00
Miller, Mahogany, restored, c.
1892 . . . . 2500.00
Pianos
Blasius & Sons, 64 note, mechani-
cal 1500.00
Franklin Ampico, c. 1923 . . . . . . 2000.00
Meister, oak, c. 1904 . . . . 750.00
Morgan Davis, Pianoforte, c. 1910 900.00
Steinway, Duo Art-style, walnut,
carved legs and molding 7500.00
Steinway, square grand, rose-
wood, fruit carved legs 3500.00
Van Dyke, 88 note, upright, me-
chanical, restored 2500.00
Saxophone, Tenor, brass,
"Buescher," c. 1935 . . . . 850.00
Trombone, Campo, nickel over
brass, case 85.00
Trumpet, brass, MOP keys 75.00
Viola, one piece back construction,
Germany, 18th century 350.00
Violins
"Edward Reichert Dresden," bowl
with MOP inlay, case, complete . 150.00
Primitive-type, 7 x 21" 50.00
"Stradivarius, Cremona," A Sears
Roebuck importation of early 1890
–1900 period 50.00
Zither, late 1800's 85.00

MUSTACHE CUPS AND SAUCERS

Mustache cups were popular in the late Victorian period (1880–1890). The majority were
made and decorated by the transfer method
in Germany. The rarest items in this group at
are the left-handed cups. They are rare and
have been reproduced.

White china with gold decoration,
bottom of letters accented in blue,
marked B.S./C & M $38.00

Decal, portrait decor, Austrian 35.00
Decal, mother and child decor,
heavy gold trim 60.00
Floral decorated, ring handle, Carls-
bad 25.00
Floral decor, "A Present," Germany 45.00
Hand painted, floral decor, "Papa"
in gold letters, Germany 50.00
Floral spray, German inscription,
gold letters 50.00
Floral decor, lettered "Brother" . . . 45.00
Handpainted floral on pale green
background, lots of gold, Nippon . 50.00
Pink lustre, gold leaves decor, bead-
ed edges 50.00
Pink lustre flowers on white back-
ground 50.00
Gold and white embossed decor,
Grindley, England 30.00
Royal Worcester, handpainted flow-
ers on peach background 125.00
Silverplated
Engraved florals, dated 1891 . . . 75.00
Engraved, left handed 150.00
Staffordshire, ironstone, flowing blue
decor 55.00
Sterling, American 125.00
White background, gold banded bor-
der, "Wedding Band," no mark . . 50.00
White ironstone, with copper lustre
decor, c. 1850 . . . . 275.00

NAILSEA GLASS

Although glass was made in Nailsea, England,

"Nailsea-type glass" was made during the late 18th and early 19th centuries by several glass makers, including glass works in America. Characteristics of Nailsea glass are its white loopings, swirls or spatters on clear or colored glass. Therefore, it is more appropriate to apply the name "Nailsea" to the decoration and technique rather than the provenance.

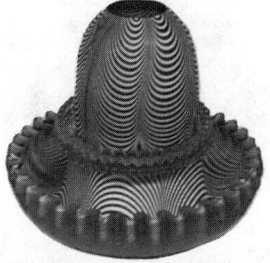

Fairy Lamp, pink and white, Clarke signed insert, 5" $275.00

Bell, 12", cranberry, clear handle and stopper 195.00
Bottles
  Barber, red and white 95.00
  Bellow, 8¾", clear with white looping 275.00
  Gemel, 10", clear with pink and white looping 235.00
Bowl, 5½", blue with white looping, ruffled rim 95.00
Carafe, 7", clear with white looping 135.00
Cruets
  6", blue with white looping, applied clear handle and base 150.00
  6¼", clear with pink and white looping, applied frosted handle and base 175.00
Epergne, peach satin with white looping, single lily 345.00
Fairy Lamps, See FAIRY LAMPS
Flasks
  8", pink and white 85.00
  Double red and white looping, blue ring around spout 95.00
Lamp Shades
  6", clear with white looping, blue rim 75.00
  8½", ball shape, deep rose with white looping 300.00
Pipes
  10½" long, curved stem, clear with white loopings 125.00
  14" long, clear with red and white loopings 175.00

Pitchers
  8", cranberry with white loopings, clear applied handle 175.00
  9½", clear with white loopings, clear applied handle 250.00
  10", blue with white loopings, applied handle 275.00
Rolling Pin, clear with blue and white loopings 95.00
Rose Bowl, cranberry satin with white loopings, applied camphor satin ribbon edge 225.00
Tumbler, white with blue looping .. 75.00
Vases
  9", white with blue loopings 100.00
  10½", blue and white, clear base, pair 155.00

NAKARA
See WAVECREST

NANKING

Nanking is a type of Chinese export porcelain made in Canton, China, from the early 1800's into the 20th century for export to America and England. It is often confused with the Canton pattern.

Three elements help distinguish Nanking from Canton. Nanking has a spear and post border, as opposed to the scalloped line style of Canton. The blues may tend to be darker on the Nanking ware. Second, in the water's edge or Willow pattern, Canton usually has no figures. Nanking features a standing figure with open umbrella on the bridge. Finally, Nanking wares often are embellished with gold.

Green and orange variations of Nanking survive, although they are scarce. Copies of Nanking ware currently are being produced in China. They are of inferior quality and decorated in lighter rather than the darker blues.

Plate, water edge scene, c. 1780-1800, 9½" $80.00

Bottle, water, 8″	375.00
Bowl, fruit, oval, reticulated, matching underplate, 6 x 9″	675.00
Cups and Saucers	
Baroque Handle	55.00
Handleless	75.00
Loop Handle	45.00
Dish	
6″, leaf shape, c. 1840	125.00
9″, petal form, scalloped rim	180.00
Jar, Ginger, 6″	130.00
Jug, Cider, 9⅛″, c. 1800	450.00
Plates	
8″	75.00
10″, oval, reticulated border	275.00
Platters	
12″, square, c. 1880	175.00
15″, c. 1800	500.00
18″, well and tree, c. 1840	625.00
Tureens	
10″, oval, acorn knop on lid, gilt trim, late 18th C.	575.00
12″, rectangular, acorn knop on lid, early 19th C.	430.00

NAPKIN RINGS

Silverplated figural napkin rings were popular in the late 1800's into the early 1900's. For other types of napkin rings, see specific categories.

Silver plated, Derby, Birmingham, CT, 3½ x 2¼″ $85.00

Barrel on leaves and twigs	45.00
Bird in flight, sits beside ornate ring, Queen City Silver	95.00
Cat pushing hoop ring	125.00
Cherub with wings, Meriden	125.00
Chick, sits beside ornate ring, oval base; Rogers, Smith & Co.	125.00
Cupid, wishbone and claw, heart shaped base inscribed "Best Wishes"	95.00
Dog chasing bird up ring	100.00
Doves, oblong base	55.00
Eagles, small one on each side of	

ring, Meriden-Britannia Co., #146	95.00
Fans, two, with butterfly, Meriden-Britannia Co., #208	100.00
Flowers on oval base	55.00
Fuchsia	70.00
Horseshoe, floral details	70.00
Kangaroo, ostrich and boomerang	95.00
Kate Greenaway, girl pushing ring	165.00
Lily pad with bud	65.00
Parrot, outstretched wings	80.00
Pear	65.00
Rabbits, two, one standing, one sitting, Pairpoint	250.00
Rooster	70.00
Sailor boy, pushing embossed ring. Rogers Bros. Co.	125.00
Squirrels with nuts	90.00
Soldier holding shield on base	115.00
Turtle	125.00
Turtles, two, round tiered base	150.00
Water Lily, Rogers Bros. Co.	55.00
Water Lily, barrel, cherries and leaves against ornate ring, Toronto Silver Plate #732	95.00
Wheelbarrow, Pairpoint #10	125.00
Wishbone, 4 ball feet	45.00
Wishbone, double	40.00

NASH GLASS

Arthur Nash and his sons, Leslie and Douglas, were employed by Tiffany Furnaces, Corona, Long Beach Island, in the early 1900's. It has been reported that the Nash family was responsible for designing, producing and promoting the iridescent glass for which Tiffany's received recognition.

Arthur Nash was a former member of the Woodall Gem Cameo team of Thomas Webb, England.

See LIBBEY GLASS.

Bowl, 5¾″, inverted rim with leaf design, signed	125.00
Candlesticks, 3¼″, 3 leaf design, signed, pair	250.00
4½″, blue iridescent, signed and no'd, pair	500.00
5″, gold iridescent, pair	275.00
Plates	
4½″, amber iridescent, scalloped edge, signed and no'd	300.00
6″, "Chintz," clear with orange	75.00
6½″, Spiral, orchid and clear, signed	130.00
8″, "Chintz," Green and blue	165.00
Salt, 1¼ x 4″, gold iridescent, ruffled top, signed and no'd	350.00
Stemware, "Chintz"	
5″ high	80.00
6½″ high	90.00
Vases	
6¼ x 3½″ dia. at top, trumpet-	

Vase, gold iridescent, labelled 544 Nash, 4¼" $350.00

shape, "Chintz," signed and no'd	350.00
8", blue iridescent, signed	375.00
9", "Chintz," blue-green, silver iridescent, signed	390.00

NAUTICAL ITEMS

The sea always has held a strong fascination for collectors. The objects listed focus on the historic period of the sailing and clipper ships along with the related aspects of naval warfare and whaling.

Naval supplies were manufactured in the United States and abroad. They represent the highest quality of workmanship. The instruments and implements had to withstand heavy use. In addition, many hand made objects survive as sailors, ship carpenters, or ship blacksmith's perfected items to individual taste.

See also BELLS, SCIENTIFIC INSTRUMENTS, SCRIMSHAW, and SWORDS.

Binnacles
  Brass, compass and kerosene burner for night viewing, 8" **175.00**
  Brass, compass and kerosene burner night lamp, made by Sestrel
    London, round iron side weights,mounted on octagonal mahogany base, 50" **1200.00**
Compass, card, mounted in glass covered brass bowl on gimbels, dovetailed walnut box with sliding lid, 6 x 6" **285.00**
Figure Heads
  Admiral Adam Duncan, Vicount of Camperdown (1731–1804), from frigate and later ships, blue jacket with cream colored waistcoat, black tricorn hat, 61 x 27" **3500.00**
  Lady, full busted with long flowing hair, oak, faded paint, 48" **2800.00**
Lanterns
  Brass, 3" font weighted with iron ball at base and mounted on gimbel ring, 10" glass globe **175.00**
  Brass, starboard, triangular shape, rounded green glass reflector, round kerosene burner, 15" **250.00**
Logs
  Barque Annaconda, Pacific whaling voyage beginning and ending in Mass., 1852–1856, hand stamps, drawings **3000.00**

(Top) Percussion Whaling Bomb Lance Gun, 40" $750.00

(Bottom) Percussion Whaling Bomb Lance Gun, 36½" $750.00

Grand Turk of Salem, privateer Brig of War, fifth cruise, 1815, 3½ months 2500.00

Granges, merchant, Boston to India to Canton, 1801 .... 425.00

Models

Cannon, deck, 8″ brass barrel mounted on walnut deck platform, oak wheels, 12″ 175.00

Ship, clipper, half hull, marked "Coppida," Bristol, Captain Hamlin, natural wood mounted on painted plaque 450.00

Ship, schooner, fishing, marked "Fishing Schooner Vessel No. 78, Eastbank Steam Fishing Co., 1904," mounted on sea painted plaque 375.00

Ship, schooner, *Marion Sprague*, three masted, wood hull painted black and copper, full rigging, 14″ ... 275.00

Octant, Spencer Browing & Co., English oak case, New Bedford label ... 650.00

Sextants

Browing & Co., Spencer, London, mahogany case, New Bedford label 600.00

Holt, I. L., Tonsberg, mahogany case 400.00

Telescopes

Two draw, leather wrapped, Joseph Brothers, San Francisco, day or night glass 275.00

Two draw, brass, barrel covered in mahogany, unmarked, 10″ 95.00

Three draw, brass, barrel covered in leather, Cox, London, 17″ 225.00

Five draw, brass, barrel covered in mahogany, Browing, London, 45″ ... 400.00

Trumpet, ship's hailing, brass, 15″ . 275.00

Whaling Implements

Blubber cutting spade, iron mounted on 60″ wood shaft, 6″ wide blade 200.00

Harpoons

34″, forged iron, Artic double flue 175.00

35½″, forged iron, Greener-type hand thrown 350.00

36″, forged iron, steel toggle head 225.00

Wheels

Clipper Ship, mahogany, ten spokes, brass hub, 52″ dia. 700.00

Ship, mahogany, six spokes, brass hub, 20″ dia. 150.00

NAZI ITEMS

This field has enjoyed immense popularity over the last few years. It also has attracted those firms and individuals who specialize in reproduction equipment. In fact, several military price guides carry listings of reproduction items. Know your dealer or have the item checked for you by an established collector.

Knife, place setting piece belonging to Adolph Hitler, "A.H." and swastika $250.00

Armbands

Africa, palm trees on end 55.00

Medical Personnel, Wehrmacht .. 10.00

Swastika on white ground, red, 4 x 10½″ 7.50

Badges

Infantry, Assault, bronze 24.00

Luftwaffe, Pilot, marked 200.00

Panzer, Assault, bronze 22.50

Banners

12″, Post Office 65.00

18″, triangle, black swastika on red ground 50.00

Bayonets

Army dress, long model 40.00

Fireman's sawtooth, short model . 50.00

Police, slotted service, long 150.00

Belt Buckle, Army Officers, silver .. 35.00

Binoculars, Wehrmacht 82.50

Bugle, Wehrmacht, brass 60.00

Cross, Mother's, blue and white enamel, "Der Deutschen Mutter," original ribbon, 1½ x 1¾″ 50.00

Daggers

Army Officers, engraved blade ... 250.00

Hitler Youth 65.00

Labor Service, Hewer 200.00

Luftwaffe, 1st Model 240.00

Red Cross, leaders 300.00

SS, Elite Guard 275.00

Finial, RAD, for flag pole 125.00

Flags

Afrika Korps 42.50

Hitler Youth 325.00

Luftwaffe Squadron 40.00

National War Flag, swastika 110.00

Goggles, tanker's, amber lens, type used in Africa 35.00

Gorgets

Political leaders 300.00

SS or Schutzstaffel 500.00

Hats

Army, officers, M-43, field cap ... 80.00

Army, other ranks, M-38 .... 40.00

Luftwaffe, officers 100.00

SS, officers	700.00

Helmuts

Fire Police	90.00
M-35, decals	75.00
M-43, decals	60.00
SS, M-35	425.00
Tropical	125.00
Luger, H. Krieghoff Waffenfabrik, Suhl, Model 1936	1500.00

Medals

Iron Cross, 1st Class, cased	55.00
Service Metal, 12 years, matte gilt finish, round	30.00
Service Metal, 18 years, silver maltese cross	50.00
Mess Kit, Wehrmacht, three sections	20.00
Overcoat, motorcyclist, waterproof, Wehrmacht	110.00
Stickpin, enameled swastika on silverplate	35.00

Swords

Army Officer	150.00
Luftwaffe	200.00
Navy Officer	300.00
Transfer, helmut, 14 per sheet	30.00
Tunic, camouflage, Wehrmacht	225.00

NETSUKES

The traditional Japanese kimono has no pockets. Daily necessities such as keys, money purses, tobacco supplies, etc., are carried by hanging them from a cord with a netsuke toggle. Netsuke comes from "neroot" and "tuske"— to fasten.

A netsuke has two holes drilled at an angle so they come together at the bottom. The holes usually are of different sizes. The netsukes are made from a wide variety of materials —bone, horn, ivory, lacquer, metal, porcelain, semi-precious stones, and wood. Average size is 1 to 2 inches.

CAUTION! Recent reproductions are on the market. Many are carved from African ivory.

Carved Ivory, 19th century ...$80.00

Actor, holding sring of beads and fan, ivory	235.00
Badger, study, ivory	750.00
Bat on leaf, bone	125.00
Bat on tile roof, ivory	500.00
Boar, resting on leaves, signed Mitsuharu, ivory	900.00
Cannon, brass fittings, ring attachment	175.00
Carp, white with brown eyes, porcelain	625.00
Chicken in egg, signed, African ivory	45.00
Child, ivory	450.00
Child, playing drum, ivory	240.00
Darkoku, group, seated on shoulders of Fukurujoku, ivory	280.00
Dog, front paws on ball, wood	230.00
Dragon, coiled, brass eyes, ivory	700.00
Elephant, standing, base, inlayed eyes, ivory	450.00
Erotic figure, ivory	550.00
Fox, study, guise of farmer, wood	450.00
Frog on tree stump, ivory	200.00
Horse, recumbent, coral, pink	245.00
Horse, winged, African ivory	85.00
Hotei at his toilet, Hoshin, ivory	1100.00
Hunter, standing, carrying sword, ivory, 18th C.	800.00
Kabuki dancer, holding fan, ivory	180.00
Kitten, sleeping on cushion, ivory, Garaku, 18th C.	4000.00
Lotus pad, ripe, Nagasaki, glass	350.00
Man, European, long beard, stagshorn	600.00
Man, pouring tea in cup, ivory	260.00
Monkey, "See No Evil, etc.," signed, 19th C.	375.00
Monkey, pod, African ivory	65.00
Monkey, rock, Gyokko, ivory	700.00
Mouse, scratching ear, hornbill	160.00
Octopus in barrel, head moves, ivory	425.00
Rabbit, seated, Kogyoku, ivory	850.00
Sage, holding brush, lounging, 18th C., ivory	550.00
Samurai warrior, leaning on sword, ivory	260.00
Shishi head, porcelain	225.00
Snail, signed, 19th C., ivory	350.00
Snake, coiled, inlayed eyes, signed Tomonobu, ivory	1200.00
Squirrel, bunch of grapes, Hosai, ivory	400.00
Turtle, group, on lotus leaf, two babies on back, Bazan, wood	2400.00
Woman, nursing child, ivory	530.00

NEW HALL

From 1781–1835 the New Hall China Manufac-

tory made both Hard Paste Porcelain and Bone China using many of the same patterns and forms on both bodies, with some variations. Less famous in its day than many English factories making similar wares, New Hall was the only firm to make the transition from Hard Paste to Bone Porcelain. All others went from Soft Paste to Bone.

Unseasoned collectors should approach New Hall with caution since imitators abound as David Holgate warns in his book, *New Hall and Its Imitators*. Although this definitive reference lists New Hall pattern numbers up to 1681, many patterns are not illustrated. However, pattern alone cannot be used to date a particular New Hall item. Shape, and in some cases nature of paste and glaze, are the only true guides.

It is possible that New Hall patterns exist that have not been documented. Such pieces, including a complete tea service, have been found recently in pattern 1278.

Tea pot, white ground, blue flowers, orange trim, 6¼ x 11" $150.00

Coffee Cans, pattern 1278, set of 4	425.00
Creamer, pink lustre decor	75.00
Cream Jug, unknown pattern	165.00
Cups and Saucers	
Blossom band decor	50.00
Family scene in pink, blue, green and brown	65.00
Flower decor in green, red, yellow	60.00
Oriental figures, flowers	60.00
Pattern 195, early	80.00
Mug, small, oriental decor	45.00
Plates	
7¼", rose decor	60.00
8", deep with center bouquet and single floral motifs at intervals around border, c. 1790, marked . .	125.00
Platter, 16½ x 21", two scenes— one with sailboat, other with stream and trees	155.00
Sugar Bowl, pink lustre decor	100.00

Tea Bowl and Saucer, Pat. 195, set	75.00
Tea Pots	
Chinese pattern	150.00
Chippendale shape	165.00
Flower spray	150.00
Pink lustre decor	165.00
Oriental figure, Swan finial	250.00
Teapot, pattern 173, silver shape . .	225.00
Tea Services	
15 pieces, pattern 139	750.00
26 pieces, pattern 1064	1075.00
29 pieces, pattern 1278	1250.00

NEW MARTINSVILLE GLASS

New Martinsville Glass Manufacturing Company began operation in 1901. Art glass produced during the early years of the company rivaled, in beauty and design, foreign products. Unfortunately, these pieces had limited production when a fire destroyed the plant in 1907. Thereafter, the fragile Peachblow and other types of art glass were never again produced.

Four periods of production are noteworthy: 1901–1907, Art and opaque glass including "Peachblow;" 1907–1937, pressed pattern glass; 1937–1944, crystal wares including the animal line; 1944, contemporary novelties and tableware.

When the company went into receivership in 1931, the plant was sold and the business was reopened as the New Martinsville Glass Company. In 1944 the entire stock was purchased by G. R. Cummings and the name was changed to The Viking Glass Company under which it still operates today.

Swan, Janice pattern, crystal, 11½ x 7½ x 8½" $30.00

Animal Figurines
Bear, baby, 3"	40.00
Dog, Bulldog, 2½"	28.00

Dog, Police, 5″	55.00
Hen, small, frosted	45.00
Pelican, 8″	75.00
Rooster, 8½″	60.00
Squirrel, 5½″	45.00
Basket, 9″, cobalt handle, "Janice"	50.00
Basket, Bride's, 9″, "Peachblow," footed holder	250.00

Bookends
Cornucopia, crystal, pair	50.00
Gazelle, pair	65.00
Ship, pair	30.00

Bowls
5″, crystal, embossed squirrels	45.00
10½ x 3½″ deep, "Peachblow," glossy finish	180.00
12 x 4″ deep, "Janice," crystal	30.00
Box, covered, 8″, 3 compartments, crystal	30.00

Candlesticks
6½″, crystal, pair	35.00
7¼″, high, crystal, pair	45.00

Creamers and Sugars
"Berry Cluster"	25.00
"Moondrops," ruby	25.00
"Radiance," blue	30.00
Jam Jar, covered, with underplate, "Janice," blue	40.00
Pitcher, large, etched	55.00
Spooner, "Japanese Iris"	30.00
Sugar, "Star in Bull's Eye," emerald green	20.00
Sugar Castor, "Peachblow"	90.00

Swans
5½″, open back, crystal	18.00
5½″, black bowl, crystal neck	20.00
5½″, green bowl, crystal neck	22.50
13″, red bowl, crystal neck	65.00
Vase, 7½″, "Peachblow," ruffled top	150.00

NEWCOMB POTTERY

The brilliant achievements of Newcomb pottery began in 1885 in Tulane University art classes and then at the Art Pottery Co. in New Orleans. Later in 1886, the pottery was operated in conjunction with the Art Department at Sophie Newcomb Memorial College for Women in the same city.

William and Ellsworth Woodward were the founders. The two brothers directed an elective arts program at the college which was funded generously by Josephine Louise LeMonnier Newcomb and joined to Tulane University in 1887.

Students at Newcomb College worked in the pottery, producing and painting a quality art pottery with the distinctive high gloss glaze. Designs on Newcomb wares have a decidedly Southern flavor such as myrtle, jasmine, sugar cane, moss, cypress, dogwood and magnolia.

Of particular interest to collectors are the early, highly glazed pieces. The later matte glazed pieces are usually decorated with carved-back floral designs, but pieces depicting murky, bayou scenes are most desirable.

Vase, blue, artist signed, Sadie Irvine, 6″ **$650.00**

Bowls
4 x 8″, rim slightly closed, cut back floral design round opening, artist signed	275.00
8″ dia., pink morning glories, artist signed	400.00
Candleholder, 5 x 3″, ring handle, pink flowers on blue, artist signed	325.00

Plaques
9½″, incised fish decor, high glaze	725.00
9 x 6″, Spanish moss hanging from cypress trees, artist signed	1500.00

Vases
4 x 3″, undecorated, thin, green glaze	100.00
4 x 4¾″, glossy purple glaze, artist signed	275.00
5 x 5″, bulbous, carved blue swamp scene on light blue ground	550.00

5½", pale green and blue, artist signed 350.00
6 x 4", carved back pink and yellow flowers on matte blue ground ... 350.00
7 x 5½", blue floral border decor on beige ground, high glaze, early ... 900.00

NILOAK POTTERY

Niloak (Kaolin spelled backwards) Pottery was made in Benton, Arkansas, from 1911 to 1946. The hand thrown marbleized pottery developed by J. H. Hyten and his two brothers is of the greatest interest to collectors of American pottery. Molded or cast pottery was also made at the factory.

Planter, blue, paper label $12.00

Bowls, Marbleized
5 x 2¾" deep 30.00
5½ x 6" deep 42.50
10 x 3¼" deep 75.00
12 x 4" deep 85.00
Cup and Saucer, square, yellow glaze 25.00
Ewer, 7¼", pink glaze 25.00
Figurine, "Southern Belle," 9½", paper label 40.00
Pitchers
6½", pink 15.00
3 pt., blue 25.00
Planters
Clown, White 20.00
Dog, White 10.00
Dutch Shoe 12.50
Elephant on Drum 12.00

Swan, Blue 15.00
Vases, Marbleized
4½" 30.00
6½" 35.00
8", bud 45.00
Wall Pocket, 7" 30.00

NIPPON CHINA

Much of the Nippon porcelain seen today was manufactured by the Noritake Company, Ltd., in Nagoya, Japan. In 1891, when Congress passed a law that all imported articles must be marked as to country of origin, Japan chose to use their own name for Japan, "Nippon."

In 1921 it was decided "Nippon" was no longer acceptable and all Japanese wares must be marked with the English word "Japan," thus the end of the "Nippon" period. There are over fifty different marks used on Nippon pieces, some identical except colored differently. They identify different qualities of the piece, workmanship, decoration, importers' marks, maker, or artist. Serious collectors should familiarize themselves with these marks. During the last five years, the demand for this ware has increased greatly, thus raising prices.

Berry set, master bowl, 9", six 5¼" serving bowls, hand painted raspberries and leaves, gold trim, set 95.00
Bowls
Berry with underplate, 8¾", pink flowers, gold trim, M in wreath .. 150.00
Lillies, 9", gold trim 55.00
Floral border, 7", rising sun mark 45.00
Hand painted harbour sunset, handled, gold band, beaded, blue leaf mark 65.00
Box, covered, heart-shaped, hand painted pink roses 37.50
Cake Set, 10" plate, six 7¼" plates, scenic decor, green M 85.00
Candy Dish, 7", jewelled, handles, Noritake-Nippon mark 45.00
Celery Dishes
Blue flowers, gold trim, M in wreath 38.00
Dish, 5 individual salt dips, dainty floral decor, 6 pieces 75.00
Chocolate Pots
Molded body, 8 gold ball feet, 12¼", 8 panels, wide scalloped bands of gold and beige; yellow, pink shaded roses, encrusted with jewels, beads and gold 395.00
Soft, floral colors, gold and gold butterflies 95.00

Scenic, matte finish, 8¼"	38.00
Gaudy, gold beads, colored jewels, base and top, signed	295.00

Cookie Jars

Cobalt blue and gold, swans and lake scene	250.00
Floral decor, 8", gold trim and beading	155.00

Creamer and covered sugar, hand painted roses, gold trim, pair	75.00

Cups and Saucers

Roses, pink with white beading, rising sun mark	27.50
Swans on blue background, jewelled, gold, pink trim, green mark .	35.00
Gold band, hand painted pink and green single rose border, gold trim and scrolling, hand painted Nippon mark	28.00

Figurine, "Little Nipper, His Master's Voice," RCA souvenir novelty item	200.00

Humidors

Scenic, man, woman, buggy and horse	295.00
Old automobile decor, hand painted	400.00
Smoking set, humidor has pipe finial, 4 pieces	450.00

Vase, roses, gold trim, 7" ...$125.00

Mayonnaise set, covered, attached underplate, ladle, hand painted flowers, blue leaf mark	45.00
Mug, 5¾", owl with glass eyes, on blue background	225.00
Mustard Pot, and spoon, white, gold scroll trim, no mark	30.00
Nut Set, footed, four piece set, ornate and gold trimmed	75.00
Pancake Dish, covered, 10", cobalt blue and gold, no mark	30.00

Pin Box, 3¼", gold leaves and flowers, M in wreath	25.00

Plates

Berries, 6½", soft orange, grey, green leaves, marked Nippon ...	14.00
Beaded and gold border, 8½", two owls in tree	48.00
Cherry blossoms, 7", gold, rising sun mark, set of six	25.00

Powder Box, 4", footed, floral border, green M in wreath	40.00
Relish, 7", Indian head cut out for handles	95.00
Salt and Pepper shakers, handled, pink roses, gold, rising sun mark .	24.00
Sugar, covered and creamer, roses, green leaves, gold, set	75.00

Tea Set, cherry trees, pagodas, gold handles, egg-shell thin, 7 pieces . | 295.00

Tea Pot, cobalt blue and gold, signed	198.00

Toothpicks

Scenic view, three handles, 2½", colorful	25.00
Windmill scene, 3", gold and beading	18.00

Vases

Double-handled, hand painted roses, gold and green	125.00
Winter landscape and church building, handled, wide gold neck and trim, 8½", hand painted, M in wreath	175.00
Sunset scene, gold trim, 10½", cow and bull	295.00
Geese in water	35.00
Handled, flowers, 5¾", gold outlining and beading	40.00
Boat scene, handled	50.00
Pink flowers, 7", cobalt, gold trim on white ground, blue leaf mark ..	80.00
Poinsettia decor, handled, gold beaded trim, blue leaf mark	80.00
Scenic decor, handled, 14", green ground, heavy gold beading	175.00

NODDERS

Nodders are figurines with heads and/or arms attached to the body with wires to enable them to move. Nodders are made from a variety of materials—bisque, celluloid, paper mache, porcelain, and wood.

Most nodders date from the late 19th Century with Germany being the principal source of supply. Among the American made nodders, those of Disney characters and cartoon figures are most eagerly sought.

Andy Gump, 4", Germany	65.00
Boy, 6½", bisque, blue & white ...	125.00

Monkey, terra-cotta, glaze on pink vest, 3¾" high $125.00

Chinaman, 8", bisque	350.00
Donkey, standing, 3 x 2", celluloid .	9.00
Farmer, standing, 8", paper mache	45.00
Girl, 3", bisque, Germany, dressed in green and red	50.00
Girl, riding chicken side saddle, 3 x 2½", bisque	75.00
Grandmother with hat, 6½", bisque, pink-blue cape and glasses	175.00
Horse, 3 x 2¾", leather	75.00
Horse with man's clothing, standing, paper mache	47.50
Man, sitting, 9", paper mache with twig chair	85.00
Man and Woman, sitting, 4", paper mache	45.00
Monkey riding black mule on platform with wooden wheels, 9½", wood and wire composition	175.00
Orphan Annie, 3½", bisque, Germany	65.00
Rabbit, standing, 7½", paper mache	45.00
Rabbit, sitting, 8", paper mache, light brown	65.00
Santa Claus, 3", bisque, Germany .	100.00
Santa Claus, 9½", paper mache, Germany, red & blue	175.00

NORITAKE CHINA

Noritake china, still in production in Japan, has been exported in large quantities to the United States since late in 1880. In 1904 they started to use the name "Noritake" on their china. They also made blanks for other companies and for the amateur china painters prolific at that time.

Relish Dish, Tree in Meadow pattern $45.00

Ashtray, hand painted lake, tree, and sky scene	35.00
Baskets	
4½", handled, orange, lavender and blue floral decor	50.00
6", hand painted, purple on chartreuse background	55.00
Bowls	
5¼", "Tree in the Meadow" pattern	35.00
8", leaf handles, hand painted nuts and leaves decor	65.00
10¼", oval, pierced handles, water scene, with tree and house ..	60.00
Chocolate Pot, melon ribbed, rose decor on white to pale green ...	85.00
Chocolate Set, oval pot and four cups and saucers, large floral decor, leaves outlined in gold	175.00
Compote, water scene, houses and Japanese fisherman	70.00
Creamer and Sugar Bowl, hand painted sailboat scene	29.00
Creamer, 5", and Sugar shaker, 6", cream color, ship, pagoda, heavy gold trim, pair	45.00
Cups and Saucers	
Demitasse, orange and blue flower decor	12.50
Demitasse set, 7½", octagonal teapot, creamer sugar, four octagonal cups and saucers, orange, black, gold diamond design, Art Deco style, marked "Noritake," set	95.00
Dresser Set, gold and cobalt blue, overlay design on white background, 7 pieces, set	65.00
Olive Dish, hand painted petunias,	

gold trimmed handles	28.00
Mustard Jar, with scalloped edge tray, original spoon, blue and white, fruit and foliage	25.00
Planter, handles molded as grape clusters, hand painted lake scene, with cottage, trees, heavy gold border	60.00
Plates	
Child's "Hickory, Dickory, Dock" .	12.50
9", pansy decor, artist signed . . .	18.50
Platter, 10", oval, white with gold designed wide edge	25.00
Service for six, "Black Bliss" pattern, 48 pieces	600.00
Six matching service pieces for above set	150.00
Slant topped cheese dish, white with gold trim, gold handle	45.00
Snack Set, "Baskets and Butterflies" decor, 21 pieces, Red Wreath mark	87.50
Tea Set, teapot, creamer, covered sugar bowl and cookie plate, floral decor on cream background with maroon border and red and yellow birds on lid, four pieces	58.50
Tile, hand painted scene, water, willow tree, rushes, man in boat . . .	35.00
Vegetable Dishes	
Covered, three gold handles, and three gold feet, Monterey pattern	75.00
Open, triangular shaped, with fluted edge, two gold handles and gold feet, gold, wide border on white background	48.00
10", oval footed, with cover, red poppies on cream background . .	50.00
9", open, yellow and purple violets, gold handles and feet	48.00
Vase, 13", white and gold collared neck, panelled blue and gold body, hand painted roses in panels, outlined in gold	95.00

NORITAKE-AZALEA PATTERN

One of Noritake's most commonly known patterns was "Azalea." The dinnerware was widely distributed by the Larkin Tea and Coffee Co. from the 1920's to the 40's as premiums and by a mail order plan. The Larkin Club Plan enabled those on a limited budget to purchase fine china on a piece-by-piece basis.

Four different marks were used during production. The earliest was simply "Hand-Painted Nippon." Two succeeding green and red marks were "M" in a wreath with the words "Noritake" and "Made in Japan" followed by symbols and the numbers "19322." The latest mark reads "Azalea Pattern" with an Azalea sprig.

Vegetable, covered, gold finial $375.00

Basket, 2½ x 4¼"	80.00
Bouillon Cup and Saucer	12.00
Bowls	
6¼"	10.00
Shell shaped	120.00
Butter chip	24.00
Butter, covered, with drain, 5⅛" . . .	35.00
Cake plate, 9¾"	30.00
Celery Tray	30.00
Creamer, tall	38.00
Cup and Saucer	18.00
Dish, handled, for lemons	13.00
Fruit Dish, 5¼", ea.	6.50
Grapefruit dish	135.00
Gravy Boat, with tray	35.00
Grill plate	75.00
Jam Jar, covered, original server and underplate	115.00
Oatmeal Dish, 5½", ea.	12.50
Pitchers	
1 quart	90.00
Milk	135.00
Plates	
6½"	7.00
7½"	7.00
8½"	15.00
9¾"	18.00
Relish dishes	
8¼", oval	12.00
10", 4 divisions, handled	68.00
Roll tray, 12½"	75.00
Salt and Pepper	
Single shaker, gold top	10.00
Tray, condiment set	35.00
Sugar and Creamer, set	25.00
Spoonholder	55.00
Syrup, covered, with underplate . . .	115.00
Tea Pot	55.00
Tea Tile, 6"	35.00
Vase, fan shaped, 6"	120.00

NUTCRACKERS

Since primitive man first cracked nuts with his teeth or with stones, inventors have been devising ways to make the task simpler and easier. Examples listed below are the fruits of their ingenuity.

Wood, carved, 6¾" **$85.00**

Alligator, cast iron, 7½"	35.00
Bear's Head, wood, 7", glass eyes, 1850's	85.00
Chicken's Head, brass	30.00
Dogs	
Cast iron, red and gilt paint, wooden base, 11½"	35.00
Wooden	35.00
Dragon, brass	50.00
Eagle, brass	20.00
Elephant, cast iron	55.00
Fish, 5", brass	30.00
Ladies' Legs	
Brass, 4"	30.00
Cast iron, 6"	75.00
Lion's Head, brass	30.00
Monkey's Head, brass	35.00
Parrots	
Brass	42.00
Cast iron, 6 x 9½", painted black, red and gilt trim	35.00
Regis, Dickens' character, silver plate	35.00
Rooster, brass, 2 handles	50.00
Snail, wooden, hand carved	85.00
Squirrels	
Cast iron	20.00

Wooden, hand carved	100.00
Twist and Screw type, cast iron, chrome plate, 1910	20.00

OCCUPIED JAPAN ITEMS

Items marked "Occupied Japan" were made after the surrender of Japan in World War II in 1945 and during the occupation by the Allied Forces.

Ashtrays	
2¼", heart-shaped, white with handpainted floral sprays	10.00
6¾", chrome plate, pierced floral rim	10.00
Bookends, 5½", oriental lady and gent, pair	30.00
Box, jewelry, piano-shaped, silvered metal	15.00
Cigarette Lighters	
3", Gun shaped	7.50
3¼", cobalt, white, red and gold .	25.00
Chocolate Set, Victorian style, floral, 6 cups and saucers, set	50.00
Clock, 5⅛", Grandfather-style, bisque, floral trim	8.50
Condiment Set, 2⅝ x 5¾", oranges in basket, 6 pieces, set	20.00
Cream and Sugar, covered, pink roses, green leaves, red trim, set	18.50
Cups and Saucers, hand painted, marked "Orion"	20.00
Fan, 8½", red lacquered bamboo sticks, painted roses on silk, gold trim	20.00

Figurines, dancers in 17th C. dress, 4", pair **$12.50**

Figurines	
Betty Boop, 6", blond hair, celluloid, moveable arms	20.00
Boy, singing, 4", Hummel-type . .	12.50
Cat, fishbowl climber	12.50

Cherub, 3", with drum and symbol, pierced pedestaled base	8.00
Girl, oriental, 4¾", shelf sitter, green	10.00
Lady, oriental, 7¼", white and gold	15.00
Lady and Gentleman, 8", oriental dress, pair	30.00
Monkeys, 3" long, "The Three Wise Ones."	8.50
Harmonica, butterfly-shaped	20.00
Humidor, covered, rust color with mums, Foo dog finial	35.00
Nappy, with gold handle	10.00
Parasol, 4" long, paper and bamboo	5.50
Planters	
Coolie, pulling rickshaw, 3½ x 5"	10.00
Duck, 5 x 8"	15.00
Kitten, 3¼"	7.50
Plate, 4½", pierced scalloped fancy rim, silvered metal	10.00
Plate, grill, 10", "Blue Willow."	8.50
Shakers, Salt and Pepper	
Ducks, 2½", original box	10.00
Flower Girls, 4¼", Hummel-type .	20.00
Tomatoes in basket, handled tray, 2½ x 4¼", 3 pieces	18.50
Shelf, curio, 19" high, black lacquered wood, gold decoration . . .	35.00
Smoke set, lighter, urn, tray, silvered metal, 3 pieces	20.00
Tea infuser, teapot-shaped, metal .	5.00
Teapot, 5" high, violets on white . .	30.00
Tea Set, demi-size, blue lustre ground, handpainted decor, 16 pieces	60.00
Tobys	
Happy Hooligan, 5"	25.00
Indian Chief, 2¾"	16.50
Jailer, Full figure, 7½"	35.00
Man, Full figure, 2¼"	12.50
Pirate, 3¼"	16.50
Tray, 5 x 8¼", papier mache, brown with multicolored handpainted flowers	12.50
Vases	
3", urn-shaped, floral bouquets . .	5.00
6⅛", ewer-type, handpainted flowers in relief	15.00
Miniature, swan-shaped	10.00
Wall Pockets	
Colonial Lady in balcony, 1½ x 2¾ x 4", high	12.00
Cuckoo Clock, 5", orange lustre, pine cone weights	10.00

G. E. OHR,
BILOXI.
OHR POTTERY

Ohr pottery was produced by George E. Ohr

in Biloxi, Mississippi. There is some discrepancy as to when Ohr actually established his pottery. Some suggest 1878; but, Ohr's autobiography indicates 1883. In 1884 Ohr exhibited 600 pieces of his work, indicating that he had been working for some time.

A primary characteristic of Ohr's pottery is extremely thin walls, often no thicker than an egg shell. Ohr's techniques of twisting, crushing, folding, denting, and crinkling clay into odd, grotesque and sometimes graceful ware was ridiculed by the critics. They called him "The Mad Pottery of Biloxi."

Critics of his day were considerably more enthusiastic about his use of glazes which were rich and varied. Ohr carefully signed all his work, and most of it bears the town designation. The markings are either incised or impressed.

In 1906, Ohr closed the pottery and stored over 6,000 pieces as his legacy to his family. He hoped it would be purchased by the U.S. Government. This never happened. The entire collection remained in storage until it was rediscovered in 1972.

Reproductions of Ohr pottery are being made.

Bank, pear shape, nonglazed, 4" . .	200.00
Bowls	
4½", pinched, blue mottled glaze	300.00
4¾", footed, crimped rim, gun metal glaze	240.00
5½", mottled yellow and brown glaze, applied caterpillar	350.00
Chamberstick, conical, crimped rim, gun metal and green glaze, 3¼ x 3¾"	250.00
Inkwells	
Donkey's Head, green glaze, 3 x 4½"	325.00
Shoe, mottled brown glaze, 3" . .	200.00
Symmetrical, oxblood glaze, 4⅜"	225.00
Tiger's Head, 3½", bright blue glaze	400.00
Mugs	
3½", puzzle type, iridescent brown	220.00
5½", mottled gun metal and green glaze	240.00
Pitchers	
3¾", yellow and brown glaze . . .	250.00
6½", folded neck, blood red glaze	450.00
Planter, hanging, coiled snake inside, mottled brown glaze on exterior, 3½ x 6½	
Teapot, dark blue glaze, serpentine spout and handle, 5½"	700.00
Vases	
2¾", twisted, green-brown glaze .	225.00
3¼", seaweed green, speckled with light green and orange, han-	

dled	300.00
3¼", pinched rim, dimpled sides, raspberry color glaze exterior, dark brown interior	350.00
3¾", pinched sides, ruffled edges, green-brown glaze	200.00
5", pleated rim, dark brown glaze, speckled with yellow	325.00
5", spherical, speckled green glaze, marked	900.00
7½", ovoid, gun metal glaze, marked	400.00

OLD IVORY 84

OLD IVORY CHINA

This china derives its name from the ground color of the ware. The difference in patterns is indicated by a number on the base. It was made in Silesia, Germany, in the latter part of the 1800's. Marked pieces usually bear the Crown Silesia mark.

Plate, floral decor, "VIII," 8" . . $45.00

Berry Set, #63, 9½", bowl, six saucers, set	250.00
Bouillon Cup and Saucer	45.00
Bowls	
5", #28	25.00
6½", #15	30.00
9¼", #200, #113	75.00
Butter, covered, #16	150.00
Butter Pat, #11	35.00
Cake Plates	

9½", pierced handles, marked Silesia	55.00
10", #11	65.00
Pot, Hot chocolate size	36.00
Cookie Jar, covered, #82	225.00
Creamer and Sugar	
#82	100.00
#10, #75	85.00
#69	150.00
#84	150.00
Cups and Saucers	
#15	45.00
#7, #28, #200	40.00
Mustard, covered, #84	85.00
Plates	
7", #14	35.00
8", #315	40.00
Chop Plate, #2	50.00
Relish Dish, 6½", #15	32.50
Sauces	
#15	20.00
#32	20.00
Shakers, Salt and Pepper, #16, set	100.00
Sugar, covered, #84, #200, #202	95.00
Teapot, full size, #34	45.00
Tea Tile, 6½", #15, round	75.00
Toothpick, #16	75.00

OLD PARIS CHINA

Old Paris is a generic name for fine quality porcelain made by French factories during the 18th and 19th centuries. Some pieces are marked but the majority of the ware was not. Its main characteristics are fine quality porcelain and beautiful decorations; a favorite color was dark maroon, also cobalt blue, and much gold trim. Open work was often present but not common.

Plate, Boy and Girl, multicolored pale blue border, 8⅛" $45.00

Bowl, 11½″, oval floral decor	90.00
Card Receiver, 6″, floral	50.00
Cologne bottle, Square, deep blue and white, pink flowers	85.00
Cups and Saucers	
Floral decor	55.00
Magenta floral on white to seagreen, gold trim, c. 1800	65.00
Figurine, 6½″, lady seated on reclining camel, palm trees, marked "Asia"	295.00
Gravy boat, covered, blue bird decor, anchor and rope finial	100.00
Snuff box, enamelled, cobalt, signed Swan, fitted with inkpot and sander, gold decor	225.00
	140.00
Tureens	
11½ x 13″, cobalt on white, handpainted, unmarked	165.00
13″, oval, covered, molded fruit finial, white, with wide maroon bands and gold trim around body, no mark	175.00
Vases	
4¼″, spill, portrait decor, pair ...	145.00
12″, with figures of goat, and tree trunks	225.00
12″, portrait of girl, flaring top ...	180.00
13″, blue with floral decor, griffon handles, pair	220.00
DuBarry Rose color, handpainted scene, molded leaves, pair	185.00
17″, hand painted decor, gold at neck and base	240.00

OLD SLEEPY EYE

In the early 1900's, Sleepy Eye, Minnesota was the milling center of the world for production of flour in barrels. The town was named for Chief Sleepy Eye, a Sioux Indian. The pottery, which is decorated with a likeness of Chief Sleepy Eye, was made by Monmouth Pottery and Western Stoneware for inclusion as premiums in bags of Sleepy Eye flour. Although the pottery is the most collectible, other articles associated with the town and mill are also attracting Old Sleepy Eye collectors.

Butter Jar, blue on gray	380.00
Centennial Items, c. 1972	
Calendar	10.00
Newspaper, Sleepy Eye Herald Dispatch, 114 pages	15.00
Trivet	25.00
Cookbook	100.00
Pitchers	
4″, cobalt on cream, Indian on handle	130.00
5½″, cobalt on cream, Indian	

Mug, Indian head on handle, one side with Indian, other side Indian village, 7½″ $325.00

head handle	160.00
6¼″, cobalt on cream, Indian head handle	180.00
8½″, cobalt on white, Indian head handle	185.00
Postcard	50.00
Salt Bowl, 6½″ dia., blue on gray, marked "Old Sleepy Eye."	327.00
Stein, Indian head on handle, signed "Old Sleepy Eye"	450.00
Vases	
8½″, cobalt on cream, cattails and dragonflies	150.00
9″, cobalt on gray	220.00

ONION MEISSEN

Blue Onion or Bulb pattern is of Chinese origin and depicts peaches and pomegranates and not onions. It was originally made in the 18th century by the German Meissen factory, thus the name Onion Meissen.

This popular pattern was made by several other factories in other countries including England and Japan and is still in production today. Onion Meissen is marked with the familiar Crossed Swords. Other makers marked their wares accordingly, and those made after 1891 with the country of origin.

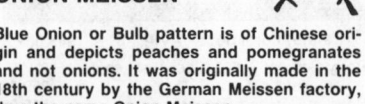

**Plate, soup, Meissen, star mark, scal-
loped edge, late, 9¾″** $45.00

Bowls
7″	35.00
9½″	65.00
11″	65.00

Bread board 35.00
Butter, covered, rose finial 125.00
Cheese Dish, covered 130.00
Coffee Pot, 9″, rose finial 150.00
Compote, 8¼ x 9″ high 185.00
Cream and Sugar, Set 125.00
Creamers
3½″	35.00
5½″	48.50

Cruets, Oil and Vinegar, pair 100.00
Cups and Saucers
Bouillon	35.00
Coffee	30.00
Demitasse	30.00
Tea	25.00

Egg Cup 25.00
Fruit Knives, set of 6 .... 85.00
Grater, vegetable, 5 x 9″ 35.00
Gravy Boat, 10″, with underplate .. 85.00
Invalid feeder 27.50
Knife Rest 30.00
Match Holder 35.00
Meat Tenderizer, wooden handle .. 32.50
Melon Mold, handled 30.00
Mustard, 4¾″ high, with ladle and
 underplate, set 50.00
Pie Crust crimper, wooden handle .. 22.50
Plates
6″	25.00
9″	45.00
9″ leaf-shaped	75.00
10″, soup	50.00
12″	60.00
14″	85.00
14″, with hot water jacket	125.00

Platters
11″	85.00
15″	100.00
21″	175.00

Pot de Creme 45.00
Rolling Pin 50.00
Salt Box, covered 75.00
Sauce, 5½″ dia. 20.00
Scoop, 9″ long 35.00
Sugar, covered 65.00
Teapot, 5¼″ high 85.00
Tea Strainer, wooden handle 20.00
Tureen, Soup, 10½ x 14″, rose finial 350.00
Vase, 5½″, spill-type, scroll feet ... 60.00
Vegetable dishes, covered
8½″ dia.	85.00
10″ square	125.00
14″ dia., divided	225.00

ONYX GLASS

This rare glassware was produced in 1889 in Findlay, Ohio by the Dalzell, Gilmore and Leighton Co. and is often called "Findlay Onyx." Onyx ware is plated or cased and may consist of two or three layers of glass. The interior layer is generally an opaque white. Each of the succeeding layers are of similar color and in the end it may contain a variation of colors.

There are five basic colors of onyx; however, no two pieces have exactly the same coloring due to varied temperatures in the manufacture. Consequently, shades of Findlay onyx are often described as cream, rose, cranberry, raspberry and cinnamon. Onyx was made for only a short time because of high production costs. It is a fragile, delicate glass.

**Salt and Pepper Shakers, cream
ground, 3″** $500.00

Bowl, 8″, cream 400.00
Butter, covered, raspberry 725.00
Celery, 6½″, cream 400.00
Creamer, cream 450.00
Salt, shaker, amber 110.00

Spooner, raspberry	375.00
Sugar, covered, cream	450.00
Syrup Jug, 7″, original lid, cream	550.00
Toothpicks, cream	225.00
Tumblers	
Barrel shape, cream	225.00
Raspberry	210.00

OPALESCENT GLASS

Opalescent glass is a clear or colored glass with milky white decorations. When held to the light, the whitened portions show a fiery or opalescent quality; thus the name. The glass falls into two basic categories: blown or mold blown such as Coin Spot and Spanish Lace, and pressed pattern glass such as Hobnail. On blown items, the pattern is made in white. On pressed glass pieces, the opalescent effect is found on the embossed and rim edges.

Novelties, Corn Vase, Pump and Trough, and Cabbage Leaf made of opalescent glass are listed as a separate category but are pressed glass. Their main distinction is that they were only made in one unique form and never a complete table set as in other pressed patterns.

Opalescent glass was produced in England in the 1870's. It gained wide popularity in America at the turn of the 20th century. It was made by several glass companies, including the early Boston and Sandwich Glass Company. Opalescent glass is currently being produced but very few of the items should be called reproductions, because many of the 'new' patterns were not originally produced in opalescent.

Also see OPALESCENT PATTERN GLASS SECTION, for additional pressed glass patterns.

BLOWN

Bowls
Spanish Lace, 9½″, blue	85.00
Seaweed, 9″, white	50.00

Butters, covered
Seaweed, cranberry	250.00
Spanish Lace, blue	250.00

Celerys
Lattice, cranberry	85.00
Seaweed, blue	95.00
Swirl, cranberry	95.00

Cruets
Daisy & Fern, blue	85.00
Ribbed Opal Lattice, cranberry	150.00
Finger Bowl, Spanish Lace, blue	35.00

Pitchers, Syrup
Lattice, white	70.00
Reverse Swirl, yellow	125.00

Blown, Miniature Lamp, Spanish Lace, 4″, blue $210.00

Spanish Lace, blue	75.00
Stripe, blue	75.00
Pitchers, water	
Reverse Swirl, yellow	175.00
Seaweed, blue	275.00
Spanish Lace, ruffled rim, blue	250.00
Spanish Lace, white	125.00
Swirl, Bulbous, ruffled top, cranberry	130.00
Swirl, square top, blue	125.00
Rose Bowls	
Daisy and Fern, blue	40.00
Seaweed, yellow	50.00
Spanish Lace, yellow	60.00
Salt Shaker, Seaweed, cranberry	35.00
Sugar Shakers	
Ribbed Opal Lattice, blue	75.00
Lattice, blue	65.00
Toothpick, lattice, white	35.00
Tumblers	
Poinsettia, blue	35.00
Reverse Swirl, cranberry	50.00
Spanish Lace, cranberry	35.00
S-Repeat, blue	45.00
Stripe, blue	28.00
Windows, plain, blue	32.50

NOVELTIES

Cabbage Leaf, blue	75.00

Corn, 8", blue 100.00
"Pump and Trough," pump, 7" high, trough, 5" long, blue, pair 165.00

PRESSED

Berry Sets
Northwood's Block, blue, 7 pieces 350.00
Regal, green, 7 pieces 225.00
Wreath and Shell, white, 4 pieces 100.00
Bowls
Cabbage, Winter, green, 3 twig-feet 75.00
Ruffles and Rings 75.00
Shell and Wild Rose, 7½", footed, green 28.50
Many Loops, blue, 6¼" 35.00
Butters, covered
Circled Scroll, blue, (rare) 200.00
Regal, vaseline 125.00
Wreath & Shell, vaseline 151.00
Celeries
Thousand Eye, white 75.00
Wreath and Shell, green 95.00
Compotes, Jelly
Circled Scroll, blue, (rare) 85.00
Maple Leaf (Northwood's) blue .. 60.00
Panelled Holly, with gold 75.00
Scroll with acanthus, green 58.00
Creamers & Sugars
Circled Scroll, blue 165.00
Diamond Spearpoint, blue 175.00
Double Greek Key, yellow 150.00
Duchess, blue 160.00
Fan, white 150.00
Cuspidor, Wreath and Shell, blue .. 95.00

Pitchers, Water
Panelled Holly, no gold 350.00
Scroll with acanthus 325.00
Rose Bowl, beaded fan, blue 50.00
Salt and Pepper Shakers
Circled Scroll, pair 65.00
Flora, (rare) 75.00
Sauces
Circled Scroll, blue 40.00
Daisy & Greek Key, blue 27.50
Trailing Vine, white, (rare) 48.50

Spooners
Gonterman Swirl, clear opal, amber top 80.00
Idyll, blue 75.00
Regal, green 50.00
Toothpicks
Bubble Lattice, (rare) 75.00
Seaweed, cranberry, (rare) 125.00

Tumblers
Idyll, white 40.00
Lustre Flute, blue 40.00
Drape (Fenton's) 30.00
Twist, blue 40.00

Rose Bowl, footed, Pearl and Scale, green, 4¾" dia. $50.00

OPALINE GLASS

Opaline or Opal glass was a popular mid-to-late 19th century European glass. The glass has a certain amount of translucency. The finished wares were often decorated with painted enamels and trimmed in gold.

Box, hinged, French, pale green, gold enamel, 4 x 2½" $125.00

Basket, small, with deep blue and gold trim 135.00
Bottles
Perfume, 5" high, jade green, enamel decor 85.00
Perfume, 5½", gold trim around

neck, pair	150.00

Bottles, Perfume

5", white, gold trim	55.00
7", blue, gold trim, in Art Nouveau-style metal holder	75.00

Bowls

8 x 2" deep, rose coloring	35.00
6" dia., low	80.00
Finger, light blue	65.00
10 x 1½" deep, flared, pink, gold trim	75.00
Cheese dish, white with enamel decor in gold	175.00
Cruet, applied handle, aqua, gold trim	85.00
Cup and Saucer, green	69.50
Finger Bowl, with underplate, blue ..	50.00

Goblets

5", white	25.00
7", blue	35.00
Lamp Base, 12", white, French	100.00
Mug, white, enameled florals, gold trim	40.00
Pitcher, 7", high, French, ground pontil, soft pink ground, signed by "Anne"	200.00
Toothpick Holder, lavender color, on small ball feet	65.00

Vases

5½", globular body, slender neck, pink, yellow flowers, green leaves	95.00
6", plain, no decor	85.00
6¾", French, mauve with gold trim, pair	150.00
10", bud vase, pink with gold enamel decor	100.00
6", globular body, slender neck, pink, yellow flowers, green leaves, butterflies	95.00
6¾", mauve, gold rims, French, pair	150.00
8", Jack-in-the-Pulpit, white	150.00
9½", bulbous, handpainted peacock, flowers, beaded pedestaled base, gold trim	165.00
11", footed, white, pale green turned down rim	150.00
16", blue, quilted	175.00

ORIENTAL RUGS

The history of these rugs or carpets dates 3000 B.C. but it was in the 16th century that they became prevalent. Commonly referred to as "Orientals" because of their origin from regions east of Europe comprised of central Asia, Iran (Persia), Caucasus and Anatolia, these rugs can be classified into basic categories of Iranian, Caucasian, Turkoman, Turkish and Chinese. Later, India, Pakistan and Iraq produced similar rugs after the fashion of the Persians, Chinese and Turks.

The pattern name is derived from the tribes or people of these regions who produced the rugs, e.g., from Iran we have the designs of Hamadan, Herez, Sarouk, Tabriz and others.

When evaluating an oriental carpet, age, design, color, weave and knots per square inch are very important. These factors plus the condition of the carpet determine the final value. Silk rugs and prayer rugs commonly command higher prices.

Examine rugs carefully; there are repainted rugs on the market.

Persian, Senna, late 19th C., 46 x 55" $850.00

The Prices Given are Approximate and Calculated on a Per Square Foot Basis.

Afghan	30.00
Baktiari	30.00
Baluchistan	30.00
Bergamo	50.00
Bijar	50.00
Bokhara	40.00
Cabistan	50.00
Dagestan	75.00
Ersari......................	40.00
Fereghan	60.00
Ghiordes, Prayer, Turkish	100.00
Hamadan	50.00
Herez	40.00
Ispahan	125.00
Kashan, silk	250.00
Kashan, wool	100.00
Kasvin	60.00
Kazak, Caucasian	125.00
Kerman	50.00

Kilim, Caucasian	40.00
Kilim, Turkish	30.00
Kuba, Caucasian	80.00
Peking	60.00
Salor	50.00
Saraband	60.00
Sarouk	75.00
Senna	
Shiraz	70.00
Shirvan, Caucasian	70.00
Tabriz, silk	
Tabriz, wool	
Animaliers	150.00
Geometric	80.00
Tekke	50.00
Tientsin	60.00

ORIENTALIA

Orientalia is a term used to apply to objects made in the orient which encompasses the Far East, Asia, China, and Japan. The diversity of cultures produced a variety of objects and styles.

This category deals with objects which do not have individual categories in our guide. See also Canton, Celadon, Cloisonne, Fitzhugh, Nanking, Netsukes, Rose Medallion, and other categories for specific oriental objects.

Armchair, carved, rosewood .$550.00

Bottle, 6", Bizen ware, Japanese, deep brown, 19th C.	250.00
Bowls	
Arita, Japanese, blue and white, landscape, 10"	90.00
Korean, Yi Dynasty, greenish blue, tinted white glaze, 5½"	190.00
Ming Dynasty, Chinese, glazed in pale blue-white tint, 7", 16th C.	650.00
Carpet, Chinese, 144 x 108", blue field with central pagoda, gold outer border	1300.00
Costume, Chinese	
Coat, gold quilted silk, trimmed with key fret pattern, early 19th C.	300.00
Dragon robe, black satin, 8 medallions of peonies, gold border	800.00
Dragon robe, five clawed dragon, 20th C.	275.00
Skirt, black and red silk, floral motif panels	230.00
Creamer, Chinese export, helmut shape, 4"	175.00
Cup and Saucer, handless, Chinese export, horn of plenty, wide pink border	125.00
Desk Set, brass, engraved, 3 pieces —tray, letter opener, blotter, lined wooden box, 3½"	110.00
Figurines	
Buddaha, Gautma, brass, Indian, lion's throne, circular halo	80.00
Sage, Chinese Export, porcelain, holding child, enameled, 24"	200.00
Suryea, bronze, Nepalese, arms entwined in lotus blossom	100.00
Furniture	
Cabinet, Chinese, black lacquer doors, inlaid in ivory, gild painted, children at play, 39"	1100.00
Chair, arm, Japanese, pierced carving, cabriole legs, late 19th C.	600.00
Chair, side, Chinese, back of swirling dragons, 39"	850.00
Chest (Tarsu), carved red cinnabar lacquer, inlaid in Shibayama, 64 x 40"	3000.00
Chest on Chest, Korean, each chest with two doors and brass mounts, 71 x 29"	250.00
Mirror, Chinese, inlayed with shell, 39" wide	325.00
Screen, Japanese, four fold, falcon motif, 65 x 25", 19th C.	1500.00
Stand, Chinese, inlayed marble top, frieze pierced with pomegranate sprays, 23"	340.00
Table, Chinese, lacquer, gold and black landscape scenes, square legs, 44"	525.00
Table, Thai, top of elephant motif, cabriole legs, 16 x 66"	475.00

Ginger Jars
  Chinese Export, white, pair, decorated with ladies, gentlemen, and horses, 5″ 200.00
  Famille Jaune, insects and flower motif, 9″ 300.00
Fans
  Chinese, ivory brise carved with dragons, bats, etc., 11½″, c. 1850 . . . . 160.00
  Japanese, lacquered, floral motif, c. 1880 . . . . 500.00
Incense Burner, brass, Chinese, square tapering form, pierced cover of Buddhistic lion 90.00
Kimono, ivory ground, dragon 150.00
Lamps
  Bronze, Japanese, pair, relief of birds in flight, ovoid, 19th C. 375.00
  Famille Jaune, porcelain, reticulated, 13¼″ 1250.00
Mug, Chinese export, cylindrical shape, woman and children in garden, Famille rose colors, 5″ 400.00
Printing Set, Chinese, 100 pieces, handcarved wood 200.00
Rice Mold, Chinese, wood, 13½ x 2 x 1½″ 75.00
Rice Pot, covered, Chinese, geometric motif, jade finial, c. 17th C., 4½ x 6 x 6″ 250.00
Tea Caddy, Japanese, pottery, red ground with silver overlay of dragon and phoenix 80.00
Teapots
  Banko, Japanese, grayware, Mt. Fuji with snow capped peak, c. 1890 . . . . 135.00
  Bizen ware, Japanese, tortoise form lid, 19th C. 300.00
  Copper, Tibetan, dragon spout and handle, 19th C., 10¾″ 340.00
  Nineteenth Century, Chinese, cadogan, yellow and green glaze, rustic motif, 5″ 100.00
  Tokoname, Japanese, reed handle, landscape scene 150.00
Tureen, Chinese export, figural in shape of pig, two panels of archers, late 19th C. 700.00
Vases
  Clair de Lune, Chinese, rectangular body, 8 relief panels, 11″ 19th C. 675.00
  Coralene, Japanese, scenic houses and trees, 9″, 1909 . . . . 280.00
  Flambe, Chinese, balaster form, deep crimson glaze, 15″ 600.00
  Lapis Lazuli, covered, baluster form, elephant handles, 8″ 550.00
  Mirror Black, Chinese, rouleau shape, gilt of floral and scroll design, 17″, 19th C. 500.00

Wedding box, Chinese, polychrome leather, original hardware, floral and bird motif, 11 x 15½ x 25″ . . 250.00

OWENS POTTERY

J. B. Owens began making pottery in 1885 near Roseville, Ohio. In 1891 he built a plant in Zanesville and in 1897 began producing art pottery. It is not likely that much art pottery was produced at Owens after 1907, most of their production being centered on the output of tiles.

Owens pottery, employing many of the same artists and designs of its two crosstown rivals, Roseville and Weller, can appear very similar to that of its competitors (i.e., Utopian—brown glaze; Lotus—light glaze; aqua verde—green glaze, etc.).

There were a few techniques used exclusively at Owens, however, and these included red flame ware (slip decoration under a high, red glass); Mission (over-glaze, slip decorations in mineral colors) depicting Spanish Mission scenes. Obese pieces often came with wooden stands; Opalesce (semi-gloss designs in lustred gold and orange); Coralene (small beads affixed to the surface of decorated vases).

Vase, Aborigine, 6″ $200.00

Candlestick, 7″, Utopian, berry and leaf decor 80.00
Mug, 5″, Utopian, berry and leaf de-

| cor . . . . | 55.00 |
| Pitcher, 6″, red flame ware, clover blossoms, 3 footed . . . . | 350.00 |

Vases

6″, Aborigine, Indian decor on brown ground, signed, JBO	85.00
6″, bisque glazed slip decorated floral on blue to brown blended bisque ground, matte line, artist signed	100.00
7″, aqua verde, embossed floral decor	50.00
7″, Utopian, vintage decor, artist signed, 3 handles	125.00
8″, Lotus, slip decorated florals on grey ground, clear hi-glaze	125.00
9″, Art Nouveau, incised design of woman's head on brown, bisque ground, Henri Deux	200.00
10″, Venetian	175.00
11″, coralene beads with slip decorated floral design	250.00
11″, Utopian, Indian portrait by A. F. Best, perfect but crazed	1750.00
12″, opalesce tulips on swirling gold ground	300.00

PADLOCKS

Padlock collecting has become one of the fastest growing hobbies in America. People are collecting old locks not only for nostalgia and signs of the past, but are intrigued with the mechanisms from simple designs to ingenious and elaborate works of art.

Padlocks are made in numerous varieties. In a span of over 100 years, approximately 75 American manufacturers have been recorded. Some makers listed hundreds of types in production at one given time.

Brass Tumblers

A. E. Dietz, "252," 2¾″	12.00
Eagle, 3¼″	10.00
Mallory Wheeler & Co., 2½″	5.00
Winchester, 3″	25.00

Chinese (Sliding-type)

| Engraved, 3″ long, oriental or floral designs . . . . | 10.00 |
| Plain, 4″ long, brass . . . . | 7.50 |

Combinations

| W. A. Harrison, Inc., "Insurance Lock," 2½″, brass . . . . | 10.00 |

Miller

| 2″, four lettered brass cylinder dial, iron frame, changeable-type . . . . | 25.00 |
| 3″, Pat. Nov. 29, 1910, nickel-plated steel . . . . | 2.00 |

Gate

| Hand forged steel, various sizes | |

B & O Railroad, Key, Rt 1963 . . $25.00

and shapes, common variety	25.00
Hand wrought iron, various sizes and shapes, American, 18th C. . .	150.00
Kit Bag, 5″ long, brass	10.00

Levers (Push Key)

Eagle, "Favorite," 2½″, brass . . .	7.50
Miller, "Champion," 2″, 4-lever, brass	10.00
Yale, 2⅞″, steel	5.00

Levers (Six and Eight)

Six

Edwards, Pat. mark, steel	5.00
Sargent, steel	3.50
Winchester, steel, early 1900's .	20.00

Eight

| Armory, steel, early 1900's . . . . | 6.00 |
| Corbin, Samson, brass . . . . | 8.50 |

Eagle, Mammoth

| Brass . . . . | 10.00 |
| Steel . . . . | 6.50 |

Levers (Wrought Iron)

Davenport, Mallory & Co., 3¼″, Barrel key-type	6.50
Mallory Wheeler & Co., 3½″, flat double key-type	8.50
Sargent & Co. 3½″, flat-key-type .	6.50
United States, 3½″, barrel key-type	7.50

Pin Tumblers

Sargent, 3″, brass	6.50
Segal, 4″, brass, rotating bolt-type	12.50
Yale, "USN," 2″, brass, push key-type	8.00
Zeiss Ikon, 3″, brass	6.50

Railroad

| Adlake, "Union Pacific," 3½″, brass, switch-type . . . . | 15.00 |

Dayton Mfg. Co. "A & V," 3½", brass, shank key-type	20.00
Shank key-type	20.00
Yale	
"PRR," 3", brass, signal	12.50
"Santa Fe," 3", steel	6.50
Scandinavian (Barrel, Jail or Store)	
J.H.W. Climax Co., 2½", iron	6.00
Fraim, 2¼", iron	8.50
Russel & Erwin Co., "USA," 2½", iron	8.50

PAIRPOINT

In 1880, Pairpoint Manufacturing Co. was organized as a silverplating firm in New Bedford, Mass. The company merged with Mt. Washington Glass Co. in 1894 and became known as Pairpoint Corporation. The new company produced specialty glass items, often accented with metal frames. Pairpoint Corp. was sold in 1938 and Robert Gunderson became manager; it operated until his death in 1952 as Gunderson Glass Works. Robert Bryden became manager of Pairpoint-Gunderson Glass Works until its closing in 1957. In 1970, Bryden reopened the factory of Cape Cod under the famous Pairpoint name. In 1978, Pairpoint Glass Company returned to its New Bedford birthplace.

Hat, deep red and white with controlled bubbles, original paper label, 4¼" $60.00

Baby's Cup, engraved	25.00
Bell, Table, 5½", cut crystal	35.00
Biscuit Jars	
Green, etched vintage decor, silverplated frame	225.00
Yellow, floral decor, reticulated silverplated frame	250.00
Bowls	
11 x 3½", leaf shape, full bodied squirrel, silverplated, gold wash interior	175.00
Blurina bowl, signed	60.00
Boxes	
6" dia., beige ribbed opal glass with enamel decor, footed silver body	175.00
6½", hinged cover, blue, purple violets, signed in diamond	275.00
4½ x 3½", footed, painted porcelain, insert on cover, silk lining, marked "Pairpoint Mfg. Co."	250.00
Butter, covered, with knife rest, silverplated	150.00
Candlesticks	
5½", clear paperweight base	95.00
11½", amber, crystal bubble-ball stems, bell-shaped bases, pair	175.00
Champagne, 5½", "Flambo," crystal	50.00
Compotes	
6 x 6" high, crystal, etched leaf and floral decor on underside	85.00
7" high, amber, bubble-ball stem	125.00
7 x 8½" dia., "Wexford."	135.00
Console Sets	
Bowl, 9½", lamps 16¾" high, with coralene shades, c. 1900-20, signed	500.00
Bowl, 14", candlesticks 12", light green with bubble-ball stems, cut & etched vintage decor	350.00
Creamer and Sugar, Silvered pattern on green with white tops, Gothic shape, set	75.00
Figurine, Peachblow Hat, with enameled sprig of flowers	125.00
Inkwell, 2¾" dia., crystal, paperweight-type, hinged lid	35.00
Ladle, Punch, 14", silver with cut glass handle	350.00
Lamps	
7", blownout flowers on shade, tree trunk base	895.00
14", blownout roses on shade, tree trunk base	2500.00
Napkin Ring, figural & leaves, domed base	48.00
Plateau Mirror, baroque silverplated base, beveled mirror	125.00
Shaving Mug, silverplated, engraved florals, lift-out soap insert	85.00
Sherbet, with underplate, "Flambo"	125.00
Swan, opalescent and pink, paper label	125.00
Tray, 7¾ x 5", painted porcelain insert	350.00
Vases	
3½", Delft Mini, melon-ribbed, white glossy ground, windmill	

scene on one side, sailboat on reverse, signed **175.00**
8", goblet-shape, cobalt, crystal bubble-ball stem **75.00**
85 ", bud, iridescent amber, silver holder, signed "P," c. 1895 .... **275.00**
10", trumpet-shape, deep blue, bubble base **95.00**

Wine

Red bowl, black glass base **75.00**
12", trumpet-shape, crystal bubble-ball stem **150.00**

PAISLEY SHAWLS
See TEXTILES

PAPERWEIGHTS

Although paperweights had their origin in ancient Egypt, it was in the mid 19th century that· this art form reached its zenith. The classic period for paperweights was 1845–55 in France where the Clichy, Baccarat and Saint Louis factories produced the finest examples of this art. Other weights, made in England, Italy and Bohemia during this period and later in America, rarely match the quality of the French weights. Popularity peaked during this classic period and faded toward the end of the 19th century.

Paperweights were rediscovered nearly a century later in the mid 1900's. Contemporary weights are still made by Baccarat, Saint Louis, Perthshire and by many studio craftsmen in the U.S. and Europe.

Some collectors prefer to limit their collections to antique weights while others collect both contemporary and earlier editions; fine examples are available in both areas. Today, interest in paperweights is greater than ever and values have increased accordingly.

Baccarat
Fruit, 2 cherries, 1 pear **600.00**
Millefiori, patterned **550.00**
Primrose, star cut base **950.00**
Wallflower, blue and white **1250.00**

Baccarat, Modern
American Beauty, star cut base .. **475.00**
L'Escargot **490.00**
Millefiori, patterned **275.00**
Millefiori, circular garlands **200.00**
Monkey Gridel, white **180.00**
Seahorse **310.00**

Baccarat, Modern, Sulfides
Bonaparte, Napoleon, overlay ... **225.00**
Kennedy, John F., white overlay .. **500.00**
Paine, Thomas **75.00**
Rogers, Will **100.00**
Wilson, Woodrow, clear and tur-

Baccarat, Zodiac-Leo pattern, cobalt blue ground, signed $125.00

quoise base **100.00**
Banford
Cabbage Rose **250.00**
Pansy **350.00**
Pears on leafy branch **300.00**
Boston and Sandwich
Clematis, double, blue petals **475.00**
End of Day **200.00**
Wheatflower **685.00**
Clichy
Cameo, portrait of a Gentleman .. **850.00**
Millefiori, stylized bouquet **475.00**
Millefiori, trefoil garlands **450.00**
Millefiori, interlacing trefoil garlands **1800.00**
Pansy in crystal **600.00**
Scrolls "C," concentric rings of florets **850.00**
D'Albret, Sulfides
Columbus, Christopher, regular .. **150.00**
Chief Sitting Bull, Terra Cotta ... **95.00**
Gustaf VI, H.M. **70.00**
Jones, John Paul, overlay **170.00**
Lindberg, Charles, overlay **180.00**
Schweitzer, Albert, regular **70.00**
Twain, Mark, regular **80.00**
Gillinder & Sons, Memorial Hall, camphor glass **350.00**
Kaziun
Morning Glory, opaque pink ground **850.00**
Rose, classic, yellow **850.00**
Perfume Bottle, floral design on blue and gold ground faceted, 3". **1300.00**
Lundberg
Butterfly **135.00**
Fish, opaque **75.00**
Orchid **150.00**

Peacock Feather, pulled	60.00
Underwater Seascape	150.00

Orient and Flume

Butterfly with Millefiori scarab and flower	75.00
Marbrie	75.00

Pairpoint

Controlled air bubbles	170.00
Swan, amethyst, original label . . .	195.00

Perthshire

Clematis, double	220.00
Christmas Bells	200.00
End of Day, scrambled	75.00
Fruit on latticinio ground	380.00
Millefiori, Formal Garden	140.00
Millefiori, Nosegay, 4 Forget-me-nots	180.00
Scottish Bluebell	230.00
Scottish Heather	195.00

St. Louis

Crown weight, 2 colorful twists radiating from central cane	1800.00
End of Day, hand cooler	400.00
Nosegay, 5 flowers, 6 green leaves	600.00
Pelargonium on white latticinio . .	2200.00

St. Louis, Modern

Amour	385.00
Cherries, Pears, Plums	390.00
Opaque and Latticinio Twists, hand cooler	200.00
Queen Elizabeth, 1953, sulfide . .	350.00
Washington, George, regular	325.00

Stankard

Flax Blossom	330.00
Sippewissett Bouquet	600.00
Spider Orchid	350.00
Wild Rose, single flower	385.00
Steuben, Luminaire, signed	300.00
Tarsitano, Pink Primrose	200.00
Trabucco, Yellow Bell Flower	100.00

Whitefriars

Millefiori, concentric, central floret	350.00
Owl	300.00
Snowflake	250.00
Whittemore, Calla Lillies	240.00

Ysart

Butterfly on flowering branch	750.00
Clematis, double	300.00
Fish, Tropical	350.00
Parrot on leafy branch	600.00

Miscellaneous

Advertising

Bryant Gas Heating, metal dog . .	45.00
Hartford Fire Insurance Co., 1810–1921, bronze	30.00
Mohawk Tires, frog, iron	50.00
Smith Bros. Coughdrops, in shape of coughdrop	15.00
Apple, applied leaves and stem, St. Claire	30.00
Bear, standing, snow type	18.50

Bell, 3", brass	15.00
Chinese, Millefiori, red, white, yellow	20.00
Crystal, clear, 1¾" cube, faceted . .	25.00
Donkey, brass	75.00
Fort Dearborn, 1933 World's Fair . .	20.00
Gemini Twins, 4"	35.00
Kingfisher, cast iron	25.00
Niagara Falls, mother-of-pearl in falls	10.00
Obelisk, multi-color, glass	35.00
Pear, iridescent yellow and red	85.00
Pig, sitting, cast iron	12.00
Pirate Pistol, 9½"	35.00
Plymouth Rock, 1876 with inscription	65.00
Snowman, snow type	17.00
Statue of Liberty	7.00
Submarine, brass	12.00
Telephone, 3½", cobalt, glass	40.00

PAPER MACHE

The literal translation of the French term "chewed paper," paper mache is a mixture of ground paper, glue, resin and fine sand which is subjected to great pressure, then dried. The finished product is tough, durable and heat resistant. Various finishing treatments were used — lacquers, japanning, painting, enameling, and inlaying with mother-of-pearl. Paper mache articles such as boxes, trays, and tables were in high fashion during the Victorian era.

Candy container, orange body,
5½" $70.00

Basket, 10" dia., brass handle, MOP inlay, signed Jemmens, c. 1860	125.00
Bell, 4"	12.00

Boxes

Applied silver decor on black lacquer, 1 x 2"	25.00
MOP inlay, 1 x 1½ x 3"	25.00
Snuff, silver inlay on hinged lid, 1 x 3 x 1¼"	25.00
Cat, bead eyes, and filled with sand	50.00
Chicken, life size	100.00
Crumb Tray and brush	20.00

Dogs

Bull, 25"	75.00
Bull, seated in harness, 6½"	25.00
With removable head	20.00
Easter Eggs, (candy container type), Germany	18.50
Easter Eggs, with red rabbits	20.00
Figurine, bird, glass eyes, 4"	27.00
Funnel, 11"	25.00
Horse, 20"	25.00
Lap Desk, pearl inlay, slant top	200.00
Mask, clown's head, original polychrome decor, 17"	110.00
Model of watermelon, hinged lid, painted, 15½"	400.00
Napkin Ring, tartan of clan McBeth around outside, marked	25.00
Owl, 16"	100.00

Plates

Oriental design, gold, red, black	45.00
Scene of family around table, man playing lute, Russian 19th century, 8½"	400.00
Tea Caddy, black with gold, MOP inlay	250.00

Trays

Shaped edge, hand painted, color floral red, gold green on black background, 32 x 25¼"	200.00
On stand, dished top, chinoiserie decor, warriors, Regency style base, 26½ x 18"	150.00
Chippendale decor, exotic bird, MOP inlay 24 x 31"	125.00
Round, MOP decor, gold wire rim border, 6½"	75.00
"Sweet Caporal," advertising type, Victorian lady decor, oval, 11 x 20"	120.00

PARIAN WARE

Both Minton and Copeland have been credited for developing Parian around 1842 in England. There is controversy about which of the two actually did invent this ware and it was subsequently made in both England and United States in the Victorian era. America's best production came from Bennington Pottery and Copeland, Charles Meigh, Minton, Wedgwood, Boote, Rose, T. Booth, William Adams and Samuel Alcock all made it in England.

Bust, John Bright (1811–1889), by Robinson Leadbetter, 6½" $80.00

Box, pin, 2¼", oval, floral on blue	30.00

Busts

Beethoven	65.00
Dickens	75.00
Disraeli	60.00
George Washington	125.00
Gladstone, 6"	60.00
Miranda, 6", Bell, c. 1872	60.00
Milton, Wedgwood, designed by Wyon	800.00
Mozart	65.00
Queen Victoria, Robinson and Leadbetter	350.00
Sir Robert Peel	80.00
Tennyson	60.00
Shakespeare, 8", T. and R. Boote, c. 1890	100.00

Creamers

Cow	45.00
Molded Iris in relief	38.00
Water Lily	50.00

Figurines

Apollo, 15", Bing and Grondhal	295.00
Cupid and Venus, 20", Charles Meigh and Sons	350.00
Flower vase, supported by Dolphin	200.00

Harvest maiden, with sickle, holding wheat sheaf, oval base	200.00
Little Red Riding Hood	300.00
Mercury, Wedgwood, designed by Wyon	800.00
Prometheus, 20″	200.00
Puck and Companions, John H. Rose and Co.	300.00
Two hunting dogs, flushing a quail, 8½″	115.00

Jugs

8″, molded panels, classical figures on green, gold trim, c. 1862, Brownfield	110.00
8″, water lily on lavendar, Charles Meigh and Son	140.00

Pitchers

4¼″, bulbous body, trefoil scalloped top, ivy leaves, berries decor, Minton	45.00
Columbian Exposition, figures of Columbus and his men, molded, marked Copeland	300.00
Cupid and Psyche	275.00
7½″, gypsy scenes in relief, twig handle	275.00
Love and War, knight and his lady, (rare)	300.00
Palm Tree, Bennington ribbon mark	375.00
8½″, water lily, white on blue	200.00
8½″, molded figures, with figural handle	225.00
Plate, 8″, pond lily	50.00
Platter, 13″, basketweave, wheat sheaf handles, GUTDODB, etc.	125.00
Sugar Shaker, figural owl	45.00
Syrup Jug, Rose design, raised, all white, pewter top	75.00
Tumbler, 4″, classical figures	35.00

Vases

5⅛″, molded hand holding ear of corn	150.00
5⅛″, molded hand holding a pineapple	150.00
6″, in shape of girl's head, on oval base	40.00
6″, applied grapes and leaves, acanthus leaves and medallions	50.00
7½″, floral and berries, on blue	35.00
10″, vintage pattern, bulbous shape	225.00

PATE DE VERRE

Pate de Verre can be translated simply as "Glass Paste." More precisely, it is a molded glass form. The process is to grind lead glass into a powder or crystal form. The ground glass is then made into a paste by adding a 2% or 3% solution of sodium silicate. The re-sulting mixture can be molded, fired and carved. This type of glass was known to the Egyptians as early as 1500 B. C.

In the late 19th and early 20th centuries, Pate de Verre was again revived by advanced glass makers in France. Cros, Dammouse and the Daum Brothers were active in leading this movement. Within the past ten years, contemporary artists have rediscovered Pate de Verre as a medium for sculpturing.

Clock, made for J. E. Caldwell & Co., by G. Argy Rousseau, France, orange and black, 4½″ square $2500.00

Atomizer, 4″, turquoise with brown pine cones, "A. Walter, Nancy"	650.00

Bowls

5⅝″, signed "A. Walter, Nancy"	375.00
3″, cream and yellow with orange sunflower, rayed interior, "A. Walter, Nancy"	350.00
5½″, octagonal, green and brown, "Decorchement"	650.00
Box, 3 x 3″, round, violet decor, "G. Argy Rousseau"	1000.00

Figurines

3¼″, monkey reading book, green, "A. Walter, Nancy"	795.00
3¾″, monkey sitting on stump, light amber to green, second signature of A. Mercie	500.00
Inkwell, 1½″, bee cover, yellow to russet, twig and berry trim, signed, "A. Walter"	650.00

Lamps

4½″, flowers, leaves and berries, orange, lavender, gold and white, bronze base, "A. Walter, Nancy"	750.00
9″, figural motif, 3 panels, tree trunks, figures, yellow, red,	

browns, all original, "G. Argy
Rousseau" 1450.00
11", Nude in white, red back-
ground, Art Deco, silvered metal
base, "A. Walter, Nancy" 1250.00
Leaf Dishes
2 x 5½", blue and green, "A. Wal-
ter, Nancy" 500.00
3 x 11", iguana on leaf, yellow, orange and green berries, "A. Wal-
ter, Nancy" 1100.00
Pen and Ink holder, 12", yellow
and orange insert on leaf decor,
flowers, "A. Walter" 225.00
Pendants
2", brown and black beetle on
grey background, "Walter" 225.00
2¼", pine cone decor in green,
browns, "G. Argy Rousseau" . . . 200.00
Plaque, 4¾ x 10¾", Madonna and
Child surrounded with roses in re-
lief 1000.00

PATE-SUR-PATE

Pate-sur-pate (paste on paste), an outstanding 19th century porcelain, has become
unmistakenly synonymous with Marc Louis
Solon. About 1863, Solon and other artists
employed at the Sevres manufactury in
France experimented with this process of
porcelain decoration, inspired by a Chinese
Celadon vase in the Ceramic Museum at
Sevres.

Just prior to the outbreak of the Franco-
Prussian War in 1870, Solon suffered a se-
vere illness and ultimately was unable to aid
in the defense of his country. He migrated to
England, worked at the Minton factory at
Stoke-on-Trent, and during this time he made
most of his masterpieces in this ware.

This type of ware features designs in relief
which are obtained by successive layers of
the thin pottery paste, painted one on top of
the other.

Lamp Base, 2½", semi translucent
floral design on tinted grey green
background 575.00
Plaques
4¼ x 7", Limoges, draped figure
on blue, signed Crolerot, pair . . . 350.00
5 x 7", Minton, draped figure of
Neptune on blue, framed 250.00
8 x 9", five reclining nudes with
swan, scalloped border with fo-
liage, blue-green 300.00
Plate, blue, figures in white, gold
borders, each panel different,
Signed Tiffany Co. 495.00
Vases

**Plaque, Wedgwood green, French, 4⅜
x 7½"** $295.00

4½", blue and white narcissus,
green leaves 65.00
4½", white floral with butterflies
on brown background, signed
Geo. Jones and Son 250.00
5", celadon green with panel of
children playing, silver deposit flo-
ral, design 350.00
6", emerald green with fernery, on
gold ball feet 375.00
7", sea green with mauve medal-
lion, dancing lady, 14k gold 350.00
7", Minton, blue and white medal-
lions, floral, artist signed 275.00
7", white narcissus on pale green
background 95.00
8¼", blue with lavender back-
ground, nude maiden holding
large shell filled with four cherubs 650.00
8½", Limoges, blue and white de-
cor signed Tovy, pair 500.00
9½", blue and white, figures 180.00
11½", blue and white decor, gold
band around top and base 700.00
Pilgrim shaped, Brown and white
decor marked "Schenk" 285.00

PATENT MODELS

Patent Models are one of the most important
documentations of the creative genius and
inventiveness of the American people. The
Patent Act of 1836 required every patentee
to furnish a model of his invention. Two
disasterous fires, the last in 1877, destroyed
the early models and over 70,000 models
from the 1840 to 1877 period. Many models
did survive; and, inventors kept submitting
models through the early 1900's.

Many of the models were built by professional model builders, thus often making
them aesthetic statements in themselves. In
1926 the patent models were sold and still

remain in private hands. A series of public sales in the 1970's and catalogue sales since 1980 have made these models available to collectors.

Models can be collected by subject, geographic area, aesthetic characteristics, and inventor. Each model can be researched by obtaining a copy of the patent application. A high percentage of the categories in WARMAN'S have a corresponding patent model available in the current market.

Patent models range in size from a few inches to slightly over a foot. The listing pattern is name of patent, number, date, patentee, location of patentee, and construction materials.

Reclining Dentist Chair, No. 270724, Jan. 16, 1883, M. O. Baldwin . $1420.00

Barrel Bung, #70024, 10/22/1867, J. Ruegg, St. Louis, MO, iron . . .	110.00
Fireplace, #31785, 3/26/1861, B. F. Cowan, Memphis, TN, brass and tin	160.00
Flour Sifter, #47056, 3/28/1865, Howard Tilden, Philadelphia, PA, wood, mesh, and rubber	95.00
Fly Trap, #118852, 9/12/1871, Louis Grim, Ft. Branch, IN, tin . . .	45.00
Horse Nail Machine, #202824, 4/23/1878, J. T. Hough, Pittsburgh, PA, wood	200.00
Ink Stand, #45498, 12/20/1864, Philip Holbrook, Malden, MA,	

wood	130.00
Letter Boxes, #197849, 12/4/1877, Robert Hale, Minneapolis, MN, tin	135.00
Manufacture of Weldless Chains, #224659, 2/17/1880, Augustin O. David, Paris, France, iron	115.00
Pill Machine, #14904, 5/20/1856, H. E. Chapman, Albany, NY, wood, brass, iron, and tin	540.00
Pincer for Applying Fence Barbs, #199965, 2/5/1878, John Edwards, Oswego, IL, iron	500.00
Rotary Plows, #158482, 1/5/1875, William H. Foye, San Francisco, CA, steel	270.00
Sewing Machine, #72574, 12/24/1867, Wm. Weitling, New York, NY, iron	800.00
Speaking Tube, #140539, 7/1/1873, Andrew Rankin, Philadelphia, brass and iron	500.00
Steering Apparatus for Canalboat, #32296, 5/14/1861, Jefferson, John, and James McCausland, Rondout, NY, wood and brass . .	240.00
Sugar Boiling Apparatus, #92932, 7/27/1869, Bonnin & Escudler, Iberia, LA, wood and tin	250.00
Telephone Exchange Apparatus, #235056, 11/30/1880, James See, Hamilton, OH, wood, brass, and wire	400.00
Washing Machine, #43508, 7/12/1864, H. P. Jones, Davenport, IA, wood, brass, and tin	190.00
Watchman's Register, #169378, 11/2/1875, David Shive, Philadelphia, PA, wood and brass	150.00
Water Closet, #199233, 1/15/1878, John H. Stevens, Cambridge, MA, wood and iron	180.00

S.E.G.

PAUL REVERE POTTERY

Paul Revere Pottery, Boston, Mass., was an outgrowth of a club known as "The Saturday Evening Girls." The S.E.G. was a group of young female immigrants who met on Satur-

day night for reading and crafts such as ceramics.

Regular production began in 1908; and the name Paul Revere was adopted because the pottery was located near the Old North Church. The firm moved to Brighton, Mass., in 1915. Known also as the "Bowl Shop," the pottery grew steadily. In spite of popular acceptance and technical advancements the pottery required continual subsidies. It finally closed in January, 1942.

Items produced ranged from plain and decorated vases to tablewares to illustrated tiles. Some decorated ware was incised and glazed in Art Nouveau matte shades and occasionally a high glass glaze.

Paper "Bowl Shop" labels were used prior to 1915 in addition to the impressed mark. Pieces can also be found dated and P.R.P. or S.E.G. painted on the base.

Teapot, artist signed — S.E.G. . .$65.00

Bowl, 4½x 2¼″ deep, deep pink band with grapes in relief on light pink	100.00
Butter, Covered, hen and chick decor, twig handles, S.E.G., c. 1918	250.00
Candlesticks, 8″, glossy dark blue glaze, S.E.G., pair	85.00
Charger, 12″ dia., 7 colors, incised scene of 2 Galleons, S.E.G., c. 1912	800.00
Creamer, 3¼″, chick decor on cream, S.E.G.	75.00
Desk Set, floral decor on pink, S.E.G., 4 pieces	225.00
Paperweights	
5″ dia., 6 colors, Paul Revere on horseback	150.00
Octagonal, scenic décor, S.E.G., 1916	100.00
Plates	
6″, buff "O Don't Bother Me . . . ," S.E.G.	85.00
8″, tree decor, blue, green, white, black	100.00
9″, stylized water lily on green ground, S.E.G.	100.00

Tile, 4¼″ dia., scenic woodland decor on yellow ground	65.00
Vases	
5″, incised scenic on blue ground	250.00
11″, incised blue iris on green ground	450.00
11″, incised 5 color scenic, overall, S.E.G.	500.00

PEACH BLOW

Peach Blow is an art glass which derived its name from a fine Chinese glazed porcelain — described as the color of crushed strawberries or resembling the color of the peach.

Three American glass manufacturers and two English firms produced Peach Blow Glass in the late 1880's. Each firm's final product possessed its own characteristics. The following list will be helpful in identifying the makers.

Gunderson Glass Co. About 1950 they began producing "Peach Blow" type art glass to order. Their wares shade from an opaque faint tint of pink, which is almost white, to a deep rose.

Mt. Washington Peach Blow. Trade name for New Bedford Works. A homogeneous glass that shades from a pale gray blue to a soft rose color. Many decorative items were further enhanced with glass appliques, enameled and gilded.

New England Peach Blow, New England Glass Works. The advertised name of their art glass was "Wild Rose," but the factory name was "Peach Blow." The glass is translucent, shading from rose to white acid finished or left in the original glossy state. Some of the wares were also enameled and gilded.

Thomas Webb & Son, Stevens and Williams, England. Around 1888, these two English glass makers were both making a similar art glass which they termed "Peach Blow" or "Peach Bloom." It is a cased glass shading from yellow to red. Both firms occasionally employed cameo-type designs in relief on the basic objects.

Wheeling Peach Blow, Hobbs Brockunier & Co. An opalescent glass that was plated or cased with a transparent amber glass and shades from yellow at the base to a deep red at the top. The finish can be either glossy or satin.

In the price listings below, all pieces are satin finish unless noted to be glossy finish.

GUNDERSON

Cologne Bottle	175.00
Cup & Saucer	225.00

Vase, Wheeling, acid finish, 7¾" **$925.00**

Goblet	225.00
Tumbler	115.00
Vase, 5"	150.00

MT. WASHINGTON

Bowl, tricorner	1125.00
Cream & Sugar	3200.00
Vase, 4½", bulbous, applied rigaree around neck	2750.00

NEW ENGLAND

Bell, 6½"	495.00
Bowls	
4½ x 8¼", fluted edge, glossy finish	325.00
4⅜", finger, glossy finish	395.00
Creamer, 2½", ribbed	375.00
Darner, 5¼" long, glossy finish ...	225.00
Peak, 5", glossy finish	200.00
Pitcher, 7", bulbous, ribbed, applied handle	495.00
Punch Cup	175.00
Spooner, 4½", square ruffled top, glossy finish	400.00
Toothpick, tricorn	325.00
Tumbler	275.00
Vases	
5¾", gourd shape	250.00

8¼", lily form	295.00

WEBB

Bottle, 6", silver lid, gold oriental decor	795.00
Ewer, applied camphor handle	300.00
Punch Cup	250.00
Sweet Meat Jar, 4½ x 3¾", gold floral decor, silver plated top, rim and handle	450.00
Tumbler, enamel floral decor	150.00
Vases	
3½", petal top, floral decor	350.00
6½", stick, gold prunis decor ...	250.00
8", gold leaves and floral decor, glossy finish	295.00
11½", stick, English ivy decor ...	850.00
15", gourd, floral and bee decor .	1700.00

WHEELING

Cruet, applied glossy amber handle .	900.00
Pitcher, 7½", bulbous, ruffled top .	900.00
Salt & Pepper, pewter tops	325.00
Sugar Bowl, 2¾" dia., open, glossy	350.00
Tumbler	300.00
Vases	
2⅜", bulbous, glossy finish	190.00
3½", bulbous, glossy finish	275.00
"Morgan" replica	1400.00

PEARLWARE

Introduced by Josiah Wedgwood in 1779, Pearlware was a fashion of the late 18th century but not a technical improvement as such. Ladies of that period tired of cream-colored china and demanded a change in coloration, so cobalt was added to the glaze formerly used for Creamware and the result was Pearlware.

This ware bridged the gap between hard-paste porcelain, soft-paste porcelain, Creamware, and the advent of bone china. This bridge covered a span of years from 1740 to 1791, and Pearlware continued until about 1830. Marked pieces are uncommon; there appear to be examples of Pearlware made earlier than 1779, including Bristol pottery which could not have been made later than 1778.

Collectors should look for collected pools of blue or bluish green glaze on the footrim of Pearlware. Among the finest examples of this ware is the blue Staffordshire of the 1803–1820 period. Leeds, Liverpool and Swansea are among the best known makers and good examples of Pearlware include many pieces of Mocha and all Gaudy Dutch items.

See also SWANSEA.

16½″, blue edge, Hall		45.00
Sauce, polychrome, chipped		45.00
Shakers		
4½″, green, Leeds		110.00
4¾″, mocha, "Seaweed"		165.00
Sugars		
Blue decoration		125.00
Ochre draping, swan finial, Bristol, damaged		65.00

PEKING GLASS

Peking Glass is a type of cameo glass of Chinese origin. Its production began in the 1700's and continued well into the 19th century. It is currently being reproduced, but readily identified when compared to the earlier glassware.

Plate, Water Nymph, impressed Wedgwood Pearl, c. 1840–65, 9½″ $45.00

Bowls	
5″, blue chinoiserie, Leeds	200.00
5¾″, polychrome, Leeds	125.00
6″, blue chinoiserie, Leeds	210.00
8½″, square, polychrome, Botanical series, Swansea	175.00
11½″, oval, polychrome, Botanical series, Swansea	325.00
Coffee Pots	
Polychrome, repaired	350.00
Staffordshire, blue, repaired	225.00
Cups and Saucers	
Polychrome, Leeds, repaired	110.00
Polychrome, "Queen's Rose"	85.00
Staffordshire, blue, small	65.00
Jugs	
2½″, polychrome	85.00
4½″, pink scale, slight damage	125.00
4¾″, silver shape	135.00
8½″, polychrome, repaired	275.00
Mugs	
2¾″, baluster-shaped	135.00
4¾″, polychrome, Spatterware, "Peafowl," Leeds	365.00
5¾″, polychrome, Leeds	200.00
5¾″, polychrome, Leeds, damaged	120.00
Plates	
7⅞″, polychrome, reticulated rim, Swansea	185.00
8¼″, polychrome, "King's Rose"	200.00
Plates, Soup	
10″, blue edge, Clews	55.00
10″, blue edge, Stubbs and Kent	45.00
Platters	
9″, purple edge, Wedgwood	110.00
11½″, green edge	85.00

Snuff bottle, blue, 3¼″ $200.00

Bottle, 3½″, white, cobalt foliage	175.00
Bowls	
4½″ dia., translucent white, green prunus and rockwork	275.00
6″ dia., translucent white, purple ducks and lotus plants	150.00
7″ dia., lemon yellow, red branches in bloom	175.00
7″ dia., translucent white, red frogs and lotus	280.00
Jar, covered, 5¾″ high, urn shaped, carved blue geometric pattern	575.00
Vases	
6″, coral to white, red dragons	180.00
6½″, turquoise, dark striations	225.00
7″, double gourd shape, opaque violet, blue cut bottom rim	500.00
8″, white, Imperial yellow butterfly, flowers, leaves	295.00
10″, baluster shape, white, red	

bands and florals **225.00**
12", baluster shape, translucent
deep blue, white cranes **450.00**

PELOTON

Wilhelm Kralik of Bohemia patented this novelty art glass in 1880 and later patented it in both America and England. For the base piece, both transparent and opaque glass were used, with opaque glass most common. The hot glass was removed from the furnace either before or after it was worked into shape and opaque colored glass filaments (strings) were applied by dipping or rolling. Generally the threads are pink, blue, yellow and white (rainbow colors) but can be all a single color. Items can also be satin finished and have enamel decoration.

Cruet, light blue ground, clear stopper, 7" $250.00

Biscuit Jars
Ribbed, soft blue satin, rainbow colored strings, silver plated mountings **750.00**
Glossy white, rainbow colored strings, silver plated mountings . . **650.00**
Bowl, ribbed, opaque white satin, rainbow colored strings, silver plated top rim **650.00**
Cruets
6½", clear overshot, rainbow colored filaments, clear applied han-

dle and cut stopper **295.00**
6½", amber with embossed swirl, rainbow colored strings, clear applied handle and cut stopper **350.00**
Pitchers
7", cranberry with embossed swirl, rainbow colored strings, clear reeded handle **350.00**
7½", clear, cranberry strings, clear handle **225.00**
Rose Bowl, opaque white, rainbow colored strings, 4 point top, shell crystal feet **295.00**
Sweetmeat Jar, 4½", squatty, fine ribbed, opaque white, rainbow colored strings, silver plated top mountings **595.00**
Tumbler, juice, clear with royal blue strings **65.00**
Vases
3½", lavender cased, rainbow colored strings **265.00**
4", ribbed, cased white, rainbow colored strings **350.00**
6", bulbous, thin neck stick, yellow cased, rainbow colored strings . . **295.00**
7", bulbous, clear, royal blue colored strings **245.00**
fan, lavender pink cased, rainbow colored strings, ruffled **450.00**

PENS AND PENCILS

The steel pen point or nib was invented by Samuel Harrison in 1780. It was not commercially produced in quantity until the 1880's when Richard Esterbrook entered the field. The holders became increasing elaborate. Mother of pearl, gold, sterling silver, and other fine materials were used to fashion holders of distinction. Many of these pens can be found intact with velvet lined presentation cases.

Lewis Waterman invented the fountain pen in the 1880's. Three other leading pioneers in the field were Parker, Sheaffer (first lever filling action, 1913), and Wahl-Eversharp.

The mechanical pencil was patented in 1822 by Sampson Mordan. The original slide-type action developed into the spiral mechanical pencil. Wahl-Eversharp was responsible for the automatic "clic" or repeater type pencil which is used on ball points today.

The flexible nib that enabled the writer to individualize his penmanship came to an end when Reynolds introduced the ball point pen in October 1945.

Conklin
1923, pen, Model 25P, ladies filigree-cap ribbon, black, crescent

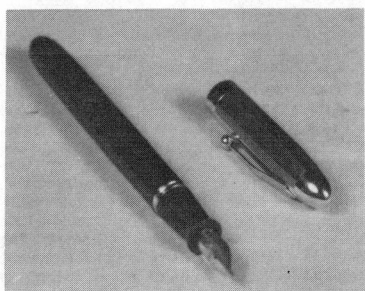

Morrison Fountain Pen, black with chrome plated cap, 14KT tip, lever filled **$8.00**

filler	**30.00**
1925, pen, Endura, ladies, blue lapis ribbon, 14 KT gold point . . .	**40.00**
1920's, pen and pencil set, lime green, spring pocket clips	**30.00**
Dunn, 1920, pen, black with red barrel, goldplated trim	**6.00**
Epenco, pen, black case, goldplated trim	**10.00**

Eversharp

1920, pencil, silverplated	**6.00**
1932, pen, Doric, man's, Gold Seal	**70.00**
1935, pen, Midget, mottled green with goldplating	**7.50**
1944, pen and pencil, $64, 14 KT gold caps, level filled	**50.00**
Laughlin, 1905, pen, silver overlay case, eyedropper filled	**40.00**

Moore

1906, pen, ladies ribbon style, black hard rubber with three narrow gold bands on cap, side lever fill	**10.00**
1910, pencil, green ribbon with brass goldplated cap and tip	**5.00**
1915, pen, maroon-rose body with fancy etched band on cap, marked 14 KT, warrented nib, side level fill	**12.00**

Parker

1915, pen, Model 48, ring top, gold filled barrel and cap, button filled	**45.00**
1917, pen, Lucky Curve, push-button filler	**20.00**
1923, pencil, Duofold Senior, red, propel-repel mechanism	**40.00**
1927, pencil, Duofold, Model 78M, ladies, fuchsia color, gold color cap and tip, originally sold for $3	**10.00**
1929, pen and pencil set, Duofold	

Deluxe, black and pearl, three narrow gold color bands on cap, push button fill	**125.00**
1942, pen, Blue Diamond—51, black with goldplated cap, button filled	**20.00**
1944, pen, Blue Diamond—Vacumatic, blue and black with goldplated trim, button filled	**20.00**
1956, pen, Model 61, first edition	**17.50**
Reynolds, pen, original ball point, Model 2 (1945–46)	**12.00**

Sheaffer

1923, pen, White Dot, green jade with goldplated trim, lever filled . .	**45.00**
1936, pen, White Dot, black with goldplated trim, level filled	**35.00**
1946, pencil, Fineline 4000, novel point with platinum plating	**5.00**
1953, pen, White Dot, snorkel, black with 14 KT gold cap and band, plunger filled	**12.50**
Swan (made by Mabie, Todd & Co., NY and London)	
Pen, Eternal model, orange with gold clip, gold color band top and bottom, lever fill, 5½"	**20.00**
Pen, ladies, 16 KT plated, lever filled	**20.00**
Pen, Swallow, black & white marbled, single gold color band, lever filled, #2 14 KT nib	**12.00**

Wahl

1918, pen, silver overlay case, eyedropper filled	**25.00**
1928, pen, goldplated case, ball clip, lever filled	**25.00**

Wahl-Eversharp

1923, pencil, ring top, goldfilled case	**7.50**
1924, pencil, sterling silver, engraved case	**22.50**

Waterman

1886, pen, Model #12, mottled brown with 14 KT gold bands . . .	**35.00**
1918, pen and pencil, Model #454, sterling silver engraved case, lever filled pen	**175.00**
1925, pen, Model #71, ripple red hard rubber case, goldplated trim, wide clip, lever filled	**60.00**
1928, pen, Lady Patricia, sterling silver case, lever filled	**40.00**
1943, pen, Commando	**10.00**

PETERS AND REED POTTERY

J.D. Peters and Adam Reed founded their pottery company in South Zanesville, Ohio, in 1900. Common flower pots, jardinieres and cooking wares comprised their major output

in the beginning. Occasionally, art pottery was attempted, but it was not until 1912 that their "Moss Aztec" line was introduced and widely accepted. Other art wares included "Landsun," "Chromal," "Montene," "Pereco" and "Persian."

Peters retired in 1921 and Reed changed the name of the firm to "The Zane Pottery." Marked pieces of Peters and Reed Pottery are unknown.

Also see ZANE POTTERY and GONDER POTTERY.

Vase, shallow, Peraco, 5½" dia., 3¼" h. $45.00

Bowls

6½", "Pereco," matte green glaze, butterfly decor	35.00
8½", "Landsun," blue, yellow, green	35.00
8½", "Pereco," berry decor	55.00
Jardiniere, 6½ x 7½", green lion's head decor on beige ground	65.00
Jug, 10½", decorated with portraits of George Washington in slip	125.00
Mug, 5¾", floral sprigs, high glaze	30.00

Pitchers

6½", tankard, "Moss Aztec," artist signed	35.00
Sprigged on heads, brown glaze	80.00

Vases

4¾", "Landsun"	30.00
7", Portraits of George Washington	95.00
7¾", blackberry decor	40.00
9¾", "Moss Aztec," pine cone decor	55.00
12", "Landsun," blue glaze	85.00
Wall Pocket, 7¾", "Pereco," Egyptian decor	70.00

PEWTER

Pewter is a metal alloy, consisting mostly of tin with small amounts of lead copper, antimony and bismuth added to improve form-

ability and hardness. The metal can be cast, formed around a mold, spun, easily cut and soldered to form a wide variety of utilitarian articles.

Pewter ware was known to the ancient Chinese, Egyptians, the Romans and later the Medieval European continent. English pewter supplied the major portion of the needs of the American Colonies for nearly one hundred and fifty years before the American Revolution. The Revolution ended the embargo on the basic pewter making material, raw tin, which had been imposed by England. The American pewter industry, small before the Revolution, then flourished and thrived up until about the Civil War period. The listing that follows concentrates on the American and English pewter forms most often encountered by the collector.

Pewter Makers — Location — Period

American

Austin, Nathaniel, Charleston, Mass., 1763–1800

Austin, Richard, Boston, Mass., 1792–1817

Badger, Thomas, Boston, Mass., 1737–1815

Barns, Blakslee, Phila., Pa., 1812–1817

Bassett, Frederick, New York & Hartford, Conn., 1761–1800

Boardman, Thomas Danforth, Hartford, Conn., 1805–1850

Calder, William, Providence, R.I., 1817–1856

Capen & Molineux, N.Y., 1848–1854

Danforth, Edward, Middletown, Conn., 1788–1790

Danforth, Joseph, Middletown, Conn., 1780–1788

Danforth, Josiah, Middletown, Conn., 1825–1837

Danforth, Thomas, III, Stepeny, Conn. & Phila., Pa., 1777–1818

Dunham, Rufus, Westbrook, Maine, 1837–1861

Gleason, Roswell, Dorchester, Mass., 1822–1871

Griswold, Ashbil, Meriden, Conn., 1802–1842

Hamlin, Samuel, Hartford, Conn., 1767–1801

Hamlin, Samuel, Jr., Providence, R.I., 1801–1856

Jones, Gersham, Providence, R.I., 1774–1809

Lee, Richard, Mass., New Hampshire & Vermont, 1770–1823

Leonard, Reed and Barton, Taunton, Mass., 1835–1840

McQuilkin, William, Phila., Pa., 1845–1853

Morey & Ober, Boston, Mass., 1852–1855

Putnam, James, Malden, Mass., 1830–1835

Richardson, George, Sr., Boston, Mass., 1818–1828

Savage, William, Middletown, Conn., 1830's

Sellew and Co., Cinn., Ohio, 1830–1860

Sheldon & Feltman, Albany, N.Y., 1847–1848
Trask, Israel, Beverly, Mass., 1807–1856

English

Dixon, James & Son, Sheffield, mid 1800's
Duncomb, Samuel, Birmingham, 1780–1811
King, Richard, Jr., London, 1707–1738
Towsend, John, London, 1748–1801
Towsend & Compton, London, 1780–1811
Yates, Lawrence, London, 1740–1774

Basins

Badger, Thomas, 8″ dia.	475.00
Barns, Blakslee, 6½″ dia.	675.00
Boardman, Thomas D., 12″ dia. . .	550.00
Brunstrom, John A., 11¾″ dia. . .	900.00
Calder, William, 10″ dia.	425.00
Danforth, Josiah, 6″ dia.	475.00
Lightner, George, 10″ dia.	600.00
Towsend & Compton, London, 10½″ dia.	300.00

Beakers

Boardman, Timothy, 5″ high	700.00
Dixon, James, Sheffield, England, 4½″ high	200.00
Hamlin, Samuel, 3″ high	900.00
Unmarked (European) 5″ high . . .	125.00
Unmarked (American) 4½″ high .	275.00

Candlesticks

Dixon, James, Sheffield, England, 5″ high, single	150.00
Dunham, Rufus, 6″ high, pair	600.00
Gleason, Roswell, 8″ high, pair . .	750.00
Morey and Ober, 8″ high, pair . . .	475.00
Putnam, James, 8½″ high, pair . .	525.00
Reed and Barton, 5½″ high, single	125.00
Unmarked (18th century European) 12½″ high	1100.00

Castors

Smith, Eben, holder with 4 bottles	325.00
Trask, Israel, holder with 4 blown bottles	475.00

Chargers

Austin, Nathanial, 13½″ dia., repaired	450.00
Hamlin, Samuel, 13½″ dia.	700.00
Leffer, Samuel, London, 15″ dia. .	275.00
Townsend & Compton, London, 12¾″ dia.	250.00
Weldon & Feltman, 13½″ dia. . . .	400.00
Yates, Lawrence, London, 14″ dia.	300.00

Coffee Pots

Danforth, Josiah, 11″ high	425.00
Dixon & Son, Sheffield, England, 11½″ high	150.00
McQuilkin, William, 11½″ high . . .	350.00
Palethorp, John, 12″ high	500.00
Porter, Freeman, 12″ high	325.00
Richardson, George, 12½″ high .	375.00
Savage, William, 11″ high	275.00

Cuspidors

Curtis, Daniel, 9″ dia.	300.00

Gleason, Roswell, 10″ dia.	350.00

Flagons

Boardman, Thomas D., lidded, 14″ high	1400.00
Calder, William, lidded, 11″ high .	700.00
Reed & Barton, lidded, 12½″ high	350.00
Towsend, John, London, no lid, 10″ high	425.00
Trask, Israel, lidded, 10½″ high . .	650.00

Inkwells

English, 7½″ dia., 5 pen holes . .	225.00
English, 4½″ dia., 4 pen holes . .	150.00
Whitcomb, George, 2″ high, school desk type	100.00

Lamps

Boardman, Thomas D., 4½″ high	550.00
Capen & Molineaux, 9″ high	375.00
Gleason, Roswell, 7″ high	450.00
Morey & Smith, 6″ high	275.00
Sellew & Co., 5½″ high, pair	800.00
Unmarked (American) 9½″ high .	325.00

Pitchers

Boardman, Thomas, D., open, 10″ high	900.00
Dunham, Rufus, 7″ high, small repairs	325.00
Gleason, Roswell, lidded, 9″ high	600.00
Putnam, James, no lid, 9″ high . .	450.00
Richardson, George, lidded, 10″ high	700.00
Unmarked (American) 9″ high . . .	475.00

Plate, American, B. Barnes, 8″ $275.00

Plates

Austin, Nathanial, 9½″ dia.	425.00
Badger, Thomas, 8″ dia.	275.00
Boardman & Hart, 9¾″ dia.	325.00
Boardman & Hart, 11″ dia.	400.00
Boardman, Thomas, D., 9¾″ dia.	375.00
Brunstrom, John, 6″ dia.	600.00
Calder, William, 9½″ dia.	475.00
Curtis, Daniel, 9½″ dia.	425.00
Danforth, Samuel, 7¾″ dia.	275.00
Gleason, Roswell, 9″ dia.	325.00
Hamlin, Samuel, 8¼″ dia.	525.00

Jones, Gershom, 8" dia. 350.00
King, Richard, London, 10¾" dia. 225.00
Kilbourn, Samuel, 11" dia. 335.00
Lee, Richard, 5¾" dia. 575.00
Melville, David, 8¾" dia. 400.00
Palethorp, Robert, 9" dia. 450.00
Smeets, John, London, 11" dia. . . 150.00
Towsend & Compton, London,
8½" dia. 75.00
Towsend & Compton, London,
10½" dia. 250.00
Weldon & Feltman, 12" dia. 250.00
Yates, Lawrence, London, 10" dia. 225.00

Porringers

Boardman, Thomas, D., crown
handle, 5" dia. 500.00
Gleason, Roswell, crown handle,
3¾" dia. 450.00
Hamlin, Samuel, flower handle,
5½" dia. 700.00
I.G. (American) crown handle, 5"
dia. 350.00
Lee, Richard, flower handle, 4¾"
dia. 600.00
Whitmore, Jacob, flower handle, 5"
dia. 900.00

Tankards

Austin, Richard, quart, lid with fini-
al, 7" high 4000.00
Boardman, Thomas, D., quart, 7½"
high 1750.00
English, 6½" high 125.00
English, Imperial, one pint, 5½"
high 100.00
Smith & Co., 8" high 275.00
Unmarked (American) 6" high . . . 350.00
Yates, London, 7" high 150.00

**Teapot, American, D. L. Farnam, c.
1825, 11"** $350.00

Teapots

Boardman, Thomas, D., 6½" high 575.00
Boardman, Luther, 7" high 1150.00

Dixon & Son, Sheffield, England,
10" high 175.00
Dunham, Rufus, 8½" high 350.00
Munson, John, 9" high 250.00
Morey & Smith, 10" high 275.00
Porter, Freeman, 9" high 325.00
Richardson, George, 9½" high . . . 475.00
Savage, William, 8" high 350.00

PHOENIX BIRD PATTERN

**The Phoenix Bird pattern is a blue and white
Japanese porcelain. There are seven patterns
known using the Phoenix bird as a focal
point. The two most popular patterns are
"Flying Phoenix" (Phoenix almost always
looking over his left wing) and "Flying Turkey" (looking straight ahead).**

**The pattern reached its peak in the early
1900's and continued until the 1930's and
1940's. After World War II, a few pieces were
made and marked "Made in Occupied Japan." Newly designed items with the Phoenix
Bird Pattern are currently being produced.
Variations in size, design and pattern exist
between the old and the new.**

Plate, 7¼" $10.00

Bowls

5½" 25.00
7½" 30.00
8¾" 40.00
Butter Dish, covered, with drain, 5",
handled, pierced disc insert 45.00
Cake Set, large plate, 4 smaller
plates, 5 pieces 30.00
Cup and Saucer, "Japan" 12.50
Dish, oval 3.50
Egg Cup, single 10.00
Ginger Jar, covered, 4½" 25.00
Gravy Boat, with underplate 25.00
Nappy, "Noritake," 5" 10.00

Plates

7" 6.00
9½", "Occupied Japan" 18.00

Salt and Pepper Shakers, pair	15.00
Sauce Dish	3.00
Teapot, covered	50.00
Tea strainer, with stand	35.00
Tumbler, 2¾"	20.00
Vase, 8 x 7"	60.00

PHOENIX GLASS

Phoenix Glass Company, Beaver, Pa., was established in 1880. Although the firm was known primarily for commercial glassware, it began producing a molded, sculptured, cameo-type line in the 1930's. This decorative ware was discontinued in the 1950's and is widely collected today.

Basket, 4½", pink, dogwood	40.00
Bowls	
9", frosted and clear, nudes	65.00
10 x 5½ x 4" oval, blue	125.00
14 x 4¼" deep, frosted and clear, lily	175.00
Box, 6", covered, blue, floral decor .	45.00
Candlesticks	
3¼", blue, bubbles and swirls, pair	40.00
4", blue, frosted, pair	35.00
Compote, 8½", butterscotch, dragonflies and water lilies	85.00
Jar, ginger, covered, bird finial	70.00
Planter, 3¼ x 8½", green, lion	45.00
Plates	
6¾", frosted and clear, dancing nudes	35.00
8¼", yellow, dancing nudes	50.00
8½", clear and frosted, cherries .	55.00
14", blue, white daffodils	85.00
18", green, dancing nudes	125.00
Vases	
6", frosted and clear, cattails	40.00
6¼", white pink peonies, green leaves	60.00
7", custard, pine cones	65.00
7", dogwood	85.00
7¼ x 8" wide, white, blue praying mantis	95.00
8", cosmos, salmon	85.00
8¼", grasshoppers, blue	90.00
10", madonna	125.00
10", lovebirds, blue	120.00
11 x 10" dia., blue, seagulls	140.00
12", white, dancing nudes	150.00
12", flying geese, blue	150.00
17½", thistle, white & peach	180.00

PHONOGRAPH RECORDS

With the advent of more sophisticated re-

Vase, turquoise with pink carp, 8 x 9" $110.00

cording materials, such as 33⅓ RPM long playing records, 8-track tapes and cassettes, earlier phonograph records have become collectors' items. These records are also sought by collectors of memorabilia for past artists who recorded on different labels.

Brunswick, 10"	4.00
Capitol, 12"	4.00
Columbia, 10"	3.50
Decca, 10"	3.50
Decca, Judy Garland	15.00
Decca, Al Jolson	25.00
Edison Blue Amberol Cylinder, 4 minutes	10.00
Edison Cylinder, 4 minutes	10.00
Edison Diamond Disc	7.50
Indestructible Cylinder, 2 minutes . .	7.50
Little Wonder, 5½"	5.00
Shore, Dinah, 10"	8.50
Sinatra, Frank, 10"	10.00
MGM, Yellow Label, 10", 78 RPM . .	5.00
Opera Disc, (German), 12", single sided, Caruso	15.00
Pathe, 10", 10½", 11½"	4.00
RCA Victor, 10", Black Label	
Krupa, Gene, each	8.50
Shaw, Artie, each	10.00
RCA Victor, 10", Bluebird	5.00
RCA Victor, 12", Black Label	4.50
RCA Victor, 12", Red Seal, single sided	7.50
RCA Victor, 12", Red Seal, double sided	7.50
RCA Victor, 45 RPM, Elvis Presley .	10.00
Victrola, 10", 12"	5.00

PHONOGRAPHS

Early phonographs were commonly called 'talking machines.' Thomas A. Edison invented the first successful phonograph in 1877. Other manufacturers followed with their variations.

Edison, Amberole, Model 30, 4 minute cylinder, oak case, 11 x 12½ x 14¼" $285.00

Amberola, model 75, Diamond reproducer	300.00
Baltiphone, console, 38" high, plays 78 RPM's	250.00
Britannia, Key wind, open mechanism, c. 1910, Germany	175.00
Brunswick, console, 47" high, golden oak cabinet, plays 78 RPM's .	250.00
Columbia Gramaphone, 2 minute-type	350.00
Edison Standard, disc-type, built in horn in cabinet	300.00
Edison Standard, disc-type, model A, black and gold horn	500.00
Edison Standard, 14" brass horn ..	350.00
Edison Standard, Morning Glory horn, painted black and decorated, 2 minute or 4 minute cylinders	500.00
Edison Triumph, plywood horn, brass, bell end, 2 minute cylinders	950.00
Excelsior, two minute gearing, c. 1904–08, Germany	275.00
G.C. & Co., spun aluminum horn, c. 1900	375.00

Gramophone, very rare table model, c. 1900, all original, plays cylinders	1500.00
Kameraphone, 4½ x 6½", portable .	125.00
Keeno-Lo-Phone, double doors conceal 2 drawers with record pockets, bonnet is amplifier	500.00
Lyrophonwerke, c. 1908, Germany .	300.00
Mira Mahogany console, floor model, music box, 15¾" discs, fully restored	3800.00
Pathe, model no. O, c. 1904, French	350.00
Polyphon disc music box, upright models play 22½" discs, original condition	5000.00
Reginaphone, model 150, mahogany case	4000.00
Robeyphone, disc-type, large horn, English	500.00
Symphonium table model, walnut case, 9½ x 16½ x 20" disc, 13⅝" with 20 records, Sublime-Harmonie combs, good mechanical playing condition, cabinet condition fair ..	1500.00
Victor, Type III	500.00
Victor, Type V, table model with morning glory horn, oak cabinet ..	750.00

PIANO AND ORGAN ROLLS

Player piano rolls were introduced at the turn of the 20th century. The first pianos were 65-note players, i.e., the rolls had 65 notes punched across the 11¼" wide paper roll. In 1901, the Melville and Clark Piano Company manufactured the 88-note player.

U.S., Imperial, Vocal style, Recordo, Cannonized and International were among the first piano-roll companies. The largest was QRS who issued over 1000 titles a year. However, piano-roll sales diminished when people began to seek entertainment out of their homes.

In the 1950's, player pianos were restored and returned to the family room. A new, smaller spinet-type player piano was introduced. Two companies, Aeolian and Melodee, began producing new rolls until 1967. Music Rolls are still being made today but it is the earlier ones that music collectors seek.

This list is comprised mainly of piano rolls, but other types used with mechanical playing musical instruments are also included.

Aeolian, 65-note	2.00
Aeolian Pipe Organ, 116-note	8.00
Aeolian Reed Organ, 46-note ...	5.00
Ampico Reproducing A or B	7.50
Apollo Concert Grand	5.00
Automusic, 65-note	3.50
Cecilian Organ	10.00

Columbia, 88-note	3.50
Deluxe Reproducing	7.50
Duo Art Reproducing, organ	15.00
Gem, organ cob	6.00
Ideal, 88-note	2.50
Imperial, 88-note	3.50
Metrostyle, 65-note	3.50
Nickelodeon, A, O, or G	20.00
Pianostyle, 88-note	3.50
Q.R.S., 88-note	2.00
Recordo	5.00
Rollmonica	6.50
Simplex	2.50
Tanzbar, 2½"	15.00
Tanzbar, 4⅛"	20.00
Tel-Electric, 65-note	5.00
U.S., 88-note	1.50
Vocalstyle, 88-note	2.50
Welte Philharmonic Organ	15.00
Wurlitzer Band Organ, 165-note . . .	20.00

Organ Rolls: QRS — $1.50 to 2.50; Imperial — $3.00 to 5.00; Vocal style — $2.00 to 4.00; Melodee — $3.00 to 5.00

PICKARD

The Pickard China Company was founded in 1894. They were known for their fine handpainted porcelains. Originally they acquired blanks from other sources, namely Limoges, but now produce their own. The firm is presently located in Antioch, Illinois.

Berry Set, 10" bowl, six 5½" bowls; orange and yellow tulips; heavy gold trim, artist signed, set	300.00
Bowls	
6", pierced rim, gold florals inside, allover gold exterior	40.00

Plate, pink floral on cream ground, gold trim, marked, 8¼" $35.00

10", yellow shaded ground, violet decor; gold and red patterned band; artist signed and dated 1898	150.00
Box, covered, 2¾ x 5¾" dia., stylized florals in gold, black and ivory	85.00
Candlesticks, 9", floral decor, Limoges blanks, artist signed, pair .	100.00
Chocolate Pot, 11½" high, white pearlized ground, orchids and leaves decor	150.00
Coffee Pot, 8½", allover floral, much gold, signed Wagner, 1905 mark .	155.00
Compotes	
5 x 9", floral center	80.00
10½", handled, fruit and flower decor, gold border and pedestal, artist signed	165.00
Creamers and Sugars	
Allover gold, on tray, set	65.00
Gold beaded rims on white, set .	60.00
Pink blossoms, artist signed and dated 1905, set	85.00
Cup and Saucer, enamel beading, artist signed	75.00
Hatpin Holders	
Allover gold, etched florals, c. 1925	35.00
Florals, gold band top, artist signed and dated 1905	45.00
Lemonade Set, 5 Tumblers, Tall pitcher, lemon color with bluebells	85.00
Marmalade Jar, covered, 6" high with underplate, pink dogwood, gold trim, artist signed	75.00
Mug, 6", Dutch Girl decor, artist signed, c. 1908	95.00
Pitchers	
6", cider, allover etched gold decor, gold interior, c. 1930's	100.00

8", Aura Argento linear, artist
signed 200.00
10", tankard, dark green ground,
gold grapes, gold trim, artist
signed and dated 1905 . . . .   250.00

Plates
5½", etched all over in gold 20.00
8", humming birds and orchids, 2"
embossed gold border, Hutschenreuther blank, signed E. Challinor   100.00
8½", reds, greens and browns
with decor of gooseberries, artist
signed, c. 1905–1910 . . . .   65.00
8½", scalloped with gold, strawberries and white blossoms,
signed E. Challinor, c. 1905 . . . . .   100.00
9", yellow cherries on green
ground, artist signed and dated
1905 . . . .   75.00
10¼", overall gold, ornate Art
Deco border 50.00
11", cake, open handles, Mum de-
cor, artist signed, c. 1910–1912 . .   125.00
11", service, yellow roses in center, Bavarian blanks, c. 1930. Set
of 4 . . . .   150.00

Salt and Pepper Shakers
Stylized floral decor, gold tops,
artist signed, c. 1912. Pair 35.00
Allover gold, pair 30.00
Sugar Bowl, large, 2 handled, all
gold encrusted 45.00
Stein, 7", tankard-shape, red poinsettias on iridescent pearlized
ground, signed N.R. Coutall, 1898–
1904 mark 165.00
Swan, 3" long, heavy allover gold,
inside and out 30.00

Tea Sets
3 pieces, scenic decor, gold handles, spouts and finials, artist
signed, set 350.00
4 pieces, teapot, creamer, sugar,
16" tray, pierced handles, allover
gold 250.00
Tray, 6½ x 12" long, handled, gar-
den scene, signed E. Challinor . . .   195.00
Urn, 11½", allover gold, 3" band of
grapes and strawberries, Belleek
blank, artist signed 500.00

Vases
5½", footed, tropical scene, gold
handles, artist signed 195.00
7", scenic, signed E. Challinor, c.
1905–1910 . . . .   250.00
7", allover gold floral, Shield mark   40.00
8¼", garden scene, artist signed,
c. 1912–1919 . . . .   235.00
10", classic oriental scene, artist
signed 275.00
15", peonies on pastel ground,
gold scalloped rim, base, artist
signed 295.00

PICKLE CASTORS

A pickle castor is a novelty table accessory
used to serve pickles. It consists of a
silverplated frame fitted with a glass insert
and metal tongs. These were very popular in
the Victorian period and are quite collectible
today.

**Pressed glass, castle scene in re-
serve, metal frame $85.00**

Amber Cane pattern insert, resilvered frame, cover and tongs . .   85.00
Amber, Finecut and Penal insert, ornate silverplated Tufts frame, cov-
er, and tongs 225.00
Clear Finecut pattern insert, ornate
silverplated frame, lid and fork . . .   150.00
Clear, Daisy and Button insert,
silverplated frame 100.00
Amber Inverted Thumbprint insert,
with swirled rim, resilvered ornate
holder and fork 125.00
Clear pressed Flute insert, resilvered
cover, frame and tongs 95.00
Cranberry Inverted Thumbprint in-
sert, ornate silverplate footed
frame, with ball grip handle and
openwork galleried base 225.00
Cranberry Opalescent Coin Spot insert, silverplated frame and cover   250.00
MOP Satin Diamond Quilted insert,
shading from deep fuchsia to pale
pink, white lining, silverplated
frame and cover 325.00

Sapphire blue insert with enameled
daisies, ornate silverplated frame
with maple leaves **225.00**

PIGEON BLOOD GLASS

**Pigeon Blood refers to the orange-red col-
ored glass ware produced around the turn of
the century. Do not confuse it with the many
other red glass wares of the period. Pigeon
Blood has a very definite orange glow.**

**Pickle Castor, Empire Mfg. Co., qua-
druple plate, 8″** $250.00

Bowls
  9″, beaded rim **160.00**
  10″, boat shape **250.00**
Butter, covered, metal trim **175.00**
Candlesticks, 7½″, twisted stem,
  pair **150.00**
Compote, 7″, scalloped edge **185.00**
Cracker Jar, melon ribbed, silver
  plated, scroll embossed collar,
  cover, 2 handles **250.00**
Creamer, clear applied handle, metal
  top **130.00**
Creamer & Sugar, covered, em-
  bossed silver plate borders & han-
  dles **275.00**
Cruet, bulbous, ruffled top, clear
  reed handle **90.00**

Pitchers
  11″, clear applied handle **260.00**
  Tall, quilted **150.00**
Salt & Pepper, pewter tops, pair . . .   **100.00**
Syrup, Torquay **145.00**
Tumbler, water **70.00**
Vases
  4½″, urn, clear applied handles . .   **75.00**
  7¼″, enameled decor **130.00**
  12″, pedestal, applied clear glass
  rigaree **225.00**

PINK LUSTRE CHINA

**Pink Lustre derived its name from the color
of the decoration. In 1790, Josiah Wedgwood
began to experiment in decoration with a thin
film of metal applied by various methods.
Successors followed by using silver, platinum
and gold (pink). Lustre decorations were often used in conjunction with enamels and
transfers. Transfers used for lustre decorations covered a wide range of public and domestic subjects. These were often accompa-
nied by pious or sentimental doggerel as well
as the humours of everyday life. Also see
SUNDERLAND LUSTRE.**

Plate, House, 8½″ $55.00

Biscuit Barrel, 4½″, lid and verse, c.
  1860 . . . .   **135.00**
Bowls
  7¾″, shallow, House pattern . . .   **120.00**
  6½″, pink lustre, red and green
  enamelled strawberry vine border
  exterior, Staffordshire, c. 1820 . .   **175.00**
Creamers
  5 petal flowers, green leaves . . .   **65.00**
  House pattern **75.00**

Cups and Saucers
Schoolhouse pattern	65.00
Child with lamb	45.00
Handleless, Pink lustre	35.00
Mug, 3½", c. 1850	75.00

Pitchers
3½", House pattern	60.00
6", House pattern	110.00
Vintage, Lustred band and handle	175.00

Plates
6"	30.00
9¼", soup	40.00
Sauce Boat, Vintage pattern	55.00
Sugar Bowl, House pattern	125.00

Tea Pots
Floral medallion	120.00
House pattern	160.00

Bowl, 4½ x 2½" deep, footed	600.00
Butter, covered	1000.00
Compote 6½"	600.00
5"	750.00
Condiment Set, handled holder, covered pepper, covered mustard and open salt, set	110.00
Jam Jar	850.00
Lamp, miniature, shape of swan	870.00
Pitcher, 8"	1000.00
Punch Cup, footed	375.00
Sauce, footed	295.00
Sugar	650.00
Syrup	850.00
*Toothpick	450.00

PINK SLAG

The molded pattern regarded as true Pink Slag is that of an Inverted Fan and Feather. Pieces recently have come into the market in the Inverted Strawberry and Inverted Thistle. The two patterns were made in the molds of the now defunct Cambridge Glass Co., and are not considered "true" Pink Slag. The price of these late patterns are only a fraction of the true Pink Slag. Quality pieces shade from pink at the top to white at the bottom. This is the most sought after of the slag wares. The glass is extremely scarce and commands a good price.

PIPES

Tobacco was first introduced in England by Sir Walter Raleigh. The use of tobacco quickly became popular on the continent and the need for pipes developed. Many were produced in Holland in the Gouda vicinity and were exported throughout the world.

Briar
Amber stem, velvet cast, French	45.00
Bulldog, 7"	50.00
Stag's head, glass eyes, 9"	75.00

Clay
Acorn	18.00
Dog's head	15.00

Corncob
Advertising	5.00
Reed handle	15.00
Horn, deer painted on bowl, wood stem, 28"	100.00
Majolica, dog at base of bowl, wood stem, 11"	75.00

Tumbler, Inverted Fan & Feather, 3⅞" tall, 2¾" dia. $395.00

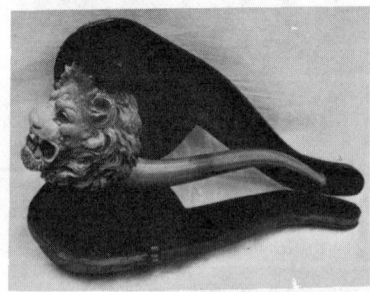

Italian, Lopoldo Weiss, Genoa, carved Meerscham bowl $300.00

Meerschaum
Boy, girl, 2 dogs, case	150.00
Cherott, acorn cluster, 3¾"	65.00

Deer, antlered, 14½″	250.00
Deer, chased by dog, 7″	135.00
Devil, leather case	175.00
Elk, standing, amber stem, case, 10″	500.00
Fox and shield, amber stem, 5″ . .	150.00
Hand holding running horse	120.00
Horse's head, case, 7½″	250.00
Horse running, 5″	85.00
Knight with armour, 9″	90.00
Maiden, Art Nouveau style, case, 8¼″	175.00
Monk smiling, case	165.00
Monkey, glass eyes	150.00
Nicholas II, case, 4⅝″	220.00
Scholar, tasseled cap, 7″	75.00
Shepherdess holding lamb, ram, 4″	140.00
Suede covered bowl, leather case	60.00
Viking head	80.00

Opium

Brass, Chinese, 10″	50.00
Porcelain, transfer scene of deer, German	40.00

Porcelain

Delft type, blue and white, 20″ . .	80.00
Hand painted deer scene, silver rim and cover	45.00
Water, porcelain, devil's head	75.00

PLAYING CARDS

The motifs found on playing cards are varied and offer the collector many organizing options. One can concentrate on cards manufactured by a single company such as Congress, DeLaRue, or Western Publishing Co. A thematic approach might focus on advertising cards or cards featuring royal figures. Country of origin is a third alternative.

In addition to decks, uncut sheets and single cards are sought by collectors. Since playing cards date to the 16th century, the early examples are often found only in single form.

The number of cards depends on the game to be played. An American straight deck has 52 cards and usually a joker. Pinochle requires 48 cards; Tarcot decks have 78. When buying a deck make certain to check that all cards are present.

We have organized our list by both topic and country. Although concentrating heavily on cards by American manufacturers, we have included foreign makers. Prices for decks of the late 19th and 20th century remain modest.

Advertising

Anheuser Busch, wide gold edge, 52 cards, c. 1900	100.00
Cigarette, Skat Express, German, A.S.S., 32 cards	8.00
Golden Nugget Gambling Hall, Las Vegas, 54 cards	10.00
Tobacco, Old English Curve Cut, hunter in red coat, c. 1900	25.00
United Fruit Company, Great White Fleet, 52 cards, c. 1932 . . .	27.50

Exposition

Columbian Exposition, Clark, 1892, 52 cards	65.00
Columbian World's Fair, Winters, 1892, 54 cards	45.00
Century of Progress, 1934, 52 cards	20.00
Pan American Exposition, 1901, 53 cards	25.00

Games

Block, Parker Bros., 1905, 58 cards	30.00
Flags, c. 1900	12.50
Gulliver's Travels, English, 36 cards	17.50
Old Maid, trades, c. 1890, 53 cards	32.50
Star Baseball Game, Wm. Ulrich, c. 1941, 56 cards	25.00
White Squadron, Fireside Game Co., 1896, 52 cards	45.00

Souvenir

C & O Railroad, 1908, 53 cards . .	42.50
California, Waters, c. 1900, 53 cards	32.50
Florida East Coast Railroad, U.S.P.C., 1922, 53 cards	30.00
Panama, U.S.P.C., 1912, 53 cards	40.00
Pittsburgh, W. J. Gilmore Co., c. 1901, 53 cards	40.00
Yellowstone Park, wide, 52 cards	17.50

Transportation

Farrel Lines, U.S.P.C., 54 cards . .	16.00
Prudential Lines, B. & B., 54 cards	8.00
S.A.S. Airlines, Oberg, 52 cards . .	10.00

Austria and Hungary

Arab, Piatnik, 1978, 54 cards	8.00
Regional Customes, Piatnik, 1955, 53 cards	16.00
Rococco Series, Piatnik, c. 1950, 54 cards	12.00

China and Orient

Lion, Lion P. C. Co., Shanghai, China, 54 cards	9.00
Rosier, Nintendo, Japan, 1967, 54 cards	27.50
Ukiyo-E, Sanyo Enterprise Ltd., Japan, c. 1950, 54 cards	27.50

England

Bezique, DeLaRue, c. 1900, 33 cards	24.00
Coronation, Elizabeth and Philip, 1953, DeLaRue, 54 cards	35.00
Patriotic, Kimberley, 1897	125.00

France

Casanova, Philibert, 1961, 54 cards	140.00
Hand stencilled, Gatteaux, 1853, 52 cards	60.00

Germany

Casanova Skat, A.S.S., 1969, 32 cards, risque	9.00
Frolic, A.S.S., 1977, 32 cards	6.00
Simultane, Bielefelder, 1964, 52 cards	10.00

Spain and Italy

Monuments of Spain, Fournier, 1955, 53 cards	12.00
Neoclassics, Fournier, reprint of 1810 Clemente Roxas deck, 48 cards	15.00

United States

Cupid on Bicycle, Bicycle, Pinochle, c. 1920, 48 cards	10.00
Autumn, Congress, 53 cards	12.50
Marilyn Monroe, pin up photo, 53 cards	50.00
National Whist, National, c. 1890, 53 cards	20.00
Sportsman, U.S.P.C., c. 1925, 52 cards	7.00
Steamboat O, Dougherty, c. 1890, 52 cards	35.00

POCKET KNIVES

The three leading companies manufacturing pocket knives are Case, Ka-Bar and Remington. There is a wide variety of knives which are collected not only along functional lines but also by decorative elements.

CASE

Case uses a numbering code for its knives. The first number (1–9) is the handle material; the second number (1–5) designates the number of blades; the third and fourth number (0–99) the knife pattern. Stag (5), pearl (8 or 9), and bone (6) are most sought in handle materials. The most desirable patterns are 5165—folding hunters, 6185—doctors, 6445—scout, muskrat—marked muskrat with no number, and 6254—trappers.

In the Case XX series a symbol and dot code is used to designate year.

1920–1940

5265	250.00
*5394	1000.00
6185	200.00
6254	300.00
6465, four blade hunter	1000.00
Muskrat	250.00

1940 to 1964

4200, mellon tester	100.00

5165, stag, hunter	130.00
6165, stag, hunter	130.00
5254, trapper	100.00
6254, trapper	75.00
6275, moose	90.00
C61050, Coke bottle	125.00

1964–1969

6165, hunter	90.00
62131, canoe	75.00
6250, Bradford Bonanza, elephant toe	100.00
6265, hunter	90.00

1970's, XX series

6165	40.00
62131	40.00
6250	50.00
6265	40.00

1980's, XX series

6165	22.00
62131	30.00
6250	37.00
6265	30.00

KA-BAR

The company was founded by Wallace Brown at Tidioute, Pa., in 1892. It was relocated in Olean, N.Y., in 1912. The products have many stampings including Union [inside shield], U-R Co. Tidioute [variations], Union Cut Co. Olean N.Y., Alcut Olean N.Y., Keenwell Olean N.Y., and Ka-Bar. The larger knives with a profile of a dog's head on the handle are most desirable. Pattern numbers rarely appear on a knife prior to the 1940's.

KA-BAR (Union Cut)

02118, Bicentennial, red, white, and blue	100.00
21107, dog's head	500.00
21107, little grizzley	1200.00
35119, tool kit, 5 blade	125.00
42027, office	75.00
61161, metal, fish folder	125.00
62156, boy scout shield	350.00
62156, imitation pearl	150.00
6360, knife, fork, spoon	175.00
6244, doctors	100.00
72110, abalone, pumpkin seed	200.00

REMINGTON

The Remington is the most collectible of all pocket knives. They were last made in 1940.

R 293, bullet	1000.00
R 433, doctors	125.00
R 953, toothpick	125.00
R 1128, bullet	1000.00
R 1240, Daddy Barlo	150.00
R 1273, bullet	1500.00
R 3322, scout	100.00
R 4233, girl scout	100.00
R 4353, bullet	900.00

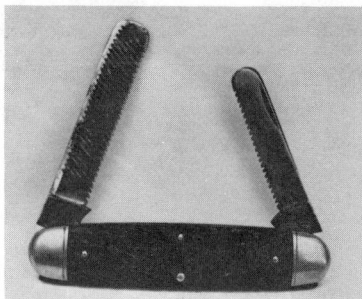

Remington, Dog Grooming Knife, Staghorn handle, 3¾" $115.00

OTHER MANUFACTURES

To provide a comparison for pricing, a folding hunters knife is used for all manufactures.

Barry Wood, Colt	**250.00**
Cattaraugus, #12819	**200.00**
Keen Kutter	**200.00**
Maher & Grosh, #109	**125.00**
Napanoch	**200.00**
Robeson	**100.00**
Schrade, Custer's Last Fight	**125.00**
Smith and Wesson	**150.00**
Winchester, #1920	**1000.00**
G. Wostenholm, #IXL, Gen. Taylor	**1200.00**

POMONA GLASS

Pomona glass, patented in 1885 by Joseph Locke, was produced only by the New England Glass Works. Pomona glass is a delicate type of blown art glass which has a pale soft, beige background and a top band of honey amber that is approximately one inch deep.

There are two distinct types of backgrounds: first grind, made only from April 1885 to June 1886, was produced by fine cutting through a wax coating followed by an acid bath; second grind was a less time consuming method that consisted of rolling the piece in acid resisting particles and acid etching. Both methods produced a soft frosted appearance, but on first grind pieces fine curlicue lines are visible.

Designs were used on some pieces. These were etched and then stained in color; the most familiar design is blue cornflowers.

No reproductions are known. Do not confuse it with a type of glass known as Mid-

western Pomona which is a pressed glass with a frosted body and amber band.

Bowl, N.E. Glass Co., c. 1884, 4½ x 2" $120.00

Bowls

4½ x 2¼" deep, crimped rim, first grind	130.00
8", cornflower, crimped rim, second grind	400.00
Cream and Sugar, crimped tops, first grind	380.00

Pitchers

6", trefoil top, first grind	225.00
8", bulbous, cornflower, diamond optic, second grind	275.00
Water, cornflower, first grind	395.00
Plate, ruffled, second grind	85.00

Punch Cups

Cornflower, first grind	175.00
Cornflower, second grind	140.00
Diamond quilted, first grind	100.00
Rose Bowl, 2½", footed, crimped top, second grind	140.00

Tumblers

Acanthus, first grind	145.00
Cornflower, first grind	200.00
Cornflower, second grind	135.00
Diamond quilted, second grind ..	115.00

Vases

3", fan, second grind	150.00
6½", sheaves of wheat, second grind	285.00

PORTO BELLO WARE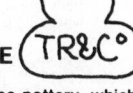

This is a commemorative-type pottery, which was made at Porto Bello Pottery Midlothian, Scotland, in remembrance of Admiral Vernon's victory over the Spanish at Puerto Bello, Panama, November 23, 1739. It was also made by John and Thomas Astbury of Shelton in mid 18th century.

It is brownish-red pottery, glazed with figures of ships and human figures. The glaze is deep brown with allover paisley design in ochre. The ware found today was made in Tunstall, England, after 1830.

Bowl, 4"	155.00
Jug, 7"	195.00
Pitchers	
Large	200.00
Small	185.00
Plate, 7", English Coat of Arms	155.00
Platter, 11½", view of Porto Bello	120.00
Tray, octagonal, signed	255.00

PORTRAIT PLATES

Portrait plates, in the Victorian era, were very popular in decorating the home. Usually they were pictures of beautiful women. However, there are also plates with portraits of Napolean, Queen Victoria, etc., that are very collectible today. Some are artist signed, some are not, and were made by almost all the well known American and European potteries.

Napoleon, marked Bonaparte, Haviland, Limoges, 12½" $60.00

5", center of classic figures, gold borders, signed Kauffmann, pair	185.00
8", Pittsburgh Commandery Plate, girl with roses, blue border gold trim	32.50
8½", transfer picture of lady and cherub	27.50
8½", signed, Madam Sans Gene	60.00
9", Madam LeBrun and daughter, gold border	32.50
9¼", woman with rose in hair, dark brown rim, gold trim, G. Bonfits	40.00
9½", brunette woman, in deep rose and gold	32.50
9½", Madonna and child, brown to tan tints	25.00
9½", Marie Louise, Royal blue, gold and white	42.50
9¼", dark green rim, lady in black hat, signed copyright, 1909, by Phillip Boileau	85.00
9¾", woman with brown hair, yellow background, brown rim, signed, Innocence, Cress Wiollett	35.00
9⅝", Dresden Art #201, tin, Ariadne	35.00
10", farmer, dog, cows, irregular edge, deep colors, gold trim, marked Z. S. Bavaria	55.00
10", divided with gold handle; in center, Napoleon and Josephine; four portraits around edge, R. S. Germany	250.00
11½", Queen Louise, full figure, heavy gold edge, Bavaria	200.00
11", Queen Louise with scarf	67.50

POST CARDS

Post card collecting is technically known as deltiology and a post card collector is called a deltiologist. Austria was the first country to put a post card in the mail in 1869. England followed suit in 1870. The well known Raphael Tuck cards were a result of Queen Victoria's request. The first colored photographic post cards were issued in 1939.

Prices listed are approximate. Artist, subject, condition, circa and desirability must be considered.

Actors or Actresses, pre-1915	3.50
Airplanes, early	3.50
Automobiles, pre-1930	3.50
Billikens, c. 1908	10.00
Capitols, (U.S. State), with seals	5.00
Christmas, embossed, pre-1915	5–10.00
Christmas, general	3.50
Clapsaddles, signed	5–10.00
Courthouses, pre-1925	3.50
Disasters, (Floods, Tornadoes, etc.), pre-1930	2.50
Easter, embossed, pre-1925	3.50
Expositions, 1900's	5–10.00
Florals	1.00
Foreign, early	1.00
Fraternal Organizations	2.00
Gelatin, (Processed type)	1.75
Hall Mfg.	1.50
Humorous	2.50–5.00
Indians, pre-1915	5–10.00
Leather	2.50–7.50
Martin Luther, biographical	5.00

Leather, Autumn Girl, Gartner & Bender (publ.), Chicago $5.00

Lithophanes	7.50–10.00
Mitchell, fruit, flowers, c. 1900's ...	1.50
Series famous musicians cards, set of 10, maker unknown, complete set, c. 1890	40.00
Patriotic	2.00
People, famous	2–5.00
Presidents, pre-1915	5–10.00
Religious, pre-1930	2.50
Royalty	3.50–10.00
Santa Claus	
Bergman	3.50–5.00
Nash	3.50–5.00
Stechner	3.00
Tucks	7.50–15.00
Whitney	3.50–5.00
Winsch & Winsch	3–10.00
U.S.A. (Made)	1.75
Ships, pre-1930	1.50
Souvenir Folders, pre-1925	2.00
States, pre-1930	1.50–5.00
Thanksgiving	2.00
Trains, early	2–10.00
Trolley Cars	2.50–10.00
Tucks	
Dickens	5–7.50
Four Seasons Bears, set of 4 ...	18.00
Greetings, general	3.50–5.00
Greetings, holidays	7.50
Nursery Rhymes	3.00
School Days	5.00
Women	5.00
Valentines, general	2–5.00
Valentines, sentimental, early	5–10.00
World War I	3.00

POSTERS

Posters are commercially produced art works for the purpose of advertising products or services, announcing events or introducing people. They were seldom considered serious works of art, even when executed by accomplished artists. Today, posters are a recognized art form and have attracted art connoisseurs.

Prices given are approximate. Condition is important and affects the final price considerably.

ADVERTISING

"Babbitt's Soap," Tom Sawyer type boy catching fish, 1892, 27 x 14".	150.00
"Dandy For Home Made Candy," Karo, Leyendecker, c. 1920's ...	295.00
"De Laval Cream Separators," 41 x 30", 5 different pictures, farm girl hugging cow, framed, 1905	1250.00
Hires Root Beer, 13 x 37", self-standing, Maxfield Parrish	275.00
"Nabisco," 11 x 22", baker with box of cookies, c. 1910	65.00
National Phonograph Co., 32 x 24", old man & woman listening to Edison Phonograph, 1905	375.00
"Pompeian Beauty," 7½ x 28", Forbes, metal, autographed, "Sincerely, Mary Pickford." Dated 1917	75.00
"Red Cross Cotton," 33 x 24", Negroes picking cotton, wagons, 1894	375.00

ADVERTISING-TOBACCO

"Briar Pipe," 31 x 23", man smoking, framed, 1910	195.00
"Cloth of Gold Cigarettes," 14 x 30", Victorian blonde with fan, framed poster, 1895	295.00
"Flyer 5c Cigar," 9 x 20", Lindberg Commemorative, c. 1920's	10.00
"Kool Cigarettes," 12 x 18", Willie the Penguin, c. 1940	25.00
"Old English," 31 x 24", 18th century Englishman by fireplace with dog, framed, 1900	225.00
"Red Indian Tobacco," 20 x 30", tin rim	225.00

CIRCUS

Cooper Bros., 8 x 22", double sided pictorial, c. 1920's	10.00
Hamid Morton, 'Featuring Clyde Beatty,' litho, late 1940's	50.00
Ringling Bros. Barnum & Bailey, Landing of Columbus, c. 1896 ...	150.00

**Circus, Canadian, 1970's, 17 x
24″ $5.00**

Ringling Bros. Barnum & Bailey, 28 x
40″, litho, c. 1928–30 .... 60.00
Ringling Bros. Barnum & Bailey, 20 x
30″, Col. Tim McCoy, litho, c.
1935 .... 50.00
France, 33 x 44″, Cirque D'Hiver,
Winter Circus, c. 1890 .... 115.00

POLITICAL

Blaine, James G., President and
John A. Logan, Vice-president, 15
x 20″, c. 1884, pair 75.00
"Johnson & Humphrey for the
USA," 20 x 28″, black and white
photos, folded, c. 1964 .... 25.00
McCarthy, 25 x 38″, "Peace," Ben
Shahn, c. 1968 .... 100.00
"Nixon's The One," 20 x 28″, Offi-
cial Nat'l Youth For Nixon—Ag-
new, J. Michailson, c. 1968 .... 35.00
Roosevelt, F.D., A Gallant Leader,
39 x 59″, black and white portrait,
c. 1940 .... 85.00
Wallace, 14 x 22″, c. 1948 .... 35.00

THEATRICAL

African Queen, 40 x 80″, folded, c.
1952, original 175.00
Alice In Wonderland, Disney, 14 x
22″, French 30.00

A Star Is Born, 30 x 45″, Judy Gar-
land and James Mason, c. 1954 . 75.00
Bus Stop, 27 x 41″, Marilyn Monroe,
c. 1956 .... 35.00
Equus, 40 x 60″, Clive Barnes
quote, Broadway edition 55.00
Godspell, 30 x 45″, David Byrd,
Broadway edition 25.00
Gone With The Wind, 27 x 41″,
Classic reissue, 1968–1974 ..... 15.00
Jesus Christ, Superstar, 40 x 80″,
Broadway edition, original 25.00
Red Dragon, The, 14 x 22″, Charlie
Chan, French, c. 1937 .... 25.00
Santa Fe Trail, 14 x 22″, Errol Flynn,
litho, French 30.00
Three Penny Opera, 40 x 80″, Paul
Davis, Broadway edition 60.00

TRAVEL

Air France, 27 x 40″, c. 1935 ..... 40.00
Ile De France, litho, c. 1915 ..... 85.00
Pa. RR, 27 x 42″, Pittsburgh in the
Beginning — Fort Prince George,
1754, linen mounted, N.C. Wyeth,
c. 1925 .... 200.00

WORLD WAR I

"Clear the Way," 20 x 30″, H.C.
Christy, bond 125.00
"Food is Ammunition — Don't Waste
It," 20 x 30″, J.E. Sheridan 80.00
"I Want You for the Navy," 28 x 40″
, H.C. Christy 350.00
"Order Coal Now," 20 x 30″,
Leyendecker 350.00
"Treat 'em Rough," 14 x 22″, Ahgiet
Hutof 175.00
"Weapons For Liberty," Leyen-
decker, bond 200.00
"Your Country Needs You, Join the
Navy Now," 20 x 30″ 100.00

WORLD WAR II

"Buy War Bonds," 28 x 40″ 60.00
"Give 'em Both Barrels," 28 x 40″,
Jean Carlu, mint 275.00
"Keep 'Em Flying," 28 x 40″, Ivan
Dimitri 45.00
"Remember Dec. 7th," 28 x 40″,
Saalburg 65.00
"This Is the Enemy," 20 x 30″ 65.00
"We Have Just Begun to Fight!" 30
x 40″ 35.00

POT LIDS

Pot lids are just 'that' . . . lids from pots or

containers. The pots originally held oint-
ments, pommades or soap. The lids were
decorated with transfers of various scenes.

The majority of these ceramic containers
were made by Pratt, Fenton, Staffordshire
between 1845–1888. Although a complete set
of pot and lid is desirable to some collectors,
lids are the most collectible.

It has been reported that some of these
lids with the original designs have been reissued by Kirkman Pottery, England.

Ceramic, German, 5⅝" $40.00

Bear Pit, (scarce)	100.00
Best Card	110.00
Blue Boy	100.00
Cavalier, The	75.00
Charing Cross	85.00
Crabbing on Ordic Beach	65.00
Cries of London	60.00
Crystal Palace	125.00
Game Bag, The	75.00
Garibaldi	75.00
Golden Hour, Constantinople	100.00
Good Dog	65.00
Hamlet and His Father's Ghost	125.00
Harbour of Hong Kong	65.00
Hide and Seek	75.00
Landing the Fare, Peawell Bay	125.00
Late Prince Consort	110.00
Master of the Hounds	95.00
Natchez Riverboat scene	65.00
Ning Po River	65.00
On Guard	100.00
Pair, A	100.00
Persuasion	75.00
Picnic, The	110.00
Residence of Ann Hathaway	85.00
Rifle Contest, Wimbledon	100.00
Sandringham, The Seat of HRH, The Prince of Wales, 4¼"	65.00
Second Appeal	85.00
Seven Stages of Man, "As You Like It," Act II; also Dr. Johnson, pair, wooden frames	130.00

Shakespeare's Home	95.00
Shepherdess with Dog, 3 sheep . . .	100.00
Shrimpers, The	75.00
Thirsty Soldier, The	55.00
Uncle Toby, 4⅜"	65.00
Village Wedding	125.00
War	95.00
Westminster Abbey	150.00
Wolf and Lamb	75.00

POTTERY, EARLY
See STONEWARE.

POWDER FLASKS AND HORNS

Early containers for carrying gun powder
were made of animal horns, especially those
of cattle and buffalo. In their idle moments,
soldiers and hunters added decorative elements to their horns to distinguish them from
others.

In the mid-19th century manufactured containers of copper, brass, pewter, and other
metals entered the market. The leather and
brass containers were oriented toward the
sport shooter and often had dispensers
which measured the exact charge of powder
needed.

**Horn, inscribed with man with
pipe, dog, eagle and deer, 1858,
8½"** $675.00

Brass

Dead Game, James Dixon Co., 8½"	75.00
Eagle, gun and flask, 4½"	150.00
Feather, embossed	65.00
Hanging Game, American Flask & Cap Co.	50.00
Hanging Game, James Dixon & Sons	80.00
Floral, 5"	50.00
Rabbit, 8"	65.00

Shell, American Flask & Cap Co. . . 75.00
Wreath and Shell, American Flask
& Cap Co. 60.00
Copper
Basketwork & Leaf 90.00
Eagle, brass dispenser, 5″ 85.00
Hunter shooting over dog, James
Dixon & Sons 75.00
Old Powder Horn 62.50
Ribbed 50.00
Stars and disk 85.00
Undecorated 45.00
Horn
5¼″, engraved with spread-
winged eagle, "E. B. Holden,
1834" 250.00
11¼″ engraved with Am. eagle
and shield, Battle of Tippecanoe,
c. 1840 . . . . 900.00
12″, engraved with soldier, sailing
vessel, and animals, "Ruben
John, 1776" 400.00
12¼″, Revolutionary War, en-
graved with soldiers, fish, flowers,
etc., patriotic slogans, "Elijah
Case, 1775" 1200.00
13″, plain, wood plug 60.00
29½″, dark brown, hinged lid
mount in silvered metal, silvered
link chain 75.00
Leather Covered
Flora and Fauna, 9″ 70.00
Plain, James Dixon & Sons, 9″ . . 37.50
Pewter, brass dispenser, 7″ 75.00

PRATT

PRATT WARE

PRATT
FENTON

The earliest Pratt earthenware was made by
William Pratt, Lane Delph in the late 18th century.

In 1810–1818, Felix and Robert Pratt, sons
of William, established their own firm known
as F. & R. Pratt, Fenton, Staffordshire. The
wares consisted of relief molded jugs, commercial pots and tablewares with transfer
decoration. Much of the early ware is
unmarked. The mid-nineteenth century wares
bear several different marks in conjunction
with the name Pratt, including "& Co."
See also POT LIDS.

Candlestick, 7⅜″, figures, Roman
Key border 75.00
Cereal dish and creamer, gilt edges,
white chariot scene on matte
black, pair 180.00

**Plaque, Christ in Wheat Field, signed
J. Austin, c. 1851, 13″ dia. $85.00**

Compote, 9¼″ dia., 5″ high, transfer
of English castle 150.00
Creamer, 3″, basalt, white figures in
relief 65.00
Cream and Sugar
4″, scenic transfer decor, set . . . 100.00
Etruscon, black & white, signed,
pair 125.00
Dessert Set, eight 5½″ plates, oval
handled bowl, scenic transfers . . 350.00
Jar, covered, Uncle Toby 110.00
Mugs
Frog, 5¼″ 125.00
Satyr Mask, 4¼″, c. 1810 . . . . . . 225.00
Pitchers
4¾″, "Mischievous Sport," poly-
chrome 225.00
5¼″, Wellington, pink lustred trim 195.00
6″, The "Greek" Scholars and
Athletes decor, on black, gold
Greek key border 150.00
6½″, transfer of hunt scene, blue
and gold, c. 1850 . . . . 125.00
11″, pewter cover, beige back-
ground, colorful seashells in relief,
c. 1810 . . . . 500.00
Plates
7″, animals and people at tavern,
rust border, artist signed 75.00
Battle of the Nile, basketweave
border, 9½″ 65.00
Game Bag, basketweave border,
9½″ 65.00
Hop Queen, acorn and oak bor-
der, 10″ 150.00
Laundry Woman, tan border, 8½″ 60.00
Philadelphia Exposition 1876, 8½″ 110.00
Picnic, The, maroon border, 8½″ . 60.00
Roman Ruins, Roman Key border,
8½″ 55.00

Shakespeare's Birthplace, basketweave border	**75.00**
7", Shrimper's plate	**160.00**
Times, The, 7"	**55.00**
Trooper, The, basketweave border	**65.00**
Pot Lids, See "Pot Lids"	
Snuff Jar, 4", blue with tan and black transfer of men, animals . . .	**30.00**
Toby Jug, Englishman, 3½", multicolored	**85.00**
Vase, urn-shaped, handles, 4½", classical figures, orange with gold	**95.00**

PRIMITIVE PAINTINGS

The portrait, miniature and silhouette were the prime ways to capture personal images in the early 19th century. Demand, especially in rural areas, exceeded the pool of academic trained artists. The portraits of the primitive or folk artist often are out of proportion or contain unusual facial expressions. The palette also ranges greatly.

Some of these portraits were painted in stages. The artist would prepare the background and body of a subject in his studio. Then he would travel the countryside seeking prospective clients. The head and additional body features, e.g., decoration to clothing and jewelry, were added to complete the portrait. Seldom are these paintings signed by the artist. Recent scholarship has focused on trying to identify these individuals.

Primitive type painting continues. Twentieth century artists, namely Grandma Moses, are bringing record breaking prices at auction.

Prices are for paintings sold. Prices vary according to desirability, quality and condition.

Boy, Young, with Hobby Horse, oil, 19th C., 11½ x 9½"	**800.00**
Boy, Young, with Toy Cat, oil, early 19th C., 24½ x 19"	**13000.00**
Child, watercolor, landscape, dog, 19th C., 12 x 8¾"	**175.00**
Child in Pink Gown, pastel, budding rose, 19th C., 15⅝ x 11½"	**800.00**
Girl, young, pastel, ¾ view, carrying basket of flowers, 19th C., 22½ x 17¼"	**275.00**
Hoffman, Charles, oil, View of the Schuylkill County Almshouse Property, at the Year 1881, 30 x 41¾"	**90000.00**
Landscape with figures, oil, two gentlemen standing before landscape with lakes, shipping, mountains, etc., 19th C., 21½ x 29"	**550.00**
Maentel, Jacob, watercolor, Boy with Parrot, 6¼ x 7½"	**15000.00**

Prior, William Matthew, oil, Captain Littlejohn, 33½ x 28"	**2750.00**
Stone, F. H., oil, View of Hudson River, 19th C., 17 x 25¼"	**135.00**
Three children in Interior, oil, c. 1855, 17¼ x 19½"	**1650.00**

PRINTS

Prints serve many purposes. They can be a reproduction of an artist's paintings, drawings, or designs. Prints themselves often are an original art form. Finally, prints can be developed for mass appeal as opposed to aesthetic statement. Much of the production of Currier & Ives fits this latter category. Currier & Ives concentrated on the genre, urban, patriotic, and nostalgia scenes.

Prints are beginning to attract a wide following. This is partially because prices have not matched the rapid rise in oil and other paintings.

Reproductions are a problem, especially of the Currier & Ives prints. Check the dimensions before buying any print.

Wall, W. G., View of the Canal at the Little Falls, Mohawk River, engraved by Fenner, Sears, & Co. **$45.00**

Audubon, J. J.

American Goldfinch, 1832, 19½ x 12½"	**800.00**
Owls group, 1838, 21¾ x 26" . . .	**900.00**
Savanah Finch, 1831, 19¼ x 12½"	**550.00**
Snowy Owl, 1837, ¾ x 25⅛" . . .	**3000.00**

Baille, J.

Eliza	**30.00**
Iron Steamship	**140.00**

Christy, Howard Chandler

Four in Hand, 1901	**60.00**
Gold is Not All	**50.00**
Poaching, 1903	**55.00**

Currier and Ives

American Country Life, October Afternoon, large folio	**500.00**

Burning of the Clipper Ship Golden Light, 8¼ x 12¼″ 135.00
Great East River Suspension Bridge, 1881, 9 x 12⅞″ 300.00
Life of Hunter, Catching a Tartar, 1861, 18½ x 27⅛″ 2750.00
Portraits, small folio, each 35.00
Presidents, Washington to Polk, small folio, each 90.00
Through Express, 6⅞ x 13⅜″ . . 650.00
Velociped, 1869, 8¼ x 12¾″ . . . 550.00
Godey, fashion print 17.50

Haskill and Allen
Fannie 27.50
Smuggler 67.50

Icart, Louis
Amazonia 2250.00
Autumn Leaves 375.00
Blue Buddha 325.00
Butterfly Falls 1000.00
Cassanova 400.00
Cat with paw in fish bowl 430.00
Dollar 300.00
Finlandia 550.00
French Doll 325.00
Intimacy 475.00
Lovers 2700.00
Milkmaid 240.00
On the Beach 300.00
Red Riding Hood 425.00
Sleeping Beauty 650.00
Tosca 450.00
View of Montmarte 275.00
White Wings 550.00
Woman holding little red cage . . 315.00
Woman with cat 1100.00
Zest 700.00

Kellog, E. C., Uncle Tom and Little Eva 60.00

Kellog and Thayer, The Soldier's Adieu 75.00

Nutting, Wallace, matted and framed
Berkshire Cross Roads 25.00
Brookside Blossoms, 9 x 12″ . . . 35.00
Cliff Clingers 17.50
Flowering Time, 4½ x 13″ 30.00
Mohawk Drive 30.00
Polishing the Sheffield, 10 x 18″ . 50.00
Road to Far Away 30.00
Rock Bound Coast 40.00
Stitch in Time 70.00
Unbroken Flow, 12″ x 21″ 35.00
Where the Road Turns 25.00

Parrish, Maxwell
Brazen, The Boatman, 10 x 12″ . 37.50
Canyon (maiden in the canyon), 14 x 17″ 60.00
Dawn, Mazda print 42.00
Daybreak, 18 x 30″, c. 1954 . . . . 55.00
Enchantment, 9½ x 20½″ 140.00
Fishermen and the Geni, 10 x 12″ 40.00
Garden of Opportunity 55.00

Hilltop, small size 75.00
King of Black Isles, 10 x 12″ 40.00
Little Princess 17.50
Night Call, 6 x 8″ 25.00
Pandora's Box 45.00
Potpourri 18.00
Prosperina, 10 x 12″ 42.50
Sandman, 6 x 7½″ 30.00
Singing Tree, 10 x 12″ 35.00
Walls of Jasper, 12 x 14″ 90.00
Waterfall, large Edison Mazda calendar 250.00

Rockwell, Norman—see "Norman Rockwell"

Sarony and Major
Death of Montgomery 75.00
Wedding Day 50.00

PRINTS, JAPANESE

Japanese woodblock prints currently are very popular. Prices have risen dramatically during the past four years.

Values ranges from a few dollars to thousands of dollars depending on an artist, subject, quality and condition. A popular print has many editions. First and second editions command the highest price.

Abbreviations:

H = Horizontal	C = Chuban, 7″ x 10″
T = Triptych	K = Koban, 6″ x 9″
V = Vertical	O = Oban, 10″ x 15″

Azechi
Portrait of woman, 46/100, 1955, VC 80.00

Chikuyo
Portraits of actors Ichimura, Uzaemon, and Nakamura Shikon, 1860, VO 250.00

Choki
Courtesan with fancy hairdo and kimono, H 175.00

Eisen
Shrine and tea house at Atagoyama, Toto Meisho, Zukushi, 1830, HO 325.00
Woman carrying a biwa, VO 250.00

Eishi
Man, boy, two girls, eight bijin, O . 1200.00

Eisho
Two women bringing tachi, O . . . 2250.00

Eizan
Courtesan with towel, VO 225.00
Geisha reading hand scroll, scroll 600.00

Goyo
Nude drying after bath, O 3000.00

Hausi
Moonlight on canal, 1931, O 450.00
Sado Kamomura, 1920, O 1000.00

Hiroshige I, Gyosho, Tokaido series, c. 1840 . . . . $400.00

Hiroshige I
Cliffs at Konotai and Tonegawa River, 100 Views of Edo, 1856, VO 650.00
Drinking in garden at night, HK . . 400.00
Famous Views of the 60 Odd Provinces, 1853–1856, VO
Chikuzen, boats 450.00
Omi-Moonlit night scene 600.00
Figures on cliff with cherry trees and sailboats (Gotenyana Hanami), OV 1000.00
Rain at Oiso, 1832, Hoeido Takaido, HO 900.00

Hiroshige II
Ekoin Temple Complex at Ryogaku, TO 900.00
Mountain Village by River, 1862, VC 350.00

Hiroshige III
View of Fuji, 36 Views of Tokoyo, 1870, VO 200.00

Hokusai
A View of Mt. Fuji from Totsuka, from 36 Views of Fuji, c. 1813, HK 1500.00

Kampo
Morning at Sanjobashi, 1925, O . . 225.00

Kunisada
Bijin and her attendant, O 175.00
Mother and child, 1830, VO 650.00
Princess Genj and his lover watch boat, TO 400.00
Theatrical Scene with three actors, TO 420.00
Warrior climbing out of box, 1840, HO 300.00

Kuniyoshi
Actors in various roles, 1865, VO . 225.00
Farmer showing waterfalls to travelers, One Hundred Poem Series, O 475.00
Sage with golden cat and six children beneath willow tree, VO . . . 550.00

Young Lovers at Oyashiro Shrine, Iwami — Medicine Vendor, c. 1852, VO 1500.00
Shinsui
Distant Mountain, sunset, 1949, O 225.00
Man in boat, misty marshes, 1919, C 2000.00
Woman adjusting hairpin, 1923, O 450.00
Shunsen
Actor hiding parasol, O 200.00
Ichikawa Enjaku against curtain, O 150.00
Shunsho
Actor as Samurai, H 1200.00
Toyohiro
Hotei crossing stream, O 350.00
Two bijin playing with hobbyhorses, H 1100.00
Toyokuni I
Actor as Woman, viewing party, 1800, OV 400.00
Interior scene of a green house with courtesans, OT 1500.00
Raiko punishing Oni, VO 725.00
Toyokuni II
Boys and women in garden, 1854, VC 275.00
Nobleman in a villa looking out at a lake, TO 450.00
Yoshida, Hiroshi
Avenue of Cherry Trees, 1935, Cherry series, HO 600.00
Grand Canyon, 1925, HO 425.00
Niagara Falls, 1925, American series, HO 390.00
Zeshin
Stick of bamboo with fishing net, C 350.00

QUEZAL Quezal

Quezal Art Glass was a very fine quality blown iridescent glassware produced by Martin Bach, a former Tiffany employee, in his factory in Brooklyn, N.Y., from 1901–1920. The company was called the Quezal Art Glass and Decorating Co. After the death of Bach, his son-in-law, Conrad Vohlsing, opened a small shop near Elmhurst, L.I., New York, where he produced the same type of ware until 1929. Vahlsing marked his glass "Lustre Art Glass."

Named after the Central American bird, Quezal Glass has an iridescent finish featuring contrasting colored glass threads. While still in the cooling stage, the threads were pulled up and drawn into various designs, often a drape with a peacock eye at the end of the feather. Gold, green and white colors are most often found.

Candlestick, 10″, blue iridescent . . . 400.00

Shade, pulled feather motif, gold, green, and white, marked, c. 1910, 5¾" $200.00

Cologne, gold iridescent, red high-lights	175.00
Compote, 6 x 8" high, gold irides-cent	550.00
Lamp Shades—See "Lamp Shades"	
Nut Dish—gold-blue iridescent, signed	200.00
Rose Bowl, 4", gold iridescent	500.00
Salts	
Blue-gold iridescent, signed	175.00
Gold-rimmed	180.00
Vases	
4½", classical, gold iridescent ...	225.00
4¾", ovoid, two shades of green, cream top, lily pad decor, signed .	1000.00
6", gold iridescent, pulled feather on calcite	350.00
6¾", gold iridescent, green leaf and vine decor, signed	500.00
7" blue-gold iridescent, silver overlay, signed	1400.00
8¼", white, blue, gold swirl decor, 3 footed, signed	1800.00
9", dark blue, silver King Tut de-cor, signed	750.00
9¾", gold iridescent, violet high-lights, silver overlay, signed	650.00
11", Jack-in-the-Pulpit, dark blue, gold swirl decor, blue-gold irides-cent lining, signed	1050.00
Flower form, calcite with green and yellow pulled feather decor, gold lining	1700.00

QUILTS

Quilts have been passed down as family heirlooms for many generations. Each is an individual expression as patterns of like style have risen hundreds of variations both in color and design.

The advent of the sewing machine increased, not decreased the number of quilts which were made. Quilts still are being sewn today.

The key considerations for price are age, condition, aesthetic beauty and design. The latter point is especially important. Pricewise, quilts have risen dramatically over the last ten years. The market now is glutted, causing a leveling in prices. The exception is the very finest examples which continue to bring record prices.

Bowtie, pieced calico, multicolored, 80 x 76"	400.00
Crazy Quilt, Victorian, pieced silk, quarter circle pattern, 76 x 75" ..	350.00
Double Irish Chain, pieced cotton, light blue, maroon, and lavendar, c. 1930, 78 x 76"	675.00
Duck's Foot in Mud, pieced cotton, red and yellow, 80 x 92"	625.00
Feathered Star, multicolors, 72 x 96"	320.00
Flower Basket, pieced cotton, medium blue solid, 70 x 80"	525.00
Friendship, appliqued, N.E., numerous printed and solid cut outs, late 19th C., 88 x 89"	2750.00
Kansas Troubles, pieced calico, multicolored, 84 x 88"	200.00
Masonic, appliqued, masonic symbols, 80 x 102"	1500.00
Mosaic, wool, Amish, Pa., hexagonal shapes, multicolored, 80 x 84" ..	1200.00
Oak Leaf, pieced calico, N.E., tasseled swag border, 19th C., 80 x 98"	610.00
Penny and Bud, appliqued cotton, N.Y. or Pa., red and green, 82 x 100"	725.00
Princess Feather, appliqued cotton, Pa., red and green, eagle borders, 92 x 94"	3500.00
Roman Stripe, multicolors, 62 x 61"	225.00
Saw Tooth, pieced calico, Pa., red, green, yellow, 72 x 84"	250.00
Star, pieced cotton, red, green, white, 84 x 92"	660.00
Star of Bethlehem, pieced linslev woolsey, multicolored, 76 x 76" ..	2500.00
Tulip, pieced calico, Pa., red, green, yellow, 84 x 88"	425.00
Turkey Track, red, yellow, green, c. 1900, 100 x 85"	1350.00

Whig Rose, appliqued and trapunto,
Pa., red, green, yellow, mid-19th
C., 84 x 84" **1200.00**

QUIMPER

Quimper pottery is a tin-glazed earthenware
that has been produced in and around the
town of Quimper in Northwest France since
the late 17th century. Three factories sur-
vived through the 19th century with items
from these three found most frequently on
the market today.

Jules Henriot used the HR mark from 1886
through 1926 when the familiar Henriot mark
appeared. The Porquier-Beau "Golden Period" occurred in the 1880's. This mark is most
prized by collectors.

The Hubaudiere-Bousquet HB covers most
of the 1880's and into the present period and
exists in many styles and forms. In 1968 the
Henriot and HB faienceries consolidated
and began producing the modern dinnerware
seen today.

Plate, fish shape **$85.00**

Basket, small, greyish glaze with
blue handle, Henriot mark **95.00**
Bell, fleur-de-lis handle and floral de-
cor, unglazed clapper **70.00**
Bookends, boy and girl figurals on
gun metal, color bases, artist
signed **450.00**
Bottle, 14½" with stopper, HB
Quimper mark **275.00**
Bowls
Fruit, 9", yellow and blue striped
pattern, pierced for hanging **50.00**
Mush, floral decor, tight rope han-
dles **45.00**
Soup, wide rim with border of yel-
low and blue stripes **48.00**
Butter Pat, ruffled edges, HR Quim-
per mark **25.00**

Chamberstick, clover shaped base
with ring handles, slotted for raising candle, Henriot mark **85.00**
Cider Jug, 6½", two bale handles,
tiny pouring spout, peasant decor **80.00**
Cigarette Box with pair of matching
ash trays, blue sponging with or-
ange circles **85.00**
Cream and Sugar, pear color glaze
with wide looping handles **55.00**
Cruets, joined at base with crossed
necks, tan glaze, HB Quimper
mark **75.00**
Cup and Saucer, blue fleur-de-lis
pattern on white background,
wishbone handle **25.00**
Egg Cup, blue and yellow stripes,
strutting rooster **28.00**
Figural, dancing couple in peasant
dress, artist signed **185.00**
Figural, three old women gossiping **650.00**
Fish Plate, 10½", outline of fish
molded into pattern, male peasant
in center, strong red and blue col-
ors **58.00**
Gravy Boat, attached underplate,
single pouring handle, yellow bor-
der with blue inner bands **85.00**
Hotplate, footed, with yellow glaze,
peasant decor **60.00**
Inkstand, 15", two covered wells on
base with four small feet, fleur-de-
lis opening in backplate, Henriot
mark **275.00**
Inkwell, heart shaped, yellow glaze,
peasant and floral **125.00**
Knife Rest, blue sponged ends with
peasant in center, Henriot mark . **32.00**
Pencil Holder, orange glaze, geometric pattern, pierced top **75.00**
Pitchers
4", green dragon handle, Henriot
mark **70.00**
6¼", pinched spout and bulbous
body **65.00**
8¼", helmut shaped on narrow
footed base, blue and yellow
striped **75.00**
Planter, footed, diamond shape,
seated peasants, HR Quimper
mark **145.00**
Plates
1¾", geometric pattern **18.00**
5", scalloped border, red and blue
dashes, HR Quimper mark on
front **35.00**
8", yellow border, blue inner
bands, peasant motif **25.00**
9¼", botanical pattern for English
trade, Porquier-Beau mark **375.00**
9¼", mustard background, blue,
yellow and green florals in bunch-

es 38.00
9½", octagonal, yellow glaze,
peasant decor 25.00
Porringer, 6", double blue sponge
handles, yellow and blue stripes,
peasant, pierced for hanging 25.00
Powder Jar, greyish glaze, floral decor, Henriot mark 65.00
Ramekin, clover shaped with vertical
ribbing on sides, male peasant .. 28.00
Salt and Pepper, figurals, cork stop-
pers 50.00
Salts, pair, seated peasants figurals
with open baskets at sides, HB
Quimper mark in brown 195.00
Sauciere, covered with blue sponge
handle, yellow border, blue inner
rings 55.00
Syrup Jug, wide loop handle, match-
ing cover, HB Quimper mark 85.00
Teapot, panels outlined in blue, late
HB Quimper mark 55.00
Teaset, three piece, Deco Apple
Blossom pattern, HB Quimper
mark 150.00
Trays
Pin, shaped like bagpipe, HB
Quimper mark 25.00
Relish, 15", three sections (two
cabbage rose, middle peasant),
fan shaped, HB Quimper mark .. 85.00
Relish, rectangular, two small
open handles, yellow glaze, raised
red and blue daisy-like flowers,
Henriot mark 48.00
Serving, 15", oval, blue border, al-
ternating green and rust dashes . 85.00
Vase, pair, fan shaped with round
feet, male and female peasant on
front, Henriot mark 150.00
Vase, 5", dark blue and grey geometric pattern, HB Quimper Odetta
mark 45.00
Wall Pocket, cone-shaped, front
view of male peasant 88.00
Wine Casket, 5", Henriot mark 210.00

R.S. GERMANY
R.S. POLAND
R.S. PRUSSIA
R.S. SUHL
R.S. TILLOWITZ
See SCHLEGELMILCH PORCELAIN.

RADIO RECEIVERS

A growing number of collectors have taken
an interest in early items from the radio
broadcasting field. At present, radio receivers are one of their favorites. Old radio programs are also popular remembrances of the
pre-TV era.

**Zenith, Trans-Oceanic Wave Mag-
net $55.00**

Atwater Kent, Cathedral 65.00
Clapp Eastman, R4 .... 95.00
Crosley, Ace B3 .... 50.00
Crosley, Bandbox 45.00
Eveready, table model, metal cabi-
net, c. 1932 .... 100.00
Grebe, table model with separate
speakers, type CR5, c. 1920's .. 275.00
Magnavox, TRF, c. 1925 .... 250.00
Marconiphone, model 42, table top,
c. 1930's 125.00
Philco, Beehive-type, c. 1930's ... 75.00
Philco, Transitone 35.00
RCA, Aeriola, Jr., c. 1922 .... 125.00
RCA Radiola, 3A 165.00
RCA Victor, Traveler, battery operat-
ed, complete, c. 1925 .... 125.00
Stromberg Carlson, table model, 125 155.00
Westinghouse, 3 tube 60.00
Zenith, VIII 180.00

RAILROAD ITEMS

Railroad collectors have existed for decades.
The merger of the rail systems and the end
of passenger service made many objects
available for private collections. The Pennsylvania Railroad sold its archives at public sale.
Railroad enthusiasts have organized into
regional and local clubs. Join one if interested. Your local hobby store can probably
point you to the right person. The best
pieces pass between collectors and rarely
make it into the general market place.

Adlake Nonsweating Lantern, Chicago, four color lights, 17½″ . . $125.00

Baggage and Brass Checks

B & O, round	10.00
Erie, octagonal	8.00
Pennsylvania, square	3.00

Badges

Baggageman, PRR, gold colored	25.00
Police, C & NY, 3¼″	175.00

Book, Rules and Instructions, c. 1915–1930, average . . . . — 2–5.00

Buttons, Uniform, brass

1870–1900	5.00
1900–1952	3.00

Dining Car, Tablewares

Ashtray, Norfolk and Western, 4¾ x 6¾″ 17.50

Bowls

6¼″, C & O, George Washington, Buffalo China 50.00

8″, Chicago, Milwaukee, St. Paul, Pacific Traveler 90.00

Butter Pat, Atlantic Coast Line, Carolina, Sterling China Co. 12.50

Caster, 2 crewets, GN, silverplate, International 125.00

Celery, Erie, Susquehanna, Buffalo China 65.00

Coffee Pot, PRR, Keystone Herald, silverplate 50.00

Cream and Sugar, covered, NY, NHRR, silverplated, Reed & Barton 80.00

Cups and Saucers

Bouillion, CB&O, Chuck Wagon, Syracuse China 60.00

Demitasse, UP, Winged Streamline, Sterling China 25.00

Flatware, silverplated

Bouillion spoon	8–12.00
Cocktail fork	6–10.00
Dinner fork	10–17.50
Knife	12–20.00
Tablespoon	15–30.00
Teaspoon	10–20.00
Serving Spoon	15–30.00

Goblet, UP 7.50

Menu Holder, PRR, applied Keystone crest 30.00

Plates

5½″, CN, Queen Elizabeth, Royal Doulton 25.00

5¾″, Alaska, McKinley logo, Shenango China 150.00

6¼″, C & O, George Washington 27.50

7½″, soup, MRR, Traveler, Syracuse China 17.50

8″, soup, MRR, Peacock, Syracuse China 22.50

10½″, D & H, Adirondeck, Syracuse China 85.00

10½″, NYC, Country Gardens, Buffalo China 60.00

Platters

8½″, oval, GN, Mountains and Flowers, Syracuse China 30.00

9½″, C & O, George Washington, Buffalo China 85.00

11¾″, Southern, Peach Blossom, Buffalo China 40.00

Relish, NYC, Vanderbilt, Limoges, 5¾ x 8½″ 65.00

Sauce boat, L & N, International . 50.00

Tablecloth with logos

36 x 36″, square	15.00
42 x 58″	20.00

Tray, bread, silverplate, SOO, Gorham, 13¼ x 6″ 55.00

Tumbler, LVRR, 3¼″ 17.50

Vegetable, Washington Terminal, Shenango China, 7¼″ 30.00

Firebucket, canvas, folding metal frame, bail handle 40.00

Lanterns, Hand

Adams & Westlake, etched globe, ring bottom 40.00

Adlake Reliable, embossed globe, ring bottom 75.00

Dietz Vesta, clear globe, single

ring 65.00
M. M. Buck, clear globe, brass
   top, bell bottom, c. 1908 . . . .   125.00
Lanterns, Marker
   Adlake, blue lens, brass plated, c.
   1906 . . . .   125.00
   Handlan, amber lens 85.00
Lanterns, Switch
   Armspear, 4 lenses, two red, two
   green 125.00
   Dressel, 4 lenses 70.00
Oil Can, large spout, copper, 24″ . .   60.00
Paperweight, grizzly bear, bronze fin-
   ish, Chicago, Milwaukee & St.
   Paul 75.00
Passes, c. 1890–1915, average . . . 7.50–12.50
Switch Key 10.00
Telegraph Key, brass, early 25.00
Tickets, c. 1890–1930, average . . . 5–10.00
Timetables
   Pre-1900 . . . .   10–15.00
   1900–1930 . . . . 7.50–12.50
   1930–1965 . . . .   4–9.00
Water Dispenser, NY, NH, H, gallon,
   milk can shape, tin with brass
   spigot 55.00
Way Bills
   First Half 19th C. 25–75.00
   Second Half 19th C. 7.50–30.00
Whistle, Caboose, brass, steam op-
   erated, Sherbourne Co., c. 1930 .   75.00

RAZORS

Razors date back several thousand years.
Early man used sharpened stones. The Egyptians, Greeks, and Romans had metal razors.
   Early metal razors were made of hand-
hammered steel such as Damascus steel.
Later, in the 19th century, razors were made
of machine steel and hard tempered to hold
their edges. Germany (Solingen) and England
(Sheffield) blades were popular. Often foreign
blades were imported for American manufactured razors. By the last quarter of the 19th
century, American made blades were available.
   In collecting razors the fancier the handle
or more intricately etched the blade the
higher the price. Ivory and pearl handles are
especially desirable. Beware of imitations.
Several American knife and gun manufacturers made razors — Case, Kabar (Union Cutlery Co.), and Winchester.

AMERICAN BLADES

A. F. Bannister Co., Newark, N.J.,
   blade etched with eagle, green
   marbleized handle with nickle inlay   45.00
Case, "133 Red Imperial," red celluloid handle with raised decoration   18.00

(TOP) Reliance Cutlery Co., two col-
ored celluloid handle, $65.00; (BOT-
TOM) German, distributed by J. P.
Alcamizi, Schenectady, N.Y., marked
Lincoln, imitation wood grain celluloid
handle $75.00

De Moines Barber Supply Co., "La
   Fiesta," brown, wood grain style
   celluloid handle 18.00
Genco, Henry's, Geneva, N.Y., or-
   ange and yellow marbleized raised
   filigree handle, marked $1.00 on
   tang 15.00
Shumate Razor Co., St. Louis, Mo.,
   "Schumate Barber's Deluxe," yel-
   low bone ivory handle 19.00
Simmons Hardware Co., "K 83 Keen
   Kutter," black celluloid handle,
   serrated tang top and bottom . . .   15.00

DUTCH BLADES

Najaeb Malluk, etched blade of Statue of Liberty and ship, marbleized
   celluloid handle 55.00

ENGLISH BLADES

"John Barber," raised sterling silver
   handle with cabin, river, castle,
   stag and dog, possible blade re-
   placement 100.00
John Roger & Sons, wedge blade,
   pressed horn handle with mother
   of pearl and silver inlay, c. 1830 .   55.00
Sheffield blade, "The Admirals,"
   black celluloid handle 20.00
George Wostenholm & Son, horn
   handle, weight on top of blade,
   etching worn 15.00

GERMAN BLADES

S. Baltuch, etched blade, black celluloid handle with silver tip, mother
   of pearl tang 35.00
Bartman, Solingen, yellow celluloid
   handle with silver inlay 25.00
Halma, Shear & Co., Razor Works,
   Solingen, "105 — PEP," brown,
   wood grain style celluloid handle .   21.00

T. Hessen-Bruch & Co., "Perfection," bone handle, blade inserted into top 12.00

J. Hollinger & Bros., "Barber's Leader, No. 410," black celluloid handle with raised pair of sissors and name, serrated on bottom of tang. 12.00

Imperial Razor, "America's Steel King," black celluloid handle . . . 20.00

Imperial Razor, "Horticultural Building," (1876 Centennial), black celluloid handle 20.00

Steinbruck & Drucks, Solingen, "Mozart Spezial," imitation ivory handle with silver embellishment . 20.00

"Tennis, K4," marbleized red celluloid handle with shield, serrated tang top and bottom 12.00

Wedge blade etched with Masonic symbols, pressed buffalo horn handle 65.00

Weiner Schaber, No. 7, black celluloid handle with silver diamond shaped inlay of Puma 12.00

Wilkes-Barre B. S. Co., "Silver Steel," yellow celluloid handle inlayed with silver end caps and insignia 12.00

UNIDENTIFIED BLADES

"Galvanic," black celluloid handle with art deco woman with flowing hair 30.00

Yellow celluloid handle with acanthus style end, pearl tang 15.00

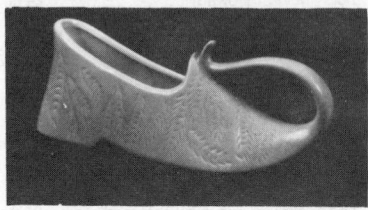

RED WING POTTERY

There were several potteries located in Red Wing, Minnesota, in the late 1800's. The parent company was the Red Wing Stoneware Co. A merger with other local potteries resulted in the formation of the Red Wing Union Stoneware Co. in the early 1900's. The firm was one of the largest producers of stoneware utilitarian wares — crocks and jugs — in the United States.

In 1930, when the desirability for stoneware items diminished, a line of art pottery was introduced and the company was renamed **Red Wing Potteries, Inc.** Production of stoneware continued in limited quantities until 1947. The art line flourished until 1967 when the stockholders voted to liquidate the establishment due to labor disputes.

Planter, rose color, 9″ **$35.00**

Bean Pot, covered, interior glaze, Provincial ware 25.00

Beater Jar, Stoneware 35.00

Bowl, 8 x 3¼″, deep, tab handles, matte green 15.00

Canning Jar, 1 quart, Stoneware . . 35.00

Coffee Server, 12¾″, green, "Waffle" 25.00

Compote, 6 x 9″ dia., green matte . 17.00

Console Sets
Square-shaped, bowl 9″, candlesticks 3¾″, white with pale green interior 25.00
Bowl 10″, candlesticks 2 x 5″ long, ivory with brown accents, vintage decor 30.00

Cookie Jars, figural
Apple, turquoise 25.00
Baker, blue 35.00
Yellow 28.00
French Chef 25.00

Crock Pot, 4 x 5″, handles, unglazed tan exterior, glazed interior 25.00

Crocks
3 gal., stoneware 25.00
5 gal., grey stoneware 35.00

Jugs
1 gal., grey, Minnesota stoneware 25.00
½ gal., white, Minnesota stoneware 35.00

Pitchers
4″, "Waffle" 10.00
Sponge Band 55.00

Planter, 14″, aqua glaze 20.00

Teapots
Rooster, green 20.00
Handpainted florals on cream ground, flower finial 25.00

Vases
6″, geometric design 12.00
6½″, ivory, gardenia in relief, brown stain 27.50
7½″, fan, pink 10.00

8", green, Bird of Paradise in relief	28.00
8", yellow, free form	12.00
10½", five finger-type, brown and green	30.00
11", stippled exterior, glazed interior, Union Stoneware	45.00
Wall Pocket, 8", flower form, white .	15.00

REDWARE

From the late 1600's on, the availability of clay, the same used to make bricks and roof tiles, accounted for the great production of red earthenware pottery in the American colonies. Redware pieces are mainly utilitarian — bowls, crocks, jugs, etc.

Lead glazed redware retained its reddish color, but a variety of colored glazes were obtained by the addition of metals to the basic glaze. Streaks and mottled splotches in redware items resulted from impurities in the clay and/or uneven firing temperatures.

"Slipware" is a term used to describe redwares decorated by the application of slip, a semi-liquid paste made of clay. Slipwares were made in England, Germany and elsewhere in Europe for decades before becoming popular in the Pennsylvania Dutch country and elsewhere in colonial America.

Crock, Strassburg, Va., green slip $125.00

Banks

3¼", dog's head, brown glaze . .	65.00
5¾", frog, brown glaze	150.00
6½", seated dog, green and brown glaze	570.00
Beaker, 3⅝", tooled rim, speckled brown glaze	105.00

Bowls

9½" dia., brown glaze, manganese sponging on rim	115.00
11¾" dia., brown slip lines, green splash decoration	580.00
Shaving bowl, yellow slip, 1779, worn	395.00
Butter Tub, marked "John Bell, Waynesboro," mottled orange and brown glaze	1100.00
Candlestick, 5", marked "M.A. & A.A. #22-1866," brown glaze . . .	210.00

Crocks

2½", miniature, brown glaze . . .	45.00
4", impressed C. Link, inside glaze	57.50
5", brown glaze	17.50
5", green glaze in spots and stripes	150.00
12½", with lid, green and yellow slip, brown glaze	295.00
Apple butter, one handle, inside glaze	35.00

Figures

Lion, Shenandoah, 8½", brown speckled glaze	4500.00
Man Sitting on Dog, attributed to Bell, red glaze	5700.00
Sitting Dog, basket around neck, attributed to John Bell, mottled glaze	2100.00
Flask, manganese splash, brown glaze	190.00

Flower Pots

3¾", attached saucer, mottled cream glaze	165.00
5", attached saucer, green and brown glaze	75.00
7¼", unattached saucer, crimped rim, cream and brown glaze	155.00
7¾", marked S. Bell & Son, green, cream and brown glaze . .	525.00
Hanging pot, reddish brown glaze	70.00
Hot Plate, marked "John Bell, Waynesboro," embossed urn of flowers, brown with manganese splash	555.00

Jars

Jelly, 5", mottled green and red glaze	80.00
Jelly, green mottled glaze	55.00
Ovoid, 15½", with lid, incised designs, high open handles, yellow slip and green glaze	550.00

Jugs

6", ovoid, brown splotches on green glaze	125.00
7", ovoid, dark brown	45.00
7¼", marked John Bell, brown glaze	205.00
8½", ovoid, green glaze	275.00

Loaf Dishes

Crow's feet in yellow slip	410.00
Four line yellow slip	290.00
Mold, curved fish, 12⅝", clear glaze	160.00

Mugs

5¾", marked John Bell, brown running glaze	435.00
6", brown speckled glaze	65.00
6½", bands of manganese sponge, red glaze	395.00

Pitchers

5½", strap handle, brown glaze	60.00
6", New Geneva, Pa., brushed brown flowers and scallops, unglazed body	500.00
7¾", incised bands, green and brown glaze	225.00
10", marked S. Bell & Son, Strasburg, cream slip on brown and green glaze	515.00
10", Medinger type, embossed eagle and banner, brown glaze	300.00
Shenandoah type, green, cream and brown glaze	475.00

Plates

6", four line yellow slip	150.00
6½", brown and yellow wavy slip lines	225.00
7¼", brown glaze	55.00
8", crow's feet in yellow slip	180.00
9¼", marked "John W. Bell, Waynesboro," brown glaze	185.00
9¼", star design in yellow slip	700.00
11½", four line yellow slip	325.00
12", ABC in yellow slip script	500.00
13½", JPD in yellow slip script	900.00
14", two line slip	230.00
Soap Dish, marked "John Bell, Waynesboro," brown glaze	360.00
Sugar Bowl, lid with bird finial, brown glaze	900.00
Spittoon, 5¼" marked "John Bell, Waynesboro," brown spone glaze, hairline	140.00

Turksheads

8", fluted sides, manganese splash on rim, brown glaze	65.00
9", fluted sides, brown glaze	50.00
9¾", marked "John Bell, Waynesboro," light brown glaze	210.00
Wall Pocket, Shenandoah, applied flowers and bird	750.00
Whistle, 3", rooster on top, reddish brown glaze	1300.00

RELIGIOUS ITEMS

Objects for the worshipping or expression of man's belief in a superhuman power are being collected by many people for many reasons.

Icons are included in this category, as they are religious momentos; usually paintings with a brass encasement. They have been collected dating from the earliest time of Christianity. What is available in shops today are usually from the mid-1880's.

Italian, polychrome, wood, 18th C., 14" $1100.00

Bible, leather-covered, brass locks, mid-1800	70.00
Cross, ivory, on chain, hand carved	40.00
Fonts, Holy Water	
Angel, 3½", porcelain, French	100.00
Cross, 2½", porcelain, hand painted	65.00
Madonna, 14", Parian	150.00
Icons	
6", brass, Greek Saints, enamel background	325.00
Three-panelled Cathedral scene, 16" high, Russian, 17th century	1400.00
Hymnals, any denomination, good condition	3.00
Pews from old churches	220.00
Rock of Ages, Bread Plate, glass, with milk glass center	125.00

REVERSE PAINTING ON GLASS

Reverse painting on glass was produced in parts of Europe in the 17th century and a similar technique was applied by the Chinese as early as the 13th century. However, reverse painting on glass did not reach any significance in America until the 18th century.

European artists preferred classical and mythological scenes. In America, the subject matter was usually confined to patriotism, family mourning pictures and traditional still life.

Quality and demand for such paintings decreased with the advent of less expensive methods of print making. By the 1850's, most reverse paintings on glass were executed by non-professionals and are rarely signed.

Genre scene, late 19th C. or early 20th C., 16½ x 20" $40.00

Blarney Castle, gilt frame 25 x 30" .	90.00
Checkerboard, gilt frame, 17½ x 17 ¾"	125.00
Floral with birds, red painted frame, 18¼ x 22½"	350.00
Jackson, Portrait, framed, 6⅞ x 9½"	645.00
Lady in Blue Gown, framed, 7½ x 10"	225.00
Lafayette, framed, 12½ x 15 ½" . .	350.00
Niagara Falls, framed	25.00
Sweet Little Dear, full length portrait of girl, framed, 6½ x 10"	250.00
U.S. Capitol Building, c. 1916, 17½ x 23"	45.00
Washington, George, portrait, framed, 7 x 10"	300.00
Washington, George, full length portrait, framed, 10 x 12"	500.00
Young Gentleman, framed, 8 x 10" .	200.00

RIDGWAY

The name Ridgway has been prominent in English pottery since the early 1800's. Two firms, J. and W. Ridgway and William Ridgway, operated in Shelton during the 1800's, producing a series of historical scenes. Most early wares marked "Ridgway" were made by one of these two firms. Ridgway Potteries, Ltd. continues the operation today in England.

See also STAFFORDSHIRE

Creamer and Sugar, white ground with gray shading, gold trim . . $65.00

Bowl, "A Clandestine Interview," silver lustre rim, lettered "Porridge"	55.00
Chocolate Pot, 9", portrait of girl and on reverse, brown and yellow high glaze, silver sculptured spout, handle and finial	90.00
Creamer, 2½","Coaching Days and Ways—Changing Horses"	45.00
Dish, "Devonshire Park, Bermuda," sepia	35.00
Jug, 7", salt glaze, Drab Ware, pewter top, tavern scene decor, marked "Ridgway, Oct. 1, 1835" .	150.00
Mug, 3½", "Coaching Days and Ways," silver lustre rim and handle	45.00
Parian bust of Handel, 8¾"	65.00
Pitchers	
3½", "Mr. Pickwick," silver lustre rim and handle	55.00
10½", Jousting knights on blue grey stoneware, dated 1840	165.00
6¼", grey salt glaze	95.00
8½", grey Parian, molded cattails, dated Oct. 1835	165.00
Plates	
9", "It's a Long Way to Tipperary," dated 1914	35.00
9", "Coaching Days and Ways— Paying Toll," brown with silver lustre trim	45.00
11", "Coaching Days and Ways— A Snowdrift," brown, with silver lustre trim	45.00
Platters	
13", "Asiatic Plants," green border, purple center	95.00
19½ x 16", "Hawthorne," blue and white, c. 1843	165.00
Syrup Pitcher, 6", pewter top, dated 1835	150.00
Tea Pot, blue and white, "Catskill Moss" pattern (rare)	200.00

Tea Service, floral decor, blue and gold border, teapot, covered, 2 plates, covered sugar, creamer and waste bowl, 6 pieces **250.00**

RING TREES

Small, objects of glass, metal or porcelain with branches or spokes for hanging or storing finger rings are known as "ring trees."

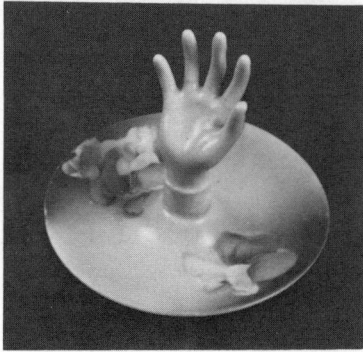

Hand, porcelain, German, 3¾" dia. $25.00

Glass
Cobalt, gold decor of flowers and leaves, 4¼" **60.00**
Cranberry, white enamel decor, gold trim, 4" **55.00**
Crystal, pear-shape, blue rose in center **110.00**
Cut glass, blue **95.00**
Gray, bristol-type, handpainted florals **40.00**
Leprechaun, green, with red hat ... **36.00**
Milk, pink roses, green leaves, 3" .. **40.00**

Metal
Silver, Sterling, Tiffany and Co. 2½ x 3½" diam. **125.00**

Porcelain
Austrian, handpainted floral decor .. **30.00**
Austrian, with attached hatpin holder, white with pink roses, gold trim **50.00**
Bavarian, handpainted floral decor, gold trim, 3" **30.00**
Copeland, Morning glory, bee decor **45.00**
Haviland, handpainted floral sprays on white, gold trim **30.00**
Limoges, hand-shaped, gold ring, bracelet, pink roses, gold trim ... **45.00**

Nippon, hand-shaped, handpainted roses **30.00**
Parian, Hand **42.50**
Shape of hand, heart shaped tray .. **45.00**
Shape of pear, crystal with large blue rose in center **75.00**
Tiffany Silver, 3½" **85.00**

ROCKINGHAM WARE

Rockingham earthenware was first produced on the estate of the Marquis de Rockingham, Yorkshire, England in 1745. A succession of potters followed for almost 100 years. The well known dark brown high glaze pottery known as "Rockingham," was introduced by Brameld and Co., Swainton, England, in 1788. Porcelain of great artistic beauty was also made at the same factory in the 1820's and continued until the firm was dissolved in 1842.

The Rockingham-type glaze was used in the United States by various potteries including the Bennington, Vermont works.

See also BENNINGTON

Pitcher, unmarked, mocha and gold, floral decoration, 6½" $125.00

Bed Pan, brown glaze **100.00**
Bird Whistle, 3", brown glaze **65.00**
Bowls
  9¾", brown glaze **65.00**
  6½" **50.00**
Creamers
  *Cow, covered **150.00**
  Silver lustre on white **75.00**

Cuspidor, brown glaze	120.00
Dish, 11½", oval	65.00
Foot Warmer, brown glaze	125.00
Mug, 3¾", brown glaze	50.00
Pitcher, 7¼", hanging game, brown glaze	200.00
Plates	
9¾", pie, brown glaze	55.00
11", pie, brown glaze	75.00
Soap Dish, embossed foliage design	37.50
Shoe bottle, 6½", brown glaze	25.00
Tea Pot, "Rebecca at the Well," 10¼"	75.00
Tea Service, teapot, sugar, creamer 6 cups and saucers	650.00
Tureen, covered, 6 x 6½", flower panels, gold trim, c. 1825	200.00

ROCKWELL, NORMAN

Norman Rockwell's influence on many forms of creative production — from bells and plates to coins and figurines — requires this separate category of Rockwell "collectibles." These items are not antiques as such; but they demand attention because of the popularity of the artist and the increased demand for reproduced versions of his work since his death on November 8, 1978.

Born in 1894, Norman Rockwell was America's best known and prolific artist and illustrator. He produced over 3000 works, including 323 "Saturday Evening Post" covers, "Boy's Life" covers and calendars, plus over 1,500 paintings for various advertisers. Rockwell works with the most value are the original illustrations and limited edition lithographs.

In the months following his death, prices began to skyrocket. In 1979, they tended to fluctuate. In 1980 and 1981, prices stabilized and in many instances have fallen drastically.

Bells

Danbury Mint Series No. 1, 1975–1977 issues, each	55.00
Gorham	
1976, Young Love	30.00
1978, Vintage Times	25.00
Grossman Designs, Bicentennial	25.00
River Shore, Ltd. 1978, set of four	150.00

Coins

Ford Motor Company, 50th Anniversary	20.00
Four Freedoms, Kennedy Mint, set of four	150.00

Print of *Saturday Evening Post* cover, 7/7/57, signed by Rockwell, 11 x 14" $300.00

Four Seasons, Hamilton Mint, L.E., set of four	80.00

Figurines

Gorham Fine China	
At the Vets, RW-4	45.00
Batter Up, RW-6	45.00
Pride of Parenthood, RW-18	85.00
Tiny Tim, RW-3	40.00
Weighing In, RW-1	45.00
Gorham Fine China, "Four Seasons," sets of four.	
1972, Puppy Love	500.00
1973, Four Seasons Childhood	500.00
1974, Four Ages of Love	500.00
1975, Grandpa and Me	450.00
1976, Me and My Pal	450.00
1977, Grand Pals	425.00
1978, Going on Sixteen	400.00
1979, Tender Years	350.00
Franklin Mint, porcelain	
1976, Joys of Childhood, series of ten, L.E., each	150.00
Grossman Designs, Inc. L.E.-1000	
1974, Baseball, NR102, (Closed)	250.00
1975, Barbershop Quartet, NR23	150.00
1976, Tom Saywer Series No. 1, (Closed)	75.00
1977, Tom Sawyer Series No. 2 or No. 3, (Closed)	75.00

1978, Tom Sawyer Series No. 4,
(Closed) 75.00
Grossman Designs, Inc. (Retired)
1973, Lazy Bones, NR8 . . . . 80.00
1973, Leapfrog, NR9 . . . . 190.00
1973, Marble Player, NR11 . . . . . 95.00
1973, Red Head, NR1 . . . . 35.00
1973, Schoolmaster, NR10 . . . . . 75.00

Ingots
Franklin Mint
Mark Twain
Bronze, set of ten 175.00
Sterling, set of ten 350.00
Hamilton Mint
Christmas
1974, sterling 30.00
1975, 24K gold on fine silver . . 40.00
1976, sterling 30.00
1977, 24K gold on fine silver . . 55.00
1978, sterling 40.00
Fondest Memories, sterling, set of
ten 450.00
Four Freedoms, fine silver, set of
four 225.00
Portraits of America, fine silver,
set of 24 . . . . 850.00

Medals
Franklin Mint
Boy Scouts of America, Spirit of
Scouting, sterling, set of 12 . . . . . 300.00
Girl Scouts of America
Bronze, set of 12 . . . . 250.00
Sterling, set of 12 . . . . 350.00

Ornaments
Hallmark Cards, Inc.
1975 . . . . 20.00
1976 . . . . 10.00
1977 . . . . 10.00
Gorham, Four Seasons, 1976 . . . . . 20.00
Grossman Designs, Inc.
1975 . . . . 20.00
1976 . . . . 25.00
1977 . . . . 10.00
1978 . . . . 10.00
1978, The Carrolers, NRX-3, L.E.
(Closed) 30.00
1979, Drum for Tommy, NRX-24,
L.E. 20.00

Plates
Brown and Bigelow
1977, F.E., Runaway, Clown Se-
ries 60.00
1978, The Runaway 50.00
1979, F.E., Grand Pals, Grandpa
and Me Series 55.00
Franklin Mint
1970, F.E., Bringing Home the
Tree, sterling 600.00

1971, Under the Mistletoe, sterling 100.00
1972, The Carrolers, sterling 60.00
1973, Trimming the Tree, sterling 60.00
1977, American Sweethearts,
crystal, set of six 900.00
Gorham Fine China
1970, F.E., Family Tree 125.00
1974, F.E., Christmas, Tiny Tim . . 40.00
1976, Dwight D. Eisenhower 40.00
1976, Four Freedoms, set of four 200.00
1976, John F. Kennedy 40.00
Gorham Fine China, "Four Sea-
sons," sets of four.
1971, A Boy and His Dog 415.00
1972, Young Love 155.00
1973, Ages of Love 265.00
1974, Grandpa and Me 145.00
1975, Me and My Pal 150.00
1976, Grand Pals 209.00
1977, Going on Sixteen 180.00
1978, Tender Years 90.00
1979, Helping Hand 70.00
1980, Dad's Boy 112.00
1981, Old Times 98.00
Grossman Designs, Inc.
1976–1979, Tom Sawyer Series,
set of four 200.00
Lake Shore Prints
1973, F.E., Butter Girl 175.00
River Shore, Ltd.
1976–1979, Famous American Se-
ries, copper, set of four 900.00
Rockwell Museum, Baby's First
Step, 1978 . . . . 45.00
Rockwell Society of America
1974, F.E., Christmas, Scotty Gets
His Tree 100.00
1976, F.E., Mother's Day, A Moth-
er's Love 60.00
Royal Devon
1975, F.E., Christmas, Downhill
Daring 50.00
1975, F.E., Mother's Day, Doctor
and Doll 70.00

Prints
Circle Gallery, Ltd.
Children At the Window, 20 x 26",
lithograph 1100.00
Critic, The, 28 x 32", collotype . . . 2800.00
Doctor and Doll, 29 x 35", collo-
type 5000.00
Family Tree, 20 x 35", lithograph . 3000.00
Four Seasons, Folio, 20 x 21",
lithograph, set of four 6500.00
Freedom From Fear, Religion,
Speech, Want, 29 x 35", collotype
each 11000.00
Marriage License, 28 x 32", collo-
type 3200.00
Prescription, 24 x 30", lithograph . 2400.00
Save Me, 15 x 18", lithograph . . . 1200.00

Tom Sawyer Folio, 20 x 26″, lithograph, set of eight 12500.00
Wet Paint, 24 x 30″, collotype . . .   1300.00
Eleanor Ettinger, Inc.
After the Prom, 24 x 26¾″, lithograph 3000.00
Ben Franklin, 21 x 28″, lithograph   3600.00
Buttercup, 21 x 24″, lithograph . .   2000.00
Gilding the Eagle, 21 x 25½″, lithograph 2200.00
Puppy Love Folio, 20 x 21½″, lithograph 7500.00
Sports Folio, 20¼ x 24½″, lithograph 6000.00
Swing, The, 20 x 21″, lithograph .   2000.00
Young Lincoln, 19 x 34″, lithograph 6500.00

Miscellaneous
Ads, individual, approximate value, in excellent condition 3–5.00
Bowl, Yankee Doodle, Danbury Mint   75.00
Display Cards, individual ads, approximate value, each 125.00
Magazine Covers, S.E.P. including other publications, approximate value, in excellent condition.
  1920–1930, each 20.00
  1930–1940, each 15.00
  1940–1960, each 10.00
Posters
  Freedom From Fear, Religion, Speech, Want, one sheet, World War II, each 100.00
Steins, Gorham
  1976 . . . .   45.00
  1977 . . . .   35.00
  1978 . . . .   30.00
  1979 . . . .   25.00
Toby Mugs, Grossman Designs, Inc.
  1979, NR1 thru NR6, each 40.00
Trays
  1975–1976, various designs and producers, approximate value, each 20.00

ROGERS STATUARY

John Rogers, born in America in 1829, studied sculpturing in Europe and produced his first plaster-of-paris statue, "The Checker Players," in 1859, followed by "The Slave Auction" in 1860.

His works were popular parlor pieces of the Victorian era. He published at least 80 different subjects and the total number of groups produced from the originals is estimated to be over 100,000. One of his best and largest pieces is "The Council of War," which shows President Abraham Lincoln, Gen. U. S. Grant and Edwin M. Stanton.

It has been determined that "Romeo and Juliet," "Is That You, Tommy?" and "A Capitol Joke" were never listed in Rogers' catalogue. They were the work of Casper Hennecke, one of Roger's contemporaries, who operated in Milwaukee, Wis., and appeared in the Hennecke catalogue.

"Checkers Up At The Farm" . $550.00

Balcony 525.00
Bath 525.00
Henry Ward Beecher 400.00
Bubbles 500.00
Bushwacker 425.00
Camp Life 525.00
Charity Patient 525.00
Chess 600.00
Council of War 850.00
Elder's Daughter 450.00
Fugitive Story 650.00
Hide and Seek 600.00
Home Guard 650.00
John Alden and Priscilla 600.00
Mail Day 625.00
Miles Standish 350.00
Matter of Opinion 500.00
Mock Trial 650.00
One More Shot 600.00
Referee 600.00
School Days 695.00
Taking the Oath-Drawing Rations . .   700.00
Washington 950.00
Wrestler 1000.00

ROOKWOOD POTTERY

Mrs. Marie Longworth Nicholas Storer, Cincinnati, Ohio, founded Rookwood Pottery in 1880. The name of this outstanding American art pottery came from her family estate "Rookwood," named for the rooks (crows) which inhabited the wooded grounds.

There are five elements to the Rookwood marking system — the clay or body mark, the size mark, the decorator mark, the date mark, and the factory mark. Rookwood art pottery can best be dated from factory marks.

In 1880–1882 the factory mark was the name "Rookwood" incised or painted on the base. Between 1881 and 1886 the firm name, address, and year appeared in an oval frame. Beginning in 1886, the impressed "RP" monogram appeared and a flame-mark was added for each year until 1900. After 1900 a Roman numeral, indicating the last two digits of the year of production, was added at the bottom of the "RP" flame-mark monogram. This last mark is the one most often found on Rookwood pottery today.

From 1880 to 1941 when the pottery was sold, Rookwood wares changed with the times. The variety of wares is endless, in part because of the large variety of glazes and designs. In the 1930's over 500 different glazes were used.

Ashtray, Mermaid On Seashell, 9½" dia., 1915, white glaze	150.00
Ashtray, Rook with wing extended, 8½", 1921, blue glaze	125.00
Bookends	
5½", Girl Seated on Bench, 1920, brown	195.00
6½", Rook, 1924, blue	165.00
7", Colonial Girls, matte pink and green glaze	195.00
Bowls	
Dinnerware, 4", white with blue sailing ships	50.00
Stylized Floral, 8" x 3", artist W. Henschell, 1923, matte glaze	175.00
Candlesticks, commercial, 8½", 1924, blue molded design	125.00
Creamer & Sugar, dinnerware, 2½", white with blue sailing ships	125.00
Cup & Saucer, Holly & Berries, 2½", artist "CCL," 1887, standard glaze	275.00
Ewers	
6", Floral, artist K. Hickman, 1898, standard glaze	300.00

Vase, Adventurine glaze, 7¼" $195.00

9", Primroses, artist Lonore Asbury, 1899, standard glaze	550.00
Figurals	
3", Rook, 1909, black	150.00
3 x 6", Panther, 1930, brown matte glaze	195.00
3½", Ship Paperweight, 1928, white	95.00
4", Geese paperweight, 1930, 4", green	125.00
5", Child kneeling, flower frog, 1922, blue	125.00
Jar, covered, floral, 9", artist Laura A. Fry, 1885, standard glaze	700.00
Jugs	
4", Honey Jug, Limoge style, Birds in Flight, 1884	350.00
5½", Ear of Corn, artist S. Toohey, 1897, standard glaze	450.00
Lamps	
9½", flowers, pink and blue with white background, artist S. E. Coyne, 1915, vellum glaze	500.00
23", flowers, pink and green on matte blue background, artist H. Wilcox, 1903, matte glaze	750.00
Mugs	
4½", Ear of Corn, artist Lenore Asbury, 1902, standard glaze	385.00
5", Indian portrait, artist M. Daly, 1898, standard glaze	2000.00

Pitcher, 8", flowers, salmon and white on tan background, artist A. R. Valentien, Limoge style, 1882 . . . . 1200.00

Plaques

5¼ x 9¼", snowy river and landscape scene, artist S. E. Coyne, 1919, vellum 850.00

10 x 12", pastoral scene, artist E. T. Hurley, 1912, vellum 1400.00

Plates

7¼", Daisies, painted on background of salmon shading to white, 1891 . . . . 225.00

8", dinnerware, white with blue sailing ships 60.00

9", floral, delicate on salmon colore, 1885 . . . . 325.00

Teapot, floral decoration of crocuses, 5", artist A. M. Valentien, 1882, standard glaze 750.00

Tiles

6", architectural, tulips, impressed Rookwood Faience 55.00

6", tea tile, birds, 1924 . . . . 95.00

6", tea tile, ship, 1935 . . . . 125.00

Vases

5", magnolia blossoms on green and blue background, artist E. Lincoln, 1925, matte glaze 250.00

5½", commercial, green molded Butterflies, 1945 . . . . 55.00

5½", silver overlay by Gorham Mfg. Co. on underglaze of daisies, artist N. Lincoln, 1892, standard glaze 1800.00

6", floral, yellow and white on blue background, artist K. Shirayamadani, 1925, wax matte (curdled matte glaze) 450.00

6½", pastoral scenic in blues and greens, artist "SEC," 1920, vellum glaze 600.00

7½", floral in matte green and red, artist S. Toohey, 1904, carved matte glaze 320.00

8½", floral on white to gray shaded background, artist L. Asbury, 1907, high iris glaze 700.00

9", commercial, Banded, pink shading to green, 1906 . . . . 75.00

9", thistle, artist Sara Sax, 1895, standard glaze 450.00

9½", flowers, blue on white background, artist "LH," 1946, high jeweled porcelain glaze 250.00

9½", cherry blossoms, artist Laura Fry, 1892, standard glaze 650.00

10", commercial, geometric, matted blue and molded, 1933 . . . . . 100.00

12½", daffodils, artist A. Sprague, 1920, standard glaze 750.00

14½", floral, artist "LE," 1925, vellum glaze 750.00

ROSALINE GLASS
SEE STEUBEN

ROSE BOWLS

A Rose Bowl is a decorative open bowl with a crimped or pinched top used to contain fragrant rose petals and a potpourri. The bowl was placed on a table top and the pleasant aroma scented the room. A popular room accessory in the late Victorian period, Rose Bowls were made in a variety of patterns by practically every glass manufacturer of the period, including fine art glass.

See specific categories for additional listings.

Opalescent Swirl, green, Fenton, 4½ x 5½" **$75.00**

Amethyst, 4½", fine cut and roses, footed 50.00

Bristol, 4½", decorated 30.00

Blue, applied green leaves and feet . . . 125.00

Cased

3½", lavender, crimped 35.00

4½", yellow, crimped top 35.00

6", ovoid, rose to pink, white lining, 6 applied frosted feet 175.00

Crystal, 4", cut 45.00

Porcelain, 5", handpainted floral decor 45.00

Spangled, 5", crimped, cream and yellow, silver mica 105.00

Vaseline, opalescent, applied flower decor 90.00

White, reverse swirl, opalescent . . . 25.00

ROSE CANTON, ROSE MANDARIN, ROSE MEDALLION

The pink rose color has given its name to three related groups of Chinese export porcelain. Rose Mandarin was produced from the late 18th century to approximately 1840. Rose Canton began somewhat later extending through the first half of the 19th century. Rose Medallion originated in the early 19th century and was made through the early 20th century.

Rose Mandarin derives its name from the Mandarin figure(s) found in garden scenes with women and children. The women often feature gold decorations in their hair. Polychrome enamels and birds separate the scenes.

Rose Medallion has alternating panels of figures and birds and flowers. The elements are four in number, separated evenly around a center medallion. Peonies and foliage fill voids.

Rose Canton is similar to Rose Medallion except the figure panels are replaced by flowers. People are present only if the medallion partitions are absent. Some patterns have been named—Butterfly and Cabbage, Rooster, etc. The category actually is a catchall for all pink enamel ware not fitting into the first two groups.

Rose Medallion still is made, although the quality does not match the earlier examples.

Plate, 20th C., 6″ $20.00

ROSE CANTON

Basin, straight sides, flat rim, children playing, green ground, 14″ . .	775.00
Bowls	
5¾″, foliate scrolls, lemon yellow ground, Tao Kuang seal	1500.00
10″, quadrifoil shape, floral	80.00
11½″, figures and floral, alternating sections, green ground	280.00
Creamer, figures in pavillion, relief floral motif, twisted handle, 4″ . . .	160.00
Dish	
8½″, celadon ground, late	75.00
10½″, celadon ground	110.00
13″, figures in landscape, reticulated border in iron red	475.00
Jardinier, square form, 16″	750.00
Mug, cylindrical form, seated dignitaries, rim of flowers and fruits with gilt bands	350.00
Plate, court official and two women with child, 9″	375.00
Teapot, covered, ladies and attendants at tea in garden, 7″	575.00
Vases	
9½″, trumpet neck, splayed foot .	95.00
12¾″, floral on yellow ground . . .	250.00
27½″, baluster form, mid-19th C., gilt dragon handles	860.00

ROSE MANDARIN

Bowl, shallow, border of mellons and flowers, 12″ dia.	450.00
Brush Pot, 5″	275.00
Mug, mandarins and lady, 5½″	250.00
Plates	
10″, garden setting	170.00
11″, five mandarins	275.00
Punch Bowl, mandarins and women in court scene, 11″ dia.	825.00
Vegetable dish, scalloped edge, boating scene, 10″	600.00

ROSE MEDALLION

Basin, 15½″ dia.	900.00
Bowls	
7″	65.00
8″	75.00
11″	225.00
11⅝″, c. 1850	450.00
Creamer, hellmut shape	110.00
Cup, handleless	30.00
Dishes	
Kidney shape, figures, 11⅜″	350.00
Scalloped, 10¼″	325.00
Square, 9¼″	325.00
Fruit Stand, slightly tapered foot, 15⅛″	600.00
Garden Seat, 18⅝″	1750.00
Ginger Jar, 8″	130.00
Hot Water Dishes	
10¾″, scene on terrace	100.00
11″, scene in garden	110.00
Pitcher, 7″, late 19th C.	100.00
Plates	
6″	30.00
7¾″, set of 10, figures at various pursuits	950.00
8″	50.00
9¾″, set of 12, initials	900.00

Platter

12″	175.00
14½″, oval, dignitaries, ladies on terrace	325.00
15″, oval, well and tree, gilted rim edge	310.00
17¼″, oval, figures of various pursuits	425.00
Punch Bowl, 16⅛″	475.00
Teapot, 7″	150.00
Tureen, cover and stand, figures in lotus garden	250.00
Umbrella Stand, 24½″	1250.00

Vase

6″	55.00
8″	125.00
13⅞″, gilt dragon applied handles, Ku-form	1600.00
15½″, figures and birds, Ku-form	700.00

ROSE O'NEILL ITEMS

Rose O'Neill created "Kewpie" in the early 20th century. The pixie-like character was first introduced to the public in the "Ladies' Home Journal." An immediate success, Kewpie dolls and various items decorated with the 'imps' were soon in wide production. Early dolls and china decorated with "Kewpies" were produced in Germany. Later, other manufacturers followed. The popularity of the frolicking figures continues as a decorative motif.

Bank, 3″, glass	95.00

Bowls

6″, cereal, 6 kewpies, Royal Rudolstadt	82.50
6″, shallow, 6 kewpies, ABC border, Germany, signed	125.00
7½″, shallow, 8 action kewpies, Royal Rudolstadt, signed	150.00
Box, 3″, green Jasperware, pink kewpies, signed	250.00
Candlestick, 4″, applied kewpie	125.00
Christmas Card, 4 x 2″, kewpies, signed "R. O'Neill"	30.00
Clock, blue jasper, signed	275.00
Cream and Sugar, 2½″, green lustre on white	165.00

Creamers

2½″, blue Jasperware, 7 kewpies, signed	195.00
3″, action kewpies	85.00
Cup and Saucer, Royal Rudolstadt, signed Rose O'Neill Wilson	135.00
Dish, 7¾″, kewpies	95.00

Figurines

Baby on Scale, 5¼″, Bisque, signed	95.00

Bride and Groom

2½″, Bisque, signed	85.00

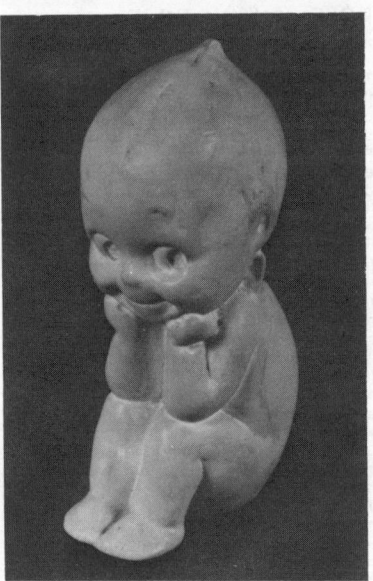

Chalkware Kewpie, late, brass insert on bottom, unsigned, 6¼″ $65.00

4½″, Bisque, signed	150.00
Doll, 4½″, Celluloid, signed	45.00
Doll, 5″, Bisque, Germany, signed	100.00
Doll, 10½″, Bisque, signed heart label	350.00
Doll, 14″, kewpie, Penna. Dutch, red velvet hat and suit, compo.	150.00
Farmer, The, 4″, with rake, Bisque, signed	250.00
Huggers, The, 2½″, Japan, c. 1912	45.00
Huggers, The, 3⅝″, German, original bouquet	150.00
Soldier, 4¾″, dressed, signed	225.00
Thinker, The, 6¼″, original heart label	185.00
Traveler, The, 3½″, Bisque, signed	135.00
Flannels, 5 x 5¾″, signed, c. 1914, each	20.00
Hair Receiver, green Jasperware, pink kewpies, signed	175.00
Hat Pin Holder, blue Jasperware, signed	175.00
Mug, 3″, pearl lustre, signed	85.00
Paperweight, 1¼ x 2″, cast iron	35.00
Pin, 1½ x 1¾″, porcelain, pink kewpie with tennis racket	75.00
Plaque, 8 x 10″, wood, Callus, c.	

1973 .... 20.00
Plates
  5", Two kewpies, Royal Rudolstadt, signed 60.00
  6", Six action kewpies, Royal
  Rudolstadt, signed 75.00
  7½", deep, Eight action kewpies 125.00
  8", Nine action kewpies 150.00
  10", Christmas Plate, Callus, c.
  1973 .... 25.00
Post Card entitled "The Wedding,"
  signed Rose O'Neill 22.50
Poster, 7⅜ x 18", framed, "Kewpie
  Baseball Team," signed 175.00
Sand Bucket, 3" high, tin, litho-
  graphed "Kewpie Beach." 60.00
Shakers, Salt and Pepper, 3",
  silverplated, signed, pair 185.00
Stickpin, signed R. O'Neill 15.00
Tea Set, Teapot, covered sugar,
  creamer, 6 cups and saucers,
  green lustre bands, signed 500.00
Toothpick Holders
  Glass 50.00
  Porcelain, signed 75.00
Trays
  Dresser, cloverleaf-shape, 5 kew-
  pies on green Jasperware, signed 250.00
  Ice Cream, 11¼ x 17½", advertis-
  ing-type 175.00
Vase, 6½", blue Jasperware with 4
  kewpies, signed 150.00

ROSE TAPESTRY
See ROYAL BAYREUTH.

MARKE

ROSENTHAL

**Rosenthal Porcelain Manufactory began op-
erating at Selb, Bavaria, in 1880. Specialties
were tablewares and figurines. According to
recent reports, the firm is still in operation.**

Biscuit Jar, 7", Pate-sur-Pate, white
  flowers on green 175.00
Bowls
  10", Portrait, c. 1900 .... 150.00
  13", handpainted roses on shaded
  green, white ground 75.00
Candlesticks, 2¾", white with gold
  trim, pair 35.00
Chocolate Set, pot, creamer, covered sugar, violets in relief on
  white, gold finials and handles ... 150.00
Condiment Set 55.00
Compote, 10 x 4" high, handpainted
  floral center, fruit border 85.00

**Cup and Saucer, Donatell pattern,
chocolate color $12.00**

Cream and Sugar, pink florals, gold
  trim 35.00
Cups and Saucers, Demitasse.
  Ivory with gold bandings and han-
  dles 28.00
  Silver Overlay, Art Nouveau 35.00
Dinnerware, "Alda," 5 piece place
  setting 35.00
Figurines
  Boy with lamb, 6" 125.00
  Dragonfly, 1¼ x 3" 60.00
  Finch, 4½", artist signed 45.00
  Goat, 7½", orange glaze 150.00
  Horse, 7", "Dapple Grey" 85.00
  Nude, woman, 4 x 5 x 8", white
  signed L.F.G. 115.00
  Rabbit, 2½" 35.00
  Street Musician, artist signed 125.00
  Wire-haired Terrier, sitting, 5",
  signed 125.00
Mug, 5½", blackberries 60.00
Pitcher, 5½", pink roses on white .. 40.00
Plates
  8½", handpainted grapes and
  roses 45.00
  9", Art Nouveau 65.00
  14", Marie Theresia 35.00
Tureen, covered, 10", gold trim on
  white 65.00
Vases
  5", handpainted orchids on black
  ground, gold trim 95.00
  7", handpainted jonquils 30.00
  9", Art Nouveau style decor, artist
  signed 160.00

Roseville
U.S.A.

ROSEVILLE POTTERY

Incorporated in 1892 at Roseville, Ohio, Roseville Pottery originally produced only utilitarian wares at plants in Roseville and, after 1898, in Zanesville, Ohio. In 1910 work ceased at the Roseville plant and continued in Zanesville until 1954.

In 1900, art pottery was introduced and the popular glazed "Rozane" line was developed. Roseville art wares were made with many types of decoration, slip, decals, free hand, incised and embossed designs. In 1918, a new trademark, "Roseville U.S.A." was adopted.

In 1920, machine-made pottery replaced the hand made wares and very little free hand decoration was used.

Much of the early Roseville production is decorator signed. Factory marks, impressed, ink stamped or paper stickers, may be used to date Roseville art wares.

Vase, Blackberry, 1933, 8¼" . .$175.00

Ashtray, 3", Donatello, cherubs in relief, 1915, rv. ink stamp	50.00
Baskets	
6", Pinecone, handled, blue, 1931, impressed mark	55.00
7", Dogwood I, hanging, 1918	65.00
8", Wincraft, handled, blue, 1948	55.00
10", Peony, hanging, yellow, 1942	65.00
Futura, hanging, 1928	75.00
Bookends	
5", Columbine, blue, 1940, pair	65.00
5½", Peony, yellow florals on pink background, 1942, Roseville in relief, pair	55.00
Bowls	
2½ x 7", Mostique, geometric design on pebbly grey background, 1915, no mark	20.00
3 x 12", Wisteria, 1933, paper label	75.00
4", Bushberry, green, 1948	18.00
Candlesticks	
2½", Ming Tree, white, 1949, pair	35.00
4", Futura, 1928 pair	65.00
4½", Magnolia, blue, 1943, pair	35.00
Cookie Jar, 10", Waterlily, brown, 1943	85.00
Cornucopia, 6", Bushberry, blue, 1948	25.00
Cups and Saucers	
Juvenile, chicks on cream background, pre-1916	25.00
Raymor, brown, 1952	15.00
Cuspidor, 5½", Donatello, cherubs in relief, 1915, no mark	100.00
Ewers	
7½", Rozane, artist TS., floral decor, brown glaze, 1900's, Rozane seal	200.00
15", Waterlily blue, 1943	95.00
Jardinieres	
4", Imperial I, 1916	40.00
8½", Donatello, 1915	125.00
Jardinieres and Pedestals	
29", Jonquil, 1931	700.00
30", Peony, 1942, Roseville in relief	350.00
Lamps	
10", Rosecraft Panel, panels of nudes on green background, 1920	300.00
10", Rozane, floral decor brown glaze, 1900's	195.00
Mugs	
5", Dutch, decal, pre-1916, no mark	45.00
6", Rozane, floral decor, brown glaze, Die stamp Rozane RPCo.	125.00
Pitchers	
7½", Cow, utilitarian, embossed	75.00
7½", Owl, utilitarian, pre-1916, no mark	200.00
7½", Tulip, utilitarian, embossed	45.00
8", Fuschia, blue with icelip, 1939	100.00
Plates	
Dinner, shape #152. Raymor, white, 1952	10.00
8", Juvenile baby plate with rolled edge, rabbits decor	35.00

Tankards

12", Creamware, transfer decal of Quaker men	200.00
15½", Rozane, artist Myers, floral decor on dark brown background 1900's, Rozane wafer mark	300.00
Tea Set, Bittersweet, brown, 1940, 3 pieces	125.00

Vases

4", Ferrella, 1931	125.00
5", Blackberry, 1933, Ni mark	95.00
5 x 7", pillow shape, Dahlrose, 1924, Rv. sticker	35.00
6¼", twisted shape, Woodland, Thistles decor, 1905, no mark	650.00
7", Cherry Blossom, 1932, no mark	95.00
8", Bleeding Heart, 1938	35.00
8", Falline, handled, 1933	150.00
8", twisted shape, Futura, 1928, no mark	65.00
9", Laurel, yellow, 1934, Rv. sticker	50.00
9¼", Rozane, artist EA., floral decor, Rozane seal	200.00
10", Pinecone, brown, 1931	65.00
10", pillow shape, Rozane Royal, artist Myers, iris decor on cream to grey glaze, 1900's, Rozane wafer	450.00
12", Mostique, 1915	65.00

Wall Pockets

8", Carnelian I, 1910	40.00
8", Futura, 1928	65.00
8", Iris, 1938, impressed Roseville	50.00
9", Donatello, 1915	60.00

ROYAL BAYREUTH CHINA

The Royal Bayreuth factory was founded in Tettau, Bavaria, in 1794 and has continued production to the present. Currently the factory is producing dinnerware with no attempts to duplicate their earlier wares, primarily the figural line.

The figural series were introduced in 1885 as inexpensive souvenir items. Designs included animals, people, fruits, vegetables and others in a wide array of tablewares.

Not all the wares were marked or the stamped mark did not prove permanent. The Royal Bayreuth crest mark varied in design and color over the years and it is impossible to verify the chronological years of production due to the lack of authentic records.

The pattern "Rose Tapestry" was made by Royal Bayreuth, Germany, in the late 19th century. The surface of the ware feels and looks like woven cloth. It was created by covering porcelain with a piece of fabric tightly stretched over the surface, then decorated and glazed. It is very expensive when found by collectors now. There were other patterns made with the tapestry background but Rose Tapestry seems to be most popular with collectors.

See also SUNBONNET BABIES.

CORINTHIAN PATTERN

Ashtray	65.00
Box, black and white	75.00
Creamer	85.00
Sugar, open	85.00

DEVIL AND CARDS PATTERN

Ashtray	150.00
Creamer	165.00
Demitasse, set	200.00
Match Holder	200.00
Tobacco Humidor, 8¼", green mark	385.00

LOBSTER PATTERN

Dish, figural, red lobster	85.00
Mustard Jar, covered, lobster	60.00
Water pitcher, lobster	175.00

MOTHER-OF-PEARL FINISH PATTERN

Candy dish, shell shaped, handled	22.50
Creamer, scuttle shape	47.50
Hatpin Holder, Oyster and Pearl pattern	225.00
Match Holder, hanging type	100.00
Pitcher, water, figural grape cluster	350.00
Planter, Murex shell	295.00

ROSE TAPESTRY PATTERN

Ashtray, 6", with cigarette rests	120.00
Baskets	
5 x 5", roses, braided handle	350.00
5½ x 4½", yellow roses, pink roses inside	350.00
Box, 4 x 1¾", pink and yellow roses	275.00
Cake plate, 11", handled, pink roses	225.00
Creamer, pink roses, yellow background	165.00
Dresser Tray, 11¼", three-color roses, green mark	220.00

Dish, leaf shaped, pink and white roses	165.00
Hair Receiver, three-color roses, three gold feet	175.00
Hatpin Holder, three color roses ...	225.00
Match Holder, hanging type	175.00
Pin box, 4½"	235.00
Plate, 4½", roses	75.00
Powder Box, covered	150.00
Relish tray, 8"	295.00
Toothpick	85.00
2⅝", two-handled, four-footed ..	275.00
4½", roses, signed	485.00
5", three color roses	250.00
Whimsey, ladies' laced shoes with French heels, three-color roses .	300.00

TAPESTRY PATTERN, VARIOUS

Basket, birch leaf decor	150.00
Box	
Castle scene, oblong	120.00
Egg shaped, woodland, scenic ..	400.00
Bowl, 5¾", sheep, mountain scene .	225.00
Chocolate Pot, mountain goats, pastoral scene	400.00
Creamer, goose girl	325.00
Dresser tray, 10" courting scene ...	275.00
Ewer, 11½"	295.00
Hair Receiver, 3", floral, gold trim ..	180.00
Humidor, 6¾", scenic, mushroom finial, gold trim	335.00
Plate, scenic, man fishing, blue mark	260.00
Shoes, Lace-up slipper, vivid colors, blue mark	290.00
Vases	
3½", Chrysanthemums decor ...	395.00
8½", Garden scene, dancers ...	180.00
Sand Babies	
Candleholder, children at beach .	90.00
Creamer, children at beach	115.00
Inkwell	225.00
Pitcher, 4½", beach and children	80.00
Snow Babies	
Creamer, Snow babies on sled ..	125.00
Cup and Saucer, demitasse	135.00
Pitcher, 4½", Snow babies sliding down hill	125.00
Plate, 9"	165.00
Tea Tile, 6⅛"	115.00
Sunbonnet Babies	
Bowls	
3¼", Babies cleaning	180.00
6", Babies ironing	150.00
Creamer, Babies fishing	150.00
Cup and saucer, Babies fishing, gold handle	175.00
Mug, Babies cleaning	150.00
Plate, 7½", Babies ironing	130.00

TOMATO PATTERN

Bowl, 9"	90.00
Creamer	50.00
Dish, covered	40.00
Sauce boat with underplate	50.00
Sugar, handled	42.50
Tea Set, 3 pieces	225.00

Pitcher, Bull $175.00

MISCELLANEOUS PATTERNS

Ashtray	
Figural elk	105.00
Goat scene 5⅜"	45.00
Basket, handled, peasant couple decor	52.50
Bowls	
5", Floral decor, gold handles ...	45.00
8", Figural poppy	60.00
Creamers	
Apple, figural, red	65.00
Cat, figural, black	105.00
Head of lettuce, lobster handle ..	35.00
Little Jack Horner	65.00
Polar bears in moonlight scene ..	125.00
Storks on green background	65.00
Cup and Saucer, Brittany girl decor .	65.00
Plate, 9", hanging type, hunting scene with hunter and dog in marsh	60.00
Rose Bowl, Little Bo-Peep decor ..	80.00
Sugar Bowl, Jack and Jill decor ...	82.50
Tea Pot, covered, Figural pansy ...	480.00
Toothpick, Figural elk	110.00
Vase, "Ring Around the Rosie" decor, silver top and handles	75.00

ROYAL BERLIN
See KPM CHINA

ROYAL BONN

Bonn

The Bonn Factory was established by Clemers August in the mid-eighteenth century in Bonn, Germany. Subsequently known as Royal Bonn, the majority of this porcelain encountered on today's market is from the late 19th century. These later wares are usually marked Mehlem, a castle or with the initials FM.

Teapot, red, black, and light blue with gold gilding, marked 1755, 9¼ x 4½ x 3½" $50.00

Biscuit Jar, 5", multicolored florals on ivory ground, gold trim	95.00
Bone Dish, blue and gold	15.00
Bowls	
9", "Wild Rose"	75.00
10 x 5" deep, handpainted roses, heavy gold trim	200.00
Cheese Dish, covered, wedge-shaped, roses on white, gold trim	125.00
Ewer, 14", red and white roses, brown foliage, gold handle	150.00
Fish Set, platter and 6 plates, different fish on each plate, peach shading to blue-grey ground, artist signed, set	225.00
Jam Jar, 5", silverplated lid and bail, floral decor on beige ground	55.00
Jardiniere, 6½ x 7½", "Persian Cashmere"	125.00
Mantel Clock, Ansonia china, 9¼", pale blue background, pink roses, foliage, square base, gold feet, large molded floral bead on top, porcelain face, marked Royal Bonn	350.00

Plates		
8", "Wild Rose"		40.00
9½", portrait		75.00
8¼", sprays of florals, gold edges		42.50
14", portrait, fruit border, artist signed		150.00
Relish, 10", handled, 3 sections, handpainted florals, gold trim		125.00
Urn, 13½", handpainted florals, tapestry finish, gold handles and base		225.00
Vases		
4", red roses on green ground, gold trim		35.00
5", garden scene, tapestry finish		100.00
9½", handpainted pastel florals, animal head handles in gold		175.00
12", cavalier portrait, gold trim, artist signed		225.00
12", floral decor, transfer with handpainted accents		125.00
15", portrait, leaf stem gold handles		285.00
17", multicolored floral decor, ornate gold handles, base		225.00

ROYAL COPENHAGEN

Royal Copenhagen was established in 1773 when Franz Mueller produced his first piece of porcelain. In 1779, the Danish king acquired ownership of the factory, named Mueller manager and adopted the name Royal Copenhagen. The Crown sold its interest in 1867 and the company remains privately owned to this day.

Royal Copenhagen's most famous pattern "Blue Fluted" was created in 1780. It is of Chinese origin, comes in 3 types: (1) smooth edge (2) closed lace edge (3) perforated lace edge (full lace), and was copied by many other factories. "Flora Danica," named for a famous botanical work and introduced in 1789, remains Royal Copenhagen's most unique and exclusive pattern. Botanical illustrations were done free-hand and all edges and perforations were cut by hand.

All Royal Copenhagen porcelain is marked with three wavy lines which signify ancient waterways and a crown which was added in 1889; the stoneware does not carry the crown.

Basket, 7½"	45.00
Bon Bon, blue Fluted	40.00

**Vase, floral, marked, 1584-271,
4½" $52.00**

Bottle, 10", medallions, "Fredercks-borg Castle"	90.00
Butter Pat, 3"	22.00
Candlesticks, full lace, 4" pair, 2" pair	140.00
Cruet, Stoppered, blue Fluted	125.00
Cups and Saucers, blue Fluted	
Demi, full lace	80.00
Dinner	60.00
Figurines	
Boy with Goose, 7"	90.00
Cat, 5½", sitting, gray, white, green eyes	85.00
Goose Girl, 9½"	150.00
Lovebirds	75.00
Scottie, 4"	80.00
Squirrel, 3½"	50.00
Woman knitting	250.00
Inkwell with Tray, 6 x 8½" long, blue Fluted	100.00
Jar, covered, 9", white, figures in re-lief, milkmaid finial	95.00
Jardiniere, 7", bulbous, blue fluted, snail handles, c. 1897	175.00
Plates	
7¾", soup, blue fluted, full lace . .	45.00
8", fruit center, hand decorated . .	35.00
9", leaf-shape, handled, blue fluted	45.00
9¼", blue, full lace	80.00
10¾", portrait, Josephine, 1923 .	85.00
Plates, Christmas, see COLLEC-TOR'S PLATES	
Platters, blue Fluted	
10"	105.00
12", full lace	250.00
19"	270.00

Syrup, blue fluted, spring-type lid . .	125.00
Tile, 5 x 6", blue fluted	40.00
Trays, blue fluted, 9½ x 15"	125.00
Tureen, covered, 18" long, blue flut-ed, c. 1897	250.00
Vases	
5", florals, green and white, crack-le glaze	50.00
6", bulbous, molded leaves, ap-plied frog on celadon ground, 19th century	175.00
8", sailboat, blue on white	100.00
12", gold decor on green, crackle glaze, pair	300.00
13", lake scene	145.00

ROYAL CROWN DERBY

Derby Crown Porcelain Co., established in 1875 in Derby, England, had no connection with earlier Derby factories which operated in the late 18th and early 19th centuries. In 1890, this new and distinct company was appointed "Manufacturers of Porcelain to Her Majesty" (Queen Victoria); from that date to the present it has been known as "Royal Crown Derby".

Derby porcelains from 1878 to 1890 carry only the standard crown printed mark. From 1891 on, the mark carries the "Royal Crown Derby" wording, and in the 20th century, "Made in England" and "English Bone China" were added to the mark.

A majority of these porcelains, both table-ware and figures, were hand-decorated, but a variety of printing processes were used for additional adornment. Today, Royal Crown Derby is a part of Royal Doulton Tableware, Ltd.

Bowl, 11 x 3¾" deep, handpainted florals, cobalt rim	85.00
Box, covered, 4½ x 5" dia., multicol-ored flowers on white	55.00
Cups and Saucers	
Demitasse, florals, blue, gold and green decor	55.00
Demitasse, sailboat, cobalt	45.00
Tea, blue chinoiserie decor	50.00
Tea, Imari-type decor	55.00
Dessert Set, Imari-type decor, 35 pieces	450.00
Ginger Jar, 10½", berry branches on red ground, gold trim	250.00

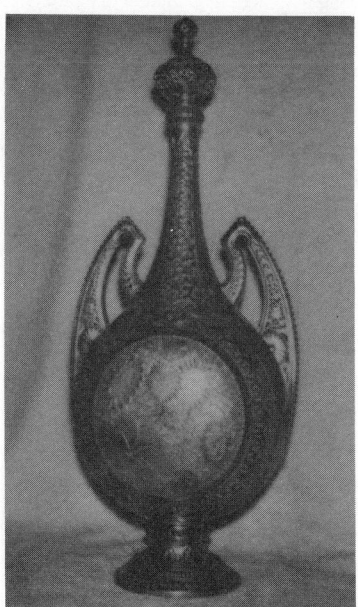

Pedestal Vase, reticulated handles, and cover, gold on gold, decor, 1889, 14½" $2000.00

Mug, 2¼", gold handle, Imari-type decor	65.00
Plates	
9", floral medallions, green border	50.00
9½", Imari-type decor	65.00
Platter, 8½ x 11½", "View of North Wales," cobalt with gold trim ...	175.00
Service Plates, 10½", floral centers, rose and green borders, gold bands, set of 12	1000.00
Tea Service, Imari-type decor, c. 1919, 18 pieces	350.00
Tea Set, pot, covered sugar, creamer, ovoid-shaped, Imari coloring, heavy gold	225.00
Tray, 13 x 17", closed handles, blue flowers in swag design on white, gold trim	165.00
Vases	
4½", gold handles, flowers and insects on yellow, gold trim, c. 1900	125.00
7½", Imari-type decor	150.00
9", blue and ivory panels, overlay design, gold trim	295.00

ROYƵL
DOULTON
FLƵMBE

ROYAL DOULTON

Doulton pottery began in 1815 under the direction of John Doulton at the Doulton & Watts pottery in Lambeth, England. Early output was limited to salt-glazed industrial stoneware. John Watts retired in 1854; the firm became Doulton and Company and production was expanded to include hand decorated stoneware such as figurines, vases, dinnerware and flasks. In 1872, the firm began marking their ware "Royal Doulton."

In 1878, John's son, Sir Henry Doulton, purchased Pinder Bourne & Co. in Burslem and the companies became Doulton & Co., Ltd. in 1882. Decorated porcelain was added to Doulton's earthenware production in 1884 and the Royal Doulton mark was used on both wares.

Most Doulton figurines were produced at the Burslem plants from 1890 until 1978, when they were discontinued. A 'new' line of Doulton figurines was introduced in 1979.

Beginning in 1913, an "HN" number was assigned to each new Doulton figurine design. The "HN" numbers refers to Harry Nixon, a Doulton artist. "HN" numbers were chronological until 1940, after which blocks of numbers were assigned to each modeler. From 1928 until 1954, a small number appeared to the right of the crown mark; this number added to 1927 gives the year of manufacture of the figurines.

Dickensware, in earthenware and porcelain, was introduced in 1908. The ware was decorated with characters from Dicken's novels. The line was withdrawn in the 1940's, except for plates which continued until 1974.

Character jugs, a 20th century revival of early Toby models, were designed by Charles J. Noke for Doulton in the 1930's. They come in 4 major sizes and feature fictional characters from Dicken's, Shakespeare and other English and American novelists, and historical heros.

Doulton's Rouge Flambee (also Veined Sung) is a highly glazed, strong colored ware noted most for the fine modeling and exquisite colorings, especially in the animal items. The process used to produce the vibrant colors in this ware is a Doulton secret.

Production of stoneware at Lambeth ceased in 1956; production of porcelain continues today at Burslem.

Animal Models

Airdale, 1023	55.00
Bloodhound, 176	265.00
Bull Dog, white, 1074	35.00
Huntsman Fox, 6448	25.00
Kittens, various, 2579–2584, each	28.00
Lion on Rock, 2641	600.00
Pekingese, 1012	35.00
Siamese, various, 2655, 2660, 2662, each	45.00

Bowls

5", Cat and the Fiddle	15.00
8½", The Gleaners	65.00
9¼", Dr. Johnson at Temple Bar	50.00
9½", Two Babes in Woods	195.00

Candlesticks

Welsh Ladies, pair	125.00
8¾", Battle of Hastings, pair	175.00

Character Jugs, tiny, 1¼"

'Arriet	140.00
Auld Mac	180.00
Fat Boy	90.00
John Peel	160.00
Old Charlie "A"	70.00
Paddy	85.00
Sairey Gamp	65.00

Character Jugs, miniature, 2¼ to 2½"

'Arriet	85.00
Captain Henry Morgan	20.00
Cardinal "A"	35.00
Fat Boy "A"	45.00
Fortune Teller	225.00
Gardener	25.00
John Barleycorn "A"	50.00
Mine Host	18.00
Paddy	45.00
Regency Beau Rip Van Winkle	18.00

Character Jugs, small, 3½ to 4"

'Arry	55.00
Farmer John	60.00
Fortune Teller	225.00
Gladiator	385.00
Jester "A"	85.00
Merlin	25.00
Old King Cole "A"	65.00
Parson Brown "A"	55.00
Ugly Duchess	140.00

Character Jugs, large, 5¼ to 7"

Captain Hook	225.00
Cardinal "A"	90.00
Cavalier "A"	80.00
Clown, Red hair	2500.00
Jockey "A"	125.00
Lord Nelson	225.00
Mr. Pickwick "A"	90.00
Robin Hood	100.00
Sam Johnson	190.00
Scaramouche	305.00

Creamers and Sugars

The Cardinal	110.00
Welsh Ladies	128.00

Cups and Saucers

Coaching Days	40.00
Jack Daw of Rheims	100.00
Nursery Rhyme Series	25.00
Welsh Ladies	55.00

Decanters

Old Crow	65.00
Zorro	40.00

Dickensware

Bowls

Bill Sykes, 6¾"	35.00
Barkis, 6"	65.00
Mrs. Bardell	95.00
Butter Pat, Tony Weller, 3¼"	25.00
Cream and Sugar, 5", Bill Sykes	140.00
Creamer, Tony Weller	70.00
Cup and Saucer, Cap'n Cuttle	75.00
Pitcher, Fagin, 6¼", brown mark	65.00

Plates

Dick Swiveller, 10"	55.00
Fat Boy, 8"	45.00
Tom Pinch, 10"	55.00
Tony Weller, 8"	45.00
Teapot, Fagin	80.00
Tray, Mr. Squeers, 9 x 7½"	60.00
Tray-Pin, Mr. Pickwick, 8"	35.00
Vase, Sam Weller, 3¼"	55.00

Figurine, The Judge, HN 2443 matte finish, 6" $200.00

Figurines

Alice in Wonderland Series, each	25.00
Beatrix Potter Series, each	20.00
Bunnykins Series, each	20.00
Child (Williamsburg) 2154	55.00
Christmas Parcels, 2851	90.00
Dickens Series, each	22.00
Elsie Maynard 639	600.00
Fair Lady, 2193	115.00
Grace, 2318	75.00
Helmsman, 2499	150.00
Jester, 1295	500.00
Kate Greenaway Series, each	60.00
Little Jack Horner, 2063	220.00
Make Believe, 2225	70.00
My Love, 2339	120.00
Old Balloon Seller, 1315	110.00
Picnic, 2308	65.00
St. George, 2051	225.00
Sweet Seventeen, 2734	140.00
Victorian Lady, 1345	275.00
Viking, 2375	150.00
Votes for Women, 2816	185.00

Flambee

Animals

Cat, 9	55.00
Duck, 112	40.00
Elephant, 489A	98.00
Fox, 14	50.00
Hare, 656A	35.00
Penguin, 84	62.00
Penguin, 8½", Veined Sung, signed Noke	350.00
Rabbit, one ear up, 113	55.00
Bowl, 10", Veined Sung	900.00

Vases

4¼", Veined Sung	50.00
5", Veined Sung, 1605	40.00
6½", Woodcut	55.00
7", Woodcut, Castle scene	125.00
8½", Desert Scene	345.00
11⅛", Woodcut, Pastoral scene, signed Noke	195.00

Humidors

Birds, dogwood branches, brown salt glaze, F. Barlow	210.00
Cardinal Archbishop of Rheims	100.00
Three Musketeers, cream	150.00

Jardinieres

Babes in Woods, 10"	475.00
Tapestry, 10 x 11"	250.00

Jugs

Midsummer Night's Dream, 5¾"	85.00
Old Curiosity Shop, figures in relief	115.00
Oliver Twist, figures in relief	125.00

Mugs

Dr. Johnson at the Cheshire Cheese	30.00
Fox Hunting	25.00
Take Ye a Cup of Kindness	35.00

Pitchers

Battle of Hastings, 6"	75.00
Canterbury Pilgrims, 7½"	65.00
Dutch, 5½"	45.00
The Gleaners, 7"	150.00
Jolly Drinker, signed Noke	295.00

Plaques

The Gleaners, 13"	150.00
The Gypsies, 13"	140.00
Jackdaw of Rheims, 15"	175.00

Plates

All the Way from Zummerset, 10"	45.00
Gondoliers, 8½"	25.00
Old Curiosity Shop, 7" square	120.00
Robin Hood, 8¾"	45.00
Shakespeare, Falstaff, 10"	55.00
Teapot, 4½", Tudor Rose	90.00

Tile

Much Ado About Nothing	45.00
Sir Winston Churchill, 9"	50.00

Tobacco Jars

Battle of Hastings, covered	90.00
Here's A Health Unto His Majesty, blue and white	85.00

Toby Jugs, Full Seated

Captain Cuttle, 4½"	180.00
Falstaff, 5¼"	35.00
Jolly Toby	75.00
Old Charley, 5½"	125.00
Sir Winston Churchill, 9"	50.00
Squire, 6"	235.00

Tumblers

Coaching Days, 4¼"	40.00
Leatherware, sterling rim, 10"	90.00

Vases

Babes in Woods, Two Children under Tree, 8¾"	125.00
Gleaners, 6½"	65.00
Monk in Sandals, 11½"	425.00
Wall Mask, Sweet Anne, 8"	450.00

ROYAL DUX

Royal Dux was porcelain made in Dux, Bohemia (Czechoslovakia) at the Duxer Porzellan-Manufaktur established in 1860. Many items were imported to the United States. A relatively inexpensive porcelain in the beginning, the ware is gaining in recognition to the point of being reproduced.

Basket, 2¼ x 4 x 4½", brown basketweave pattern, applied cherries	125.00

Vase, white Bisque, 15½″ ...$150.00

Bowls

6 x 9½″, open handles, applied rose spray on green ground	100.00
7″, full figure maiden reclines on edge	160.00
Bust, Lady, 17″, flesh tones, pink and green	850.00

Centerpieces

Atlantis Survivors, 11 x 12″, man holding woman, waves form bowl	375.00
Girl with basket and umbrella, flower bowl base, 7¼ x 8″	350.00
Maiden holding seashell, sea waves forms base, 8½ x 11″ ...	350.00
Dish, 12″ footed, figural Cupid on seashell with frogs on sides	355.00
Ewer, 10″, applied fruits and flowers, natural coloring	185.00

Figurines

Bird Dogs, 8 x 10½″, pink triangle mark	100.00
Boy with Basket, 5½ x 7½″	150.00
Boy with Fish, Girl with Basket, 10⅜″, natural coloring, gold highlights, pink triangle mark, pair ...	450.00
Camel, with rider, 17½″	350.00
Dancers, Tango, blue and white costumes, gold trim, 14″	175.00

Horse, rearing, 8″	125.00
Woman with Water Jar, 11½″, Ivory with gold base and trim ...	135.00
Tobacco Jar 8″, Figural head of man smoking pipe with night cap	150.00
Tray, Centered by girl holding a basket on her back, iridescent blue .	300.00

Vases

5″, handled, applied roses on green ground	50.00
11″, maiden holding conch shell, green, rose and ivory	300.00
16″, ornate handles, applied plums	185.00
19″, ornate twig handles, pale green with applied roses and foliage	250.00

ROYAL FLEMISH

Royal Flemish was produced by the Mt. Washington Glass Co., New Bedford, Mass. It has heavy raised gold enamel lines on frosted transparent glass that separates areas into sections, colored in russet tones. It gives the appearance of stained glass windows with elaborate florals or coin medallions in the design. The process was patented by Albert Steffin in 1894.

Vase, Roman heads, signed in medallions, original label, 6″ dia. ..$2500.00

Biscuit Jars, 8″, ancient Roman coins in heavy gold, colored, sectioned background, plated silver mountings, marked MW under lid .	2250.00
Bowls	
6⅞″, footed, panels of birds with heavy gold outlines	2450.00
16″, round in tall, figural cupid silver plated bride's basket holder, fancy mums outlined in heavy gold, gold trim, signed	5000.00

Ewer, 12", chrysanthemum and
leaves, center light blue crosses
on field of cerise 3500.00
Pitcher, 8½", heraldic like emblems
in heavy raised gold, sectioned
stained glass window background,
gold rope handle 3500.00
Rose Jar, 10", bulbous, lid with
spearpoint finial, pastel pansies
outlined in heavy gold, gold trim . 3500.00
Vases
7", bulbous, corset waist neck,
flared three way top, coin-like gold
medallions against deep toned
section background, unsigned . . . 2700.00
8", bulbous with small round neck,
heavy gold winged dragon against
russet toned section background . 2850.00
12", bottle shape, pastel chrysanthemums, heavy gold outlining
and sectioning 1450.00

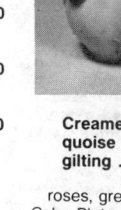

ROYAL RUDOLSTADT

**This hard paste porcelain was made in
Rudolstadt, Thuringen, East Germany. The
first factory was established by Ernt Bohne
in 1854. A second factory was opened by L.
Straus & Sons, Ltd. in 1882.**

**The ware was never originally labeled
"Royal Rudolstadt" but the word 'Royal' was
probably added by dealers because of the
connotation of the word.**

**The early mark was a hayfork representing
the arms of Johann Fredrich von
Schwarzburg-Rudolstadt, the patron. Later,
crossed two-prong hayforks were used to
imitate the Meissen or Dresden mark. In
1800, the letter "R" was used. Still later, variations of the hayfork were used. Modern
marks show a shield with the latters "RQ", a
crown on top, with the word "Crown" above
and the name "Rudolstadt" below the shield.
Another mark has the word "Germany" in
place of the word "Crown" which indicates
the ware was made after 1891.**

Basket, 4½ x 6¾", gold handle, flo-
ral design on ivory 85.00
Biscuit Jar, 8", corset-shaped,
paneled with multicolored flowers 125.00
Bowls
9" long, shell-shaped, Cupid seat-
ed on edge 150.00

9" scalloped rim, Deco style decor
in multicolors, artist signed 65.00
9⅝", purple flowers and gold
highlights 55.00
11", cream ground, pink, yellow

**Creamer and Sugar, covered, tur-
quoise and pink, cream ground, gold
gilting $55.00**

roses, green foliage, artist signed 125.00
Cake Plate, 12", gold handles, pink,
white roses, gold trim 50.00
Candlesticks, 7", ivory embossed
aconthies leaves, petal shaped
cups marked on base with Crown
Mark, pair 50.00
Cheese Dish, wedge-shape, rose
decor 95.00
Chocolate Set, pot, 4 cups, saucers,
handpainted roses on cream
ground, gold trim 250.00
Cup and Saucer, handpainted roses,
gold trim 20.00
Dresser Set, tray, hatpin holder, hair
receiver, ring tree, covered jar,
Rose decor, 6 pieces 250.00
Ewer, 9½", floral decor, scrolled
gold handle 75.00
Hatpin Holder, decor in lavender and
roses 25.00
Pitchers
4½", flower spray medallions,
gold serpent handle 65.00
11", bulbous, floral decor, gold
handle 125.00
Plates
6", handpainted multicolored
roses, gold trim 25.00
8½", handpainted poppies, gold
trim 45.00
11", rose decor, gold trim 75.00
Shakers, Salt and Pepper, handpainted floral decor, pair 50.00
Trays
8¼ x 11½", pink roses on ivory
ground 55.00
10" dia., "Corn," gold trim 65.00

Vases

7¼", gold handles, handpainted florals on ivory ground **60.00**

9", bulbous, gold handles, handpainted florals **125.00**

11½", baroque style, flowers, berries, foliage on ivory ground **150.00**

ROYAL VIENNA

Production of this hard paste porcelain began in 1720 with Claude Innocentius du Paquier, a runaway employee of the Meissen Works. The factory was located in Vienna. In 1744, Empress Maria Theresa brought the factory under royal patronage and subsequently the ware became known as Royal Vienna. The establishment went through many administrative changes until its closing in 1864 but the quality of workmanship was always maintained. The majority of this ware encountered on today's market was probably made by other Austrian or German firms who continued to produce a reasonable facsimile of Royal Vienna including using the distinctive and distinguished 'Beehive' mark.

Pitcher, marked Vienna, Austria, 13" $265.00

Bowl, 5", handled, portrait, blue with gold trim **135.00**

Box, Cherubs, hinged **150.00**

Chocolate Pot, 10", cupids on shaded purple ground **275.00**

Compote, 8¼ x 4½" high , floral decor in blue and green on white .. **175.00**

Cup and Saucer, Demitasse, portrait, maroon with gold, artist signed .. **150.00**

Ewers

4¼", "Trauman," green lustre, gold handle, signed Wagner **475.00**

12", "Die Hochzeit," red ground, gold handle, signed Huber **800.00**

15½", mythological scene, maroon ground, signed Schulers ... **1000.00**

Figure of Cupid as Scholar, 4⅝" ... **275.00**

Jar, covered, 12", portrait, burgundy ground, gold trim, jeweled, signed Wagner **850.00**

Plates

8", Tannhauser Opera Scene, artist signed **395.00**

9½", "Amorosa" **715.00**

9½", 2 maidens, in front of fire .. **250.00**

11¾", Portrait **440.00**

13¾", mythological scene, artist signed **495.00**

Service Plates, floral center, burgundy rims, gold trim, set of 12 ..... **1500.00**

Tea Caddy, 7" high, "Amor Und Cephiste" and "Rinaldo Und Almeido," signed, C. Herr, c. 1820 **500.00**

Tray, 8¼ x 12", handpainted violet decor on pale green ground, gold trim **175.00**

Urns

6½", "Erbluht," burgundy, gold trim, signed Wagner **400.00**

10", covered, "Josephine," green ground, 18K gold trim, signed Wagner **750.00**

11¼", covered, "Ann Gitana," signed Wagner **850.00**

13", portrait of sleeping lady, cupids, gold beading **275.00**

15¼", classical scene **375.00**

Vases

4½", portrait of lady, signed Wagner **300.00**

5", Portrait **400.00**

7¼", bottle-shaped, portrait center, heavy applied allover gold, signed Wagner **500.00**

8½", bulbous, scenic, Story of Moses, Mother holding child, children riding lions **550.00**

ROYAL WORCESTER

This works was established in 1751 by Dr. John Wall and 14 partners. Dr. Wall died in

1776 and the entire business was sold to Thomas Flight in 1783. Martin Barr was admitted as a partner in 1793 and the firm was known as Flight and Barr. In 1807 the name was changed to Flight, Barr and Barr. It was changed again in 1813 to Barr, Flight and Barr, or "B.F.B." and continued as such until 1840 at which time Chamberlin and Son and Barr, Flight and Barr were consolidated. The works moved to Dighlis, the home of Chamberlin and Son. The company was sold to Kerr and Binn in 1852. Most of the earlier ware encountered are of the 1870–1900 period. Current Royal Worcester wares are available on the modern market.

Vase, reticulated top, cream ground, gold trim handles, 8¾" **$385.00**

Basket, 6", floral decor, 1903	185.00
Biscuit Barrel, handpainted florals, silverplated lid and bail	245.00
Bone Dish, blue floral decor	40.00
Bowls	
4¾ x 2¼" deep, swags of fruits, insects and butterfly decor, gold border	500.00
9" square, floral spray decor, 19th century	250.00
Butter, covered, blue and white, c. 1770	375.00
Cache Pot, 2¼ x 2½" deep, white with decor of roses, blue bells, berries, dragonfly, etc., gold trim, Three gold feet, c. 1908	200.00
Cake Stand, 10¼" dia., 5¼" high, lilac with narrow gold bands, scalloped edge, c. 1908	200.00

Candle Snuffers	
Granny Snow	110.00
Toby and Punch, c. 1882, Pair . . .	350.00
Chocolate Pot, 8¾", floral decor on beige satin ground, gold handle and trim, c. 1894	250.00
Cup, handleless, blue and gold, c. 1770	95.00
Cups and Saucers	
Demitasse, cream ground, rust flowers, c. 1890	60.00
Handleless, brown lines, flowers, leaves, c. 1770	195.00
Ewers	
7", florals on front and reverse, beige ground, gold handle	185.00
11½", serpent handle, multicolored floral decor, c. 1908	475.00
12½", bulbous base, ornate gold handle, floral decor on quilted base, c. 1920	400.00
Figurines	
April Girl	75.00
Children, Days of the Week, (Monday, Tuesday, etc.) 7½", F. Doughty, each	75–130.00
Flower Seller, 4", F. Doughty	250.00
Girl with Apron Spread, 8½"	350.00
Joy and Sorrow, 10½", pair	500.00
Spring, 8½"	145.00
Humidor, sabrina ware, c. 1906	195.00
Leaf-shaped Dish	25.00
Mug, 5", blue and white, c. 1770 . .	300.00
Pitchers	
5", bulbous, gold on beige ground, gold reeded handle, c. 1891	120.00
8½", bulbous, gold handle and ring base, allover gold florals	195.00
8¾", bulbous, ornate gold handle, florals in blue, pink, lavender, purple mark	300.00
Plates	
7½" multicolored	35.00
9", handpainted florals	60.00
Rose Bowl, 3", handpainted bluebird, gold trim	125.00
Sweetmeat, covered, 8", pedestaled, beige to gold, c. 1903	250.00
Teapots	
5", bulbous, floral decor, c. 1770 .	375.00
6 x 7½", blue and white, c. 1770 .	275.00
6", Cobalt, gold decor	225.00
Tureens, covered	
4½ x 9½" long, blue, white oriental decor, gold finial, gold feet, gold elephant head handles, c. 1880	225.00
14½" x 10½" long, blue and white, crow's feet, elephant handles, with underplate, c. 1880	550.00

Vases
4¼", bulbous, floral decor on beige, gold trim, c. 1912 . . . . **115.00**
4¼", handled, florals on beige ground, gold trim, c. 1902 . . . . . . **125.00**
7", bulbous base, natural colored flowers, c. 1908 . . . . **225.00**
10½", blue molded cabbage leaves in relief, c. 1760 . . . . **450.00**
12", white, gilded & colored florals, signed **775.00**

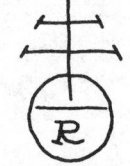

ROYCROFT ITEMS

Elbert Hubbard, founder of the Roycrofters in East Aurora, New York, during the turn of the 19th and 20th centuries, was considered a genius in his day. He was author, lecturer, manufacturer, salesman and philosopher.

Hubbard established a campus, including a printing plant where he published "The Philistine," "The Fra" and "The Roycrofter." His most famous book was "A Message to Garcia," 1899. His 'community' also included a furniture manufacturing plant, a metal shop and a leather shop.

See also FURNITURE.

Footstool, leather cover, 10 x 15" $175.00

Ashtray, 3½", copper, octagon **20.00**
Bench, Ali Baba, 42" long, oak slab **900.00**
Bookends, metal
4", leather inserts, pair **95.00**
5", sailing ship, brass finish, pair . **65.00**
6", round with owls heads, brass finish, pair **65.00**
Books
1901, "Little Journeys," Great Musicians I, leatherbound, signed by Hubbard, illum. **40.00**

1912, "The Myth in Marriage," leatherbound, by Alice Hubbard . . **12.00**
1915, Scrapbook **8.00**
1927, "The Man of Sorrows," leatherbound, by Elbert Hubbard . **15.00**
Candlesticks, 8", copper, tubular stem with square base, pair **65.00**
Card tray, 6" dia., copper with leaf decor, dark finish **40.00**
Chairs
Morris, 24 x 22" seat, oak **850.00**
Rocker, 29" high, oak, leather seat **250.00**
Crumb Tray and Scraper, 8", hammered copper **35.00**
Desk, Lady's, slant front, 46" high, oak **1500.00**
Jug, pottery, brown glaze **15.00**
Letter Opener, hammered copper . . **15.00**
Lamp, 14" high, mushroom shade, hammered copper, dark brown patina **400.00**
Stand, Little Journies, 30" high, 15 x 26" top, oak **200.00**
Tables
Library, 30" high, 2 drawer, oak . . **600.00**
Serving, 36 x 44", single drawer, oak **600.00**
Tray, Serving, 16" dia., copper, brass finish **75.00**
Vase, 6", hammered copper, chased design **40.00**
Wastebasket, 13" high, slat sides, oak **200.00**

RUBENA GLASS

Rubena crystal is a transparent blown glass made in the late 1800's by several of the glass companies. One of the first to produce it was Hobbs, Bracunier & Co., Wheeling, West Virginia. Rubena glass shades from clear to red.

Basket, thorn handle **110.00**
Bottle, Cologne **65.00**
Compote, 5½" dia., floral decor, wheel engraved **225.00**
Finger Bowl with underplate **65.00**
Pitchers
5¼", overshot **95.00**
5½", bulbous, fluted tri-corner rim, IVT enamel decor **125.00**
9", IVT **150.00**
9¾", overshot **165.00**
Rose Bowls **95.00**
IVT, floral decor **110.00**
Overshot **95.00**
Sugar Castor **95.00**
Syrup Pitcher, optic pattern with etching **100.00**
Toothpick, bulbous, IVT **60.00**

Vase, enameled, 6″ **$35.00**

Tumblers
Hobnail, frosted	75.00
Threaded	125.00

Vases
7″, swirl	65.00
10″, enamel floral decor	135.00
12¾″, lily pads and floral enamel decor	125.00

RUBENA VERDE GLASS

Rubena Verde is a blown art glass made by Hobbs, Brocunier & Co., Wheeling, West Virginia, in the late 1800's. It is a transparent glass that shades from red in the upper section to a yellow-green in the lower. It is often found in the inverted thumbprint (IVT) pattern termed "Polka Dot" by Hobbs.

Bowls
8″ dia.	175.00
9¾″, ruffled rim	200.00
Cruet, IVT, applied crystal handle . .	150.00
Epergne, 12″, 2 pieces	250.00
Finger Bowl	85.00

Pitchers
4″, hobnail opalescent	200.00
5¾″, hobnail	235.00
8¼″, IVT	185.00

Bride's Basket, miniature, 4½ x 6½ ″ ....:**$85.00**

Miniature, IVT, honey reeded amber handle	165.00
Rose Bowl	95.00
Sauce, 4½″ square hobnail	65.00
Tumbler, IVT	75.00

Vases
6″, egg shape, footed	185.00
7½″, hobnail, ruffled top	180.00
10″, bulbous, enamel floral decor	195.00

RUBY STAINED GLASS (SOUVENIR TYPE)

Ruby stained glass, a late Victorian introduction used to decorate souvenir items, was produced primarily in Pittsburgh, Pa., during the 1880's and 1890's. These items were fashioned from clear glass, pressed in one of several thousand patterns, and then a ruby-red staining material was painted on the annealed glass for a decorative effect.

Patterns used for this purpose were many but "Button Arches," "Heart Band" and "Almond Thumbprint" were three of many popular ones. Often a factory would press the glass and sell it to various decorating companies where different parts of the pattern would be stained. Ruby stained glass souvenir items were sold at fairs and expositions, and often etched with the name of a place, person, date or event.

A few years ago there was a tendency to down-grade a piece of pattern glass if it carried souvenir-markings. With the increasing interest in memorabilia, souvenir marked pieces have increased in value.

See also the Pattern Glass sections in this guide.

Cordial, "Syracuse Fair," 1905	35.00

Tumbler, marked William Frederick from F. W. C. 1909, 3⅞″ $35.00

Goblets
Plymouth, Pa.	35.00
Eau Claire, Wisconsin	37.50

Mugs
Atlantic City and Fred	45.00
Cincinnati, Ohio	35.00
Clinton, Oklahoma	35.00
Gettysburg, Pennsylvania	45.00
Winona, July, 1910	35.00
World's Fair, 1893	48.50
World's Fair, plain, blown, souvenir, 1876, applied handle, pontil, made at the Gillinder Pavillion at Centennial Exposition. Reads "To My Daughter"	85.00

Pitchers
Cedar Rapids, Iowa	40.00
Gettysburg	45.00
Mt. Clemens, 1901	40.00
Ocean City, N. J., 1912	37.50
Ogonquit, Maine	35.00
Virginia Beach, Virginia	45.00

Toothpicks
Christmas, 1906	40.00
Mother, 1901	45.00
Philadelphia, 1905	45.00

Tumblers
Asbury Park, N. J., 1907	35.00
Green Bay, Wisconsin	40.00
Scranton, Pa., Mother	40.00

Wine, Asbury Park, N. J. 35.00

RUSSIAN ITEMS

Works of Russian artists and craftsmen are highly regarded by collectors. Russian enamels are one of the most exquisite examples of the Russian arts executed during the Czarist period. The items were fashioned of precious metals, elaborately enameled and encrusted with precious and-or semi-precious stones.

Presentation Goblet and Tray, 4 Hallmarks, engraved — Moskau small den 20, May 1879, tray — 8⅜″ dia., goblet — 5⅜″ high $4000.00

ENAMELS

Basket, Strawberry, 4¼ x 1½″ deep, multicolored enamels, bail handle, signed	2700.00
Blotter, rocker type, knob holder ..	600.00
Bowl, 2½ x 1″ deep, sloped sides, bead trim, multicolored enamels, signed	1600.00
Boxes	
1¾″ dia., covered, red, green, white rose decor sunburst bottom	1200.00
2½″ dia., domed, hinged lid, multicolored florals and scroll decor, c. 1890	1850.00
3¾ x 7″ rectangular, multicolored florals and scroll decor	3000.00
Brandy Tester, signed	1500.00
Cane Head, 4¼″ long, multicolored scroll decor	1250.00
Cigarette Case, 2¾ x 4″, allover scroll work, amethyst clasp	3000.00
Demitasse Cup, 3½″, multicolored enamels, marked H.C. 84, St. George	1250.00

Egg Cup, 3″, multicolored scrolls, marked Saltykov, 84, St. George 950.00

Eggs

2½ x 4″ hanging-type, allover decor on gold 10000.00

2 x 3⅓″, multicolored enamels on silver gilt, marked Kucmitchev, c. 1890 . . . . 6500.00

Fork, 5″, blue and white enameling on gold washed sterling, Gustav Klingert 750.00

Glass holder, Vodka miniature shape of Tea glass holder, multicolored . 425.00

Letter Opener, 3″ enameled handle, 12″ wooden blade, marked on handle 750.00

Napkin Ring, 2″ oval, multicolored enamels 750.00

Salts

1 x 2″ dia., enamels on silver gilt, marked F.R. 88 . . . . 600.00

2¾″ dia., enamels on silver gilt, marked 84, St. George 750.00

2¾″ multicolored, maker's mark . 425.00

Scoop, 4½″ 5 colors, cobalt, lavender, white, red and turquoise 1950.00

Spoons

2½″, multicolored enamels 350.00

4¼″, multicolored pastel enamels, marked Kokoshnik, 11 Attel, 84, St. George 450.00

5″, red, white, blue enamels on gold wash 750.00

6¾″, pastel florals and scrolls on silver gilt, marked Khelebnikov, Kokoshnik, 88 . . . . 850.00

Spoon Set, 13 spoons in original satin lined leatherette case, 12 four inch long spoons; one 6″ long spoon; multicolored enamels, marked 84, St. George 4500.00

Sugar Scoop, 6″, pastel enamels, marked 84, St. George 850.00

Tie Pin, 1 x 2¼″ long, multicolored enamels, marked 84, St. George . 1250.00

Tongs, 5″, blue and white on silver gilt, signed 750.00

Tumbler, 4¾″, coronation of Nicholas II, c. 1896, signed 500.00

Vodka Cup, 2½″, multicolored enamels on body and base, marked 84, St. George, signed . . 1500.00

SILVER

Belt Buckle, Niello, dagger clasp, marked AA, 84 . . . . 450.00

Candlesticks, pairs 12″, c. 1885 . . . 850.00

15″, ornate bases and stems, engraved with grapes and leaves . . 950.00

Dispatch Case, 4 x 5½″, shield-shape, hinged lid, chased with silk tassel 350.00

Match Safe, pocket-type, chased, marked 84, St. George 250.00

Napkin Rings

Niello, hallmarked 250.00

1½″ dia., bird decor 175.00

Pin, Bow Knot, 2½″ long, marked 84, St. George, KL 350.00

Salt Dip, ball feet, etched florals, marked 84, St. George 150.00

Spoon Set, Six 4¼″ long spoons in original satin lined box, twisted handles, engraved bowls, c. 1886 600.00

Russian Orthodox Cross brass, 3¼″ $125.00

MISCELLANEOUS

Box, 3⅝″, brass, troika in relief . . . 200.00

Bread Plate, 11″ dia., carved wood . 85.00

Candlesticks, 9″, brass, Cossack stems, pair 150.00

Coffee Pot, 9 x 12″ high, brass, double eagle mark 300.00

Cup and Saucer, white with delicate gold floral rims, ribbed and swirled, Lamanosox Factory 85.00

Eggs

Porcelain, 3¼″, handpainted decor of Bible in panel, heavy gold borders, signed 650.00

Wood, 3″, hand decorated in allover pattern 65.00

Tea Caddy, 2½ x 3 x 4", papier
mache, scenic decor, three medallion seal **450.00**
Tray, 14 x 23", hammered copper,
double eagle mark **350.00**
Umbrella Stand, 8 x 21" high, brass,
ring handle, double eagle mark .. **500.00**
Vases
10", covered, woodpecker handle,
pine cone finial, Gardner, c. 1850 **750.00**
12", copper, tankard-shape, step
joint construction, two handles,
hallmarked **300.00**

SABINO GLASS

Sabino glass is a type of art glass that originated in Paris, France, in the 1920's. A wide
range of decorative glasswares was produced in frosted, clear, opalescent and colored glass by blown and pressed moldings.
Production was interrupted during and after
WW II.

In 1960, Sabino introduced a line of opalescent glass figurines, as well as a few other
items from hand sculptured molds in the Art
Deco style. Sabino died in 1971 and left no
record of his original fiery opalescent glass
formula. Attempts to duplicate this glass
failed and the family considered discontin-
uing glass production. At present, Sabino
items are again being made for export only.
All items are signed "Sabino France."

Scent Bottle, 6 nudes inscribed
Sabino, France $85.00

Ashtrays
Shell, 3½ x 5½" **25.00**
Swallow, 3½" **20.00**
Swallow, 4¾" **35.00**
Violet, 4½" **30.00**
Birds
Branch of 5, 7 x 8" **500.00**
Cluster of 2, 3½ x 4½" **100.00**
Cluster of 3, 5 x 5" **165.00**
Feeding, 1½ x 2" **25.00**
Fighting, 2 x 2¾" **25.00**
Jumping, 3¼ x 3½" **35.00**
Kingfisher, 4½", on stump **60.00**
Mini, ½", wings up or out **15.00**
Mocking, 4½ x 6" **70.00**
Teasing, 2½ x 3", wings down or
up **40.00**
Wren, 1½" **20.00**
Bowls
Beehive, 7 x 7" deep **150.00**
Berry, 5¾". Shallow **50.00**
Fish, 5" **50.00**
Box, Powder, 3" diam. **45.00**
Butterflies
2¾", wings closed **25.00**
2¾", wings open **30.00**
6" **125.00**

Cherub, 2" **20.00**
Chick, drinking, 3¾" **30.00**
Dogs
German Shepherd, 2" **25.00**
Pekinese, 2¾ x 3¾" **60.00**
Scotty, 1½ x 3 x 4" **60.00**
Dove, 1¾", head up or down **20.00**
Dragonfly, 5¼ x 6" **80.00**
Fish
2 x 2" **25.00**
4 x 4", swimming **55.00**
Heron, 7½" **100.00**
Knife Rest, various-types, each ... **22.00**
Madonnas
3" **30.00**
5" **65.00**
Mouse, 3" **45.00**
Napkin Ring, birds, 2¼" diam. **20.00**
Nudes
6", kneeling **235.00**
6½", woman with long flowing
hair **125.00**
Panthers, grouping, 5¾ x 7¾" **200.00**
Pigeon, 6¼" **120.00**
Rabbit, 2" **20.00**
Roosters
3½" **25.00**
7" **200.00**

Snail, 1 x 3″	30.00
Squirrel, 3″	25.00
Statues	
Draped, 7¼″	225.00
Nude, 6¾″	150.00
Stork, 7¼″	125.00
Swan, 2″	20.00
Turkey, 2″	25.00
Turtle, ¾ x 2″	20.00
Venus de Milo, 4½″	50.00
Zebra, 5½ x 5½″	125.00

Ⅽ Ⓢ SALOPIAN

SALOPIAN WARE

Salopian Ware was made at Caughley Pot Works, Salop, Stropshire, England, in the 18th century by Thomas Turner. The ware is polychrome on transfer. At one time it was classified as Polychrome Transfer but regained the more popular name of Salopian. Wares are marked with an "S" or "Salopian," impressed or painted under the glaze. Much of it was sold through Turner's Salopian warehouse in London.

Cup and Saucer, handleless, Bird on Branch, saucer — 4¾″ dia., cup — 2⅞″ dia. **$175.00**

Bowls	
6¾″, black transfer with blue edging, couple at tea in garden with blackamoor pouring	130.00
Blue and white	300.00
Milkmaid and Cow	400.00
Creamers	
House pattern, brown and blue	390.00
Deer, single	390.00
Cup and Saucer, handleless	
Deer pattern, blue and white, pair	300.00
House pattern	225.00
Oriental, handleless	250.00

Mug, Milkmaid and Cow	240.00
Plates	
4⅛″, Cottage	325.00
8½″, Cottage	400.00
8¾″, oriental, octagonal	200.00
Sauce, 4⅞″, Cottage	325.00
Sugar, covered, 4¾″, Milkmaid and Cow	400.00
Teapots	
Birds and Flowers	475.00
Cottage	525.00
Deer, double	600.00
Milkmaid and Cow	425.00

SALT GLAZED WARES

Salt glazed wares have a distinctive "pitted" surface texture, made by throwing salt into the hot kiln during the final firing process. The salt vapors produced sodium oxide and hydrochloric acid which react on the glaze.

Many Staffordshire potters produced large quantities of this type of ware during the 18th and 19th centuries. A relatively small quantity was produced in the United States. Salt glazed wares continue to be made today.

Syrup, cleadon hue, pewter lid, 7″ **$125.00**

Bowl, 8 x 4½″ deep, white, undecorated, English, c. 1860	125.00

Jugs

10½", white, Bacchanalian decor in relief, hinged pewter lid, Chas. Meigh, c. 1845 . . . . 400.00

15¼", gray, blue stylized floral decor, hinged pewter lid, unmarked 200.00

Pitchers

7½", white, lily and foliage in relief, American, c. 1890 . . . . 125.00

Apostle pitcher, Gothic design, ornate handle 400.00

8", bulbous, white, hunt scene in relief on base, blue banded top with vintage decor in relief, Wedgwood, c. 1780 . . . . 750.00

8¼", pale green, game in relief, Envitte 150.00

9", putty colored, embossed vintage, foliage, satyrs and Dionysus handle, impressed anchor and urn mark with W. Ridgency & Co., hinged pewter lid 225.00

11½", white, Muenster-type, c. 1846 . . . . 500.00

Plates,

9", "Success to The King of Prussia & his forces," clear center, embossed rims, c. 1760, pair . . . 1000.00

Sauce Boats, relief molded with scrolls and plumage, pair 950.00

Syrups

7", white, berries and foliage in relief, c. 1890 . . . . 150.00

7½", melon ribbed, white with blue bands, hinged pewter lid, W.B. Flouger 195.00

9½", white, Bacchanalian decor in relief, hinged pewter lid, English, c. 1860 . . . . 225.00

Teapot, 8", white, Neptune in relief, shell finial, c. 1835 . . . . 425.00

Tea Set, white, Apostle-type, Chas. Meigh, c. 1842, 3 pieces 750.00

Vase, 7¾", white, blue vintage decor in relief 175.00

SALTS

In the days of the Roman Empire, salt was very scarce and expensive. Roman soldiers were posted to guard the Via Salaria (salt road) to protect the supply. Salt was procured from saline plants, inland streams, and ocean waters. Even with this limited supply of salt, the need arose for a receptacle in which to serve it. The first open salt was a hand carved wooden trencher, probably the size of a small master salt.

From this humble beginning until the late 1800's when the shaker was invented, master and individual salts (the latter becoming popular by the 1500's) were on the tables of royalty and peasants alike. The finest salts were at the head of the table, the lesser ones for those sitting "below the salt."

By 1700 salts of many shapes and materials were being made. By the 18th century master silversmiths and glass makers in America were producing silver and blown flint glass salts. During the 1800's and to a small extent into the 1900's, many china, cut glass and pressed glass salts were made.

The use of open salts has decreased since the shaker was invented. The collection of salts has been very popular for many years with the number of collectors steadily increasing.

The numbers in parenthesis refer to the plates in the eight volumes of books on open salts and master salts by Allan B. and Helen B. Smith, Topsham, Maine. In the Lacy section of Master Salts the references from L. W. and D. B. Neal's *Pressed Glass Salt Dishes of the Lacy Period, 1825–1850* also are given.

SALTS, INDIVIDUAL

China

Belleek, Irish, shell and coral pattern, second black mark (250) . . 25.00

Belleck, Lenox, white with floral motif, signed Kucher 10 (42) 18.00

Belleek, Willett, blue with floral decoration (42) 18.00

Celery Dip, platter type, Leuchtenburg, Germany (259) 5.50

Celery Dip, platter type, Nippon (259) 4.50

Crown Milano, Mt. Washington, shiney (46) 125.00

Dresden, footed, floral (258) 20.00

Doulton, Lambeth, hallmarked silver ring, 1876 (264) 95.00

Kate Greenaway, basket weave, two seated figures (46) 45.00

Portrait of three ladies, signed Angela Kaufmann (38) 28.00

Quimper, Henroit, round with floral decoration, 1926 . . . . 45.00

Royal Austria, acorn and oak leaf (251) 15.00

Royal Austria, O. & E. G., set of 6 salts with tray (269) 135.00

Royal Bayreuth, blue mark, pedestal, girl with geese (87) 65.00

Satsuma, figures inside (249) . . . 32.00

Wedgwood, Jasperware, hallmarked silver band, classical figures and trees (91) 140.00

Colored Glass

Aurene, blue, fluted edge, teardrop feet, signed (256) 530.00

Atterbury, milk glass with handle, dated (40) 28.00
Burmese, Mt. Washington, footed, blue enamel flowers (256) 550.00
Button Daisy pattern, blue, triangular (37) 22.00
Cambridge, Mt. Vernon (40) 28.00
Cameo, Daum Nancy, rain scene (256) 550.00
Cameo, Webb, citron color, silver band, oak leaves and acorn motif (256) 550.00
Cranberry, enamel flowers (306) . 65.00
Custard, four blue glass feet (306) 50.00
Jersey Swirl, blue (36) 28.00
Mercury, pedestal (8) 18.00
Moser, unsigned, deep blue, applied flowers, gold decoration (305) 65.00
Plique-a-jour, Viking ship, marked 930S and M (252) 500.00
Portland, electric blue, fine cut and block pattern (261) 50.00
Sandwich, attr., amethyst, rectangular (33) 20.00
Slag, purple, double, embossed Sowerby peafowl (300) 55.00
Staffordshire, hen on nest (44) . . 60.00
Tiffany, gold iridescent, witch pot (92) 185.00
Vallerysthal, hen on nest, amber (44) 32.00
Vaseline, boat, cathedral pattern (262) 30.00
Vaseline, leaf and rib pattern (37) 22.00

Cut Glass

Baccarat, attr., etched, scalloped, pedestal (265) 15.00
Diamond and Fan motif (270) . . . 15.00
Hawkes (15) 55.00
Playing Card symbols, set (274) . . 125.00
Tub, with tray (270) 30.00
Tub, oval (13) 15.00
Tub, round (13) 12.00
Waterford (22) 35.00

Metal

Brass, stonestudded with two green intaglios (252) 65.00
Cloisonne, covered, matching spoon (260) 45.00
Enamel, French, with spoon (253) 95.00
Enamel, French, with spoon (252) 65.00

Pressed Glass, clear

Cable, Sandwich, commemorating laying of Atlantic Cable (8) 17.00
Dated, knife rests (52) 35.00
Early Washington, N.E. Glass Co., 1860's (23) 15.00
Hickman pattern (26) 8.00
Krystop, embossed, scalloped top (26) 9.00

Individual, pressed glass, pedestal with Chippendale handle, embossed Krystol $12.00

Liberty Bell, mint, both dates legible (4) 65.00
Old Moon and Star pattern, Sandwich (275) 45.00
Palm Leaf and Fan (29) 9.00
Round, plain (6) 4.00
Round, plain, swirl pattern (6) . . . 6.00
Round, sixteen orbed (5) 9.00
Star, five pointed (5) 6.00
Sunburst, medallion (30) 10.00
Thistle, Higbee, paneled, bee and H I G (15) 22.00
Torpedo (23) 12.00
Tub, paneled (13) 8.00
Tulip (19) 6.00

Silver

Gorham, sterling, ruby glass liner, 1892 (247) 85.00
Steiff, sterling, hand cased, 1910 (230) 75.00
Tiffany, sterling, three ball feet, 1892 (227) 85.00
Coach with coachman and footman, Dutch, c. 1890 (245) 400.00
Ricksha, Chinese, hallmarked (226) 125.00
Ruffled, three ball feet, London, 1884 (228) 50.00
Set, six, sterling, cobalt liners, c. 1910, boxed (227) 220.00

Wood

New England covered Shaker treen (255) 75.00
Round, plain, hand carved in uneven rows (232) 12.00

SALTS, MASTER

China

China, white, blue icicle pattern (320) 35.00
Dresden, double, floral (320) 45.00

English Yellow-Glaze, border decoration (322) 30.00
Sunderland, pink, pedestal (320) . 45.00

Colored Glass

Black, Steuben, threading on colorless pedestal (322) 200.00

Blue
Anvil, button daisy pattern (325) 30.00
Tub, Vallerysthal (313) 35.00

Blue, light, pedestal, popcorn pattern (318) 30.00
Cranberry, horizontal ribs (316) .. 50.00

Green
Frog (325) 25.00
Lily Pad (315) 125.00
Swirl pattern (318) 30.00
Greenish, milk glass, Portieux, fan motif (316) 40.00
Mercury, pedestal, floral decoration (321) 30.00

Lacy

Clear
Beaded Scroll (BS2: 328) 95.00
Beaded Scroll (BS4: 327) 95.00
Cornucopia (OL16: 327) 90.00
Diamond Star and Scroll (OL17: 327) 95.00
Eagle (EE1a: 328) 100.00
Eagle (EE3: 328) 70.00
Oblong (OO22: 327) 90.00
Staghorn (SN1: 328) 175.00
Blue, opaque, Basket of Flowers (BF1c: 324) 325.00
Citron, light, Mt. Vernon (MV1a: 324) 225.00
Green-yellow, Strawberry Diamond (SD7: 324) 225.00

Metal

Pewter
Dickson & Son, Sheffield, pedestal 40.00
English, round, footed (349) ... 45.00

Silver
Holder, blue glass liner, E.P.N.S. (312) 40.00
Holder, pale green glass liner, early (312) 30.00
Holder, leaf shaped feet, Cranberry liner (312) 50.00
Holder, ram's head feet, Pairpoint, blue glass liner (312) 50.00

Pressed Glass

Bull's Eye variant, scalloped rim (332) 11.00
Cordova (341) 15.00
Lion, reclining, frosted base (346) 75.00
Nova Scotia, diamond pattern, fan ends (339) 30.00
Oblong, blown in mold, ribbed sides (339) 40.00
Oval, ribbed bowl (339) 8.00
Square, hobstar sides (335) 12.00

Master, pressed glass, Jacobs Ladder pattern, pedestal base $30.00

Valise (346) 25.00
Waffle, rectangular (339) 8.00

Pressed Glass, Pedestal

Bellflower (345) 28.00
Bleeding Heart (345) 28.00
Buckle and Star (275) 30.00
Bull's Eye and Prism (345) 25.00
Cabbage Rose (345) 45.00
Deer and Pine Tree (346) 35.00
Diamond Rosette (345) 28.00
Electric (334) 15.00
Frosted Leaf (343) 50.00
Lincoln Drape (345) 30.00
Oak Leaf (346) 30.00
Round, blown in mold (339) 50.00
Sandwich Loop, covered (346) .. 35.00
Stiegel, blown in mold (343) 100.00
Stippled Chairn (345) 25.00
Stippled Swag, early (345) 28.00
Strawberry (344) 30.00
Tulip, variant, early (346) 25.00
Waterford, boat shaped, 1890 (275) 90.00

SAMPLERS

Samplers served many purposes. For a young child they were a practice exercise and permanent reminder of stitches and patterns. For a young woman they demonstrated her skills in a "gentle" art and preserved key elements of family genealogy. For the mature woman they were a useful occupation and functioned as gifts or remembrance, e.g., mourning pieces.

Schools for young ladies of the early 19th century prided themselves on the needlework skills they taught. The Westtown

School in Chester County, Pa., and the Young Ladies Seminary in Bethlehem, Pa., are two examples. These schools changed their teaching as styles changed. Berlin work was introduced by the mid-19th century.

Examples of samplers date back to the 1700's. The earliest ones were long and narrow, usually done only with the alphabet and numerals. Later examples were square. At the end of the 19th century the shape tended to be rectangular.

The same motifs were used throughout the country. The name is a key element in determining region.

In January, 1981, Sotheby's sold the Theodore H. Kapnek Collection of American Samplers. This sale badly distorted the market since many record prices were realized. Recent auctions have not maintained this price level. Prices from the Kapnek sale are marked (K) at the end of the listing.

Samplers are assumed to be on linen unless otherwise indicated. English examples bring two-thirds to one-half American examples.

Dated 1862, cross stitch on homespun linen, 16 x 20½" $525.00

1757, 16¾ x 10⅝", Abigail Byles, Boston, variety of stitches, alphabet separated by horizontal bands of birds and flowers (K)	2500.00
1773, 12¾ x 12", Mary Grant, alphabet, trees, animals	650.00
1796, 8¼ x 7⅝", Sarah Cochran, Derry, Mass., alphabet, numerals (K)	825.00
1799, 16½ x 13¼", Sally Sandborn, Pa., alphabet, floral border	2100.00
1807, 17 x 17", alphabet, numerals, trees	250.00
1811, 12 x 11¾", Rachel James, Phila., North School, alphabet, pious verse (K)	880.00
1815, 12¾ x 17", Adam and Eve, biblical quotation	425.00

1815, 16 x 12½", Eliza Pikering, Balch School, R.I., dark linen ground, alphabet, pious verse, column, embroidered floral spray border	325.00
1815, 18½ x 18½", Catherine Schrack, Phila., Mount Vernon and grounds (K)	25000.00
1826, 17¼ x 15¼", Ann Hoff, Pa., family record, dates, house	200.00
1827, 9 x 18", Margaret Steen, alphabet, numbers, "S" backwards	270.00
1830, 9¾ x 18", Margaret Bryth, alphabet, peacocks, flowers, birds .	115.00
1830, 22¾ x 17", Matilda Filbert, Pa., young girl, American eagle, house, elaborate decoration, strawberry border (K)	41500.00
1831, 17 x 18", Carolina A. Andrus, N.E., family register, pious verse, columns, floral border	400.00
1836, 15¼ x 16¾", Martha Southwick, Dublin, N.H., alphabet and numerals above green house with white trim, bud and berry border (K)	3000.00
1841, 29½ x 25¾", Mary Ann LeSeur, house flanked by woman, animals in yard, upper two thirds floral sprays, plants, and birds, geometric border	500.00
1843, 15¾ x 15½", Rachel Gratz, Va., alphabet bands, floral sprays, baskets of fruit	900.00
1844, 5 x 17¾", Mary Craigie, alphabet, numerals	320.00
1850, 25½ x 27½", Leach Barlow, mother with children, verse, strawberry border	250.00
1858, 18¾ x 20¾", Emily Hall, punched paper, house, trees, pots of tulips and roses	150.00
1879, 12½ x 12½", Franciska Wilhelm, alphabet, verse, vine border	150.00

SANDWICH GLASS

The term Sandwich Glass applies to the large variety of glass, including lacy (1825–1850), made by The Boston and Sandwich Glass Company from 1822 to 1888. Although the company is best known for its pressed glass, it also manufactured art glass in the 1870's and 1880's.

Bottles, see "Bottles"
Bowls, shallow

Acanthus, clear, 6¼"	125.00
Daisy & Button, canary	95.00
Oak Leaf, clear, 8¼"	115.00
Princess, clear, 6¼"	125.00

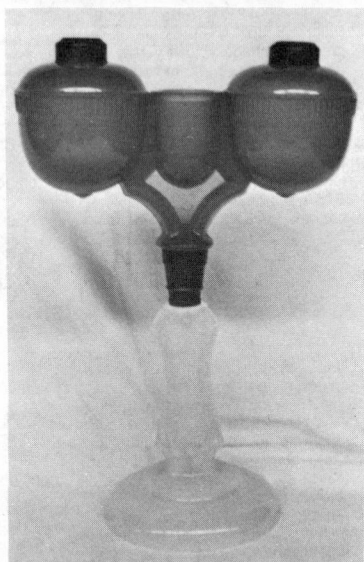

Lamp, blue with clambroth base, Riley & Co., c. 1870 .... $1000.00

Rayed Peacock Eye, clear, 6½" .	75.00
Roman Rosette, clear, 6½"	50.00
Tulip, clear, 6¼"	135.00

Candlesticks

2", canary, hexagonal base	225.00
6¾", canary, Petal and Loop, pair	325.00
7", blue, Petal and Loop, pair ...	650.00
7", clambroth, Petal and Loop, pair	300.00
7", clear, trefoil paw foot base, lacy socket	450.00
8¼", white and blue opaque, petal top, pair	550.00
9¼", white and blue opaque, Acanthus leaf, pair	800.00
9½", blue translucent top, white fluted base	500.00
10", canary, Dolphin, double stepped base, single	275.00
10", clear Dolphin, pair	450.00
10½", clear Dolphin, single	150.00
10¾", white and blue clear, Acanthus leaf, pair	800.00
12½", fiery opalescent, Crucifix .	300.00
Carafe, 9½", overlay blue to white to clear, Star-cut stopper, enamel decor in panels	250.00
Casket, covered, clear, Lee, Plate 168	350.00

Celery Vases

Blue Amethyst, octagonal base with wafer	550.00
Diamond Thumbprint, pair	400.00
Gothic Arch, flint	90.00
Cream and Sugar, Ivy, clear, miniature	100.00

Creamers

Lacy, clear, miniature	95.00
Star and Punty	125.00
Cruet, clear, Overshot	50.00
Decanter, clear, blown	150.00

Dishes

Double Horn of Plenty, clear, 5½ x 8"	150.00
Gothic, clear, 8⅜"	85.00
Ewer, 12½", Swirled Rib, Amber thorn handle	295.00
Finger Bowl, 5", Overshot	75.00
Goblet, Star & Scroll, 6"	75.00
Honey, fiery opalescent, 3½"	65.00
Inkwell, Star, brass hinged top	140.00

Lamps, Also see "Lamps"

Clambroth, Ellipse, brass collar and double whale oil burned	180.00

Amethyst

8½", brass base	395.00
12", tulip shape font, milk glass base	450.00

Clear

5½", crackle, frosted and clear	80.00
10½", Star and Punty	225.00
11", Sweetheart, pair	300.00
19", Peg, pair	185.00
Peacock Blue, 8½", Petal and Loop, square base	950.00
Paperweight, 2½", candy-type	225.00

Pitchers

1⅞", clear, miniature	250.00
6½", clear	95.00
7", blue overshot glass, square mouth, bulbous body, applied amber handle in ribbed shell, blown .	250.00
7", Syrup, Star and Buckle, clear, hexagonal body, applied handle .	185.00
8", bulbous, cranberry and clear .	235.00
8½", Overshot amber glass, cloverleaf-shaped top, amber, ribbed shell applied handle, blown	250.00
10½", Overshot clear, reeded handle	180.00
11", tankard-shape, Overshot cranberry, applied crystal ribbed handle	295.00

Plates, clear

Beehive, 9¼" hexagon	140.00
Bust of Victoria & Albert	90.00
Hairpin, 6"	65.00
Heart, 6"	55.00
Leaf and Scroll, 6"	55.00
Oak Leaf, 6"	35.00
Peacock Eye, 7"	60.00

Peacock Eye and Thistle, 8″	125.00
Thistle and Beehive, 9¼″ octagonal	150.00
Pomade, 3¾″ high, bear, black amethyst	275.00

Pulls, drawer

Canary, set of six	225.00
Clear, Raised Petal and Loop, set of six	80.00

Salts, see "Salts"

Sauces

Beaded Scale and Eye, daisy center, clear	65.00
Oak Leaf, clear	35.00
Peacock Eye, clear	40.00
Roman Rosette, fiery opalescent .	90.00
Shell Medallion, octagonal, clear .	65.00
Variant Eye, clear	15.00

Sugars, covered

Acanthus, clear	175.00
Gothic, clear	135.00
Sugar Shaker, diamond quilted, clear, original top	125.00

Tie Backs

Amber opalescent, 4¼″, pair . . .	60.00
Canary, 3″, pair	75.00
Clear, 4½″, pair	40.00
Cobalt, pair	40.00
Tray, 5 x 6½″, scrolled Leaf and Fleur de Lis, clear	65.00

Tumblers

Clear, cranberry threading	85.00
Cranberry and clear, Overshot, Roman Key	65.00

Vases

7½″ Bigler, canary, Circle and Ellipse	290.00
7½″, loop, green	600.00
9″, paneled, amethyst	750.00
10″, Three Punty, canary	450.00

Whiskey Tasters

Lacy, fiery opalescent	150.00
Loop, canary	225.00

SARREGUEMINES

SARREGUEMINES CHINA

Sarreguemines ware is a faience type, i.e., tin-glazed earthenware. The factory was established in Lorraine, France, in 1770, under the supervision of Utzcheider and Fabry. The factory was regarded as one of the three most prominent manufacturers of French Faience. Most of the wares found today are of the 19th century. Later wares are impressed Sarreguemines and Germany due to a change of boundaries and location of the factory.

Bowls

10″, fruit decor	45.00
10″, roses and leaves, gold trim .	45.00

Dish, shallow, oval, strawberries and leaves, brown interior, marked, 5 x 9¼″ **$22.00**

Character Jugs

"Lawyer"	100.00
Head of jolly man, green hat, black handle	90.00
Coffee Pot, 8″, Dresden type, floral decor, c. 1850	100.00

Pitchers

8″, floral decor	35.00
9¾″, molded in relief, scene of villagers dancing and drinking, dark green glaze exterior, aqua interior	160.00
8″, sceneic decor, artist signed . .	90.00
Hunting scenes, 10″	95.00

Plates

Asparagus, molded majolica type, round	35.00
4½″, flower decor, reticulated edge, marked	30.00
7½″, Napoleon, portrait	40.00

Vases

13½″, tan and green, floral and geometric design, slip decor	95.00
12″, blue and green, geometric design	85.00
Wine Jug, 11″, cherubs and trees .	70.00

SATIN GLASS

Satin Glass refers to an opaque colored glass that has a soft velvety surface finish. The glass was treated with hydrofluoric acid to produce the dull satin finish. It was produced by many glass companies in the late Victorian era. The large majority of Satin Glass pieces were cased or had a white lining. Favorite items were vases and rose bowls which were most often produced in shaded tones of rose, yellow or blue. Plain satin glass was at times enamel decorated or had applied glass ornamentation.

Mother-of-Pearl (MOP) Satin Glass was perfected in 1885 by Joseph Webb while he was working at the Phoenix Glass Co., Beaver, Pa. Similar to plain satin glass in respect to the plating (or casing), Mother-of-Pearl

Satin Glass differs in that it displays integral or indented designs in the glass and has a distinctive surface finish. The most common design was the diamond quilted pattern. Mother-of-Pearl Satin Glass was made in a variety of items such as tableware, fruit bowls, vases, rose bowls, pickle jars, night lights, etc. The most common colors were yellow, rose or blue with the beautiful rainbow coloring being considered choice.

Satin Glass, both plain and Mother-of-Pearl, have been widely reproduced.

For 'Coralene'' and ''Cut Velvet'' see the specific categories.

Lamp, miniature, pink, 8½″ . $1350.00

Basket, 8″, cranberry, MOP, ruffled camphor edge and camphor thorn handle 395.00
Biscuit Jars
  6⅝″, yellow, blue enamel floral decor, gold trim, silver plated top rim and handle 195.00
  Ribbon, blue, MOP, silver plated rim, lid and handle 495.00
Bobeches, blue, ruffled, clear rims, pair 45.00
Bride's Basket, 10 x 11″, purple, pie-crust edge, enamel floral decor, no holder 235.00

Compote, 5⅝″ x 7⅜″, pink, silver plated foot 125.00
Creamers and Sugars
  Herringbone, blue, MOP, rose lining, ruffled rim, pair 325.00
  Ribbon, blue, MOP, pair 350.00
Cruet, diamond quilted, blue, MOP, frosted triangular handle, knobby clear stopper 585.00
Dishes
  9″, cheese dish, herringbone, pink, MOP, clear faceted knob ... 525.00
  Purple to lavender, pink and lavender enamel floral decor 235.00
  Diamond quilted, pink, MOP, ruffled, ornate ormalu holder 300.00
Ewers
  5½″, diamond quilted, pink, MOP 160.00
  8½″, pink to rose, applied frosted thorn handle 175.00
  9″, pink to rose, ruffled top 175.00
  9″, blue, enamel bird decor, camphor handle 245.00
Fairy Lamps—See ''Fairy Lamps''
Jars, Sweetmeat, diamond quilted, pink, MOP, silver plated top, rim and handle 295.00
Inkwell, herringbone, blue, MOP, hinged metal jockey cap cover .. 450.00
Pitcher, 7 x 6″, melon, pink to white, applied celery handle 250.00
Rose Bowls
  2½″, ribbon, butterscotch, MOP . 275.00
  3⅛″, ribbon, pink, MOP, frosted wafer foot 335.00
  3½″, diamond quilted, yellow, MOP 195.00
  4″, blue 65.00
  4″, yellow 65.00
  4½″, blue, enamel decor, frosted feet 135.00
  4½″, pink, enamel decor 115.00
  6″, pink, enamel and gold decor . 165.00
  6″, oval shape, enamel bird decor, footed 135.00
  6″, diamond quilted, rainbow, MOP 385.00
Tumbler, diamond quilted, pink, MOP, enamel floral decor 225.00
Vases
  3½″, fan, ribbon, blue, MOP, frosted foot 235.00
  5⅛″, herringbone, gold, MOP, frosted amber rigaree around neck 225.00
  5½″, herringbone, pink, pleated top 125.00
  5½″, ribbon, red, MOP 325.00
  6″, raindrop, blue, MOP 175.00
  8″, raindrop, peach, MOP, pinched, ruffled top, pair 640.00
  10″, raindrop, green, MOP, enamel morning glories decor 475.00

SATSUMA

Satsuma, named for a war lord who brought skilled Korean potters to Japan in the early 1600's, was a hand-crafted Japanese faience glazed pottery. It is finely-crackled, has a cream, yellow-cream or gray-cream color and is decorated with raised enamels in floral geometric and figural motifs.

Figural Satsuma was made specifically for export in the 19th century. Later Satsuma, referred to as Satsuma-style ware, is Japanese porcelain also hand-decorated in raised enamels. From 1912 to the present, this Satsuma-style ware has been mass-produced and much of the ware on today's market is of this later period.

**Vase, Kinkozan, Mandarin duck,
5¾"** **$300.00**

Basket, 8", children and old men, c.
1850 .... 975.00
Bottles
  8½", peonies and clouds, c. 1885 200.00
  10½", Phoenix bird and clouds,
  Awaji, c. 1830 .... 1000.00
Bowls
  4" square, Arhats with phoenix
  bird, c. 1920 .... 275.00
  4¾ x 2" deep, overall floral motif,
  early 19th century 650.00
  6", Arhats and Kwannon, crack-
  led, gold trim, c. 1925 .... 175.00
  12¼", signed in blue on base,
  19th century 1400.00

Boxes
  2¼ x 5", fan-shaped, figural and
  floral decor, c. 1935 .... 65.00
  3 x 5", melon-shaped, florals and
  butterflies, c. 1840 .... 300.00
  Buttons, 1" dia., face on each, set
  of six 85.00
Brush Holder, 5", decor of colorful
  flowers and butterflies on cream-
  colored ground 45.00
Buddha, seated, small 100.00
Buttons
  ¾" dia., purple wisteria, gold rims,
  set of 6 .... 15.00
  1½" dia., floral motif, early 45.00
Charger, 12½", Thousand Warriors,
  diapered border of dragons in
  multicolors, c. 1850 .... 1500.00
Cups and Saucers
  Arhats on black, 19th century ... 60.00
  Scenic, diapered, 3-legs, c. 1900 . 75.00
Dish, shallow, scalloped rim, 14",
  painted duetiters formed border,
  later 19th century 1000.00
Figurines
  Elephant, 3", c. 1935 .... 25.00
  Hotel, 3½", c. 1935 .... 35.00
Incense Burners (Koro)
  2½", bulbous, birds and peonies
  on oxidized cobalt, c. 1875 ..... 450.00
  6", bulbous, 3-legs, wisteria decor
  on black, lion dog handles and finial, c. 1900 .... 375.00
Jars, covered
  3½", Thousand Faces, 19th century 85.00
  8½", 3-legs, scenic decor with figures, heavy gold, c. 1875 ...... 450.00
  10", 3-legs, lion dog handles and
  finial, c. 1920 .... 75.00
  17½", 3-legs, peonies in medallions, Awata, c. 1900 .... 300.00
Pitchers
  4½", fruit and flower decor on tan
  ground, c. 1840 .... 85.00
  4½", warrior scene, gold scrolled
  handle, c. 1920 .... 225.00
Plate, 4", jeweled iridescent scrolling, c. 1800 .... 175.00
Teapots
  4½", bulbous, peony decor, tortoise finial, c. 1800 .... 350.00
  7", elephant-shaped, pagoda finial, c. 1930's 75.00
  8½" Samurai Warriors, decor, c.
  1870 .... 70.00
Tea Sets
  7 pieces, enameled florals on
  white, handleless cups, c. 1920 .. 225.00
  21 pieces, Arhats, Kwannon, dragon scales, dragon handles,
  spouts, finials, handled cups, c.
  1925 .... 500.00

27 pieces, Thousand Faces, gold dragon handles, 19th century ... **2250.00**

15 pieces, enamelled bamboo trees on beige ground, 20th century, set **290.00**

Vases

5", square-shaped, Arhats with halos in panels, c. 1930 .... **150.00**

6", double gourd-shaped, figures in reserves, late 19th century ... **595.00**

7¼", baluster-shaped, peacock with trees in background, white ground, heavy gold trim, early 19th century **650.00**

7½", jeweled leaf decor, C. 1800 **450.00**

8½" ovoid, carp swimming, gilt feather scrolls, iron red neck **1500.00**

10", enameled flowers and leaves on pale ground, gold clouds, c. 1810 .... **1000.00**

12½", baluster-shaped, chrysanthemums and foliage on white ground, heavy gold trim, c. 1910 . **125.00**

15", baluster-shaped, Arhats with halos, c. 1925 .... **250.00**

18", ring handles, figures, dotted enamel trim **300.00**

23", sleeping sage, attendants, court people, diaper borders, c. 1850 .... **1500.00**

SCALES

Prior to 1900, the simple balance scale was commonly used for measuring weights. Since then, scales have become more sophisticated in design and more accurate. Scales in a variety of styles and types, used by farmers, storekeepers and druggists, include beam, platform, postal and pharmaceutical.

Candy, 4 lbs., 14½ x 18" long, cast iron, painted and stenciled, brass pan **125.00**

Egg, cast iron, "Zenith," **15.00**

Fairbanks Morse beam scale, ceramic platform, Fairbanks logo ... **150.00**

Fairbanks, small, beam **22.00**

Jeweler

Brass pans, marble-top base with drawer **125.00**

Original lined green velvet case, brass pans and 12 different measures, brass chain **112.00**

Letter, desk-type, tin **15.00**

Money, 2 x 7", complete, all original, 18th century **250.00**

Pelouze milk scale **15.00**

Pharmaceutical, 15½ x 16½", cast iron, marble pans, brass weights . **150.00**

Photographer, German silver pans, brass weights **125.00**

Platform, 50 lbs. counter-top-type, cast iron **75.00**

Platform, 300 lbs., floor model-type, cast iron, single or double beam . **150.00**

Pocket, folding, English, 18th century **200.00**

Postal, brass, includes nest of weights, ½ oz. to 4 lbs., wooden base **175.00**

Postal, cast iron, brass beam, sliding weight **75.00**

Spring balance

5 lbs., hanging-type, brass **25.00**

10 lbs., tin, brass dial **50.00**

15 lbs., hanging-type, steel **25.00**

25 lbs., hanging-type, with tray, brass dial **65.00**

30 lbs., hanging-type, tin with white porcelain dial **75.00**

Spring Platform Postal Scale **16.00**

SCHLEGELMILCH PORCELAIN

From 1861–1918, production of this porcelain (marked R.S. Germany, R.S. Poland, R.S. Prussia, R.S. Suhl and R.S. Tillowitz) was directed by two brothers, Erdmann and Reinhold Schlegelmilch at their respective factories in the Germanic provinces of Prussia, Thuringia and Silesia.

All Schlegelmilch porcelain is of the finest quality with exquisitely molded forms and unique decoration. A majority of it was factory-decorated, but blanks were produced for home-decorating and occasionally, artist-signed examples are found.

In the past, the famous "red mark" R.S. Prussia was valued above the "green mark" pieces. Today, as prices soar on R.S. Prussia, so it is also with the R.S. Germany scenic, portrait and floral examples, plus the R.S. Suhl and R.S. Tillowitz items. R.S. Poland is commanding high prices due to the scarcity of the red mark which was manufactured only from 1916–1918.

The "animal" pieces are much sought after by collectors because production of these particular patterns were limited.

CAUTION: A great many "fake" Schlegelmilch are appearing on the market. These reproductions have new decal marks, transfers or recently handpainted animals on old, authentic R.S. pieces.

R.S. GERMANY

Ashtray, 1½ x 3¾", Pinecone decor **25.00**

Berry Set, 9¼" master bowl, four 5" bowls, floral decor, set **75.00**

Bowls

7¼", pedestaled, handpainted orange, white flowers, green ground **35.00**

8¼", hexagonal, underplate 9½", floral decor, gold trim, set **75.00**

9¼", wild rose decor, lustred ground **45.00**

10", cottage scene, gold lustred top **150.00**

10" Four feet, satin with roses . . **95.00**

10", "Harvest Basket" **60.00**

Cake Set, 10" plate, Six 6" plates, handpainted floral decor, satin finish, set **125.00**

Cake Plate, three handled, roses and gold trim, R.S. red mark **410.00**

Candlestick, 5", lilies on beige, green ground **35.00**

Celery Tray

12¼", lily decor **35.00**

Pierced handles, Water lily decor **37.50**

Cheese and Cracker Plate, lilies on gray ground **45.00**

R. S. Germany, Sugar Bowl, covered, 5" $35.00

Chocolate Pots

5", blue, pink florals on light green ground, gold handle and trim . . . **55.00**

9", handpainted carnations on cream ground **75.00**

Chocolate Set, pot, 6 cups and saucers, tulips, blue with gold trim . . **250.00**

Cracker Jars

Geometric decor in aqua, black, gold trim **85.00**

Tulips, satin finish **65.00**

Creamers and Sugars, covered

Lilies on off-white ground, set . . . **50.00**

Silver Lustre, hexagonal-shape, set **85.00**

Creamer, sugar and teapot, fruit decoration with blown-out iris mold **850.00**

Creamer and sugar with Tiffany border, jewelled, roses **700.00**

Demitasse set, pot, 6 cups and saucers, rose decoration **650.00**

Hatpin Holder, orange poppies **35.00**

Jam Jar, covered, orchids **25.00**

Mustard Pot, "Harvest Basket" . . . **90.00**

Nappies

5½", handpainted daisies, gold trim, green mark **25.00**

6¾", pink roses, green to beige background, scalloped rim, satin finish **35.00**

Pitchers

Cider, pink roses on blue-green ground **85.00**

Syrup, white hydrangea, gold trim, satin finish, 14½" **45.00**

Tankard, blown out molded roses, snowballs and water lillies **1125.00**

Plates

6", orange poppy on green **8.50**

7½", scenic, shepherd boy, farmhouse, tree **38.50**

8½", white clematis, gold trim . . . **25.00**

10", classical scene, Saxe mark . . **75.00**

10", petaled flowers with raised centers **50.00**

11", open handles, multicolored poppies on white, gold trim **60.00**

Relish, 9", three sections, handpainted pink blossoms, gold handle and trim, signed L. S. Huxley . **45.00**

Sauce, with tray, pink roses, gold leaves, gold trim **30.00**

Shaving Mug, with soap drain, undecorated **35.00**

Sugar Castor, white dogwood on green, gold trim **45.00**

Tea Service, 16 pieces, pink roses on tan lustre, set **250.00**

Toothbrush Holders

Pink roses on green **55.00**

White, undecorated **35.00**

Toothpicks

2 handles, roses, gold trim **25.00**

3 handles, pansies on pastel ground, gold trim **40.00**

Trays

3¼ x 5½", white dogwood, scalloped edges, gold trim **35.00**

5 x 14", handled, white flowers with gold centers, green leaves on tan **50.00**

Pin tray, with Easter lily **70.00**

Vase, 4½", iris on white ground . . . **30.00**

R.S. POLAND

Bowl, crane, 9" **900.00**

Hatpin Holder, floral decor on shaded ground **95.00**

Plate, portrait, 9½" **1000.00**

Vases

7", Lion and Lioness **1000.00**

9", Scenic decor **850.00**

R. S. Poland, Vase, floral, 12",
pair $550.00

R.S. PRUSSIA

Berry Sets
    7 pieces, 11½" bowl, six 5¾"
    bowls, handpainted orchids, gold
    trim, set **425.00**
    7 pieces, master bowl, six serving
    bowls, swan decor, icicle molded
    edges, set **1000.00**

Bowls
    5", green ground, white, yellow
    poppies **475.00**
    5½", red ground, floral center,
    portrait medallions **225.00**
    7½", roses **75.00**
    9½", green, multicolored flowers,
    gold trim **150.00**
    10", boat scene, pearlized finish .   **600.00**
    10", cabbage mold, satin finish . .   **500.00**
    10½", Melon Eaters, jewel mold-
    ed edge **1000.00**
    10½", portrait center **850.00**
    Berry bowl, red mark, raspberries
    and green flowers, melon rib and
    gold trim, footed **225.00**
    Oval bowl, roses **259.00**

Whipped Cream Set, Baine under-
    plate and ladle, white poppies de-
    cor, 3 pieces **75.00**
    11", floral center, shaded green
    ground, gold trim **225.00**
    11", stage center, beaded molded
    edge, gold trim **1800.00**
    12" oval, open handles, roses . . .   **175.00**

Boxes, covered
    Jewel, pink and white flowers . . .   **125.00**
    Powder, rose decor on white **95.00**

Chocolate Pots
    Castle Scene, ball feet **1250.00**
    Florals, all white flowers on shad-
    ed green ground, gold beaded
    trim **350.00**

Snowbird, icicle molded edge . . .   **1750.00**
Swan, gold beaded edge **500.00**
Chocolate Sets, 7 pieces
    Farmyard, icicle molded edges . .   **2750.00**
    Floral, carnation molded edges
        Gold trim **850.00**
        Portrait **3000.00**
        Swallows **1200.00**
Compote, 6½" dia., 7" high, roses
    on shaded green ground **200.00**
Cracker Jars
    6½", pink and white flowers, scal-
    loped base **175.00**
    7", green florals, satin finish **300.00**
Creamers and Sugars, covered
    Castle, ball feet **600.00**
    Floral, ball feet **275.00**
    Swans **350.00**
Dishes
    Jewelled Bon Bon, gold colored
    flowers, molded, three feet **125.00**
    7⅝", oval, handles, floral red
    mark **120.00**
Hair Receivers
    Florals, diamond-shape, pearlized   **150.00**
    Roses, shaded green ground **95.00**
Hatpin Holder, roses on shaded yel-
    low-green ground **95.00**
Humidor, with jewels, red mark **325.00**
Jam Jar, with underplate, pink roses,
    gold trim, beaded edge **150.00**
Mug, roses on yellow ground **125.00**
Pitchers, Tankard-shaped
    Fall Season, carnation molded
    edges **4000.00**
    Lilies, shaded violet ground, satin
    finish **500.00**
    Roses, pink and yellow on shaded
    green ground **325.00**
    Swans, icicle molded edges **1500.00**
Plates
    Castle, petaled edges, gold trim 8
    ¾" **500.00**
    9", iris border and fan **135.00**
    Embossed lily border, much gold .   **55.00**
    Farmyard scene, 10½" **950.00**
    Floral, shaded ground, carnation
    molded edge, 10" **300.00**
    Melon Eaters, jeweled molded
    edge, 10½" **1000.00**
    Mill Scene, 10" **400.00**
    Portrait, plain rim, 10" **650.00**
    Sheepherder, 10½" **700.00**
    Ship, orange, 10½" **650.00**
Ring Tree, florals, gold trim **110.00**
Sauce, 5", Mill Scene **55.00**
Shaving Mug, roses, yellow and
    pink, beaded edge **125.00**
Sugar Castors
    Apple Blossoms, shaded green
    ground, gold trim **135.00**
    Roses, three handles, satin finish   **175.00**

R. S. Prussia, Plate, red mark, green wreath, 8½" $95.00

Syrup, with underplate, pink roses on shaded green ground, gold trim ... 175.00
Tea Sets, 3 pieces
  Daffodils, shaded green ground .. 300.00
  Swans, icicle molded borders ... 1000.00
Toothpick Holder, floral decor, 2 handles 125.00
Trays
  6 x 12", Swans 500.00
  6 x 12½", open handles, Waterlilies 250.00
  7½ x 11", pink roses on green ground 175.00
  7½ x 12", Snowbirds 1500.00
  Frosted platinum finish, Daisies and cattails 185.00
Vases
  Cage, The, handles, 8" 1000.00
  Cottage Scene, 4½" 250.00
  Farmyard Scene, 9" 950.00
  Florals, pink and white on yellow ground, 8" 175.00
  Hummingbirds, 5" 625.00
  Melon Eaters, handles, jeweled, 10" 1500.00
  Mill Scene, handled, cobalt, gold trim, 9" 1000.00
  Peace Bringing Plenty, green, 7" . 950.00
  Roses, pink, handles, 9" 325.00
  Ships, handles, 9" 600.00
  Winter Season, 8½" 650.00

R.S. SUHL

Bowl, Mill and Sheepherder (combination), 10" 850.00
Box, covered, Nightwatch 650.00
Plate, Lion and Lioness, 9" 750.00
Tea Service, Nightwatch, 15 pieces . 1000.00
Vases
  Nightwatch, 12" 850.00
  Three by Dawn, 8" 600.00

R. S. Tillowitz, Relish Dish, oblong, 9¼" $20.00

R.S. TILLOWITZ

Basket, 5 x 2½" high, octagonal, handpainted multicolored florals, gold handle and trim 60.00
Bowls
  7½", shallow, handled, poinsettias on white 60.00
  9¼", roses on shaded green ground, gold trim 40.00
Cake Plate, 10", open handles, orange poppies 55.00
Cake Set, 7 pieces, blue handpainted roses, gold trim 175.00
Cream and Sugar, 3" high, poinsettia decor on white ground, set ... 45.00
Teapot, pastel florals 40.00
Tea Tile, 6", white sweetpeas on orange 45.00
Tray, 6¼", handled, handpainted florals, artist signed 30.00
Tray 9 x 13" oval, pastel peonies on blue ground 50.00
Vase, 6" ovoid, roses on shaded tan ground 45.00

Schneider

SCHNEIDER GLASS

Charles and Ernest Schneider founded the firm known as Christalerie Schneider in Epinay-sur-Siene, France. Their art glass can be identified by the distinctive mottled colors. This type of Schneider glass was made from 1913 to 1933. The firm is currently producing crystal tableware.

Bowl, Centerpiece, 13¾" dia., blue frosted glass etched leaf design on rim 210.00
Compotes
  3½ x 5" dia., mottled orange, wrought iron frame 150.00
  5 x 14", mottled rose, amethyst stem, iron and glass base 345.00
  9½" dia., mottled orange and blue 275.00

Vase, light amber, signed, 7″ dia., 4½″ high $125.00

Ewer, 6½″, mottled blue and gray, applied black amethyst handle ..	200.00
Finger Bowl, with underplate, smoked glass	135.00
Pitchers	
Roses with vari-colored twisted handle	250.00
6″, raspberry body, mottled handle and spout	325.00
Plate, 4″, mottled deep pink	60.00
Vases	
7½″, spherical, deep violet, etched, footed	220.00
7½″, bulbous, mottled blue with amber	125.00
9¾″, ovoid, mottled rose with green	145.00
12″, ovoid, mottled pink, bubble glass, c. 1930	125.00

SCHOENHUT TOYS

Albert Schoenhut, son of a toymaker, was born in Germany in 1849. In 1866, he ventured to America to work as a repairman of toy pianos for Wanamaker's, Philadelphia, Pa. Finding the glass sounding bars inadequate, he perfected a toy piano with metal sounding bars. His piano was an instant success and the A. Schoenhut Company had its beginning.

From then on, toys seemed to flow out of the factory. Each of his six sons entered the business. The business prospered until 1934, when misfortune forced the company into bankruptcy. In 1935 Otto and George Schoenhut contracted to produce the Pinn Family Dolls.

At the same time, the Schoenhut Manufac-

turing Company was formed by two other Schoenhuts. Both companies operated under a partnership agreement that eventually led to O. Schoenhut, Inc. which continues today.

Some dates of interest: 1872-toy piano invented; 1903-Humpty and Dumpty and Circus patented; 1911–1924-wooden doll production; 1928–1934-composition dolls.

Elephant, glass eyes $125.00

Animals	
Alligator, glass eyes	235.00
Alligator, painted eyes	175.00
Bear, brown painted eyes	125.00
Buffalo, glass eyes	225.00
Buffalo, painted eyes	135.00
Bulldog, brown painted eyes, (rare)	225.00
Camel, glass eyes, one hump ..	250.00
Camel, painted eyes, two humps .	175.00
Camel, painted eyes, one hump ..	200.00
Deer, glass eyes	275.00
Donkey, large, glass eyes	125.00
Donkey, small, painted eyes	45.00
Elephant, painted eyes	50.00
Giraffe, 11″ high, painted eyes ..	240.00
Goat, glass eyes	110.00
Goose, painted eyes	200.00
Hippopotamus, glass eyes	250.00
Hippopotamus, painted eyes	185.00
Horse, painted eyes	150.00
Lamb, painted eyes	150.00
Leopard, glass eyes	225.00
Lion, glass eyes	160.00
Monkey, painted eyes	150.00
Ostrich, painted eyes, (rare)	200.00
Pig, glass eyes	150.00
Poodle, glass eyes	180.00
Poodle, painted eyes	115.00
Spark Plug, all original	150.00
Tiger, glass eyes	225.00
Tiger, painted eyes	150.00
Zebra, glass eyes	225.00

Blocks	
"A,B,C"	80.00
"Building Blocks," original box, complete	150.00

Circus, "Humpty Dumpty," glass-eyed figurines, poster, original box, incomplete, 22 pieces **1000.00**
Circus, "Humpty Dumpty," animals with glass eyes, complete with tent, 52 pieces **5500.00**
Circus Accessories
Barrel **7.00**
Chair **9.00**
Platform **10.00**
Tent, 25 x 35" **400.00**
Circus Performers
Acrobat, Lady **140.00**
Acrobat, Lady, bisque **225.00**
Clown, cotton suit, large **95.00**
Bare back rider on white horse, 6½" **250.00**
Lion Tamer, wooden head **175.00**
Ringmaster, 8", bisque head, all original, complete **275.00**
Ringmaster, 8½", wooden head . **135.00**
Strong Man, bisque head **275.00**
Dirigible, 13", original box, c. 1929 . **50.00**
Doll House—Garage, 14 x 19 x 20" high, two stories, stairway, hinged roof, swing-away sides, c. 1920's . **350.00**
Dolls
Baby Face, 14", baby body, wooden head, painted hair, eyes, dressed **225.00**
Baby Face, 16", toddler body, wooden jointed body, painted hair, eyes, closed mouth **250.00**
Clothespin Boy, yarn hair, painted features, suitably dressed **85.00**
Character, 16", wooden, Intaglio eyes, molded hair with pink ribbon **475.00**
Nature, 11", sitting, original wig . . **175.00**
Walking, 14", all wood, painted eyes, mohair wig, open mouth, suitably dressed **425.00**
Personalities
Barney Google **150.00**
Farmer **125.00**
Hobo **125.00**
Jiggs **300.00**
Maggie with rolling pin **400.00**
Max and Moritz, replaced coats, pair **500.00**
Teddy Roosevelt with hat **350.00**
Teddy Roosevelt without hat **300.00**
Pianos
8½ x 9½ x 16", 15 keys **100.00**
11 x 21 x 23", brass pedals **150.00**
17 x 24 x 27", grand **275.00**
17 x 29 x 31", 29 keys **200.00**
Piano Stools
Double **150.00**
Single **65.00**
Roly Dolly, baby **250.00**
Trinity Chimes **125.00**

SCIENTIFIC INSTRUMENTS

Chemists, doctors, geologists, navigators and surveyors used precision instruments as tool of their trade. Such objects are well designed and beautifully crafted. The principal medium is brass. Fancy hardwood cases also are common.

Balance, Laboratory, Fisher Co., brass beam scale and brass weights, nickel plated pans, wood and glass case, c. 1920 . . . . **350.00**
Barometers
Aneroid marine, mounted in 5" dia. brass case, adjustable for altitude **150.00**
Brass, Short & Mason, London, 1890, 4" dia. **80.00**
Mercurial, U. S. Signal Corps, mercury tube mounted on brass plate, 43" **225.00**
Generator, Electrostatic, Central Scientific Supply, 12" dia. fiber discs, brass discharge rods, glass tube condensors, mounted on walnut base, c. 1920 . . . . **550.00**
Levels, Surveyor
Elliot, London, 1830, brass, walnut case, 12" **695.00**
Warren Knight, Phila., 1920, brass, 12" **595.00**
Stackpole & Brothers, New York, 1850, brass, walnut case, 18" . . . **1295.00**
Microscopes, brass
C. Reinert, Wein, 1870, single object lens, student type, 10" **375.00**
C. Reinert, Wein, three objective lense, laboratory type, walnut case, 13" **550.00**
Single Object lens, student field type, 4" **85.00**
Octants
Imray, London, c. 1840, ebony and brass, ivory vernier scale . . . **450.00**
Spencer & Barrett, London, c. 1830, ebony and brass, ivory vernier scale, oak case **600.00**
Sextants
Thomas A. Anisley, London, c. 1840, brass, brass vernier scale, mahogany case **650.00**
Lenadrice & Co., London, brass, silver vernier scale, mahogany case **950.00**
Unmarked, c. 1820, ebony and brass, ivory vernier scale, mahogany case **800.00**
Transits, Surveyors
Brandeis and Son, Brooklyn, N.Y., brass, large compass, oak case, 15" **1500.00**

W. & L. Gurley, Troy, N.Y., 1850, brass, large compass, cherry case, 12" 1250.00
Keuffel & Esser, Germany, 1891, brass, large compass, 14" 1500.00

SCONCES

A sconce is a wall bracket used to hold candles or lights.

Wall, French, copper, 13¼" ..$135.00

Brass
  1-candleholder, Dolphin finial, mirrored back 100.00
  2-candleholders, American, pair . 250.00
  2-candleholders, drip cup, pair .. 150.00
  2-candleholders, Queen Anne-style, English, pair 350.00
  3-candleholders, prisms & beads 140.00
Cast Iron, 2 candleholder, crimped top 145.00
Glass, 2 candleholder, cut prisms, pair 250.00
Tin, strap, 9¾" 145.00
Tole, single candleholder 8¼" 150.00
  10", back plates, rounded crimped tops, small reflector, pair 425.00

SCRIMSHAW

Scrimshaw carving had its origins in the early 19th century and is generally associated with the whaling industry. Sailors occupied their idle hours by carving or engraving whale and walrus tusks, bone and other forms of ivory. Eskimos also used this means to express their artistic endeavors.

The most common designs are ships, whaling scenes, patriotic themes, or women, perhaps a wife or sweetheart. While some of the articles had a utilitarian purpose, most were purely ornamental and presented as homecoming gifts.

Interest in scrimshaw lessened in the first half of the 20th century. It is being revived today by skilled craftsmen. Unfortunately, modern technology also has created a large number of reproductions and outright fakes. Lists of reproduction teeth and tusks are being published by antique trade papers. *Note:* Whale and walrus ivory are included in the modern import ban. If you are engaged in trading in any of the "endangered species," you must familiarize yourself with the bill of November, 1978.

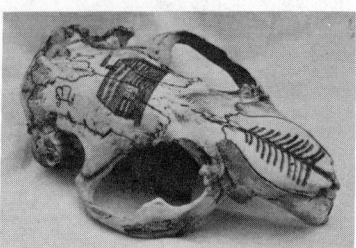

Beaver Skull, N.Y., c. 1910, 5½" long $150.00

Candlesticks, pair, turned, 6¾" 600.00
Clothes Pins, set of 4, 5" 225.00
Corset Busk, flowers, flag, hearts, etc., 13¹¹⁄₁₆" 425.00
Cribbage game, Eskimo, relief carving of Eskimo scene, 22½" 400.00
Dipper, coconut shell bowl, turned bone & ivory handle, 14¾" 350.00
Gravel, whalebone, 8½" 275.00
Jagging Wheel, star and crescent carved wheel, simple turned handle, 6⅜" 300.00
Rolling Pin, lignum vitae roll, turned whale ivory handle, 16" 725.00
Swift, whale ivory and bone, double, carved center support, 15½" ... 1350.00

Walrus' Tusk
    15½", one side with four separate
    human subjects, other with name
    Samuel Shurlock **450.00**
    27½", James Parker, late 19th C.,
    Bark *Superior*, arctic whaling
    scene **600.00**
Whale's Tooth
    5⅛", Victorian Lady **450.00**
    5½", actor in Scottish costume
    holding sword **550.00**
    6½", sailing ship with native ca-
    noes, island in background **950.00**

SEBASTIANS

Sebastians are handpainted, lightly glazed figurines of characters from literature and history. They range in size from 3 to 4 inches. Each figurine is made in limited numbers. Other series include children and scenes from family life.

Prescott W. Baston, the originator and designer of Sebastian figures, began production in 1938 in Marblehead, Mass. His son, Woody Baston, has begun designing, with his first figures becoming available in 1981. Sebastian Studios is located in Hudson, Mass.

Baby Buggy, 6303	**22.50**
Becky Thatcher, 6131	**20.00**
Bell, First Annual, 6603	**30.00**
Ben Franklin, 6218	**20.00**
Clown, 6205	**100.00**
Collector Plaque, 1976–78, green label, each	**30.00**
Colonial Lace Maker, 6301	**18.00**
Dickens Collection, 6119	**275.00**
Dicken's Cottage, 6116, green label	**26.00**
Family Picnic, 6602	**30.00**
Family Reading, 1202	**30.00**
Farmer, 6226	**16.00**
Fisherman, 6228	**20.00**
George Washington, 6001	**25.00**
Little Mother, 6231	**22.00**
Little Sister, 6238	**22.00**
Mark Twain, 6137	**20.00**
Mrs. Rittenhouse Square, 2199	**45.00**
Nativity Scene, 6314	**95.00**
Old Salt, 6242	**16.00**
Paul Bunyon, 6250	**250.00**
Pilgrim, 6324	**25.00**
Pioneer Village, 6252	**20.00**
Rub-a-Dub Dub, 6404	**24.00**
Sailing Days, Girl, 2104	**20.00**
Shoemaker, 6217	**30.00**
Snow Days, Boy, 6262	**25.00**
Swan Boat, 6244	**27.00**
Town Crier, 6247	**16.00**
Uncle Sam, 6206	**15.00**
Wall Display, 6987	**30.00**

SEVRES

Sevres is a superb porcelain made in Sevres, France since the middle 1700's. Originally sanctioned by royalty, some of the finest porcelain ever made was produced in the early years. The name now applies to all wares made in Sevres, France.

Urns, pair, cobalt blue and gold, courting scene, bouquet of summer flowers, c. 1870, 17½" **$1250.00**

Bowl, 13" long, ornate handles, white with multicolored roses . . .	**500.00**
Box, hinged, 5" dia., white with floral decor, c. 1771	**300.00**
Compote, 8¾", classical scene, signed Watteau	**400.00**
Condiment Set, 8", Trefoil-shaped, three containers, white with floral sprays, gold trim, c. 1760	**500.00**
Cup and Saucer, demitasse, cobalt and gold	**35.00**
Figurine, 12", cherub, lavender, gray, gold trim, c. 1880	**300.00**
Pen Tray, 11¼", hand painted bouquets of garden flowers, gilt borders	**325.00**
Plates	
8", four diamond-shaped reserves with "LP", three oval reserves with floral bouquets, gold trim . . .	**135.00**
9", classical scene of lady and gentleman, blue rim with florals, gold trim, signed Watteau	**200.00**

9½", "LP" crown in center, gold vines around celeste blue border, c. 1844, set of 6 .... 750.00
9½", portrait, "Mme Elisabeth, Duc de Burgogne," signed Debrie 195.00
Salt, Master, white, turquoise, gold jeweled, gold interior, c. 1850 ... 150.00
Tazza, 10½ x 17½", portrait center plate, ormolu frame 450.00
Urns
14½", cobalt with gold scrolls, flowers, center medallion of young girl and boy, signed Callard 375.00
19", cobalt, lady and gentleman on front, scenic design on reverse, ormolu base and handles . 600.00
Vase, 28", baluster-shaped, multicolored roses on cobalt, heavy gold trim, artist signed 750.00

SEWING ITEMS

As late as 50 years ago, a wide variety of sewing items were found in almost every home in America. Women, of every economic and social status, were skilled in sewing and dress making.

Even the most elegant ladies practiced the art of embroidery with the aid of jeweled gold and silver thimbles. Sewing birds, an interesting convenience item, were used to hold cloth (in the bird's beak) while sewing. Made of iron or brass, they could be attached to table or shelf with a screw-type fixture. Later models featured pin cushions.

Baskets
Victorian, 2 tiers, 38½ x 15½" .. 100.00
Victorian, 12", fitted with scissors, pins, lined, 3 legs 85.00
Woven splint, pockets, scissors attached 145.00
Beading Tool, sterling, 6" 45.00
Bodkins
MOP, 3" 7.50
Sterling, fish-shaped, set of three in silk case 35.00
Boxes
Attachments, oak 15.00
Leather, silver trim, lined 22.00
Shaker style, domed 275.00
Buttons, approximate 1" dia.
Brass, English .... .75
Enameled 2.00
Glass 3.00
Crochet Hook, ivory 10.00
Darning Eggs
Glass, "End-of-day," blown 95.00
Ivorine 10.00
Wood, embossed sterling handle 30.00
Wood, ebony 15.00

Machines
Busy Bee, hand-type, 3¼ x 6" base, New England 50.00
Minnesota, in cabinet 195.00
Wilcox & Gibbs, clamp on 70.00
Needle Cases
Bone 15.00
Ivory, umbrella-shaped, carved .. 40.00
Pewter, key-shaped 40.00
Sterling, scroll work design, handled 28.00
Wood, Urn-shaped, mechanical . 15.00

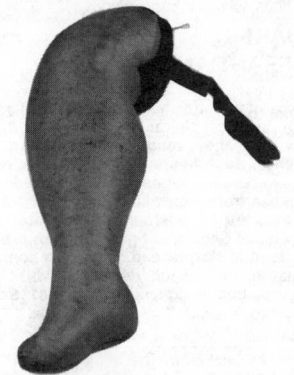

Pincushion, 9" long, silk encased $20.00

Pincushions
Beaded, 7½", floral center 30.00
Patchwork pillow, 8" 15.00
Shoe, pewter, velvet cushion ... 25.00
Punches
Ivory 20.00
Sterling, with gauge 22.00
Scissors
Brass, 7", Art Nouveau motif ... 85.00
Steel, 3½", H. Boh, 19th century 30.00
Sterling, 4¼", embossed handles, c. 1890 .... 50.00
Sewing Birds
Brass, one cushion 90.00
Brass, two cushions, 1853 ..... 155.00
Cast Iron, two cushions 45.00
Silver, two cushions 95.00
Shuttles
Silver, Sterling 25.00
Wooden, 11" Netting 15.00
Tape Measures
Alarm clock, footed with large bell 20.00
Bone case, ivory knob, pink measure 25.00
Brass, paddle wheel boat, c. 1830 80.00
China clown 15.00

Thimbles
Brass	**15.00**
Cloisonne, 20th century	**30.00**
Ivory, scrimshaw	**15.00**
Thimble Holder, sterling pierced cylinder	**65.00**
Thread Holder, cat	**45.00**

Thread Winders
Bone	**7.50**
Ivory, pierced, scalloped border	**35.00**
MOP, scalloped border	**35.00**

SHAKER

The Shakers, so named because of a dance used in worship, are one of the oldest communal organizations in the United States. This religious group was founded by Mother Ann Lee who emigrated from England and established the first Shaker community near Albany, N.Y., in 1784. The Shakers reached their peak in 1850 with 6,000 members. Less than ten Shakers are living today.

Shakers lived celibate and self-sufficient lives. Their philosophy stressed cleanliness, order, simplicity, and economy. Highly inventive and motivated, the Shakers created many utilitarian household forms and objects. Their furniture reflects their striving for quality and purity in design.

In the early 19th century, the Shakers produced many items for commercial purposes. Chairmaking and the packaged herb and seed business thrived. In every endeavor and enterprise, the members followed Mother Ann's advice: "Put your hands to work and give your heart to God."

Collecting Shaker items is expensive. The furniture is among the most sought after in the American country style. A number of popular house design books published recently have added to this craze.

Almanac, 1886	**35.00**
Bag, flour, Shaker Mills, New Gloucester	**155.00**
Bandbox, wood, oval, tongued	
5", plain	**60.00**
5⅝", green	**200.00**
6⅜", Harvard, green	**300.00**
6¾", J. Fenno, green	**225.00**
7⅞", plain	**120.00**

Baskets
9⅛", oval, handled	**70.00**
21", Laundry, Maine	**175.00**
Basket Mold, wood	**20.00**
Bonnet, No. 5	**55.00**

Bottles
4⅛", Shaker Anodyne, North Enfield, N.H., blue	**40.00**

Butter Churn, Strap hinges, old red paint	**$350.00**
6", Imperial Rose Baum, Mt. Lebanon, blue, thin elongated form	**70.00**
7¾", Shaker Hair Restorer, amber	**125.00**
Bucket, Sap, N.E. Shakers, Enfield, N.H., 9¼"	**100.00**
Cheese Press, box, 5" square	**25.00**
Candleholder, Hancock, Mass., cherry and maple with red wash, 24"	**1400.00**
Candle Stand, Harvard, Mass., cherry and birch, adjustible	**3750.00**

Chairs
Mt. Lebanon, side, 3 beveled edge slats, acorn finials, 36½"	**450.00**
Side, 3 slats, bulb finials, 39½"	**325.00**
Work, 2 slats, 33"	**375.00**

Chests
Enfield, Conn., bonnet drawer on top, yellow, c. 1850–60, 18 x 44 x 45"	**4000.00**
Watervliet, N.Y., cherry, pine, and birch, 6 drawers, 1827, 18 x 40 x 62"	**7000.00**

Cupboard
Harvard, pine, cupboard on chest of 6 drawers, refinished	**3900.00**

Mt. Lebanon, N.Y., jelly, red paint, c. 1820–30	1250.00
Tyringham, Mass., red, 11 x 17 x 23″	1500.00
Drying Rack, Enfield, 4 legs, ten arms	450.00
Firkin, Canterbury, N.H., gray	150.00
Hangers	
14¾″, bowed slat	35.00
17½″, South Family, yellow	75.00
Knife Box, Mt. Lebanon, N.Y., yellow	375.00
Mirror Rack, cherry, 5 brush pegs	900.00
Rake, wood teeth, metal support	110.00
Rockers	
Alfred, Me., four slat, chrome yellow paint (record price)	8000.00
Mt. Lebanon, Shaker's No. 6, four slats, acorn finial 41½″	650.00
Stand, black cherry, black, one drawer with brass pull, 17 x 17 x 26″	1200.00
Spinning Wheel, flax, Alfred, made by Samuel Ring	275.00
Stocking Form, Sister Miriam, Canterbury, N.H., 29″	70.00
Swift, Hancock, Mass., yellow	300.00
Tables	
Canterbury, N.H., sewing, pine and cherry, green, 2 drawers, c. 1830, 27 x 28 x 50″	6000.00
New England, maple, tapered legs, 49 x 27½ x 29″	2500.00
Sabbathday Lake, Me., table, from kitchen of trustees' house	11500.00
Trencher, oval, blue paint, 9¼″	100.00
Tailcring Stick, cherry, W. Balfour	525.00
Wool Winder, 4 adjustible arms, marked W. W. Wyman, West Waterville, Me.	175.00

SHAVING MUGS

A shaving mug was an essential item in the Victorian gentleman's toiletry. The container held soap and hot water to be used with a soft bristled brush to lather the face before shaving. During the period of 1870–1924, shaving mugs of porcelain or pottery were manufactured and decorated with the owner's name and occupation. They were usually kept at the owner's favorite barber shop for his exclusive use.

Scuttle shaving mugs get their name from their general appearance, resembling somewhat the early European coal scuttles. Most scuttles were European imports and few were handpainted, but had transfer decorations. A few were American made. Scuttles are 2-compartment receptacles (one for water and one for soap). The earliest ones are without drain holes in the soap (top) com-partment. **The lower compartment has a spout for pouring off the water after use. Note: Many reproductions are currently imported from England and Japan.**

Fraternal, Masonic	$50.00

Fraternal Emblems (with owner's name)

A.O.U.W.	40.00
B.P.O.E., handpainted	50.00
F.O.E.	45.00
G.A.R.	65.00
I.O.O.F. (Odd Fellows)	35.00
K.K.K.	90.00
K.G.E.	65.00
K. of C	45.00
K. of L	65.00
K. of P	35.00
K.T.	35.00
L.O.O.M	35.00
M.W.A	30.00
O. of I.A.	90.00
Shrine	80.00
W.O.W.	35.00

Occupational

Architect Emblem	135.00
Artist, painting picture	135.00
Athlete, track runner	130.00
Bakery Wagon	165.00
Baseball Players, batter and catcher	185.00
Blacksmith, anvil and hammer	155.00
Boy on bike	125.00
Butcher, steer head and tools of trade	130.00
Carpenter at work	115.00
Coal Wagon	125.00
Cowboy, lassoing steer	130.00
Dairy Wagon	140.00
Dentist, pulling teeth	185.00
Dentist, false teeth	145.00
Drayman, horse drawn cart	100.00

R.S. Prussia	95.00
Seashell-shaped	30.00
Silverplated, pairpoint	90.00
Swan-shaped	45.00

SHAWNEE POTTERY

Organized in 1935 in Zanesville, Ohio, Shawnee Pottery was not an art pottery. The factory produced inexpensive commercial pottery, kitchenware, dinnerware and premium items for the American mass market until early 1961. At first, Shawnee pieces carried an Indian-on-an-arrowhead trademark. Later production was marked "Shawnee" or "Kenwood," and many items were marked with paper labels.

Shakers, Salt and pepper, Corn, King $15.00

Occupational, Bartender $225.00

Express Wagon	120.00
Farmer, instructing son	160.00
Fireman, 2 horses	190.00
Fireman, steam engine	200.00
Fisherman	100.00
Florist with wagon	160.00
Grocery Wagon	150.00
Harness Maker, working	160.00
Hunter, with bird-dog	165.00
Jockey in sulky	175.00
Milkman, horse and wagon	165.00
Miner, with tools	155.00
Minister, in pulpit	200.00
Mortician, horse-drawn hearse	475.00
Musicians	120.00
Notary, pen in hand	110.00
Painter	125.00
Pharmacist, mortar and pestle	125.00
Photographer, with camera	125.00
Policeman	180.00
Printer, at case	115.00
Railroad, caboose	100.00
Railroad, locomotive engine	135.00
Seaman, captain of sailng vessel	170.00
Stationary Engine	175.00
Surveyor, with instruments	150.00
Tailor, 5 men	160.00
Telegrapher, with key	125.00
Watch Maker, watch and chain	100.00
Whiskey Distributor, with wagon	150.00

Scuttles

Cream pitcher-shaped	28.00
Fish-shaped	35.00
Floral decor	30.00
Ironstone, floral transfer	35.00
Ironstone, plain	28.00
Lady's Portrait, transfer	48.00
Porcelain, pat. Sept. 20, 1870	38.00
Porcelain, with drain hole in handle	35.00

Bowls

8", Corn King	15.00
8", basketweave	15.00

Casseroles, covered

Corn King, large	30.00
Corn Queen, large	25.00

Cookie Jars

Cat	19.00
Corn King	30.00
Dutch Boy	25.00
Lady Pig	28.00
Raggedy Ann	16.00
Winnie Pig	25.00
Cream and Sugar, Corn King	20.00

Creamers

Bo-Peep	15.00
Cat	8.50

Pitchers

Chicken	20.00
Corn	25.00
Elephant, 4"	4.00
Little Boy Blue	18.00

Planter, train, 4 pieces, set	32.50	Jolson, Al, regular format, c. 1920's	7.50
Platter, 11¾", Corn King	11.00	Marches, Waltzes, Fox Trots, small format, c. 1900–1940	1.00
Salt and Peppers		Movie Melodies, small format, c. 1925–1950	2.00
Dutch Boy and Girl, 5"	12.50	Piano Solos, small format, c. 1925–1945	2.00
Fruits, 3½"	10.00	Western, small format, c. 1930–1950	1.50
Winnie Pig	12.00	World War I, large format	5.00
Teapots		World War I, small format	1.50
Corn King	27.00	World War II, regular format	3.00
Granny Ann	30.00		
Tom, The Piper's Son	25.00		

SHEET MUSIC

Even if you can't play a note or sing on key, collecting sheet music can be an informative and rewarding experience. Much of our history is recorded in music . . . time of war, depressions, fashions and glimpses of our romantic trends. People collect sheet music by composers, favorite stars, musicals, movies, colorful covers or just for memories. A few years ago old sheet music could be bought for a "song." Today prices range from one dollar for the ordinary to several dollars for the earlier lithographed covers.

Group of three, each $1.00

Ballads, large format, star on cover, c. 1900–1920	2.00
Berlin, Irving, large format, c. 1910–1915	10.00
Campaign Songs	10.00
Crosby, Bing, regular format, c. 1935	10.00
Dixieland, large format, c. 1900–1915	5.00

SHIRLEY TEMPLE ITEMS
See CHARACTER AND PERSONALITY ITEMS

SILHOUETTES

Silhouettes (or shades) are shadow profiles. They were very popular during the 18th and 19th century. Silhouettes are either hollow cut, mechanically traced, or painted.

The name silhouette came from a French Minister of Finance, Etienne de Silhouette, who tended to be tight with money and cut "shades" as a pastime. In America, the Peale family was one of the leading makers of silhouettes. An impressed stamp marked "PEALE" or "Peale Museum" identifies them.

Silhouette portraiture dropped in popularity prior to the Civil War with the introduction of the daguerreotype. In the 1920's and 1930's, this art form had a brief revival when it became popular for tourists to Atlantic City and Paris to have their profiles cut as souvenirs of their visit.

Lady and Gentleman, 4 x 3¼", hollow cut, pair $140.00

Children	
Drummer Boy, hollow cut, watercolor landscape background, 1840, 7½ x 5½"	550.00
Girls, two, Agnew and Lindsay, hollow cut, double, Auguste Edouart, 1831, 4½ x 5¾"	425.00
Gentlemen	
3¾ x 4¾", oval, James Monroe	150.00

4½", hollow cut, pencil details .. **90.00**
4½ x 3½", hollow cut, P: Eddy, Peale Museum **145.00**
5 x 6", military officer **80.00**
5⅛ x 6", inked, gold, brushwork details **125.00**
Family Group
Adams [William, John, Abigail, John Quincy, Louise Catherine], 1809, 12⅛ x 10¼" **3250.00**
Conversation group, crayon and pencil, room setting, 6¾ x 8¾" .. **600.00**
McClure Family, hollow cut, 4 figures, Auguste Edouart, 1832 10 x 14" **500.00**
Ladies
4⅞ x 4³/₁₆", outline filled in with ink, Mary Rhoads, Thomas Gilpin copy of Joseph Samson silhouette **175.00**
5 x 4¹/₁₆", hollow cut, M. Tatnall, "MUSEUM" **130.00**
6½x 5¼", hollow cut, Esther Isaacs, c. 1800 .... **275.00**
7 x 9", hat, high neck gown with cut work, 1904 .... **80.00**
10½", full skirt, blouse with leg-o-mutton sleeves, bonnet **125.00**
Ladies and Gentleman, hollow cut, ink details, F. P. Jones artist, pair, 4 x 5" **175.00**

SILK PICTURES
See STEVENGRAPHS

SILVER

The natural beauty of silver lends itself to the designs of the artist and craftsman. It has been mined and worked into an endless variety of useful and decorative items. Pure silver is too soft to be fashioned into strong, durable and serviceable utensils. Therefore, a way was found to give silver the required degree of hardness by adding alloys of copper and nickel.

Silversmithing in America goes back to the early 17th century in Boston and New York. It began in the early 18th century in Philadelphia. Boston was influenced by the English styles; New York by the Dutch.

SILVER, COIN

Coin silver is slightly less pure than sterling silver. Coin silver has 900 parts silver to 100 parts alloy; sterling silver has 925 parts sil-

Tablespoon, Brenise, J., York County, Penn., 9¾" **$60.00**

ver. American silversmiths followed the coin standards. Coin silver also is called Pure Coin, Dollar, Standard, or Premium.

Beaker, A. E. Warner, slightly bulbous, tapered form, c. 1810, 3⅝" . **250.00**
Bowl, hemispherical, pedestal foot, early 19th C., 6" **475.00**
Cann, Joseph Downes, tapered barrel form, c. 1810, 3¾" **550.00**
Coffeepot, Thomas Fletcher, vase shape form, leaf tip rim, c. 1825, 11¼" **1100.00**
Christening Mug, baluster form, William Gale & Son, N.Y., c. 1850 .. **125.00**
Creamer, J. D., vase shape on square foot, c. 1785, 6⅜" **400.00**
Creamer and Sugar, covered, Wm. Haverstick, Phila. and Lancaster, Pa., c. 1820 .... **400.00**
Flatware
Demitasse Spoons
Coles, Albert, NYC, twisted handle, c. 1850 .... **20.00**
Kirk, Repousse, earliest mark . **55.00**
Dessert Spoons
Shoemaker, Phila., fiddleback, Wheat design, c. 1840 ...... **60.00**
Twedy and Barrows, fiddleback, basket of flowers, 1850 ...... **60.00**
Forks
Gordon, George, Augusta, dinner, fiddle thread **40.00**
Hood & Tobey, monogram, 1848 .... **25.00**
Kinsey, D., Cincinnati, serving, c. 1865 .... **125.00**
Lowe, Daniel, serving, engraved, 6¼" **35.00**
Knives
Bacon & Co., butter, grape pattern, c. 1850 .... **30.00**
Lewyn, Gabriel, Baltimore, pair, hollow handles, coin silver blade, c. 1795 .... **175.00**

Ladles
Buff, Thomas, Easton, Md., c. 1800, 14¾" 310.00
Coles, Albert, NYC, mustard, twisted stem 50.00
Duhme, Medallion, gold wash fluted and scalloped bowl, 16½" 375.00
Krider, Peter, honey, gold wash bowl, engraved handle, c. 1855 45.00

Marrow Spoon, Irish, bull's head crest, c. 1750, 7¾" 175.00

Serving Spoon, pie, N. Harding & Co., Boston, c. 1850 .... 62.50

Stuffing Spoon, English, oval bowl with double drop, c. 1750, 11½" . 175.00

Sugar Shells
Child, W. W., c. 1830 .... 55.00
Duhme & Co., c. 1860 ...... 50.00

Sugar Tongs, R. & W. Wilson, Phila., Shell, c. 1830 .... 125.00

Tablespoons
Curtis, Joel & Co., Cairo, N.Y., fiddle thread, engraved, c. 1840 30.00
Cutler, A., Boston, fiddleback, c. 1840 .... 40.00
Hastings, B. B., Cleveland, fiddleback, c. 1830 .... 55.00
Hill, E. H., Ky., pinched waist, fiddleback, c. 1840 .... 45.00
Hood & Tobey, monogram, 1848 .... 22.00
Kinsey, David, Cincinnati, fiddleback, c. 1840 .... 45.00
Moulton, J., Newberry, Mass., pointed handle, engraved, c. 1820, 8½" 45.00
Sargent, Jacob, Hartford, Conn., 1761 .... 40.00
Tucker, J. W., San Francisco, beaded oval and shell, c. 1860 . 90.00

Teaspoons
Coles, Albert, N.Y., set of 6, Jenny Lind style, c. 1860 ..... 125.00
Elliott, John Aaron, Sharon, fiddleback, c. 1810 .... 25.00
Faris, William, Annapolis, Md., c. 1760 .... 100.00
Lynch, L., Baltimore, fiddleback, c. 1820 .... 25.00
Tanguy, John, Phila., fiddleback with rounded edges, engraved, c. 1830 .... 35.00
Wilson, R. & W., Phila., set of 8, sheaf of wheat, c. 1830 ...... 450.00
Flatware Set, Lewis Kimball, J. N. Lindsay & Co., leaf and scroll pattern, monogram, 22 pieces (8 tablespoons, 4 dinner forks, 10 entre forks), c. 1860 .... 325.00

Lemon strainer, bowl pierced, flowerhead pattern, c. 1770, 4" dia. 250.00
Mugs
Boyce, G. C., c. 1835, 3½" 185.00
Lownes, Joseph, Phila., tapered cylindrical form, reeded horizontal bands, c. 1790, 4½" 1400.00
Napkin Ring, pair, unknown maker, boxed 300.00
Pitchers
Gardiner, Baldwin, urn form, pedestal foot, foliage motif, c. 1830, 12½" 650.00
Lewis, Harvey, bulbous body, eagle's head handle, c. 1820, 10½" 2000.00
Porringers
Burt, Samuel, Boston, c. 1740, 5¼" 650.00
Richardson, Jospeh, Sr., Phila., c. 1760, 8" 2000.00
Winslow, Edward, Boston, c. 1760, 7½" 800.00
Salvers
English, James Morrison, London, pie crust border and crest, 1756, 11¾" dia. 1450.00
Forbe, Wm., for Ball, Black and Co., N.Y., circular, engraved crest in center surrounded by engraved flowers, grape motif on rim, mid-19th C., 13" dia. 600.00
Sugar Bowl, covered, inverted pear shape, dome cover, c. 1775, 7¼" 2250.00
Tankard, covered, double scroll handle, tapered sides, engraved, late 18th C., 11" 2500.00
Tea Caddy, eagle on cover, ball and claw feet, c. 1820, 6¼" 950.00
Tea Sets
Cox, J. J., NYC, 3 pieces, c. 1840, 61 oz. 1800.00
Sayre, Joel, 4 pieces, paneled oval shape, c. 1800, 45 oz. 2750.00
Tray, English, Richard Sibley, London, gadrooned scalloped rim, fluted handles, arms and center crest, 28½" 3000.00

SILVER, PLATED

Plated silver production by an electrolytic method is credited to G. R. and H. Elkington, England, in 1838.

In electroplating silver, the article is completely shaped and formed from a base metal and then coated with a thin layer of silver. In the late 19th century, the base metal was Britannia, an alloy of tin, copper, and antimony. Other bases are copper and brass. Today the base is nickel silver.

In 1847 the electroplating process was introduced in America by Rogers Bros., Hartford, Conn. By 1855 a number of firms were using this method to mass produce silver plated items in large quantities.

The quality of the plating is important. Extensive use or polishing can cause the base metal to show through. The prices for plated silver items are low, making it a popular item with younger collectors.

Creamer (6029) and Sugar (6039), oval tray, 6¼ x 9¼", Inter. Silver Co., Camille $26.00

Ashtray, Barbour, square shape, match holder on top, ball feet, shell handle, embossed with human figures 16.00
Basket
  Barbour, stationary handle, embossed tavern scene, 6¼" 40.00
  Rodgers, Wm., bride's type cut glass insert 260.00
Beaker, maker unknown, ornate tavern scene 22.00
Bell, maker unknown, wooden handle, 7" 50.00
Bowls
  Maker unknown, plain, Paul Revere shape 30.00
  Meriden, Art Nouveau, ornate, monogram, 10" 45.00
Bread Tray, Rodgers, flair, 1847 . . . 35.00
Butter Dishes
  Meriden, dome type, pineapple finial, embossed ornate design, liner missing, resilvered 30.00
  Tufts, round dome type, ornate chasing on lid, liner, monogram . . 25.00
Cake Stand, Meriden, Art Nouveau design 100.00
Candelabra
  Maker unknown, pair detachable scones and branches, square base, raised and chased leaf and scroll design, c. 1860, 24" 420.00

Rodgers, Victorian Rose, pair . . . 125.00
Candle Snuffer, Meriden, embossed floral design 15.00
Cigarette Case, maker unknown, ornate design with Lady Godiva motif 45.00
Compote, maker unknown, Art Nouveau style, standing maiden holding bird plus flowers and bowl of compote, 8" 165.00
Cup and Saucer, Pairpoint, nautical engraving 75.00
Flatware
  Baby spoon, Community, Adam, long handled 6.00
  Berry Fork, DeSancy 12.00
  Berry Spoon, Deep Silver, Laurel Mist 16.00
  Butter Knives
    Benedict, Shell, twisted handle . 9.00
    Gorham, Lady Caroline 7.00
  Dinner Forks
    Community, Adams 5.00
    Holme and Edwart, Nassau . . . 5.00
  Tablespoons
    Oneida, Louis XVI 8.00
    Rogers and Co., Flemish 8.00
  Teaspoons
    American Silver Co., Rosalie . . 6.00
    Reed and Barton, Oxford 4.00
Flatware set, 46 pieces, 8 five piece place settings (dinner fork, dinner knife, teaspoon, salad fork, oval soup spoon), 6 servers (butter knife, sugar shell, gravy ladle, lemon fork, two serving forks), monogram 170.00
Goblet, Crescent Silver Co., Vintage, set of 6, 5½" 75.00
Gravy Boat, maker unknown, embossed ornate floral motif 35.00
Humidor, Derby Silver, 3 compartments, 1887 . . . . 95.00
Inkstand, maker unknown, double inkwells, 7" 85.00
Nut Bowl, maker unknown, squirrel figural 35.00
Pastry Server, Community, Patrician, master pastry fork type 20.00
Pitchers
  Barbour Bros., syrup size, tavern scene, reed wrapped handle 30.00
  Maker unknown, syrup size, beading on rim, cherub finial, ornate handle, 1865 . . . . 65.00
Punch Bowl, maker unknown, shell motif with 12 pedestal cups, pedestal base, tray and ladle, 3 gallon capacity, monogram 300.00
Shaving Mug, Hartford Silver Plate . 45.00
Sugar and Creamer set, Rogers, Wm., Eagle, footed 15.00

Tea Caddy, Barbour, embossed
house, ladies, and child **45.00**
Tea and Coffee Service, International, 6 pieces (coffeepot, teapot,
sugar bowl, creamer, waste bowl,
tray), plain motif, monogram **175.00**
Teapot, Wilcox, bright cut motif **35.00**
Trays
 Maker unknown, rectangular,
 plain, 17" **37.50**
 Maker unknown, round, ornate
 trim, 17" **35.00**
 Reed and Barton, Georgian styling, scrolls and flowers in relief,
 ribbing on inner rim **37.50**

SILVER, SHEFFIELD

**Sheffield Silver, or Old Sheffield Plate, was
made by a fusion method of silverplating
used from the mid-18th century until the
mid-1880's when the silver electroplating process was introduced.**

**Sheffield plate was discovered in 1743
when Thomas Boulsover of Sheffield, England, accidentally fused silver and copper.
The process consisted of sandwiching a
heavy sheet of copper between 2 thin sheets
of silver. The result was a plated sheet of silver which could be pressed and rolled to a
desired thickness. All Sheffield plate articles
were worked from these plated sheets.**

**Most of the silverplated items found today
marked "Sheffield" are not early Sheffield
plate. They are later wares made in Sheffield,
England.**

Argyle, cylindrical, ball finial, c. 1790,
4½" **375.00**
Basket, cake, boat shaped, swing
handle, c. 1800, 12¾" **120.00**
Candelabra, 3 lights, pair, reeded
borders, 17" **225.00**
Candlestick, chamber, Matthew Boulton Co., c. 1810, 4¼" dia. **270.00**
Candlesticks, table, pair, column
form, c. 1775, 12⅜" **300.00**
Candlesticks, pair, American, ribbed
tapering stem, c. 1800, 10" **200.00**
Candlesticks, set of four, American,
ribbed baluster stems, early 19th
C., 7½" **175.00**
Coasters, wine, set of 4, T. & J.
Creswick, decorated with grapevines, c. 1820, 6¾" **475.00**
Dish, cross, sliding support, crest, c.
1765, 11¼" **275.00**
Dish, entree, pair, rectangular,
rounded angles, c. 1810, 11½" . . **400.00**
Epergne, plated frame, central cut
glass bowl, c. 1830, 12" **550.00**

**Vase, 8½", opalescent fluted
top $95.00**

Inkstand, octagonal, blue glass liners, c. 1790, 11" **625.00**
Jug, hot water, octagonal urn shape,
reeded border, urn finial, c. 1795,
10" **200.00**
Kettle, Swinging, plain, ivory handle,
18" **350.00**
Salver, circular, gadroon, foliate rim,
c. 1875, 18⅛" **200.00**
Sugar Coaster, octagonal shaped,
8" **90.00**
Trays
 11", candle snuffer, American,
 wrought leaves, scrolling, 19th C. **50.00**
 16", c. 1850 . . . . **350.00**
 23", American, two handled, c.
 1820 . . . . **225.00**
 27¼", tea, two handled raised
 gallery, engraved, Hall & Co.,
 1880 . . . . **300.00**
Tankard, quart size, tapered cylinder, c. 1780, 9⅞" **300.00**
Tureen, sauce and cover, lobed and
bombe oval form, c. 1830, 8" . . . **275.00**
Tureen, soup and cover, leafy scroll
feet and handles, T. & J.
Creswick, 1825 . . . . **800.00**

Urn, hot water, American, reeded
body and handles, c. 1790, 14½"   600.00
Wine cooler, circular form, rim
scrolls, c. 1820, 9¼" 575.00
Wine coolers, pair, campana shape,
twig handles, c. 1810, 11" 1200.00

SILVER, STERLING

There are two possible sources for the origin
of the word sterling. The first is that it is a
corruption of the name Easterling.
Easterlings were German silversmiths who
came to England in the Middle Ages. The
second is that is named for the starling (little
star) used to mark much of the early English
silver.

Sterling silver has 925/1000 parts pure silver. Copper comprises most of the remaining
alloy. American manufacturers began to
switch to the sterling standard about the
time of the Civil War.

**Tea Set, 6 piece, Shreve & Co., San
Francisco, 317 oz. $4500.00**

Animal Figures
Cat, sitting, 2" 125.00
Horse, standing, 3½ x 4" 225.00
Ash Tray, Kirk, repousse, individual .   35.00
Basket, Cake, Gorham, oval, pierced
lattice work, grape and vine motif
on border, c. 1908 ....   525.00
Beakers
Smith, Frank W., flared cylinder
shape, engraved crest, set of 6,
5" 220.00
Steffins, E., & Co., plain, tapered
form, rounded sides, c. 1890, 3⅛"   200.00
Bell, Reed & Barton, Pointed An-
tique 40.00
Boot Hooks, Kirk, repousse, monogram 65.00
Bowl
Gorham, berry, applied fruit border, 10" 350.00
Unknown maker, Art Deco,
vertical engraved line, c. 1930,
6½" 145.00
Bread Tray, Gorham, pierced border,
monogram in center 250.00

Brushes
Gorham, floral pattern 35.00
Unknown maker, Art Nouveau,
lady with flowering hair, set of 3 .   145.00
Butter Dish
Gale & Willi, circular, dome cover,
c. 1858 ....   225.00
Kirk, underplate and pierced liner
of plain design, cow finial, mono-
gram 350.00
Button Hook, unknown maker, or-
nate design 30.00
Cake Stand, Black, Starr & Frost, 3
tiered, arch framework, c. 1924,
17⅞" 350.00
Candelabra, Gorham, pair, 3 light
type, upper section detachable,
weighted 275.00
Candlesticks, pair, Gorham, square
base, beaded trim, weighted, 6" .   50.00
Card Case, Leonard and Wilson,
U.S. Capitol, c. 1850 ....   125.00
Centerpieces
Gorham, oval shape, flowers and
sprays, c. 1910, 17⅛" 2000.00
Unknown maker, Art Nouveau, ap-
plied lily pads and flowers, stems
meet to form handle, c. 1900,
14½" 3000.00
Child's Set, 3 pieces, scenes are
verses of nursery rhymes, c. 1900   450.00
Cocktail Shaker, Gorham, girdled
body and cover, applied handle, c.
1925, 9" 200.00
Coffee and Tea Sets
Tiffany, 6 pieces, rectangular
shape, c. 1920, 143 oz. 5500.00
Unknown maker, 6 pieces, octag-
onal shape, Art Deco, 149 oz. ...   4500.00
Creamers
Gale & Willis, pear shape, molded
rim, c. 1859, 7¼" 150.00
Unknown maker, helmut shape, c.
1870, 6½" 100.00
Demitasse set, 3 pieces, chased de-
sign 800.00
Dresser Set
Tiffany, 8 pieces, plain design ...   850.00
Unger, Evangeline, 3 pieces 300.00
Flatware
Demitasse spoon, Tiffany, Renais-
sance 33.00
Desert Spoon, Kirk, Repousse ...   40.00
Dinner Fork, Towle, Georgian ...   43.00
Dinner Knife, International, Riche-
lieu, stainless blade 28.00
Salad Fork, Wallace, Normandy ..   32.00
Soup Spoon, Gorham, Willow ...   28.00
Flatware, Place Settings
Adam, G. A., Fiddle and Thread,
English, 5 pieces, c. 1800   1000.00

Gorham, Sovereign, 5 pieces ...	300.00
International, Prelude, 6 pieces ..	350.00
Flatware, Serving Pieces	
Asparagus Servers, Tiffany, Chrysanthemum	375.00
Asparagus Tongs, individual, Reed and Barton, 'Les Cinq Fleurs ...	85.00
Basting Spoon, G. A. Adams, English, c. 1800	450.00
Berry Spoon, Gorham, King George, 9"	95.00
Bouillon, Ladle, Lunt, Chatelaine .	125.00
Carving Set, Frank Smith, Chippendale	140.00
Cheese Scoops, Whiting, Dresden, enamel work on handle, 6⅛"	80.00
Coffee Spoons, Whiting, Empire	20.00
Cold Meat Fork, Reed & Barton, Francis I, c. 1907	140.00
Cracker Scoop, Tiffany, English King, pierced	300.00
Cream Ladle, Lunt, Monticello ..	42.50
Fish Fork, Oneida, Versailles	37.50
Grape Shear, Tiffany, Olympian ..	500.00
Gravy Ladle, International, Crystal	95.00
Ice Tongs, Whiting, Lily	125.00
Jelly Server, Durgin, Fairfax	25.00
Pastry Tongs, Tiffany, English King	175.00
Salad Set, Alvin, Raphael, 2 pieces, 9"	450.00
Glasses, cocktail, female figures Udall & Ballou, 1920	800.00
Gravy Boat, Georgian style	175.00
Hurricane Lamp, pair, 12"	95.00
Ice Bucket, chased design, 8"	325.00
Jardinieres, pair, Tiffany, rectangular, shaped sides, c. 1880, 9⅝"	1000.00
Letter Openers	
Art Nouveau, pierced handle	85.00
Sword shape, 11"	100.00
Mugs	
Bailey Co., tapered cylindrical form, c. 1850, 4¾"	325.00
International, plain design, monogram and date, child's size	50.00
Pitcher	
Black, Starr & Frost, spherical body, cylindrical top, 7½"	200.00
Tiffany, embossed with floral motif, cartouche with monogram, 10"	1250.00
Platter, Chester Billups & Son, oval, scroll work rim, c. 1905, 20"	475.00
Porringer, Reed & Barton, plain design, pierced handle	135.00
Salt and Pepper Shaker, Baltimore Sterling Silver Co., c. 1895	175.00
Salvers	
Gorham & Co., circular applied shell work, c. 1901, 12⅞"	260.00
Kirk, border repoussed, c. 1900, 14½"	450.00

Wallace, Rosepoint, 17"	500.00
Sugar Caster, S. Kirk, urn shape, Repousse, 6½"	130.00
Tea Infuser, Gorham, Cambridge ..	80.00
Tea Set, Unger Bros., Art Nouveau style, 3 pieces	725.00
Tray	
Footed, oval, shaped crest, armorial, c. 1850, 24"	1450.00
Gorham, oval, rim chased with daisies, roses and other flowers, c. 1896, 18½"	780.00
Vase, Gorgan Co., slender cylindrical design, c. 1920, 15¼"	375.00
Vegetable dishes, pair, oval form, foliate scrolled edges, c. 1890, 12" .	425.00
Waiter, S. Kirk & Son Co., circular form, scrollwork rim, 1910, 6" ...	125.00

SILVER DEPOSIT GLASS

Silver Deposit Glass, so-named because a thin coating of silver was actually deposited on glass by an electrical process, was popular at the turn of this century. The process was simple: glass and a piece of silver were placed in a solution; and an electric current was introduced which caused the silver to decompose, pass through the solution, and remain only on those parts of the glass on which a particular pattern had been outlined previously.

Bonbon, 7", crystal, footed, handled	50.00
Bottles, Perfume	
4", emerald	45.00
5½", crystal	35.00
Bowls	
5½ x 3" deep	45.00
9 x 2" high, crystal, flared turned over rim	85.00
Box, Puff, 4¼ x 3½" high, crystal .	50.00
Cream and Sugar, crystal, set	75.00
Cruet, 6¾", fluted stopper, crystal .	60.00
Decanter, 9", emerald	100.00
Mustard Jar, 4¾", crystal	48.00
Pitcher, 8", cobalt	65.00
Plates	
7", crystal	35.00
7½ x 10", handled, footed	50.00
12", crystal, floral decor	75.00
Sherbets, with underplates, crystal, set of 6	250.00
Toothpick Holder, 2½", crystal ...	35.00
Tumblers, 4⅝", crystal, flared tops, 6	75.00
Vases	
4¼", emerald	35.00
5½", flared top, crystal	40.00
6", cobalt	50.00
8", bud, crystal	45.00

SILVER LUSTRE

This metal-surfaced earthenware was made in large quantities in the Staffordshire district of England between 1805 and 1840. In this process the item was first covered completely with a thin coating of a "steel lustre" mixture containing a small quantity of platinum oxide; then an additional coating of platinum, worked in water, was laid on before the item was fired.

With the introduction of electroplating in 1840, there was a sharp decline in the demand for such metal-surfaced earthenwares.

Pitcher, 3⅝"	**$50.00**
Bowl, festoon and shell decor	80.00
Coffeepot, 10¼"	300.00
Creamers	
4½", Fine Rib design	65.00
Dolphin handle	80.00
Goblet	75.00
Sugar, covered, Ribbed Design	75.00
Teapot, Ribbed, Queen Anne style .	100.00
Tea Set, Ribbed, Queen Anne style,	
teapot, covered, creamer, covered	
sugar, waste bowl, 4 pieces	375.00
Toby Jug, 6"	250.00

SILVER OVERLAY

Silver overlay is applied directly to a finished glass or porcelain object. The pieces is cut and decorated, usually by engraving, prior to being molded around the object.

The glass usually is of high quality, either crystal or colored. Lenox employed silver overlay on some of their decorative wares. Most of the design are indicative of the Art Nouveau and Art Deco periods.

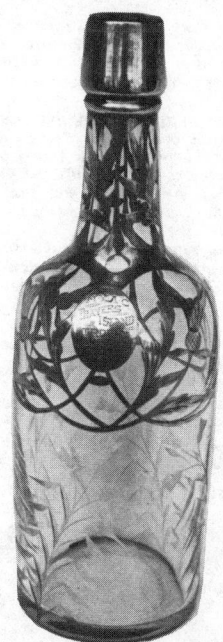

Trophy Whiskey Decanter, sterling overlay, New York Athletic Club Travers Island, 1/24/14, 10½", no stopper	**$90.00**
Bottles, Pinch	
10½", amber	150.00
10½", amethyst	175.00
Bowls	
10", crystal, Clematis motif, turned	
down, ruffled top	90.00
10", shallow, emerald, tapered	
sides	400.00
Chalice, cranberry, vine and blooming flowers, 8"	235.00
Decanter, crystal, Wheat, stopper, monogram, 8½"	250.00
Nut Dish, white porcelain, oval, footed	45.00
Teapot, dark brown porcelain, 8" ..	200.00
Vases	
4½", crystal, gourd shape, iridescent	150.00
8", emerald, floral	200.00
10", cranberry, floral	260.00
12½", cobalt, vines and flowers .	450.00

Bottles, Perfume stoppered
2⅛", crystal, rose motif	37.50
3¼", emerald	75.00
4¾", cranberry	85.00

SILVER RESIST

Silver Resist ware was first produced about 1805. It is similar to Silver Lustre in respect to the silvering process. It differs from Silver Lustre in that a pattern appears on the surface.

The outline of the pattern was drawn or stenciled on the body of the ware. A glue or sugar-glycerin adhesive was brushed over the part which was not to be lustred. The lustering solution was applied and allowed to dry. The glue or adhesive was then washed off.

The glue or adhesive had caused the pattern to "resist" the lustering solution. When fired in the kiln, the lustre glaze covered the entire surface except for the pattern.

Pitcher, doghandle, Wedgwood, made in Eng., 4KL/C5224, c. 1942 . . . $45.00

Creamer, floral motif	175.00
Cup and Saucers	
Berry and Leaf	90.00
Greek Key, handled, 2½"	75.00
Jugs or Pitchers	
4½", floral and leaf motif, tan ground	200.00
5", floral and leaf motif, bulbous shape, applied handle, c. 1815 . .	260.00
5½", Commodore Decatur and Major General Brown transfers, floral motif under spout	850.00
6¼", floral medallions, flutes and flowering vine motif	300.00
Mug, floral vine motif, green ground, 5"	120.00
Plate, soup, Greek Key motif, sunburst center	135.00
Tea set, miniature, 6 cups and saucers, covered sugar, and creamer	120.00
Teapot, vine and floral motif, 5½" .	300.00
Toothpick holder	30.00

SINCLAIRE GLASS

H. P. Sinclaire and Company was founded in 1904. It was the twelfth glass works to locate in the "Crystal City," Corning, N.Y. In 1920, H. P. Sinclaire began his own glass blowing factory in Bath, N.Y. Prior to this, Sinclaire's cut and engraved designs were done on other glassmaker's blanks.

Sinclaire produced some of the most beautiful glass of the "Brilliant Period." Many of his designs were based on nature—fruits, flowers, and foliage—and he approached them from an architectural viewpoint.

Only a small amount of Sinclaire glass is marked.

Candlestick, cut decor, blue, 7", signed $130.00

Bowls	
9¾", hexagon, engraved panels, signed	325.00
13", canary, etched florals	185.00
Box, 3½" square, grapes and bands	280.00
Candlesticks	
10", twisted blown stems, topaz, pair	150.00
10", amber	100.00
10¾", hollow stem, topaz, pair . .	250.00
Cologne Bottle, 6", floral etch, signed	140.00
Compote, floral etch, small	50.00
Console Set, amethyst compote and candlesticks, signed	300.00
Cruet, 8½", crystal, engraved and cut	175.00

Goblet, grapes	50.00
Plate, 8½", green, signed	40.00
Sugar Bowl and Creamer, Queen Louise, signed	240.00
Tray, 11¾ x 10", amber, etched, center handle	60.00

Tumblers

Copperwheel engraved	50.00
Etched	35.00

Vases

6½", Holly	150.00
8", bud vase, engraved	80.00
13½", Tulips, crystal, etched, signed	250.00

SMITH BROS. GLASS

After establishing a decorating department at the Mt. Washington Glass Works in 1871, Alfred and Harry Smith in 1875 moved to their own location in New Bedford, Mass., to operate a firm that soon became known worldwide for fine opal decorated wares similar to the Mt. Washington products. Their glass often carried a red shield enclosing a rampant lion and the word "Trademark" on the base.

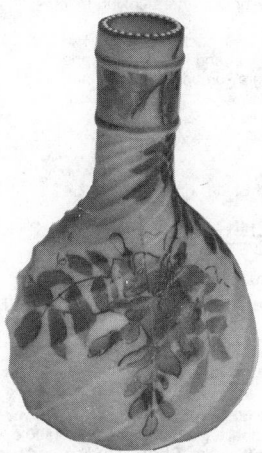

Vase, Swirl with floral and leaf decor **$575.00**

Biscuit Jars

8", melon ribbed, cream satin with heavy gold florals and foliage	395.00
8", shaded pink with dainty blue florals and foliage, silver plated mountings	225.00
Bowl, 10", melon ribbed, beige satin with white shasta daisies and foliage, silver plated top rim	350.00
Box, 4" dia., covered, melon section, beige satin with blue florals, signed	325.00
Mustard Pot, 3½", melon ribbed, white satin with pink florals	85.00
Rose Bowl, 5¼", melon section, cream satin with purple morning glories, beaded top rim, signed	245.00
Shakers, 2½" squatty, melon sectioned, cream with pink florals, original metal tops, pair	145.00
Sugar Castor, ribbed, white satin, heavy gold florals, metal top	195.00
Toothpick, melon ribbed, pastel florals, beaded top rim	75.00

Vases

4½", cream satin with carnations, beaded enamel dot trim around top, signed	325.00
6", melon ribbed, beige satin with white daisies, signed	250.00

SNOW BABIES

Snow Babies are small bisque figurines, originally made in Germany, that came onto the market in the early 1900's. There are several theories on their origin. One is that German doll makers copied the designs from their traditional Christmas candies. Another theory, the most accepted, is that they were made to honor Admiral Peary's daughter who was born in Greenland in 1893 and was called the "Snow Baby" by the Eskimos.
CAUTION: Reproductions abound.

2⅞" high, red, blue and maroon **$150.00**

Babies

Hiking, 4½"	65.00
Hugging, two, 3"	65.00
Lying on tummy, 3½" long	95.00

Playing accordion, 2¾"	50.00
Playing drums, 2¾"	50.00
Playing musical instruments, seven babies, 2"	300.00
Playing trumpet, 2¾"	50.00
Pulling sled, 2"	60.00
Santa's helpers, red hats and coats, 2½"	65.00
Seated	
1"	35.00
2"	65.00
3¼"	125.00
Skater, 1½"	55.00
Skier, 1½"	55.00
Sledding	
1½"	45.00
1½ x 3", baby turns on wooden peg	175.00
2"	50.00
2¾", pulled by huskies	75.00
3"	65.00
Bear, 2¼"	50.00
Elf, 1½"	45.00
Kitten, 1½"	35.00
Matchholder, 3½"	125.00
Snow Man	45.00
Sheep, 2"	40.00

SOAPSTONE

The mineral steatite, used in producing all sorts of soapstone wares, has a greasy feel, and has been utilized, among other things, for carved figurine groups by the Chinese and others. These were very popular during the Victorian era. It has also been fashioned into utilitarian pieces.

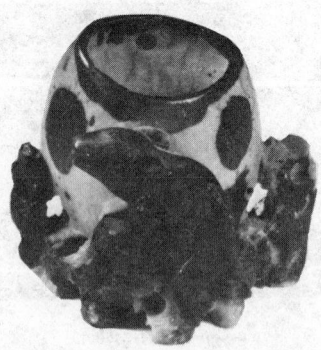

Vase, tan and brown, carved rodent, 2½" $65.00

Basket, 8 x 9", grotesque monkeys, bats and flowers, grey and cream	45.00
Bookends, 4 x 5", carved oriental mountain and house, black rust, green gray	35.00
Candleholder, 8½", Foo dog	50.00
Centerpiece, covered urn, flanked with vase each side, carved birds flowers, and open work, five colors	185.00
Figurines	
Elephant, 4½", on engraved base	40.00
Fisherman, 14", shaded grey . . .	100.00
Horses, two, in motion, 8"	45.00
Man, with beard, green on chocolate brown base	75.00
Storks, three, 3½ x 5"	85.00
Woman, Chinese, seated on mound, 5 x 4"	35.00
Flower holder, 10 x 5", monkey and birds, open work	60.00
Incense burner, Foo dog finial, black	70.00
Jardiniere, 8 x 6", three carved birds, and foliage, grey-green to brown	65.00
Planter, double, berry and leaf carving	55.00
Toothpick holder, three carved monkeys	30.00
Urn-form wall pockets, 7¾ x 4¼", carved leaf and fruit designs, open work, grey-green with rose striations, pair	65.00
Vases	
Adjoining type, 4½ x 2½", China, c. 1890	35.00
Carved leaf and open work, marked China	35.00

SOUVENIR-TYPE GLASS
See RUBY STAINED GLASS

SOUVENIR SPOONS
See COMMEMORATIVE AND SOUVENIR SPOONS

SPANGLED GLASS

Spangled glass is a blown or blown molded variegated art glass of the late 1800's very much like Spatter Glass with the addition of flakes of mica or metallic looking green aventurine. It can be cased with a white or clear layer of glass.

There has been much confusion about Spangled Glass, as it had been previously attributed only to the Vasa Murrhina Art Glass Company of Hartfort, Connecticut, which advertised Factory Cape Cod Works, Sandwich, Mass. However, the production of Spangled Glass included many companies in the United

States, England, and Europe and it is impossible to attribute any specific piece to any source.

Spangled Glass has continued to be made by many companies and is being made at present.

Fairy Lamp, multi-color, gold mica, 6⅜" $190.00

Baskets
4¾ x 6½", melon ribbed, maroon and pink, mica flakes, cased 165.00
8½ x 10 x 8½" high, exterior white, interior gold with gold mica flakes, crimped rim, fishscale handle 350.00
cranberry, silver mica, applied clear rope twist handle 145.00
Yellow, gold mica flakes, crimped edge, applied thorn handle 125.00
Bowls
4⅞ x 6⅞", lavender and pink, mica flakes, cased, 3 crystal feet . 245.00
Pink and cranberry, silver mica flakes, applied thorn feet 165.00
Candlesticks, 9¼", pink and white, green aventurine flakes, embossed swirls, pair 110.00
Condiment Set, 3 pieces, cranberry, green flakes, silver plate holder . . 195.00
Ewer, 7½", blue, mica flakes, applied thorn handle 115.00
Pitchers
8¾", cranberry with silver mica flakes, applied reeded handle . . . 155.00

10", ruby and peach, gold flakes, cased, applied amber thorn handle 185.00
Rose Bowls
3¾", blue and clear, crimped top, mica flakes 120.00
4", egg shape, yellow, gold flakes 100.00
5", cream and yellow, silver mica . 120.00
Salt and Pepper, 4", pink, silver mica, cased, pair 275.00
Syrup, 6", green, pink and white, silver mica flakes, pewter lid, applied clear handle 150.00
Toothpick, 2", blue, gold flakes 65.00
Tumblers
3¾", 4 colors, cased 135.00
green, silver mica flakes 35.00
red and white, gold flakes 50.00
Vases
5", green, silver mica 50.00
6", pink, silver mica 110.00
8", yellow, swirl, cased 110.00
8¼", mica flakes in striped pattern, clear handles 75.00
8¾", pink, silver mica, ruffled top 100.00
9½", white lining, gold mica overlay 90.00
9½", apricot, gold flakes 95.00

SPANISH LACE GLASS
See OPALESCENT GLASS

SPATTER GLASS

Spatter Glass is a variegated blown or blown molded art glass produced at the end of the 19th century by many of the glass factories both in the United States and abroad. The collection of various colored pieces of glass onto the glass blower's gather produced the combinations of colors seen in the glass. It can be cased either in white or clear glass.

Spatter Glass has been known previously as "End-of-Day Glass" as it was felt the pieces were made with leftover bits of glass at the end of the day. However, it is now known that this glass was a specific line of glass in production. It is still being produced.

Baskets
5¾", pink and yellow, crimped top, applied thorn handle 85.00
7¼ x 5½", tri-corn, rose, pink, yellow, gold, applied twisted thorn handle 210.00
13", brown and gold, cased, applied clear thorn handle and clear feet 295.00
Bowl, 3 x 7", multicolored, cased . . 85.00

Miniature Lamp, green, brown, clear swirl, 8½" $275.00

Condiment Set, open salt, pepper, mustard pot, maroon, white, blue, silver plate holder 165.00

Cookie Jar, white, brown and red, applied clear finial on lid 150.00

Cream and Sugar, maroon, white and green, creamer applied clear handle, sugar applied clear feet and ruffle 110.00

Cruet, blue and white, applied blue handle and stopper 75.00

Pitchers
Green and white, tri-corn, reed handle 85.00
7½" x 5⅞", multicolored, cased, dimpled sides 195.00
10", amber, gold and white 130.00

Rolling Pins
Shades of blue 50.00
Dark amber variegated 125.00

Sugar Castor, pink and white, metal top 50.00

Toothpick, yellow and white 45.00

Tumbler, red and white 35.00

Vases
6⅛", melon ribbed, pink, maroon and green, crystal handles 50.00
7", fan shape, blue, white and maroon 95.00
7", bowl shape 60.00
8", swirl and ribbed, white interior, clear applied fluted handle, ruffled top 195.00
10", red, green, blue and brown . 95.00

SPATTERWARE

The earliest examples of English Spatterware were made about 1780. Spatterware is made of common earthenware, although occasionally creamware was used. The peak period of production was 1810–1840. Marked pieces are rare. Firms known to have made Spatterware are Adams, Barlow, and Harvey and Cotton.

Collectors today focus on the patterns— Cannon, Castle, Fort, Peafowl Rainbow, Rose, Thistle, Schoolhouse, etc. On flat ware the decoration is in the center. On hollow pieces it occurs on both sides.

Color is a key to price. Blue and red are most common. Green, purple, and brown are in a middle group. Black and yellow are scarce.

The amount of spatter decoration varies from piece to piece. Some objects simply have decorated borders. These are often decorated with a brush, requiring several hundred touches per square inch to achieve the spatter effect. Other pieces have the entire surface covered with spatter. Aesthetics of the final product is another key to value.

Like any soft paste, Spatterware was easily broken or chipped. Prices are for pieces in very good to mint condition.

Bowls
Vegetable, blue, 6⅝" long 135.00
Waste, Thistle, yellow, 6⅝" dia. . . 1500.00

Creamers
Peafowl
Blue 375.00
Green 400.00
Rainbow, blue and red 130.00
Thistle, yellow 1000.00

Cups and Saucers
Blue 75.00
Castle, purple 175.00
Fort, blue 275.00
Peafowl
Blue 275.00
Green 275.00
Pink 280.00
Peafowl on bar, green 600.00
Rainbow, red and green 165.00
Rose
Purple 165.00
Rainbow, red and green 190.00
Thistle
Purple 225.00
Rainbow, red and yellow 350.00
Yellow 475.00
Tree, blue, miniature 210.00
Tulip, yellow 800.00
Schoolhouse, three color, green . 500.00
Shield, red 475.00

Miscellaneous Forms

Dish, shell shaped, Peafowl, blue, marked Adams, 9″	550.00
Mug, Peafowl, blue, 2½″	475.00
Mustard Pot	
Blue, 2⅞″	400.00
Peafowl, green, 2¾″	750.00
Salt Cellar	
Blue, 3″	200.00
Rainbow, red and green, 3″	300.00
Pitchers	
Peafowl, blue border, 6⅝″	750.00
Thistle, yellow, 8½″	3250.00

Plate, Peafowl, blue sponging, bird, light blue, yellow belly, red tail, 8¼″ $215.00

Plates

Acorn, purple, 6¼″	250.00
Castle, green, 8⅜″	240.00
Fort, blue, 5⅛″	150.00
Peafowl	
Blue, 9¼″	325.00
Green, 8¼″	350.00
Red, 9½″	350.00
Yellow, 9½″	3000.00
Pineapple, blue, 8″	700.00
Rainbow	
Blue and red, 5⅛″	150.00
Red, blue, and green concentric circles, white center, 10¼″	160.00
Thistle, yellow, 8⅝″	625.00
Tulip	
Purple, 6¼″	250.00
Yellow, 8½″	375.00
Schoolhouse	
Three color, green, 7½″	600.00
Five color, blue, 8⅜″	1000.00
Star, blue, 8½″	220.00
Platters	
Peafowl	
Blue, 15⅝″	2250.00
Red, 15⅝″	2000.00
Red, 15¾″	500.00

Rainbow, red and blue, cross design	475.00
Thistle, yellow, 15¾″	2500.00
Sugar Bowls	
Blue	110.00
Fort, blue, miniature	260.00
Peafowl, blue	450.00
Rainbow, red and purple	200.00
Schoolhouse, green, chip on foot	1100.00
Teapots	
Fort, blue, 4½″	280.00
Peafowl, green	900.00

SPONGEWARE

Spongeware indicates a specific type of decoration, not a type of pottery or glaze. The decoration was not applied with a sponge as is commonly believed.

Spongeware decoration is found on many types of pottery bodies—ironstone, redware, stoneware, etc. It was made in both England and the United States. Marked pieces indicate a starting date of 1815, with manufacturing extending to the 1860's.

Decoration is varied. In some pieces, the sponging is minimal with the white underglaze dominant. Other pieces appear to be sponged solidly on both sides. Pieces from 1840–1860 have sponging which appears in either a circular movement or a streaked horizontal technique.

Examples are found in blue and white, the most common color. Other prevalent colors are browns, greens, ochres, and greenish-blue. The greenish-blue results from blue sponging which has been overglazed in a pale yellow. A red overglaze produced a black or navy color.

Other colors are blue and red (found on English creamware and American earthenware of the 1880's), gray, grayish green, red, dark green on stark white, dark green on mellow yellow, and purple.

Spongeware should not be confused with Spatterware or Design Spatterware, both of which are listed separately.

Baking Dishes

7″, round, greenish blue, red outerglaze, redware	145.00
7½″, oval, greenish blue, red outerglaze	120.00
Banks	
Pig, blue and brown, cream ground, 6″	150.00
Pig, green, stoneware	175.00
Tudor, red and blue, c. 1800, 6 x 6¾″	400.00
Bowls	
5½″, blue and white	80.00
8″, blue and white	90.00

Pitcher, cobalt and tan sponge, 8″ $160.00

Bowls, Mixing
Large, blue and white, 10″ 140.00
Large, relief exterior 225.00
Medium, blue and white 125.00
Small, blue and white 110.00

Bean Pots
Green, brown, ochre 150.00
4 quart, blue and white 225.00

Butter Crock
Large, blue and white, no lid 165.00
Small, blue and white 200.00

Chamber Pot, blue and white 125.00

Compote, shallow, blue and white, 8½″ 300.00

Creamer, blue and brown, cream ground, 6″ 80.00

Crocks
7½″, blue and white, wire bail .. 100.00
8½″, grayish green, straight sides, wire bail 185.00
10½″, covered, blue and white, wire bail 200.00

Cups and Saucers
Curved Side, blue and white 100.00
Straight Side, blue and white ... 110.00

Custard Cup, blue and white, 4″ ... 105.00

Gypsy Kettle, lid, blue and white .. 85.00

Honey Jar, covered, handles, blue and white, scarce 125.00

Inkwells
Blue and white, scarce 225.00
Green 175.00

Jugs
3″, green, ochre, brown 130.00
4″, bluish green 60.00
5¼″, baluster, blue and white ... 170.00
5½″, baluster, purple, creamware 250.00
8½″, deer in relief on two sides, blue and white 185.00

9″, baluster, blue and white 125.00
9″, barrel shape, grayish green .. 135.00
9″, tankard, blue and white 135.00

Match Holder, blue and white, 2⅜″ 185.00

Mugs
1¾″, red 125.00
3½″, vase shape, blue and white with green stick dots 105.00

Mustard Pot, covered, blue and white 150.00

Nappy, rectangular, blue and white, sponged interior only, 8½″ 165.00

Pitchers
6″, bulbous body, extended neck, blue and white 195.00
6¾″, slightly tapered sides, rect-angular handle, blue and white .. 140.00

Plates
6¾″, blue cobalt, scalloped rim, Ott and Brewer type 85.00
10¼″, blue and white, scalloped rim 110.00
10½″, blue and white, sponged interior only, no interior rim 130.00
10½″, blue and white, sponged both sides, interior rim, plain edge 115.00

Plates, Soup
Red and green, early 300.00
9¼″, blue and white 100.00
10″, blue and white, marked 140.00

Platters
6½″, rectangular, blue and white . 120.00
11¼″, oval, blue and white, scal-loped rim 135.00
13¼″, oval, blue and white, wide rim 90.00
13½″, oval, blue and white 130.00
15½″, rectangular, chamfered corners, blue and white, star cen-ter, ironstone mark 160.00

Pots
Coffee, blue and white, unmarked 275.00
Tea, blue and white, bulbous body, flat lid, curved handle, 7¼″ 360.00
Tea, blue and white, spatter paneled, high dome, rectangular handle, 9″ 335.00

Razor Box, blue and white, lid, 7½″ 175.00

Salt Crock, blue and white, hanging type 200.00

Spittoon, blue and white, blue bands 75.00

Soap Dish, red and blue 125.00

Sugars
Blue and green 220.00
Blue and red 170.00
Blue and white, covered, minia-ture, 3¼″ 110.00

Umbrella Stand, blue and white, blue bands, 21¼″ 450.00

Wash Bowl and Pitcher, blue and white, blue strips 475.00

SPOONS
See COMMEMORATIVE AND SOUVENIR SPOONS

STAFFORDSHIRE, HISTORICAL

The Staffordshire district of England had an abundance of fine clay for pottery making. There were 80 different potteries operating there in 1786, with the number increasing to 149 by 1802. The district included Burslem, Cobridge, Eturia, Fenton, Foley, Hanley, Lane Delph, Lane End, Longport, Shelton, Stoke and Tunstall. Among the many famous potters were Adams, Davenport, Spode, Stevenson, Wedgewood, and Wood.

In historical Staffordshire the view is the most critical element. Because of the variety, collection can be organized around a single theme, e.g., maker, Pennsylvania or transportation. Most collectors focus on the dark blue, but lighter views do seem to be gaining in popularity.

Prices are for proof examples. Adjust prices by 20% for an unseen chip, a faint hairline, or an unseen professional repair; by 35% for knife marks through the glaze and a visible professional repair; by 50% for worn glaze and major repairs.

W. ADAMS & SONS   ADAMS

ADAMS

The Adams family has been associated with ceramics from the mid-17th century. In 1802 William Adams of Stoke-upon-Trent produced American views.

In 1819 a fourth William Adams, son of William of Stoke, became a partner with his father and was later joined by his three brothers. The firm became William Adams & Sons. The father died in 1829 and William, the eldest son, became manager.

The company operated four potteries at Stoke and one at Tunstall. American views were produced at Tunstall in black, light blue, sepia, pink, and green in the 1830–40 period. William Adams died in 1865. All operations were moved to Tunstall. The firm continues today under the name of Wm. Adams & Sons, Ltd.

Hudson River Series

Fort Edwards, Hudson River, pink, 5¼" plate	85.00
View Near Sandy Hill, Hudson River, pink, 4" cup plate	75.00

Adams, U.S. Views Series, Headwaters of the Juniata, U.S., plate, pink, 10½" $130.00

Log Cabin, medallions of Gen. Harrison on border

Teapot, pink	275.00
Waste Bowl, brown	240.00

Seal of United States, dark blue, pitcher, 7½" 850.00

U. S. Views

Lake George, U.S., brown, vegetable dish	125.00
Shannondale Springs, Virginia, U.S., pink, 8" plate	75.00

CLEWS

From sketchy historical accounts that are available, James Clews took over the closed plant of A. Stevenson in 1819. His brother Ralph entered the business later. The firm continued until about 1836 when James Clews came to America to enter the pottery business at Troy, Ind. The venture was a failure because of the lack of skilled workmen and the proper type of clay. He returned to England but did not re-enter the pottery business.

Cities Series, dark and medium blue

Albany, 10" plate	325.00
Baltimore, vegetable dish	1700.00

Clews, States, building, fishermen with nets, plate 10½″ $225.00

Chillicothe, 10½″ platter	1300.00
Philadelphia, 5½″ plate	400.00
Quebec, 9″ plate	175.00
Washington, 7¾″ plate	250.00

Doctor Syntax, dark blue

Doctor Syntax setting out on his first tour, 12″ covered dish	425.00
*Doctor Syntax Disputing his bill with landlady, 10″ plate	165.00
*Doctor Syntax mistakes a Gentleman's house for an inn, 10″ soup	135.00
Doctor Syntax with the dairy maid, 3⅞″ cup plate	400.00
Doctor Syntax and the gypsies, soup tureen	800.00
Doctor Syntax turned nurse, 7¾″ plate	140.00
Doctor Syntax, advertisement for a wife, 16″ platter	475.00

Don Quixote Series, dark blue

Don Quixote's Library, vegetable dish	280.00
Don Quixote, repose in woods, 6″ plate	150.00
Sancho Panza and the priest and barber, 7½″ plate	165.00
Sancho Panza's debate with Teresa, 9″ plate	150.00

Landing of Lafayette at Castle Garden, dark blue

Cup Plate, 3½″, oval medallion ..	350.00
Pitcher, 5½″	750.00
Pitcher, 8″	875.00
Plate, 7½″	225.00
Plate, 10″	250.00
Platter, 15″	700.00
Platter, 21¼″, well and tree	950.00

Teapot	825.00
Soup, 9″	200.00
Vegetable Dish, 10″, square	725.00

Picturesque Views Series

Bakers Falls, Hudson River, pink, 9″ plate	90.00
Fort Edward, Hudson River, light blue, 4⅛″ cup plate	100.00
Hudson, Hudson River, black, gravy tureen	300.00
Hudson, Hudson River, brown, 10½″ soup	85.00
Near Hudson, Hudson River, brown, 7″ plate	75.00
Penitentiary in Allegheny, near Pittsburgh, Pa., pink, 15½″ tray ..	280.00
Troy From Mount Ida, light blue, 6″ pitcher	225.00

Pittsfield Elm, dark blue

Plate, 8″	170.00
Platter, 15″	650.00
Soup, 10½″	200.00

Peace and Plenty, dark blue

Cup Plate, 4½″	525.00
Plate, 10″	240.00
Platter, 17″	650.00

States or America and Independence Series, dark blue

Building, Deer on Lawn, 10½″ plate	225.00
Building, Sheep on Lawn, 9″ plate	220.00
Dock, large building and ships, 19½″ platter	2750.00
Mansion, circular drive, vegetable dish	625.00
Mansion, small boat with flag in foreground, 13½″ bowl	850.00

J.&J. JACKSON

J. & J. JACKSON

Job and John Jackson began operations at the Churchyard Works, Burslem, about 1830. The works formerly were owned by the Wedgwood family. The firm produced transfer scenes in a variety of colors, such as black, light blue, pink, sepia, green, maroon, and mulberry. Over 40 different American views of Conn., Mass., Pa., N.Y., and Ohio were issued. The firm is believed to have closed about 1844.

American Scenery Series, all colors

Albany, N.Y., 20″ platter	300.00
At Richmond, Va., 7″ plate	125.00
Bunker Hill Monument, 6½″ plate	250.00
Deaf & Dumb Asylum, Phila., 7″ plate	160.00
Fort Ticonderoga, N.Y., gravy tureen with cover	225.00

Jackson, American Scenery series, Upper Ferry Bridge over the River Schuylkill, platter, brown, 10″ .$275.00

Hartford, Conn., 10″ soup	130.00
Iron Works at Saugerties, 12″ platter	270.00
State House, Boston, 10½″ plate	80.00
Water Works, Phila., 9″ plate	75.00
View of the Canal, Little Falls, Mohawk River, 10½ ″ plate	130.00
Yale College, deep dish	210.00

Miscellaneous

New York, select sketches series, 17″ platter	900.00
Schenectady on Mohawk River, 8″ pitcher	300.00

THOMAS MAYER

In 1829, Thomas Meyer and his brothers, John and Joshua, purchased Stubbs' Dale Hall Works of Burselm. They continued to produce a superior grade of ceramics.

Arms of the American States, dark blue

CT, gravy tureen	2500.00
DE, 17″ platter	3000.00
GA, 11¾″ vegetable dish	2250.00
MA, 9½″ platter	2500.00
PA, 21″ platter	8500.00
Lafayette at Franklin's Tomb, dark blue, sugar bowl	575.00
Lafayette at Washington's Tomb, dark blue, sugar bowl	550.00
Lafayette at Washington's Tomb, dark blue, waste bowl	450.00

Mayer, Arms of the American States series, New York, plate, 10″ .$1250.00

CHARLES MEIGH

Job Meigh began the Meigh pottery in the Old Hall Pottery, Hanley, in 1780. Later his sons and grandsons entered the business. The firm's name is recorded as Job Meigh & Sons, 1823; J. Meigh & Sons, 1829; Charles Meigh, 1843.

The American Cities and Scenery series was produced by Charles Meigh between 1840 and 1850. The colors are light blue, brown, gray, and purple. Sometimes the colors appear in combination.

Albany, 7½″ Pitcher	225.00
Baltimore, washbowl	175.00
Capitol at Washington, tureen, round, cover	250.00
City Hall, NY, 10¼″ plate	62.50
Hudson City, 10¼″ soup	55.00
Utica, cup plate	150.00
Village of Little Falls, 8¼ ″ plate	65.00
Yale College, New Haven, 9½″ plate	77.50

MELLOR, VENABLES & CO.

Little information is recorded on Mellor, Venables & Co. except that they were listed as potters in Burselm in 1843. Their Scenic Views series with the Arms of the States Border does include the arms for New Hampshire. This state is missing from the Mayer series. However, the view was known in England and collectors search for a Mayer example.

Arms of States, white body, light color transfers

MD, teapot	475.00
PA, sugar bowl	325.00

Scenic Views, Arms of States Border, light blue, pink, brown, purple

Albany, 15″ platter	300.00
The President's House from the River, 14″ pitcher	300.00
Tomb of Washington, Mt. Vernon, 7½″ plate	100.00
View of Capitol at Washington, 11″, vegetable dish	275.00

W. RIDGWAY J.W.R.
Stone China

J. & W. RIDGWAY AND WILLIAM RIDGWAY & CO.

John and William Ridgway, sons of Job Ridgway and nephews of George Ridgway who owned Bell Bank Works and Cauldon Place Works, produced the popular Beauties of America series at the Cauldon plant. The partnership between the two brothers was dissolved in 1830. John remained at Cauldon.

William managed the Bell Bank works until 1854. Two additional series were produced based upon the etchings of Bartlett's *American Scenery*. The first series had various borders including narrow lace. The second series is known as Catskill Moss.

Beauties of America is in dark blue. The other series are found in the light transfer colors of light blue, pink, brown, black and green.

Ridgway, American Scenery series, Harper's Ferry from the Potomac Side, plate, light blue, 9¼″ $70.00

American Scenery

Albany, washbowl	230.00
Columbia Bridge on the Susquehanna, pitcher	275.00
Columbia Bridge on the Susquehanna, soup tureen	550.00
Peekskill Landing, Hudson River, teapot	250.00
Peekskill Landing, Hudson River, vegetable dish	160.00
Valley of the Shenandoah from Jefferson's Rock, 7″ plate	80.00
Wilkes-Barre, Vale of Wyoming, coffee pot	240.00

Beauties of America, dark blue

Almshouse, Boston, soup tureen	1400.00
Almshouse, New York, 16″ platter	700.00
Bank, Savannah, gravy tureen	800.00
City Hall, New York, 10″ plate	160.00
Exchange, Baltimore, cup plate	400.00
Exchange, Charleston, vegetable dish	300.00
Library, Phila., 8″ plate	175.00
Octagon Church, Boston, 10″ soup	185.00

Catskill Moss

Anthony's Nose, 6″ plate	135.00
Caldwell, Lake George, 5″ sauce dish	50.00
Kosciusko's Tomb, 10″ plate	85.00
Kosciusko's Tomb, 10″ soup	77.50
Meredith, 9½″ plate	85.00
President's House, tray	150.00
Valley of Wyoming, cup	35.00

Columbia Star, Harrison's Log Cabin

End View, plate	100.00
End View, soup	110.00
Side View, cup with handles	55.00
Side View, sugar bowl	230.00
Side View, plowing, 10¼″ plate	95.00

ROGERS ROGERS

John Rogers and his brother George established a pottery near Longport in 1782. After George's death in 1815, John's son Spencer became a partner and the firm operated under the name of John Rogers & Sons. John died in 1816. His son continued the use of the name until he dissolved the pottery in 1842.

Boston Harbor, dark blue

Cup plate	475.00
Cup and Saucer	375.00
Sugar Bowl	525.00
Waste Bowl	450.00

Boston State House, dark blue

Creamer	275.00
Plate, 10″	120.00
Platter, 14″	300.00
Platter, 19″	700.00

Pitcher, Boston State House, dark
blue, 7½" $425.00

Soup Tureen	650.00

Shells and Seaweed, medium blue

Chesapeake and Shannon, 22½" platter	550.00
Shannon, 10" plate	100.00
Shannon, 10" soup	120.00

R. S. W.

STEVENSONS

As early as the 17th century the name Stevenson has been associated with the pottery industry. Andrew Stevenson of Cobridge introduced American scenes with the flower and scroll border. Ralph Stevenson, also of Cobridge, used a vine and leaf border on his dark blue historical views and a lace border on his series in light transfers.

The initials R. S. & W. indicate Ralph Stevenson and Williams are associated with the acorn and leaf border. It has been reported that Willis was Ralph's New York agent and the wares were produced by Ralph alone.

Acorn and Oak Leaves Border, dark blue

Baltimore Exchange, 5½" plate . .	675.00
Columbia College, N.Y., 7½" plate	425.00
Harvard College, 10" soup	250.00
Octagon Church, Boston, 4½" cup plate	600.00
Park Theater, N.Y., 10" plate . . .	190.00
State House, Boston, 5" plate . .	425.00
Water Works, Phila., 10" soup . . .	360.00

Floral and Scroll Border, dark blue

Almshouse, New York, 10" plate .	400.00
Catholic Cathedral, New York, 7½" plate	625.00
City Hall, New York, 7" plate	375.00
Columbia College, New York, 6½" soup	425.00
Troy from Mt. Ida, 9¾" platter . . .	1450.00
View of New York From Weehawk, soup tureen	3250.00

Stevenson, Lace Border series, Erie
Canal at Buffalo, plate, purple,
9¾" $175.00

Lace Border

Erie Canal at Buffalo, 10" soup . .	130.00
New Orleans, cup and saucer . . .	140.00
New Orleans, teapot	325.00
New Orleans, sugar bowl	225.00
Riceborough, Ga., washbowl	650.00

Vine Border

Almshouse, Boston, 14" platter . .	575.00
Almshouse, New York, 7" pitcher	775.00
Battery, New York, 7¾" plate . . .	475.00
Capitol, Washington, 10" soup . .	300.00
Columbia College, NY, 8" plate . .	475.00
Hospital, Boston, 9" plate	250.00
Pennsylvania Hospital, Phila., soup tureen	4500.00

STUBBS

STUBBS

In 1790 Stubbs established a pottery works
at Burslem, England. He operated it until 1829

when he retired and sold the pottery to the Mayer brothers. He probably produced his American views about 1825. Many of his scenes were from Boston, New York, New Jersey, and Philadelphia.

Stubbs, Spread Eagle Border series, Mendenhall Ferry, platter, 18¾" $550.00

Rose Border, dark blue

Boston State House, 7" pitcher ..	550.00
City Hall, New York, 6" plate	450.00
City Hall, New York, teapot	525.00
City Hall, sugar bowl	325.00

Spread Eagle Border, dark and medium blue

City Hall, New York, 6½" plate . .	220.00
Fair Mount Near Phila., 10" soup .	220.00
Fair Mount Near Phila., 22" platter	1100.00
Highlands, North River, 10" plate .	525.00
Hoboken in New Jersey, salt shaker	300.00
Mendenhall Ferry, 4½" cup plate .	400.00
State House, Boston, 14½" platter......................	575.00
Upper Ferry Bridge over the River Schuylkill	
Dish, round	350.00
Plate, 8¾"	185.00
Platter, 19"	550.00
Vegetable Dish	340.00
Wash Pitcher	500.00

S. TAMS & CO.

The firm operated at Longton, England. The exact date of its beginning is not known, but believed to be about 1810–1815. The company produced several dark blue American views. About 1830 the name became Tams, Anderson, and Tams.

Capitol, Washington, deep bowl . .	900.00
Capitol, Washington, wash pitcher	950.00
United States Hotel, Phila., 10" plate	350.00
United States Hotel, Phila., 10" soup	325.00

BURSLEM

WOOD

Enoch Wood, sometimes referred to as the Father of English Pottery, began operating a pottery at Fountain Place, Burselm, in 1783. A cousin Ralph Wood was associated with him. In 1790 James Caldwell became a partner and the firm was known as Wood and Caldwell. In 1819 Wood and his sons took full control.

Enoch died in 1840. His sons continued under the name of Enoch Wood & Sons. The American views were first made in the mid-1820's and continued through the 1840's.

It is reported that the pottery produced more signed historical views than any other Staffordshire firm. Many of the views attributed to unknown makers probably came from the Woods.

Marks vary, although always with the name Wood. The establishment was sold to Messrs. Pinder, Bourne & Hope in 1846.

Wood, Celtic China series, Fairmount Waterworks on the Schuylkill, plate, 9" $120.00

Celtic China, light transfer colors

Buffalo on Lake Erie, vegetable dish	225.00
Columbus, Ga., 3⅞" cup plate ..	325.00
Harvard College, 10" plate	125.00
Natural Bridge, Va., 9¼" plate ...	95.00
Pass in the Catskill Mountains, 7" plate	85.00

Shipping Port on the Ohio, KY, 12" platter 375.00
Transylvania University, Lexington, KY, 10" soup 130.00
Trenton Falls, 8" plate 100.00
West Point, Military Academy, openwork dish 400.00

Floral Border, irregular, dark blue
Commodore MacDonnough's Victory
  Coffee Pot 925.00
  Cup and Saucer 325.00
  Plate, 9" 300.00
Entrance of the Erie Canal into the Hudson at Albany
  Plate, 6" 750.00
  Soup, 10" 825.00
Erie Canal, Aqueduct Bridge at Rochester, pitcher, with first canal view, 5½" 675.00
Erie Canal, View of the Aqueduct Bridge at Little Falls
  Pitcher, with one of the views, 7" 775.00
  Pitcher, wash 900.00
Wadsworth Tower, sugar bowl ... 250.00

Four Medallion, Floral Border Series, light transfers
Castle Garden, 8" plate 110.00
Monte Video, 7½" plate 170.00
Race Bridge, Phila., gravy tureen . 425.00

General Jackson
Cup Plate 575.00
Pitcher, lustre, 4" 725.00
Plate, 7" 625.00

Shell Border, circular center, dark blue
Belleville on the Passaic River, soup tureen 2000.00
Castle Garden Battery, New York, 18½" platter 925.00
Catskill Mountains, Hudson River, custard cup with handle 350.00
City of Albany, State of New York, 10" plate 260.00
Highland, Hudson River, vegetable dish 550.00
Mount Vernon, 5¾" plate 350.00
Mount Vernon, 7½" plate 300.00
Railroad, Baltimore and Ohio, level, 10" plate 600.00
Railroad, Baltimore and Ohio, incline, 9" plate 650.00
West Point Military Academy, 12" platter 675.00
White House, Washington, cup plate 625.00

Shell Border, irregular center, dark blue
Cadmus, 10" soup 300.00
Commodore MacDonnough's Victory
  Coffee Pot 1200.00
  Plate, 9" 300.00

Teapot 740.00
Constitution and Guerriere, 10" plate 675.00
Erith on the Thames, vegetable dish 450.00
Union Line, 9¼" plate 300.00
Union Line, 10" soup 275.00
Wadsworth Tower
  Coffeepot 1050.00
  Cup and Saucer 350.00
  Pitcher, 4½" 460.00
  Waste Bowl 350.00

Washington's Tomb, dark blue
Creamer 400.00
Soup, 10" 350.00
Sugar Bowl 550.00
Teapot 800.00

Unknown Maker, Utica Inscription and Clinton Eulogy, pitcher, 6½" .$675.00

UNKNOWN MAKERS

Anti-Slavery, light blue, 9¼" plate .. 130.00
Erie Canal Inscription
  Cup Plate, 3¾" 700.00
  Pitcher, 5¼" , damaged spout ... 475.00
  Plate, 10" 450.00
Famous Naval Heroes, 7; pitcher .. 725.00
Famous Naval Heroes, washbowl .. 800.00
Franklin Flying a Kite, light blue, 3¾" platter, miniature 50.00
Great Fire, City of New York, series, plates, each 125.00
Mount Vernon, Washington's Seat, 8" pitcher 850.00

STAFFORDSHIRE ITEMS

A wide variety of ornamental pottery items came from the pottery district of Staffordshire, beginning in the 17th century and extending to today. The high point of production was the 19th century.

The objects are many — trinket boxes, pastille burners, animal figures, and figurines (called chimney ornaments). The key to price is age and condition. The older items clearly are most desirable, in part because the quality of workmanship is much higher.

Cottage Bank, 5″, c. 1885 . . . . $195.00

Animals
Cats	
7¼″, pair, sitting on cobalt cushions	250.00
12″, gray, green glass eyes, late	175.00
Cow, russet spots on cream colored body, green base	85.00
Dogs	
4″, pair, spaniel, russet spots on white	125.00
5½″, pair, dalmations, black markings on white	165.00
8″, pair, spaniels, red and black	200.00
9¼″, pair, spaniels, black and white	300.00
Hawk, c. 1780, 5¼″	400.00
Hens	
6½″, brilliant coloring, caramel nest	200.00
8¾″, white hen on light brown base	250.00
Leopards, pair, cream colored, c. 1790, 8¼″	2750.00
Lion, c. 1825, 12¼″	425.00
Lion and Lamb, mid-19th C., 4¾″	375.00

Banks
Cottage, orange, white roof, 3 stories, green grass	195.00
Cottage, white, brown roof, black outlining	150.00

Chimney Ornaments
Baden Powell, standing in front of	

cannon	135.00
English Queen, crown and ermine	175.00
Franklin, Benjamin, The Old English Gentleman, 15″	650.00
Huntsman, 15″	175.00
Man, old, lame with crutch and walking stick, brown clothing, Walton, c. 1810	295.00
Milkmaid, suckling calf, 5″	110.00
Peace on Earth, Good Will Toward Men, 12¾″	175.00
Prince of Wales, Edward VIII, orange robe, c. 1875	210.00
Uncle Tom and Eva, 8½″	175.00

Pastille Burners
Castle, 3 turrents, grey, green grass	175.00
Cottage, 1 chimney, hexagon shape, open door	100.00
Cottage, beige, 2 chimneys, white roof, green grass	135.00
Cottage, white, yellow roof, green grass	140.00
Slippers, high heeled, white with colored flowers, heels rest on pillow	80.00
Spill Holder, cow and calf, pair, russet with green accents, 6″	250.00

Trinket Boxes, covered
Anchor and Hooks	65.00
Lamb and Baby Lamb, oval, white with green, footed	70.00
Marriage Bed Series	75.00
Spaniel, reclining	62.50
Watch and ring	57.50

STAFFORDSHIRE, ROMANTIC

This is perhaps one of the most overlooked collecting areas. This popular dinnerware was produced in the Staffordshire district of England between 1830 and 1860. A large number of potters were involved and over 800 patterns have been identified.

The services often come in a variety of colors with light blue and pink perhaps the most popular. Usually the pattern is identified on the back of the piece. It was not uncommon for two potters to issue pieces with the same design. Therefore, check not only pattern name, but maker as well.

Petra William's *Staffordshire: Romantic Transfer Patterns* is an excellent source for identifying views.

It would be impossible to list all patterns. A representative selection follows. Some price ranges to keep in mind are Cups and Saucers (handleless) $35–60; Plates, cup $40–75; Plates, 9″ to 10″ $5–50; Platters $25–75.

Abbey, light blue
Cups and Saucers, handleless . . .	40.00

Plate, Parisian Chateau, R. Hall, 10¼″ dia. $42.00

Dish, condiment, 5″	10.00
Plates	
7″	15.00
8″	18.00
9½″	20.00
Relish, oval shape	15.00
Sauce, 4″	10.00

Archipeligo, Adams and John Ridgway, light blue

Cups and Saucers, handleless . . .	50.00
Plate, 9½″	25.00
Platter, 18 x 11½″	50.00
Relish, oblong	20.00

Bologna, William Adams & Son

Pitcher, pink, 10″	125.00
Plate, mulberry, 9½″	45.00
Vegetable, pink, 8 x 10″	110.00

Caledonia, William Adams

Plates	
7½″, pink	60.00
8½″, dark blue	125.00
10½″, pink	65.00

Cyrene, William Adams & Son, pink

Cups and Saucers, handleless . . .	35.00
Plates	
7″	25.00
8″	30.00

Gondola, probably William Davenport & Co., pink

Cups and Saucers, with handles .	18.00
Plate, scalloped edge, 8″	25.00

Mongul Scenery, T. Mayer, pink

Cups and Saucers, handleless . . .	40.00
Plate, 8″	30.00
Platter, 18 x 24″	75.00

Palestine, William Adams, also Ridgway

Creamer, pink	100.00
Plates	
6″, med. blue	50.00
7½″, pink	40.00
10½″, pink	50.00

Rhone Scenery, T. & J. Mayer, light blue

Cups and Saucers, handleless . . .	40.00
Plate, 8″	18.00
Vegetable, square, open	20.00

Sydenham, J. Clementson, medium blue

Creamer	35.00
Cups and Saucers, handleless . . .	40.00
Custard Cup, two handles	15.00
Dish, wire frame, handle	25.00
Gravy Boat with tray	45.00
Plates	
7″	12.00
8″	15.00
9″	18.00
10″ . . . . : . .	20.00
Relish, oblong	18.00
Sugar, covered	40.00
Teapot	55.00
Tureen, cover, and tray	75.00
Vegetable, open	30.00
Waste Bowl	12.00

Venus, Podmore Walker & Co., light blue (also polychrome — add 25%)

Creamer	45.00
Dish, condiment	15.00
Egg Cups	35.00
Gravy Boat with tray	50.00
Oatmeal Bowl, 4½″	25.00
Plates	
Cup	50.00
7″	30.00
8″	35.00
10″	40.00
Relish, scoop shape	35.00
Sugar, covered, pagoda shape . .	85.00
Teapot, pagoda shape	150.00
Tureen, lid	175.00
Vegetable, open	45.00

Vintage, J. & G. Alcock, light blue

Creamer	50.00
Cups and Saucers, handleless . . .	55.00
Plates	
Cup	50.00
7″	25.00
8″	30.00
10″	40.00
Relish Dish	20.00
Tureen, lid	50.00
Teapot, collar	75.00
Vegetable, open	35.00
Waste Bowl	15.00

STAINED AND/OR LEADED GLASS PANELS

The Egyptians are credited with using the first stained glass windows. With the advent of Christianity, stained glass windows became a major expression in religious art. The best known 20th century stain artist is Louis C. Tiffany.

Stained glass can be transparent, translucent or opaque. The panels are held together with lead cames. This lead often is soft. When purchasing a panel, check the lead and have any necessary repairs made to protect your investment.

14 × 33″ panel **$250.00**

22 x 42″, semi-circular, torch center, original frame	275.00
2½ x 6′, railroad station window . . .	415.00
34¾ x 80½″ high, plant in pot, 3 large blossoms, green leaves, green and pink border, minor cracks	400.00
3 x 6′ church window	650.00
Leaded glass windows for each side of front door, c. 1890, pair	500.00

STANGL POTTERY

Stangl Pottery acquired Fulper Pottery in the late 1920's. Stangl birds are their most collectible items; but other objects such as planters, vases and bowls were produced.

Cardinal, # 3444 . . . .**$55.00**

Birds
Blackbird, 3591	45.00
Cockatoo, 3580	85.00
Hummingbird, 3634	40.00
Orioles, double, 3402 D	75.00
Rooster, 3445	80.00
Warbler, Parula 3583	45.00
Warbler, red faced, 3594	40.00
Wren, 3401	40.00

Bowls
6 x 2¼″ deep, leaf handle, terra rose	10.00
7 x 4″ deep, covered, terra rose .	15.00
8″, petal-shaped, white	15.00
Candlesticks, calla lily on blue leaf, pair	30.00
Carafe, stoppered, 8″ high, ribbed, yellow and blue, wooden handle .	20.00
Cigarette Box, covered, 5¾″, leaf-shaped	10.00
Cornucopia, 8¾″, terra rose, green	15.00
Creamer, 2½″, thistle, brown and white	5.00
Dinnerware, terra rose, 38 pieces . .	150.00
Nut Set, Starflower, 7 pieces	40.00
Planter, 5¾ x 6″, open blossom, terra rose	20.00

Vases
7″, Milk can, terra rose, tan	8.00
7″, handled, turquoise	10.00
9½″, sunflower-shaped, terra rose	20.00
11″, Urn-type, black and gold . . .	55.00
Wall Pocket, Alacite	50.00

STATUES AND FIGURES

The technical difference between a statue and a figure is the material. A statue is made of stone or metal. A figure is composed of wood or clay (porcelain or pottery). Large or important figures are sometimes classified as statues. The terms figurine and statuette are used to distinguish size. Using the human figure as a guide, if the statue measures one-fourth life size, it is known as a statuette. If a figure is less than approximately one-fourth life size it is referred to as a figurine. See BRONZES.

Bronze
Classical, mythological female figure	700.00
Satan, 12″, Bronze, c. 1500	650.00
Wild Horses of Mallet, man in loin cloth holding rearing horses, French bronze, signed	200.00
Woman, 13½″, semi-nude, ivory head, hands and bust, bronze skirt washed in gold, marble base, tiara in gold with rubies, pearl earrings, serpent arm decoration, French, signed by artist	550.00
Woman, 22″, metal, signed Moreau	90.00

Wood
Figure, 16″, carved, ivory insets,

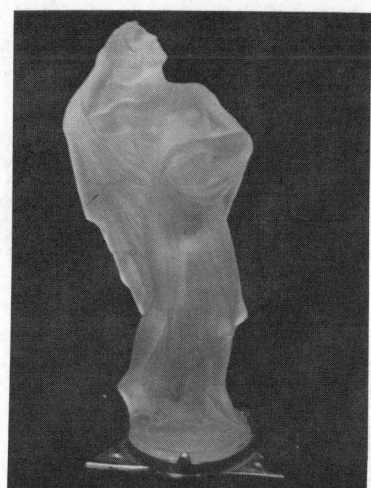

Glass, brass base, Art Deco, 9″,
unmarked $175.00

Italian, 19th century	185.00
St. Joseph with Christ Child, carved, 5″	275.00
Porcelain	
Boy and Girl, 13″, Germany, c. 1900, pair	175.00
King and Queen, 8″, Meissen, pair	375.00
Rabbit, 7″, Meissen	275.00

STEIFF

This company is known as Margarete Steiff, GmbH, and has been in business in Germany since 1880. It is known for very fine quality stuffed animals as well as other beautifully made collectible toys; it is still in business today and its products are highly respected.

The company's first products were wool-felt elephants made by Margarete Steiff. In a few years the elephant line was expanded to include a donkey, horse, pig and camel.

By 1903, the company was also producing a mohair, jointed Teddy Bear and production of that toy was dramatically increased to 974,000 in 1907. Margarete's nephews took over the company at this point; the bear's head became the symbol for its label, and the famous "Button in the Ear" round metal trademark was added.

Newly designed animals also were added: Molly and Bully, the dogs, and Fluffy the cat. Pull toys and kites were also produced, as well as larger animals on which children could ride or play.

The wary buyer can now see the familiar metal button attached to animals that are not Steiff, so it is wise to become familiar with the genuine products before purchasing an antique stuffed animal. Plush in old Steiff animals was mohair; trimmings were usually felt or velvet.

Steiff has become collectible in recent years not only because it is well made but because of the appealing and realistic expressions and the general appeal of the animals themselves.

See also TEDDY BEARS.

Dog, white, 11″ $125.00

2½″, Elephant	35.00
3″, early fluffy Cat with metal rimmed paper tag	100.00
4″, Beagle dog	40.00
4″, Owl	50.00
4″, Monkey, "Coco"	45.00
4″, white Lamb, "Lamby"	35.00
5″, Fawn, "Bambi"	25.00
5″, Penguin	45.00
5″, black Cat with arched back	35.00
5″ long, Turtle	25.00
5½″, Pony, saddle and bridle	55.00
6″, Squirrel, holding acorn	65.00
6″, Boxer dog	75.00
7″, Wire Haired Terrier dog, fat	75.00
7″, Giraffe	35.00
12″ long, crouched Cat	125.00
20″, Kangaroo with baby in pouch	475.00

STEINS

A stein is a mug especially made to hold beer or ale. Most steins are fitted with a metal hinged lid with thumblift. The earthenware character-type steins are attributed to German origin. See also METTLACH.

**Cat, Germany, DRGM 154927-
701B** **$235.00**

Art Nouveau-style decor, 14″, copper and brass, Germany	100.00
Bacchus, 11½″, silverplated, English	150.00
B.P.O.E., Germany	75.00
Bike Rider, painted scene	170.00
Bismarck, 1½ l., porcelain, radish finial, Musterschutz	400.00
Clown, ½ l., lithophane	350.00
Drinking Scene, ¼ l., Germany . . .	25.00
Field Artillery, 1 l., regimental	275.00
Flower, 1 l., Gesetzlicht	295.00
Indian, ¼ l., Musterschutz	450.00
Mandarin, ½ l., Merkelbach & Wick	175.00
Monks, ½ l., Gesetzlicht	175.00
Monkey, ½ l.	230.00
Munich Maid, ½ l.	275.00
Nun, 7″, lithophane	250.00
Owl, blue and grey	230.00
Pixie, 1 l., Musterschutz	850.00
Ram, seated, 1 l., Musterschutz . .	650.00
Rolandbrannen Park, 1 l., lithophane, Dresden	400.00
Satan, ½ l., Musterschutz	500.00
Scull	280.00
Stoneware, ½ l., Germany	75.00
Village Dancers, ½ l., Musterschutz	225.00

STEREOSCOPE VIEWERS AND CARDS

First marketed in 1854, the stereoscope was a popular Victorian parlor ornament; almost every home in America had one. This optical instrument had two eyeglasses which enabled the viewer to see the double picture cards as a single view with true feeling of depth and distance. Stereoscopes were hand held and fitted to the face; the picture cards were contained in a slide (or rack) 10 inches away at the other end of the instrument.

Scenes of far away places and people, foreign cities, cathedrals and other architectural wonders were popular subjects. Millions of stereoscopic views were published, often in large issues of hundreds or thousands. As the first truly pictorial medium, stereoscopes remained available into the late 1930's; however, interest in the medium had begun to decline with the advent of the picture postcard, movies and radio.

Hand type	$45.00
Cards, each	$2.00

Viewers

Binocular-type, with light bulb	30.00
Double-type, 18 x 10″ wide, American	150.00
Double-type, 10½ x 6½″, French . .	150.00
Eye Comfort, with stand	40.00
Keystone, Junior	35.00
Keystone View Co., Leather, velvet trim	50.00
Stereosconse	50.00
Tin, pocket box	45.00

Cards

Sets

Countries, 75	75.00
Egypt, with map and book, 100 . .	50.00
Germany, 100	50.00
Holy Land, 50 views	75.00
Italy, with maps and book, 100 . .	50.00
London, 8 views	25.00
San Francisco Earthquake, 50 . .	75.00
Sears Roebuck, 50	35.00
World War I, 100	65.00

Singles. Prices quoted are approximate for cards in good condition. Folded, mutilated or badly soiled cards are of little or no value to collectors.

Advertising-type	.75
Alaska Gold Rush	3.00
Battleships	1.25
Civil War	10.00
Comics	1.50
Disasters	1.50
Expositions	2.00
Indians	3.50
Panama Canal	1.50
Presidents	3.00
Railroads	5.00
Sentimentals	1.00
Ships	2.00
Spanish American War	2.50
States	1.00
Teddy Roosevelt, Rough Riders	3.50
Tissues, American and French	5.00
Transportation, early	2.50

STERLING
See SILVER

STEUBEN GLASS

The Steuben Glass Works began in 1904 with Frederick Carder, an Englishman, and Thomas G. Hawkes of Corning, New York. In 1918 the Corning Glass Co. purchased the Steuben Works. Carder remained with the company and designed many of the pieces bearing the Steuben mark. Probably the most widely recognized wares are "Aurene," "Verre de Soie" and "Rosaline," but many other types of wares were produced. For "Aurene" see "Aurene."

The firm continues operating, producing glass of exceptional quality.

Basket, 4½ x 4½" Verre de Soie, raspberry prunts on handle, etched monogram	85.00
Bon Bon, 5", green jade, signed	85.00
Bottle, vinegar, Verre de Soie, sterling top, signed Hawkes	145.00

Bowls

7¾", white, aurene interior	150.00
8", ribbed, pomona green, topaz swirl, pedestal foot, signed	75.00
10", Rosaline, signed	200.00
11¾", Silverene, amethyst, diamond air trap pattern	450.00
12", ribbed, topaz with aquamarine rim and pedestal	125.00
12", Verre de Soie, inverted bell form with applied pink glass trailing	250.00

19", centerpiece, Verre de Soie, melon ribbed, rims applied Rosaline	265.00
19", console, melon center, Rosaline edge	195.00

Candlesticks, crystal with black base, 8 prisms, 9", signed, pair $225.00

Candlesticks

6", green, pair	225.00
12", ribbed, marina blue, signed and numbered, pair	250.00
12", topaz, domed foot and wafers, pomona green stem and top, signed, pair	250.00
12", Rosaline, alabaster wafer, pair	575.00
Champagne, lavender and purple specks, twisted stem, signed	95.00

Compotes

5¼", blue, teardrop stem, reeded rim, signed	115.00
7 x 20" dia., Rosaline, alabaster stem, base and finial	575.00
8¼", jade, signed	147.00
10¼", Rosaline, alabaster stem and foot	300.00
14", deep purple with stem	325.00
Creamer and Open Sugar, topaz, applied blue handle and feet	110.00
Cup and Saucer, Citron, alabaster	110.00

Finger Bowls

4", Calcite, Peche Melba with underplate	320.00
5", 7" underplate, Verre de Soie, flared, garlands, bows medallion decor, signed Hawkes	185.00
light green, panelled with underplate, signed	35.00

Goblets

5", Selenium ruby	40.00
5¾", Flemish blue	40.00
7", jade, twisted alabaster stem	140.00
7", crystal, tear drop stem	45.00

Crystal, controlled bubbles, blue threading	55.00
Water, Rosaline	225.00
Jars	
5⅜", square, dresser, Citron, threaded covers, swirl, pair	175.00
7", pomona green, footed, signed	125.00
7", Luminar, signed	750.00
9½", pale blue, leaf etching, signed Steuben and Carder	200.00
Mug, 6", jade, black applied handle, signed	75.00
Nut Dishes	
3½", Verre de Soie, optic swirl . .	50.00
5", black Cluthra, signed	175.00
Pitchers	
5 x 6", IVT, amber, fleur de lis, 6 sided top, applied handle with cross twirl, signed	225.00
10¼", crystal with black threading and stopper, signed and numbered	150.00
Plates	
9", Rosaline, copper wheel decor	200.00
9", amethyst, fleur de lis, copper wheel decor	200.00
amethyst, etched border, signed, 6	160.00
Salts	
1¾", Verre de Soie, copper wheel engraved, sterling pedestal	55.00
1¾", Verre de Soie, pedestal . . .	35.00
Sherbets	
Crystal, yellow stem, yellow rimmed underplate, signed	85.00
Deep purple with underplate	95.00
Jade with underplate	90.00
Verre de Soie with underplate . . .	65.00
Shot Glass, crystal, fleur de lis, green threading, footed, signed . .	50.00
Tumblers	
4½", Verre de Soie, engraved, signed Hawkes	70.00
6", crystal, amethyst twisted handle, Cintra amethyst trim	250.00
Vases	
5", green blue, optical ribbing, signed	150.00
5", Ivorine	175.00
5¼", Verre de Soie, pedestal base	60.00
6", ribbed, amethyst, crystal ring handles, pedestal base, signed . .	250.00
6", Rosaline, handled	140.00
6", dark amethyst, self-reeding at top, flared rim, signed	110.00
6½", swirl ribbed, French blue, signed	95.00
6½", jade, alabaster raised foot .	85.00
6½", Verre de Soie, Rosaline threading	175.00
8", ribbed, topaz, signed Carder .	165.00

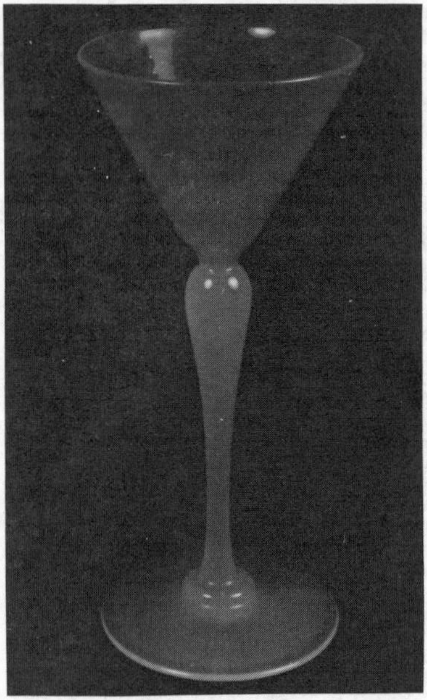

Sherbet, Rosaline, 6¼" $185.00

8", crystal, pink cast, 3 blue applied shell feet, signed	85.00
8½ x 10¼" dia., yellow jade	1200.00
9", folded handkerchief shape, crystal to red, pedestal foot	175.00
10", fan, ribbed, pomona green top, topaz foot	170.00
10¼", bud, bulbous base, Rosaline to alabaster cutback, flowers, leaves, swag decor	395.00
10½", Verre de Soie, signed Hawkes	295.00
Thorn vase, 3 prong, forest green, signed	215.00
Cluthra, blue, classic urn, signed .	395.00
Wisteria, 3 handled, signed	325.00
Wines	
Crystal, green threading around top	25.00
Gold, ruby bowl, crystal twist stem	60.00
Optic rib, celeste blue bowl, rose stem, signed	70.00
Optic rib, topaz, signed	55.00

STEVENGRAPHS

Thomas Stevens of Coventry, Warwickshire, England, first manufactured woven silk de-

signs in 1854. His first bookmark was produced in 1862, followed by the first Stevengraph in 1874. Stevengraphs are miniature silk pictures, matted, framed, and made by Stevens. Other companies copied his technique; their efforts should not be confused with Stevens' products.

The bookmarks are longer than they are wide, have mitred corners at one end, and are finished with a tassel. Stevens' name *always* is woven into the silk at a mitred corner.

True Stevengraphs are miniature silk pictures, matted, framed and produced by Stevens. Stevens' name *never* is woven into a Stevengraph. His name may appear on the mat near the title, but is usually found on the trade announcement on the back of the mat. Stevengraphs in original mat and with the trade announcement are the most desirable.

American collectors favor the Stevengraphs of the Declaration of Independence and Columbus expedition from the 1892-93 World Exposition in Chicago. Stevengraphs were never sold at the New York Crystal Palace Exposition in 1853, simply because they did not exist at that time.

BOOKMARKS

Birthday Blessing, A	85.00
Birthday Gift, A	85.00
*Centennial, Washington	165.00
Faith, Hope, and Charity, on original advertising card	110.00
Home Sweet Home	125.00
Last Rose of Summer, The	75.00
Lord Watch Between Me and Thee, The	65.00
Remember Me	70.00
Unchanging Love	55.00
Wish (With Best Wishes), A, on original advertising card	110.00
With Best Wishes	65.00

The Lady Godiva Procession .$275.00

STEVENGRAPHS

Are You Ready	150.00
Called to the Rescue	275.00
Death, The	225.00
Death of Nelson, The	195.00
Declaration of Independence	385.00
Finish, The	195.00
First Touch, The	335.00
For Life or Death	325.00
Good Old Days, The	175.00
Hands Across the Sea	40.00
Landing of Columbus, The	375.00
Madonna and Child	1500.00
Present Time, The	300.00
Spanish Bull Fight	350.00
Start, The	195.00
Water Jump, The	260.00
Wellington and Blucher	195.00
William, Prince of Orange	350.00

STEVENS AND WILLIAMS

In the late 19th century, Stevens and Williams, Stourbridge, England, become one of the pioneers in producing a less expensive and commercial cameo glass. Earlier cameo glass was handcarved. It was produced mainly for exhibition purposes or for the wealthy, but as demand increased, Stevens and Williams revised the old method by employing the wheel and acid for the engraving. This hastened the production and subsequently made the glass available to more people.

While the earlier cameo glass was of the classical design. Stevens and Williams' designs were influenced by the Orient. One of their foremost artists was also a botanist, which accounts for the many beautiful nature designs.

Biscuit Jar, blue interior, white exterior, applied flowers and leaves. Amber thorn handle and feet	350.00
Bowls	
6", green, intaglio cut thistles & leaves, clear cut stem	258.00
7", Tortoise shell coloring. Scalloped rim. Applied birds and flowers	350.00
12", pull-up, butterscotch zipper, pink lining, clear foot	550.00
Cologne Bottle, intaglio cut	245.00
Compote, 5¼", blue cut to crystal	395.00

Miniature Rose Bowl, gold and white vertical stripes, 2½" h., ...$65.00

Cruet, Arabesque	165.00
Parfait, 5½", jade green with alabaster stem and foot, signed	75.00
Perfume Bottle, amber cut to clear .	435.00
Pitcher, 9", amber, blue handle and feet, applied green leaves	350.00
Rose Bowl, 3", green, pullups	195.00
Sauce, 5½", crystal with red strawberries, gold leaf	150.00
Syrup, cranberry threaded	150.00

Vases

5", Jewel, amber	150.00
5¾", ruffled top, pink and white loop pattern, applied frosted rigaree, three feet	450.00
8", blue & pink, pull up, yellow interior, footed	550.00
9½", amberina, "Swirl"	1000.00
11", applied rigaree, florals	280.00

STIEGEL TYPE GLASS

Baron Henry Stiegel founded America's first flint glass factory at Manheim, Pa., in the 1760's. The principal products were clear bottles and flasks, glasses, and salts. Also attributed to Stiegel is enamel decorated ware. Prosperity was short lived. Stiegel's extravagant living forced the factory to close.

Enameled glass ware, American or European, is designated as Stiegel type. An overwhelming majority is of European origin. Beware of modern reproductions.

Bottles

5", clear, woman carrying water on shoulder yoke, floral motif on remainder, pewter collar	275.00

Bride's Bottle, script one side, fox with basket of birds on back on other, 5⅞", ...$375.00

6⅛", clear, floral motif on all sides, pewter collar	350.00
6¼", opaque blue, red coated British officer on white horse, floral motif on remainder, pewter collar for screw top	650.00
Creamer, cobalt blue, 16 vertical ribs, applied circular foot, 4½" . .	425.00
Cruet, clear, extended neck on Bride's bottle base, applied handle, floral motif on all sides, 7" . .	500.00

Flip Glasses

3½", clear, King of Prussia, floral sprays	275.00
4⅜", clear, sprays of flowers, inscription Liberty in floral wreath .	600.00
4⅞", clear, bird perched on red heart, floral motif	250.00
Finger Bowl, cobalt blue, expanded diamond pattern, scarred pontils, 4¾" dia.	175.00
Flask, Pocket, amethyst, attributed to Stiegel, diamond over vertical flutes, 5⅛"	2500.00

Mug, pint, clear, strap handle, decorated with berries and bird, 5″ ... **400.00**

Salts

Clear, diamond quilted, applied foot **85.00**

Cobalt blue, diamond quilted, applied foot **150.00**

Sugar Bowl, cobalt blue, expanded diamond, circular foot, scarred pontil, 5⅞″ **1300.00**

STOCK AND BOND CERTIFICATES

Stock and bonds are collected for a variety of reasons — the graphic illustrations, the history of romantic times in America including gold and silver mining, railroad history, and early automobile pioneers.

Some of the factors that affect price are (a) dates [with pre-1900 more popular and pre-1850 most desirable], (b) autographs of important persons [Vanderbilt, Rockefeller, J. P. Morgan, Wells and Fargo, etc.], (c) number issued [most bonds have number issued printed in text], and (d) the attractiveness of the vignette.

BONDS

Blue Ridge Railroad Co., SC, 1869, $1,000, three imprinted revenue stamps, signed by Henry Clews .. **175.00**

Cairo and Norfolk Railroad, KY, 1908, $100 .... **90.00**

Chicago and Alton Railroad, IL, 1899, $1,000 .... **60.00**

Consolidated Railway Co., CT, 1905, $10,000 .... **15.00**

Holly, Wayne, and Monroe Railroad, 1871, $1,000, two imprinted revenues **165.00**

London Mining Co., NY, 1882, $500 **15.00**

Louisville and Nashville Railroad Co., KY, 1880, $1,000 .... **120.00**

Providence Security Co., CT, 1907, $10,000 .... **20.00**

Yosemite Short Line Railway, CA, 1905, $100 .... **85.00**

STOCKS

Bank of America, NY, 1850's **45.00**

Bellvue Land and Improvement Co., NY, 1890's **10.00**

Canada Southern Railway Co., Canada, signed by Vanderbilt, 1880's **270.00**

Charles Jacquin et. Cie, Inc., 1960's **9.00**

Delaware, Lackawanna, and Western Railroad Co., PA, 1950's **10.00**

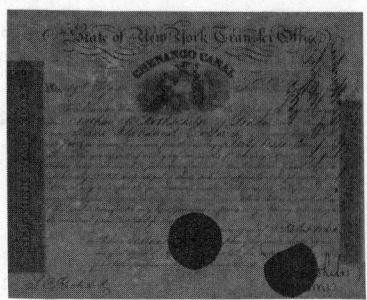

New York, Chenango Canal, 1836, issued to Nathan M. Rothschild of London $135.00

Demoine Navigation and Railroad, IO, 1850's **125.00**

Gallatin Valley Electric Railway, MT, 1900's **35.00**

Illinois Central Railroad, 1880's **10.00**

Kaiser Frazer Corp., 1940's **5.00**

Lehigh Valley Transit Co., PA, 1910 **9.00**

Lion Country Safari, FL, 1970's **12.00**

Louisville Railway, KY, 1895 ...... **25.00**

Mahoning and Shenango Railway and Light Co., PA, 1910's **20.00**

New York, New Haven, and Hartford Railroad Co., 1940's and 50's ... **12.00**

Peoria and Bureau Valley Railroad, IL, 1850's **125.00**

Philadelphia and Reading Railroad, PA, 1870's, one imprinted revenue **65.00**

Pullman Co., NY, 1910's and 20's .. **12.00**

Rio Grande Southern Railroad, CO, 1890's, signed by Otto Mears ... **150.00**

Western Union Telegraph Co., NY, 1960's **3.00**

Yankee Girl Gold Mining Co. of Bullfrog, NV, 1907 .... **25.00**

STONEWARE

Made from dense kaolin clay and commonly salt-glazed, stonewares were hand-thrown and high fired to produce a simple, bold vitreous pottery. Stoneware crocks, jugs and jars were produced for storage and utility purposes. This use dictated shape and design — solid, thick-walled forms with heavy rims, necks and handles with little or no embellishment. When decorated, the designs were simple ... brushed cobalt oxide, incised or slip trails; also stamping or tooling.

Stoneware has been made for centuries. Early American settlers imported stoneware items at first. As English and European potteries refined their earthenwares, colonists began to produce their own wares. Two major North American traditions emerged based mainly on the location or type of clay. North Jersey and parts of New York were the first area; the second was eastern Pennsylvania spreading westward and into Maryland, Virginia and West Virginia. These two distinct locations, style of decoration and shape are discernible factors in classifying and dating early stoneware.

By the late 18th century, stoneware was manufactured in all sections of the country. During the 19th century, this vigorous industry flourished until glass 'fruit jars' appeared and the wide spread use of refrigeration. By 1910, commercial production of salt-glazed stoneware came to an end.

Batter Jugs

1 gal., Sipe, Nichols & Co., Williamsport, Pa., blue flowers, both tin lids missing	420.00
1½ gal., Cowden & Wilcox, Harrisburg, Pa., blue flowers, original tin lid and spout cap	625.00

Butter Crocks

John Bell, Waynesboro, blue leaves, matching lid	575.00
F. H. Cowden, Harrisburg, Pa., blue two blossom floral design, lid missing	310.00
Unknown maker, 5 x 8″, fully decorated with blue leaves, matching lid	350.00
Unknown maker, 10″ dia., blue leaf design, lid missing	225.00

Canning Jars

Solomon Bell, 8″, Strasburg, no decoration	55.00
Unknown maker, three bands of blue	45.00
Churn, unknown maker, 5 gal., blue 5 and leaf decoration	75.00

Coolers

14″, N. Clark & Co., Lyons, blue filled incised leaf	475.00
19″, Somerset Potters Works, flared base, urn shaped top, applied side handles, blue filled incised birds on branches, chip and hairline	2225.00

Crocks

7¼″, F. H. Cowden, apple butter crock with handle, no decoration	40.00
8¾″, Evan Jones, Pittston, Pa., blue flower	70.00
9¼″, unknown maker, ovoid, blue foliage	155.00
10″, unknown maker, blue flower and leaves, full decoration	120.00

11″, C. Crolius Manufacturer, Manhattan Wells, N.Y., ovoid, incised flower and foliage filled with blue, short lines	425.00
11″, N. A. White & Son, Utica, N.Y., large blue bird on branch	235.00
1 gal., Cowden and Wilcox, blue flower	125.00
1½ gal., J. & E. Norton, Bennington, Vt., blue bird looking backwards	420.00
2 gal., Cowden and Wilcox, cluster of four flowers in blue	265.00
2 gal., F. H. Cowden, stenciled blue geometric design	90.00
2 gal., Fulper Bros., Flemington, N.J., crock with lid, blue stylized flowers	180.00
2 gal., New York Stoneware Co., pale blue bird on branch	185.00
2 gal., T. F. Reppert, Greensboro, Pa., blue freehand and stenciled design	95.00
2 gal., unknown maker, blue flower and leaves	85.00
2 gal., F. T. Wright & Son Stoneware, Taunton, Mass., blue stenciled bunch of grapes	85.00
3 gal., Cowden and Wilcox, ovoid, blue spray of flowers	285.00
3 gal., Swank, Johnstown, Pa., blue flower	140.00
3 gal., unknown maker, number 3 in blue slip	35.00
4 gal., T. F. Reppert, Greensboro, Pa., blue stenciled design	110.00
4 gal., unknown maker, blue running rooster design	310.00
5 gal., H. & G.G.P., York, Pa., blue stencil decoration	110.00
5 gal., W. Roberts, Binghamton, N.Y., blue bird on floral branch	400.00
5 gal., unknown maker, blue running chicken design	250.00
6 gal., James Hamilton & Co., Greensboro, Pa., blue stenciled and freehand design	110.00
8 gal., A. Eberhart & Co., New Geneva, blue stenciled and freehand design	250.00
Footwarmer, marked "Goodwill's Bed and Foot Warmer"	40.00

Ink Wells

C. Crolius, dated July 12, 1773, heart shaped, beaded edge, blue highlights	15000.00
unknown maker, brown glaze, tooled, serrated edge	45.00

Jugs

3¼″, miniature, "Bennington, Augt 1877" scratched inscription, exterior Albany slip	45.00

Jug, 2 gal. American, unsigned $150.00

8″, John Bell, Waynesboro, blue brushed on handle terminals	115.00
9¼″, C. Crolius Manufacturer, Manhattan Wells, N.Y., ovoid, blue brushed over mark	350.00
9¾″, Hamilton and Jones, Greensboro, name stenciled in blue	45.00
10¾″, J. & E. Norton, Bennington, Vt., blue stylized flowers	265.00
10¾″, L. Norton & Son, ovoid, blue brushed over label	250.00
11¼″, Norton & Son, ovoid, brown stylized bird	1250.00
11¾″, T. Crafts & Co., Whately, no decoration	50.00
13″, unknown maker, ovoid, blue flower	95.00
14″, A. Clark, Jr., Athens, N.Y., simple blue floral design	120.00
1 gal., F. H. Cowden, Harrisburg, Pa., blue stenciled medallion	80.00
1 gal., A. M. Dipple, Lewistown, Pa., simple blue flower	120.00
1 gal., Whites, Utica, N.Y., blue bird looking backwards	350.00
2 gal., Cowden & Wilcox, Harrisburg, Pa., blue flower	110.00
2 gal., Cowden & Wilcox, Harrisburg, Pa., fine bird on a branch ..	725.00
2 gal., J. Fisher, Lyons, N.Y., blue 2 and flourish	45.00
2 gal., J. Norton & Co., Bennington, Vt., blue spray of flowers	310.00
2 gal., W. Roberts, Binghamton, N.Y., blue bird on branch	290.00
2 gal., D. P. Shenfelder, Reading, Pa., blue leafage	115.00
2 gal., F. Woodworth, Vt., no decoration	30.00
3 gal., S. Purdy, Portage Co., Ohio, ovoid, blue brushed over name	115.00
3 gal., unknown maker, blue slip design of two leaves	170.00

Milk Bowls

12¼″ dia., unknown maker, salt glaze, no decoration	40.00
12½″ dia., unknown maker, blue three petal flowers, pouring spout	200.00
1½ gal., Sipe & Sons, Williamsport, Pa., blue flower	275.00

Pitchers

8⅜″, Cowden & Wilcox, Harrisburg, Pa., blue flowers	500.00
9¼″, unknown maker, exterior Albany slip	55.00
10″, unknown maker, simple blue leaf design	375.00
10½″, unknown maker, salt glaze, no decoration	75.00
1 gal., Sipe Nichols & Co., Williamsport, Pa., blue single leaf design	525.00
1½ gal., unknown maker, blue leaf spray	550.00
Snuff Jar, 9″, "Fine Maccoboy" in blue stencil	45.00

Spittoons

F. H. Cowden, Harrisburg, Pa., no decoration	30.00
Unknown maker, blue design of simple three petal flowers	145.00
Unknown maker, blue slip leaves .	190.00

STRAWBERRY CHINA

This ware takes its name from the distinctive decorative motif, the Strawberry. There are three primary types: strawberries and strawberry leaves (often called Strawberry Lustre), green feather-like leaves with pink flowers (often called Cut Strawberry, Primrose or Old Strawberry) and a third type with the decoration in relief. The first two types are characterized by rust red moldings. All examples of this ware are handpainted on Creamware.

Strawberry was produced by many manufacturers, but Davenport created some of the finest forms of excellent quality. Marked pieces are uncommon.

"Strawberry" ranges from complete tea services to serving pieces, including platters. While the hollow wares are highly prized, flat pieces are more rare.

Handleless Cup and Saucer, Cut Strawberry $325.00

Bowl, 6½" top dia., 3½" deep	350.00
Creamers	
4½" long, strawberries in relief . .	450.00
6¼" long, "Cut Strawberry"	300.00
Plates	
5½"	225.00
6½"	275.00
8¼"	450.00
8¼", "Cut Strawberry"	275.00
10"	400.00
Soup Plate, 8¼"	295.00
Sugar, covered, footed, "Cut Strawberry"	250.00
Teapots	
4¼ x 9½"	450.00
6 x 10½", strawberries in relief, repaired finial	400.00
7½ x 11", footed, sculptured handle	500.00

STRETCH GLASS

Stretch glass was produced by many glass manufacturers in the United States from the early 1900's through the 1920's. The most prominent makers were Cambridge, Fenton (who probably manufactured more Stretch glass than any others), Imperial, Northwood and even Steuben. Stretch glass can be identified by its iridescent, onionskin-like effect. Look for mold marks. Imports are blown and show a pontil mark and are not American Stretch Glass.

Basket, 10¼", white	125.00
Bobeches, scalloped, vaseline, pair	35.00

Vase, white iridescent, 5" $325.00

Bowls	
6½ x 2½" deep, ribbed, blue, rolled edge	50.00
10", gold	55.00
10 x 4½" deep, yellow iridescent, Imperial	85.00
13", blue, wide rim, collared base	100.00
Candlesticks 11", blue, pair	80.00
Compote, covered, 9½ x 6" dia., green, Imperial	60.00
Perfume Bottle, stoppered, 5½", bulbous, footed, blue	75.00
Plates	
6", red, paneled, Imperial	50.00
6", green	20.00
Rose Bowl, 3½ x 5", melon ribbed, pink	50.00
Sherbet, 4", red, melon ribbed	50.00
Tray, 9½", vaseline, center handle .	35.00
Vases	
5½", pink, signed Imperial	65.00
8½", Amberina, signed Imperial .	150.00
11¾", bud vase, pink	30.00

STRING HOLDERS

Grocery and dry goods stores found string holders to be useful items. Usually made of iron, there were two common types: the hanging holder and the counter-top type.

Glass

Beehive, 4¾", tin closure	35.00
Beehive, 4¾" x 5½", base, clear with applied cobalt rim and collar .	150.00
Free blown, domed, 5", applied blue rim and blue around string hole, wheel floral engraving around body	265.00

Tin, enamel decor, 4½″ high, 4″ dia. $10.00

Flint glass, 4½″	60.00
*Pattern glass, Thousand Eye, in apple green	57.00
Sandwich	150.00
Zipper and Prism, cut, sterling top	85.00

Iron

Apple	25.00
"Bulman," attaches to counter, marked	45.00
Man in top hat, smoking pipe, figural wall type	50.00

SUGAR CASTORS

Muffineers, sugar shakers or sugar castors, all served the same purpose: to 'sugar' muffins, scone or toast. They were much in vogue in the late Victorian era. Larger than salt or pepper shakers, ranging in sizes from four to six inches high, they were made in a variety of materials.

See also, specific glass categories.

Bisque, floral decor	60.00

Cranberry

Cut Bands, silverplated top	55.00
Hobnail	175.00
Ribbed, twelve, silverplated top .	70.00
Venetian Diamond, ornate silverplated top	85.00
Cut Glass, allover crosscut, sterling top	90.00

Emerald Green

Cut	180.00
Ribbed, enameled flower decor, silverplated top	75.00

Floral motif, hand painted $55.00

Frances Ware, frosted swirl and amber	125.00

Leaf Mold

Blue satin, Northwood	150.00
Cranberry	115.00
Yellow, cased, original top, Northwood	145.00

Milk Glass

Acorn

Blue	75.00
Pink	125.00
Blackberry	55.00

Forget-me-not

Blue	125.00
Green	85.00
Pink	95.00
Nettled Oak	55.00
Opalescent, See OPALESCENT GLASS	

Quilted Phlox

Amethyst	95.00
Pink	75.00
Sapphire blue	85.00
Rubina, crackle, frosted	225.00
Ruby	45.00

Satin Glass

Green, egg-shaped, blue and purple decor, original top	165.00
Pink, shading to yellow, decorated with white florals, green leaves, original pewter top	175.00

Silver

Sterling, signed Theodore B. Starr	125.00
Silverplated, English, hallmarked . . .	55.00

SUNBONNET BABIES

Molly and Mae, the Sunbonnet Babies, were created in the early 1900's by Bertha Louise Corbett. Although she was a talented artist, Miss Corbett had no confidence in her ability to draw faces, so she tried hiding the faces of her people under large bonnets and the Sunbonnet Babies were born. The "Babies" were an instant success. Illustrations of them were first used on postcards and greeting cards; then story books, quilts, porcelains and prints. "The Sunbonnet Babies Primer" was the first school primer printed in four colors. Royal Bayreuth China Co. in Germany produced most of the porcelain. Interest in all these items continues to this day; in recent years, Royal Bayreuth has brought out new Sunbonnet Babies plates and bells. Postcards are being reproduced and applique-embroidery patterns have been reprinted.

Door Stop, cast iron, marked "72", 6" $35.00

Books
ABC, 1935 edition	50.00
At Work, 1906 edition	85.00
In Holland Grove, 1915 edition . .	85.00
In Mother Goose Land, 1936 edition	50.00
Book Ends, metal, pair	65.00

Bowls
1¾", miniature, "Mending," R.B. .	135.00
6", "Washing," R.B.	150.00
8", three ball feet, gold trim, "Ironing," R.B.	195.00

Candlestick, "Mending," pair	185.00
Creamer, "Mending"	175.00
Cup and Saucer, "Ironing & Mending," R.B.	235.00
Egg Cup, double, "Sewing"	75.00
Feeding Dish, "Washing"	250.00
Mug, R.B.	115.00
Nut Dish, "Working," R.B.	150.00

Pitchers
3", "Fishing," R.B.	125.00
5¾", "Washing," R.B.	185.00

Plates
6¼", "Washing," R.B.	95.00
7", "Fishing," R.B.	115.00
8", "Ironing," R.B.	155.00
10½", cake, open handles, "Ironing," R.B.	245.00

Post Cards
Days of the Week, Ullman Mfg. Co., c. 1905, set of 7	150.00
Months of the Year, set of 12 . . .	200.00

Prints
Days of the Week, series 106, signed Corbett, set	275.00
Months of the Year, 6 x 8", Ullman Mfg. Co., c. 1906, each . .	35.00
Relish Dish, 4 x 9½", "Fishing," R.B.	195.00
Rose Bowl, 4", "Cleaning," R.B. . . .	150.00
Saucer, 5½", R.B.	95.00
Sugar, open, "Fishing," R.B.	135.00
Tile 6", "Fishing," R.B.	150.00
Toothpick, "Cleaning," R.B.	150.00

Trays
5½", diamond-shaped, "Mending," R.B.	100.00
7 x 10", "Washing," R.B.	250.00

Vases
2¾", "Sweeping," handled, R.B. . .	115.00
4¼", "Ironing," R.B.	185.00
6¼", "Mending," R.B.	275.00

SUNDERLAND LUSTRE

Sunderland ware is a coarse type of cream colored earthenware with a marbled or spotted pink lustre decoration which shades from pink to purple. A solution of gold compound applied to a white body developed the many shades of pink lustre; shades were determined by the thickness of metallic film.

Decorated with transfer prints of commemorative and sentimental scenes and inscriptions, these wares were produced by Adams, Bailey and Batkin; Copeland and Garrett; Wedgwood; Enoch Wood and many others. Also see PINK LUSTRE CHINA.

Box, 2½ x 3½ x 5", Comic, black transfer on top of cover and in bottom	90.00

Jug-Pitcher, High Level Bridge, Sailor's Farewell, 7¼" $395.00

Bowls
10", Sailor's Farewell and Sailor's Return, verses inside and out ...	275.00
10", 4½", view from the cast iron bridge	250.00
Waste bowl	55.00
Cake plate	135.00

Cups and Saucers
Babes in the Woods	85.00
Black and white transfer commemorating death of Princess Charlotte	85.00
Cloud	85.00
Handled, Allerton and Son	75.00
Mustache, black transfer of ship on front, sailor's poem on back ..	95.00
Goblet, allover lustre decor	120.00

Pitchers
5⅝", Baluster shape, strap handle, black transfer print of the bridge over the river, Wear and Ancient Order of Foresters coat of arms, pink splash lustre, c. 1825 .	300.00
6½", scene and rim in pink lustre, Davenport	275.00
6", hunting scene in black, allover pink lustre	175.00
6½", Wilkie comic scene, lustre inside and out	300.00

Mugs
Faith, Hope	175.00
4½", Iron bridge transfer, ships, peace and plenty	175.00
4", Sailor's tears and ship flying British flag	155.00

Plaques
Farmer's Prayer	110.00
Prepare to Meet Thy God	110.00
Thous God See'st Me	45.00

Plates
7", pink and floral decor	50.00
8", lady with trees harp, child ...	85.00
9", Babes in the Woods	110.00
Platter, 7½ x 8½", picture of Adam Clark, Wesleyan minister	185.00

Shakers
Pepper	85.00
Salt, round footed	75.00
Sugar	75.00

Teapots
Large, "Cloud"	265.00
Medium, "Cloud"	185.00
Wash Bowl set, bowl and pitcher, Ship Caroline	400.00

SWANSEA

This superb pottery and porcelain was made at Swansea (Glamorganshire, Wales) as early as the 1760's and production continued until 1870; but the most highly collectible examples are those made before 1830.

Marks on Swansea vary; the earliest was SWANSEA impressed under glaze to DILLWYN under glaze after 1805. CAMBRIAN POTTERY was stamped in red under glaze from 1803-1805. Many fine examples, including the Botanical series in Pearlware, are not marked but may have the botanical name stamped under glaze.

Dark brown mouldings at the rim of plates and serving dishes is a characteristic of Swansea porcelain, but not a sure mark of identification. Often, fine examples of Swansea may show imperfections such as firing cracks; these pieces must be considered mint because this is the way they left the factory.

Documented examples have not appeared in enough numbers to make Swansea popular, although it is eagerly sought by advanced collectors.

Plates
7¾", Creamware, reticulated, handpainted flowers, marked Dillwyn, c. 1805	185.00
9", "Gaudy Welsh," marked Dillwyn, c. 1810	125.00
Punch Bowl, Earthenware, in manner of Oriental porcelain, marked Cambrian Pottery, c. 1803-05 ...	950.00

Serving Dishes, Botanical Series.
Pearlware
Lily, Pink, 11½", oblong, c. 1805	325.00
Nightshade, 8", square, c. 1805	175.00
Sweetpeas, 8", square, c. 1805	165.00
Tray, Dessert, 9½", Creamware, handpainted, polychrome with gilding, marked Swansea under glaze, c. 1780	275.00

Plate, floral, signed Swansea under glaze, c. 1815, 8½″ $110.00

SWORDS

The first swords in America came from Europe. The chief cities for sword manufacturing were Solingen in Germany, Klingenthal in France, and Hounslow and Shotley Bridge in England. Among the American importers of these foreign blades was "Horstmann" whose mark is found on many military weapons.

New England and Philadelphia were the early centers for American sword manufacturing. By the Franco-Prussian War, the Ames Manufacturing Company was exporting American swords to Europe.

Sword collectors concentrate on a variety of styles — commission vs. non-commission officers' swords, presentation swords, naval weapons, and swords from a specific military branch such as cavalry or infantry. The type of sword helped identify a person's military rank and, depending on how he had it customized, his personality as well.

Following the invention of repeating firearms in the mid-19th Century, the sword lost its functional importance as a combat weapon and became a military dress accessory. Condition is a key criteria determining value.

AMERICAN

Artillery Officers', 1810, 36½″, brass
horse head pommel, checkered
ivory grip, gilded blade with Eagle
and "E. Pluribus Unium," leather
scabbard **1800.00**

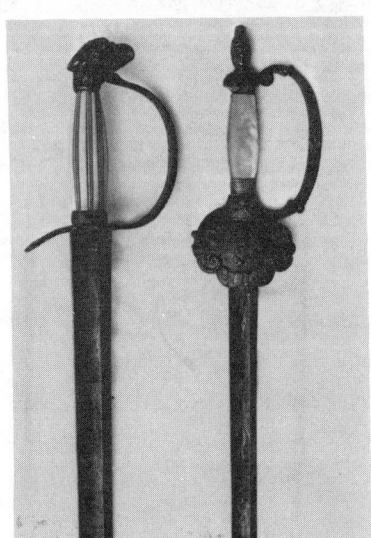

(Left) Artillery Officer's Sword with Indian head pommel, 1821–1850, $250.00; (right) Foot Officer's Saber, non-regulation, 1810 . . . . . .$350.00

Artillery, Foot, 1832, 25″, Roman
type short sword, brass Eagle
pommel, "Ames Mfg. Co.
Chichopee, Mass.," leather scab-
bard 350.00
Artillery, Light, Saber, 1840, 38″,
brass hilt, wood grip with leather
and brass wire 250.00
Artillery Officers', Mounted, 1840,
37½″, brass Eagle head pommel,
wood grip with leather and brass
wire, "Horstmann" (Philadelphia),
leather scabbard 600.00
Cavalry, Saber, Starr contract, 1818,
cast iron hilt, wood grip with leather, "N. Starr and U.S./P/LS," iron
japanned scabbard 300.00
Cavalry, Saber, heavy, 1840, 41½″,
brass half basket hilt, wood grip
with leather and brass wire, iron
scabbard 225.00
Cavalry, Saber, light, 1860, 30¾″,
brass half basket hilt, wood grip
with leather and brass wire, iron
scabbard 175.00
Cavalry, Saber, light, 1860, 30¾″,
brass half basket hilt, wood grip
with leather and brass wire, "Tiffany Company," iron scabbard 300.00

Dragoon, Saber, Ames contract, 1833, 39", iron hilt with half basket guard, wood grip with leather and brass wire, blade with "N. P. Ames, Springfield" and "United States," iron scabbard 500.00

Infantry Officers', 1821, 37½", brass Eagle head pommel, ribbed ivory grip, blade etched with Eagle and military motif, leather scabbard . . 375.00

Infantry Officers', 1820–1850, 35", brass hilt and Indian head pommel, mother of pearl or ivory grip with brass wire, blade etched with Eagle and military motif, brass scabbard 450.00

Light Horse Saber, 1790, 40½", iron hilt with lions head pommel, blade etched "American Light Horse" and Eagle motif, blade marked "Germany" 1400.00

Marine Officers', 1826, 34½", Maneluke (Turkish style) hilt, blade gilded with anchor, ship, and Indian head, high engraved brass scabbard 1500.00

Militia Staff Officers', 1840, 32¾", brass Knight's head pommel, checkered ivory grip, blade gilded with military motif, engraved brass scabbard 600.00

Militia Infantry Officers', 1830–1850, 34¼", brass hilt, pistol grip ivory pommel, military motif cast in knuckle guard, gilded blade, brass scabbard 550.00

Musicians, 1840, 34", brass hilt, leather scabbard (similar to Non-Commissioned Officers', Model 1840) 150.00

Naval, Cutlass, Starr contract, 1808, 35¼", cup shaped iron guard, wood grip, "N. Starr" and "U.S." . 900.00

Naval Cutlass, 1841, 26¼", brass hilt and grip, half basket guard, "N. P. Ames/Springfield" and "U.S.N./1843/RC," leather scabbard 450.00

Naval, Cutlass, 1860, 36", brass full basket guard, wood grip with leather and brass wire, "Ames Mfg. Co./Chicopee" and "U.S.N./DR/1862," iron scabbard 300.00

Non-Commissioned Officers', Starr contract, 1818, 31", wood grip with leather and brass wire, "N. Starr" and "U.S./P/LS," iron japanned scabbard 400.00

Non-Commissioned Officers', 1840, brass hilt, ribbed grip, kidney shaped counter guard, leather scabbard 800.00

EUROPEAN

British, Infantry, 1742, 31½", brass hilt, brass grip in spiral pattern, blade slightly curved, good condition 125.00

German, Duelling, mid-19th Century, iron basket hilt, "Solingen," iron scabbard 150.00

TEA CADDIES

Tea was a precious commodity in the past. Special boxes or caddies were used as containers to accommodate different teas, including a special cup for blending.

Around the turn of the 18th century, silver caddies appeared in England. There were also other materials used, from Sheffield plate to tin, wooden, china, and pottery. They became quite ornate and are collectible today, and are expensive when found.

Rosewood, brass hinges, dome top, inlaid fruitwood all sides, 1 compartment, 4⅛ × 4⅝ × 5 " $495.00

Apple Wood, pear shaped body with lidded top, George III Period late 18th century 350.00

Brass, square with enameled scenic side panels, cobalt blue glass knob on cover 50.00

Ceramic, melon-shaped, chinoiserie gold decor on black with original pewter fittings 350.00

Mahogany, 10½", rectangular with hinged inverted bell top, with two tole tea cannisters within, early 19th century	100.00
Paper mache, 7 x 4", with MOP inlaid cover	75.00
Pewter, globe-shaped on pedestal base, Chinese	68.00
Sterling silver, octagon, repouse of overall florals and two panels with children	80.00
Wieldon-type, oblong, rounded corners, motif and scrollwork, mottled green, brown, yellow tortoise shell glaze, c. 1765	297.50
Worcester porcelain, fluted ovoid form, painted sprays of enameled florals below turquoise trellis, diaper border outlined in gold, C-scrolls, First Period	200.00
Wooden, apple form body, with cover, late 18th century	525.00

TEA LEAF LUSTRE

A type of gold lustre decoration on ironstone china, which is more or less a stylized form of the oriental tea leaf. It was also known as "Lustre Band with Sprig." The ware was produced by a number of English and American potteries. A large amount was made by J. and G. Meakin, and it was produced by Wedgwood, Shaw, Clementson, Mayer and Grindley, and others.

Cup and Saucer; Cup 2¼" dia.; Saucer, 5¾" dia. $45.00

Bacon Rasher	15.00
Bone Dish, with scalloped rim	40.00
Bowl, 10", fruit Shaw	50.00
Bread plate, round, Mayer	32.50
Butter, covered, with insert, Meakin	75.00
Butter Pat, square, Meakin	10.00
Cake Plate, square, Meakin	35.00
Coffee Pot, 9", Meakin	100.00

Chamber Pot, covered 12-sided, Shaw	150.00
Creamer and covered sugar bowl, pair	100.00
Cups and Saucers, handleless	
Meakin	50.00
Shaw	55.00
Wedgwood	65.00
Pitchers	
Milk, 8", Mayer	45.00
Water, Meakin	85.00
Plates	
7¼", Shaw	8.00
8½", Wedgwood	10.00
9", Grindley	15.00
10", Shaw	18.00
Platters	
13", square, Meakin	37.50
14", oblong, Meakin	35.00
16½", Wedgwood	50.00
Sauce dish, oblong, Meakin	18.00
Soap dish with cover, and drain insert, oval, Shaw	75.00
Sauce boat with underplate, Shaw	50.00
Shaving Mug, Shaw	60.00
Teapot, covered, Meakin	90.00
Vegetables	
Open, square, Meakin	45.00
Covered, Meakin	65.00
Wash Bowl and Pitcher, hot water pitcher, waste jar, covered, cham-	

TEDDY BEARS

Originally thought of as "Teddy's Bears," the name comes from President Theodore Roosevelt. These stuffed toys are believed to have originated in Germany and in the United States during the 1902–1903 period.

Most of the earliest Teddy Bears had humps on their backs, elongated muzzles and jointed limbs. The fabric used was usually mohair; the eyes were either glass with pin backs or black shoe buttons. The stuffing was generally excelsior. Kapok (for softer bears) and wood-wool (for firmer bears) also were used as stuffing materials.

Quality older bears often had elongated limbs, sometimes with curved arms, oversize feet and felt paws. Noses and mouths were black and embroidered onto the fabric.

The earliest Teddy Bears are believed to have been made by what is now the Ideal Toy Corporation and a German company, Margarete Steiff, GmbH. Bears made in the early 1900's by other companies can be difficult to identify because they had a strong similarity in appearance and because most tags or labels were lost through childhood play.

Teddy Bears are rapidly increasing as collectibles and their prices are increasing proportionately. As in other fields, desirability should depend upon appeal, quality, uniqueness and condition. One modern bear has already been firmly accepted as a valuable collectible among its antique counterparts: the Steiff Teddy put out in 1980 for the company's 100th anniversary. This is a reproduction of that company's first Teddy and has a special box, signed certificate and numbered ear tag. Eleven thousand of these were sold worldwide.

20″, mohair, fully jointed, hump on back, elongated muzzle $300.00

8½″, mechanical roller skater, German	275.00
9″, mohair jointed clown with original hat and ruffle, Steiff	200.00
11″, jointed mohair "bellhop" with red felt jacket and hat, mechanical tail moves head, German	300.00
12″, mohair jointed bear with hump and long nose, early vintage	225.00
14″, wool fabric, jointed limbs and head, shoe button eyes	150.00
15″, gold long mohair, "Character" label	60.00
17″, brown mohair, jointed limbs and head, working condition bellows music box inside stomach	250.00
17″, brown plush body, tan paws, molded muzzle, Ideal Toy Corporation	45.00
20″, brown mohair, jointed, flat face, Knickerbocker	100.00

21″, brown mohair, fully jointed, open felt mouth, Knickerbocker .	250.00
22″, mohair, jointed limbs, mechanical tail moves head, English "Roddy"	400.00
24″, jointed arms, light bulb eyes that go on when stomach is pressed	225.00
20″, mohair wheeled bear with operating large growler activated by wire pull, Steiff	350.00
15″, gray mohair muff swivel head, felt paws	300.00
15″, mohair bear pair, fully clothed and jointed, attached as if dancing, Steiff	850.00
23″, white mohair, fully jointed, long muzzle, hump on back	300.00
3¾″, mohair, jointed limbs; head is removable to show glass perfume bottle inside body	150.00
3¾″, mohair, jointed limbs; head is removable to reveal hinged compact body with mirror	150.00
Horsman paper dolls including original paper envelope, bear, five costumes and two hats	350.00
20″, fully jointed, hump on back, elongated muzzle	300.00
17″, 100th anniversary limited edition issued in 1980, Steiff	300.00 +

TELEPHONES

The basic principle of the telephone was developed in Germany as early as 1854. Alexander Graham Bell was granted the first American patent in 1876 for his electromagnetic telephone. Since that time, the telephone has gone through many evolutions, improving in structure, design and function. Many so-called improvements occurred earlier than is commonly thought — in 1892, Automatic Electric Co. developed the first push-button phone using telegraph keys.

Also in 1892, Almon Strowger invented the dial phone and his patent for automatic switching still holds today. By 1900 there were over 300 phone manufacturers including such companies as Ericsson, B&B, Chicago and Western Electric.

Early telephones came in two basic model types — the candlestick phone and the cased wall phone.

Candlestick-type

Brass	120.00
Kellogg, dial	65.00
Kellogg, non-dial	85.00
Stromberg-Carlson, nickelplated trim, dial	125.00

Candlestick, brass, West. Elec. Co. Pat. Aug. 16, 1904, non dial, 1900–1913 Pat. on speaker, 11¼" ... $55.00

Desk-type

Cradle, black bakelite, c. 1930's .	10.00
French-style, c. 1920's	50.00
Lineman's, Western Electric, oak case, complete with leather strap	75.00

Wall-type

American Electric, oak case, plain front	200.00
Automatic Electric, improved rotary, c. 1905	450.00
Centralia, Chicago Parts, wet battery, carved oak case	1000.00
Centralia, Ericsson Parts, wet battery, carved oak case	3000.00
Chicago Gibson Girl, glass front .	1500.00
Ericsson, Fiddleback, copper plated, plain front, Sweden	350.00
Ericsson, Fiddleback, copper plated, chrome trim, Sweden	400.00
J.E. Atkinson, oak case, all original, Swedish-American, c. 1910 .	400.00
Kellogg, oak case, brass trim . . .	225.00
Monarch, straight walnut case, plain front	175.00
Stromberg, oak case, plain	200.00
Western Electric, Fiddleback, hook and switch and hand set . .	650.00

Western Electric, #4, with cow bells	450.00
Western Electric, oak case with cathedral top, double box	375.00
Western Electric, straight oak case, single box	200.00

TEPLITZ CHINA

Teplitz wares were manufactured in the Bohemian province of Czeckoslavakia, where Teplitz is located. In early 1900, there were 26 ceramic manufacturers in the city of Teplitz. The wares were molded, cast and hand-decorated. Most of these wares are of Art Nouveau or Art Deco style. Most items found today are marked "Teplitz" or "Turn-Teplitz" or "Turn" a city nearby, and prices recently have increased.

Vase, Amphora type, marked Crown Oak Ware Teplitz/Austria, B.B. 3803 Signed, G. Klint, 15" $1300.00

Box, covered, oval, green jasper
ware, basket-weave base, large
figural rose on cover 39.00
Busts
8″, girl, porcelain, polychrome finish, raised base 180.00
Woman, 20th century marked
"Turn-Teplitz, Bohemia" 300.00
Ewers
9″, decorated in grey and green
enameling, boy with duck, marked
"Teplitz, Stellmacher" 125.00
7″, lizard handle, hand painted florals, raised gold decor 100.00
Jug, three handled, decorated, in
brown and green, boy with dog,
marked "Teplitz, Stellmacher" . . . 70.00
Vases
4″, pinched sides, curled gold
handles, orchid decor 80.00
4½″, grey-green decor, girl with
balloon 65.00
6″, conical shape, berries and
leaves in relief 200.00
8″, amphora type, stylized birds . . 150.00
8¼″, conical shape, painted de-
sign of Arab 100.00
8″, amphora type, molded with
marigolds, polychrome glaze 280.00
9″, Pink body, white flowers, gold
neck and foot, "Turn-Teplitz, Bo-
hemia" 80.00
9″, molasses-drip glaze, applied iridescent leaves 100.00
9″, handled, yellow and pink Art
Nouveau florals on green and
white background 85.00
Twin-amphora type vase/bowl, 10
x 7″, gold handles, bunches of
grapes in high relief 95.00
11¼″, amphora-type, portrait
vase, ovoid, Byzantine maiden . . . 1900.00
12¼″, amphora type, in form of
maiden with flowing robes 220.00
14″, avacado green, violet and
gold 150.00
14″, hand painted, lavender flow-
ers outlined in red and gold on
pale yellow background, artist
signed 160.00

TERRA COTTA WARE

Terra Cotta is another name applied to wares
made of a hard, semi-fired ceramic clay. The
color of the pottery ranges from a light or-
ange-brown to a deep brownish red. It is usually unglazed, but some pieces can be found
partially glazed, or decorated with slip designs, incised or carved. All kinds of utilitarian objects have been made for centuries as

have statuettes and large architectural
pieces. Fine early Chinese terra cotta pieces
have recently brought substantial prices.

Figurine, 4½″, Italian $48.00

Busts
Chopin, black, dated 1879, V and
C, Germany 125.00
Geronimo, 8″, artist signed 150.00
Candlestand, enameled in Chinese
motif 85.00
Figurines
Beggar, 16″ 375.00
Holy Family group, Flight into
Egypt, Italian, 18th century 400.00
Horse, standing, T'ang Dynasty . . 5000.00
Inkstand with sander and inkpot, re-
clining whippet, impressed B and
Co. 180.00
Teapot
6″, Chinese, enameled people
and florals 35.00
4″, Foo dog finial 40.00
Urn, 12 x 13″, India, enameled, c.
1900 . . . . 80.00
Water pitcher 55.00

TEXTILES

Textiles are cloth or fabric items, especially
anything woven or knitted. Those that survive usually represent the best since these

were the objects that were carefully used and stored by the housewife.

Textiles are collected for many reasons — to study fabrics, understand the elegance of an historical period, and for decorative and modern use. The renewed interest in clothing has sparked a revived interest in textiles of all forms. A number of textile items have their own categories — clothing, quilts, and samplers. This category is a catchall for what remains.

Coverlet, Jacquard, blue and white, 72 x 85", woven by Samual Meily $350.00

Bedspreads
Crochet, medallion pattern, 90 x 90"	175.00
Linen, matching pillow covers, white, embroidered cut work	125.00

Coverlets, woven
Crewel, embroidered, NE, white linen, vine and leaf motif, late 18th C.	2500.00
Jacquard, blue and white, double woven, center seam, NY	475.00
Jacquard, red and white, floral, mid-19th C.	375.00
Jacquard, red, green, yellow, floral, Fehr, Emmaus, PA	525.00

Trapunto, NE, all white, tasseled fringe, 1808	2750.00

Lace
3 yds, 2½", banding with scalloped edges	30.00
3 yds, 7", small scalloped edge, fully covered with darned floral design on fine net	50.00

Lace, Battenburg
Handkerchief, 12" square	15.00
Runner, 18 x 54"	40.00
Table Cover, 49" dia.	60.00
Pillow, charity sheltering two small children, 7½ x 12"	450.00

Pillow Shams
Embroidered, ruffled eyelet borders, pair	15.00
Muslin, ruffled edge, pair	10.00
Pocketbook, Irish stitch, 18th C.	575.00
Rug, braided, wool, reversible, multi-colored, 54 x 82"	75.00

Rugs, Hooked
Crazy Quilt, 50 x 100"	800.00
Dog, brown and tan, landscape, late 19th C., 31¼ x 55"	600.00
Geometric pattern, 21 x 38"	75.00
Lion, strolling, sawtooth border, 19th C., 20½ x 61½"	1200.00
Ship, fully rigged, American ensign, 29¼ x 45"	550.00
Welcome, two cats, 19th C., 30"	475.00

Shawls, Paisley
62 x 63", self fringed	125.00
65" square, Scotland, wool, c. 1860	100.00
Sheet, homespun, seamed center	110.00

Tablecloths
Belgium linen, hand crocheted inserts and corners, 64 x 84"	100.00
Damask, red, fringed, 60 x 90"	60.00
Irish linen, hand stitched, 66 x 104", 12 napkins	80.00
Towel, cotton, wide end border in red and white with narrow side stripe, knotted fringe, 25 x 43"	

Wall Hangings
Crewel, pair, floral, 18th C., 14 x 11½"	450.00
Crewel, floral, late 19th C.	225.00
Needlework, Rebecca at the Well, wool, 24½ x 32"	275.00

THREADED GLASS

Glass decorated with applied threads is called Threaded Glass. The process was used extensively both in the United States and abroad during the 19th Century.

In the beginning, the glass threads were applied by hand. In 1876, an Englishman patented the first apparatus to apply the threads mechanically.

Threaded Glass was produced in quantity and in varying degrees of quality by practically every major glass factory and definite attribution is almost impossible. It continues to be made to the present.

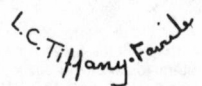

TIFFANY ITEMS

Louis Comfort Tiffany (1849–1934) established a glass house in 1878 primarily to make stained glass windows. It was here he developed a unique type of colored iridescent glass called Favrile. His Favrile glass differed from other art glass in manufacture as it was a composition of colored glass worked together while hot. The essential characteristic is that ornamentation is found within the glass. Favrile was never further decorated; different effects were achieved by varying the amount and position of colors which project movement in form and shape.

In 1890, in order to utilize surplus materials, at the plant, Tiffany began to design and produce "small glass," such as iridescent glass lamp shades, vases, stemware and tableware in the Art Nouveau manner.

Almost all of the early blown glass went to museums. Commercial production began in 1896. Most Tiffany wares are signed with the name L.C. Tiffany or the initials L.C.T. Some pieces also carry the word "Favrile" as well as a number.

Tiffany items marked with an "X" were not for sale. An "O" indicated a special order, and "A-Coll" indicated Tiffany had selected that piece for his own collection.

Prefix and suffix marks can be used to date Tiffany pieces. Prefixes A through N (1896–1900), P through Z (1901–1905) and suffixes A through N (1906–1912), P through Z (1913–1920).

Louis Tiffany and the artists in his studio are also well-known for fine work in other art areas — bronzes, pottery, jewelry, silver and enamels.

Pitcher, 6″, pink and yellow swirl, possibly Stevens and Williams $175.00

Atomizer, blue on red	60.00
Basket	100.00
Biscuit Jar, rose on clear, applied feet	135.00
Bowl, applied clear feet	140.00
Dish, cranberry on clear, opalescent interior, ruffled edge	65.00
Finger Bowls with Underplates	
Cranberry on clear, gold trim ...	65.00
Cranberry on clear, fluted edge, Sandwich	175.00
Blue on clear	55.00
Jam Jar, pink on clear, silver plated lid and handle	90.00
Pitcher	
5¼″, cranberry on clear, applied handle	125.00
12″, cranberry on clear, applied clear handle	175.00
Syrup, cranberry on clear	150.00
Tumblers	
Juice, green on clear	25.00
Water, cranberry on clear	85.00
Vases	
3″ bulbous, cranberry on green, clear rigaree top	95.00
5″, pink on clear, ruffled top ...	75.00

Bowls	
6″, gold, intaglio etched, leaves, signed	675.00
6¼″, gold iridescent, dimpled edges	495.00
Butter Pat, 3″, blue iridescent, signed	175.00
Candlesticks	
4″, gold and blue iridescent, signed, single	195.00
4½″, gold and blue iridescent, ball stem, signed, pair	260.00
16¾″, gold shade with green pulled feather design, bronze stem with purple favrile cabochons inset, shade and stem signed	1900.00

Compotes
    6½ x 6¾", pink iridescent to clear, stretched edge, rice grain decor, stem clear to iridescent white, signed 650.00
    6¾ x 7", green iridescent to clear, rice grain decor in center, stretched edge, signed 650.00
    13½ x 10½", blue iridescent, signed, 1891 .... 1850.00
Cup, gold iridescent, lily pad decor . 265.00
Dish, 3¾" dia., gold rainbow iridescent, dimpled edges 350.00
Finger Bowls
    Gold, lavender and blue iridescent, ruffled rim 465.00
    Gold iridescent, signed 500.00
    Pastel yellow opalescent, signed . 150.00
Flower Form, gold iridescent, corset form with rows of loops, signed . 150.00
Goblets
    7½", yellow, hollow Venetian stem 385.00
    7¾", pastel pink, hollow green Venetian stem 425.00

Candlelamp, gold iridescent, 12", signed "L.C.T." $1800.00

Ink Well, original insert, signed 225.00
Lamps
    Acorn, 10", oil can style, green, signed shade and base 3250.00
    Desk, 14½", turtleback, gold iridescent tiles, Dore' base 4000.00
    Floor, 5' 3½", 23" dia. leaded glass shade, Nasturtium, bronze base 35,000.00
    Lily, 20½", 6 lite, opalescent lily form shades with green pulled feathers, circular base with molded leaves and stems, bronze ... 2500.00
    Table, 22", 3 lite, gold iridescent with feather decor shades, (2 signed), green finish bronze base 3000.00
    Table, 24", 25½" dia. leaded glass shade, Lotus pattern, bronze base 14,000.00
Lamp Shades
    5 x 4", gold and blue iridescent, petal fluted top, signed 300.00
    candle, gold iridescent, signed ... 325.00
Nut Cup, 3¼", gold iridescent, ribbed, signed 125.00
Parfait, pastel blue, rice grain decor 485.00
Pendant, butterfly, 10" wing span, 6" body 1250.00
Perfume, 5¾", ribbed body, 8 sided stopper, signed 550.00
Plate, 7½", gold, stretched edge, signed 160.00
Rose Bowl, 3", gold iridescent with green leaves, white florettes, signed 1750.00
Salts
    2¼", gold iridescent, footed, signed 215.00
    2¼", gold iridescent, 2 handles, signed 225.00
    Rainbow iridescent, pulled out twists overall 210.00
Sherbets
    3¼", gold iridescent, knob stem, with underplate 300.00
    6½", green pastel onion skin, ribbed, onion white foot 435.00
    Rainbow iridescent, 8 applied lily pads, long stem 275.00
Shot Glasses
    Gold iridescent, dimpled sides ... 135.00
    Gold phantom lustre, signed 130.00
Toothpick, 1½" sq., gold iridescent, dimpled sides, signed 175.00
Vases
    3", squatty, gold iridescent, raised design, signed 425.00
    3¼", gold, cone shape, thick round base, signed 295.00
    4½", narrow neck, flared rim, 2 handles pulled from base, signed 375.00
    5", blue iridescent, signed 350.00

Vase, Favrile, signed "1067-9673L L.C. Tiffany, Favrile" $775.00

6½", cream with green palmettes, signed	550.00
6⅝", black oily iridescent ground, threaded white, lava top, signed .	650.00
8", bud vase, opalescent clambroth, gold iridescent pulled feathers, pedestal foot, signed	525.00
8", gold iridescent, signed, experimental X165	450.00
9", flower form, rainbow iridescent, ribbed, signed	775.00
10½", urn shape, brown and ochre with purple, pink, gold and green feathered decor, signed . . .	4250.00
12½", gold iridescent, 4½", round etched bronze base, signed	650.00
15", flower form, opalescent iridescent top with green feathering, green stem, gold foot with opalescent border	3500.00
Stick vase, gold iridescent shade signed, bronze base, signed	1500.00
Wines	
7¾", blue iridescent, rice grain decor, clear stem	425.00
Gold, carved leaves, signed	185.00
Pastel green iridescent, signed . .	265.00

TIFFIN GLASS

The Tiffin Glass Co., Tiffin, Ohio, a subsidiary of the U. S. Glass Co., discontinued operation in 1980.

From 1923 to 1926, they produced a line of black glassware, sometimes referred to by collectors as "Black Satin." This is very popular with collectors, and is quite collectible now. They also produced other colored glass, manufactured blanks for other concerns, and did a limited amount of cutting themselves.

Vase, black, "Poppy," 5" $35.00

Basket, 10", Black Satin	55.00
Bottle, perfume, brass plunger, Black Satin	35.00
Bowl, 4", Black Satin	35.00
Box, covered, 5", Black Satin	35.00
Compote, crystal stem, Black Satin	40.00
Console Set, bowl, with base, two candlesticks, frosted yellow	95.00
Cornucopias	
8 x 13", Blue	45.00
7 x 13", Crystal	35.00
Jar, covered, 4½", Black Satin, with red and yellow coralene	95.00
Pheasant 13", Blue	95.00
Rose Bowls	
Canterbury, Crystal	30.00
Poppy, Black Satin	40.00
Stemware, Optic, Blue, and crystal, 36 pieces	350.00
Tumblers	
Black Satin, plain	15.00
Black Satin, set of 8	100.00
Vases	
7", flower decor in gold trim	50.00
6½", gold decoration around top	50.00
10", Iris Black Satin	45.00
11", Poppy Black Satin, bulbous shape	80.00
Urn shape, 5½"	45.00
Wine Set, 6 wines and decanter, Black Satin	90.00

TILES

Decorative and utilitarian tiles have been made throughout the years by various potteries in the United States and abroad. Their usages are varied from small tea tiles or table top protectors to fireplace facings, floors and walls.

Reverse of Calendon, 1915, white with sepia, 4½ x 3¼" **$35.00**

Austrian, tea, dandelion decor	15.00
Bavarian, 6¾", basket of flowers ..	12.00
California Faience, white with blue fleur-de-lis	55.00
Copeland, country scenes, 6 x 12", signed, pair	150.00
Delft type, 6"	12.00
Grueby Faience & Tile Co.	
6 x 6", flower	100.00
6 x 6", knight	225.00
6 x 6", mermaid	225.00
Longway, 8 x 8", bird among flowers	175.00
Moravian Pottery & Tile	
4", castle and verse	35.00
4", zodiac	30.00
Mosaic Tile Co.	
Black Bear	80.00
Geometric	15.00
Paul Revere Pottery, Paul Revere riding horse, c. 1926	68.00
Proventential Tile Works, 6", girl's portrait	55.00
Staffordshire, 9 x 6", Indian woman, sepia	320.00
Stoneware, tea, horse and rider ...	15.00

Wedgwood	
8" Demetrius, c. 1880	80.00
Johnathan	85.00

TIN CONTAINERS

Tin containers were used in the early part of the 20th century for the packaging of tobacco, medicines, chemicals, powders and foodstuffs. Tins were manufactured in countless shapes, sizes and colors by U. S. and foreign companies.

Many were made plain and companies would put on their own labels. On others, the name was embossed or stamped on the tin.

Tin container collecting has become popular in the last several years. Old tins can be found almost everywhere. Prices vary greatly depending on the age and condition of the tin, and the location in which the tin is found.

CAUTION: A variety of tin containers are currently being reproduced in England exclusively for a U. S. firm. They are marked accordingly.

Tea, black with gold decor, 1 lb. $15.00

Baking Powder

Calumet, Indian Head embossed in lid, 12 oz.	7.50
Royal Baking Powder, c. 1940, with label	8.00

Biscuits — Huntley and Palmer

Artist's Studio, 7¼ x 9"	150.00
Books, bound with straps, 8" ...	135.00
Wicker hamper, c. 1904	125.00

Biscuit, Loose-Wiles

George Washington portrait, octagon 35.00
1939 World's Fair 75.00

Candy

"Burn's English Toffee," S. S. Queen Mary, 2½ x 4 x 7" 15.00
"DeWitt," round, Valentine candy, lid drawing, Colonial lady and gentleman, by Leyendecker, unsigned, red, c. 1920, 11 x 3"deep ... 35.00
Hershey's Chocolate cannister, 5 x 12½" 25.00
"Novia Popular Mixture," oval, blue and gold, hard candy pictures in color around sides, c. 1918 ... 12.50
Schraft's, large chest, lid has color map of Manhattan Island, scenes of New York harbor all around, blue and gold, hinged lid and fastening, excellent condition, 11 x 13 x 6½" 75.00
Whitman
Prestige Chocolates, 1 lb. 7.50
"Salamagundie Assortment," portrait of girl by I. Mucha, 1 lb. box, c. 1927 .... 30.00

Cigars

Mayo Roly Polys
Dutchman 500.00
Mammy 300.00
Satisfied Customer 500.00
U. S. Marine Storekeeper 650.00
"Orange Flower," 5¢ cigars, guaranteed imported, Sumatra wrapped, "Henry B. Grauley, Quakertown, Pa.," foral decor, very colorful, round, with lid, 5" .. 27.50

Cigarettes

Old Gold pocket tin 18.00
"Melachrino Egyptian Cork Tipped," blue and gold hinged lid 9 x 3½ x 3", c. 1923 .... 45.00
Murad pocket tin 18.00
Cocoa, Droste's, Haarlem, Holland, square cannister, picture Dutch boy and girl, 5½ x 3¼" 18.00

Coffee

Caddy-type, with small cover, "Perfect Coffee," japanned, bronze worn, c. 1890 .... 25.00
Capital Coffee, red store cannister, printing is upside down 275.00
Hotel McAlpin, picture of hotel .. 15.00
"Mammy's Favorite" cannister, picture of Mammy, bail handle, 4 lbs. 45.00
Royal Dutch cannister, red and white 12.00
Cough Drops, Moses, round tin, "Will Cure Coughs and Colds" .. 90.00

Crackers, Educator-Krackerland, lunch pail, animal scenes 95.00
Drawing Pencils, A. W. Faber, "Castell," colored picture of Knights Jousting, made in Bavaria, c. 1920, 6 x 2" 20.00
Gun Powder, Hazard Powder Company, original paint and label 19.00

Peanut Butter

Monarch, with Teeny Weenies, 1 lb. 95.00
Pickininny, pail 95.00
Sultana, pail 30.00

Peanuts

"Mother's Salted," cannister 40.00
Planter's, pennant, 10 lb. container 55.00
Potato Chips, "Saratoga" 16.50

Spices

Durkee's Ginger, paper label 25.00
Rich's Canton Ginger, 5 lb. 25.00
Red Pepper, "J. Harkness, Little Rock, Arkansas," girl in color on front (with pepper), 5 x 2", c. 1920 10.00

Tea

Arbuckle 15.00
"Ming Jasmine" covered, orange and gold, Oriental figures, 3½", c. 1925 .... 20.00
Sears, Roebuck, "Montclair," 3 lb. 25.00
Tetley, red, royal blue and gold, trade mark in three places, elephant holding bag of tea bags, with trunk, hinged lid, 5 x 3 x 2½" 25.00

Tobacco

Bagley's Old Colony pocket tin, picture of woman 50.00
Dan Patch Cut Plug box, 3 x 4 x 6" 35.00
Dill's Cut Plug 10.00
Edgeworth Pocket tin 10.00
Edgeworth Cannister 14.00
Half and Half pocket tin 8.00
Maryland Club pocket tin 260.00
Prince Albert, cannister, sponge in lid 12.00
Prince Albert, pocket tin 8.00
Union Leader pocket tin, with eagles 12.50
Velvet, sample pocket tin 45.00

TINSEL PICTURES

Tinsel pictures (or 'paintings') are basically a form of "cottage art" which enjoyed great popularity during the mid-19th century. The 'painting' was created by using bits and pieces of colorful foil as the primary media. A mother and her children worked on tinsel pictures as a family project.

Designs are usually simple — still life, fruit, flowers and birds. Occasionally, an exceptionally talented artist produced a more sophisticated design. The prices quoted below are general since the value of a particular 'painting' is determined by quality of the artwork and intricacy of design.

Vase of Flowers, orange, black and purple, with butterfly, walnut frame, original label $145.00

Bowl of Flowers, 9½ x 12"	85.00
Butterflies and Flowers, 8 x 10" . . .	75.00
Floral Arrangement in urn-shaped vase, 15½ x 20"	175.00
Peacock on Rock	125.00
Roses	80.00
Wild Roses, with buds and leaves, 10¼ x 22½"	95.00
Wreath with Birds, 17½ x 21½" . . .	100.00

TINWARE
See TOLE

TOBACCO CUTTERS

Before pre-packaging, tobacco was delivered to merchants in bulk form. A special tool was used to cut the tobacco into desired sizes.

Arrow	28.50
*Black Beauty	45.00
Brown Mule	35.00
*Drummond Tobacco Co., St. Louis	40.00
Five Brothers Tobacco Co., Louisville, Kentucky	50.00
*Imp	80.00

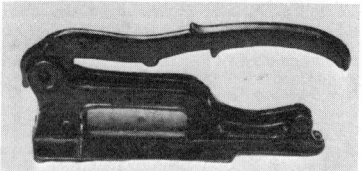

Brighton 3, cast iron	$30.00
P. Lorillard & Co.	50.00
Piper Heidsieck Tobacco Works, bottle-shaped	85.00
Spearhead, P.J. Sorg & Co.	75.00
Standard	45.00
Star	60.00
Triumph	35.00

TOBACCO JARS

A tobacco jar is a container for storing tobacco. Early tobacco humidors were made of various materials and in various shapes including figural types.

Indian Head, Majolica type, marked "No. 6628" on bottom, 8" . . . $125.00

Baker, majolica	75.00
Black Boy	85.00
Black Girl	85.00
Castle, majolica	125.00
Cossack Man	90.00
Cut Glass, zipper, silver plate lid . .	85.00

Elephant, majolica	100.00
Fisherman	65.00
Frog, smoking pipe, majolica	85.00
Gnome, wood tone	75.00
Hand Painted	
Autumn colored decor on white, Bristol	75.00
Cottage, mountains and trees, Noritake	95.00
Country scene with deer, gold trim, Nippon	275.00
Pine cones on yellow, applied pipe on lid, Austrian	125.00
Jockey, majolica	100.00
Man with Derby, Austrian	65.00
Monkeys, papier mache	150.00
Owl, majolica	65.00
Pirate, majolica	100.00
Sea Captain	70.00
Skull	70.00
Tobacco in gold letters on front, pink with floral decor, Nakara	450.00

TOBY JUGS

A Toby Jug is a drinking vessel usually depicting a full-figured, robust, genial drinking man. They originated in England in the late 18th century, and the term "Toby" probably related to the character Uncle Toby from "Tristam Shandy" by Laurence Sterne.

Within the last 100 years or more, tobies have been copiously reproduced by many potteries in the United States and England. The early ones are quite expensive while later versions are available in a wide price range.

England

Chelsea toby jug, 10", anchor mark	300.00
Delft ware, "Jolly Good Fellow"	160.00
Delft ware, full figure, blue and white, creamer size	45.00
Falstaff, impressed, 5¼"	70.00
Friar Tuck, Royal Doulton	48.00
Lord Nelson, early jug	320.00
Man holding beer glass, copper lustre decor, Allerton	50.00
Staffordshire, "Hearty Good Fellow"	250.00
Staffordshire, Squatting and holding pitcher and mug, blue coat and yellow trousers, 5½"	180.00

United States

Coachman Toby, Bennington, c. 1849	300.00
6", General Stark, seated, 1848 mark, Bennington, Rockingham glaze	375.00

Old Staffo Toby, Shorter & Son, Ltd., Staffordshire, 5⅜" **$25.00**

6¼", long haired man, seated, glass in one hand, pipe in other, loop handle, grapes, Bennington, Rockingham glaze	275.00
9¾", Toby holding mug, Bennington, Rockingham glaze	225.00
George Washington Toby, squatty, polychrome, Higgins and Seiter, mark	175.00
9", about 5½" diam. across base, water pitcher, blown glass, aqua, pontil mark, believed made in South Jersey area, c. 1925, full figure Toby, applied handle on his back	75.00

TOLE (Tinware)

Tole is the original name given to tinwares used for many household items such as boxes, pots and trays. The complete name is to'le peinte, French for sheet iron. Today collectors use "tole" as a generic name applied to stenciled or hand decorated tinwares. See **KITCHEN COLLECTIBLES** for unpainted tinwares.

**Milk Can, black with original stencilling, red and gold flowers, 8½″ .....
$150.00**

Boxes

1 x 2 x 3¼″, polychrome likeness of General Jackson, salmon pink ground 625.00

2½ x 4″, ME, rectangular form, red and green berries and leaves on white ground, early 19th C. 250.00

3½ x 6¾″, deed box, CT, rectangular form, dome lid, cherries and leaves in white banded border, early 19th C. 300.00

6 x 9¾″, deed box, NY, rectangular form, dome lid, swags & tassels, cross hatching, c. 1830 . . . . 1250.00

Candlemold, oval crimped top, 3 tapering tubes, c. 1820, 5¼″ 130.00

Cannister, CT, circular form, hinged lid, white band with cherries, brown varnish ground with flowers and leaves, early 19th C., 7½″ . . 625.00

Coffee Pots

PA, conical form, straight tapered side spout, multi-colored flowers on red ground, c. 1830, 11″ 2250.00

PA, conical form, straight tapered side spout, multi-colored flowers on black ground, c. 1830, 11″ . . . 1000.00

PA, punched work decorated, urn of flower and band motif, circular lid, outward curving spout, c. 1820, 10½″ 1250.00

Unknown, tapered cylinder, flat lid, straight spout, free hand motif, brown varnish ground 675.00

Foot Warmer, stenciled, complete with pan, c. 1850, 6½ x 8½ x 8½″ 250.00

Inkwell with sander, oval, yellow fretwork, four lion feet, 4½″ 175.00

Match Safe, wall type, shaped edges, stenciled, rural village scene, 6″ 140.00

Mugs

Advertising, red ground, stenciled label, "Wm. S. Rapp, Tin wares, stoves and roofing, 213 N. Eight St., Reading, Pa." 50.00

PA, cylindrical form, strap handle, floral and leaf motif in white band, black ground, 4″ 750.00

Sander, circular form, leaf motif against black ground, 2¾″ dia. . . 90.00

Spice Box, 6 stenciled cans, gold and red letters on black ground, rectangular wood box with sliding lid 85.00

Sugar Bowl, covered, circular, slight dome lid, bands of flowers and leaves, early 19th C., 4½″ 450.00

Sugar Shaker, circular form, pierced lid, strap handle, swag & tassels, black ground, early 19th C., 4″ . . 175.00

Tea Caddy, English, claw feet, floral on white ground, shaped hinged top, turned wood finial, 5¾ x 4¾″ 175.00

Tea Pot, oval form, strap handle, fruit and leaves on black ground, early 19th C., 6″ 1100.00

Trays

3 x 8″, oblong, interior with tulip, floral and leaf against white band 625.00

19 x 25″, Chippendale type, gold leaf and scroll border, floral center 325.00

TOOLS

Before the advent of assembly line, mass production, practically everything required for living was hand made at home or by a local tradesman or craftsman. The cooper, the blacksmith, the cabinet maker all had their special tools. Early examples of these hand tools are collected for their workmanship, ingenuity or design.

Adzes

Bowl, C. Whitehouse 80.00

Gutter, hand-forged, early 78.00

Broad Axe, Wm. Beatty & Son, Chester, Cast Steel, 23½″ $40.00

Auger, hand-forged	10.00
Axes	
Felling, Black Raven	50.00
Goosewing, hand-forged, early Pa.	300.00
Hewing, Beatty	75.00
Mortise, sample	150.00
Side, Cooper	75.00
Belt Slitter, rosewood and brass, Osborn	75.00
Brace	12.00
Brace Bits, each	3.50
Broommaker's shears	62.00
Bung Hole Bore and Reamer	25.00
Caliper, 20″, unmarked	25.00
Chisel, Corner, hand-forged, early Pa.	40.00
Croze, sawtooth-type, brass wear plates	65.00
Fence Stretcher, complete	35.00
Gauges	
Primitive, cherry	45.00
Stanley, G-4	85.00
Woodmarking	9.00
Hacksaw, hand-forged, rosewood handle	45.00
Hammers	
Brass, head	75.00
Snow Knocker, hand-forged	35.00
Howel, Cooper, small	75.00
Jointer, 4″ square x 5′ long, Cooper	175.00
Knives	
Crooked, drop handle, early	40.00
Draw, 13″, hand forged	25.00
Farrier's Hoof, bone handle	25.00
Levels	
Marples & Sons, Sheffield, England	35.00
10″, Stanley, 1896, brass trim . . .	30.00
12″, adjustable, brass filagree, Davis	85.00
Line Reel, box-type, early Pa.	30.00
Mallets	
Bookbinder's, Burl	75.00
Carpenter's, Lignam Vitae	15.00
Mitre Box, large, Stanley 2′ saw . . .	125.00

Planes	
Beltmaker's, Maple	65.00
Bullnose, ⅝″, rosewood and brass	175.00
Circular, Stanley #113, c. 1897 .	65.00
Dado, ½″ width, Stanley #39 . .	25.00
Plow, adjustable, boxwood	75.00
Rabbit, side, cast brass, mahogany handle	225.00
Rabbit, side, Stanley #98	45.00
Sun, Cooper	75.00
Tongue and Groove, Cherry	50.00
Witchet, adjustable	200.00
Plumb Bob, brass	12.00
Router, snaggle tooth, mahogany . .	35.00
Rules	
24″, folding, boxwood, brass edge and fittings	38.00
36″, folding, boxwood	45.00
36″, straight, tiger maple	50.00
Saws	
Bow	50.00
Frame, early	35.00
Scraper, Veneer, rosewood handle, Stanley	45.00
Squares	
7″, W. Marples Sheffield, rosewood, brass trim	35.00
7″, 45° angle, rosewood, brass trim	20.00
Travelers	
Brass disc, Connolly, English	150.00
Hand-forged iron	50.00
Wood disc, early Pa.	50.00
Wrench, hand-forged	8.00

TOOTHPICK HOLDERS

Toothpick holders are small containers used to hold toothpicks. They were an important table accessory during the Victorian era. They have become very popular as collectibles during the last fifty years because of their size, and because they are often a souvenir item.

Atlas	15.00
Banded Portland (Virginia #1), clear, with gold	20.00
Button Arches, Ruby top, souvenir .	14–35.00
Coal Scuttle, blue, with wire handle	22.50
Colorado, green with gold, souvenir	50.00
Cordova, green	15.00
Cut Crystal, ornate cut	45.00
Daisy and Button, vaseline, urn shape, with silver rim and base . .	55.00
Frog, holding cornucopia	37.50
Hat, Blue Finecut, top hat	37.50
Minnesota, clear with gold, three handles	27.50
Monkey, clear opalescent	65.00

Roller Skate, amber, dated 1886 . . . . $15.00

Ribbed Opal (Beatty's Rib), blue . .	50.00
Royal Ivy, frosted rubina	65.00
Ruby Thumbprint, vintage etching .	27.50
Silverplated, rabbit beside egg	16.00
Silverplated, eggshell, chick, on wishbone "Best Wishes"	28.00
Silverplated, Victorian lady beside holder, Reed and Barton	30.00
Texas, clear with gold	18.00
Thousand Eye, vaseline	40.00
Virginia #2 (Galloway)	20.00
Water Pail, glass, like old oaken bucket, bail handle, clear	45.00
Wild Bouquet, green opalescent . . .	120.00

TORTOISE SHELL ITEMS

For many years, amber and mottled colored tortoise shell has been used in the manufacture of small items such as boxes, combs, dresser sets and trinkets, which are today quite collectible.

Note: Anyone dealing in the sale of tortoise shell objects should be familiar with the Endangered Species Act and Amendment in its entirety. As of November, 1978, antique tortoise shell objects can be legally imported and sold with some restrictions.

Baby comb, tiny, folds into sterling silver case	45.00

Bracelet, 6″ $25.00
Boxes	
7 x 3″, lined	100.00
4″, covered, round, clear swirled ball finial	125.00
Combs	
4¼″, amber and brown butterfly .	50.00
4½″, amber set with red stones .	55.00
6″, amber top with rhinestones . .	75.00
Dish, 4½″, round, oriental scene in gold	85.00
Dresser Sets	
8 pieces, tray, mirror, comb, 3 brushes, shoehorn, buttonhook . .	96.00
4 pieces, powder box, hair receiver, shoehorn, cuticle knife	65.00
Fork, Pickle	55.00
Jewelry Box, grand piano shape, red velvet lining	87.50
Match holder	35.00
Mirror, hand	50.00
Tea Caddy, domed hinged cover with chamfered corners, two compartments, with ivory claw feet, first quarter 19th century	250.00
Vanity case, gold plated	57.50

TOYS

There always have been toys. They are a reflection of what is happening in any given era. Archaeologists have unearthed the remains of a 5,000 year old toy factory in India. Centuries ago, Asian and Egyptian children enjoyed dolls and toy animals.

The earliest American toys were handmade. Very few survive today. By the mid-19th century toymakers established themselves in larger American cities. The advent of industrialization coupled with the mail order catalogue made toys available to a mass market.

By 1900 toys were easily available. They tended to be of high quality. The Europeans, especially the Germans, also turned to toy manufacturing. Tin toys from Germany are among the most sought after by collectors.

Every toy is collectible. The key to a toy is condition and working order if mechanical. Toys made prior to 1955 are rising in price rapidly.

Popeye Pushing Cart, Windup **$275.00**

Arcade

Ambulance, "City Ambulance," 6"
long, 1920 .... 105.00
Auto, 1933 Plymouth, 4¾" long,
white rubber tires 24.00
Brink's Armored Truck 1875.00
Bus, 8" long, 7 side windows, c.
1930 .... 90.00
Coal car with horse 60.00
Coupe, 2 side windows, 6¾" long,
c. 1922 .... 90.00
Fageol Safety Coach, 12½" long,
rubber tires, 1920 .... 150.00
Fire engine, 9" long, 1930s 60.00
Manure spreader with team of
horses, "McCormick-Deering" .. 90.00
Plow, one horse, 10½" 120.00
Steam roller, 4½" 72.00
Yellow Cab, 5" long 285.00

Auburn Rubber

Cadillac, 1936 .... 15.00
Oldsmobile sedan, 4 door, 6"
long, 1940 .... 25.00
Tank, 4½" long 5.00

Buddy L

Curtis Candy Truck 140.00
Greyhound Lines bus 95.00
Robotoy dump truck, with driver,
remote control 550.00
Station wagon, 15½" long, 1950s 15.00
Stock car, 10½" 30.00
Trencher, 1928–31 .... 250.00

Champion

Gas & Motor oil truck, 8", cast
iron, c. 1930 .... 50.00
Race car, 9" long, 1930s 65.00

Dent

Bus, 6¼" long, cast iron, sample 100.00
Fire truck, 7" long, cast iron, sample 65.00

Hose reeler with men, cast iron,
large 275.00
Ox cart, stake sides, one ox 18.00
Steam roller, 6" long, cast iron .. 70.00

Hubley

Bell Telephone truck, 9" long, with
implements 225.00
Bus, 5½", rubber wheels, c. 1938 45.00
Cart, 8" long, horse and driver .. 30.00
Fire engine, No. 526, 10½" long,
c. 1936 .... 55.00
Huber road roller 100.00
Milk and cream truck, 3½" long,
white rubber tires, 1920 ...... 125.00
Railroad Express Truck, 5" long,
rubber tires 115.00

Ives

Dog pulling stake cart 175.00
Horseless carriage runabout, 6½"
long, 6" high to top of jockey cap
on driver 1500.00
Steamer, 19½" long, 2 drivers,
cast iron 325.00

Kenton

Band wagon, musicians, driver,
rider on horse 160.00
Buckeye ditching machine 300.00
Dump cart, mule 95.00
Plantation cart, 10" long, black
driver, mule 70.00
Steam roller, "Gallon Master,"
6½" long 50.00
Tow auto, 9½" long, 1920s 1200.00

Kingsbury

Caterpillar, 8½" long, windup ... 175.00
DeSoto, 14½" long, pressed
steel, windup, c. 1938 .... 60.00
Ladder truck, 13" long, cast iron,
tin & wood, 1900 .... 175.00
Rack truck, 16" long, pressed
steel, windup 275.00

Lehmann

"Africa," ostrich pulling cart, tin,
friction toy 195.00
Bucking Broncho, Wild West, 6½"
long 275.00
Climbing Miller, cardboard blades 250.00
"Express," porter pulling cart, 6"
long, c. 1927 .... 185.00
"Lu-Lu," 2" 9.00
OHO, patented 1903 .... 200.00
Rooster pulling egg cart, rabbit
perched on top, tin, friction 350.00
"Tom," climbing monkey, 8" long 120.00

Marx

Acrobatic Marvel, early 50.00
Air Mail monoplane, 2 engine,
1930 .... 125.00
Balky Mule, pre-1940 .... 55.00
Dump truck, No. 1084 .... 20.00
Gang Buster Car No. 7200, 14"
long, 1930s 70.00

Marx, car, windup $87.50

Jalopy pickup truck, 7″	28.00
Main Street, 1929	90.00
Panel wagon	15.00
Rex Mars tank, windup	55.00
Siren Police Car No. 8300, 14″ long, 1930s	100.00
Tricky Taxi, 4½″ long, friction ...	23.00

Strauss

Big Trixo, climbing monkey, 10″ long	45.00
Black Porter pulling wheelbarrow, 6¼″	125.00
Jackee the Horn Pipe Dancer, 8½″ long	275.00
Speedwagon	70.00

Structo

Army truck with canvas top, 21″ long	50.00
Dump truck, open cab, 18″ long, c. 1930	90.00
Garbage truck, 21″ long	40.00
Steam shovel, 16″	50.00

Tootsietoy

Armored car	20.00
Automobiles	
Buick Roadster, 1926	25.00
Buick sedan, 1926	20.00
Cadillac coupe, 1926	30.00
Chevrolet roadster, 1926	28.00
Oldsmobile Brougham, 1926 ..	27.00
Fire engine water tower	25.00
Funnies Set "Andy Gump" roadster, standard version	125.00
Mack Insurance Patrol in garage .	40.00
TransAmerica bus, in set only, 1941	85.00

Unique

Bombo the Monk, 1940s	45.00
Dandy Jim, dancer, 1921	190.00
Krazy Kar, litho	180.00
Musical Sail-Way	14.00
Rollover Motorcycle Cop, 1935 ..	100.00
Skyranger's Plan and Zeppelin, revolving from tower, 1933	85.00

Miscellaneous

Buster Brown, cast iron, painted ...	125.00
Cap Guns, cast iron	
Buddy	18.00
Daisy, Pat. Apr. 1873	50.00
Ohio, Kenton, 1930	14.00

Dog Patch Lil Abner Band, windup .	450.00
Erector Set, A.C. Gilbert, Set No. 9, complete	50.00
Ford Tri-Motor, 25″ wingspan, pressed steel, 1930s	85.00
Foxy Grandpa roly poly, painted papier mache	55.00
My-T-Fine Grocery Store, folds out to 8 x 3″, 1930	40.00
Riverboat, 7½″ long, cast iron, c. 1910	185.00
Soldiers	
Auburn, rubber, each	5–10.00
Barclay, lead, each	5–10.00
Composition, each	2–4.00
Manoil, lead, each	5–10.00
Playwood Plastics, each	2.50–5.00
Stove, Eagle, 4¼″ high, cast iron ..	50.00
Spirit of America, 14″ long, steel and litho, pull toy	24.00

TRAINS, TOY

Railroading was an important part of any youngster's childhood, largely in part because of the romance associated with the railroad and the emphasis on toy trains. Almost everyone had a train layout. Basements, back rooms, or attics allowed the layout to remain up year-round.

The first toy trains were cast iron and tin. The wind-up motor added movement to the trains. The Golden Age of toy trains was from 1920–1955 when electric powered units were widely available. The construction and details of the rolling stock were of high quality. The advent of plastic in the late 1950's lessened this quality considerably.

Toy trains are designated by a model scale or gauge. The most popular are HO, S, and O. Gauge affects price as does age and condition. American Flyer and Lionel are the two firms which dominated the market during the golden period.

Lionel, No. 10, Electric standard gauge; #332, bag car; #339 pullman; #341 observation; Peacock illuminated cars, c. late 1920's–1930 .. $300.00

AMERICAN FLYER

Cars

625, Tank, Gulf, S	7.00
629, Cattle, red, S	8.00
639, Box, yellow, S	12.00
928, Log Carrier, S	7.50
941, Gondola, S	6.00
3007, Gondola, lithographed, O	9.00

Locomotives

300, 4-4-2, S	40.00
307, Reading, black with plastic tender, S	20.00
322, 4-6-2, NYC, smoke unit	80.00
350, B & O, S	65.00
1218, 0-4-0, Streamliner, O	65.00

Sets

Silver Bullet, 356, S	100.00
Streamliner, 556, two coaches 495, and two baggage cars 494, O	200.00

LIONEL

Cars

214, Box, orange, S	50.00
217, Caboose, red, S	65.00
309, Pullman, blue, S	45.00
529, Pullman, green, O	25.00
652, Gondola, yellow, O	12.00
653, Hopper, green, O	12.00
657, Caboose, O	25.00
817, Caboose, O	10.00

Locomotives

224, 2-6-2, 2245 tender, O	125.00
225E, 225W tender, O	225.00
238E, steam, tender, O	125.00
249, tender, black and nickel trim, O	150.00
318E, green, electric, S	175.00
384, 2-4-0, black with green stripe, steam, S	275.00
1688, tender, O	40.00

Sets

Flying Yankee, 616 with two 9167 coaches, and 618 observation car, gun metal	300.00
Junior, wind-up engine, tender, and two cars	200.00

TRAMP ART

Tramp Art was prevalent in the United States from about 1875 into 1930. These items were made by itinerant artists, who left no record of their identity. They used old cigar boxes, fruit and vegetable crates, and edges of items were chip-carved and layered, which created a unique effect. Finished items were usually given an overall stain, and they are collectible today as an example of a special type of crafted wood work.

Picture Frame, 26 x 20" $150.00

Boxes

Covered, layers, of chip-carved designs	50.00
Jewelry, (or sewing), hidden compartment in lid, trick locking device, inlaid names on lid, "Edith and Amy"	300.00
Jewelry, 9¼ x 11½", old gilding with green cloth insert panels in very good condition interior, lid and mirror	65.00
Sewing, octagonal, 13 x 13", 4 drawers and open top with 8 thread spindles and large central pincushion	42.50
Wall hanging, 6½ x 11", chip carved layers of wood	57.50
Clock, case with layers of chip-carved designs, original works	175.00
Corner shelf, chip carved edges and applied ornaments	175.00
Doll chest of drawers, made of wooden cigar boxes, original mirror, brown alligator finish	65.00
Foot stool	35.00

Frames

10 x 12", layers of chip-carved wood	25.00
16 x 34", overall, layers of chip-carved wood in "crown of thorns" design	100.00
Letter Opener, "Christmas 1906"	10.00

TRIVETS

A trivet is a three-legged stand used to support hot vessels, either in an open fireplace, in workrooms or on table tops. The popular collectible trivets are those which were used to hold the early hand irons. These trivets were usually very ornate, incorporating designs of animals, birds, flowers, fruits, etc.

All listed are cast iron, unless otherwise designated.

Jenny Lind, cast iron **$50.00**

Bar and Holes, Open railings	15.00
Cathedral	22.00
Chevrons	25.00
Christmas Tree	25.00
Colt	20.00
Crown and Cross	15.00
Eastern Star	35.00
Enterprise Mfg. Co.	15.00
Fern & Urn	20.00
Fireplace, 8½ x 23″, adjustable . . .	150.00
Fox and Geese Tracks	45.00
Fox and Grapes, brass	75.00
Good Luck (no horseshoe), brass .	65.00
Harp	40.00

Harp, brass	95.00
Hearts	
Circle	25.00
Double, 2 stars	140.00
Single, hand wrought, 18th century	200.00
Single, with star center	45.00
Triple, brass	125.00
Hex Sign, hand wrought	175.00
Horseshoes	
Brass & Iron, hickory handle	90.00
Good Luck, eagle	30.00
Masonic emblem	45.00
Masonic emblem, brass	125.00
Rose	35.00
Lacy Lantz	35.00
Lacy Urn, wavy railing	50.00
Leaf and Scroll, brass	95.00
Letters, in center	20.00
Love Birds, brass	140.00
Lyre, brass, English	75.00
Sensible	40.00
Spade, lacy	75.00
Star, brass	75.00
Star, open handle	40.00
Sunflower	25.00
Swastika	25.00
Target	35.00
Triple-eight, brass	75.00
Turtle	35.00
Turtle, brass	75.00
Waffle, octagonal, no railing	35.00
Washington, George	100.00
Wilton	40.00

TRUNKS

Trunks are portable boxes or containers that clasp shut for the storage or transportation of personal possessions. Many trunks arrived in America during the immigration movement. These early trunks are now being sought, restored and used for a multitude of purposes. Prices will vary considerably depending on size, shape and condition.

Dome Top

Metal covered pine or poplar, wooden slats	75.00
Wood, ladies' hat trunk, fitted interior	125.00
Wood, metal slats	85.00
Wood, wooden slats, completely refinished, new leather handles, relined with cloth	125.00 +

Flat Top

Canvas covered pine, wooden slats, c. 1910	75.00
Leather covered pine, metal slats, brass studs, corner protectors and handles, Chinese	150.00

Dome Top, leather covered, initialed with nail heads, iron hardware and rivets, 26½ x 15 x 12½″ $150.00

Paper covered poplar, iron hardware	50.00
Wood, oak, dovetailed and pegged construction	350.00

TUCKER CHINA

William Ellis Tucker, (1800–1832), was the son of a Philadelphia schoolmaster who had a small shop on Market Street, where he sold china which he imported from France. William helped in the shop and became interested in the manufacture of china.

In 1820, a sample of the white-clay kaolin, from a Pennsylvania Chester County farm, was discovered, and the business started in earnest for William. Kaolin is the prime ingredient for translucence in porcelain, and they had a plentiful supply close at hand. The business prospered but not without many trials and financial difficulties. He had many partners, and the marks found on Tucker china are "William Ellis Tucker," "Tucker and Hulme" and "Joseph Hemphill." Workmen's incised initials are sometimes found.

The business operated between 1825 and 1838, when Thomas Tucker, William's brother, was forced by business conditions to close the firm. There are very few pieces available for collectors today and almost all known pieces are in collections or museums. But you never can tell!

Pitchers
White, floral decor all over, large square handle, "Walker" type . . .	1750.00
White, floral spray decor, gold trim "Walker" type	1750.00
White, fruit and leaves decor, "Walker" type	1750.00
White, floral decor, banded, jug shape type, c. 1830–1836	2000.00

Pitcher, sepia landscape on both sides, 9⅝″, unsigned $1250.00

White, sepia, polychrome scene decor	2000.00
White, colored wide band, and floral decor	2000.00
Teapot, boat shaped, polychrome scene decor	2500.00

VAL ST. LAMBERT

Val St. Lambert Cristalleries of Belgium was established in the early 1800's. They feature exquisite cased glass, heavily cut and engraved. The company is still in existence and produces many types of glass.

Ashtray, clear crystal, signed	45.00
Bowls	
6″, cranberry swirl	85.00
11½″, crystal and cranberry	175.00
Boxes	
4″ square, blue, cameo cut rose poppies	270.00
Powder, Art Deco, frosted	38.00
Perfume Bottles	
6½″, crystal cut to yellow	275.00
6½″, etched	95.00
Blue frosted, red flowers, signed .	225.00
Tray, 6″, crystal, gold trim	100.00
Vases	
6″, cranberry swirl	80.00
Cameo, blue and purple frosted .	425.00
Cameo, red to clear	340.00

Vase, cameo cut, purple tulip,
9½″ $475.00

VALENTINES

Esther Howland was the first American artist to create Valentine Day messages commercially. As the custom to send affectionate greetings on this special day developed, other artists and printers followed. The Victorians delighted in receiving and sending elaborately decorated cards and the majority of the collectible cards are from this era.

The price range for early Valentines is wide, from a few dollars to hundreds of dollars. Quoted prices listed are general and will vary according to composition, condition and size.

Artists

Addenbrooke	35–50.00
Brundage	15–20.00
Dobb	50–100.00
Greenaway	25–50.00
Howland	50–100.00
Meek	10–20.00
Nester	15–25.00
Tuck	15–25.00
Whitney	10–15.00

Sailor's Valentine, dresser piece, mirrored, shell encrusted, 4¾″ wide, 5¾″ high $75.00

Types

Comic	3–5.00
Comic, mechanical	10–15.00
Fold-out	15–25.00
Handmade	5–10.00
Lithographed	10–20.00
Mechanical, lacy	15–20.00
Sailor's	25–75.00
Theorems	100–200.00

VALLERYSTHAL GLASS

Vallerysthal (Lorraine), France, has been a glass producing center for centuries. In 1872, two major factories merged and produced art glass from 1898. Later pressed glass covered animal dishes were introduced. The factory continues operation today.

Box, 3½ x 4″, covered, blue milk glass	65.00
Candlestick, Grecian Girl, frosted, single	45.00
Dishes, covered	
Beehive, 5″, clear glass	65.00

Duck, 4½″ high, brown top, green base $75.00

Cow and pasture scene on cover, 7″, clear glass	75.00
Dog, 4½″, blue	45.00
Dog, 4½″, white milk glass	55.00
Hen, 2½″, cobalt	20.00
Swan, milk glass	95.00
Dish, Jam, 4½ x 3½″, covered, deep blue	22.50
Goblet, footed, blue	50.00
Jar, Jam, Grape and Leaf	60.00
Pitcher, Grape and Leaf, vaseline, frosted	22.00
Plates	
6″, Thistle	75.00
7″, floral decor, blue	32.00
Salt Dip, Ram's Head	40.00
Salt Shaker, Chicken on Nest	35.00
Tumbler, 4″, cobalt	40.00

VAN BRIGGLE POTTERY

Born in 1869, Artus Van Briggle was a talented Ohio artist who studied in Paris for three years prior to working at Rookwood. In 1901, he moved to Colorado for his health and established his own pottery in Colorado Springs. In that year, he produced his famous "Despondency" vase.

Van Briggle's work was heavily influenced by the Art Nouveau "school" he saw in France and he produced a great variety of matte glazed wares in this style. Glazes varied, but the most famous were Ming and Persian Rose.

In the beginning, "AA" mark was incised by

hand on each piece along with the date and words "Van Briggle." Later, stock numbers were stamped on items and the letters "U.S.A." followed the mark from 1922 to 1929. After 1920, the words "Colorado Springs, Colorado" (or an abbreviation) were added. When Artus died in 1904, his wife Anne continued the pottery operation. Van Briggle Pottery continues to be made today.

Vase, molded pattern, purple mauve glaze, 4½″ $32.00

Bookends	
Puppies, brown	125.00
Peacock, Ming, pair	150.00
Bowls	
2¾ x 8¾″, dragonflies, Persian Rose, c. 1922	70.00
3 x 5½″, acorn and oak leaves, green and brown, c. 1910	175.00
5 x 10″, triangular leaves, Ming, c. 1917	120.00
7 x 11″, four handles, daisy, Ming	85.00
10½ x 11 x 15″, kneeling nude, maroon and blue	195.00
Candlesticks	
2¾″, leaf base, brown, pair	45.00
3½″, tulip-shaped, Persian Rose, pair	65.00
4¼″, high glazed black with blue and white drip, signed Anne Van Briggle, pair	1500.00
10½″, flowers and vines, Ming, c. 1906	200.00
Console Set, Siren of the Sea, with frog, two dolphin candlesticks ...	600.00
Figures	
Dog, 2″, Persian Rose	75.00
Indian Girl, 6″, turquoise	70.00
Rabbit, 2½″, plum, c. 1917	150.00
Flower Frog, 1¾ x 4″, dome-shaped, oak and leaf, Ming	25.00
Lamp Bases	
6″, Mission-style, bluish gray, c. 1914	150.00

Mulberry Moth	135.00
Planter, 4¼ x 12½", Dragonfly, Persian Rose	70.00
Vases	
3", royal blue, c. 1917	75.00
3", bulbous, mistletoe, deep green and brown, c. 1907	300.00
5", plum, c. 1919	65.00
7", vertical line, yellow and green, shape #690, c. 1915	225.00
8", urn-shaped, floral decor, Ming, c. 1917	175.00
9¼", Lorelei, Ming, c. 1919	150.00
10", Daffodils, c. 1920	140.00
11½", Indian heads, Persian Rose	150.00
12", urn-shaped, two handles, maroon, c. 1920	200.00
13", maroon and dark blue, shape #748, c. 1930	175.00
Wall Pocket, Lotus	55.00

Mug, mottled blue and green	45.00
Rose Bowl, mottled white and lavender	50.00
Tumbler, blue and white	40.00
Vase, 8½", mottled blue shading to pink	95.00

VENETIAN GLASS

Venetian glass has been made on the island of Murano, near Venice, since the 13th century. Most of the wares are thin walled. Many types of decoration have been used — embedded gold dust or lace work and applied fruits or flowers. Venetian glass continues to be made today.

VASA MURRHINA GLASS
See SPANGLED GLASS

VASART *Vasart*

Vasart is a contemporary art glass made in Scotland by the Streathearn Glass Co. The colors are mottled and sometimes shade from one hue to another. It is readily identified by an engraved signature on the base.

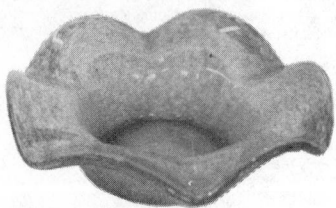

Ashtray, mottled light blue, 4½" dia., signed $48.00

Paperweight, blue and goldstone millefiori accents, crystal base, 13" $195.00

Baskets	
4 x 6", mottled blue	65.00
6" high, blue, yellow, loop handle	70.00
Bowls	
4" dia., yellow at base, speckled at top	70.00
4 x 6", mottled pink at bottom, green at rim, handles	55.00
9 x 3½" deep, orange, black and clear	75.00
Hat, signed	25.00

Basket, 5½ x 8 x 10½", crystal . . .	195.00
Bowls	
9½", crystal, gold decor	85.00
4 x 7 x 10", rubena, footed base, applied amber flowers	165.00

Candlesticks
5", dolphin, crystal with gold dust	55.00
12", crystal with gold dust, pair . .	125.00

Candy Jar, covered, 10½", enameled floral decor	70.00
Cologne Bottle, 7½", crystal with applied rigaree	75.00
Compote, 7", cranberry, crystal dolphin stem	150.00
Cruet, lavender, double swirled . . .	95.00
Cup and Saucer, demi-tasse, multi-colored	70.00
Finger Bowl with Underplate, diamond optic	50.00

Goblets
4", dolphin, mica flakes	30.00
8", ribboned and gold dust	125.00
Pitcher, crystal, gold flecked	125.00

Plates
7½", pink, gold dust	25.00
8½", pink, diamond optic	20.00
Salt, open, pink, gold trim	25.00
Sherbet, 7", pink and green blown .	50.00
Toothpick, pastel ribboned and lacy, handled	45.00

Vases
7½", blue swirl, fluted top	75.00
9½", rose shading to peach, ruffled top, applied green leaves . . .	165.00
11", urn shape, pink, gold dust . .	195.00
18", red shading to clear, white enameled floral decor, gold trim .	225.00

Wines
Dolphin, pink and green, gold dust	30.00
Pink, diamond optic	30.00

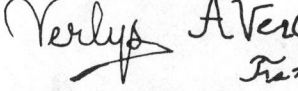

VERLYS GLASS

Verlys Glass is a type of art glass originally made in France after 1930. For a period of a few months, Heisey Glass Co., Newark, Ohio, produced the identical glass, having obtained the rights and formula from the French factory. The French-produced glass can be distinguished from the American product by the signature; the French is mold marked, the American is etched script signed.

Ashtrays
3", swallows, script signed	35.00
3½", florals, script signed	40.00
4½", frosted doves, floral border, script signed	40.00

Bowls
5", frosted roses, mold signed . .	35.00
8¾", thistle, script signed	65.00
9", thistle, mold signed	90.00

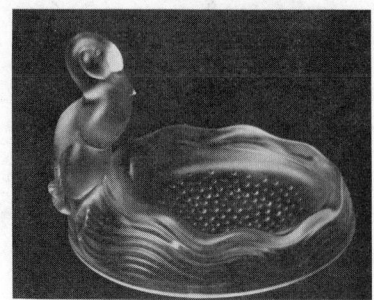

Ashtray, 6" oval, mold marked, signed French $40.00

13", frosted angel fish, mold signed	180.00
13", wild ducks, script signed . . .	115.00
14", dragonflies, script signed . . .	160.00

Boxes
3¾ x 5", horses, script signed . .	65.00
6½", butterflies, script signed . . .	95.00
hinged, florals, script signed	70.00

Dishes
4½ x 6½", lovebirds	45.00
6", candy, frosted pinecones . . .	30.00

Plates
5", clear and frosted fish	50.00
6¼", pinecones, mold signed . . .	55.00
14", birds and fish	75.00
Trivet, 11", oval, amber, aquatic plants	150.00

Vases
5", lovebirds, mold signed	105.00
6½ x 6½", opalescent, large blown out berries, script signed . .	175.00
7", florals, script signed	80.00
10½", frosted forest	125.00

VERRE DE SOIE GLASS
See STEUBEN

VILLEROY & BOCH

The founder of one of the original potteries that eventually became Villeroy and Boch was Pierre Joseph Boch who established a factory near Luxemburg, Germany, in 1767. His son, Jean Francis, attained the distinction of introducing the first coal fired kiln in Europe and perfecting a water power driven potter's wheel. Other potteries in the area

were those of Mettlach, managed by Pierre's grandson, Eugene, and Nicholas Villeroy's factory.

A consolidation of these three firms was effected in 1841 and became known as Villeroy and Boch. Early production included a hard paste earthenware comparable to English Ironstone. This ware continues to be made today for their line of tablewares.

It was the combined talents and efforts of this organization that initiated decorated stonewares known the world over as Mettlach.

See also METTLACH.

Platter, 12¾", "Villeroy & Boch/ Mettlach/Gesehutzt", Remagen, Dec. 158, impressed 1044 ......$245.00

Bowls
8", floral decor	50.00
10½", handled, blue floral decor .	95.00
Bread Board, 5½ x 8½", white ...	95.00
Butter, covered, design in relief, tan and green	125.00
Cider Set, tankard pitcher, 6 tumblers, baseball theme, set	225.00
Cruet, 8½", blue and white	55.00
Fish Mold, 8" long, brown and white	60.00
Mug, figural leaves, twig handle, 6", cream with raised blue lines	55.00

Pitchers
Vintage decor, blue on white ...	50.00
7½", florals in relief, handpainted	75.00
9", light to dark green	95.00
Plaque, 13¾", blue with white portrait center, tan decorated border, c. 1885	395.00
Plate, 12", blue and white	55.00
Platter, 12 x 18" blue and white, deer scene	120.00
Ramekin, with underplate, blue and white	30.00
Syrup Jug, lidded, 4", blue and white	45.00
Teapot, 6¼", white with blue decor	100.00

Tile, 6 x 6", Dutch scene, blue on white	50.00
Tureen, Soup, covered, 12½", with underplate, blue and white	275.00

Vases
5½", Amphora-type, apples and leaves, "Yorkshire"	55.00
7½", beige figures in relief on tan ground, silver lustre trim	225.00
9", cherubs in relief, white	125.00
10", Art Deco	130.00

WARWICK CHINA

Warwick China Manufacturing Co., Wheeling, W. Va., began operation in 1887 and continued until 1951. They were one of the first manufacturers of vitreous glazed wares in the United States. The date 1887 is when the incorporation papers were issued; there is some question that some pieces may have been made before then. There are pieces of experimental eggshell type of porcelain made before 1887 that are very rare.

Hand painted Warwick is more valuable than pieces decorated by decals. The most desirable are portrait items and special pieces for fraternal organizations such as the Elks, Eagles, and Knights of Pythias.

Their production lines were extensive, including tableware, garden ornaments, decorative and utilitarian items.

Pitcher, brown with rose motif, "IOGA", 10½" $90.00

Ale set, tankard and six mugs, dog portraits, 7 pieces **325.00**

Bean pot, covered, double handled, florals **58.50**

Cheese dish, covered, roses decor with gold swirled trim and gold handle **38.50**

Jar, Marmalade, covered, handled, earth brown, and pale yellow . . . **85.00**

Jardiniere, large, scene, signed "Beck" **385.00**

Mugs

  Hobo, wearing top hat and playing guitar **65.00**

  Scene of lady waving goodbye to calvary man, brown background . **65.00**

  Picture of fisherman, "IOGA" . . . **55.00**

Pitchers

  Lavender flowers and gold trim . . **43.00**

  Lemonade, pinched spout, monk on shaded brown background . . **165.00**

Punch bowl and 12 matching cups, (rare) **225.00**

Plate, 10¼", "Poppy" pattern, artist signed **85.00**

Vases

  11", hand painted, roses and foliage on brown, shading to tan background, pair **235.00**

  13", wide across base, portrait of monk sipping from mug **300.00**

  12", stick vase, arranged poppies **75.00**

  10", two handled, pointsetta on reddish background, excellent glaze **65.00**

  10", "Lady of the Night" portrait, Gray, IOGA **145.00**

Umbrella Stand, 21", portrait and scene **500.00**

WASH BOWL AND PITCHER SETS

Before the advent of indoor plumbing, the wash set was an essential part of every household. The water pitcher and wash basin were the basic set. More complete sets of other essentials were available, and a full set would contain a wash bowl and pitcher, toothbrush holder, soap dish with drain and cover, (which were sometimes round, and sometimes oblong in shape), shaving mug, and large waste jar with lid, and a smaller pitcher for hot water.

Very few complete sets are still intact. They were made by practically every major ceramic manufacturer in the United States and abroad in varying degrees of quality. Many are imported today from Europe, and they are also being reproduced.

Miniature, 5 pc. white with multicolor floral decor, dark blue rims, gold trim, c. 1830 . . . . **$300.00**

All white, embossed florals, ironstone, 2 pieces **75.00**

All white, embossed and figural elephant-head on chamber pot lid, and handle on soap dish, 4 pieces **200.00**

Clematis, transfer on white, brown decor, bowl and pitcher, marked "T. G. Booth" **95.00**

"Cyprus" Davenport, washbowl and pitcher, mulberry **600.00**

Flowing Blue, florals interior and exterior, Mason's Patent, pitcher and bowl **300.00**

Flowing Blue, gilt, embossed and scalloped rims, oblong bowl and bulbous pitcher, marked Royal Doulton **350.00**

Flowing Blue, wash bowl and pitcher, "Nile" **260.00**

Flowing Blue, wash bowl and pitcher, "Pelew" **595.00**

Flowing Blue, wash bowl and pitcher, "Scinde" **650.00**

Mason's wash bowl and pitcher, white with orange-red rims, and dragon handle blue flowers, marked "Ashworth" **450.00**

Medium blue, Staffordshire transfer pattern, English scenery, floral border, no mark, 2 pieces **125.00**

Transfer, English Staffordshire, "Eagle," no mark, wash bowl and pitcher, light grey-blue, 2 pieces . **350.00**

Weller pottery bowl, pitcher, toothbrush holder, soap dish **95.00**

White ironstone, wash bowl, pitcher, soap dish, toothbrush holder, with gold borders, 4 pieces **210.00**

WATCH FOBS

A watch fob is a useful and decorative jewel-

ry item attached to a man's pocket watch. Fobs have been of interest to men since the Victorian age. The advertising-type fob became popular in the 1870's and continues today. The majority of these fobs are metal that have been die-struck. Companies gave these fobs as a media of advertising.

Special fobs were also designed to commemorate events, places and people. Watch fobs continue to be made today some are restrikes of the earlier ones, others are totally new designs.

State Farm Mutual Auto Ins. Co., black leather strap $18.00

Art Nouveau Maiden, advertising on reverse	30.00
Atlas Life Insurance Co., Tulsa, Okla	30.00
BPOE, c. 1912	35.00
Betsy Ross, gold mesh strap	45.00
Bottle opener	20.00
Bred in Kentucky	25.00
Buick, enameled, c. 1920	75.00
Caterpillar, c. 1954	15.00
Century of Progress	20.00
Columbia Expo. 1893	50.00
Copper Clad Ranges, original ribbon	30.00
Dr. Pepper, with Billiken	75.00
Fireman's Convention, c. 1920	19.00
Fish, enamels on sterling silver . . .	40.00
Football Player, c. 1925	15.00
Gamewell Fire Alarm Telegraph Co., copper	25.00
Gold Mesh with hanging crown . . .	50.00
Indian, Sterling	45.00
Initials, cut-out, brass	20.00
International Harvester, c. 1960 . . .	18.00
Iowa Dairy Assoc., 1911	27.00
Mack Trucks, c. 1960	20.00
McCormick	25.00
Memphis Furniture Mfg. Co., enameled, original strap	35.00
Minneapolis Tractor	15.00
100F	10.00
OVB, souvenir-type	30.00

"Over Sea . . . to Give Kaiser Hell," c. 1917	45.00
Pennsylvania, c. 1915	25.00
Pepsi Cola	25.00
Pioneer Coal & Timber Co., Oklahoma City, Okla	35.00
Roosevelt-Cox, c. 1919	55.00
Tractomotive	15.00
Vol. Fireman, c. 1948	15.00
Washburn, Crosby Flour	24.00

WATCHES

The first watch, basically a miniature table clock, was made in Germany in 1500. Nuremberg, Germany and Blois, France, became early production centers. Later Geneva and London were prominent watchmaking centers while in the United States, watchmaking was practiced by the clockmakers of the period on a very small scale.

Early watches were regarded more as jewelry than time pieces. When the balance spring was introduced in 1675, accuracy increased and watches achieved a new image.

Abraham Louis Brequet, a Swiss born genius who worked in Paris in the late 18th century, is called the finest watchmaker of all times. He developed, invented and improved many watch components and changed the appearance of the pocket watch. Since then, the watch has gone through a metamorphosis of dramatic change culminating in the quartz-crystal electric watch.

Abbreviations used: S-size, gf-gold filled.

Fils Rosskopf, railroad, open face, Russian silver, ornate hands, 2″ dia. $275.00

POCKET WATCHES

Ball (Hamilton) 16 S, 17 jewels, open face, gf case, lever set . . .	175.00
Ball (Waltham) 16 S, 21 jewels, gf hunter case, lever set	220.00
Bunn (Illinois) 16 S, 19 jewels, open face, lever set	140.00
Bunn (Illinois) Special, 16 S, 23 jewels, open face, lever set	325.00
Columbus Watch, Railroad Monarch, 18 S, 17 jewels, gf case, open face	125.00
Columbus Watch, Time King, 18 S, 21 jewels, gf case, Damaskeened	250.00
Elgin, Father Time, 18 S, 21 jewels, open face, gf case, stem wind, Damaskeened	130.00
Elgin, Veritas, 16 S, 23 jewels, gf case, Damaskeened	400.00
Elgin, Frances Rubie, 10 S, 7 jewels, gf case, key wind	165.00
Hamilton, #929, 18 S, 15 jewels, gf hunter case	150.00
Hamilton, #979, 16 S, 16 jewels, gf hunter case	75.00
Hamilton, #922, 12 S, 23 jewels, open face, gf case	250.00
Hampden, Gladiator, 18 S, open face, gf case	140.00
Hampden, New Railway, 16 S, 21 jewels, open face, gf case	130.00
Home, 17 jewels, blue enamel ball case	200.00
Howard, III, 18 (N) S, 15 jewels, open face, gf case, key wind . . .	450.00
Illinois, B & O R.R. Special, 18 S, 21 jewels, open face, gf case	600.00
Illinois, Interstate Chronometer, 18 S, 17 jewels	260.00
Lancaster, Keystone, 18 S, 15 jewels, gilt case	200.00
Manhattan, 18 S, chronograph, open face	95.00
Marion, Fayette, Stratton, 18 S, 15 jewels, gilt case, key wind	400.00
N. Y. Standard, Dan Patch, 16 & 18 S, 7 jewels, stop watch	395.00
Rockford, Iroquois, 16 S, 17 jewels, double roller	200.00
Seth Thomas, Liberty, 18 S, 7 jewels, eagle on back plate	85.00
Seth Thomas, Henry Molineux, Model #2, 17 jewels, gold jewel settings	995.00
U.S. Watch, Dome Plate Model, 16 S, 7 jewels, gilt case	200.00
Waterford, non-jeweled, common . .	65.00
Waterbury, 6 S, duplex escapement	95.00

MISCELLANEOUS WATCHES

Character

Barbie	25.00
Cinderella, Grosgrain strap, c. 1940	85.00
Dick Tracy, c. 1940	140.00
Donald Duck	65.00
Elvis Presley, limited edition, c. 1978	75.00
Lil Abner, animated	125.00
Mickey Mouse, c. 1930	200.00
Mickey Mouse, c. 1940	75.00
Mickey Mouse, pocket-type, c. 1935	225.00
Snow White	35.00

Lapel, Lady's

14K gold, open face	160.00
Blue enamel bow pin, blue enamel ball	150.00

Wristwatch, Lady's

Enameled rose gold, Art Deco-style	200.00

Wristwatch, Man's

Patek Phillippe, 14K, gold c. 1900	600.00

WATERFORD

Waterford crystal is quality flint glass commonly decorated with cuttings. The original factory was established at Waterford, Ireland, in 1729. The early glass made before 1830 was darker than the brilliantly clear glass of later production. The factory closed in 1852 and after 100 years reopened and continues production today.

Fruit Bowl, clear turned down rim, 5¾″ high, 6¾″ inside dia. $275.00

Biscuit Jar, band of cuttings, silver plated cover and bail	275.00
Butter, covered, ovoid, mushroom finial, early	250.00
Celery, diamond point	55.00
Cruet, 9″, stoppered, applied handle	100.00

Decanter, 7", mushroom stopper . .	150.00
Egg, covered	65.00
Hock Glass, cut	43.00
Jar, covered, 7"	175.00
Mustard Jar	45.00
Paperweight	45.00
Perfume Bottles	
Large	75.00
Small	55.00
Pitcher, 10½", applied handle	195.00
Plate, 8", center cut	65.00
Relish Dish	54.00
Salts	
Individual, boat shaped, c. 1820 .	85.00
Master, diamond shaped	50.00
Sugar Castor	45.00
Tumbler, all over cutting	65.00
Vases	
7¾", cylindrical	110.00
10¾", all over cutting, c. 1810 . .	500.00
Wine, 5½", diamond cut	25.00

WAVE CREST

WAVE CREST WARE

The C. F. Monroe Co. of Meriden, Conn., produced the opal glassware known as Wave Crest from 1898 until World War I. The company bought the opaque blown molded glass blanks from the Pairpoint Manufacturing Co. of New Bedford, Mass., and other glass makers including European factories. The pieces were then decorated, usually with floral designs. Trade names used were "Wave Crest Ware," "Kelva" and "Nakara."

Box, blue floral decor, covered, hinged, 4" high, 7" dia. $425.00

Biscuit Jars	
8", floral decor, silver lid signed	
CTM Co.	475.00
Cream, floral decor, brass lid and	
bail handle	250.00
Bon-Bon, covered, blue with brass	
bail handle	475.00

Bowl, 8 x 6", cream brown and yellow rose decor	195.00
Boxes	
3" dia., swirl, blue, daisy decor, hinged	225.00
4½" dia., turquoise base, blownout zinnia lid	690.00
4½" dia., cream, floral decor, signed	195.00
4½" dia., deep yellow and pink, scenic, hinged, signed	295.00
5½" dia., puffy, "Tobacco" on front	450.00
6¾" dia., pink to green, floral decor on lid, hinged, paper label . .	650.00
8 x 6¾", cream, red and blue floral decor, ormalu base and legs . .	775.00
8" dia., pink, azalea decor, hinged, signed	350.00
14½" circ., portrait, beading, ormalu collar, rose lining	650.00
Card Holder, 4 x 2½", floral decor, ormalu frame	280.00
Cigar Humidor, 5 x 4½", eggcrate mold, "Tobacco" in gold, floral decor, brass lid	495.00
Clock, Easel, green, floral decor . . .	450.00
Ferner, floral decor, original brass liner, signed	360.00
Jar, Mustard, yellow, pansy decor . .	50.00
Jardiniere, white, cherry blossom decor, signed	325.00
Jewelry Stand, 3¼ x 3¼", blue floral decor, handled pedestal	125.00
Letter Holder, 3¼ x 4 x 6", violet decor, ormalu frame	360.00
Photo Receiver, 5¾ x 4¼", puffy egg crate mold, floral decor with beading, ormalu top rim	350.00
Planter, 4½ x 5¼", puffed, floral decor, ormalu rim	240.00
Salt and Pepper Shakers, pair, scenic decor	195.00
Spooner, 4½", swirl, Helmschmied, 2 handled	295.00
Trays	
4", pin, floral decor, handled, signed	85.00
4¾" dia., bon-bon, lavender, blue floral decor, handled	115.00
Pin, swirl, ormalu trim	135.00
Vases	
5", coral pink, floral decor, heavy ormalu mounting	345.00
12½", cream, heavy floral decor .	700.00
13½", cream, pink mum decor, gold handles and feet, ormalu mountings, signed	995.00

WEATHERVANES

A weather vane indicates wind direction. The

earliest known examples were found on late 17th century structures in the Boston area. The vanes were handcrafted of wood, copper, or tin. By the last half of the 19th century, weathervanes adorned farms and houses throughout the nation. Mass produced vanes of cast iron, copper, and sheet metal were sold through the mail order catalogues or at country stores.

The champion vane is the rooster, in fact the name weathercock is synonymous with weathervane. The styles and patterns are endless. Weathering can affect the same vane entirely different. For this reason, patina is a critical element in collecting vanes.

Whirligigs are a variation of the weathervane. Constructed of wood and metal, often by unskilled craftsmen, whirligigs not only indicate the direction of the wind and its velocity but their unique movements served as entertainment for children, neighbors, and passersby.

Note: Reproductions of early models exist, are being aged, and sold as originals.

"Blackhawk", signed Harris & Co., 26" $1700.00

WEATHERVANES

Arrow, molded copper, late 19th C., 22 x 42"	850.00
Automobile, copper, full bodied, c. 1920, 26"	700.00
Bull, molded copper, 19th C., 19¼ x 23"	1850.00
Captain Ahab, sheet copper, peg leg sea captain, William Paris maker, 19th C., 36 x 31"	1100.00
Cow, tin, painted black, copper bar, 15"	250.00
Eagle, molded and gilded copper, 19th C., directional arrow, 36 x 54½"	1800.00
Fish, wood, original silver paint, 27"	900.00

Grasshopper, molded copper and brass, 19th C., 26 x 42"	3500.00
Horse, running, copper, on large wood pedestal, 19th C.	800.00
Horse, standing, molded copper, painted, 19th C., 27 x 24½"	875.00
Horse, trotting, sheet metal, wood dial, 44 x 40"	3250.00
Indian, molded copper, 19th C., 31¾ x 37"	10500.00
Locomotive, sheet metal, painted, 19th C., 9 x 19"	475.00
Rooster, cast iron, original gold paint, NE, 20 x 22"	800.00
Rooster, James Lombard, Bridgton, ME, wood, pine, late 19th C., 17 x 18"	12000.00
Sailing Ship, molded copper, 1888, twisted copper baluster shape base, 62"	2250.00

Whirligig 14" high, 18" long . . . $95.00

WHIRLIGIGS

Dutchman, wood, painted, 19th C., 10½"	1200.00
Farm scene, wood and metal, painted, barn, horses, and figures, c. 1900, 30 x 32"	750.00
Fireman, wood, carved, painted, 19th C., 12"	1700.00
Fish, wood, carved, painted, c. 1900, 16 x 39½"	750.00
Indians in canoe, wood, carved, painted, 19th C., 8 x 23"	1100.00
Washerwoman, wood, painted, c. 1930, 23 x 23"	310.00

WEDGWOOD

WEDGWOOD

Josiah Wedgwood founded the famous Wedgwood Pottery at Burslem, England, in 1759. Wedgwood's history is complex. Although Wedgwood is probably associated more with the production of Basalt and Jasperware, the factory produced many wares including Creamware, Drabware, Redware and a fine quality porcelain.

In 1920, Fairyland Lustre was introduced. This porcelain is decorated with colorful, fantasy-like decals with gold detail. Lustreware production ceased in 1932. The firm in Wedgwood, England, is still active and produces fine quality dinnerware and accessories.

Also see BASALT, JASPERWARE and PEARLWARE.

Teapot, Drabware, smear glaze, 4½" high, relief molded architectural pattern **$175.00**

Ashtray, Terra Cotta, 4½", scene
  with laurel border 40.00
Beakers
  Basalt, 4", enamel decor 90.00
  Jasperware, 4", blue, classical decor, early 190.00
Biscuit Jars, Jasperware
  7", lavender, classical decor,
   "Wedgwood England" 390.00
  7½", blue, classical decor 140.00
Book Cover, tropical wood, mounted
  with Jasperware, blue oval medallion 70.00
Bowls
  Basalt, 10", engine turned, c.
   1790 .... 325.00
  Creamware, 4¾", grape & leaf
   decor, with ladle 275.00

Flame, 11¼", multi-colors, gold
  outlining 2500.00
Lustres, Dragon
  3 x 4¾", octagon shape, oriental decor 350.00
  5" 350.00
Lustres, Fairyland
  8", Z5360/2, Fiddler in Tree,
   Ship & Mermaid 1600.00
  11", Z4968/11, Chinese Garden, Elves & Birds 2600.00
Boxes
  Lustre, Hummingbird, 5¾" dia. .. 400.00
  Lustre, Dragon, 6" dia., blue 650.00
  Jasperware, 5", blue, classical decor 80.00
Butters, covered, Jasperware, blue
  classical decor, "Wedgwood" ... 90.00
Busts
  Aristotle, 12" 1150.00
  Venus, 13¾" 715.00
  Milton, Parian, E. W. Wyon,
   "Wedgwood" 850.00
Candlesticks, Jasperware, 6¾",
  classical decor, "Wedgwood", pr. 265.00
Chocolate Pot, Queensware, 4",
  green leaf decor 110.00
Clock, Basalt, 5½", classical figures 150.00
Coffee Pot, Caneware, 9", glazed,
  early 225.00
Compote, Majolica, oval, reticulated
  border, Satyr stem 160.00
Condiment Set, mustard, salt and
  pepper in silver plate holder,
  green, white, yellow, bamboo lattice design 425.00
Creamers
  Jasperware, 4", dark blue 70.00
  Silver resist 16.00
Creamers and Sugars
  Nippon, 3 pieces 185.00
  Basalt, engine turned design,
   "Wedgwood" 95.00
Cup, handleless, bird decor, "Wedgwood, England" ....
Cups and Saucers
  Jasperware, blue, classical decor,
   "Wedgwood" 100.00
  Terra Cotta 75.00
Dishes
  Creamware, 9⅜" oval, painted by
   Emile Lessore, "The Vintage",
   1865 .... 800.00
  Lustre, Moonlight, shell form,
   "Wedgwood", pair 280.00
  Majolica, covered game dish, rabbits and game birds 200.00
  Majolica, 10", emerald green, leaf
   shape 90.00
Ewers
  Basalt, 15", gilded, early 2250.00
  Basalt, 15½", early 1300.00

Figure, Basalt, Polar Bear, J. S. Keaping, ebonized base 400.00
Heels, Jasperware, lady's, blue, 1950's 200.00

Jars
Basalt, covered sweet meat (1907) 50.00
Terra Cotta, 6½", tobacco, oviform, classical decor, "Wedgwood, made in England" 170.00

Jardiniers
Jasperware, 4½ x 5¼", blue, mythology decor, "Wedgwood," pair 440.00
7 x 7", black Grecian figures on yellow, white bands 440.00

Stoneware, Jug, blue cobalt glaze, brown top, marked "Wedgwood" $295.00

Jugs
8", Cambridge ale, c. 1870 ..... 110.00
6¼", Toby, brown glazed, "Elihu Yale", c. 1933 .... 90.00
Medallion, Jasperware, 2" dia. "Portrait of Bearded Scholar," "Wedgwood" 175.00
Paper Knife, brass, mounted with Jasperware medallion 45.00

Pitchers
Basalt, 3", souvenir 20.00
Creamware, 7", raised hunt scene, hound handle 45.00
Jasperware, 8", blue, classical decor, "Wedgwood, England" 115.00
Queensware, 5", white with pink . 50.00

Plaques
Drabware, 4½", blue raised figures, "Wedgwood" 300.00

Jasperware, 4½ x 6½", framed, black, white, gold 795.00
Jasperware, 9" oval, classical decor, ormalu frame 425.00
Lustre, 7½", light yellow, green, with white figures 250.00

Plates
Creamware, 8½", decorated, c. 1820–40 .... 45.00
Ivanhoe, "Rebecca Gives Purse to Gurth" 35.00
Jasperware, 10", green, "Wedgwood, Made in England" 45.00
Lustre, Dragon, 9⅛", Portland Vase Mark 350.00
Platter, Queensware, oval, reticulated, "Wedgwood" 500.00
Sherbet, Fairyland Lustre, flying cranes and temple dog 525.00

Sugars, covered
Basalt, 4", c. 1810–20 .... 290.00
Caneware, 6" 245.00
Drabware, 7", glazed, gilded bands 150.00

Teapots
Basalt, Famile Rose, enameling, c. 1880 .... 250.00
Drabware, raised blue band of flowers 100.00
Redware, relief molded with lotus blossoms, bamboo form handle .. 150.00
Stoneware, relief molded flowers, leaf scroll, spaniel knob, with stand 200.00
Tile, "The Mayflower Approaching Land," brown tones, 1910 ...... 55.00
Tureen, Queensware, covered, 8¾", enamel floral decor, attached stand, "Wedgwood" 80.00

Vases
Cream, 4", 20th Century, pair ... 65.00
Jasperware
4¾", bulbous, classical decor, "Wedgwood" 115.00
5⅛", blue, classical decor 80.00
10¼", blue, large handled, classical decor, "Wedgwood" 625.00
Lustre, Dragon, trumpet vase, turquoise 345.00

WELLER POTTERY

In 1873 Samuel A. Weller opened a small factory in Fultonham, Ohio, to produce stoneware jars and flower pots. In 1882 he moved his facilities to Zanesville and in 1893 formed a partnership with W. A. Long. Within the year, they began to produce "Lonhuda," a shaded brown ware with decoration underglaze.

After Long left the company in 1895, Weller continued to make similar art ware under the name "Louwelsa," and a large variety of other art pottery lines. By 1915 Weller claimed to be the largest pottery in the world.

At the end of World War I, many prestige lines were discontinued and Weller concentrated on more commercial wares. During the Depression the art lines became even less elaborate. Even though business prospered again briefly during World War II, foreign competition forced the factory to close in 1948. Many lines were offered by Weller and it is impossible to list all here. Most of the pottery was marked "Weller," either impressed, incised or rubber stamped; some art pottery was also artist signed.

Vase, Hudson, signed Hester Pillsbury, 10" $275.00

Basket, 7½", handled, Cameo, blue, 1930's 20.00
Bowl, 3½ x 12", Silvertone, molded yellow flowers on lavender background with flower frog, 1920's .. 100.00
Candlesticks, 2½", Warwick, molded leaves and berries, pair 45.00

Ewers
  6½", Louwelsa, artist MT, yellow floral decor, brown glaze, impressed Weller 150.00
  8½", Oakleaf, beige, Weller in script, 1930's 35.00
  10½", Floretta, relief molded grapes, brown glaze, 1904 ..... 250.00
Figurals
  4", Pop-eye Dog 250.00
  4", Coppertone Frog, mottled brown and green, 1920's, ink stamp Weller 125.00
  6½", Muskota, nude with swan, early 1900's, block letters Weller 125.00
  19½ x 17", Pelican 1500.00
Jardinieres
  7½", Ivory, embossed geometric decor, early 1900's, no mark .. 45.00
  8", Knifewood, molded daisy decor, early 1900's, impressed Weller 150.00
  8½", Roma, cream 50.00
  9", Dickensware, 1st line, floral decor on dark green background, Dickensware seal 200.00
  9½", Louwelsa, floral decor, brown glaze; Louwelsa, Weller seal 125.00
Jardiniere and Pedestal, 26", Forest, molded trees, matte glaze 750.00
Jug, 6½", Aurelian, floral decor, 1890–1900's, marked "Aurelian, Weller" by hand 275.00
Mug, 6", Louwelsa, artist M, floral decor, dark brown 100.00
Pitchers
  7½", Zona, blue 65.00
  8", Zona, molded decor of Kingfisher, hand decorated in color, 1920's 200.00
Planter, 6", Woodcraft, round tree trunk with fox cubs, 1920–1930's 150.00
Plate, 8", Zona, apples 20.00
Tankards
  15½", Barcelona, ink stamp Weller 250.00
  17", Louwelsa, artist Ferrell, grape clusters and leaves decor, brown glaze, impressed half-circle Louwelsa, Weller 650.00
Tobacco Jar, 7", Dickensware, Turk's Head, marked "Dickensware" by hand 450.00
Umbrella Stand, 26", Louwelsa, pansy floral decor, brown glaze 450.00
Vases
  3½", Louwelsa, double gourd shape, floral decor 85.00
  4½", Etna, floral decor, marked Weller, Etna by hand 85.00
  4½", Lustre, pink, 1920 .... 35.00

5″, Roma, comport, pink florals on ivory background, block letters Weller 30.00

6″, Bonito, lily decor, late 1920's, signed Weller 45.00

6 x 8″, Sicard, floral decor, purple iridescent glaze 550.00

6½″, LaSa, bud vase, tree decor on red & gold iridescence 125.00

7″, Glendale, double bud vase, bird on nest, 1920's 125.00

7½″, Louwelsa, pillow shape, artist signed Timberlake, Indian portrait 1200.00

7½″, Louwelsa with silver overlay, artist MM. floral decor 1000.00

7½″, Turkis, green and gold drip over red, marked Weller by hand . 50.00

8″, Coppertone, figural frog handles, molded leaves 275.00

8″, LaSa, palm tree decor, red and gold iridescent lustre glaze, signed LaSa, Weller 275.00

8″, Sicard, bulbous bottom, tapered top, hollyhock decor, iridescent glaze, 1902–1907 .... 400.00

8½″, Burntwood, birds and branches decor in brown bisque, 1910 .... 200.00

8½″, Chase, fan shape, horseman and hounds in molded relief, blue, late 1920's 250.00

9″, Ardsley, slender, cattails, 1920's, ink stamp Weller 35.00

9½ x 10″, Baldin, molded applies in relief, 1915–1920 .... 175.00

9½″, Hudson, artist H. Pilsbury, hand decorated iris, ink stamp Weller 275.00

10″, Louwelsa, bulbous shape, handles and foot, artist H., Nasturtiums decor 200.00

11½″, Eocean, artist EB, floral decor on grey background 350.00

13″, Jap Birdimal, oriental figure on orange background, 1904 .... 2500.00

13½″, Forest, molded trees, matte glaze 150.00

16″, Woodcraft, tree trunk with owl figural on side 400.00

Wallpockets

7″, Roma 45.00

8½″, Zona, floral 40.00

9″, Glendale, bird on branch feeding babies, no mark 125.00

9″, Woodcraft, with figural of squirrel, block letters Weller 100.00

WHIELDON

WHIELDON POTTERY

The Staffordshire potter, Thomas Whieldon, established his shop in 1740. He is best known for his mottled ware, molded in forms of vegetables, fruits and leaves. Both Josiah Spode and Josiah Wedgwood were connected with him, in different capacities, during these years.

Whieldon ware is a generic term, because his items were never marked and other potters made similar type of items. The ware is agate-tortoise shell earthenware, in limited shades of green, brown, blue and yellow, usually utilitarian items such as dinner ware, plates, etc., but they also made figurines, and other decorative type items.

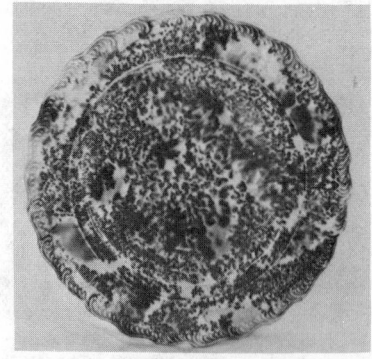

Plate, 9½″, feather edge $295.00

Cradle, 3¾″, whimsy type, in three colors, mottled, c. 1760 .... 325.00

Creamer, floral decor, lid attached by metal chain, c. 1750 .... 425.00

Milk Jug, covered, pear shaped on three lion-mask and paw feet, oriental figures in garden, mottled blue, green, ochre and brown tortoise shell glaze, c. 1760 ...... 450.00

Model of cockerel, standing, splashed in brown, green, c. 1770 165.00

Plates

7⅞″, molded rims, grey, green, blue, ochre and brown tortoise-shell glaze, pair 400.00

9″, octagonal, grey tortoise-shell glaze, splotches of blue, green, ochre, pair 600.00

10″, pheasant design, mottled brown 300.00

Teapot, covered, twig finial, molded with fruiting, grapevines, crabstock handle and spout, mottled blue and brown tortoise-shell glaze, c. 1755 .... 1550.00

WHITE PATTERNED IRONSTONE

Ironstone is a heavy earthenware first patented by Charles Mason, Staffordshire, England, in the late 18th century. The range of patterns seems endless; a few better-known ones dominate the market. The earliest patterns were natural motifs: florals, berries, vegetables and geometrics; "Sydenham Shape," "Washington Shape," etc. Later patterns from 1870–1890 tend to be on the plainer side, e.g., "Cable and Ring." Some all white ironstone patterns were decorated with touches of color, such as "Ceres," with gold, green, or blue, (known as "Blue Wheat"). Some patterns were all white, with lustre decor, such as "Lustre Sprig" and "Lustre Pinwheel." There is much white ironstone that is not marked at all.

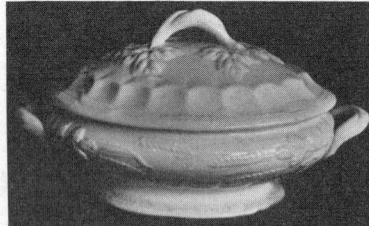

Tureen, Vegetable, Wheat and Leaf, marked, "Stone China/W. Taylor/Hanley," 11½" **$70.00**

Butter pats, 3", Johnson Bros., ea. . **5.00**
Coffee or Tea Pots
  Acorn, J. & G. Meakin and Co. . . **125.00**
  Grape and Medallion, E. and C. Challinor, 1865, ring finial **125.00**
  Prairie Flower, Livsey and Powell, 1862, (wheat stalks and poppy flower, large bud finial) **190.00**
  Wheat and Blackberry, (raised flowers and leaves) Meakin, 1865 **200.00**
Creamer, Lustre Pinwheel, 6", paneled, impressed "W" in base, all white with lustre decor **60.00**
Cups and Saucers
  Ceres, Turner and Goddard and Co., handleless **55.00**
  Oak Leaf, Pankhurst, 1863, handleless **40.00**
  Sydenham Shape, T. and R. Boote, 1853, handleless **60.00**
Egg Cups, Johnson Bros. **7.50**
Pickle or Relish Dishes
  Ceres, oval **25.00**
  Grape and Medallion, 9", oval, open handles **20.00**

Leaf shaped, 5 x 4½", no mark . **15.00**
Lily of the Valley, no marks **22.00**
President shape, J. Edwards, 1856, oval **25.00**
Octagon, T. and R. Boote, relish shaped like a shell **35.00**
Plates
  Bamboo, Meakin **12.00**
  Blackberry, Davenport **27.50**
  Corn, Wedgwood, October, 1863 **20.00**
  Dallas, J. Clementson, 1850 . . . **25.00**
  Lustre Pinwheel, 8" gold lustre decor, panelled edge **18.00**
  Lustre Sprig, 8", Reg. E. G. Walley, Niagara Shape, November 29, 1856 . . . . **18.00**
  Morning Glory, 8¾", Turner and Tompkinson **20.00**
  Sydenham Shape, 7½" **15.00**
  Washington Shape, 9", J. Mier and Son **18.00**
  Wheat and Clover, Turner and Tompkinson **20.00**
Platters
  Large, 10¼ x 14¾", plain, "Prince of Wales" marked Royal Patent Ironstone, Burgess and Goddard **15.00**
  Acanthus Leaf, cold meat, Johnson Bros. **25.00**
  Gothic, 14 x 9½", Ridgeway, c. 1840 . . . . **55.00**
  Sydenham Shape, 12" **42.50**
Service for six, Edward Walley, 1845–1856, white, copper lustre borders, coffee pot, creamer, covered sugar, water pitcher, 2 platters dinner and luncheon plates, handleless cups and saucers, set . . . **600.00**
Sugars, covered
  Baltic, Mier and Son, 1855 . . . . . **20.00**
  Bonaventure, T. & R. Boote, 1890 **18.50**
  Cable, 1866–1890, various makers **18.50**
  Oak Leaf, Pankhurst, 1863, acorn finial **25.00**
  Prairie Flower, Livsey and Powell, 1860 . . . . **32.50**
  Sydenham Shape, T. & R. Boote, 1850–1854, bud finials on 1854 pieces. **30.00**
Tureen, Sauce, or Gravy Boats
  Lily of the Valley with tray, 1860, no marks **55.00**
  Prairie Flower, matching handled tray, Livsey and Powell, 1860 . . . **55.00**
  Wheat, no tray **14.00**
Tureens, Vegetable
  Cable and Ring, Maddock, 1872 . **45.00**
  Ceres, Elsmere and Foster, 1859, twig finial, with touches of color, green and gold **100.00**
  Prairie Flower, handled and leaves

around finial, 1860 . . . . 80.00
Wash Bowl and Pitcher, Blackberry,
no mark 150.00

WILLOW WARE

This popular ware derives its name from a design which is in the Chinese tradition. Willow ware had its inspiration from early Canton ware brought to Europe from China in the 16th century. An early willow transfer pattern, said to be the first ever transfer-printed, is credited to either Thomas Tucker or his apprentice Thomas Minton, both of whom worked at Caughley Pottery in the Staffordshire district of England.

The first (1780) under-glaze transfer design did not contain all the Chinese legend motifs found in the later "standard" willow pattern developed in 1810 by Josiah Spode. The "standard" willow pattern has several distinctive features—a willow tree, two pagodas, a rail fence with finials, two birds and a three-arch bridge with three figures crossing it.

In the late 18th century, Willow Ware was made in England and Germany. By the 19th century it was produced in the United States, France, Japan, Holland and Ireland; it is still produced today in many countries.

Most commonly produced in blue; occasional pieces can be found in pink and green.

Plate, 9″, Allerton **$17.00**

Bowl, 5½″ dia., Buffalo Pottery 10.00
Butter, covered, Brown & Stevenson 50.00
Butter Pats
  Allerton 7.00
  Grindley 3.00
Coffee Pot, Booth 55.00
Compote, 9″ dia., Ashworth 65.00

Cup & Saucer, Homer Laughlin
  (1958) 5.00
Mug, Japan 5.50
Plates
  9⅛″, Wood 20.00
  9½″, Buffalo China 11.00
  10″, Buffalo Pottery 18.00
Platters
  14″, oval, Copeland 82.00
  15¾ x 12½″, Buffalo Pottery . . . 75.00
Sauce Dish, unmarked 3.00
Tureen, Covered, Allerton 35.00
Vegetables, 11 x 8½″, Allerton 45.00

WITCH BALLS

A witch ball simply is a hollow sphere of colored or multicolored glass. There are various myths surrounding the origin and purpose of the witch ball. Some say they were displayed by the fireplace to catch demon spirits as

Nailsea Type, clear with white looping, 6″ dia. matching vase, 12″ **$450.00**

they descended the chimney. They could then be taken outside for cleaning. Others contend they were used to store salt by the chimney to keep it dry.

In all probability a witch ball was a glassmaker's whimsey, used strictly for decorative purposes atop an unfilled flower vase.

Don't confuse witch balls with Christmas tree ornaments, target balls, floats, or early glass fire extinguishers. Witch balls come in a variety of sizes. They can not be attributed to one specific glass maker or company.

Amethyst, 4½" dia.	75.00
Cranberry, 4½" dia.	55.00
Nailsea Type	
Aquamarine with white loopings, 6½" dia.	200.00
Clear with white and cranberry loopings, 3½", possibly south N.J.	200.00
Clear with opalescent loops, 4½" dia., matching vase, 8", possibly Pittsburgh, pair	750.00

WOODENWARES

Many utilitarian household objects and farm implements were made of wood. Although they were used heavily, these implements were made of the strongest woods and well taken care of by their owners. This category serves as a catchall for wood objects which do not fit into other categories in our book.

Sugar Bucket, painted, 9" high, 9½" dia., C.S. Hershey $50.00

Barbells, hand, walnut, lady's	40.00
Barrel, sap	30.00
Bootjack, one piece	40.00
Bottle corker, 10½"	20.00
Bowls	
7 x 2½" deep	220.00
13½ x 6" deep	280.00
20½", red exterior paint	250.00
Boxes	
Cheese, diamond	5.00
Pantry, handled, blue, 11½"	50.00
Broom, birch	135.00
Buckets	
Berry, brass bands and handle	85.00
Grease, tankard	95.00
Pickle	65.00
Water, bentwood handle	45.00
Butter Churn, floor model, plunger, oak	195.00
Candle Box, pine, 16"	70.00
Cider Funnel, poplar	30.00
Cigar Mold, 11"	15.00
Cranberry Scoop	70.00
Egg Carrier, 24 dozen size, slat construction	35.00
Gavel, 12", turned handle, maple	25.00
Grain Scoop	25.00
Grain Shovel, one piece	175.00
Hat Stretcher	20.00
Hay Forks	
2 prong	75.00
4 prong	95.00
Kegs	
Root beer, 24"	230.00
Rum, wood staves, metal bands	80.00
Mill Spindles, 7"	2.50
Mortar and Pestles	
7¼"	80.00
8½", maple	95.00
Ox Yokes	
Calf, with bows	150.00
Training	90.00
With bows, large	225.00
Paddles	
Butter, 11", curved handle, walnut burl	150.00
Soap, 16½"	40.00
Scoop, 1 quart, c. 1850	50.00
Shoulder Yoke, pine	100.00
Shuttle, 18", maple	15.00
Smoothing Board, American, 7½ x 10½", hand carved maple	40.00
Hay Forks	
2 prong	75.00
4 prong	95.00
Kegs	
Root beer, 24"	230.00
Rum, wood staves, metal bands	80.00
Mill Spindles, 7"	2.50
Mortar and Pestles	
7¼"	80.00
8½", maple	95.00

Ox Yokes
Calf, with bows	150.00
Training	90.00
With bows, large	225.00

Paddles
Butter, 11," curved handle, walnut burl	150.00
Soap, 16½ "	40.00
Scoop, 1 quart, c. 1850	50.00
Shoulder Yoke, pine	100.00
Shuttle, 18," maple	15.00
Smoothing Board, American, 7½ x 10½," hand carved maple	40.00
Soap Mold, 3 x 3½ x 6"	30.00
Tallow Dipper, 23½" long, walnut	200.00

WORLD WAR II COLLECTIBLES

If you are fifty years old or younger, World War II is probably a distant or unknown memory. It is the war in which our parents or grandparents fought. As modern children are looking through the drawers of their parents, it is World War II memorabilia that is being found.

This category is an acknowledgement of the inevitability of the passage of time. Time occasionally adds value to objects along with sentiment. This is what is happening with the World War II collectible area. Don't throw those old war souvenirs out.

Poster, 12½ x 9", by Dan V. Smith **$35.00**

Airplane, Model, B-24, made by pilot who flew it, names of crew members written in their positions, one engine shot out	100.00
American identification ship models, 1 to 1/2000 scale, 14 ships, made by Framburg Co., Chicago, wood carrying case	250.00
Armband, oilcloth, U.S. flag, worn on arm during Normandy landing, slight staining	25.00
Ashtray, 50mm shell casing, English coins bent to hold cigarettes	10.00
Bomb, practice, made into ashtray, silk screened Team member, 10th Olympic, C.A.A.F., Dec. 19, 1943, 26"	75.00
C-1 emergency sustenance vest, A.A.F., insignia left breast, 15 pockets, holster for pistol, no contents	75.00
Flag, Man in Service, 1 star, marked Air Force	3.75
Helmet, Civil Defense Air Raid Warden's, white-painted steel with decal intact	10.00
Jacket, high altitude, leather flying, fleeze-lines, type B-6, handpainted 8th Air Force Patch, The Mighty 8 on breast and various other symbols	200.00
Jacket, same, type D-1, blood chit on back, rayon, seven far Eastern languages asking safe return of pilot if shot down	195.00
Lapel Pin, Air Raid Warden Civil Defense	2.50
Life Vest, Mae West, yellow, Army Air Force, 1944, type B-4	25.00
Mess Kit, marked USA, knife, fork, spoon	7.50
Model airplane portfolio, 3 flying models of allied fighting planes by Judd Reed, plus American Ace Spotter, 1944, originally sold for 25¢	10.00
Model Airplane series, Kellogg's Pep, premium, 5 in set, uncut	12.00
Plates, commemorative china, military and political leaders, 8 in set, 1946, Salem, OH	150.00

Posters
A Careless Word . . . a Needless Loss, A. O. Fischer, 22 x 28"	45.00
Because Someone Talked, Wesley, 20 x 28"	90.00
Enemy Ears are Listening, 13¾ x 26"	90.00
Having seen the quality of the work and the workers on the production line, FDR quote, 28 x 40"	20.00
Let's Give Him Enough and on	

Time, N. Rockwell, 28½ x 40" . . .	350.00
Polish War Relief, "Inasmuch as ye have done it unto one of the least of these . . . ," W.T. Benda, black and white, 30 x 44"	200.00
Stop Him and the Job's Done, H. A. Meyers, 28½ x 40"	350.00
This is Nazy Brutality, Ben Shahn, 28 x 38"	375.00
United We are Strong, United we will Win, H. Koerner, 28 x 40" . . .	70.00
Tumbler, silk-screened, "Remember Pearl Harbor, December 7, 1944," picture of battleship on seas, 7"	15.00

YELLOW WARE

Yellow Ware is a fairly heavy earthenware of varying weight and strength. Not to be confused with English Yellow-Glazed Earthenware; Yellow Ware, when broken, will show yellow completely through, not just a yellow overglaze. Pieces of this ware vary in color from a rich pumpkin to lighter shades with more tan than yellow. Kitchen pieces are most prevalent although plates, nappies and custard cups can also be found. There are both English and American examples available; however, the English pieces appear to have had additional ingredients added to the earthenware to make a harder body.

Derbyshire and Sharp's were foremost among English manufacturers and the Bennington, Vermont, factory was one of the first among American producers. Yellow Ware is widely collected and used. Prices of this ware are rising.

Humidor, banded, 6", c. 1830–40 . . . .$65.00

Baking Dishes	
10", oblong, white interior	72.00
11", oval	80.00
Bowls, Milk	
5¼"	15.00

10"	45.00
14"	65.00
Bowls, Mixing, relief exterior	
7½"	25.00
12"	40.00
13½"	45.00
Butter, covered, brown rings	45.00
Crocks, covered	
Medium, brown bands	55.00
Medium, white bands	65.00
Custard Cups	
Extra Large	20.00
Medium	18.00
Small	10.00
Ginger Jar, 8", rare form	35.00
Humidor, 6", banded	65.00
Molds	
Corn, large	40.00
Geometric	35.00
Rabbit	38.00
Mortar, 5½", white bands, rare form	65.00
Mugs	
Brown bands	35.00
Plain	30.00
White bands	40.00
Nappy, 9¾", oval, scalloped edge .	45.00
Pie Plates	
8"	40.00
8½"	30.00
9¼", pie crust edge	65.00
9½"	45.00
Plate, 8½", rare form	55.00
Rolling Pin, wooden handles	85.00
Soap Dish, round, rare form	45.00

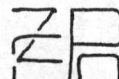

ZANE WARE
MADE IN U.S.A.

ZANE POTTERY

Adam Reed and Harry McClelland bought the Peters and Reed Pottery located in Zanesville, Ohio in 1921. The firm continued production of garden wares and introduced several new art lines: "Sheen," "Powder Blue," "Crystalline" and "Drip." The factory was sold in 1941 to Lawton Gonder.

See PETERS AND REED and GONDER

Bowls	
5", blue & brown	20.00
6", Landsun glaze	25.00
Jardiniere, 14½", 2 handles, variegated green semi-matte glaze, Montene	125.00
Vases	
8", Aztec	38.00
8", handled, ribbed body, powder blue, c. 1925	50.00

Vase, unglazed terra cotta, glazed green interior, 6" $25.00

LA MORO
ZANESVILLE POTTERY

Zanesville Art Pottery, one of several potteries located in Zanesville, Ohio, began production in 1900. A line of utilitarian products was first produced. Art pottery was introduced shortly thereafter. The major line was La Moro — handpainted and decorated under glaze. The impressed block print mark La Moro appears on the high glazed and matte glazed decorated ware. The firm was bought by S.A. Weller in 1920 and became known as Weller Plant No. 3.

Tea Pot, dark green, souvenir type, 2¾" high, Tyces Pottery, Zanesville, Ohio $28.00

Bowl, 7", with flower frog, dark blue matte glaze **35.00**

Jardiniere, 9", brown and gold glaze	120.00
Plate, 4½", applied floral decor . . .	15.00
Tankard, floral decor, artist signed .	300.00
Vases	
6", 3 handles, floral decor, La Moro	125.00
7", clover blossoms, artist signed, La Moro	175.00
9½", pansy decor, La Moro	225.00
9½" floral decor on brown high glaze, unmarked	140.00
Whiskey Jug, 5½", floral decor, La Moro	125.00

ZSOLNAY POTTERY

Zsolnay is a Hungarian ceramic ware. Vilmos Zsolnay (1828–1900) took over his brother's factory located in Pe'cs, Hungary, in the mid 1800's. Zsolnay's son, Miklos, became manager in 1899.

Characteristically, the ware possesses a cream colored ground and is highly ornamental and is glazed. "Eosin" glaze, a deep rich play of colors, reminiscent of Tiffany's iridescent wares, was developed by Zsolnay in 1820. This technique was awarded the Gold Medal at the 1900 World Exhibit in Paris.

No trademark was used in the beginning. From 1878 on, the blue mark depicting the five towers of the Cathedral at Pe'cs was used. The letters, "T. J. M." incorporated into the other known trademark, are reported to be the initials of Miklos Zsolnay's three children.

Of more recent origin are the iridescent glazed figurines appearing on the market. These figurines initially sold for small sums; however, after catching the attention of Zsolnay collectors, they are beginning to increase in value.

Bon Bon dish, irregular shape, reticulated	55.00
Box, horizontally ribbed, covered, bronze-lustred, green, purple ...	120.00
Bowl, 3½ x 2½", oval, reticulated rim, iridescent blue, pink with gold	55.00
Cachepot, 7¾", openwork, autumn colors	190.00
Cup and Saucer, floral decor, enameled	75.00

Figure, green/gold iridescent 6¼", castle mark, "Made in Hungry, Zolnay" $110.00

Inkwell, sgraffito decor on body of well, and molded figure of nude lady by opening of well, mottled yellow purple and green 185.00

Figurines
Bird, sitting, 2½", metallic lustre . 110.00
Cat, 2¼", iridescent blue 120.00
Deer, reclining, iridescent metallic blue-green, artist signed 150.00

Jar, covered, 4½", Cylindrical, stylized florals in blue, between latticework panels, on red ground, c. 1900 .... 75.00

Plates
8", handpainted Art Nouveau florals in red, blue, brown, gold 65.00
8", purple orchids against cobalt blue background 50.00

Platter, 11", entwined arabesques, overall lustre decor, blue, red, yellow and gold 395.00

Teapot, Pink orchids on cobalt blue background 87.50

Vases
3", pale blue radiating crystaline glaze 150.00
3½", molded figure of nude woman, mottled green and yellow with metallic iridescence 150.00
3¼", four applied prunts 75.00
10", reticulated and enameled .. 100.00
Mermaid on side of top, mottled purple, green and yellow 175.00

PHOTO CREDITS

We wish to thank those who permitted us to photograph objects in their possession. Unfortunately, we were unable to identify the sources for all of our pictures; nevertheless, we are deeply appreciative for all who contributed to this edition.

California: Butterfield's, San Francisco; Wayne Reed, Los Angeles; Cliff Peterson Collection, Los Angeles. **Canada:** Coach House Antiques, Montreal; Connoisseur Antiques, Ltd., Montreal; Kaleidoscope, Montreal; Petit Museé, Montreal. **Connecticut:** David Arman, Pompret Center; Noble Peddler Antiques, Torrington; Ell and Nellie Winterfield, Wallingford.

Delaware: Phoenix Antiques, Wilmington; Terrace Antiques, Wilmington. **Illinois:** Eureka! Antiques and Collectibles, Chicago; Riverside Antiques, Springfield. **Kentucky:** Ervan Lucas Bols Distilling Co., Louisville. **Maine:** Patricia Anne Reed, Damariscotta; Richard W. Oliver Auction & Art Gallery, Kennebunk. **Maryland:** Golden Era Antiques, Elkton; Col. B. J. Soshinsky, Clarksville; William Thomas, Baltimore.

Massachusetts: Berman's Antiques, Framingham; Richard A. Bourne, Inc., Hyannis; Alma Libby Antiques, Melrose. **Minnesota:** Temple's Antiques, Minneapolis. **New Jersey:** Barbara and Melvin Alpren, West Orange; Before My Time, Lodi; Ed and Emily Bonek, Ocean City; Colico Antiques, Washington; Don Fisher, Burlington; Evelyn Graves, Cedarville; Bruce D. Horton, Blackwood; Odd Couple's Curios, New Brunswick; David Rago, Trenton; Dorothy Sutton, Antique Mall, Montvale

New York: AA Antiques, Binghamton; Americana Antiques, Middletown; Blake's Antiques, Corning; Roger Butler, Phoenix; Myron Cohen Antiques, High Falls; Donna Davis, Fort Lee, Long Island; Exquisite Antiques, Ltd, Bellmore, Long Island; V & J Ferrante, Glen Cove, Long Island; Glass Menagerie, Yonkers; Jesse Goldberg, North Salem; Pat Guariglia, Saugerties Antique Exchange, Saugerties; Homestead Antiques, Camillus; Edward W. Leach, Wallkill; Now & Then, Latham; Oxen Hill Antiques, Binghamton; Joseph Pinto, Hudson; Otto Ramirez, Middletown Schenley Affiliated Brands, New York; Snuff Bottle Antiques, Albany; Brian Windsor, Staten Island

Ohio: Peggy and Alan Bialosky, Novelty; Lewis Bettinger, Canton; Nance Darrow, Akron; Michael B. McCray, Elyria; Private Stock, Cleveland; Irene Trittschuh, Youngstown

Pennsylvania: The Abrahams, Langhorne; Alexsandra's, Plymouth Meeting; Antiques, Better Forever, Allentown; Barby Sales, Allentown; Sylvia A. Barrish, Lahaska Antique Center, Lahaska; Jeremiah Beard, Reading; Benney's Antique Shop, Harrisburg; Helen Bereskie, Renninger's, Adamstown; Blue Marsh Antique and Gift Shop, Bernsville; C & D Pottery, Hollsopple; Grace Cannon, Rice's in Solebury; Sandra Carpenter, Renninger's, Kutztown; Chays' Curios, Hatboro; Coach and Four, Easton; The Cummings, Black Angus Antique Mall, Adamstown; Gary E. Ditty; Northumberland; Caroline E. Edleman, Royersford; Dottie Freeman and Allan Teal, Renninger's, Adamstown; Bud & Lee Graham, Pittsburg; Granny's Parlor, Williamsport; G. T. W. Antiques, Scranton; Heawatha's Antiques, Renninger's, Adamstown; Henry's Antiques, Black Angus Antique Mall, Adamstown; Historical Society of Cocalico County, Ephrata; Bonne Hohl, Black Angus Antique Mall, Adamstown; Irons Antiques, Northampton; Jim Lo Antiques, Allentown; Thomas A. Lupold, Black Angus Antique Mall, Adamstown; The Lustre Jug, Black Angus Antique Mall, Adamstown; Martha's Antiques, Black Angus Antique Mall, Adamstown; Marty & Arlene, Pottstown; Paul Maynard Antiques, Chadsford; Josephine Miller, Fleetwood; Lucy Mohr or Less, Philadelphia; Bill Morris, Williamsport; Nemeth Antiques, Orefield; Pat's Antiques & Collectibles, Moselem Springs; The Petersons, Philadelphia; Joseph Pinto, Renninger's, Adamstown; Michael Rath, Williamsport; Ann Reinert, Renninger's, Kutztown; Rinsland's Americana Mail Auction, Zionsville; Roan Bros. Auction Gallery, Cogan Station; Robesonia Antiques, Robesonia; Robert Sabol, Johnstown; Sauerkraut Hill Antiques, Macungie; Search Ends Here, Womelsdorf; Sha-Ron Antiques, Allentown; Douglas Smith, Renninger's, Adamstown; Elizabeth Sussman, Nicholson; T & L Antiques, New Hope; Walt's Collector's Corner, Broomall; Willowbrook Antiques, McMurray; Windy Hill Antiques, Renninger's, Kutztown; Niel and Clodogh Wotring, Coopersburg

Tennessee: Brian Cullity Antiques, Mountain City. **Vermont:** Brandon Antiques Center, Brandon; Country Bumpkin Antiques, Fairhaven; Iron Antiques, Brandon; Sigourney's Antiques, Cavendish. **West Virginia:** Weaver's Antiques, Salem

INDEX

HOW TO ORDER ADDITIONAL COPIES

If your local bookseller is out of *Warman's,* you may order additional copies directly from the publisher. Please use the attached coupon.

Dear Warman's:

☐ Enclosed is my check/Money Order for ____ copies of *Warman's Antiques & Their Prices, 16th Edition*, at $10.95 each .... $ _____

Add postage & handling at $1.50 each $ _____

Total amount enclosed $ _____

(Pa. residents add 66¢ per book Sales Tax. Sorry, no COD's or charges accepted)

☐ Please notify me of the 17th Edition, to be published in 1983.

NAME _____

ADDRESS _____

CITY, STATE, ZIP _____

MAIL TO: Warman's, Dept. 16, P.O. Box 26742, Elkins Park, PA 19117. Be sure to enclose payment.